ROBERT P. CARROLL

THE BOOK OF JEREMIAH

old testament library

ROBERT P. CARROLL

JEREMIAH

A Commentary

SCM PRESS LTD

British Library Cataloguing in Publication Data

Carroll, Robert P.
The Book of Jeremiah: a commentary.
1. Bible. O.T. Jeremiah——Commentaries
I. Title II. Bible. O.T. Jeremiah.
English. 1986
224'.207 BS1525.3

ISBN 0-334-02093-X

First published 1986
by SCM Press Ltd
26–30 Tottenham Road, London N1

Phototypeset by Input Typesetting Ltd, London
and printed in Great Britain by
Redwood Burn Ltd
Trowbridge, Wiltshire

In memory of my father

THOMAS FRANCIS CARROLL

1911 – 1982

one who walked in the ancient paths

CONTENTS

I want no more than to speak simply, to be granted that grace.
Because we've loaded even our songs with so much music that they're slowly sinking
and we've decorated our art so much that its features have been eaten away by gold
and it's time to say our few words because tomorrow our soul sets sail.

George Seferis, 'An Old Man on the River Bank'

PREFACE

Writing a commentary on a book as long and complex as Jeremiah incurs debts to many people. An exhaustive list of all those who contributed to the making of this book would rival the length of its introduction, but the support of friends and the kindness of strangers must be acknowledged in general and that of a few individuals in particular. Whether for listening with their tongues, supplying books, sending offprints, giving advice, or simply being there I must thank the following: Peter Ackroyd, John Ashton, Peter Asplin, Graeme Auld, the Balmore Group, Bob Coote, Robert Davidson, Alastair Hunter, William McKane, Heather McKay, the Renfield Centre Seminar Group, Angus Turner, Willie Wessels and Nick Wyatt. No blame, except by association, attaches to them for anything in this commentary. The responsibility for it is mine (aided and abetted by the writers of Jeremiah!).

A different kind of gratitude must be expressed to Mary Anne for her long period of being a book-widow: condolences and admiration for tolerance and tolerability are hers. Her assistance in a number of ways, including the fiendish task of proof-reading, must also be acknowledged.

The dedication needs no exegesis, but hints at some of the background to the writing of this book. The *marzēaḥ* for my father was modest as befits the memory of an honest man who lived according to his lights, and in dedicating this work to his honoured memory I acknowledge a debt beyond payment. 'Ah well, God rest him all road ever he offended!' (Hopkins).

Glasgow
14 July 1985

Robert P. Carroll

ABBREVIATIONS

A	Aquila
AB	Anchor Bible
ABR	*Australian Biblical Review*
AOAT	Alter Orient and Altes Testament
AThANT	Abhandlungen zur Theologie des Alten und Neuen Testaments
AV	Authorized Version
BA	*The Biblical Archaeologist*
BASOR	*Bulletin of the American Schools of Oriental Research*
BDB	*Brown, Driver, Briggs, *A Hebrew and English Lexicon of the Old Testament*
BETL	Bibliotheca Ephemeridum Theologicarum Lovaniensium
BHS	Biblia Hebraica Stuttgartensia
BJRL	*Bulletin of the John Rylands Library*
BKAT	Biblischer Kommentar, Altes Testament
BWANT	Beiträge zur Wissenschaft vom Alten und Neuen Testament
BZ	*Biblische Zeitschrift*
BZAW	Beihefte zur *Zeitschrift für die alttestamentliche Wissenschaft*
CB:OTS	Coniectanea Biblica Old Testament Series
CBQ	*Catholic Biblical Quarterly*
CHJ	*The Cambridge History of Judaism*, ed. W. D. Davies and L. Finkelstein
Comm.	Commentary
EvTh	*Evangelische Theologie*
EV(V)	English version(s)
FRLANT	Forschungen zur Religion und Literatur des Alten und Neuen Testaments
FS	Festschrift
G	Septuagint (LXX)
G*	Original Greek text

ABBREVIATIONS

G^A	Codex Alexandrinus
G^B	Codex Vaticanus
G^L	Lucianic recension
G^{min}	*codices minusculis scripti*
G^O	Origen's recension
G^S	Codex Sinaiticus
G^V	Codex Venetus
GK	*Gesenius' Hebrew Grammar*, ed. E. Kautzsch and A. E. Cowley, Clarendon Press 1910
HDR	Harvard Dissertations in Religion
HSM(S)	Harvard Semitic Monographs (Series)
HTR	*Harvard Theological Review*
HUCA	*Hebrew Union College Annual*
IEJ	*Israel Exploration Journal*
Interpr	*Interpretation*
JBL	*Journal of Biblical Literature*
JJS	*Journal of Jewish Studies*
JNES	*Journal of Near Eastern Studies*
JPSB	Jewish Publication Society Bible
JQR	*Jewish Quarterly Review*
JR	*Journal of Religion*
JSOT (SS)	*Journal for the Study of the Old Testament* (Supplement Series)
JTS	*Journal of Theological Studies*
K	Ketib (the written text)
KB^3	*Köhler, Baumgartner, *Lexicon in Veteris Testamenti Libros* (third edition)
ms(s)	manuscript(s)
MT	Masoretic Text
NCB(C)	New Century Bible (Commentary)
NEB	The New English Bible
NKZ	*Neue Kirchliche Zeitschrift*
OAN	Oracles against the nations
OTE	*Old Testament Essays* (Dept of OT, UNISA, Pretoria)
OTL	Old Testament Library
OTS	Oudtestamentische Studiën
PEQ	*Palestine Exploration Quarterly*
Q	Qere (the spoken text)
4QJer	Fragment(s) of Jeremiah text from Qumran (Cave IV)
RB	*Revue Biblique*
RHPhR	*Revue d'histoire et de philosophie religieuses*

ABBREVIATIONS

RSV	Revised Standard Version
S	Syriac
SBL DS (MS)	Society of Biblical Literature Dissertation Series (Monograph Series)
SBT (SS)	Studies in Biblical Theology (Second Series)
SEÅ	*Svensk Exegetisk Årsbok*
SOTS	Society for Old Testament Study
StTh	*Studia Theologica*
SVT	Supplements to *Vetus Testamentum*
Symm	Symmachus
T	Targum
TB	*The Tyndale Bulletin*
Theod	Theodotion
TGUOS	*Transactions of the Glasgow University Oriental Society*
TLZ	*Theologische Literaturzeitung*
UF	*Ugarit-Forschungen*
V	Vulgate
Vrs	Versions
VT	*Vetus Testamentum*
WMANT	Wissenschaftliche Monographien zum Alten und Neuen Testament
ZAW	*Zeitschrift für die alttestamentliche Wissenschaft*
ZTK	*Zeitschrift für Theologie und Kirche*

For full details of entries marked * see Bibliography.

BIBLIOGRAPHY

1. Texts, translations, dictionaries

The Holy Bible: Revised Standard Version, Collins 1973

The New English Bible with the Apocrypha, Oxford University Press/Cambridge University Press 1970

The Prophets Nevi'im: A new translation of The Holy Scriptures according to the Masoretic text. Second section, Jewish Publication Society of America 1978

sēfer yirmᵉyāh, liber jeremiae, ed. W. Rudolph, Biblia Hebraica Stuttgartensia, Württembergische Bibelanstalt, Stuttgart 1970

Biblia Hebraica Stuttgartensia, ed. K. Elliger et W. Rudolph, Deutsche Bibelgesellschaft, Stuttgart 1967/77

Ieremias, Baruch, Threni, Epistula Ieremiae, ed. J. Ziegler, Septuaginta: Vetus Testamentum Graecum XV, Vandenhoeck und Ruprecht 1957

F. Brown, S. R. Driver and C. A. Briggs, *A Hebrew and English Lexicon of the Old Testament with an appendix containing the biblical Aramaic*, Clarendon Press 1907

E. Hatch and H. A. Redpath, *A Concordance to the Septuagint and the other Greek Versions of the Old Testament (including the Apocryphal Books)*, Clarendon Press 1897

L. Köhler and W. Baumgartner (eds), *Lexicon in Veteris Testamenti Libros*, E. J. Brill 1958

Hebräisches und Aramäisches Lexikon zum Alten Testament, third edition, ed. W. Baumgartner and J. J. Stamm (et al.), I (1967), II (1974), III (1983), E. J. Brill

2. Commentaries

Bright, J., *Jeremiah: A New Translation with Introduction and Commentary*, AB 21, Doubleday & Company 1965

Condamin, A., *Le Livre de Jérémie: Traduction et Commentaire*, Études Bibliques, J. Gabalda et Cie [3]1936

Cornill, C. H., *Das Buch Jeremia*, Chr. Herm. Tauchnitz 1905

Cunliffe-Jones, H., *The Book of Jeremiah: Introduction and Commentary*, The Torch Bible Commentaries, SCM Press 1960

Driver, S. R., *The Book of the Prophet Jeremiah*, Hodder & Stoughton 1906

Duhm, B., *Das Buch Jeremia*, Kurzer Hand-Commentar zum Alten Testament XI, J. C. B. Mohr (Paul Siebeck) 1901

Feinberg, C. L., *Jeremiah: A Commentary*, Zondervan Publishing House 1982

Freedman, H., *Jeremiah: Hebrew Text and English Translation with an Introduction and Commentary*, Soncino Books of the Bible, The Soncino Press 1949

Freehof, S. B., *Book of Jeremiah: A Commentary*, The Jewish Commentary for Bible Readers, Union of American Hebrew Congregations 1977

Giesebrecht, F., *Das Buch Jeremia*, Handkommentar zum Alten Testament III, 2.1, Vandenhoeck und Ruprecht 1894

Harrison, R. K., *Jeremiah and Lamentations: An Introduction and Commentary*, Tyndale Old Testament Commentaries, The Tyndale Press 1973

Hitzig, F., *Der Prophet Jeremia*, Kurzgefasstes exegetisches Handbuch zum Alten Testament, S. Hirzel [2]1866

Hyatt, J. P., 'The Book of Jeremiah: Introduction and Exegesis', *The Interpreter's Bible* V, 775–1142, Abingdon Press 1956

Leslie, E. A. *Jeremiah: Chronologically arranged, translated, and interpreted*, Abingdon Press 1954

Nicholson, E. W., *The Book of the Prophet Jeremiah: Chapters 1–25; The Book of the Prophet Jeremiah: Chapters 26–52*, The Cambridge Bible Commentary: New English Bible, Cambridge University Press 1973; 1975

Nötscher, F., *Das Buch Jeremias*, Die Heilige Schrift des Alten Testaments 7:2, Peter Hanstein Verlagsbuchhandlung 1934

Peake, A. S., *Jeremiah and Lamentations*: I *Jeremiah I–XXIV*; II *Jeremiah XXV–LII, Lamentations*, The Century Bible, T. C. and E. C. Jack 1910, 1912

Rothstein, J. W., 'Das Buch Jeremia', *Die Heilige Schrift des Alten Testaments* I, 671–813, ed. E. Kautzsch, J. C. B. Mohr (Paul Siebeck) [3]1909

Rudolph, W., *Jeremia*, Handbuch zum Alten Testament I, 12, J. C. B. Mohr (Paul Siebeck) [3]1968

Thompson, J. A., *The Book of Jeremiah*, The New International Commentary on the Old Testament, William B. Eerdmans Publishing Company 1980

Volz, P., *Der Prophet Jeremia*, Kommentar zum Alten Testament X, A. Deichertsche Verlagsbuchhandlung 1922

Weiser, A., *Das Buch des Propheten Jeremia*, Das Alte Testament Deutsch: Neues Göttinger Bibelwerk 20/21, Vandenhoeck und Ruprecht [4]1960

3. Books and articles

Aberbach, D. (1977), '*w'tn lhm y'brwm* (Jeremiah viii 13): The Problem and its Solution', *VT* 27, 99–101
Ackroyd, P. R. (1958), 'Two Old Testament Historical Problems of the Early Persian Period', *JNES* 17, 13–27
— (1963), 'Jeremiah x.1–16', *JTS* 14, 385–90
— (1968a), *Exile and Restoration: A Study of Hebrew Thought of the Sixth Century BC*, OTL, SCM Press
— (1968b), 'Historians and Prophets', *SEÅ* 33, 18–54
— (1972), 'The Temple Vessels: A Continuity Theme', SVT 23, 166–81
— (1973), *I & II Chronicles, Ezra, Nehemiah: Introduction and Commentary*, Torch Bible Commentaries, SCM Press
— (1984a), 'Historical Problems of the Early Achaemenian Period', *Orient* 20, 1–15
— (1984b), 'The Jewish Community in Palestine in the Persian Period', *CHJ* 1, 130–61
Ahuis, F., (1981), *Der klagende Gerichtsprophet: Studien zur Klage in der Überlieferung von den alttestamentlichen Gerichtspropheten*, Calwer Theologische Monographien 12, Calwer Verlag
Aitken, K. T. (1984), 'The Oracles against Babylon in Jeremiah 50–51: Structures and Perspectives', *TB* 35, 25–63
Albertz, R. (1982), 'Jer. 2–6 und die Frühzeitverkündigung Jeremias', *ZAW* 94, 20–47
Albright, W. F. (1950–1), 'A Catalogue of Early Hebrew Lyric Poems (Psalm 68)', *HUCA* 23:I, 1–39
Alonso Schökel, L. (1981), 'Jeremías como anti-Moisés', *De la Tôrah au Messie: Études d'exégèse et d'herméneutique bibliques offertes à Henri Cazelles pour ses 25 années d'enseignement à l'Institut Catholique de Paris (Octobre 1979)*, ed. M. Carrez, J. Doré and P. Grelot, Desclée, 245–54
Alter, R. (1981), *The Art of Biblical Narrative*, Allen and Unwin
Althann, R. (1978), 'Jeremiah IV 11–12: Stichometry, Parallelism and Translation', *VT* 28, 385–91
Andersen, F. I. & Freedman, D. N. (1980), *Hosea: A New Translation with Introduction and Commentary*, AB 24, Doubleday and Company
Anderson, B. W. (1964), 'The New Covenant and the Old', *The Old Testament and Christian Faith: Essays by Rudolf Bultmann and others*, ed. B. W. Anderson, SCM Press, 225–42
— (1978), ' "The Lord Has Created Something New": A Stylistic Study of Jer. 31:15–22', *CBQ* 40, 463–78 (= Perdue and Kovacs, 367–80)
Andreasen, N.-E.A. (1983), 'The Role of the Queen Mother in Israelite Society', *CBQ* 45, 179–94

BIBLIOGRAPHY

Andrew, M. E. (1982), 'The Authorship of Jer. 10 1–16', *ZAW* 94, 127–30

Auld, A. G. (1983), 'Prophets Through the Looking Glass: Between Writings and Moses', *JSOT* 27, 3–23

— (1984), 'Prophets and Prophecy in Jeremiah and Kings', *ZAW* 96, 66–82

Avigad, N. (1978), 'Baruch the Scribe and Jerahmeel the King's Son', *IEJ* 28, 52–6

Bach, R. (1961), 'Bauen und Pflanzen', *Studien zur Theologie der alttestamentlichen Überlieferungen: Gerhard von Rad zum 60 Geburtstag*, ed. R. Rendtorff and K. Koch, Neukirchener Verlag, 7–32

— (1962), *Die Aufforderung zur Flucht und zum Kampf im alttestamentlichen Prophetenspruch*, WMANT 9, Neukirchener Verlag

Balentine, S. E. (1983), *The Hidden God: The Hiding of the Face of God in the Old Testament*, Oxford University Press

— (1984), 'The Prophet as Intercessor: A Reassessment', *JBL* 103, 161–73

Baltzer, K. (1961), 'Das Ende der Staates Juda und die Messias-Frage', *Studien zur Theologie der alttestamentlichen Überlieferungen* (FS von Rad), 33–43

— (1968), 'Considerations regarding the Office and Calling of the Prophet', *HTR* 61, 567–81

— (1975), 'Die Einsetzung Jeremias', *Die Biographie der Propheten*, Neukirchener Verlag, 113–28

Bardtke, H. (1935), 'Jeremia der Fremdvölkerprophet', *ZAW* 53, 209–39

— (1936), 'Jeremia der Fremdvölkerprophet', *ZAW* 54, 240–62

Barth, K. (1957), 'The Hiddenness of God', *Church Dogmatics* II/1, T. and T. Clark, 179–202

Barton, J. (1984), ' "The Law and the Prophets". Who are the Prophets?', *Prophets, Worship and Theodicy: Studies in Prophetism, Biblical Theology and Structural and Rhetorical Analysis and on the Place of Music in Worship*, OTS XXIII, ed. A. S. van der Woude, E. J. Brill, 1–18

Baumann, E. (1929), '*šwb šbwt*: Eine exegetische Untersuchung', *ZAW* NF 6 (47), 17–44

Baumgartner, W. (1917), *Die Klagegedichte des Jeremia*, BZAW 32, Verlag Alfred Töpelmann

Begrich, J. (1934), 'Die priesterliche Heilsorakel', *ZAW* 52, 81–92

Bernhardt, K.-H. (1961), *Das Problem der altorientalischen Königsideologie im Alten Testament unter besonderer Berücksichtung der Geschichte*, SVT 8

Berridge, J. M. (1970), *Prophet, People, and the Word of Yahweh: An*

Examination of Form and Content in the Proclamation of the Prophet Jeremiah, Basel Studies of Theology 4, EVZ-Verlag

Bettelheim, B. (1955), *Symbolic Wounds: Puberty Rites and the Envious Male*, Thames and Hudson

Beuken, W. A. M. and van Grol, H. W. M. (1981), 'Jeremiah 14, 1–15, 9: A Situation of Distress and its Hermeneutics. Unity and Diversity of Form-Dramatic Development', Bogaert 1981c, 297–342

Beyerlin, W. (1978), *Near Eastern Texts Relating to the Old Testament*, OTL, SCM Press

Blank, S. H. (1961), *Jeremiah: Man and Prophet*, Hebrew Union College Press

— (1977), 'The Prophet as Paradigm', *Prophetic Thought: Essays and Addresses*, Hebrew Union College Press, 23–34

Blenkinsopp, J. (1971), 'The Prophetic Reproach', *JBL* 90, 267–78

— (1972), *Gibeon and Israel: The role of Gibeon and the Gibeonites in the political and religious history of early Israel*, SOTS monograph series 2, Cambridge University Press

— (1983), *A History of Prophecy in Israel: From the Settlement in the Land to the Hellenistic Period*, Westminster Press

Boecker, H. J. (1980), *Law and the Administration of Justice in the Old Testament and Ancient East*, SPCK

de Boer, P. A. H. (1973), 'Jeremiah 45, verse 5', *Symbolae Biblicae et Mesopotamicae Francisco Mario Theodoro de Liagre Böhl Dedicatae*, Nederlands Instituut voor het Nabije Oosten Studia Francisci Scholten Memoriae Dicata 4, ed. M. A. Beek, A. A. Kampman, C. Nijland, J. Ryckmans, E. J. Brill, 31–7

Böhmer, S. (1976), *Heimkehr und neuer Bund: Studien zu Jeremia 30–31*, Göttinger Theologische Arbeiten 5, Vandenhoeck und Ruprecht

Bogaert, P.-M. (1981a), 'De Baruch à Jérémie: Les deux rédactions conservées du livre de Jérémie', Bogaert 1981c, 168–73

— (1981b), 'Les mécanismes rédactionnels en Jér. 10, 1–16 (LXX et TM) et la signification des suppléments', Bogaert 1981c, 222–38

— (1981c), (ed.), *Le Livre de Jérémie: Le prophète et son milieu, les oracles et leur transmission*, BETL 54, Uitgeverij Peeters/Leuven University Press

Boswell, J. (1980), *Christianity, Social Tolerance, and Homosexuality: Gay People in Western Europe from the Beginning of the Christian Era to the Fourteenth Century*, University of Chicago Press

Brekelmans, C. (1981), 'Jeremiah 18, 1–12 and its Redaction', Bogaert 1981c, 343–50

Bright, J. (1951), 'The Date of the Prose Sermons of Jeremiah', *JBL* 70, 15–35 (= Perdue and Kovacs, 193–212)

— (1966a), 'An Experiment in Hermeneutics: Jeremiah 31:31–34', *Interpr* 20, 188–210

— (1966b), 'The Prophetic Reminiscence: Its Place and Function in the Book of Jeremiah', *Biblical Essays*, Proceedings of the Ninth Meeting of 'Die Ou-Testamentische Werkgemeenskap in Suid-Afrika', 11–30

— (1970), 'Jeremiah's Complaints: Liturgy, or Expressions of Personal Distress?', Durham and Porter, 189–214

— (1974), 'A Prophet's Lament and Its Answer: Jeremiah 15:10–21', *Interpr* 28, 59–74 (= Perdue and Kovacs, 325–37)

— (1977), *Covenant and Promise: The Future in the Preaching of the Pre-exilic Prophets*, SCM Press

Brockington, L. H. (1973), *The Hebrew Text of the Old Testament: The Readings Adopted by the Translators of the New English Bible*, Oxford University Press, Cambridge University Press

Brodie, L. T. (1981), 'Jacob's Travail (Jer. 30:1–13) and Jacob's Struggle (Gen. 32:22–32): A Test Case for Measuring the Influence of the Book of Jeremiah on the Present Text of Genesis', *JSOT* 19, 31–60

Brongers, H. A. (1969), 'Der Zornesbecher', *OTS* xv, 177–92

Broughton, P. E. (1958), 'The Call of Jeremiah: The Relation of Deut 18:9–22 to the Call and Life of Jeremiah', *ABR* 6, 37–46

Brueggemann, W. (1973), 'Jeremiah's Use of Rhetorical Questions', *JBL* 92, 358–74

— (1978), 'The Epistemological Crisis of Israel's Two Histories (Jer. 9:22–23)', *Israelite Wisdom: Theological and Literary Essays in Honor of Samuel Terrien*, ed. J. G. Gammie and others, Scholars Press, 85–105

Bruno, D. A. (1954), *Jeremia: Eine rhythmische Untersuchung*, Almqvist and Wiksell

Buber, M. (1960), *The Prophetic Faith*, Harper and Row

Buis, P. (1968), 'La nouvelle alliance', *VT* 18, 1–15

Bultmann, R. (1955), 'Prophecy and Fulfilment', *Essays Philosophical and Theological*, SCM Press, 182–208

Buss, M. J. (1982), 'An Anthropological Perspective upon Prophetic Call Narratives', *Semeia* 21, 9–30

Calkins, R. (1930), *Jeremiah the Prophet: A Study in Personal Religion*, Macmillan

Carroll, R. P. (1976a), 'A Non-cogent Argument in Jeremiah's Oracles against the Prophets', *StTh* 30, 43–51

— (1976b), 'Prophecy, Dissonance, and Jeremiah XXVI', *TGUOS* 25, 12–23 (= Perdue and Kovacs, 381–91)

— (1977), 'The Aniconic God and the Cult of Images', *StTh* 31, 51–64
— (1979), *When Prophecy Failed: Reactions and Responses to Failure in the Old Testament Prophetic Traditions*, SCM Press
— (1980), 'Translation and Attribution in Isaiah 8.19f.', *The Bible Translator* 31, 126–34
— (1981), *From Chaos to Covenant: Uses of Prophecy in the Book of Jeremiah*, SCM Press
— (1983), 'Poets not Prophets: A Response to "Prophets through the Looking-Glass" ', *JSOT* 27, 25–31
— (1984), 'Theodicy and the Community: The Text and Subtext of Jeremiah V 1–6', *Prophets, Worship and Theodicy*, OTS XXIII, 19–38
Cazelles, H. (1967), 'Sophonie, Jérémie, et les Scythes en Palestine', *RB* 74, 24–44 (= Perdue and Kovacs, 129–49)
— (1968), 'Israël du nord et arche d'alliance', *VT* 18, 147–58
Charlesworth, J. H. (1983), (ed.), *The Old Testament Pseudepigrapha*: I *Apocalyptic Literature and Testaments*, Darton, Longman & Todd
Childs, B. S. (1959), 'The Enemy from the North and the Chaos Tradition', *JBL* 78, 187–98 (= Perdue and Kovacs, 151–61)
— (1963), 'A Study of the Formula "Until this Day" ', *JBL* 83, 279–92
— (1974), *Exodus: A Commentary*, OTL, SCM Press
— (1979), *Introduction to the Old Testament as Scripture*, SCM Press
Christensen, D. L. (1973), ' "Terror on every side" in Jeremiah', *JBL* 92, 498–502
— (1975), *Transformations of the War Oracle in OT Prophecy: Studies in the Oracles Against the Nations*, HDR 3, Scholars Press
Clements, R. E. (1975), *Prophecy and Tradition*, Growing Points in Theology, Basil Blackwell
— (1980), *Isaiah 1–39*, NCBC, Eerdmans/Marshall, Morgan and Scott
— (1982), 'The Ezekiel Tradition: Prophecy in a Time of Crisis', *Israel's Prophetic Tradition: Essays in Honour of Peter R. Ackroyd*, ed. R. Coggins, A. Phillips and M. Knibb, Cambridge University Press, 119–36
Clines, D. J. A. and Gunn, D. (1976), 'Form, Occasion and Redaction in Jeremiah 20', *ZAW* 88, 390–409
— (1978), ' "You tried to persuade me" and "Violence! Outrage!" in Jeremiah XX 7–8', *VT* 28, 20–7
Cogan, M. (1974), *Imperialism and Religion: Assyria, Judah and Israel in the Eighth and Seventh Centuries B.C.E.*, SBL MS 19, Scholars Press
Coote, R. B. (1981), *Amos among the Prophets: Composition and Theology*, Fortress Press
Coppens, J. (1963), 'La nouvelle alliance en Jér. 31, 31–34', *CBQ* 25, 12–21

Crenshaw, J. L. (1971), *Prophetic Conflict: Its Effect Upon Israelite Religion*, BZAW 124, Walter de Gruyter
— (1975), *Hymnic Affirmation of Divine Justice: The Doxologies of Amos and Related Texts in the Old Testament*, SBL DS 24, Scholars Press
— (1983), 'A Living Tradition: The Book of Jeremiah in Current Research', *Interpr* 37, 117–29
— (1984), 'Seduction and Rape: The Confessions of Jeremiah', *A Whirlpool of Torment: Israelite Traditions of God as an Oppressive Presence*, Overtures to Biblical Theology 12, Fortress Press, 31–56
Croatto, J. S. and Soggin, J. A. (1962), 'Die Bedeutung von *šdmwt* im Alten Testament', *ZAW* 74, 44–50
Cross, F. M., Jr (1953), 'The Council of Yahweh in Second Isaiah', *JNES* 12, 274–7
— (1958), *The Ancient Library of Qumran and Modern Biblical Studies*, rev. ed., Doubleday & Company
— (1975), 'The Evolution of a Theory of Local Texts', *Qumran and the History of the Biblical Text*, ed. F. M. Cross and S. Talmon, Harvard University Press, 306–20
Dahood, M. (1959), 'The Value of Ugaritic for Textual Criticism', *Biblica* 40, 164–8
— (1961), 'Two Textual Problems in Jeremiah', *CBQ* 23, 462–4
— (1962a), 'Philological Notes on Jeremiah 18 14–15', *ZAW* 74, 207–9
— (1962b), 'Ugaritic Studies and the Bible', *Gregorianum* 43, 55–79
— (1963), 'Denominative *riḥḥam*, "to conceive, enwomb" ', *Biblica* 44, 204–5
— (1966), 'Hebrew-Ugaritic Lexicography IV', *Biblica* 47, 403–19
— (1975), 'The emphatic double negative *m'yn* in Jeremiah 10:6–7', *CBQ* 37, 458–9
David, M. (1948), 'The Manumission of Slaves under Zedekiah (A Contribution to the Laws about Hebrew Slaves)', *OTS* v, 63–78
Davidson, R. (1964), 'Orthodoxy and the Prophetic Word: A Study in the Relationship between Jeremiah and Deuteronomy', *VT* 14, 407–16
— (1976), 'Jeremiah X 1–16', *TGUOS* 25, 41–58
— (1983), *The Courage to Doubt: Exploring an Old Testament Theme*, SCM Press
Day, J. (1979), 'The Destruction of the Shiloh Sanctuary and Jeremiah VII 12, 14', *Studies in the Historical Books of the Old Testament*, SVT 30, ed. J. A. Emerton, E. J. Brill, 87–94
— (1985), *God's Conflict with the Dragon and the Sea: Echoes of a Canaanite Myth in the Old Testament*, University of Cambridge Oriental Publications 35, Cambridge University Press

DeRoche, M. (1978), 'Is Jeremiah 25.15–29 a Piece of Reworked Jeremianic Poetry?', *JSOT* 10, 58–67
— (1980a), 'Contra creation, covenant and conquest (Jer. viii 13)', *VT* 30, 280–90
— (1980b), 'Zephaniah i 2–3: the "sweeping" of creation', *VT* 30, 104–9
— (1983), 'Yahweh's *rīb* Against Israel: A Reassessment of the So-called "Prophetic Lawsuit" in the Preexilic Prophets', *JBL* 102, 563–74
DeVries, S. J. (1975), *Yesterday, Today, and Tomorrow: Time and History in the Old Testament*, SPCK
— (1978), *Prophet Against Prophet: The Role of the Micaiah Tradition (I Kings 22) in the Development of Early Prophetic Tradition*, William B. Eerdmans Publishing Company
Dietrich, E. L. (1925), *šwb šbwt: Die endzeitliche Wiederherstellung bei den Propheten*, BZAW 40, Verlag Alfred Töpelmann
Dijkstra, M. (1983), 'Prophecy by Letter (Jeremiah xxix 24–32)', *VT* 33, 319–22
Dodds, E. R. (1973), *The Greeks and the Irrational*, Sather Classical Lectures 25, 1950, University of California Press
Driver, G. R. (1937–38), 'Linguistic and Textual Problems: Jeremiah', *JQR* 28, 97–129
— (1950), 'Difficult Words in the Hebrew Prophets', *Studies in Old Testament Prophecy: Presented to Professor Theodore H. Robinson*, ed. H. H. Rowley, T & T. Clark, 52–72
— (1951), 'Hebrew Notes', *VT* 1, 241–50
— (1955a), 'Birds in the Old Testament – II Birds in Life', *PEQ* 1954–55, 129–40
— (1955b), 'Two Misunderstood Passages of the Old Testament', *JTS* 6, 82–7
— (1960), 'Abbreviations in the Massoretic Text', *Textus* 1, 112–131
— (1963), 'Once Again Abbreviations', *Textus* 4, 76–94
Driver, S. R. (1896), *A Critical and Exegetical Commentary on Deuteronomy*, 2nd ed., T. & T. Clark
— (1913), *An Introduction to the Literature of the Old Testament*, International Theological Library, 9th ed., T. & T. Clark
Duhm, B. (1903), *Das Buch Jeremia*, Die poetischen und prophetischen Bücher des Alten Testaments. Übersetzungen in den Versmassen der Urschrift III, J. C. B. Mohr (Paul Siebeck)
Durham, J. I. and Porter, J. R. (1970) (eds), *Proclamation and Presence: Old Testament Essays in honour of Gwynne Henton Davies*, SCM Press
Ehrlich, A. B. (1912), *Randglossen zur Hebräischen Bibel: textkritisches,*

sprachliches und sachliches. IV *Jesaia, Jeremia*, J. C. Hinrichs'sche Buchhandlung

Eichrodt, W. (1970), *Ezekiel: A Commentary*, OTL, SCM Press

Eissfeldt, O. (1965), *The Old Testament: An Introduction*, Basil Blackwell

Elliger, K. (1955), 'Das Gesetz Leviticus 18', *ZAW* 67, 1–25

Ellison, H. L. (1961), 'The Prophecy of Jeremiah: IX The sin of Jerusalem', *The Evangelical Quarterly* 33, 27–35 (full sequence in vols 31–40, 1959–68)

Emerton, J. A. (1981), 'Notes on Some Problems in Jeremiah v 26', *Mélanges bibliques et orientaux en l'honneur de M. Henri Cazelles*, AOAT 212, ed. A. Caquot and M. Delcor, Neukirchener Verlag, 125–33

Emmerson, G. I. (1984), *Hosea: An Israelite Prophet in Judean Perspective*, JSOT SS 28, JSOT Press

Eppstein, V. (1968), 'The Day of Yahweh in Jeremiah 4, 23–28', *JBL* 87, 93–7

Feliks, Y. (1981), *Nature and Man in the Bible: Chapters in Biblical Ecology*, The Soncino Press

Fensham, F. C. (1962), 'Salt as Curse in the Old Testament and the Ancient Near East', *BA* 25/2, 48–50

Fishbane, M. (1971), 'Jeremiah IV 23–26 and Job III 3–13: A Recovered Use of the Creation Pattern', *VT* 21, 151–67

— (1979), 'Jeremiah 20: 7–12/Loneliness and Anguish', *Text and Texture: Close Readings of Selected Biblical Texts*, Schocken Books, 91–102

Fohrer, G. (1953), *Die symbolischen Handlungen der Propheten*, Zwingli-Verlag

— (1967), 'Jeremias Tempelwort (Jeremia 7 1–15)'; 'Prophetie und Magie', *Studien zur alttestamentlichen Prophetie (1949–1965)*, BZAW 99, Verlag Alfred Töpelmann, 190–203; 242–64

— (1970), *Introduction to the Old Testament*, SPCK

— (1981), 'Vollmacht über Völker und Königsreich', *Studien zur alttestamentlichen Texten und Themen (1966–1972)*, BZAW 155, de Gruyter, 44–52

Foucault, M. (1970), *The Order of Things: An Archaeology of the Human Sciences*, Tavistock Publications

Friedman, R. E. (1981), *The Exile and Biblical Narrative: The Formation of the Deuteronomistic and Priestly Works*, HSM 22, Scholars Press

Frost, S. B. (1968), 'The Death of Josiah: A Conspiracy of Silence', *JBL* 87, 369–82

Gaster, T. H. (1969), 'Jeremiah', *Myth, Legend, and Custom in the Old Testament: A Comparative Study with Chapters from Sir James G. Frazer's Folklore in the Old Testament*, Duckworth, 586–606

Gerleman, G. (1974), 'Der Nicht-Mensch: Erwägungen zur hebräischer Wurzel *NBL*', *VT* 24, 147–58
Gerstenberger, E. (1962), 'The Woe-Oracles of the Prophets', *JBL* 81, 249–63
— (1963), 'Jeremiah's Complaints: Observations on Jeremiah 15: 10–21', *JBL* 82, 393–408
Gevirtz, S. (1963), 'Jericho and Shechem: A Religio-Literary Aspect of City Destruction', *VT* 13, 52–62
Gibson, J. C. L., (1971), *Textbook of Syrian Semitic Inscriptions:* I *Hebrew and Moabite Inscriptions*, Clarendon Press
Gilula, M. (1967), 'An Egyptian Parallel to Jeremia I 4–5', *VT* 17, 114
Ginzberg, L. (1913), *The Legends of the Jews:* IV *Bible Times and Characters from Joshua to Esther*, The Jewish Publication Society of America
Goldmann, M. D. (1952), 'Was Jeremiah Married?', *ABR* 2, 42–7
Gouders, K. (1971), ' "Siehe, ich lege meine Worte in deinen Mund": Die Berufung des Propheten Jeremia (Jer 1, 4–10)', *Bibel und Leben* 12, 162–86
Gray, J. (1977), *I and II Kings: A Commentary*, OTL, 3rd ed., SCM Press
Gross, K. (1931), 'Hoseas Einfluss auf Jeremias Anschauung', *NKZ* 42, 241–56, 327–43
Gruber, M. I. (1983), 'The Motherhood of God in Second Isaiah', *RB* 90, 351–9
Gunneweg, A. H. J. (1967), 'Ordinationsformular oder Berufungsbericht in Jeremia 1', *Glaube, Geist, Geschichte: Festscrift für Ernst Benz zum 60, Geburtstage am 17, November 1967*, ed. G. Müller and W. Zeller, E. J. Brill, 91–8
— (1970), 'Konfession oder Interpretation im Jeremiabuch', *ZTK* 67, 395–416
— (1983), '*'m-h'rṣ*: A Semantic Revolution', *ZAW* 95, 437–40
Habel, N. (1965), 'The Form and Significance of the Call Narratives', *ZAW* 77, 297–323
Haran, M. (1963), 'The Disappearance of the Ark', *IEJ* 13, 46–58
— (1978), *Temples and Temple Service in Ancient Israel: An Inquiry into the Character of Cult Phenomena and the Historical Setting of the Priestly School*, Clarendon Press
Harris, S. L. (1983), 'The Second Vision of Jeremiah: Jer. 1.13–15', *JBL* 102, 281–2
Harvey, J. (1962), 'Le "rib-pattern", réquisitoire prophétique sur la rupture de l'alliance', *Biblica* 43, 172–96
Hayes, J. H. (1968), 'The Usage of Oracles against Foreign Nations in Ancient Israel', *JBL* 87, 81–92

Hermisson, H.-J. (1980), 'Jeremias Wort über Jojachin', *Werden und Wirken des Alten Testaments: Festschrift für Claus Westermann zum 70. Geburstag*, ed. R. Albertz, H.-P. Müller, H. W. Wolff and W. Zimmerli, Vandenhoeck und Ruprecht, 252–70

Herodotus, The Loeb Classical Library, 4 vols, translated by A. D. Godley, William Heinemann/G. P. Putnam's Sons 1925ff.

Herrmann, S. (1965), *Die prophetischen Heilserwartungen im Alten Testament: Ursprung und Gestaltwandel*, BWANT 85, W. Kohlhammer Verlag

— (1977), 'Forschung am Jeremiabuch: Probleme und Tendenzen ihrer neueren Entwicklung', *TLZ* 102, 481–90

— (1984), 'Overcoming the Israelite Crisis: Remarks on the Interpretation of the Book of Jeremiah', Perdue and Kovacs, 299–311 (= 'Die Bewältigung der Krise Israels. Bemerkungen zur Interpretation des Buches Jeremia', *Beiträge zur Alttestamentlichen Theologie: Festschrift für Walther Zimmerli zum 70. Geburtstag*, 1977, ed. H. Donner, R. Hanhart und R. Smend, Vandenhoeck und Ruprecht, 164–78)

Herrmann, W. (1983), 'Jeremia 23, 23f. als Zeugnis des Gotteserfahrung im babylonisches Zeitalter', *BZ* 27, 155–66

Heschel, A. J. (1962), *The Prophets*, Harper & Row

Hertzberg, H. W. (1952), 'Jeremia und das Nordreich Israel', *TLZ* 77, 595–602

Hicks, R. L. (1983), '*DELET* and *MᵉGILLAH*: A Fresh Approach to Jeremiah xxxvi', *VT* 33, 46–66

Hillers, D. R. (1965), 'A Convention in Hebrew Literature: The Reaction to Bad News', *ZAW* 77, 86–90

Hobbs, T. R. (1972), 'Some Remarks on the Composition and Structure of the Book of Jeremiah', *CBQ* 34, 257–75

— (1974), 'Jeremiah 3 1–5 and Deuteronomy 24 1–4', *ZAW* 86, 23–9

— (1979), 'Some Proverbial Reflections in the Book of Jeremiah', *ZAW* 91, 62–72

Hoffmann, H.–D. (1980), *Reform und Reformen: Untersuchungen zu einem Grundthema der deuteronomistischen Geschichtsschreibung*, AThANT 66, Theologischer Verlag, Zürich

Holladay, W. L. (1958), *The Root ŠŪBH in the Old Testament with Particular Reference to its Usages in Covenantal Texts*, E. J. Brill

— (1960), 'Prototype and Copies: A New Approach to the Poetry-Prose Problem in the Book of Jeremiah', *JBL* 79, 351–67

— (1961), 'On Every High Hill and Under Every Green Tree', *VT* 11, 170–6

— (1962a), 'The so-called "Deuteronomic Gloss" in Jer. 8:19b', *VT* 12, 494–8

— (1962b), 'Style, Irony, and Authenticity in Jeremiah', *JBL* 81, 44–54

— (1963), 'Jeremiah's Lawsuit with God: A Study in Suffering and Meaning', *Interpr* 17, 280–301

— (1964), 'The Background of Jeremiah's Self-Understanding: Moses, Samuel, and Psalm 22', *JBL* 83, 153–64 (= Perdue and Kovacs, 313–24)

— (1965), ' "The priests scrape out on their hands," Jeremiah v 31', *VT* 15, 111–3

— (1966a), 'Jeremiah and Moses: Further Observations', *JBL* 85, 17–27

— (1966b), 'Jer. XXXI 22b Reconsidered: "The Woman Encompasses the Man" ', *VT* 16, 236–9

— (1966c), 'The Recovery of Poetic Passages of Jeremiah', *JBL* 85, 401–35

— (1972), 'The Covenant with the Patriarchs Overturned: Jeremiah's Intention in "Terror on Every Side" (Jer. 20:1–6)', *JBL* 91, 305–20

— (1975a), 'A Fresh Look at "Source B" and "Source C" in Jeremiah', *VT* 25, 394–412 (= Perdue and Kovacs, 213–28)

— (1975b), 'Jeremiah II 34bβ – A Fresh Proposal', *VT* 25, 221–5

— (1976a), *The Architecture of Jeremiah 1–20*, Bucknell University Press, Associated University Presses

— (1976b), 'Structure, Syntax and Meaning in Jeremiah iv 11–12A', *VT* 26, 28–32

— (1980), 'The Identification of the Two Scrolls of Jeremiah', *VT* 30, 452–67

— (1981), 'A Coherent Chronology of Jeremiah's Early Career', Bogaert 1981c, 58–73

— (1983), 'The Years of Jeremiah's Preaching', *Interpr* 37, 146–59

Honeyman, A. M. (1954), '*Māgōr mis-sābīb* and Jeremiah's Pun', *VT* 4, 424–6

Hopper, S. R. (1956), 'The Book of Jeremiah: Exposition', *The Interpreter's Bible* 5, 794–1142

— (1978), 'The "Terrible Sonnets" of Gerard Manley Hopkins and the "Confessions," of Jeremiah', *Semeia* 13/2, 29–73

Hossfeld, F. L und Meyer, I. (1973), *Prophet gegen Prophet. Eine Analyse der alttestamentlichen Texte zum Thema: Wahre und falsche Propheten*, Biblische Beiträge 9, Verlag Schweizerisches Katholisches Bibelwerk

— (1974), 'Der Prophet vor dem Tribunal: *Neuer Auslegungsversuch von Jer. 26*', *ZAW* 86, 30–50

Hubmann, F. D. (1978), *Untersuchungen zu den Konfessionen Jer. 11, 18–12, 6 und Jer. 15.10–21*, Forschung zur Bibel 30, Echter Verlag

— (1981), 'Jer. 18, 18–23 in Zusammenhang der Konfessionen', Bogaert 1981c, 271–96

Huffmonn, H. B. (1959), 'The Covenant Lawsuit in the Prophets', *JBL* 78, 285–95

Hume, D. (1976), *The Natural History of Religion and Dialogues concerning Natural Religion*, ed. A. W. Colver and J. V. Price, Clarendon Press

Hyatt, J. P. (1941), 'The Original Text of Jeremiah 11 15–16', *JBL* 60, 57–60

— (1942), 'Jeremiah and Deuteronomy', *JNES* 1, 156–73 (= Perdue and Kovacs, 113–27)

— (1951), 'The Deuteronomic Edition of Jeremiah', *Vanderbilt Studies in the Humanities* I, ed. R. C. Beatty, J. P. Hyatt and M. K. Spears, Vanderbilt University Press, 71–95 (= Perdue and Kovacs, 247–67)

Isbell, C. D. (1978), '2 Kings 22:3–23:24 and Jeremiah 36: A Stylistic Comparison', *JSOT* 8, 33–45

— and Jackson, M. (1980), 'Rhetorical Criticism and Jeremiah VII 1–VIII 3', *VT* 30, 20–6

Ittmann, N. (1981), *Die Konfessionen Jeremias: Ihre Bedeutung für die Verkündigung des Propheten*, WMANT 54, Neukirchener Verlag

Jahnow, H. (1923), *Das hebräisches Leichenlied im Rahmen der Völkerdichtung*, BZAW 36, Verlag A. Töpelmann

Janssen, E. (1956), *Juda in der Exilszeit: Ein Beitrag zur Frage der Entstehung des Judentums*, FRLANT 69, Vandenhoeck und Ruprecht

Janzen, J. G. (1967), 'Double Readings in the Text of Jeremiah', *HTR* 60, 433–47

— (1973), *Studies in the Text of Jeremiah*, HSM 6, Harvard University Press

Janzen, W. (1972), *Mourning Cry and Woe Oracle*, BZAW 125, Walter de Gruyter

— (1981), 'Withholding the Word', *Traditions in Transformation: Turning Points in Biblical Faith*, ed. B. Halpern and J. D. Levenson, Eisenbrauns, 97–114

Jellicoe, S. (1968), *The Septuagint and Modern Study*, Clarendon Press

Jobling, D. K. (1978a), 'Jeremiah's Poem in III 1–IV 2', *VT* 28, 45–55

— (1978b), 'The Quest of the Historical Jeremiah: Hermeneutical Implications of Recent Literature', *Union Seminary Quarterly Review* 34, 3–12 (= Perdue and Kovacs, 285–97)

Johnson, A. R. (1962), *The Cultic Prophet in Ancient Israel*, 2nd ed., University of Wales Press

— (1967), *Sacral Kingship in Ancient Israel*, 2nd ed., University of Wales Press

Johnstone, W. (1967), 'The Setting of Jeremiah's Prophetic Activity', *TGUOS* 21, 47–55

Jones, D. R. (1963), 'The Cessation of Sacrifice after the Destruction of the Temple in 586 BC', *JTS* 14, 12–31

Jüngling, H.-W. (1973), 'Ich mache dich zu einer ehernen Mauer: Literarkritische Überlegungen zum Verhältnis von Jer. 1, 18–19 zu Jer. 15, 20–21', *Biblica* 54, 1–24

Kaiser, O. (1974), *Isaiah 13–39: A Commentary*, OTL, SCM Press

— (1975), *Introduction to the Old Testament: A Presentation of its Results and Problems*, Basil Blackwell

— (1983), *Isaiah 1–12: A Commentary*, OTL, 2nd ed., SCM Press

Kant, I. (1963), 'Idea for a Universal History from a Cosmopolitan Point of View', *On History*, ed. L. W. Beck, Bobbs-Merrill

Katzenstein, H. J. (1983), ' "Before Pharaoh conquered Gaza" (Jeremiah xlvii 1)', *VT* 33, 249–51

Kaufmann, Y. (1972), *The Religion of Israel: From Its Beginnings to the Babylonian Exile*, Schocken Books

Kenik, H. A. (1983), *Design for Kingship: The Deuteronomistic Narrative Technique in 1 Kings 3:4–15*, SBL DS 69, Scholars Press

Kessler, M. (1966), 'Form-Critical Suggestions on Jer. 36', *CBQ* 28, 389–401

— (1968), 'Jeremiah Chapters 26–45 Reconsidered', *JNES* 25, 81–8

— (1972), 'From Drought to Exile: A Morphological Study of Jer. 14:1–15:4', *Proceedings of the Society of Biblical Literature*, 501–25

Kierkegaard, S. (1967), 'The Disciple at Second Hand', *Philosophical Fragments or A Fragment of Philosophy*, Princeton Paperback, Princeton University Press

Kingsbury, E. C. (1964), 'The Prophets and the Council of Yahweh', *JBL* 83, 279–86

Klein, R. W. (1974), *Textual Criticism of the Old Testament: The Septuagint after Qumran*, Guides to Biblical Scholarship: OT Series, Fortress Press

Klopfenstein, M. A. (1964), *Die Lüge nach dem Alten Testament: ihr Begriff, ihre Bedeutung und ihre Beurteilung*, Gotthelf

Koch, K. (1969), *The Growth of the Biblical Tradition: The Form-Critical Method*, Adam and Charles Black

— (1983), *The Prophets*: II *The Babylonian and Persian Periods*, SCM Press

Köhler, L. (1909), 'Beobachtungen am hebräischen und griechischen Text von Jeremia Kap. 1–9', *ZAW* 29, 1–39

— (1934), 'Vom alttestamentlichen Wörterbuch', *Monatsschrift für Geschichte und Wissenschaft des Judentums* 78, 1–6

— (1956), *Hebrew Man: Lectures Delivered at the Invitation of the University of Tübingen December 1–16, 1952*, SCM Press

Krašovec, J. (1984), *Antithetic Structure in Biblical Hebrew Poetry*, SVT 35, E. J. Brill

Kraus, H.-J. (1964), *Prophetie in der Krisis: Studien zu Texten aus dem Buch Jeremia*, Biblische Studien 43, Neukirchener Verlag

— (1966), *Worship in Israel: A Cultic History of the Old Testament*, Basil Blackwell

Kremers, H. (1953), 'Leidensgemeinschaft mit Gott im Alten Testament: Eine Untersuchung der "biographischen" Berichte im Jeremiabuch', *EvTh* 13, 122–40

Kselman, J. S. (1970), 'A Note on Jer. 49, 20 and Ze. 2, 6–7', *CBQ* 32, 579–81

Kugel, J. L. (1981), *The Idea of Biblical Poetry: Parallelism and its History*, Yale University Press

Kuschke, A. (1961), 'Jeremia xlviii, 1–8: Zugleich ein Beitrag zur historische Topographie Moab', *Verbannung und Heimkehr: Beiträge zur Geschichte und Theologie Israels im 6. und 5. Jahrh. v. Chr.* (FS W. Rudolph), 181–96

Kutsch, E. (1973), *Verheissung und Gesetz: Untersuchungen zum sogenannten 'Bund' im Alten Testament*, BZAW 131, Walter de Gruyter

— (1981), 'Weisheitsspruch und Prophetenwort: Zur Traditionsgeschichte des Spruches Jer. 9, 22–23', *BZ* 25, 161–79

Labuschagne, C. J. (1966), *The Incomparability of Yahweh in the Old Testament*, E. J. Brill

Landsberger, F. (1949), 'The House of the People', *HUCA* 22, 149–55

Landes, G. M. (1956), 'The Fountain at Jezer,' *BASOR* 144, 30–7

Lang, B. (1983), *Monotheism and the Prophetic Minority: An Essay in Biblical History and Sociology*, The Social World of Biblical Antiquity 1, The Almond Press

Langkammer, H. (1965), 'Der übernaturliche Charakter des Berufungserlebnisses des Propheten Jeremias: Ein Beitrag zu den Erklärungen der Prophetenekstaste', *Freiburger Zeitschrift für Philosophie und Theologie* 12, 426–38

Lehmann, M. R. (1953), 'A New Interpretation of the Term *sdmwt*', *VT* 3, 361–71

Lemche, N. P. (1976), 'The Manumission of Slaves – The Fallow Year — The Sabbatical Year – The Jobel Year', *VT* 26, 38–59

Lemke, W. E. (1966), 'Nebuchadrezzar, My Servant', *CBQ* 28, 45–50

— (1981), 'The Near and the Distant God: A Study of Jer. 23:23–24 in its Biblical Theological Context', *JBL* 100, 541–55

Levenson, J. D. (1984a), 'The Last Four Verses of Kings', *JBL* 103, 153–61
— (1984b), 'The Temple and the World', *JR* 64, 275–98
Levin, C. (1981), 'Noch einmal: die Anfänge des Propheten Jeremia', *VT* 31, 428–40
Limburg, J. (1969), 'The Root *ryb* and the Prophetic Lawsuit Speeches', *JBL* 88, 291–304
Lindars, B. (1961), *New Testament Apologetic: The Doctrinal Significance of the Old Testament Quotations*, SCM Press
— (1979), 'Rachel Weeping for her Children – Jeremiah 31.15–22', *JSOT* 12, 47–62
Lindblom, J. (1962), *Prophecy in Ancient Israel*, Basil Blackwell
Lindström, F. (1983), *God and the Origin of Evil: A Contextual Analysis of Alleged Monistic Evidence in the Old Testament*, CB:OTS 21, C. W. K. Gleerup
Lohfink, N. (1981), 'Der junge Jeremia als Propagandist und Poet: Zum Grundstock von Jer. 30–31', Bogaert 1981c, 351–68
Long, B. O. (1976), 'The Stylistic Components of Jeremiah 3.1–5', *ZAW* 88, 386–90
Loretz, O. (1970), 'Die Sprüche Jeremias in Jer. 1, 17–9, 25', *UF* 2, 109–30
Lundbom, J. R. (1975), *Jeremiah: A Study in Ancient Hebrew Rhetoric*, SBL DS 18, Scholars Press
Lust, J. (1981), ' "Gathering and Return" in Jeremiah and Ezekiel', Bogaert 1981c, 119–42
Lys, D. (1979), 'Jérémie 28 et le problème du faux prophète ou la circulation du sens dans le diagnostic prophétique', *RHPhR* 59, 453–82
McCarthy, C. (1981), *The Tiqqune Sopherim and Other Theological Corrections in the Masoretic Text of the Old Testament*, Orbis Biblicus et Orientalis 36, Vandenhoeck und Ruprecht
McCarthy, D. J. (1972), '*b^e^rīt* in Old Testament History and Theology', *Biblica* 53, 110–21
— (1978), *Treaty and Covenant: A Study in the Ancient Oriental Documents and in the Old Testament*, Analecta Biblica 21A, new edition completely rewritten, Biblical Institute Press
McKane, W. (1965a), 'The Interpretation of Jeremiah xii 1–5', *TGUOS* 20, 38–48
— (1965b), *Prophets and Wise Men*, SBT 44, SCM Press
— (1970), *Proverbs: A New Approach*, OTL, SCM Press

— (1972), 'Jeremiah II 23–25: Observations on the Versions and History of Exegesis', *OTS* XVII, 73–88

— (1974), 'Observations on the TIḲḲÛNÊ SÔPᵉRÎM', *On Language, Culture, and Religion: In Honor of Eugene A Nida*, ed. M. Black and W. A. Smalley, Mouton, 53–77

— (1978), 'Jeremiah 13:12–14: A Problematic Proverb', *Israelite Wisdom (FS Terrien)*, 107–19

— (1980a), '*mś'* in Jeremiah 23, 33–40', *Prophecy: Essays presented to Georg Fohrer on his sixty-fifth birthday 6 September 1980*, BZAW 150, ed. J. A. Emerton, Walter de Gruyter, 35–54

— (1980b), 'Poison, Trial by Ordeal and the Cup of Wrath', *VT* 30, 474–92

— (1981), 'Relations Between Poetry and Prose in the Book of Jeremiah with Special Reference to Jeremiah III 6–11 and XII 14–17', *Congress Volume: Vienna 1980*, SVT 32, ed. J. A. Emerton, E. J. Brill, 220–37 (= Perdue and Kovacs, 269–84)

— (1982), 'The Construction of Jeremiah Chapter XXI', *VT* 32, 59–73

McKay, J. W. (1973), *Religion in Judah under the Assyrians 732-609 BC*, SBT SS 26, SCM Press

Mackie, J. L. (1982), *The Miracle of Theism: Arguments for and against the Existence of God*, Clarendon Press

Malamat, A. (1966), 'Prophetic revelations in New Documents from Mari and the Bible', *Volume de Congrès: Genève 1965*, SVT 15, E. J. Brill, 207–27

— (1968), 'The Last Kings of Judah and the Fall of Jerusalem', *IEJ* 18, 137–56

March, W. E. (1970), 'Jeremiah 1: Commission and Assurance. A Study of the Form, Composition, and Some Theological Implications of Jeremiah 1', *Austin Seminary Bulletin: Faculty edition* 86/1, 5–38

Margaliot, M. (1980), 'Jeremiah X 1–16: A Re-examination', *VT* 30, 295–308

Margalit, B. (1980), *A Matter of 'Life' and 'Death': A Study of the Baal-Mot Epic (CTA 4–5–6)*, AOAT 206, Neukirchener Verlag

Marrow, S. (1965), 'Ḥāmās ("violentia") in Jer. 20, 8', *Verbum Domini* 43, 241–55

Martin, J. D. (1969), 'The Forensic Background to Jeremiah III 1', *VT* 19, 82–92

Martin-Achard, R. (1974), 'Quelques remarques sur la nouvelle alliance chez Jérémie (Jérémie 31, 31–34)', *Questions disputées d'Ancien Testament: Méthode et Théologie*, BETL 33, ed. C. Brekelmans, Leuven University Press, 141–64

Mauser, U. (1971), 'Jeremia', *Gottesbild und Menschwerdung: Eine Untersuchung zur Einheit des Alten und Neuen Testaments*, Beiträge zur historischen Theologie 43, J. C. B. Mohr (Paul Siebeck), 78–114

May, H. G. (1942), 'Towards an Objective Approach to the Book of Jeremiah: The Biographer', *JBL* 61, 139–55

— (1955), 'Some Cosmic Connotations of *Mayim Rabbim*, "Many Waters" ', *JBL* 74, 9–21

— (1956), 'Some Historical Perspectives', *A Stubborn Faith: Papers on Old Testament and Related Subjects Presented to Honor WILLIAM ANDREW IRWIN*, ed. E. C. Hobbs, Southern Methodist University Press, 100–16

Mayes, A. D. H. (1979), *Deuteronomy*, NCBC, Oliphants

— (1983), *The Story of Israel between Settlement and Exile: A Redactional Study of the Deuteronomistic History*, SCM Press

Mays, J. L. (1976), *Micah: A Commentary*, OTL, SCM Press

Mendecki, N. (1983), 'Die Sammlung und die Hineinführung in das Land in Jer. 23, 3', *Kairos* 25, 99–103

Mendelsohn, I. (1949), *Slavery in the Ancient Near East: A Comparative Study of Slavery in Babylonia, Assyria, Syria, and Palestine from the Middle of the Third Millennium to the End of the First Millennium*, Oxford University Press, New York

Mendenhall, G. E. (1973), *The Tenth Generation: The Origins of the Biblical Tradition*, The Johns Hopkins University Press

Mettinger, T. N. D. (1982), *The Dethronement of Sabaoth: Studies in the Shem and Kabod Theologies*, CB:OTS 18, CWK Gleerup

Meyer, I. (1977), *Jeremia und die falschen Propheten*, Orbis Biblicus et Orientalis 13, Vandenhoeck und Ruprecht

Michaud, H. (1960), 'La vocation du "prophète des nations" ', *Maqqēl shāqedh: la branche d'amandier – Hommage à W. Vischer*, Causse Graille Castlenau, 157–64

Migsch, H. (1981), *Gottes Wort über das Ende Jerusalems: Eine literatur-, stil- und gattungskritische Untersuchung des Berichtes Jeremia 34, 1–7; 32, 2–5; 37, 3–38, 28*, Österreichisches Biblische Studien 2, Österreichisches Katholisches Bibelwerk

Milgrom, J. (1955), 'The Date of Jeremiah, Chapter 2', *JNES* 14, 65–9

Millar, W. R. (1976), *Isaiah 24–27 and the Origin of Apocalyptic*, HSMS 11, Scholars Press

Miller, J. W. (1955), *Das Verhältnis Jeremias und Hesekiels sprachlich und theologisch untersucht mit besonderer Berücksichtung der Prosareden Jeremias*, Van Gorcum's theologische Bibliothek 28, Van Gorcum

Miller, P. D. Jr (1982), *Sin and Judgment in the Prophets: A Stylistic and Theological Analysis*, SBL MS 27, Scholars Press

— (1983), 'Trouble and Woe: Interpreting the Biblical Laments', *Interpr* 37, 32–45

Moore, C. A. (1977), *Daniel, Esther and Jeremiah: The Additions. A New Translation with Introduction and Commentary*, AB 44, Doubleday and Company

Moran, W. L. (1958), 'Ugaritic *ṣîṣūma* and Hebrew *ṣîṣ* (Ecclus 43, 19; Jer. 48, 9)', *Biblica* 39, 69–71

— (1969), 'New Evidence from Mari on the History of Prophecy', *Biblica* 50, 15–56

Mottu, H. (1975), 'Jeremiah vs. Hananiah: Ideology and Truth in Old Testament Prophecy', *Radical Religion* 2.2/3, Community for Religious Research and Education, Berkeley, 58–67 (= *The Bible and Liberation: Political and Social Hermeneutics*, ed. N. K. Gottwald, Orbis Books 1983, 235–51)

Mowinckel, S. (1914), *Zur Komposition des Buches Jeremia*, Jacob Dybwad

— (1942), 'La connaissance de Dieu chez les prophètes de l'Ancien Testament (1)', *RHPhR* 22, 69–105

— (1946), *Prophecy and Tradition: The Prophetic Books in the Light of the Study of the Growth and History of the Tradition*, Avhandlinger utgitt av Det Norske Videnskaps-Akademi i Oslo II. Hist.-Filos. Klasse 1946 No. 3, Jacob Dybwad

— (1962), *The Psalms in Israel's Worship*, 2 vols, Basil Blackwell

Muilenburg, J. (1970), 'Baruch the Scribe', Durham and Porter, 215–38

Mullen, E. T., Jr. (1980), *The Assembly of the Gods in Canaanite and Early Hebrew Literature*, HSM 24, Scholars Press

Neher, A. (1960), *Jérémie*, Libraire Plon

Neumann, P. K. D. (1973), 'Das Wort, Das Geschehen Ist . . . zum Problem der Wortempfangsterminologie in Jer. I–XXV', *VT* 23, 171–217

— (1975), *Hört das Wort Jahwäs: Ein Beitrag zur Komposition alttestamentlicher Schriften*, Stiftung Europa-Kolleg Hamburg 30, Fundament-Verlag Dr Sasse and Co

Nicholson, E. W. (1970), *Preaching to the Exiles: A Study of the Prose Tradition in the Book of Jeremiah*, Basil Blackwell

— (1977), 'Blood-spattered Altars?', *VT* 27, 113–6

Niditch, S. (1983), *The Symbolic Vision in Biblical Tradition*, HSM 30, Scholars Press

Nötscher, F. (1953), 'Zum emphatischen lamedh', *VT* 3, 370–80

Ochshorn, J. (1981), *The Female Experience and the Nature of the Divine*, Indiana University Press

Oded, B. (1977), 'Judah and the Exile', *Israelite and Judaean History*, ed. J. H. Hayes & J. M. Miller, OTL, SCM Press, 435–88

Ogden, G. S. (1982), 'Prophetic Oracles Against Foreign Nations and Psalms of Communal Lament: The Relationship of Psalm 137 to Jeremiah 49: 7–22 and Obadiah', *JSOT* 24, 89–97

Ong, W. J. (1982), *Orality and Literacy: The Technologizing of the Word*, New Accents, Methuen

Orr, A. (1946), 'The Seventy Years of Babylon', *VT* 6, 304–6

Osswald, E. (1962), *Falsche Prophetie im Alten Testament*, Sammlung gemeinverständlicher Vorträge und Schriften aus dem Gebiet der Theologie und Religionsgeschichte 237, J. C. B. Mohr

Overholt, T. W. (1965), 'The Falsehood of Idolatry: An Interpretation of Jeremiah x.1–16', *JTS* 16, 1–16

— (1968), 'King Nebuchadnezzar in the Jeremiah Tradition', *CBQ* 30, 39–48

— (1970), *The Threat of Falsehood: A Study in the Theology of the Book of Jeremiah*, SBT SS 16, SCM Press

— (1971), 'Some Reflections on the Date of Jeremiah's Call', *CBQ* 33, 165–84

— (1979), 'Rhetorical Questions in Jeremiah 2', *CBQ* 41, 262–73

Paul, S. (1969), 'Literary and Ideological Echoes of Jeremiah in Deutero-Isaiah', *Proceedings of the Fifth World Congress of Jewish Studies* I, ed. P. Peli, World Union of Jewish Studies, 102–20

Pearce, R. A. (1973), 'Shiloh and Jer. VII 12, 14, and 15', *VT* 23, 105–8

Perdue, L. G. (1984), 'Jeremiah in Modern Research: Approaches and Issues', Perdue and Kovacs, 1–32

Perdue, L. G. and Kovacs, B. W. (1984) (eds), *A Prophet to the Nations: Essays in Jeremiah Studies*, Eisenbrauns

Perlitt, L. (1961), *Bundestheologie im Alten Testament*, WMANT 36, Neukirchener Verlag

— (1971), 'Die Verborgenheit Gottes', *Probleme biblischer Theologie: Gerhard von Rad zum 70. Geburtstag*, ed. H. W. Wolff, Christian Kaiser Verlag, 367–82

Petersen, D. L. (1977), *Late Israelite Prophecy: Studies in Deutero-Prophetic Literature and in Chronicles*, SBL MS 23, Scholars Press

— (1985), *Haggai and Zechariah 1–8*, OTL, SCM Press

Pfeiffer, R. H. (1941), *Introduction to the Old Testament*, 2nd ed., Harper and Brothers

Phillips, A. (1975), 'NEBALAH – A Term for Serious Disorderly and Unruly Conduct', *VT* 25, 237–42

Plöger, O. (1968), *Theocracy and Eschatology*, Basil Blackwell

Pohlmann, K.-F. (1978), *Studien zum Jeremiabuch: Ein Beitrag zur Frage nach der Entstehung des Jeremiabuches*, FRLANT 118, Vandenhoeck und Ruprecht

Polk, T. (1984), *The Prophetic Persona: Jeremiah and the Language of the Self*, JSOT SS 32, JSOT Press

Polley, M. E. (1980), 'Hebrew Prophecy within the Council of Yahweh, Examined in its Ancient Near Eastern Setting', *Scripture in Context: Essays on the Comparative Method*, ed. C. D. Evans, W. W. Hallo, and J. B. White, Pittsburgh Theological Monograph Series 34, The Pickwick Press, 141–56

Pope, M. (1977), 'Notes on the Rephaim Texts from Ugarit', *Essays on the Ancient Near East in Memory of Jacob Joel Finkelstein*, Memoirs of the Connecticut Academy of Arts and Sciences 19, ed. M. de Jong Ellis, Archon Books, 163–82

Porten, B. (1968), *Archives from Elephantine: The Life of an Ancient Jewish Military Colony*, University of California Press

Pritchard, J. B. (1969) (ed.), *Ancient Near Eastern Texts Relating to the Old Testament*, 3rd ed. with Supplement, Princeton University Press

von Rad, G. (1962), *Old Testament Theology*: I *The Theology of Israel's Historical Traditions*, Oliver and Boyd (reissued SCM Press 1975)

— (1965), *Old Testament Theology*: II *The Theology of Israel's Prophetic Traditions*, Oliver and Boyd (reissued SCM Press 1975)

— (1972), *Wisdom in Israel*, SCM Press

Rahlfs, A. (1935), (ed.), *Septuaginta*: II *Libri poetici et prophetici*, 7th ed., Württembergische Bibelanstalt, Stuttgart

Raitt, T. M. (1977), *A Theology of Exile: Judgment/Deliverance in Jeremiah and Ezekiel*, Fortress Press

Ramsey, G. W. (1977), 'Speech-Forms in Hebrew Law and Prophetic Oracles', *JBL* 96, 40–58

Rast, W. E. (1977), 'Cakes for the Queen of Heaven', *Scripture in History and Theology: Essays in Honor of J. Coert Rylaarsdam*, ed. A. L. Merrill and T. W. Overholt, The Pickwick Press, 168–80

Rendtorff, R. (1954), 'Zum Gebrauch der Formel *n^{e}'um jahwe* im Jeremiabuch', *ZAW* 66, 27–37

Reventlow, H. G. (1962), *Das Amt des Propheten bei Amos*, FRLANT 80, Vandenhoeck und Ruprecht

— (1963), *Liturgie und prophetisches Ich bei Jeremia*, Gütersloher Verlagshaus Gerd Mohn

— (1969), 'Gattung und Überlieferung in der "Tempelrede Jeremias", Jer. 7 und 26', *ZAW* 81, 315–52

Rhodes, A. B. (1977), 'Israel's Prophets as Intercessors', *Scripture in History and Theology* (Essays Rylaarsdam), 107–28

Richter, W. (1970), *Die sogenannten vorprophetischen Berufungsberichte: Eine literaturwissenschaftliche Studie zu 1 Sam. 9, 1–10, 16, Ex. 3f. und Ri. 6, 11b–17*, FRLANT 101, Vandenhoeck und Ruprecht

Rietzschel, C. (1966), *Das Problem der Urrolle: Ein Beitrag zur Redaktionsgeschichte des Jeremiabuches*, Gütersloher Verlaghaus Gerd Mohn

Robinson, H. W. (1944), 'The Council of Yahweh', *JTS* 45, 151–7

Robinson, T. H. (1918), 'The Structure of Jeremiah 50, 51', *JTS* 19, 251–65

— (1924), 'Baruch's Roll', *ZAW* 42, 209–221

Rowley, H. H. (1962), 'The Early Prophecies of Jeremiah in Their Setting', *BJRL* 45, 198–234 (= Perdue and Kovacs, 33–61)

Rudolph, W. (1963), 'Jesaja xv–xvi', *Hebrew and Semitic Studies presented to Godfrey Rolles Driver in celebration of his seventieth birthday 20 August 1962*, ed. D. W. Thomas and W. D. McHardy, Clarendon Press, 130–43

Saggs, H. W. F. (1978), *The Encounter with the Divine in Mesopotamia and Israel*, Athlone Press

Sarna, N. (1973), 'Zedekiah's Emancipation of Slaves and the Sabbatical Year', *Orient and Occident: Essays presented to Cyrus H. Gordon on the occasion of his sixty-fifth birthday*, AOAT 22, ed. H. A. Hoffner, Neukirchener Verlag, 143–9

Sawyer, J. F. A. (1978), 'A Note on the Brooding Partridge in Jeremiah xvii 11', *VT* 28, 324–9

Schafer, B. E. (1971), '*mbḥwr/mbḥr* = Fortress', *CBQ* 33, 389–96

Scharbert, J. (1964), *Heilsmittler im Alten Testament und im Alten Orient*, Quaestiones disputatae 23/24, Herder

Schechter, S. (1961), *Aspects of Rabbinic Theology*, new ed., Schocken Books

Schmidt, K. W. (1982), 'Prophetic Delegation: A Form-Critical Inquiry', *Biblica* 63, 206–18

Schmidt, W. H. (1965), 'Die deuteronomistische Redaktion des Amosbuches: Zu den theologischen Unterschieden zwischen dem Prophetenwort und seinem Sammler', *ZAW* 77, 168–93

— (1984), *Introduction to the Old Testament*, SCM Press

Schmitt, J. (1983), 'The Gender of Israel', *JSOT* 26, 115–25

Schoneveld, J. (1976), *The Bible in Israeli Education: A Study of Approaches to the Hebrew Bible and its Teaching in Israeli Educational Literature*, Van Gorcum

Schottroff, W. (1966), 'Horonaim, Nimrim, Luhith und der Westrand des "Landes Ataroth", ein Beitrag zur historischen Topographie des Landes Moab', *Zeitschrift des Deutschen Palästina-Vereins* 82, 163–208

— (1970), 'Jeremia 2, 1–3: Erwägungen zur Methode der Prophetenexegese', *ZTK* 67, 263–94

Schulz, H. (1969), *Das Todesrecht im Alten Testament: Studien zur Rechtsform der Mot-Jumat-Sätze*, BZAW 114, Verlag Alfred Töpelmann

Seebass, H. (1970), 'Jeremias Konflikt mit Chananja: Bemerkungen zu Jer. 27 und 28', *ZAW* 82, 449–52

Seeligmann, I. L. (1977), 'Die Auffassung von der Prophetie in der deuteronomistischen und chronistischen Geschichtsschreibung (mit einem Exkurs über das Buch Jeremia)', *Congress Volume: Göttingen 1977*, SVT 29, 254–84

Seidl, T. (1978), *Formen und Formeln in Jeremia 27–29: Eine literaturwissenschaftliche Untersuchung* 2, Arbeiten zu Text und Sprache im Alten Testament 5, Eos Verlag

Simon, U. (1960), 'The Mysticism of Jeremiah', *Church Quarterly Review* 161, 270–9

Skinner, J. (1922), *Prophecy and Religion: Studies in the Life of Jeremiah*, Cambridge University Press

Smit, E. J. (1966), 'Death and Burial Formulas in Kings and Chronicles relating to the Kings of Judah', *Die Ou-Testamentiese Werkgemeenschap van Suidaafrika*, 173–7

Smith, G. V. (1979), 'Use of Quotations in Jer. xv.11–14', *VT* 29, 229–31

Smith, J. Z. (1982), 'Fences and Neighbors: Some Contours of Early Judaism', *Imagining Religion: From Babylon to Jonestown*, The University of Chicago Press, 1–18

Smith, M. (1971), *Palestinian Parties and Politics That Shaped the Old Testament*, Columbia University Press

— (1975), 'The Veracity of Ezekiel, the Sins of Manasseh, and Jeremiah 44 18', *ZAW* 87, 11–16

— (1984), 'Jewish Religious Life in the Persian Period', *CHJ* 1, 219–78

Snaith, N. H. (1966), 'The Cult of Molech', *VT* 16, 123–4

Soggin, J. A. (1960), 'Der prophetische Gedanke über den Heiligen Krieg als Gericht gegen Israel', *VT* 10, 79–83 (= 'The Prophets on Holy War as Judgment against Israel', Soggin 1975, 67–77)

— (1975), *Old Testament and Oriental Studies*, Biblica et Orientalia 29, Biblical Institute Press

— (1975a), ' "Your Conduct in the Valley": A Note on Jeremiah 2, 23a', Soggin 1975, 78–83

— (1975b), 'The "Negation" in Jeremiah 4, 27 and 5, 10a, cf. 5, 18b', Soggin 1975, 179–83

— (1981), 'The Ark of the Covenant, Jeremiah 3, 16', Bogaert 1981c, 215–21

— (1984), *A History of Israel: From the Beginnings to the Bar Kochba Revolt, AD 135*, SCM Press

Southwood, C. H. (1979), 'The spoiling of Jeremiah's girdle (Jer. XIII 1–11)', *VT* 29, 231–7

Sparks, H. F. D. (1984) (ed.), *The Apocryphal Old Testament*, Clarendon Press

Steck, O. H. (1967), *Israel und das gewaltsame Geschick der Propheten: Untersuchungen zur Überlieferung des deuteronomischen Geschichtsbildes im Alten Testament, Spätjudentum und Urchristentum*, WMANT 23, Neukirchener Verlag

Steiner, G. (1985), 'Our Homeland, the Text,' *Selmagundi* 66, 4–25

Steinmann, J. (1952), *Le prophète Jérémie: Sa vie, son oeuvre et son temps*, Lectio divina 9, Editions du Cerf

Stoebe, H.-J. (1964), 'Jeremia, Prophet und Seelsorger', *TZ* 20, 385–409

Streane, A. W. (1896), *The Double Text of Jeremiah (Massoretic and Alexandrian) Compared Together with an Appendix on the Old Latin Evidence*, Deighton Bell and Co., Cambridge; London, George Bell and Sons

Sturdy, J. V. M. (1980), 'The authorship of the "prose sermons" of Jeremiah', *Prophecy* (Essays Fohrer), BZAW 150, 143–50

Swetnam, J. (1965), 'Some Observations on the Background of *ṣaddīq* in Jer. 23:5a', *Biblica* 46, 29–40

— (1974), 'Why was Jeremiah's New Covenant New?', *Studies on Prophecy: A Collection of Twelve Papers*, SVT 26, 111–5

Tadmor, H. (1966), 'Philistia Under Assyrian Rule', *BA* 29/3, 86–101

Thiel, W. (1970), '*Hēfēr b*ᵉ*rīt*: Zum Bundbrechen', *VT* 20, 214–29

— (1973), *Die deuteronomistische Redaktion von Jeremia 1–25*, WMANT 41, Neukirchener Verlag

— (1981), *Die deuteronomistische Redaktion von Jeremia 26–95*, WMANT 52, Neukirchener Verlag

Thomas, D. W. (1938), 'A Note on *w*ᵉ*lō yāda'ū* in Jeremiah 14:18', *JTS* 39, 273–4

— (1952a), '*ml'w* in Jeremiah IV.5: A Military Term', *JJS* 2, 47–52

— (1952b), 'A Note on *mū'ādīm* in Jeremiah 24, 1', *JTS* 3, 55

Tov, E. (1972), 'L'incidence de la critique textuelle sur la critique littéraire dans le livre de Jérémie', *RB* 79, 189–99

— (1975), (ed. and trs), *The Book of Baruch: Also called I Baruch (Greek and Hebrew)*, Texts and Translations 8: Pseudepigrapha series 6, Scholars Press

— (1976), *The Septuagint Translation of Jeremiah and Baruch: A Discussion of an Early Revision of the LXX of Jeremiah 29–52 and Baruch 1:1–3:8*, HSM 8, Scholars Press

— (1979), 'Exegetical Notes on the Hebrew Vorlage of the LXX of Jeremiah 27 (34)', *ZAW* 91, 73–93

— (1981), 'Some Aspects of the Textual and Literary History of the Book of Jeremiah', Bogaert 1981c, 145–67

Trible, P. (1976), 'The Gift of a Poem: A Rhetorical Study of Jeremiah 31:15–22', *Andover Newton Quarterly* 17, 271–80

— (1978), *God and the Rhetoric of Sexuality*, Overtures to Biblical Theology 2, Fortress Press

van Rossum, J. (1970), 'Wanneer is Silo verwoest?', *Nederlands Theologisch Tijdschrift* 24, 321–32

Van Seters, J. (1972), 'Confessional Reformulation in the Exilic Period', *VT* 22, 448–59

— (1975), *Abraham in History and Tradition*, Yale University Press

van der Woude, A. S. (1969), 'Micah in Dispute with the Pseudo-prophets', *VT* 19, 244–60

van Zyl, A. H. (1960), *The Moabites*, E. J. Brill

Vawter, B. (1985), 'Were the Prophets *nābī's*?', *Biblica* 66, 206–20

Vermeylen, J. (1981), 'Essai de Redaktionsgeschichte des "Confessions de Jérémie" ', Bogaert 1981c, 239–70

Vincent, J. M. (1977), *Studien zur literarischen Eigenart und zur geistigen Heimat von Jesaja, Kap. 40–55*, Beiträge zur Biblischen Exegese und Theologie 5, Peter Lang

Wambacq, B. N. (1974), 'Jérémie, X, 1–16', *RB* 81, 57–62

Wanke, G. (1971), *Untersuchungen zur sogenannten Baruchschrift*, BZAW 122, Walter de Gruyter

— (1980), 'Jeremias Besuch beim Töpfer: Eine motivkritische Untersuchung zu Jer 18', *Prophecy* (Essays Fohrer), BZAW 150, 151–62

Watson, W. G. E. (1984), *Classical Hebrew Poetry: A Guide to its Techniques*, JSOT SS 26, JSOT Press

Watters, W. R. (1976), *Formula Criticism and the Poetry of the Old Testament*, BZAW 138, Walter de Gruyter

Weidner, E. F. (1939), 'Jojachin, König von Juda, in babylonischen Keilinschrifttexten', *Mélanges syriens offerts à Monsieur René Dussaud* II, 923–35

Weinfeld, M. (1969), 'The Moloch cult in Israel and its background'

(Hebrew with English summary), *Proceedings of the Fifth World Congress of Jewish Studies*, 37–61, 227–8
— (1972a), *Deuteronomy and the Deuteronomic School*, Clarendon Press
— (1972b), 'The Worship of Molech and the Queen of Heaven and its Background', *UF* 4, 133–54 (based on 1969 lecture)
— (1976), 'Jeremiah and the Spiritual Metamorphosis of Israel', *ZAW* 88, 17–56
Weippert, H. (1971), 'Jahwekrieg und Bundesfluch in Jer. 21:1–7', *ZAW* 83, 396–409
— (1972), 'Die "deuteronomistischen" Beurteilungen der Könige von Israel und Juda und das Problem der Redaktion der Königsbücher', *Biblica* 53, 301–39
— (1973), *Die Prosareden des Jeremiabuches*, BZAW 132, Walter de Gruyter
— (1979), 'Das Wort vom neuen Bund in Jeremia XXXI 31–34', *VT* 29, 336–51
— (1981a), 'Der Beitrag ausserbiblischer Prophetentexte zum Verständnis der Prosareden des Jeremiabuches', Bogaert 1981c, 83–104
— (1981b), *Schöpfer des Himmels und der Erde: Ein Beitrag zur Theologie des Jeremiabuches*, Stuttgarter Bibelstudien 102, Verlag Katholisches Bibelwerk
Weippert, M. (1972), ' "Heiliger Krieg" in Israel und Assyrien: Kritische Anmerkungen zu Gerhard von Rads Konzept des "Heiligen Krieges im alten Israel" ', *ZAW* 84, 460–93
Welten, P. (1977), 'Leiden und Leidenserfahrung im Buch Jeremia', *ZTK* 74, 123–50
Wessels, W. J. (1984), 'Towards a Historical-ideological Understanding of Jeremiah 22:13–19', *OTE* 2,61–80
Westermann, C. (1964), 'The Way of the Promise through the Old Testament', *The Old Testament and Christian Faith*, ed. B. W. Anderson, 200–24
— (1967), *Basic Forms of Prophetic Speech*, Lutterworth Press
— (1969), *Isaiah 40–66: A Commentary*, OTL, SCM Press
— (1979), *Genesis*, BKAT I, Neukirchener Verlag
— (1981a), *Praise and Lament in the Psalms*, T. and T. Clark
— (1981b), *The Structure of the Book of Job: A Form-Critical Analysis*, Fortress Press
Whallon, W. (1969), *Formula, Character, and Context: Studies in Homeric, Old English, and Old Testament Poetry*, The Centre for Hellenic Studies, Washington, DC
Whitley, C. F. (1954), 'The Term Seventy Years Captivity', *VT* 4, 60–72

— (1957), 'The Seventy Years of Desolation – A Rejoinder', *VT* 7, 416–18
— (1964), 'The Date of Jeremiah's Call', *VT* 14, 467–83
Wiesel, E. (1981), 'Jeremiah', *Five Biblical Portraits*, University of Notre Dame Press, 97–127
Wijngaards, J. (1965), '*hwsy*' and *h'lh*: A Twofold Approach to the Exodus', *VT* 15, 91–102
Wiklander, B. (1978), 'The Context and Meaning of NHR 'L in Jer. 51:44', *SEÅ* 43, 40–64
Wildberger, H. (1942), *Jahwewort und prophetische Rede bei Jeremia*, Zwingli Verlag, Zürich
— (1979), *Jesaja*, BKAT X/16, Neukirchener Verlag
Williams, P. H. (1965), 'The Fatal and Foolish Exchange: Living Water for "Nothings". A Study of Jeremiah 2:4–13', *Austin Seminary Bulletin: Faculty Edition* 81, 3–59
Williams, W. G. (1956), 'Jeremiah's Vision of the Almond Rod', *A Stubborn Faith* (Papers Irwin), 90–9
Williamson, H. G. M. (1977a), 'Eschatology in Chronicles', *TB* 28, 115–54
— (1977b), *Israel in the Books of Chronicles*, Cambridge University Press
— (1982), *1 and 2 Chronicles*, NCBC, Eerdmans/Marshall, Morgan and Scott
Wilson, J. V. K. (1982), 'Medicine in the Land and Times of the Old Testament', *Studies in the Period of David and Solomon and other essays*, ed., T. Ishida, Yamakawa-Shuppansha, 337–65
Wilson, R. R. (1980), *Prophecy and Society in Ancient Israel*, Fortress Press
— (1984), *Sociological Approaches to the Old Testament*, Guides to Biblical Scholarship: OT Series, Fortress Press
Wimmer, D. H. (1978), 'The Sociology of Knowledge and "The Confessions of Jeremiah" ', *Society of Biblical Literature: Seminar Papers* 114, 393–406
Winckler, H. (1903), E. Schrader, *Die Keilinschriften und das Alte Testament*, 3rd ed. by J. Zimmern and H. Winckler, Verlag von Reuther und Reichard
Wiseman, D. J. (1956), *Chronicles of Chaldaean Kings (625–556 B.C.) in the British Museum*, The Trustees of the British Museum
— (1958), 'The Vassal-Treaties of Esarhaddon', *Iraq* 20, 1–99
Wisser, L. (1983), *Jérémie, critique de la vie sociale: Justice sociale et connaissance de Dieu dans le livre de Jérémie*, Le Monde de la Bible, Labor et Fides, Genève
Wolff, C. (1976), *Jeremia im Frühjudentum und Urchristentum*, Texte und

Untersuchungen zur Geschichte der altchristlichen Literatur 118, Akademie Verlag, Berlin
Wolff, H. W. (1974), *Hosea: A Commentary on the Book of the Prophet Hosea*, Hermeneia, Fortress Press
— (1975), 'The Kerygma of the Deuteronomic Historical Work', W. Brueggemann and H. W. Wolff, *The Vitality of Old Testament Traditions*, John Knox Press, 83–100
— (1983), 'How Can We Recognize False Prophets? Criteria for the Difficult Task of Testing the Spirits', *Confrontations with Prophets: Discovering the Old Testament's New and Contemporary Significance*, Fortress Press, 63–76
Yamauchi, E. (1983), 'The Scythians: Invading Hordes from the Russian Steppes', *BA* 46/2, 90–9
Yaure, L. (1960), 'Elymas-Nehelamite-Pethor', *JBL* 79, 297–314
Yeivin, S. (1948), 'The Sepulcher of the Kings of the House of David', *JNES* 7, 30–45
Zenger, E. (1968), 'Die deuteronomistische Interpretation der Rehabilitierung Jojachins', *BZ* 12, 16–30
Zevit, Z. (1969), 'The Use of *'ebed* as a Diplomatic Term in Jeremiah', *JBL* 88, 74–7
Ziegler, J. (1958), *Beiträge zur Ieremias-Septuaginta*, Nachrichten der Akademie der Wissenschaften in Göttingen aus dem Jahre 1958: Philologisch-Historische Klass, Vandenhoeck und Ruprecht
Zimmerli, W. (1979), *Ezekiel 1: A Commentary on the Book of the Prophet Ezekiel, Chapters 1–24*, Heremeneia, Fortress Press
— (1981), 'Frucht der Anfechtung des Propheten', *Die Botschaft und die Boten: Festschrift für Hans Walter Wolff zum 70. Geburtstag*, ed. J. Jeremias and L. Perlitt, Neukirchener Verlag, 131–46 (= 'The Fruit of the Tribulation of the Prophet', Perdue and Kovacs, 349–65)
— (1982), 'Visionary Experience in Jeremiah', *Israel's Prophetic Tradition* (Essays Ackroyd), 95–118

INTRODUCTION

1. GENERAL REMARKS ON THE BOOK OF JEREMIAH

Placed between the books of Isaiah and Ezekiel, the book of Jeremiah is the longest of the three. According to 1.1–3 it purports to be the words of Jeremiah ben Hilkiah, who is identified as one of the priests who lived in Anathoth in Benjaminite territory. He is represented as being active in the period when the Assyrian imperial power was waning and Babylon was emerging as the new imperium in the ancient Near East. The book presents the downfall of the kingdom of Judah and the city of Jerusalem in the sixth century BCE in terms of the work and sayings of Jeremiah. Presented at certain points in the book as a prophet, Jeremiah emerges as a counterpoint to the collapse of Judaean culture. The few details of his life which appear in the text are tantalizingly incomplete and open to a variety of interpretations. At times he is associated with the temple in Jerusalem (e.g. 7.2; 19.1–2, 10–11, 14; 22.1; 26.2; 35.2), but more generally his movements are obscure and it is difficult to locate him in Jerusalem society with any degree of confidence. Neither a birth nor a death notice is provided for him, so the book cannot be considered to be a biography of Jeremiah (cf. Baltzer 1975, 113–28, for a different analysis of Jeremiah using an *Idealbiographie* genre).

The brevity of this introductory summary of the book of Jeremiah contrasts with the lengthy biographical accounts of the life of Jeremiah produced by many commentators on the book (e.g. Berridge, Bright, Holladay, Thompson) and pinpoints one of the central problems in the contemporary interpretation of Jeremiah. What status does the presentation of Jeremiah have in the book traditionally associated with his name? Is it historical, biographical, theological, imaginative, fictional or what? How may the genre(s) of the material be determined? The problem generates many questions, but few answers are forthcoming because the interpretation of the data is underdetermined by corroborative evidence. Commentaries follow a traditional or *a priori* position and analyse the different strands of material in the book in accordance with the option exercised. Thus the book is read by many exegetes as a historically accurate portrayal of the man Jeremiah and as representing a record of his sayings, deeds, adventures, and travels. On this reading it is firmly believed that in the book of Jeremiah we possess more information about the life and innermost thoughts of a prophet than from any other book in the Bible. This is the view of the majority of writers on Jeremiah, though dissenting voices have been heard in recent decades. The book may indeed be read in this fashion, but it is only one approach, and different readings may be obtained if the interpretative perspective is changed.

An *a posteriori* reading of the text may yield a very different understanding of the book of Jeremiah if certain features of the material are allowed to shape the interpretation. What these features are and how they may be read are the central issues in this introduction and inform the commentary which follows. To simplify a complex matter, the different approaches to the interpretation of the book of Jeremiah may be reduced to two categories: the life, words and deeds of the 'historical' Jeremiah approach and the editorial assemblage of many discrete levels of tradition constitutive of the book reading. These two distinctive analyses represent the core of contemporary Jeremiah studies (cf. Perdue 1984; also Crenshaw 1983), though there are many different readings of the text within the spectrum constituted by these two positions. If the first approach is virtually self-explanatory, the alternative reading of the tradition requires explanation and justification.

The fundamental difference between the two approaches is, in the first instance, due to the recognition that the anthologies traditionally known as the prophetic books are collections of discrete and disparate sayings. These sayings acquire their shape and force through the work of editors who have provided the *secondary* stages of the traditions by supplying details of speakers, places and occasions of utterances. Such details are *not* an integral element of the sayings and poems collected together, but are clearly editorial. It is in the development of the individual traditions that the so-called biographical elements appear (lacking in many of the anthologies) and at this level the 'life' of the speaker may be constructed to carry the tradition or appear as an epiphenomenon of the anthology. That this is the case will become apparent in the following analysis of the book of Jeremiah, but it may be seen in the editorial introductions to the prophetic collections and especially in Isa. 6–8; 36–39; Amos 7.10–17. These examples illustrate the way such material breaks up the flow of poems as well as raising serious problems of interpretation for the individual traditions. A counter-argument to this approach is made by some exegetes who regard the prophets as the editors and arrangers of their own material (e.g. Holladay, Lundbom), but this fails to make allowance for the development of motifs within the traditions due to changing circumstances and the passage of time. It also tends to homogenize discrete levels of tradition within a collection by harmonizing contrary and contradictory elements.

A cursory reading of the book of Jeremiah will demonstrate the fundamental point being made here (further readings may exacerbate the problem but should confirm this analysis). Collections of discrete poems are broken up by prose discourses in 2–25, with very little information provided to indicate when and where each individual item may have been spoken. Certain thematic collections may be detected (e.g. 4.5–6.26; 7.1–8.3; 21.11–23.6; 23.9–40), but prose and poetry switch back and forward and themes occur and recur. Then in the second half of the book (26–45) prose narratives dominate and the figure of Jeremiah emerges as a central actor in the life of the community. Only the occasional editorial note identifies Jeremiah as the speaker or actor in 2–25, so the two halves of the book are a stark contrast in presentation. What is the relation between these two parts of the tradition? Is everything to be determined by the redactional introduction to the book in 1.1–3 which attributes all the words to Jeremiah ben Hilkiah? The linguistic differences between the poems and the prose raise questions about the identity of the speaker of both types of material. That many of the prose discourses reflect a similar linguistic and semantic style to the writing found in Deuteronomy and the collection of Joshua – II Kings only complicates the problems of analysis. Further problems arise from a consideration of substantive elements within the tradition. In 2–25 the speaker is very hostile towards Judah and Jerusalem (the occasional fragment contradicts this attitude, cf. 3.14–18; 12.14–17; 16.14–17; 16.14–15; 23.5–6, 7–8), but in 30–31 (cf. 32–33) he is very friendly towards them. In 27–29 Jeremiah is represented as a friend and advocate of Babylon, but in 50–51 as its implacable enemy. The speaker of 2–23 is a vituperative opponent of the people of Judah and Jerusalem, yet in 24.5–7 speaks highly of and comfortingly to those people exiled to Babylon. Those who remain behind are denounced in even more extreme terms (cf. 24.8–10; 29.16–19), yet after the fall of Jerusalem are spoken to with kindness (42.7–12). Whether the setting is Jerusalem, Babylon or Egypt Jeremiah is represented as the one in control constantly proclaiming the divine word (cf. 27–29, 40–44). If the speaker of 2–25 appears to give the impression of being persecuted by the authorities (e.g. 20.1–6) or of being ignored, he is also presented as commanding the leaders of society to accompany him on some of his excursions (e.g. 19.1–2; cf. 35.1–11). Much of his movement is related to the temple (e.g. 7.2; 19.1–2, 10–11, 14; 22.1; 26.2; 29.25–29; 35.2), which suggests a figure of authority, yet on other occasions he appears to be barred from it (cf. 36.5; but contrast 35.2). The narratives show him as a man with powerful friends (e.g. 26.24; 36.4; 38.7–13, 14–16; 39.11–14; 40.1–6), yet some of the poems may be interpreted as the complaints of a solitary figure (e.g. 15.17). In 40.7–41.18 he is entirely absent from the narrative! The repetition of elements in different parts of the book complicates any account of the editing of the tradition (e.g. 6.22–24/50.41–43; 10.12–16/51.15–19; 16.14–15/23.7–8; 23.5–6/33.14–16; 23.19–20/30.23–24; 30.10–11/46.27–28; 49.19–21/50.44–46), but underlines the fundamental role of redaction in the construction of the book.

When to these examples are added the differences between the MT and G editions of the book (see 3, below), the case for a redactional analysis and interpretation of Jeremiah is overwhelming. A scrutiny of the book will reveal editorial divisions of it into four major blocks: 2–25; 26–36; 37–45; 46–51; with a prologue (1) and an epilogue (52; cf. II Kings 24.18–25.30). Further divisions may be detected, especially in 2–25 (see 7, below). Each division and subdivision is introduced by an editorial note identifying the contents of the section with the divine word spoken by Jeremiah. Thus the creation of the book of the words of Jeremiah as representing his inspired utterances is very much the work of the editorial schemata used to present the different levels of tradition grouped together in the book. Remove the editorial framework from the book, especially 2–25, and the figure of Jeremiah disappears from much of it. Only in a few narratives would he remain as an important element in the stories (e.g. 26; 28; 32.1–15; 35; 37–38; 40.1–6; 42.1–43.7). This feature of the way the book of Jeremiah is constructed may point to the origins of the figure of Jeremiah in the narratives rather than the poetry, and the history of the development of the tradition may need to be traced in terms of the prose material to which the poems have been added (cf. Kaiser 1983, 45 n.34). Such a hypothesis, which can only be suggested here rather than developed into a fully worked-out thesis, would help to account for the conflicting images of Jeremiah which abound in the tradition. Much of the conflict arises out of the conjunction of the different sub-divisions in the one book and the difficulty of reconciling the disparate *personae* of Jeremiah represented by the various levels of tradition in it. A redactional analysis, i.e. one which emphasizes the editorial contributions to the construction of the book, helps to explain the untidiness of the text and the problem created by the conflicting images of Jeremiah better than alternative approaches.

There is no dearth of alternative interpretations of the book of Jeremiah, and many of these do not recognize the importance of the role played by the editors in the creation of the figure of Jeremiah. Traditional accounts of Jeremiah remain popular (e.g. Blank, Bright, Feinberg, Thompson), and complex explanations which attempt to reconcile the difficulties in providing a consistent account of the prophet also thrive (e.g. Holladay, Raitt). Deuteronomistic editions of the book are allowed (e.g. Hyatt), but these are not considered to negate substantially the image of the prophet as fixed by conventional thought. Holistic readings of the book as one might read a modern novel (e.g. Fishbane, Polk) also gloss over the difficulties of relating the different images of Jeremiah to a coherent reading of the tradition. Many of the problems in reconstructing the 'historical' Jeremiah from a reading of the text are surmounted by the assumption that this is the way to read the book and by appeals to a form of argumentation initiated by the phrase 'it is not impossible that . . .' or 'there seems no reason to doubt that . . .' (cf. Bright, Thompson). All these approaches provide alternative readings of the book of Jeremiah to the one presented in this commentary and the wise reader will consult many different writers in order to gain insights into the *probable* interpretation of the text. But the problems of the composition and editing of the book remain the key to the interpretative approach to Jeremiah.

2. THEORIES OF COMPOSITION AND REDACTION

To the modern reader the books of Isaiah, Jeremiah and Ezekiel are virtually incomprehensible as *books*. This is especially the case with Isaiah and Jeremiah, where poetry and prose alternate or interrupt each other in commingled forms. Often the material lacks apparent order or arrangement, does not have the kind of contextualizing information necessary for interpretation, and is quite unlike the artefacts known as books produced in modern civilization since the time of Gutenberg. The term 'book' is a misleading description of these congeries and they might be described better as a miscellany of disparate writings – a gallimaufry of writings suggests itself as an entirely adequate categorization of this type of collection, except that it lacks a certain technical sophistication. The more prosaic 'a collection of shorter "books", plus miscellaneous material' (Bright, LVII) is equally accurate. Such a miscellaneous collection of discrete and disparate writings describes well the book of Jeremiah. Dismantled into their constituent parts the 52 chapters of Jeremiah form a series of independent elements. 1 and 52 form prologue and epilogue (themselves collections of smaller units); 2.1–3 are a preface to the 'books' contained in Part I (2–25) and especially to the first collections of poems in 2–6 (made up of smaller collections e.g. 2.4–4.4; 5–6.26; with 6.27–30 forming a closure with 1.17–19); further collections are constituted by 7.1–10.25; 11.1–13.27; 14.1–17.27; 18.1–20.18; with an appendix to Part I in 21.1–24.10 and a concluding summary in 25.1–14; Part II begins in 25.15–38 (here MT and G differ in order of sequence) and is continued in 46–51; Part III (26–36) is made up of two collections 27–29 and 30–31 (appendices in 32–33) and a series of individual narratives in 26, 34, 35, 36; Part IV (37–45) consists of 37–38; 39.1–40.6; 40.7–41.18; 42–44; 45. These many 'books' melded into one large work and held together by a redactional framework explaining the individual parts as the work of Jeremiah constitute the Jeremiah tradition. But what were the origins of the processes which gave rise to such a collection and why does the tradition have the shape and order which appear in MT or G? Data are lacking for direct answers to such important questions, but there is no lack of speculative theories about the origins and editing of the book of Jeremiah in twentieth-century biblical scholarship. The most important features of these theories must be considered here as a necessary introduction to the interpretation of the book of Jeremiah, but brevity rather than comprehensiveness will be the aim of this section (for further details cf. Bright, LV–LXXXV; Herrmann 1977; Hobbs 1972; Perdue 1984, 14–22; Rietzschel 1966; Rudolph, XIV–XXII; Thompson, 27–50).

The 1901 commentary on the book of Jeremiah by Bernhard Duhm may be taken as a convenient starting point for the history of Jeremiah studies in the twentieth century. In his analysis of the book three major strands account for the poetry and prose sections constituting Jeremiah: the poems of Jeremiah, the book of Baruch containing Jeremiah's biography, and the supplements added to these two writings by later hands (XI–XX). Using MT Duhm allocates approximately 280 verses to the poems, 220 verses to Baruch's book, and the other 850 verses to the supplements (XVI; cf. his 1903 translation of the text). Thus the dominant element in the book of Jeremiah is the later supplementation of Jeremiah's poetry and Baruch's biography, and this reflects the fiction of Jeremiah as a preacher, using midrash and prophetic legend (XVII–XX). The writers of these supplements write theology rather than history (XVIII) and the influences of Deuteronomy, Ezekiel, Second Isaiah and Third Isaiah may be discerned in their work (XX). Although modern scholarship has moved considerably from the time of Duhm and would hardly now regard the book of Jeremiah as the product of three kinds of material, it seems to me that much of what Duhm has to say about the supplements and their relation to later literature is quite sound.

The work of Sigmund Mowinckel perhaps has been more influential in shaping Jeremiah studies because his analyses of the book (1914; 1946) have dictated the basic approach of many subsequent writers – Duhm being regarded as too drastic in his attribution of so much material to non-historical sources and in limiting Jeremiah to being a poet. Mowinckel's 1914 book offers a much lengthier and more precise analysis of the sources of Jeremiah than Duhm's commentary affords. He isolates four sources: A, B, C, D and posits redactors for each source (i.e. R^{A}, R^{B}, R^{C}, R^{D}), so that 1–45 are the work of R^{ABCD}. Chapters 46–52 are a later appendix, somewhat like Isa. 40–66 (1914, 14), and the completed book (1–52) is the work of R^{J}. Source A consists of the poetic oracles to be found in 1–25 and as these show little redactional work they must be regarded as 'ipsissima verba Jeremiae' (1914, 21). Source B is made up of historical tales reflecting the activities of the prophet, similar to those to be found in the books of Samuel, and appears in 19.1–2, 10–11a, 14–20.6; 26–44 (1914, 24–5). C, the third source, comprises those speeches which do not belong to A or B and which are found in 7.1–8.3; 11.1–5, 9–14; 18.1–12; 21.1–10; 25.1–11a; 32.1–2, 6–16, 24–44; 34.1–7, 8–22; 35.1–19; 44.1–14 (1914, 31). Formulaic introductions and characteristic phrases identify source C as similar to the Deuteronomistic language of Deuteronomy, Joshua, Judges, Samuel and Kings and sharing the concerns of Deuteronomistic thought (cf. 1914, 33–8). The fourth source D is a later collection inserted into the book and consists of the oracles in 30–31 which envisage a good future for the people (1914, 45–8). A number of later additions appear in this source (e.g. 31.29–40; 33). The chronological order of these sources is, according to Mowinckel, A–B–C–D: A (sixth-fifth century); B (somewhat later than A); C (by end of fifth century); D is undatable. In his later book, which is a more general work about prophecy rather than a study of Jeremiah, Mowinckel is more inclined to talk about 'tradition complexes' than sources (e.g. 1946, 48–51, 62–7). Indeed, he acknowledges the point as a change from his previous position (1946, 62, 105 n.61), and this more sophisticated approach allows him to recognize the greater degree of complexity in the development of new prophetic sayings as an essential element of tradition history. The transmission of prophecy in traditionary circles 'is at the same time a living stream of living and topical prophecy' (1946, 67). Thus levels of tradition rather than sources is the proper approach to the study of Jeremiah (cf. Schmidt, 1984, 236).

Much of recent research on Jeremiah consists of the development or modification of the views of Duhm and Mowinckel. Debate continues about the relation of the poetry of Jeremiah to the prose contained in the book (cf. McKane 1981) and the extent to which the levels of tradition represented by Mowinckel's sigla A, B, C (D has been dropped in contemporary discussions) are independent of each other (cf. Bright 1951; 1966b; Holladay 1960; 1962b; 1975a; Weippert 1973; 1981a). Thus Duhm and Mowinckel effectively have set much of the agenda for modern Jeremiah studies. The two issues cited here illustrate the development of scholarship on Jeremiah in directions initiated by Duhm and Mowinckel but now considerably advanced in sophistication from those two authorities. Source C or the Deuteronomistic level of tradition is one of the key critical areas of modern study which divides scholars in their evaluations of the nature and degree of Deuteronomistic influence in the construction of the book of Jeremiah. Hyatt regards the Deuteronomistic involvement in the book as an editorial one producing a Deuteronomic edition of Jeremiah in which Jeremiah is presented as a prophet in agreement with that school's outlook (1951; cf. Hyatt 1942). In his opinion this has led to some distortion in the presentation of Jeremiah and made the task of discovering the historical Jeremiah that much more difficult. Hyatt's position has been developed by Siegfried Herrmann (1965, 159–241) and the approach to the book in terms of the Deuteronomistic editing of Jeremiah given its most thoroughgoing treatment in the work of Winfried Thiel (1973; 1981). Thiel's analysis is not only the most complete examination of every aspect of Deuteronomistic influence on the construction of the book of Jeremiah, but is also unlikely to be surpassed because it is the end-stage of that particular approach. Produced in Judah in the sixth century, the Deuteronomistic redaction of Jeremiah 1–45 is said to include a number of statements reflecting the central ideas of Deuteronomistic theology: e.g. the juridical interpretation of the exile as retribution for the nation's sins, the position of Deuteronomy as the rule for the conduct of the people, the prophet as the preacher of the law following Moses as the prototypical interpreter of the Deuteronomistic laws, sermons with conditional formulations of alternatives facing the people, the subordinate role of the shrine and the sacrificial cult in contrast to the demand for obedience, and a marked expectation of salvation in which return from exile and a new covenant play an important part (cf. Thiel 1973, 301–2; 1981, 107–12). Thiel's location of the Deuteronomistic redaction of Jeremiah in the land of Judah (1981, 113) contrasts with Hyatt's view that it may have been made in Egypt (Hyatt, 788). Both scholars recognize a fair amount of post-Deuteronomistic material in the book of Jeremiah.

There can be little doubt that the book of Jeremiah shares certain linguistic features in common with the Deuteronomistic corpus (i.e. Deuteronomy and the Deuteronomistic history of Joshua-Kings; cf. Thiel 1981, 93–9; Weinfeld 1972a, 320–61), but the significance of these shared elements is a matter of much debate. Thiel's comprehensive analysis argues for a very systematic production of a Deuteronomistic edition of the book of Jeremiah, even to the point where words only found in Jeremiah are attributed to Deuteronomistic activity (cf. McKane 1981 for criticisms of Thiel's approach). This may be to posit too rational a basis for the construction of the book and to discern too coherent a work in the finished product. The conclusion of McKane's important critique of Thiel's analysis is to the point here:

> Those who claim a systematic theological activity for a Deuteronomistic editor and identify compositions in which this is realized are perhaps professing to know more of the inner workings of his mind than can be gathered from the text. They are in danger of creating systematic theological aims for the editor whom they postulate rather than extracting these from the text. In general they exaggerate the coherence of the book and underestimate its lack of cohesiveness and obscurities (1981, 237).

It may also exaggerate the Deuteronomistic influence on the production of the book. Allowance should be made for the existence of post-Deuteronomistic material in the book which may have been influenced by Deuteronomistic ideas but not have emanated from such circles (cf. the discourses against false religious practices in 2.4–4.4).

A very different account of level C is given in the analyses of the prose of Jeremiah in the work of Helga Weippert and William Holladay. Weippert's main contribution to the discussion is an intensive study of certain linguistic features of the book of Jeremiah intended to demonstrate that the prose speeches are the utterances of the prophet Jeremiah rather than the product of Deuteronomistic circles (1973; cf. Weippert 1981a). She achieves this aim by an exegetical consideration of 7.1–15; 18.1–12; 21.1–7; 34.8–22 and an examination of certain words and phrases peculiar to the Jeremiah tradition. Her work is a good example of finely-honed lexical analysis producing valuable information on the distinctiveness of some of the language in the book of Jeremiah. But her conclusion that the prose comes from Jeremiah rather than the redactor (1973, 228–34) is surely wrong-headed. What her analysis does suggest is that we must allow for a more sophisticated and complex account of the redaction of Jeremiah and be less inclined to attribute so much of it to Deuteronomistic sources. Perhaps within Deuteronomistic circles there were those who worked specifically on a production of Jeremiah, or post-Deuteronomistic sources contributed nuances of language which went beyond the Deuteronomistic lexical range. Weippert provides evidence for the transcendence of Deuteronomism in

Jeremiah, but her judgment commits her to look in the wrong direction and turns her gains into losses. To cite McKane once more:

> . . . the extra-linguistic perception which puts her conclusions out of court is that they imply a view of the inner relations of the constituent parts of the book of Jeremiah and of the processes of growth and composition which is altogether incredible. We are dealing with a long, complicated, untidy accumulation of material extending over a very long period, to which many people have contributed. The supposition that a major part of it, including much of the prose, was already in existence in the lifetime of the prophet Jeremiah is a literary judgement which seems to take no account of the problems which arise when one considers in detail the baffling inconcinnities of the constituents of the book (1981, 228).

Holladay, whose contribution to Jeremiah studies is a prolific one which regularly changes its interpretation of the book, regards Weippert's work as solving the issue of the poetry-prose relationship in Jeremiah (cf. Holladay 1975a, 403, 408). His work spans three decades and develops the view held by a number of scholars (e.g. Robinson 1924, Eissfeldt, Reventlow, Weiser) that Jeremiah himself used prose sermons which had a Deuteronomistic style. Poetic elements can be detected in the prose (Holladay 1960; 1962b; 1966c), and this kind of prose (Weippert's *Kunstprosa* 'formal' or 'artistic' prose) reflects a new mode of recorded prophetic discourse. When Jeremiah dictated his paraenetic addresses to Baruch, the scribe used the patterns of writing to which he had become accustomed and therefore the prose sermons conform to the scribal conventions of the period (cf. 1975a, 411). Presumably Jeremiah made very clear to Baruch that when he was transcribing poetry he must not lapse into the formal patterns of his training but must write each word as he heard it and in the order in which he heard it! Having resolved this problem to his own satisfaction, Holladay's more recent work involves the construction of a coherent chronology of Jeremiah's preaching career (cf. Holladay 1981; 1983). This he achieves by presenting Jeremiah's sermons as counter-proclamations to the recitation of Deuteronomy every seven years (cf. Deut. 31.9–13). According to Holladay (1983, 147), Deuteronomy was recited in the years of 622, 615, 608, 601, 594 and 587, and Jeremiah probably received his call to be a prophet at the recitation of 615. The thesis is ingenious but depends upon the traditional view of the discovery of Deuteronomy and the belief, for which there is no evidence, that Deuteronomy was *actually* read in public every seven years. The neatness of Holladay's thesis is such that he can date Jeremiah's sermons with a precision which would surprise many commentators and astound the careful reader of the text. As a contribution to the traditional reading of the book of Jeremiah Holladay's work is formidable, but it solves none of the substantive problems of complexity and interpretation to which the book gives rise.

There is no lack of scholars who have argued for a close connection between Jeremiah and the prose sermons. Bright regards the style of the sermons, though akin to Deuteronomistic literature, to be a reflection of the standard rhetorical prose style of the period (1951; 1966b). The words of these sermons belong to the editors but they represent the gist of what Jeremiah himself said. Thus there is no fundamental difference between what Jeremiah said by means of poetry and what the sermons present him as saying. For Bright the B and C prose sayings are identical (1966b, 16) and the different strands should not be regarded as separate sources or circles of tradition: 'They are all parts of a single interlocking stream of transmission through which Jeremiah's words have been handed down' (1966b, 23). Muilenburg (1970) favours the view that the prose narratives are to be attributed to Baruch and conform to conventional scribal compositions (the same style used in Deuteronomistic contexts). The Deuteronomistic connection is accepted by many scholars but the degree to which the sermons have any direct link with Jeremiah is much debated.

Equally debated is the role and significance of Baruch the scribe. Baruch appears in 32.1–13, 16; 36; 43.3, 6; 45. He is credited with writing the oracles of Jeremiah for a public reading on a particular occasion (36.4–6) and is associated with Jeremiah on three other occasions. Many exegetes (e.g. Duhm, Bright, Hyatt, Rietzschel, Rudolph, Weiser, Thompson) have taken 36 literally, even to the point of reconstructing the contents of the *two* scrolls written by Baruch (cf. Holladay 1980). Furthermore, they have assumed from the sparse information in the book about Baruch's association with Jeremiah that he was a constant companion, amanuensis and *biographer* (May 1942 is an exception to this view of Baruch as biographer). Whatever justification there may be for interpreting Baruch as Jeremiah's amanuensis on the strength of a literal reading of 36, there is none for viewing him as a creative writer, biographer or lifelong companion. He is associated with Jeremiah during and after the fall of Jerusalem (as deeds trustee of the property transaction in 32.12; as the recipient of an oracle in 45; and is accused of being a bad influence on Jeremiah in 43.3) and is represented as going to Egypt with Jeremiah (43.6). There may be a certain logic to extending these roles beyond what the text says (cf. the development of Baruch in post-biblical literature), but the elevation of Baruch into the writer of the tradition begs the question of genre in 36. Baruch appears in a number of stories which reflect different levels of tradition in the book (cf. Wanke 1971). They do not belong to a uniform strand within the book nor should they be taken literally. A scrutiny of 36 will reveal a highly structured story that parallels the account of the discovery of the lawbook in the temple in Josiah's time (II Kings 22.8–13; cf. Isbell 1978) and which closes the part (III) that opens with the story of Jeremiah before the tribunal (26). Such structured accounts are literary and theological constructs rather than eye-witness reports of historical events. The roots of the creation of the figure of Baruch are to be found in the Jeremiah tradition (as are those of Jeremiah), but that figure develops considerably in later literature (as does Jeremiah, cf. 4, below). It would be unwise to assume that the biblical stories must be historical, when the later stories are regarded as legendary by all scholars. The characters behind the stories may be historical (though that is a matter for debate in view of the lack of *prima facie* evidence), but it does not follow that stories about real people are necessarily historical accounts. Archaeological evidence for a Baruch the scribe (cf. Avigad 1978) does not validate the tales of the book of Jeremiah as true or historical stories, any more than the existence of real people called Macbeth, Richard the Third, Amled, Alexander Selkirk or Eleanor Rigby confirms the literal truth of the plays of Shakespeare (*Macbeth, Richard the Third, Hamlet*), Defoe's novel *Robinson Crusoe*, or the Beatles' song. The extent to which the real and the imaginary can be separated in the Bible is beyond our knowledge because we lack the primary data which would establish such modern distinctions.

A different approach to the prose sermons is taken by Nicholson, who argues for an interpretation of the prose tradition in the book of Jeremiah in terms of the theological issues facing the circle which transmitted the sayings of Jeremiah (1970, 12–13). The sermons go beyond Bright's notion of the gist of Jeremiah's preaching and represent a conscious and deliberate development of the prophet's teaching. 'It is as the product and deposit of a living, active tradition that these sermons must be interpreted rather than as the creations of a purely literary activity at the hands of authors and editors' (1970, 14). Nicholson identifies the circle of tradition as Deuteronomistic and places the location of their activity in Babylon during the exile (e.g. 1970, 122–3, 131–3). In his presentation the figure of Baruch disappears and the obsession with historical biography characteristic of much research on Jeremiah gives way to a more convincing exposition of the book as theological in its concerns. It is recognized that some of the discourses are *ad hoc* creations of the Deuteronomists and that their primary aims are kerygmatic and didactic. Perhaps Nicholson retains too strong a connection between the prose discourses and sermons and the ministry and preaching of Jeremiah himself, but his account of the matter is a balanced one which may be regarded as an advance on the arguments of previous decades. His locating the tradition in Babylon rather than Judah may be questioned, but identifying the place where the different levels of tradition were put together is very difficult, and necessarily an inferential reading of the text.

So many different approaches to the prose material in the book of Jeremiah indicate the difficulties inherent in establishing the modes and history of composition and redaction in the tradition. McKane's argument about 'a type of enlargement and elaboration which operates within narrow contextual limits' and 'a type of expansion through commentary or exegesis which attaches itself to pre-existing elements of the *corpus*' (1981, 237) should be taken into account when analysing the text. It has the advantage of identifying the neglected aspects of the text, which hardly fit any general thesis about the book's redaction, and highlights the untidiness of the book, which is seldom commented on in Jeremiah studies. The book of Jeremiah is at times a sprawling, untidy and exasperating collection of discrete and disparate units whose order and meaning baffle the exegete. A competent commentary must also reflect this aspect of the book or fail to deal adequately with all its variegated elements.

The poetry of the book of Jeremiah (source or level A) raises fewer controversial discussions because many scholars are agreed on attributing it to the prophet Jeremiah (for formal analysis of the poetry cf. Bruno 1954; different aspects of parts of the book are analyzed in Krašovec 1984, 76–95, 108–10; Loretz 1970; Watson

1984). Jeremiah is seen as a poet in the first instance; hence the majority of poems in Part I are accepted as his work (the few in 30–31 and those in 46–51 are more difficult to attribute). Recent controversy over the nature of biblical poetry (cf. Kugel 1981) foreshadows further debate about the poetry-prose distinctions observed in the book of Jeremiah (e.g. Kugel 1981, 76–84). Such distinctions between poetry and prose in ancient literature (cf. Whallon 1969, 173–210 who argues for a complete separation of styles in the Old Testament) will continue to divide scholars in their judgments about the nature of biblical language and cannot be considered here without consuming more space than is warranted in a commentary (cf. Bright, CXXV–CXXXVIII for a general introduction to biblical poetry, with some examples drawn from Jeremiah). However, the attribution of all the poetry in the book to the prophet Jeremiah conceals an unwarranted assumption which should be questioned (cf. Herrmann 1977, 488–9). It is the redactional framework which attributes the poems to Jeremiah; there is nothing inherent in the poetry to identify who the speaker might be (a function of the prose). It is a dogma of Jeremiah studies that the prophet is the poet of the tradition. That dogma cannot be established by argument; it can only be believed. Yet much of the poetry of the book of Jeremiah is similar to poetry to be found elsewhere in the Hebrew Bible and has a stereotypical quality which frustrates identifying it with a specific author. The association of Jeremiah with the book of Lamentations in later tradition (cf. T Lam. 1.1) illustrates the way a named individual may be linked to a specific work. Laments appear in Jer. 4.19–21; 10.19–20; 14.17–18 (and a number of other places) which may justify a common authorship of these poems and Lamentations (cf. Jeremiah's reputation in II Chron. 35.25), but there are other explanations which would link the genre of poem with situation rather than speaker. After the fall of Jerusalem the lament for the destroyed city must have become a popular type of song (cf. Ps. 137). Only the redaction justifies the identification of the lament speaker with Jeremiah. Without the instruction provided by the rubrics of redaction the poems remain anonymous. We have no *reason* to believe the poems of 1–25 to be other than anonymous utterances from a variety of sources. The editors of the book have put them into the mouth of Jeremiah and we read them as his utterances. But the status of Jeremiah as a poet is no more secure than his status as the author of the prose traditions now constituting the rest of the book associated with his name. Thus the 'historical' Jeremiah disappears behind the activities of redactional circles and levels of tradition which have *created* the words and story of Jeremiah ben Hilkiah of Anathoth!

This reading of the book is not due to radical scepticism about the figure of Jeremiah but is a recognition of the function of the redactional framework in creating a link between the persona of the narrative (Parts III and IV) and the unidentified speaker of the poems and the prose sermons. Without 1.1–3 the 'me' of 1.4; 2.1 is anonymous. The framework identifies the speaker in 7.1; 11.1; 14.1; 18.1; 21.1; 25.1; 27.1; 29.1; 30.1; 32.1, 26; 33.1, 19, 23; 34.1, 8; 35.1, 12; 36.1; 37.6; 40.1; 42.7; 43.8; 44.1; 45.1; 46.1, 13; 47.1; 49.34; 50.1. It also allows the 'me' of 13.1; 15.1; 16.1; 17.19; 18.5; 24.1 to be related to the central figure of the tradition. In the narratives (e.g. 26; 28; 37–38; 40.2–6), Jeremiah has an integral role to play and again the question arises as to whether the origins of the tradition are not to be found in the stories rather than the utterances. If the redactional framework is removed, the figure of Jeremiah disappears from the poetry and the prose. Thus the framework provides the kind of information necessary for understanding who the speaker of these utterances is and, on occasion, the circumstances in which such statements are made. 'The prose assigns to the poetry its speaker and occasion' (Whallon 1969, 184), and this principle holds good especially for the collections associated with the prophets (cf. Whallon 1969, 191–3). Furthermore, the redactional framework also furnishes the interpretation of Jeremiah as the speaker of the divine word (analysis in Neumann 1973; 1975; Wildberger 1942; see 4, below). The anonymous word and speaker are both identified by the editing which specifies Jeremiah as the one to whom the word comes and Yahweh as the source of that word. Specification and legitimation are achieved by the framework and both poetry and prose are given an authority within a community where the recital or proclamation of these words took place. The regular interruption of the units, especially in MT, by the phrase 'says Yahweh' (*ne'um yhwh*) indicates the liturgical or recitative function which the tradition developed at some stage in its transmission (cf. Rendtorff 1954 for analysis of this formula). With the addition of editorial elements to the collection of poems and prose pieces the oral origins of the material (cf. Schmidt 1984, 173–4, on prophets as speakers rather than writers) are transformed and the fully edited work becomes something quite different from its beginnings in the spoken word (cf. Ong 1982, 31–116, for an investigation of the structural differences between orality and literacy). The full significance of such a transformation in the development of biblical traditions is as yet far from clear, and further research needs to be carried out on the processes involved in turning the spoken and recited word (*miqra*) into the written, recited word (*scripture*).

The diversity of opinions on the composition and redaction of the book of Jeremiah set out in this section demonstrates the difficulties inherent in the interpretation of the book. Few exegetes agree on the weight to be given to the role of the editors in the production of the book, and there is no consensus of scholarly opinion on such matters as the extent to which the Deuteronomists worked on the different levels of tradition, the relation between the poetry and the prose, the connections between a 'historical' Jeremiah and the tradition, the figure of Baruch as amanuensis, biographer, creator of the tradition or creation of one level of tradition, and the dating of the book or its parts. Such a lack of consensus means that disagreements about every aspect of the book are inevitable and no appeal can be made to one dominant line of exegesis (cf. 6, below). Further problems of interpretation are caused by lack of background information which would corroborate a particular reading of the book, and widely differing opinions on matters relating to Jeremiah but not exclusively concerned with it. The prime example of this latter interpretative problem is the question of the structure and date of the Deuteronomistic history and their bearing on the book of Jeremiah. Different answers on this subject will provide significantly variable interpretations of Jeremiah. Thus Bright represents Jeremiah as speaking a form of prose characteristic of the late seventh century and shared by him and the Deuteronomists. Holladay takes the Deuteronomistic historians' account of Josiah's reform at face value and reads the prose as counter-proclamations to the reading of the Deuteronomic law. Others see a Deuteronomistic adaptation of Jeremiah's preaching (cf. Rudolph), but also regard the account in II Kings 22–23 as a factual report of events in the time of king Josiah. If a radically different view is taken of the Deuteronomistic history in which the reform movements are seen as a pattern imposed on the past from a later period (i.e. during or after the exile), then the discussion about Jeremiah's attitude to Josiah's reform or his response to a hypothetical reading of the law on a septennial basis is irrelevant (cf. Hoffmann 1980, 264–70). As this commentary takes a view of the Deuteronomistic history closer to Hoffmann's thesis of reform as a Deuteronomistic idealized interpretation of history (cf. Mayes 1983, 13–14, for criticisms of Hoffmann's thesis about the unity of the history), other positions are less persuasive. But the problems surrounding the composition and redaction of the book of Jeremiah persist and are unlikely to be resolved in favour of one overarching theory.

3. THE TEXT OF JEREMIAH

The most striking feature of the text of Jeremiah is the difference between the MT and G versions of the book. G is a significantly shorter text, with many variations from the MT version and a different position and arrangement of the OAN material (G 25.14–20; 26–32 = MT 46–51; 25.15–38). According to Giesebrecht (XIX) it lacks 2700 words which are to be found in MT and may be regarded as being about one-eighth shorter (cf. Giesebrecht, XIX–XXXIV, for analysis of the differences). This is a remarkable variation in length, especially in view of the tendency of the G translation of the Hebrew text to be expansionistic for most of the books of the Bible. Such a contracted text requires explanation. Some of the variations in G also call for comment because they affect the interpretation of the book of Jeremiah: e.g. the lack of developed epithets of Yahweh (cf. Klein 1974, 32–3) in comparison with MT, fewer redactional introductions to units of text, some fifty fewer occurrences of the formula 'says Yahweh' (*n*^{e}*'um yhwh*), and hardly any uses of the epithet 'the prophet' (*hannābî'*) to qualify the name Jeremiah. All of these examples point in the direction of a greater degree of redactional activity in the production of MT and confirm the argument of §2, that the key to the interpretation of the book of Jeremiah is the analysis of its redactional history. Differences in the order and placing of the OAN indicate a source for G at variance with MT. As the placement of the OAN collection in G conforms to the pattern of the books of Isaiah and Ezekiel, it is their position in MT which requires explanation (cf. Janzen 1973, 115–16).

The study of the G text of Jeremiah is a complex business, and a comparison of the text and the critical apparatuses represented by Rahlfs 1935 and Ziegler 1957 will demonstrate some of the complexities of the matter. A commentary is not the place for a comprehensive introduction to biblical scholarship on G (cf. Jellicoe 1968; Klein 1974); nor does space even permit an expansive treatment of the plethora of recent work on the G edition of Jeremiah (see Janzen 1967; 1973; Tov 1972; 1976; 1979; 1981; cf. Perdue 1984, 10–14). Central questions here are the relation of the shorter (G) to the longer (MT) text and which is the more original text of Jeremiah. The discovery of four fragments of Jeremiah among the texts found at Qumran has contributed to the clarification of the issues involved in the debate about the two texts (cf. Cross 1958, 120–45; Janzen 1973, 173–84). These fragments from cave IV (4QJer[a], 4QJer[b], 4QJer[c]) and cave II (2QJer) testify to the existence of Hebrew texts similar to MT and to a shorter Hebrew text representing the *Vorlage* (i.e. the text used by the translator) behind G* (4QJer[b]). The presence at Qumran of the long and short texts of Jeremiah indicates the fluidity of the two traditions and the independent development of them from the fifth to the second century BCE. Dating the fragments and the *Vorlage* each may represent is fraught with difficulty (cf. Cross 1975; Janzen 1973, 128–35). However, the developing consensus of scholarship now is that the shorter text on which G* is based represents the more original and superior textual tradition of the book of Jeremiah (e.g. Cross, Janzen, Klein, Tov). 4QJer[b] is identified by Cross with a shorter Egyptian Hebrew text and the other fragments with Palestinian proto-MT textual families. Typical of these textual groups is the expansionistic style found also in the MT of Jeremiah. Concluding his study of the text of Jeremiah, Janzen characterizes the main features of MT as follows:

> The text of M has undergone much secondary expansion. Names are filled out frequently to their full form, and titles and epithets are added to them, while pronoun objects and subjects of verbs are made explicit. The text is heavily interpolated from parallel, related, or nearby passages. Many of these interpolations are innocuous, but many others are of such size and character as to reflect conscious scribal notation and harmonization. Particularly striking are the large doublets, and the interpolations from O.T. passages outside Jeremiah (1973, 127).

If MT is a revised text, G contains few secondary expansions and preserves a superior text to that of MT. One area where this superiority becomes clear is in the matter of the conflation of variant readings typical of MT. These double readings, as they are called (Janzen 1967, 434; 1973, 10), appear frequently in MT (e.g. 1.15; 7.24; 10.25; 14.3b, 4b; 25.6–7; 29.23; 41.10; fuller lists in Janzen 1967, 435–45; 1973, 10–25). They represent the changes and developments of the MT *Vorlage* and the attempts to make divergent texts conform to each other. Double readings in G (cf. Janzen 1973, 25–32; Ziegler 1958, 87–113) are more difficult to interpret and some may represent the influence of later G recensions (closer to MT) on the G* tradition (cf. Janzen 1973, 32–3). However, the G-*Vorlage* would appear not to have undergone large-scale recensional activity (Janzen 1973, 128).

> The Hebrew text from which the Greek translation was made was prerecensional in character, and stood at the end of a relatively inactive transmission history. That is, relatively few manuscript generations separated G-*Vorlage* from the Egyptian Hebrew archetype; the stream of transmission was narrow, allowing haplography to go undetected and therefore uncorrected; and very little collation of variant readings was carried out, since narrow transmission did not produce many. On the other hand, the stream of transmission behind M was wide and long, giving rise to much glossing and expansion from parallel and related passages, and to numerous minor variants (often of the synonymous or stylistic variety) which later were conflated in the process of recensional activity (Janzen 1967, 447).

The significance of the G tradition for the study of Jeremiah is developed further in the work of Emanuel Tov (e.g. Tov 1972; 1979; 1981). In his analysis the two textual traditions (G, MT) reflect particular stages in the editing of the book of Jeremiah. G represents the first edition of Jeremiah in which an editor adds his comments to levels A and B. MT is the second edition made by a later editor from a similar (but not identical) text to that used by the first editor. This second editor knew or made a different arrangement of the text and added new verses and sections (cf. Tov 1981, 153–7). As an exegete, editor II clarified details, made explicit implicit elements in the story, and stressed ideas to be found elsewhere in the book (Tov 1981, 158). According to Tov both editors belonged to the Deuteronomistic school, and their work on Jeremiah demonstrates that the Deuteronomistic revision of Jeremiah is more complex than previously thought (1972, 199). Level C in Jeremiah is therefore the product of two redactional stages in the development of the tradition and may be compared to the editorial stages of Deuteronomy and the Deuteronomistic revision of Joshua–II Kings (Tov 1972, 199).

The work of Janzen and Tov in establishing that G and MT represent two editions of the book of Jeremiah is important for the understanding of the complexities of the text and fundamental to the interpretation of the book offered in this commentary. Differences between the editions are observed in the Notes and, though often of a trivial nature, have a direct bearing on the exegesis of the text. Between the two editions variations in the development of the story may be detected and the *persona* of Jeremiah is considerably enlarged in the second edition. A good example of this editorial enlargement is to be seen in the formulaic phrase 'Jeremiah the prophet' (*yirmᵉyāhū hannābî'*). In the first edition this formula only appears four times (42.2; 43.6; 45.1; 51.59), but in the second edition it occurs a further twenty-six times (20.2; 25.2; 28.5, 6, 10, 11, 12, 15; 29.1, 29; 32.2; 34.6; 38.8, 26; 37.2, 3, 6, 13; 38.9, 10, 14; 42.4; 46.1, 13; 49.34; 50.1). This massive increase of references to Jeremiah as '*the prophet*' may be surprising (cf. Tov 1981, 161); it is certainly 'most noteworthy' (Auld 1983, 6). Such multiple insistence on Jeremiah's prophetic status in contrast to its almost entire absence in the first edition indicates the direction in which the tradition developed between editions (cf. 4). Older authorities may regard the attachment of the title 'the prophet' to Jeremiah's name as 'unimportant' (e.g. Driver 1913, 269), but more recent approaches to the interpretation of prophecy have detected in this redactional development of the tradition an important clue to the delineation of the categories of prophet and prophecy (e.g. Auld 1983; 1984; cf. Vawter 1985).

The complex pattern of variations discernible in the second edition (cf. analysis in Tov 1981, 152–67) is but one significant feature of the differences between G and MT. Another important aspect of the comparison between the two editions is the arrangement of the OAN material. In the first edition the order of the nations denounced is different from that in MT and the collection of OAN follows the summary of Part I in 25.1–13. The second edition breaks the connection between Parts I and II by placing the OAN after Part IV (MT 46–51) and has a different order of the nations. It does, however, recognize the association between Parts I and II by adjoining a magical act against the nations and a listing of the nations (25.15–38) to the summary of Part I. The reference to 'everything written in this book' (25.13) suggests an independent collection of OAN and is more pertinent in G than MT. Added to the poems and appendix of Part I, Part II forms in G the pattern of judgment against Judah-judgment against the nations-salvation for Judah (to some extent) to be found in the other heavily developed traditions of Isaiah and Ezekiel. Whether MT's order represents the independent development of the collections of material constituting the tradition in different periods and places or is an attempt to maintain 'the close connection between the oracles in chs. 1–25 and the biographical events in chs. 26–45' (Childs 1979, 352) is a moot point. The different arrangements of the two editions have hermeneutical implications for the interpretation of the book because the sequences and emphases are related differently to each other in G and MT (cf. Bogaert 1981a). At the end of G Baruch is the recipient of an oracle, whereas MT ends with Jeremiah writing a book against Babylon – the epilogue of 52 may mask these concluding stories as the termination of particular traditions but they should be read as giving different slants to the shape of the book. In the first edition Baruch's oracle concludes the redaction 'like a signature' (Bogaert 1981a, 173); in the second edition Jeremiah, without Baruch, stands as the eponymous prophet of his own book.

The interpretative differences between the editions and the hermeneutical consequences arising out of them indicate something of the complexities of the interpretation of the book of Jeremiah facing the exegete of the text who takes seriously *both* versions of Jeremiah. Behind G and MT are many complex developments of language and tradition which cannot be explained adequately in a general commentary. This is because the two editions represent the accumulation of centuries of development, reflection, supplementation and variation which requires patient and sophisticated analysis by *many* scholars in order to display the rich levels of tradition contained in G and MT. The conflation of variant readings and the presence of a large collection of Ketib-Qere interpretations (a particular feature of the book of Jeremiah) in MT demonstrate something of the complexity and rich texture which characterize the book of Jeremiah. At times the Hebrew of MT is difficult, confused or unsatisfactory (e.g. 5.26; 8.13; 15.11), requiring emendation using the Vrs (cf. RSV margins) or puzzling analysis by modern sophisticated linguistic techniques. Such difficulties reflect the long transmission history of the text which inevitably develops corruptions, lacunae and variations over the course of time. The MT of Jeremiah is by no means as unsatisfactory a Hebrew text as that of Samuel, Hosea or Ezekiel. In the case of G, the main feature to be noted of that text in terms of inner-Greek problems is the relationship between the different sections of the book. Between 1–28 and 29–52 there are significant lexical differences which have persuaded some scholars that two translators worked on the text (i.e. Jerα and Jerβ). Theories of two or multiple translators of Jeremiah have held the field of studies in the G text of Jeremiah until recently. Tov's 1976 investigation of the matter offers a more sophisticated account of the differences between α and β which accounts for the similarities as well as the variations. According to him the first translation of Jeremiah into Greek is to be identified with G* (1976, 5–6). This version would account for the similarities between α and β. By postulating a revision of G*, preserved only in part now, the differences between the two halves of the book may be explained. The revision aimed at a more precise, consistent translation of the Hebrew. It is, however, only preserved in Jerβ. In Tov's thesis G* represents a translation not only of Jeremiah but also of Bar. 1.1–3.8; this part of the book of Baruch was revised as well. Tov dates the revision of G* to the period between 116 BCE and *c.* 50 CE (1976, 165–8) and claims that his theory demonstrates that G 'is a heterogeneous collection of translations, original and revised, early and late, free and literal' (1976, 168). This judgment is undoubtedly true, as many studies of G have shown the complexities of G as translation(s) of the Hebrew. Nowhere are these features of G more evident than in the text of Jeremiah, though the main importance of G for Jeremiah studies is its witness to a *Vorlage* different from the one presupposed by MT.

4. THE FIGURE OF JEREMIAH

The conventional approach to the figure of Jeremiah in the book associated with his name sees in him the paradigmatic *prophet* of the Bible and reads the book as providing *prima facie* evidence for the innermost thoughts of such a prophet. This reading of the book has given rise to many dramatic and hyperbolic presentations of Jeremiah, his life, thought and times (e.g. Blank 1961; Leslie 1954; Neher 1960; Skinner 1922; Steinmann 1952). In these rhetorical portrayals of the prophet's struggles against inner doubts and external conflicts there is often a tendency to treat Jeremiah as an exemplar whose experiences and reflections provide guidance for those hearing his story (cf. Crenshaw 1984, 31–56; Davidson 1983, 121–39; Polk 1984, 151–2, 167–74). Such readings make interesting connections between an ancient book and the history of Western thought, literature and spirituality (e.g. Hopper 1956) and represent the influence of the story of Jeremiah on a wide variety of religious and literary reflections (poems by Burns, Hopkins and Rilke are outstanding examples of the latter). The legendary association of Jeremiah with the authorship of the book of Lamentations and the reading of certain poems of lament in Jer. 11–20 as 'confessions' of his have assisted the creation of a persona of gloom, tension, debate and imprecation for the figure behind the text. His apparent sufferings and the tortured state of his mind have made him for many modern readers of the book a classic figure of promethean strivings with the deity. All this is in keeping with a gloomy existentialism (cf. Neher, xii: 'unquiet life . . . absurd life') once fashionable in this century which identifies Jeremiah with some of those deep and disturbing geniuses who have shaped the intellectual contours of modern thought. Thus Jean Steinmann writes:

> Mais Jérémie fut vraiment le génie du tourment et du désaccord, l'Euripide, le Pascal ou le Dostoïevsky de l'Ancien Testament (1952, 296).

Less graphically, others have regarded Jeremiah as the greatest poet among the prophets (e.g. Nötscher, 24; cf. Volz, XXXVI).

All these descriptions and evaluations are the fruit of reading the book of Jeremiah as a combination of autobiography and historical narrative sanctioned by more than two millennia of such a reading (cf. NT; Wolff 1976). Modern variations on such an approach (e.g. Polk 1984) do not materially affect the interpretation of the book, and the recognition of additional editorial elements in the text does not frustrate the conventional reading of Jeremiah (cf. Bright, Holladay, Thompson). As such, the approach may be recognized as a majority report on the book of Jeremiah which will continue to flourish wherever the Bible is read. It is therefore quite safe from alternative readings of Jeremiah and may be accorded the respect due to ancient landmarks.

A different approach to the reading of the book of Jeremiah is taken in this commentary. It is neither unique nor novel, but reflects a developing trend in the interpretation of the many levels of tradition contained in the book (cf. Carroll 1981; Herrmann 1984; Perdue 1984). Unlike the traditional or conventional account of Jeremiah, it does not start off from an autobiographical or historical narrative reading of the text, but focuses on the redactional organization of the many units and blocks of material constituting the book. It sees a greater degree of development and a longer period of gestation in the construction of the text and recognizes the essentially creative role of the editors in the production of the two editions of the book. The developmental differences between G and MT also indicate the importance of the factors of time and editing. As the product of several or more generations the book of Jeremiah requires a different interpretative approach from that assumed by commentators who regard it as the production of Jeremiah himself and aided by Baruch (e.g. Holladay, Lundbom), with only a few additions from other hands. Furthermore, a view which sees the book as the product of more than the few decades between 580–550 (cf. Clements 1982, 122–6; see §5) will interpret it in ways quite different from an approach which relates the book to '*a* specific historical situation' (Clements 1982, 125). The different situation*s* and issues addressed by the book of Jeremiah (e.g. 27–29; 30–31; 42–44; the additions of 17.19–27; 34.8–22) point to the need for a more complex account of the disparate levels of tradition constituting that book (cf. McKane 1981 on the untidiness of the editing of Jeremiah). One consequence of this approach to the redactional analysis of the text is the quite different interpretation of the figure of Jeremiah it entails.

As a character in the book Jeremiah appears in the narrative sections (except for 40.7–41.18) and, without the editorial rubrics prefacing the various collections of poems in 2–23; 30–31, there is no necessary connection between him and the poetry. Although the biblical prophets are often regarded as poets (cf. Carroll 1983), this impression is misleading with reference to Jeremiah. By attributing the poetry in the book to him it is possible to interpret the poems in conjunction with the prose sermons and the narratives so as to limit their interpretation to conform to the figure presented in the stories. This has the effect of narrowing down the very broad generalizations of much of the poetry (cf. 2; 5; 10; 13.15–27) and concealing the fact that many of the poems may refer to a number of different situations and periods. Only the narrative figure of Jeremiah gives a specificity to the poetry, and this is imposed on the poems from the redaction. One example of how this affects (distorts?) the interpretation of various poems is the tendency of many exegetes to identify the laments scattered about 11–20 as 'confessions' of Jeremiah. As laments they may represent a number of different things (see commentary), but to read them as utterances of Jeremiah introduces the *possibility* that they may be self-referring individual laments. The same process is to be found in the book of Psalms, where editorial headings attribute specific poems to David. That modern scholarship can read such psalms without associating them with David is a practice not yet fully integrated into Jeremiah studies. Whether the editors intended the laments in the book to be read as the personal utterances of Jeremiah or as responses to disaster by the community is a moot point, because we do not know the order in which the prose was added to the poetry or vice versa. The editorial clues are too few and far from clear for modern exegetes to insist on a monolithic reading of the laments or to maintain that they must represent the utterances of the 'historical' Jeremiah. Thus the reading of the tradition as autobiographical or biographical or even as the presentation of Jeremiah as prophetic *persona* (e.g. Polk 1984) may be too modern an approach to the text. The figure of Jeremiah may only be an editorial link between different elements in the tradition, with the emphasis on the teaching addressed to the community rather than on the bearer of that proclamation.

The figure of the speaker is not significant in *most* of the anthologies making up the collection of prophetic texts in the Bible. Only in First Isaiah, Jeremiah, Ezekiel, Jonah, and Amos 7.10–15; Hos. 1; 3 are there narratives which purport to be about the speakers. Few of these stories are unproblematic and they all raise questions about the nature and dating of the levels in which they appear. To judge from Jeremiah, Ezekiel and Isa. 6–8 the sixth century would seem to be the period when such stories began to be told about the bearers of various traditions, and this story-telling continued for many centuries. In the book of Jeremiah a number of narratives concern Jeremiah and in a few of them the figure of Baruch appears. Subsequent literature represents a richly developed tradition of Jeremiah and Baruch, the roots of which can be discerned in the Bible. These stories (cf. the Apocalypses of Baruch in Charlesworth 1983, 615–79; Sparks 1984, 835–914; the Book of Baruch in Moore 1977, 255–316; Tov 1975; the Paraleipomena of Jeremiah in Sparks

1984, 813–33; the Epistle of Jeremiah in Moore 1977, 317–58; the Midrash to Lamentations; and assorted legends in Ginzberg 1913, 291–326) display a lively and imaginative development of the speeches and activities of Jeremiah and Baruch. They do not, however, present a consistent picture of the two figures and in this they are very similar to the canonical stories. In some of the accounts Baruch takes over from Jeremiah and makes the great speeches – a tendency which may be discerned in Jer. 36 and possibly in 43.2–3. Nor are the stories always consistent with those in the biblical tradition. A good example of this variability in the story-telling concerns the sacred vessels of the temple. According to the Deuteronomistic history these were plundered by Nebuchadrezzar and taken to Babylon as loot. In other biblical stories (e.g. II Chron. 36.18; Ezra 1.5–11; Dan. 1.2; 5.2–4) the vessels survive as cult objects in Babylon and are returned to Jerusalem. The first edition of Jeremiah has no interest in them (see on 27.16–22), whereas the second edition hints at their return (27.22). According to the later stories Jeremiah is commanded by Yahweh to hide the vessels in the earth so that they may survive the destruction of Jerusalem (cf. Paraleipomena Jer. 3). What is most interesting about *all* these stories is that they quite happily contradict each other without any attempt to provide a coherent or consistent account of the fate of the temple vessels. More important than this independent development of different story-lines (whatever these may signify) is the fact that we have no reason to believe that the stories represent historical reminiscences of Jeremiah and Baruch. Why then should we suppose that similar stories to be found in the book of Jeremiah are any the less fabricated? The construction of stories about how Jeremiah behaved during the fall of Jerusalem and afterwards appears to be part of a long oral and literary activity stretching from the sixth century (?) to the early centuries of this era (cf. Paraleipomena Jer. 9.12–14, where the resuscitated body of the 'dead' Jeremiah confesses faith in Jesus Christ and predicts his coming in 477 years time!). If biblical characters can live and develop in literature so far removed from the original traditions, it would be unwise to treat the stories in the Bible as belonging to a different genre from the apocryphal writings. All the stories appear to belong to the art of storytelling at home in circles which produced the Bible and much later literature. The legends of the prophets appear in the Deuteronomistic history (esp. I Kings 17–II Kings 13), II Chronicles, the narrative sections of Isaiah,

Jeremiah and Ezekiel, and an even larger collection of writings not recognized as canonical by most Jewish or Christian authorities. It is in these legends that we learn of Jeremiah being stoned to death in Egypt or elsewhere (cf. Heb. 11.37; The Lives of the Prophets 2.1). Are the stories about Jeremiah or Baruch anything more than examples of this legendary story-telling activity in the life of the second temple communities?

The question is left unanswered because it applies only to genre. Other factors play a part in the construction of the book of Jeremiah, and these relate to theological propaganda designed to make sense of the collapse of Judaean society and the fall of Jerusalem in the sixth century. Stories can convey such teaching as effectively as any other means and it would be foolish to insist that only history provides the genre for reading the story of Jeremiah or that the theological insights of a group can only be put across by historical accounts of the past. The matter may be more complicated than space permits an introduction to a commentary to discourse on, but the force of narrative and story for making important claims is not derived from approximation to historical reality (whatever that may mean) but from the imaginative power of the storyteller to make connections between many discrete matters. In the story of Jeremiah it is the interplay of many traditions which carries the teaching and proclamation for the communities to which it is addressed, and the narrative art serves these purposes as well as the poems and other genres in the book. Robert Alter's judgment on the art of biblical narrative is worth citing here:

> The Hebrew writers manifestly took delight in the artful limning of these lifelike characters and actions, and so they created an unexhausted source of delight for a hundred generations of readers. But that pleasure of imaginative play is deeply interfused with a sense of great spiritual urgency. The biblical writers fashion their personages with a complicated, sometimes alluring, often fiercely insistent individuality because it is in the stubbornness of human individuality that each man and woman encounters God or ignores Him, responds to or resists Him. Subsequent religious tradition has by and large encouraged us to take the Bible seriously rather than to enjoy it, but the paradoxical truth of the matter may well be that by learning to enjoy the biblical stories more fully as stories, we shall also come to see more clearly what they mean to tell us

about God, man, and the perilously momentous realm of history (1981, 189).

Baruch appears in only a few places in the book (32.12–13, 16; 36.4–32; 43.2–3, 6; 45) and, though he looms large in the accounts some scholars give of the composition of the book, the inchoateness of this strand in the tradition may illustrate the growth of the story of Jeremiah. Apart from 36 Baruch's role is very passive and more hinted at than fully realized. Even in 36 he is but the mouthpiece of Jeremiah – a feature developed in the later apocalypses where his speeches and those of Jeremiah are virtually interchangeable. An analysis of the blocks of material where Baruch appears shows them to belong to three different and independent sets of texts: (i) 19.1–20.6; 26–29; 36; (ii) 37–43; (iii) 45; 51.59–64 (cf. Wanke 1971). Each set represents a distinctive tradition, and there is no concrete evidence for attributing any of them to Baruch as author. What Baruch represents in these strands is difficult to determine, though his role in 36 might reflect a scribal or Deuteronomistic involvement in the production of part of the book of Jeremiah. In 32.12–13, 16 he is a witness to Jeremiah's transaction, and in 45 he functions as the recipient of one of Jeremiah's oracles (cf. Ebed-melech in 39.15–18). When it is realized that these inchoate glimpses of a figure in the story of Jeremiah are developed in the later literature into a character who receives his own revelations and gives instructions to Jeremiah (see the Apocalypses of Baruch; cf. Jer. 43.3), it is worth speculating whether the figure of Jeremiah might not have developed also from equally modest beginnings. Absent from the story of Gedaliah's community (40.7–41.18), he becomes an adviser to the remnant of that group (42). Only in Part IV and a few other places (e.g. 19.1–2, 10–11, 14; 20.1–3; 26–29; 36) do narratives about him appear and only Part IV in the first edition presents him as a prophet. In the second edition his role as prophet is greatly increased and this may reflect the development of the tradition in circles which came to view Jeremiah *as a prophet*. The editing of the book accordingly illustrates the way expansions shape the interpretation of Jeremiah as a prophetic figure. Both editions know him as a prophet *to the nations* (1.5, 10), but between the two traditions there is a considerable expansion of his role as prophet. Given the attitude expressed towards prophets in the book of Jeremiah (e.g. 14.13–16; 23.9–40) it is ironic that Jeremiah should be presented as a prophet, but by this stage of the tradition's growth such an epithet may not have been an execrable one. But it is against a background of the development of the title 'prophet' as a term of approbation (Deuteronomistic circles?) that the production of MT must be seen and it is difficult to put a date on such a trend (after Zech. 13.2–6?). The redactional framework functions to transform many of the poetic sequences and some of the narratives into utterances of the divine word, and this transformation reflects the growth of the 'prophetic' reading of the tradition.

Many factors, some problematical, bear on the analysis of the figure of Jeremiah in the book associated with his name and it would be to oversimplify the matter to suggest that a straightforward and consistent line of interpretation could be derived from the highly edited and already interpreted data available in the book. Editorial inconsistency is an important principle for interpreting the Bible and especially the book of Jeremiah (cf. McKane 1981; Tov 1981, 151), so a consistent, linear account would be a misconceived approach to the interpretation of Jeremiah. The problems of determining the relationship between a tradition and the figure to whom it is attributed are such that few scholars could venture confidently to delineate the growth of books such as Isaiah, Jeremiah or Ezekiel. Understanding the multiple levels of tradition in such books as syncytial in nature hardly assists the determination of what the relation between original speaker and developed work might be. Many exegetes wish to maintain a definite connection between a named figure as speaker and the development of the tradition handling that speaker's utterances. In the case of Jeremiah a wide divergence of opinion exists on the question of this connection. Behind the tradition, it is assumed, stands the figure of the 'historical' Jeremiah, whose utterances are contained in the book and whose influence shapes many of the other statements. The degree of connectedness is disputed by most commentators, but there is no corroborative evidence available to determine the issue in favour of one position or another. Each exegete must produce a reading of the text consistent with the inconsistencies of the book and dependent on sophisticated interpretative judgments. To the question 'what is the relation of the book of Jeremiah to the historical Jeremiah?' no answer can be given. The question assumes too many things which require prior arguments before they can be incorporated into a formal query about the 'historical' Jeremiah. For it is not clear that 'historical' prophets can be reconstructed from books associated with their names, nor is it established that such 'historical' figures are *not* the products or even the epiphenomena of the traditions in which they appear!

These judgments allow a wide variety of opinions to exist on the relation of Jeremiah ben Hilkiah to the work associated with his name, but they undermine the certitude with which any one view may be held. It is relatively easy to believe or to assert that Jeremiah must have said this poem or that sermon, but the connections cannot be made in such a grand manner without firmer evidence than the book affords. The complex editorial constructions and the multiple levels of disparate traditions in the book militate against easy solutions to the problems of authorship and association with a 'historical' Jeremiah. It is assumed that Jeremiah did exist (like Macbeth or Richard III), but that assumption does not underwrite the attribution of everything in the book to his authorship. Whether it permits anything to be assigned to him with certainty is questionable and a matter for interpretation and debate. A close scrutiny of the poems or the prose will reveal inconsistencies and inconcinnities which point to the shaping forces of redaction and accumulative inner-textual exegeses. These distance the tradition from whatever origins are posited for it and loosen the connection hypothesized between it and Jeremiah. Simple hypotheses which may be entertained include the view that Jeremiah uttered certain poems in the period between 605–587 which warned of the dangers constituted by the Babylonians or that he was a figure active in the time of Zedekiah and the aftermath of the fall of Jerusalem (as in Part IV). But these are not unproblematic positions, and as remarkably little else may be put forward without serious debate, it is clear that locating the 'historical' Jeremiah is, at least, as difficult as finding the historical Jesus (cf. Carroll 1981, 5–30; Jobling 1978b, 6–10; Schottroff 1970, 294).

Reference to the presentation of Jesus of Nazareth in the Synoptic Gospels provides an analogy for Jeremiah studies. In the Gospels there is an interpenetration of the stories of Jesus (sayings, parables and deeds) with material reflecting the Christ of faith and the post-resurrection theology of the churches. No serious New Testament scholar would read the Gospels without allowing for the influence of early church theology and the development of the traditions about Jesus to meet the needs of the nascent churches. So it must be in the reading of the book of Jeremiah. The refraction of the figure of

Jeremiah due to the editing and developing of many discrete traditions over a long period of time must be recognized as creating Jeremiah in a different image from whatever may have been the case before the tradition developed. Thus *now* he is a prophet who commands all strata of society, speaks for and to the kingdom (Judaean) and the empire (Babylonian), announces the fate of individuals, groups and nations, stands in judgment over everything, speaks the word of restoration over all (except Babylon), sides with Babylon *and* against it, identifies with the deportees of 597 and with the survivors of 587, stands for the people in Babylon *and* for those in Judah after 587, speaks against the communities in Egypt, condemns the worship of the Judaean communities (2–3) and encourages the fidelity of their worship (10.1–16). He is a protean figure who bestrides all contradictions and overcomes the problems of time and place. He is a prophet to the nations (1.5, 10), yet his work is addressed to the 'house of Jacob, and all the families of the house of Israel' (2.4). His words and deeds embrace the communities of the sixth and fifth centuries along with all the problems facing them. Though set in a particular forty-year period (1.2–3), he is timeless – without birth or death! For him everything resonates with the divine word, and over all things he pronounces the word of Yahweh. This is not a real person but a conglomerate of many things, reflecting the fortunes of various Jewish communities during and after the Babylonian period. The 'historical' Jeremiah may still be there hidden by or weighed down under the additions and interpretations of countless editors and transformed beyond recognition, so that we cannot now rediscover him with any assurance. The extent to which this is thought to be the case will vary with each reader of the text, but that it has happened can hardly be denied. Hence the figure of Jeremiah which is discerned in the text must not be confused with a hypothesized real person, but must be interpreted as the production of the various levels of tradition making up the text. This figure will, on examination, turn out to be a very complex amalgam of social, political, and theological elements which, though lacking consistency or coherence, reflects the hermeneutically rich strands which constitute the book of Jeremiah.

5. FUNCTION, SETTING AND DATE OF THE BOOK

Collections of material as complex and complicated as the Isaiah, Jeremiah and Ezekiel traditions defy scholarly attempts to determine matters as precise as function, setting and date. Yet scholars have decided views on all three aspects of the book of Jeremiah, and these must be considered as further elements in the interpretation of the text. The difficulties of establishing these matters should not be understated. A book like that of Jeremiah or Isaiah is the product of lengthy processes of editing and accumulation, and few traces of the history of such processes can be detected clearly from the text itself. Without an acute knowledge of the social and religious background it is difficult to determine why such collections were made or given the shape they possess in the Bible. Nor do we know how such books (once their oral stages have become written documents) functioned in the communities where they were regarded as important or why they should have existed in writing in the first place. If ignorance is stressed here it is because it is important to be aware of how little we really know and how uncertain that little knowledge is. Without such agnosticism too little evidence will have to bear too much weight and the level of claims made for the material will be determined by assumed knowledge rather than controlled by an awareness of our deep-seated ignorance.

According to the redactional introduction of the book, Jeremiah's utterances belong to the forty-year period which saw the final collapse of the Judaean state (1.2–3). Thus the book may be read as commentary on the events of the years *c.* 627–587. Within this period the editors identify 605 (the fateful year of Babylonian victory at Carchemish) as a turning point in the fortunes of Judah and represent Jeremiah as summarizing twenty-three years of work in terms of the popular rejection of Yahweh as the grounds for the Babylonian destruction of the state (25.1–7, 8–11; cf. 36). Apart from 1.2 and its echoes in 25.1, 3; 36.2 (cf. 3.6), all other editorial dating refers to the reigns of Jehoiakim and Zedekiah rather than to the time of Josiah; the sharpest focus is on the period of Zedekiah. Whatever the problems of the Josiah datings, the edition of Jeremiah represented by these redactional headings must be read as a statement about the fall of Judah and Jerusalem set in a particular period. The period is determined by Deuteronomistic considerations (cf. II Kings 22–25) and reflects the style and concerns of that school of thought. From the irredentist policy of Josiah (II Kings 23.15–20; cf. II Chron. 34.6–7) to Nebuchadrezzar's destruction of Jerusalem represents a period of radically changing fortunes in the political life of Judah, and some account is required to explain the sharp decline in the nation's performance. One such account is to be found in the Deuteronomistic redaction of the book of Jeremiah which is an attempt to justify what happened in 587 by exposing the false worship of the pre-587 people of Judah and Jerusalem; it may also be seen in the Deuteronomistically edited sermons in Jeremiah (e.g. 7.1–8.3; 11.1–13; 16.10–13; 19.3–9, 11b–13). These sermons betray the same concerns with cultic purity as are used in the Deuteronomistic history to denounce the kings of Israel and Judah, and demonstrate a Deuteronomistic influence in the construction of the book of Jeremiah. The extent of that influence is much debated among scholars, but the fact of it seems difficult to deny. What it signifies is also debatable: did a special group of Deuteronomists take over the editing of Jeremiah material or add a layer of edited sermons to a work in progress, or did the Jeremiah tradition go through a period when Deuteronomistic ideas and terminology were fashionable? The questions multiply and only scholarly theories exist as data to answer them. Each theory chases too little information for too much text to be able to provide a coherent or persuasive answer. Too many fundamental problems of interpretation remain with reference to Jeremiah and the Deuteronomistic history for a solution to the central questions to commend itself to a consensus of opinion. Even if a Deuteronomistic element in the construction of the Jeremiah tradition were to be agreed on, it would not resolve the debate about the larger issues of what constituted the material to which the Deuteronomists added their contribution or the extent to which they shaped the tradition.

The Deuteronomistic edition of Jeremiah focuses on the fall of Jerusalem as the punishment of the nation for impurity of worship. Such a thesis provides a function and a setting for the book at one level of its development, but it does not give a date for this stage of the tradition. The setting is Deuteronomistic, but where? The function is a critique of the cultic life of Judah and Jerusalem, but for whom? When should the Deuteronomistic corpus be dated, and what date is to be put on the editing of this strand of Jeremiah? Each question raises another set of problems and disputed interpretations of the date. A late date for the Deuteronomistic history and a theory of it having only one edition rather than the more popular two-edition theory (e.g. Hoffmann 1980; cf. Mayes 1983) would have serious implications for dating the Deuteronomistic level of tradition in the book of Jeremiah. Furthermore, it should not be assumed that Deuteronomistic circles operated for a brief period and then disappeared; nor should the possibility of a much later (i.e. fifth-century) date for Deuteronomistic activity be ruled out *a priori*. The termination of the history with an episode from *c*. 560 (II Kings 25.27–30; cf. Jer. 52.31–34) does not necessarily date the history to the mid-sixth century. It may simply represent a positive ending of the story of the kings of Israel and Judah with a detail from the life of the *last* living Judaean king. After his death (alluded to but not recorded because too negative?) there were no more kings, and the gesture of kindness towards him from the Babylonian authorities closes the record on a note of benevolence (contrast Jer. 22.24–30). Such a story hardly constitutes evidence for dating the history, because the lack of a successor to the throne requires no recording and centuries later Jehoiachin remains *the last king of Judah* (in II Kings 25 Zedekiah is displaced by Jehoiachin presumably because he died first or for ideological reasons).

If function, setting, and date of the Deuteronomistic level of the editing of Jeremiah cannot be determined with any certitude – beyond the generality of cultic criticism, Judaean or Babylonian background, and from the mid-sixth century onwards – it should be noted that these indeterminacies accurately reflect our state of knowledge. The general vagueness of opinion matches the information conveyed by the Deuteronomistic sermons in the book. They are broad denunciations of communal practices reflecting ideology and propaganda, but lacking in precise detail corroborated by independent data. This vacuity of reference is best illustrated by the fact that, in spite of relating the critique of the cult to the fall of Jerusalem, there is so little real information about the actual fall of the city in the book of Jeremiah! The accounts in 39.1–10; 52.3–11 provide a few details (far from clear) about the capture of the king and his officers and the fate of various strata of people, but of the eighteen months period of siege, deprivation and defeat virtually nothing is recorded. The immediacy of the destructive consequences of the Babylonian invasion is conveyed by the poems in the tradition (e.g. 4.19–21, 29; 5.16–17; 6.22–26; 8.14, 16; 10.19–20; 12.10–13) but not by the Deuteronomistic elements. Such lack of immediacy in the Deuteronomistic strand suggests a distance between the events of 597–587 and the reflections on them of the Deuteronomists. For the latter, the fall of Jerusalem is in the past and provides the justification of their theological propaganda, but the extent of that distance between events and warrants is a moot point. It could be as early as 550 but it equally could be a century further on from that. Theological vagueness is undatable.

The tendency of many scholars to date the book of Jeremiah *c.* 550 is caused by the belief that much of it must have been written before the fall of Babylon in 539 and the subsequent return of a few exiles to Jerusalem after the Persian take-over of power. This view only has force if it can be shown that the fall of Babylon impinged directly on the consciousness of the Judaeans (whether in Babylon or the land of Judah). Babylon was not destroyed, but taken over by the Persians. The return of exiles to their own land and the rebuilding of Jerusalem were features of Palestinian life for centuries after the 'fall' of Babylon (cf. Ezra-Nehemiah). Elements of both can be detected in the book of Jeremiah (e.g. 16.14–15; 30.18–21; 31.7–9, 12–14, 38–40), but no date can be put on these texts. The tradition knows of the defeat of Babylon because it can date the Babylonian period of power to seventy years (25.11–12; 29.10; cf. Zech. 1.12) or three generations (27.7), but some of these references may be additions to the second edition (e.g. 27.7; cf. G). The complex collection of material directed against Babylon in 50–51 cannot be read as necessarily coming from the period before the defeat of Babylon, though elements in it appear to predate the Persian conquest of the empire. Certain aspects of the representation of Babylon in 50–51 point to the development of 'Babylon' as a symbol for the imperial powers ranged against Israel (and Yahweh), and the lack of realism in the descriptions of Babylon's defeat suggests a post-539 extension of the anti-Babylonian material in the direction of a final battle between Yahweh and the nations under the guise of 'Babylon' (cf. 25.30–38; Ezek. 38–39; Rev. 17–18). Thus the dating of this level of tradition in the book is far from clear and, though a post-539 date seems the more likely, the evidence must be regarded as ambiguous for putting a specific date on the completion of the book of Jeremiah.

The function and purpose of the Deuteronomistic redaction of Jeremiah are clear, but setting and date remain unknown. Dating depends on prior decisions about the Deuteronomistic corpus, though the independent Deuteronomistic elements (Jer^{Deut}) which worked on the Jeremiah tradition may be later than the production of the history (i.e. fifth century?). The setting of the Deuteronomistic school(s) of editing is a matter of debate among scholars. An Egyptian background is unlikely (cf. 42.13–22; 44.12–14, 26–30 for Deuteronomistic hostility towards Egypt), so the choice is between Babylonian or Palestinian settings for the production of this important strand in the book. Nicholson (1970) favours the preaching circles among the Babylonian exiles for the prose sermons, but a Palestinian background is as likely (cf. Janssen 1956). The emphasis on Jerusalem or the temple in the sermons (e.g. 7.2–4; 11.2, 6; 16.2–4; 19.3–9; 22.1–5; 26.2–6) makes better sense in a Judaean setting than in a Babylonian context. Such preaching is more appropriately delivered to the worshipping community in Jerusalem (or throughout Judah) where references to the past would have more than historic interest for the hearers than would be the case in Babylon. The extent to which the cult functioned in Judah during the Babylonian exile is debatable (cf. Janssen 1956, 94–104, for a positive assessment of the evidence), so a Palestinian setting for the Deuteronomistic sermons may also imply a late sixth-fifth century dating for the strand. Disagreements about the relation between Jeremiah and the Deuteronomistic material also affect questions of dating. For those scholars who posit a direct connection of influence and development between the two sources an earlier date is likelier than is the case among those who see little or no connection between the two. Whether the sermons represent the extension of Jeremiah's preaching by the Deuteronomists (Nicholson) or the work of hypothesized disciples of Jeremiah (Sturdy 1980), the connections between the two serve to date the material in the mid-sixth century. However, neither approach does justice to the distinctiveness of the Deuteronomistic material nor allows for the development of new responses to different situations facing the Jerusalem community in the Persian period. A later dating of the Deuteronomistic level of redaction provides a more adequate account of the matter and recognizes the creative contribution to the formation of the book made by the Deuteronomists.

In my opinion the complex issues of date and setting can only be settled in an approximate way by reference to the different *interests* represented by the various traditions in the text. These interests fracture the monolithic theory of editing and suggest a longer period for the development of the text than is allowed for by many exegetes.

The different cycles of material in the book reflect distinctive interests, and these may be identified with various social circles active after the fall of Jerusalem and during the Persian period. Specific cycles of texts relate to the Judaean kings (21.11–23.6), the prophets (23.9–40; 27–29), the return of exiles and the reconstruction of the land (30–31; 32–33), ideological criticisms of the cult (6.20; 7.1–8.3; 11.9–13; 19.3–9, 12–13), the foreign nations (46–51), the Jewish communities in Egypt (42.7–44.30), the Judaean community under Gedaliah (40.7–41.18), and relations between Jeremiah and important social strata (26; 36; 37–39). Other features in the book which betray the influence of special interests include the theologization of the poetry by means of the redactional framework (transforming it from responses to events in the socio-political world to divine words proclaimed to the community), the denigration of the Judaean communities in favour of the exiles in Babylon (24.4–10; 29.10–19), the favouring of the Judaean communities over against the Jewish exiles in Egypt (42.7–44.30), and the differentiation of various strata of people in Jerusalem (e.g. 21.3–10; 35; 38.2; 39.15–18; 45). Each cycle or set of texts reveals certain religio-political factors at work and a diversity of influences shaping the editing of the book. No consistent, coherent pattern can be established which would unite all these diverse elements into one large body of work reflecting a unity of editing and background. They must be seen as the product of different groups within the Judaean territory struggling for power and position over a long period after the fall of Jerusalem.

Defining the aims of some of these groups is easier in certain cases because it is not difficult to detect their interests behind the text. Thus the denunciations of the Jewish communities in Egypt (44.1, 15) reveal a bitter hostility towards the flourishing groups in that part of the world and, in view of 42.10–12, must reflect a pro-Judaean anti-Egyptian polemic among the Jews of the post-catastrophe period (cf. the attitude of the Jerusalem religious authorities towards the Jews of Elephantine in the fifth century). Conflict between the Judaean and Babylonian communities evidenced by 24.4–10; 29.10–19 is seen by some exegetes as an indication of the Babylonian background to the production of the tradition, but it could be read quite differently. It reflects conflict between the communities to some extent but, as the lateness (i.e. fifth century?) of the strand suggests, the conflict relates to the power struggle between the Judaeans and the returning exiles in the time of Ezra and Nehemiah. This reading is justified in terms of treating the anti-Judaean stance of the Ezra-Nehemiah traditions as the background to the struggle. All those who remain in the land (and the land of Egypt, 24.8) are written off, and only those who return from Babylon have a place in Yahweh's schemes of *šālōm* (29.11). As many people remained in the land and only a few ever returned from Babylon, it is necessary to read these pieces as elements in a fierce polemic about the legitimacy of power in Jerusalem and the land. The Babylonian power group under the aegis of the Persian empire appears to have won power in the time of Ezra and Nehemiah and its interests are represented by these texts in the Jeremiah tradition. Elements of a similar power struggle may be detected in the material on king Jehoiachin (22.24–30), which expresses an aggressively rhetorical rejection of his kingship and any future dynasty associated with him. In the cycle of texts on the kings (21.11–22.30; 23.5–6) so much invective against a minor king who hardly reigned for more than three months is remarkable, and contrasts starkly with the more benevolent attitude taken by the Deuteronomistic conclusion to the book of Jeremiah (52.31–34). If the rejection of Coniah is read against the background of the political struggle to make Zerubbabel, his grandson, the leader of the community in the time of Haggai and Zechariah (see Comm.), then the harshness of 22.24–30 may become comprehensible. The oracles in the cycle represent the anti-Zerubbabel faction and have been incorporated into a collection of disparate pieces now linked to the pre-catastrophe kings. By producing oracles against his ancestor king, the anti-Zerubbabel group denied the legitimacy of Zerubbabel's claim to high office.

Reading the texts in this manner provides known backgrounds against which to interpret them and uncovers the interests served by them. The question of interests is very important to the interpretation of the book of Jeremiah because it provides insights into various features incorporated into it. These features give the book a greater depth than the flat reading of it as all the work of one man in four decades. They also match parts of the book with socio-religious settings provided by other books in the Bible and reveal the Jeremiah tradition to have connections with the reconstruction period of the second temple. The collections of salvation material (30–31; 32–33; cf. 12.14–17; 16.14–15; 23.7–8; 29.10–14) in the tradition run counter to the general tendency of the book to denounce and may be regarded as representing rather different factors in the production of

Jeremiah. They are concerned with rebuilding the city and the economy and with bridging ancient rifts between communities (cf. 3.14–18; 31.31–34) and are rather idyllic expressions of hope about the future (cf. 30.18–21; 31.2–6, 7–9, 10–14). Few exegetes attribute them to Jeremiah (cf. Weinfeld 1976 for this approach), and they are better assigned to a period when a resurgence of optimism expressed in terms of nostalgia became possible (i.e. after the collapse of Babylon). The interests served by this strand of tradition may be akin to those reflected in the Chronicler's eirenic account of the history of the monarchy aimed at unifying all the political parties and tribal factions in a dominion of 'all Israel'. Such an interpretation of this material in Jeremiah points to a date in the fifth or fourth century and moves away from the tendency of some scholars to relate 30–31 (also 3.12–18) to the Hosea tradition and date them accordingly (cf. Rudolph). Similarities between parts of Jeremiah and the book of Hosea can hardly be denied (cf. Gross 1931), but the blanket assumption of an early dating for everything in Hosea is a questionable feature of modern biblical studies and certainly does not necessitate the reading of 30–31 as elements in the *early* preaching of Jeremiah. The similarity between the two traditions at this point is of a piece with the general editing of the book of Jeremiah using material to be found in many of the other biblical books (details in Notes), and has no bearing on the dating of material in Jeremiah. A general conservatism in dating traditions is hardly warranted by the data in the prophetic books, for there are no controls on the material which necessitate an early date for *everything* in the collections of Amos, Hosea, Isaiah, Jeremiah and Ezekiel. But dates and interests are difficult to determine for the positive traditions in the book of Jeremiah and can only be related to the rebuilding of Jerusalem after the depredations of the Babylonian period. The editing of these pieces in the book may reflect a tendency to combat the harshness of the negative material (a feature more obvious in the editing of Isa. 1–12), but they appear too infrequently in the book to sustain this argument. At best they represent a more positive view of the community and the future (cf. 50–51) than the bulk of the tradition, and may be regarded as reflections of the interests of the people in general rather than of factional interests in particular.

Detecting the interests concealed behind various levels of tradition in Jeremiah is not an easy task, and disagreement among exegetes is inevitable over the interpretation of specific texts. According to

Herrmann (1984, 308–10) certain stories may be read as arguing that guilt for the downfall of the city and land should not be assigned to everybody indiscriminately. Certain individuals and classes were more guilty than others: king Jehoiakim and his nobles, the priests and the prophets are singled out as the guilty parties (cf. 26; 36), and other groups are presented in a better light (e.g. the princes and people who defend Jeremiah in 26; Baruch, Ahikam, Ebed-melech). The vacillating Zedekiah appears in a sympathetic light in 37–38 (cf. 34.2–5), but it is hard to say what significance this point has in the tradition (a reflection of the high view taken of Zedekiah in 23.6?). The Deuteronomistic epilogue offers a harsher judgment on Zedekiah (52.1–3). If any one group is marked out in the book of Jeremiah as the guilty party it is the prophets (14.13–16; 23.9–40; 27.14–18; 28; cf. 27.9–10; 29.8–9, 21–23; 'priests and prophets' 2.8, 26b; 4.9; 5.31; 6.13b = 8.10b). This motif is different from that which attaches blame to the kings or the poems which accuse the whole community of being guilty for the catastrophe. It singles out an unidentified group (associated with the temple in 23.11; 26.7; cf. 28.2) for obloquy and in the cycle of 23.9–40 denounces them as the *cause* of the evil in society: 'for from the prophets of Jerusalem ungodliness (*ḥănuppāh*) has gone forth into all the land' (23.15b; cf. Lam. 2.14). In the critique they are associated with evil and all their actions, attitudes, and techniques are described as 'false' (*šeqer*). Their falseness is at the heart of society's collapse and their self-willed evil stands between the people and salvation. The cycle in 27–29 is dominated by the exposure of the prophets as false and warnings to different communities against their prophets (27.9, 14, 16, 17; 29.8; cf. 28.15; 29.21–23). By any standard of measurement there is a remarkable amount of material directed against the prophets in the book of Jeremiah, and the question of interests inevitably arises with reference to the denunciations of the prophets in the tradition.

Most exegetes interpret the cycles against the prophets as evidence of intense prophetic conflict in the decades before the collapse of the Judaean state (cf. Ezek. 13.1–14.11). This interpretation includes the view that the essence of the conflict is the antagonism between Jeremiah and the other prophets. It is a case of Jeremiah against the prophets: an opposition between the bearer of the word and the official mantic functionaries of court and cult. The overall redaction of the book may warrant this interpretation, though there are factors which counsel against such a bland reading of the cycles. Nothing connects Jeremiah with 23.9–40, a cycle with minimal Deuteronomistic editing (cf. Thiel 1973, 249–53), and the cycle of 27–29 represents an independent collection in the book (see Comm.). The blaming of the prophets for the disintegration and deception of society does not sit well with the traditions in the book which make the kings responsible for the Babylonian seizure of the city (e.g. 36.20–31; 37.1–2; 38.17–23) or which specify the people as the culprits (e.g. 5.1–5, 7–8, 20–25; 6.6–8, 9–15, 16–21; 8.4–7). These different traditions of accusation demonstrate the presence in the book of Jeremiah of many, disparate explanations of what caused the downfall of Judah and Jerusalem and reveal the lack of a coherent and consistent account of the period leading up to the catastrophe. Such multiple explanations indicate the search for a justification of what happened combined with a theodicy which would exonerate the deity from culpability. The Deuteronomistic redaction may represent a single strand of explanation (i.e. cultic offences brought the divine anger against city and cult), but it is only one level of tradition in the book. A different level blames the prophets (4.10 hints at the deity manipulating the prophets, cf. Ezek. 14:9). But the lack of a unitary explanation should be noted because it demonstrates the multiple-layered nature of the book of Jeremiah. Like modern explanations of the Shoah (Holocaust), no one account could be given of the disaster which befell Judah and Jerusalem in 587. The book of Jeremiah can be read as a collection of stories and accounts which attempt to explain 587, and the traditions hostile to the prophets belong to one favoured explanation of where blame was to be placed.

A holistic interpretation of the book of Jeremiah as a *series* of explanations of the fall of Judah and Jerusalem (40–44; 46–51 do not fit this approach) raises questions about the retrospective element in the traditions collected together in the book. To what extent do these traditions represent historical features of the period before the collapse of Judah and how much of later periods is incorporated into them? Quantifying such matters is beyond the task of the exegete, but the questions undermine a sanguine approach to the text as the product of pre-587 factors. Too many guilty parties are identified and castigated for these levels of tradition to be other than post-catastrophe deliberations and reflections. This being the case, it must be asked whether the diatribes against the prophets necessarily represent the activities of prophets before the fall or do not include material from a later period (see on 23.33–40)? The history of the Babylonian and Persian periods is not easily written because of the lack of reliable information (cf. Ackroyd 1968a; 1984a; 1984b), so questions of this kind are difficult to answer. Zech. 13.2–6 may be regarded as the final stage in a series of prophetic activities from the time of Haggai and Zechariah (late sixth century) which testifies to bitter hostility against prophets in the fifth century (or later). Behind the cycles against the prophets in the book of Jeremiah may be elements of this ideological conflict which ends in the banning of prophets (Zech. 13.3; note the projection of a different kind of prophetic activity into the future in Mal. 4.5–6 [MT 3.23–24]). The association of the prophets with the period of the catastrophe and the saddling of them with the responsibility for that disaster which constitute the gravamen of the cycles against the prophets in the book of Jeremiah may well be part of the anti-prophetic polemics of the Persian period. Such a reading of the cycles points to interests hostile to prophets behind the material gathered together in the Jeremiah tradition, but can hardly define them more precisely. What interests would be served by such anti-prophetic hostility? Specific quarrels within the Judaean community (cf. Zech. 13.2, 'I will remove *from the land* the prophets') may be reflected in the cycles but whether on behalf of the temple (cf. Jer. 23.11), a militant priesthood, or movements to control the prophets in the period of the second temple (cf. Deut. 13.1–5; 18.20–22) can only be mooted here. With reference to the integration of the cycles into the book of Jeremiah it is possible to put forward a different reading of the denunciations of *all* the prophets (with the notable exception of Uriah ben Shemaiah in 26.20–23) in terms of interests served by the tradition.

It is one of the ironies of the book of Jeremiah that in the name of the *prophet* Jeremiah it denounces the *prophets* of Judah and Jerusalem. An irony because the motif of one prophet denouncing another prophet (cf. 28.13–16; I Kings 22.5–28) exposes the fragility of the genuineness of any prophet. The assertions and counter-assertions of encounters between prophets (e.g. 28; I Kings 13; 22) undermine any attempt to demonstrate the truth of one speaker and the falseness of the other and reveal the prior commitment of the editorial presentation of the stories (see on 28). If this be a correct judgment of the matter, then the hostility directed against the prophets in the book of Jeremiah is part of the editorial claims on behalf of the authenticity of the *prophet* Jeremiah. This may be only the function of the cycles rather than the intention behind the original material, but it fits the presentation of Jeremiah as the bearer of the divine word. He *alone* is the speaker of the word in the community and therefore there is a striking contrast between him and the prophets. This is especially the case in the cycle of 27–29, where the word he speaks is always opposed to the proclamation of the other prophets (27.9–10, 14–15, 16–18; 28.13–16; 29.8–9, 21–23, 30–32). The other prophets in the tradition provide a foil for Jeremiah and by their falseness endorse him as the one speaking the word of Yahweh. The interests served by this contrast are those of the editors of the tradition who, in an undefinable period, wish to present Jeremiah's words as the divine words for their time. It is in conformity to his words that obedience to Yahweh is to be expressed rather than by listening to other prophets (whatever they may represent). To read the cycles in this way is to make an interpretative leap from the text to the interests behind the text, and such an approach is inevitably open to question. However plausible it may seem, it can only be a hypothetical reading of certain levels of tradition within the book, but it is based on making connections between different parts of the text. The representation of Jeremiah as a prophet is a minor feature of the first edition which is enlarged considerably in the second edition. This development shows a movement of the tradition towards the presentation of Jeremiah as the prophetic source of the words of Yahweh and concomitantly as the opponent of all other prophetic voices. The prologue, which is common to both editions, makes him a prophet to the nations (incorporating 25.15–38; 46–51 into the defining of Jeremiah process), but the narratives, cycles about the prophets and the redactional framework develop that figure well beyond the role of a prophet with the oversight of the nations (1.5, 10). Whatever the origins of the man Jeremiah or the cores constituting the tradition (cf. Part IV) may be, the fully developed work focuses on him (the editions vary on the prophetic designation) as the one to whom the word of Yahweh comes to the exclusion of all other sources proclaiming the divine.

This analysis leads on to a consideration of the *theological interests* served by the book. The theologization of the poems and narratives by means of the redactional framework has been noted already and represents a transformation of disparate material into a relatively unified stereotypical proclamation to later communities. Such a transformed level of discrete traditions has significant implications for a number of elements in the book, including the role of the prophet, the setting of the sermons and the religious ideology behind much of Part I. Here the exegete must face the problem of determining the relation between the text and the theological interests served by it. This relationship is an inferred connection rather than a plain reading of the substance of different texts. With regard to the role of the prophet much more is said by way of condemning prophets whose work is described as *šeqer* than is stated in positive terms. Apart from 1.4–10 in the prologue and the formulas for the reception of the divine word represented in the editorial framework, the analysis of prophets in the book is a critical one. What the prophets do and say is false, the imagination of their own minds and the self-willed deception of themselves and the people. The active participation of the prophets in the performance of the prophetic role is emphasized and condemned: they run, they speak, they lead the people, they strengthen the hands of evildoers, they reassure those who despise the word of Yahweh, they dream, they manipulate oracles, they make the people trust what is false, they commit adultery (cf. 23.9–40; 28.15; 29.23). They are profoundly active, and as activists they are condemned for not having the divine word and lacking the divine commission. Their voluntary enthusiasm for the prophetic role marks them as false! In contrast to all this frenzied activity is the representation of Jeremiah as a prophet. In the prologue the brief account of his commission presents him as passive; i.e., receiving the word, not volunteering for it. A formal protest (1.6) underlines his lack of enthusiasm. The divine words are *put* in his mouth (1.9) and he is set over the nations by Yahweh. Yahweh speaks to him and sends him (1.4, 7) and thus a structural contrast is established between Jeremiah and the other prophets (cf. 14.14; 23.21; 28.15; 29.23, 31). When the framework in which the poems, speeches, sermons and narratives are set is analysed, the figure of Jeremiah emerges as one who only speaks or acts when Yahweh commands him to do so. Like a robot he is programmed to act only on divine command and thus represents the paradigmatic prophet (cf. Balaam; the conventional interpretation of the laments as 'confessions' militates against this exemplary role reading of the text and must be regarded as a misreading of the tradition). On the few occasions when he appears as an individual in the community he is clearly at a loss until the divine word comes to him after a period of waiting or consultation (e.g. 28.12; 42.7). He is the bearer of the word and has no existence apart from that word. This theological construction of much of the tradition makes biographical readings of it misconceived. In the narratives, especially in 37–45, Jeremiah appears simply 'as the expression of the divine word' (Ackroyd 1968b, 52). Thus the presentation of the other prophets, with their self-willed activities and deluding visions, serves to emphasize the passive qualities of the true bearer of the word.

The theological interests of an ideology of the word are served by the images of Jeremiah in the tradition, but what setting is to be posited for such an ideology? Whose interests are promoted by this construction of the book? Deuteronomistic circles are the most likely candidates for locating an ideology of the word which would serve their purposes in the second temple period (note the location of Jeremiah in the temple in so many sermons and narratives: e.g. 7.2; 19.1, 14; 22.1; 26.2; 29.26–29; 35.2). A more diversified setting might be hypothesized among post-Deuteronomistic circles which combined Deuteronomistic ideology with prophetically influenced ideas. Part of the problem in determining the question of interests here is the word 'prophet', which is used equivocally in the book of Jeremiah. It is a word used to describe Jeremiah *and* all the other prophets, though not necessarily by the same levels of tradition. Yet in the first edition Jeremiah is rarely called a prophet (1.5; 42.2; 43.6; 45.1; 51.59). It is in the second edition that his role as prophet, i.e. the description of him *as a prophet*, is greatly developed. Between the editions there is a glossing of the tradition which reflects the use of the term 'prophet' to indicate an approved role. This may reflect different circles and locations for the development of the editions or it may represent a period when the title has become neutral or honorific, rather than pejorative (after Zech. 13.2–6?). It may simply be from an era which regarded all great men of the past as 'prophets' (cf. Barton 1984, 7) and which made no distinction between speaking and acting or associated scandal with the epithet 'prophet'. Such a shift in terminological usage would help to explain the differences between the two editions and the confusion likely to arise by designating Jeremiah a 'prophet' when that term appears in the tradition to describe the false mantics who brought about the destruction of Jerusalem by their lying visions. Jeremiah is only called a prophet in two strands of the first edition: 51.59 in conjunction with the denunciation of Babylon (i.e. a prophet against the nations) is to be associated with the prologue 'a prophet to the nations' (1.5) as one strand and in Part IV (42.2; 43.6; 45.1) he is a prophet in a context where there are no other prophets. Hence the first edition does *not* juxtapose Jeremiah *the prophet* and the other prophets, but presents the bearer of the word over against the prophets whose behaviour is false (pseudo-prophets in G). In the second edition social changes have affected nomenclature to the point that Jeremiah may indiscriminately be termed a prophet without being confused with the prophets condemned in the tradition. But in the first instance Jeremiah's status as a prophet arises from the presentation of him as a speaker against the nations (a role akin to the prophets of *šālōm*, see on 28.8–9) and from narratives which have been edited to vindicate the attitudes of the exiled community in Babylon (cf. Pohlmann 1978, 183–97). The interests behind the presentation of Jeremiah *as a prophet* therefore would appear to reflect conflict between different ideologies in the reconstruction period and the origins of the prophet motif to be part of the struggle to impose a *gōlāh*-type outlook on the Judaean community.

This tentative analysis of the influences of the *gōlāh* community, or elements of it, on the construction of parts of the Jeremiah tradition points to a fifth century dating for such features as the prophetic status of Jeremiah and the defence of certain values associated with the exiles in Babylon (cf. the treatment of the reconstruction period in the Ezra-Nehemiah traditions). An earlier date may be mooted for the origins and development of an ideology of the word because the collapse of the central institutions of Judaean and Jerusalem life facilitated the rise of abstract motifs such as the word (of Yahweh). The loss of temple, court, king, statehood, with the concomitant destruction of life and property, must have undermined many Judaean values and exposed the transitoriness of all human matters. Hardly surprising, then, is the emphasis put on the divine word in Deuteronomistic circles and other traditions of reflection on the meaning of the catastrophe:

All flesh is grass,
  and all its beauty is like the flower of the field.
The grass withers, the flower fades,
  when the breath of the LORD blows upon it;
  surely the people is grass.

The grass withers, the flower fades;
but the word of our God will stand for ever (Isa. 40.6b–8).

In contrast to human experience the divine word stands for ever and transcends the catastrophes and setbacks to which flesh is heir (cf. the generality, even vagueness, of Isa. 55.10–11). As the bearer of the word Jeremiah represents one development of a theologized surrogate for human institutions in the Persian period and reflects a movement of considerable importance in the evolution of Judaean religion in the direction of early Judaism. It is difficult to locate the social roots of such a movement, though a number of writers have posited connections between the Jeremiah tradition and the origins of the synagogue (e.g. Duhm; Volz; Janssen 1956, 105–15). It may well be the case that the preaching circles which contributed to the development and transmission of various levels of tradition in the book of Jeremiah became in time the prototypes of the gatherings and activities later associated with synagogues, but no data are available to confirm this hypothesis.

The religious discourses in 2.4–4.4 and the Deuteronomistically influenced sermons reflect a combative ideology designed to denigrate the practices and beliefs of the cultic communities of Judah and Jerusalem (contrast 10.1–16). Merely as records of the past and 'battles long ago' these strands would have neither value nor significance in the circles which constructed and transmitted them, so they must be read as reflecting interests current in the period of their development. Read as polemics against alternative views of Yahweh and his relation to other gods they would appear to belong to the utterances of the Yahweh-alone party intent on disputing the legitimacy of other Yahwists of a more inclusive type (cf. Smith 1971; 1984; Lang 1983, 13–59). Placed at the beginning of Part I (curiously prefaced at a later date by 2.2b–3), the discourses have the effect of smearing the opposition with the blame for the catastrophe of 587. In this sense the fall of Jerusalem in 587 greatly strengthened the ideology of the monist party by discrediting their opponents' claims to control the cult centre because of their association with temple practices of the past (cf. Ezek. 8; 44). Such a reading makes some sense of the conflicting accounts given of worship in the book of Jeremiah (cf. 2.4–3.5 with 14.7–9, 19–22) and accounts for the invective so characteristic of many strands in Part I. It also allows for the element of turning advocated in 3.12–14, 21–4.4a to be interpreted as the cajoling side of the abusive ideological stance aimed at winning converts from the opposition.

So many different interests are reflected in the many levels of tradition contained in the book of Jeremiah that only a multiple-explanations approach can deal with them adequately. But if the interpretation of the text itself is often difficult, the attempt to read behind it in order to penetrate the interests giving rise to it is fraught with greater difficulties. Attempting explanations of the meaning of such large sweeps of tradition may be foolhardy because the modern reader is inclined to think that accumulated traditions must have a coherent meaning and one that will yield to careful scrutiny. On the contrary, biblical texts are untidy masses of disparate material which are often

> like the mounds of ancient near-eastern cities, layer over layer of deposits from generation after generation of nameless persons who lived in these structures, added, destroyed, remodelled, and left the complex to their successors for further alterations (Smith 1984, 256).

This is especially true of collections such as the Pentateuch, the book of Psalms, Isaiah, Jeremiah, Ezekiel, Chronicles, Ezra and Nehemiah. Hence a coherent, consistent reading of a lengthy book is undoubtedly a mistaken one. Allowance must be made for the contribution made by different traditions to the shape of a book and the changes of meaning brought about by editing over a long period of time. In analysing the factors behind the function, setting, and date of the book of Jeremiah an interpretation of the tradition as a whole has not been attempted, but the analysis inevitably bears on a hermeneutical approach to the book. It is tempting to read the setting of the tradition in the period from Josiah to the fall of Jerusalem (1.2–3) as the creation of a special period in the past having a paradigmatic status for the treatment of ideological issues in the period when the traditions were being shaped into the book of Jeremiah. This reading of the editorial introduction to the prologue may be correct, but it is not possible to determine whether this was the intention of the editors. Even if it were what they had in mind, it would not take into account the presence of the post-catastrophe material in the book (e.g. 40–44; 50–51), nor would it apply to the ultimate conclusion of the tradition in 52. Every level of tradition incorporated into the book extends its interpretation and vitiates the attempt to provide a consistent reading of Jeremiah. Thus the wise reader will note the many different interpretations of the text offered by commentators and will pay due attention to the conflicting meanings suggested by various readings of the book without seeking to avoid the questions and lack of certitude which remain after the hermeneuts have had their say.

6. *APOLOGIA PRO LIBRO SUO*

A book as long, complex and difficult as Jeremiah warrants a very long commentary. Limits of space, not to mention more congenital limitations, have contributed to making this commentary shorter than is adequate for a proper account of the matter. Limits on the time available for writing it have curtailed the sophistication and depth of comment on individual sections. Yet if space and time did permit, no commentary would ever be completed to the satisfaction of the commentator, for always there would be further secondary literature to be consulted and arguments to be polished. Kierkegaard comments in his *Philosophical Fragments* that 'the monks never finished telling the history of the world because they always began with the creation' and because 'history continues to grow'; if we were 'to begin by first recounting what has previously been said' we would not be able to begin, let alone finish (1967, 138). So it is with writing commentaries on biblical books: too many exegetes have passed this way before and their accumulated writings fill the libraries of Christendom and other cultures. But what commentator would be so bold as to ignore everything previously written and plunge into commenting on a text without benefit of dragomen! Hence every modern commentary is an uneasy compromise between assimilating as much previous work as possible and transcending the past by striking out in new directions. This commentary on Jeremiah is no exception to such a pattern of writing.

The arrangement of the commentary is a simple one of Text – Notes – Commentary. The English text used is the RSV, but the Notes employ the NEB and the JPSB as alternative renderings of the text into English. As translating the biblical text is a complex business (cf. Bright, CXIX–CXXVI), the Notes include references to the work of other exegetes and their decisions on how the text of Jeremiah should be translated in particular instances. However, the main concern of the Notes is with the two editions of Jeremiah: G and MT; and also with the critical apparatus of BHS. This gives the Notes a philological and exegetical slant, though by no means is a comprehensive account given of the language of the book of Jeremiah. The amount of repetition in Jeremiah is considerable, and some attempt has been made in the Notes to provide adequate cross-references where necessary. After the Notes, where appropriate, reference is made to specific studies bearing directly on a section of the text. Often these studies are incorporated into the Commentary following the Notes, but the specification of them is intended to inform the reader of the whereabouts of further or alternative treatments of the text and issues raised by it. The Commentary, within the limits of space set for it, is a general, discursive approach to the text. It is *not* an exhaustive exegesis of the text, but is intended as a reading of the book of Jeremiah following the general lines of recent research on Jeremiah. Fifty-two chapters constitute a long book and my reading of it is only *one* interpretation of what is a particularly difficult and complex book. Many different readings of Jeremiah are to be found in other commentaries and monographs and, where necessary, I allude to such interpretations. But I have not attempted to provide a comprehensive account of what every other scholar or exegete imagines the meaning of the text may be. What has been said so often before will not bear too much repeating, so I have limited the space devoted to reciting the views of other writers on the book of Jeremiah. Cognizance has been taken of alternative interpretations of the book, but whether the balance is right between my reading of the text and the citation of the opinions of other exegetes is a moot point. In the final analysis the Commentary must be judged as a reading of the *text* of the book of Jeremiah rather than as a refereeing of contrary opinions about its meaning.

In the Commentary I have tried to keep faith with the twentieth century at certain points by asking questions of the text. Such questioning is a move away from the tendency to enshroud the Bible, or parts of it, in mystification whereby the reader is bound to believe whatever it is purported to say. Apart from the serious problems of establishing what precisely the text means (or its *levels* of meaning), the text reflects the period of its production and is a series of responses to the (new) issues of that time. Between then and now there have been many changes (cultural and noetic), radical discontinuities, and what may be regarded as a profound 'epistemic break' (cf.

Foucault 1970, xxiif., 17–45). A commentary is not the place for an exposition of these important shifts in human consciousness, but it would be less than honest to read ancient texts as if the world in which we now hear them had not changed. A hermeneutic of the changes would make a fascinating project for biblical scholars, but in the meantime a responsible commentator must acknowledge the distance between the contemporary world and the ancient traditions without minimizing the *alien* quality of the Bible. In the case of the book of Jeremiah, the critical stance is often simply a matter of noting the relativity of its theological judgments by reference to other biblical books (e.g. Qoheleth, Job). It is important that such comparisons should be made because it is part of the modern understanding of the Bible that the multiple stances, theologies and viewpoints in it are not harmonious. Recognition of this truth means that the exegete will read the text without absolutizing the opinions to be found in it and will not make the mistake of thinking the denunciations which abound in the book of Jeremiah are necessarily the whole truth or a well-balanced account of ancient controversies. In these senses, then, the Commentary keeps faith with the present state of knowledge and allows for the distance between the biblical era and our own.

The Bibliography contains all the works cited or referrred to in the Notes and Commentary. As footnotes have been eschewed, names appear with a date to indicate the specific work under discussion, except in the case of commentaries, where only the name is used. General arguments or viewpoints are usually attributed to a name without a date because it is only the identification of the holder of the position which is required to be acknowledged. No attempt has been made to produce a comprehensive bibliography of the secondary literature on Jeremiah. Only works actually used in the text of this commentary are listed in the Bibliography. That means that books and articles consulted but not used do not appear here. This distinction is a practical one which compromises between a splendidly comprehensive bibliography of every known piece of work on Jeremiah and the Bibliography as a substitute for footnotes. It will become apparent to the reader that sufficient secondary sources have been used to make the Bibliography a fair representation of current literature on the subject.

If the Bibliography represents the art of compromise, it is intended also to indicate the sources where the arguments of the Notes and

Commentary are to be found in more extended form or where quite different positions are maintained. Dependence on the work of others is inevitable in the production of a commentary and I have used, in particular, the commentaries of Duhm, Volz, Rudolph, and the translation, notes and comments of Bright. The work of Ackroyd, Holladay, McKane and Thiel has been indispensable also. However, as every commentary represents the individual reading of the commentator, it needs to be balanced by reference to other commentaries, and the wise reader will consult a number of different commentaries in order to gain a fair understanding of the book under scrutiny. In this commentary, within the limits set by the series, I have tried to combine an individualistic reading of the text with an acknowledged use of other exegetes' work. At times my approach to the text is a minimalist one and hardly does more than paraphrase a unit where others find rich deposits of theological ore. A minimalist approach may be a necessary corrective to the imaginative schemes of some commentators for the biblical text is often in danger of sinking under the weight of theological embellishments. At other times I have expanded comment in search of the sub-text in order to find the proper frame of reference for interpreting the text. Finding the balance between a minimalist and an expansive approach to the text is not an easy hermeneutic exercise, and fluctuations between the two are not uncommon in this commentary.

The book of Jeremiah is not only a lengthy text; it is also a complicated and difficult one. I have therefore allowed many questions to appear in the Notes and Commentary in order to draw the reader's attention to the range of possible interpretations of a particular text. The query mark may well be the most important sign used in this commentary. A text as full of metaphors as the book of Jeremiah does not present the interpreter with an easy task, and the number of abstruse or ambiguous elements are such as to require a multiple-explanations approach to interpretation. Where ambiguities abound (as they do in Jeremiah), scholars least of all are entitled to firmness of opinion. An ancient text in an alien language from a culture far removed from our own demands an undogmatic approach and a generous allowance for diversity of opinion on its meaning. When reading the book of Jeremiah (or any book of the Bible) it would be wise to keep in mind the counsel of, I believe it was, Maimonides: 'Teach your tongue to say I don't know.' Occasions for such confessions of ignorance are frequent in the study of Jeremiah and warrant the consideration of as many commentaries and other sources as possible. An occupational hazard of the commentator's trade is the desire to clarify the meaning of the text to the point of explaining away every view except the one favoured by the writer. The tendency to offer too many alternative meanings is its twin hazard. Whether either hazard has been avoided in this commentary remains to be discovered. But between the tedium of the exhaustive comment and the irritation of the all too brief exegesis is the area of the ideal commentary to which all competent exegetes aspire. This commentary is but *one* account of the task and *one* reading of the book of Jeremiah. To chart the territory properly, go read *all* the other commentaries!

7. OUTLINE OF THE BOOK OF JEREMIAH

Prologue: 1.1–19
1.1–3 redactional title to book; 4–10 commissioning of Jeremiah as prophet to the nations; 11–14 two visions; 15–16, 17–19 additional material

Part I: 2.1–25.14. Poems and sermons against Judah and Jerusalem
A. 2.1–6.30
2.1–3 preface to the cycle of poems; 2.4–4.4 discursive poems on false cults; 4.5–6.26 cycle of poems on 'the foe from the north' and other motifs; 6.27–30 coda
B. 7.1–10.25
7.1–8.3 sermons against cultic practices; 8.4–9.26 collection of individual poems; 10.1–16 polemic against idols and hymn of praise to Yahweh; 10.17–25 independent fragments
C. 11.1–13.27
11.1–14 the preacher of the covenant; 11.15–12.13 various poems and laments; 12.14–17 prose fragment about the nations; 13.1–11 the waistcloth incident; 13.12–14 a saying about jars of wine; 13.15–27 sundry poems
D. 14.1–17.27
14.1–15.4 the drought; 15.5–21 poems, laments and prose fragments; 16.1–9 sermon against the social practices of the people; 16.10–17.18 miscellany of poetic and prosaic pieces; 17.19–27 rulings about the sabbath

E. 18.1–20.18

18.1–12 Jeremiah at the potter's; 18.13–17 poem about the nation's apostasy; 18.18 prose fragment; 18.19–23 a lament; 19.1–20.6 incident with a ceramic flask, sermon against false cults, and matters arising; 20.7–18 laments

F. 21.1–24.10 (appendix to I)

21.1–10 Zedekiah and the fate of Jerusalem; 21.11–23.6 cycle of material about the kings and the city; 23.7–8 oracle of future restoration; 23.9–40 cycle of material about the prophets; 24.1–10 vision of the two baskets of figs with explanation

Summary of Part I. 25.1–14

Part II: 25.15–38; 46–51. Oracles against the nations

25.15–29 dramatic performance with wine cup and list of nations doomed; 25.30–38 poetic denunciations of the nations; 46.1 title; 46.2–26 poems against Egypt; 46.27–28 restoration of Israel; 47.1–7 against the Philistines; 48.1–47 poetic and prose denunciations of Moab; 49.1–6 concerning the Ammonites; 49.7–22 against Edom; 49.23–27 against Damascus; 49.28–33 against Kedar and the kingdoms of Hazor; 49.34–39 concerning Elam; 50.1–51.58 poems and prose denouncing Babylon; 51.59–64 incident with a book against Babylon

Part III: 26–36. Miscellaneous narratives and cycles of material

26 Jeremiah before the tribunal; 27–29 independent cycle of material directed against the prophets; 30.1–31.22 cycle of poems about the restoration of the nation; 31.23–33.26 prose additions to the cycle; 34.1–7 interview between Jeremiah and Zedekiah; 34.8–22 emancipation of the slaves and a sermon; 35 incident with the Rechabites; 36 the writing and reading of the scroll by Baruch in the temple, the princes' chamber, and before the king

Part IV: 37–45. The fall of Jerusalem and aftermath

37.1–2 titular summary; 37.3–38.28 Jeremiah during the siege of Jerusalem; 39.1–10 the fall of Jerusalem; 39.11–14 the release of Jeremiah; 39.15–18 words of deliverance to Ebed-melech; 40.1–6 another release of Jeremiah; 40.7–41.18 Gedaliah's governorship and assassination; 42.1–6 community appeal to Jeremiah; 42.7–22 sermon against going to Egypt; 43.1–7 response to sermon and retreat to Egypt; 43.8–13 incident in Egypt; 44 denunciations of communities in Egypt, with popular responses and further denunciations; 45 words for Baruch

Epilogue: 52.1–34
1–3a summary of Zedekiah's reign; 3b–11 the fall of Jerusalem and the fate of Zedekiah; 12–16 destruction of Jerusalem and deportation of the people; 17–23 transportation of the temple furnishings; 24–27 execution of the leading citizens; 28–30 statistics of the three deportations; 31–34 the release of king Jehoiachin from prison

COMMENTARY

PROLOGUE 1.1–19

1.1–3

1[1] The words of Jeremiah, the son of Hilkiah, of the priests who were in Anathoth in the land of Benjamin, 2 to whom the word of the LORD came in the days of Josiah the son of Amon, king of Judah, in the thirteenth year of his reign. 3 It came also in the days of Jehoiakim the son of Josiah, king of Judah, and until the end of the eleventh year of Zedekiah, the son of Josiah, king of Judah, until the captivity of Jerusalem in the fifth month.

---

[1] MT *dibrē yirm^e yāhū*, 'the words of Jeremiah': the closest parallel to this formal introduction is Amos 1.1 (*dibrē ʿāmos*, 'the words of Amos'); Rudolph, 2, translates it as 'the story of Jeremiah'. G *to rhēma tou theou, ho egeneto epi Ieremian*, 'the word of God which came to Jeremiah'; this is closer to MT introduction to a number of sections (e.g. 7.1; 11.1; 18.1; 34.1, 8; 35.1; 40.1) and other prophetic collections (cf. Hos. 1.1; Joel 1.1; Micah 1.1; Zeph. 1.1). 'Jeremiah' (meaning uncertain: perhaps 'Yahweh loosens [the uterus]' or 'Yahweh exalts'; even 'Yahweh hurls' or 'Yahweh justifies'): the name is not an infrequent one in the Bible; two other Jeremiahs appear in 35.3; 52.1 (others in I Chron. 5.24; 12.4, 10, 13; Neh. 10.2; 12.1, 34). 'Hilkiah': an equally common name, cf. 29.3; II Kings 18.18, 26; 22.4, 8, 10, 12, 14; I Chron. 6.13 (MT 30); 26.11; Neh. 12.7, 21. MT *min-hakkōh^a nīm ʾ^a šer baʿ^a nātōt*, 'from the priests who (were) in Anathoth': cf. Amos 1.1, 'who was among the shepherds from Tekoa'; for the Anathoth connection cf. 11.21, 23; 29.27; 32.7–9. T Lam. 1.1 *kah^a nāʾ rabbāʾ*, 'the great priest', makes Jeremiah the senior priest, presumably a deduction from his family background in Anathoth. **[2]** MT *ʾ^a šer hāyāh debar-yhwh ʾēlāyw*, 'to whom the word of Yahweh came': a second (and probably secondary) title using a formulaic reception of the divine word notice = 14.1; 46.1; 47.1; 49.34 (though Rudolph treats it as a simple relative clause, cf. I Kings 18.31 for the same phrase). G *Amōs* for 'Amon' (cf. G Isa. 1.1). Cf. 3.6; 25.3 for other references to the period of Josiah in Jeremiah; Josiah's thirteenth year would be 627. **[3]** G lacks *tōm*, 'the end of': MT is incoherent in view of the final clause 'in the *fifth* month' (hardly the *end* of Zedekiah's eleventh year); cf. 52.4, 12 for the datings here (587).

Thiel 1973, 49–61

These verses form one of the longest (cf. Ezek. 1.1–3) and most complicated introductions to the anthologies traditionally known as the prophetic collections. The closest parallel is with Amos 1.1, but the form here provides a closure with 25.1–3 and may be regarded as a post-Deuteronomistic editorial introduction to the book of Jeremiah (cf. Thiel, 56). It introduces and identifies the speaker of the collected materials in 2–20 (plus 21–24) as Jeremiah ben Hilkiah, one of the priests of Anathoth in the territory of Benjamin. It dates his speaking career in the service of the divine word to the period 627–587. A forty-year period such as this is a conventional figure and indicates the significance of the speaker and the importance of his work – similar periods of activity are ascribed to Moses for his leadership of the people from Egypt to the edge of the land of Canaan (cf. Deut. 34.7) and to David as king over Israel (I Kings 2.11). Thus the son of Hilkiah (to be identified with Josiah's high priest?) is represented by the editorial heading as a very important figure in the fateful decades which led to the exile of Jerusalem.

As the editorial title to the prologue which introduces the words of Jeremiah, vv. 1–3 present Jeremiah as a priest (his status is elevated further in T Lam. 1.1) who began his work in 627. As a Benjaminite he may not necessarily have been a member of the official cult in the Jerusalem temple (cf. Hananiah from Gibeon in 28.1), but much of the book of Jeremiah represents him as operating in or from the temple (e.g. 7.2; 19.1–2, 14; 22.1; 26.2; 28.1; 29.26; 35.2; cf. 36.5–6), so it may well be the case that the editors regarded Jeremiah as a priest active in the temple. The association of Jeremiah with the priests of Anathoth is general enough to leave open the precise nature of his involvement with the priesthood of Anathoth but, given the Deuteronomistic-style influences in vv. 1–3, some allusion to Anathoth, the place to which king Solomon banished Abiathar the priest (I Kings 2.26–27), cannot be ruled out. This banishment fulfilled the divine word against the house of Eli in Shiloh and it is difficult to avoid detecting a whiff of irony here in view of the use of Shiloh as an analogy of the destruction of Jerusalem and its temple in 7.14. Thus from the place to which Abiathar was banished in the days before the temple was built comes a man who will speak the word against Solomon's edifice and preside over the destruction of Jerusalem. The word has come full circle. It is, however, much less likely (even an illegitimate leap of interpretation) that 1.1 should be read as indicating that Jeremiah's family were descended from Abiathar *the priest*. The Anathoth connection figures very slightly in the rest of the tradition: cf. 'Jeremiah of Anathoth' (29.27; 27–29 are an independent section in the book), 'the men of Anathoth' (11.21, 23), and the family property there (32.7–9; cf. 37.12). It is a marginal element in the book and may be regarded as part of the later additions to the developing tradition, typified by 1.1.

The claim that Jeremiah (first) received the divine word in the thirteenth year of king Josiah (i.e. 627) raises a problem for the interpretation of the book. This is because there is virtually nothing in the tradition which may be *clearly* attributed to Josiah's period (627–609): a possible allusion to the death of that king in 2.16 and an oblique reference to a dead person in 22.10 (identified as Josiah in the prose commentary of 22.11) do not constitute material from the time of Josiah but possible reflections on Josiah of a later period. Two pieces are dated to Josiah's reign (3.6–10; 25.3–7), though only 3.6–10 is explicitly set in his time and it is generally regarded by commentators as a later development of the tradition (cf. McKane 1981, 229–33). 25.3 reflects the editing of 1.1–3 and, though consistent, is hardly *evidence* of activity on Jeremiah's part in the period when Josiah was king. It is, of course, possible to read much of Part I (e.g. 1–6, cf. Rudolph, 1) as coming from Josiah's time, but as these chapters may be read equally well for later periods, the reading is determined more by considerations other than the exegesis of the text. A dominant feature of 2–20 is the complete lack of even editorial guidance about when each section is to be dated, and 1.1–3 cannot be used to make good that lack because it allows a forty-year period for the work (perhaps limited to twenty-three years by 25.3). The timelessness of the oracles and discourses of 2–20 is important theologically because it allows them to be used in different periods and with reference to communal affairs other than those perhaps envisaged originally in the oracular utterances.

If nothing in 2–20 necessitates a date in the time of Josiah, what is to be made of the editorial introduction setting Jeremiah in the period 627–587? The conventionality of the forty-year motif has been noted, and it may explain why the thirteenth year of Josiah marks the beginning of Jeremiah's work (i.e. counting backwards from 587!). As the introduction is also quite conventional (cf. the various titles prefacing the collection of prophetic anthologies; discussion of 1.1–3 in Thiel, 49–61), it is very difficult to determine what relationship there is between 'the words of Jeremiah' and the rest of the preface. Conventions conceal particularity, and the presentation of Jeremiah in quasi-Deuteronomistic terms turns him into a stereotypical figure rather than a real person. What can be said with some certitude is that the editors of the book of Jeremiah wish to present the period of Jeremiah's activity as 627–587. The fall of Jerusalem is the limit of his work (does this imply that 40–44 were not part of the editors' original collection?) and the time of Josiah its beginning. For Deuteronomists and those influenced by them Josiah's period is the one redeeming feature of the closing decades of Judaean statehood, and they may have placed Jeremiah there in order to associate him with the great reforming activities of that king (cf. Hoffmann 1980, 169–270, on the ideological nature of that reform). Thus Jeremiah's work may be read as a continuation of Josiah's reform by other means. However, this may be to read too much into vv. 1–3, and it would be wiser to admit that there is *no* necessary connection between the title and the work which follows. The prologue may be intended as a guide to the reading of 2–20 (i.e. vv. 4–19), but the title need not be read in such a fashion. It specifies certain 'facts' about Jeremiah and uses a conventional indication of the period of his activity (cf. Isa. 1.1; Hos. 1.1; Amos 1.1; Micah 1.1; Zeph. 1.1). It would, however, be wrong to read such stereotypical introductions to the various anthologies as affording biographical information. That is not their intention, and to attempt to read what follows as the biography of the individual named in 1.1 is to misunderstand the nature of the material collected together in the tradition. The association of the speaker named in the titular introduction with the reigns of specific kings is conventional, and reflects the Deuteronomistic presentation of prophecy and monarchy as twin institutions in the history of Israel (cf. Ezek. 1.2; the anthologies of Joel, Obadiah, Jonah, Nahum and Habakkuk lack such introductions).

The other two kings mentioned in v. 3 are less problematic as the material contained in Parts III and IV is set mainly in the time of Zedekiah, with an occasional story placed in Jehoiakim's reign (e.g.

26, 36, 35). To judge from the stories contained in the tradition, Jeremiah is to be associated with king Zedekiah in the period 597–587 and perhaps with king Jehoiakim during 605–597. Yet there are no encounters between Jeremiah and Jehoiakim in contrast to his relationship with Zedekiah, and the only occasion on which they might have met introduces the figure of Baruch so as to remove Jeremiah adroitly from the possibility of such a confrontation (cf. 36).

1.4–10

4 Now the word of the LORD came to me saying,
5 ‘Before I formed you in the womb I knew you,
and before you were born I consecrated you;
I appointed you a prophet to the nations.’
6 Then I said, ‘Ah Lord GOD! Behold, I do not know how to speak, for
I am only a youth.’ 7 But the LORD said to me,
‘Do not say, “I am only a youth”;
for to all to whom I send you shall go,
and whatever I command you you shall speak.
8 Be not afraid of them,
for I am with you to deliver you,
says the LORD.’
9 Then the LORD put forth his hand and touched my mouth; and the
LORD said to me,
‘Behold I have put my words in your mouth.
10 See, I have set you this day over nations and over kingdoms,
to pluck up and to break down,
to destroy and to overthrow,
to build and to plant.’

---

[4] MT *way^{e}hī d^{e}bar-yhwh ’ēlay lē’mōr*, ‘and the word of Yahweh came to me saying’: G *pros auton* ‘to him’; the reception of the divine word formula used here appears also in vv. 11, 13; 2.1; 16.1; G 32.26; G 35.12 (cf. 42.7) and represents one of the few such first-person accounts in the tradition. **[5]** K *’ṣwrk* (ṣūr, ‘fashion’); Q *’eṣṣār^{e}kā*, ‘I formed you’ (*yṣr*, ‘form, fashion’); cf. Gilula 1967 for an Egyptian parallel to the images and ideas expressed here; Isa. 49.1, 5b. MT *hiqdaštīkā’*, ‘I set you apart’: *qdš* (‘sanctify, make holy’) can also have the sense of ‘ritually prepare’ (cf. 6.4; 22.7; 51.27, 28), a sense well suited here for a priest (cf. v. 1). MT *nābī’ laggōyim*, ‘a prophet to the nations’: cf. 25.15–38; 46–51. **[6]** MT *kī-na‘ar ’anōkī*, ‘for I am a child’: *na‘ar* has a wide range of meanings from child, lad, boy, youth to apprentice, retainer, squire; here it is a conventional response and reflects the Deuteronomistic presentation of Solomon (I Kings 3.7, *wᵉʾānōkī naʿar qāṭōn*, 'but I am a small child') and Samuel (cf. I Sam. 3.1, 8, where *naʿar* describes the youthful apprentice to Eli the priest); cf. Kenik 1983, 104–8, on the 'little child' motif. **[7]** G has the deity repeat the full statement '*for* (*hoti*) I am a child'. The motif of sending (*šlḥ*) is important in the sections on prophets (e.g. 23.21, 32; 28.15; cf. 43.2). MT *wᵉʾēt kol-ʾᵃšer ʾᵃṣawwᵉkā tᵉdabbēr*, 'and all which I command you shall speak': cf. Deut. 18.18, *wᵉdibbēr . . . kol-ʾᵃšer ʾᵃṣawwennū*, 'and he shall speak . . . all which I command him'; Ex. 7.2, *ʾattāh tᵉdabbēr ʾēt kol-ʾᵃšer ʾᵃṣawwᵉkā*, '*you*, you shall speak all which I command you'; discussion in Broughton 1958. **[9]** G *pros me* '(put forth his hand) to me'. MT *wayyaggaʿ ʿal-pī*, 'and he touched my mouth' = Isa. 6.7aα. MT *hinnēh nātattī dᵉbāray bᵉpīkā*, 'look, I have put my words in your mouth': cf. Deut. 18.18 *wᵉnātattī dᵉbāray bᵉpīw*, 'and I will put my words in his mouth'; a similar phrase occurs in Isa. 51.16aα (using *śīm*, 'put', for *ntn*). A different set of images is used in Ezek. 2.8–3.3 for the reception of the divine words. **[10]** The six terms (*ntš*, *ntṣ*, *ʾbd*, *hrs*, *bnh*, *nṭʿ*) used here appear throughout the tradition (12.14–17; 18.7, 9; 24.6; 31.28, 38, 40; 42.10; 45.4), though never all six together (except in 31.28). 1.10 differs from all the other occurrences of these motifs in that it represents Jeremiah as the agent, whereas Yahweh is the performer in all the other references. Some exegetes delete the middle couple, 'to destroy and to overthrow' (e.g. Volz, 3; Rudolph, 4; cf. BHS), as it destroys the chiastic form of the statement, though it accurately reflects the range used throughout the book (cf. Carroll 1981, 55–8). G lacks *wlhrws*, 'and to overthrow'. Cf. Bach 1961 for the meaning of the terms as shorthand for prosperous community life or the destruction of civilized living. Cf. Eccl. 3.2–8 for a similar, but longer, series of polarities.

Berridge 1970, 26–62; Carroll 1981, 31–58; Gouders 1971; March 1970; Reventlow 1963, 24–77

The prologue presents as the first oracular statement in the tradition a divine commissioning of Jeremiah (cf. vv. 1, 11) to be a prophet to the nations (vv. 5, 10). No occasion is specified for this reception of the divine word and its placing in the prologue must be understood as an affirmation of the status of Jeremiah *as a prophet* (*nābīʾ*). In the first edition (G) Jeremiah is seldom referred to as a prophet, but the second edition (MT) frequently identifies him as *the prophet*. Both editions contain 1.4–10 and therefore the section must come from a period when the reading of the tradition as the output of *a prophet* was beginning to establish itself. Yet such a prologue is required to make it clear that the utterances of Jeremiah are to be read as the divine word mediated through a legitimate prophet. Hence v. 9 represents Yahweh as putting *his words* in Jeremiah's mouth and other elements in vv. 4–10 cover the necessary ideological requirements of Yahweh's sending (*šlḥ*), commanding, commissioning, appointing and enabling. These are prerequisites of the authorized prophet in a period of ideological conflict between different factions of prophets over the polemical issues of authority and legitimation (cf. 23.9–40; 27–29; Deut. 13.1–5; 18.9–22; Zech. 13.2–6). At the outset of their work the editors assert the authorization of Jeremiah ben Hilkiah of the priests of Anathoth to be Yahweh's prophet.

Less clear is the force of the term 'to the nations' (*laggōyim*). The appointment of Jeremiah to be a prophet to the nations and the setting of (*pqd*) him over the nations and the kingdoms must be read as a statement about his oversight of the foreign nations (cf. 25.15–38; 46–51) and identifies his sphere of influence. As such, the commissioning reflects a period when the nations hold dominance over Judah and subtly reverses that domination by representing Yahweh's prophet as the one with real power over these apparent dominant forces. He it is who, at Yahweh's command, exercises control over the fortunes of the nations – *he* plucks up and breaks down and *he* builds and plants. The misfortune or well-being of nations depends upon him (cf. 29.7) and against him the nations struggle in vain (cf. v. 8). How these roles are worked out may be detected in the material on the foreign nations: Jeremiah serves them with the cup of the wine of Yahweh's wrath (25.15–17, 27–29) or proclaims their destruction (46–51). Subtle hints of the restoration of the fortunes of the nations appear in 46–51 (e.g. 46.26; 48.47; 49.6, 39) and in 12.14–17; 18.7–10. But the real force of v. 10 is derived from the tradition, where the six terms appear in various permutations (12.14–17; 18.7, 9; 24.6; 31.28, 38, 40; 42.10; 45.4) referring to Jerusalem, Judah and the nations. These are used here to summarize the work of Jeremiah as an activity guiding the destinies of the nations. What is curious about the form of v. 10 is the fact that only here is a human agent made the subject of these verbs; every other use of them has Yahweh as the one who destroys or builds. This variation of usage indicates how 1.4–10 uses terms from the tradition but in a rather different way from how 2–51 employs them. Other examples of this derivative, yet distinctive, employment of terms include the preparation (*qdš*) of Jeremiah in v. 5, a word used in the tradition for the sacral preparation of the nations to go to war (e.g. 6.4; 22.7; 51.27, 28), and the appointment (*pqd*) of Jeremiah over the nations and kingdoms in v. 10, a motif frequently employed to describe Yahweh's appointment of Judah's enemies (e.g. 6.15; 9.24 [EV 25]; 15.3; 21.14) or his punishment of offenders.

These features of vv. 4–10 suggest that the commissioning of Jeremiah is constructed to reflect certain aspects of the tradition and reflect an elevation of the prophet to the position where he is not simply Yahweh's representative but acts as Yahweh in the affairs of the nations. This divine role is demonstrated in 51.59, where it is Jeremiah who commands and Seraiah ben Neriah who obeys in the matter of destroying Babylon (cf. Ex. 4.16; 7.1 for a similar relationship between Moses as god and Aaron as his mouth, i.e. his prophet). No longer is it Yahweh who plucks up or plants (cf. 17.5–8 for different arboreal imagery), but Jeremiah the prophet to the nations who engages in these tasks. But why a prophet to the nations? Why not a prophet to Judah or, even, Israel? Why is Jeremiah not like Ezekiel who is sent to the house of Israel and *not* to many peoples of foreign speech (Ezek. 3.4–6)? It is difficult to answer these questions, especially as the Isaiah and Ezekiel traditions contain as much material against the nations as 46–51 (e.g. Isa. 13–23; Ezek. 25–32). Perhaps the sweep of different traditions about the Jewish communities in Palestine, Babylonia, Egypt and elsewhere during the period of Babylonian domination justifies this designation of Jeremiah. After 597 and 587 the scattering of Palestinians all over the empire and the rise of hopes for their return (e.g. 31.8, 17; 40.11–12; 44.1) created a climate of opinion orientated towards the communities outside Palestine. As the overseer of the nations Jeremiah belongs to this climate and is appropriately represented as such in 1.4–10. In the light of the catastrophe of 587 any introduction to the book of Jeremiah would need to appeal to those who suffered the most by the fall of Jerusalem and in order to do that must address itself to the contemporary context of such social groups. This is achieved in vv. 4–10 by the presentation of Jeremiah as *a prophet to the nations*, an achievement more readily observed in the MT, where the beginning and ending of the tradition are direct statements about the nations (1.5, 10; 51.59–64). This symmetry is spoiled to some extent by the additions of 1.1–3; 52 and because it is lacking in G, but it remains a significant feature of the second edition and should be read as an important perspective on the tradition.

Many exegetes take a different view from the one expressed here and include Judah in the nations over which Jeremiah is appointed prophet and overseer (e.g. Michaud 1960, 160–2; Rudolph, 6; Thompson, 146). That possibility cannot be ruled out, but it is less likely for two reasons. The term *gōyīm*, 'nations', when used in the *plural*, invariably applies to the foreign nations (the singular *gōy* is occasionally used of Judah *or* Israel, cf. 5.9, 29; 7.28; 9.8 [EV 9]; unless *both* are intended, e.g. Ezek. 35.10; 37.22) and in contrast to Judah or Israel (e.g. 10.2). The other reason is more persuasive because it relates to the pattern of commissioning to be found in the prophetic collections. In each case where there is a commissioning motif the individual is sent (*šlḥ*) to speak or prophesy to Israel or Judah (cf. Amos 7.15; Isa. 6.8–9; Ezek. 2.3–7; 3.4–11). Thus the absence of a specific reference to Judah in 1.4–10 is noteworthy and makes the commissioning of Jeremiah an act with reference to the foreign nations. The closest analogy to this may be the burning bush commission of Moses where he is sent (*šlḥ*) to the Pharaoh (Ex. 3.10), though his mission is to deliver the people of Israel from Egypt. That Jeremiah is not specifically commissioned to act on behalf of or against (cf. Isa. 6.8–13) Judah is strange and necessitates the development of the second vision in vv. 15–16 in order to incorporate some such reference in the prologue.

The lack of an occasion for the commissioning of Jeremiah in vv. 4–10 may be explained by the hyperbole in v. 5, which places his formation to be a prophet to the nations before his birth (or even his conception!). This uterine setting where he was consecrated to or prepared for his task (*qdš* may reflect his priestly status, cf. 1.1) has an Egyptian parallel in which the god Amun addresses king Pianchi (XXVth Dynasty: eighth century) with similar words:

> It was in the belly of your mother that I said concerning you that you were to be ruler of Egypt; it was as seed and while you were in the egg that I knew you, that (I knew) you were to be Lord (Gilula 1967; other examples in Beyerlin 1978, 27–30).

Similar imagery is used of Israel, the servant of Yahweh, in Isa. 49.1b, 5, where the context makes the metaphors difficult to interpret (cf. Westermann 1969, 208). Two examples of such hyperbolic assertions of divine approval do not constitute a pattern, but the force of each statement represents the validation of a claim to office. In view of the anti-prophetic polemics which dominate parts of the book of Jeremiah, v. 5 must be read as an introductory authentication of Jeremiah as a genuine prophet, appointed by Yahweh, whose task it is to speak the divine words to the nations. Its place in the prologue is therefore a necessary counter to any challenge to Jeremiah's authenticity and to the sceptical question, unexpressed but implicit in the necessity for including such an assertion as this, 'when did he become a prophet?' it responds 'before he was born!' This priest's sacred task is being a prophet and he is sent and commanded by Yahweh to speak as ordered by the lord Yahweh.

The brief moment of dialogue constituted by vv. 5–7 registers a formal protest by the speaker on the grounds of his youth (the occasion of this exchange is not recorded). Such an objection is stereotypical and forms part of the pattern of commissioning narratives to be found in Ex. 3–4; Judg. 6; Isa. 6; cf. I Sam. 10.20–24 (analysis of these stories in Baltzer 1968; Buss 1982; Carroll 1981, 31–44; Habel 1965; Richter 1970). It would appear to be the case that part of the authenticity of the commissioned one is indicated by a formal reluctance to take on the commission. But the objection is a conventional response and should not be interpreted in a literal manner. The various objections of Moses permit a pyrotechnical display by the deity, and the formal evasions of Gideon, Saul, Isaiah or Jeremiah are easily swept aside without impairing the commissioning.

Jeremiah's protest that he is a youth need not be taken literally because the same objection is used by *king* Solomon at his accession, where it reflects conventional humility rather than the king's youth (I Kings 3.7; Solomon was old enough to be married and may have been about twenty, cf. I Kings 11.42; 14.21; Gray 1977). In Egyptian royal ideology the king was chosen in infancy and the Deuteronomistic historians have adapted this motif for Solomon and, conceivably, for Jeremiah (cf. Kenik 1983, 104–6; Beyerlin 1978, 27–30). It is a moot point whether in the absence of the monarchy after 587 the commissioning of Jeremiah to be a prophet to the nations is a replacement of kingship with prophecy. Such a possibility would close the circle begun with Samuel when, according to the Deuteronomistic historians, kingship replaced prophecy.

This reading of the formal objection 'I am a youth' as a conventional show of humility and reluctance and as a parallel to king Solomon's prayer for wisdom when Yahweh appeared to him in a dream at Gibeon (I Kings 3.5–15) negates the need to become involved in a lengthy and complex discussion about when Jeremiah might have been born. Many exegetes have struggled with Jeremiah's reference to his youthfulness in conjunction with the editorial note of v. 2 which dates the beginning of his work in 627 and have argued for his birth in the period 650–640 (e.g. Bright; Rudolph; Levin 1981; Overholt 1971). Others take 627 as the year of his birth and 609 or 605 as the beginning of his work (e.g. Holladay; Hyatt; Whitley 1964). All these arguments are based on the biographical approach to the book of Jeremiah and make no allowance whatsoever for the conventionalist reading of the text. Jeremiah's protest is understood as a literal assertion of youthfulness and his age calculated in relation to v. 2. However, the reading of v. 5 as a formal protest characteristic of a commissioning narrative removes the question of Jeremiah's age from the agenda of interpretation and relegates it to the minutiae of scholarly debate.

The presence in vv. 7, 9 of elements to be found in Ex. 7.2; Deut. 18.18; Isa. 6.7 (see Notes) indicates the influence of other sources in the construction of vv. 4–10. A common pattern of commissioning and sending may be detected for Moses and Jeremiah (cf. Holladay 1964; 1966a for one view of this pattern) and, though many exegetes favour a one-way influence of the Moses story on Jeremiah, this suggests a common origin for this section of the prologue to Jeremiah and the construction of the commissioning of Moses using a prophetic model. The extent to which Jeremiah may be considered the prophet of Deut. 18.15, 18 or an instantiation of it is difficult to determine because Deut. 18.15–18 are a late addition to the Deuteronomistic law on the prophet (cf. Mayes 1979, 279–80). The influence could be the other way and the producers of 1.7, 9 might have belonged to the circles which contributed to the formulations of Deut. 18.9–22. A pattern of placing the divine words in the prophet's mouth (Moses, Jeremiah, the sequence of prophets in Deut. 18.15, 18) represents the Deuteronomistic view of prophecy as the mediation of the divine word, and much of the redactional framework in the book of Jeremiah presents a Jeremiah who only speaks in order to declare the word of Yahweh. The touching of the mouth (cf. Isa. 6.7) symbolizes the transference of the words from Yahweh to Jeremiah (cf. Ezek. 2.8–3.3). Thus the man whose words are gathered together in the tradition is presented as a prophet to the nations, one set apart for this sacred task from before his birth, commissioned and sent, given the words with which to speak, and set over the nations to break and build, pluck up and plant. A veritable prophet for all seasons!

One major question of interpretation remains: to whom are these words addressed? That question may be rephrased as: on what occasion would such information be made available? 1.4–10 cannot be read as the *private* experience of the prophet Jeremiah, for in declaring it in the prologue the editors make it public knowledge (cf. Langkammer 1965 on ecstasy and psychology in relation to this story). As an account designed to authenticate Jeremiah's work, vv. 4–10 by their very nature are a public proclamation declaring Jeremiah to be a prophet of Yahweh, commissioned to speak his words to the nations. But no occasion is indicated for this declaration, either in the life of Jeremiah or the community. In a book where there are many indicators of time and place for Jeremiah's utterances (though by no means a comprehensive account of such details), it is surprising that no information is provided here (the transference of v. 2 to replace v. 4 is hardly warranted as an attempt to make good the omission). However, the lack of a rubric for the commission is to be explained in terms of the declaratory nature of vv. 4–10. They are an introduction to the reading of the Jeremiah tradition, whether in the second temple, the prototypes of the synagogue, or wherever such matters were read or recited to the communities of Jews in Palestine (or elsewhere). Accompanying extracts from the book whenever it was used, vv. 4–10 do not require a rubric because they already form part of the introductory prologue. That is why they set out the validation of Jeremiah's commission to be a prophet to the nations and declare that the utterances which follow are the authenticated words of Yahweh delivered by his consecrated prophet.

The public nature of 1.4–10 is readily acknowledged by exegetes (cf. March 1970, 14), but a different explanation is offered by Reventlow (cf. Gunneweg 1967). In a very comprehensive analysis of these verses he interprets them as representing the *ordination* ritual for a person becoming a cult prophet. It is an attractive thesis, confirming the view expressed here that vv. 4–10 afford no insights into Jeremiah's personality or outlook, but lacks substantiation from other sources for the existence of such an ordination process in the temple cult. The temple is an important matrix for the construction and maintenance of the Jeremiah tradition, but it does not follow from such a setting of the book that Jeremiah was a cult official. The editors regularly set Jeremiah in a temple context, but that reflects their interests rather than a historical awareness of what Jeremiah might have been.

Many exegetes treat vv. 4–10 as the 'call' of Jeremiah to be a prophet (e.g. Berridge). Such a 'call' makes Jeremiah a prophet and authenticates his ministry. However, the story is better read as an account of his commissioning to a specific task: being a prophet *to the nations*. This interpretation fits the pattern of the *commissioning* narratives and it is more appropriate to describe such accounts as commissions to perform certain tasks (e.g. Moses is sent to Egypt to confront the Pharaoh and deliver the people from there; Gideon is commissioned to defeat the enemy; Amos is sent to prophesy to Israel; Ezekiel is commanded to go and confront the rebellious house of Israel). Being a prophet may be a by-product of obeying such commissions or a perspective introduced into the stories by the editors, but a 'call' does not make a prophet. What makes a prophet is the possession and delivery of the divine word at the divine command (cf. Wildberger 1942, 34, 39). The distinction between a commission and a 'call' may be regarded as rather subtle, but a commission is a very specific task whereas a 'call' is an abstraction. Subtle distinctions are recognized in the narratives where such commissions appear (e.g. Amos 7.14–15) and it is not an easy matter to interpret these stories (e.g. Isa. 6 does not represent the speaker *as a prophet* at all) without reading a great deal of non-textual information into them (cf. Auld 1983; 1984). The category of commission is an adequate description of all the narratives parallel to 1.4–10 and is better suited to the interpretation of all the stories than the more ideologically loaded word 'call'. With the declaration of his commission to be a prophet to the nations made public the editors introduce Jeremiah as one to whom the word of Yahweh comes and who therefore may legitimately proclaim on specific occasions 'thus says Yahweh' to the nations round about.

1.11–12

11 And the word of the LORD came to me, saying, 'Jeremiah, what do you
see?' And I said, 'I see a rod of almond.' 12 Then the LORD said to me, 'You
have seen well, for I am watching over my word to perform it.'

---

[11] Cf. vv. 4, 13; 2.1; 16.1; 24.4; G 39.26 (cf. MT 32.26); G 42.12 (cf.

MT 35.12) for this version of the formulaic reception of the divine word. Cf. 24.3 for the same question (cf. Amos 7.8; 8.2). MT *maqqēl šāqēd*, 'a rod of almond': a branch rather than the tree (cf. Gen. 30.37–41); cf. the story of Aaron's rod (*maṭṭeh*) which blossomed in the tent of meeting and bore almonds (*šeqēdīm*), Num. 17.16–26 (EV 1–11). **[12]** MT *kī-šōqēd 'anī 'al-debārī la'asōtō*; for I am watching over my *word* to perform *it*': a word play on *šāqēd*, 'almond', and *šōqēd*, 'watching'; cf. 5.6; 31.28; 44.27 for the motif 'watching' (*šqd*). G . . . *epi tous logous mou poiēsai autous*, '. . . over my *words* to perform *them*' = *'al-debāray la 'asōtām*: cf. *debāray*, v. 9.

Niditch 1983, 41–2; Williams 1956; Zimmerli 1982, 104–9

The vision is not a major feature of the Jeremiah tradition (contrast Zech. 1–8; Amos 7.1–8; 8.1–2; 9.1), but appears at the edges of the work (e.g. 1.11, 13; 24.1–3), where editorial elements dominate (cf. 38.21–23). The very few examples of the genre are increased by some exegetes who interpret certain passages as visions: e.g. 4.23–26 (Zimmerli, 99–104); 13.1–7; 25.15–29 (Rudolph, 93, 163). There may be some textual justification for reading 4.23–26 as a vision, but the other two accounts may be interpreted in a number of different ways without being read as visions. The two visions which appear in the prologue are part of the editorial conversations between Yahweh and Jeremiah, though they are not a continuation of vv. 4–10 (as 'a second time' in v. 13 demonstrates). They supplement the authentication of Jeremiah in vv. 4–10 by attributing visions to him (cf. the conjunction of visions and commissioning narrative in Amos 7.1–8.3) and, at the same time, manoeuvre the focus of the prologue from the commissioning of Jeremiah to be a prophet to the nations to the word of judgment against Jerusalem and Judah.

The form of the first vision could hardly be simpler: a question is directed to Jeremiah by Yahweh with reference to what he sees, Jeremiah replies that he sees an almond rod, the deity commends his acuity of perception, and explains the significance of what is seen by means of paronomasia. Amos 7.7–8; 8.1–2 provide parallels to the form used here, including the element of word-play (Amos 8.1–2). In this instance the meaning of the almond rod seen by Jeremiah is given as evidence of Yahweh's watchfulness over his word (G 'words' may refer back to vv. 9–10). Whether Jeremiah saw a branch cut from an almond tree and stripped (cf. Gen. 30.37) by the side of the road or in a village or had a vision of such an item by means of his imagination cannot be determined from the text nor is it important to be able to decide such a matter. It is unlikely that the vision, however understood, concerned a whole almond tree, whether flowering or otherwise (cf. NEB; Thompson, 153). The interpretation of the word-play is difficult: what does Yahweh mean by saying he is watching over his word to perform it? Over what word is he watching? Part of the interpretative problem is caused by the use of word-play. Such techniques sacrifice meaning for similarity of sounds (assonance), puns or associations of words and ideas. Hence the idea of watching over a word is less than clear: in 5.6 a leopard watches the cities, intent on devouring anyone foolish enough to venture forth from the security of civilized life; in 31.28 the watching motif is combined with some of the elements of 1.10; and in 44.27 it refers to Yahweh's determination to do evil. So in v. 12 Yahweh is determined to perform his word – but the content of the word is not specified (hence the need for a second communication in v. 13). It must therefore be understood in the most general of ways: Yahweh makes a connection between the almond rod and his word by means of homophonic similarities. The almond rod conjures up (Volz, 9, allows for the possibility of a divinatory connotation of the rod; cf. Hos. 4.12 and the magical use of rods in Gen. 30.37–43) the notion of intent observation and oversight. The word presses towards its realization (Zimmerli, 107). But what word? The redactional context suggests v. 9 (hence G) and that would make v. 12 an assurance to Jeremiah that the divine word(s) spoken by him would materialize (i.e. pluck up and break down, destroy and overthrow, build and plant). But the addition of vv. 13–16 changes the context of vv. 11–12 and refers the word to the destruction of Jerusalem and Judah (cf. 44.27 rather than 31.28). Perhaps vv. 11–12 should be allowed to retain their essential ambiguity in order to illustrate the need for further elucidation within the text itself.

The hint of mantic divinatory practice detected in the allusion to the rod (Volz) would fit the numerous traces of magical activity in the tradition (e.g. 19.1–2, 10–11; 43.9; 51.59–64) but is too tenuous to develop as the meaning of the vision. An almond rod with magical properties could be a reflection of the legendary rod associated with Aaron which, on one particular occasion (Num. 17.1–11 [MT 16–26]), magically blossomed and produced almonds! But this is a very unlikely connection between two stories which only share the motif 'almond' (even different terms are used for the rods) and absolutely nothing else. However, Williams in his interpretation of the vision makes precisely that connection and argues that Jeremiah's vision was a recapturing of the original meaning of Aaron's rod. Trained as a priest, Jeremiah revolted against the interpretation which had been put on the rod and recovered its original significance (cf. 8.8; 31.31–34). This rejection of a corrupt priesthood which had twisted the symbol of the rod to its own purposes led Jeremiah to become a prophet and preach against the political ambitions of the priests. Hence the association of the almond rod vision with the commissioning section of the prologue. Interesting though Williams' interpretation is as an example of misguided exegesis, it is too fanciful to have any force and lacks that close scrutiny of the text which is the *sine qua non* of responsible hermeneutics. The almond rod features in v. 11 and appears nowhere else in the tradition. What it signifies – the word over which Yahweh watches to perform (cf. Isa. 55.11) – dominates that tradition, and its abstract, unqualified nature in v. 12 makes it an excellent bridge between vv. 4–10 and 13–16 in the prologue introducing 'the words of Jeremiah'.

1.13–16

13 The word of the LORD came to me a second time, saying, 'What do you see?' and I said, 'I see a boiling pot, facing away from the north.' 14 Then the LORD said to me, 'Out of the north evil shall break forth upon all the inhabitants of the land. 15 For, lo, I am calling all the tribes of the kingdoms of the north, says the LORD; and they shall come and every one shall set his throne at the entrance of the gates of Jerusalem, against all its walls round about, and against all the cities of Judah. 16 And I will utter my judgments against them, for all their wickedness in forsaking me; they have burned incense to other gods, and worshipped the works of their own hands.'

---

[13] See Notes on v. 11 for formulaic introduction: it is expanded here by *šēnît*, 'a second time' (cf. 13.1; 33.1), indicating a supplementary word to that in v 11. Cf. v. 11 for the question (here lacking 'Jeremiah'); 24.3; Amos 7.8; 8.2. MT *sîr nāpûaḥ*, lit. 'a pot blown': i.e. a pot heated and boiling (cf. Driver 1937–38, 97; NEB 'A cauldron . . . on a fire, fanned by the wind'); G *lebēta hupokaiomenos*, 'a cauldron on the fire'. Harris 1983 translates *sîr* as 'thorn' (thorn bush): 'I see kindled thorn . . .' cf. Isa. 34.13; Hos. 2.8; Nahum 1.10; Eccles. 7.6 (all *sîrîm*, 'thorns'); this would make the second vision also use a flora metaphor (*šqd:syr*). MT *ûpānāyw mippᵉnê ṣāpōnāh*, lit.

'and its face from the face of the north': NEB 'it is tilted away from the north'; the image is uncertain and may reflect the way the wind is blowing or a pot tipped over from the direction of the north. Driver proposes *ūpānūy* 'tipped, turned', i.e. the pot is tilted to one side and threatens to spill its contents; Harris's kindled thorn is 'facing from the north'. **[14]** MT *tippātaḥ*, 'shall be let loose': G *ekkauthēsetai*, 'shall flame forth'; this unusual use of *ptḥ*, 'open', has given rise to various emendations (cf. BHS *tuppaḥ*, 'shall be blown'; *tipᵉneh* 'shall be turned'), but MT may be retained (cf. Driver 1937–38, 98). **[15]** G lacks 'the clans of' (*mišpᵉḥōt*): cf. 25.9, where the phrase 'all the clans of the north' appears (G 'clan'), but lacking 'kingdoms'. **[16]** MT *wᵉdibbartī mišpāṭay 'ōtām*, 'and I will speak my judgments (to) them': many mss read *'ittām* 'with them'; the idiom *dbr mšpṭ 't*, 'to speak judgment with', means to pass sentence on a guilty party (cf. 39.5; 52.9). MT *wayᵉqaṭṭᵉrū lē'lōhīm 'ᵃḥērīm*, 'and they sacrificed to other gods': *qiṭṭēr* is better translated as the more general 'burn' (i.e. sacrifice) than 'burn (incense)', see Notes on 44; the phrase appears in 19.4; 44.3, 8; II Kings 22.17; cf. Thiel 1973, 74–6, on the Deuteronomistic language of v. 16.

Niditch 1983, 43–52

The second vision is as oblique as the first and requires considerable explanation by means of additional material (vv. 15, 16). A similar format to v. 11 introduces the object seen by the one to whom Yahweh addresses his question, though on this occasion there is no commendation of the speaker's perceptivity. As the vision is a response to the word of Yahweh which comes *a second time* (*šēnīt*), it must be understood as an attempt to clarify the first vision (cf. the clarification of Isa. 7.10, 'again Yahweh spoke to Ahaz . . .'). In this case what the speaker sees is less clear than on the first occasion, and the explanation, lacking for the almond rod except in the most perfunctory sense, is developed by the editing to the point of obfuscation.

The object seen is a pot boiling on a fire (cf. G). The wind blows from the north, so the steam from the pot and the smoke of the fire are blown from that direction. This interpretation of the vision makes the key motif the phrase 'from the north' (*ṣāpōnāh*, cf. v. 15). An alternative reading of v. 14 understands the pot to be tilted or tipped over from the direction of the north. Such a reading suggests an image of a village raided by brigands coming from the north: an overturned pot symbolizes the invasion. It is a poignant object telling the story without words. The upturned cauldron – the interrupted meal in preparation – bespeaks pillage. However, the precise image indicated by v. 13 cannot be determined clearly, and exegetes differ in the nuances they detect in the text (e.g. the vision may be of a pot boiling and bubbling on the fire, with its mouth facing from the north [cf. Rudolph]). As in v. 12, the deity provides an explanation of the sight. In this instance the meaning of the vision is disaster being let loose from the north: the whole land will be invaded from the north.

The two visions taken together mean that Yahweh is watching over his word to perform it and that that word is disaster looming out of the north against all the inhabitants of the land. Following on from vv. 4–10, where the speaker is appointed to be a prophet over the nations, vv. 11–14 would appear to be the word of judgment spoken against those nations. Out of the north destruction comes against the (enemy) nations, of which Babylon must be considered the foremost (cf. 50.3, 9, 41). To announce this fearlessly is why Jeremiah has been set apart as a prophet to the nations (vv. 5, 8, 10). During the sixth century the land of Israel was controlled by the Babylonians and thereafter by other nations, so the vision of trouble out of the north against the land uses a motif familiar from the oracles against the nations and the foe from the north cycle to herald the liberation of the conquered land. Thus the visions of the prologue, along with the commissioning of vv. 4–10, form a closure with 50–51 (MT) and announce hope to the exiled and the dominated of the land. Jeremiah's oversight of the nations proclaims the imminent destruction of the enemy.

The interpretation of vv. 13–14 is complicated by the additional material appended to the vision. Question, response, explanation is the form of vv. 11–12, 13–14 and, whatever the difficulties of interpreting the precise meaning of the object seen, the brief exchanges constitute the genre (cf. Amos 7.7–8; 8.1–2). What follows in vv. 15, 16 must be regarded as differing significantly from vv. 11–14 (cf. Niditch) and as an addition which obscures rather than illuminates. Influenced by 25.9, v. 15 envisages all the clans of the north coming against Jerusalem and Judah (in 25.9 they come against all the nations round about *as well*) and the kings of these clans will set up their thrones at the entrance to the gates of Jerusalem (a Jerusalem with only one set of gates!). This striking image of the foreign kings setting up their thrones before the gates of Jerusalem hardly reflects the siege of 588–7 (cf. 39.3, but see Comm. on 39.1–10; 52.4–11), but it may be an echo of the mythological future when all the nations will come up against Jerusalem (e.g. Ezek. 38–39; Joel 3 [MT 4]; Zech. 12.1–9; 14.1–9). Before Jerusalem and Judah can enjoy the permanent salvation of Yahweh, the nations must assemble against them and be struck down by Yahweh. Hence the word of judgment is spoken against them at the beginning of v. 16. The assembled kings with their clans gathered before the gates of Jerusalem must hear Yahweh's sentence against them. Only with the defeat of the enemy can Jerusalem and Judah be saved (in 50–51 the defeat of Babylon has as its counterpoint the deliverance of Israel). This reading of vv. 15–16a makes them an expansionary explanation of vv. 13–14 and understands vv. 11–14 to be a further statement about the fate of the nations implicit in the appointment of Jeremiah as a prophet over the nations (vv. 4–10). Read against a background of the post-587 period the prologue consists of a series of statements addressed to the scattered communities of Jews throughout Palestine and Babylon (and Egypt?) and encouraging them to expect Yahweh's judgment against the nations.

Many exegetes read the prologue in a very different way and their reading is based on the further additions to the text of vv. 16–19. The idomatic 'I will pass sentences upon *them*' in v. 16a is ambiguous: 'them' may refer to the clans which come from the north or to the cities of Judah. The rest of v. 16 is stereotypical (cf. Thiel 1973, 75) and reflects the Deuteronomistic style of denouncing Jerusalem and Judah for pursuing the worship of other gods. It transforms the meaning of the overturned pot image from a word of judgment against the nations (the sense necessitated by vv. 5, 8, 10) to one against the Judaean people. The pot image is obscure and the explanation in v. 14 does not identify the victims of the evil let loose from the north. As the book of Jeremiah uses this motif to describe the destruction of Jerusalem (4.6; 6.22) *and* also of Babylon (59.3, 9, 41), the pot image may be understood as a statement about Jerusalem or Babylon. Nothing in vv. 4–14 suggests that Jerusalem is the object of discourse, but much indicates that the nations are the subject of Jeremiah's activity, and a consistent reading of the prologue favours this interpretation. However, the additions of vv. 15, 16, 17–19 represent a more parochial reading of the prologue and indicate an understanding of v. 15 as a statement of judgment against Jerusalem rather than the assembled nations.

It is only with the coming of the clans of the north against Jerusalem that the people of Judah make their first appearance in the prologue (apart from the editorial title in vv. 1–3). Thus the additions in vv. 15–19 make good a notable lack in the prologue: the words of Yahweh which come to Jeremiah (unlike the words of Yahweh which he speaks in the body of the tradition) say nothing about Jerusalem and Judah (as is to be expected after 587). The commissioning of Jeremiah to be a prophet is an act with reference not to them but to the nations. Only with the expansion of the explanation of the pot image is Jerusalem introduced into the prologue. Further additions develop that reference along different lines and shape the way the chapter is read by modern exegetes. The worship of other gods motif is a theme of the prose elements in the tradition and its occurrence here indicates an editorial history of the prologue which includes a Deuteronomistically influenced explanation for the catastrophe of 587.

1.17–19

17 'But you, gird up your loins; arise, and say to them everything that I command you. Do not be dismayed by them, lest I dismay you before them.
18 And I, behold, I make you this day a fortified city, an iron pillar, and bronze walls, against the whole land, against the kings of Judah, its princes, its priests, and the people of the land. 19 They will fight against you; but they shall not prevail against you, for I am with you, says the LORD, to deliver you.'

---

[17] G includes v. 8b at the end of v. 17 (cf. v. 19b); 17bα = 7bβ. **[18]** G lacks 'and an iron pillar'; many mss read 'bronze *wall*' rather than 'bronze *walls*', cf. 15.20a. G *pasi tois basileusin Iouda*, 'all the kings of Judah', for MT, 'against the whole land, against the kings of Judah'; cf. 34.19 for a similar listing of officials. MT *ūlᵉʿam hāʾāreṣ*, 'and against the people of the land': a technical phrase with a number of meanings; e.g. the landed gentry, representatives of the people in government, rural people in contrast to urban folk, the whole body of citizens, or religious illiterates. Given the list of officials here it probably means landowners; cf. 34.19; 37.2; 44.21; Gunneweg 1983. **[19]** 19a = 15.20b; 19b = 8b. Volz, 11, deletes *nᵉʾum (yhwh)* 'says (Yahweh)' as a copyist's error for 'I, Yahweh . . .', but the phrase is dependent on v. 8b (cf. 15.20c) and may be original here.

Jüngling 1973

The prologue ends with another shift of reference and subject matter. Yahweh turns to Jeremiah (presumably) and orders him to prepare himself for the task of speaking everything he is commanded (cf. v.7b). Those to whom he must speak are not identified, but in vv. 7–8 they are the nations whereas in v. 18b they are the people of Judah (or the ruling classes). Thus the editing of the prologue has transformed the prophet of the nations into a speaker and fighter against his own people (if 18b is originally part of 17–19). It is possible to read vv. 17–19 as a qualification of v. 15 in the light of vv. 7–8, 10 (i.e. the prophet is sent to speak to the nations and warned against being terrified by them), but v. 18b identifies the mission as one against Judah, and this may be an intentional incorporation of Judah into the prologue.

The imagery of v. 18 presents an obdurate figure who stands like a fortified city against the community (an ironic reflection of the fortified Jerusalem of 588–7?). Such imagery appears also in 15.20, where it represents a divine reassurance of deliverance to the righteous in their warfare with the wicked (see on 15.19–21). A similar motif of obduracy, using different images, occurs in Ezek. 3.7–9, but there it reflects a hard-headedness shared by people and prophet alike. Here Jeremiah is made impervious to the people: thus ruining the thesis of those exegetes, such as Stoebe (1964) and others, who read a pastoral ministry (*Seelsorge*) for Jeremiah in the book. He is to be a fighter not a pastor and thus the prologue is turned into 'an aggressive document' (Jüngling, 24) rather than a series of reassurances to the people. Such a transformation may reflect certain elements in the tradition (e.g. 11.21–23; 20.1–3; 37–38), but they are minor features of the book and, if related to the story of Jeremiah, must be regarded as a late development in the construction of that book and running counter to 1.10.

Yet the image of Jeremiah as a fighter is not quite an accurate reading of 1.19; 15.20. Whoever the figure fought against may represent, it is the people who do the fighting. The one fought against is to be a passive object of resistance to that fighting. Both occurrences of the imagery of walled resistance and fighting have the community as the object to be resisted. If in 15.20 that which resists the fighting is the righteous group of community, might not the same be true of 1.18–19? There is here a problem of interpretation which goes beyond the letter of the text to the more fundamental hermeneutical issues involved in the understanding of the book of Jeremiah. The tendency to read the book as a biographical account of the prophet Jeremiah obscures the meaning of much of the text by predisposing the exegete to read into that text what may not be there in the first place. If the book of Jeremiah is the product of conflicting communal forces during the sixth century and later, the prologue may contain reflections of those tensions. One such reflection may be vv. 17–19, where the opposition to the ruling classes may be an outright rejection of the Judaean community on behalf of another group (e.g. the exiles). This reading of the text would make 'the people of the land' a technical term in opposition to the returned exiles from Babylon (*b^enē haggōlāh* or *'am haggōlāh*, cf. Gunneweg 1983). Such a reading suggests that the opposed groups of wicked and righteous to be found in the laments in the tradition (11–20) may well represent the social conflicts of the fifth century when Jerusalem society was under reconstruction.

The supporting evidence for such a reading of vv. 17–19 lies in the overview of the tradition and in the stereotypical nature of the language used in the laments. The command to gird up the loins in v. 17 indicates an individual addressed in the prologue and points to the transformation of the conflict motif into the beginnings of a story about Jeremiah. But this feature only appears at the fringes of the tradition (e.g. 11.21–23; 20.1–3; 37–38), and it is not possible to extract from the book of Jeremiah a confirmation of v. 19 in relation to the life of Jeremiah. A divine promise of deliverance is a conventional part of reassurances to the righteous in the lament psalms; used of Jeremiah in v. 19 it may be regarded as a transference from such a convention, but the Jeremiah of the tradition never experiences a deliverance. The book has no interest in his life and he disappears from sight as enigmatically as he appears in 1.5. Legend has him stoned to death in Egypt, but nothing indicates that the divine promise of v. 19 was ever fulfilled in his lifetime. It would therefore be a better reading of vv. 17–19 to relate them to social conflict within the Jewish communities, reflecting the period of the prologue's construction and expansion. However, the more popular exegetical understanding of them as the fortification of Jeremiah against the opposition of the people is unlikely to lose its appeal for many readers of the book.

The prologue ends on a note of deliverance and makes connections between its ending (v. 19) and its beginning (v. 8). In the context of the nations the bearer of the word (prophet or community) enjoys divine protection, though what follows is concerned solely with that word. Remarkably little of the tradition is reflected in the prologue, but what is used is transformed in ways which must make the exegete ponder the art of interpretation.

PART ONE

Poems and Sermons against Judah and Jerusalem 2–25.14

The book of Jeremiah may be divided into four parts, with a prologue (1) and an epilogue (52; cf. II Kings 24.18–25.30). Part I coincides with the first half of the book (2.1–25.14); Part II consists of the OAN (MT 25.15–38; 46–51); Parts III and IV take up 26–45. These divisions are a convenient organization of a long book which displays little order in the material collected and much repetition of verses and phrases.

Part I is the longest and most complex of the four parts and many commentators include the prologue in it (there are redactional links between the introduction to the prologue in 1.1–3 and the opening section of the summary of Part I in 25.1–3). It consists of six blocks of material (labelled A–F in this commentary), with a brief preface in 2.1–3 and a summary in 25.1–14. The sixth block (F. 21–24) is an appendix to Part I and uses material more at home in Parts III and IV (e.g. 21.1–10; 24). Block A is almost entirely a collection of poems (3.6–12a, 15–18 are prose), but the other blocks are a mixture of prose (sermons) and poetry. The only way to describe the contents of Part I is by the exegesis of each section because there is no unifying theme, other than the general negative tone of denunciation against the people of Judah and Jerusalem (with minor exceptions to this attitude in 12.14–17; 16.14–15; 17.12; 23.5–8; 24.4–7). As a variegated collection of poems and prose pieces, Part I states the case against Judah and Jerusalem and seeks to justify the destruction of Jerusalem in 587 (i.e. it constitutes a theodicy).

A. 2.1 – 6.30

The first block of material in Part I is a collection of disparate poems forming two thematic cycles of criticism of Israel (i.e. the Jerusalem community, cf. 2.2). The first cycle (2.5–4.2 with a coda in 4.3–4) focuses on the nation's apostasy and draws its argument from aspects of Israel's history. It includes material which allows for the possibility of the nation's turning to Yahweh (3.12, 14, 22–23; 4.1–2). The second cycle (4.5–6.26) is built around the motif of 'disaster from the north' (4.6; 6.1, 22) and depicts a Jerusalem disintegrating in the face of an advancing and implacable enemy. The two cycles are enclosed between brief editorial pieces (2.1–3; 6.27–30). The first piece functions as a preface to the whole block and incorporates a post-Deuteronomistic poem (cf. Deut. 32.10–14) as an optimistic statement about the status of the community by way of introduction. As this is very different from the tone of the cycles, it must be regarded as an adjustment of the theology of the poems to meet the needs of the editorial presentation to the community of a later period (cf. Schottroff 1970). The concluding section in 6.27–30 deals with the attitude of the speaker to the community and has connections with 1.18–19.

Many commentators treat the material in 2–6 as the earliest preaching of Jeremiah, assigning the apostasy cycle to his ministry to northern Israel and the foe from the north cycle to Judah (e.g. Albertz 1962; Neumann 1975, 349–62). The period of this activity is usually dated from 627 to after 609, and some exegetes identify the enemy as the Scythians (e.g. Cazelles 1967; cf. Yamauchi 1983 on the more general features of the Scythians as marauding hordes from the Russian steppes). This opinion is less popular now, and the modern approach to the enemy depicted in the poems is to leave its identity unspecified and to reject the Scythian hypothesis. This view allows the material to be early yet capable of reinterpretation at a later period. Thus some external threat in the 620s gave rise to the poems in the first place and then with the emergence of Babylon after the battle of Carchemish in 605 they were reinterpreted in the light of the new enemy. So failed prophecy was transformed into fulfilled prophecy! This is an interesting but unnecessary interpretation of the text. Although the identity of the enemy is never specified, Babylon is the only historical candidate for the role and the poems should be interpreted against the background of Babylonian imperial designs on Palestinian and Egyptian political affairs. This approach would date the poems between 605 and 587 and explain why Jeremiah's work was summarized by the statement 'the king of Babylon will certainly come and destroy this land' (36.29; cf. 21.3–7; 25.9). It is also very much in keeping with that view of Jeremiah which sees the period of his earliest work as being between 609 and 605 and the crisis which produced him as the appearance of Babylon on the stage of world politics.

What then is to be made of the apostasy cycle? The predilection of scholars for treating 2.1–4.4 as Jeremiah's preaching between 627–621 (eg Rudolph; Thompson; Rietzschel 1966) reflects the influence of 1.2 with its redactional inflection of the whole tradition. It may not be necessary to accept such redactional shaping of the material, but arguments have been put forward for dating the oracles in 2–6 to the period of Josiah's reform (e.g. Milgrom 1955; Rowley 1962). There is no *prima facie* evidence for dating the poems, but the reference to Assyria in 2.18 is thought by some to presuppose the existence of the Assyrian empire (e.g. Fohrer 1970, 390). That is a possible interpretation of the verse (in contrast to 2.36), but not a necessary one. The term 'Assyria' continued to be used to describe the ruling power even in the Persian period (Ezra 6.22) and appears to have functioned as a word-pair with Egypt in contexts where Babylon might have been more fitting (e.g. Lam. 5.6; Zech. 10.10–11). As will be seen in the exegesis of 2.18, the most likely explanation of the allusion to Assyria is as a conventional word-pair usage. Nothing else in the poems necessitates a dating earlier than 605, and it is arguable that in the light of the similarity between 2.2–13 and Deut. 32 the discourse in ch. 2 is exilic, if not later.

The rhetorical nature of the discourse defies identification with a specific historical occasion and functions as a generalized denunciation of the nation for idolatrous rejection of Yahweh. It is a charge which would fit any period of Israelite history, including the fifth century (cf. Isa. 57.1–13; 65.1–7; Zech. 10.2; 13.2). Too general to be assigned to a particular era, the apostasy cycle makes an ideal introduction to the condemnation of the community characterized by the Jeremiah tradition. It identifies the cause of the nation's ruin with its religious practices, taking examples from its past history as arguments to prove the point. Similar arguments in ch. 44 provide with ch. 2 a polemic against religious behaviour which forms an inclusive device holding together the whole Jeremiah tradition. This inclusive feature is much better brought out in G (51) than in MT (44). As an encapsulating motif it reveals a dominant concern with religious ideology; a concern explicitly devoted to exposing false forms of religious practice. Such a polemic dismisses the religion of the Jerusalem and Egyptian communities in favour of a different ideology of religion. That alternative ideology is made explicit in the Deuteronomistic sections of the book, in ch. 44, and is most likely present in ch. 2.

The occurrence of a 'complaint' (*rīb*) motif in 2.9, 29 has led a number of scholars to see in ch. 2 a covenantal lawsuit prosecuted by Yahweh against Israel (e.g. Harvey 1962; Huffmon 1959; Limburg 1969). It is argued that such a lawsuit derives from legal and international treaty procedures and its pattern is discernible in Isa. 1.18–20; 3.13–15; Micah 6.1–5; Hos. 2.4–17; 4.1–6; 5.3–15; Jer. 2.5–29 (cf. Westermann 1967, 199–200). However, an examination of the relevant passages in the light of the supposed pattern will reveal at best a fractured pattern and, in relation to Jer. 2, a misleading analysis (cf. Blenkinsopp 1971; Lundbom 1975, 9–12). It is unnecessary to reconstruct an imaginary courtroom procedure in order to provide a social setting for the *rīb* metaphor of conflict between Yahweh and Israel. It may simply be derived from a stock of metaphors describing 'the personal bilateral level of quarrel between Yahweh and Israel' (DeRoche 1983, 574). The complaint explains why disaster befell Jerusalem in 587.

The preliminary investigation of chs. 2–3 raises questions which will inevitably shape the interpretation of the text and account for the divergence of opinions among commentators. Few commentators agree on the point at which each unit begins or ends (the choice made here is partly subject-matter and partly convenience for exegesis) and the peppering of the text with oracular indicators (*n*e*'um yhwh*, 'says Yahweh', esp. 2.9–22; 3.12–14) points in the direction of editorial emphases. The combination of so many rhetorical questions and a number of quotations of popular response (in some cases clearly fabricated for theological purposes, cf. Overholt 1979) gives the impression of a sustained dialogue between speaker and community. Yet it does reveal the rejection of what the speaker regards as popular religion (Brueggemann 1973). There are elements in ch. 2 which hint at a liturgical structure to the discourse (whatever the origins of the individual units): the multiple descriptions of the desert in v. 6 (cf. Deut. 8.7–9, 15–16), the repeat of children in v. 9 (cf. Joel 1.3), the address 'O generation' in v. 31 (cf. Ps. 24.6). But positing a liturgy of community denunciation is very different from demonstrating that such a thing existed in post-catastrophe times. Allied to the liturgy of turning in 3.12–14, 19–4.2 (with its Hosea-Deuteronomistic connections), it is possible to see in the early chapters of Jeremiah a theological handling of the disaster which provides explanation and hope within some teaching-liturgical setting (however dimly we may discern it). Its purpose is to write off the past and everything associated with it and to call the contemporary generation to devote itself to Yahweh (cf. 4.4).

2.1–3

2[1] The word of the LORD came to me, saying, 2 'Go and proclaim in the hearing of Jerusalem, Thus says the LORD,
I remember the devotion of your youth,
your love as a bride,
how you followed me in the wilderness,
in a land not sown.
3 Israel was holy to the LORD,
the first fruits of his harvest.
All who ate of it became guilty;
evil came upon them,
says the LORD.'

[1–2] G lacks the introductory formula of 1 and the directional instructions of 2. It introduces the oracle with 'and he said, Thus says the lord'. **[2]** G has 'following the holy one of Israel, says the lord' for the last two clauses. **[3]** K, *tbw'th;* Q, *tᵉbû'ātō*, 'his produce'.

Schottroff 1970

The preface to the lengthy discourse in 2.4–37 introduces the block of materials in 2.4–6.30 and makes Jerusalem the recipient of the prophetic address. The formulaic introduction is typical of the late redaction of the tradition (lacking in G) and reflects a concern with establishing the source of the speaker's statements as well as indicating divine instructions for the speaker's movements. Unlike other such rubrics in the book (e.g. 7.1–2; 11.6; 18.1–3; 19.1–2; 22.1) no precise details are given here as to location in the city or classes of people to be addressed. There is just a general instruction, 'Go and proclaim in the hearing of Jerusalem . . .'. But it makes Jerusalem, whether as city or community (cf. Isa. 40.1–2), the focus of what is to be said. All that follows in the block is now addressed to Jerusalem and this suggests that we should read that material as part of a complex argument intended to persuade the community of the truth of the assessment offered. Jerusalem's past is about to be held up for scrutiny and its future determined by its response to that judgment.

An idyllic image of the past is used as a preface to the indictment. Israel is depicted as a young bride, loyally following Yahweh, in the wilderness, the place of barrenness. Dedicated to him, she is herself the fruit of his work. In an unsown place, she is the beginning of his harvest. Subtle images are at play here: loyalty and love produce fruitfulness, status and relationship guarantee protection. The language and images may reflect the influence of the Hosea tradition (cf. Hos. 2.15; 9.10; 13.4–5; Deut. 32.10–14), but their real force is derived from what follows. Throughout the succeeding chapters images abound of disloyalty, misplaced love, fruitlessness and lack of protection from external sources. Thus a stark contrast is set up by this poem between the idyllic origins of the community and its recent experience. The honeymoon was wonderful but the marriage – a complete failure!

Two very different metaphors are used in 2.2–3 to describe Israel. In v. 2 Israel is viewed as a bride (cf. NEB's 'bridal days') and the devotion of the young nation as equivalent to the passion of the period of espousals. The marital metaphor is very important for describing the relationship between Israel and Yahweh in Hosea, Jeremiah, Ezekiel and Third Isaiah and gives rise to a whole cluster of symbolic descriptions of and reflections upon the nation, especially during the sixth century. Having its origins in Canaanite thought, the adaptation of such erotic language into Yahwistic terms poses certain problems for the interpretation of the early chapters of the book of Jeremiah (see below on 3.1–5; 5.7–8). Yet as a metaphor it works very well for describing the history, however imaginary, of a community, because marriages often start well and then turn sour. Its occurrence in 2.2 may be more optimistic than elsewhere in the Jeremiah tradition and may reflect the more positive content of the metaphor in the post-exilic period (cf. Isa. 62.1–5). In v. 3 the metaphor used is an agricultural one. Israel is the beginning of Yahweh's harvest, the first-fruits of his produce (cf. the image of Israel as Yahweh's first-born son in Ex. 4.22). If the word *rē'šīt* is understood as 'best' (cf. its use in Deut. 33.21; Amos 6.6), then Israel is the best of Yahweh's agricultural products. If the various rulings about the first fruits belonging to Yahweh (cf. Ex. 34.26; Lev. 23.10; Deut. 26.1–4; but contrast Num. 18.12f.; Deut. 18.4) are behind this metaphor here, then Israel's protected status is the point being made. As the shadow of the fall of Jerusalem (1.3) is everywhere in the book this point becomes a subtle counterpoint to what follows.

The preface only speaks of a good time in the past and is intended to make explicit the disparity between the nation's origins and its current state. A similar contrast between Jerusalem's past and present is made in the redactional prefaces to the Isaiah tradition in Isa. 1.21 (Kaiser 1983, 41f.). Both allusions to an imaginary past are theological constructs designed to make a point against contemporary society and conceivably raise hopes of a future return to that idyllic state (cf. Isa. 1.26b). The tendency to idealize the past (cf. 6.16), so characteristic of a period of disintegration and ruin, is given its strongest expression in Deut. 32.10–14, a post-Deuteronomistic addition to Deuteronomy (Mayes 1979, 382; cf. Fohrer 1970, 189–90). Yet this idealized view of the past is in striking contrast to the Deuteronomistic account of the desert period as one of deep apostasy (7.22–26) and the history of Jerusalem-Israel as depicted by Ezekiel (chs. 16; 20; 23). The primary narrative itself (Genesis-Numbers) presents the wanderings in the wilderness as a time of constant rebellion against Yahweh. The formal contradiction between these diverse accounts of the desert behaviour of the nation arises in the first place because so many different traditions have been combined to create the biblical writings. Seen side by side the stories are contradictory. Such contradictions are a normal feature of the Bible in relation to historical matters because the essential point of such traditions is not their historical accuracy but their theological function. The negative view of the desert period stresses the weaknesses inherent in the community, whereas the positive view holds promise for the future (cf. Hos. 2.14–23).

The G of v. 2 omits any reference to the wilderness period, but its account of the nation's past is as idyllic as that of the more developed MT. The reference to Israel's youth provides a parallel to the youthfulness of the prophet in 1.6. Further parallels between prophet and nation are to be found in the common motif of being holy (*qdš*) or consecrated (1.5) and the idea of a relationship to other people which affords a protected status (1.7–8; 2.3). The deity delivers the fearful prophet from those to whom he is sent and in the desert period any who dared to attack Israel (the probable meaning of the metaphor 'eat' in 2.3) incurred guilt and ensuing disaster. The youthfulness of the prophet may well occur in the tradition as a deliberate parallel to the nation's youth in 2.2, and in the introductory material in 1.1–2.3 the editors may be making connections between the prophet and the nation (but see on 1.6). Because of the lapidary nature of biblical statements and allusions it is difficult to be certain of just what is being expressed in the text. It is equally difficult to determine the relative order of textual units, so that it remains unclear whether 2.1–3 preceded 1.4–10 or vice versa in order of construction. As the book of Jeremiah now stands, we should read 2.1–3 in the light of 1.4–10, but originally 1.4–10 may have owed something to the metaphors used of the nation in 2.2–3. A possible reading of the fully edited text suggests that the prophet has replaced the nation in a time of destruction and that the focus of divine action has become the prophetic word.

2.4–9

4 Hear the word of the LORD, O house of Jacob, and all the families of
the house of Israel. 5 Thus says the LORD:
'What wrong did your fathers find in me,
that they went far from me,
and went after worthlessness, and became worthless?
6 They did not say, "Where is the LORD
who brought us up from the land of Egypt,
who led us in the wilderness,
in a land of deserts and pits,

in a land of drought and deep darkness,
in a land that none passes through,
where no man dwells?"
7 And I brought you into a plentiful land
to enjoy its fruits and its good things.
But when you came in you defiled my land,
and made my heritage an abomination.
8 The priests did not say, "Where is the LORD?"
Those who handle the law did not know me;
the rulers transgressed against me;
the prophets prophesied by Baal,
and went after things that do not profit.
9 Therefore I still contend with you, says the LORD,
and with your children's children I will contend.'

---

[6] G has *akarpō*, 'barren', for MT *ṣalmāwet*, 'deep darkness'. The last phrase may be a gloss, cf. 51.43. For the repeated phrase 'in a land . . .' cf. the repeated 'I looked . . .' in 4.23–26. **[8]** 'rulers': MT 'shepherds', a standard Semitic term for leaders. **[9]** Some mss, V, BHS omit *bᵉnē* and read 'your children'; this makes a better contrast with 'your fathers' in v. 3. However, the MT reading may well indicate a three-generation period of divine judgment (cf. 27.7) or, with the fathers of v. 3, a third-fourth generation target of god's anger (cf. Ex. 20.5; Deut. 5.9).

Lundbom 1975, 70–4; Williams 1965

The lengthy discourse in 2.5–3.5 is introduced by an editorial note addressing it to the families of Israel (cf. 3.14; 31.1). It is unnecessary to make the phrases 'house of Jacob', 'house of Israel' refer to Israel rather than to Judah and treat the discourse as extracts from Jeremiah's early preaching to the northern clans (*contra* Albertz 1982 and many commentators). The rhetorical nature of the material hardly permits such interpretative precision and the demise of Israel in 722 allowed the Judaean state to use its epithets freely without opposition. The use of the epithet 'Jacob' to refer to Judah-Jerusalem-the exiles is a feature of the oracles in Second Isaiah (Isa. 40.27; 41.8, 14; 43.1; 48.1–2, 20). This more generalized use of the terms 'Jacob' and 'Israel' to refer to the community centred on Jerusalem seems to be confirmed by the allusions in 2.16, 18, 28 (cf. 3.14; 4.4).

The element holding together the different units in the discourse is a series of rhetorical questions. Such questions probe the history and consciousness of the community and demonstrate its persistent apostasy. The lack of firm evidence to date this material or to locate it in the history of the community makes it difficult to determine its precise purpose. It may represent preaching against the religious practices of the community over a long period or it may be a discourse deliberately constructed from discrete units and intended to confront a contemporary situation with the need for radical change in its religious attitudes.

The first unit in the discourse skilfully expresses the argument between Yahweh and Israel. It is a family quarrel, hence the familial references in vv. 5, 9 (and also most likely in v. 4). In spite of the complicated scholarly arguments for treating ch. 2 as a covenant lawsuit, it is unnecessary to read into the metaphors of the discourse concepts derived from modern legal terminology. It is unnecessary because to introduce the notion of covenant into the text is to go beyond what that text says. The editors of the book of Jeremiah were quite capable of expressing covenantal ideas where relevant or necessary (e.g. 11.1–10; 22.8–9; 31.31–34), but have not so presented the critique of Israel's religion in 2.5ff. The quarrel (*rīb*) between Yahweh and Israel is about the breakdown of a relationship (cf. Isa. 1.2–3), and that is why so much of the material in chs. 2–6 describes that breakdown in marital terms. The rupture is represented as having taken place in the past ('your fathers') and going on into the future ('your children's children'). The fathers distanced themselves from Yahweh (cf. Ezek. 8.6 for a similar image of the deity distancing himself from the community because of cultic corruption) and became worthless. The fathers are not identified, but presumably a vague reference to the exodus generation is intended (contrast Deut. 5.3). Such generalized references to 'fathers', 'you', 'children' are characteristic of Deuteronomistic sermons and, in spite of the paucity of specific Deuteronomistic phrases in the chapter (cf. Thiel 1973, 80–3), the section should be treated as a Deuteronomistic-type sermon (in agreement with Duhm, 17). The whole history of the nation is one of apostasy, and the relationship between Yahweh and Israel one of squabbling (*rīb*).

The poetic balance of the poem in 5–9 draws a parallel between the activities of the fathers in the past and the generation addressed in the sermon. Both groups have pursued other gods (the word-play in v. 5 *hahebel wayyehbālū* is difficult to capture in English): the fathers sought *hebel* 'vanity' (Qoheleth's word), the children Baal. The fathers did not seek Yahweh, neither did the leaders of the later generations. The repeated question, 'Where is Yahweh?', is shorthand for the correct approach to and understanding of Yahweh. The formal question itself may be a sceptical response to suffering (cf. Ps. 42, 3, 10; 79.10) but here it is intended to indicate a failure of correct procedure. Failing to ask themselves this question, the various communities demonstrate the falseness of their worship. The charge that the fathers pursued the worthless and became worthless is the same accusation as that made against the people of Israel in II Kings 17.15. As the theological commentary in II Kings 17 comes from the exilic Deuteronomistic editing of Kings (Mayes 1983, 125–7), the sermon in 2.5–9 must be associated with Deuteronomistic influence or editing. The characterization of other gods as worthless (*hebel*) or the indictment of the community for such idolatrous practices occurs elsewhere in the Jeremiah tradition at 8.19; 10.15; 14.22; 16.19; 51.18. The question about the location of Yahweh in 2.6, 8 should be contrasted with the public assertion of his presence in 8.19. For a more complicated treatment of this type of question the prohibition against asking such questions (Ex. 17.7) should be investigated.

The characteristics of the deity from whom the nation distanced itself are given in vv. 6–7. He is the one who led the people through the terrible wilderness (the six qualifications of the desert in v. 6 probably reflect liturgical usage) and into a fruitful land. The garden-land (*karmel*) of Israel (Canaan), however, was profaned by the people: presumably a reference to involvement with the local baals. This is a curious accusation in that it seems to ignore the fact that the land would have been profaned already by the idolatrous practices of the pre-Israelite occupants! Such glossing over reality is probably typical of sermons and in keeping with the idyllic nature of Israel's past as presented in the discourse. The responsibility for the profanation of the land is laid at the door of the priests, rulers and prophets (or possibly just the priests and the prophets, so Berridge 1970, 140), cf. 2.26. The phrase 'those who handle the law' (v. 8, *tōpšē hattōrāh*) may simply refer to the priests (poetic parallelism) or a sub-division of the priesthood (Hyatt).

Precision of meaning should not be sought in such rhetorical discourses where the gravamen is carried by emotion rather than argument. The leadership is to blame: priests, scribes (cf. 8.8), shepherds (cf. 23.1–2) and prophets (cf. 23.9–40). They have shown themselves to be unsound ideologically. That is, they have either lacked knowledge of Yahweh or have pursued divine knowledge by false means (Baal). Another word-play is used to describe this pursuit of the worthless (v. 8 *ba'al . . . lō'-yō'ilū*). Here the religious ideology of the ruling classes is written off, and in the corruption of the nation those who are to blame are clearly defined. Those two themes, the corrupt nation and the corrupting leadership, will echo throughout the whole Jeremiah tradition and especially in the narratives of 26–29, 34–39, where the folly of the leaders will even eclipse the role of the nation in the disaster of 587.

So the quarrel between Yahweh and Israel will go on for generations (v. 9). The three generations here probably parallel the three generations of Babylonian domination (27.8–9). For the tradition reflects the belief that the fall of Jerusalem would entail a substantial period of servitude (cf. 13.27; 25.11; 28), and this belief the discourse in 2.5–37 sets out to justify. The profanation of the land by the hearers of the sermon (the 'you' of v. 7 or v. 9) and the false consciousness of the leadership would be punished severely by Yahweh.

2.10–13

10 'For cross to the coasts of Cyprus and see,
  or send to Kedar and examine with care;
  see if there has been such a thing.
11 Has a nation changed its gods,
  even though they are no gods?
But my people have changed their glory
  for that which does not profit.
12 Be appalled, O heavens, at this,
  be shocked, be utterly desolate,
    says the LORD,
13 for my people have committed two evils:
  they have forsaken me,
the fountain of living waters,
  and hewed out cisterns for themselves,
broken cisterns,
  that can hold no water.'

---

[11] MT *k^{e}bōdō*, 'its glory', is one of the eighteen *tiqqūnē sōp^{e}rîm*, 'corrections of the scribes', in the Hebrew Bible (on these cf. McKane 1974). For similar changes, though in plural form (*k^{e}bôdām*), cf. Hos. 4.7; Ps. 106.20. The original form would have been *k^{e}bôdī*, 'my glory'; i.e. the deity himself. Cf. McCarthy 1981, 97–105 on such corrections. **[12]** G has *epi pleion*, 'greatly', for MT *ḥorbū*, 'desolate'; BHS follows S and reads *ḥirdū*, 'tremble', cf. NEB.

The next unit in the discourse asserts the same charge as 2.5–9 but using different terms and images. Further rhetorical questions are asked and charges made. The nation has changed its god, has forsaken Yahweh, the source of life. The hyperbolic level of the accusation is clear: what has happened in the life of the nation is something unthinkable and without parallel or precedent in the history of nations. As proof of this claim the people are invited to travel to the west (Cyprus) and to the east (Kedar). Such travel will convince them that no nation has ever changed its gods, therefore Israel is unique in having changed its god. Not only has Israel changed its god but it has changed the real for the unreal (the one of substance for the unprofitable). This double change constitutes two evils: abandoning Yahweh, the fountain or source of fresh water, and the construction of faulty cisterns.

The sense of vv. 10–13 is very clear and is very similar to the poem in 18.13–17. Equally evident is its rhetorical nature. It is highly improbable that no other social group ever changed its beliefs or gods. That is just the hyperbole of preaching. The equation of abandoning Yahweh and making faulty cisterns indicates the stance of the speaker as one belonging to a different outlook from the national position. For no group would ever abandon its water supply in favour of becoming waterless; nor would a group change its ideology from a successful one to such a manifestly useless one. For these evaluations to be made in such a fashion requires understanding the discourse as a highly ideological statement directed against a different ideology. The critique of the nation's religious history as apostate, idolatrous and baalistic is made from the standpoint of a Yahweh-alone group which was not prepared to tolerate certain kinds of syncretistic religion (cf. Smith 1971). Their position was greatly strengthened by the collapse of Jerusalem because that disaster allowed them to associate their opponents' position with worn-out creeds and failed policies (cf. 44.16–19 for a similar critique but from the opposite ideological stance). In so far as Israelite religion can be discerned in the Bible in its original form, it conforms to a Canaanite type of belief and practice, but the account of that religion produced by post-587 biblical writers is dominated by their Yahweh-alone ideology. The fall of Jerusalem was the greatest boon to that ideology, for it discredited all the other religious and political parties. It also so changed political and social structures that it afforded the first real opportunity to the Yahweh-alone ideologies to reshape the Jerusalem community in the succeeding centuries. Part of this reshaping process can be seen in the lengthy discourse in 2.5 – 4.4. The discrediting of the past is an essential feature of ideological change (contrast 6.16), and the various units in the discourse achieve that by denouncing all previous practices and values. But not without incurring some ironic twists in the argument. Thus the change the nation is accused of in 2.11 is precisely what the ideologues themselves wished for from the nation – to change their baalistic understanding of Yahweh to a different concept of him. In a manner of speaking, this was a change of gods. The view of Yahweh as the source of living water will find an ironic echo in 15.18b.

2.14–19

14 'Is Israel a slave? Is he a homeborn servant?
Why then has he become a prey?
15 The lions have roared against him,
they have roared loudly.
They have made his land a waste;
his cities are in ruins, without inhabitant.
16 Moreover, the men of Memphis and Tahpanhes
have broken the crown of your head.
17 Have you not brought this upon yourself
by forsaking the LORD your God,
when he led you in the way?
18 And now what do you gain by going to Egypt,
to drink the waters of the Nile?
Or what do you gain by going to Assyria,
to drink the waters of the Euphrates?
19 Your wickedness will chasten you,
and your apostasy will reprove you.
Know and see that it is evil and bitter
for you to forsake the LORD your God;
the fear of me is not in you,
says the Lord GOD of hosts.'

[15] MT 'will roar', *yiš'ᵃgū*; cf. BHS. MT 'in ruins', *niṣṣᵉtāh* (K), but *niṣṣᵉtū* (Q), 'burned'. Note Q–K on Tahpanhes in v. 16, a scribal error in the MT. **[16]** RSV 'have broken the crown of your head' = MT *yir'ūk qodqōd*, 'have pastured (i.e. devastated) crown (of head)'; Duhm, Cornill, Rudolph prefer *yᵉ'ārūk*, 'have stripped'; G *egnōsan se kai katepaizon sou*, 'have known you and mocked you'. **[17]** MT 'Yahweh your god'; G '(forsaking) me said the lord your god'; delete last phrase with G, BHS, NEB. **[18]** 'Nile'; MT *šiḥōr*, G *Gēōn* (cf. Gen. 2.13); *šiḥōr* is a branch of the Nile on the border of Egypt. **[19]** Cf. note on v. 17; for MT *paḥdātī 'ēlaik*, 'fear of me in you', G has *eudokēsa epi soi*, 'I take (no) pleasure in you'.

The metaphors and images change yet again but the message remains the same. Israel's present state of ruin is due entirely to its (the gender is considerably fluid in the Hebrew) having forsaken Yahweh. In vv. 14–19 the nation's involvement with other gods is not the bone of contention but its past history of political alliances with the great powers of Egypt and Assyria. In the Deuteronomistic history of the kingdoms of Israel and Judah such foreign alliances constitute apostasy from Yahweh. Such a xenophobic concept reflects the Deuteronomistic ideology that to seek aid from foreign powers is to become involved with alien gods, and if Judah is to live in fidelity to Yahweh it must shun all tendencies towards such cultural assimilation (on the cultural ramifications of vassalage to Assyria see Cogan 1974). So in vv. 14–19 such political involvement is equivalent to idolatry and expresses the same charge of apostasy as the other units in the discourse. Because the Deuteronomistic outlook is an ideology, it refuses to recognize the *Realpolitik* of the period of Assyrian domination when all small states inevitably became the vassals of the empire. This was not a matter of morality or a case of religious infidelity but a question of powerlessness in the face of superior political forces. The shape of political existence changed for all the small nations once the Assyrian empire came to power and Judah was to become ever after subject to such domination. It was ruled over first by Assyria, then Babylon and beyond that, Persia, Greece and Rome until it was extinguished as a political entity in the second century CE. It would take the loss of statehood, monarchy and the fall of Jerusalem before such political realities penetrated certain forms of Yahwism, and theology was adjusted accordingly (cf. Ezra 6.14). Given this analysis, v. 14 is a case of special pleading and becomes quite ironic when compared to the advocacy of servitude to the Babylonians as the will of Yahweh in chs. 27–28.

Looking back at a history of military invasions and a devastated land the speaker can only raise the question 'Is Israel a slave?'. Slave, house-born servant, prey are all images of creatures lacking freedom and in the power of others. This has been the experience of the nation for a long time and the explanation is simply that Israel has abandoned Yahweh. No complex political analysis is provided in this sermon. Even the Egyptians have humiliated the people. The reference to Tahpanhes in v. 16 may reflect the experiences of the people who fled there after the fall of Jerusalem (43.7) but the reference is too allusive to be given a specific meaning. The general principle enunciated in v. 18 makes the pursuit of aid from Assyria and Egypt futile activities (cf. Isa. 8.6 for a similar metaphor).

The image of going to Egypt or Assyria to drink water, having forsaken Yahweh (the fountain of living waters), suggests that the broken cisterns of v. 13 may well be an image of such imperial powers as Egypt or Assyria. If the experiences described in vv. 15–16, 18 refer to historical events in the life of the nation, then the Israel referred to in v. 14 is most definitely Judah. But the language of the unit is sufficiently general and abstract to require no precise identification with actual events. Judah remains the subject of the diatribe, and the general experiences of the past underwrite the theology of the speaker. Reliance on other nations is symptomatic of Judah's apostasy and that has been a bitter experience (v. 19; cf. Isa. 30.1–5).

The reference to Assyria in v. 18 has led many commentators to assume that Assyria was still powerful at this period and that therefore the unit should be dated to the 620s, at the beginning of Jeremiah's ministry. This is to ignore the rhetorical nature of such poetry. Egypt and Assyria are word-pairs in biblical poetry (Isa. 7.18; 19.25; 52.4; Hos. 7.11; 9.3, 6; 11.5; 12.1; cf. 8.9, 13; Isa. 10.24; 11.11, 16; 19.23–24; 20.4; 27.13). Word-pairs are formulaic and stereotypical and suggest a traditional diction with a stockpile of pairs and phrases (see Watters 1976; Whallon 1969). The use of such pairs aids the poet in the construction of poems, but they are clichés and lack meaning (cf. Homer's 'wine-dark sea'). As a formal element in a poem the word-pair carries the thought along, but each member of the pair need not have its semantic force in operation. 'Assyria' is such a formal element here (cf. its cipher status in Lam. 5.6; Zech.

10.10–11; Ezra 6.22) and does not necessitate dating 2.14–19 in the Assyrian period (745–605).

2.20–22

20 ‘For long ago you broke your yoke
and burst your bonds;
and you said, “I will not serve.”
Yea, upon every high hill
and under every green tree
you bowed down as a harlot.
21 Yet I planted you a choice vine,
wholly of pure seed.
How then have you turned degenerate
and become a wild vine?
22 Though you wash yourself with lye
and use much soap,
the stain of your guilt is still before me,
says the Lord God.’

---

[20] MT’s *šābartī* and *nittaqtī* are old feminine endings, cf. G. Q *’e‘ebōr* for K *’e‘ebōd* is curious. MT *ṣō‘āh*, ‘bowed down’, is an obscene word, cf. NEB: ‘sprawled in promiscuous vice’. The reader’s imagination will serve better than a translation. **[21]** MT *lī sūrē haggepen* probably corrupt, cf. BHS, which follows Duhm and reads *lesōrīyyāh gepen*, ‘foul-smelling vine’. Cf. *gepen sōraḥat*, ‘a low spreading vine’, in Ezek. 17.6. **[22]** G has ‘lord’ but lacks *’adōnāy*.

Holladay 1961

The feminine form of address begun in v. 16 continues in vv. 20–22. Three sets of images are used here to convey the same message as in the other units. In v. 20 the image is that of a rebellious woman who long ago refused to obey her overlord and broke away from his service in order to become an energetic whore (*ṣō‘āh zōnāh*). Her ‘I will not serve’ is in striking contrast to the accusation in v. 14 that the community is a slave. As a man the community is a slave, but as a woman it is riotously free from restraint. Both figures describe the same community, using very different metaphors in order to make the same point. The nation is in revolt against Yahweh.

The phrase 'upon every high hill and under every green tree' is almost repeated in 3.6 (the assonance of *gib'āh g^ebōhāh* in v. 20 is lost); 17.2 and echoed in 3.13. The same phrase occurs in I Kings 14.23 and II Kings 17.10, and there are a number of variants of it elsewhere in the Hebrew Bible (cf. Deut. 12.2; Hos. 4.13; Isa. 30.25; 57.5, 7; Ezek. 6.13; II Chron. 28.4; full listing in Holladay 1961, 170–1). It would appear to be a Deuteronomistic phrase here (so Thiel 1973, 82–3), but Holladay argues 'with real confidence' for it having a family tree of Hos. 4.13, then Deut. 12.2, and Jeremiah standardizing it in the form it has in 2.20. In spite of such confidence, and although the phrase appears to fit quite well in this verse, it is most likely a Deuteronomistically influenced addition which disrupts the point of the metaphors being used. It makes v. 20 overlong in comparison to vv. 21, 22 and overloads the metaphor of 20b with other associations.

An entirely different set of metaphors is used in v. 21 to describe the decline of the nation from its great past. Yahweh planted it a choice species of vine (*śōrēq*) but it has turned into a wild vine. The genuine quality of the original vine has degenerated into something alien. A similar project with precisely the same results is described in Isa. 5.1–7. The claret has turned into vinegar! The vine is a common figure for Israel (Hos. 10.1; Ezek. 17.6–8; Ps. 80.8–14), but the image of its degeneration into something worthless appears to be 'a retrospective *theology of history* standing in the shadow of the Deuteronomistic movement' (Kaiser 1983, 93). That assessment of Isa. 5.1–7 would fit the use of the image here in 2.21. In the light of the destruction of Jerusalem the history of Israel is a complete failure and Yahweh's wine-making enterprise a disaster. Just as the bridal loyalty turned to infidelity, the choice grapes turned rotten ('lilies that fester . . .').

A third image occurs in v. 22. The stain of Israel's guilt cannot be washed off (cf. 13.27). No matter what cleansing agents are used the stain remains before the deity's eyes. All the images used in vv. 20–22 represent an unchangeable state; a state frozen by the fall of Jerusalem. Rebellion, degeneracy and pollution characterize the state of the nation.

2.23–25

23 'How can you say, "I am not defiled,
I have not gone after the Baals"?
Look at your way in the valley;
know what you have done –
a restive young camel interlacing her tracks,
24 a wild ass used to the wilderness,
in her heat sniffing the wind!
Who can restrain her lust?
None who seek her need weary themselves;
in her month they will find her.
25 Keep your feet from going unshod
and your throat from thirst.
But you said, "It is hopeless,
for I have loved strangers,
and after them I will go." '

---

[23] MT 'in the valley': G *en tō polyandreiō*, 'in the burial ground'; at this point G is quite different from MT. The Hebrew metaphors are lost in an expansion of 'activity in the way'. **[24]** MT *pereh limmud midbār*, 'a wild ass used to the wilderness', is understood differently by G; some commentators following Köhler 1909 read *pōrṣāh lammidbār*, 'breaking loose in the desert', thus losing the figure of the wild ass (ct. NEB). K *napšū*; Q *napšāh*. MT 'in her month', but G 'in her humiliation'. **[25]** K *wgwrnk* a scribal error for Q *ūgᵉrōnēk*, 'your throat'.

McKane 1972

In this unit the community is represented as responding to the charge of being stained. It denies the polluting effect of its behaviour but confesses to the compulsive nature of its pursuit of other gods. This exchange is a rhetorical device rather than an actual conversation between the speaker and some representative of the nation. But the form and content of the exchange are complicated, and posed many problems for the early translators of the piece (exhaustively examined in McKane 1972). It is not clear whether the nation is denying the pursuit of the *baalim* in v. 23 or simply denying that pollution has been caused by such activity. The phrase 'your way in the valley' is ambiguous. Does 'valley' refer to the valley of Ben Hinnom where a fire cult was practised (7.31–32; 19.5–6;

many commentators) or some valley associated with baal worship (cf. Num. 25.1–5; Rashi, Kimchi)? Although G appears to refer to the Ben Hinnom practice, MT is better understood as a non-specific reference to baalistic worship and not an allusion to Ben Hinnom (Soggin 1975a favours G as a reference to 'cult of the dead'). 'Your way in the valley' becomes shorthand for involvement with baalism throughout Israel's history.

Two graphic images are used to describe this history: a restive young camel (she-camel) and a wild ass. Both are presented as victims of their own lust, behaving crazily in the desert and driven by sexual appetite. It is a picture of uncontrollable lust and promiscuity. That is about the only element in vv. 23–25 on which translators and commentators can agree. G lacks the two images and a number of modern scholars read the text in such a way as to lose the wild ass image (e.g. Rudolph, Bright; NEB inevitably follows Driver 1937–38). The wild ass in heat is an image of the accessibility of the animal to all male animals of the species and serves here as a statement about Israel's availability for the service of other gods. The frantic activity of the animals seeking sexual satisfaction is paralleled in v. 25 by the prohibition to keep the feet unshod and the throat dry. Although 'feet' is a standard Hebrew allusion to genitals it is not used here in that sense but appears to be a reference to frantic journeys (in the desert) which wear out the shoes and cause thirst. 'Avoid such restless journeys' is probably the best interpretation of v. 25a. As such it restates the meaning of the images in 23–24. Yet it is not a command containing an element of hoped for change in the community so much as a rhetorical way of indicating the people's deep inability to change. 'It is hopeless' is the response. The frantic woman is driven by her passions and cannot do otherwise. It is a compelling image of a person swept away by a commitment to a particular way of life and incapable of doing other than that. Israel's condition in v. 25 is the same as that described in vv. 20–22.

The gender of much of the imagery in the discourse is feminine. This is particularly true of the terms used in vv. 16–25, where the nation (or city cf. 2.2) is personified as a woman. Cities and lands are feminine in Hebrew, so Israel and Jerusalem are regularly addressed as women (cf. 'daughter Zion' 6.2; 'daughter my people' 8.19). The relationship between Yahweh and Israel is often represented in terms of the man-woman/husband-wife set of metaphors. In the biblical world a married man had a greater degree of sexual freedom than a married woman had. A woman was bound to her husband and any sexual activity outside the marriage branded her a whore and liable to serious punishment. Strong emotions were aroused by such matters and the Bible contains a good deal of abusive language directed at women who failed to conform. Other cultures appear to have had somewhat different practices, especially in connection with the cult, though adultery as a major offence appears to be a common feature of all ancient Near Eastern societies. The precise degree to which sacred prostitution was practised among Israel's neighbours is impossible to determine, but its presence contributed to making sexual references terms of abuse for Yahwistic ideologues. Since Hosea, religious pornography has become a standard form of abusing opponents. Once the metaphors of marriage are transferred to describing the relationship between Yahweh and Israel, then all the abuse that might be heaped on a faithless wife will become part of the arsenal of religious denunciations. This transference will explain the degree of emotion generated in such statements as appear in 2.20, 23–25; 3.1–3, 13; 5.7–8. Theological metaphors have allowed strong emotions to be expressed. Recent feminist theological writing has complained about the misogynistic nature of this biblical element (e.g. Ochshorn 1981, 160–3). Without knowing the psychological make-up of the biblical writers it is not possible to evaluate the degree to which their writings may be characterized as misogynistic or otherwise. But given the metaphoric nature of the language used (masculine as much as feminine) caution is warranted before jumping to the wrong conclusions (see below on 3.1–5; 5.7–8).

2.26–28

26 'As a thief is shamed when caught,
so the house of Israel shall be shamed:
they, their kings, their princes,
their priests, and their prophets,
27 who say to a tree, "You are my father,"
and to a stone, "You gave me birth."
For they have turned their back to me,
and not their face.
But in the time of their trouble they say,
"Arise and save us!"

28 But where are your gods
   that you made for yourself?
 Let them arise, if they can save you,
   in your time of trouble;
 for as many as your cities
   are your gods, O Judah.'

---

[26] G has 'sons' for MT 'house'. Many commentators (e.g. Duhm, Rudolph, Weiser) treat the second half of the verse as a later addition. **[27]** K *y^{e}lidtinī*, cf. G, BHS rather than Q *y^{e}lidtānū*. **[28]** Cf. 11.13; G has 'and as many as the streets of Jerusalem they sacrificed to Baal'.

The metaphorical nature of the language of vv. 23–25 is made clear by vv. 26–28, which have the same point to make. Israel (i.e. Judah, cf. v. 28) has turned from Yahweh to serve other gods and this turning will be a cause of deep shame (just like a thief's shame when caught). A Deuteronomistic gloss in 26b (cf. 1.18; 32.32; Thiel 1973, 83) specifies the leading classes of the community which will be shamed. It is indicative of an editorial concern to spotlight certain strata of society as the ones responsible for the state of the nation which brought about the catastrophe of 587. The nation's idolatry is the root cause of that disaster. Its involvement in the nature cults – the numina of trees and stones (on these cf. Gaster 1969, 586) – is equated with turning the back on Yahweh (cf. Ezek. 8.16). Yet in spite of such apostasy Israel expects Yahweh to save it in time of trouble. The irony of the response to that request is very clear in v. 28, where Judah is castigated for the sheer number of its gods.

The rhetorical question, 'Where are your gods that you made for yourself?', so reminiscent of 2.6, 8, conceals a different kind of irony. The question itself appears to be a standard response to disaster or suffering (cf. Ps. 42.3, 10; 79.10), but implying a sceptical view of the victim. The powerlessness of the gods to deliver those who worship them is part of the logic of defeat: 'Where are the gods of Hamath and Arpad? Where are the gods of Sepharvaim, Hena, and Ivvah? Have they delivered Samaria out of my hand?' (II Kings 18.34). The defeat of Jerusalem in 587 must have raised the question 'where is Yahweh?' in its most serious form. Because, in point of fact, neither Yahweh nor the gods could save city or people. In the fall of Jerusalem Yahweh's status as god must have been questioned seriously by many people. That such questioning took place is demonstrated by the production of the book of Job, the tenor of the liturgical poems constituting Second Isaiah and the ideological handling of the exile in the book of Jeremiah. It is the desperate need of the Yahwistic ideologues to pin the blame for the catastrophe on other cults which is behind the shaping of the discourse in 2.5 – 37 as an introduction to the Jeremiah tradition. As well as developing a theodicy for the exile, the ideologues are engaged in a polemic against alternative understandings of the nature of Yahweh. He is not the nature god of the older cultic ways of Israel; he cannot be worshipped in forms associated with fertility or ‘on every high hill and under every green tree’. Multiplicity (of altars or sacred places cf. 11.13) and diversity are not characteristics of his (hence the formal ruling about his unity in Deut. 6.4). Whatever the beliefs and practices of the temple cult in Jerusalem before 587 (cf. Ezek. 8), the destruction of the city with its cult was a godsend for these ideologues because it allowed them to blame previous administrations for the disastrous state of affairs prevailing after 587. It would take a different kind of theological reflection to move away from a theology of blame for disaster and develop a sensitive understanding of the truth expressed in Job's question ‘Shall we receive good at the hand of God, and shall we not receive evil?’ (Job 2.10; cf. Isa. 45.7).

2.29–32

29 ‘Why do you complain against me?
  You have all rebelled against me, says the LORD.
30 In vain have I smitten your children,
  they took no correction;
your own sword devoured your prophets
  like a ravening lion.
37 And you, O generation, heed the word of the LORD.
Have I been a wilderness to Israel,
  or a land of thick darkness?
Why then do my people say, “We are free,
  we will come no more to thee”?
32 Can a maiden forget her ornaments,
  or a bride her attire?
Yet my people have forgotten me
  days without number.’

---

[29] G ‘Wherefore do you speak to me? All of you are ungodly and all of you have transgressed against me, says the lord.' **[30]** MT 'your children': BHS prefers 'fathers and sons', cf. 6.21. G '*you* took' for MT 'they took'; G concludes v. 30 with 'but you did not fear'. **[31]** MT *haddōr 'attem rᵉ'u dᵉbar-yhwh*, lit., 'the generation (are) you see the word of Yahweh': G *akousate logon kuriou Tade legei kurios*, 'hear the word of the lord Thus says the lord'. Cf. Ps. 24.6a for a similarly peculiar form of address to the worshipping community (*dōr*, cf. Ps. 14.5; 73.15). Many commentators delete v. 31a as a marginal comment or later gloss (cf. BHS). MT *radnū*, 'we are free' (i.e. to move about): G *ou kurieuthēsometha*, 'we will not be ruled over'; BHS favours *māradnū*, 'we have rebelled'. **[32]** MT *'edyāh* 'her ornaments': meaning what in this context? Perhaps 'first period' is the sense (cf. *'iddīm*, 'menstruation' Isa. 64.5 [EV 6]; Ezek. 16.7).

The discourse continues with a unit of rhetorical questions which demonstrates the homiletical nature of the whole section. The community is represented as complaining against the deity (a reversal of v. 9) and that is swiftly countered with the principle 'the accused has no right to accuse the accuser'. If there is more than rhetoric behind v. 29, it may refer to some communal lament in which the people complain to the deity about recent disasters or suffering in general (cf. 12.1–4; Ps. 44; 73; 74; 79). To this the deity responds, 'I am the one behind the striking down of your children and the slaying of your prophets.' Disasters which have proved to be ineffective (cf. the longer recital of such deity-controlled catastrophes in Amos 4.6–11). The reference to the killing of the prophets is too general to permit identification with any historical episode (it hardly can refer to the isolated incident in 26.20–23) and is in stark contrast to the dominant line in the Jeremiah tradition on the prophets as the enemy of the people (see on 23.9–40). It reflects the late tradition (cf. Neh. 9.26) of the killing of the prophets by earlier generations, a belief which had become a dogma by NT times (cf. Matt. 23.29–31; Luke 11.47–48; Acts 7.51–53; on the development of the legend see Steck 1967). However, it should be noted that, the killing of the prophets of Baal apart, there is very little killing of prophets in the Hebrew Bible. Apparently the people of ancient Israel were not nearly as vicious as the prophetic traditions depict them (people seldom are!). The futility of this divine destruction of the people by way of correcting their behaviour (as also in Amos 4) underlines the ideological obtuseness of the speaker.

Although v. 31a is generally recognized as a later addition to the text, it indicates that the discourse is addressed to the worshipping community (the sense of *dōr*, cf. Ps. 14.5; 24.6; 73.15) and the community is expected to respond to the preaching against it. It is a fragment of the history of the discourse. The sermon went on being preached to subsequent generations of worshipping Judaeans so that they might learn the lessons of history as presented in this ideological account of the past. In view of v. 30 (cf. Amos 4.6–11) the question in 31b might well be answered in the affirmative! A god who destroys his own people is a thick darkness, a desert and a demoniacal force. Small wonder that the people should shun him. However, that is not the intention of the speaker: it is not Yahweh's behaviour which is being questioned but the people's religious affiliations. That the speaker is unaware of the theological difficulties raised by vv. 30–31 (contrast the lament psalms or the book of Job) reveals just how ideologically committed the discourse is to a one-dimensional interpretation of the exilic disaster. To maintain such a line of argument it is necessary to represent the people as deliberately rejecting their own god. It is highly unlikely that any group would so dismiss its central cult figure (cf. v. 11a) that it becomes necessary to interpret the discourse in terms of an ideological dispute about the cultic representations of Yahweh. The community's account of their beliefs and practices may so differ from the speaker's that their way of life is tantamount to a rejection of his theology. This is an inner community argument rather than a description of reality. Ideological interpretation (misrepresentation?) is at work here and the hyperbole of v. 32 bears that out. The images in v. 32, obscure though they may be, make the same point. It might be illuminating to have access to the community's account of the matter, but that is not possible because ideology makes all opposition silent.

2.33–37

33 'How well you direct your course
to seek lovers!
So that even to wicked women
you have taught your ways.
34 Also on your skirts is found
the lifeblood of guiltless poor;
you did not find them breaking in.
Yet in spite of all these things
35 you say, "I am innocent;
surely his anger has turned from me."

Behold, I will bring you to judgment
  for saying, "I have not sinned."
36 How lightly you gad about,
  changing your way!
You shall be put to shame by Egypt
  as you were put to shame by Assyria.
37 From it too you will come away
  with your hands upon your head,
for the LORD has rejected those in whom you trust,
  and you will not prosper by them.'

---

[33] MT *'et-hārā'ōt limmadtī* (K), better translated 'with evil deeds you have trained your ways'; cf. G 'you have done wickedly in corrupting your ways'; cf. *hārā'ōt* in 3.5. It is unnecessary to posit a special class of 'evil women' in Judaean society! **[34]** G has 'hands' for MT 'skirts' and lacks 'poor'. The 'guiltless' (*n^eqīyyīm*) is probably a parallel reference to 'prophets' in v. 30 (cf. BHS). The last clause in MT *kī 'al-kol-'ēlleh*, 'but upon/because of all these', is incomprehensible; G 'I have not found them by searching but on every oak', cf. NEB 'but by your sacrifices under every oak'. This understanding of *'lh* as 'oak' suggests the garden cults of Isa. 1.29; 17.10 with overtones of human sacrifice; BHS, Rudolph prefer to treat the clause as *kī 'ālaik l^e'ālāh kol-'ēlleh*, 'for upon you for a curse are all these', with the first *'ālāh* omitted due to haplography. Holladay 1975b reads *'lyk* as 'yoke': 'your yoke is execrable'. **[36]** MT *tēzlī*, 'gad about', suggests *'zl*, 'go', but Vrs imply *tāzēllī*, *zll*, 'scorn, make light of'.

The theme of vv. 23–25 is continued in vv. 33–37 with its use of erotic metaphors to describe political alliances with other countries (the strangers of v. 25 are such as Egypt and Assyria in vv. 13, 36). The units between these two (vv. 26–28, 29–32) are concerned with idolatry but the sexual imagery is about alien alliances. These two themes appear to be mixed together in the original poems and it is difficult to determine whether political or religious apostasy is intended as the charge against Israel. The two are not necessarily the same thing and it is symptomatic of the discourse that it fluctuates between two different, but equally vague, themes. Judah has lightly gadded about seeking political security among the nations or it has indulged in the worship of gods without number. The pejorative tone of these poems indicates a highly xenophobic, narrowly defined ideological group castigating extremely imprecise practices. The past, characterized by the quest for political stability in conjunction with the empires, is proof of lack of fidelity to Yahweh. Its constant changing of allegiances will only be a cause of shame rather than security. The unit shares the same spirit as Isa. 30.1–5 with its diatribe against relying on Egyptian help. Whether that reliance on Egypt refers to the past in general, Jehoiakim's subjection to Egypt or the escape to Egypt after the destruction of Jerusalem (cf. 43.7; 42.13–22) cannot be determined from this unit. Great hostility toward Egypt appears to have been a feature of the early exilic period (cf. Isa. 19.1–15; Ezek. 29.1–20).

Within the tirade against seeking Egyptian help is an attack on the community for killing the innocent (v. 34) and for claiming to be innocent itself (v. 35). In the MT the innocent are the poor (cf. Isa. 3.14–15) but the original form (cf. G) may have referred to the same class of victim as in v. 30. The oppression of the poor is not a main theme in the Jeremiah tradition, so its appearance here is probably a secondary development. The allusion to 'breaking in' (v. 34) reflects the ruling of Ex. 22.2–3 that a thief may be killed if found breaking in during the hours of dark. So the charge is one of premeditated killing. The claim of being innocent is echoed in 2.23 and is akin to the sense of having done nothing wrong expressed elsewhere (cf. 5.24; 8.6; contrast 3.21, 24–25; 14.7, 19–22). Given the general tenor of the tradition it is difficult to believe that there were any innocent people in the community (cf. 5.4–5; 9.4–6), but it is the mark of an ideological analysis to be able to absorb seemingly contradictory points of view.

3.1–5

31 'If a man divorces his wife
  and she goes from him
and becomes another man's wife,
  will he return to her?
Would not that land be greatly polluted?
You have played the harlot with many lovers;
  and would you return to me?
    says the LORD.
2 Lift up your eyes to the bare heights, and see!
  Where have you not been lain with?
By the waysides you have sat awaiting lovers
  like an Arab in the wilderness.

You have polluted the land
with your vile harlotry.
3 Therefore the showers have been withheld,
and the spring rain has not come;
yet you have a harlot's brow,
you refuse to be ashamed.
4 Have you not just now called to me,
"My father, thou art the friend of my youth -
5 will he be angry for ever,
will he be indignant to the end?"
Behold, you have spoken,
but you have done all the evil that you could.'

---

[1] MT begins with *lē' mōr*, 'saying', which may be a fragment of the introductory formula, 'the word of Yahweh came to me . . .' (cf. 1.4; 2.1): G begins with the next word *hēn*, 'if', *ean*. MT *hayāšūb 'elēhā 'ōd*, 'shall *he* return to her again?': G 'shall she return to him any more at all' makes better sense here. MT is influenced by the argument of Deut. 24.4, but Mayes (1979, 323) takes the opposite view. G has 'that woman' for MT 'that land'; possibly a Greek error of *gunē* for *gē*. For land pollution cf. v. 9. **[2]** MT *šuggalt*, 'been ravished', K but Q *šukkabt*, 'lain with'; K is an obscene term well translated by Margaret Kohl as 'Where have you not been fucked?' (Koch 1983, 22). Bright's 'tumbled' may save a few blushes and continues the Masoretic task of making the biblical text fit for genteel consumption. G has 'as a deserted crow' for MT 'like an Arab in the desert'. **[3]** The first two clauses are quite different in G: *kai esches poimenas pollous eis proskomma seautē*, 'and you retained many shepherds for a stumbling-block to yourself'. MT *'iššāh zōnāh*, 'woman whore', contains a redundant term: BHS suggests reading the phrase as (*ūmēṣaḥ*) *neḥušāh*, 'brazen (brow)', cf. Isa. 48.4; Ehrlich 1912, 243; Volz, Rudolph. **[4]** MT *halō' mē'attāh*,' is it not just now'. NEB 'Not so long ago', but G *ouch hōs oikon me ekalesas*, 'have you not called me as it were a house'. BHS 'nevertheless you called me . . .', omitting 'my father' (misplaced from v. 19, cf. Duhm, Rudolph) on the grounds that *'āb* does not refer to 'husband'. Q corrects old feminine ending of *tī* in *qr'ty*, cf. 2.33. **[5]** MT *hinnēh*, 'behold', might be better as *hēnnāh*, 'these things', so BHS. Q–K correction of *dbrty*.

Hobbs 1974; Long 1976; Martin 1969

After the long and repetitive discourse on apostasy there follows a series of reflections and discussions built around the term *šūb*, 'turn, return' (on *šūb* in the Jeremiah tradition see Holladay 1958, 128–39).

Both apostasy and the possibility of returning are discussed in vv. 1–5 so that it continues the first theme and introduces the new theme. Apart from v. 1, the unit makes the same points as are made in 2.5–37. Judah has played the whore against her husband Yahweh and has done it so persistently and so brazenly that drought has beset the land (v. 3; cf. 14.1–6; 12.4). Yet there is no sense of shame in the community (cf. 6.15 = 8.12). The image of the faithless woman waiting by the wayside for lovers suggests the political alliances condemned in 2.36, yet the language about the pollution of the land points to involvement with the baalistic cults. Both notions appear to be interwoven throughout the discourse and its additions in ch. 3. The ambiguity of the language is very much caused by the metaphors drawn from erotic relationships to describe Judah's bond with Yahweh, its political alliances with other powers, and some of its religious practices. Too few terms have to serve too many purposes and the result is inevitably confusing to readers who are not party to the original discussions which gave rise to the text. It is not always possible to determine whether the text is referring to political, religious or sexual activities (or to all three at once!). What does emerge from texts such as 3.1–5 is the very strong emotion behind the accusations, typified by the obscene language used. If the language were not so stereotypical (cf. Hosea or Ezekiel), its verisimilitude would suggest that it is derived from the timeless quarrels of husbands and wives. The whining hysteria of vv. 1–5, lapsing into sentimentality in vv. 4–5 (also vv. 19–20), is hardly rescued by being attributed to the deity. Here is part of the problem of this kind of language. The cuckold god comes across as pathetic and ranting. As he pleads continually with a wife who clearly is not interested in him at all but in all the young men about the place, he becomes the butt of ribald remarks. Now there may be the basis for a theology of the pain of God here, but cuckoldry is more a matter for ribaldry than a serious foundation for doing theology. In the context of ancient Semitic society, a god who cannot depend upon his wife's fidelity is a wretched figure. Here then is the thrust of these passages: Judah, like a faithless wife, has made Yahweh look foolish and impotent. He, like an outraged cuckolded husband, can only retaliate by smashing up the place and destroying everything (cf. 4.5 – 6.26).

This analysis may take the rhetoric too seriously, but the rage and violence is detectable in the text, and the events which gave rise to the literary activity of the exile were themselves bloody. The language is of course metaphorical and inherited from the Hosea tradition, though with variations and developments, and the Deuteronomistic writers. It may gain its force from human emotions, but it seldom describes real sexual activities (5.8; 29.23 may be exceptions to this rule). Yet metaphors drawn from human sexuality and applied to human-divine relationships are fraught with misunderstanding and misapplications. They tend to devalue sexual behaviour and associate it with alien cults and apostasy. The long tradition of treating one's opponents as 'an adulterous generation' has its roots here, and much real human suffering has been caused by it.

The rhetorical questions of v. 1 are followed by a disputation in vv. 2–5 (cf. Long 1976), with elements derived from the wisdom tradition (Hobbs 1974). Such a mixture of formal features may suit the ambiguities inherent in the unit, but does not facilitate interpretation. The question in v. 1 reflects a common background with Deut. 24.1–4 but in reality only shares one feature with it. A man may not take back his former wife if she has married another man between leaving and returning to her first husband. Such behaviour would pollute the land (a land already polluted according to 2.7). The meaning is clear: Judah cannot return to Yahweh. That point has already been made a number of times in 2.5–37. The questioning technique simply reiterates the contention of the discourse. A wife who has behaved the way Judah behaved with other gods would never be taken back by her former husband, nor will Yahweh take back Judah. The destruction of Jerusalem is the historical correlative of this metaphorical analysis. The connection between harlotry and drought in v. 3 is ironic: the fertility cults of Canaan were designed to guarantee the cycle of nature. Sowing the fields, rain in due season, growth of crops, reaping the harvest were all under the aegis of the local baals representing the god Baal. Except that in Israel and Judah the role of Baal was attributed to Yahweh (cf. Hos. 2.8). Yet many of the rituals may have been the same (e.g. sacrifice, unleavened bread festivals). This interpenetration of Yahwism and Baalism was anathema to the Deuteronomistic writers, and the exile was viewed as the result of such a syncretistic religion. So droughts were blamed on it and therein lies the irony. The very cult which was supposed to guarantee crops and fertility was the cause of aridity and blight. It is an ideological point, because supporters of the mixed religious outlook would have argued the case the other way around (cf. 44.16–19).

The 'just now' of v. 4 is difficult. It may refer to some specific event or statement to which the speaker is responding with a divine word (vv. 5, 19–20). But there is no information available to indicate what it might have been. A more likely explanation is that it is one more rhetorical device in the speaker's presentation by which he puts words into the nation's mouth in order to rebut them (the clearest example of this technique is 13.12). In response to the drought the nation seeks Yahweh's help (cf. the fast in 36.9 or the liturgy in 14.7–9) in the hope that his anger will not last for ever (cf. Ps. 44.23–26; 89.46; Lam. 5.20–22). 'Mere words' is the speaker's response to such behaviour. The gap between words and actions is too great (cf. 7.9–10; 12.2b). Although an important point is being made here (see below on 7.8–11), it is also necessary to step back from the text and ask questions. What did the community imagine it was doing in its worship of Yahweh? Did it think it was unfaithful to him? Would it have described its behaviour in such pejorative terms? We do not possess the data to answer such questions, but in asking them we raise the much more important question about the degree of ideological bias in the texts we do possess. If they are not scrutinized for ideological distortion then our exegesis of them is vacuous.

3.6–11

6 The LORD said to me in the days of King Josiah: 'Have you seen what she
did, that faithless one, Israel, how she went up on every high hill and under
every green tree, and there played the harlot? 7 And I thought, "After she
has done all this she will return to me"; but she did not return, and her false
sister Judah saw it. 8 She saw that for all the adulteries of that faithless one,
Israel, I had sent her away with a decree of divorce; yet her false sister
Judah did not fear, but she too went and played the harlot. 9 Because
harlotry was so light to her, she polluted the land, committing adultery with
stone and tree. 10 Yet for all this her false sister Judah did not return to me
with her whole heart, but in pretence, says the LORD.' 11 And the LORD
said to me, 'Faithless Israel has shown herself less guilty than false Judah.'

---

[7] Q–K on *wtr'h*, 'and she saw'. **[8]** MT reads 'and I saw'; some G mss read 'and she saw', cf. BHS; followed by RSV, NEB but not JPSB. G has 'into her hands', after 'a bill of divorce', cf. Deut. 24.1. **[9]** G lacks 'she polluted the land'.

McKane 1981, 229–33; Thiel 1973, 83–91

A prose section now follows which appears to be an exegetical piece built around the motifs of 'divorce' in v. 1 and 'faithless Israel' in v. 12. Its place here may be due to a Deuteronomistic editor (Hyatt, Holladay, Thiel), though there is little evidence of Deuteronomistic clichés in the passage. The setting of the verses in the time of Josiah indicates that it is a very late addition to the tradition coming from the redactional strand which provided 1.1–3; 25.1–7. The author has misinterpreted the reference to divorce in v. 1 and applied it to northern Israel (cf. the editorial note in v. 12a). The same misinterpretation holds for 'faithless Israel' (*mᵉšubāh yiśrā'ēl*) in v. 12a. Failing to understand that 'Israel' in the discourse refers to Judah, the later exegete, influenced by the views behind Ezek. 16.51–52, offers some thoughts on the relative merits of northern Israel and Judah. After the fall of Jerusalem there developed opinions among the exiles that to be in exile was virtuous and to have remained behind in Judah was to be subject still to the judgment of Yahweh (cf. 24.4–10; 29.1–7, 15–19; Ezek. 11.14, 21). This outlook included the construction of a paradigm of comparative wickedness in which Israel/Samaria, for all its evil, was superior to Judah (3.6–11; 23.13–14; Ezek. 16.51–52; for the exilic dating of the Ezekiel passage see Zimmerli 1979). The sins of Judah make Samaria appear righteous (Ezek. 16.51) and less guilty (in both texts *ṣdq* is used of Israel/Samaria). Such a presentation of the kingdom destroyed some centuries previously would border on the absurd were it not for the ideological struggle underpinning it. The conflict between the different communities (exilic and Palestinian) is an important strand in the Jeremiah tradition, and this comparative praise for Israel is intended to support the exilic claim over the Judaean position.

What makes Judah worse than Israel is the fact that she had the example of Israel's fate to warn her, but ignored that dire warning. Judah's response to Israel's divorce (i.e. destruction and deportation by the Assyrians) was to behave in the same way (i.e. to play the whore with false gods) and to view such behaviour in a frivolous manner. Hence her epithet *bāgōdāh*, 'false' or 'faithless' (*mᵉšubāh* would be better translated 'apostate' so as to distinguish it from Judah's 'faithless' epithet, cf. v. 20). Such treacherous behaviour even extends to her returning (*šābāh*, v. 10) to Yahweh. What this 'turning' to Yahweh refers to is unclear. As the piece is dated in the time of Josiah, it may be a reference to Josiah's reform (II Kings 22–23). But if it is, it is a very oblique reference to that event and highly dismissive at that. The statement 'Judah did not return to me with her whole heart, but in pretence (*kī 'im-bᵉšeqer*)' combines two key motifs (*šūb*; *šeqer* – for the use of *šeqer* in Jeremiah see Overholt 1970) in a most strange way. The 'turning' motif of 3.1 – 4.2 is generally (apart from v. 1 and the epithet *mᵉšubāh*) a positive term, whereas *šeqer* describes all that is false in the community. To concede that 'turning' (or repentance) may itself be false is to undermine the importance attached elsewhere to such 'turning' (cf. 18.7–11). However, the purpose here of such a combination is to do down Judah (whatever its incidental relation to Josiah's reform may be) and to dismiss its efforts at turning back to Yahweh (after the fall of Jerusalem?). Judah is so wicked that even its turning to Yahweh is false. The ideological masking by that judgment of the promotion of another group's status should be noted.

3.12–13

12 'Go, and proclaim these words toward the north, and say,
"Return, faithless Israel,
says the LORD.
I will not look on you in anger,
for I am merciful,
says the LORD;
I will not be angry for ever.
13 Only acknowledge your guilt,
that you rebelled against the LORD your God
and scattered your favours among strangers under every green tree,
and that you have not obeyed my voice,
says the LORD." '

---

[13] MT *wattᵉpazzᵉrī 'et-dᵉrākaīk*, 'and scattered your ways', cf. use of *derek* in 2.23; NEB 'confess your promiscuous traffic with foreign gods', where RSV takes *lazzārīm* as 'among strangers'. Rudolph follows Cornill by reading *dōdaīk*, 'love', for *drkyk*, cf. BHS. The phrase 'under every green tree' may be a gloss from v. 6 (cf. BHS, Rudolph) or a Deuteronomistic element cf. 2.20 (Thiel 1973, 86). MT *šᵉma'tem*, 'you obeyed'; GV 2 sing.

The original poem has a preface directing the speaker to address the north with a message of Yahweh's forgiveness on condition that its guilt for apostasy is acknowledged. This editorial instruction is probably a late identification of the 'faithless Israel' with the northern kingdom rather than Judah and may come from the same circle which produced the exegetical piece in vv. 6–11. Although many scholars refer the poem to Israel and not Judah because they believe Jeremiah was active in preaching to the north during the 620s (e.g. Bright, Hertzberg 1952), this view is dependent upon a very early date for Jeremiah's ministry and the belief that Israel still existed as a distinctive entity. A more likely explanation of the poetic and prosaic uses of *šūb* material in 3.12 – 4.2 is to attribute them to circles which preached turning-repentance after the catastrophe and which had links with Deuteronomistic thinking on the subject of Israel's return (see below on 30–31). The units are loosely grouped together here around the *šūb* motif and are too general to afford any specific dating or location information. The Jerusalem community as addressee of the discourse in 2.5–37 and the enemy from the north cycle in 4.5 – 6.26 is the most obvious referent of this material.

A word-play on *šūb* (*šūbāh m*ᵉ*šubāh*) introduces the poem in 12b, but it is not clear whether *šūb* here refers to repentance or return from exile. The pious sentiments of the poem suggest that repentance (i.e. turning to Yahweh) is the appropriate understanding of *šūb* here (though in v. 14 the ambiguity may allow both ideas to be intended). If apostate Judah will only turn back to Yahweh and acknowledge its guilt, all will be well. Yahweh is merciful (*ḥāsīd* is indicative of loyalty and devotion rather than mercy) and will not be angry for ever (this point answers the question in v. 5a). We are in a different world here from that so repeatedly presented in 2.5–37. Hope and divine devotion are here, but entirely absent in the discourse.

Having established that in the matter of a divorce the divorcing party cannot concede to the return of the erring spouse and having created numerous images of a state of the community beyond help, the appended material on turning is quite incompatible with what precedes it. Now it is possible to theologize away this incompatibility by observing 'that what is impossible from a human, legal point of view is yet possible with God' (Martin 1969, 92), but that is to fail to grasp the absoluteness of the divine rejection of Judah spelled out so categorically in 2.5–37. That absoluteness may owe something to the actual destruction of Jerusalem, but its centrality to the Jeremiah tradition must be the key to understanding that tradition. If there are strands which appear to modify the word of absolute judgment, then they must be treated as discrete streams flowing into the tradition and coexisting with it rather than changing it. In the light of the fall of Jerusalem these other strands came into existence and received their importance as a way back to Yahweh for those who survived the disaster and for future generations. The theme of 'return' is an important one in the late edition of the Deuteronomistic history work and presupposes the exile (see Wolff 1975) – only after the disaster has happened can the work of repentance and restoration begin (cf. Deut. 29.29–30.14) – so the occurrence of a set of 'return' passages in 3.12 – 4.2 indicates that the disaster (divorce in the metaphor of 3.1) has already occurred. This response to the disaster over the next century has been edited into the book as the preaching of Jeremiah and grounds the future hope in his oracular utterances (note the frequency of *n*e*'um yhwh*, 'says Yahweh', in vv. 12–13).

3.14–18

14 ' "Return, O faithless children,
says the LORD;
for I am your master;
I will take you, one from a city and two from a family,
and I will bring you to Zion.
15 And I will give you shepherds after my own heart, who will feed you
with knowledge and understanding. 16 And when you have multiplied and
increased in the land, in those days, says the LORD, they shall no more say,
'The ark of the covenant of the LORD.' It shall not come to mind, or be
remembered, or missed; it shall not be made again. 17 At that time Jerusalem
shall be called the throne of the LORD, and all the nations shall gather to it,
to the presence of the LORD in Jerusalem, and they shall no more stubbornly
follow their own evil heart. 18 In those days the house of Judah shall join
the house of Israel, and together they shall come from the land of the north
to the land that I gave your fathers for a heritage." '

---

[14] RSV treats this verse as poetry and 15–18 as prose; NEB, Bright, Rudolph make 14–18 prose; JPSB takes 3.6–20 as all prose; BHS prints the Hebrew of 14–18 as prose, resuming the poetry at 19; Thompson takes 14–15 as poetry and 16–18 as prose, but works with 12–18 as the unit. **[15]** MT *dē'āh*, 'knowledge': G *poimainontes* = *rā'ōh*, 'will certainly feed'. **[16]**

BHS, Rudolph posit a missing *'ē*, 'where is?', before 'the ark . . .' **[17]** MT *kol-haggōyīm*, 'all nations', but BHS *mikkol-haggōyīm*, 'from all nations': here Rudolph, 29, follows Volz, 46, in limiting the return to only some of the nations. RSV 'presence' translates MT *šēm*, 'name', but loses the Deuteronomistic motif of name theology; cf. NEB. G lacks 'to the name of Yahweh to Jerusalem'. **[18]** MT 'your fathers'; Vrs 'their fathers'.

Cazelles 1968; Haran 1963; Mettinger 1982, 62–6; Soggin 1981

If *šūb* in 12–13 invites the community to repent of its idolatrous ways, its occurrence in 14 introduces a prose statement about the return of exiles to Zion. Yet the repentance nuance of *šūb* is retained in the word-play 'return . . . faithless' (*šūbū . . . šōbābīm*, a variant word-play to that of 12b). The relationship between Yahweh and Israel is that between children and master (cf. 31.32, where the phrase *'ānōkī ba'altī*, 'I am husband . . .', also occurs), though husband-wife relation is also conveyed by the term *ba'al* (cf. vv. 19–20). The bringing to Zion theme occurs in the oracles of consolation in 30–31 (cf. 31.6, 12; Hos. 3.5) and so this prose insertion should be attributed to that strand of the tradition. Why a fragment of it should appear here is not known, but it may be because an exegete wished to modify the harshness of the discourse denouncing the nation. It also extends the summons to turn in 12b to those in exile, and promises them a return to Zion where they will enjoy better leadership than used to be the case (cf. 23.4). The limited return ('one from a city and two from a district') is unusual (cf. the few who will return from Egypt in 44.14, 28), but may well reflect a late and realistic assessment of the few who did return to Jerusalem. However it cannot be ruled out that it may be a more localized appeal to people to leave their cities to go up to Jerusalem to help repopulate the once great city.

To what kind of Zion will the return take place? It will be a city run by good leaders, who will look after their citizens properly and feed them true insight. In other words, it will be very different from the corrupt leadership of the old city (cf. 2.8). The impression conveyed by this prosaic inset is that of a modest exegete envisaging specific and desirable changes in the future organization of Zion. The return to Jerusalem will be necessary to build up its population (cf. 30.19), and once that has happened certain old losses will no longer be felt. The example given is that of the ark, described here in Deuteronomistic terms (on the post-Deuteronomistic nature of this section see Thiel 1973, 91–3), which had disappeared at some stage in the past. The question of the fate of the ark may be the background to this piece. A very practical question – 'whatever happened to the ark?' or 'will the ark be made again?' – gives rise to this statement. Assuming the ark had ever had a role to play in the temple worship, it appears to have disappeared and was never rebuilt. The most likely period for its disappearance would have been the fall of Jerusalem, but the Bible is silent on the matter (why would it not have been taken by Nebuchadrezzar to Babylon along with all the other valuable vessels and returned in due course? cf. 27.16–22; 28.3 and see below on 27–28). According to II Chron. 35.3 the ark was still in operation in the time of Josiah but there are some difficulties with the interpretation of this verse (cf. Williamson 1982, 405). It has been argued that the ark was destroyed in Manasseh's time (Haran 1963), in fact that king Manasseh had substituted an image of Asherah for ark and cherubim in the temple (Haran 1978, 281f.). Whatever may have been the case, the silence of the Bible on the subject may well indicate how unimportant the ark was as a cult object in the temple cult. The Deuteronomistic treatment of the ark (Deut. 10.1–3) may certainly be viewed as a demotion of a once sacred object. The observation in v. 16 about its loss not being missed in the future is in keeping with such a demythologized bit of ancient wood. It may also (this we do not know) be a fragment of a contemporary discussion about the prospects of a rebuilt temple and what furniture should be in it. The ruling that the ark would not need to be replaced is included here as one of the features of the future ('in those days'). The fate of the ark question is resolved: it will not even be missed! Deuteronomistic demythologization proved to be less radical than the Babylonian invasion.

Two other fragments about the future are included in this prose exposition of what the turning would entail for Zion. The thought in v. 17 follows on logically from v. 16 because the ark had at one time been thought of as Yahweh's throne, where he sat flanked by the cherubim. No longer will people talk about the ark (cf. 16.14; 23.7 for the motif *lōʾ-yōʾmᵉrū ʿōd* cf. Weinfeld 1976) because the city will be the throne (in 17.12 the temple is the throne). To it will gather the nations, to Yahweh's name in Jerusalem. The reference to the name betrays Deuteronomistic influence (cf. Mettinger 1982), though here it may be a post-Deuteronomistic usage (cf. Isa. 18.7; 60.9). The pilgrimage of the nations to Jerusalem belongs to a futuristic strand (cf. 'at that time') of belief that the nations would visit Jerusalem to learn of and serve Yahweh (cf. Isa. 2.2–4 = Micah 4.1–3; Zech. 14.16–19). The moral change in the nations is more absolute than that suggested by 12.16f., but both statements must be regarded as post-exilic. In the future all the old problems – exile, loss of cult objects, hostility from the nations – will be resolved. These expectations appear to be linked here to the turning of the nation back to Yahweh, though the link may be purely editorial. The final fragment ('in those days', the same as v. 16) concerns the joining of the houses of Judah and Israel and their joint return to Palestine. Clearly exilic or later, this hope comes from a circle (cf. 31.2–6, 16–20; Ezek. 37.15–22) which refused to recognize that Judah and Israel were two discrete nations and which looked forward to a time when they would be reunited (cf. Zech. 11.7–14 for a rather different expectation). Both nations are represented as having been exiled to 'the land of the north' (Israel to Assyria, Judah to Babylonia). The joint venture of their return is one more consequence of the turning to Yahweh of vv. 12–13. With this prose collation of future hopes about Jerusalem and the reunification of Judah and Israel, with the other nations in attendance, the direness of the discourse is temporarily arrested and the Book of Consolation (30–31) anticipated.

3.19–20

19 ' "I thought
how I would set you among my sons,
and give you a pleasant land,
a heritage most beauteous of all nations.
And I thought you would call me,
My Father,
and would not turn from following me.
20 Surely, as a faithless wife leaves her husband,
so have you been faithless to me,
O house of Israel,
says the LORD." '

---

[19] MT *wᵉʾānōkī ʾāmartī ʾēk*, 'and I, I thought how . . .', but G *kai ego eipa Genoito, kurie hoti*, 'and I said, so be it, lord, for . . .' suggests MT *ʾēk* is an abbreviation for *ʾāmēn yhwh kī*, cf. BHS. For MT 'sons' G^B has 'nations'.

RSV 'my' is interpretative, cf. NEB 'how gladly would I treat you as a son'; 'among sons' will do as a fair translation of the Hebrew. MT *ṣᵉbī ṣib'ōt*, 'most beauteous': G *theou pantokratoros*, 'god almighty'. K–Q on *tqr'w* and *tswbw*: 2 pl (K), fem. sg (Q). **[20]** G 'but as a wife acts treacherously against her husband'; BHS reads *'ak kibgōd* for MT *'ākēn bogdāh*, following G. MT *bᵉgadtem*, 'you have acted treacherously', but G *ēthetēsen* = *bāgad* and suggests 'the house of Israel has acted treacherously against me'.

This brief oracular statement appears at first sight to be a continuation of 3.1–5 (in fact Bright treats 3.1–5, 19–24; 4.1–4 as a continuous unit). Although most commentators take it with 1–5 it is most unlikely that an editor would have inserted vv. 6–18 into the middle of a long poem. The usual technique is to append additions, and as this chapter is made up of a series of *šūb* pieces (3.1, 7, 10, 12, 14, 19, 22; also 4.1) 19–20 should be viewed as one more independent piece. There are gender problems in v. 19: the 'you' addressed, i.e. Israel, is feminine, but the object of 'set' is masculine (cf. BHS for proposed corrections). Daughter Israel is to be set among Yahweh's sons. Although daughter inheritance was not a common feature of Israelite social practice (for exceptions cf. Num. 27.1–8; Job 42.15), it is unnecessary to insist that poetic metaphors must be precise and socially accurate. The unvocalized Hebrew text (K) avoids the problem altogether, restores gender equilibrium and may be the best way to understand the text's meaning. The image is that of the deity setting one of his children among all his children but giving it the best of all lands. There is a hint of universalism here with all the nations being Yahweh's sons (cf. Deut. 32.8–9), but with Israel enjoying something like favourite status. As a response to such special treatment Israel was expected (*'ōmar* in 19b could be translated as a command cf. NEB 'I said, You shall call me Father'; Thompson, 207) to treat Yahweh as father and not turn (*tāšūb* Q) from following him loyally. The negative use of *šūb* in this unit defines what should have been Israel's way of life.

The image changes in v. 20 from familial metaphors to marital ones. It is a general comparison between a woman who leaves (*bgd*, 'acts treacherously') her lover (*mērē'āh*) and Israel's behaviour towards Yahweh. It is not the indiscriminate pursuit of lovers condemned in v. 1 but the betrayal constituted by a woman who departs from her friend. Faithless Israel has turned from the privileged position planned for her by Yahweh. A further difference between 19–20 and 1–5, within the general similarity which explains their proximity to one another, is the pleasant land of v. 19 in comparison to the polluted land of vv. 1–2. Although not developed, the unit expresses the point that the family has broken up, the lovers parted.

The different units in the chapter expound the motifs of turning, treachery, faithlessness and return. These are all metaphors for the fractured relationship between Yahweh and Israel and, although sexual terms are frequently used, they seldom have a sexual connotation. Yet their strength of feeling is gained by the transference of terms from human relationships. Yahweh is presented as showing all the jealous rage and wounded pride of a husband-lover, especially in response to the breach of proprietary rights. This is in keeping with the Semitic view of a man exercising such rights over his children or his wife. As a husband or lover Yahweh displays the frenetic outrage of a man betrayed by his woman. It could hardly be otherwise, for theology reflects society. Yet the language *is* metaphorical, and alternative metaphors, which reflect masculine foibles (e.g. 5.8), are used. Ambivalence about women (Ochshorn 1981) may be behind some of these metaphors, but a balance is maintained by the biblical writers which much feminist theology is blind to for ideological reasons.

3.21–25

21 A voice on the bare heights is heard,
the weeping and pleading of Israel's sons,
because they have perverted their way,
they have forgotten the LORD their God.
22 'Return, O faithless sons,
I will heal your faithlessness.'
'Behold, we come to thee;
for thou art the LORD our God.
23 Truly the hills are a delusion,
the orgies on the mountains.
Truly in the LORD our God
is the salvation of Israel.
24 But from our youth the shameful thing has devoured all for which our
fathers laboured, their flocks and their herds, their sons and their daughters.
25 Let us lie down in our shame, and let our dishonour cover us; for we have

sinned against the LORD our God, we and our fathers, from our youth even to this day; and we have not obeyed the voice of the LORD our God.'

---

[21] For MT 'on the bare heights' G has 'from the lips'; the same variation is found in 7.29. **[22]** MT 'we come to thee'; G 'we will be thy servants'. **[25]** MT *miggᵉbāʿōt hāmōn*, regarded as incomprehensible by commentators; G 'the hills *and* the strength of the mountains were a lying refuge', cf. BHS, Duhm, Rudolph. Driver 1937–38, 99, is happy with MT and translates 'surely the hilly places are treacherous (i.e. no safe refuge), the mountains a noise (i.e. all noise and no help).' *hāmōn*, 'crowd', 'hubbub' (Bright), a dismissal of alien worship in terms of the noise it makes; 'hills', metonymy for the nature cults. **[24]** MT *wᵉhabbōšet 'ākᵉlāh*, 'the shame has devoured', probably a substitution for 'Baal has devoured'. RSV prints vv. 24–25 as prose, NEB as poetry (though 25a is an overloaded line in NEB). Rudolph; Holladay 1976a, 48; Jobling 1978 all treat 24–25 as poetry. Provided that the line 'their flocks and their herds, their sons and their daughters' (inserted from 5.17) is removed, a case can be made for a poetic core here. **[25]** In his translation Rudolph omits 25b, treating it as a liturgical expansion which destroys the strophic structure of the verse. Quite so!

The tone of 21–25 is very different from the denunciations of the nation in the discourse. There it is presented as wicked and incapable of realizing its true state (2.8, 23, 25, 30, 31, 35; 3.3); here it is fully aware of its perverted way and, weeping and entreating, seeks Yahweh's healing. All the metaphors used to describe a hopeless condition are vitiated by this poem. It has a reversal effect on what has preceded it as great as the Book of Consolation in 30–31 has in its context. In the light of the next cycle (4.5 – 6.26) it is equally disjunctive here. To account for it requires positing some editing procedure which has broken the pattern in the discourse and enemy from the north cycle by using fragments of a liturgy of repentance from a different period to lessen the horrors of the past. The poem provides a response to the appeal in v. 13 and utilizes the *šūb* motif (v. 22 *šūbū bānīm šōbābīm . . . mᵉsūbōtēkem*). It has affinities with the post-exilic liturgies of confession and repentance (cf. Ezra 9.5–15; Neh. 9.6–37; Dan. 9.3–19), but is clearly not nearly as developed or prolix as they are. It may therefore represent an early form of exilic response to the past (cf. Hos. 14), but because concrete information on its setting is entirely lacking, the possibility that it has been created for its present location cannot be ruled out.

The poem depicts a nation deeply conscious of the wrong it has done, hence the divine invitation to turn and the promise of healing for such waywardness. In Hos. 14 the central point is the healing motif (so Wolff 1974, 233); here it is one element, and the acknowledgment of past mistakes the central feature. The nation responds to the divine call by acknowledging Yahweh as its god and confessing the falseness of its previous commitment to other gods – the high hills and green trees are false (*šeqer*) – Yahweh is Israel's salvation. It had taken a long time to learn this and it was a hard lesson: cities had been wasted, families destroyed and much suffering endured. The prose coda in vv. 24–25 (whatever its original poetic form might have been) spells out the wasted years. From its youth (cf. 2.2) onwards the nation's substance has been devoured by the baals and great shame brought upon it. From the exodus 'even to this day' shame and dishonour have befallen the nation because it did not obey Yahweh (cf. v. 13). We are back in the world of 2.5–9 but with one fundamental difference: now Israel is aware of the falseness of her whole history and is seeking Yahweh's healing. Destruction and exile have worked and things are changing – thus we hear echoes of a later generation's response to past catastrophe and the word of hope is let loose in the midst of dismal cycles of impending disaster.

4.1–2

41 'If you return, O Israel,
says the LORD,
to me you should return.
If you remove your abominations from my presence,
and do not waver,
2 and if you swear, "As the LORD lives,"
in truth, in justice, and in uprightness,
then nations shall bless themselves in him,
and in him shall they glory.'

---

[1] MT *wᵉlōʾ*; Vrs *lōʾ* = 'do not waver': a more forceful command. *tānūd*, 'wander', 'waver'; cf. Gen. 4.14 for the sense of wandering from Yahweh's presence; Bright 'nor stray from my presence'. **[2]** MT *bō . . . ūbō*, 'in him . . . and in him', cf. BHS. NEB, JPSB, Rudolph favour *bᵉkā . . . ūbᵉkā*, 'in you and in you'. 2b is a citation from the late verses Gen. 22.18 or Gen. 26.4 (so Duhm, 45); for similar notions cf. Gen. 12.3; 18.18.

Yet another short poem on *šūb* setting out the object of the turning, namely to Yahweh, and the way in which it must be done. The 'abominations' (*šiqqūṣīm*) are idols or the alembic of the false cults (cf. II Kings 23.13, 24; Ezek. 20.7). The turning to Yahweh necessarily involves the putting away of false gods (cf. Gen. 35.1–4; Josh. 24.14–15), especially from the divine presence, i.e. sanctuary (cf. Ex. 20.3; Deut. 5.7). Here the programme of the Yahweh-alone party is the standard of turning, for it believed that to worship Yahweh properly meant a radical restructuring of worship. Various manifestations of Yahweh, e.g. multiple altars, fertility associations, Canaanite rituals, had to be banned as they compromised what the Yahwists stood for and also diversified power far too freely in the Jerusalem temple. The prohibition against wandering may refer to going after other gods (Thompson), though it could mean 'do not waver in your resolve to put away your abominations'. For the Yahweh-alone group, such practices meant divided loyalties and therefore they had to be rejected. Turning in this sense has a very practical connotation. No more swearing by other gods but by Yahweh 'in truth, in justice and in righteousness' (for a similar triple cf. 9.24 with *ḥesed* instead of *'emet*). If turning could be false (3.10, though not specified), this is true turning and has a distinctively cultic definition to it. Now if the nation can sort out its cultic matters, discover exclusive devotion to Yahweh, then the nations round about will benefit greatly from such a turning. The gathering of the nations to Jerusalem has already been mooted in 3.17, but here the well-being of the nations is made dependent upon Israel's turning. This motif of the nations blessing themselves is connected with the royal ideology of the temple (cf. Ps. 72.17) and after the exile came to be associated with the patriarchs (Gen. 12.3; 18.18; 22.18; 26.4; cf. Van Seters 1972). So we must assume that this treatment of *šūb* in vv. 1–2 belongs to a late strand in the tradition. The fate of the nations is not usually tied into the cultic reformation of Israel, so this poem represents a variation on a theme. Israel's turning means the transformation of the nations.

4.3–4

3 For thus says the LORD to the men of Judah and to the inhabitants of Jerusalem:
'Break up your fallow ground,
and sow not among thorns.
4 Circumcise yourselves to the LORD,
remove the foreskin of your hearts,
O men of Judah and inhabitants of Jerusalem;
lest my wrath go forth like fire,
and burn with none to quench it,
because of the evil of your doings.'

---

[3] MT 'to the men of Judah and Jerusalem', so NEB; RSV influenced by the phrase 'men of Judah and inhabitants of Jerusalem' in 4a and by G. MT *nīrū lākem nīr*, 'break up your fallow ground' = Hos. 10.12c. **[4]** MT *layhwh*, 'to Yahweh'; G *tō theō humōn*, 'to your god'; BHS suggests *lī* 'to me', which makes sense in a divine speech. MT *'orlōt*, 'foreskins', but many mss, GS *'orlat*, 'foreskin' (G *sklērokardian*, 'hardness of heart'). BHS suggests omitting 'men of Judah and inhabitants of Jerusalem' (it spoils the rhythm, according to Rudolph). **[4b]** = 21.12c.

The discourse, with its addenda of *šūb* pieces, is concluded with a final instruction to the people of Judah-Jerusalem (cf. 2.2). Its sentiments are similar to 4.1–2 but the images used are quite different and there is no use of *šūb*. The influence of Hosea (never far away from 3.12–25 or 30–31) is clear in 3b where Hos. 10.12c is cited. Addressed to the people of Judah and Jerusalem (closing the cycle at virtually the same point as it began in the editorial 2.2), it summons the people to change their ways with a radical new start. This new beginning sets aside the past and opens up the future. The possibility of such a changed course of direction suggests that the catastrophe is now behind the community and that it is time for setting a new course. It is therefore an appropriate conclusion to the liturgy of turning in 3.21 – 4.2. The turning idea remains, but different motifs express it (ploughing and circumcision). The ground to be broken up is the untilled land (*nīr*). Whether that refers to land unploughed for a long time or virgin soil cannot be established from the two occurrences of the word here and in Hos. 10.12 (*nīr* also occurs in Prov. 13.23, where it may mean 'marginal land, newly broken in for growing crops', McKane 1970, 462). The ploughing metaphors are used more extensively in Hos. 10.11–13, whereas in 4.3 they refer to moral activity. 'Sow not among thorns' may refer to the ploughing enterprise (poetic parallelism), though Thompson offers an explanation deriving from ancient techniques of ploughing which concludes 'Judah's own field was so infested with the thorn seeds of past evil deeds that her only hope was to reclaim new ground' (Thompson, 215).

The same advice is now repeated, but using a different image. Circumcision, a common practice in the ancient world, is used as a metaphor and is a good example of masculine metaphors being used to describe the community. The phrase 'foreskins of your mind' (v. 4) refers to the hardness (cf. G) or badness of the community, and the act of circumcising that mind means a change of ways. If the 'whore' metaphor (inherited from the Hosea tradition) is used frequently of the community under the figure of a woman, then the circumcision metaphor (derived from the Deuteronomistic tradition, cf. Deut. 10.16; Thiel 1973, 94) depicts that community as a man. Thus there is a balance between feminine and masculine metaphors of abuse of the community. Judah-Jerusalem is an uncircumcised man – an abomination to Yahweh (hence the command 'circumcise yourselves *to Yahweh*'). The mind of the people has a foreskin (cf. 9.26). These metaphors are definitely masculine, but they hardly reveal a misanthropic bias, just as the 'whore' metaphors do not betray misogynistic values. Both sets of metaphors are also too stereotypical to permit such presuppositional analysis. Hence in this matter feminist theology has allowed ideology to produce naive exegesis.

Circumcising the mind is a metaphoric extension of an ethnic practice, but whereas the social practice is one of tribal identification this symbolic use of the term is far from clear. In biblical metaphors different parts of the body are said to possess foreskins: lips (Ex. 6.12); ears (Jer. 6.10); minds (Lev. 26.41; Deut. 10.16; Jer. 4.4; 9.26; Ezek. 44.7, 9). Difficulty with hearing and with speaking are the meanings of two of these parts, so difficulty of understanding may be the meaning of 'foreskins of the mind'. Unreceptivity to divine instruction or warning may be the force of the metaphor here (cf. 'The Israelite's heart is not to be unreceptive of godlike affections', the comment of Driver 1896, 125 on Deut. 10.16). The command has no content built into it, so must derive its meaning from the issuing authority. That meaning is implicit in the ideological programme of the party behind the statement. That the piece comes from the Deuteronomistic editing of the tradition appears to be the case, because of the form of address 'men of Judah and inhabitants of Jerusalem' (cf. 11.2, 9; 17.25; 18.11; 32.32; 35.13; II Kings 23.2; II Chron. 34.30), and the cliché 'the evil of (your) doings' (cf. 21.12; 23.2, 22; 25.5; 26.3; 44.22; Thiel 1973, 95). 4.4b = 21.12c. The figure 'circumcise your mind' is also Deuteronomistic (cf. Deut. 10.16; 30.6). If *nīr* refers to virgin soil (so Andersen and Freedman 1980, 568) rather than fallow ground (the commentaries seem to confuse these two terms), then the circumcision image is a good parallel to tilling the soil for the first time. Both actions refer to something happening for the *first* time. The call is not to renewal, but to begin finally to serve Yahweh lest his fire destroy the community (the unquenchable fire image appears also in 7.20; 17.27). The hint of possibility in 4b should not be taken to mean that the discourse analysis allowed room for repentance, it did not. The destruction of Jerusalem is in the past here and the call to the nation to begin to be receptive to Yahweh is intended to prevent future outbursts of divine anger. The Deuteronomistic enterprise of persuading the nation to turn is a consequence of that destruction and runs through the tradition as a counterpoint to the people's incorrigibility which brought about the catastrophe in the first place. Those who survived the disaster (or their descendants) might still encounter the fire of Yahweh's anger.

4.5–8

5 Declare in Judah, and proclaim in Jerusalem, and say,
'Blow the trumpet through the land;
cry aloud and say,
"Assemble, and let us go
into the fortified cities!"
6 Raise a standard toward Zion,
flee for safety, stay not,
for I bring evil from the north,
and great destruction.
7 A lion has gone up from his thicket,
a destroyer of nations has set out;
he has gone forth from his place
to make your land a waste;
your cities will be ruins
without inhabitant.

8 For this gird you with sackcloth,
lament and wail;
for the fierce anger of the LORD
has not turned back from us.'

---

[5] BHS deletes the first 'and say' as a gloss from 5b and then suggests reading *mah^{a}rū*, 'hurry', for the second 'and say'. All the verbs in vv. 5–6 are plurals, so addressed to the people rather than a herald (*pace* Thompson). Q 'blow' for K 'and blow'. Cf. Thomas 1952a on *ml'w*, 'aloud', as a military term meaning 'muster, mobilization'; hence 'proclaim mobilization'. **[6]** G *pheugete*, 'flee' (*nusū*), for MT *nēs*, 'standard'. **[7]** The last two clauses are taken as an addition from 2.15 by Duhm, Rudolph; cf. BHS. They may be additional to v. 7, but they are also a variation in the Hebrew of 2.15.

The generality of the apostasy cycle gives way to the particularity of a mercilessly invasive and destructive army bringing terror and devastation to the territory of Judah and the city of Jerusalem. Images of invasion, siege, despair and defeat abound in these poems and their background is the Babylonian threat to Palestine after 605. Dividing the cycle into individual poems and editorial comments is difficult and a scrutiny of the commentaries will reveal a degree of disagreement about where units may begin or end (esp. in chs. 4–5). Such divergency of opinion allows for differences of interpretation and underlines the principle that exegesis, like translation, concerns choices, not rules. The poems about the enemy from the north are the focus of the cycle, but other elements provide a dialectic within the collection between the poems and later voices theologizing the disaster.

The first poem announces that great destruction is coming out of the north, 'a destroyer of nations has set out', and the communities are summoned to flee into their cities. The raising of a standard towards Zion (MT v. 6) may indicate a warning signal to Jerusalem (cf. Isa. 18.3), but the G 'flee' fits the context better. Fleeing, putting on sackcloth, mourning and lamenting are the responses to this threat behind which lies the unrestrained anger of Yahweh.

4.9–10

9 'In that day, says the LORD, courage shall fail both king and princes; the priests shall be appalled and the prophets astounded.'

10 Then I said, 'Ah Lord GOD, surely thou hast utterly deceived this people and Jerusalem, saying, "It shall be well with you"; whereas the sword has reached their very life.'

[9–10] Treated as prose by RSV but poetry by BHS, Rudolph, Bright, Thompson, Volz, JPSB (in part), NEB (v. 9 but not v. 10). **[10]** Cf. 14.13; for MT, 'and I said'; G^{A} 'they said', followed by BHS, Duhm, Rudolph, etc. MT is probably influenced by *wā'ōmar* in 14.13. The corrected form makes v. 10 the utterance of the classes specified in v. 9. BHS deletes 'this people and Jerusalem' as an addition from v. 11, reading 'us' with Cornill.

Two responses to the devastating invasion follow the first 'enemy from the north' poem (9–10, 11–12). Both are introduced by time indicators ('in that day', 'at that time'), which suggests that they are late supplements (cf. 8.1; 31.1; DeVries 1975, 317f.) appended to the poem by way of response to it. The first supplement is an oracular statement about the reactions of the ruling classes to the disaster. They are so shattered by the invasion and destruction of Jerusalem that they (corrected text) confess to having been deceived completely (*haššē' hiššē'tā* cf. 29.8; 37.9; 49.16; Gen. 3.13) by the lord Yahweh. This divine deception has happened to them via the prophets (the 'they said' may refer to the prophets of v. 9), whose preaching of *šālōm* (cf. 14.13–16; 23.17) during a period of dire emergency has misled them about the true nature of the situation (destruction not salvation). In the MT it is the speaker (presumably Jeremiah is who the editor intended to be the speaker here) who recognizes that Yahweh has thoroughly deceived the community. Such deception has been achieved by the medium of the prophets.

The Jeremiah tradition has much to say against the prophets (e.g. 14.13–16; 23.9–40; 27–28; 29.21–23) but only here is it admitted that the prophets were themselves deceived rather than the deceivers. It is an admission quite alien to the tradition, but in line with the theology of I Kings 22.19–23; Ezek. 14.6–11; Deut. 13.1–3. The deity wished to bring destruction to the community and gave it prophets whose message of *šālōm* was gladly received and blinded it to the reality of the Babylonian threat. Because the prophetic mode of communication was one of inspirational revelation, whatever the prophets said would have been received as the divine truth. So when they preached 'it shall be well with you' (*šālōm yihyeh lākem*, 4.10; 23.17; contrast its use in 29.7), they lured a nation to its destruction.

The supplement reflects the view taken after the catastrophe that the prophets had played a part in the nation's misfortune (cf. Lam. 2.14), but it goes deeper and recognizes behind the activity of the prophets the sinister hand of Yahweh. Where there is or will be terrible suffering and devastation, the activity of Yahweh is recognizable (cf. Eli's response to Samuel's horrible tale of destruction in I Sam. 3.11–18: 'It is Yahweh . . .'; the creator of such mayhem is instantly identifiable to the experienced eye or ear). Yet the theology of 4.10 appears to play no part in the attack on the prophets in 23.9–40; 27–29.

4.11–12

11 At that time it will be said to this people and to Jerusalem, 'A hot wind from the bare heights in the desert toward the daughter of my people, not to winnow or cleanse, 12 a wind too full for this comes for me. Now it is I who speak in judgment upon them.'

[11–12] Many scholars and some translations treat these verses as poetry (e.g. NEB, JPSB, Volz, Bright, Rudolph, Thompson; Althann 1978; Holladay 1976b). **[11]** MT *ṣaḥ šᵉpāyīm*, 'hot bare heights'; G *pneuma planēseōs*, 'a spirit of error'. MT *bammidbār* 'in the desert'; BHS, following Cornill, suggests *bā' mimmidbār*, 'comes from the desert', though MT *b* may have the force of 'from'. MT *bat-'ammī*, 'daughter of my people', should be understood as two words in apposition: 'my daughter, my people' (cf. Bright; also *bat-bābel*, *bat-kaśdīm*, Isa. 47.1). **[12]** G lacks MT *mē'ēlleh*, 'from these' (a duplication of *mālē'*, 'full', cf. BHS). MT *lī*, 'for me', i.e. at my bidding (Rudolph; NEB). MT *mišpāṭīm*, 'judgments', or 'charges' (JPSB), is better than RSV.

Althann 1978; Holladay 1976b

The second response to the invader poem addresses the people personified as Jerusalem. Although the phrase 'this people' has a contemptuous nuance to it (cf. Isa. 6.9–10), too much cannot be made of such an editorial use of it, because the saying introduced by it refers to the community as 'my people' (cf. 6.14; 8.11; 'my daughter, my people', 6.26; 8.19, 21, 22; 9.1; 14.17; Lam. 2.11; 3.48; 4.3, 6, 10). The figure which describes what has happened to the people is that of the sirocco wind, a hot, sand-laden wind, sweeping across the sand dunes and through the city. This is not the kind of wind which can be used for winnowing or cleansing. It is too fierce, too hot, too oppressive to contribute positively to the life of the people. Completely destructive, it offers no hope to cultivated territory. Contrary to much modern general interpretation of biblical prophecy which likes to balance positive and negative aspects of judgment and salvation, the metaphors used in 4.11–12 allow no such diplomatic balancing acts. Such a sirocco-like wind sweeps away the grain with the chaff; or, to translate the metaphors, the good with the bad are swept away by this invading force. Armies of invasion (of which the hot wind is a metaphor) usually do not distinguish between good and bad elements in the communities they destroy – they sweep everything aside. Hence the oracular statement in Ezek. 21.3: 'Thus says the LORD: Behold, I am against you, and will draw forth my sword out of its sheath, and will cut off from you *both righteous and wicked*' (see vv. 1–5). Yet it is not simply the invading army which carries out this destructive enterprise; it is Yahweh who destroys the community. 'I bring charges upon them' (cf. 39.5, where the same idiom is translated 'and he passed sentence on him', with reference to Nebuchadrezzar's treatment of the captured Zedekiah) means that Yahweh has executed his judgments on the people and destroyed them. That is the real meaning of the enemy coming from the north (cf. 1.14–16), and the supplement here underlines it at the beginning of the cycle.

4.13–14

13 Behold, he comes up like clouds,
his chariots like the whirlwind;
his horses are swifter than eagles –
woe to us, for we are ruined!
14 O Jerusalem, wash your heart from wickedness,
that you may be saved.
How long shall your evil thoughts lodge within you?

A brief poetic statement describes the invading army ('he comes up' refers back to v. 7) in meteorological figures: 'clouds', 'whirlwind'. The invader's chariots are drawn by horses swifter than eagles

– the speed of the onslaught is frightening and elicits the communal response 'woe to us, for we are destroyed'.

A further fragment reflects upon the meaning of the invasion (at least it does in this context). The community as Jerusalem is called upon to cleanse itself (cf. Isa. 1.16) in order to be saved. Lodging in the city are evil schemes (*maḥšebōt 'ōnēk*), though what these might be is not defined (contrast Isa. 1.21, where murderers now lodge in the city). Equally vague is the command 'wash the evil of your mind'. Such vacuous commands indicate a pious source for this verse, which wishes to condemn the community's way of life in favour of its own. The verse is a secondary element here (Duhm) and incompatible with the sentiments expressed in vv. 11–12. The call to change and be saved sees the invasion as an opportunity for the community to alter its ways. That is to make the invasion a wind which winnows or cleanses rather than a devastating force which sweeps all in front of it. It is out of keeping with the other fragments in the chapter and must represent a later pietist's response to the threat or, more likely, is of a piece with the turning material in ch. 3. It is then an appeal to the post-catastrophe community to change its ways (of the kind found in Isa. 1.10–20) and may be associated with 4.3–4. As such it indicates something of the history of the cycle as it was developed after the events of 597 and 587. It is unnecessary to claim that 'it would seem that Jeremiah never thought an appeal to repent was too late' (Thompson, 225) on the strength of v. 14, for that would be to contradict the many statements in the tradition which make the incorrigibility of the community a dominant element in the preaching of Jeremiah. The oddness of the verse in its present context is to be accounted for along the lines that in creating and preserving the collection of poems, various hands have added pieces relevant to their own situation by way of commenting on the text (cf. the turning elements in 3.12–14, 19–23 as comment on 3.1–5).

4.15–18

15 For a voice declares from Dan
 and proclaims evil from Mount Ephraim.
16 Warn the nations that he is coming;
 announce to Jerusalem,

'Besiegers come from a distant land;
  they shout against the cities of Judah.
17 Like keepers of a field are they against her round about,
  because she has rebelled against me,
    says the LORD.
18 Your ways and your doings
  have brought this upon you.
This is your doom, and it is bitter;
  it has reached your very heart.'

---

[16] MT *hazkīrū laggōyīm hinnēh*, 'report to the nations, behold'; Driver 1937–38, 100, treats *hinnēh* as *hēnnāh*, 'these things' (cf. JPSB); cf. 'Report these things to this nation' (Thompson); 'warn Benjamin' (Rudolph) or 'inform Judah' (Volz), cf. BHS. Bright leaves blank but approves of the reading *laggōy hazzēh* (enclitic *mem*), 'report it to this nation'. For MT *nōṣrīm*, 'besiegers', Volz *ṣārīm*, 'foes', followed by Rudolph (cf. BHS), Bright, etc. As *nṣr* means 'watch' rather than 'besiege', Driver revocalizes it to *nāṣōrīm*, 'banded together' (cf. G *sustrophai* 'bands'), from *ṣrr*. **[18]** MT *darkēk*, 'your way', but some mss, Vrs read plural. Rudolph treats MT *'āśō* as an infinitive absolute in his commentary, but in BHS offers alternative readings (*'āśōh*, *'āśū*). MT *kī mār kī*, 'for it is bitter for . . .'; BHS suggests *meryēk*, 'your rebellion' (cf. 17b), though again Rudolph's commentary is different ('it is so bitter'); cf. NEB 'your rebellion'.

The next poem depicts the response to the invaders of the local inhabitants. Warnings are sent through the land to Jerusalem and the cities of Judah from the north that the adversaries from a distant land are on their way. From Dan and the hill country of Ephraim the warnings come as the invaders travel southwards (for a more detailed itinerary of such an invasion see Isa. 10.27a–32, though eschatological overtones make that a much less historical description than is often thought to be the case; cf. Kaiser 1983, 245–51). Like those who watch a field (i.e. guard its produce from thieves), so the foes gather round Jerusalem (v. 17 *'āleyhā*, 'against her', but the 'her' is not identified so it could refer to the cities of Judah, so Rudolph, Thompson). The cause of this invasion and siege is made clear in 17b 'because she has rebelled against me' (with the stress on 'me' in that sentence). Jerusalem-Judah has revolted against Yahweh, so he has sent foreign armies against her to destroy her. This oracular explanation is reinforced by the following verse, which blames the catastrophe on the nation's own behaviour. Its way of life and its activities (not specified) have brought these things (MT *ʾēlleh*) upon it and they constitute its disaster (*rāʿātēk*). A disaster which has penetrated to its very core (cf. v. 10, where the sword penetrates to the very life of the people). The disaster is indeed bitter, but it is all the community's own fault – its way of life has resulted in this invasion.

4.19–22

19 My anguish, my anguish! I writhe in pain!
  Oh, the walls of my heart!
My heart is beating wildly;
  I cannot keep silent;
for I hear the sound of the trumpet,
  the alarm of war.
20 Disaster follows hard on disaster,
  the whole land is laid waste.
Suddenly my tents are destroyed,
  my curtains in a moment.
21 How long must I see the standard,
  and hear the sound of the trumpet?
22 'For my people are foolish,
  they know me not;
they are stupid children,
  they have no understanding.
They are skilled in doing evil,
  but how to do good they know not.'

---

[19] MT *mēʿay*, 'bowels', 'intestines': the seat of the emotions in Hebrew thought, cf. 31.20. MT *ʾḥwlh* K; Q *ʾōḥīlāh*, 'I writhe', cf. BHS. BHS deletes *libbī*, 'my heart', and transposes *napšī* from the next line to here (cf. G). MT *šāmaʿat* (Q) *napšī*, 'I hear', but K *šmʿty* is probably the old feminine 2nd sing. ending (cf. 4.30; 2.20); JPSB margin 'you, O my being, hear'. **[20]** MT *regaʿ*, 'in a moment', but Driver 1937–38, 100, insists on finding a verbal form here (cf. G *diespasthēsan*, 'have been torn asunder'): *rugg*^{e}*ʿū*, 'are violently agitated'. **[21]** MT *nēs*, 'standard', but G *pheugontas*, 'fugitives' (*nās*, cf. BHS). **[22]** MT *bānīm* . . . *n*^{e}*bōnīm*, 'children . . . understanding' a hint of wordplay? (so Rudolph). G *hoi hēgoumenoi*, 'the princes of . . .' (= *ʾēlē*) for MT *ʾ*^{e}*wīl*, 'foolish'.

The next poem presents an emotion-charged response to the

invasion. The speaker cries out in pain and anguish (cf. II Kings 4.19, 'my head, my head') in reaction to the alarms of war. But who is the speaker here? The land (Judah) or the city (Jerusalem) would be the most fitting subject of the lament in vv. 19–21 (cf. 30.12–15), and the poem should be understood as an expression of the community's disturbance and disintegration under the onslaught of the enemy from the north. However, some commentators prefer to see the speaker as Jeremiah (e.g. Rudolph, Bright, Thompson, Berridge 1970, 169f.; cf. Polk 1984, 49–53) and the poem as one of his 'confessions' (for this category see on 11.18–20). The 'I' of the poem represents Jeremiah's identification with his people, so that he can call their homesteads 'my tents . . . my curtains'. A similar poem in 10.19–20 uses this type of language, and of that Reventlow writes 'as the mediator he represents the people in the lament before God, he is in this virtually the opponent of God for the people; his I and the I of the people to a certain extent merge into one another' (1963, 200). This analysis is a much disputed one and dependent upon a particular interpretation of the role of Jeremiah in the community. If the hypothesis behind Reventlow's statement is not accepted, then the case for making Jeremiah the speaker here is much weakened. Nothing in the text indicates who the speaker might be, and the redactional framework of 1.1 ('the words of Jeremiah') can hardly be extended to the point where it must necessarily provide reliable information about the original meaning of the individual poems in the collection.

To this poem of communal anguish in a time of war has been added in v. 22, a comment on the people. It is similar to 10.21, but identifies the whole people as stupid (only the leadership is so castigated in 10.21; G makes both verses condemn the rulers). Whether this is an explantion for the disaster or for their reactions is not clear. But its fairly stereotypical dismissal of the community as foolish children suggests that it is one more gloss explaining why the nation suffered such destruction (cf. 5.21). The addition certainly treats the subject of vv. 19–21 as the people, but may be more of an addition to the poem than an understanding of it. It is in keeping with the general editing of the cycle: poems about the invader have later reflections, comments and theological points added to them to form a commentary (cf. treatment of *šūb* in 3.1 – 4.2). This commentary provides the lessons from the past for the community addressed by the editors.

4.23–26

23 I looked on the earth, and lo, it was waste and void;
and to the heavens, and they had no light.
24 I looked on the mountains, and lo, they were quaking,
and all the hills moved to and fro.
25 I looked, and lo, there was no man,
and all the birds of the air had fled.
26 I looked, and lo, the fruitful land was a desert,
and all its cities were laid in ruins
before the LORD, before his fierce anger.

---

[23] MT *tōhū wābōhū*, 'formless and void', cf. Gen. 1.2; G *outhen* lacks *wābōhū*. Rudolph deletes *wābōhū* (cf. BHS) and translates *tōhū* as Chaos; MT does overload the metre (Rudolph), but in view of Gen. 1.2 the Hebrew phrase might be a citation here. **[26]** Some mss read 'burned' (*yṣt*) for 'laid in ruins' (*nṣh*); cf. 2.15; 9.10, 12 (MT 9, 11); 46.19. G 'they were destroyed' after 'his fierce anger'.

Childs 1959, 193–5; Eppstein 1968; Fishbane 1971

A vivid and very distinctive poem now reflects upon the invasion of the land but is not a product of that onslaught. Though many commentators attribute the poem to Jeremiah, it is better viewed as a later apocalyptic insertion into the cycle (Eppstein). The style is very different and the destruction depicted is cosmic, so those commentators who have questioned its Jeremianic authorship are to be followed (e.g. Giesebrecht, Volz, Hyatt). The poem reflects the disaster of Jerusalem's destruction, but elements of a transhistorical, apocalyptic outlook influence it (cf. Childs 1959, 195). The great day of Yahweh motif (cf. its expanded form in Isa. 2), with its terrible shaking (*r'š*) of the world, has expanded the enemy from the north tradition so that it has become a figure of the return of chaos (Childs). From the historical experiences of the devastating invasion of Nebuchadrezzar and Jerusalem's fall and the mythology of chaos, later communities constructed their apocalyptic visions. Out of the primordial chaos Yahweh created order and the world as late Israel knew it (Gen. 1.1–3; 2.1–3), but in the conflict of nations and the forces of nature lay the return of that order to chaos. Israel's theologizing of this cosmic drama made Yahweh the creator and destroyer of order and life. 4.23–26 reflects some of the subtle shifts from prophecy to apocalyptic, but without affording any insight into how they came about (see on 50–51).

The poem's presentation of widespread chaos is very graphic. In four stanzas the speaker looks and sees various elements of nature and humankind in a state of disintegration (in spite of Zimmerli 1982, 99–104, the poem is not a prophetic vision as such). There are similarities between the elements listed in the poem and the view of creation presented in Gen. 1 (but hardly the pattern described by Fishbane). Earth, chaos, heavens, light, mountains, hills, mankind, birds, fertile land (*karmel*), desert and cities: not all these entities appear in Gen. 1 or in that order (e.g. birds, mankind). The poem could be a meditation on the creation story but supplemented by the experience of catastrophe and emanating from circles where the exegesis of texts or traditions was an important element in visionary declarations (i.e. apocalyptic or visionary groups which produced material such as Isa. 24–27; Joel; Zech. 12–14; see Plöger 1968). The cosmic upheaval of vv. 23–24 is clear and suggests that a devastating earthquake has destroyed the earth's stability. In vv. 25–26 the images are drawn from a war-torn or earthquake-shattered landscape where the most noticeable feature is the absence of humans and birds. Civilization is also absent: the cultivated or fertile land has returned to wilderness, the constructed cities in ruins. Culture and people were once here but not any longer. Yahweh's fierce anger has swept everything away.

Whatever the traditional or worked elements in the poem may be, its presence here makes a stark impact. As comment on the enemy from the north theme, it extends the horror of that invasion by embracing later ideas and incorporating them into the cycle. Whether singing birds were 'objects of special interest to Jeremiah' (so Skinner 1922, 50) cannot be established from the text, but the birds motif is used in a number of different ways in the tradition. Their absence signifies terrible destruction and suffering (9.10; 12.4); their presence as consumers of carrion indicates widespread death (7.33; 15.3; 16.4; 19.7; 34.20); and they are also used in similes in the exposition of principles (5:27; 8.7; 17.11). Their disappearance in 4.25; 9.10 conjures up Keats's words 'the sedge is withered from the lake *and no birds sing*'. Yet 4.25 goes deeper than that. It is about a catastrophe on a massive scale which undoes creation; a veritable holocaust which can only be described in broad terms but hardly understood because it is so breathtaking in its scope. Words of Elie Wiesel perhaps capture the appalling import of the poem:

> As for the birds of the sky that have fled, I understood the prophet's imagery only when I returned to Auschwitz and Birkenau in the summer of 1979. Then and only then did I remember that, during the tempest of fire and silence, there were no birds to be seen on the horizon: they had fled the skies above all the death-camps. I stood in Birkenau and remembered Jeremiah (Wiesel 1981, 126).

4.27–28

27 For thus says the LORD, 'The whole land shall be a desolation;
yet I will not make a full end.
28 For this the earth shall mourn,
and the heavens above be black;
for I have spoken, I have purposed;
I have not relented nor will I turn back.'

---

[27] MT *wᵉkālāh lōʾ ʾeʿᵉśeh* 'but I will not make a complete end', cf. 5.10, 18, raises the problem of whether a contradiction is involved. BHS suggests *lāh*, 'for her', i.e. 'I will put an end to her'; cf. 28b. Others take *l* as an emphatic 'I will surely make an end . . .' (e.g. Soggin 1975b). A similar problem arises in Amos 7.14. **[28]** MT repeats *ʿal* from v. 27 (cf. BHS). G has a different order in 28b; 'I have spoken and I will not repent; I have purposed, and I will not turn back from it.'

A divine word interrupts reflection on the dreadful scene of 23–26 and reassures the community that the destruction will not be total. Such an understanding of v. 27 suggests that it is an editorial interpolation here (cf. Duhm; JPSB puts the verse in parenthesis) from a later period which knew of a survival of the destruction. However, it is possible that the Hebrew should be understood as an emphatic statement rather than a negative one. In view of a similar assertion in 5.10 the verse is better taken as a later gloss. The cosmic extent of the destruction is graphically depicted in terms of the universe draped in black. In its present position v. 28 reflects on vv. 23–26, but may originally have been a comment on the invading enemy from the north. The cosmic funeral is inevitable and irrevocable because it is Yahweh's doing and he will not repent (both *šūb* and *niḥam* are used). The invasion is his scheme (as also is the apocalypse) and he will not deviate from it. Elsewhere the tradition has a different understanding of divine action and allows the deity to repent (*niḥam*, 18.7–10; cf. Jonah 3.9 for a combination of both *šūb* and *nḥm* with reference to the deity). There can be no turning back from the destruction of the land or the world. This addition to the cycle may need to be balanced by the other reflections which make the invasion the responsibility of the community, but the absoluteness of its theology should not be ignored completely. The process whereby the cycles of material in the tradition came into being is unknown, but clearly the cycles picked up many different strands of thought in the course of their development. They have the appearance of patchwork quilts, but during their construction they probably incorporated elements from many different discussions and only the vestiges of those debates survive in the text. Hence the difficulty of interpreting all the nuances present in that text.

4.29–31

29 At the noise of horseman and archer
   every city takes to flight;
they enter thickets; they climb among rocks;
   all the cities are forsaken,
   and no man dwells in them.
30 And you, O desolate one,
what do you mean that you dress in scarlet,
   that you deck yourself with ornaments of gold,
   that you enlarge your eyes with paint?
In vain you beautify yourself.
   Your lovers despise you;
   they seek your life.
31 For I heard a cry as of a woman in travail,
   anguish as of one bringing forth her first child,
the cry of the daughter of Zion gasping for breath,
   stretching out her hands,
'Woe is me! I am fainting before murderers.'

---

[29] G *pasa hē chōra*, 'the whole land', for MT 'every city' (possibly an anticipation of *kol-hā'īr* in 29b). G 'they have gone into the caves, and have hidden themselves . . .' for MT *bā'ū be'ābīm*, 'they enter thickets'. RSV 'all the cities' hardly translates *kol-hā'īr ʿᵃzūbāh* (cf. NEB), though a plural is implied by *bāhēn*, 'in them'. **[30]** Q-K on *w'ty*: feminine form (K) with masculine adjective *šādūd*, 'desolate' (lacking in G); better with G, NEB, 'and you, what are you doing?'. **[31]** MT *kᵉḥôlāh*, 'as one in labour': BHS vocalizes it from *ḥyl* rather than MT *ḥlh*. MT *ṣārāh*, 'anguish'; modern commentators prefer *ṣeraḥ*, 'scream' (Ehrlich 1912, 251), cf. G *tou stenagmou sou*; NEB 'sharp cry'. MT *lᵉhōrgīm*, 'murderers'; G *anērēmenois*, 'the slain'.

A further fragment about the invasion (v. 29 would make a suitable continuation of v. 21) is followed by two very divergent images of the city or nation. In response to the invasion the people in the cities flee (quite a different picture from other images of cities under siege, cf. 5.6; 6.3–6; 8.14; 10.17) and hide wherever they can (cf. Isa. 2.19–21). As a result the cities are all left abandoned. Appended to the brief statement are two metaphorical descriptions of Jerusalem (daughter Zion in v. 31). They are such different images that they must have had discrete origins. In the first the city is represented as a tart or courtesan dressing herself for her lovers. Seeking to stimulate them by her appearance, she goes to great lengths to beautify herself. But it is all to no purpose. Her lovers reject her and seek her life. The image is highly metaphorical and, although quite realistic as social comment (whores always run the risk of their clients beating them to death), cannot be related to the Babylonian invasion in any sense. Jerusalem sought no alliances with Babylon. The verse stems from the rhetoric of the apostasy cycle (cf. 2.33–37). In the second image the city is a young woman in labour giving birth to her first child and terrified by the experience. She gives birth among the corpses slain by the invaders – a terrible experience! The MT reading combines both images at this point (i.e. giving birth among murderers). If the images are taken together, the woman titivating herself for her lovers and the girl giving birth for the first time, they convey the sense of the city's shock, horror, danger and pain at the onslaught of the invading forces. Too late Jerusalem, tart and mother, realizes the mortal danger she is in and can now only capitulate in terror and anguish, screaming and fainting. They are very graphic images of fear and destruction and well reflect the kind of panic induced by the violence of invasion.

Some modern readers will take offence at the biblical use of feminine *metaphors* to denigrate or describe the collapse of the city (cf. Schmitt 1983). Such metaphors are used frequently in Jeremiah and Ezekiel as images of a community or city hell-bent on destruction or corrupted beyond redemption, but they hardly imply an undervaluing of women in the society from which they emanate. Fewer masculine figures may be used (the relative proportions are debatable) because the denunciations of men (cf. 22.10–19, 24–30; 23.9–40; 36.29–31) tend to be less metaphorical and more direct, but masculine values are as severely denounced (e.g. 5.7b–8). The ideological readings of the prophets which detect breaches of twentieth-century notions of equality (e.g. Ochshorn, Trible) are not only misguided but are often exegetically unbalanced. Thus the images in 31.2–22 resonate with feminine virtues and strengths and the poems of Second Isaiah also represent the deity as possessing and practising feminine qualities (cf. Gruber 1983). The negative and positive images need to be integrated without imposing an alien ideology on them, and their metaphorical status must be recognized as removing them from the sphere of direct comment on the valuation of real people.

5.1–6

5[1] Run to and fro through the streets of Jerusalem,
look and take note!
Search her squares to see
if you can find a man,
one who does justice
and seeks truth;
that I may pardon her.
2 Though they say, 'As the LORD lives,'
yet they swear falsely.
3 O LORD, do not thy eyes look for truth?
Thou hast smitten them,
but they felt no anguish;
thou hast consumed them,
but they refused to take correction.
They have made their faces harder than rock;
they have refused to repent.
4 Then I said, 'These are only the poor,
they have no sense;
for they do not know the way of the LORD,
the law of their God.

5 I will go to the great,
  and will speak to them;
for they know the way of the LORD,
  the law of their God.'
But they all alike had broken the yoke,
  they had burst the bonds.
6 Therefore a lion from the forest shall slay them,
  a wolf from the desert shall destroy them.
A leopard is watching against their cities,
  every one who goes out of them shall be torn in pieces;
Because their trangressions are many,
  their apostasies are great.

---

[1] G has *legei kurios* at the end of the verse (= *n*ᵉ*'um yhwh*, 'says Yahweh'). This serves to indicate that the speaker is Yahweh rather than Jeremiah or another party. BHS inserts it into the MT. **[2]** MT *lākēn*, 'therefore': RSV 'yet'; many mss, S read *'ākēn*, 'surely'; Driver 1937–38, 100f., argues for the adversative use of *lākēn*, 'but', cf. NEB. **[3]** Driver treats *ḥālū*, 'they felt anguish', as from the root *ḥālāh*, 'thought, reflected', and *killītām*, 'you consumed them', as *k*ᵉ*lītām*, 'thou holdest them in check'; BHS suggests *kull*ᵉ*hem*, 'all of them' (Rudolph), or *hiklamtām*, 'you humiliated them'. **[4]** BHS punctuates the text differently from MT: *hēm* is taken with the next clause, '*they* have no sense', and the first clause read 'I said "Only the poor" ' (Rudolph). **[6]** MT *z*ᵉ*'ēb* ᶜᵃ*rābōt*, 'a wolf of the desert': G *lukos heōs tōn oikiōn*, 'a wolf even to the house (has destroyed)'; Vrs 'evening wolf', cf. Hab. 1.8; Zeph. 3.3.

Carroll 1984

The theme of the enemy from the north is suspended until vv. 15–17 and a number of discrete units are used to present a justification of the destruction of the nation by that enemy. Such a justificatory exercise may be defined as an attempt at producing a theodicy (cf. Carroll 1984). The ways of Yahweh in the matter of the destruction of Jerusalem require vindication and the various commentaries on the foe cycle provide these. Although the original poems may have referred to the first Babylonian invasion which led to defeat in 597, the shadow of the second and more devastating defeat in 587 has shaped the whole tradition. It is now impossible to separate the two events in relation to the text.

The first unit in explaining 'why the war?' is vv. 1–6 (following

Duhm, Giesebrecht, Rudolph, Weiser rather than commentators who opt for 1–8 or 1–9). It purports to be a dialogue between Yahweh and an unnamed speaker (possibly Jeremiah), but the plural form of address in v. 1 renders this interpretation problematical. A dialogue would describe the poem from v. 2 or v. 3, but the rhetorical nature of the whole piece hardly permits a precise categorization. The vivid images of v. 1 depict a search being made through the streets of Jerusalem for one good person (defined as a practitioner of justice and a seeker of truth). The speaker is Yahweh (G; 'That *I* may pardon her' MT), but to whom does he address the command to search? It cannot be Jeremiah (Hyatt) because of the plurals; it may be the people (Thompson) or, if behind this verse there is an allusion to the divine council, members of the heavenly assembly (Carroll, 22; see on 23.22). The image of searching Jerusalem also occurs in Zeph. 1.12. This search (akin to Diogenes going through the streets of Athens looking for an honest man) is designed to reveal the presence or absence of grounds for divine forgiveness.

In vv. 2–5 the community of Jerusalem is exposed as incapable of producing *one* loyal devotee of Yahweh. This sweeping condemnation of the entire people makes 5.1–6 convey the same point as 9.2–8. The poem may not define what 'one who does justice and seeks truth' is but it provides a negative account of its meaning in portraying what the opposite is like. There is here the antithesis between *'ᵉmūnāh*, 'truth', and *šeqer*, 'falsehood' (Wisser 1983, 32). The people are ostensibly Yahwists (they swear by Yahweh), but their Yahwism is merely vocal (cf. 12.2). In spite of punitive actions taken against them by Yahweh they have not responded to him (cf. 2.30). They have refused to accept instruction, have become adamant and refuse to turn (*šūb*). This insensitivity may be due to their social status: they are the poor and have no knowledge of Yahweh's way or law (*mišpāṭ*). Perhaps the ruling classes know better; but they too are as ignorant of Yahweh's way as the poor. Together the classes have broken the yoke which linked them to Yahweh (cf. 2.20). Hence the deadly fate awaiting the community, graphically portrayed as wild animals watching cities in order to devour any who dare leave the security afforded by the towns.

The view of society in the poem is unreal and the rhetoric overwhelming in its hyperbolic dismissal of everybody. The result of the search instigated in v. 1 is a complete failure to find one righteous person in the community. Yet there must have been good people in

Jerusalem during whatever period this poem reflects. The narratives in 26, 34–39 reveal acts of human goodness (if these stories are to be read as straight historical accounts) and warn against 'accepting Jeremiah's pessimistic evaluation of his people . . . without qualification. There *were* good men in Judah!' (Bright, 172). It is certainly unnecessary to accept the rhetoric at face value (as Ellison 1961, 34 does), though Duhm's account of the young prophet moving from Anathoth to Jerusalem and being shocked by the corruption of city life after the simplicities of rural life is a touching explanation of his intemperate outburst (Duhm, 56). Nor is it necessary to follow Kimhi's exegesis which explains that there were no righteous on the streets because they were afraid to go out for fear of the wicked who were there (Freehof, 43 accepts this explanation). The image of a Jerusalem in a state of permanent 'passover night' cautiousness with the righteous cowering indoors is as graphic as the original poem's claim that the streets and squares of Jerusalem were empty of good people. There were righteous people in the Jerusalem of the period before its destruction (cf. Ezek. 9.4–6), so the claim should be treated as an exaggeration (Freedman, 34). Much of the language of the Jeremiah is hyperbolic, and it is a mistake to interpret it other than as rhetorical. However, beyond that rhetoric it may be possible to uncover functions which are as important as the meaning of the language and which point to activities behind the text.

Two such functions may be mooted here. The principle hinted at in v. 1, namely that the existence of a man of approved behaviour or attitude would permit the deity to forgive the city, suggests that the poem may have its background in exilic discussions about the role of the righteous in protecting the community. The *locus classicus* of this debate is Gen. 18.22–33, the story of Abraham's dialogue with Yahweh over the fate of Sodom. This reflective piece of theological writing works with the principle that the righteous have an apotropaic role in the community and their presence can ward off great evil. It was probably produced after the catastrophe of 587 (Westermann 1979, 348f.) and should be read as a reflection upon that disaster. The equation Sodom is Jerusalem (Isa. 1.10; 3.9; Jer. 23.14; Ezek. 16.45f.) makes that reading of the story even more likely. Why was Sodom destroyed? Because *all* the men of Sodom were wicked (Gen. 19.4). Why was Jerusalem destroyed? Because all her men were false. The fact of destruction precedes the explanation, but requires a warrant because Yahweh is believed to be righteous and therefore ought not to destroy the good (Gen. 18.25). Could Jerusalem have been saved? Theoretically 'yes', but in fact 'no' because her people were hardened sinners who 'refused to turn'. Thus 5.1–6 looks like an attempt at theodicy from a period when the subject was a matter of urgent discussion. It was not the only answer given to the problem, but it was one line of *theological* explanation (for others cf. Carroll, 26–33; see on 15.1).

Another function is served by the poem. The terms used are general ones without much specification of content: 'one who does *mišpāṭ* and seeks truth', 'you have smitten them . . . they refused to take correction', 'they do not know the way (*derek*) of Yahweh, *mišpāṭ* of *their* god', 'they have broken the yoke . . . burst the bonds'. Commentators disagree about the precise meaning of these terms. 'Religious ordinances' (cf. 10.2) may be the best way to understand them (Driver, 344; Hyatt). Here are people who are Yahwists but who do not know (i.e. practise) their religion properly. Their way of life is false (*šeqer*) and they cannot grasp the significance of recent hard times. They refuse to turn, to submit to the ordinances approved of by the speaker. Is there here a clash of ideological understandings of what constitutes religious observance? It would fit the argument of ch. 2 and especially 4.2 with its stress on proper swearing (in contrast to 5.2). It would also mean that the phrase 'one who does *mišpāṭ*' in v. 1 refers to correct religious behaviour rather than 'justice'. The disaster befell Jerusalem because her people were ignorant of the correct form and content of Yahwistic religion. The content may be filled in by reference to Deuteronomistic ideology (in line with commentators who relate the poem to the period after Josiah's reform) but need not be restricted to it. The poem then is the work of a group who believed that the cause of the disaster (the lack of divine forgiveness for Jerusalem) was the community's false sense of religion. The waiting animals are the result of many rebellions and great apostasies (*m^e^šūbōt*). Such an ideological dispute about religious practices reflects the post-catastrophe struggles for dominance in organizing the community's religious life (cf. 44.15–23).

5.7–9

7 'How can I pardon you?
Your children have forsaken me,
and have sworn by those who are no gods.
When I fed them to the full,
they committed adultery
and trooped to the houses of harlots.
8 They were well-fed lusty stallions,
each neighing for his neighbour's wife.
9 Shall I not punish them for these things?
says the LORD;
and shall I not avenge myself
on a nation such as this?'

---

[7] K *'slwḥ*, Q *'eslaḥ*, 'I forgive'. MT *yitgōdādū*, RSV 'trooped', suggests derivation from *g^edūd*, 'a troop'; G *kateluon*, 'lodged'; some mss also read *yitgōrārū*, 'stayed'; cf. NEB 'haunted', Bright 'tarried'. MT means 'they gashed themselves' (cf. 16.6; 41.5; 47.5; Deut. 14.1); used with reference to religious practices of a Canaanite nature in I Kings 18.28. A few mss read *š* for *ś* in *wā'aśbi'a*, 'when I fed them', making it 'I took (their) oath' (preferred by Weiser, 42). **[8]** MT *sūsīm m^eyuzāznīm maškīm* (K Occ has *mūzānīm*): a difficult line; G 'they became as wanton horses'. If *m^eyuzāznīm* is derived from *zūn* (cf. *māzōn*, 'food') it means 'well-fed' (hence RSV); if related to Arabic *naza*, then 'to be lustful', i.e. 'lusty' (Köhler 1934, 5); in view of *maškīm* (a variant?), it probably should be derived from *yzn* 'to have heavy testicles'. MT *maškīm* is regarded as incomprehensible by Volz, Rudolph; possibly related to post-biblical *'ešek*, 'testicle', i.e. *ma'^ašikīm*, 'testicles', cf. BHS. Bright (a Masorete in whom is no guile) has no comment to make on this difficult word (nor has Driver or Thompson). The combination of the two nouns suggests that *maškīm* is an explanatory variant indicating that *myznym* should be understood as 'testicles': the stallions are 'well hung', is the sense of the phrase. The RSV pun '*neigh*ing for his *neigh*bour's wife' is only an accident of English; it does not represent any paronomasia in the Hebrew. See range of translations of 8a in Boswell 1980, 336. **[9]** = 5.29; 9.9 (MT 8), with the addition of *bām* 'on them' in 9.9 (8). RSV reverses the order of the clauses in 9b.

To confirm the understanding offered of 5.1–6, the next element is an attack on the community for its idolatrous practices. It has some similarities to vv. 1–6 (e.g. the question of forgiveness, the false swearing of the people), and these explain why vv. 7–8 follow 1–6.

The community cannot be forgiven because of its religious practices. These have alienated the deity beyond the point of forgiveness. The images in 7b–8 are not easy to understand (as the lengthy textual notes above indicate). They are a combination of sexual and metaphorical terms which obscure the precise sense of the attack. Is the community being condemned for its religious or sexual practices? Does the brothel (*bēt zōnāh*) refer to such houses of ill-repute used by prostitutes or to Canaanite places of worship? Is the speaker combining both ideas or could he distinguish between them in the first place? (Andersen and Freedman 1980, 160 refer it to the house of a married woman.) Is this just one more example of pejorative language abusing opponents from a xenophobic viewpoint or is there a kernel of shrewd observation and criticism here? The use of such metaphors invites these questions, but answering them is a difficult interpretative task.

Part of the difficulty is caused by not knowing what is being described in the text. The ancient world of the Near East practised sacred prostitution (the holy women and men of Deut. 23.17; cf. Hos. 4.14) as well as ordinary, secular prostitution (*znh* as opposed to *qdš*; on *znh* cf. Andersen and Freedman 1980, 157–70). According to Herodotus every woman in that area once in her life had to offer her body to a stranger at the temple of Aphrodite (details and discussion in Wolff 1974, 86–8). Cultic sexuality took place under the shade of green trees on the hills. The Hosea, Jeremiah, Ezekiel and Deuteronomistic traditions all refer to these practices but without much distinction between them. The extent to which the ordinary Israelite indulged in fornication or adultery cannot now be established, but as such forms of domestic sexuality are universal they must be included in the practices condemned. Furthermore, as the making of alliances with other nations or the recognition of foreign cultural practices is also termed 'whoring after false gods', it is not easy to unravel the strands of allusion in 5.7–8. Idolatry, adultery, sacral prostitution and the pursuit of each other's wives are all mentioned. If allowance is made for rhetoric, exaggeration, prejudice and ideological abuse (as well as the stereotyped forms used), then it is next to impossible to be precise about the meaning of vv. 7–8. The logic of religious abuse allows for condemnation by association and extension: e.g. a rabid Ulster Presbyterian will condemn Catholics as cannibals because of their doctrine of the real presence in the Mass, or a doctrinaire, unreconstructed Catholic will regard all

Protestant marriages as invalid and their children as therefore illegitimate. So the speaker of these lines may be lumping together many discrete practices, including the confusion of brothels and Canaanite sanctuaries (hence *bēt zōnāh*; Andersen and Freedman 1980, 160, understand this to be 'not a brothel, but the home of a married woman'), in order to condemn religious parties by such association. Hence the further editorial condemnation of 5.9 (cf. 9.9; for a different application of the same obloquy, cf. 5.29).

The image of the community 'gashing themselves' in the sacred brothel and pursuing one another's wives like well-hung stallions vividly mixes rather different metaphors. Whatever confusions abound in the polemic, the disparagement of male activity in the community is apparent. Contrary to modern feminist rhetoric, biblical condemnation of sexual activity, whether real or metaphorical, is a balanced matter of condemning male as well as female behaviour (epitomized in Hos. 4.14). If feminine images of sexuality appear to be more numerous, that is because it is masculine behaviour which is being condemned: 'whoring after . . .' is a male activity. The figure of 'well-hung stallions' denigrates males, not females, though it would be wrong to deduce from that criticism that the speaker was 'poorly hung' himself or disliked men. It is absurd to argue from stereotypical phrases to psychological motivations or value judgments. Adequate information is not available to make such imaginative leaps, nor is it sound exegesis to suppose that metaphors of ancient polemics can be imbued with modern ideology. The social world of ancient Israel differs considerably from that of advanced industrial societies, and reading its writings from a modern ideological perspective can be very misleading. The biblical writers were very much against most forms of sexual behaviour outside marriage and used that disapproval to generate metaphors of other kinds of activities equally condemned.

5.10–11

10 'Go up through her vine-rows and destroy,
but make not a full end;
strip away her branches,
for they are not the LORD's.

11 For the house of Israel and the house of Judah
have been utterly faithless to me,
says the LORD.'

---

[10] MT *bᵉśārōtehā*, 'among its walls' (from *šûr*), or 'her (vine-)rows' (*šûrāh*), so BDB, 1004; but Rudolph makes it a hapax legomenon *šārāh*, 'rows, terraces' of a vineyard. G has a quite different understanding of the verse: 'Go up upon her battlements, and break down; but make not a full end; leave her buttresses; for they are the lord's.' MT *wᵉkālāh 'al-taʿᵃśû*, 'but do not make a full end': cf. 4.27; 5.18; BHS, Rudolph delete the negative.

A number of fragments appear here, and it is difficult to determine the extent to which they belong together (commentators group them together, but ideally they might be dealt with as five individual pieces: 10, 11, 12, 13, 14). Nor is it easy to discern who is speaking or to whom. The fragments appear to reflect other editorial strands in the tradition (e.g. cf. v. 10 with 2.21; 6.9; v. 11 with 3.6–11), but in too disjointed a manner to form a coherent statement.

The image in v. 10 is that of a group of people (Hebrew is plural) going through the vineyard and stripping the vines of their branches (a quite different activity is indicated by G). A full end of the nation is to be made (assuming the deletion of MT's *lō'*, 'not', or reading it as an asseverative). The vineyard, i.e. Judah-Israel, does not belong to Yahweh any more, so it must be destroyed (cf. the image of the degenerate vine in 2.21 and the destruction of the wine-making enterprise in Isa. 5.5–6). It would be unwise to make a distinction between the vine and its branches and so render the image one of a severe pruning of Yahweh's choice vine (Thompson, 243). The figure is that of complete destruction (*kālāh*), and the terms 'rows', 'branches', are poetic metonyms for the vine itself (the poetic balance is well judged, but should not mislead the exegete into differentiating between the vine and its branches). The image in G refers the verse to the destruction of the city (more in keeping with the siege of Jerusalem aspect of the invasion from the north), but permits a survival of its buttressing. This survival motif would explain the present MT's *lō'*, 'do *not* make a full end'. Those who survived the disasters and those who rebuilt the city (or the vineyard) knew a full end had not been made and perhaps allowed an echo of their own experience to inflect the meaning of the verse.

Verse 11 may be taken on its own or with vv. 10, 12. It simply states that the two houses of Israel and Judah (cf. 3.18 for this association) have acted treacherously against Yahweh (Rudolph deletes 'and the house of Judah'). Whether that action refers to apostasy (cf. 3.6–11) or to what follows (the speaking falsely of v. 12) is not clear. The nation's behaviour towards Yahweh has justified its complete destruction.

5.12–14

12 'They have spoken falsely of the LORD,
and have said, "He will do nothing;
no evil will come upon us,
nor shall we see sword or famine.
13 The prophets will become wind;
the word is not in them.
Thus shall it be done to them!" '
14 Therefore thus says the LORD, the God of hosts:
'Because they have spoken this word,
behold, I am making my words in your mouth a fire,
and this people wood, and the fire shall devour them.'

---

[12] MT *lōʾ-hū*, 'it is not he': G *ouk esti tauta*, 'these things are not so'; NEB 'he does not exist'; JPSB 'It is not so'. Contrast the phrase *ʾanī hūʾ*, 'I am he' (Deut. 32.39; Isa. 43.13). **[13]** MT *wᵉhaddibēr*, 'and who says': G 'the word of the Lord'; EVV treat *hdbr* as a noun 'the word'. MT 'thus shall it be done to them', lacking in G^A; BHS would transfer to after 'God of hosts' in v. 14. **[14]** MT *dabberkem*, 'you have spoken', probably should be *dabbᵉrām*, 'they have spoken', in order to differentiate between the 'you' of 14b and the 'them' of 14a.

Three fragments held together by the motif of things said but lacking clear indications as to who is saying what to whom. The 'they' of v. 12 is presumably the people but, depending upon the interpretation of v. 13, might be the prophets. The editors may have connected vv. 11–12 by the similar notions of treacherous action (*bgd*) and false speaking (*kḥš*), but originally the verses appear to have been distinct compositions. The false speaking (NEB 'denied' cf. Isa. 59.13) refers to the statement 'it is not he' or 'it is not so', and presupposes some prior assertion which is here being combated. Presumably the proclamation of divine judgment (via the invading enemy?) is here rebutted with a counter-assertion 'it is not the case'. Disaster will not come upon the people ('us'), nor will invasion (sword) or famine hit the people. The denial of this threat is also found in 14.15, which may point to the prophets as the speakers of v. 12 (hence v. 13). Rather than treating the phrase 'it is not he' (*lō'-hū'*) as a statement about Yahweh's existence or as an expression of practical atheism (cf. Zeph. 1.12; Ps. 94.7), it may be better understood as a dismissal of the claim that disaster is coming upon the people. From the speaker's standpoint such a rejection of impending disaster is 'to speak falsely' ('lie' *kḥš*) with reference to Yahweh. The present context of the counter-claim is the enemy from the north cycle (where it sits very poorly with the expressions of terror and fear caused by the invasion), but it was probably constructed for a very different debate.

The RSV understanding of v. 11 makes it the continuation of the people's rejection of the threatened disaster. The prophets who speak of such a terrible fate will become wind because they lack the word. What that word is is not specified but presumably it refers to the word of hope or *šālōm* (see on 17.15). Prophets who prophesy disaster are mere wind (a possible play on *rūaḥ*, 'wind' or 'spirit' of inspiration) lacking the divine word. It is a specification of divine action as positive on behalf of the community rather than destructive of Yahweh's people. That is one interpretation of vv. 12–13 (see Duhm), but there is an alternative way of reading the text. If v. 13 is an independent statement, then it may be a reflection on the saying in v. 12 and, identifying the speakers as the prophets of *šālōm*, a dismissal of such windbags because they lack the word. In the context of the conflict between the prophets and the editors of the Jeremiah tradition the key distinguishing mark is possession of 'the word' (cf. 23.25–29). That word dominates the tradition, and all alternative prophetic activities are dismissed as sound and fury without signification. In spite of the ambiguity in understanding vv. 12–13 (a similar ambiguity exists for Hos. 9.7, where prophets are dismissed as windbags), this interpretation is closer to the tradition and may be preferable to the RSV's reading of it. Yet the ambiguity should be noted and due allowance made for the difficulty in distinguishing 'spirit' from 'wind'!

A further independent element comments on the (false) speaking of the people and makes a distinction between the people and the speaker (the prophet?). The 'this word' (v. 14) may refer to 12 or

12–13. The divine word in the speaker's mouth (in contrast to the lack of the word in the prophets of v. 13) now becomes 'fire' and the people 'wood', so that it consumes the community. Thus it demonstrates the falseness of the assertion in v. 12. The prophetic word is like fire in 23.29, so this is probably a reference to the prophetic word directed against the community (in the enemy from the north context).

5.15–17

15 'Behold, I am bringing upon you
  a nation from afar, O house of Israel,
      says the LORD.
It is an enduring nation,
  it is an ancient nation,
a nation whose language you do not know,
  nor can you understand what they say.
16 Their quiver is like an open tomb,
  they are all mighty men.
17 They shall eat up your harvest and your food;
  they shall eat up your sons and your daughters;
they shall eat up your flocks and your herds;
  they shall eat up your vines and your fig trees;
your fortified cities in which you trust
  they shall destroy with the sword.'

---

[15] G lacks 'it is an enduring nation, it is an ancient nation'; for the last two clauses in MT it has 'a nation the sound of whose language one shall not understand', cf. Deut. 28.49b. **[16]** MT *'ašpātō*, 'its quiver'; G lacks this sentence, only reading 'all mighty men'. The MT figure is a strange one; BHS suggests *ś*^{e}*pātō*, 'its lips', or *'*^{a}*šer pīhū*, 'whose mouth' (Volz), cf. NEB, JPSB. If MT is a metaphor for deadly weapons, it fits *gibbōrīm*, 'warriors', better than the emendations. But Rudolph reads the phrase *kullām gibbōrīm*, 'they are all mighty men', as *killū miggōbīm*, 'they consume more than grasshoppers', cf. v. 17; BHS. **[17]** MT *w*^{e}*'ākal . . . yō'k*^{e}*lū . . . yō'kal*: as collectives *yō'k*^{e}*lū* should be sing. MT *y*^{e}*rōšēš*, 'beat down', only elsewhere Mal. 1.4 (*ršš*); BHS prefers *yōriš*, 'dispossesses'.

The theme of the invading army is resumed in vv. 15–17. It is an ancient, perennial, distant, foreign-language-speaking, irresistible nation. It comes against Israel to devour all its possessions like locusts wiping out the harvest. Just as such insects settle down on and devour every particle of vegetation, so will this mighty army consume the land of Israel and wipe out its fortified cities. Whether the people flee *from* the cities (4.29) or *into* the cities, they will be devastated by this invading force. Like a mobile grave this machine will terrorize the land. The repeated phrases of v. 17 (*'kl* four times) and v. 15 (*gōy* four times) indicate a liturgical shape to this unit, and its origins are probably to be found in some curse ritual of the period (cf. Thiel 1973, 97). But it is Israel which is cursed rather than its enemies. A similar threat appears in Deut. 28.49–52 and common elements are to be found there and in 6.22–24; Isa. 5.26–29; Hab. 1.5–11. A common tradition describing the powerfulness of an enemy is behind all these pieces and it is used here to depict the fearsome Babylonians invading the land. Behind the invasion is Yahweh who brings the enemy against Israel. This is the word become fire in the speaker's mouth (v. 14) and thus (v. 17) the people become fuel for that fire. Sword and famine are precisely what the people denied would happen (or at least their prophets did 14.15), so sword and famine will be the outcome of the invasion. Although the language is stereotypical, v. 17 is an accurate description of the effects of an invading army sweeping through the land and devouring everything in sight. A divine curse indeed!

5.18–19

18 'But even in those days, says the LORD, I will not make a full end of you.
19 And when your people say, "Why has the LORD our God done all these things to us?" you shall say to them, "As you have forsaken me and served foreign gods in your land, so you shall serve strangers in a land that is not yours." '

---

[19] MT *tō'mᵉrū*, 'you say'; an impersonal *yō'mᵉrū* is more suitable here: 'When they say . . .', i.e. 'when people say . . .'. S, BHS insert after 'you shall say to them . . .' 'thus says the lord'.

Thiel 1973, 97–9

The placing of vv. 15–17 allows for a Deuteronomistic reflection on the disaster (note *'āśāh*, 'he *has* done', in v. 19). In a fictive future

(Thiel's phrase), when some of the people have survived the invasion they will ask (the prophet?), 'why did Yahweh do these things to us?'. What is the meaning of such a destruction of the nation? A full end (*kālāh*) cannot be made of the nation, otherwise there would be none left to learn any lesson (cf. the reason for survival of the wicked in Ezek. 6.8–10). Here the phrase 'I will not make a full end' is more likely to be genuine and an integral part of the verse than in 4.27; 5.10. The survivors live to tell the tale and thereby point up the moral lesson of the disaster. Having served alien gods in their own land, now they must serve strangers in a foreign land. Poetic justice!

5.20–25

20 Declare this in the house of Jacob,
proclaim it in Judah:
21 'Hear this, O foolish and senseless people,
who have eyes, but see not,
who have ears, but hear not.
22 Do you not fear me? says the LORD;
Do you not tremble before me?
I placed the sand as the bound for the sea,
a perpetual barrier which it cannot pass;
though the waves toss, they cannot prevail,
though they roar, they cannot pass over it.
23 But this people has a stubborn and rebellious heart;
they have turned aside and gone away.
24 They do not say in their hearts,
"Let us fear the LORD our God,
who gives the rain in its season,
the autumn rain and the spring rain,
and keeps for us
the weeks appointed for the harvest."
25 Your iniquities have turned these away,
and your sins have kept good from you.'

---

[22] MT *wayyitgā'ᵃšū wᵉlō' yūkālū*, 'they toss and cannot prevail', makes the waves the subject (as in EVV); but G singular verbs make the sea that subject; 'though it rages it cannot prevail', cf. BHS. **[23]** Rudolph omits 'rebellious', a gloss from Deut. 21.18, 20, as destroying the rhythm, and reads with Ehrlich *wayyukālū* for MT *wayyēlēkū*, cf. 3.5. The sea could not break Yahweh's eternal law, but this people could (Ehrlich 1912, 254). **[24]**

K *wyrh*, Q *yōreh*. BHS regards *yōreh ūmalqōš*, 'autumn rain and spring rain', as an addition (Rudolph deletes it following Rothstein as a 'pedantic gloss'); BHS also deletes *šᵉbuʿōt*, 'weeks', as a dittography (presumably of *bᵉʿittō*).

The subject-matter of ch. 5 is idolatry and false forms of worship, with only a hint of the enemy from the north theme and a few fragments on the divine word. The lesson to be learned from the destruction of the nation is about serving alien gods. It is followed by a late piece (Cornill) reflecting upon nature and the community's unnatural ways. Although the passage is addressed to Jacob-Judah, the identity of those doing the addressing is unknown (plurals are used, so a solitary speaker should not be envisaged). The people are described (again plurals are used to designate the community) as foolish, lacking mind and, although possessing eyes and ears, blind and deaf. This kind of language is associated with the rejection of 'this people' (v. 23) in Isa. 6.10 and with idols in Ps. 115.4–7; 135.15–18 (used frequently in the NT; cf. Lindars 1961, 159–67). Although allusive, it connects foolishness with idolatry or rejection of true understanding of Yahweh (cf. Ps. 94.7–9). Given over to idolatry, the individual people of Judah cannot see the obvious; they cannot understand nature. Two examples of nature's laws are given as part of the argument against the nation, as evidence of its blindness and deafness.

Technically neither nature nor the laws of nature form part of biblical thought, but the examples given in the argument here are classified as *ḥoq-ʿōlām*, 'a permanent limit' (v. 22), and *šᵉbuʿōt ḥuqqōt*, 'weeks appointed for . . .'. The terms represent limits and appropriate periods rather than the laws of modern physics, and neither example given constitutes a law as such. But the Hebrew *ḥōq* or *ḥuqqāh* refers to decrees, statutes, limits and enactments (whether human or divine) and so the arguments from the natural world (the sea) and the social world (harvest) speak of a permanence in contrast to Judah's unstable behaviour. It is metaphorical language (the sea is hardly a good example of permanent limits, except to those not familiar with it, for soil erosion and land reclamation demonstrate just how impermanent a limit has been set for it) and serves the purpose of denouncing the nation for its failure to understand and fear Yahweh. As a stubborn, rebellious people Jacob-Judah has transgressed the limits set for it (not specified, but something similar to *mišpāṭ* in vv. 4–5 is probably meant). The incomprehension of

Judah is further demonstrated by its failure to understand Yahweh's role in sending rain (note 'do not say in their minds', v. 24, cf. v. 2; 12.2). As giver of rain (cf. Hos. 6.3), Yahweh is the one to be feared, not the baals. Yet the rains have not come because of the people's sins (v. 25; whether the drought of 12.4; 14.2–6 is the background to this piece cannot be determined from the text); the very worship which was designed to produce rain and thereby prosperity has prevented it. The failure of harvest may be implied by v. 17 and 'good' (v. 25 *ṭōb*) refers to fertility of produce or rain. Similar arguments are to be found in Isa. 59.1–2; Hos. 2.8–9.

5.26–29

26 'For wicked men are found among my people;
    they lurk like fowlers lying in wait.
  They set a trap;
    they catch men.
27 Like a basket full of birds,
    their houses are full of treachery;
  therefore they have become great and rich,
28   they have grown fat and sleek.
  They know no bounds in deeds of wickedness;
    they judge not with justice
  the cause of the fatherless, to make it prosper,
    and they do not defend the rights of the needy.
29 Shall I not punish them for these things?
                says the LORD,
  and shall I not avenge myself
    on a nation such as this?'

---

[26] MT *yāšūr k^{e}šak y^{e}qūšīm*, 'he watches as the bending (?) of fowlers', meaning quite uncertain (cf. Bright); BHS *yiśr^{e}kū ś^{e}bākā k^{e}yōqšīm*, 'they set a net like fowlers', cf. NEB; 'who lurk, like fowlers lying in wait' JPSB; by transposition Driver 1937–38, 101f., arrives at *'āš^{e}rū w^{e}kaśū k^{e}yāqōšīm*, 'they grow rich and are gorged; like fowlers'; G 'they have set snares to destroy men'. Emerton 1981 treats *sōk* as 'a hide' and translates 'they watch, as in a fowler's snare'. **[28]** G lacks 'they have grown fat and sleek . . . deeds of wickedness . . . to make it prosper . . .' and for 'needy' has *chēras*, 'widow'. Driver, 102, treats 28c as a gloss on 'they judge not with justice'; BHS prefers 'they transgress my words to do evil' for *'ābrū dibrē-rā'*. **[29]** = v. 9.

Wisser 1983, 42–64

A late piece which recognizes the community as 'my people', in contrast to the preceding unit which dismisses the nation contemptuously as 'this people' (Duhm attributes it to a post-exilic writer with lament elements in it). A division among the people between good and evil, rich and poor, is presupposed in vv. 26–28, whereas in most of the poems and discourses of the tradition no such division is mooted. It is a polemic directed against 'the guilty men' (*rᵉšāʿîm*) lurking in the community and preying off its weaker elements. These people have grown rich at the expense of the poor. The argument is similar to Isa. 1.23 (a post-exilic attack on the authorities of the city, Kaiser 1983, 43). It reflects a situation of exploitation among the different social strata rather than that of an apostate society or one filled with warring factions (cf. 9.2–6). No indication of dating or social setting is given for the unit, but a corrupt leadership in the time of Ezra-Nehemiah would suit, though many commentators prefer an earlier dating in the later reign of Josiah or the early years of Jehoiakim (Bright, Thompson). The judgment of v. 29 is a refrain included here because the editors wished to record their disapproval of this situation, but it has no inherent connection with vv. 26–28. It does not suit this context because it is directed against the nation, whereas vv. 26–28 are a denunciation of 'fat and sleek' exploiters of the poor. Against them the deity will act. But in the destruction of Jerusalem both rich and poor, exploiter and exploited alike, were destroyed. Duhm is right to connect these verses with the post-exilic division of the community into the pious and the godless (cf. Isa. 29.19–21; Ps. 64).

5.30–31

30 An appalling and horrible thing
has happened in the land:
31 the prophets prophesy falsely,
and the priests rule at their direciton;
my people love to have it so,
but what will you do when the end comes?

---

[31] MT *baššeqer*, 'falsely'; some modern commentators prefer to treat *šeqer* here as a personification of Baal (cf. Klopfenstein 1964, 394); cf. 2.8; 23.13. MT *yirdū*, 'rule', but BHS prefers *yōrū* or *hōrū*, 'teach' (following Cornill); Duhm *y^eraddū*, 'scrape out' (a living), cf. Judg. 14.9. MT *'al-y^edēhem*, 'at their hands', RSV 'at their direction', cf. 27.16; Johnson 1962, 63f. The Hebrew is ambiguous and may mean 'at their direction', 'beside them', 'by their authority' (cf. 29.26); Holladay 1965 regards it as a consecration formula antonym 'deconsecrate'.

The cultic leaders of the community are attacked here (the combination 'prophets and priests' occurs in 2.8, 26b; 4.9; 6.13 = 8.10; 23.23; 26.7, 8, 11, 16). Their joint leadership is described as 'an appalling and horrible thing' (*ša'^arūrāh*, 'disgusting', cf. the disgusting figs of 29.17), yet as something the people love (*'āh^abū*). There is no division between people and leadership here (as there is in vv. 26–28); they are at one in the religious life of the community (cf. Amos 4.5). The precise relationship between priests and prophets is not clear in v. 31, nor is the nature of the false (*šeqer*) prophesying, but both are condemned by the editor and also the people when the end (unspecified) comes. Duhm puts the piece in the time of Third Isaiah; it would fit, but the terms are too vague for confidence in any dating of the unit.

6.1–5

61 Flee for safety, O people of Benjamin,
from the midst of Jerusalem!
Blow the trumpet in Tekoa,
and raise a signal on Beth-hac-cherem;
for evil looms out of the north,
and great destruction.
2 The comely and delicately bred I will destroy,
the daughter of Zion.
3 Shepherds with their flocks shall come against her;
they shall pitch their tents around her,
they shall pasture, each in his place.
4 'Prepare war against her;
up, and let us attack at noon!'
'Woe to us, for the day declines,
for the shadows of evening lengthen!'
5 'Up, and let us attack by night,
and destroy her palaces!'

[1] Elements of word-play are found here: *b^{e}nē binyāmīn*, *t^{e}qōʿa tiqʿū*, *ś^{e}ʾū maśʾēt*; cf. 4.6 for a similar statement. **[2]** MT *hannāwāh w^{e}hamm^{e}ʿunnāgāh dāmītī*, EVV unlikely: following Cornill, Volz read with BHS *h^{a}linwēh maʿ^{a}nāg dām^{e}tā(h)* (also Rudolph), cf. Bright, 'are you like a beautiful meadow?'. **[4]** MT *qadd^{e}šū*, 'prepare', cf. 1.5; *qdš* may refer to commencing battle with a sacral rite (Weiser; cf. Soggin 1960; Bach 1962).

The foe from the north theme reappears in a poem warning people to flee from Jerusalem. This 'fleeing' motif (cf. 4.6; 50.8) is part of the prophetic proclamation of a holy war (analysis in Bach 1962) but it has some unusual features in 6.1–5. The reference to Benjaminites is peculiar (cf. 1.1; 17.19), and Jerusalem as the target of the enemy rather than the foreign power as Yahweh's object of attack is an inversion of normal holy war concepts. The Babylonian threat to Jerusalem necessitated changing traditional modes of thought, and in this period Judaeans had to learn to flee – first from Jerusalem when Babylon invaded (4.6; 6.1) and then as exiles from Babylon when that great power itself faced the enemy from the north (50.8–10; 51.6, 45; cf. Isa. 48.20). It is hardly necessary to make the appeal to the Benjaminites to flee evidence of Jeremiah's concern for his own countryfolk (cf. Volz, 71; Duhm) because the formal language of v. 1 and its rhetoric of assonance and word-play militate against the place names (Benjamin, Tekoa, Beth-hakkerem) having any particular semantic force. The actions of fleeing, blowing the trumpet and raising the war signals all convey the single idea of an invading force threatening Jerusalem. Daughter Zion, a beautiful meadow, is about to become the object of unwelcome attentions. In vv. 2–3 the images used are those of grassy meadow land and shepherds pasturing their flocks in it, with their tents surrounding the meadow. An idyllic picture! Each shepherd grazes his flock in his own strip of pasture (NEB understanding of *yādō*, 'his hand'; JPSB's 'under his care' is equally suitable; cf. *ṣōʾn yādō*, 'sheep of his hand', Ps. 95.7). But these terms also are only metaphors, metaphors standing for the invading army about to besiege Jerusalem (cf. 1.15). The beautiful meadow infested with shepherds grazing their sheep is in reality a city under siege from a formidable enemy. Sheep may *not* graze safely here.

In vv. 4–5 a dramatic dialogue is used to represent the beginning of the attack on the city (RSV understanding of Hebrew; other translations read the verses as a statement by the invaders, cf. NEB, Bright, Thompson). Preparations for battle are made using sacral rites and noontide is set as the time for attack. But it is too late for that plan (perhaps the rituals went on too long), so the attack is rescheduled to begin during the night. This is a determined enemy which will not be put off by the exigencies of having to fight in the dark. An alternative understanding of vv. 4–5 is as an exchange between invaders and defenders or, more likely, other attackers who regret the loss of daylight. This attack motif suggests a battle rather than a siege and it is possible that the image of the shepherds and their flocks is intended to convey a literal description of the territory around Jerusalem as the place where ideal pasturage is to be found (cf. NEB, Bright). The attack dialogue then breaks into this lovely picture and shatters its peacefulness. It is not necessary to match the metaphors exactly with the reality of the siege and later destruction of Jerusalem. The language is stereotypical and reflects holy war ideas and may well be derived from the poems against the foreign nations (see on 46–51). The poem represents the enemy from the north attacking Jerusalem in terms drawn from the stock of holy war terminology.

6.6–8

6 For thus says the LORD of hosts:
'Hew down her trees;
cast up a siege mound against Jerusalem.
This is the city which must be punished;
there is nothing but oppression within her.
7 As a well keeps its water fresh,
so she keeps fresh her wickedness;
violence and destruction are heard within her;
sickness and wounds are ever before me.
8 Be warned, O Jerusalem,
lest I be alienated from you;
lest I make you a desolation,
an uninhabited land.'

---

[6] Cf. Deut. 29.19 for the irony of hewing down trees for a siege; read *'ēṣāh*, 'her trees', for MT *'eṣāh*, 'trees', with some mss, Vrs. MT *hī' hā'īr hopqad*, 'this is the city to be punished': verb masc. but noun fem. G *ō polis pseudēs* = *hōy 'īr haššeqer* 'woe O false city'; Driver, 102, 'alas! city of licence'. **[7]** K *bwr*; Q *bayīr* = *b*ᵉ*'ēr* 'well'; K 'cistern'. G takes *ḥolī ūmakkāh*, 'sickness and wounds', with v. 8 'you shall be disciplined with pain and scourging . . .'. A marginal note in MT indicates that v. 7 is the middle verse of the Hebrew Bible.

An oracle follows the poem of disaster from the north and explains why Jerusalem is under siege. The siege machines of the Babylonians are represented as responses to Yahweh's command. The enemy from the north is there by Yahweh's invitation, and the reason for this reversal of the deity's patronage of Jerusalem is the city's evil ways. This is the false city (*šeqer*, G) harbouring oppression. A striking image describes the state of the city. As a well keeps water fresh (Rudolph prefers to understand *hāqīr* from *qwr*, 'bubbling'), so does the city keep fresh its evil (*rā'ātāh*; for the container image of the city cf. Ezek. 11.7, 11). Evil is like a source of water constantly renewing itself in the city (the K tradition makes it just a container of water, i.e. a cistern). The phrase 'violence and destruction' (*ḥāmās wāšōd* function as a word-pair in 20.8; Amos 3.10; Isa. 60.18; Ezek. 45.9; Hab. 1.3) is a cry of outrage, the shout of those set upon by thugs (cf. Bright, 48), and here conveys the atmosphere of social oppression in Jerusalem. The city is full of battered and broken bodies, 'sickness and wounds', though the reference could be to the state of the city in the deity's eyes (cf. Isa. 1.5–6). The poem is a hyperbolic statement of the city's wrongdoing, depicted vividly as a well gushing with fresh, sparkling water. For this the siege works are thrown up against the city's walls.

The warning in v. 8 about the possibility of divine alienation (*tēqa'*, a term meaning 'dislocation', cf. Gen. 32.26, or a strong sense of revulsion, cf. Ezek. 23.17) may suggest a note of hope but, rhetoric apart, should be referred to the later application of the material. The community addressed by the editors is warned to learn from what happened to the city in the past lest they also disgust Yahweh. Other commentators treat it as an early poem holding out hope to the city (e.g. Bright, Thompson).

6.9–11

9 Thus says the LORD of hosts:
'Glean thoroughly as a vine
  the remnant of Israel;
like a grape-gatherer pass your hand again
  over its branches.'

10 To whom shall I speak and give warning,
that they may hear?
Behold, their ears are closed,
they cannot listen;
behold, the word of the LORD is to them an object of scorn,
they take no pleasure in it.
11 Therefore I am full of the wrath of the LORD;
I am weary of holding it in.
'Pour it out upon the children in the street,
and upon the gatherings of young men, also;
both husband and wife shall be taken,
the old folk and the very aged.'

---

[9] MT *'ōlēl yᵉ'ōllū*, 'they shall thoroughly glean'; in view of the sing. *yādᵉkā*, 'your hand', better as imperative sing. MT may be a reference to the Babylonians of vv. 4–6. MT *salsillōt*, 'branches', hapax legomenon cf. *sal*, 'basket'. **[10]** MT *'ᵃrēlāh 'oznām*, 'their ears have a foreskin', i.e. are uncircumcised. **[11]** MT *wᵉ'ēt ḥᵃmat yhwh mālē'tī*, 'with the wrath of Yahweh I am full': Ehrlich 1912, 257, suggests *wa'ᵃnī*, 'but as for me'; cf. Micah 3.8 (BHS). G 'and I allowed my wrath to come to the full'; here Yahweh is the speaker. **[11]** MT *šᵉpōk*, 'pour out', but G *ekcheō*, 'I will pour it out' (= *šāpōk*). MT *gam . . . 'im* should read *gam . . . gam*, 'both . . . (man) and (wife)'. BHS adds *lō*, 'not', before 'very aged' (haplography), making a contrast between the old and those *not* full of years. It is an unnecessary change in view of the grouping 'man and wife . . . old and aged' ascending from children and youths.

Many commentators divide ch. 6 into five sections (1–8, 9–15, 16–21, 22–26, 27–30), but those who follow a different division have problems determining where units start or finish (e.g. Lundbom 1975 works with the units 1–7, 8–12). Part of that problem is concerned with identifying the speaker in various pieces. There is a case for a piecemeal division of the chapter, but even such a radical operation cannot be certain of having identified each speaker correctly. A further part of the problem in ch. 6 is the fact that vv. 12–15 are very similar to 8.10–12 and may well be an editorial insertion in the chapter. I have divided this section up in a way different from most commentators in order to focus upon different voices in the text, but v. 11 is quite problematic (Volz settles for 9–11a, 11b–15). If v. 12 and 8.10 were not variants of each other, it would have been tempting to make this unit 9–12. Dissatisfaction with whatever division of units is made can only be overcome by treating the whole chapter as one unit. That is an even less satisfactory way of handling the text. The different ways of dividing the text into units can make a significant difference to the interpretation of that text.

The oracular statement in v. 9 refers to the harvest vintage as a figure for the final destruction of Israel. It is final because the harvesting of the grapes is the final stage of the summer's work when the late fruits and the vintage are gathered. It is also the final act because what is here gleaned is what is left of Israel (*šᵉʼērīt yiśrāʼēl*, 'remnant of Israel'). As a vine Israel is to be harvested and, just in case any grapes remain, the hand is to be passed over its branches again (*hāšēb yād*, 'return the hand'). The utter destruction of Israel is envisaged by this image of the thoroughly gleaned vine. It is the equivalent of the destroying of the terraces and stripping of the branches of the vineyard in 5.10. It is not clear from the text who is to do the gleaning. The MT's plural reading suggests that the Babylonians are here described as harvesting the grapes (cf. the divine command to them in v. 6). The suggested reading 'glean thoroughly' leaves the subject of the action uncertain, but in view of v. 10 the editors may intend Jeremiah to be that subject. The verse is probably best treated as an isolated unit with subject unclear but now incorporated into a section which appears to be a dialogue between Yahweh and the speaker (presumably Jeremiah).

In its present context the command to glean is understood as a command to speak. But to whom is he to speak? The remnant of v. 9? Is the use of that term indicative of a prior defeat of Israel (i.e. 597) and should the figure of further gleaning be understood as a reference to the period prior to 587? The questions must be asked, but the text affords no clear evidence to answer them. The implication of v. 10 is that there are no people capable of listening to the warnings, so to whom is the speaker to address himself? The people's ears have a foreskin (cf. 4.4 for this figure with reference to the people's minds), so they are incapable of comprehending what is being said. The metaphor of ears with a foreskin points to a community unable to receive the divine word because that word is an object of scorn to them. The notion of a community beyond the reach of the word is similar to that expressed in Isa. 6.9–10, though the language used is different and the role of the speaker quite distinctive. The association of the vine metaphor with a statement about the people's relation to the divine word in vv. 9–11a makes the unit a parallel one to 5.10–14. There a similar command about destroying the vineyard is followed by a number of statements condemning the people/prophets because their words are wrong and they lack the divine word. That word then becomes a fire in the mouth of the speaker (5.14) and devours the people. Here the speaker is filled with the wrath of Yahweh, and it is poured out on the people.

Is then the speaker the gleaner of the grapes? He is not in 5.10 but might be in 6.9. Or is the gleaning a rather different figure from that of destruction? It is because the people will not receive the divine word that they are destroyed; yet that incapacity is the reason that grapes cannot be gathered (assuming the present conjunction of vv. 9–10). A different interpretation of v. 9 is suggested by Duhm, who relates the search for remaining grapes to Abraham's question about the fate of the righteous in Sodom (Gen. 18.23–33). Will the whole city be destroyed? No is the answer – glean the grapes which remain (cf. the image in Isa. 27.12; Duhm treats the reference to the remnant as a later eschatological gloss). To this instruction the reply is as given in v. 10. So the quest for finding righteous people in the city fails as it did in 5.1–5. This understanding of v. 9 (Duhm, 67) is interesting and worth considering in view of the fact that the text is too allusive to allow one definitive meaning. Whatever the original meaning of v. 9 may have been, its place here inevitably means that it will be read in conjunction with v. 10.

The people find no pleasure in the divine word, in fact they scorn it. On the other hand, the speaker is full of Yahweh's wrath (cf. 15.17). This presumably refers to the proclamation of divine anger against the nation (a rather different understanding of v. 9 from Duhm's). Tired of holding this anger within him (the fire of 5.14?), he appeals to the deity (or the enemy from the north?) to pour it out on the whole community: the children in the streets, the group (*sōd*, cf. 23.18, 22) of young men, husbands and wives and the very old. This demand for the execution of wrath upon the people because he is full of that anger contrasts the speaker with the prophets of vv. 13–14 who are full of *šālōm*. It also raises questions about 17.16 if both statements are taken as coming from the prophet Jeremiah. Some commentators (e.g. Rudolph) see 11b as the point at which the speaking switches from Jeremiah to Yahweh. It is thus Yahweh who asserts 'I have to pour out . . .', and his wrath flows forth upon every age-group in the community because they have rejected his word.

Not the social oppression but the people's attitude to Yahweh's word is the clue to their destruction (as in 5.12–14). Thus two distinctive strands (false religious concepts and false notions about the divine word) are interwoven with the enemy from the north motif.

6.12–15

12 'Their houses shall be turned over to others,
their fields and wives together;
for I will stretch out my hand
against the inhabitants of the land,'
says the LORD.
13 'For from the least to the greatest of them,
every one is greedy for unjust gain;
and from prophet to priest,
every one deals falsely.
14 They have healed the wound of my people lightly,
saying, "Peace, peace,"
when there is no peace.
15 Were they ashamed when they committed abomination?
No, they were not at all ashamed;
they did not know how to blush.
Therefore they shall fall among those who fall;
at the time that I punish them, they shall be overthrown.'
says the LORD.

---

[12] 8.10a is a variant of this verse; vv. 13–15 = 8.10b–12, with very minor linguistic variations. In 8.10 their wives are given to others, their fields to conquerors; no mention is made of houses and 12b is absent. **[14]** MT *wᵉ'ēn šālōm*, 'but there is no peace'; G *kai pou estin eirēnē*, 'and where is peace?' (= *wᵉ'ayyēh*). **[15]** MT *haklīm*, 'blush', cf. 8.12 *hikkālēm*. MT *pᵉqadtīm*, 'I punish them', but G *episkopēs autōn*, 'their visitation' = *pᵉquddātām* as in 8.12.

The editorial 'says Yahweh' at the end of v. 12 suggests that vv. 11–12 were taken together and vv. 13–15 (also concluded with the editorial indication of oracular status) are a separate poem. But the presence of a variation of v. 12 in 8.10a, followed by a repeat of 6.13–15 in 8.10b–12, points to the necessity of treating 6.12–15 as an independent unit here added to v. 11. It expands the word of judgment in v. 11 by elaborating on the fate of the community and explaining why everybody must suffer in the time of divine visitation. Although some commentators (e.g. Rudolph, 45) regard the common poem as original to ch. 6 but secondary in ch. 8, it is preferable to treat the unit as independent of its present contexts. It may appear to fit 6.11 better than 8.9 (so Bright, 50, 'they fit the present context splendidly'), but in fact it fits 8.8–9 just as well (what precedes the unit in each case is a statement about the rejection of the divine word). As the unit can hardly be original to both contexts yet is as suitable in the one as in the other, treating it as an independent piece seems justified.

The property of the people – houses, fields, wives (in contrast to the grouping of husband and wife in v. 11) – will become that of the invading forces (cf. 8.10), because Yahweh will turn his hand (i.e. power) against those who live in the land (cf. v. 8). Why? Because they are *all* in pursuit of unjust gain (cf. 22.17). The invading armies will seize the land with its houses and rape the women (cf. Amos 7.17 for a similar threat). Such seizures and sexual exploitation of women are the normal features of military invasions (cf. Lam. 5.11).

The whole community suffers because everybody in it has been party to oppression (*bṣ'*, 'unjust gain', hints at violence and plunder but may in this rhetorical setting simply refer to the eager pursuit of profit at the expense of others, cf. 22.17). Although everybody ('from the smallest to the biggest', cf. 5.4–5, 'poor and great alike') is to blame, the cult officials are especially guilty (13b–15 concentrates on prophets and priests). If the whole community pursues gain, the cult leaders practise falsehood (*šeqer*). The definition of falsehood in this context is: in a community where everybody is eager for ill-gotten goods there can be no justification for prophets responding to society's brokenness ('the wound of my people') with reassurances of well-being. To proclaim *šālōm* at such a time is to be false. In the larger context of the enemy from the north cycle the people's wound (*šeber*, cf. *šeber gādōl*, 'great destruction', 4.6; 6.1) may be the invading forces. To proclaim *šālōm* (equivalent perhaps to 'all will be well') in the face of such danger is disgraceful (15a). The incantatory *šālōm šālōm* receives the response 'there is no *šālōm*' (G is better in that it poses the pertinent question 'but whither peace?'). Wounds must be treated realistically, not ignored (cf. Isa. 1.5–6). As a metaphor for a society tearing itself apart (cf. vv. 6b–7), the people's wound requires treatment other than reassurances of well-being, however theologically well grounded such *šālōm* may be. The frivolous (*n^eqallāh* describes trivial or contemptuous activity) healing offered by the prophets (i.e. *šālōm*) is useless. So when the nation is destroyed these quacks will fall among the slain. *šālōm*, indeed!

6.16–21

16 Thus says the LORD:
'Stand by the roads, and look,
and ask for the ancient paths,
where the good way is; and walk in it,
and find rest for your souls,
But they said, "We will not walk in it."
17 I set watchmen over you, saying,
"Give heed to the sound of the trumpet!"
But they said, "We will not give heed."
18 Therefore hear, O nations,
and know, O congregation, what will happen to them.
19 Hear, O earth; behold, I am bringing evil upon this people,
the fruit of their devices,
because they have not given heed to my words;
and as for my law, they have rejected it.
20 To what purpose does frankincense come to me from Sheba,
or sweet cane from a distant land?
Your burnt offerings are not acceptable,
nor your sacrifices pleasing to me.
21 Therefore thus says the LORD:
"Behold, I will lay before this people
stumbling blocks against which they shall stumble;
fathers and sons together,
neighbour and friend shall perish." '

---

[16] MT *'im^edū 'al-d^erākīm ūr^e'u*, 'stand by the ways and see', is unclear as to meaning and hardly parallel with the next line (NEB treats 16–21 as prose). BHS suggests *'āmartī 'al-darkē mērō'š* (cf. Rudolph, who retains *'im^edū*), 'I said . . . concerning the ways of old'; cf. Driver 1937–38, 103, 'stand by the ways of old'. **[18]** MT *ūd^e'ī 'ēdāh*, 'know O congregation'; G 'they that feed their flocks'. BHS suggests *ūd^e'ū dē'āh* (following Giesebrecht), 'really know'. MT *'et-'^ašer-bām*, 'that which against them': something like *'e^eśeh* may be implied or have fallen out (cf. BHS). G lacks any equivalent of the clause. All Bright translates of v. 18 is 'Therefore hear, O nations!'; he leaves the rest blank because it is corrupt and the suggested emendations are unconvincing. **[19]** MT *maḥšᵉbōtām*, 'their schemes'; G *apostrophēs*, 'apostasies' = *mᵉšūbātām*. **[20]** MT *tābō'*, 'comes'; G *pherete*, 'you bring' = *tābī'ū*. **[21]** K *y'bdw* (*yō'bēdū*, 'they shall perish'); Q *wᵉ'ābādū*, 'and they perished'.

Thiel 1973, 99–101

The text of this unit is problematical and not well preserved. It has a number of Deuteronomistic elements in it (analysed in Thiel 1973, 100f.) and gives the appearance of being a mosaic of distinctive motifs (e.g. directions and warnings, a polemic against the sacrificial cult, criticisms of the community for rejecting Yahweh's *tōrāh*). These different fragments may have been put together by a Deuteronomistic editor as part of a preaching programme against the community fitting in with the incorrigibility theme of v. 15. The fabricated dialogue of vv. 16–17 (so similar to elements in 2.5 – 4.4) represents the people as rejecting all the directions and warnings given to it. This feature may have its conclusion in v. 21: having refused to walk in the old ways, the people must now face the stumbling blocks put in the way chosen by them. Once again the rhetoric of paired groups (cf. vv. 11, 12, 13) is used to identify the victims of divine punishment. The nostalgia behind v. 16 ('walk in the old ways, inquire of the ancient paths') is indicative of a society disintegrating and lacking direction. The recommendation to go back to the past (ironic in view of 2.5–20; 7.25–26!) is typical of Deuteronomistic thought (cf. the representation of Deuteronomy as a sermon by Moses). The people will find rest if they return to the good old ways. But they refuse (cf. 2.20, 25, 31). The pattern of vv. 16–17 is recommended action and popular rejection of it. The watchmen (*ṣōpīm*) of v. 17 are probably prophets (cf. Ezek. 3.16–21; 33.7), though in view of the scathing remarks about the prophets in the tradition the term may simply be a metaphor for those who warn. Those who blow the trumpet give warning of attack (cf. 4.5; 6.1), watchmen just report what they see or hear (cf. Isa. 21.6–8; unless they are derelict of duty as in Isa. 56.10). In Hos. 9.8 the prophet is the watchman. The Deuteronomistic belief that the prophets were never listened to (see on 7.25–26) appears here. In spite of advice about the proper paths or warnings of danger the community *deliberately* refused to pay attention. For this refusal disaster will come upon the community (in spite of v. 18's lack of clarity, v. 19 provides a further statement of consequence for the nation).

The coming disaster is the fruit of the people's own schemes; it is the result of rejecting the divine law (a favourite motif of Deuteronomistic writings). If each element in the collection is scrutinized, the vagueness and generality of the language used will emerge. Roads, paths, sound of the trumpet, disaster, my words, *tōrāh*: they have no specific content and acquire their meaning from the group using them. In the context of the enemy from the north cycle they may be referred to the Babylonian invasion, but the origin of the pieces (or the sermon-like editorial) could be attributed to any period, especially after the fall of Jerusalem. Since it has rejected Yahweh's *tōrāh* (cf. 2.8; 8.8), the community's sacrificial cult is useless. This need not be a dismissal of the pre-catastrophe cult but could be a polemic against the temple authorities of a later period (cf. Isa. 65.3). The sweet cane and frankincense may be ingredients in cult worship, but the passage could also be a dismissal of foreign imports. These were required not only for the rituals of worship but for making life tolerable in a hot climate (without the wafting of incense about the place, especially in the temple, the stench would be too unbearable). But for all their aesthetic pleasure there is no point to their importation from distant lands (such trade hardly took place during the invasion!), nor is the complex sacrificial system at all effective. No amount of beautiful scents and licit offerings (the old ways of mankind!) could please a deity offended by the community's rejection of his words (on the rejection of sacrifice see 7.21–23). The opposition between divine *tōrāh* and the sacrificial approach (in terms of relative merit) indicates the partisan nature of this unit. Without the protection of sacrifice (useless in the circumstances) the people are for destruction. The nature of the stumbling blocks is not specified, but this can hardly be a reference to the invading Babylonians (cf. Isa. 8.14–15).

6.22–26

22 Thus says the LORD:
'Behold, a people is coming from the north country,
a great nation is stirring from the farthest parts of the earth.
23 They lay hold on bow and spear,
they are cruel and have no mercy,
the sound of them is like the roaring sea;

they ride upon horses,
set in array as a man for battle,
against you, O daughter of Zion!'
24 We have heard the report of it,
our hands fall helpless;
anguish has taken hold of us,
pain as of a woman in travail.
25 Go not forth into the field,
nor walk on the road;
for the enemy has a sword,
terror is on every side.
26 O daughter of my people, gird on sackcloth,
and roll in ashes;
make mourning as for an only son,
most bitter lamentation;
for suddenly the destroyer
will come upon us.

[22–24] = 50.41–43 (with minor variations); except that one is addressed to Zion and the other to Babylon. **[23]** MT *hū'*, 'he' (is cruel); some mss and 50.42 read *hēmmāh*, 'they', as do EVV. MT *ke'īs*, 'as a man': G *hōs pur*, 'as fire' (= *ke'ēš*); BHS, Rudolph prefer *kol-'īs*, 'every man'. Modern commentators favour translating *kīdōn*, RSV 'spear', as 'sword, sabre'; cf. NEB, Bright, Rudolph, comparable to the Roman *gladius*. **[25]** K *tṣ'y* fem. sing. 'go out'; Q *tēṣe'ū* plur; 'you go out'; K represents the city as the one addressed, Q the individual people. In view of v. 26 K seems the more appropriate. The same K–Q differentiation is made for *tlky tēlēkū*, 'walk'. **[26]** MT *haššōdēd*, 'the destroyer': G *talaipōria*, 'hardship, pain', suggests *haššōd*, 'destruction'.

The final poem in the collection about the enemy from the north uses a poem also found in the oracles against the nations cycle (50.41–3). One is directed against daughter Zion, the other against daughter Babylon. The occurrence of the same poem in different contexts should underline the stereotyped nature of this material. Forms and patterns are used interchangeably in the construction of the tradition and wise exegesis will not overemphasize the semantic element or underplay the formal aspect of such features. The form for announcing the imminent threat to a city is used of the Babylonians attacking Jerusalem and of the Persians (assuming 50.41–3 is not purely formal) attacking Babylon. Hence the poems should not be understood as literal descriptions of the invading armies but as conventional proclamations. It is therefore not possible to determine the relation of such poems to the events themselves, whether as anticipations, accompaniments or later reflections (see on 51.54–58). In later eschatological and apocalyptic writings the language of such battles is retained, but now it refers to purely mythological events, without any historical referent. The poems in 4.5 – 6.26 belong to the earlier stage of that development but give some indication of how they will evolve (hence the presence of 4.23–26 in the collection).

In this poem the enemy comes from the north, from a distant part of the earth (*yark^e^tē-'āreṣ*, 'the farthest parts of the earth', is hyperbole, though there may be traces of the mythological north here, cf. Ps. 48.2). It is a mighty army, armed and cruel, whose movements sound like the sea roaring (it is difficult to know whether such terms as *'akzārī*, 'cruel', cf. Job 30.21 [God the cruel one]; Prov. 5.9; or *yām*, 'the sea' [Canaanite Yam], have mythological connotations here). It is ready for battle and its target is Zion. Verses 24–26 give the responses of city and people to this terrible news (cf. 4.31 for the woman in labour image, though here it is only a general figure as in 30.6). The city is advised to stay indoors because outside the enemy is abroad. The phrase used to describe this state of affairs, 'terror is on every side' (*māgōr missābīb*), is almost a Leitmotiv in the Jeremiah tradition (cf. 20.3, 4, 10; 46.5; 49.29; see also Lam. 2.22; Ps. 31.13). Here it is the motive for staying in the city (cf. 5.6). In view of such a destructive force in the land, Zion is commanded to dress in mourning, that kind of deep, bitter mourning characterized by lamenting the loss of an only son (G beloved son). The city as a woman weeping over the death of her children (cf. 31.15) is a figure drawn from real life: in a time of invasion, with its ensuing skirmishes, all that women can do is weep over their dead (cf. Isa. 3.25–26). Most bitter lamentation!

6.27–30

27 'I have made you an assayer and tester among my people,
 that you may know and assay their ways.
28 They are all stubbornly rebellious,
 going about with slanders;
they are bronze and iron,
 all of them act corruptly.

29 The bellows blow fiercely,
the lead is consumed by the fire;
in vain the refining goes on,
for the wicked are not removed.
30 Refuse silver they are called,
for the LORD has rejected them.'

---

[27] MT *mibṣār*, 'fortress', is probably a gloss that should be deleted (BHS); some (e.g. KB, 142) revocalize as *m^ebaṣṣēr*, 'one who searches through' (cf. Bright, Thompson). Duhm treats it as *m^ebaṣṣēr*, 'gold tester', a synonym for *bāḥōn*, 'assayer'. Better omitted with NEB. **[28]** MT *sārē sōr^erīm*, 'the most rebellious of rebels'; G lacks *sārē*: *pantes anēkooi*, 'they are all disobedient'. Many mss, also Vrs, read *śārē*, 'princes', i.e. 'rebellious princes'. MT *n^eḥōšet ūbarzel*, 'bronze and iron', a gloss, possibly influenced by 1.18 where the terms *mibṣār*, *n^eḥōšet*, *barzel* all occur (cf. Ezek. 22. 18, 20 where such figures are used of the house of Israel). Thompson transfers the phrase 'copper and iron' to the next verse, cf. NEB. **[29]** MT *nāḥar* from *nḥr*, 'snort' (referring to bellows), rather than *ḥrr*, 'burn', cf. BHS, Rudolph. K *m'štm* Q *mē'ēṣ tam* (cf. G), 'from the fire complete'; Bright 'comes whole from the fire'; some read *tittōm* (as in Ezek. 24.11). MT *rā'īm*, 'wicked', but it may mean 'ore' here (Driver 1955b, 86), hence NEB's 'lead, copper and iron . . .' (Driver + transposition from v. 28). **[30]** MT 'they are called', but G 'call them . . .'.

A coda brings the enemy from the north cycle to a close. The final unit is textually unclear and it appears to have been influenced by 1.18. This influence may be due to the transmission of the text but it may also point to conscious editorial linking of the prologue and the first block. The presence of similar elements in both suggests a quite late date for vv. 27–30. In view of such a conclusion to the cycle it is worth stressing that the motif 'enemy from the north' is in fact only a minority element in 4.5 – 6.30. It does, however, provide a focus for a number of developments within the cycle and may therefore justifiably be used as a heading for introducing the material, diverse though it may be.

The 'you' of v. 27 is part of the strand already encountered at 5, 14, 19 (cf. 'me' in 2.1; 3.6, 11; 'I' in 4.10; 5.4–5; 6.10–11). It refers to a figure (unless it is taken as purely a figure of speech) that is never defined in the block and only appears in the redactional framework (e.g. 1.1; 7.1; 11.1; 14.1; 18.1) and the narratives. Such a shadowy figure should be seen as the development of the speaker in the tradition. The combination of the poem cycles with the narratives will allow that speaker to be identified with Jeremiah but whether the 'you' of these fragments should so be identified is a moot point.

The deity makes the speaker an assayer of the people. Images from the processes of refining metal are used to define the purposes of this task. Similar figures from metallurgy are used in 1.18 but understood in a quite different way (hence the direction of influence may be from 6.27–30 to 1.18 but it is more likely that the influence has come about through the transmission of the text). What is strange about the image of the speaker as assayer is the fact that, although the speaker is so designated in v. 27, the conclusion of his task is given alongside the commissioning! He is made a tester and then informed of the results of his testing. This sounds like prejudice but should perhaps be taken as the apocopated form of stereotyped statements in the tradition. Unless vv. 28–30 are taken as the results of the speaker's investigations, the piece reads like a verdict given against the people and not the commissioning of an assayer. It is such a verdict because it closes the block of material and underlines the true nature of the people destroyed by the Babylonians.

Under the figure of a refining process the nation is exposed as worthless. What that refining process refers to is not known nor is it explained in the text. Speculation may posit a prophet going around trying to persuade people to change their ways, but such a speculative interpretation fails to grasp the significance of the smelting process image. The people cannot be saved because they are rubbish. A smelting enterprise aims to remove the dross and produce the pure metals. Judah is not a pure metal, hence the refining techniques are in vain. The assayer is designated in order to confirm that this is the case. 'Rejected silver' is the verdict because Yahweh has rejected them. The unit summarizes the whole cycle and announces the result of the refining process: my people, rebellious and slanderous (cf. 9.4), are dismissed as scum by Yahweh.

B. 7.1 – 10.25

7.1–15

7[1] The word that came to Jeremiah from the LORD: 2 'Stand in the gate of the LORD's house, and proclaim there this word, and say, Hear the word of the LORD, all you men of Judah who enter these gates to worship the LORD. 3 Thus says the LORD of hosts, the God of Israel, Amend your ways and your doings, and I will let you dwell in this place. 4 Do not trust in these deceptive words: "This is the temple of the LORD, the temple of the LORD, the temple of the LORD."

5 For if you truly amend your ways and your doings, if you truly execute justice one with another, 6 if you do not oppress the alien, the fatherless or the widow, or shed innocent blood in this place, and if you do not go after other gods to your own hurt, 7 then I will let you dwell in this place, in the land that I gave of old to your fathers for ever.

8 Behold, you trust in deceptive words to no avail. 9 Will you steal, murder, commit adultery, swear falsely, burn incense to Baal, and go after other gods that you have not known, 10 and then come and stand before me in this house, which is called by my name, and say, "We are delivered!" – only to go on doing all these abominations? 11 Has this house, which is called by my name, become a den of robbers in your eyes? Behold, I myself have seen it, says the LORD. 12 Go now to my place that was in Shiloh, where I made my name dwell at first, and see what I did to it for the wickedness of my people Israel. 13 And now, because you have done all these things, says the LORD, and when I spoke to you persistently you did not listen, and when I called you, you did not answer, 14 therefore I will do to the house which is called by my name, and in which you trust, and to the place which I gave to you and to your fathers, as I did to Shiloh. 15 And I will cast you out of my sight, as I cast out all your kinsmen, all the offspring of Ephraim.'

[1–2] G lacks 1–2a and most of 2b: it simply has 'Hear the word of the lord, all Judah'. This indicates that MT is a second edition with expanded redactional framework, developing the role of Jeremiah (cf. 11.1; 14.1; 18.1;

30.1 for the formulaic reception of the word introduction). **[2]** MT 'stand in the *gate* of the house of Yahweh'; cf. 26.2, 'stand in the *court* of the house of Yahweh'. **[3]** MT *wayʾašakkenāh ʾetkem*, 'and I will cause you to dwell', but A, V, Ehrlich, Volz, Rudolph, BHS vocalize it as *weʾeškenāh ʾittkem*, 'I will dwell with you'. The original consonantal text would permit either reading (*wʾšknh ʾtkm*). **[4]** G has 'for they will not profit you at all' after 'deceptive words'. MT *hēkal yhwh hēkal yhwh hēkal yhwh hēmmāh*, 'temple of Yahweh, temple of Yahweh, temple of Yahweh (are) they'; for the triple incantatory phrase, cf. 22.28; Isa. 6.3; Ezek. 21.27. *hēmmāh*, 'they', may refer to the complex of buildings constituting the temple but is probably an abbreviation for *hammāqōm hazzeh*, 'this place', cf. NEB. **[6]** For the phrase 'or shed innocent blood in this place', cf. 22.3. **[7]** MT *wešikkantī ʾetkem*, 'I will allow you to dwell', see note on v. 3. **[10]** MT *lemaʿan ʿaśōt*, 'in order to do . . .' RSV 'go on doing'; Rudolph suggests reading *šenōt* for *ʿaśōt*, 'continue doing', cf. BHS. **[11]** G 'my house'. MT *gam ʾānōkī hinnēh rāʾītī*, 'also I, look, I have seen', cf. Volz, 91, for range of possible meanings: 'I have seen, I am not blind', 'so I have experienced it', 'I have seen that it is so.' **[13]** G lacks *neʾum yhwh*, 'says Yahweh', and the Hebrew idiom *haškem wedabbēr*, 'rising early and speaking', RSV 'persistently'; the idiom (with various verbs) occurs in 7.25; 11.7; 25.4; 26.5; 29.19; 32.33; 35.14, 15; 44.4.

Fohrer 1967, 190–203; Reventlow 1969, 325–41; Thiel 1973, 105–19

The temple sermon is built around the ambiguous term 'place' (*māqōm*), meaning 'temple' (v. 12) or 'land' (v. 7) or possibly 'city' (v. 14; v. 3 could refer to temple or city; cf. v. 20 where city or land, as in v. 17, rather than temple, is the object of divine threat; v. 32 and 8.3 refer to unspecified places). The narrative in ch. 26, which has some similarities to 7.1–15, combines the notions of 'temple' and 'city' (26.2, 6, 9, 12; vv. 11, 15 refer only to the city and v. 20 has Uriah's preaching directed against city and land). If ch. 26 concentrates on the threat to the city, 7.1–15 uses that threat to make observations on matters relating to temple worship. It is therefore much more of a 'temple' sermon than the story in 26. There the narrative focuses on the public reaction to a sermon against temple and city, whereas 7.1–15 provides a number of statements about the role of social behaviour in relation to the temple (see on 26).

The editorial framework makes the sermon a divine word proclaimed in the temple (dated in 26.1) and addressed to the men of Judah who worship Yahweh there. There are four elements in the sermon: a first admonition (vv. 2–4), a second admonition (vv. 5–7), invective (vv. 9–11), and threat (vv. 12–14; cf. Fohrer 1967, 195). The nation is called upon to mend its ways in order to be allowed to live in the land (or city, hardly temple) or for the deity to remain with them (in the temple; following the alternative understanding of *w'šknh 'tkm*). What it must not do is trust in the words of a lie (*dibrē haššeqer*). That lie is contained in the incantation 'the temple of Yahweh, the temple of Yahweh, the temple of Yahweh', uttered with reference to the complex of buildings believed to be the home of Yahweh. This trust is misplaced. The amendment of life will provide the people with what they want, i.e. guaranteed security. But the buildings and what they stand for (Yahweh's place among his people) guarantee nothing – hence the application of *šeqer* to the trust shown in the temple. The sermon is in opposition to the object of public trust (*bṭḥ*, 'trust', is used in vv. 4, 8, 14) and may therefore be associated with that strand in the tradition which opposes the things trusted by the people (e.g. foreign allies in 2.37; fortified cities in 5.17). Cult ideology reflected in the magical formula 'the temple of Yahweh' is false (*šeqer*). It is false because the people's security is not to be found in the possession of a divine house. Everything in which the nation puts its trust may become the source of false consciousness if it is divorced from amendment of life: temple, city, cultic officials, king, religion, history. Such is the essential critique of ideology in the book of Jeremiah. The fall of Jerusalem exposed the falseness of all such beliefs, and not even possession of Yahweh's temple could protect an evil people (it would take a Job or a Qoheleth to expose the false ideology behind the amendment of life notion of divine protection but the editors of the Jeremiah tradition are not that radical).

But what is meant by amendment of life? That is spelled out in vv. 5–6. The practice of justice, non-oppression of alien, orphan or widow, the refusal to shed innocent blood and the avoidance of following other gods (to the detriment of the community). Such demands may be found in many biblical traditions (Exodus, Deuteronomy, Isaiah, Amos, Hosea, Micah, etc.) and are, in some ways, quite conventional, but presumably are here opposed to a different ideology. In contrast to this definition of amendment of life the people are represented as trusting in the words of a lie (*dibrē haššeqer*, v. 8): the lie is not defined but may refer back to v. 4 or to v. 10, 'and say, "We are delivered!" '. The admonition in vv. 9–11 is heavy with irony (or is it outrage?). The community is accused of stealing, murdering, committing adultery, false swearing, serving Baal and other gods and *then* taking refuge in the divine temple and praising Yahweh for being saved, only to go back to doing all these bad things. However rhetorical the picture may be, it is a striking illustration of mindless worship. This type of behaviour turns the temple, Yahweh's house, into a robbers' cave.

This trenchant criticism of the people's way of life in relation to their attitude to the temple is presented in Deuteronomistic language (analysis in Thiel 1973, 105–19). The stress put on certain rules (v. 9) does not reflect the Decalogue (Ex. 20.3–17; Deut. 5.7–21) but points to a period when such formulations as the Decalogue were emerging as special summaries of behaviour expected of the community (hence the dislocation of the Decalogue in Exodus and Deuteronomy). Had the Decalogue been in a fixed form with special status at the time of the editing of 7.1 – 8.3 it would have been cited here. Reventlow treats the instructions in the temple sermon as a *tōrāh* for entry to the temple (cf. Pss. 15; 24.3–6) proclaimed by the prophet speaking as a cult official and using a mixture of priestly and prophetic forms of speech. That analysis is dependent upon Reventlow's interpretation of Jeremiah as a representative of the community figure in the cult. The mixture of forms may lie behind the sermon, but the unit as it now stands is more likely to be directed against a particular ideology of the temple than to be a clarification of the entry requirements for worshippers. This view of the sermon is reinforced by its position at the head of a collection of further criticisms of cultic behaviour (7.16 – 8.3). Taken together these polemical pieces constitute a thoroughgoing critique of Jerusalem's cultic ideology and identify the destruction of the city with false cultic practices accompanied by false ethical attitudes.

The sermon is not a statement against temple worship. The tradition is not at all hostile to cultic practices as such (cf. 17.12) and the use of the Deuteronomistic motif 'this house, which is called by my name' (vv. 10–11; cf. vv. 12, 14) indicates its acknowledgment that the temple belongs to Yahweh. What the critique here does offer is a quite radical account of the relationship between ethics and worship. Unlike the *tōrōt* for entry to the temple (e.g. Ps. 15; 24.3–6), which specify the qualifications of those who wish to gain entrance to the holy place, v. 11 suggests that the temple acquires its status from the quality of the worshippers who gather there. It is but a suggestion, a question raised: 'a cave of robbers has this house become?' But it makes the connection between the worshippers' lives and temple service work in the other direction. The holy place does not save people, but how they live outside the temple gives the holy place its real quality. In typical Deuteronomistic fashion this is to desacralize the temple. It does not confer holiness on people, thereby protecting them, but they can pollute it and render it liable to destruction.

The question behind the speech is 'what provides protection?' (so Volz, 89), hence the declaration in v. 10, 'we are delivered'. In time of trouble turn to Yahweh and all will be well: 'the temple, the temple, the temple'. The final unmasking of the false consciousness behind such a belief comes in vv. 12–14. An analogy is drawn between the fate of the sanctuary at Shiloh (I Sam. 1–4) and the fate of the Jerusalem temple (and city). If Yahweh could destroy his own temple once, he could do it again. Just because it is *his* house does not give it any protected status – it is not a magical entity, and no chants, incantations, formulas or slogans can conceal its vulnerability. When Shiloh was destroyed is debatable (see van Rossum 1970; Pearce 1973; Day 1979), but its destruction in the time of Eli the priest is the point here (coming from the Deuteronomistic history). Shiloh affords a precedent for what will happen to Jerusalem (the use of a precedent also occurs in the narrative account in 26.18). The wickedness of Israel caused the fall of Shiloh then and now the wicked deeds (v. 13, 'all these things', refers to vv. 8–10) of the men of Judah will cause the fall of temple and city. But there is a second charge laid against the community. Not only has it behaved outrageously, it has also rejected the divine word.

The Deuteronomistic theme of the sending of the divine word and its continual rejection by the people occurs in v. 13. Throughout its history the deity has sent that word via the prophets (although they are not referred to in v. 13, it should be understood as the implication of the figure used, cf. v. 25; 25.3–4; 26.5; 29.19; 35.14–15; 44.4), but that word has not been heard. The statement uses a metaphor here (*haškēm wᵉdabbēr*, 'rising early and speaking', cf. also 11.7; 32.33) which is translated variously in EVV (RSV 'persistently', NEB 'I took pains'). The image depicts the deity rising early in the morning to load up the pack animals (*škm* 'to shoulder'): a figure which may convey diligence, intent on getting a particular task done, persistence (cf. 'day after day', v. 25). Its occurrence so frequently in the Jeremiah tradition with reference to Yahweh's activity (apart from

II Chron. 36.15) indicates a distinctive strand of linguistic usage peculiar to the tradition (cf. Weippert 1973, 123–7, for analysis of *škm*). The figure of a deity who rises up early in the morning to send his messengers to his people is a touching one but only a metaphor. Elsewhere in the Bible God sleeps and his worshippers have to urge him to wake up (Ps. 44.23), or he never sleeps and thus protects Israel (Ps. 121.3–4). Each metaphor of sleeping is an image of divine activity or its absence. In the Jeremiah tradition it relates to a history of prophetic activity from the exodus down to the destruction of Jerusalem. It is essentially a prophetic view of history and one that ignores the alternative strand in the tradition which sees the prophets as the people who misled the nation to its doom. The Deuteronomistic view of history as a series of prophetic messengers rejected by the people is used here to explain the destruction of Jerusalem.

The history of not listening and not responding to the divine word comes to an end with the destruction of temple and city (as it is the land which is given to the fathers in v. 7, the land may be referred to in v. 14). What Yahweh gives he can take away: no divine promise is for ever. If the community will not respond regularly to his word, then all previous divine commitments are cancelled (cf. 18.7–9; Isa. 50.2; 65.12; 66.4). So Judah will be cast out just as Ephraim was. The conclusion in v. 15 makes the destruction of Shiloh equivalent to the casting off of Ephraim, and therefore puts it in the period of 722. The history of non-hearing explains the fall of Jerusalem but does not account for the section recommending amendment of life (vv. 3–7). The two sections, admonition and destruction, do not belong together. They are about very different matters. This is not the tension between Yahweh's absolute word of judgment and the conditional possibility of hope (so loved of Buber 1960), but two discrete elements brought together by the editors (cf. Skinner 1922, 170f.). The word of denunciation explains why destruction has befallen Jerusalem; the call to amendment of life is addressed to those of the period after that fall and constitutes 'an earnest exhortation to them that they themselves should live in accordance with the requirements of the Law which would assure them Yahweh's blessing' (Nicholson 1970, 71). Jerusalem fell, but those who survived that fall, and their descendants, needed to be taught the lessons of that fall. Wherein lay security? Not in false beliefs about cultic security but in following a certain ethical way of life. If that conviction also appears false (*šeqer*) to the modern reader, then it is not because of the hermeneutics of suspicion but because Job, Qoheleth and the lament psalms (e.g. Ps. 44.17–22) have exposed it, too, as being ideologically based and therefore capable of becoming *šeqer*.

7.16–20

16 'As for you, do not pray for this people, or lift up cry or prayer for them, and do not intercede with me, for I do not hear you. 17 Do you not see what they are doing in the cities of Judah and in the streets of Jerusalem? 18 The children gather wood, the fathers kindle fire, and the women knead dough, to make cakes for the queen of heaven; and they pour out drink offerings to other gods, to provoke me to anger. 19 Is it I whom they provoke? says the LORD. Is it not themselves, to their own confusion? 20 Therefore thus says the Lord GOD: Behold, my anger and my wrath will be poured out on this place, upon man and beast, upon the trees of the field and the fruit of the ground; it will burn and not be quenched.'

---

[16] Cf. 11.14; 14.11 for comparable prohibitions against prayer. **[18]** Cf. 44.17–19. MT *kawwānīm*, 'cakes' (cf. Akkadian *kamānu*), i.e. cakes bearing the image of the goddess on them (44.19; cf. Rast 1977). MT *limᵉleket haššāmayīm*: G *tē stratia tou ouranou*, 'to the hosts of heaven', but other Greek versions have *tē basilissē*, 'the queen', which suggests that *mlkt* should be vocalized as *malkat*, 'queen' (many mss have *lml'kt*, 'works . . .' = 'hosts of heaven'). **[20]** G lacks *'ᵃdōnāy*, 'lord'.

The second item in the attack on false cultic attitudes and practices singles out the cult of the queen of heaven as the grounds for the destruction of Jerusalem (the 'this place' of v. 20). This is just one particular cult in the more general service of 'other gods' (v. 18). The cult is described in vv. 17–18, and a longer discussion of it appears in 44.15–23 (see on ch. 44). Enveloping the description are divine comments which put the cult into perspective. The introductory prohibition against prayer being made for the people indicates the gravity of the practice about to be described. The 'you' of v. 16 is unspecified but presumably is covered by the editorial 'Jeremiah' of v. 1. The prohibition also appears in 11.14 (context of idolatrous practices) and 14.11 (in a shorter form and different context). Such editorial repetitions present the nation as beyond help. That Jeremiah is represented as an intercessor on behalf of the people who is now not permitted to exercise that role is the conventional interpretation of the triple prohibition. It is based on the view that one of the fundamental roles of a prophet is that of intercession (cf. Gen. 20.7; Amos 7.1–6; Rhodes 1977; Scharbert 1964, 153–224) and that Jeremiah in particular exemplifies that function (cf. Reventlow 1963, 140–205). Yet there are problems with such a viewpoint and there is probably much less to be said about the intercessory role of the prophet than is often imagined (cf. Balentine 1984). In so far as the prophets had such a role it was hardly a routine one, and may have been confined to northern prophets (Balentine 1984, 169–72). Whether 7.16 represents a shift away from such activity (Balentine) or is simply a hyperbolic way of saying that the people are beyond help is difficult to determine. The Deuteronomistic notion of a prophetic figure interceding for the people (I Sam. 7.5–11; 12.19–23) may be behind this prohibition, but it is used in the tradition to underline the wickedness of the nation. The same point is made in 15.1. In v. 13 the nation would never listen to Yahweh; here Yahweh will not listen on their behalf (cf. v. 27).

Prayer, lament, supplication and intercession are all useless because the deity will not hear. The explanation for this refusal to respond to special entreaty is a reference to a popular cult being practised throughout Judah ('cities of Judah . . . streets of Jerusalem', cf. v. 34; 11.6; 33.10; 44.6, 9, 17, 21; a Deuteronomistic phrase, Thiel 1973, 120). It is represented as a family cult: the children collect the firewood, the fathers light the fires, and the women make the dough for turning into cakes. An idyllic picture of egalitarian religion with strong emphasis on the family worshipping together! The cakes have impressed on them the image of the queen of heaven, the mother goddess of the ancient world (so 44.19), or they may be cakes in the shape of a star (cf. Rudolph, 55). The precise identity of the goddess is unknown (various candidates have been suggested: Ishtar, Astarte, Isis, Anat, the goddess of the Venus star), but different names tend to describe the one goddess, whatever her particular cultural manifestation. In this account of the matter (in contrast to 44.15–23) it is presented as a family practice and combined with libations offered to other gods. Such idolatrous cults provoke Yahweh to great anger, though v. 19 suggests that any provocation (to anger, *k's*) is caused to themselves (to their shame). In this sense the worship of false gods humiliates the worshippers (cf. 'to your own hurt', v. 7), because people become like what they worship (Ps. 115.8; 135.18).

Yet it also does anger Yahweh, as the brief oracle in v. 20 asserts. The whole land will burn because of that wrath. In the context of cultic criticisms 'place' (*māqōm*) should indicate 'temple', but here it seems to mean 'land' (cf. v. 17). The influence of 44.22 may account for this conclusion to the unit.

7.21–26

21 Thus says the LORD of hosts, the God of Israel: 'Add your burnt offerings
to your sacrifices, and eat the flesh. 22 For in the day that I brought them
out of the land of Egypt, I did not speak to your fathers or command them
concerning burnt offerings and sacrifice. 23 But this command I gave them,
"Obey my voice, and I will be your God, and you shall be my people; and
walk in all the way that I command you, that it may be well with you." 24
But they did not obey or incline their ear, but walked in their own counsels
and the stubbornness of their evil hearts, and went backwards and not
forward. 25 From the day that your fathers came out of the land of Egypt
to this day, I have persistently sent all my servants the prophets to them,
day after day; 26 yet they did not listen to me, or incline their ear, but
stiffened their neck. They did worse than their fathers.'

---

[22] K *hwsy'*, 'brought out'; Q *hōṣī'i*, 'I brought out'. **[24]** MT *b^emō'ēṣōt bišrirūt libbām*, 'in the counsels of, in the stubbornness of their own minds': the incorporation of a variant into MT; G *enthumēmasin tēs kardias*, 'the schemes of their hearts'. MT addition of *b^emō'eṣōt* may be a gloss influenced by Ps. 81.12 (MT v. 13); so Cornill, cf. BHS. MT *wayyihyū l^e'aḥōr*, 'they were for backwards', some mss *wayyēl^ekū*, 'they went (backwards)'. **[25]** MT 'your fathers'; Vrs 'their . . .'. MT 'to you (I sent . . .)', S 'them'. MT *yōm*, 'today': RSV 'day after day', cf. 25.4, where *yōm* does not appear; S *yōm yōm*, 'day by day'. BHS omits *yōm* as dittography.

There is disagreement among commentators about how the next unit should be divided: 21–26 (cf. Bright), 21–28 (e.g. Rudolph), 21–29 (Thiel). If vv. 21–26 are the divine address to the nation and vv. 27–28 an address to the speaker, it is better to treat them separately in order to emphasize the different features of each speech. It is not an important issue, but may be noted in passing as a point of exegetical decision. The oracular statement (v. 21a) is directed against the sacrificial system and introduced by an ironic command: put your sacrifices together and eat the flesh (cf. Amos 4.4f.). This is not a command to do something illicit, such as eating the holy flesh, but an indication that sacrifice is now no more than a domestic meal. It has no greater significance than eating meat. Such a loss of signification has come about because the people have failed to understand the divine priority of obedience to the word. Obedience, a key concept in Deuteronomistic thought, is primary. Sacrifice is no substitute for obedience and as evidence of this the oracle describes the origins of the nation in terms of the command to obedience rather than to sacrifice. This demand is presented as having been mediated through the prophets from the day of the exodus and equally as having been rejected by the people from that time onwards. The fathers of the nation were commanded to obey Yahweh's voice but disobeyed; later generations also disobeyed and were a stiff-necked people (*wayyaqᵉšû 'et-'orpām*, 'but they stiffened their neck', cf. 17.23; 19.15; *'am-qᵉšeh-'ōrep*, 'a people of stiff neck', i.e. 'a stubborn people', Deut. 9.6, 13; Ex. 32.9; 33.3, 5; 34.9). They were worse than their fathers (v. 26 does not state who 'they' were, but presumably the generation living at the time of the fall of Jerusalem is intended). Although the nation is presented as having been uniformly disobedient, it is still necessary to suggest that one instantiation of it was worse than the others (cf. 3.11). That would explain why it was that only one generation was punished (i.e. the destruction of Jerusalem) rather than each and every generation.

The unit is full of Deuteronomistic phrases and concepts (analysis in Thiel 1973, 121–8) and dominated by the idea of a history of uniform disobedience (cf. 2.5–8). A contrast is set up between sacrifice and obedience which, though representing the Deuteronomistic evaluation of sacrifice as a minor matter (see the place of sacrifice in the Deuteronomic code), is quite problematic. The primary narrative (Genesis – Numbers) presents the exodus story within a predominantly cultic orientated account (e.g. Ex. 19.10–25; 24.3–8; 25–31; 35–40; Lev. 1–16). The place of sacrifice in this presentation is fundamental: 'indeed, under the law almost everything is purified with blood, and without the shedding of blood there is no forgiveness of sins' (Heb. 9.22). How then can the oracle speak of the exodus as a time when Yahweh did *not* speak to or command the fathers concerning burnt offerings and sacrifices? It can do so for a number of reasons. Apart from the inevitable tendentiousness of argument and the Deuteronomistic attitude to sacrifice, two other considerations should be noted. The historical-critical approach to biblical interpretation regards the massively detailed instructions on sacrifice in the primary narrative as being much later than the period into which they are set. In many cases the regulations on sacrifice and its pre-eminence in the life of the community may reflect the cultic arrangements of post-exilic Jerusalem. That would explain why v. 22 claims that sacrifice was not spoken about in the exodus event. A similar denial of the institution of sacrifice in the wilderness period appears in Amos 5.25 and belongs to the Deuteronomistic redaction of the prophets (Schmidt 1965, 188–91). These criticisms of the Jerusalem sacrificial cult (whenever they may be dated) accurately point out that originally such a system was not part of the nation's past. Commentators who prefer to combine the incompatibility of this criticism with the belief that there was such a system instituted by Yahweh at the time of the exodus interpret the statement in v. 22 to refer to the relative importance of sacrifice in comparison to obedience (e.g. Feinberg, 75f.; Thompson, 288). As v. 23 makes clear, obedience was the divine command of the period, not sacrifice. In the Deuteronomistic understanding of the exodus the revelation of *tōrāh* at Sinai is prefaced with a divine statement about obedience (Ex. 19.3b–8, cf. Childs 1974, 360–1). It is part of the Deuteronomistic desacralization of the community's life in order to concentrate its attention on the divine word – an example of the theology of the word rewriting the nation's history. Obedience, not sacrifice, was the original command, and by that standard the nation's history has been one of complete and continual rebellion against Yahweh. Hence its destruction is warranted.

A hostile attitude to sacrifice is evinced in a number of biblical traditions (Isa. 1.11–13; Hos. 6.6; Amos 5.22; Micah 6.6–8). This tendency to disparage the sacrificial cult is limited to editorial or additional sections of these traditions (apart from Hos. 6.6) and should not be interpreted as a major element in the prophetic preaching of ancient Israel. Although Micah 6.7 rejects the fundamental principle of sacrifice, namely the concept of exchange, it is probable that all the other statements represent a rejection of a specific regimen of sacrifice rather than sacrifice *per se*. They are not statements of principle but polemics against the upholders of a system of sacrifice. Because sacrifices are rejected, everything associated with them is also condemned (cf. 6.20; Isa. 66.1–4). Not sacrifice but those who sacrifice are the object of scorn. This interpretation would explain why the rejection of sacrifice appears so often in the editorial additions to various traditions and may even point to the period of editing as the social context of the polemic. In the reconstructed community of Jerusalem during the Persian period fierce polemics abound between different factions (cf. Isa. 56–66; Ezra-Nehemiah), and those who maintained the cult were the object of much criticism. This is the world of partisan politics, and it is unnecessary to deduce from the controversies that the rejection of sacrifice must be entailed by the denunciations of those who offered such things to Yahweh (e.g. Isa. 66.3). The fact that *others* offered sacrifices is sufficient for the speakers to reject those offerings. It is a matter of ideology: correct sacrificial procedure includes ideological purity, and those who were not obedient to the Deuteronomistic rulings were by definition impure and their sacrifices worthless. This ideological perspective is behind the material in 7.1 – 8.3.

The history of the rejection of the divine word mooted in v. 13 is repeated and clarified in v. 25, 'I have persistently sent (*haškēm wᵉšālōaḥ*) all my servants the prophets'. The rising up early and speaking-sending figure, so characteristic of the Jeremiah tradition, has already been explained as a metaphor. Its repetition throughout the Deuteronomistic sections of the tradition makes it a cliché and it may be treated simply as a linguistic trigger of statements about the theology of the word. In this clarification of the term the mode of divine speaking, unspecified in v. 13, is defined as the sending of the prophets. The epithet 'my servants the prophets' is a further characteristic of the Deuteronomistic strand of writing (cf. 26.5; 29.19; 35.15; 44.4; 'his servants', 25.4; also II Kings 9.7; 17.13, 23; 21.10; 24.2; Amos 3.7) and later writings (Ezek. 38.17; Zech. 1.6; Ezra 9.11; Dan. 9.6, 10). It is a tendentious view of history in terms of the prophets as spokesmen-messengers sent constantly to the nation to deliver Yahweh's word. The rejection of that word from the very exodus (a belief in conflict with 2.2) presents Israel's history as one of continual opposition to the word. Thus the Deuteronomistic theology of the word (hence their interest in and editing of prophetic traditions) is the ideology shaping much of the material in Jeremiah. Yet it is not the only shaping ideology behind the tradition because its curious view of 'my-his servants the prophets' contradicts the anti-prophets strand also to be found in the book (see on 23.9–40). One strand (typified by Lam. 2.14) blames the prophets for what happened (they misled the people), another blames the people for not listening to the prophets. Separate strands, no doubt, but capable of confusing the intelligent reader into making equivocal interpretations.

7.27–28

27 'So you shall speak all these words to them, but they will not listen to you. You shall call to them, but they will not answer you. 28 And you shall say to them, "This is the nation that did not obey the voice of the LORD their God, and did not accept discipline; truth has perished; it is cut off from their lips." '

---

[27] G 'and you will speak this word to them', followed by v. 28 without the MT introductory phrase 'and you shall say to them'. **[28]** S only has 'truth has perished; it is cut off from their lips'. MT *'āb^{e}dāh ha'^{e}mūnāh w^{e}nikr^{e}tāh mippīhem*, 'truth has perished, cut off from their lips', could be a snatch of poetry (treated as such by Bright, Thompson).

An editorial comment provides instructions for the delivery of 'all these words' (presumably 21–26 if not the previous two units) and the reactions of the people to them (cf. 16.10 for a similar treatment of material). The people will not listen to the speaker (Jeremiah as in v. 1?), but then as they have not listened to Yahweh (v. 13), why should the messenger receive any different response? The unit is shaped by v. 13 and demonstrates its truth by having the speaker ignored. Hence the verdict of v. 28: 'this is the nation . . .'. Its refusal to obey is the equivalent of not receiving instruction or discipline (cf. 17.23; 33.32; 35.13). Presumably *mūsār*, 'discipline', here means the Deuteronomistic interpretation of history (cf. Deut. 11.2), i.e. the explanation of events occurring in the life of the community as Yahweh's positive or negative treatment of the nation (cf. 2.30; 5.3). However, as there is no reference to any such events here, *mūsār* may just function as a Deuteronomistic cliché accompanying the statement about the people not obeying the divine word. A brief poetic fragment concludes the verdict on the people: 'truth (*'^{e}mūnāh*) has perished, cut off from their mouth'. It hardly fits the context, but ancient editorial methods use such devices without too much concern for appropriateness of fit. Originally it may have been a statement about people who no longer told the truth (cf. 9.3), but here it is simply one more phrase dismissing the nation as obdurate. The term *'ᵉmūnāh* can mean 'fidelity, faithfulness' (cf. Hab. 2.4), but 'truth' is better in this context because it is a reference to something gone from their mouths. They no longer speak the truth. In 5.1 it had been impossible to find in Jerusalem society one person who practised true religion or sought truth, hence the verdict here 'truth is perished'. Within the context of 7.1 – 8.3 'truth' may be more constrained than in the original poem, having as its meaning a view of cultic matters akin to Deuteronomistic ideology. By such a standard the nation was gravely defective and insensitive to instruction (a point made more clearly in the other references to the refusal to accept discipline).

7.29

' "Cut off your hair and cast it away;
raise a lamentation on the bare heights,
for the LORD has rejected and forsaken
the generation of his wrath." '

MT *gāzzī nizrēk*, 'cut off your hair': *nēzer*, 'crown, consecration, Naziriteship', cf. Num. 6.19 ' . . . upon the hands of the Nazirite, after he has shaven *the hair of his consecration (nizrō)*'. Symm *tēn komēn tēn hagian tēs naziraiotētos sou*, 'the sacred hair of your naziriteship', cf. NEB, 'cut off your hair, the symbol of your dedication'; Rudolph, 'your long hair'. MT *'al-šᵉpāyīm*, 'on the bare heights'; G *epi cheilōn*, 'on your lips', cf. 3.21. MT *'et-dōr 'ebrātō*, 'the generation of his anger': G *tēn genean tēn poiousan tauta*, 'the generation which does these things' (= Aramaic *'ābād dᵉnāh*, cf. 33.6; BHS).

This brief poem could be a conclusion to vv. 27–28 or the beginning of vv. 30–34 (cf. Isbell and Jackson 1980), but I take it as one more fragment which has been introduced editorially in the transition from vv. 21–26 to vv. 30–34. Treated as one of the editorial fragments which the history of the text has incorporated into the text (note G on 27–28a) and as isolated from vv. 28, 30, it may be allowed to conclude and introduce what precedes and follows it. The community which has failed to grasp Yahweh's discipline is a doomed one and the society which indulges itself in the terrible rites described in v. 31 is a place of death. Funeral lamentation is in order.

The feminine figure addressed in the poem is the city Jerusalem (cf. NEB, 'O Jerusalem'). She is depicted as a woman who now must cut off her long hair in mourning for the death of her people (cf. 6.26; 31.15). The dirge (*qīnāh*) must be lifted up on the bare heights – Jerusalem has become a mourning woman (cf. 9.17) and must seek out the hills and there mourn the loss of her children (cf. Judg. 11.37–38 for weeping in the mountains). The cause of this funeral dirge is Yahweh's rejection of the people; he has forsaken 'the generation of his wrath'. His anger has devastated the community to the point that Jerusalem is a woman shorn of her hair wailing for the dead. The people who experienced the Babylonian onslaught and the destruction of the city were a generation *constituted* by divine anger.

7.30–34

30 'For the sons of Judah have done evil in my sight, says the LORD; they have set their abominations in the house which is called by my name, to defile it. 31 And they have built the high place of Topheth, which is in the valley of the son of Hinnom, to burn their sons and their daughters in the fire; which I did not command, nor did it come into my mind. 32 Therefore, behold, the days are coming, says the LORD, when it will no more be called Topheth, or the valley of the son of Hinnom, but the valley of Slaughter: for they will bury in Topheth, because there is no room elsewhere. 33 And the dead bodies of this people will be food for the birds of the air, and for the beasts of the earth; and none will frighten them away. 34 And I will make to cease from the cities of Judah and from the streets of Jerusalem the voice of mirth and the voice of gladness, the voice of the bridegroom and the voice of the bride; for the land shall become a waste.'

---

[30] MT *n'wm* should be *n'm*. **[31–33]** Cf. 19.5–7. **[31]** MT *ūbānū*, 'and they will build': probably *wayyibᵉnū*, 'and they built', as in 32.35, or delete *ū* as dittography of previous letter. MT *bāmōt*, 'high places': G sing. (*bōmon*) as required by place name Topheth. MT *hattōpet*: G *Taphet*; original form may have been *tepet* (Rudolph), but *tpt* supplied with vowels of *bōšet*, 'shame', to indicate disapproval of practice. MT *ṣiwwītī*, 'I commanded'; G 'commanded them'. **[32]** MT *hahᵃrēgāh*, 'slaughter'; G *anērēmenon*, 'slain'. **[34]** G 'the *whole* land shall become a desert'.

Dirge rather than prayer is raised for the nation (vv. 16, 29) and a number of fragments (30, 31–32, 33–34) set out further causes for that lamentation. In the first fragment the sons of Judah are accused of having set 'abominations' (*šiqqūṣīm*) in the temple. These are probably cult objects (Thompson) of a kind disapproved of by the Deuteronomists (they are referred to in 4.1; 13.27; 16.18; 32.34). They are not identified here or in any of the references in Jeremiah, but clearly refer to objects regarded as unclean or illicit by priestly or ideological standards (cf. Lev. 7.21; 11.10–12; Deut. 7.26; Ezek. 5.11; 7.20; Dan. 9.27; 11.31; 12.11). Some commentators have seen here a reference to the cult objects set up by Manasseh (II Kings 21.1–15) or, in view of Josiah's destruction of such things (II Kings 23.4–20), the resurrection of such articles by Jehoiakim. Whatever the way *šiqqūṣīm* is used in the tradition, it is a term of abuse freely employed against a much disliked cultic community (e.g. 32.33–35 is a variation of 7.28, 30–31) and therefore may not have very much specific meaning. The picture of the temple depicted in Ezek. 8 suggests that Josiah's reform had no effect at all on Jerusalem's cultic life and raises the question whether 'reform' is the right word for the Deuteronomistic story of Josiah (II Kings 22–23). However, that is too controversial and difficult a matter to resolve here (see Hoffmann 1980; Smith 1975). The image in v. 30 of a temple with idols in it (in 16.18 it is the land which is filled with such detestable things) is hardly in keeping with the sermon in vv. 2–7. However, the theme holding the fragments together is that of pagan practices, so the mention of the defiling of the temple by such detestable things is appropriate here.

A second piece focuses on a cultic practice outside Jerusalem in the valley of ben Hinnom (see on 19.5–7). A high place has been built south-west of Jerusalem, and there the people burn their sons and daughters (to Baal according to 19.5; 32.35). This place, Tophet (a form indicating strong disapproval), appears to have housed a fire cult where children were offered 'in the fire' to nature gods. This fire cult demanded human sacrifice and may have been associated with the astral powers (attacked in the next unit 8.1–3; cf. Koch 1983, 46–51). Because of the horrific practices out in the valley at this fire-place (Aramaic *tĕpat*) there will come a time when the valley will be renamed to match its fate as one huge burial ground. It will become such a grave 'because there is no room elsewhere' (v. 32 *mē'ēn māqōm* is ambiguous): either because everywhere else will also be full of corpses (unlikely) or until it, Tophet, has no more room left for burial (Bright). Whatever the cult may have celebrated, it will become the place of the dead.

The account of the fire cult at Tophet is not an easy unit to understand. The cult is not described but abused and condemned. There is some evidence in the ancient world for cults of human sacrifice, but it should not be assumed that the abuse of opponents necessarily is to be taken literally (*contra* Koch 1983, 49). Writings influenced by the Deuteronomists have a tendency to substitute abuse for argument and contempt for description. Nowhere is this tendency more at work than in the imputation to their opponents of practising child sacrifice in the valley or in the city of Jerusalem (cf. II Kings 16.3; 17.17; 21.6; 23.10; II Chron. 33.6). The polemics against the community in Jeremiah and Ezekiel (16.20–21; 20.26, 31; 23.37, 39) also make such accusations, and in stronger language. The technical phrase used in the Deuteronomistic history is *ha'ᵃbīr* (or various Hiphil forms of *'br*), 'cause to pass through', and may have the force of 'dedicate' in the context of fire cults. Passing children through the fire was probably some form of dedication service whereby they were offered symbolically to the god and then received back into the community. The prohibition against the practice in Lev. 18.21, given its context of forbidden sexual practices, may indicate the sexual nature of some of the forms and possibly the dedication of children to prostitution (cf. Weinfeld 1972b). It has also been suggested that the Molech cult involved the sacrifice of newborn children which were the result of cultic prostitution (Elliger 1955; Zimmerli 1979, 344, 411f.; Eichrodt 1970, 270–3). If the references in the Deuteronomistic history can be translated to describe a non-lethal fire cult involving dedication (whether to the god, prostitution or whatever), the statements in Jeremiah and Ezekiel assert that the children were burned (*liśrōp*, 'to burn', 7.31; 19.5), slaughtered (Ezek. 16.21; 23.39) or sacrificed as food (Ezek. 16.20; 23.37). From *rite de passage* to ritual slaughter, the biblical writers appear to have combined a number of discrete notions in their attack on the practices of pre-catastrophe Jerusalem. It may be the case that two very different cults have been confused in the polemics in Jeremiah and Ezekiel: a divinatory fire cult of Molech which did not involve child sacrifice and a common Canaanite cult of child sacrifice (so Cogan 1974, 77–83). A metaphorical expression for the dedication of children to a god (Adad according to Weinfeld 1969) has become, under the impetus of hostility towards the community of the past, a pejorative description of great evil. The original practice may not have been theologically licit from the

Deuteronomistic viewpoint, but it was hardly as harmful as portrayed in Jeremiah and Ezekiel. A purification rite has been turned into a pollution ritual causing great harm to city and land. This is an ironic reversal, but characteristic of propaganda in the Bible. Whatever the crimes of old Jerusalem may have been, it would be wise not to impute to it such fiendish practices as the burning to death of children in the service of pagan gods (on the correct understanding of 'passing children through fire' see Carroll 1981, 303–4; Gaster 1969, 586–8; Snaith 1966, 123–4; cf. McKay 1973, 39–41 for the 'sacrifice by burning' viewpoint).

The fire cult in the valley is described as a practice not commanded by Yahweh, one which never occurred to him (v. 31b; even more strongly denied in 19.5b). Why such stress on the lack of warrants for the cult? It suggests that a divine command was regarded as the authority for such practices, so that this denial is an attempt to combat an alternative explanation. That Yahweh should order the burning of children (to keep to the text of 7.31–32) is not as inconceivable as some commentators appear to imagine. The exchange of ideas about what Yahweh requires in Micah 6.6–8 allows the possibility that he might demand human sacrifice but counters it by rejecting the principle of such exchange. The story of Abraham's attempt to offer Isaac as a sacrifice (Gen. 22) makes that endeavour obedience to a divine command. Yahweh was also believed to require the firstborn of people and animals (Ex. 22.29–30; 13.1–2, 11–16) and failure to slaughter people designated for killing by the deity could be a serious offence (cf. I Sam. 15.1–3, 8–33). Ezekiel specifically states that Yahweh gave the people statutes which were not good and ordinances by which they could not live and defiled them by making them pass their children (through the fire? 20.25–26). So what is not commanded by Yahweh in Jer. 7.31 is regarded as a divine action in Ezek. 20.26. Clearly, whatever the practice may have been, divine commands played some part in the matter. The formal contradiction between the different accounts in Jeremiah and Ezekiel should underline the relative nature of the arguments in the different traditions. The Deuteronomists are at pains to persuade the community that such cults do not have Yahweh's approval; the Ezekiel tradition develops the matter in the direction of aversion therapy. It is ironic that in a chapter about disobedience there should be a reference to a cult where participation in it was believed to be *obedience* to a divine command! A further irony, though not the responsibility of the editors, lies in the fact that later generations were to turn the linguistic element 'valley of Hinnom' (*gē' hinnōm*, NT Greek *geenna*, 'Gehenna') into a synonym for hell. The transformation may perhaps be appropriate but theologically it is ironic: for many who would condemn human beings for burning their children would also praise god for burning his children for ever!

The last element in the unit depicts the fate of city and land: bodies without burial (in contrast to Tophet) constituting food for the birds and beasts. All human activity will cease from Judah and Jerusalem (cf. 16.9) and the land will become a desert. This is a dreadful picture of the consequences of cultic misconceptions and malpractices (reversed in 33.10–11).

8.1–3

81 'At that time, says the LORD, the bones of the kings of Judah, the bones
of its princes, the bones of the priests, the bones of the prophets, and the
bones of the inhabitants of Jerusalem shall be brought out of their tombs;
2 and they shall be spread before the sun and the moon and all the host of
heaven, which they have loved and served, which they have gone after, and
which they have sought and worshipped; and they shall not be gathered or
buried; they shall be as dung on the surface of the ground. 3 Death shall be
preferred to life by all the remnant that remains of this evil family in all the
places where I have driven them, says the LORD of hosts.'

---

[1] K *wysy'w*; Q *yōṣī'u*, 'shall be brought out'. **[3]** MT repeats *hanniš'ārīm*, 'who remain', after 'in every place'; EVV all omit. G lacks 'says Yahweh of hosts'.

The section concludes with a sarcastic reflection on the burial theme introduced by vv. 32–33. In v. 32 there is burial in Tophet to such an extent that the place is turned into one large grave; in v. 33 dead bodies lie everywhere so there is no burial; and now in 8.1 there is unburial. The bones of all the great citizens and the other inhabitants are brought out of their tombs and spread out on the ground like manure. This motif of dead bodies or bones spread out as dung occurs a number of times in the tradition (*dōmen* 9.22; 16.4; 25.33; cf. II Kings 9.37; Ps. 83.10). It contrasts the fate of the long dead with those in 7.33 whose unburied corpses provide food for birds and beasts (in 16.4 both motifs, dung and food, are used to describe the fate of the dead). In a period of widespread death the treatment of the corpses is indicative of the community's dishonourable ways. Even those who died before the invading armies humiliated the city will share in this fate. Their bones will be spread out in full view of the sun, moon and stars ('host of heaven') and in this grotesque posture they will continue to worship those they loved when alive. Irony and sarcasm are at work in this ghoulish picture. Those who do the bringing out of the bones are presumably the invaders, hence the image must be seen as hyperbole. Invaders are hardly likely to waste their time plundering the family tombs in order to display the bones; though the unit may represent a fanciful explanation of why the tombs were disturbed. Grave robbing is an ancient custom and a good source of acquired wealth: invasions provide ample opportunity for such plundering and the unit may well be a reflection on the practice with a Deuteronomistic interpretation attached. In this sense the verses should be viewed as coming from a period after the fall of Jerusalem (contrary to the view expressed by some commentators that they must pre-date that fall because in the event the bones were not exposed).

The reason for this dishonouring of the dead (for dishonouring dead kings see on 22.19) is given as the community's involvement in astral cults. The MT of 7.18 condemns this practice (probably a specific 'queen of heaven' astral cult), but here it is the generality of worship offered to the heavenly bodies that is condemned. Those who survive the destruction of the period and who are driven away from Jerusalem (an implicit contrast between *māqōm*, 'the place', i.e. city, temple, land, and *mᵉqōmōt*, 'the places', i.e. all other places) will be worse off than the dead. They will envy the dead. Hence deportation will be an even worse fate for the survivors of the invasion (contrast 29.1–9). The community is described as 'this evil family' (v. 3) and in its extended sense it covers the generations of the dead (now exposed to the elements and before the sun, moon and stars) and those deported. With this grim picture of the miserable living and the dishonoured dead the collection of pieces hostile to the community's cultic attitudes and practices concludes.

7.1 – 8.3 combines a number of reflections on cultic matters in Jerusalem and its environs. Starting off with the crowds flocking to the temple in Jerusalem, it finishes with images of the ground covered in corpses and the survivors driven away to alien parts. Silence and desolation cover the temple mount, and the fate of that shrine indicates the incorrectness of the worship offered there. That progression from crowds to corpses apart, there is no real progress in the collection. It is made up of discrete units and put together because of its common focus on cultic practices. 'Section by section, in a downward spiral, the various improper forms of religious practice upon which the people in their perversity have relied are chronicled and even parodied. Beginning with Temple worship, which above all would have been deemed acceptable, the passage as a whole winds swiftly down . . . to the point of the basest possible kind of idolatry, worship of the creature rather than the Creator' (Isbell and Jackson 1980, 26). This is to overstate the degree of development between the units. All the abuses of the collection are delineated in 7.9, and so there is no progress from bad to worse. The rottenness of the worshipping community is to be found in the temple of Yahweh in Jerusalem as much as in the valley of ben Hinnom. The corpses that are strewn about the place in 8.1–2 reflect the murdered in the streets of Jerusalem. The families who gaily celebrate the queen of heaven and her cult of family religion (a development from the feminine cult of 44.15) are the families who burn their children in the valley. Those who readily bring sacrifices to Yahweh are the ones who refuse to hear the word of Yahweh mediated by his prophets. Each practice condemned exposes the community as the generation of Yahweh's wrath. Everything is false: temple worship, family religion, sacrifice and the fire cult. False ideology and attitudes warp the nation's understanding of Yahweh, hence 'the land shall become a waste'. All the social celebrations of marriages which are the basis for the production of families will be cut off from the streets of Jerusalem. In the nation's cultic life can be seen the justification for the destruction of Judah. Such is the force of the collection in 7.1 – 8.3, and it offers one more variation on the theme of why Jerusalem and Judah were destroyed. 'Wherein is security to be found?' – not in temple, sacrifice or service of Yahweh, but only in obedience to the word proclaimed.

8.4–7

4 'You shall say to them, Thus says the LORD:
When men fall, do they not rise again?
If one turns away, does he not return?

5 Why then has this people turned away
in perpetual backsliding?
They hold fast to deceit,
they refuse to return.
6 I have given heed and listened,
but they have not spoken aright;
no man repents of his wickedness,
saying, "What have I done?"
Every one turns to his own course,
like a horse plunging headlong into battle.
7 Even the stork in the heavens
knows her times;
and the turtledove, swallow, and crane
keep the time of their coming;
but my people know not
the ordinance of the LORD.'

---

[4] MT 'and you will say to them', lacking in G. It is a redactional introduction linking the poem with the speaker. **[5]** MT *šōbᵉbāh hā'ām hazzeh yᵉrūšālem*, '. . . this people slid back Jerusalem . . .', read *šōbab hā'ām hazzeh*; MT includes a variant reading, hence *šbbh*. G lacks 'Jerusalem'. **[6]** G plur. forms of *qšb*, *šm'*, 'give heed and hear' (imperatives). K *bmrṣwtm*, Q *bimrūṣātām*, 'in their own courses'; G sing. Driver 1937–38, 105, prefers to take *šab*, 'turns', from *šīb*, 'run about', rather than *šūb*, 'turn'. **[7]** MT *ḥᵃsīdāh . . . tōr . . . sīs* (K *sws*) . . . *'āgūr*: all names of birds but difficult to match with English names (see EVV).

A poem about the people's turning away from Yahweh to their own ways. An editorial introduction makes it a statement addressed to the people. The use of *šūb*, 'turn', in the tradition is seen at its best in vv. 4b–5:

> If one turns away (*yāšūb*) . . . one returns (*yāšūb*) . . . turned away (*šōbāb*) . . . backsliding (*mᵉšubāh*) . . . to return (*lāšūb*).

Such word-play allows a contrast to be made between normal human behaviour and the state of the nation. Its turning away and refusal to turn back is unnatural. This kind of argument, apart from the rhetorical questions of v. 4b, is also found in 5.1–3 (both poems use the same phrase *mē'ᵃnū lāšūb*, 'they refuse to turn'). The unnaturalness of the community's behaviour (cf. 5.21–25) is argued from the behaviour of birds. A number of migratory birds are named as examples of creatures which know (instinctively) when to fly away and when to return. In contrast to these, Yahweh's people do not know his ordinance (*mišpāṭ* as in 5.4–5). Here 'ordinance' must mean 'Yahweh's set pattern of life for the community'. In contrast to the movements of instinctive behaviour, the community's actions are like that of a horse plunging, out of control, into battle. It is the opposite of orderly behaviour. What is worse, nobody in the community is aware of what he is doing. None acknowledges wrongdoing or turns from it (cf. 2.35; 5.24).

8.8–9

8 'How can you say, "We are wise,
and the law of the LORD is with us"?
But, behold, the false pen of the scribes
has made it into a lie.
9 The wise men shall be put to shame,
they shall be dismayed and taken;
lo, they have rejected the word of the LORD,
and what wisdom is in them?'

---

[8] MT *'āśāh*, 'has made'; EVV presuppose a mappiq in *h*, hence *'āśāh*, 'has made *it*'. **[9]** MT *w^ehokmat-meh lāhem*, 'and wisdom what (is it) to them?'; BHS, following Ehrlich 1912, 264, Volz, reads *ḥokmātām*, 'their wisdom' (*m* lost by haplography).

An independent piece attacking the wise men follows the condemnation of the nation for not knowing Yahweh's *mišpāṭ*. Perhaps it is intended as a response to the assertion of v. 7, but it is really about a different matter. It is an attack on the *tōrāh* of the wise, rather than about the people's knowledge of the divine order of things. It posits an assertion (presumably by the wise, but the imaginary speakers are not identified) of wisdom because Yahweh's *tōrāh* is possessed by the group. But this claim to wisdom is dismissed because it is based on a false (*šeqer*) *tōrāh*. The *tōrāh* is false in the sense of having been falsified by the scribal activity which produced it (both *tōrāh* and the scribes' pen are qualified by the term *šeqer*, 'false'). What precisely this means is not clear from the text. The *tōrāh* may be false because it is written, or because this particular group's scribal activities have somehow made it false. Whether by interpretation, additions or commentary can only be speculated about. What the *tōrāh* may be is also not stated, but we must imagine a situation in which there may have been rival groups, each with its own *tōrāh*, in conflict. This then is a partisan statement on behalf of the divine word (v. 9) against the written *tōrāh* of the wise men. As one stratum in society (cf. 18.18), the wise men had their own divine *tōrāh* (the claim made for their document is that it is *tōrat yhwh*, 'Yahweh's law'). Whatever the exact details of the conflict may be, it is clearly a quarrel about the respective merits of a written divine *tōrāh* and the spoken word of Yahweh (told from only one side!). Because the wise men's *tōrāh* is false (*šeqer*), they will be put to shame when the invasion occurs and will be captured by the enemy. Having rejected Yahweh's word, what possible wisdom could they have?

The short poem is deceptively simple in appearance, but so underdetermined is its meaning that a great deal may be written about it without any certitude of its meaning. All the terms used are clear and there are no difficult or obscure words, but what does the poem mean? The simplest way to understand it is to treat it as a straightforward ideological clash between a written *tōrāh* and the spoken word. It is an attack on the attitude that possession of the divine *tōrāh* in written form is the basis of wisdom (cf. Deut. 4.6). To the written law it opposes the spoken word, and where these are in conflict then the spoken word of Yahweh is the final arbiter of opinion. What is meant by the statement, 'they have rejected the word of Yahweh' is not stated, so the poem has to be understood in this very general way (see on 11.1–13; cf. Friedman 1981, 71–5 for 8.8 as an attack on alternative priestly *tōrōt*).

Commentators have seen in this attack on wisdom an attack on the circles which produced Deuteronomy and a rejection of the way wisdom thought has manipulated the divine law (discussion in McKane 1965, 102–12). The Deuteronomic movement certainly fused wisdom and law as the product of the wisdom schools' appropriation of religious instruction (cf. Weinfeld 1972a), but the extent to which 8.8 should be seen as an attack on that phenomenon is dependent upon prior views about the relation of the Deuteronomic code to Josiah's reform (cf. Skinner 1922, 89–107). The principle of a written *tōrāh* of Yahweh is called in question by v. 8, and this may be extended to include Deuteronomy (or any such written *tōrāh*), but it cannot be established from vv. 8–9 that Deuteronomy is the target of these remarks. Without access to the larger discussion, of which

8–9 may be a part, only the principle expressed in the poem may be taken as the meaning of the unit. Those who control the *tōrāh* have made it false (cf. 2.8 'those who handle *tōrāh* do not know me') and are counted as having rejected the divine word. The attack on the written *tōrāh* should be associated with the rejection of other forms of false security in the community (e.g. temple, priests, prophets). Security is not even to be found in the possession of Yahweh's *tōrāh*. Only the spoken word of Yahweh can provide that possibility of wisdom. How ironic, then, that the spoken word should eventually be turned into writing (36.2).

8.10–12

10 'Therefore I will give their wives to others
and their fields to conquerors,
because from the least to the greatest
every one is greedy for unjust gain;
from prophet to priest
every one deals falsely.
11 They have healed the wound of my people lightly,
saying, "Peace, peace,"
when there is no peace.
12 Were they ashamed when they committed abomination?
No, they were not at all ashamed;
they did not know how to blush.
Therefore they shall fall among the fallen;
when I punish them, they shall be overthrown,
says the LORD.'

8.10–12 is a variant of 6.12–15; for Notes see on 6.12–15.

Minor variations apart, this poem also appears in 6.12–15, and its occurrence in two different parts of the tradition indicates the stereotypical nature of its contents. To priest and prophet may now be added wise man ('a word to the wise'!) as victims of the misfortunes of invasion. The generality of the criticisms gives little indication about what the various social strata are guilty of, but assigns them all a place in the divine visitation against the community.

8.13

'When I would gather them, says the LORD,
there are no grapes on the vine,
nor figs on the fig tree;
even the leaves are withered,
and what I gave them has passed away from them.'

MT *'āsōp 'ᵃsīpēm* allows a confusion between *'sp*, 'gather', and *sūp*, 'make and end of, consume' (cf. AV, RSV): word-play using assonance can be too clever. Commentators tend to revocalize to *'e'ᵉsōp 'ᵃsīpēm*, 'I will gather their harvest', cf. G 'they shall gather their produce' or *'āsōp 'ōsᵉpēm*, 'I will thoroughly harvest them', or even *'ᵉsōp 'sīpām*, 'gather their harvest'. MT *wa'etēn lāhem ya'abrūm*, 'and I gave to them they shall pass them': obscure, lacking in G. A later marginal note according to Duhm; Bright leaves blank; NEB omits; Volz treats as a fragment relating to Yahweh's *tōrāh* (for other views see commentaries). Aberbach 1977 redivides *y'brwm* as *y'r 'rwm*, 'naked forest', cf. Ps. 29.9. BHS *mᵉba'ᵃrūm*, '(I gave them) destroyers and they have destroyed them'; Driver 1937–38, 105 *wᵉ'etnēm lᵉmab'ērāh*, 'and I will give them to be burned'; DeRoche 1980a is happy with MT which he regards as a variation on Zeph. 1.2–3 and refuses to emend the text: 'In-gathering I shall destroy them . . . I gave to them, they pass by them.' On Zeph.1.2–3 cf. DeRoche 1980b.

DeRoche 1980a

Commentators disagree on whether v. 13 should be treated with what precedes it (e.g. Reventlow 1963, 190) or what follows it (e.g. Rudolph). By making it the answer to the question in v. 9, Duhm links it to the preceding discussion (with vv. 10–12, unlike Reventlow's view, as an interpolation). Volz's treatment of vv. 13–17 as fragments makes better sense of the text. It is therefore taken as a fragment here and its position after vv. 10–12 may be accounted for in terms of an editing process similar to 6.9–15, where an individual verse about grape-picking introduces a section not unlike 8.8–12, but with the grape-picking verse concluding the unit.

The imagery used is that of Yahweh as harvester picking grapes and figs (see on 6.9) but finding no harvest. Even the leaves are withered and the task is futile. There will be no harvest this year (cf. v. 20). It is a tragic picture, representing the community as a barren place incapable of producing fruit and therefore as good for nothing.

The image here may be behind the NT parable of the man who planted a fig tree in his vineyard (Luke 13.6–9, but cf. Matt. 21.18–20; Mark 11.20–21). The gloss at the end of the verse may be a reference to the destruction of the community for its uselessness, but is too obscure in its present condition for certainty of meaning. DeRoche's treatment of the text as a variation on Zeph. 1.2–3 and linking both texts with Gen. 1.29, with Zech. 3.10 reversing the Jeremiah text, is too subtle a treatment of this fragmentary statement. The vineyard as an image of Israel is a familiar one in the Hebrew Bible (e.g. 2.21; 5.10; 6.9; Isa. 5.1–7; Hos. 9.10; 10.1), but most of the occurrences of the figure are critical assessments of the performance of that enterprise. As a vineyard Judah-Jerusalem is a miserable failure.

8.14–15

14 Why do we sit still?
Gather together, let us go into the fortified cities
and perish there;
for the Lord our God has doomed us to perish,
and has given us poisoned water to drink,
because we have sinned against the Lord.
15 We looked for peace, but no good came,
for a time of healing, but behold, terror.

---

[14] MT 'we have sinned against Yahweh': G 'against him'; cf. 14.20b. **[15]** = 14.19b.

A fragment put in the mouth of the people as a response to the invading armies. Volz takes it with v. 16, making the unit vv. 14, 16, but the stance of the speaker is somewhat different in v. 16 (cf. 'let us go into the fortified cities . . . they come and devour . . . the city and those who dwell in it'), so the two verses should be treated as independent units. The last clause of 14 and v. 15 are an addition to the fragment from the confession of sin in 14.19b, 20b (see on 14.19–22).

A sense of despair is conveyed by v. 14 and continues the depressing tone of v. 13. In despair the peasants in the fields gather up their stuff (*hēʾāspū*, 'gather together', links 14 with 13 by association of *ʾsp*, 'gather') and reluctantly retreat to the fortified cities in order to die there. This devastating prospect has come about because Yahweh has silenced the people (*h^a^dimmānū*, 'he has silenced us', i.e. 'caused us to perish'). A different figure is then used to assert this point. Yahweh has given them 'a draught of bitter poison' (NEB; *mē-rō'š*, cf. 9.15; 23.15; a potion made from a poisonous plant, cf. McKane 1980b). This may just be a specific figure for a deadly situation, but a number of commentators have seen in it an allusion to the trial by ordeal (Num. 5.11–31) whereby the suspected unfaithful wife must drink waters of bitterness to test her fidelity (e.g. Rudolph, Duhm). The cup of the wine of Yahweh's wrath (25.15) may also be behind this reference (so Duhm, 91; McKane 1980b, 491). If this understanding of the metaphor is correct, then the people must die because they have failed the test of fidelity to Yahweh (hence the confession which follows). Here fidelity is hardly a reference to adultery but to apostasy. Having demonstrated their guilt the people must resign themselves to death and so, gathering together (cf. 10.17 for a similar figure but with a different significance), they shuffle off to the cities to die there.

The confessional statements which follow indicate an awareness of having sinned against Yahweh: the outcome of the ordeal was terror rather than healing, disaster rather than *šālōm*. Although they belong to the liturgy of confession in 14.7–9, 19–22, the presence of such comments here should warn against accepting the rhetoric of the people's incorrigibility at face value. Whatever the origin and setting of such confessions, the community (of any period) could hardly have been as obtusely wicked as presented in the tradition.

8.16–17

16 'The snorting of their horses is heard from Dan;
at the sound of the neighing of their stallions
the whole land quakes.
They come and devour the land and all that fills it,
the city and those who dwell in it.
17 For behold, I am sending among you serpents,
adders which cannot be charmed,
and they shall bite you,'
says the LORD.

[17] G lacks 'says Yahweh'. Reventlow 1963, 139n., finds a word-play in *ṣip'ōnīm*, 'adders', on *ṣāpōn*, 'north' (implicit in the poem about invaders). The first word in MT of v. 18, *mablīgītī*, is incomprehensible. If the consonants are redivided with emendation to *mibbᵉlī gᵉhōt*, 'without healing', and the phrase transferred to the end of v. 17, good sense is achieved, cf. BHS: '(they shall bite you) beyond recovery' i.e. 'fatally' (Bright); cf. G *aniata*, 'incurably'.

An element of the enemy from the north motif appears in v. 16. The invading army is heard in the region of Dan in the north and comes from there through the land to destroy the city and its inhabitants (a probable reference to Jerusalem, though *'īr*, 'city', may be in apposition to *'ereṣ*, 'land'). The whole land quakes at the sound of its horses, a quaking which may point to the later development of the enemy from the north motif in the direction of the final shaking of the world at the return of chaos (Childs 1959).

To this fragment is added a divine oracle (editorially indicated as such in MT). Poisonous snakes are being sent against 'you' (presumably the nation). These are not snakes which can be charmed (cf. Eccles. 10.11), there is no magic against this type of disaster (cf. Isa. 47.11–12). The poison of these snakes has no antidote; it is incurable, and when the people are bitten there will be no healing for them. The venomous snakes image is not the same as the poisoned drink of v. 14, but the editors may have linked these two fragments together because of a general similarity of ideas. They parallel one another but use very different metaphors and offer a number of reflections on the falsity of the claim expressed in v. 11 (*šālōm, šālōm*).

8.18–9.1

18 My grief is beyond healing,
   my heart is sick within me.
19 Hark, the cry of the daughter of my people
   from the length and breadth of the land:
 'Is the LORD not in Zion?
   Is her King not in her?
 Why have they provoked me to anger with their graven images,
   and with their foreign idols?
20 The harvest is past, the summer is ended,
   and we are not saved.'

21 For the wound of the daughter of my people is my heart wounded,
I mourn, and dismay has taken hold on me.
22 Is there no balm in Gilead?
Is there no physician there?
Why then has the health of the daughter of my people
not been restored?
9[1] O that my head were waters,
and my eyes a fountain of tears,
that I might weep day and night
for the slain of the daughter of my people!

---

[18] As the first word has been transferred to v. 17, MT now reads *'ālay* (*'ālāh* or *ya'aleh*) *yāgōn 'ālay*, 'grief has overcome me', and the repunctuated MT *libbī dawwāy*, 'my heart is sick', cf. BHS, Bright. **[19]** MT *mē'ereṣ marḥaqqīm*, 'from a land of distances', i.e. 'a distant land', cf. NEB. The phrase occurs in Isa. 33.17 where it means 'a land that stretches afar' (but cf. the comments of Kaiser 1974, 338), cf. BHS. Others prefer to read *merḥābīm*, 'expanses of the earth' (cf. Hab. 1.6), or *merwāḥīm*, 'spacious' (cf. 22.14), meaning 'far and wide through the land' (cf. Rudolph, Bright). 19c can hardly be an answer to the rhetorical question of 19b; it is better treated as a Deuteronomistic addition (Thiel 1973, 135f.; cf. Holladay 1962sa). **[21]** MT *hošbārtī*, 'I am broken'; RSV 'my heart wounded' is more an interpretation than a translation, cf. NEB 'I am wounded'; G lacks it but reads 'I am gloomy; pangs have seized me as a woman in labour', as in 6.24. **[22]** MT *'arukat*, 'the health', lit. 'lengthening' (of flesh), i.e. new flesh growing over the wound cf. 39.17; 33.6; NEB 'why has no new skin grown over their wound?' **[9.1]** = MT v. 23.

The fragments give way to a lamentation for the city's plight. But who is the speaker? The lament for the city has already been encountered in 4.19–22 and there it was suggested that city or community might be the speaker. As this poem is very similar to that one, again the most likely speaker is the city (or the community speaking as the city). However, the city as speaker is but a metaphor; in reality somebody has to do the speaking. That somebody might be a priest, a prophet or a poet, and therefore a number of commentators treat the speaker as the prophet Jeremiah. Jeremiah speaks for or *as* the city. This is quite possible, but the logic of such an explanation requires it to be the city which is doing the speaking (Jeremiah is but the mouthpiece). It is therefore the city's pain which is spoken of rather than the individual speaker's pain. The people who are wounded (i.e. the community) are the wound of the city (cf. 30.12,15; 31.15). The personification of the city (a regular feature of the tradition) in such poems does not mean that the speaker speaks of his own feelings; he speaks of the city's responses to the disaster. The fictive mode of representation does not allow for two speakers – just as in 31.15 Rachel is a personification of the community, not the matriarch Rachel mourning for the community. So in these laments there are not two figures involved, the speaker Jeremiah and the figure represented, but just one – the city Jerusalem. It is an illegitimate move to argue from these poems to the personal feelings of Jeremiah or to cite them as evidence for the oneness of feeling and identity between Jeremiah and his people. The many poems and statements critical of the community indicate quite clearly just how alienated that speaker felt from the community (i.e. not at one with it).

The speaker is overcome with grief and sick because all over the land is to be heard the cry for help of daughter Zion. Desperately she asks the question, 'Is Yahweh not in Zion?', for the cry is directed at Yahweh from whence help is expected. 'Is her king not in her?' may be a reference to Yahweh or whichever king was on the throne. King Yahweh is the more likely meaning of the question because the disaster has struck and only Yahweh could have helped to prevent it. The lament is of a city whose god has let her down when she was blithely of the opinion that 'all is well, Yahweh is in Zion, the king is here'. This is ironic in view of 2.6, 8 but the rhetoric of both passages points to stereotypical responses to situations rather than clearly analysed evaluations. A later hand has replied to the rhetorical question in v. 19 by adding an explanation for the disaster. The people of Jerusalem have angered Yahweh by their graven images and foreign idols (in spite of 7.19 where it is implied that Yahweh is not provoked to anger by such matters but it is the people who suffer such provocation). This interpolation may have been influenced by 7.18–19 (cf. Volz, Rothstein, Nötscher), but if so the glossator has not quite understood the point of 7.19. Others prefer to treat the addition as a response to the question, turning the poem from a monologue into a dialogue (cf. Holladay 1962a; Berridge 1970, 170; Weiser, 76). It explains the disaster as being due to idolatry, but spoils the poem as a lament of the fallen city.

The images change slightly, but their significance remains the same. Harvest is over, summer ended, but the people are not delivered. The probable meaning of v. 20 is: the time when grains and fruits should be gathered in is over, the season of growth and ripening over, and there is nothing in the granaries (cf. v. 13). The prospect now is a winter without food, so we are lost. The wound of the people is the city's wound, and she mourns their loss. Again the image changes (v. 22), and the figure of the wound (*šeber*, 'breaking') conjures up its healing process. Is there neither balm (odiferous resin of the styrax tree) nor physician in Gilead? Rhetorical questions which reflect the trade with Gilead (Gen. 37.25; Ezek. 27.17) and the belief that balm helped pain (cf. 46.11; 51.8). Whether the balm was used to heal wounds or to conceal the smell of festering wounds is a moot point. The questions are rhetorical because the wound is incurable (i.e. the city is destroyed), as the intense emotion of 9.1 shows. Such strong response to the people's wound highlights the triviality of the nostrums used by prophet and priest (8.11).

9.2–6

2 O that I had in the desert
a wayfarers' lodging place,
that I might leave my people
and go away from them!
For they are all adulterers,
a company of treacherous men.
3 They bend their tongue like a bow;
falsehood and not truth has grown strong in the land;
for they proceed from evil to evil,
and they do not know me, says the LORD.
4 Let every one beware of his neighbour,
and put no trust in any brother;
for every brother is a supplanter,
and every neighbour goes about as a slanderer.
5 Every one deceives his neighbour,
and no one speaks the truth;
they have taught their tongue to speak lies;
they commit iniquity and are too weary to repent.
6 Heaping oppression upon oppression, and deceit upon deceit,
they refuse to know me, says the LORD.

[2–6] = MT 1–5. **[2]** MT *m^elōn 'ōrḥīm*, 'travellers' lodging place': G *stathmon eschaton* suggests 'a most distant lodge'. **[3]** RSV follows G and repunctuated text for MT's 'they bend their tongue; their bow is false and not for truth have they grown strong in the land'; if MT *gābrū*, 'they have grown strong', is read as *gāb^{e}rāh*, 'it has grown strong' (cf. BHS), sense is obtained in the new reading. The *l* of *le'^{e}mūnāh* may be an emphatic (cf. Nötscher 1953, 380), though BHS omits it. MT *w^{e}'ōtī*, 'and me (they do not know)', makes the speaker Yahweh, but this is unlikely in view of v. 2, so perhaps it is an abbreviation of *w^{e}'t-yhwh*, 'and Yahweh (they do not know)', cf. BHS, Bright. G lacks *n^{e}'um yhwh*, 'says Yahweh'. **[4]** RSV 'every brother is a supplanter' = MT *kol-'āḥ 'āqōb ya'qōb*, a word-play on *ya'^{a}qōb*, 'Jacob', but difficult to convey in English; cf. Bright's 'for every brother's as crafty as Jacob'; NEB margin 'Every brother is a supplanter like Jacob', cf. Gen. 27.36. BHS, Rudolph transfer v. 8 (7) to the end of v. 4 (3), where it makes a better fit. **[5]** RSV 'they commit iniquity and are too weary to repent' involves certain changes in MT *ha'^{a}wēh nil^{e}'ū*, 'to act perversely they weary themselves'; next verse *šibt^{e}kā b^{e}tōk mirmāh b^{e}mirmāh mē'^{a}nū*, 'your sitting is in the midst of deceit, in deceit they refuse . . .'. A redivision of the consonants yields *he'^{e}wū nil^{e}'ū šūb: tōk b^{e}tōk mirmāh b^{e}mirmāh*, (cf. G) 'they act perversely, they are too weary to turn; oppression on oppression, deceit on deceit (they refuse . . .)', cf. NEB. JPSB translates MT but recognizes the meaning of the Hebrew as uncertain; cf. Berridge 1970, 175. **[6]** MT *da'at-'ōtī n^{e}'um-yhwh*, 'to know me says Yahweh': cf. end of v. 3 (2) and note above. *'ōtī* may be an abbreviation for *'et-yhwh*; G lacks 'says Yahweh'.

A very different piece follows the lament over the slain of the people. Although it is also spoken in the first person, the speaker is quite distinct from the speaker of the previous poem. Both speakers have very different viewpoints about the nature of the community, and their responses reveal distinctive attitudes to the people. The poems appear together because they have certain associated elements in common. One is a lament, the other begins as a lament; both are soliloquies. The cry from distant places in 8.19 is echoed in the speaker's wish to flee well away from the people in 9.2. But they are very different poems and reflect dissimilar situations. In this poem the speaker disparages the community for its social behaviour in terms as inclusive as in 5.1–5 (contrast 5.26–28). No setting is provided for the poem, so it may refer to any period in the community's existence, though commentators are keen to place it in the early period of Jehoiakim's reign.

The poem represents the community as an entity disintegrating under the force of its own corruption: adultery, treachery, falsehood, evil actions, supplanting, deception, lies, oppression and lack of knowledge of Yahweh. A society characterized by such activities is one at war with itself; hence the speaker's wish to leave it and live in a shack in the desert. The terms used to describe the people's behaviour are stereotypical and used elsewhere in the tradition, so it is difficult to determine the extent to which the poem is descriptive or rhetorical. 'They are all adulterers' (cf. 23.10; Hos. 7.4) in this context suggests sexual activity but, given its use in Hosea as 'idolatrous passions' (Wolff 1974, 124–5), may hint at idolatry. However, the hyperbolic nature of the poem's rhetoric should warn against seeking to match the terms of abuse with real social activities. The charge in 4b 'every brother is a supplanter' may contain a word-play on the name Jacob ('every brother is a thorough Jacob') and an allusion to that patriarch's reputation for conflict with his brother (cf. Hos. 12.3; Gen. 25.21–34; 27, 29–31). The precise force of *'āqōb ya'qōb* is not clear: the phrase may refer to supplanting or overreaching or being crafty (all rather different activities), hence the story of Jacob may be the simplest way of understanding it. A society of cheats, just like Jacob, is the force of the statement; though the relative order of the text of Jeremiah in relation to the patriarchal stories remains a moot point (cf. Brodie 1981). The masculinity of the terms of abuse 'adulterers', 'brother', 'jacob', should be noted in order to remind naive exegetes that polemic and abuse in the Bible are expressed frequently using masculine imagery. The gender of the terms is irrelevant because it is the *whole* community which is condemned, not a particular gender, and it is not a case of misogynistic values at work in the text when feminine images are used to make the same point.

The rhetoric of the poem portrays a deceitful society where no individual is safe from another. Language is used as a weapon, falsehood thrives, lies and slander abound, deceit and oppression vie with one another, and the community is too tired to turn from such activities. Such a state of affairs reveals a people who do not know Yahweh, where knowledge of Yahweh means orderly social relations (*da'at yhwh* is too clichéd a term in biblical language for it to have a specific meaning; cf. Wisser 1983 for a general treatment of it in the Jeremiah tradition). The redaction of this poem has tended to turn the speaker's statements into divine utterances (cf. 'says Yahweh', vv. 3, 6), perhaps as part of the development of the tradition in the direction of making Jeremiah the speaker of all the poems.

9.7–9

7 Therefore thus says the LORD of hosts:
'Behold, I will refine them and test them,
for what else can I do, because of my people?
8 Their tongue is a deadly arrow;
it speaks deceitfully;
with his mouth each speaks peaceably to his neighbour,
but in his heart he plans an ambush for him.
9 Shall I not punish them for these things? says the LORD;
and shall I not avenge myself
on a nation such as this?'

[7–9] = MT 6–8. **[7]** MT *kī-'ēk 'e'aśeh mippᵉnē bat-'ammī*, 'for how will I do because of the daughter of my people': G *hoti poiēsō apo prosōpou ponērias thugatros laou mou*, 'for I will do because of the wickedness of the daughter of my people'. Either *bat* should be read as *rā'at* 'evil' (G) or words have fallen out; BHS reads as *rā'ātām*, 'their evil', cf. Volz. Driver 1937–38, 106, 'how (else) should I act in view of their going astray?' understanding *'ēkākāh . . . bᵉtā'āyām*. **[8]** K *swḥṭ*; Q *sāḥūṭ*, 'deadly' (passive for active). MT *lᵉšōnām*, 'their tongue', perhaps should be *lᵉšōnō*, 'its tongue', because everything else in v. is singular; if v. 8 belonged originally after v. 4 (as BHS proposes) the plural might suit here. MT *mirmāh dibbēr*, 'it speaks deceit', but G 'the words of their word are deceitful' suggests a redivision of the Hebrew clauses to *mirmāh dibbēr bᵉpīw*, 'deceit it speaks with its mouth'. **[9]** = 5.9, 29.

Many commentators treat 9.2–9 as the unit, though there is some disagreement over v. 9 because of its appearance in 5.9, 29. I follow Bright here in regarding vv. 2–6 as a soliloquy and vv. 7–9 as separate from it. However, vv. 7–9 are not so much a unit as a mishmash of fragments appended to the poem about chaotic social relations (Volz's division consists of 2–7 with 8, 9 omitted). The incorporation of v. 8 into the poem would make sense (e.g. Rudolph) but it may equally be regarded as a marginal note reflecting on vv. 4–5 (cf. Volz). It develops the notion of the tongue as a weapon, but along the lines of a concealed weapon for use in an ambush. The distinction between speech and intention noted elsewhere in the tradition (e.g. 5.2; 12.2) is here a good example of the tongue as weapon. The speaking of *šālōm*, hiding the intention of doing the neighbour a mischief, makes an interesting contrast with the speaking of *šālōm* which characterizes the prophets who have not understood the gravity of the situation they confront (4.10; 6.14; 8.11; 14.13; 23.17). But the way the speakers of *šālōm* are denounced in the tradition may point to an equation between such speaking and deceitfulness (with the exception of 29.11?).

The editorial introduction to v. 7 makes it a divine oracle, but originally the statement may have been a reflection on 6.27, where the speaker is made a tester of the people. It does not fit here, which may explain why it has been turned into a divine oracle – not the speaker but Yahweh refines and tests the people. Presumably to filter out of them the men of violence and deceit, but the figure is not developed (cf. 6.30). The editorial conclusion in v. 9 provides what is missing in the material. Given such a society, small wonder the speaker wishes to flee from it (cf. Ps. 55.6–8).

9.10

'Take up weeping and wailing for the mountains,
 and a lamentation for the pastures of the wilderness,
because they are laid waste so that no one passes through,
 and the lowing of cattle is not heard;
both the birds of the air and the beasts
 have fled and are gone.'

---

[10] = MT 9. MT *'eśśā'*, 'I will take up'; G *labete* = *śᵉ'ū* plur.: an address to the community rather than to the individual speaker. G lacks *wānehī*, 'and wailing'. MT *niṣṣᵉtū* from *yṣt*, 'burned', cf. NEB 'scorched', BDB, 428 sense of 'desolated'. Duhm, Rudolph read *niṣṣū*, 'devastated', from *nāṣāh*, 'fall in ruins'. Cf. Notes on 2.15; the same point may be made about 9.12 (11); 46.19.

A fragment of a lament for the general devastation of the land appears here. At least it is a fragment in its present position, but some commentators link it with vv. 17–22 (e.g. Volz) or even with v. 11 and vv. 17–22 (e.g. Rudolph). MT and G differ in their understanding of the speaker of the lament: the individual speaker (MT) or the community instructed to take up a lament for the disaster which has befallen the country (G). The lament focuses on the consequences of the great destruction (the *šeber* of 8.21 rather than the self-inflicted wounds of 9.2–6) of the nation for the territory round about. No pastoral animals are heard there because no humans are left to pasture sheep and herds (contrast Isa. 7.21–25). Nor are birds or beasts heard (cf. 4.25), for they have fled – it is a lament for a landscape *emptied* of all sound.

9.11

'I will make Jerusalem a heap of ruins,
  a lair of jackals;
and I will make the cities of Judah a desolation,
  without inhabitant.'

---

[11] = MT 10. Cf. 51.37, where there are some similarities between the two verses: 'Babylon shall become a heap of ruins, the haunt of jackals, . . . without inhabitant.'

Another fragment (linked to vv. 15–16 by Volz) on the subject of great destruction. This one refers to Jerusalem and the cities of Judah and reflects the view that the deity (implied rather than stated) is the one who destroys the city and its territory. The terms used – 'heaps' (*gallīm*; 'ruins', are implied; cf. *'īyyīm*, 'ruins', 26.18), 'lair of jackals' (10.22; 49.33; 51.37), 'without inhabitant' – are too stereotypical for the lament to be understood literally. In its position here (cf. 51.37) it parallels v. 10's description of a desolate land without animals with a statement about Jerusalem and the Judaean cities lacking people. Only the jackals will roam through the heaps of stone (cf. Zeph. 2.13–15 for a much more graphic depiction of the takeover of a city by animals). Conventional elements provide the terms of the lament (Jerusalem, Hazor, Babylon). These fragments belong to the post-catastrophe redaction of the tradition and make connections between the poem of vv. 2–6 and the fall of Jerusalem.

9.12–16

12 Who is the man so wise that he can understand this? To whom has the mouth of the LORD spoken, that he may declare it? Why is the land ruined and laid waste like a wilderness, so that no one passes through? 13 And the LORD says: 'Because they have forsaken my law which I set before them,

and have not obeyed my voice, or walked in accord with it, 14 but have stubbornly followed their own hearts and have gone after the Baals, as their fathers taught them. 15 Therefore thus says the LORD of hosts, the God of Israel: Behold, I will feed this people with wormwood, and give them poisonous water to drink. 16 I will scatter them among the nations whom neither they nor their fathers have known; and I will send the sword after them, until I have consumed them.'

[12–16] = MT 11–15. RSV, NEB treat this section as prose but some commentators prefer to see some poetry in it: BHS prints 12b (11b) as poetry, JPSB treats all v. 12 as poetic; Bright 12b, 15b as poetry and Thompson 12b, 15b, 16 as poetic. There is a case for treating 12b, 15b as fragments of poetry. **[12]** MT *w^{e}yābēn*, 'understand'; Rudolph understands this as a Hiphil, 'explain'. **[14]** G 'their evil hearts' = *š^{e}rirūt libbām hāraʿ*, cf. 7.24. **[15]** MT *maʾ^{a}kīlām ʾet-hāʿām hazzeh*, 'feed *them* this people': 'this people' lacking in G and redundant in Hebrew.

The question-and-answer format of this prose section (cf. 5.19; 16.10–13; 22.8–9; Deut. 29.24–28) is a product of the Deuteronomistic strand in the Jeremiah tradition (Thiel 1973, 136–8). Two poetic fragments (12b, 15b) are woven into a brief theological discourse on the significance of the fall of Jerusalem, using Deuteronomistic terminology and theology. The first fragment, 'why is the land ruined, laid waste as a wilderness without traveller?', allows for an answer which will conform to a particular ideology of exile. It is a didactic piece which associates being wise with knowing the right answer to this question. The question about the wise man is not formulated in terms of the old wisdom techniques of observation and experience but reflects a prophetic type of inquiry. Knowing the answer to this question is a matter of having had a word from Yahweh – 'to whom has Yahweh spoken?' It is that combination of wisdom and prophecy which characterizes Deuteronomistic thought. The answer to the question is then given in v. 13 as a divine statement. When Yahweh speaks, he does so in Deuteronomistic language (just like the foreign nations in 22.9 or the Babylonian general in 40.2–3). The land lies in ruins because the people forsook Yahweh's *tōrāh* and followed after the baals. Idolatry caused the fall of Jerusalem and the exile of the nation's citizens. This way of life they learned from their fathers (cf. 7.26; 16.12). To be truly wise is to understand this account of the disaster; it is to be capable of reflecting on history and learning its lesson. A similar approach to wisdom is found in Hos.

14.9 (cf. Ps. 107.43), indicating a movement, in exilic times and later, of wisdom and prophecy being integrated in such a manner as to provide an answer to the question 'who is wise?' (cf. Wolff 1974, 239f.).

The other fragment of poetry, 'look I am feeding them wormwood, and will give them poisonous water to drink', describes the disaster using a different set of images (cf. 8.14; 23.15). The figure is that of a deadly potion made from poisonous herbs (cf. McKane 1980b, 484) and fed to the people. The result of this fatal meal is the destruction of the nation. The two items in this vegetarian diet are herbs: the drink has already been referred to in 8.14, where it is related to a trial by ordeal metaphor for apostasy (Weiser, 74, relates it there to the golden calf story in Ex. 32,20). The food is described as *laʿ^a^nāh*, usually translated as 'wormwood' (Latin *absinthium*; the modern drinks, absinthe and vermouth, related to this word only mislead if applied to the biblical word) but it probably indicates some poisonous plant. It is used as a metaphor of destruction here and in 23.15, for the bitterness of suffering in Lam. 3.15, 19, for describing the effect of a prostitute on a man (Prov. 5.4), for the social transformation of justice and right into their opposites (Amos 5.7; 6.12) and for the fruit of idolatry (Deut. 29.18 [MT v. 17]). According to the Deuteronomistic usage the service of other gods is equivalent to the production of this poisonous plant. Hence the people are fed the fruit of their serving other gods and die as a result. They are scattered among the nations (cf. Deut. 4.27; 28.64; 30.3 for the scattering [*hēpîṣ*] motif and 29.16–28 for the Deuteronomistic understanding of the relation between exile and idolatry). The sending of the sword after those scattered is part of the hyperbolic treatment of the fall of Jerusalem as an annihilation of everybody and should not be understood in a literal way: 'until I have consumed them' (v. 16) is contradicted by 30.11. This second fragment of poetry is also presented as a divine oracle, hence the two separate sections may be treated as one unit.

9.17–22

17 Thus says the LORD of hosts:
'Consider, and call for the mourning women to come;
send for the skilful women to come;

18 let them make haste and raise a wailing over us,
that our eyes may run down with tears,
and our eyelids gush with water.
19 For a sound of wailing is heard from Zion:
"How we are ruined!
We are utterly shamed,
because we have left the land,
because they have cast down our dwellings." '
20 Hear, O women, the word of the LORD,
and let your ear receive the word of his mouth;
teach to your daughters a lament,
and each to her neighbour a dirge.
21 For death has come up into our windows,
it has entered our palaces,
cutting off the children from the streets
and the young men from the squares.
22 Speak, 'Thus says the LORD:
"The dead bodies of men shall fall
like dung upon the open field,
like sheaves after the reaper,
and none shall gather them." '

[17–22] = MT 16–21. **[17]** MT *hitbōnᵉnū wᵉ*, 'consider and . . .', lacking in G; probably a later editorial direction to the audience, along with the transformation of the poem into a divine oracle effected by adding 'thus says Yahweh of hosts'. MT *ūtᵉbō'enāh . . . wᵉtābō'nāh*, 'and let them come . . . and let them come'; BHS deletes the first occurrence which would yield a tighter text: 'summon the keeners, send for the mourners' (*haḥᵉkāmōt*, 'the skilled women', i.e. professional mourners in this context). For MT *wᵉtābō'nāh*: 17 *ūtᵉmahērnāh*, 'let them come and let them make haste'; G *kai phthegxasthōsan*, 'and let them utter their voice'. **[19]** MT *miṣṣīyyōn*, 'from Zion': a few mss and G 'in Zion'. MT *kī hišlīkū*, 'for they have hurled down (our home)': G 'we must cast aside (our homes)' = *hišlaknū*; Bright suggests *hošlaknū*, 'we are cast (from our homes)'. **[21]** MT *bᵉ'armᵉnōtēnū*, 'in our palaces': G *eis tēn gēn humōn*, 'into your land'. **[22]** G lacks 'Speak, "Thus says the LORD:" '; some G Vrs understand MT *dabbēr*, 'speak', as *deber*, 'pestilence'. MT *wᵉnāpᵉlū*, 'and shall fall'; G *kai esontai*, 'and shall be'. For MT *kᵉdōmen*, 'as dung': G *paradeigma*, 'example', cf. II Kings 9.37, 'and the corpse of Jezebel shall be as dung upon the face of the field'; the dung image also appears in 8.2. Bright follows vv. 17–22 with 10.17–25 and treats 9.23 – 10.16 as miscellaneous sayings interrupting the connection between 9.22 and 10.17.

The dirge element in v. 10 is taken up again in two separate poems in vv. 17–19, 20–22. Although they may have been separate poems originally, they may be treated together here because they are essentially parallel poems about lamentations over the death of the community. In the editing of the poems they have been turned into divine oracles and presented as statements from Yahweh. This editorial transformation probably reflects the process whereby much of the book of Jeremiah (esp. in 1–25) was developed from human statements into the divine word.

The professional mourning women are summoned to come and raise a wailing in the community so that the people may join in the weeping. The performance of such keeners at a funeral in the ancient world was rather different from the restrained grief of modern funerals in the Western world (though it may still be seen in the Middle East today). The black-clad (cf. 4.28) groups of wild, noisy women shrieking and screaming, howling and yelling, would trigger off the grief of mourners and bystanders (cf. 9.1). A noise to waken the dead! The city is destroyed, the homes pulled down and the land abandoned (cf. 13.18–19; 38.22–23 for similar responses to the disaster). The disaster is so great that the women of the community are invited to teach their daughters the art of wailing because death stalks the land (G). The images of death in v. 21 are vivid: death (*māwet*) comes in the windows, enters the palaces, cuts off children and youths in the streets and squares of the city (cf. Zech. 8.4–5 for the reverse image of salvation as the streets full of old people and children playing there). In Canaanite mythology there is a story about Baal's reluctance to have windows put in his palace in case Yam, his arch-enemy, should enter through them; he overcomes that hesitancy and the serpentine henchmen of Mot (the Canaanite god of death) do enter at the windows (cf. Margalit 1980, 45–50). Whether v. 21 is an allusion to that story or a transformed use of it cannot be determined. It may just be a metaphor which happens to be similar to an ancient mythical story. The figure changes in v. 22 to the corpses of the dead lying in the open fields like manure or abandoned sheaves of grain. Whether in city or field the dead lie all around – the cause of great wailing and lamentation.

9.23–24

23 Thus says the LORD: 'Let not the wise man glory in his wisdom, let not the mighty man glory in his might, let not the rich man glory in his riches;
24 but let him who glories glory in this, that he understands and knows me, that I am the LORD who practise steadfast love, justice, and righteousness in the earth; for in these things I delight, says the LORD.'

[23–24] = MT 22–23. **[23]** MT *yithallēl*, 'boast, glory', cf. 4.2. **[24]** MT *'ōśeh ḥesed mišpāṭ ūṣᵉdāqāh*: 'who practises loving kindness, justice, and righteousness'. Vrs have 'and' before 'justice'; cf. the triple terms in 4.2, *'ᵉmet mišpāṭ ṣᵉdāqāh*; and the quadruple terms in Hos. 2.19 (MT) *bᵉṣedeq ūbᵉmišpāṭ ūbᵉḥesed ūbᵉraḥᵃmīm*.

Brueggemann 1978; Kutsch 1981

A brief statement reflecting on the proper grounds for human boasting. It has no connection with what precedes or follows it, but its place in the miscellany following the laments may be due to v. 12. There the wise man is the one who understands the meaning of what has happened because he has access to Yahweh's word. Here the wise man is warned about his wisdom. But triple elements dominate the piece: the wise, the powerful and the rich; wisdom, might and wealth; *ḥesed* (virtually untranslatable), justice and righteousness. Possession of wisdom, power or wealth is not the proper ground of boasting, but the one who boasts must boast in understanding and knowing Yahweh. The statement is enclosed by indicators that it is an oracular statement representing the divine view of values.

So true wisdom, power or wealth is the knowledge of Yahweh. What is meant by such knowledge? Presumably as Yahweh is identified as the one who practices kindness to his own people (*ḥesed* as devotion), justice and righteousness, the proper grounds for boasting must be the practice of these three virtues. Their content is not defined, so it is difficult to be more precise about the human qualities which permit legitimate boasting. The terms used are so common to the Bible that specific meaning can hardly be supplied for them here. They appear to represent a displacement of wisdom, power and wealth in favour of piety, and their content would then be defined in terms of the ideology of the group employing them. The piece looks like an ideological declaration of a group determined to undermine the values of other groups and as such would fit that strand in the tradition which criticizes wisdom and offers contrasts between proper and improper attitudes (e.g. 8.8–9; 17.5–11). It is a theological knowledge rather than a practical one (Volz). It has been described as 'a harmless unimportant saying' (Duhm, 97) and attributed to later piety circles. Its piety can hardly be doubted, and its use of terms which are so common and undefinable suggests a pious glossing of the tradition at this point. It is both harmless and pious. Using hurrah words, it allows the wise, the powerful and the wealthy to retain all they possess provided they boast only in their piety, i.e. their understanding of Yahweh. It may be viewed as a statement from pious circles developing a line of thought which may be traced in G of I Sam. 2.10, pre- and post-exilic ideas, into NT times (I Cor. 1.31; II Cor. 10.17; James 1.9) and beyond (cf. I Clement 13.1). Jer. 9.23–24 is a branch of that line (discussion in Kutsch 1981).

Such an evaluation of vv. 23–24 is not held by all commentators (e.g. Weiser, 83–4; Thompson, 318–21). Some would regard them as 'a succinct summary of the religion of Israel at its highest' (Thompson, 321), or as providing 'a screen through which Jeremiah can be understood more generally' (Brueggemann 1978, 99). This latter opinion views the piece as the expression of an alternative epistemological framework to that of wisdom's epistemology of continuity and consensus. The verse may not be as banal as Duhm and others think, but Brueggemann overstates his case and uses polarizing categories which are misleading. The banality of 23–24 needs to be emphasized, even if only to balance the view that 'in categories of Christian faith, Jeremiah here presents a theology of the cross in protest against a theology of glory' (Brueggemann 1978, 99). Apart from Josiah (22.15) and the future king (23.5), no one practices *ḥesed*, justice or righteousness in the nation (e.g. 5.1; 9.2–6; though stereotypical statements, they illustrate how alien the thought of 9.24 is to the tradition). If there is no justice in the community and Yahweh is the one who practises justice on the earth, then he is inactive! But the critical poems only know a justice which is practised by people or not at all (how else would Yahweh do justice in the earth?). So 23–24 use these terms in a distinctive and theological sense.

The best way to read vv. 23–24 would seem to be *ḥesed*, *mišpāṭ*, *ṣᵉdāqāh* in a theological sense, i.e. as attributes and activities of

Yahweh. Grounds for boasting are only to be found in acknowledging (the force of *yādō'a*, 'knows') Yahweh. Such knowledge of the deity is essentially a confessional one (cf. 12.1, *ṣaddīq 'attāh yhwh*, 'righteous are you, Yahweh') which views history as the sphere of Yahweh's activity, an activity characterized by loyalty (to his followers cf *'ōśeh ḥesed*, Ex. 20.6; Deut. 5.10), justice and right. Understanding of or insight into (*haśkēl*) this confession is what constitutes a person's right to boast. Yahweh delights in these qualities. There may be an implicit point here that human boasting can only legitimately be in the practice of such godlike qualities, but it is neither stated nor spelled out. Yahweh delights in *ḥesed*, *mišpāṭ*, *ṣᵉdāqāh* – so should humans, rather than in wisdom, power or wealth. The statement is not so much an advocacy of these practices (cf. Isa. 5.7; Amos 5.24; Micah 6.8) as a putting into perspective of such values as wisdom, power and wealth. The world it emanates from is very different from those circles which denounced the wise, the powerful and rich on behalf of the poor in the community. It is a world of piety at peace with its surroundings: it attributes the justice and right-doing in the world to Yahweh. It appears to know nothing of that state of existence characterized by the lament psalms, Job or Qoheleth. Alien to it is the possibility that evil and injustice in the world might come from Yahweh (cf. Isa. 45.7; Job 9.22–24) or the realization that only if humans behave in certain ways will there be any justice or right on the earth. In view of its sanguine outlook, Duhm's judgment on it would appear to be nearer the truth than that represented by Brueggemann, Weiser or Thompson.

9.25–26

25 'Behold, the days are coming, says the LORD, when I will punish all those who are circumcised but yet uncircumcised – 26 Egypt, Judah, Edom, the sons of Ammon, Moab, and all who dwell in the desert that cut the corners of their hair; for all these nations are uncircumcised, and all the house of Israel is uncircumcised in heart.'

[25–26] = MT 24–25. **[28]** MT *'al-kol-mūl bᵉ'orlāh*, 'against all who are circumcised in the foreskin': G *epi pantas peritetmēmenous akrobustias autōn*, 'upon all the circumcised their circumcision'. RSV seems to understand MT as 'circumcised, with a foreskin', i.e. circumcised but retaining the foreskin! NEB 'all the circumcised'; JPSB regards the force of the Hebrew as uncertain. Bright's 'circumcised physically' is probably the correct way to understand MT. **[28]** MT *kol-qᵉṣūṣē*, lit. 'all who cut the corner' (hair implied) cf. 25.23; 49.32; an epithet of desert tribes. For *pē'āh* meaning 'hair' cf. Lev. 19.27; 21.5. NEB 'all who haunt the fringes of the desert', but cf. marg. MT *kī kol-haggōyim ʿᵃrēlīm*, 'for all the nations are uncircumcised', lit. 'have foreskin'; G *aperitmēta sarki*, 'uncircumcised in flesh', making a better contrast with 'uncircumcised in heart'. BHS reads *hā'ēlleh*, 'these', for *ʿᵃrēlīm* 'foreskins', yielding 'all these nations and the whole house of Israel are uncircumcised of heart' (Rudolph).

A further fragment echoing a lost polemic about the nature and meaning of circumcision. It is cast as a futuristic reference ('days are coming') and addressed to the nations, including Judah (house of Israel). It justifiably follows vv. 23–24 because it is also about the proper understanding of common matters. In spite of the fact that the group of nations referred to all practised circumcision, they would be the object of Yahweh's punishment. To make sense of this statement requires positing a background of the belief that circumcision is the fundamentally important tribal mark which distinguishes the true from the false. Such a background would include the Babylonians as the enemy, the uncircumcised. It is possible that a coalition of circumcised groups in league against the Babylonians could have used circumcision as their rallying point (cf. 27.3, where a number of these groups seem intent on opposing the Babylonians; see on 27–28). The list of groups also appears in the OAN (46–49, but such uncircumcised nations as the Philistines and the Babylonians also are included there). An Egyptian plot against the Babylonians and incorporating all these smaller nations into the conspiracy would make sense (cf. Bright, 78). But information is not available to make this suggestion more than a reasonable hypothesis.

The significance of the unit is that circumcision is no protection against Yahweh's anger. Circumcision is not a special qualification. It is a practice shared with other ethnic groups, and they are all lumped together here as warranting the judgment of Yahweh. The RSV 'circumcised but yet uncircumcised' is a good phrase for exposing the underlying point, though it hardly translates the Hebrew. It allows a distinction to be drawn between circumcision of the flesh, i.e. the cutting off of the foreskin of the penis, and circumcision of the heart, i.e. the receptivity of the mind to Yahweh (cf. 4.4; 6.10). In a culture where being circumcised was important but automatic, its symbolic status was weakened because what it stood for was automatically achieved. In a Babylonian context its symbolic status became much stronger because now it differentiated between the chosen and the godless. In the later literature circumcision is a symbol of Yahweh's covenant (Gen. 17.9–14), its absence a mark of the enemies of Yahweh (I Sam. 17.26, 36). The Deuteronomistic tendency to turn circumcision into a metaphor of receptivity to Yahweh's *tōrāh* indicates the move away from circumcision as a mark of tribal identity to a special meaning for it. Not to be circumcised is unthinkable in such cultures which practise the cutting of the penis, but where everybody is circumcised only its symbolic force can be made into a differentiating mark. Such a move is typified by the concept 'circumcised but yet uncircumcised'. It allows even those who are circumcised to be criticized on the grounds that they are not *really* circumcised. In later polemics Samaritans and Christians used precisely this argument against Jews (cf. Smith 1982, 8–14, for a discussion of the taxonomic role of circumcision).

Originally circumcision was an initiatory rite associated with puberty and marking the passage from childhood to manhood (a *rite de passage*). It prepared the youths of the tribe for marriage and identified them as full members of a particular tribe (on its range of meanings see Bettelheim 1955). Its theologization as a mark of the covenant meant that the covenant was automatically kept by every circumcised male. Now this view of circumcision may be underlying 9.25–26 and the opposition to it may come from those who disapproved of the group holding such a belief. For their purposes Judah may be ranked with all the other circumcised nations and face Yahweh's judgment in spite of being circumcised. It is an echo of a conflict which is otherwise lost now but which needs to be reconstructed in order to understand such a fragment.

The assertion in MT that 'all these nations are uncircumcised' is technically untrue. The nations listed did practise circumcision. However, the point of the claim may be that all nations except Judah were 'uncircumcised' as opposed to the 'circumcised' Judah: meaning that the chosen people were special and differentiated from other cultures (the influence of a Babylonian environment?). For the purpose of this argument other nations have foreskins, Israel does not (analogous to a legal fiction). But even allowing for this special status, Israel shares with the other nations an 'uncircumcised' status: it is uncircumcised of heart. So the visitation of Yahweh, believed to be the fate of all the 'uncircumcised' nations, would also befall Israel. It is the world of the godly versus the godless (e.g. I Sam. 17), but the unit offers a radical critique of such assumptions. Only the circumcised heart can protect from Yahweh's wrath. The unit should be considered along with the critique of cultic means of security in 7.1 – 8.3 (though not necessarily coming from the same source). Even circumcision cannot protect. This may be a late addition to the tradition, but it is in the same spirit as much in the book which strips bare the assumptions of the community about its sacred institutions, beliefs and practices.

10.1–16

10 1 Hear the word which the LORD speaks to you, O house of Israel.
2 Thus says the Lord:
'Learn not the way of the nations,
nor be dismayed at the signs of the heavens
because the nations are dismayed at them,
3 for the customs of the peoples are false.
A tree from the forest is cut down,
and worked with an axe by the hands of a craftsman.
4 Men deck it with silver and gold;
they fasten it with hammer and nails
so that it cannot move.
5 Their idols are like scarecrows in a cucumber field,
and they cannot speak;
they have to be carried,
for they cannot walk.
Be not afraid of them,
for they cannot do evil,
neither is it in them to do good.'
6 There is none like thee, O LORD;
thou art great, and thy name is great in might.
7 Who would not fear thee, O King of the nations?
For this is thy due;
for among all the wise ones of the nations
and in all their kingdoms
there is none like thee.

8 They are both stupid and foolish;
the instruction of idols is but wood!
9 Beaten silver is brought from Tarshish,
and gold from Uphaz.
They are the work of the craftsman and of the hands of the goldsmith;
their clothing is violet and purple;
they are all the work of skilled men.
10 But the LORD is the true God;
he is the living God and the everlasting King.
At his wrath the earth quakes,
and the nations cannot endure his indignation.
11 Thus shall you say to them: 'The gods who did not make the heavens
and the earth shall perish from the earth and from under the heavens.'
12 It is he who made the earth by his power,
who established the world by his wisdom,
and by his understanding stretched out the heavens.
13 When he utters his voice there is a tumult of waters in the heavens,
and he makes the mist rise from the ends of the earth.
He makes lightnings for the rain,
and he brings forth the wind from his storehouse.
14 Every man is stupid and without knowledge;
every goldsmith is put to shame by his idols;
for his images are false,
and there is no breath in them.
15 They are worthless, a work of delusion;
at the time of their punishment they shall perish.
16 Not like these is he who is the portion of Jacob,
for he is the one who formed all things,
and Israel is the tribe of his inheritance;
the LORD of hosts is his name.

---

[2] MT *'el-derek*, 'to the way of . . .'; BHS *'et*, cf. 12.16. Driver 1937–38, 106 understands MT as *lmd 'l*, 'addicted to'; Dahood 1966, 410, takes *'el* as *yhwh*. **[3]** MT *ḥuqqōt . . . hū*: 'customs . . . is'; the plural is hardly correct. BHS and others suggest *ḥittat*, 'fear', i.e. the idol described in 3b–4 (cf. Gen. 35.5); cf. Gen. 31.42 *paḥad yiṣḥāq*, 'the fear of Isaac' (Giesebrecht, 62). **[4]** MT *yᵉyappēhū*, 'beautify it': T *yᵉṣappēhū*, 'cover it', cf. BHS. Some read v. 9 after 4a (e.g. Rudolph, Bright), hence BHS reading *yapīqū*, 'they (cannot) move'. **[5]** MT *kᵉtōmer miqšāh hēmmāh wᵉlō' yᵉdabbērū*, 'as a scarecrow in a cucumber field are they, they cannot speak'; G *argurion* (= *ketem*, 'gold'?) *toreuton estin, ou poreusontai*, 'it is worked silver, they will not move'. G has v. 9 here. MT *yinnāśū'* is a scribal error for *yinnāśᵉ'ū* (Rudolph). MT *'ōtām*, 'them'; perhaps it should be *'ittām*, 'with them' (BHS), i.e. it is not in their power to do good. **[6]** MT *mē'ēn*, 'there is none . . .'; double negative, but BHS treats the *m* as a dittography. Dahood 1975 translates the double negative as 'absolutely no one . . .'. G lacks 6–8. Rudolph reads 8 here and relegates 6–7 to the end of the poem. **[7]** MT *mē'ēn*, 'there is none . . .', see note on 6. Theod reads 'their kings' for MT 'their kingdoms'; it provides a better balance to 'O king of the nations'. **[8]** MT *mūsar ḥᵃbālīm 'ēṣ hū'*, 'instruction of idols is wood': difficult. Hebrew is unintelligible (Bright). BHS reads *'eṣ* as *mē'ēṣāh*, 'lacks counsel' (privative use of *mīn*, 'from'). **[9]** Tarshish: a location in the west, possibly Spain (cf. Rudolph) cf. Ezek. 27.12. Uphaz: location unknown; some Vrs read Ophir, G Mophaz. G lacks 'the work of the craftsman'; BHS transposes the last clause to replace MT *ma'ᵃśēh ḥārāš*. **[10]** G lacks v. 10. **[11]** This verse is in Aramaic (variant spellings appear in it) and is regarded by many commentators as a gloss (marginal or otherwise). Rudolph consigns it to the end of the poem along with 6–7. It is in G. **[12–16]** = 51.15–19. In 12 G has 'it is the lord who made . . .'. **[13]** MT *lᵉqōl tittō*, 'at the sound of his giving forth'; G lacks the phrase. BHS, following Duhm, reads *lᵉqōlō nittak*, 'at his command pour forth (the tumult of waters)'; NEB 'at the thunder of his voice . . .' cf. Driver 1937–38, 106, *yehemāyūn*. K *'rṣ*, 'earth'; Q *hā'āreṣ*, '*the* earth', cf. 51.16. For MT, 'wind', G has 'light'. Cf. Ps. 135.7 for this verse. **[14]** RSV 'idols . . . images', MT *pesel . . . niskō*, sing. BHS makes *niskō nᵉsākāw*, 'his images'. **[16]** G lacks 'of hosts', 'and Israel is the tribe'; 51.19 lacks 'Israel'.

Ackroyd 1963; Bogaert 1981b; Davidson 1976; Margaliot 1980; Overholt 1965; Wambacq 1974

A lengthy poem interpolated here is addressed to the nation on the subject of the customs of the nations. It is a hymn of praise to Yahweh the incomparable and a polemical dismissal of the cult of idols practised by other nations. Like much else in the book it includes a section (vv. 12–16) which appears elsewhere (51.15–19) and has links with the Psalms and the liturgical poems of Second Isaiah. Commentators are generally agreed that the poem does not come from Jeremiah, though a few dissenting voices attribute it or parts of it to Jeremiah (e.g. Weiser, Overholt, Margaliot, Thompson). The ethos of the poem is so very different from that of the rest of the book that it is difficult to see how Jeremiah could have uttered it. The community condemned for idolatry, apostasy, social injustice and abandoning Yahweh in many of the poems is here addressed in eirenic tones which aim to warn them about the falseness (*šeqer*) of the nations' religious ways. The poem is sympathetic to Israel and encourages it to be independent of the false cults in a period when such independence may have been hard to achieve (cf. Andrew 1982, 130). Such a supportive attitude may be akin to the Jeremiah of 29.1–14, but unless it is argued that the poem is addressed to the exiles in Babylon this is not an attitude ever displayed towards the people of Judah. Margaliot dates the poem in the period between 627 and 605 and demonstrates the connections between the language of the poem and the Jeremiah tradition. However, it would require a substantial leap of the imagination to match the tenor of the poem with the angry voices denouncing the community for its idolatrous practices. The speaker of this poem is not the voice we hear in the other strands of the tradition: neither may belong to Jeremiah, both certainly do not. That the poem has connections with the tradition (cf. Overholt) is to be expected, but the links point as much to redactional circles or to the liturgical elements in it as they do to an ideal form of the prophet.

There is considerable difference between MT and G versions of the poem. G is much shorter and has a different arrangement of the verses. Both seem to represent different developments of the tradition, and the presence at Qumran of a fragment preserving parts of vv. 4, 9, 11, in that order (4QJer^{b}), confirms the independent G recension (the longer recension represented by MT is also present at Qumran; cf. Cross 1958, 139). Whether the longer or the shorter text should be the focus for exegesis is a matter dividing commentators and many exegetes do rearrange the text in the light of G. Yet others have argued for the coherence and order of MT (e.g Ackroyd, Overholt, Margaliot) upon which the RSV is based. Examples of the former include Duhm (1–3a, 5b, 10, 12–16), Volz (1, 2, 3, 4, 5, 10, 12–16), Rudolph (1, 2, 3, 4a, 9, 4b, 5, 8, 10, 12–16) and Bright (1, 2, 3, 4a, 9, 4b, 5, 6, 7, 8, 10, 12–16). Weiser, though he belongs to this group, has a different approach in that he sees genuine words of Jeremiah behind the paraenetic section in 1–5, 8, 9 (Wambacq only allows v. 2 to Jeremiah), which inevitably he associates with the covenant cult of the pre-exilic period. They represent the renunciation of the gods in the festival of that cult. The rest of the poem is made up of discrete elements: v. 11 is a late liturgical piece, 6–7 a liturgical hymn, 12–16 are exilic and come from the composer of 51, and 10 is also a cult hymn (his order is 1, 2, 3–4a, 9, 4b, 5, 8, 11, 6–7, 10, 12–16). Considering all these different rearrangements of the text the judgment that 'in its present state (10.1–16 is) a terrible confusion' (Duhm, 98) seems appropriate.

The alternative approach to this reliance upon G as a first edition of the poem discerns a logical structure in the present arrangement of the verses (e.g. Overholt, Margaliot). It is a straightforward contrast between Yahweh and the gods: they are weak, he is powerful (3–5, 6–7); they are 'dead', he is the living god (8–9, 10); they do not create but he does (11, 12–13); a contrast between the worshippers of the gods and the worshippers of Yahweh (14–15, 16). This pattern (Margaliot's) may be discerned loosely in the poem, but it lacks sharpness and is accountable for by means of the other approach. There is a contrast between Yahweh and the gods but the force of the original poem is more a denigration of the other gods. MT has developed the contrast in terms of the incomparability of Yahweh (on this aspect see Labuschagne 1966) and interwoven the two themes.

The Aramaic v. 11 is an unusual feature in the poem. Dan. 2–7; Ezra 4.8–6.18; and a few phrases apart, the Bible is written in Hebrew, so some explanation is required for this foreign language fragment in a Hebrew poem. Because Aramaic was spoken by neighbouring peoples it could have been known by some Israelites in the time of Jeremiah. Margaliot explains it in terms of the Israelites living in the Assyrian empire and accepts it as coming from Jeremiah (so also does Overholt). Most commentators see it as a gloss coming from a later period when Aramaic had become the *lingua franca* of the empire (Persian period). On the content of the statement 'the gods who did not make the heavens and the earth shall perish from the earth and from under the heavens' various explanations have been offered: a banal point about the contrast between Yahweh and the gods, a chauvinistic assertion of superiority, a marginal echo of the poem's sentiments. A different kind of argument about its significance may carry more force. It is a curse uttered against the gods of the nations (cf. Overholt, 5), or it is a protective formula (Duhm). In this latter sense it functions as an incantation directed against foreign cults and may have been believed to operate magically against opponents. This explanation (very much Duhm's) would fit the context of a struggle between the cult of Yahweh and the much more powerful cults of its Babylonian overlords. Against such frightening powers (cf. v. 2) the hurling of incantatory formulas may have been the only defence available to a weaker cult (hence v. 11 'thus *you* shall say to *them* . . .').

A Babylonian or Persian period background is here assumed for the poem (cf. Bogaert). A number of arguments justify such an assumption. The difference between the attitude towards Israel in the poem and elsewhere in the tradition removes the context of the poem from a Canaanite setting and the people referred to from association with the pre-catastrophe community addressed by the other poems. The construction of the idols and their instrumental participation in processions point in the direction of Babylonian practices rather than the numina of Canaanite religion. The theme of creation and the conflict between which gods created are something the Israelites learned from the Babylonians (see Saggs 1978, 41–50; contrast the approach of Weippert 1981b). The incantation of v. 11 is a denial of the cosmic creative powers of the Babylonian gods in favour of Yahweh. The same approach is to be found in the poems of Second Isaiah where the very claims of Babylonian religion are denied and asserted of Yahweh. A similar polemic against the idols is based on the techniques of idol construction (cf. Isa. 44.9–20), and this makes the ethos of Second Isaiah one of the coordinates of 10.1–16. Many commentators see striking affinities between this poem and the polemics against idols in Second Isaiah (e.g. Overholt, Bright). However, it is not necessary to make 10.1–16 a derivative of Second Isaiah circles. It has sufficient linguistic independence of Isa. 44.9–20 to make it similar but distinctive in its descriptions of the making of idols (analysis in Davidson). The Babylonian background asserted here for the poem is but the necessary condition for this kind of polemic; it is not a sufficient condition. The polemic may have had its setting in the post-exilic Jerusalem cult (for the Palestinian liturgical setting of the poems of Second Isaiah, cf. Vincent 1977), but that cult was constructed by those who had learned much from the Babylonians. The lampooning of other gods, especially in terms of how their idols are made, is to be found in Ps. 115.3–8; 135.13–18; and 10.1–15 may have links with that activity as well as the Jeremiah tradition.

The chauvinism of 10.1–16 is very clear. What is less obvious is the irony engendered by the poem. By way of encouraging the people the divine oracle warns against the religion (for *ḥuqqōt* as 'religious customs', cf. Lev. 18.3) of the nations by asserting the superiority of their own god over those of others. But the gods of the other nations had regularly conquered Israel and demonstrated the powerlessness of Yahweh (the whole Jeremiah tradition is a desperate attempt to explain that powerlessness). The satire on the making of idols is not a cogent argument against what the images represent nor is there any force in equating the significance of something with the process of its manufacturing. The criticism that the idols cannot move, speak, walk or do either good or evil is one that may be made against any cult object: the ark of the covenant in the Jerusalem temple, the *tōrāh* scroll in the synagogue, the Bible in a church or the host in a chapel. All these things *have to be carried* and the processes of their manufacturing can be delineated exhaustively. As for the criticism that the gods do nothing, it is one often heard in the Bible but directed against Yahweh (e.g. Zeph. 1.12, 'Yahweh will not do good, nor will he do ill'). The shape and force of the polemic against the idols will serve to disparage any and all gods (including Yahweh). What prevents it becoming such a two-edged weapon is the confessional context within which it is maintained. The cult of the incomparable Yahweh could take these views of the gods of their neighbours because his worshippers did not believe in such gods but did believe in Yahweh. Without that prior affiliation there could be no polemic. The defeats of the nation had to be absorbed into theological accounts of disobedience and punishment (accounts very similar to those of their neighbours, see on 25.12) and xenophobic satires mask the fragility of their own belief system. The precariousness of this form of argumentation and the misrepresentation of paganism have long been recognized (e.g. Kaufmann 1972, 7–20; von Rad 1972, 177–85; Carroll 1977). Attention is drawn to it here in order to underline the degree to which 10.1–16 represents the expression of a small cult huddled together to preserve its ideological distinctiveness against considerable pressures to learn the way of the nations. It is therefore an inset in the Jeremiah tradition which is itself quite distinctive.

The exegesis of 10.1–16 is parallel to this necessarily discursive introduction to the unit. The poem is presented as an oracular statement addressed to the house of Israel (cf. 2.4). Israel must not learn the way of the nations (for the reverse idea cf. 12.16), because their customs, i.e. religious instruction (cf. v. 8), are false (*šeqer* as in v. 14). The making of their idols is then delineated as an exposure of the folly behind them. They are no more than the material out of which they are made – the medium is the message! In contrast to these stupid things is the living god, Yahweh. The aesthetic appeal of the richly clad and ornate idols is nothing beside the cosmic power of Yahweh displayed in nature (vv. 10, 12–13). If Yahweh is the true, the living god, then he is also the true creator of the heavens and the earth. So the community may say to the other cults 'the gods who did not create . . . shall perish'. Israel has learned well from its encounter with Babylon (travel broadens theology!) and incorporated that lesson into its liturgy (hence Ps. 115; 135). The incantation hurled at the opposing cult will prove effective and it will perish (cf. v. 15). That vv. 12–16 also appear in 51.15–19 is further evidence for a Babylonian context for the origins of this polemic. Bound up with the identity of the true god is the fate of the worshipping community (who is the true one to fear?). Because the idols are stupid, their worshippers are stupid: both are false (*šeqer*). Again the tradition offers a description of what is false and thereby removes any sanction from cults using images. In contrast to the idols is Yahweh, and therefore the fate of Israel is quite different from that of the nations. Jacob's portion (*ḥēleq*, 'possession': a primitive view of god, cf. Ps. 15.5; 73.26; 119.57; Deut. 32.9; Lam. 3.24) is Yahweh, so Israel is protected. By having Yahweh as its property Israel has nothing to fear from the nations and their stupid iconic religions.

10.17–18

17 Gather up your bundle from the ground,
O you who dwell under siege!
18 For thus says the LORD:
'Behold, I am slinging out the inhabitants of the land
at this time,
and I will bring distress on them,
that they may feel it.'

---

[17] MT *'ispī*, 'gather', cf. *mᵉ'asēp*, 'gather' in 9.22 (21), suggesting an original association of these two units (last word of 9.22, first word of next unit). MT *'ispī mē'ereṣ*, 'gather from the ground': G *sunēgagen exōthen*, 'he has gathered from outside'. MT *kin'ātēk*, 'your bundle', hapax legomenon. G *hupostasin*, 'substance'. MT could be understood as 'Gather your bundle! Out of the land!', cf. NEB, Bright, 72. K *yšbty*; Q *yōšebet*, 'one who lives'. MT *bammāṣōr*, 'under siege': G *en ekletois*, 'in choice (vessels)' = *bᵉmibḥar*, cf. 22.7; 48.15. **[18]** G lacks *bappa'am*, 'time', i.e. 'this (land)'. MT *wahᵃṣērōtī lāhem*, 'and I will distress them': G *en thlipsei*, 'with affliction' = *baṣṣārāh*.

MT *l^e^ma'an yimṣā'ū*, 'in order that they may find': difficult. G 'that your plague (*plēgē*) may be discovered'. BHS suggests *yimmāṣē'ū*, 'they may be found' (cf. GV); Rudolph *l^e^mān'ām miṣṣē't*, 'to refuse them exit'. Driver 1937–38, 107, reads *yimmāṣē'ū* from *mṣh*, 'squeeze', not *mṣ'*, 'find': 'and I will squeeze them tight that they may be drained dry', cf. NEB; followed by Bright, Thompson.

A brief poem which should be read in conjunction with 9.17–19, 20–22. The community, addressed as a woman (i.e. the city Jerusalem), is told to prepare for departure. The text is rather obscure, so the details of the poem elude precise exegesis. An oracular statement refers to divine pressure being put on the community as part of the process it is now ('at this time') undergoing. It is Yahweh who is slinging the inhabitants out of their land (or uprooting them, NEB under the influence of Driver), Yahweh who is making the experience even more painful. Commentators favour referring this piece to the siege of 598/7 and the deportation which followed it. It may refer to that period or the subsequent siege and deportation of 587. Nothing in the text permits a definite identification of the period referred to, though the presence of exilic material in the chapter and the redactional splitting of the units may point to a post-587 reference.

10.19–21

19 Woe is me because of my hurt!
    My wound is grievous.
  But I said, 'Truly this is an affliction,
    and I must bear it.'
20 My tent is destroyed,
    and all my cords are broken;
  my children have gone from me,
    and they are not;
  there is no one to spread my tent again,
    and to set up my curtains.
21 For the shepherds are stupid,
    and do not inquire of the LORD;
  therefore they have not prospered,
    and all their flock is scattered.

---

[17] MT *ḥolī*, 'affliction', Vrs 'my affliction' (*y* missing through haplography?). **[20]** MT *y^e ṣā'unī*, 'have gone from me': G *kai ta probata mou*, 'and my flocks' = *w^e ṣō'nī*. BHS suggests transposing the verbs 'spread', 'set up' (following Volz).

An individual lament similar to 4.19–20; 8.18–9.1 represents the response of the city or community to the disaster hinted at in vv. 17–18. The disintegration of the community renders the speaker heartbroken and sick with pain. The breaking (*šeber*) of the people is a metaphor of the destruction of city and community. The city as bereaved parent bemoans the terrible loss of people caused by the Babylonian invasion, siege of Jerusalem and its eventual capture. Again it is not possible to determine whether 597 or 587 is the occasion of the lament. The dominant meaning of *šeber*, 'breaking', is the destruction of the nation (8.21; 14.17; 30.12, 15), though the tradition also uses the term to describe that condition of the nation which prophet and priest have failed to heal (6.14; 8.11). The broken community must bear its wound, for it is too late to do anything but suffer. The figure changes in v. 20 to that of a bedouin family whose tent has been wrecked and the children taken away. There is no one left to pitch the tent again. It is a picture of disaster and desolation: the nomadic dwelling has been pulled down, the family scattered and none left behind to reconstruct the home.

To this brief lament has been added an explanation of the disaster. Some exegetes see v. 21 as the divine response to the lament of 19–20 (e.g. Reventlow 1963, 202; Berridge 1970, 176), though it lacks any indication of being a divine saying. It should be understood as an attempt to explain the destruction of the community but not as an oracular pronouncement attributed to Yahweh (spoken of in the third person rather than the first). The finger of blame (Rudolph's phrase) for the disaster points at the leadership (under the figure of 'shepherds' cf. 2.8; 23.1–2). Since they have failed to seek Yahweh (*drš*, 'consult'), their policies have not succeeded, and as a result of such failure the people ('their flock') have been scattered. Not the people but the leadership are to blame.

10.22

Hark, a rumour! Behold, it comes! –
  a great commotion out of the north country
to make the cities of Judah a desolation,
  a lair of jackals.

A fragment of the enemy from the north motif appears in v. 22. It is the report of the great uproar (*ra'aš*, 'earthquake, shaking') caused by the invasion from the north. Its purpose is defined here as the turning of the cities of Judah into a wasteland (*šᵉmāmāh* 4.27; 9.11; cf. 51.37). It belongs to the period after the devastation of the land and is attached here to indicate the extent to which the policies of the leadership have not prospered (v. 21; the leaders are stupid, just like the idols and idol-makers of vv. 8, 14). As a summary of the period the verse reads as if it has been put together from phrases to be found throughout the tradition (cf. the opinion of Volz, 126, that it has a compilatory character). Its various elements appear in 4.7, 15; 6.8, 22, 24; 8.16; 9.11; 18.16 (Volz). But for vv. 23–25 it would close off the second cycle of poems (cf. the similar penultimate ending of the first cycle in 6.22–26).

10.23–25

23 I know, O LORD, that the way of man is not in himself,
  that it is not in man who walks to direct his steps.
24 Correct me, O LORD, but in just measure;
  not in thy anger, lest thou bring me to nothing.
25 Pour out thy wrath upon the nations that know thee not,
  and upon the peoples that call not on thy name;
for they have devoured Jacob;
  they have devoured him and consumed him,
and have laid waste his habitation.

---

[27] MT *yāda'tī*, 'I know'; BHS reads this as *yāda'tā*, 'you know' (*y* due to dittography, Rudolph following Cornill; Ehrlich 1912, 272). Vrs have 'and' before 'not' in 23b ('and it is not for man who walks . . .'). MT *wᵉhākīn*, 'and to direct . . .'; EVV, BHS omit *wᵉ*. **[24]** MT *yassᵉrēnī*, 'correct *me*'; G 'correct *us*'. MT *tam'itēnī*, 'make me few, diminish me', rather than RSV, 'bring me to naught'; cf. NEB 'almost to nothing'. **[25]** = Ps. 79.6–7 (for *mišpāḥōt* 'families, clans' in v. 25, Ps. has *mamlākōt* 'kingdoms'). MT *wa'ᵃkāluhū wayᵉkalluhū*, 'and they have devoured and consumed him', lacking in Ps. 79.7.

The cycle of 7.1 – 10.25 is concluded with a lament for the disaster befallen Jacob. Some exegetes treat the unit as vv. 22–25, making the lament a response to the invasion of v. 22 (e.g. Weiser, 91–2; Berridge 1970, 194–8; Reventlow 1963, 196–205 takes vv. 19–25 as a lament liturgy). Although the lament is spoken in the first person singular (cf. G of v. 24), its subject is a collective one. This interpretation is confirmed by the phrase 'lest you make me few' (24b) and the appended v. 25 from the communal lament of Ps. 79, which identifies the subject of vv. 23–24 as a reference to Jacob. The speaker is anonymous but must be understood as the community or city lamenting its fate (cf. 4.19–20; 8.18–9.1). Others see the speaker as the prophet, speaking as the representative of the people (Reventlow 1963, 201). A cult figure as speaker would fit the lament in so far as such statements require an actual speaker, but the speaking itself is done as the expression of the group's position and is in no sense an autobiographical statement. Yet the occurrence of a short piece focusing on 'I', 'me' at the end of the cycle should be noted because the editing of 2.4–6.30 concludes that cycle in a similar way (cf. 6.27). The addition of v. 25 may just distort our understanding of vv. 23–24.

The speaker acknowledges the incapacity of mankind (the collective *'ādām* balanced by the particular *'īš*) to direct, i.e. establish, its steps. Such a confession of human inadequacy links vv. 23–24 with the wisdom sayings of 17.5–11 as statements about the human condition (see on 17.9–10). This being the case, the speaker appeals to Yahweh for discipline in due proportion (*'ak-bᵉmišpāṭ*, 'within reason', so Bright). The alternative to such 'just' discipline is Yahweh's anger, and that would dangerously diminish the speaker (for a contrast between such appropriate correction and complete annihilation cf. 30.11). Translated into communal terms, the lament appears to be a prayer for justice from Yahweh (not mercy!) rather than anger. His anger would be too diminishing of the community for it to survive the experience. Justice (*mišpāṭ*) in the sense of what is due to people would allow the nation the possibility of survival, but Yahweh's wrath would reduce it to so few that its survival would be endangered. This plea for justice is similar in its hoped-for consequences to oracular expressions of Yahweh's will to increase the nation (29.6; 30.19). It is, however, questionable whether such a concern with the survival of the nation should be regarded as being 'rooted in the patriarchal traditions' (Berridge 1970, 196). More likely is the case that such exilic problems of population levels contributed to the form taken by the patriarchal stories, especially in relation to increase of numbers (cf. Isa. 49.19–21; 51.2; 54.1–3). Israel began as the fewest of all peoples (cf. Deut. 7.7; 26.5), but became a great nation (a process reversed, according to the Deuteronomists, because of disobedience, Deut. 28.62). In this lament the nation prays for justice so that it does not return to being too few for survival. As such, the lament must be seen as coming from a time after the fall of Jerusalem and representing (cultic?) concern about the nation's future.

This interpretation of vv. 23–24 helps to explain why an extract from a lament psalm appears at this point. Israel (Jacob) is devastated by the nations (the result of Yahweh's anger Ps. 79.5) and now prays for Yahweh to redirect his anger against the nation's enemies. In view of the satire on the customs of the nations in 1–16, the conclusion to the chapter has an ironic undertone (without knowing the editorial history of the chapter it is not possible to determine whether the irony is intentional or otherwise). These stupid nations with their stupid little idols have devoured and consumed Jacob. So much for the powerlessness of their gods! Unintentional irony is also to be found in the contrast between 24 and 25: 'do not treat me with your anger . . . but treat the others with that anger' (see on 18.19–23). It is ironic because it has no awareness that once the anger of Yahweh is released it destroys good and bad alike, his own people and aliens. So to pray for that anger to be poured out on the nations, quite understandable in the context of Ps. 79, while pleading for justice for oneself, is to be exposed to great danger. That irony only arises out of the redaction of the text here and need not be laid at the door of the speaker of v. 24. What is certainly strange in the context of the tradition is the conviction that justice rather than anger is the mode of Yahweh's dealings with his people. Throughout the tradition the anger of Yahweh is the divine response to the community and the cause of its destruction – a destruction which leaves the country a wasteland and the cities uninhabited. Verses 23–24 know nothing of this analysis of the situation, and therefore we may be justified in questioning whether they should be described as a lament (other than in the context here and assuming the holistic approach to interpreting the tradition). Their wisdom elements make it more a statement about the human situation, perhaps here utilized to represent the community of a later period expressing its piety (similar to 9.23–24). The quotation from Ps. 79.6–7 would then conclude the cycle with an expression of animosity against the nations.

C. 11.1 – 13.27

11.1–14

11[1] The word that came to Jeremiah from the LORD: 2 'Hear the words of
this covenant, and speak to the men of Judah and the inhabitants of
Jerusalem. 3 You shall say to them, Thus says the LORD, the God of Israel:
Cursed be the man who does not heed the words of this covenant 4 which
I commanded your fathers when I brought them out of the land of Egypt,
from the iron furnace, saying, Listen to my voice, and do all that I command
you. So shall you be my people, and I will be your God, 5 that I may perform
the oath which I swore to your fathers, to give them a land flowing with
milk and honey, as at this day.' Then I answered, 'So be it, LORD.'

6 And the LORD said to me, 'Proclaim all these words in the cities of
Judah, and in the streets of Jerusalem: Hear the words of this covenant and
do them. 7 For I solemnly warned your fathers when I brought them up
out of the land of Egypt, warning them persistently, even to this day, saying,
Obey my voice. 8 Yet they did not obey or incline their ear, but every one
walked in the stubborness of his evil heart. Therefore I brought upon them
all the words of this covenant, which I commanded them to do, but they
did not.'

9 Again the LORD said to me, 'There is revolt among the men of Judah
and the inhabitants of Jerusalem. 10 They have turned back to the iniquities
of their forefathers, who refused to hear my words; they have gone after
other gods to serve them; the house of Israel and the house of Judah have
broken my covenant which I made with their fathers. 11 Therefore, thus
says the LORD, Behold, I am bringing evil upon them which they cannot
escape; though they cry to me, I will not listen to them. 12 Then the cities
of Judah and the inhabitants of Jerusalem will go and cry to the gods to
whom they burn incense, but they cannot save them in the time of their
trouble. 13 For your gods have become as many as your cities, O Judah;
and as many as the streets of Jerusalem are the altars you have set up to
shame, altars to burn incense to Baal.

14 Therefore do not pray for this people, or lift up a cry or prayer on their
behalf, for I will not listen when they call to me in the time of their trouble.'

[1] Cf. 7.1; 14.1; 18.1; 30.1 for the reception of the word formula. **[2]** MT *šimᵉʿû . . . wᵉdibbartām*, 'hear . . . and speak', plurals: BHS reads *wᵉdibbartem* (G sing). Rudolph omits, 2, 3a ('you shall say to them . . .'). **[4]** MT *waʿăśîtem ʾôtām kᵉkōl . . .* 'and do *them* all . . .': delete *ʾôtām* (with G), due here to *waʿăśîtem ʾôtām*, 'and do them', in v. 6. **[6]** G lacks 'all (these words)'. **[7]** G lacks all of v. 7 and only has 'but they did not' of v. 8 (*kai ouk epoiēsan* = *wᵉlōʾ ʿāśû*). MT *haškēm wᵉhāʿēd*, 'warning persistently', lit. 'rising early and warning', cf. on 7.13, 25. **[9]** RSV 'Again', an interpretative point rather than the translation of a corresponding word in MT. MT *qešer*, 'conspiracy', rather than 'revolt'. **[10]** MT *wᵉhēmmāh*, 'and they': G *kai idou autoi* = *wᵉhinnēh hēmmāh*, 'and behold they'. **[13]** MT 13a = 2.28b. G lacks 'altars to shame'; MT is probably a variant of 'altars to burn incense to Baal'; the euphemism *bōšet*, 'shame', is unnecessary given the direct reference to Baal. Thompson, 340n., offers a poetic arrangement of vv. 13–14. **[14]** Cf. 7.16, which is almost the same as 11.14. MT *bᵉʿad rāʿātām*, 'on behalf of their trouble', read *bᵉʿēt*, 'at the time of . . .', with Vrs.

Thiel 1973, 139–57

This lengthy section presents Jeremiah as a preacher of the covenant. Apart from the secondary unit in 3.16, this is the first reference to covenant in the book and it inevitably occurs in a Deuteronomistically constructed sermon (cf. 7.1–8.3 for other Deuteronomistic strands). That the language and ideas of vv. 1–13 are a Deuteronomistic composition can hardly be disputed: 'the words of this covenant' (2, 3, 6, cf. Deut. 29.1 [MT 28.69], 9 [8]; II Kings 23.3); 'cursed be . . . Amen' (3, 5, cf. Deut. 27.15–26); 'from the iron furnace' (4, cf. Deut. 4.20; I Kings 8.51); 'a land flowing with milk and honey' (5, cf. 32.22; Deut. 6.3; 11.9; 26.9, 15; 27.3; 31.20); 'to go after other gods' (10, cf. 7.6, 9; 13.10; 16.11; 25.6; 35.15; Deut. 6.4; 8.19; 11.28; 13.2; 28.14). The repetitiveness of the phrases used throughout the sermon also reveals the mark of the Deuteronomists (analysis in Thiel; cf. Nicholson 1970, 67–8). The presentation of Jeremiah as a preacher of the covenant and spokesman of the law is characteristically Deuteronomistic (in Deuteronomy Moses has these roles). In this sermon the catastrophe has already happened (8, 'therefore I brought upon them all the words of this covenant . . .', though G lacks 7–8), so it is too late to warn the community. However, that is not the point of the sermon: it is preached to those living after the disaster and is intended to warn them about the consequences of disobedience. It 'represents the actualization for a later generation of the Word of Yahweh spoken by the prophet Jeremiah to an earlier generation' (Nicholson 1970, 67).

The unit may be divided into a number of sub-sections: 1–5, 6–8, 9–13 with 14 as a redactional addition (Duhm divides it into 1–3a, 3b–5, 6–8, 9–14). The triple division follows the occasions of the divine speaking (1, 6, 9), even though these are editorial markers. Nicholson finds a threefold pattern in the sermon: proclamation of Yahweh's law (3–7); Israel's disobedience (8–10); Yahweh's judgment on Israel (11–17). This threefold structure he also finds in the temple sermon and 34.8–22 (cf. 1970, 64, 68–9). It follows the Deuteronomistic presentation of history as the sphere of the divine word, its proclamation to Israel and the reception of that word (usually a negative reception). The main focus of the Deuteronomistic sermons in Jeremiah is the reception of the word and its rejection by Judah (e.g. 7.13; 11.10; 17.23; 34.14, 17). Originally the sermon may have been preached by a number of speakers (as the plural verbs in MT 2 demonstrate and the reference to 'cities . . . streets' in 6 indicates, though it may be a stereotypical phrase from the editing), but in its final form here it is made into the preaching of Jeremiah (v. 1). This movement from communal activity to solitary individual action may typify the process whereby the many forms and genres of the tradition were reshaped into the presentation of Jeremiah as a paradigmatic figure. In the prose sermons he is edited into the material: thus v. 1 makes all that follows Yahweh's word to Jeremiah and the other two sections become a command to him (v. 6) and information conveyed to him (v. 9). Apart from v. 5, 'then I answered, "So be it, Yahweh" ', there is neither response nor movement from Jeremiah throughout the section. It is clear from these factors that the Deuteronomistic sermon carries the figure of Jeremiah rather than that the present shape of the sermon developed from words originally preached by him.

A different analysis of 11.1–14 is offered by other commentators who, although acknowledging that the sermon is Deuteronomistic in language and style, believe 'there is no reason to doubt that it reflects Jeremiah's actual sentiments and activity' (Bright, 89). This approach then requires a discussion of the probable occasion on which Jeremiah may have preached this kind of sermon. The similarity between v.2 and II Kings 23.3 suggests that it should be related to Josiah's reform and represents Jeremiah as a preacher of that reform (e.g. Feinberg, 95–8; Harrison, 94–6). However, in view of the breakdown of the covenant and the conspiracy among the men of Judah, some exegetes prefer to relate the sermon to the time of Jehoiakim (e.g. Bright, 89; Thompson, 343). Questions about the identity of the covenant, i.e. whether it refers to the covenant made by Josiah or at Sinai, are irrelevant in that there is only one covenant: the covenant made at Sinai as presented by the Deuteronomists. If the editors intended 11.1–13 to represent Jeremiah as the preacher of the covenant at Josiah's reform, then they have failed singularly to indicate that information in their presentation here. What they have done is to present him as a covenant preacher, but in such general terms that no precise historical setting can be established for his activity. This is what is to be expected from writers whose interests are theological rather than historical. It is the proclamation of the word and its rejection as the grounds for Jerusalem's destruction and the nation's fall which interest the Deuteronomists and allow them to maintain their ideological interpretation of why the catastrophe happened.

The quest for history behind the sermon is a fruitless one because sermons are not statements of exactitudes but repetitive, rhetorical matters. That this is the case may be demonstrated by observing the various elements in vv. 1–13. The phrase 'land flowing with milk and honey' is a cliché in the Bible. It is derived from Canaanite ritual descriptions of the land and, as used in this sermon, indicates nothing about the situation of the people. In fact its presence here in the tradition is ironic in view of the material on drought (e.g. 5.24; 8.13; 12.4a; 14.2–6) and invasion. The stereotypical phrase 'in the cities of Judah, and in the streets of Jerusalem' (6) hardly indicates a peripatetic teaching role for the individual speaker. In v. 7 the rhetoric of preaching may be seen in the repeated idea of 'solemnly warned . . . warning them persistently'. The fathers so warned and destroyed by the curses of the covenant are in fact the generation of Jerusalem's destruction (a point obscured by the further statement in 9–11 but clearer in G). The conspiracy of v. 9 refers to the community's turning back (*šūb*) to the sins of their forefathers (i.e. former fathers). For this breaking of the covenant inescapable evil will come upon them (v. 11). But, it may be asked, if their fathers behaved in such a covenant-breaking manner, why was Jerusalem not destroyed in their time? Why is it only after centuries that the curses attached to breaking the covenant should suddenly become operative? Questions begin to multiply. In v. 11 it is hard to see why the people would bother crying to Yahweh if in fact they had turned from him and were busy worshipping other gods. The rhetorical nature of the sermon is manifestly clear in v. 13, where hyperbole is used. The powerlessness of the gods (v. 12) demonstrated by their failure to help in time of trouble is an ideological point. For the collapse of the community in 587 demonstrated Yahweh's lack of power to protect as much as it exposed the weakness of the gods. In the events of 587 neither Yahweh nor the gods were able to save (that point is made in 44.15–19). The sermon is designed to explain why such a double-edged interpretation is not the case.

Rhetoric apart, the key to understanding the sense of unreality engendered by this sermon is the motif of covenant. As a theological concept the term *b^erīt*, conventionally translated as 'covenant', though perhaps better understood as 'obligation' (cf. Kutsch 1973), is very much the creation of the Deuteronomists (cf. Perlitt 1969; McCarthy 1972). Used as a regulative principle to organize and present the history of the nation from the exodus to the fall of Jerusalem, it suffers considerably from the normal defects of any theory used to explain too much. A covenant enacted by Moses on the plains of Moab as a renewal of an original covenant formed at Sinai and then renewed in every generation until the destruction of the nation, some eight hundred years later, is too little theory for too much reality. The further claim that it was continually broken but all the curses attached to its breaking (e.g. Deut. 28.15–68) were not implemented until centuries after the covenant was breached (i.e. 587) strains credulity to breaking-point and demands a rethinking of the whole subject. The concept makes sense as an attempt to explain the disasters which befell the nation in 587 (or 722 if an Israelite prototype is allowed for) but as a *description* of centuries of history it is unreal. Its reality is an ideological one, and as a retrospective explanation for disaster it serves a theological purpose. Covenant describes the programme of the Deuteronomistic ideology, and the fall of Jerusalem gives it its force. That disaster demonstrated the truth of its claims and allowed sense to be made of an otherwise inexplicable catastrophe. By recasting the nation's history in terms of the covenant the Deuteronomists were able to capture that history for their ideology but to ignore that ideological construction for the belief that it describes 'what really happened' is to allow ideology to distort reality. The sense of unreality generated by the sermon is evidence of such distortion and indicative of how misleading a concept covenant is in modern biblical studies (for the Deuteronomistic treatment of history cf. Hoffmann 1980).

The attachment of v. 14 to the sermon is not necessary; it may be taken with the following verses or treated on its own. In its present context it allows preaching to the community (e.g. 1–13), but not praying for it. The community which serves other gods puts itself beyond the reach of prayer, whether individual or liturgical. The fate of such a community is sealed. Those who heard such sermons would have been warned of what might happen if idolatrous practices were tolerated because of what had happened to Jerusalem in the past.

The importance of the sermon in 1–13 lies in its position at the head of the cycle of material in 11.1 – 13.27. It shapes the way the cycle is read as a series of statements about the community which broke the covenant (10 *hēpērū . . . b^e^rītī*, 'they broke my covenant': see on 31.32; cf. Thiel 1970). The broken covenant is to be explained in terms of idolatrous practices (the many altars) and serves as shorthand for Deuteronomistic notions of the disobeyed word, the history of rebellion and the rejection of the prophets. The image of the broken covenant is used here and in 31.32 to make the same point about the community's failure in the past. In the communal lament of 14.19–22 the motif occurs, but in an appeal to Yahweh not to break the covenant. It is important to recognize that the Deuteronomistic notion of the broken covenant is only one side of the argument; on the other side is the community's hope that Yahweh will not break that covenant or the affirmation that the covenant has not been broken (cf. Ps. 44.17; 74.20). In later strands in the tradition the deity affirms his loyalty to specific covenant which are regarded as unbreakable (33.20–21). Thus there is a cluster of notions associated with *b^e^rīt* in the Jeremiah tradition and, although the Deuteronomistic concept of the broken covenants is given at greatest length, it would be unwise to take the Deuteronomistic ideology as the heart of the matter. There is more to be said about *b^e^rīt* than is apparent in 11.1–13, and the tradition clearly embodies elements which require to be dealt with in a dialectical manner.

11.15–17

15 'What right has my beloved in my house, when she has done vile deeds?
Can vows and sacrificial flesh avert your doom? Can you then exult? 16 The
LORD once called you, "A green olive tree, fair with goodly fruit"; but with
the roar of a great tempest he will set fire to it, and its branches will be
consumed. 17 The LORD of hosts, who planted you, has pronounced evil
against you, because of the evil which the house of Israel and the house of
Judah have done, provoking me to anger by burning incense to Baal.'

[15–16] NEB, JPSB, Rudolph, Bright, Driver, Thompson treat as poetry. There are many textual problems here and the various reconstructions offered by scholars are necessarily conjectural. Cf. Hyatt, 911; 1941, 57–60; Driver 1937–38, 108–11 for reconstructions. **[15]** MT *meh līdīdī*, 'what to my beloved?': BHS, Rudolph read *lī dūdaik*, 'what concern of mine are your baskets . . . ?', cf. 24.1; II Kings 10.7. MT *'^{a}śōtāh*, 'her doing'; BHS *'āśītā*, 'you have done', cf. G. MT *ham^{e}zimmātāh*, 'schemes': G *bdelugma*, 'abomination'. MT *hārabbīm*, 'the many'; RSV 'can vows . . .?': G *mē euchai*, 'will vows . . .', followed by BHS *han^{e}dārīm*; Driver *hab^{e}rīyyīm*, 'shall fatlings . . . ?', also Hyatt. MT *ya'ab^{e}rū*, 'they shall pass': revocalize with G, Giesebrecht and others *ya'^{a}bīrū*, 'remove, avert'. MT *mē'ālāik kī rā'ātēkī*, 'from you because of your evil': Driver reads as *mē'ālekā rā'ōtekā kī*, 'thine evil deeds from upon you? Surely . . .', cf. G. MT *'āz ta'^{a}lōzī*, 'then you may exult': G 'will you escape by these things?' (= *'im 'al zō't tā'uzī?* Bright); Driver *kī 'āz ta'^{a}lōz*, 'surely then wouldst thou exult'. BHS (*ha*)*'^{a}zakkeh 'al-zō't*, 'shall I declare you pure', cf. Rudolph; Hyatt treats as a marginal gloss. BHS transposes 16b to the end of 15 'when the great tempest roars'; NEB transposes end of 15 to the middle of 16. **[16]** MT *y^{e}pēh p^{e}rī-tō'ar*, 'fair of fruit form': G lacks 'fruit'. MT may represent variants 'fair of form' (a common phrase)/'fair of fruit' (a unique phrase), cf. Driver. Hyatt reads *y^{e}pēpēh tō'ar*, 'beautiful in form', followed by BHS, Rudolph, cf. 46.20. MT *qārā' yhwh š^{e}mēk*, 'Yahweh called your name': Hyatt omits *yhwh*, as does Driver, who reads *qōre' š^{e}mekā* 'was thy name called' (making the gender agree with *y^{e}dīdī*). MT *l^{e}qōl h^{a}mūllāh g^{e}dōlāh*, 'with the roar of a great tempest': Hyatt omits, Driver shifts to end of v; *h^{a}mūllāh*, meaning uncertain, but probably refers to the wind fanning the flames of the fire in the tree; cf. the noise of the wings described by the word in Ezek. 1.24. MT *hiṣṣīt 'ēš 'ālehā*, 'he kindles a fire against her': G pass. 'was kindled'; BHS reads *b^{e}'ālēhū*, 'in its leaves', cf. Bright. MT *w^{e}rā'ū*, 'breaks' (from *r''*); Driver derives it from *r'h*, an archaic form of a *lamedh-he* verb, 'feed', i.e. a reference to the fire consuming the branches. BHS *bā'^{a}rū*, 'burned', with V, Volz.

Two brief poems and a statement about Yahweh's anger are

appended to the sermon. The first poem questions the people's right to be in the temple (assuming the 'beloved' to be the people referred to in v. 14). It is in a poor state of preservation, so its interpretation is far from clear. Driver's explanation makes sense here:

> The difficulty in interpreting this little poem has been due to the abrupt changes of person which were made clear to an ancient listener by the tone of the speaker's voice but can be indicated only by inverted commas to a modern reader and to the use of irony which too was indicated by voice or gesture at the time of delivery but now requires a mark of exclamation (1937–38, 111).

The image of Judah as Yahweh's beloved also appears in 12.7 (cf. Isa. 5.1). The sense of the poem seems to be an ironic questioning of the beloved's activity in the temple (Rudolph also takes the view that v. 15 has ironic elements in it). The community's schemes are not defined, but by placing the poem here the editors may wish to indicate idolatry as the cause of the questioning. What does Judah imagine it is doing in the temple offering sacral flesh? Given its behaviour, such offerings cannot avert disaster. If this is the correct way to interpret the poem, then it pairs well with v. 14. In 14 liturgical prayers and entreaties cannot be made for the people because the deity is no longer receptive to such activities. In 15 the same may be said about sacrifices. They cannot ward off evil; they have lost their apotropaic power. The rites in the temple are ineffectual because of what the people do (whether in the temple or outside is not clear, cf. 7.9–10). Each occurrence of the prohibition on praying for the people is placed beside a criticism of cultic behaviour (sacrifice in 11.15; 14.12; general temple behaviour in 7.1–15), so the ban should be related to temple services. The pointlessness of sacrifice has already been stated in 6.20, and the Deuteronomistic view that obedience outranks sacrifice (7.22–23) is served here by the incorporation of this brief poem illustrating its preaching (cf. Thiel 1973, 156).

The second brief poem refers to Judah under the image of a green olive tree (cf Ps. 52.8; 92.12–14 for similar images but generalized as a reference to the righteous). At least, that is what Judah used to be called (MT 'he called . . . your name' may not imply a past state now lost). The reference to Yahweh in 16 is omitted by some exegetes because Yahweh is viewed as the speaker in the poem. The beautiful green tree is now to be struck by lightning and consumed (cf. the bride turned whore in 2–3). The tree image is a common one in the Bible (see on 17.5–8), but usually a green tree stands for a positive image. Here it describes a state about to be transformed by the judgment of Yahweh when he fires it and a great wind fans the flames so that the leaves and branches are all consumed. This image of the nation as a once green olive tree blazingly alight with its branches and twigs aflame is an impressively vivid figure of catastrophic destruction.

Why? Why such destruction? Why such useless sacrifices? Because the one who planted the tree (i.e. Yahweh of hosts) has spoken evil against the people. The divine speaking of evil against the nation is a common motif in the Deuteronomistic editing of the tradition (cf. 16.10; 19.15; 26.13; 35.17; 36.31; 40.2). Why should he have spoken evil (i.e. pronounced disaster) against it? Because (*biglal*, cf. 15.4; Deut. 15.10; 18.12; I Kings 14.16) of the evil done by Israel and Judah. The evil here refers to sacrifices (*qṭr* may refer to burning sacrifices or incense) offered to the baals of Canaanite religion (cf. 44.3). This cultic practice provokes Yahweh to anger (in spite of 7.19), so the tree must burn (the image of the green tree and its burning may have subtle overtones of cultic matters – for it was under every green tree that sacral prostitution was supposed to have taken place!). Syncretistic practices have invalidated the offering of sacred flesh and ruined the growth of the green tree.

11.18–20

18 The LORD made it known to me and I knew;
then thou didst show me their evil deeds.
19 But I was like a gentle lamb
led to the slaughter.
I did not know it was against me
they devised schemes, saying,
'Let us destroy the tree with its fruit,
let us cut him off from the land of the living,
that his name be remembered no more.'
20 But, O LORD of hosts, who judgest righteously,
who triest the heart and the mind,
let me see thy vengeance upon them,
for to thee have I committed my cause.

[18] MT *wayhwh*, 'and Yahweh': GS lack *wa*; MT is a redactional link with v. 17 which also begins with *wayhwh*. MT *hōdī'anī*, 'he made known to me': G 'make me know'. MT *wā'ēdā'āh*, 'and I knew': BHS reads *wā'ēdā'ehā* 'and I knew it'. MT *hir'ītanī*, 'you showed me': G *eidon*, 'I saw' = *rā'ītī*; BHS inserts *yhwh* here, treating *y* as haplography. Rudolph (hence BHS) transposes 12.6 to the end of 11.18 as the explanation of what Yahweh showed the speaker. Bright, following Cornill, Peake, transposes 12.1–6 to before 11.18–20; Reventlow 1963, 240–2, uses a similar transposition but limits it to 12.1–4. **[19]** MT *našḥītāh 'ēṣ belaḥmō*, 'let us destroy the tree with its flesh': G *deute kai embalōmon xulon eis ton arton autou*, 'come and let us put wood into his bread', a nicely literal translation of the Hebrew. BHS suggests *belēḥō* for *belaḥmō*, following Hitzig, 91–2, i.e. 'in its sap', cf. Deut. 34.7 where *lēḥōh* means 'his vigour, natural force'; Ezek. 20.47 (MT 21.3) *'ēṣ-laḥ*, 'green tree', as opposed to *'ēṣ yābēš*, 'dry tree'. Dahood 1962, 66, treats the *mem* as enclitic. **[20]** Cf. 20.12: essentially the same verse with the variations: *bōḥēn ṣaddīq*, 'tests the righteous', for *šōpēt ṣedeq*, 'judges righteously', and *rō'eh*, 'sees', for *bōḥēn*, 'tests (heart and mind)'. MT *kelāyōt wālēb*, lit. 'kidneys and heart', i.e. 'affections and mind'. Rudolph inserts 12.3 after 20a (cf. BHS). MT *gillītī*, 'I have revealed (my cause)': BHS *gallōtī*, 'I have rolled on to . . .' cf. Ps. 22.8; 37.5. NEB treats vv. 18–19 as prose, v. 20 as poetry; cf. Thiel 1973, 158f.

The separate problems of distinguishing poetry from prose and determining the relationship of proximate verses to each other are combined when attempting to interpet vv. 18–20. 18 is linked to 17 by the introductory 'and Yahweh' and 19 shares the tree motif with 16–17. Such connections may be sufficient to account for the placing of 18–19 here. The presence of 20 here and in 20.12 points to editorial activity making some association between the two units. The appeal to the deity to wreak vengeance on the enemy identifies what precedes it as a lament about persecution and plots (cf. 20.7–11). But the lament in 18–19 does not provide adequate information for identifying speaker or those spoken about. In its present context what is revealed by Yahweh to the speaker are the evil deeds which account for the destruction of the green tree in 16 (the curse of v. 3 bearing fruit). That meaning is changed by 19, which makes the evil deeds revealed schemes directed against the speaker. The speaker was blithely unaware that he was the target of their plans. This sudden realization of what is afoot has only come to him via divine revelation. Before the reception of this information he was like a tame lamb being led to the slaughter, unaware that it is the meal or sacrifice.

The figure graphically describes blissful ignorance (cf. Isa. 53.7 for a somewhat different use of the image of a lamb led to the slaughter). He may have known about the schemes of destruction, but he did not realize 'it was against *me* they devised schemes'. The plot is simple, but uses the image of a tree (cf. vv. 16–17; 12.2; 17.7–8) and its destruction to summarize the scheming. The intention is to wipe out the name of the victim from memory, to cut him off from the land of the living. The tree is a flourishing one (green with sap), so its annihilation is all the more surprising and shocking. In response to this dastardly plot the speaker appeals to Yahweh, the righteous judge, for protection because he has committed his case (*rīb*, cf. 12.1) to him. Such protection is expected to take the form of divine vengeance against the plotters.

What does it mean? In view of the tree image used of the nation in a context of destruction, the unit looks like a lament for what is about to happen to the people. The enemy has plans to destroy the whole nation and wipe its name from the community of the living (cf. Isa. 10.7 for a similar overreaching plan of destruction by the foreign invader). The community (the 'I' of the speaker already encountered in 4.19–20; 8.18–9.1; 10.23–24) appeals to Yahweh the judge for vindication lest it be blotted out entirely (cf. 10.24) and because its case is now Yahweh's case. Such an interpretation makes sense of 11.18–20.

The matter is more complicated than just making sense of units of text. The next unit in the redaction offers an entirely different interpretation of 18–20 and that understanding of the text has to be taken into account. Whatever the original meaning of 18–20 may once have been, it is changed by its position in the text: what precedes it and what follows it change its meaning. That can cause problems of distortion and infinite regression, so that a text's meaning becomes the history of that text's redaction. If that history were known it would be helpful, but the lack of adequate information on the subject renders interpretation an even more speculative activity than it need be. Such general considerations about the interpretative process have a direct bearing on 18–20.

A number of commentators regard the proper division of units here to be 11.18 – 12.6 and treat the twelve verses as a unit for interpretation purposes. Some exegetes are prepared to rearrange them in order that meaning may become clearer (e.g. Volz, followed by Rudolph, inserts 12.3 into the middle of 11.20; Bright, following

Cornill and Peake, reads 12.1–6 before 11.18; Reventlow follows a similar tactic, but excludes 12.6 from the unit). The justification for such changes of the order of the text is that they make greater sense of it and render it more intelligible. Whether Western standards of sense and intelligibility are adequate warrants for changing the text around is a debatable matter, but such changes are themselves an interpretative move. The meaning of the text will be determined in part by reorganizing the order of the verses.

A more general interpretative problem confronts the exegete when dealing with 11.18–12.6. Some of the laments in the book of Jeremiah (e.g. 11.18–12.6; 15.10–21; 17.12–18; 18.19–23; 20.7–18) are understood as personal statements of the prophet Jeremiah and used to construct aspects of his autobiography (cf. Berridge 1970). The theological struggles and reflections of these poems are sometimes entitled 'the confessions of Jeremiah' (e.g. Hubmann 1978; Ittmann; Skinner 1922, 201–30). As such they are viewed as evidence of Jeremiah's mystical experiences (e.g. Simon 1960) or his prayers (e.g. Blank 1961, 105–42); even as part of his proclamation spoken in public (Berridge 1970, 157) or as 'prayer plus discovered response' communicated to others in a paradigmatic way (like Ezekiel's communications with the elders of Judah – Blank 1977, 31). They are seen also as sophisticated statements of a theological nature about god's passion (pathos) in relation to his own people (e.g. Heschel 1962; Mauser 1971, 102–13). In such treatments of the poems Jeremiah appears as an Augustine or a Rousseau offering his innermost thoughts and feelings as theological commentary on his life and times. He emerges, in these poems, as a man struggling with self-doubt and doubts about god, a man fearful of failure, persecution and dryness of soul, a man caught between them and hell in a struggle with and for faith (e.g. Davidson 1983, 121–39; cf. Crenshaw1984, 31–56). In all the chaos of the period, when the state was disintegrating and the nation was in hot pursuit of other gods in the brothels under the green trees, one man stood faithful to Yahweh and, in spite of terrible suffering and severe doubts, maintained the proclamation of the sacred word to the community. Such a brief summary of extensive writings on these poems allows the mythic nature of the picture of a heroic Jeremiah to emerge as the end-result of reading the laments as 'confessions'. How very modern and existential an image of Jeremiah it produces!

The autobiographical approach to the poems in 11.18–12.6;

15.10–21; 17.12–18; 18.18–23; 20.7–18 is too anachronistic to be correct. Writing biographies and autobiographies is not a feature of ancient Semitic cultures, and the practices of a minority in later Greek and Roman civilization should not be assumed for the earlier period. The presentation of the prophet through the vehicle of these poems is one possible interpretation of the material, but it points in a direction different to biography. A holistic approach to the tradition is capable of interpreting the poems in terms of the created persona of the prophet (e.g. Polk 1984). This persona carries the theology of the editors and instructs the community of a later day. A different approach allows the poems to be seen as communal laments in which the prophet acts as spokesman in the cult (e.g. Reventlow 1963). In this view the poems allow some insight into the community at worship in response to the disintegration of their world. The use of individual laments more frequently than communal ones accounts for the 'I' of the poems. Whether the poems are described as 'laments', 'complaints', or 'confessions' makes a difference to the line of interpretation taken on them. That they should be interpreted as laments seems to be a correct assessment (e.g. Baumgartner 1917; cf. Ahuis 1981), but it does not follow from this that Jeremiah should be treated as a cult spokesman. That view depends upon a prior theory for which adequate data are not available. Yet to characterize the poems as laments is to place them in the same category as many of the psalms and the book of Job (cf. Westermann 1981a; 1981b). Anonymity or fictive representation is the mark of these works and the laments in the Jeremiah tradition probably should be seen in similar terms.

The link with the book of Psalms is in fact stronger than just the common element of anonymous laments. Many of the psalms are attributed to king David and have titles which relate them to incidents in the life of the king (e.g. Ps. 3, 7, 18, 34, 51, 52, 54, 56, 57, 59, 60, 63). Given the title in 1.1 and the occasional editorial framework reference (e.g. 7.1; 11.1; 14.1; 18.1), the anonymous laments in the tradition have become identified as Jeremiah's laments in a way similar to the titles of the psalms (cf. Carroll 1981, 109). An examination of the individual lament psalms will reveal stereotypical language (clichés) that is metaphorical and capable of many meanings but unlikely to have a single referent (cf. Miller 1983). The lament has three dimensions: it is directed at god (accusation or complaint), towards others (the enemy), and towards the speaker

('I' or 'we'). These are so woven together that existence in the community, relationship to god and the meaning of life are inseparable (cf. Westermann 1981a, 267–8). Conflict, the enemy, suffering, incomprehension, complaint, hope, prayer, sickness, bitterness and the treachery of friends are only some of the elements in these outbursts against the exigencies and contingencies of life. There is such an overload of language and emotion in these laments that we cannot reconstruct a biography of the speaker from them. To do so would be to diminish them, to reduce them to a particularity which would rob them of significance and render them incapable of serving the whole community.

To return to the text of 11.18–20 after such a brief consideration of the issues involved in interpreting the lament elements in the tradition allows the analysis to be applied to specific texts. The form of vv. 18–20 hardly follows that of a lament (hence the need some exegetes have to transpose 12.1–6 before it). Yet the sudden interruption of the flow of the text by a fragment lacking sufficient indicators to permit its precise interpretation is a major feature of Jer. 1–25. As a prose statement (Thiel 1973, 157; cf. NEB) it asserts a response of an unidentified speaker to information received that there is a plot against his life. The image of the tame lamb could refer to the speaker's innocence or gullibility, but it could also be a simile for the community unaware that it is about to be slaughtered (cf. Ps. 44.22 for the image of the community as sheep). The tree image is capable, too, of being interpreted of individual (cf. 17.8; Ps. 1.3) or community (11.16; cf. 2.21). If an individual interpretation is given to it and Jeremiah is identified as the tree (the view taken by v. 21), then a certain irony is achieved by the redaction. What Yahweh is planning to do to the community (v. 16), Jeremiah's enemies are planning to do to him (like god, like community!). The appeal to Yahweh in v. 20 reflects an element of the lament form but it may be eisegetical to see vv. 18–19 as a lament because of its presence here. In order to clarify the meaning of vv. 18–20 it is necessary to consider the other pieces associated with it in the editing of the whole section.

11.21–23

21 Therefore thus says the LORD concerning the men of Anathoth, who seek your life, and say, 'Do not prophesy in the name of the LORD, or you will

die by our hand' – 22 therefore thus says the LORD of hosts: 'Behold, I will punish them; the young men shall die by the sword; their sons and their daughters shall die by famine; 23 and none of them shall be left. For I will bring evil upon the men of Anathoth, the year of their punishment.'

---

[21] G 'my life', making Jeremiah the speaker rather than Yahweh. For MT *wᵉlō*, 'and (you will) not', G has *ei de mē* = *wᵉ'im lō'*, 'but if not . . .'. **[22]** G lacks 'therefore thus says Yahweh of hosts'. Rudolph deletes *habbaḥūrīm*, 'the young men', on the grounds that it is the children of the people of Anathoth who will die rather than the children of the young men; he explains its occurrence as a dittography of *baḥereb* 'by the sword' (following Volz), and *ym(tw)* 'shall die'.

A further brief prose piece now identifies the *dramatis personae* in v. 19. Jeremiah (not named as such but implied by the reference to Anathoth) is the target of the plot to kill and the men of Anathoth, his home town (1.1), the conspirators. The reason for the plot is his prophesying in the name of Yahweh (cf. 26.9, 16). What he is prophesying is not stated, but the meaning of the obscure metaphors in v. 19 is narrowed down considerably to the matter of prophesying. The plot to kill is also modified because the divine statement attributes to the men of Anathoth the intention not to kill Jeremiah if he will cease prophesying. A further divine word (only in MT as such) denounces the men of Anathoth and specifies their punishment ('the year of their punishment'): the death of their sons by invasion and their daughters by the concomitant starvation. Thus those who set out to kill one of the sons of Anathoth must bear as their punishment the death of all the children of Anathoth (bar one!). None shall survive.

The explanation provided by vv. 21–23 is a good example of the concretization of stereotypical statements in the life of an individual (e.g. David in the psalms' titles). Jeremiah of Anathoth (29.27; cf. 1.1) and the men of Anathoth (11.21), with property in Anathoth (32.7–7), belong to a minor strand in the tradition which is used infrequently to explain conflict in the life of the *prophet* (it is always in the context of his 'prophesying'). In all the occurrences of this motif (i.e. Anathoth), except for here, Jeremiah is in prison or threatened with some such disciplinary measure (cf. 29.26–27) for prophesying unpleasant things about the community (whether Jerusalem or the one in exile). In 11.21 it is his life which is at stake, and one may assume that his crime, though not stated, is that of prophesying against the city, though that would not explain why the men of Anathoth sought to kill him. Beyond such a patterned explanation speculation must take over: his preaching in Josiah's reform did his family out of their livelihood! An unlikely reason (see on 1.2), if only because the offer of property in 32.7–9 hardly suggests such hostility. Indeed, it would be difficult to reconcile 11.21–23 with 32.7–9 if either or both were treated as referring to historical events. They are stories constructed around the motifs 'do not prophesy' and 'the men of Anathoth' (see on 32.7–9).

The motif 'the men of Anathoth' represents a late strand in, and is peripheral to, the tradition. That it is late is clear from its occurrence only in the prose sections and the redactional framework of 1.1–3, its connection with Jeremiah as 'prophesying', its construction here as an explanation for a lament (12.1–5; cf. psalms' titles), and the Deuteronomistic elements in 11.21–23. The word of judgment is characterized by Deuteronomistic language (cf. Thiel 1973, 159; Vermeylen 1981, 248–50): the introductory formulation 'thus says Yahweh concerning . . .' (cf. 12.14; 14.15), the sword and hunger motifs (cf. 5.12; 14.13, 15, 16; 18.21; an abridged form of the triad 'sword, hunger, pestilence' 14.12; 21.7, 9; 24.10; 27.13; 29.17–18), and the reference to prophesying *in the name of Yahweh* (cf. 14.14–15; 23.25; 26.20; 27.15; 29.9, 21). The final element in the judgment (v. 23b) is similar to 23.12b, except that it has the added specification 'the men of Anathoth'. The strand containing the motif 'the men of Anathoth' may be regarded as one of those minor features in the tradition which developed over the long period of its redaction and which is similar in that respect to the emergence of the Baruch strand (cf. 32.12). In subsequent Jewish traditions Baruch became a major apocalyptic seer and the men of Anathoth an example of the possibility of repentance in spite of the heavy divine decree ordained against them (cf. Schechter 1961, 326).

The penalty for opposing Jeremiah's prophesying is annihilation (*šᵉʾērīt lōʾ tihyeh lāhem*, 'and a remnant shall not be left to them'). The specific reference to not even a remnant remaining is strange. It may be understood as hyperbole typical of the tradition and as intended to underline the fatal consequences of opposing one of Yahweh's prophets (e.g. Amos 7.16–17; 2.12). But it should be considered in the light of the statement that 128 'men of Anathoth' returned from exile (Ezra 2.23; Neh. 7.27). Far from a remnant not being left to them, they would appear to have flourished in exile, and a substantial body of their men could return to the homeland. Is 11.23a then just one more failed prediction of a biblical prophet? Technically the answer must be 'yes'; but the failure of predictions is not a serious problem in the Bible (cf. Carroll 1979). A better understanding of the issue here would be to see 11.21–23 as a polemic against 'the men of Anathoth', reflecting some controversy in the Jerusalem of the reconstruction period (i.e. Persian) incorporated into the tradition as an element in the construction of the opposition to Jeremiah theme (cf. on 22.28–30). That theme is an important element in the tradition, and to it each of the laments or 'psalms of the book of Jeremiah' (Vermeylen 1981, 268) makes a contribution. The motif 'the men of Anathoth' only occurs here and is not therefore a major element in the poems. At best it may only be an echo of some inner community struggle long forgotten but for this vestige of it – or a trace of events contemporaneous with the redaction of the tradition.

12.1–6

121 Righteous art thou, O LORD, when I complain to thee;
yet I would plead my case before thee.
Why does the way of the wicked prosper?
Why do all who are treacherous thrive?
2 Thou plantest them, and they take root;
they grow and bring forth fruit;
thou art near in their mouth
but far from their heart.
3 But thou, O LORD, knowest me;
thou seest me and triest my mind toward thee.
Pull them out like sheep for the slaughter,
and set them apart for the day of slaughter.
4 How long will the land mourn,
and the grass of every field wither?
For the wickedness of those who dwell in it
the beasts and the birds are swept away,
because men said, 'He will not see our latter end.'
5 'If you have raced with men on foot, and they have wearied you,
how will you compete with horses?
And if in a safe land you fall down,
how will you do in the jungle of the Jordan?

6 For even your brothers and the house of your father,
even they have dealt treacherously with you;
they are in full cry after you;
believe them not,
though they speak fair words to you.’

---

[2] MT *yēl^{e}ku*, ‘they go’, i.e. ‘grow’ (cf. *hlk*, Hos. 14.7 [EV 6]): G *eteknopoiēsan*, ‘they have begotten children’ = *yāl^{e}dū*; Volz, 140, reads *yēlaḥū*, ‘they are fresh’ (i.e. ‘sappy’). MT *mikkilyōtēhem*, ‘from their kidneys’, i.e. ‘their true feelings’, cf. 11.20; 20.12a. **[3]** MT *w^{e}‘attāh yhwh y^{e}da‘tānī tir’ēnī*, ‘but you, O Yahweh, you know me, you see me’, cf. 11.18 (a variant?). Rudolph, Weiser follow v. 2 with 4 because they transpose 3 to between 11.20a and 20b. G lacks ‘you see me’ and ‘pull them out like sheep for the slaughter, and’. **[4]** Volz, Rudolph, Bright omit the verse except for the last clause on the grounds that it is out of place here, cf. BHS. MT *lō’ yir’eh ’et-’aḥ^{a}rītēnū*, ‘he will not see our latter end’: G *ouk opsetai ho theos hodous hēmon*, ‘god will not see our way’, thus providing a non-ambiguous subject for ‘he will see’ and reading *’orḥōtēnū*. **[5]** MT *ūb^{e}’ereṣ šālōm ’attāh bōṭēaḥ*, ‘and in a peaceful land you are confident’: Volz inserts ‘not’ before *bṭḥ*; Driver 1937–38, 111f., treats *bṭḥ* as ‘tumble down’, cf. NEB ‘fall headlong’. Bright understands it as ‘not on your guard’, i.e. ‘are unsuspecting, feel secure’. MT *big^{e}’ōn hayyardēn*, ‘in the jungle of Jordan’, lit. ‘in the majesty of Jordan’: ‘referring to the green and shady banks, clothed with willows, tamarisks, and cane, in which the lions made their covert Je 49.19; 50.44; Zc 11.3, and therefore dangerous Je 12.5’ (BDB, 145). **[6]** MT *qār^{e}’ū ’aḥ^{a}rekā mālē’*, ‘they are in full cry after you’: cf. 4.5, ‘they cry aloud after you’ (cf. Driver 1937–38, 99f.). BHS follows Volz in reading *qāš^{e}rū ’aḥ^{a}rekā kullām*, ‘they have all conspired after you’, cf. G *episunēchthēsan* ‘they have conspired against’. This verse is transposed to between 11.18 and 19 by Rudolph (cf. Bright, who places 12.1–6 before 11.18–20); other scholars (e.g. Reventlow 1963, Berridge 1970) treat v. 6 separately from 11.18 – 12.5.

Holladay 1963; McKane 1965a; Reventlow 1963, 242–51; Vermeylen 1981

The wide range of disagreement among scholars about which verses constitute the unit here and the nature of its relation to 11.18–23 should warn the reader against expecting simple interpretations of a rather complex text. Neither speaker nor situation is identified in the poem, though 11.18–23 provide both if taken with 12.1–5(6). The late elements and discrete pieces making up 11.18–23 militate against taking such a view *simpliciter*. If the history-of-redaction approach is taken (cf. Vermeylen), then a very complicated structure is uncovered and a rather different picture emerges of the meaning of 11.18 – 12.6. The more conventional approaches to the text understand it as a lament (cf. Baumgartner 1917, 52–60; Berridge 1970, 160–6), and because it is an individual lament attribute it to Jeremiah. Reventlow regards it as a communal lament in individual dress (vv. 1–4 with the divine answer in v. 5; 1963, 249). Baumgartner stresses the point that Jeremiah speaks here not as a prophet but as an individual pietist (1917, 54). Holladay organizes the material into two confessions of Jeremiah (11.18–20; 12.1–3) with two divine answers (11.21–23; 12.5–6; excising v. 4 as secondary, cf. 1976a, 138–42). Weiser, Rudolph, McKane all treat 12.1–5 as a confession of Jeremiah (though there are variations in the content and order of the verses in their accounts). Vermeylen offers the most radical treatment of 11.18 – 12.6. He sees the core of the unit in 12.4abα.5, an oracle of Jeremiah. This was inserted into a series of oracles about the same subject (8.13–17; 9.9–11 [EV 10–12], 16–21 [EV 17–22]; 10.18–22; 12.4–5*, 7–13) which may have formed a small collection in this part of the book. Its present location in 11.18 – 12.1–3, 6 came about by a number of editorial and post-exilic additions. A second ancient kernel is preserved in 11.21–22, a Deuteronomistic text associated with vv. 1–17, and answers the question of why the Israelites were rejected by Yahweh (because they rejected the prophetic word). From the Persian period an editor interpreted 11.21–22 in relation to the communal menace posed by the betrayal of unfaithful Israelites and, with the addition of vv. 18–19*, introduced a note of complaint. A second post-exilic editor added 11.18b*, 20, 23 and 12.1–3, 4bβ, 6, thus giving the unit its present appearance. Hostility towards the 'bad Jews' of the period (i.e. their prosperity being a scandal to the godly and calling in question the justice of Yahweh) puts the accent on vengeance rather than oppression. This analysis results in the text being read as the product of a complex literary history rather than as the discourse of Jeremiah's sense of being a persecuted prophet (Vermeylen, 264).

Gerard Manley Hopkins' famous sonnet 'Thou art indeed just, Lord, if I contend . . . Mine, O thou lord of life, send my roots rain' brilliantly transforms elements of 12.1–4 into a statement of personal spiritual anguish, but has no bearing on the exegesis of the text (cf. Hopper 1978 on Hopkins and the confessions). Forensic as well as lament overtones are to be found in the initial statement, indicating a dispute (*rīb*) between speaker and deity. Yahweh is admitted to be right (cf. Ps. 119.137), but the speaker wishes to pass judgment on him (*dibbēr mišpāṭīm*, 'pass sentence', cf. 1.16; 4.12 [both with Yahweh as subject]; 39.5 = 52.9 [Nebuchadrezzar implied as subject]). The argument is about the prosperity of the guilty (*rᵉšā'īm*), i.e. those who are really treacherous (*bōgᵉdē bāged*, cf. 9.2). Like the complaints of the book of Job (e.g. Job 21), the speaker is deeply disturbed by the apparent well-being of this group. The deity plants them, they grow and yield fruit (the horticultural metaphors dominating the unit may explain why 11.16–12.6 have been linked together). Made prosperous by Yahweh, they are in fact godless: apparent godliness (they mouth the right words,cf. 23.31) conceals their real feelings. This assessment of a class of people reflects a strand of piety in the tradition (cf. 7.9–10; 9.8, 25–26). It is the differentiation between outer appearances and inner realities: e.g. the people whose social lives are oppressive but who go to the temple and claim to be saved; the neighbours speaking *šālōm* to each other but planning ambushes in their hearts; the peoples whose penises are cut but whose minds are unreceptive. The protestation of innocence (v. 3) indicates the speaker's separate status from the godless. Yahweh, who can penetrate beyond appearances, knows and sees the innermost being (cf. I Sam. 16.7) and can differentiate between righteous and wicked (this the wicked appear to deny if 'he will not see our latter end' belongs to v. 2; cf. Ps. 73.17; Weiser, 103f.). The sentiment here is essentially that of 11.20; 20.12, except that the appeal for vengeance is expressed metaphorically. The wicked are to be treated like sheep (cf. 11.19), i.e. ritually prepared (*haqdīš*) for killing.

The lament changes at this point because the prosperity of the wicked (real or imagined) does not fit the motif of the land suffering from terrible drought, so vv. 1–3 should be viewed quite separately from vv 4–6. The first lament is a very general rehearsal of a conventional lament theme: the well-being of the wicked (cf. Ps. 73.1–14; Job 24) with its corollary of the suffering of the righteous unstated. The speaker affirms Yahweh's rightness, so must be counted among the righteous. The plea for vengeance in v. 3b is also the appeal for vindication of the speaker. So the poem should be understood as an element in the righteous-wicked conflict characteristic of many psalms and later piety. Identifying the wicked of v. 1 is as difficult as specifying who the wicked are in the psalms. They may be the nations in general, that nation in particular which is attacking Israel, the personal enemies of the speaker, a group within the community or a clash between different ideological groups. In its present context the poem may be put in Jeremiah's mouth and the wicked may be identified as his personal enemies. Who might they be? The nation as a whole, the leaders of the community, a particular group within the community (e.g. prophets) or perhaps his family? If Jeremiah stands as spokesman for the community (e.g. Reventlow's view) then the enemies are Judah's enemies, i.e. Babylon. The range of possibilities is considerable. The redaction may give the impression that Jeremiah's family constitute the wicked here, but that is only one possible reading of the text. It does not resolve the problem of whether the redaction has not distorted the original poem by associating an element of later piety with a late fragment of a social controversy which now contributes to the persona of Jeremiah.

The drought motif of v. 4 blames the state of the country on the wickedness of the people living in it. Whether it should be associated with other drought elements in the tradition (e.g. 14.2–6) or be understood as a metaphor of the results of invasion is difficult to determine. Beasts and birds are swept away in the drought or invasion (cf. 9.10). It is a gruelling experience for the whole land and it has been caused by human wickedness. Does v. 5 extend this point? Is the speaker addressed in mid-sentence or does he continue speaking? Who is the 'you'? Is it an individual or the community? Commentators who favour the individual interpretation (Hebrew is singular) treat v. 5 as a divine statement and Jeremiah as the recipient of it as the answer to his lament in v. 1 (where *madūʿa*, 'why' is a term characteristic of the Jeremiah tradition but never used in a lament psalm). The text gives no indication that v. 5 is a divine word (contrast 11.21, 22), so it should be read as a continuation of v. 4. The drought as punishment of the wicked certainly renders v. 1 questionable as part of 4–5. How can the wicked be said to prosper if the land is toiling under the horrors of a drought which has killed off beasts and birds? It would make better sense to keep 1–3 and 4–5 quite separate, though many commentators simply eliminate the drought reference on the grounds that it is completely out of place here. Retaining it spoils the line of interpretation pursued by such hermeneutical moves. Whether 4 and 5 should be read together is also a problem. The two could be read as discrete fragments but taken together they make an interesting, if somewhat obscure, point.

The community, i.e. 'you', has wearied itself racing against runners, so how will it manage to compete (*t^e^taḥ^a^reh*, cf. 22.15; Job 19.11; Neh. 3.20 'to be a rival') against horses? The same point is made using different figures in 5b: if you are secure in a land of peace (ironic? cf. alternative translations) how will you cope in the dangerous jungle of Jordan? The point of this strange set of images seems to be: 'If you think this is a difficult situation, just wait and see what is going to happen next!' However the unit is understood, v. 5 is not easy to relate to any of it. The drought is bad enough, but worse is coming (i.e. invasion from the north?). The image of the horses may be the clue for relating v. 5 to the Babylonian invasion (cf. Vermeylen, 247). In 4.13; 6.23; 8.16 it is part of the enemy from the north cycle, so it is possible that here it refers to the same event. A wicked people must face further punishment for its wicked ways and, in spite of the harshness of the drought, there is much worse to come.

Exegetes who read v. 5 as the divine response to the individual lament interpret it as a warning to Jeremiah that things are going to become much tougher for him. In other words, 'stop complaining about trivialities and prepare to face real problems!'. This interpretation would make it unique among responses to laments. Silence would be preferable to such an answer. This is an unlikely understanding of v. 5 and, though much pastoral counselling may be derived from it, not one which can be matched with subsequent elements in the tradition. Weiser relates it, as Jeremiah's personal problem, to 'the tension between belief and thought' (105), whereas McKane thinks it means he must 'hammer out another theology' (1965a, 48). It is difficult to see how either analysis is produced from these verses without assuming a good deal of post-biblical theological reflection in the handling of the text.

Discerning the significance of v. 6 is no less difficult than it is for all the verses in this section. Those exegetes who connect it with vv. 1–5 make it parallel 11.21–23, i.e. an identification of the conspirators against Jeremiah. It is his own family who are plotting against him. This interpretation causes some to transpose v. 6 to a position after 11.18 (e.g. Rudolph) or even to read 12.1–6 before 11.18 (e.g. Bright). Such a radical reversal of the order of the units may yield 'an excellent sense' (Bright, 89), but it is a feature of most of the wide variety of ways of interpreting and rearranging the text that they yield sense. Making sense of the text *as it is* is a real problem for the exegete, and it is for that reason that access to the history of the text's redaction would be so valuable.

12.6 is a difficult verse to understand, especially as an isolated one (cf. Reventlow, 257). Attached to 12.1–5, it can distort the different meanings of the pieces making up that unit, and perhaps it is better understood as forming the unit vv. 6–13 (cf. Berridge 1970, 127). However, its place here may be due to the use of *bgd* in vv. 1 and 6. Accounting for v. 6 in relation to vv. 1–5 may yield sense along the lines that it is about family, i.e. communal, conflict and concerns treacherous acts masked by fair words. In vv. 1–2 similar faults are identified as marks of the wicked. This kind of communal conflict (treacherous acts combined with false speaking) is referred to in 9.2–6, 8. So v. 6 may be an additional comment on a category of people classified as the wicked. The household reference indicates inner community conflict, but the cause is not specified. Household conflict is a motif in 23.33–40 (see on 23.34; cf. Zech. 13.2–6), where disputes about the prophetic word are the concern of the unit. It does not follow that v. 6 should be read as such a dispute, though it would provide a good parallel for the prohibition on prophesying motif in 11.21–23. The stress in v. 6 is on the group opposing the 'you' (i.e. the righteous of v. 3?), 'even your brothers and the house of your father, even they . . . even they . . .' (note *gam . . . gam-hēmmāh . . . gam-hēmmāh . . .*). Similar motifs are to be found in Micah 7.5–6, and many of the psalms (e.g. Ps. 5.10; 28.3; 52.1–7; 55.12–15, 20–21; 62.4; 120). Indeed, the themes of the opposition of friends and neighbours, of tongues speaking one thing while the mind plans something quite different, and of the enemy being members of one's own household (e.g. Zech. 13.6b) appear so frequently in biblical texts that they are clearly too stereotypical to permit precise identification of a specific situation to which they may allude. Connecting v. 6 with v. 5 may have the effect of turning v. 5 into a warning to the righteous to be on their guard against the wicked, because even when they feel secure, danger awaits them (cf. Vermeylen, 264). At the same time it is not difficult to see some justification for the variety of interpretations offered of v. 6, especially in relation to the construction of the persona of Jeremiah. The continual conflict between the pious and the wicked (a central theme of the book of Psalms) has left its mark on the Jeremiah tradition, even to the extent of having some of its interpreters make Jeremiah a spokesman for the pious.

12.7–13

7 'I have forsaken my house,
 I have abandoned my heritage;
I have given the beloved of my soul
 into the hands of her enemies.
8 My heritage has become to me
 like a lion in the forest,
she has lifted up her voice against me,
 therefore I hate her.
9 Is my heritage to me like a speckled bird of prey?
 Are the birds of prey against her round about?
Go, assemble all the wild beasts;
 bring them to devour.
10 Many shepherds have destroyed my vineyard,
 they have trampled down my portion,
they have made my pleasant portion
 a desolate wilderness.
11 They have made it a desolation;
 desolate, it mourns to me.
The whole land is made desolate,
 but no man lays it to heart.
12 Upon all the bare heights of the desert
 destroyers have come;
for the sword of the LORD devours
 from one end of the land to the other;
 no flesh has peace.
13 They have sown wheat and have reaped thorns,
 they have tired themselves out but profit nothing.
They shall be ashamed of their harvests
 because of the fierce anger of the LORD.'

---

[9] MT *ha'ayiṭ ṣābū'a*, 'is . . . a variegated bird of prey?'; G *mē spēlaion huainēs*, 'is not . . . a hyena's cave?'. The difficult word is *ṣābū'a*, 'dye, dyed stuff', cf. Judg. 5.30, BDB, 840; but KB, 741, understands it as 'hyena' (cf. 'valley of hyenas' [*gē haṣṣᵉbō'īm*] I Sam. 13.18). Rudolph, 84, favours 'colourful'; NEB 'Is this land of mine a hyena's lair?'. JPSB 'My own people act toward Me/Like a bird of prey [or] a hyena; let the birds of prey surround her!'. Volz omits the first occurrence of *ha'ayiṭ* as a dittography or a marginal note. MT *lī*, 'to me': BHS and others read as *kī*, 'for'. MT *ha'ayiṭ sābīb 'ālehā*, 'are birds of prey round about against her?': *hā-*, 'the', better read with G, BHS. MT *'isᵉpū*, 'gather . . .': BHS *hē'āsᵉpū* passive, 'let (the beasts) be gathered . . .' (cf. V, Cornill). **[10]** MT *ḥelᵉqātī*, 'my portion': some mss *naḥ^a^lātī*, 'my heritage'. **[11]** MT *śāmāh*, 'he made it' plural required, *śāmuhā*. Assonances in the Hebrew are impossible to convey in English: *š^e^māmāh* (10) *śāmāh lišmāmāh . . . š^e^mēmāh nāšmmāh . . . śām*. MT *kī 'ēn*, 'for no . . .': Duhm, Cornill, Rudolph *w^e^'ēn*, 'and no . . .'. **[12]** NEB treats verse as prose. BHS omits 'for the sword of Yahweh devours' as an eschatological expansion (Rudolph). **[13]** G imperatives for MT perfects: 'Sow . . . reap'. MT *mitt^e^bū'ōtēkem*, 'your harvests', read *-hem*, 'their . . .'. G reads last sentence as 'be ashamed of your boasting, because of reproach before the lord'.

A poem responding to the destruction of temple, people and land. As such it should be related to the period around 587, though some commentators prefer the period of 597 (cf. 35.11). If v. 7 is understood as a very general reference to divine anger against the people and not read as Yahweh's withdrawal from the temple and city (cf. Ezek. 11.23), then 597 may be the context of the poem, but that is a less likely reading of the poem. Yahweh is the speaker here, and he announces his actions and the reasons for them (the motifs of 'house' and 'beloved' allow for links with 11.15, but are interrupted by the build up of units now constituting 11.18 – 12.6). Many different images are used in the poem to describe the disasters which have befallen the nation. The cause of its destruction is given in the figure of the roaring lion in the forest in v. 8. Jerusalem, as a lion, has roared against Yahweh, so he hates her. The significance of the figure is not clear: is the roar an act of defiance (from a lion!) or an act of aggression indicating a dangerous animal? The images of v. 9 are difficult: like a very colourful bird Jerusalem is attacked by other birds of prey (RSV); or like a hyena she is surrounded by birds of prey (JPSB; cf. G, NEB). Whatever the precise image may be, its general sense is that the land is the prey and the wild beasts have gathered to devour it. Thus the invading forces have destroyed the land (cf. 6.3) and turned it into a desert (cf. 2.21 for the degeneration of the vineyard). As a result of such devastation no one pays any attention to the land any more; throughout the land there is no peace (*šālōm*) for anyone. The final comment in v. 13 may come from a later source (so Duhm) reflecting on the wasted harvests (cf. 8.13, 20), though it may be an observation on the fact that the people did the sowing but the invasion has frustrated the harvesting of it.

12.14–17

14 Thus says the LORD concerning all my evil neighbours who touch the heritage which I have given my people Israel to inherit: 'Behold, I will pluck them up from their land, and I will pluck up the house of Judah from among them. 15 And after I have plucked them up, I will again have compassion on them, and I will bring them again each to his heritage and each to his land. 16 And it shall come to pass, if they will diligently learn the ways of my people, to swear by my name, "As the LORD lives," even as they taught my people to swear by Baal, then they shall be built up in the midst of my people. 17 But if any nation will not listen, then I will utterly pluck it up and destroy it, says the LORD.'

---

[14] MT *'al-kol-š^e kēnay*, 'concerning all my neighbours'; G lacks 'my'. **[16]** MT *darkē 'ammī*, 'the ways of my people': G *tēn hodon tou laou mou*, 'the way of my people' = *derek 'ammī*, cf. *derek haggōyīm*, 'the way of the nations', 10.2. **[17]** MT *w^e 'im lō' yišmā'ū*, 'but if they will not listen': G *ean de mē epistrepsōsin*, 'if they will not return' (= *yāšūbū*); *yiššāb^e'ū*, '(if they will not) swear', cf. BHS following Ehrlich 1912, 277. To make sense of the unit NEB rearranges it thus: 14 (up to 'from their land'), 16, 17, 14, 15.

McKane 1981, 233–7

A prose section follows the poem about the devastated heritage and offers some reflections on 'my evil neighbours' (cf. 'my house' v. 7). It is not easy to follow the argument of the unit (hence NEB's rearrangement of the text) or to determine what its background may be. Most commentators regard it as not coming from Jeremiah, though a few think there may be a genuine kernel of his work in it (e.g. Cornill, Giesebrecht; Rudolph relates v. 14 to his thought in 1.5, 10). There are a number of Deuteronomistic elements in it which point away from Jeremiah to editorial circles (cf. Thiel 1973, 162–8). The unit uses terms to be found in the tradition (cf. 1.10 for *ntš*, 'pluck up'; *'bd*, 'destroy'), but they are handled in a strange way. This is not a statement about Yahweh's intention to have mercy on his people whom he has destroyed, but is about his intentions towards Israel's neighbours. These neighbours are not specified except for the phrase 'as they taught my people to swear by Baal', which suggests a Palestinian setting for them. They are not the Assyrians or Babylonians (as might be expected if vv. 7–13 refer to the Babylonian invasion and destruction of city and land), but the nations listed in 9.26; 48–49. Yet v. 14, 'I will pluck up the house of Judah from among them', hardly makes sense in this context. All these nations are envisaged as having been plucked from their own lands (*ntš* is used five times) and as experiencing Yahweh's compassion in being restored to their own lands. Then they are represented as living in the midst of Yahweh's people, built up by Yahweh (for *bnh* cf. 1.10) because they have become Yahwists (on swearing by Yahweh's name, cf. 4.2). Not permanent Yahwists, for they may still be plucked up yet again and destroyed. Their security depends upon conforming to Judaean religious standards.

The reference to any nation in v. 17 turns the piece into a general ruling about the alternatives of 'obeying' or 'plucking up'. It makes the unit a practical application of the general principles about turning (*šūb*) in 18.7–10. If a nation responds to the divine will, it will survive and be able to maintain a thriving existence in the land (the sense of *bnh* in v. 16, cf. Bach 1961), but if it refuses to obey Yahweh, it will be plucked up (i.e. loss of normal living conditions). The neighbours are the peoples among whom Judah lives after its restoration to its own land, hence the unit is about post-exilic times and proselytizing among the heathen (cf. Duhm, 119). In such a period there developed among some Judaeans the practice of admitting people from other nations into their religion. All the nations having suffered under the boot of the Babylonians, they could look forward to some form of divine restoration (cf. 46.26; 48.47; 49.6). Here the restoration is tied into whatever is entailed by swearing 'as Yahweh lives'. The nations were also expected to make pilgrimages to Jerusalem (Isa. 2.2–4; Zech. 14.16–21) or to worship Yahweh in their own land (Isa. 19.19–25). This unit should therefore be seen as a fragment belonging to such discussions, but couched in terminology derived from the Jeremiah tradition and its Deuteronomistic redaction. McKane argues that vv. 14–15 are a late, artificial prophetic composition to which have been added vv. 16–17 (235). He also associates the piece with the post-exilic community. It encourages the people not to fear their neighbours who, though in the past they had gloated over Judah's misfortunes (cf. Obad. 10ff.; Zeph. 2.8), also had suffered exile and, like Judah, would be restored to their own lands by Yahweh. Thus the exegetical expansion of a motif from the tradition shows Jeremiah in the role of a prophet to the nations!

13.1–11

13 1 Thus said the LORD to me, 'Go and buy a linen waistcloth, and put it
on your loins, and do not dip it in water.' 2 So I bought a waistcloth
according to the word of the LORD, and put it on my loins. 3 And the word
of the LORD came to me a second time, 4 'Take the waistcloth which you
have bought, which is upon your loins, and arise, go to the Euphrates, and
hide it there in a cleft of the rock.' 5 So I went, and hid it by the Euphrates,
as the LORD commanded me. 6 And after many days the LORD said to me,
'Arise, go to the Euphrates, and take from there the waistcloth which I
commanded you to hide there.' 7 Then I went to the Euphrates, and dug,
and I took the waistcloth from the place where I had hidden it. And behold,
the waistcloth was spoiled; it was good for nothing.
8 Then the word of the LORD came to me: 9 'Thus says the LORD: Even
so will I spoil the pride of Judah and the great pride of Jerusalem. 10 This
evil people, who refuse to hear my words, who stubbornly follow their own
heart and have gone after other gods to serve them and worship them, shall
be like this waistcloth, which is good for nothing. 11 For as the waistcloth
clings to the loins of a man, so I made the whole house of Israel and the
whole house of Judah cling to me, says the LORD, that they might be for me
a people, a name, a praise, and a glory, but they would not listen.'

---

[1] Same formula as 17.19; cf. 15.1. **[3]** G lacks 'a second time'; for MT *šēnīt*, cf. 1.13; 33.1. **[4]** MT *pᵉrātāh*, 'to Perat', i.e. the Euphrates; A *eis Pharan*, 'to Farah'. **[9]** MT *'ašḥīt*, 'I will destroy'; BHS reads *nišḥat*, 'was destroyed', as in 7b. **[10]** G lacks 'who stubbornly follow their own heart'. **[11]** MT 'the whole house of Israel and': probably an addition, as the piece is about Judah-Jerusalem (v. 9). The phrase is in G.

Southwood 1979; Thiel 1973, 169–76

A prose section now introduces the speaker as actor. The word which comes to him from Yahweh is not a message for the nation but a command to do something (cf. 7.2; 19.1–2; 22.1 which combine both). He is to go and buy a girdle (its linen quality indicates its value) and wear it in its unwashed state. He does as commanded. The word comes to him a second time and commands him to take the girdle to the Euphrates and hide it there. Again he obeys. Much later ('many days', v. 6) the word comes yet again and commands him to return to the Euphrates in order to retrieve the girdle. This he does by digging up the hidden girdle (hidden in the rock v. 4). It is ruined, useless.

What does this series of actions mean? An explanation is provided in vv. 9–11, but like the interpretations of the parables in the synoptic gospels it throws less light on the matter than could be wished for. It is a Deuteronomistic interpretation which associates the spoiling of the girdle with the nation's idolatry. It is an oblique explanation demonstrating the concerns of the Deuteronomists more than illuminating the action under scrutiny. From their viewpoint Israel and Judah were intended to be Yahweh's possession, functioning as his reputation, praise and glory (cf. Deut. 26.18–19). Their involvement with other gods ruined them as Yahweh's possession and made them useless to him. As a gloss on the action it is an unconvincing interpretation, but it does conform to the ideology of the Deuteronomists. The explanation in v. 9 makes sense but clarifies very little. The pride (*g*[e]*'ōn* is used of territory in 12.5, but here it is more likely to be a reference to the nation's wealth and possessions symbolized by the cloth being linen) of the nation will be destroyed by Babylonian influences. Exile in Babylon will ruin the people, or the invasion of the Babylonian hordes will destroy the land. Yet the point of v. 9 is that Yahweh does the destroying rather than Babylon (hence BHS emendation). Such a statement leaves the meaning of the story unclear and makes it a banal interpretation of a complicated set of moves: *kākāh*, 'thus . . .', will Yahweh destroy the nation's pride – yes, but how? In what way will Yahweh's destructive power be the equivalent of what the actor does in vv. 1–7? What force can *kākāh* have here?

This unit has been described as belonging to 'the most disputed and discussed texts of the book of Jeremiah' (Thiel 1973, 169). It has that reputation because commentators disagree on what the account of the actor's movements means. The destruction of the nation by the invading Babylonian forces (political) or as a result of idolatrous behaviour (theological) are two explanations readily available in the tradition. They are frequently stated, and often at great length. But the details of the story itself do not represent either motif in any obvious way. That is one set of problems with the story. Another set of problems which is fundamental to its interpretation concerns the genre of the piece.

Is the story a factual account of journeys made by the speaker? On the surface that would appear to be its meaning (cf. Leslie, 87f.).

But the distance between Jerusalem and the Euphrates is at least 400 miles and the return journey there twice would have involved a very lengthy period of travelling (according to Ezra 7.7–9 it took about four months to make the journey from Persia to Jerusalem). The journeys and the 'many days' (v. 6) would probably cover about a year, which would make the action comparable to one of Ezekiel's prolonged symbolic acts. An alternative explanation is favoured by some exegetes (e.g. Bright): *p^erat* should be understood as Parah rather than the standard Hebrew reference to the river Euphrates. It would then be an allusion to a town in Benjaminite territory (cf. Josh. 18.23), reckoned to be within easy reach of Anathoth. Both these explanations take a literal view of the story, but should it be understood as the descriptive account of journeys undertaken by the speaker? There are no clues in the story itself about how it should be read (unlike the details in 19.2; 24.1; 35.2). It could therefore be a story about an imaginary journey: a dream (cf. Weiser), a vision (e.g. Rudolph), a spoken parable (Volz, Cornill), or simply a proclamation of divine judgment (cf. Miller 1955, 49f.). It may also be viewed as a dramatic performance or enacted parable (e.g. Carroll 1981, 131). All of these possible explanations render it some form of preaching to the community. As there are no rubrics attached to the story, it may be an editorial explanation of what exile in Babylon achieved (i.e. loss of pride).

Whatever the genre and meaning of the story may be, the unit introduces the category of the symbolic act. This category appears frequently in the book of Jeremiah (cf. 16.1–4; 19.1–2, 10–11; 25.15–29; 27.1–3, 12; 28.10–11; 32.1–15; 43.8–13; 51.59–64) and should be associated with the visions (1.11–14; 24) and extended metaphors (18.1–11) in it. They are described as symbolic because they are actions or ideas which point beyond themselves to other matters. Their roots are in the world of magic and they belong to an epistemological framework where divination and incantation represent power transmitted through words and gestures (for general discussion cf. Lindblom 1962, 137–48, 165–73; Fohrer 1953; 1967, 92–112). These are not just actions which illustrate words with gestures but are part of the creation of the thing itself – they make things happen. The performed action, accompanied by the ritualized words and gestures, is causal (e.g. 19.10–11). 51.59–64 is a good example of such magical behaviour: all the words damning Babylon are written down in a book which is taken to Babylon; there they are read out by a delegate, then the book is tied to a stone and cast into the Euphrates. Accompanying this action are the words 'thus (*kākāh*) shall Babylon sink, to rise no more . . .'. The action and the words are bound up together and bring about the thing spoken of (see on 36.23, 32). Biblical exegetes prefer a more rationalized account of these matters, and favour treating them as symbolical rather than magical (e.g. Fohrer distinguishes carefully between the magical and the symbolical). They also tend to invoke a theological justification for this distinction. However, more sophisticated accounts of the matter, whether from a theological perspective or an analytic philosophical viewpoint, often fail to allow for the extent to which belief in magic dominated the ancient world. To evade the magical connotations of prophetic actions (e.g. 51.59–64) in favour of a 'word of god' rational scheme of warrants is simply to trade one defective explanation for another. It will not explain the breakdown of expectations in some cases (cf. Ezek. 26.7.14; 29.17–20) nor the different uses of the same formulas (e.g. 27.4; 28.2). The Jeremiah tradition is full of magical elements such as word-plays, incantations, gestures, performances, curses, and delegated actions. It would be unwise to allow anachronistic systems of explanation to obscure that fact or to rationalize the mantic world.

The meaning of the story in 13.1–7 remains open to question. The possible word-play on *pᵉrāt* may obscure its meaning, but the Euphrates remains the more likely candidate and Babylon the agent of destruction (51.59–64 should be read along with 13.1–7 as its reversal, i.e. the destruction of Babylon, and as the clearest example of this kind of story). In what sense Babylon should be regarded as the destroyer remains difficult to determine. Some exegetes see the cultural influences of Assyria and Babylon on Judaean life as causing its ruin, and the story as Yahweh's judgment on such influences (cf. Rudolph, 94). Southwood sees the story as a variant of the foe from the north motif and argues that the key to understanding it is the phrase 'and hide it there in a cleft of the rock' (v. 4). This he connects with a similar phrase in 16.16 and Isa. 7.19 (*nᵉqīqē hassᵉlā'īm*, 'the clefts of the rocks') as an allusion to invading forces (cf. 4.29). It is too subtle an argument, but it is possible that the story does refer to the Babylonian invasion as the destroyer of Judah's pride, though in a less than clear manner. In support of these two different interpretations of the story the proximity of 13.1–7 to 12.14–17 (corruption from foreign ways) or to 12.7–13 (destruction by invading forces) may be adduced. The Deuteronomistic understanding of the story favours the first explanation.

A third opinion is recommended here. The actor performs his strange drama before a mystified audience (whether as mime or with words may be surmised but without backing evidence): marking out the ground to represent the mighty Euphrates, parading around in his splendid girdle, trudging off to the river to bury the girdle, returning and waiting, then off to the river again and . . . lo and behold, the garment is ruined! What does it all mean? '*Thus* (*kākāh* 'in *this* way') shall Yahweh ruin the pride of Judah and the (even) great(er) pride of Jerusalem.' It is a dramatic enactment of exile in Babylon and quite good theatre at that! The magical content or force of this drama is difficult to determine because of the uncertainty of the interpretation of the story (Lang 1983, 88, would dissociate street theatre, his term for some prophetic actions, from the symbolism of quasi-magical performances). Did the actor by his actions contribute to Judah going into exile? In other instances of such behaviour Jeremiah was promptly beaten for his performance (e.g. 19.10–11, 14–15; 20.1–2; cf 26.8–9, 11), so blame was attached to behaving in this manner. Such blame identifies actor with action and makes him the cause of what is threatened. In a world where the divine word is believed to be effective (cf. Isa. 55.10–11), the speaker of it must suffer the consequences of uttering it. But insufficient information in 13.1–7 prevents a more precise analysis along these lines.

13.12–14

12 'You shall speak to them this word: "Thus says the LORD, the God of Israel, 'Every jar shall be filled with wine.' " And they will say to you, "Do we not indeed know that every jar will be filled with wine?" 13 Then you shall say to them, "Thus says the LORD: Behold, I will fill with drunkenness all the inhabitants of this land: the kings who sit on David's throne, the priests, the prophets, and all the inhabitants of Jerusalem. 14 And I will dash them one against another, fathers and sons together, says the LORD. I will not pity or spare or have compassion, that I should not destroy them." '

[12] G 'and you will say to this people' for longer MT. G *kai estai ean eipōsin pros se*, 'and it shall be if they say to you' = *w*^{e}*'im yō'm*^{e}*rū*, 'and if they say'. **[13]** G has 'and Judah' before 'and all the inhabitants of Jerusalem'.

McKane 1978

An independent unit made up of a proverb (*māšāl*) with explanatory application and an additional verse developing the image in a rather different direction. Originally the form of v. 13 may have been 'Look, I am filling all the inhabitants of this land with drunkenness', but Deuteronomistic editing has expanded it into a statement against the various classes and strata of society (cf. Thiel 1973, 177). The artificiality of v. 12 should be noted: the deity plays the parts of speaker and audience (G is better here). Duhm classifies it as a midrash, noting the childishness characteristic of the Elijah-Elisha sagas and how a trivial sentence 'every jar shall be filled with wine' is given the pompous introduction 'thus says Yahweh, the God of Israel' (119, 122). The proverbial saying *kol-nēbel yimmālē' yāyin* may refer to jars or skins for wine (comprehensive review of scholarly opinions in McKane). In vv. 12–13 the force of the saying relates to the drunkenness of the citizens, whereas in v. 14 the figure is that of shattering. These are two different understandings of the saying and indicative of exegetical activity developing the image in different ways.

The core of the unit is the drinkers' witticism, 'every jar is full of wine' (Giesebrecht), and the message turns that drunkards' jest into a figure of Yahweh's judgment of the nation. The hard men of drink (cf. Isa. 5.11, 22) readily agree with the use of their favourite shout in the taverns without realizing that it is an ironic play on their destruction. Yahweh will fill the nation with drunkenness. The motif of intoxication is an image of Yahweh's anger which results in death (cf. 25.15–16, 27): when Yahweh provides the drink it is fatal (cf. 48.26). Yahweh's giving drink to the nation is a similar image to that of his giving poison (8.14; 9.15; 23.15); both are figures of the nation's death. The whole land is poisoned or drunk, i.e. destroyed. The expansion of v. 13 specifies the various strata of society (cf. 22.4 for the phrase 'kings who sit on David's throne'; similar are 17.25; 22.2, 30; 29.16).

The additional v. 14 understands *nēbel* as 'jar' and the drunken citizens as jars Yahweh will smash against each other (for *nāpaṣ* cf. 51.20–23). Whether the figure is that of inebriated drinkers smashing their jars together in their drunken stupor (the English word 'smashed' makes a very good pun here for drunk and *npṣ* but has no equivalent in the Hebrew) or of drunks reeling about and bumping into each other is not clear. But the force of the figure appears to be the shattering of wine jars as an image of internecine strife (though *yaḥdāw* can mean 'together'). Such communal conflict appears in 9.2–6; 12.6 and may therefore be a reflection of later struggles within the community (cf. Zech. 13.2–6). The divine refusal to show any mercy in order to refrain from destroying them uses Deuteronomistic language (21.7 uses the same three terms but in a slightly different order), echoing the motif addressed to the nation 'you shall not pity or spare' (cf. Deut. 7.16; 13.8 [MT 9]; 19.13, 21; 25.12). The echo suggests that v. 14 understands the reason for the divine intoxication of the community to be on account of its idolatry (cf. v. 10). The divine withholding of mercy allows the work of destruction to continue until the whole community is destroyed. Some commentators understand the fragmentation of the community implied by v. 14 to refer to civil strife in the time of Zedekiah and attribute the piece to Jeremiah (e.g Weiser, Rudolph; cf. Weippert 1973, 83), but a better case can be made for treating the unit as the product of a later period (e.g. Duhm, McKane, 117).

13.15–17

15 Hear and give ear; be not proud,
for the Lord has spoken.
16 Give glory to the Lord your God
before he brings darkness,
before your feet stumble
on the twilight mountains,
and while you look for light
he turns it into gloom
and makes it deep darkness.
17 But if you will not listen,
my soul will weep in secret for your pride;
my eyes will weep bitterly and run down with tears,
because the Lord's flock has been taken captive.

---

[16] MT *wᵉśāmāh lᵉṣalmāwet*, 'and he turns it to gloom', G *kai ekei skia thanatou*, 'and there the shadow of death' = *wᵉšām* . . . Driver 1937–38, 112 reads *wᵉśāmō*, 'and he makes it . . .' (*'ōr* is masc). K *yšyt*; Q *wᵉšīt*, 'and he makes'; Duhm prefers K *yāšīt*. **[17]** MT *bᵉmistārīm*, 'in secrets, hiding-places':

it could relate to clause a 'if you will not listen' (e.g. NEB) or clause b (G, RSV). NEB 'If in those depths of gloom you will not listen' renders the plural sense and relates it to the previous verse. MT is reckoned to be incomprehensible (Rudolph, cf. BHS) and is read as *b^emisrārīm*, 'in stubbornness', or *b^emisrābīm*, 'in rebellion' (cf. Aramaic *srb*, Ezek. 2.6). Duhm understands MT in relation to 36.26 (124: Jeremiah's hiding from Jehoiakim). MT *napšī*, 'my soul', but G *hē psychē humōn*, 'your soul' (also 'your eyes'). MT *mipp^enē gēwāh*, 'because of pride': cf. 15a. Volz, 153, reads *gōlāh*, 'taken captive', 'exile', cf. *nišbāh*, 'taken captive', in 17b; *hoglāt*, 'taken into exile', in 19b. G lacks *w^edāmō'a tidma'*, 'weep bitterly'. Volz treats v. 17 with 18–19.

A brief poem (among a collection of short pieces) warning the community to pay attention to the divine word before it is too late. If due praise is not given to Yahweh he will turn the hoped-for light into darkness. The phrase 'the mountains of twilight' (*hārē nāšep: nešep* may refer to dusk or dawn) suggests a mountain scene where shepherds waiting for the dawn guard their flocks. But that dawn could become the night and the community would be lost. In v. 17 MT understands the subject of the weeping to be the speaker, but G makes it the community. The reference to 'in secret places' is problematic: what does it mean and to whom does it refer? Taken with the first clause it refers to the community's refusal to listen and belongs to the terms for darkness in v. 16 (Volz; cf. NEB). Many commentators prefer to treat it as the speaker's self-reference (e.g. 'my inmost self', JPSB) but that renders it too enigmatic. The shift between G and MT is from a communal response to an individual reaction, and part of the difficulty may be in the unadjusted text. As a communal lament the weeping is done in hiding-places because the flock (cf. 6.3) has gone into exile. The tendency to read communal statements as individual ones and to transfer what makes sense when spoken of the community to a solitary figure may account for the difficulty with 'secret places'. The cause of the captivity of the flock is the community's pride (a possible link word with 13.9; cf. 'be not proud', v. 15).

13.18–19

18 Say to the king and the queen mother:
'Take a lowly seat,
for your beautiful crown
has come down from your head.'
19 The cities of the Negeb are shut up,
with none to open them;
all Judah is taken into exile,
wholly taken into exile.

---

[18] G 'say you' plur. MT *wᵉlaggᵉbîrāh*, 'and to the queen mother': G *kai tois dunasteuousin*, 'and to the princes' = *wᵉlaggibbōrîm*. MT *mar'ᵃšotêkem*, a peculiar form: G 'from your head' = *mērā'šêkem*. Dahood 1961, 462, revocalizes as *mērā'šōtêkem* (plural of *rašt*, 'head', cf. Ugaritic). **[19]** MT *hoglat šᵉlômîm*, 'exiled completely': fem. sing with masc. plur. Cf. Vrs, BHS, Amos 1.6, 9 *gālût šᵉlēmāh*, 'a complete exile'.

A brief lament (*qînāh* form) responds to the situation of siege and deportation. If vv. 15–17 are to be seen as a last warning (so Rudolph, 96), vv. 18–19 represent the defeat of the country symbolized by the abdication of king and his mother (*gᵉbîrāh* can mean 'queen', cf. I Kings 11.19). The queen mother could be a powerful figure in Judaean royal circles, having great dignity and exercizing special powers in the court (cf. de Vaux 1965, 117–19; Andreasen 1983). She was the Great Lady contributing to the stability of the royal court, but could also be involved in palace intrigues and plots (cf. II Kings 11.1; I Kings 15.13 = II Chron. 15.16). The descent from the throne is an image of defeat (cf. Isa. 47.1). The fate of the royal women is also a picture of defeat and one which can underline the nature of the disaster (cf. 38.21–3). The lament bemoans the royal loss and the fate of the nation. For the cities of the south are under siege and the people deported ('Judah, all of it' is hyperbole).

To what occasion does the lament refer? Most commentators favour the view that it refers to Jehoiachin and his mother Nehushta (cf. II Kings 24.8–17) and the period of defeat and surrender in 597. But it could also refer to Jehoiakim and his mother Zebuddah (II Kings 23.36 Q; so Duhm, 124), or even to the later period of 587 (cf. 38.22f.) The lament itself offers no precise details other than the recognition of defeat and the hopelessness of the situation in the country. It is therefore typical of much of the material in the book of Jeremiah, i.e. it may be applied to a number of different occasions because it lacks specificity. In just over two decades the defeat of the royal house in three different crises resulted in changes of monarch and deportations (609, 597, 587),so the generality of vv. 18–19 offers no clues about the identity of the king and queen mother addressed. The lament focuses on the loss of power, the humiliation of defeat (*hašppīlū šēbū*, 'make low, sit'), and the consequences of this for the nation.

13.20–27

20 'Lift up your eyes and see
those who come from the north.
Where is the flock that was given you,
your beautiful flock?
21 What will you say when they set as head over you
those whom you yourself have taught
to be friends to you?
Will not pangs take hold of you,
like those of a woman in travail?
22 And if you say in your heart,
"Why have these things come upon me?"
it is for the greatness of your iniquity
that your skirts are lifted up,
and you suffer violence.
23 Can the Ethiopian change his skin
or the leopard his spots?
Then also you can do good
who are accustomed to do evil.
24 I will scatter you like chaff
driven by the wind from the desert.
25 This is your lot,
the portion I have measured out to you, says the LORD,
because you have forgotten me
and trusted in lies.
26 I myself will lift up your skirts over your face,
and your shame will be seen.
27 I have seen your abominations,
your adulteries and neighings, your lewd harlotries,
on the hills in the field.

Woe to you, O Jerusalem!
How long will it be
before you are made clean?'

---

[20] K *ś'y* sing.; Q *śe'ū* plur., 'lift up (your eyes)': G sing. 'lift up thine eyes, O Jerusalem and see', cf. K *wr'y* (Q *ūre'ū*). **[21]** MT *yipqōd*, 'he will set' (Yahweh?): G *episkeptōntai*, 'they will visit' = *yipqedū*, 'they will set'. RSV transposes *lerō'š* 'as head' from the end of 21b to after 'set'; cf. NEB for the transposition of *'allupīm* but with a rather different translation. BHS understands *lerō'š* to be in the form *yrwš* = *yrwšlm*, 'Jerusalem', and transposes it to the end of 21a. Bright, 95, is of the opinion that the first part of the verse cannot be translated with any assurance and so leaves bits of it blank in his translation. MT lit. 'what will you say when he appoints over you and you yourself taught them, over you friends for a head.' **[22]** RSV 'and you suffer violence': MT *neḥmesū 'aqēbaīk*, 'your heels suffer violence'; 'heels' is a euphemism for genitals (like *raglaīm*, 'feet'). Euphemisms are not a feature of the Jeremiah tradition; obscene language is more often used. For the imagery of 22b cf. Isa. 47.2–3, where *gallī-šōq*, 'uncover the thigh', may be the equivalent of *niglū šūlaīk*, 'uncovered (are) your skirts', cf. v.26. **[24]** MT *wa'apīṣēm*, 'and I will scatter them': BHS *-kem*, 'you'. **[25]** MT *menāt middaīk mē'ittī*, 'your measured share from me': G *kai meris tou apeithein humas emoi*, 'and the portion of your disobedience to me'; this suggests *merēk*, 'your rebellion'; cf. NEB 'the portion of the rebel'. **[26]** MT *ḥāśaptī šūlaīk 'al-pānāīk*, 'I will strip off your skirts to your face', meaning? RSV 'I myself will lift up your skirts over your face'; the figure is one of exposure: that your shame may be seen, *nir'āh qelōnēk*, i.e. 'your genitals' ('pudenda' BDB, 886), cf. Isa. 47.2; Nahum 3.5. *ḥāśap* suggests stripping, exposing, rather than raising, cf. *ḥeśpī-šōbel*, 'strip off the robe' (Qumran *šūlaīk*), Isa. 47.2. The use of euphemisms may conceal an obscene practice of exposing women by drawing their legs over their heads in order to uncover their vulvas completely. **[27]** MT *'al-gebā'ōt baśśādeh*, 'on the hills in the field'; G *epi tōn bounōn kai en tois agrois*, 'on the hills *and* in the fields'. MT *lō' tiṭhᵃrī'aḥᵃrē mātay 'ōd*: 'you will not be clean; after how long yet.' Volz, 155, 'that (G *kī*) you will not be clean, how long will you delay to return (*šub* from S)', cf. NEB 'unclean that you are! How long, how long will you delay'. For Volz's *māh te'aḥᵃrī*, Driver 1937–38, 112 prefers *matte'aḥᵃrī 'ōd*, 'why dost thou tarry still (i.e. to repent)?'.

A difficult section and probably not a unit, as vv. 23–24 are treated separately by a number of commentators (e.g. Volz, Rudolph, Weiser). The tone of much of the section is similar to that of the discourses against the community in 2–5. Sexual metaphors are used to abuse the city for its idolatrous practices, and the tendency to rant is evidence of the rhetoric of the passage. The placing of the composite unit here may be due to connecting links such as 'flock' (vv. 17, 20), 'beautiful' (vv. 18, 20) and the humiliation of the queen mother/city as woman (vv. 18, 22, 26).

The city is addressed by a number of questions which aim to bring home to her the plight she is in. The people (i.e. the flock) under her jurisdiction have gone (into exile as in v. 19?), and over her are set as leaders those who used to be her friends (v. 21 is quite baffling in its present state). The realization of what has befallen her will be as painful as giving birth (cf. 4.31; 6.24; 30.6). If she should ask herself 'why?' (*madūʿa*, a very frequent question in the Jeremiah tradition), then the answer is very simple: 'because of the greatness of your iniquity' (*bᵉrōb ʿᵃwōnēk*). The image changes from the pains of labour to the outrage and violence of rape (vv. 22, 26). Jerusalem has become a violated woman, a typical victim of invading warriors. The images used are graphic and violent. They are metaphors of the city's humiliation and defeat, but they are drawn from the real world of horrendous aggression directed against women in time of war and invasion. In such brutal times the women are led off to the invaders (38.23), stripped naked and savagely raped – their genitals suffer violence and their shameful humiliation is made a public spectacle. Metaphors and reality combine to portray a sickening picture of battered sexuality and torn flesh, an image of a culture invaded, raped and devastated. Why? Why have these awful things happened? Why are these outrages Yahweh's portion for the city?

The vague reference to 'greatness of iniquity' (v. 22) is expanded in v. 27 by way of explanation for what has happened to Jerusalem. The sexual practices of her own people are to blame: 'your adulteries, your neighings, your licentious whorings', these are abominations to Yahweh. Again metaphor and reality may be mixed up (see on 5.7–8). The guilt of the city is its involvement in pagan cults on the hills and in the fields. These cults may have had a sexual aspect to them or they may have tolerated sexual practices which outraged the more puritanical Yahwists who thereby smeared their opponents with epithets of an abusive nature. Whatever the facts of the matter may be (and they elude us almost completely), the destruction of Jerusalem by the Babylonians is felt by the speaker here to be poetic justice for sins committed. Rhetoric and ideology are behind the denunciations of the community. For sexual-religious offences the city has been raped: in reality women have been raped brutally and all the horrors of war imposed on the citizens, the innocent as well as the guilty (e.g. Lam. 5.1–16, esp. v. 11).

The unit is disrupted by vv. 23–24, which would follow on from v. 27c quite well. The people are incapable of changing their ways: that charge is made using hyperbolic examples. If an Ethiopian could change his black skin or a leopard its marks (*ḥ^a^barburōt*, 'stripes' = a tiger?), then so easily could the people change. But they are so schooled to doing evil (*limmudē hārē'a*) that change is virtually impossible. So they will be scattered (i.e. deported or forced to flee) as the desert wind drives chaff before it (cf. the image in 4.11–12). Woe to Jerusalem, for she is not clean! In that impurity and inability to change its ways lie the explanation for the disaster which befell city and people. It is an explanation of sorts, but one highly charged with ideological matters (for balance consult the book of Lamentations).

D. 14.1 – 17.27

14.1–6

141 The word of the Lord which came to Jeremiah concerning the drought:
2 'Judah mourns
and her gates languish;
her people lament on the ground,
and the cry of Jerusalem goes up.
3 Her nobles send their servants for water;
they come to the cisterns,
they find no water,
they return with their vessels empty;
they are ashamed and confounded
and cover their heads.
4 Because of the ground which is dismayed,
since there is no rain on the land,
the farmers are ashamed,
they cover their heads.
5 Even the hind in the field forsakes her newborn calf
because there is no grass.
6 The wild asses stand on the bare heights,
they pant for air like jackals;
their eyes fail
because there is no herbage.'

---

[1] MT *'ašer hāyāh debar-yhwh*, 'which was the word of Yahweh . . .': same formula as 46.1; 47.1; 49.34; cf. 1.2. G *kai egeneto logos kuriou*, 'and the word of the lord came . . .' = *wayehī*. . . . MT a redactional title from 46.1 (Rudolph). MT *habbaṣṣārōt* plur., 'dearths, droughts', cf. 17.8 for sing. *baṣṣōret*. G *abrochia* = *baṣṣārūt*, 'drought, waterless'; MT plur. of extension(?). **[2]** BHS suggests reading *'al-habbaṣṣōret*, 'because of the drought', in the first clause; lost due to haplography. MT *šeʿārehā*, 'her gates', i.e. 'her towns', cf. NEB 'her cities' (a metonym), cf. 15.7; Rudolph 'places'. **[3]** K *ṣʿwryhm*; Q *ṣeʿīrēhem*, 'menials'; K an uncommon form. Many mss, Vrs read *welō'*, 'and do not (find water)'. G lacks last clause 'they are ashamed . . . their heads', cf. 4b. **[4]** MT *ḥattāh*, 'dismayed': G *exelipen*, 'failed', understanding *baʿᵃbūr*, 'because', as *erga*, 'labour', cf. NEB 'the produce of the land has failed'; Bright 'tilling the soil has stopped (?)' following G. Rudolph reads *heḥārāh* (cf. *ḥᵃrērīm*, 'parched places', 17.6) for *ḥattāh*, i.e. 'because of the parched ground' (for no rain has fallen on the land). Volz transposes 'farmers' from 4b 'on account of the ground the farmers are dismayed'; *'ikkārīm*, 'ploughmen' (due to the drought the ground is too hard to plough). BHS reads 'and confounded' from 3b at 4b. G lacks MT *bā'āreṣ* at end of 4a ('because there was no rain'). **[6]** G lacks 'like jackals' (in G the wild asses stand by the woods rather than on the bare heights as in MT).

Beuken and van Grol 1981; Kessler 1972; Reventlow 1963, 149–87; Thiel 1973, 178–94

The lengthy section in 14.1 – 15.4(9) has been entitled 'the great drought liturgy' (Reventlow, cf. Rudolph). It is not technically a liturgy or even a unit, and commentators are divided about the limits of the material (i.e. whether it should end at 15.3, 4 or 9). As is usual in the analysis of Jeremiah *doctores scinduntur* ('the teachers are divided'): Volz ends the unit at 15.3 but most exegetes favour 15.4 (e.g. Hyatt, Rudolph, Bright, Kessler, Thiel, Thompson) or 15.9 (e.g. Duhm, Giesebrecht, Weiser, Reventlow, Beuken and van Grol) as the termination of the section. The composition of the section has brought together a number of discrete units and given them the appearance of a unity. Two themes dominate the collection: the drought and the ravages of war. The drought theme appears in vv. 2–6, 19–22 and the war motif in vv. 12–13, 15–16, 18; 15.2–3. Yet in places the themes are mixed with each other, and it is not an easy task to separate the section into its constituent parts. The whole section may be divided into seven sub-sections: 2–6, 7–9, 10–12, 13–16, 17–18, 19–22, 15.1–4, with 14.1 as an editorial introduction (cf. Hyatt, 927–37, for similar divisions; Hitzig, 106–14, sets it out as 12.4; 14.1–9, 19–22; and 13.27; 14.10–18; 15.1–9). But the analysis may be done in a number of different ways and each variation in approach demonstrates the protean nature of the section. Thus it may be separated into two parts: 14.1–16 a lamentation with divine response in a time of drought and 14.17–15.4 a further lamentation and supplication in a time of defeat and famine (Thompson). A variation on this type of analysis is: superscription 14.1; first lament

14.2–9 with divine response in v. 10; a prophetic-divine dialogue 14.11–17aα; second lament 17.17aβ–22 with divine response in 15.1–4 (Kessler, 503). The coherence of the section and the skill of its literary execution point to an editor working on the different sub-units in a period long after any events reflected in the material. As a literary composition rather than a liturgy it does not have an external reference (cf. Kessler, 519–21) but it does have an important communal function:

> The genre, setting and intention are . . . very closely related. The genre should be designated a sermon, the setting the exilic Jewish community, and the intention, as appropriate to a sermon: to persuade the hearers that YHWH was right in meting out such severe punishments (theodicy), and indirectly, that the people are granted a new opportunity of repentance; thus, its orientation is past, present and future (Kessler, 520).

This lack of an external referent of the section is an important point in its interpretation and a principle of some consequence for the understanding of much of the book of Jeremiah. Drought and the ravages of war were (and still are) common features of life in the areas which produced the tradition. Though specific experiences of each devastation may have given rise to some poetically expressed responses, the composition represents a distillation of such responses plus theological reflections on a wider range of bitter experiences (hence *baṣṣārōt*, 'cuttings off', in title). Drought is a constant hazard of life in dry, hot climates and its effects are devastating: everything dries up, animals and humans suffer terribly, and death spreads across a culture. The ravages of war and siege are equally horrible, though perhaps more rapid in their effects. These all provide graphic images of the judgment of Yahweh on the community, and in all such catastrophes the standard response is to appeal to the deity for a withdrawal of his anger. Religious communities beg, implore, cajole their deities and seek to placate the unseen powers which have withdrawn their favours from them. Prayers and sacrifices are offered, liturgical processions take place and litanies are pronounced. Because the giving of rain and its withholding is in the power and gift of the gods, disasters in the natural world are reckoned to be caused by the sins and offences of the community. To remove the causes of the suffering entails confessing to sins committed, making the right offerings to the offended gods and the amendment of life in general. In these matters Yahwism and Judaean religion were characteristically Canaanite in outlook, and the droughts and disasters of the sixth century called forth the kinds of responses to be found in 14.1 – 15.4. That the rain might fall on or be withheld from the just as well as the unjust does not appear to have occurred to the ritual communities which maintained such reactions to disasters, though the authors of Job and Qoheleth would have been aware of that fact. The circles which produced the book of Jeremiah worked after the fall of Jerusalem and believed it necessary to produce an explanation for that catastrophe: an explanation which would clear Yahweh of doing evil (i.e. a theodicy) and, at the same time, pin blame where they wished it pinned. The parts which make up the composition in 14.1 – 15.4 do precisely both things and offer an ideology of divine action to a later generation.

The editorial introduction in v. 1 turns what follows into a divine statement. But nothing before v. 10 fits such a description, and the verse is better seen as a reflection of its origin in the preaching of a later period and of the construction of the tradition. The plight of the land in vv. 2–6 is more a description of distress than a formal lament (though described as a lament by Baumgartner 1917, 77; Weiser, 122). Such a description of the suffering caused by the lack of water prepares the way for the lament of vv. 7–9: 'It evokes the lamentableness of the situation of distress without being in itself a lament' (Beuken and van Grol, 313). The whole land, its cities and people, and Jerusalem mourn and are weak. The shepherds (*'addīrīm* may mean 'nobles, rulers', cf. 30.21; or 'shepherds, flock-masters', cf. NEB; 25.34–36) send out their menials to look for water but they return with empty buckets and in despair. The farmers are also in despair because the ground is too hard to work. In the countryside the animals leave their young for lack of herbage and on the hills the wild asses pant for breath (cf. 2.24 MT) like jackals (or make noises like owls, cf. Feliks 1981, 121). They snuff the air looking for moisture and, because there is no grass anywhere, are going blind for lack of vitamin A (grass provides carotene which converts into vitamin A for animals, cf. Wilson 1982, 362). The four pictures in vv. 3–6 spell out in a vivid way the content of v. 2. Humankind and the animal world share the awful consequences of a severe drought. What is notably absent from the place is any reference to a specific speaker or to persons addressed. Even the deity is absent, but then in the context of a drought his absence is demonstrated by the parched landscape with its dying creatures (cf. I Kings 17–18 for drought, famine and the absent god). These grim images set the stage for the rest of the composition.

14.7–9

7 'Though our iniquities testify against us,
act, O LORD, for thy name's sake;
for our backslidings are many,
we have sinned against thee.
8 O thou hope of Israel,
its saviour in time of trouble,
why shouldst thou be like a stranger in the land,
like a wayfarer who turns aside to tarry for a night?
9 Why shouldst thou be like a man confused,
like a mighty man who cannot save?
Yet thou, O LORD, art in the midst of us,
and we are called by thy name;
leave us not.'

---

[8] Some mss, G have 'Yahweh' after 'hope of Israel' (MT *miqwēh yiśrā'ēl*, 'O hope of Israel', cf. NEB). MT *ūk'ōrēaḥ*, 'and like a traveller': G *kai hōs autochthōn*, 'and like a native' = *ūkᵉ'ezrāḥ*. MT *nāṭāh*, 'turns aside' (to spend the night), may also have the meaning 'spread' (one's tent for the night), cf. NEB. **[9]** MT *nidhām*, 'astonished', hapax legomenon: G *hupnōn*, 'asleep' = *nirdām*; for sleep as a metaphor of divine inactivity cf. I Kings 18.27 (contrast the images of the deity rising early in 7.13, 25; 11.7; 25.3, etc.). MT *kᵉgibbōr*, 'like a warrior': G *hōs anēr*, 'like a man' = *kᵉgeber*; NEB 'like a man powerless to save himself?', revocalizing *lᵉhōšīa'* from a Hiphil form to a Niphal.

A communal lament expresses the perplexity of the people at the deity's inactivity. Appeals are made to him, sins are confessed, due reverence and praise ascribed to him and reminders of the relationship between people and deity stressed. The classical form of the lament question appears (vv. 8, 9 *lāmmāh*, 'why?') rather than the form peculiar to the laments in the tradition (*madū'a*, 'why?'). Yahweh is acknowledged as Israel's hope and saviour (Israel rather than Judah: indicating the discrete pieces making up the section), but four images raise questions about his abilities or his willingness.

For the community he has become like a transient alien or a traveller just stopping overnight (a native gone to ground in lodgings, cf. G), i.e. he skulks about the land like a stranger. He is a man who sleeps (cf. I Kings 18.27, where such an accusation is part of the mocking abuse hurled at the devotees of Baal) or a man incapable of saving: the saviour of Israel is unable to save. The divine presence is acknowledged in the community (cf. 8.19), and to him the people belong (cf. 15.16), hence the appeal 'do not abandon us'.

The lament is only connected to the drought by its context; nothing in it suggests the drought as the cause of the collective appeal. It may be regarded as a lament typical of temple theology (cf. Beuken and van Grol, 327). In times of disaster the community invariably appealed to the god to act on their behalf: to wake up and perform (cf. Ps. 44.23) rather than to wander through the land like a stranger with no interest in it. The images of the community berating itself and cajoling the deity all to no avail are like scenes in one of Eisenstein's films of Russian peasants flagellating themselves because the harvests have failed again.

14.10–12

10 Thus says the LORD concerning this people:
'They have loved to wander thus,
they have not restrained their feet;
therefore the LORD does not accept them,
now he will remember their iniquity
and punish their sins.'
11 The LORD said to me: 'Do not pray for the welfare of this people. 12
Though they fast, I will not hear their cry, and though they offer burnt
offering and cereal offering, I will not accept them; but I will consume them
by the sword, by famine, and by pestilence.'

---

[10] G lacks '(wander) thus' and 'and punish their sins'. MT 'therefore Yahweh does not accept them . . . punish their sins' = Hos. 8.13b (9.9); perhaps it is a formal liturgical element. RSV prints v. 10 as poetry, but many regard it as prose along with vv. 11–16 (e.g. MT, NEB, JPSB, Rudolph). **[11]** Cf. 7.16; 11.14.

The artificiality of the composition becomes clear in v. 10 and in the difficulties of determining poetic and prosaic elements in

vv. 10–16 (cf. analysis in Beuken and van Grol, 327–30). There are also problems with the division of the sub-section: should it be 10–12, 13–16 (e.g. Hyatt, Weiser, Rudolph) or 10, 11–17a (e.g. Kessler, cf. Bright) or 10–16 (e.g. Beuken and van Grol) or an even more radical splitting up of the text into 10, 11–12, 13, 14, 15–16 centred on the motif 'say'? The variations on *'mr* suggest a principle of organization: dialogue between deity and speaker (*kōh-'āmar yhwh . . . wayyō'mer yhwh 'ēlāy . . . wā'ōmar . . .* [*'ōmᵉrīm*] *. . . wayyō'mer yhwh 'ēlay . . . kōh-'āmar yhwh . . .* [*'omᵉrīm*]) in which the deity speaks of the people, then to the speaker, who responds about what the prophets are saying, the deity speaks again to the speaker and finally he speaks of the prophets and then of the people. However, I have divided the material into two sub-sections: vv. 10–12, divine statements about the nation; and 13–16, statements about the prophets. They are two separate themes, though united in v. 16.

The divine response to the lament of vv. 7–9 appears in v. 10, but instead of being a word of reassurance or an oracle of salvation it is a statement of complete rejection of the people by Yahweh. The nation is not acceptable (*lō' rāṣām*) to him because it has loved to wander. The use of *rṣh*, so often used to indicate acceptability or otherwise of sacral offerings (cf. 6.20; Lev. 1.4; 7.18; 22.25; Deut. 33.11; II Sam. 24.23), may imply temple sacrifices accompanied the lament (cf. v.12) but on this occasion failed to persuade the deity (cf. Hos. 8.13). But v. 10 has nothing to do with a drought. It represents the editor's construction of the section as a statement of distress, lament and response, but all drawn from different aspects of the nation's culture. Stitched together as they are here, they represent a hybrid form of liturgical elements and a theological reading of the situation. The people appeal to Yahweh not to behave like a stranger, they acknowledge their many turnings away (*mᵉšūbōt*) and express their deep hopes in Israel's God. In response to such a litany of breast-beating and confession the deity behaves in a churlish manner, berates the community and ignores their sincere confession. The boorishness of the deity only becomes apparent because the sub-sections are all discrete and do not reflect a common reality. The rejection of the people in v. 10 comes from a different strand of the tradition to that of the lament, but together they appear anomalous. In constructing the section the compositor has had to work with a number of discrete elements and forge them into a theodicy which will acquit the deity of viciousness whilst justifying inordinate cruelty. The fall of Jerusalem is the single germane fact behind the construction of 14.1 – 15.4, but multiple explanations are offered to explain it.

The speaker appears for the first time in v. 11, and what follows is addressed to him. He is warned not to pray for the people's good (*l^e ṭôbāh*, 'welfare', contrast 18.20): this prohibition (cf. 7.16; 11.14) is part of the Deuteronomistic strand which sees the deity's plans for the people as being 'for evil and not for good' (21.10; 39.16; 44.27; cf. Thiel 1973, 182). Whatever the people may do, whether fast (cf. 36.9) or offer sacrifice, it is not acceptable (*'ēnennī rōṣām*, 'I will not accept them'). Yahweh's plans for them involve a triad of destructive forces: sword, famine, pestilence (i.e. the ravages of invasion and war; a frequent formulation in the book, cf. 21.7, 9; 24.10; 27.8, 13; 29.17–18; 32.24, 36; 34.17; 38.2; 42.17, 22; 44.13). Nothing can be done for the nation in the sacral sphere: by themselves or by the speaker mediating on their behalf. Why? Because the city had already fallen and therefore nothing could have worked. That factor allowed the traditionists great scope for developing their theological explanations.

14.13–16

13 Then I said: 'Ah, Lord GOD, behold, the prophets say to them, "You shall not see the sword, nor shall you have famine, but I will give you assured peace in this place." ' 14 And the LORD said to me: 'The prophets are prophesying lies in my name; I did not send them, nor did I command them or speak to them. They are prophesying to you a lying vision, worthless divination, and the deceit of their own minds. 15 Therefore thus says the LORD concerning the prophets who prophesy in my name although I did not send them, and who say, "Sword and famine shall not come on this land": By sword and famine those prophets shall be consumed. 16 And the people to whom they prophesy shall be cast out in the streets of Jerusalem, victims of famine and sword, with none to bury them – them, their wives, their sons, and their daughters. For I will pour out their wickedness upon them.'

---

[13] MT *š^elōm 'emet*, 'true peace': G *alētheian kai eirenēn*, 'truth and peace'; cf. *šālōm we'^emet*, 'peace and truth', 33.6. **[14]** K *w'lwl*; Q *w^e'^elīl*, 'and a worthless thing', possibly 'an idol', cf. Isa. 10.10; Psa. 96.5; 97.7. EVV omit *w^e* and make it qualify *qesem*, i.e. 'worthless divination', cf. Rudolph (BHS).

G *oiōnismata*, 'auguries, divinations'. K *wtrmwt*; Q *wetarmīt*, 'and deceit . . .'. MT *lākem*, 'to you' (plur.), but *'ēlay* 'to me', at beginning of verse! Some mss *lāhem*, 'to them', i.e. to the people. **[15]** MT *hannibbe'īm bišmī*, 'who prophesy in my name': G (. . . in my name) *pseudēs* 'falsely' = . . . *bišmī šeqer*, as in 23.25. BHS deletes 'concerning' as in 12.14.

A rather different theme is introduced in vv. 13–16: those responsible for the present state of false security are named and condemned. The passage is linked to v. 12 by the motifs 'sword and famine'. The people believe that genuine *šālōm* is to be their fate when in reality invasion and starvation await them. The guilty men behind this delusion are the Yahwistic prophets (i.e. those who prophesy in the divine name). They have persuaded (or deluded) the people that *šālōm* is their lot 'in this place' (*bammāqōm hazzeh*, i.e. Jerusalem, cf. 7.3, 7, 14). Now this attack on the *šālōm*-preaching prophets who are said to be misleading the people has nothing to do with the drought of vv. 2–6. It clearly is a quite independent strand in the composition, for it would be absurd to preach 'not sword nor famine but guaranteed *šālōm*' in a context set by the descriptions of starvation and drought in vv. 2–6. The attack on the prophets is part of an argument constructed to explain why city and people were destroyed by the (real) enemy, i.e. the invading army (see on 23.9–40). The people failed to grasp what was happening because the prophets had misled them (cf. Lam. 2.14). It is one more explanation for the fall of Jerusalem, but quite superfluous in view of the stress in the tradition on the wickedness of the people (e.g. v. 10; 5.1–6; 6.6–7; 13.25–27). That it is an unnecessary argument indicates a different function for the theme: the prophets are blamed for their part in the nation's downfall in order to discredit them. It is part of an anti-prophetic polemic which may reflect internecine strife in the community of a later period (see on 23.33–40; cf. Zech. 13.2–6). By associating the prophets with what caused the destruction of the city in the past the prophets' standing in the community is discredited effectively. An alternative account of the strand would see it as a reflection of that later struggle incorporated into the tradition because contemporaneous with its construction (cf. 'the men of Anathoth' motif) and not necessarily blaming them for the destruction of Jerusalem.

The divine assessment of the prophesying of the prophets is: *šeqer* 'false' (v. 14, 'And Yahweh said to me: "false (are) the prophets prophesying in my name" ' = the word order of the Hebrew). Two sets of triads qualify the judgment: the deity did not send (*šlḥ*), command or speak to them; what they are prophesying is a false vision (*ḥ^a^zōn šeqer*), worthless divination, and the deceit of their own minds (cf. 23.16, 21, 25–26, 32). The order of words in v. 14b makes the second set of triads summary descriptions of the content of the prophets' words. The phrase 'nor did I command them' occurs three times in the context of prophetic conflict (14.14; 23.32; 29.23; cf. 7.31; 19.5 for a different context) and may reflect Deut. 18.20 (cf. Thiel, 186). The vision is false, and with it the prophets, because Yahweh is not behind what they say. Here stated briefly is an ideology of prophecy which distinguishes, on the grounds of possession of the divine word, the true from the false – indicating Deuteronomistic activity in the editing of the unit (Thiel, 187). In v. 15 the preaching of the prophets is reversed so that they suffer precisely what they said would never happen (cf. 11.21–22; 23.2 for a similar reversal of fates). Those to whom they preached will also suffer the same misfortunes (cf. 44.12, 18, 27): because of famine and invasion they will be flung out (*mušlākīm* a possible assonant word-play reflecting *šlh*, cf. 36.30) on the streets and left unburied (cf. 8.2).

14.17–18

17 'You shall say to them this word:
"Let my eyes run down with tears night and day,
and let them not cease,
for the virgin daughter of my people is smitten with a great wound,
with a very grievous blow.
18 If I go out into the field,
behold, those slain by the sword!
And if I enter the city,
behold, the diseases of famine!
For both prophet and priest ply their trade through the land,
and have no knowledge." '

---

[17] G lacks 'virgin' and 'great (wound)'. **[18]** MT *sāḥ^a^rū*, 'travel about', i.e. 'go about their business', cf. Gen. 23.16; 37.28 'trade'; NEB 'go begging'. BHS, Rudolph follow Condamin, 127, in suggesting *nisḥ^a^bū*, 'they are dragged off (to a land they do not know)', i.e. 'go into exile' (cf. *lisḥōb* in 15.3). MT *w^e^lō' yādā'ū*, 'and they do not know': better with other mss and Vrs *lō* '(to the land which) they know not', i.e. 'exile'. BHS following Duhm,

Volz, Weiser, etc. read *'et* for *'el*. It is not clear whether MT indicates exile or a mindless activity in the land characterized by famine and slaughter (cf. Kessler, 510f.). Thomas 1938, 273–4, treats *yd'* as 'rest' here, cf. NEB 'and never are at rest'. Bright, 101, provides sound judgment on the line with his observation 'But the meaning is so uncertain that any translation is conjectural.'

A brief description of the ravages of war is turned into a message addressed to the people by the editorial introduction in v. 17a (Kessler, 510, makes it refer to the foregoing material in vv. 11–16). The speaker bemoans the fate of the people (cf. 4.19–20; 8.18–9.1) with bitter tears. City and people have been destroyed (the epithet 'virgin' describes the great city ravished by disaster, cf. Isa. 47.1; used of the nation in Amos 5.2). Whether in the open countryside or in the city, death is everywhere. Out in the fields lie the corpses of those killed by the invading army; in the city those who have died of the terrible diseases caused by starvation rot in the streets. The sacral leaders of the community have been dragged off into exile or, reduced to penury, they must beg for a living. The meaning of the concluding clauses of v. 18 is very difficult to determine. It could be an addition to the lament designed to belittle priests and prophets (cf. 2.26; 5.31). In that case it may be a reference to venal priests and prophets who carry on their meretricious trade in a time of great suffering (e.g. Hyatt, 935). However, this gross libel against the sacral officials is a less likely meaning if for no other reason than the fact that the circumstances depicted in v. 18a would not have permitted any normal business at all. The lack of knowledge may refer to their inability to grasp what is happening or to discern the divine will in the situation (i.e. 'Assurance is impossible', Bright, 102). The devastation of vv. 17–18 is not the drought of vv. 2–6 but the impact of war on the country. The invading Babylonians have struck the nation a sickening blow, a great wound (many commentators favour 597 as the period of this utterance; it would suit 587 equally as well).

14.19–22

19 Hast thou utterly rejected Judah?
Does thy soul loathe Zion?
Why hast thou smitten us
so that there is no healing for us?
We looked for peace, but no good came;
for a time of healing, but behold, terror.
20 We acknowledge our wickedness, O LORD,
and the iniquity of our fathers,
for we have sinned against thee.
21 Do not spurn us, for thy name's sake;
do not dishonour thy glorious throne;
remember and do not break thy covenant with us.
22 Are there any among the false gods of the nations that can bring rain?
Or can the heavens give showers?
Art thou not he, O LORD our God?
We set our hope on thee,
for thou doest all these things.

[19b] = 8.15: perhaps a lament refrain. MT 'and (for a time)'; Vrs lack 'and', cf. 8.15. **[21]** MT *'al-tin'aṣ*, 'do not spurn': G *kopason*, 'abate, desist'. MT *'al-tᵉnabbēl*, 'do not treat with contempt': G *mē apolesēs*, 'do not destroy' = *'al-tᵉḥabbēl* (cf. BHS). **[22]** G lacks 'Yahweh our god'.

A further communal lament bemoans the fate of nation and city. It parallels vv. 7–9 and in the light of v. 22 may be a response to drought. As in vv. 7–9 it raises many questions about the deity's attitude to the community and acknowledges the sins of the people and their predecessors. The question about the absolute rejection of Judah is similar to Lam. 5.22 (*mā'ōs mā'astᵉnū*), and the inquiry about Yahweh's loathing of Zion reflects the association of loathing and covenant-breaking of Lev. 26 (e.g. vv. 11, 30, 44–45). The appeal to the deity not to act in certain ways 'for your name's sake' is the negative version of the positive appeal in v. 7. The 'glorious throne' of v. 21 is the temple (cf. 17.12; in 3.17 it is the city of Jerusalem). The supplication 'remember and do not break your covenant with us', coming after the confession of sins, indicates an attitude to the covenant closer to that of Lev. 26.40–45 than to the Deuteronomistic notion of the broken covenant. For the community in the situation of vv. 19–22 the covenant remains something which Yahweh may still honour in order to protect land and people from further humiliation. It is a view of the covenant which recognizes that Yahweh may break it, whether the community has or has not (cf. Ps. 44.17; 74.20). It is difficult to determine the setting of this lament because there is no acknowledgment that the covenant has been broken by the people, and this suggests that the covenant spoken of here is a protective one in which Yahweh has promised to defend the people and not break it (a popular understanding of the covenant with David applied to city and people?). In this lament wickedness and inherited sins are not breaches of the covenant invoked.

The cult of the lament is a mixture of self-denigration and flattery of the deity: sins are confessed to; the guilt of the whole community and its ancestors is acknowledged; other deities are denounced; and the god to whom the entreaties are made is assured of his magnificence, power and uniqueness. In time of desperate trouble individuals and communities seek to influence their destiny in such well-tried ways and the sycophancy and desperation of the appeals are part of the convention (cf. Neh. 9.6–37; Dan. 9.3–19). In v. 22 the other gods are denounced as 'empty things' (*hᵃbālīm*, 8.19; 10.8; cf. Deut. 32.21) and the astral powers ('the heavens') as incapable of producing rain. In a severe drought none of the gods (nor Yahweh for that matter!) can produce rain, but each cult awards its own god a special-case argument – he would provide rain if only we were faithful to him. Thus the lament expresses the community's fidelity to its god and explores the different possibilities for inducing the god to break the drought. The acknowledgment that Yahweh is he, i.e. the one who is and who produces rain (cf. 10.12–13; also 5.24), identifies the community as loyal to Yahweh. The similarity of v. 22b to vv. 7–8 allows for a symmetrical presentation of statements of distress (vv. 2–6, 17–18) and laments (vv. 7–9, 19–22) in the composition. However, the extent to which these laments have been created for the tradition or reflect actual laments of the post-catastrophe communities cannot be determined from the text. The overall editing of the composition refers to the destruction of city and people, and against that nothing was effective. It should be noted, however, that a people who were as obdurate as the tradition elsewhere asserts they were would have been too busy worshipping other gods and oppressing each other to have uttered such laments.

15.1–4

151 Then the LORD said to me, 'Though Moses and Samuel stood before
me, yet my heart would not turn towards this people. Send them out of my
sight, and let them go! 2 And when they ask you, "Where shall we go?" you
shall say to them, "Thus says the LORD:
'Those who are for pestilence, to pestilence,
and those who are for the sword, to the sword;
those who are for famine, to famine,
and those who are for captivity, to captivity.' "
3 I will appoint over them four kinds of destroyers, says the LORD: the
sword to slay, the dogs to tear, and the birds of the air and the beasts of the
earth to devour and destroy. 4 And I will make them a horror to all the
kingdoms of the earth because of what Manasseh the son of Hezekiah, king
of Judah, did in Jerusalem.'

---

[1] MT 'and Samuel': G^{A} 'and Aaron'. MT *šallaḥ*, 'send'; BHS reads *šall*^{e}*ḥēm*, 'send them', with S,V (cf. EVV), *mem* lost by haplography. **[2]** EVV more expansive than lapidary Hebrew: *'*^{a}*šer lammāwet lammāwet wa'*^{a}*šer laḥereb laḥereb wa'*^{a}*šer lārā'āb lārā'āb wa'*^{a}*šer laššebī laššebī*. **[4]** K *lizwā'āh* (cf. Isa. 28.19) from *zw'*, 'shake, tremble'; Q *l*^{e}*za'*^{a}*wāh* (cf. Deut. 28.25; Ezek. 23.46): 'an object of horror, dread or terror', cf. 24.9; 29.18; 34.17. A few mss, Vrs read 'all' before 'what (Manasseh) did in Jerusalem'.

After the lament of 14.19–22 a divine response is to be expected, but the editing of 15.1–4 hardly provides an appropriate reply (cf. Bright, 103–4, who suggests that 17.1–4 might originally have served this purpose). The unit has connections with 14.11–16 (cf. v. 1 *wayyō'mer yhwh 'ēlay*, 'and Yahweh said to me'), but is more emphatic in its dismissal of the possibility of mediation and its statement of destruction. The oracle of salvation, so typical of the divine response to the lament, is conspicuously absent from this composition and its lack demonstrates that the purpose of the section is to construct an explanatory schema for the fate of Jerusalem and the people. The laments and the divine-speaker dialogue elements run parallel without influencing each other directly, but the compositor's juxtaposing of them allows for an interpenetration of themes which gives the section a certain unity. It thereby carries 'a considerable religious thrust aimed at those who were painfully aware of the calamities suffered by their fathers' (Kessler, 514).

The denial of mediation on the people's behalf is given its most hyperbolic form in v. 1: even intermediaries of the status of Moses or Samuel would not move the deity. In the Deuteronomistic understanding of the past these figures feature as intercessors capable of protecting the nation from great harm (e.g. Ex. 32.7–14; Num. 14.13–20; Deut. 9.13–29; I Sam. 7.8–9; 12.19–25), so the reference to them here underlines the reprobate status of the nation. In the past such mediation could protect the people, but the wickedness of the generation of Jerusalem's fall was beyond the capacity of intercessors. Interest in Moses and Samuel as intercessory figures is indicative of Deuteronomistic influence on the prose unit (cf. Thiel, 189ff.). Although Moses is regarded as a model for Jeremiah's self-understanding by some exegetes (e.g. Holladay 1964; 1966a), the relationship between the two figures is better seen as part of the editorial use of Deuteronomistic motifs. Moses does not appear in prophetic traditions, except for a few occurrences in late material (e.g. Isa. 63.11–12; Micah 6.4; Mal. 4.4 [MT 3.22]). The prohibition against intercession in 7.16; 11.14; 14.11 emphasizes the incorrigibility of the nation, and the allusion to Moses and Samuel is a further illustration of that theme. In the matter of intercession Jeremiah becomes a negative replica of Moses the great intercessor (cf. Alonso Schökel 1981, 251). But the allusion to Moses in v. 1 has another echo: 'send (them) from my sight, and let them go!' is an ironic reversal of the exodus myth, where the Pharaoh is confronted by Moses demanding in the name of Yahweh 'let my people go' (*šallaḥ 'et-'ammī*, Ex. 5.1; cf. 12.31). It is ironic in that now the command comes from Yahweh and is a dismissal from the divine presence (see 44 for further reversals of the Moses-exodus theme).

The element of dialogue is continued in v. 2, where an imaginary response of the people to such a dire command is posited (cf. 13.12 for this kind of anticipated response). To the question 'Where shall we go?' the answer is a poetic incantation chanted over the doomed nation. It has a lapidary quality which may represent its character as the answer to a searching inquiry or a reply to a lament. The twin motifs of sword and famine (14.13–16; triple motifs in 14.12) now become quadruple: pestilence, sword, famine and captivity. The notion of surviving the onslaught and ravages of war is now introduced into the list of fates awaiting the population. The oracular declaration is expanded in v. 3 as four genres (*mišpāḥōt*, 'families') of destruction: killing by the sword, dragging away of the corpses by dogs (cf. 22.19; 49.20 = 50.45), and the eating of the dead flesh by the birds and beasts of the land. Thus will the inhabitants become an object of horror and disgust to all the other kingdoms.

The 'shock horror' motif (cf. 24.9; 29.18; 34.17) is justified on the grounds of what king Manasseh did in Jerusalem. This explanation is unusual in the tradition because the wickedness of the people and their leaders is advanced regularly to justify the disaster; to refer back to a previous century and to a king long dead is somewhat excessive. The verse is an additional explanation here, but it allows the Deuteronomists to settle an old score and round off the composition. The nation's destruction may seem excessively cruel, but it is justified because king Manasseh was such a vicious and corrupt ruler (cf. II Kings 21.1–16; the Chronicler offers a kinder picture of Manasseh, II Chron. 33.10–20). That such an unusual explanation as this should appear here demonstrates the purpose of the composition to be the justification of Jerusalem's fall. It may have little place in the tradition as such, but it provides one more warrant for Yahweh's action against city and people from the Deuteronomistic viewpoint. Ironically Manasseh was blamed for filling Jerusalem with innocent blood (II Kings 21.16), when in reality Yahweh, under the guise of the Babylonians, did precisely that!

15.5–9

5 'Who will have pity on you, O Jerusalem,
  or who will bemoan you?
Who will turn aside
  to ask about your welfare?
6 You have rejected me, says the LORD,
  you keep going backward;
so I have stretched out my hand against you and destroyed you; –
  I am weary of relenting.
7 I have winnowed them with a winnowing fork
  in the gates of the land;
I have bereaved them, I have destroyed my people;
  they did not turn from their ways.
8 I have made their widows more in number
  than the sand of the seas;
I have brought against the mothers of young men
  a destroyer at noonday;
I have made anguish and terror
  fall upon them suddenly.

9 She who bore seven has languished;
she has swooned away;
her sun went down while it was yet day;
she has been shamed and disgraced.
And the rest of them I will give to the sword
before their enemies,
says the LORD.'

---

[5] G lacks MT's introductory *kī*, 'for, because', or 'surely' (Beuken and van Grol, 307). G lacks 'to ask'. **[6]** MT *nil'ētī hinnāḥēm*, 'I am weary of relenting': G *kai ouketi anēso autous*, 'and I will no longer spare them'. **[7]** MT *middarkēhem lō'-šābū*, 'from their ways they did not turn': G *dia tas kakias autōn*, 'because of their iniquities'. The phrase 'in the gates of the land' means 'towns', cf. 14.2; Deut. 5.14; 12.12, 17, 18; 14.21, 27–29. **[8]** MT *'āṣᵉmū-lī 'almᵉnōtāw* (Q; K 'its'): 'they have made (more) numerous for me their widows'; a reference to the invaders (cf. G v. 7 'they have destroyed . . .') or a plural of expansion (so Rudolph, 102). BHS suggests transposing the line to the end of the verse. MT *hēbē'tī lāhem 'al-'ēm bāḥūr*, 'I brought upon them, upon the mother of the youth': G lacks 'upon them'. BHS *lᵉ'ōm maḥᵃrīb*, 'a destroying people', for 'upon the mother of the youth'; Driver 1937–38, 113, reads *hēbē'tī ᵃlēhem 'al-maḥᵃrāb*, 'I have brought against them for laying waste'. S has 'and youths'. NEB 'I brought upon them a horde of raiders to plunder at high noon'. MT *'āleha* 'upon her', EVV 'upon them', cf. ST. MT *'īr*, 'agitation', cf. Hos. 11.9; Ps. 73.20; hapax legomenon (Rudolph); Driver understands it as 'invasion'; G *tromon*, 'trembling'. **[9]** K *b'h*, Q *bā'*: both masculine and feminine forms are correct as *šemeš*, 'sun', appears as either in biblical Hebrew.

Beuken and van Grol 1981, 314–25

This poem suits its present context as a reflection on the disaster which has befallen Jerusalem. It appears to be a divine lament over having had to destroy the people and expresses both condolence and judgment, though the condolence motif is very much a negative one. There is nobody to condole or have pity on Jerusalem and the deity is tired of consoling himself (*nḥm* also has the sense of relenting or repenting, cf. 4.28; 20.16; Amos 7.3, 6). The city is depicted as a wretched woman to whom no one shows any sympathy or concern, to whom none turns aside to inquire of her welfare (*šālōm*). The poem is filled with negative elements – none turn to inquire, the deity does not relent, the people do not turn back (*šūb*) – in the first part and images of destruction in the second part (vv. 5–7, 7–9). The towns of the land have been winnowed in a harvest of killing (contrast 4.11, where the winnowing figure is regarded as too mild to describe the destruction). Yahweh the widow-maker has bereaved the nation. In keeping with the imagery of the poem the statements all concern the effects of the invasion on the women: Jerusalem the woman is devastated, distraught with grief over her losses; the women of the land are widowed and rendered childless. Hyperbole and stereotyped language are used to depict the horrors of the occasion (v. 9, cf. I Sam. 2.5). The social consequences of the disaster are touched on in v. 9, where women, whose status depends upon having sons, are disgraced by being widowed and made childless (cf. Isa. 3.25–4.1). Now as widows and without sons they are exposed to all the oppression unprotected women suffer in cultures where their status is defined in relation to their men. Thus the lament responds to the horrors of invasion and underlines the composition in 14.1 – 15.4 as a statement about that disaster.

The lengthy composition in 14.1 – 15.4, with the following lament in 15.5–9, serves to identify the destruction of Jerusalem as an event which could not be prevented. No national lamentations, confessions of sins or acknowledgments of Yahweh could ward off the disaster; nor could mediations by legendary figures (cf. Ezek. 14.12–20) avail to circumvent the nation's fate. Nothing short of the actual tragedy itself would be acceptable to the deity (e.g. 14.12, 'I will not accept them'). The images of the people turning to Yahweh and seeking his deliverance may be purely the creation of the writers of the section, but they underline the point that nothing could prevent the defeat of Jerusalem and the massacre of the people. Neither prayers nor sacrifices were operative on their behalf (cf. 7.1 – 8.3). It is important to grasp this feature of the tradition and to understand it as part of the attempt to explain what *actually* happened, i.e. the real destruction of city and people. The element in the tradition which accuses the people of not turning (e.g. 5.3; 8.5; 15.6) is part of that explanation and conflicts with the lament fragments in 14.7–9, 19–22. That conflict may be rationalized as evidence that the people turned too late, but 15.4 makes it clear that the fate of the city was sealed long before the generation which experienced Nebuchadrezzar's wrath. Nothing the people could do would have changed the fate of city, people and land. Yet there are strands in the tradition which suggest the possibility of change without suffering (see on 18.7–11; cf. the narratives of discussion between Jeremiah and Zedekiah), and these also must be seen as being in conflict with the material which bears on the destruction of the city.

15.10–14

10 Woe is me, my mother, that you bore me, a man of strife and contention to the whole land! I have not lent, nor have I borrowed, yet all of them curse me. 11 So let it be, O LORD, if I have not pleaded with thee on behalf of the enemy in the time of trouble and in the time of distress! 12 Can one break iron, iron from the north, and bronze?
13 'Your wealth and your treasures I will give as spoil, without price, for all your sins, throughout all your territory. 14 I will make you serve your enemies in a land which you do not know, for in my anger a fire is kindled which shall burn for ever.'

---

[10] MT *kī*, 'that (you bore me)': G *hōs tina* = *mī*, 'who'. MT *wᵉʾîš mādōn*, 'and a man of contention': a few mss, Symm read *ūmādōh*, 'and strife', cf. G *diakrinomenon*. MT *kullōh*, 'all of it'; BHS reads *kullᵉhem*, 'all of them' (*mem* from *mqllwny*); G *hē ischus mou exelipen* 'my strength has failed (among those who curse me)'. BHS and others insert *kī* before *kullᵉhem qilᵉlūnī*, 'yet all of them curse me'; K *mqllwny* Q *mᵉqalᵉlanī*. **[11]** MT *ʾāmar yhwh*, 'Yahweh said': G *genoito, despota*, 'Amen (so be it), lord'. K *šrwrk*, Q *šērītīkā*?: G *kateuthunontōn autōn*, 'their prosperity' (suggests *ʾšr*, but cf. Hatch and Redpath, 750); very difficult word, BHS lists variants and reads *šēratttīkā* (following Volz, Condamin), 'I have served you (with the best intentions)' (Rudolph). Holladay 1976a, 143, opts for *šrr* as the stem yielding *šōrēr*, 'enemy', and the form here as *šārōtikā*, 'I have "enemied" you (for the best)'; cf. Hitzig, 118; Ps. 5.8 (MT 9); 27.11; 54.5 (MT 7); 56.2 (MT 3); 59.10 (MT 11). Hubmann 1978, 203, 206, follows Hitzig and reads 'truly, your hostility is for good'; cf. Thompson, 391, 'Surely I have made an enemy for you for good'. NEB 'I will greatly strengthen you', cf. RV; Aramaic *šrr*, 'be firm'. AV 'it shall be well with thy remnant', reads *šᵉʾērītᵉkā* with A, T, V; cf. JPSB. Skinner 1922, 203 n. 1, favours *śrh*, 'persist' (cf. Gen. 32.29 [EV 28]; Hos. 12.4, 5 [EV 3, 4]) and translates 11a as 'Say, Lord, if I have not persisted/With Thee for the enemy's good:'. MT 'in the time of trouble and in the time of distress': G 'their (trouble) . . . their (distress)'; BHS reads 'its trouble . . . its distress'. MT ends v. 11 with *ʾet-hāʾōyēb*, 'the enemy'; S reads the phrase after *bᵉkā*, 'with you', and understands it as '(the enemy) from the north' (*miṣṣāpōn*, cf. v. 12); BHS transposes with S and reads *ʾel-hāʾōyēb* (cf. G *pros*), 'against the enemy', or 'with reference to the enemy'. BHS also transposes *'attāh yāda'tā*, 'you know', from v. 15 to the end of v. 11. NEB understands v. 11b as 'in time of distress and in time of disaster I will bring the enemy to your feet.'. **[12–14]** Regarded as an intrusion here by many commentators. They may be a variant of 17.1–4 and, if 15.11–14 and 17.1–4 stood in adjacent columns of an ancient ms, even a correction. Smith 1979 treats vv. 13–14 as a quotation from 17.3–4. Both represent conflation in MT of two mss traditions; cf. 8.10–12; 23.7–8 (Janzen 1973, 133). NEB relegates vv. 13–14 to the margin, as does Weiser, Volz. **[12]** MT *h^ayārō'a barzel barzel miṣṣāpōn ūn^eḥōšet*: 'does iron break iron from the north and bronze?' G *ei gnōsthēsetai sidēros*; *kai peribolaion chalkoun hē ischus sou*, 'will iron be known? but your strength is a copper (brass) covering'. **[13]** BHS regards vv. 13–14 as an additon from 17.3–4 (they are variants with no equivalent to 17.4a). MT *lō' bimḥīr*, 'without price': 17.3 *bāmōtekā*, 'your high places', cf. BHS, which deletes 'not' and reads 'price' in both places. MT *ūb^ekol . . . ūb^ekol*, 'and for all . . . and in all'; BHS deletes 'and', cf. 17.3. **[14]** MT *w^eha'^abartī*, 'I will make (your enemies) pass through . . .': many mss, 17.4 *w^eha'^abadtīkā*, 'I will make you serve (your enemies), so RSV. MT *b^e'ereṣ lō' yādā'tā*, 'in a land (*'^ašer*, which, 17.4) you do not know'. MT *'^alēkem tūqād*, 'against you shall burn': 17.4 *'ad-'ōlām tūqād*, 'shall burn for ever' = RSV.

Bright 1974; Baumgartner 1917, 60–3; Gerstenberger 1963; Hubmann 1978, 203–307; Reventlow 1963, 210–28

The section 15.10–21 is made up of three units (vv. 10–14, 15–18, 19–21) which may be treated separately or together (some exegetes regard the larger context of the section to be 14.1 – 15.21, e.g. Gerstenberger, 403–8; cf. Polk 1984, 77–9). Analysing the three units separately allows the interpretative difficulties to be seen more clearly and underlines the growth of the material into a complex section. The lengthy textual notes attached to vv. 10–14 indicate the problems of translation which constitute the first stage of interpreting the unit. Such a wide divergency of opinion on how the text should be translated must encourage the exegete to be modest in advocating any particular line of interpretation. The text itself is badly preserved in places and shows evidence of editorial interpolation (e.g. vv. 13–14 as a variant of 17.3–4). The difference between MT and G in v. 11 (e.g. divine speech or speaker's utterance) points to divergent developments of the tradition. Thus it may be read as a divine reassurance to a harassed individual or group or a statement about the enemy (e.g. Baumgartner, 61, understands the reference to 'the enemy' as a mistake for 'you are my friend', reading *h'yb* as *'hby*, cf.

Isa. 41.8). If translation and interpretation may yield such distinctive results, then it would be unwise to make this unit bear the heavy weight of particularized exegesis to which it is sometimes subjected (cf. Bright 1970; 1974).

The placing of vv. 10–14 after 15.5–9 is probably due to the associative motif 'mother' in vv. 8–9, 10. The lament is directed to the speaker's mother in a context of suffering and bereavement and may reflect a communal lament (Jerusalem as mother) on the grounds that the only identifiable mother in the tradition is the communal one, Rachel (31.15; cf. 50.12). Other exegetes prefer to read the statement as a reference to Jeremiah's mother and to associate v. 10 with the familial opposition of 11.21–3; 12.6 (e.g. Holladay 1976a, 138–40). However, 'mother' may have no semantic force here but simply be an apostrophized element (cf. Ps. 27.10). This may be the correct way to understand v. 10, as it is a series of rhetorical phrases. The speaker is cursed by everybody and the subject of quarrels and litigious arguments (metaphorical). Yet why should this be so when he has bothered no one? The commercial images of borrowing or lending in MT are more generalized in G's depiction of the speaker as not having helped (*ōphelēsa*) or been helped. Why should such a solitary hermit be cursed? To ask the question is to take the complaint too literally. It is to read the text as if it were the expression of an outraged innocent, the victim of public viciousness in spite of his purity of isolation. It is to seek biography instead of recognizing the rhetoric of the lament which conventionally expresses such outrage in excessive terms. It reflects the world of the innocent sufferer complaining about injustice in spite of good done to others (though here it is admitted that indifference to others characterizes the state of the complainant). The RSV understanding of v. 11 pursues this image of doing good in spite of obloquy received. The many exegetes who make this an individual lament spoken by Jeremiah and attach biographical value to it (e.g. Bright, Thompson) represent him as naive by implication. The tradition presents Jeremiah as involved in cursing the people (e.g. 11.3, 5) and delivering long tirades of cruel threats against them – why should the people not curse him in return! Such lack of awareness in Jeremiah hardly supports the conventional view of him as a profound analyst of Judaean society. But that is a problem of defective analysis of the text as biographical rather than a comment on the text itself.

The speaker is not identified in v. 10 and therefore may be interpreted as the speaker indicated by the redactional framework, i.e. Jeremiah, though there is no editorial comment on v. 10 (cf. 14.1; 15.1). However, the speaker may be viewed better as an individual speaking for the community (cf. Reventlow) or as a pietist expressing the complaint of the pious against their oppression by the community at large (hence v. 21; cf. 12.1–3; Vermeylen 1981, 256). This latter interpretation allows v. 10 to be understood as the protestation of innocence made by the pious (cf. 12.3a; 17.16). Similar asseverations of not having done wrong (Deut. 23.19 prohibits lending to or borrowing from fellow Israelites) are a feature of such defences (e.g. I Sam. 12.3–5; Job 31, note v. 30). In spite of such innocence the pious are cursed by the whole community. In response to this lament Yahweh speaks (so MT, but G develops the picture of the lament speaker standing for the community's well-being) and presumably reassures the speaker of divine protection against the enemy. The state of the text in v. 11 hardly permits a confident exegesis of it, but one line of interpretation is as follows. The deity says: 'Surely, I have strengthened you for good; surely, I have intervened on your behalf in time of evil and in time of distress' (cf. Vermeylen 1981, 266 n. 79; NEB). The addition in MT of 'the enemy' may be a marginal gloss identifying the meaning of 'a time of evil and distress' with a specific opposition or, if 'from the north' in v. 12 belongs to the gloss, with the invader motif dominant in parts of the tradition. The degree of rearrangement of the text among different commentators indicates the problem of understanding how the text should be read in the first place and also demonstrates how meaning may be gained by manipulating the text. The interpretation offered here views v. 11 as a promise of salvation to the oppressed pietists in the community and treats vv. 10–11 as similar to the laments of the book of Psalms and Job.

The cryptic question in v. 12 adds further difficulties to the interpretation of the unit. It may be a corruption of 17.1, but with only one word in common (*barzel*, 'iron') that is a less likely explanation than alternative accounts of it being an editorial development of the tradition here. If the text is treated as a code whose words may be shifted around in order to make sense of them (e.g. the approach of Holladay 1976a), then the terms 'iron' and 'bronze' may be matched with other occurrences of them. But this approach can lead to confusion: 'iron' and 'bronze' are used to describe the speaker in 1.18 and the people in 6.28, so to whom is the reference in 15.12? As the 'iron' is qualified in MT as 'from the north' it may also refer to the invader from the north (G avoids this particular complication). Decoding the terms allows one possible meaning to be 'Who will break whom? – iron from the north [the foreign foe] or iron and bronze [the rebellious people]? Yahweh is suggesting that Jeremiah turn his attention away from domestic enemies to the foreign threat' (Holladay 1976a, 144). Yet the code of v. 12 could be deciphered to yield the meaning that the speaker (the 'iron' of 1.18) would not be broken because of divine protection (v. 11; cf. v. 20; 1.19). It is not clear in Holladay's exposition why the enemy from the north should pose more of a problem to Jeremiah than his domestic enemies, especially in view of the narratives of 37–39.

The presence of vv. 13–14 in the text of 15.10–14 and 17.3–4 may allow the exegete to treat them as a variant displaced in the context of 15.10–11, 15–18. Many commentators so treat them and provide an exegesis of them in 17.1–4 (e.g. Rudolph); but some regard them as necessitating comment in their present context. Such comment is justified on the grounds that subtle differences in the two sets of variants can be elucidated if they are treated separately. The interpretation of vv. 12–14 is shaped by the concluding phrase of v. 11 'the enemy' (MT). What follows continues the theme of the speaker's protection and comments on the fate of his opponents. The wealth and treasures must refer to the community rather than an individual, and these constitute the price the people must pay for their offences. Then the deity will cause their enemies to pass through into a land unknown to those addressed because a fire (permanent in 17.4) burns against them (MT 'you'). Read this way (cf. Gerstenberger, 395) it is a statement of salvation for the oppressed group. It may, however, be extended in meaning to refer to Israel's enemies, so that it is a promise of divine vengeance against the nation which has devastated Israel (so Gerstenberger, 396). Both readings are possible interpretations of the present context of vv. 13–14, though not of 17.3–4 (nor of the RSV treatment of vv. 13–14 as the same as 17.3–4).

If the hint of salvation discerned in the late addition to 15.10–11, 15–18 is too subtle a reading of the text, then it may be read as a condemnation of the enemies of the speaker of v. 10. His complaint on behalf of himself or the community of piety is answered by a divine statement of protective intervention which will destroy his opponents, their wealth (cf. the prosperity of 12.1), and exile them to an unknown land where they will have to serve their enemies. It is then a conventional reaction to persecution, with divine judgment as the lot of the wicked and implicit vindication of the innocent. The formal structure of 15.10–14 consists of complaint (v. 10), divine answer (v. 11), with redactional addition of destruction of enemies (13–14), and v. 12 as an element which may be taken with v. 11 (impunity of speaker) or with vv. 13–14 (a cryptic allusion to the invaders from the north as a figure of the punishment of the speaker's enemies). A parallel structure is to be found also in 15.15–21 (cf. Vermeylen). Along these lines some coherence may be found in vv. 10–14, but the state of the text and the multifarious opinions of commentators must place a question mark after every interpretation.

15.15–18

15 O LORD, thou knowest;
remember me and visit me,
and take vengeance for me on my persecutors.
In thy forbearance take me not away;
know that for thy sake I bear reproach.
16 Thy words were found, and I ate them,
and thy words became to me a joy
and the delight of my heart;
for I am called by thy name,
O LORD, God of hosts.
17 I did not sit in the company of merrymakers,
nor did I rejoice;
I sat alone, because thy hand was upon me,
for thou hadst filled me with indignation.
18 Why is my pain unceasing,
my wound incurable,
refusing to be healed?
Wilt thou be to me like a deceitful brook,
like waters that fail?

---

[15] G lacks 'thou knowest'; cf. BHS, which transfers the phrase to the end of v. 11. MT *le'erek* adj. BHS revocalizes to *'ōrek* noun, 'length'; with *'appayim*, 'face', the phrase means 'forbearance, self-restraint'; cf. G *makrothumian*, 'long-suffering'. G lacks *tiqqāḥēnī*, 'take me away', so refers the lack of divine long-suffering to the persecutors. **[16]** MT *nimṣe'ū debārēkā* *wā'ōklēm wayᵉhī* . . . 'thy words were found and I ate them and they became . . .': G *hupo tōn athetountōn tous logous sou suntelesan autous, kai estai. . .* 'from those who despise your words; consume them, and it shall be . . .' = *minnōʾᵃṣē dᵉbārekā:kallēm wīhī* . . . K *dbryk*, 'your words'; Q *dᵉbārkā*, 'your word'. **[17]** MT *wā'eʿlōz*, '(nor) did I rejoice': G *alla eulaboumen*, 'but I was cautious (because of your power)'. MT *zaʿam*, 'anger (filled with)': G *pikrias*, 'bitterness'. MT and G of vv. 15–17 are subtly different at a number of points and yield significantly distinctive readings. **[18]** MT *hāyāh kᵉʾēbī neṣah*, 'my pain is enduring': G *hoi lupountes me katischousin mou*, 'those who distress me prevail over me' (*nṣh* understood in Aramaic sense, so BHS). MT *mēʾᵃnāh hērāpē'*, 'refusing to be healed': G *pothen iathēsomai*, 'whence shall I be healed?' = *mē'ayin 'ērāpē'* (cf. BHS). MT *hāyō tihyeh*, 'will you really be?': some read the infinitive absolute as *hōy*, 'woe' (e.g. Volz, Rudolph, cf. BHS). MT *a'kzāb*, 'deceitful, disappointing': 'brook' (JPSB 'spring', cf. AV 'liar') is derived from the qualifying 'waters not to be trusted' cf. Isa. 58.11. The image is of a wadi which has rain in the winter but dries up in summer; for a delineation of its features and its metaphoric usage cf. Job 6.15–20.

Literature as for 15.10–14; Baumgartner, 33–40

The speaker continues the lament of v. 10 with further expressions of persecuted suffering and protestations of innocence. Because the form of the individual lament divides the world into the innocent complainer and the company of the wicked (e.g. Ps. 26.1–6), the contrast in this unit is between the fidelity of the speaker and the hostility of those who are not interested in Yahweh (a feature more developed in G than MT). The cause of the persecution is the godliness of the speaker ('on your behalf', v. 15, cf. Ps. 44.22) and for that reason he should not be taken away. The taking away may refer to the opportunity afforded the persecutors by the delay in Yahweh's vindication of his loyal servant (cf. Bright, 110). By showing lenience to his enemies Yahweh allows the speaker to continue suffering. These opponents are the people who despise Yahweh's word (G; in the second edition it refers to the speaker's reception of the divine word) and against whom the speaker appeals to Yahweh for vengeance (cf. G). In contrast to such rejection of the word are the speaker's acquisition of and response to the divine words. That contrast is lost in MT. The identity of the speaker is indicated by the phrase 'I am called by your name' (v. 16b *kī-niqrā' šimkā ʿālay*, a formulaic phrase referring to ownership). When used with reference to the deity it points to divine ownership of the nation (e.g. Deut. 28.10; Isa. 63.19; II Chron. 7.15; cf. 14.9; Amos 9.12) or of objects such as the ark (II Sam. 6.2 = I Chron. 13.6), the Jerusalem temple (7.10–11, 14, 30; 32.34; 34.15; I Kings 8.43 = II Chron. 6.33), and the city of Jerusalem (25.29; Dan. 9.18). It is also used to identify the exiles scattered throughout the empire (Isa. 43.5–7). What is noteworthy about the idiom is the fact that it is not used to describe individuals as such, so its occurrence here in an individual lament identifies the speaker as a member of the divinely chosen nation or indicates that the lament has a collective representational meaning (cf. Baumgartner, 36; Reventlow, 220–1). So the lament speaks for a group of pietists against those who oppose them or despise the divine word.

The protestation of innocence occurs in v. 17 in the form of an assertion that the speaker has avoided the company of merrymakers (cf. 30.19; 31.4). Avoidance of the wicked is one mark of the righteous person (e.g. Ps. 1.1), though the reference here to merrymakers (*m^eśaḥ^aqīm*) may not imply that they were mockers or wicked. If vv. 15–16 present a figure persecuted by the ungodly, vv. 17–18 show that figure to be the victim of divine power and anger. They probably represent both sides of the same coin (cf. the story of Job and the arguments of his friends). The speaker's pain is incurable (*'^anūšāh*, cf. 17.9, 16; 30.12), without healing. Elsewhere in the tradition the motif of the incurable wound refers to the community's devastation (30.12 *'ānūš l^ešibrēk*, cf. 8.21), so its use here may confirm the interpretation of vv. 15–18 as an individual lament on behalf of the community. The permanent pain makes the speaker question the behaviour of Yahweh: if the righteous suffer so much and the wicked prosper (cf. 12.1–3), then the deity is a deceiver. The figure used is that of a wadi which encourages the traveller to believe that water is at hand, only for him to discover that it is a dried-up wadi. The water of such a wadi is not reliable and so provides a good metaphor of companions who are unreliable (cf. Job 6.15–20; contrast Isa. 58.11). Directed at Yahweh the assertion (such it is in MT, NEB but RSV turns it into a query) represents the bitterness (so G) of the speaker who has experienced the deity's unreliability. The figure also introduces an ironic twist into the tradition because in 2.13 the deity is described as 'the fountain of living waters' and the other gods as 'broken cisterns'. Now the pious community has discovered the unreliability of Yahweh as a source of water. The failure of the gods, including Yahweh, is at the heart of ancient laments, and throughout the psalms and Job that failure reverberates as the central theme of the complaints. The deceptive waters of v. 18 are but one image of the problem behind the lament; the hiding of the divine face is a more frequent figure of that experience (33.5; cf. Isa. 8.17; 45.15; 54.8; 64.7; see Balentine 1983).

The exegesis of 15.10–18 as a lament on behalf of the pious against their persecution by the wicked is based on its similarity to 12.1–3, many lament psalms and the book of Job. These sources demonstrate the stereotypical motifs and conventions of the lament genre which also are to be found in the Jeremiah tradition. Because the genre is such a dominant form in biblical literature it is very difficult to specify the historical situations out of which particular laments have emerged. The fall of Jerusalem is the clearest candidate for the background to many laments (e.g. Lamentations; Ps. 74; 79; 137) and also for the Jeremiah tradition (e.g. 1.3). The polarization of the post-exilic community into pietists and others (cf. the righteous and the wicked in the writings of the Qumran community) would provide a good background to the laments in Jeremiah (cf. Vermeylen 1981). However, it must be recognized that many commentators regard the laments in the tradition as the personal utterances of Jeremiah the prophet (e.g. Baumgartner, Bright, Berridge). For them the reference to finding the divine words, eating them and their joyful effect (v. 16) is a statement about his call to be a prophet (cf. 1.9; Holladay 1976a, 141). Variations on that interpretation include the view that 15.16 is a reference to the finding of the scroll in Josiah's renovation of the temple (II Kings 22.8–13; Holladay 1966a, 25) or to Jeremiah's reception of earlier prophetic words (cf. Ezek. 2.8–3.3; Berridge 1970, 119–22). All these interpretations may be justified in the light of the vagueness of the lament form. Non-specific language permits a greater degree of variation in interpretation, and metaphorical language allows a wider range of meaning. But the reception of the divine words in v. 16 (ignoring G) is not necessarily a reference to the prophetic office but a statement about the speaker's attitude to those words typical of the pietist's response to Yahweh (cf. Ps. 1.2; 119). The pious acknowledge the sweetness of Yahweh's precepts and words (e.g. Ps. 19.10; 119.103), and such an implicit metaphor of tasting should not be construed as making the psalmists prophets. The context of 15.10–18 (cf. 14.1; 15.1) may justify treating the lament as an utterance of a prophetic figure in terms of the totality of the redactional framework, but that is then a transformation of material which may originally have been quite different. It also presupposes an editorial intention to create biographical statements, which may be a very modern understanding of how ancient traditions were created and why. If that presupposition is not allowed to prejudge the text, then it is possible to read the laments in ways which do not entail a biographical or a confessional understanding of them. And such readings may be a more acute comprehension of the tradition as the record of the many layers of its composition and the social realities they represent.

15.19–21

19 Therefore thus says the LORD:
'If you return, I will restore you,
and you shall stand before me.
If you utter what is precious, and not what is worthless,
you shall be as my mouth.
They shall turn to you,
but you shall not turn to them.
20 And I will make you to this people
a fortified wall of bronze;
they will fight against you,
but they shall not prevail over you,
for I am with you
to save you and deliver you,
says the LORD.
21 I will deliver you out of the hand of the wicked,
and redeem you from the grasp of the ruthless.'

---

[19] MT *'im-tāšūb wa'ᵃšībᵉkā . . . yāšubū . . . lō-tāšūb*: 'if you turn, I will turn you . . . they shall turn . . . you shall not turn', word-play on *šūb*. **[20]** MT *lᵉḥōmat nᵉḥōšet*, 'a wall of bronze', cf. *lᵉḥōmōt nᵉḥōšet*, 1.18.

Literature as for 15.10–18; Jüngling 1973

The divine response to the lament appears in vv. 19–21 and is essentially an assurance of deliverance from the power of the wicked. But as with so many of the divine utterances in the tradition, it is cryptic and eludes clear exegesis. It addresses the speaker but not his complaint (cf. the speeches of Yahweh to Job in Job 38–41) and uses an *ad hominem* response to challenge him to turn (*šūb*). Because responses to laments are as formal as the laments themselves, it is not to be expected that the divine reply to a lament should answer the specific complaint. Both elements are fabricated from conventional forms and placed together as an editorial unit. It is therefore pointless to speculate about the possible relationship between complaint and response, other than in general terms of oppression and deliverance. It is unnecessary to construct a complicated account of how the speaker had gone astray and must now turn back to Yahweh in order to experience divine deliverance from the oppression complained about in the lament. The demand for the speaker to turn is a way of defusing the accusation of v. 18b by accusing the speaker of having gone astray (attack is the best method of defence, even for the deity!). If the speaker is prepared to turn and speak what is precious rather than worthless (for *zōlēl* cf. Lam. 1.11), then he will become the divine mouth. The others (the oppressors of vv. 15–16?) will turn to him rather than he to them. This word-play on *šūb*, 'turn', is impressive as rhetoric but lacks semantic content. It may mean that the persecutors will respond to him rather than his taking notice of them and being terrified by them (cf. v. 15). But if this is the meaning, it is a curious use of *šūb*, and suggests that paronomasia has overcome meaning. However, the promise of deliverance is clear, if not the precise details of how it is to be implemented. The pious group who face the oppression of the godless may yet experience Yahweh's salvation if they will turn to him rather than to the oppressors and will become as his mouth, speaking precious things.

The 'they' of v. 19 (*hēmmāh*) becomes 'this people' in v. 20, and a certain tension enters the unit (cf. Hubmann, 250–1). The 'turning' of v. 19 becomes 'fighting' in v. 20, which is hardly the point of v. 19 (the notion of fighting would require both parties to turn towards each other rather than one to refuse to turn). The addressee of v. 20 now becomes a brazen wall against which the people fight ineffectually, and he is saved by Yahweh. The brazen wall motif also appears in 1.18 in a similar fashion and expresses the idea of obduracy against attacks leading to divine deliverance (cf. Jüngling on the relationship between the two texts). The shift in images and the use of motifs from elsewhere in the tradition point to additional material in the unit. The enemy motif has appeared already in vv. 12–14, and vv. 20–21 may also be such an addition to the lament with its answer in vv. 10–11, 15–19 (cf. Vermeylen 1981, 266). If this is a correct assumption, then vv. 20–21 may belong to the same redactional movement which provided vv. 18–19 as a further element in the editing of ch. 1 (see on 1.18–19). The platitudinous force of v. 21 represents a standard view of the outcome of the struggle between the righteous and the wicked, and its presence here indicates the editorial understanding of vv. 10–20 as the conflict between the righteous and the wicked.

The central theme of vv. 10–21 is the conflict between the righteous and the wicked. As this is a major theme of the psalms (e.g. Ps. 3–7, 9–13, 17, 22, 43, 44), it is too general a motif to permit precise interpretation in the Jeremiah tradition. It may represent the conflict within the community of the righteous and the wicked during the sixth and later centuries, the opposition of the nations to Judah, the struggle for dominance between different prophetic groups, or part of the creation of the persona of Jeremiah by the use of individual and communal lament forms. Such a wide range of possibilities makes the lament poems in the tradition indeterminate of meaning and open to considerable variations of interpretation (cf. Gunneweg 1970). The expressions of distress made by or on behalf of the city (e.g. 4.19–21; 8.18–9.1; 10.19–20) suggest one line of interpretation for the laments. The figure sitting alone in 15.17 may well be an image of the forlorn city in its widowhood (Lam. 1.1). But whether the individual laments of the oppressed righteous were edited into the tradition as further expressions of the city's grief over the catastrophe of 587 is a matter of hermeneutical decision rather than a demonstrable case. Complex arguments are used by each exegete to demonstrate how their particular interpretation fits the text better than alternative accounts (e.g. Bright 1970; Berridge 1970; Polk 1984), and yet the textual data elude precise definition and interpretation. This is to be expected from highly metaphorical language in texts which have been heavily edited and set into discrete frameworks.

The city or the community (often interchangeable in the tradition) is one major set of interpretative moves in the reading of the laments. Another set of interpretations, perhaps the more frequent among exegetes, reads the poems as utterances of the prophet Jeremiah (historical or fabricated). Not Jeremiah as a cult prophet speaking for and on behalf of the community (e.g. Reventlow), but as an individual figure in the closing decades of Judaean political life before the fall of Jerusalem. In this interpretative approach to the laments we see Jeremiah struggling against opposition from the community, his family and even the other prophets and using traditional liturgical forms to express his inner feelings of pain, doubt and despair. Such an exposition of the laments readily turns them into 'confessions' and can lead to an analysis of Jeremiah in terms of seeing in him 'the cradle of individual religion' (Skinner 1922, 224; cf Peake, 43–8). His suffering, as expressed in these poems, is part of a pattern of life demonstrated in the narratives of the tradition (19.1–20.6; 26–29; 37–44) which provides a paradigm of the suffering of the righteous which is not based on guilt (cf. Welten 1977, 137–45). In his persecution for obedience to the divine word it is possible to see suffering as a consequence of doing Yahweh's will rather than a result of being wicked. It therefore provides a vindication of the innocent in their struggle against opposition (cf. Isa. 53). The representation of the persona of Jeremiah in this form makes the prophet a model for imitation by the righteous in every generation (cf. Polk 1984, 151–2).

The high degree of theologization attached to the interpretation of the laments as 'confessions' is not a necessary consequence of treating the poems as utterances of the historical Jeremiah. The theology may be grounded on the poems as editorial fabrications placed in the mouth of their persona Jeremiah (e.g. Polk 1984). The difficulty with the theological understanding of suffering suggested by the exposition of the laments in terms of Jeremiah's sufferings is that the tradition resolutely presents suffering as the judgment of Yahweh against the wicked. If a new understanding of suffering is to be found in the 'confessions', then it conflicts with the central theme of the book. This is but one conflict within the tradition which emerges as a result of making that tradition a unified representation of the sayings and deeds of one person (whether historical or created by the editors). Further elements of conflict may be found in reading the laments as the 'confessions' of Jeremiah: e.g. the solitary figure of 15.17 contrasts sharply with the social character surrounded by important people in 26–29, 32–39; the vindication of Jeremiah in 15.21 is an unfulfilled prediction in the light of his fate in 43–44. Many other points of conflict could be noted (see on 17.16) but each example undermines the exegesis of the poems as personal statements of the prophet. It may be objected to this line of analysis that the poems are highly conventional and should not be expected to yield a correspondence between utterance and reality. But it is precisely this use of conventional forms which provides the argument against treating the poems as personal 'confessions' in the first place. If they were personal utterances, some correspondence might be expected between them and the other parts of the tradition (which might then be regarded as authentic). In conventional forms, reality, except in a most general way, is cloaked and the exegesis of the poems inevitably becomes a statement of possible rather than of definitive meanings.

16.1–9

161 The word of the LORD came to me: 2 'You shall not take a wife, nor
shall you have sons or daughters in this place. 3 For thus says the LORD
concerning the sons and daughters who are born in this place, and
concerning the mothers who bore them, and the fathers who begot them in
this land: 4 They shall die of deadly diseases. They shall not be lamented,
nor shall they be buried; they shall be as dung on the surface of the ground.
They shall perish by the sword and by famine, and their dead bodies shall
be food for the birds of the air and for the beasts of the earth.
5 For thus says the LORD: Do not enter the house of mourning, or go to
lament, or bemoan them; for I have taken away my peace from this people,
says the LORD, my steadfast love and mercy. 6 Both great and small shall
die in this land; they shall not be buried, and no one shall lament for them
or cut himself or make himself bald for them. 7 No one shall break bread
for the mourner, to comfort him for the dead; nor shall any one give him
the cup of consolation to drink for his father or his mother. 8 You shall not
go into the house of feasting to sit with them, to eat and drink. 9 For thus
says the LORD of hosts, the God of Israel: Behold, I will make to cease from
this place, before your eyes and in your days, the voice of mirth and the
voice of gladness, the voice of the bridegroom and the voice of the bride.'

---

[1] G lacks the redactional introduction of MT's v. 1 and begins with v. 2, 'you shall not take a wife . . .'. **[2]** G has 'says the lord god of Israel' after the prohibition. **[4]** Cf. 7.33 for 4b. **[5]** MT *bēt marzēaḥ*, 'house of mourning', but G *thiason*, 'festive company', cf. Amos 6.7, 'revelry'; NEB 'house where there is a mourning-feast', JPSB margin 'religious gathering'. KB, 566, gives 'banquet, cult festival' as the meaning of *marzēaḥ* (cf. KB^3 I, 599); on Amos 6.7, cf. Coote 1981, 36–9; Porten 1968, 179–86. Pope 1977, 166 defines *marzēaḥ* as 'a sodality devoted to feasts for the dead'. MT *n^e'um yhwh*, 'says Yahweh' . . . *lō yiqqābērū*, 'they shall not be buried', lacking in G. The argument about the 'triple-duty' suffix of *š^{e}lōmī*, 'my peace' (Holladay 1966c, 418), governing *ḥesed* and *raḥ^{a}mīm* (cf. EVV), therefore only applies to the second edition (MT). **[6]** Holladay also vocalizes *yqbrw* as a Qal *yiqb^{e}rū*, 'they will (not) bury', because the statement is addressed to the survivors. MT *yitgōdad*, 'cut himself' (cf. 5.7), *yiqqārēaḥ*, 'make himself bald': Vrs read plural here in agreement with *yispᵉdu*, 'they shall lament'. **[7]** MT *wᵉlō'-yiprᵉsū lahem*, 'and they shall not break for them': a few mss, G read *leḥem*, '(break) bread . . . ', cf. EVV. MT *'al-'ēbel*, 'for mourning'; some exegetes prefer to vocalize it as *'ābēl*, '(for the) mourner', cf. BHS (Holladay, 418–9, retains MT). MT *'ōtām*, 'them'; G *auton*, 'him' = *'ōtō* as required by sense of statement (Holladay would delete *'wtm* altogether). **[8]** MT *lāšebet 'ōtām*, 'to sit them': better with some mss *'ittām*, 'with them', cf. G *met' autōn* 'with them', BHS. **[9]** Cf. 7.34.

Holladay 1966c, 412–20; Thiel 1973, 195–201

A series of highly edited pieces contributes to a prolix statement about the destruction of the community for idolatrous practices (with the exception of vv. 14–15 = 23.7–8). Deuteronomistic editing is apparent (analysis in Thiel), and the standard problem of determining what constitutes the basic unit (e.g. 1–4, 5–9, 10–13, 16–18) provides for disagreement among exegetes. The majority of commentators regard vv. 1–9 as a prose statement, but a few see it as poetry (e.g. Condamin, Holladay, Thompson) or as having a poetic original underlying it (e.g. Bright, 112; cf. Volz, 176). The editorial introduction in v. 1 (cf. 1.4, 11, 13; 13.3, 8; 18.5; 24.4) turns vv. 2–9 into a series of divine commands to the speaker rather than to the community. Yet v. 10 suggests that what precedes it is addressed to the people rather than to an individual. The various elements of prose and poetic fragments, the mixture of singular and plural forms (e.g. v. 2, 'you shall not take', *lō-tiqqaḥ*; v. 9, 'before your eyes and in your days', *lᵉ'ēnēkem ūbīmēkem*), and the Deuteronomistic shaping of the pieces all point to a highly developed section which will not yield a simple or undisputed meaning. In Thiel's analysis the original part of the chapter consists of 1–3a, 4a, 5–8, 9*, the report of Jeremiah's symbolic action, and 16–17, a prophetic word of judgment. To these have been added the Deuteronomistic redaction in 3b, 4b, 'before your eyes and in your days' of 9, and 10–13, with 18 commenting on 16–17 (cf. 2.7b), so that a redactional unity of 1–13, 16–18 has been produced. A post-Deuteronomistic hand has added 14–15 and 19–21.

The association of 1–9 with what precedes it may be due to the common motif 'mother' in 15.8–9, 10 and 16.3 (Rudolph sees 16.1–9 as an illustration of 15.17; G's 'and [*kai*] you shall not take a wife' makes vv. 1–4 look like a continuation of what precedes them). However, the pattern of Deuteronomistically edited prose interpolated into the poems of the tradition (cf. 7.1–83; 11.1–13; 18.1–12) may point more to the growth of the book than to a deliberate policy of making precise connections with key motifs and phrases. The editorial introduction of v. 1 (absent in G) transforms what follows into a statement about the speaker but should not be allowed to divert attention from the central features of vv. 2–9. They are a concern with 'in this place' (*bammāqōm hazzeh*, vv. 2, 3, 9, cf. 7.3, 7, 20), 'in this land' (*bā'āreṣ hazzō't*, cf. 7.7), and 'this people' (*hā'ām hazzeh*, vv. 5, 10). What is said (clearer in G) is said about this people in this place (Jerusalem?), in this land (the land-city identification is a major feature of the tradition), and concerns the death of children. This links vv. 2–9 with 15.8–9 (cf. the *Kindertotenlieder* of 9.20–22) and may reflect an original message (assuming that there is an original element underlying this highly edited piece) addressed to the community about the impending disaster which would destroy so many of its people. Hence the central motifs are children, their begetting and their death, and the social celebrations or mourning associated with such matters.

The extent of death in the land will be so great that the bodies will lie on the ground as dung and as food for the birds and beasts (cf. 7.33–34; 8.1–3), so marriage is to be avoided because the having of children will bring only grief and mourning. The mourning-feast is also to be avoided because the people's wellbeing (*šālōm*) has been removed by Yahweh (MT defines *šālōm* here as Yahweh's devoted loyalty [*ḥesed*] and compassion). In the absence of such qualities (contrast 9.24, where they are said to be practised '*in the earth*' by Yahweh) death is so inevitable that there can be no mourning for the people. The mourning rites include the funeral meats, the heavy drinking, the shaving of the hair, the cutting of the body and other communal practices whereby the living proclaimed their solidarity with the dead and the spirits of the ancestors (cf. Gaster 1969, 590–604). They were common practices (cf. 41.5; 48.37; Amos 8.10; Isa. 15.2–3; 22.12; Ezek. 7.18), but later Yahwistic ideology prohibited them in an attempt to differentiate between acceptable Israelite religion and pagan practices (cf. Lev. 19.27–28; 21.5; Deut. 14.1). The funereal forms of self-laceration and oblivion induced by alcoholic beverages are forbidden here because they are tacit acknowledgements of the gods and spirits of other cults (e.g.

Ps. 106.28), against which the Deuteronomistic ideologues battle in their redaction of the tradition (cf. vv. 11, 18; 7.17–19, 30–32; 8.2; 9.14; 11.9–13; 13.10). Not only are the mourning-feasts to be avoided but so also are the feasts associated with weddings (vv. 8–9). No form of communal consolation or celebration (i.e. commensality) is to be permitted because of what is going to happen to the people. The deity is removing from them all that could give rise to such occasions and will bring about such devastation that there will be no more funerals and the sound of merry-making will cease in the land. As such, the message is constituted by a set of hyperbolic statements announcing the destruction of community and land.

The present form of the text (esp. MT), however, suggests a different interpretation of the prohibition against marriage and the warnings against sharing in funeral feasts or wedding celebrations. Rather than understand the singularity of v. 2 as referring to the people (cf. 11.16 or Jerusalem in 15.5), an interpretation confirmed by vv. 9, 10, many commentators prefer to read vv. 1–9 as a prohibition forbidding Jeremiah to marry or to attend funerals and weddings. This reading of the text makes it another symbolic action (e.g. 13.1–8) and emphasizes the prophet's isolation from the people (cf. 15.17 'I sat alone' – a prohibition hardly needed if 15.17 represents his actual practice!). His lack of solidarity (a solidarity frequently expressed by some exegetes [e.g. Berridge]) is symbolized by his non-attendance at the communal festivities and lamentations and, above all, by his state of celibacy. If vv. 1–2 do belong to the report of a symbolic action (cf. Fohrer 1953, 64–5), then the account quickly moves from such a report to a series of statements about the people and does not return at any point to reporting Jeremiah's fulfilment of his instructions. The unit shows no further interest in the symbolic nature of his behaviour. Lacking such features, vv. 2–9 are closer to proclamation than symbolic action and, allowing for the high degree of editorial expansion of the text, probably should be read as such. The response of the people in v. 10 hardly suggests a statement about personal behaviour but a declaration of destruction ('why has Yahweh pronounced all this great evil against *us*?') as the meaning of the preceding material. A symbolic action, with popular inquiry and response about its significance, is a feature of the prophetic traditions, as Ezek. 24.15–24 well illustrates, but virtually all the necessary information to read the text in this way is absent from 16.1–9. If Ezekiel's curious behaviour prompted public inquiry, then Jeremiah's persistent odd way of life would most certainly have evoked questions from the people. Yet no hint of that appears in the text.

Was Jeremiah married? To that question most commentators assuredly would answer 'No', though it has been suggested that once he was married but his wife had been unfaithful to him with his friends and he had abandoned her (Goldman 1952). Evidence for this state of affairs is to be detected in 11.15; 12.7–10, in the virulence of his denunciations of adultery (e.g. 2.20–25; 3.1–5; 5.7–8; 9.2) and in his threatening of others with a similar experience as divine judgment (e.g. 6.16; 8.10). In this approach to the text 16.2 is to be understood as a prohibition against marrying (again) *in this place* (i.e. Anathoth). It is an interesting, if unconvincing, reading of certain difficult texts and would explain the intensity of the feeling expressed in the denunciations of the community by the use of sexual imagery. However such imagery is better explained as conventional (e.g. Hosea and Ezekiel also use this kind of language) and metaphorical, though it cannot be ruled out that while the speaker was out denouncing the community for its adulterous ways others were at home enjoying his wife's favours! Yet such a reading of the text ignores its rhetorical nature in order to read it as if it were a record of historical and literal events. It also ignores the constructive part played by the editors in building the tradition out of many discrete layers and producing a work which does not provide answers to questions of the kind 'was Jeremiah married?'.

Was Jeremiah celibate then? To this question I would answer: 'the text does not permit us to answer such a question because it is not the unmediated record of somebody's life.' The editing of 16.1–9 may in its final form be moving in the direction of making a statement about the life of its protagonist, but it has not transformed the rest of the material into a consistent account of this motif. It is therefore a better reading of the text as it now stands to interpret it as a series of statements addressed to the community rather than an autobiographical account of the marital status of Jeremiah. Such a reading loses the image of the celibate prophet denouncing his promiscuous compatriots using obscene language (perhaps the victim of what the poet Auden once described as 'the distortions of ingrown virginity'?). It also cannot see him as 'time's eunuch' (to use Hopkins' fine phrase) or imagine him as suffering from Søren Kierkegaard's inability to commit himself to another human being (e.g. Regine Olsen) or Franz Kafka's equally diffident relationship with women. It must forgo treating Jeremiah as similar to the Spanish anarchists who refused to marry on principle during the Spanish Civil War and cannot utilize the touching image in 38.7–13 of the eunuch and the celibate. Nor can it produce a psychoanalytical account of Jeremiah which would integrate his vision and his repressed sexuality (cf. the half-naked Isaiah of Isa. 20.2–3 denouncing the overdressed women of Jerusalem of Isa. 3.16–24). All these ornamentations of the text are lost by this reading, including the treatment of the piece as a symbolic action.

16.10–13

10 'And when you tell this people all these words, and they say to you, "Why has the LORD pronounced all this great evil against us? What is our iniquity? What is the sin that we have committed against the LORD our God?" 11 then you shall say to them: "Because your fathers have forsaken me, says the LORD, and have gone after other gods and have served and worshipped them, and have forsaken me and have not kept my law, 12 and because you have done worse than your fathers, for behold, every one of you follows his stubborn evil will, refusing to listen to me; 13 therefore I will hurl you out of this land into a land which neither you nor your fathers have known, and there you will serve other gods day and night, for I will show you no favour." '

---

[13] G lacks 'day and night'. MT *'ašer lō'-'ettēn lākem ḥnînāh*, 'for I will show you no favour': GV 'they will . . .' = *yittnû*, i.e. the gods of the strange land will show no mercy to the exiles. MT connects *'ettēn* with *hēṭaltî*, 'I will hurl . . .', and makes Yahweh the one who will show no mercy to the people.

A formal question-and-answer unit from the Deuteronomistic redaction follows vv. 2–9 as a didactic exposition of their meaning. This format of setting up answers to leading questions in order to provide an ideologically correct account of the disaster occurs in 5.19; 9.12–16 (cf. 22.8–9; Deut. 29.22–28 [MT 23–27]; I Kings 9.8–9; see Thiel 1973, 295–300, for analysis of the two styles of this format). The theology of the editors is spelled out carefully: 'disaster . . . iniquity . . . sin . . . they forsook me . . . followed other gods . . . me they forsook . . . my law they did not keep.' The fall of Jerusalem and the deportation of the citizens constitute the disaster and

Deuteronomistic ideology provides the explanation (cf. 7.1–8.3; 11.1–13). The people ask their questions in response to 'all these words', thereby indicating that vv. 2–9 are proclamation rather than symbolic action.

The questions 'why (*'al-meh*) . . . what (*meh*) . . . what (*meh*)?' are prompted by the terrible elements which constitute the disaster in vv. 2–9: 'deadly diseases . . . sword and famine . . . I have taken away my peace . . . make to cease from this place . . .' (on the terms cf. Weippert 1973, 166–8). The complex rhythms of double, triple and quadruple terms used in vv. 2–9 are drawn from the pool of terms employed throughout the tradition and allow vv. 10–13 to provide a grounding for their operation (not given in vv. 2–9). Why should the disaster of 587 have befallen the nation? Many answers might be proferred as an explanation (e.g. political policies that failed to appreciate the power of Babylon, nationalistic schemes of opposition to the imperial overlords, etc.) but the Deuteronomistic ideology offers only one all-encompassing answer to the catastrophe – idolatry. Because the nation's predecessors had followed other gods and their descendants had maintained the same customs, all the horrific features of vv. 2–9 had happened to them. Such idolatry is equivalent to forsaking Yahweh and breaking his *tōrāh*. The motif of the contemporaneous generation behaving even worse than their ancestors also appears in 7.26 (cf. 3.11) and, in spite of its inherently rhetorical force, explains why the generation of 587 suffered the catastrophe rather than previous generations. This accusation in v. 12 may also have an allusion to the nation's refusal to listen to the prophets (cf. 25.3–4; 26.4–5; 35.14–15; 44.4–5; II Kings 17.13–14; see Nicholson 1970, 58–63), because in Deuteronomistic thought the divine word is mediated through prophets. For the Deuteronomists the prophetic word is the defence against idolatry. But the refusal to listen to the word (i.e. to the prophets) is caused by the stubbornness of the people's evil mind (individualized as *šᵉrirūt libbō-hārā'*, v. 12; cf. 7.24; 9.14; 11.8; 13.10; 18.12; 23.17). It is collective self-will which frustrates the divine *tōrāh* as revealed by his servants the prophets.

For this long history of idolatry and rejection of the *tōrāh* the people will be hurled (*ṭūl*, cf. 22.26, 28; *šlk* 7.15; 14.16; 52.3) out of their own land to an unknown land (i.e. Babylon). There (ironically) they shall serve the gods but will receive no favour (*ḥᵃnīnāh*, 'grace') from them (G). In MT it is Yahweh who shows the people no favour rather than the other gods (for G cf. 8.2), so that whether it is Yahweh or the gods the people will receive no help from either. This view of the expulsion from Palestine contrasts with 24.4–7 where those who are exiled become the recipients of Yahweh's attention for good (see on 24). From the Deuteronomistic viewpoint idolatry offers no hope whatsoever, not even after the catastrophe of 587. Idolatry cuts off all future hope of divine favour.

16.14–15

14 'Therefore, behold, the days are coming, says the LORD, when it shall no longer be said, "As the LORD lives who brought up the people of Israel out of the land of Egypt," 15 but, "As the LORD lives who brought up the people of Israel out of the north country and out of all the countries where he had driven them." For I will bring them back to their own land which I gave to their fathers.'

[14–15] = 23.7–8. **[14]** MT *w^{e}lō'-yē'āmēr*, 'when it shall not be said . . .': G also 23.7 have plur. *yō'm^{e}rū*, 'they shall say . . .'. **[15]** MT *b^{e}nē yiśrā'ēl*, 'people of Israel': G *ton oikon Israēl*, 'the house Israel', also in 23.8 (G has MT vv. 7–8 at the end of 23.40). MT *hiddīḥām*, 'he had driven them': a few mss, S have *hiddaḥtīm* here and in 23.8: 'I have driven them'.

The starkness of v. 13 with its refusal of divine favour requires some counterbalance if it is not to write off the future of the nation. Such balance is provided by the appearance of vv. 14–15 (= 23.7–8), which in its present context interrupts the series of statements describing the destruction of the people (see on v. 18). The insertion of oracles of hope after words of judgment is a feature of the editing of prophetic traditions, and the question-and-answer sequence of Deut. 29.22–28 is also followed by a statement of future hope (Deut. 30.1–5; cf. Janzen 1973, 92–3). Thus the force of v. 13 is nullified by the belief that there would be a return from exile at some future time.

The model of that return is the exodus from Egypt, and the future hope is presented in such terms that its occurrence is guaranteed. Its form is that of an oath: just as people used to swear by Yahweh, who brought the nation up out of Egypt, so in the future they will swear by Yahweh, who brought Israel out of all the countries to which they had been dispersed. The north country, whither had come the enemy and to which some of the people had been deported, will be a mythic Egypt for them and from it they will come back. It is a reversal of the north country motif as it normally appears in the tradition. The promise of divine retrieval is closer to the motifs in 24.6; 29. 10–14 than the refusal of divine favour of 16.13 and indicates a late strand in the tradition which knew of the return and hoped it would be a movement comparable to the legendary exodus from Egypt (cf. Isa. 51.9–11). If the people were punished in 587 for their own offences and those of their fathers, now a future dawns for them when they will return to their land; a land gifted to their fathers by Yahweh. The cycle of history comes full circle with this hymnic word of salvation (see on 23.7–8).

16.16–18

16 'Behold, I am sending for many fishers, says the LORD, and they shall catch them; and afterwards I will send for many hunters and they shall hunt them from every mountain and every hill, and out of the clefts of the rocks. 17 For my eyes are upon all their ways; they are not hid from me, nor is their iniquity concealed from my eyes. 18 And I will doubly recompense their iniquity and their sin, because they have polluted my land with the carcasses of their detestable idols, and have filled my inheritance with their abominations.'

---

[16] K *ldwgyn*; Q *l^e dayyāgîm*: 'for fishers': Q has a better balance with *ṣayyādîm*, 'hunters'; both forms are to be found in MT (cf. Isa. 19.8 for Q; Ezek. 47.10 for K). The verbal form of *dîgûm*, 'they shall catch them', is disputed: Qal, Hiphil, Piel are all conjectured for it (BDB, 185); Rudolph, 110, opts for Piel (= *diy^e gûm*). **[17]** G lacks 'they are not hid from me'. **[18]** MT *w^e šillamtî ri'šōnāh mišnēh ^{ca}wōnām*, 'I will recompense *first* double their iniquity', cf. NEB 'I will first make them pay in full for the wrong (they have done)'. G lacks *ri'šōnāh*, 'first': it may be an explanatory gloss in MT noting that double punishment must precede the promise of return in vv. 14–15. For 'double' cf. Isa. 40.2; 61.7; Ehrlich 1912, 285, treats *mišnēh* as 'wage' rather than 'double' and understands *niblat* 'carcase . . .' to be from *n^e bālāh*, 'senseless', rather than *n^e bēlāh*, 'corpse'.

A further statement about the destruction of the nation uses the images of fishermen and hunters being summoned to catch and hunt the people (for the fishing imagery in a different context cf. Isa. 19.8). The reference to hunting in the mountains, hills and rocks may imply that some of the people have fled away from the invading army or have tried to escape after the breaching of the city's walls (cf. 39.4) and hidden themselves in these places (a different use of this imagery appears in Isa. 7.18–19). The point of the pictures in v. 16 is that none can escape and that lesson is underlined in v. 17. Because the deity sees everything, the ways of the people (*darᵉkēhem*, 'their religious ways', cf. 10.2) cannot be hid from him (cf. 23.24). Their punishment will be a double compensation for their idolatry because they have profaned the land with their disgusting idols (*šiqqūṣēhem*). The iniquity (vv. 10, 17) of the nation is idol-worship: v. 18 combines the two terms of abuse used in the tradition to describe idolatry (cf. II Kings 23.13) *šiqqūṣīm* (cf. 4.1; 7.30 = 32.34; 13.27) and *tōʿᵃbōt* (cf. 2.7; 7.10; 32.35; 44.4, 22; its occurrence in 6.15 = 8.12 may be more a general reference to disapproved-of behaviour than to idolatry). The reference to 'corpse' (*niblat*, 'carcase') in conjunction with idols may hint at cults of the dead where sacrifices were offered to or for the dead (cf. Ps. 106.28; Lev. 26.30) and would fit the prohibition against entering the funeral feasts of the community (vv. 5, 8), but may be a more general dismissal of idolatrous practices. It concludes the highly edited section on the destruction of the community and the Deuteronomistic account of why it happened. As an additional verse it ends the theme of the land bestrewn with unburied corpses (vv. 4, 6) with images of a land polluted by the carcases of idols and connects the two by means of a statement about Yahweh's adequate (a possible understanding of *mišnēh*, 'double') compensation of the people for such corruption.

16.19–21

19 O Lord, my strength and my stronghold,
my refuge in the day of trouble,
to thee shall the nations come
from the ends of the earth and say:
'Our fathers have inherited naught but lies,
worthless things in which there is no profit.
20 Can man make for himself gods?
Such are no gods!'
21 'Therefore, behold, I will make them know, this once I will make them know my power and my might, and they shall know that my name is the Lord.'

[21] RSV treats this v. as prose but BHS prints it as poetry and NEB, JPSB translate it as such; cf. Rudolph, Bright, who also view it as poetry.

A hymn about the nations turning to Yahweh and confessing the falseness (*šeqer*) and emptiness (*hebel*) of their ancestral religion. The impossibility of man (kind, *'ādām*) making gods that are not not-gods (*lō' 'ᵉlōhīm*) is acknowledged. All this within a hymn praising Yahweh as the speaker's defence and refuge in the day of trouble. The final statement (v. 21) would follow v. 18 better than v. 20 (in the view of many commentators) and vv. 19–20 would be more appropriate after vv. 14–15 (cf. Thiel 1973, 200).

This is a loosely constructed poem made up of the prayer of a pious individual, the words of the heathen approaching Yahweh, a generalized reflection on the making of gods and a divine saying (cf. Hyatt, 948). Elements from the tradition contribute to its contents (cf. 2.5, 8, 11; 3.17; 12.16) and it may function in the context of the denunciations of idolatry as a communal acknowledgment of wrongdoing and admission of the impossibility of making gods (cf. 3.21–25; 14.20–22). The saying put in the nations' mouth is remarkably similar to the accusation against the nation's ancestors in v. 11. Whether this should be understood as an oblique statement about Israel's turning to Yahweh rather than (as well as?) that of the nations is not clear. If it refers to the nations, then it reflects a late period when the nations were expected to seek Yahweh (3.17; 12.16; cf. Amos 9.12; Isa. 2.2–4; Zech. 14.16–19).

A pious speaker (cf. 17.15) seeks comfort in a god to whom all the nations will come (thus reversing the flight of Israel to the nations vv. 13, 15). This is a hope at home in the later belief in Yahweh as the only god, the only legitimate deity beyond mankind's capacity for making gods. It could also be a belief from a period of isolation among the nations and their gods which provided comfort and security for the beleaguered pietists who acknowledged only Yahweh as the true god. The belief that one day the nations would acknowledge Yahweh and turn from their own worthless imitations would provide emotional and psychological comfort and support for the group. The assertions put in the mouth of the nations (vv. 19b–20) indicate that the hymn comes from circles which did not practise the idolatry of which the nation is accused throughout vv. 10–13, 18.

If vv. 19–21 are read in conjunction with Isa. 45.20–24 (cf. Ezek. 36.23) then they may represent the response of the nations to the return of Israel from exile (cf. Rudolph, 113). The phrase 'this once' (*bappa'am hazzō't*, understood by Weiser, 142, to mean 'here and now') then refers to the occasion when Yahweh brings the deported back to their own land (v. 15) and makes of that event a demonstration of Yahweh's existence and power to the nations (cf. 4.2). A consideration of the material here and in Isa. 45; Ezek. 36 reveals the development of the belief that the turning of the nations to Yahweh was bound up with the restoration of Israel to its Palestinian homeland. It is part of the logic of the belief that Yahweh is the only god and that the gods of the nations are false and empty concepts. Yet the sentiments of vv. 19–21 are quite different from those expressed in the other section dealing with the gods (10.1–16), where those who produce the gods will perish with their stupid manufactured objects of delusion. In the return from exile (i.e. the gathering in of the diaspora) of Israel the nations will be taught (*'ōdī'ēm*, 'I will cause them to know') the name of Yahweh: a chauvinistic view of the nations as spectators of the fate of Israel (cf. Ex. 32.11–14; Deut. 9.25–29) and whose own fate is bound up with that of Israel's response to Yahweh (4.2).

17.1–4

17 1 'The sin of Judah is written with a pen of iron; with a point of diamond
it is engraved on the tablet of their heart, and on the horns of their altars, 2
while their children remember their altars and their Asherim, beside every
green tree, and on the high hills, 3 on the mountains in the open country.
Your wealth and all your treasures I will give for spoil as the price of your
sin throughout all your territory. 4 You shall loosen your hand from your
heritage which I gave to you, and I will make you serve your enemies in a
land which you do not know, for in my anger a fire is kindled which shall
burn for ever.'

G lacks vv. 1–4 but provides a variant of them at 15.12–14 (see Notes there). **[1]** MT *mizb*^{e}*ḥōtēkem*, 'your altars': many mss, Vrs 'their altars' as EVV; cf. v. 2. **[2]** MT *kizkōr b*^{e}*nēhem*, 'as their children remember': Volz, 182, reads *k*^{e}*zikrōn bāhen*, 'as a memorial sign against them' (cf. *zikkārōn*, 'a cultic memorial'); cf. NEB 'to bear witness against them' as the end of v. 1, BHS, Rudolph. Volz, Rudolph regard the rest of v. 2 as secondary material in MT. Some mss read 'every (green tree)', cf. EVV. **[3]** MT *h*^{a}*rārī baśśādeh*, 'my mountain in the field', cf. 13.27. Theod. *oreōn*, 'mountains'; BHS reads as *harᵃrē*, 'mountains of . . .', and takes the phrase as part of v. 2. See on 15.13–14 for textual comments on vv. 3–4. **[4]** MT *wᵉšamaṭṭāh ūbᵉkā*, 'and you will loosen and against you': the idiom *šmṭ yādekā*, 'loosen your hand', cf. Deut. 15.3, suggests that *ūbᵉkā* should be read as *yādᵉkā*, 'your hand', here, cf. BHS. NEB 'you will lose possession'.

A final statement about idolatrous practices focuses on 'the sin of Judah', identified here as fertility rites of the nature cults (cf. 2.20, 23, 27; 3.6, 13, 23; 13.27). The unit is a word of judgment against such practices and associates them with the expulsion of the people from their own land to serve their enemies in a foreign land (cf. 16.13). Against such idolatry the divine anger burns for ever. The original form of the statement may have been only v. 1, with the fertility rites of v. 2 a later addition now in MT (cf. Thiel 1973, 202–3). This expanded text allows an original graphic statement about the nation's sin to become a more specific condemnation of a particular cult. Such a development gives vv. 1–2 their connection with the Deuteronomistic attack on idolatry in 16.10–13, 18, but spoils the force and irony of the imagery used in v. 1. Judah's sin (unspecified) is so deep that it is engraven on the nation's heart and altars. That engraving is permanent and deep because it is made with an iron tool, a flint point (*bᵉṣippōren šāmīr*). The carving of Judah's sin on the altars mocks the sanctity of such objects by making them expressions of the nation's corrupt state and reminders to Yahweh of their sinfulness. The horns of the altar were associated with protection (cf. I Kings 1.50–51; 2.28) and the blood of sacrifices was smeared on them (cf. Ex. 29.12; 30.10; Lev. 4.25, 34; 16.18). Such symbols of cultic protection (apotropaic magic) are here made the very signs of Judah's sin.

The spoliation of the nation's wealth in vv. 3–4 has none of the ambiguity associated with the interpretation of 15.13–14 (where the context is quite different). It is a clear statement about the devastation of national resources by the invading forces as the price to be paid for Judah's sin and the loss of the homeland through deportation. The nation's grip (emended MT) on its patrimony is released as a consequence of its sin. Whatever the case may be for reading vv. 3–4 as a threat against the enemy in 15.13–14 (cf. Gerstenberger 1963, 395–6), in 17.1–4 Judah is the victim of what it threatens. The permanence of Judah's sin in v. 1 is matched by the perpetuity of Yahweh's anger (a permanent fire) in v. 4. Whatever Judah's sin may be (v. 2 turns the cultic reference into a cultic offence associated with pagan rites) it has earned Yahweh's *permanent* hostility.

17.5–8

5 Thus says the LORD:
'Cursed is the man who trusts in man
and makes flesh his arm,
whose heart turns away from the LORD.
6 He is like a shrub in the desert,
and shall not see any good come.
He shall dwell in the parched places of the wilderness,
in an uninhabited salt land.
7 Blessed is the man who trusts in the LORD,
whose trust is the LORD.
8 He is like a tree planted by water,
that sends out its roots by the stream,
and does not fear when heat comes,
for its leaves remain green,
and is not anxious in the year of drought,
for it does not cease to bear fruit.'

---

[5] G lacks 'thus says Yahweh': MT's redactional introduction turns the poem into a divine statement rather than a proverbial contrast of human types. **[6]** MT *k*^{e}*'ar'ār*, 'like a tree': the precise type of tree is disputed by translators. RSV 'shrub', cf. Bright, 'scrub'; NEB 'juniper', JPSB 'bush', margin 'tamarisk'; Rudolph 'shrub'. G *agriomurikē*, 'wild tamarisk', cf. Feliks 1981, 219–21, for photograph. The form of the Hebrew may hint at assonant word-play on *'ārūr*, 'cursed'; cf *'*^{a}*rō'ēr*, 48.6. The word may describe a tree stripped (from *'rr*, 'strip, bare') of its vegetation because of desert conditions and providing a good contrast with the luxuriant foliage of the tree planted by water in v. 8; cf. *'ar'ār* 'stripped, destitute', Ps. 102.18 (EV 17). MT *'ereṣ m*^{e}*lēḥāh*, 'salt land': cf. Deut. 29.23 (MT 22); Judg. 9.45; Zeph. 2.9 for land salted as punishment and Fensham 1962 for salting as the result of a curse. **[7]** Rudolph treats 7b as a weak repetition and deletes it from his translation. **[8]** Cf. Ps. 1.3. K *yr'*, Q *yir'eh*: 'he will (not) see', cf. v. 6; K 'he will (not) fear', cf EVV, G, BHS.

A series of wisdom sayings making a contrast between the righteous and the wicked appears in vv. 5–11. A cult saying which makes a similar contrast occurs in vv. 12–13. Both set out the polarities of approved-of and disapproved-of behaviour and their underlying attitudes. The generalizations of the section reflect the influence of the wisdom schools from their pietized period and in the service of the tradition's development. They belong to a society where proper and improper attitudes and forms of behaviour characterize the definitions of righteous and wicked, rather than the anti-community polemics of much of the tradition. That they appear at this point in the tradition may be due to the redactional history of its growth and the generalized comment on human behaviour in 16.20. In vv. 5–10 the approved forms of behaviour and attitudes have no content except that they are related to Yahweh, and a correct attitude to Yahweh may be wisdom's contribution here to the discussion about idolatry (cf. Prov. 1.7; 9.10; 15.33). It is not necessary to make firm connections between 1–4 and 5–10 because the editing processes may have been as additive as they were integrative. Each block of material may represent the accumulation of units, discrete as well as edited, which reflect the stages of the tradition's construction and also the resting places of many isolated sayings and fragments. The holistic approach to the tradition which insists on integrating every aspect of the text into one comprehensive explanation of the text's meaning may be a misreading of the tradition.

The contrast between the man (*haggeber*) who is cursed and the one who is blessed is made in terms of what they trust in: mankind (*'ādām*) or Yahweh. The one who bears the curse is like a tree in the dry, salt lands where no good is ever experienced. The one who bears the blessing is the opposite: he is like a tree transplanted (*šātūl*) by water, its roots by the stream, its foliage green, thriving in drought and always bearing fruit. There are some affinities between this poem and the wisdom poem which prefaces the book of Psalms (Ps. 1), in particular the image of the man who is blessed as a tree transplanted (*šātūl*), 1.3) by streams of water, yielding its fruit and its leaves never withering. But there are sufficient differences between the two poems for there to be no question of borrowing or dependence. The image of the green tree as a mark of the person blessed by the deity is too common for literary dependence to be invoked for vv. 5–8 (e.g. 11.16; Ps. 52.8; 92.12–14; Ezek. 19.10). The contrast between the two types of trees is dictated by the logic of the green tree as metaphor of righteous persons. The tree in the harsh desert conditions is the perfect image of the wicked in such polarized contrasts (not a figure used in Ps. 1.4 where the wicked are 'like chaff'). Conventions of socially approved contrasts (e.g. righteous-wicked, blessed-cursed, good-bad) govern the terms used and the ways in which they are handled. It would not therefore be legitimate to point out that the image of the tree in the desert could equally stand for tenacity, courage and the ability to suffer drought and terrible conditions without succumbing to defeat or despair. Such an image of the righteous (cf Hopkins' 'send my roots rain') would not fit the conventions of the genre. Yet in the world of nature both types of trees represent equally sound examples of nature's capacity to thrive no matter what the environment.

The main feature of vv. 5–8 is the contrast between the two images of human trust: that which is cursed (the desert tree) and that which is blessed (the green tree by water). That proverbial polarity of types determines the understanding of the whole section (vv. 5–11; cf. vv. 12–13, 14–18) but does not employ the range of possibilities which the figures have in the biblical traditions. In Ps. 107.33–43 the images of water and desert are used to describe the deity's ability to transform nature in response to human behaviour (e.g. because of human wickedness the fruitful land becomes a salty waste, v. 34). The lament in Ezek. 19.10–14 uses the image of a vine transplanted (*šᵉtūlāh*) in the desert to describe the fortunes and fate of the Judaean royal house (cf. Zimmerli 1979, 393–8). An allegory in Ezek. 17.7–10 employs the figure of a vine transplanted (*šᵉtūlāh*) and withering as a result of that transplantation. A different image represents the deity as transplanting (*štl*) a sprig from the top of the cedar to the mountain height of Israel where it will grow into a mighty cedar (Ezek. 17.22–23). This action demonstrates 'that I the Lord bring low the high tree, and make high the low tree, dry up the green tree, and make the dry tree flourish' (v. 24). It also makes clear how flexible the images of trees are in the biblical traditions. The static contrast of 17.5–8 is not a necessary feature of tree imagery but an arbitrary use reflecting certain conventions employed by wisdom writers to stress the polarities of blessing and curse.

The essential ambiguity of tree imagery in the Bible is further illustrated by the tree of *life* in the garden of Eden myth which leads to the expulsion of Adam and Eve from that garden and their eventual *death* (Gen. 2–3). Mediaeval iconography of the tree of crucifixion captures that death-life polarity perfectly and shows how the one tree may combine the complexities of life and death, blessing and curse, salvation and damnation in a simple image. Perhaps the best example of the ambiguity of the dry tree-green tree imagery is the allegorical painting of Hans Holbein the Younger in the sixteenth century known as 'Allegory of the Old and New Testaments' (in the National Gallery of Scotland, Edinburgh). It depicts a tree which divides the painting into two halves: on the left-hand side the tree is withered, and all the scenes in that half of the picture are from the Old Testament (symbolizing law, sin, death and the mysteries of salvation and justification); on the right-hand side the tree is green and leafy, all the scenes are from the New Testament and represent the reversal of the Old Testament images in terms of life and salvation. It is a fine example of how the image of a tree may combine a diverse range of symbolization and how convention-bound such symbols are.

The wisdom sayings in vv. 5–11 present a contrast between attitudes and states which has little bearing on the Jeremiah figure represented by most conventional accounts of the tradition. The solitary and lamenting speaker of the poems is an opposed, persecuted and cursed individual (cf. 15.10, 15–18). His experience of the deity is that of a traveller who has stumbled on a dried-up wadi and been deceived by the lack of water (15.18b). In terms of 17.5–8 the speaker appears to be a man bearing the curse rather than the one who trusts Yahweh and flourishes as a consequence. The static images do not assist in understanding the exigencies of the speaker's experiences and, from the viewpoint of the biographical interpretation of the book, 'we must note that its (i.e. the poem) general outlook is contradictory to the prophet's own experience' (Hyatt, 951). This problem does not arise for the alternative approach to the book as the amalgam of many discrete editorial strands and traditions. Some commentators interpret the unit as a reference to king Zedekiah, the man who trusted in human resources rather than Yahweh's word via Jeremiah, and his responsibility for the exile referred to in v. 4 (e.g. Cornill, 212). This would make vv. 5–8 fit the imagery of Ezek. 17.5–10 but lose their force as generalizations about human attitudes and states.

17.9–10

9 The heart is deceitful above all things,
and desperately corrupt;
who can understand it?

10 'I the LORD search the mind
and try the heart,
to give to every man according to his ways,
according to the fruits of his doings.'

---

[9] MT *ʿāqōb*, 'insidious, deceitful', cf. 9.4 (MT 3); Bright, 'crafty': G *batheia* 'deep' = *ʿāmōq*. MT *w^{e}ānuš hūʾ*, 'and it is incurable', cf. the incurable wound of 15.18; 30.12, 15; 'day of disaster' 17.16; NEB, Bright 'desperately sick': G *kai anthrōpos*, 'and man' = *we'^{e}nōš*. **[10]** MT *bōḥēn k^{e}lāyōt*, 'trying the kidneys', i.e. the emotions, cf. 11.20a; 20.12a. Hebrew *lēb*, 'heart', usually means 'mind' (EVV confusing in vv. 9–10, cf. JPSB 'heart . . . heart . . . mind') and *k^{e}lāyōt*, 'feelings, emotions' (closer to 'heart' in English). **[10b]** = 32.19b. K *kdrkw*, 'according to his way'; Q *kidrākāw*, 'according to his ways' (= 32.19b).

A general statement about the human mind with its crafty ways which make it difficult for human beings to understand it. It is a gnomic saying about what Dr Johnson called 'the anfractuosities of the human heart'. The human mind is the most crafty of things and its activities elude analysis (MT), or it is too deep for humans to grasp what humans do (G). The polarity here is the human mind and Yahweh: beyond human understanding the mind may be but Yahweh understands it because he searches the mind and examines the emotions. He therefore can give people what they deserve because he knows the thoughts and feelings behind their actions. This divine insight avoids the problem caused by the gap between innermost thoughts and outward actions (cf. 9.8, 25–26; 12.2; though in the light of 17.9 it is difficult to see how any speaker could make such judgments about inner and outer states of being!).

The generalization of vv. 9–10 must be confined to the context of a series of polarized contrasts, otherwise it will turn into another version of the Cretan liar paradox (i.e. the speaker who said the human mind is incurably deceitful is himself deceitful in what he says!). In such a context it has the force of an appeal to Yahweh and a recognition that, in spite of human fallibilities, it is possible for righteous (i.e. appropriate) judgments to be made because Yahweh knows what is beyond human capacity to know. Read in this way it may be associated with the lament of the innocent in vv. 14–18 (Cornill, 216–18, treats them together). But such an understanding of the force of vv. 9–10 makes the polar contrast of vv. 5–8 difficult to maintain: the two types of tree are easily distinguishable, but if the human mind is so devious then who can tell who is cursed and who blessed? Only the divine reward can make manifest the distinctions entailed in bearing the curse or the blessing. Perhaps then the fragmentary nature of the gnomic sayings in vv. 5–11 can be read as a reflection upon the outcry of the innocent sufferer in v. 18 and a preparation for that lament. It is because the two types *ought* (and are believed) to be distinguishable that the innocent can cry out for divine vindication.

17.11

Like the partridge that gathers a brood which she did not hatch,
so is he who gets riches but not by right;
in the midst of his days they will leave him,
and at his end he will be a fool.

EVV have difficulty expressing the terseness of MT proverb, using many words (e.g. RSV, NEB: twenty-two, JPSB: eighteen; cf. Bright: sixteen) where Hebrew has eight: *qōrē' dāgar wᵉlō' yālād 'ōśeh 'ōšer wᵉlō' bᵉmišpāṭ*. Translating *qōrē' dāgar wᵉlō' yālād* is difficult and agreement is not to be found among the commentators: 'the partridge gathers what he did not lay', cf. G *sunēgagen*, 'gathers', where *dāgar* is understood in its Aramaic sense, 'gather' (*dᵉgar*, cf. T Gen. 31.46), and the allusion is to the partridge's habit of gathering eggs from another nest (cf. Feliks 1981, 125). This is the majority view represented by RSV, NEB and many commentators. Driver 1955a, 132–3, understands *dgr* as 'heaped up' and comments on the possible onomatopoeic origin of the term *qōrē'* for 'partridge'. There are problems with *dgr* as 'gather', and the word only occurs elsewhere in Isa. 34.15 in a context of egg-laying creatures, where commentators also express uncertainty as to its meaning (cf. Kaiser 1974, 352; Wildberger 1979, 1329). KB, 203, offers three disputed meanings for *dgr*, 'quit the nest', 'gather', 'hatch'. The masc. gender of *yālād* militates against understanding *dgr* as 'lay (eggs)', as does the sequence *ūbāq'āh wᵉdāgrāh*, 'and hatch and gather', in Isa. 34.15, and renders RSV '*she* did not hatch' wrong (Kaiser's treatment of *dgr* as 'leave', cf. Arabic *daraja*, 'to leave the nest', if applied to 17.11 would increase the interpretative problems). AV '(As) the partridge sitteth (on eggs), and hatcheth (them) not' treats *dgr* as having the sense of 'incubate'; Sawyer 1978, 325–9, argues for the meaning 'brood, incubate' for *dgr* and *yld* as a general term for 'producing young', with the point of the proverb being the 'vulnerability' of the partridge rather than its treachery. Cf. the classical phrase *ptōssousin hōste peridika*, 'they cowered like partridges' (cited in Sawyer). G *ephonēsen perdix*, 'the partridge utters its voice', duplicates *qr'*. K *ymw*, 'his day'; Q *yāmāw*, 'his days'.

Sawyer 1978

A terse proverb associates the acquisition of ill-gotten wealth with the behaviour of the partridge. The fate of both bird and rich person is the same: they lose what they have. This transitory nature of what is possessed makes the one who acquires such wealth a fool. Temporarily rich, his end is that of a fool (cf. 12.4 for the possible fate of the prosperous wicked). The meaning of the proverb as set out in 11b is hardly in dispute and conforms to standard wisdom teaching about the folly of ill-gained wealth, position or fame. It is about the wrong way of acquiring substance (cf. 22.13 for a similar warning). However, the meaning of the proverbial sentence introducing the observation about the fate of such people is far from clear. It is too lapidary to be translated into English satisfactorily because too many words and inflections have to be added to it to make sense of it. Its proverbial form lacks the usual indicators of comparison (cf. *k^e . . . kēn* 'as . . . so' used in 2.26; 3.20; 6.7; 24.5, 8, cf. Hobbs 1979, 64) and the uncertainty of meaning of one of the words used (in a four-word clause) does not ease the problem of translating it. The lengthy textual note required to express some of the possible explanations of its meaning is indicative of the problem.

Various explanations have been offered as the point of the statement about the partridge's practice. Partridges occasionally remove the eggs from other nests and incubate them along with their own, with the result that there are too many eggs for hatching and they lose the brood (cf. Feliks 1981, 122–5). A variation on that explanation is the view that when the eggs of the other birds hatch out, the fledglings soon return to their proper nests (cf. Bright, 118). In either case the partridge loses its ill-gotten brood. The first explanation may be true, but the variation is ornithologically false, though it may represent popular, hence proverbial, belief. A different approach to interpreting the proverb stresses the vulnerability of the image used (Sawyer). Partridges build their nests on the ground, often in the sand (cf. Driver's sand-partridge), where they are vulnerable to predators (e.g. snakes, animals, humans). The birds produce many eggs but few survive. The vulnerability of birds' nests is an image which appears in a number of biblical traditions (cf. the metaphors in 22.23; 49.16; the general point expressed in Deut. 22.6; also Isa. 10.14; 16.2; Hab. 2.9; Obad. 4) and it may be the point of 17.11. It is the peculiar vulnerability of the ground-nesting bird which is the point of the proverb here and not the fact that the fledglings may leave the nest after hatching. In reality all birds eventually leave the nest, so that no useful comparison can be made between that fact and the fate of ill-gotten gains (except the banal observation that wealth is like hatched eggs, soon gone!). But the particular jeopardy the partridge faces makes it a good image of the person who acquires riches without legitimate claim to them (*wᵉlōʾ bᵉmišpāṭ*). The enterprise is as hazardous as the survivability rate of the partridge's eggs. It is unnecessary to insist on a literal or very close correspondence between the two parts of the proverb (i.e. the riches leave [*yaʿazᵉbennû*], so the eggs *must* hatch out and the fledglings leave the nest) because that would make it a general comparison between ill-gotten riches and the fate of *all* hatched out eggs!

In the context of wisdom sayings 17.11 makes a statement in line with the guiding principle of those states or attitudes which contrast the cursed with the blessed. Ill-gotten gains bear the mark of the cursed state and no good will come of them. Like the tree in the desert which sees no good come (v. 6), so illegitimately acquired riches do not last, and the end-state of such a person is to be a fool. As an independent proverb, though shaped by its context, it may have no further connection with the Jeremiah tradition than as part of the strand relating to the righteous and the wicked. However, some commentators suggest that it may be a reference to Jehoiakim (cf. 22.13; Weiser, 146; Rudolph, 116). The generality of such gnomic sayings hardly warrants such an identification drawn from elsewhere in the tradition, and the use of proverbs in the construction of the book need not contribute to the implication that Jeremiah 'is a highly intelligent, creative, and well-educated prophet' (Hobbs 1979, 72).

17.12–13

12 A glorious throne set on high from the beginning
is the place of our sanctuary.
13 O LORD, the hope of Israel,
all who forsake thee shall be put to shame;

those who turn away from thee shall be written in the earth,
for they have forsaken the LORD, the fountain of living water.

---

[12] MT *mārōm*, 'a height': G *hupsōmenos* = *mūrām*, 'elevated, exalted', cf. BHS. G lacks 'from the beginning', 'the place of' and has a simple sentence as the verse: 'an exalted throne of glory is our holy place'. **[13]** MT *miqwēh yiśrā'ēl*, 'hope of Israel', cf. 14.8a. K *yswry*, 'those who turn (in the earth)'; Q *yᵉsūray*, 'those who turn from me (i.e. Yahweh)': BHS suggests *wᵉsūrekā*, 'and who turn from you' (*k* for *b* [*'rṣ*]), cf. Reventlow 1963, 229. MT *bā'āreṣ yikkātēbū*, 'they shall be written in the earth': a strange figure, but possibly a reference to the underworld (cf. Dahood 1959, 164–8), i.e. listed for death. BHS suggests *yikkārētū*, 'they shall be cut off', or *yikkālēmū*, 'they shall be ashamed' but reads MT (cf. Reventlow who rejects both suggestions and retains MT). Driver 1937–38, 114, alters *yikkātēbū* into *yikkābētū*, 'they shall be prostrated', which fits the parallel *yēbōsū*, 'they shall be ashamed'; this assumes a Hebrew stem *kbt* which is unknown, but cf. Arabic *kbt* I, 'prostrated, humbled'. MT *kī 'āzᵉbū mᵉqōr mayim-ḥayyīm 'et-yhwh*, 'for they have forsaken the fountain of living water Yahweh': delete the gloss *'et-yhwh* (cf. BHS, NEB) as an explanation of the metaphor of 2.13. RSV is misleading in the way it integrates the gloss into the sentence; the necessity for such a gloss must point to a period when the metaphor of Yahweh as the source of fresh water had become obscure.

Two verses which may be separate are treated together here as a statement contrasting those who place their hope in Yahweh and those who turn from him. This contrast suits the context of vv. 5–11, but is more likely to come from a cultic source than a wisdom one. The unit can be taken with the lament in vv. 14–18 (as Reventlow 1963, 229–40, treats it; cf. Weiser, 146–9), which would make vv. 12–18 a communal lament set in the temple (hence Reventlow's title for the section 'prayer in the temple'). As an independent statement it asserts the gloriousness of the community's temple 'the place of our sanctuary' (cf. Isa. 60.13): the throne (of Yahweh) from the beginning (cf. Ps. 93.2; from the cult tradition associating the creation of the world with the lordship of Yahweh, so Weiser, 147 n. 2). The reference to the 'height' is to the temple mount (the word can refer to the land of Israel cf. Ezek. 20.40). In the temple cult Yahweh as Israel's hope (cf. 14.8) is affirmed and worshipped. Here is the true cult of which the sin of Judah (vv. 1–4, esp v. 2), with its cult on the hills and under the green trees, is but a parody. The true height is the temple mount not the pagan cults on a multiplicity of hills.

The link between vv. 12–13 and v. 11 may be the motif of 'forsaking' (*'zb*): the riches *leave* the fool, the shamed are those who *forsake* Yahweh, who are doomed because they have *forsaken* him. The confident assertions about the temple mount (some commentators read v. 12 as a reference to Jerusalem as Yahweh's throne rather than the temple, cf. 3.17; e.g. Peake, 224) are in striking contrast to the dismissal of the temple worshippers in 7.13–15 and the nation in 17.1–4, hence reflect a rather later period and setting from other strands in the tradition. The stress on those who forsake Yahweh, in contrast to those who recognize him as the hope of Israel, makes vv. 12–13 a good introduction to the lament of the righteous against the wicked in vv. 14–18. It also fits well the series of statements about the fate of both types characterized in vv. 5–11. Those who acknowledge Yahweh have hope and security, those who turn from him face shame and death because they have abandoned the source of living waters (an echo of the dry land imagery of v. 6?). The image of being written in the earth is obscure. If v. 1 is allowed a shaping influence here, then v. 13 is a contrast with its image of a permanently inscribed matter, adamant in its effect. Unlike such an irremovable mark, these people are written in the earth, writing which may easily be removed. An alternative understanding of the figure is to relate it to *'ereṣ*, 'underworld' (Dahood 1959), and treat it as an announcement of the inscribing of such people for death. They are listed for death (perhaps a contrast with registering in the book of life, cf. Ex. 32.32–33; Isa. 4.3; Dan. 12.1; Mal. 3.16–18). This interpretation allows less connection with the imagery of v. 1, but it retains the notion of the forsakers of Yahweh having their guilt registered and being punished. The differentiation between those who praise Yahweh and recognize him as their hope and those who forsake the fountain of living waters allows for a communal advance on 2.13, where it is the whole people who have forsaken Yahweh. The difference is accountable for in terms of the editorial strands which reflect discrete groups and distinctive purposes at work in the tradition.

17.14–18

14 Heal me, O LORD, and I shall be healed;
save me, and I shall be saved;
for thou art my praise.
15 Behold, they say to me,
'Where is the word of the LORD?
Let it come!'
16 I have not pressed thee to send evil,
nor have I desired the day of disaster,
thou knowest;
that which came out of my lips
was before thy face.
17 Be not a terror to me;
thou art my refuge in the day of evil.
18 Let those be put to shame who persecute me,
but let me not be put to shame;
let them be dismayed,
but let me not be dismayed;
bring upon them the day of evil;
destroy them with double destruction!

---

[14] MT *kī t^{e}hillātī 'āttāh*, 'for you are my praise': BHS *tōḥaltī*, 'my hope', following Duhm, 148. **[16]** MT *wa'^{a}nī lō'-aṣtī mērō'eh 'aḥ^{a}rēkā*, 'and as for me I did not press from being a shepherd after you': G *egō de ouk ekopiasa katakolouthōn opisō sou*, 'I have not wearied following after you'; other Vrs understand *mr'h* as *mērā'āh*, 'from evil'. BHS reads *l^{e}rā'āh*, 'for evil', cf. 'for good', 15.11; Baumgartner 1917, 40, *yōm rā'āh*, 'evil day'; Bright, 116. Weiser, 148, retains MT and relates it to the speaker's role as a pastoral intercessor (under the 'office of shepherds' i.e. pastors); cf. JPSB. Berridge 1970, 140–1, also follows MT and makes 'shepherd' a self-reference of Jeremiah's. MT *w^{e}yōm 'ānūš*, 'and the incurable day': G *kai hēmeran anthrōpou*, 'and the day of man' = *w^{e}yōm '^{e}nōš*, cf. v. 9. Commentators understand *'ānūš* as 'disaster' but Reventlow 1963, 238, relates it to 'sickness' (i.e. the sickness of the one praying); its proper sense of 'incurable' is retained by Berridge, 141, as 'the day from which there shall be no recovery'. NEB 'the day of despair'. RSV 'thou knowest' follows punctuation of MT, but BHS repunctuates the text to yield 'thou knowest what came from my lips', cf. NEB, JPSB. **[10]** MT *ūmišneh šibbārōn šāb^{e}rēm*, 'and with double destruction destroy them': NEB 'destroy them, destroy them utterly', cf. Bright, Thompson. The rhetoric of vengeance may account for the notion of 'double', cf. 16.18, but some exegetes (e.g. Weiser, 149) identify two sins deserving of punishment: the forsaking of Yahweh in v. 13 and the blasphemous mocking of the divine word in v. 15.

Baumgartner 1917, 40–5; Berridge 1970, 137–51; Polk 1984, 131–52; Reventlow 1963, 229–40

An individual lament follows the general observations of vv. 5–13, though some exegetes begin the lament with vv. 12–13 (e.g. Baumgartner). The extent to which the lament and the fragments preceding it may be integrated is debatable (cf. the reading of vv. 1–11 in the light of vv. 12–18 in Polk, 143–50) but the lament, with its conflict between speaker and opponents, provides a good example of the polarities epitomized in vv. 5–8 and hinted at in vv. 9–13. The lament may even gain force by being associated with the general truths of the wisdom and cultic sayings because it is against a background of belief in the validity of the arguments expressed in them that the innocent speaker of the lament makes his prayer. He appeals to Yahweh in the light of these truths for their fulfilment in his case (cf. Hobbs 1979, 68–9).

The hostility of the opponents (cf. 15.15; the prosperous wicked of 12.1–3?) is the occasion of the lament, though the similarity between it and the psalms appealing to Yahweh for healing from sickness has led some exegetes to interpret it in terms of the sickness of the speaker brought about by the magical practices of his opponents (e.g. Reventlow). It is also argued that the speaker prays for deliverance on behalf of the community and in the context of a cult liturgy (e.g. Weiser, Reventlow). The cultic context of the lament may be deduced from vv. 12–13, but it is not a necessary interpretation of the text, unless the holistic approach to the redaction is followed. The individual nature of the lament allows the possibility of interpreting the poem as the outcry of one person suffering from persecution or seeing in it the expression of the group's representative speaker complaining on their behalf against opposition (cf. the 'us' and 'them' of vv. 12–13). Further interpretative options are exercised by exegetes who read the individual laments in the tradition, including 17.14–18, as the personal 'confessions' of the prophet Jeremiah (e.g. Berridge, Bright; cf. Polk).

The speaker appeals to Yahweh for healing (hence Reventlow's reading of the lament as a cultic response to sickness) and salvation (cf. 14.8, which allows a communal interpretation of this individual lament). The deity is the speaker's praise (cf. the acknowledgment of Yahweh in the lament psalms as 'enthroned on the praises of Israel', Ps. 22.3). In the light of vv. 12–13 the speaker of v. 14 is a devout follower of Yahweh and not to be identified with those who turn away from Yahweh. He is to be distinguished sharply from his opponents who, by implication of the formal structure of such laments, are the enemies of Yahweh (cf. v. 18). The identification of the 'they' (*hēmmāh*) of v. 15 is open to interpretation: it may refer to the opponents of v. 18, but it may equally be a reference to the group of which the speaker is the representative. If understood as the enemy, then the citation which follows is a hostile question expressing scepticism about the divine word and bordering on the blasphemous (so Weiser). But if 'they' refers to the speaker's companions (i.e. the righteous as opposed to the wicked), then the question 'Where is the word of Yahweh?' is about trust in the divine word, and the hope in its fulfilment is expressed by the wish 'Let it come!'. The twin problems of the speaker's identity and the meaning of the speaker's utterance remain two of the most difficult features of the interpretation of the Jeremiah tradition, and nowhere are these difficulties more pressing than in the exegesis of the lament poems in the book.

Commentators who favour reading v. 15 as a quotation from hostile sources understand it as a reference to the failure of the word of judgment to materialize and the concomitant plight of the speaker of that word because he has been exposed as false. This interpretation would make the lament an expression of the quarrel between Jeremiah and the 'false' prophets (e.g. Berridge, 138), a further element in the strand berating such mantic figures for their optimistic outlook (cf. 5.12–13; also the same phrase *hēmmāh 'ōmᵉrīm*, 'they say', used in 14.15; 17.15). Such a sceptical response to the proclamation of doom is inevitable if there has been a long delay in the fulfilment of the threat, but it may also represent a normal response to the preaching of disaster from those who do not share the epistemological framework of the preachers of doom (cf. Isa. 5.19). It is not necessarily a mark of internecine prophetic struggles that the divine word should be quarrelled about and the 'word' should not be limited to the context of prophetic matters. Alternative epistemologies may be involved or the 'word' may be a more specific one than a general reference to prophecy.

A number of alternative interpretations of the meaning of 'the word of Yahweh' in v. 15 removes the exegesis of vv. 14–18 from the context of prophetic conflict (typified by 23.9–40). The 'word' in question may be a word of salvation addressed by the deity to the speaker in relation to the petition about sickness (i.e. the priestly oracle of salvation as a response to a lament [cf. Begrich 1934]). This would fit Reventlow's understanding of the lament and would mean that the speaker's companions (i.e. the righteous group) wished to know what had happened to that word. Why had it not been realized in the healing and salvation of the group? If the sickness context is too unlikely a setting for the lament, then the word may still represent the hope of salvation for the speaker and/or the group. A previous divine word had reassured them of healing and salvation, but the delay has raised the question 'where is it?' (the question 'where?' is a feature of laments, though sometimes on the lips of opponents, cf. Ps. 42.3, 10; 79.10; putting it into the mouth of others may be an attempt to distance it from the pious). The promise that the faithful will be vindicated is a feature of pious thought, though it may appear in the form of the divine destruction of the wicked (cf. 12.4b). A variation on this interpretative approach is to refer the 'word' to the principle underlying the sayings of vv. 5–13 (hence the turning of them into an oracular statement by 'thus says Yahweh' in v. 5a MT). Where, then, is the truth of such beliefs? Why is the one who trusts Yahweh not blessed? Why are those who do not trust Yahweh not cursed? Why are the illegitimately rich not deserted by their ill-gotten wealth? Why are those who forsake Yahweh not put to shame? In view of all these claims, the lament is an appeal for them to be fulfilled in the vindication of the speaker (cf. Hobbs 1979, 69).

Consistent with this line of interpretation is the exegesis of v. 16 as the speaker's assertion of innocence (cf. 12.3a). It dissociates the speaker from being implicated in the disaster of the period by recognizing Yahweh's knowledge of what has been said (in contrast to 12.2b the speaker of 17.16b allows words to represent true attitudes). It is an appeal (cf. 15.15a) to Yahweh which implicitly acknowledges the conviction that he judges the mind of people and rewards them according to what they deserve (cf. vv. 9–10). The dissociation between the speaker's desires and the day of disaster is a formal protest of innocence (cf. the qualifications for entry to the sacred sphere in Ps. 15.2–5; 24.3–6). Its presence in the lament indicates that the poem is a defence of the speaker as much as it is a plea for vengeance on the enemy (cf. 15.15). Yet it also makes the interpretation of the lament as the utterance of Jeremiah rather difficult: at numerous points in the tradition Jeremiah is credited with demanding the destruction of the nation and those who oppose him (e.g. 6.11; 15.15; 18.19–23). To claim now that these words did not represent what he desired is to admit to being false in that he has preached one thing but wished for something else (the gap between inner and outer states characteristic of the wicked in the tradition, e.g. 12.2). However, the prophet may be rescued from this charge by stressing the formal aspects of the lament, but only at the cost of losing the poems as expressions of his innermost thoughts and destroying the view that self-awareness was a part of his psychological make-up. The alternative interpretation of the laments as the utterances of the pious against persecution by their opponents (i.e. the wicked) is a better one, but not without its own minor problems.

In v. 17 Yahweh is acknowledged as the speaker's refuge (cf. 16.19), but he is also entreated not to be a terror (*m^eḥittāh*, 'terror, destruction, ruin'). Yahweh as source of terror is a constant possibility, even for the righteous, but the pious pray that their experience of him may be different and express confidence in him. If the speaker is innocent of involvement in the disaster of his time (v. 16), he is most definitely involved in demanding destruction for his opponents. Some exegetes see a formal contradiction between vv. 16 and 18 (e.g. Peake, 225), but explain it in terms of differentiating between the groups threatened (nation in 16, enemies in 18) or the occasions on which the statements were made (cf Peake; Hyatt, 958). The force of v. 16 must be the speaker's self-absolution from complicity in the disaster giving rise to the lament; an absolution to be confirmed by the deity because he knows what was said in his presence (interpreting the lament as a response to illness would make v. 16 an assertion of non-complicity in whatever gave rise to such sickness). But the enemy must be punished because there is no other way that the speaker will be vindicated. The logic of this is determined by the formal aspects of the lament which divide the world into the innocent and the guilty, the righteous and the wicked, or those loyal to Yahweh and his enemies. The day of evil which the speaker never desired but which he has experienced must now come upon his persecutors. Otherwise the righteous-innocent will not be vindicated and their belief system (e.g. vv. 5–13) will be exposed as vacuous.

The exegesis of vv. 14–18 along these lines removes the poem from the hermeneutic perspective of Jeremiah's 'confessions' and places it in the context of the conflict between the righteous and the wicked of the post-exilic period (cf. Vermeylen 1981, 266–7). This appears to be a more adequate social and theological context for the struggle than the more popular exposition of the poem as the prophet's inmost thoughts and feelings. Among the complex arguments which may justify such an interpretation is the understanding of the conflict between the two groups as capable of being resolved in a way consistent with the language and motifs of the poems. The vindication of the innocent over against the persecution of the wicked is a constant theme of many psalms (the story of Job is analogous, but the source of disaster is different, though his friends suffer some criticism in 42.7–9) and fits the poems in the Jeremiah tradition. However, the destruction of the community in that tradition is not part of the righteous-versus-the-wicked convention at all. It is the destruction of everybody and everything (because all is *šeqer*), and there is no vindication of anybody (unless it is the abstract 'word of Yahweh'). The destruction of Jerusalem is not also the vindication of Jeremiah and the narratives of the survivors' experiences after that event do not represent the vindication of Jeremiah (the opposite is the case cf. 43–44). The prayer for vindication has no referent in the tradition other than as the expression of the hopes of the pious that the deity will deliver them from their enemies. The presence of such prayers in the tradition is indicative of the redactional history of the book, and the use of them to construct a persona for Jeremiah (cf. Polk; see on 1.17, 19) creates many problems for reading the tradition. The individual 'confession' reading is maintained militantly by many exegetes (e.g. Berridge, Bright, Thompson; cf. Polk) but equally denied by others (e.g. Reventlow, Vermeylen; cf. Gunneweg 1970; Welten 1977). In opting for 'interpretation' rather than 'confession' as the approach to the laments, this commentary favours a simpler reading of the poems than the complex decoding processes required for the alternative approach.

17.19–27

19 Thus said the LORD to me: 'Go and stand in the Benjamin Gate, by
which the kings of Judah enter and by which they go out, and in all the
gates of Jerusalem, 20 and say. "Hear the word of the LORD, you kings of
Judah, and all Judah, and all the inhabitants of Jerusalem, who enter by
these gates. 21 Thus says the LORD: Take heed for the sake of your lives,
and do not bear a burden on the sabbath day or bring it in by the gates of
Jerusalem. 22 And do not carry a burden out of your houses on the sabbath
or do any work, but keep the sabbath day holy, as I commanded your
fathers. 23 Yet they did not listen or incline their ear, but stiffened their
neck, that they might not hear and receive instruction.

24 But if you listen to me, says the LORD, and bring in no burden by the
gates of this city on the sabbath day, but keep the sabbath day holy and do
not work on it, 25 then there shall enter by the gates of this city kings who
sit on the throne of David, riding in chariots and on horses, they and their
princes, the men of Judah and the inhabitants of Jerusalem; and this city
shall be inhabited for ever. 26 And people shall come from the cities of
Judah, and the places round about Jerusalem, from the land of Benjamin,
from the Shephelah, from the hill country, and from the Negeb, bringing
burnt offerings and sacrifices, cereal offerings and frankincense, and
bringing thank offerings to the house of the LORD. 27 But if you do not listen
to me, to keep the sabbath day holy, and not to bear a burden and enter by
the gates of Jerusalem on the sabbath day, then I will kindle a fire in its
gates, and it shall devour the palaces of Jerusalem and shall not be
quenched." '

---

[19] G lacks 'to me'. MT *b^{e}ša'ar b^{e}nē-hā'ām* (Q), 'in the gate of the sons of the people'; K *bny 'm*; G *laou sou*, 'your people' = *'amm^{e}kā*. The gate is unknown but the text may be corrupt. RSV, NEB 'in the Benjamin Gate'; JPSB 'in the People's Gate'. The Benjamin Gate is referred to in 37.13; 38.7, but unlikely to be the reference here. Giesebrecht, 102, relates it to the gate for the laity, cf. II Chron. 35.5, 12–13. **[25]** G has *huper tous pateras autōn*, 'more than their fathers', after 'but stiffened their neck', cf. 7.26. K *šwm'*, Q *š^{e}mō'a*, '(not) hearing'. BHS vocalizes K as *šōmē'a*?. **[24]** K *bh*, Q *bō*; lacking in G. As *šabbāt* may be masc. or fem., either reading is correct (Rudolph, 118, favours K *bāh*). **[25]** MT *w^{e}śārīm*, 'and princes': these would hardly sit on David's throne. It may be a dittography of the next word *yōš^{e}bīm*, 'sitting', or from the next line *w^{e}śārēhem*, 'and their princes' (cf. Bright, 119). For the listing 'they and their princes, the men of Judah and the inhabitants of Jerusalem', cf. 2.26b. **[26]** MT *ūm^{e}bi'ē tōdāh bēt yhwh*, 'and bringing thank-offerings to the house of Yahweh': cf. 33.11. The phrase 'bringing thank offerings' may be an expansion here, as it sits awkwardly in the text (cf. Bright; Duhm). **[27]** MT *ûbō' bᵉšaʿᵃrê yᵉrûšālaim*, 'and enter at the gates of Jerusalem'; BHS inserts *bō* after *ûbō'* lost by haplography, 'and bring it', i.e. the burden, through the gates (Rudolph suggests an alternative *wᵉhābi'*, 'and bring . . .').

Thiel 1973, 203–9

There is no divine response to the lament. What follows it is a prose sermon about the sabbath presented in the redaction as a divine word to the speaker ('to me' may be absent in G but the command 'Go and stand' implies a recipient of the divine word). The sermon appears in vv. 20–27, but the introduction (v. 19) belongs to that strand of redactional instructions which indicates the speaker's movements about the city and among the people (cf. 7.2; 11.6; 13.1; 18.2; 19.1; 22.1). The sabbath motif may be unique in the tradition here (cf. 34.8–22 for an analogous treatment of the law on slave release), but the format of the sermon belongs to the typically Deuteronomistic alternative sermons which appear in 7.1–15 and 22.1–5 (analysis in Thiel, 204; cf. Nicholson 1970, 65–6). Deuteronomistic phraseology also dominates the sermon (cf. 7.23–6; 11.7–8).

The central point of the sermon is the keeping of the sabbath (i.e. not bringing burdens into the city or working on the sabbath) and the life of the community (v. 21 *hiššāmᵉrû bᵉnapᵉšôtêkem*, 'take heed for your lives') is made dependent upon such sabbath observance. The community's fathers had been commanded to keep the sabbath holy (cf. 7.22–6 for a similar motif, but with reference to obedience rather than sacrifice), but had refused to receive instruction. Nothing is said about the consequences of such disobedience, but the sermon moves on to offer the contemporary society the possibility of establishing its future on a permanent basis by sabbath observance. As a result of keeping the sabbath day holy, the city will play host to kings on the throne of David, their retinue and royal houses, and to the thronging masses from all over the land of Israel who flock to the temple-city to offer a wide range of sacrifices. The anti-sacrifices polemic of other strands in the tradition (e.g. 6.20; 7.22; 11.15; 14.12) is absent here and the acceptability of sacrifice is grounded in keeping the sabbath. The key to the stability of city and land, royal house and people is the sabbath. Failure to keep holy the sabbath will bring a divinely kindled fire against the city and its palaces, a fire which will not be extinguished (the same motif as in 15.14; 17.4 and possibly the link between vv. 19–27 and vv. 1–18). Idolatry brings the divine fire against the land (17.1–4), so does sabbath-breaking.

The world of vv. 19–27 is very different from that of the poems and laments, though it shares some family resemblances with 7.1–15 and esp. 22.1–5 (the movement of kings). The speaker moves (from where is not stated, see on 22.1) to a particular gate (the people's gate?) and there addresses '*kings* of Judah, and all Judah, and all the inhabitants of Jerusalem' (v. 20; the 'kings' reference indicates the theoretical nature of the sermon; cf. 13.13; 19.3; 22.4). The central charge of the sermon is that burdens (*maśśā'*, cf. 23.33–40 for this motif) must not be carried on the sabbath nor brought into the city. The elements of parades and people entering the city by certain gates or bringing burdens through those gates suggest that the sermon is preached from a vantage point outside the city (among the deportees?, cf. Nicholson 1970, 125). The preservation of life and the maintenance of stability on the basis of sabbath-keeping are also quite alien to a tradition whose dominant features relate security to other matters (idolatry, oppression, etc.). The sermon reflects a world of stabilized movement of a commercial nature and not a society threatened by imminent invasion or under siege from powerful forces. People from the outlying districts come up to Jerusalem to offer sacrifice, and officials parade about the city and through its gates. The world of the sermon (allowing for a certain level of idyllic representation characteristic of preaching) is closer to that depicted in Neh. 13.15–18 than to the society facing the catastrophe of 587.

The origins and development of the sabbath in ancient Israel are not known, but whatever its pre-exilic status may have been, most biblical scholars recognize a significant development in its importance after the fall of Jerusalem (cf. Ezek. 20.12, 21, 24; 46.1–8; Isa. 56.1–8; 58.13–14; Kraus 1966, 76–88). The sermon in 17.19–27 may represent an exposition of the prohibition against working on the sabbath (cf. Ex. 20.8–11; Deut. 5.12–15) in terms of a particular practice of bringing goods into the city (cf. Neh. 13.15–18) and reflecting the situation of post-exilic Jerusalem. It certainly reflects that movement which elevated the sabbath into a mark of the special relationship between Yahweh and Israel (cf. Ezek. 20.12–21) and which saw the exile as the enforced sabbath-keeping of the land (Lev. 26.34–5; II Chron. 36.21). The fathers failed to keep the sabbath (and presumably suffered for it – a point not needing to be made in the sermon because the memory of Jerusalem's destruction remained fresh in the collective memory for a long time); their descendants are offered in this sermon the opportunity to guarantee their own well-being and the acceptability of their sacrificial offerings by making sacred that special day.

E. 18.1 – 20.18

18.1–12

18[1] The word that came to Jeremiah from the LORD: 2 'Arise, and go down
to the potter's house, and there I will let you hear my words.' 3 So I went
down to the potter's house, and there he was working at his wheel. 4 And
the vessel he was making of clay was spoiled in the potter's hand, and he
reworked it into another vessel, as it seemed good to the potter to do.
5 Then the word of the LORD came to me: 6 'O house of Israel, can I not
do with you as this potter has done? says the LORD. Behold, like the clay in
the potter's hand, so are you in my hand, O house of Israel. 7 If at any time
I declare concerning a nation or a kingdom, that I will pluck up and break
down and destroy it, 8 and if that nation, concerning which I have spoken,
turns from its evil, I will repent of the evil that I intended to do it. 9 And if
at any time I declare concerning a nation or a kingdom that I will build
and plant it, 10 and if it does evil in my sight, not listening to my voice, then
I will repent of the good which I had intended to do it. 11 Now, therefore,
say to the men of Judah and the inhabitants of Jerusalem: "Thus says the
LORD, Behold, I am shaping evil against you and devising a plan against
you. Return, every one from his evil way, and amend your ways and your
doings."
12 'But they say, "That is in vain! We will follow our own plans, and will
every one act according to the stubbornness of his evil heart." '

---

[3] K *whnhw*; Q *w^{e}hinnēh hū'*, 'and there he was . . .'; G *kai idou autos* = Q. MT *'al-hā'ābnāyim*, 'at the two stones', i.e. one stone worked by hand or feet and the other with the clay for working on it with the hand, both connected by an axle, cf. Ecclus. 38.29–30. **[4]** MT *baḥōmer*, 'with clay': some mss *kaḥōmer*, 'like clay'. G lacks 'in/with clay'; for MT 'in the hand of the potter', G has 'in his hands', cf. NEB. Cf. *kaḥōmer b^{e}yad hayyōṣēr*, 'as clay in the potter's hand', v. 7. **[6]** G lacks *n^{e}'um yhwh*, 'says Yahweh'; it is redundant in view of v. 5 but represents the glossing of the tradition in MT with such phrases stressing the oracular nature of its contents (a frequent procedure). **[7]** MT *rega' . . . w^{e}rega'* (v. 9) has the force of 'at any moment . . .', cf. NEB. Bright's 'at one moment . . . at another moment . . .' is equally good. **[8]** MT *'ᵃšer dibartī 'ālāyw*, 'which I have spoken concerning it': lacking in G. RSV relates the phrase to the nation rather than the evil cf. NEB. JPSB understands the clause to mean 'against which I made the decree'. **[10]** K *hr'h*; Q *hāra'*, 'the evil': K the same as v. 8 and a balance to *haṭṭōbāh*, 'the good', in v. 10. **[11]** G lacks *lē'mōr kōh 'āmar yhwh*, '. . . saying, thus says Yahweh . . .'. MT *hinnēh 'ānōkī yōṣēr 'ᵃlēkem rā'āh*, 'look, I am shaping evil against you': NEB's 'I am the potter; I am preparing evil for you' may preserve the analogy between Yahweh and the potter better, but is a more awkward translation. **[12]** MT *wᵉ'āmᵉrū*, 'and they will say': cf. 13.12. G *kai eipan*, 'and they said' = *wayyō'mᵉrū*. MT *nō'āš*, 'it is hopeless' cf. 2.25.

Brekelmans 1981; Thiel 1973, 210–18; Wanke 1980

The next block of material consists of two lengthy sections of prose developing the motif 'potter' and a number of lament poems. In the first prose section (18.1–12) the potter motif is used as an extended metaphor to make a statement about Israel and a generalization about the divine attitude to nations and kingdoms. The second prose section (19.1–15) develops a symbolic action relating to a piece of potter's merchandise into a criticism of a specific cult activity. In 18.1–12 the potter's house and activities are the focus for a sermon, in 19 an object created by him is the means of delivering a word of doom. The two sections are therefore associated together, apart from the redactional development which has inserted two poems between them, by matters relating to pottery.

In vv. 1–12 three sections may be discerned: 1–6, 7–10, 11–12 (cf. analysis in Thiel). The introduction determines the reading of what follows as oracular (cf. 7.1; 11.1) and clearly specifies Jeremiah as the speaker (as opposed to those redactional indicators which simply state 'the word of Yahweh came to me . . .' or 'Yahweh said to me . . .' cf. 11.6, 9; 13.1; 15.1; 16.1; 17.19). Like 17.19; 19.1–2; 22.1, what follow are the deity's instructions for Jeremiah to go and do something: in this case he is to arise and go *down* (*yārad*, cf. 22.1; from where? the temple?) to the potter's house and there he will hear the divine words. The story in this instance is slightly different from the other formulations of the reception of the divine word in that Jeremiah is not to go and speak but must go and wait (the command to speak does not occur until v. 11). Obeying the command (a point not always indicated in accounts of this nature) he goes and observes the potter at work. He notes a botched effort by the potter and how readily such work may be remade. In the potter's ability to work with inert substances such as clay is the lesson to be learned from the visit. There in the potter's house the divine word comes to the speaker and informs him (or the house of Israel through the speaker) that Yahweh is capable of working with the nation in the same way that the potter was able to mould the clay to his will. The potter's activity provides a metaphor of divine capacity. As such the piece is a positive, optimistic metaphor of hope for the future (cf. Cornill, 221–3).

A rather different understanding of the piece is provided by the inclusion of vv. 7–10 in the editing of the section. These verses set out a general point about divine attitudes, using some Deuteronomistic terminology (cf. Thiel, 214–17), which removes the image of the potter's activity as a positive one and focuses on the clay as a substance with its own capacity for choosing what will happen to it. In v. 6 the house of Israel is the clay, but in vv. 7–10 any nation or kingdom may be the clay. The divine will for such a nation or kingdom may be its destruction ('I will pluck up and break down and destroy it', see on 1.10 for such terms), but it may change that plan by turning (*šāb*) because in response to its turning the deity will repent (*niḥam*). The clay changes, the potter changes! But the principle is a symmetrical one: if the deity wills good for a nation or kingdom (the images of building and planting convey the idea of a stable, prosperous life, cf. on 1.10; Bach 1961) and it does evil, then the deity will repent (*niḥam*) of the good intended for it. National changes bring about changes in the deity, and the future of any nation or kingdom is not predestined but determined by its preparedness to change (for good or evil). National turning is matched by divine repentance (i.e. a change of mind leading to a change of plan). However, the openness of this principle is severely limited by the fixity of its reciprocity and the highly abstract nature of its terms (i.e. it is unlikely that it envisages a series of fluctuating national plans with corresponding divine switches of response).

The theoretical nature of vv. 7–10 with their image of a predictable deity contracting with nations and kingdoms a reciprocal agreement of corresponding and alternating plans for the future is idyllic and unreal. Outside the world of the book of Jonah it represents only a theological abstraction (cf. Duhm, 154). It is partly composed by the redactional variations on the motifs 'pluck up', 'break down', 'destroy', 'build' and 'plant' which run through the construction of the book (cf. 1.10; 12.14–17; 24.6; 31.28, 38–40; 42.10). In the later stages of the employment of these motifs they are applied to the nations and 18.7–10 belongs to this stage (by this stage of the tradition Jeremiah has been transformed into a prophet to the nations, hence his message to them here). The unreality of the turning motif can be seen in its symmetrical construction here and the implicit notion behind vv. 7–10 that the divine intention has been announced to the nations so that they may respond accordingly (hence Jonah as paradigm). It is also discernible in the contrast between this principle and the adamancy with which other strands in the tradition insist that turning is not a possibility for Israel (e.g. the image of Judah's sin written with a pen of iron in 17.1). An examination of the oracles against Babylon (50–51) will confirm also the abstract and unreal nature of the notion that any kingdom may turn and avoid the evil intended by Yahweh against it, for against Babylon destruction is decreed in an absolute sense. No content is given to the notion of turning, nor is it clear how a kingdom or nation may turn (which is why in the book of Jonah turning means liturgical repentance, i.e. fasting, sackcloth and ashes applied to man and beast, woman and animal [Jonah 3.6–9]).

The concern with the possibility of turning (*šûb*) is a Deuteronomistic notion developed after the fall of Jerusalem (cf. Wolff 1975; Thiel, 215–7). After the catastrophe nothing remained but the outside possibility that Yahweh would be gracious to the nation and permit it to return to him (cf. the late Deuteronomistic passages in Deut. 4.29–31; 30.1–10; I Kings 8.46–53). This possibility appears in the Jeremiah tradition in the Deuteronomistic sermons which hold out to the community the opportunity of turning or making an amendment of life so as to avoid further destruction or to be permitted to remain in the land (cf. 7.3–7; 11.2–5; 18.11; 26.2–6; 36.2–3). The potter metaphor is used in this way in v. 11 in the third stage of the section (tied into vv. 7–10 and therefore loosely connected to the point in v. 6). However, the extension of the formal turning principle to any nation or kingdom goes beyond the Deuteronomistic preaching of repentance and should be seen as an even later development within the Jeremiah tradition (cf. Brekelmans, 346–8). It is the theoretical application to the nations of a motif which appears at various points in the tradition but is here removed from the background of thought undergirding the Deuteronomistic concept of turning (i.e. after punishment for breach of the covenant, a notion not applicable to the nations). The great fluidity of motifs in the Jeremiah tradition (e.g. 1.10) provides a wide range of possible permutations of them and the occasional development of a positive attitude to the nations (e.g. 3.17; 12.14–17) allows for this principle that any nation or kingdom may turn and thereby change the deity's attitude to it. It is, however, a very mechanical idea of turning and lacks any depth of content. Not that the notion of repentance has much depth or content in its Deuteronomistic application to Israel, but there it is integrated into a set of concepts and a history of the covenant (neither the biblical tradition of repentance nor the soteriological use of the concept in rabbinic thought would understand the point of the poet Yeats's observation 'repentance keeps my heart impure').

In vv. 11–12 the point of the visit to the potter's house is resumed but now addressed to the people of Judah and the citizens of Jerusalem (cf. 4.4; 11.2, 9; 17.25). Resumed in the sense that the community is again addressed rather than any nation or kingdom, but the statement about the deity's shaping of evil plans against the nation owes as much to vv. 7–10 as it does to the potter image (it combines *yōṣēr*, 'potter', 'forming, shaping' from the semantic field of pottery and *ḥāšab*, 'plan, scheme, devise, intend', from v. 8). Given the principle enunciated in vv. 7–10, v. 11 seeks to persuade the community to turn in order that the deity may also change his mind and act towards the people in a positive fashion. Only the possibility of turning is mooted by this address, it is not yet guaranteed (contrast 24.4–7; 29.10–14). It offers hope (cf. Nicholson 1970, 81), but not certainty. The community still must change or the deity will make effective the plan for evil devised against it.

Jerusalem fell in 587, so an explanation is required. That is provided in v. 12. The people reject the opportunity to turn, refuse the possibility of amending their ways. This refusal explains why what happened to the city took place (cf. 2.25). The point-blank refusal to turn is equivalent to the clay not responding to the potter's shaping work, but the image of the potter's ability to modify and remake is arrested at the point of his rejecting the original design which has not worked out for him. In effect, the image drawn from the world of pottery is only loosely connected with the use made of it in the tradition (cf. the similar disjunction between images and interpretation in 13.1–11). Like the symbolic actions the extended metaphors can pose interpretative problems for understanding the tradition, and the potter's activity hardly serves to reinforce the theological principles drawn from it by the editors. But the images and metaphors do permit a certain degree of editorial transformation of motifs along theological lines, and these provide, with the ones in 19, a set of responses to the theme of Jeremiah in the potter's house.

18.13–17

13 'Therefore thus says the LORD:
Ask among the nations,
who has heard the like of this?
The virgin Israel
has done a very horrible thing.
14 Does the snow of Lebanon leave
the crags of Sirion?
Do the mountain waters run dry,
the cold flowing streams?
15 But my people have forgotten me,
they burn incense to false gods;
they have stumbled in their ways,
in the ancient roads,
and have gone into bypaths,
not the highway,
16 making their land a horror,
a thing to be hissed at for ever.
Every one who passes by it is horrified
and shakes his head.
17 Like the east wind I will scatter them
before the enemy.
I will show them my back, not my face,
in the day of their calamity.'

---

[13] MT *kā'ēlleh*, 'like these': EVV 'the like of this'; cf. Isa. 66.8, where singular (*kāzō't*) and plural (*kā'ēlleh*) are combined. **[14]** MT *h^{a}ya‘^{a}zōb miṣṣūr śāday šeleg l^{e}bānōn*, 'does the snow of Lebanon leave from the rock of the field?': BHS follows Volz, 193, in readin *h^{a}ya‘^{a}bōr*, 'moved, faded', for *h^{a}ya‘^{a}zōb*, and reads *śir^{e}yōn*, 'Sirion' (a name for Mount Hermon, Deut. 3.9; cf. Ps. 29.6) with Cornill, 224, for *śāday*, cf. RSV; Rudolph understands *l^{e}bānōn* as *lābān*, 'white', i.e. 'white snow', and rejects Volz's view of *śāday* as 'soil' ('humus'). NEB 'Will the snow cease to fall on the rocky slopes of

Lebanon?'. Bright follows Albright 1950–1, 23, and reads 'Do flints depart from the fields, Or the snow from Lebanon?', cf. Dahood 1962a, 207: 'Do flints leave the field, snow Lebanon?'. MT *'im-yinnāt^{e}šū mayim zārim qārīm nōz^{e}līm*, 'are strange waters plucked up, cold flowing (streams)?': NEB 'Will the cool rain streaming in torrents ever fail?', cf. JPSB 'Does one abandon cool water flowing from afar?'. BHS proposes *yinnāš^{e}tū*, 'dry up', cf. RSV, and a number of possible readings *mimmiṣrayim m^{e}qōrīm*, 'fountains from Egypt' (Rudolph, 129), *mēmē qedem qārīm*, 'cold eastern waters', *mayim zābīm m^{e}qōrīm*, 'flowing waters, streams (running)'. Dahood, 'Or do men forget flowing waters, running springs?'; other suggestions in Duhm, 155 ('waters of the northern stars', cf. Job 37.9), and Peake, 232–3. **[15]** MT *laššāw^e' y^{e}qaṭṭērū*, 'to emptiness they have sacrificed': cf. NEB 'they burn sacrifices to a mere idol'. Bright 'To the Fraud they burn offerings'. The sense of *šāw^e'* may be 'idols', cf. *hab^{e}lē šāw^e'*, 'idols', Ps. 31.7 (EV 6); Jonah 2.9 (EV 8). MT *wayyakšilūm*, 'and they have caused them to stumble': G *kai asthenēsousin*, 'they have weakened . . .', i.e. 'failed' = *w^{e}yikkāš^{e}lu* (cf. BHS 'I will cause them to stumble'). MT *š^{e}bīlē*: many mss *š^{e}būlē* (Q-K according to BDB, 987), 'path', i.e. flowing course of life; Dahood treats it as 'twisting path', cf. *šibbōlet*, 'meandering stream' (Judg. 12.6; cf. river Meander in Asia Minor) and translates the phrase 'eternal nomads'. BHS inserts *tōhū*, 'waste, barren', after *n^{e}tībōt*, 'paths' (lost by haplography). **[16]** K *šrwqt*; Q *š^{e}rīqōt*, cf. *š^{e}rēqāh*, 'whistling, hissing', 19.8. **[17]** MT *'er'ēm*, 'I will look at them'; Vrs 'I will show them' = *'ar'ēm*. MT *'ōrep w^{e}lō'-pānīm 'er'ēm*, 'neck and not face I will show them': i.e. I will turn my back on them rather than my face, cf. 48.39. This is a figure of disfavour here, but the turning of the neck is a figure of apostasy in 2.27; 32.33 (the meaning is determined by the perspective of the speaker: to turn away from Yahweh is apostasy, but for Yahweh to turn away is disaster). The phrase *q^{e}šēh-'ōrep*, 'stiff of neck', is an image of obstinacy, cf. 7.26; 17.23; 19.15.

A poem interrupts the connection between vv. 12 and 18, but may be intended to function as the divine response to the people's reply in v. 12. The redactional 'therefore thus says Yahweh' would favour this reading of the relationship between vv. 12 and 13. The argument of the poem is similar to 2.10–13 but uses more graphic images. As it shares the theological outlook to be found in the discourse of 2.10–13, it may be assumed to be an element of the post-catastrophe theologizing about the destruction of the nation. Virgin (epithet of personification of the nation of Israel, cf. 31.4, 21; Amos 5.2; of the people, 14.17; of Egypt, 46.11; of Babylon, Isa. 47.1) Israel has behaved in a most horrible and disgusting fashion (cf. 5.30; 23.14; 29.17 for variations on the term used here, *ša'^{a}rurīt*). Her behaviour is so outrageous that the nations cannot provide an example to equal it. This is an action unique among the nations and quite unnatural. The hyperbolic force of v. 13 is clear, but the rhetorical questions of v. 14 are not easily reconstructed so as to yield clarity of meaning. Many are the suggestions made by exegetes, but they tend to compound the difficulties of the text. Allowing for the conjectural nature of such reconstructions, the point of v. 14 appears to be that certain features of nature are permanent. Snow on the high mountain slopes and peaks (or flint rocks in the fields), flowing torrents and running streams: these are all permanent aspects of the world and symbolize reliability as well as the unchanging face of nature. Not so is Israel.

In contrast to the mountains and rivers, Israel has forgotten Yahweh and followed other gods (i.e. sacrifices have been offered to emptiness). If snow and water pursue their regular courses, the people of Israel have not, but have stumbled down ancient roads and paths which are not the highway. The charge is ironic in view of the advice in 6.16, where the people are encouraged to seek out ancient paths, but rhetoric and ideology hide a multitude of contradictions. The nation's involvement in this sacrificial cult has brought about the ruination of the land (this would appear to be the force of vv. 15–16, but v. 17 makes the deity the one responsible for the disaster). The equation of idolatry and invasion allows a theological lesson to be drawn from the destruction of land and people. The point is made more poignant by the reactions of those who pass by and see the ruined land. Because the people have forgotten Yahweh, he will turn his back on them in the day of their calamity (cf. 2.27), and their appeals to him for help will not come before his face. The image used for the invading force is that of the sirocco wind from the east (cf. 4.11; 13.24), a hot devastating force which will leave the land a ruin (cf. 25.9, 11).

18.18

18 Then they said, 'Come, let us make plots against Jeremiah, for the law shall not perish from the priest, nor counsel from the wise, nor the word from the prophet. Come, let us smite him with the tongue, and let us not heed any of his words.'

MT *wayyō'mᵉrû*, 'and they said': cf. v. 12 (see textual note), a redactional introduction. MT *ballāšōn*, 'with the tongue': BHS reads with S *bilšōnō*, 'with his own tongue' (*w* lost by haplography), i.e. slander him with his own words (cf. Rudolph, 122). G lacks 'not', i.e. 'and we will hear all his words', in order, presumably, to use his own words against him or to trap him.

A brief prose statement supplied by the editors as a third stage of the scheming motif (*ḥšb*). In v. 11 Yahweh schemes an evil scheme against the people, in v. 12 the people admit to having their own schemes which they plan to follow, and in v. 18 they (i.e. the people, though some exegetes prefer understanding the 'they' as a reference to the strata of authorities listed in v. 18) scheme schemes (*maḥᵃšābōt* as in v. 12) against Jeremiah. This is a concrete example of what is meant by the schemes of the people, but hardly the sense of v. 12. The insertion of the poem against idolatry in vv. 13–17 spells out what the nation's schemes are and shows the consequences of them.

For the first time in the tradition other people mention Jeremiah and the theme of direct opposition to him by important strata of society is mooted. Such a theme is fully developed in the narratives (e.g. 26–29, 36–38), but only appears in the redactional framework at a few points in 1–25 (e.g. 1.19; 11.21–23; 18.18; 20.1–3). It is part of the development of the tradition in the direction of producing a presentation of Jeremiah as a paradigmatic figure mediating the divine word in a context of persecution and opposition. The lateness of v. 18 may be indicated by the absence of royal opposition to Jeremiah, but the lack of a reference to king or princes may have no particular significance because the notion of opposition here is one between a speaker of words and those authorities who also speak words. It is an opposition of word and teaching. The solitary word over against formal priestly instruction (*tōrāh*), the counsel (*'ēṣāh*) of the wise, and the word (*dābār*) of the prophet (cf. the double triads of Ezek. 7.26, 'they seek a vision [*ḥāzōn*] from the prophet, but the law [*tōrāh*] perishes from the priest, and counsel [*'ēṣāh*] from the elders'; a further triad appears in v. 27 'king . . . prince . . . people of the land' [this triad is not fully represented in G]). The three strata of authoritative teaching in the community are represented as conspiring to plot against Jeremiah (contrast the different roles played by various social strata in 26), but no reason is given for their plans. It probably reflects a view of Jeremiah as a solitary figure standing for the divine word in opposition to the social structures which constituted the normal media of teaching authority in the community and therefore belongs to a mythic view of Jeremiah. Jeremiah now stands for a view of the authoritative word over against other legitimate forms of speaking which invalidates them, and therefore v. 18 should be read as a fragment of the struggle between different parties and opposing ideologies of a later period (see on 23.9–40).

If v. 18a has connections with vv. 11, 12 then v. 18b, apart from spelling out the nature of the plots, may be intended to introduce vv. 19–23 (many commentators treat the unit as vv. 18–23). It is not necessary to read v. 18 in this manner, but its present position inevitably means that it will be read in connection with vv. 19–23 and the lament there interpreted as a response to the information conveyed by v. 18. The plots of MT (G singular *logismon*, 'argument') are not specified, but may be understood in the more general sense of plans to speak against him and to pay no attention to his words. The figure of 'striking with the tongue' (contrast the physical striking of 20.2) may mean 'slander' or simply 'speak against' (Bright, followed by Thompson, treats it as 'bring charges against him'). It is an opposition of words. In refusing to pay attention to his words, the authorities reduce him to being a speaker of no significance (the absence of the negative in G here may indicate a plan to scrutinize his words carefully in order to gather information against him). But the statements are too terse to allow precise interpretation and much may be built on them by the imaginative exegete who wishes to develop a view of Jeremiah *contra mundum* (cf. Bright 1977, 140–70).

18.19–23

19 Give heed to me, O LORD,
　　and hearken to my plea.
20 Is evil a recompense for good?
　　Yet they have dug a pit for my life.
　Remember how I stood before thee
　　to speak good for them,
　　to turn away thy wrath from them.
21 Therefore deliver up their children to famine;
　　give them over to the power of the sword,

let their wives become childless and widowed.
May their men meet death by pestilence,
their youths be slain by the sword in battle.
22 May a cry be heard from their houses,
when thou bringest the marauder suddenly upon them!
For they have dug a pit to take me,
and laid snares for my feet.
23 Yet, thou, O LORD, knowest
all their plotting to slay me.
Forgive not their iniquity,
nor blot out their sin from thy sight.
Let them be overthrown before thee;
deal with them in the time of thine anger.

---

[19] MT *yᵉrībāy*, 'my opponents': G *tou dikaiōmatos mou*, '. . . of my plea' = *rībī*. G represents a better poetic balance, but MT may reflect what gave rise to v. 18. **[20]** MT *kī-kārū šūḥāh lᵉnapšī*, 'for they have dug a pit for my life': G *hoti sunelalēsan rhēmata kata tēs psuchēs mou kai tēn kolasin autōn ekrupsan moi*, 'for they have spoken words against my soul and have hidden their correction from me'. Cf. v. 22, where MT phrase belongs (BHS treats it as an addition in v. 20) and G there. **[21]** Cf. 15.2. **[22]** K *šyḥh*; Q *šūḥāh*, 'pit', as in v. 20. K *šiḥāh*, cf. G *logon* = *śīḥāh*, 'word, complaint, musing', cf. Ps. 69.13 (EV 12). G understands 'pit' as 'plot'. **[23]** MT *'al-temḥī*, 'do not blot out': *y* an error cf. 3.6b (*tiznī*). BHS reads *temaḥ* (Neh. 13.14) or *timaḥ*. K *whyw*; Q *wᵉyihyū*; G *genesthō*, 'let their . . .' = *yᵉhī*. MT *mukšālīm*, '(let them be) ones who have stumbled . . .': cf. JPSB 'Let them be made to stumble . . .'; NEB 'when they are brought stumbling . . .'. S *mušlākīm*, 'ones overthrown', hence RSV. G *hē astheneia autōn*, 'their weakness'; BHS reads *mikšōlām*, 'their stumbling', Rudolph translates as 'their offence'. Bright, 125, explains his translation 'let them be hurled down before thee' as 'let them, like the criminals they are, be tripped and thrown sprawling before the judge'.

Baumgartner 1917, 44–8; Hubmann 1981

An individual lament bemoaning the treachery of his opponents (MT) and seeking revenge from Yahweh against his enemies and their families. It follows the pattern of other such laments in the tradition (15.15–18; 17.14–18; 20.7–12) and combines the elements of the speaker's innocence and the wickedness of his persecutors. These two elements constitute the grounds of the speaker's appeal to Yahweh for justification and inevitably shape the contents of the lament. The speaker's protestations of innocence take the form of an affirmation of having behaved towards the others for good (v. 20; cf. 17.16 and some readings of 15.11). He has sought to protect them from Yahweh's anger by averting that wrath (how is not explained, but intercession may be the force of 'my standing before you'), but they have compensated him with evil for his good. The gravamen of v. 20 is extremely vague, but it is a formal aspect of such complaints that there should be an innocent speaker appealing to the deity and wicked evildoers opposing the speaker (among the many psalms which provide the background to the formal analysis of the lament Ps. 35; 109 afford striking parallels to 18.19–23). The speaker has sought the good of others yet they have rewarded him with evil (cf. Ps. 35.11; 109.5). When they were in trouble he prayed for them and sought to save them (Ps. 35.13–14; 109.4), but now they seek his life (for the motif of 'digging a pit' cf. Ps. 57.6; 119.85). The plots against his life take the form of pits or snares (cf. Ps. 140.1–5; 142.3) and the lament is redolent of conspiracy and outraged innocence.

The speaker's response to such persecution is to appeal to Yahweh to punish his enemies in the most appalling ways. Let the men among them die in battle or from the plague, let their women become childless and widowed, and let their children starve to death or be slain by invaders (v. 21). Standard curses upon the enemy and befitting the Jeremiah tradition as the product of a period of invasion, destruction, and the aftermath of such disasters. And all because they have opposed the speaker! By v. 23 the complaint is formulated as a plot (counsel) to kill the petitioner, and as this is known to Yahweh the plea for vengeance is justified. Yahweh's knowledge of the speaker is appealed to in vv. 20, 23 as evidence of the speaker's innocence and the enemies' guilt and, whatever the original force of 'speaking good for' may refer to, on behalf of the plea that they should not be forgiven. Under no circumstances should the enemy experience any mercy from Yahweh. That anger once averted by the speaker must now overthrow them.

In this poem we breathe the atmosphere of the laments in the book of Psalms with their polarization of innocent sufferer and wicked persecutors. The goodness of the one is highlighted in order to emphasize the wickedness of the other. Out of a situation of pain and suffering the petitioner seeks Yahweh's aid in order to turn the tables on the others and cause them great suffering. The continued suffering of the innocent is the vindication of the wicked, hence the necessity for a transformation of roles and fates. Such is the formal structure of the poems, and the story line is a fixed one. Persecution, appeal to Yahweh, overthrow of enemies, and therefore vindication of the innocent: the elements are so formal that they mask real situations which may be behind any specific use of such laments. It is not possible to deduce the states of the petitioner, other than as suffering, from the details in the poem. Formality may produce anonymity, but it increases the range of occasions for which the poem may be used.

This being the case, the interpretation of vv. 19–23 allows for many applications of the lament to the life of the community. Whether the individual speaker is representative of a group or only speaks for himself is difficult to determine because the tradition uses both collective and individual laments to express the suffering of people and city. Interpreting it of the pious group in post-exilic Jerusalem would fit the poem with no difficulty and make it part of the series of such poems in the tradition (cf. Vermeylen 1981, 267). However, the linking of v. 19 with v. 18 using *qāšab*, 'give heed', suggests an early interpretation of the lament as the expression of Jeremiah against the plots of the authorities (there are no actual links within the poem other than *qāšab*, cf. Hubmann, 290–3). If there is any intentionality in this linking (other than the linguistic association allowing for placement), then v. 18 could be read as similar to a psalm title and as providing the occasion for the lament (see on 11.18–20). It has an appropriateness about it which allows it to be read in such a way, without having had any original connection with the framework of v. 18.

In the context of multiplicity of readings of the text there can be little objection to treating vv. 19–23 as the speaker's utterance where the speaker is identified as Jeremiah. Thus various commentators read the poem as another 'confession' of Jeremiah's (e.g. Bright, Thompson, Baumgartner). Provided the formality of the lament is not ignored so as to reconstruct details of the speaker's personal life and inner psychological states, this may be a fair application of the poem as edited. But it can raise problems of a different kind: the destruction of the community (as represented by its leaders in v. 18) is caused by its opposition to Jeremiah, whereas in vv. 12–13 and in the majority of places in the tradition it is the people's own doing which brings destruction upon them. Praying for their destruction is redundant. Furthermore, the destruction envisaged in the lament is against a particular group, a judgment which will separate and distinguish between speaker and victims. The Babylonian invasion would make no such distinction. Innocent and guilty, good and bad, leaders, led and Jeremiah himself would all suffer it. This factor should make the exegete distinguish carefully between the laments and the mainstream of the tradition: they have quite different referents and speak from distinctive social settings. The application of the laments to Jeremiah as speaker is but a secondary use of them which blurs important distinctions between them and the rest of the tradition. It has other consequences: if a personal 'confession' approach is taken, then arguments about Jeremiah's solidarity with the nation are invalidated. The calling down of vengeance on others and the pleading for mercy for oneself would then make Jeremiah a premature 'Holy Willie' (the Calvinist hero of Robert Burns' poem 'Holy Willie's Prayer': 'Lord, in the day of vengeance try him . . . But, Lord, remember me and mine . . .'). Whether this problem can be avoided whatever interpretation is taken is a debatable point, but the reading of the laments as the outpourings of the innocent against the wicked preserves the distinction between two groups which is lost if they are applied to the solitary Jeremiah before the catastrophe of 587. (It should be noted that neither Berridge nor Reventlow pays much attention to 18.19–23).

19.1–13

19[1] Thus said the LORD, 'Go, buy a potter's earthen flask, and take some
of the elders of the people and some of the senior priests, 2 and go out to the
valley of the son of Hinnom at the entry of the Potsherd Gate, and proclaim
there the words that I tell you. 3 You shall say, "Hear the word of the LORD,
O kings of Judah and inhabitants of Jerusalem. Thus says the LORD of
hosts, the God of Israel, Behold, I am bringing such evil upon this place
that the ears of every one who hears of it will tingle. 4 Because the people
have forsaken me, and have profaned this place by burning incense in it to
other gods whom neither they nor their fathers nor the kings of Judah have
known; and because they have filled this place with the blood of innocents,
5 and have built the high places of Baal to burn their sons in the fire as
burnt offerings to Baal, which I did not command or decree, nor did it come
into my mind; 6 therefore, behold, days are coming, says the LORD, when
this place shall no more be called Topheth, or the valley of the son of
Hinnom, but the valley of Slaughter. 7 And in this place I will make void

the plans of Judah and Jerusalem, and will cause their people to fall by the sword before their enemies, and by the hand of those who seek their life. I will give their dead bodies for food to the birds of the air and to the beasts of the earth. 8 And I will make this city a horror, a thing to be hissed at; every one who passes by it will be horrified and will hiss because of all its disasters. 9 And I will make them eat the flesh of their sons and their daughters, and every one shall eat the flesh of his neighbour in the siege and in the distress, with which their enemies and those who seek their life afflict them."

10 Then you shall break the flask in the sight of the men who go with you, 11 and shall say to them, "Thus says the LORD of hosts: So will I break this people and this city, as one breaks a potter's vessel, so that it can never be mended. Men shall bury in Topheth because there will be no place else to bury. 12 Thus will I do to this place, says the LORD, and to its inhabitants, making this city like Topheth. 13 The houses of Jerusalem and the houses of the kings of Judah – all the houses upon whose roofs incense has been burned to all the host of heaven, and drink offerings have been poured out to other gods – shall be defiled like the place of Topheth." '

---

[1] MT *kōh 'āmar yhwh*, 'thus said Yahweh': G *tote eipen kurios pros me*, 'then the lord said to me'; a few mss have *'elay*, 'to me'. BHS inserts *'el-yirmᵉyāhū*, 'to Jeremiah', reading 'Then spoke Yahweh to Jeremiah' (Rudolph) in view of v. 14. Some such introduction is required, otherwise the piece will look like a message rather than an instruction cf. 13.1. MT *hālōk wᵉqānītā baqbuq yōṣēr ḥāreś*, 'go and buy a potter's earthen flask': potter is probably redundant here and influenced by 18.2, deleted by BHS (G *peplasmenon* = *yᵉṣūr*, 'formed'); S lacks 'earthen'. The word *baqbuq*, variously translated as 'flask, jar, jug, bottle, decanter', may be onomatopoeic (gurgling of liquid being poured out). MT *ūmizziqᵉnē hā'ām ūmizziqᵉnē hakkōhᵃnīm*, 'and from the elders of the people and from the elders of the priests': the lack of a verb is problematical (a zeugma using *hālōk* is most unlikely); G *axeis* 'take' (= *lqḥ*). BHS reads *wᵉlāqaḥtā 'ittᵉkā mizziqᵉnē* . . . 'and take with you some of the elders . . .', v. 10 implies as much with its statement ' . . . in the sight of the men who go (*hahōlᵉkīm*) with you'. G *kai apo tōn hiereōn*, 'and from the priests' (so G^BS) lacking 'elders of (the priests)': cf. NEB. Cf. II Kings 19.2 for MT phrase 'senior priests'. **[2]** MT *'el-gē' ben-hinnōm*, 'to the valley of the son of Hinnom': G *eis to poluandrion huiōn tōn teknōn autōn*, 'to the burial place of the sons of their children' (= *bᵉnē bᵉnēhem* for *ben-hinnōm*) but = MT in v. 6. The combination of two stories (magical act with flask and denunciation of fire-cult) in ch. 19 makes it difficult to follow unless the two are separated (i.e. 1, 2a, 10, 11a, 14, 15 and 2b–9, 11b–13). K *hḥrswt*; Q *haḥarsīt* (K *haḥarsūt* or *haḥᵃrāsōt*), 'potsherds': this gate was presumably where the shards were thrown. G *charsit* confirms Q reading. A few mss have 'these' after 'the words'; G *pantas tous logous* 'all the words'. **[3]** Cf. 17.20. G *kai andres Iouda*, 'and men of Judah', between 'kings of Judah' and 'inhabitants of Jerusalem'. MT *tiṣṣalᵉnāh*, 'tingle, quiver' (*ṣālal* onomatopoeic), cf. I Sam. 3.11; II Kings 21.12. **[4]** BHS deletes 'and' before 'filled' and repunctuates the verse at 'their fathers', so that it is the kings who have filled the place with innocent blood rather than the people and their fathers. EVV follow MT. Cf. gloss in Ps. 106.38 (BHS); for people and fathers cf. 16.11, 13. **[5]** Cf. 7.31, where Topheth rather than Baal occurs; *bāmōt*, 'high places', should perhaps be *bāmat*, 'high place of . . .', implied by Topheth. MT *wᵉlō' dibbartī*, 'nor decree', lacking in 7.31 and in G^BS^. **[6]** MT *hahᵃrēgāh*, 'slaughter': ST as in 7.32, 'the slain'. **[7]** MT *ūbaqqōtī*, 'I will empty,' i.e. 'make void', a wordplay on *baqbuq*, 'flask'; the deity will pour out the plans of the community, thus rendering them useless. **[7b]** Cf. 7.33; 16.4; 34.20b. **[8]** Cf. 18.16; 49.17. **[9]** G lacks final phrase 'who seek their life'. Cf. Deut. 28.53–7; also Lev. 26.29; Ezek. 5.10; Lam. 2.20; 4.10. **[11]** G lacks the last phrase 'and in Topheth they shall bury without place to bury', cf. 7.32b. MT represents the mixing of the two stories. **[12]** MT *ūlᵉyōšᵉbāyw*, 'and to its inhabitants': BHS deletes (it occurs after the formulaic *nᵉ'um yhwh*, 'says Yahweh'). G lacks 'and' before *lātēt*, 'making': the verse may once have read 'so will I do to this place, says Yahweh, making this city like Topheth'. MT *kᵉtōpet*, 'like Topheth': G *hōs tēn diapiptousan*, 'like one that has fallen down', i.e. 'like a ruin'. **[13]** The material between the dashes in RSV is the second half of MT. MT *wᵉhāyū bāttē . . . haṭṭᵉmē'īm*, 'and the houses of . . . shall become unclean': or possibly '. . . shall be . . . like the place of Topheth, unclean', cf. Bright. G *esontai kathōs ho topos ho diapiptōn ho diapiptōn tōn akatharsiōn*, '. . . shall be as a ruined place (because of G^BA^) uncleanness . . .', cf. Amos 7.17. The second part of MT then defines those houses: *lᵉkōl* . . . 'namely all . . .'.

Thiel 1973, 219–26

The pottery theme of 18.1–12 is continued in 19.1. The first treatment of the theme develops and transforms the image of the potter at work at his wheel, manipulating the clay. In keeping with such an image the flexibility of the divine attitude to nations and kingdoms and the call to the people to turn are stressed. In 19.1–11 a different emphasis is derived from the ambience of the potter's work. Not the processes of making pottery but one of the products of the potter is the focus of attention. This object, a flask, is the end-result of a process, and because the clay has been fixed or baked its shape cannot be changed. The story is therefore about an unchangeable state of affairs. The flask and its fate represent a very different message from the motif of the potter's ability to change design and purpose. The turning of 18.11 is replaced by the impossibility of mending the flask in 19.11. Possibility gives way to fatal inevitability.

This contrast using images from the potter's world is a very simple summation of the issues in 18.1–12 and 19.1–13, but 19.1–13 is far from being a straightforward presentation of the fate of the ceramic flask. The story is contained in 19.1 – 20.6, but only a small part of this lengthy section is devoted directly to the flask incident. Interwoven into the account is a much longer sermon denouncing the fire-cult at Topheth and incorporating the kings, people and houses of Jerusalem into that denunciation. The sermon is 'a rather wordy harangue' (Bright, 133) and incorporates many elements found elsewhere in the tradition which belong to the Deuteronomistic redaction (analysis in Thiel). Attached to the story and the sermon is an account of the response to Jeremiah's preaching and his reactions to the measures taken against him (19.14 – 20.6). This account is treated separately from the story and sermon here in order to focus on the distinctive features of the material and to allow certain aspects of the tradition to emerge more clearly.

Disentangling the story of the ceramic flask from the sermon is necessary in order to establish what the action of that story is. It appears to be limited to vv. 1–2a, 10–11, with vv. 14–15 functioning as commentary on its completion. It is therefore quite a simple story consisting of instructions to go and purchase (same directions as in 13.1 with reference to purchasing a linen girdle but without comment on the carrying out of the command) a ceramic flask or bottle, to take a number of senior people (elders and priests) out to a particular gate of the city, and there to break the flask in their presence accompanying the action with the words 'so will Yahweh break this people and this city . . . so that it can never be mended'.

The action is similar to the linen girdle incident in 13.1–9, though the presence of witnesses in 19.1, 10 is a very necessary element which is absent from the report of 13.1–9. The breaking of the ceramic object is the destruction of the city and its people (cf. *kākāh*, v. 10; cf. 13.9; 51.64). The broken flask remains broken because the fired clay cannot be remoulded, so the action represents and anticipates the permanent destruction of the city. As the response in 20.2 indicates, this action is recognized for the terrible deed it is – the veritable destruction of city and people. It is an action from the world of magic where the act itself constitutes what it symbolizes and the observers are there as witnesses of its occurrence (Fohrer 1953, 70–7, limits the use of magic to very few prophetic actions, e.g. 51.59–64 and I Kings 19.19–21, but classifies 13.1–11; 19.1–15; 28.10–11; 51.59–64 together as embodying the after-effects of the action). The shattered flask broken outside the city in the place of discarded shards is a stark action which owes its impact to the culture in which it takes place. Once the flask is broken there can be no mending it – once what the action represents is explained (i.e. the words accompanying the breaking of the flask) the fate of the city is sealed. The story, although masked by the interpolated sermon, is as graphic and as effective as the action carried out against Babylon in 51.59–64. Both actions consist of deeds which cannot be undone, and their irrevocability is the essence of the action. The witnesses to the action will know that and understand precisely what they have just witnessed – the destruction of their city! The possibility of hope in 18.6 is the opposite of the meaning of the shattered flask. Hope is no longer on the agenda.

Explanation and justification of the action remain for the return from the excursion to the gate of shards (vv. 14–15), but the presence of the sermon within the story indicates the editors' determination to spell out the warrants for the city's destruction. However, the role and status of the actor should be noted. In the whole account Jeremiah emerges more fully-drawn than at any point before this in the tradition. Not named in 19.1 but implicitly there (cf. v. 14; BHS), he is presented as an important figure who can command elders and priests to accompany him on his mission as witnesses to what he has to do and say. This is not the victim of plots by priests and sages (as in 18.18) but one who commands obedience and a following (cf. the image of him in the narratives of 26–29, 34–39). Some authorities may have opposed him (e.g. Pashhur the chief officer of the temple, 20.1), but he can summon important people to do his bidding. In the second part of the section he appears as *the prophet* (20.2) and his speaking is defined as *prophesying* (19.14; 20.1; hence the opposition to him in this part). Thus he is a person with status in the community and is to be distinguished from that solitary figure hiding or lurking about the city as presented by other strands in the tradition. The different representations of Jeremiah are discrete layers of tradition reflecting distinctive stages of the construction of the figure of Jeremiah and the conflict between these images of him is the result of combining independent material together into one book.

The account of the breaking of the flask in the place where ceramic wares were consigned at the end of their usefulness is greatly expanded by a complex sermon against the cult in the valley. This is an expansion of material in 7.31–2, where the fire-cult of Topheth is denounced as one of the cultic abominations warranting divine wrath. It is integrated into the flask incident in v. 2b, where the valley is the location of the delegation's trip (it is unnecessary in the text because the named gate is a specific place whereas the valley extends along the whole southern side of the city). There Jeremiah is to address his companions with words directed against the kings of Judah and the people of Jerusalem (the combination of the motifs from the two different stories is indicative of the awkwardness of the text). Yet it is not to his companions that the words are spoken but against the kings (cf. 17.20), because the cult in the valley is a Deuteronomistic motif attacking the royal houses (see on 7.30–34). The Deuteronomistic obsession with idolatry and baalistic cults is also given voice in the sermon. The motif 'this place' usually refers to Jerusalem (cf. 7.3, 7, 14, where there is some ambiguity about whether its referent is the temple, the city or the land), but in the sermon here it must refer to Topheth (e.g. v. 6), though it is probable that Topheth has been superimposed on material which originally referred to Jerusalem (cf. v. 12). Part of the charge against the kings is the accusation that they have shed innocent blood in the fire-cult (vv. 4–5). This is the ideological distortion of a nature cult which has been analysed in 7.30–34, except that here Baal is the god to whom the human sacrifices have been made. Because of such evil deeds the disaster that will befall the cult centre (Topheth? Jerusalem?) will make ears ring (the very strong aural motifs associated with the fall of Jerusalem [v. 8; 18.16; 25.9] suggest that v. 3 should be related to Jerusalem), an onomatopoeic term used by the Deuteronomists to describe the destruction of a major cult centre (*ṣālal*; cf. I Sam. 3.11; II Kings 21.12). The cultic practices of the people have alienated (*yᵉnakkᵉrū*), i.e. turned into a foreign place, the sanctuary (Jerusalem is the obvious candidate for such a process of alienation, whereas the high place of Topheth would be alien from the start, vv. 4–5).

The one point where the story of the flask-breaking ceremony and the sermon against Jerusalem-Topheth coincide is the word-play of v. 7: 'And in this place I will make void (*baqqōtī*) the plan (*ʿᵃṣat*, cf. 18.18, 23) of Judah and Jerusalem . . .'. It is an image of the deity pouring out the contents of a flask and represents the frustrating of the community's plan or counsel (not defined but a motif used along with *ḥšb* in the section 18.1 – 20.6). It cannot be determined from the text whether this word-play reflects an implicit action of Jeremiah's before he smashed the flask or is merely a connecting link between the two elements in vv. 1–13. But whatever future plans the kings(!) or the city fathers had for the community will be cancelled by this divine act against the city.

The sermon is an amalgam of phrases to be found throughout the Deuteronomistic editing of the tradition, but it contains one Deuteronomistic motif not yet encountered in the text so far. In v. 9 the practice of cannibalism is mooted (cf. Deut. 28.53–7). Due to the invasion of the land and the siege of the city the people will be forced to eat their own children and their neighbours in order to stave off the starvation brought upon them by the prolongation of that siege. Their dead will provide food for birds and beasts (v. 7); their own flesh and blood (living or dead?) will be food for themselves. No wonder that the fictional travellers of v. 8 hiss in horror (cf. 18.16) at the disaster.

In v. 11b the Topheth theme is returned to, but only to reintroduce Jerusalem as the target (v. 12). The houses in Jerusalem implicated in idolatrous practices (private cults on the roofs?) will be treated like Topheth, i.e. profaned with corpses. The filling of Jerusalem with the dead (due to invasion, siege, starvation, slaughter and pestilence) will be a grotesque mimesis of what went on in the fire-cult of Topheth.

19.14 – 20.6

14 Then Jeremiah came from Topheth, where the LORD had sent him to
prophesy, and he stood in the court of the LORD's house, and said to all the
people: 15 'Thus says the LORD of hosts, the God of Israel, Behold, I am
bringing upon this city and upon all its towns all the evil that I have
pronounced against it, because they have stiffened their neck, refusing to
hear my words.'

20[1] Now Pashhur the priest, the son of Immer, who was chief officer in
the house of the LORD, heard Jeremiah prophesying these things. 2 Then
Pashhur beat Jeremiah the prophet, and put him in the stocks that were in
the upper Benjamin Gate of the house of the LORD. 3 On the morrow, when
Pashhur released Jeremiah from the stocks, Jeremiah said to him, 'The

LORD does not call your name Pashhur, but Terror on every side. 4 For thus says the LORD: Behold, I will make you a terror to yourself and to all your friends. They shall fall by the sword of their enemies while you look on. And I will give all Judah into the hand of the king of Babylon; he shall carry them captive to Babylon, and shall slay them with the sword. 5 Moreover, I will give all the wealth of the city, all its gains, all its prized belongings, and all the treasures of the kings of Judah into the hand of their enemies, who shall plunder them, and seize them, and carry them to Babylon. 6 And you, Pashhur, and all who dwell in your house, shall go into captivity; to Babylon you shall go; and there you shall die, and there you shall be buried, you and all your friends, to whom you have prophesied falsely.'

---

[14] MT *mēhattōpet*, 'from Topheth': BHS favours changing this to *mēhappetaḥ*, 'from the door'; cf. v. 2 or *mippetaḥ hašša'ar* 'from the door of the gate' (Volz). But such changes presuppose that vv. 14–15 are part of the original act, whereas they belong to the Jerusalem-Topheth sermon complex. **[15]** K *mby*; Q *mēbī'*, 'bringing'; K due to haplography (*mby 'l*). MT *wᵉ'al-kol-'ārehā*, 'and against all her cities'; a strange expression to use: 'Jerusalem and all her cities'. G* *tas kōmas autēs*, 'and its villages', cf. JPSB; MT may refer to the cities of Judah or to the environs of Jerusalem (cf. Volz, 203, 'districts'). Duhm, 162, reads *mēbī' 'al-hā'āreṣ*, 'bringing upon (this) land', which resolves the problem of cities. NEB 'and on all its blood-spattered altars': based on a Ugaritic word meaning 'a blood-daubed stone', cf. Nicholson, 38, 166; 1977, 113–16. **[20.1]** MT *'immēr* '(son of) Immer'; S *'ᵃmarᵉyāh*, 'Amariah'. For *hakkōhēn*, 'the priest', G^{min} reads *ho pseudoprophetēs*, 'the false prophet', cf. v 6; *nibbē'tā lāhem baššāqer*, 'you have prophesied to them falsely'. Cf. 29.26 for the functions of the overseer priest. **[2]** MT *wayyakkeh pašḥūr 'ēt yirmᵉyāhū hannābī'*, 'and Pashhur struck Jeremiah the prophet': G *kai epataxen auton*, 'and he struck him'; *nkh* may have the force of 'beat' or 'have beaten' under orders, cf. NEB, 'he had him flogged'. The lack of the phrase 'Jeremiah *the prophet*' in G is indicative of the shift between the first (G) and second (MT) editions of the text in the direction of Jeremiah's emergence as a *prophetic* figure. MT *'al-hammahpeket*, 'in the stocks': G *eis ton katarraktēn*, 'in the dungeon'(?). Cf. 29.26; *hpk* suggests cramped or crooked (posture), so either stocks or confinement in cramped conditions would fit here (cf. T, 'prison'). JPSB 'in the cell'; Rudolph, 128 'stocks', etymological derivation indicates an instrument for contorting limbs. MT *bᵉša'ar binyāmin*, 'Benjamin Gate': G *en pulē oikou apotetagmenou tou huperōuo*, 'in the gate of the upper house set apart (for special use)'. BHS suggests *oikou apotetagmenou* = *bēt mᵉnī*. Cf. 37.13; II Kings 15.35; II Chron. 20.5; Ezek. 9.2 for a gate on the north side (and a new court) which may have been this Benjamin gate facing Benjaminite territory. **[3]** G lacks MT *wayᵉhī mimmāḥorāt*, 'and it came to pass on the morrow'. MT *māgōr* *missābīb*, 'terror all around': this phrase appears in 6.25; 20.10; 46.5; 49.29; cf. Ps. 31.14 (EV 13); Lam. 2.22. G *Metoikon*, 'Exile', and lacks *missābīb*; the reference to Pashhur as *māgōr* in v. 4 suggests that *missābīb* is not part of the name but a redactional development of the tradition similar to the use of the terms of 1.10 throughout the book. G connects *māgōr* with *gwr*, I 'sojourn', rather than *gwr* II, 'quarrel', or *gwr* III, 'dread'. Honeyman 1954 offers an over-subtle account of the phrase as a pun: 'not *pašḥūr* but *paššaḥ sᵉḥōr* (destruction all around)', i.e. all Pashhur's friends will fall dead around him. Holladay 1972 provides an over-sophisticated treatment of the phrase in terms of a metalanguage developed by Jeremiah and interprets it as 'a total reverse of *Heilsgeschichte*', an overthrow of the patriarchal covenant! BHS deletes *missābīb* following G and regards it as having been written into the text from v. 10 (cf. Rudolph, 128). **[4]** MT *wᵉ'et-kol-yᵉhūdāh 'ettēn*, 'and all Judah I will give . . .': G *kai se kai panta Ioudan dōsō*, 'and you and all Judah I will give . . .'. **[5]** G lacks 'and all its prized belongings', the second 'I will give' (MT *'ettēn*, lacking in RSV, NEB), and 'who shall plunder them, and seize them'. **[6]** G lacks MT *tābō' wᵉšām*, '(to Babylon) you shall go; and there . . .'.

Holladay 1972

The report of the magical action with the ceramic flask does not contain a statement of Jeremiah having carried out the divine command, but v. 14 presupposes that he did and has him return to the temple courtyard (whence he set out?). However, v. 14 is not part of the broken flask episode but a continuation of the sermon against Topheth (Jerusalem). In this story Jeremiah goes out to Topheth and preaches a sermon against the fire-cult practised there (a sermon inextricably mixed up with an attack on the Jerusalem cult). The lateness of this sermon strand is apparent in v. 14 and 20.1, where the activity of Jeremiah is described as 'prophesying', and in 20.2, where there is a reference to Jeremiah *the prophet*. These are the first references in the tradition to him as prophet and describing his work as prophesying (the prologue of 1.4–10 is equally late and belongs to the redactional framework). He is a prophet who works in the temple, whence the deity sends him to address people and places with a word of destruction (e.g. 19.3–9) or warning (e.g. 7.3–7; 22.1–5). He commands the attention, respect and cooperation of priests and other leaders (19.1; 26.16, 24; 35.2). In such circumstances we may detect a figure who is both priest and prophet (cf. 1.1–2), who comes and goes at the divine command (cf. 13.1, 4;

19.1–2), and who therefore opposes priest-prophets who are false because they oppose him (e.g. 20.1, 6; 29.24–32). It is in a context of Jeremiah *as prophet* that we encounter his conflict with other named individuals (e.g. 20.1–6; 28–29). The movement at the divine command motif makes this strand of the tradition present Jeremiah as a figure in the Elijah mould of prophets (cf. I Kings 17.1–10; 18.1–19; 19.15–18; 21.17–19). He is one who comes and goes, but only when the deity speaks, who delivers the commanded word and then returns to the point of departure. The anonymity of the speaker of the oracles and laments suits this presentation and allows an ahistorical reading of the tradition (for further analysis of poetry and narrative into prophecy, cf. Auld 1983; 1984).

The denunciation of the fire-cult of Topheth in 7.31–32 (also set within the context of attacks on Jerusalem and temple practices 7.30–34) is given the semblance of a narrative account in 19.3–13, and v. 14 implies a visit out there. Thus the development of the tradition may be glimpsed in the turning of statements into stories and the construction of narratives to carry the message and activities of Jeremiah. In v. 15 his address to all the people is an application of the Topheth denunciation to the city of Jerusalem (it is only an application by virtue of the present context of v. 15) but the three strands in the section (ceramic flask act, anti-Topheth speech, denunciation of Jerusalem cultic practices) are independent motifs here combined by the history and development of the tradition (cf. Thiel 1973, 228). The cause of the divine destruction of Jerusalem and all its villages (see Notes) is due to the refusal to hear Yahweh's words rather than to cultic practices (for the stiffening of the neck motif, cf. 7.26; 17.23; II Kings 17.14; Deut. 10.16). That refusal to listen to the divine words is an oblique reference to the rejection of the prophetic word, because the divine word is mediated through prophets (cf. the Deuteronomistic figure of the deity's wakeful sending of the prophets 7.25; 25.3–4; 26.5; 35.14–15; 44.4). Because of this refusal the divine evil pronounced against the city will now be activated (cf. 35.17; 36.31).

For the first time the epithet prophet is applied to Jeremiah (lacking in G) and occurs in a context of conflict with another official figure (a prophetic one according to 20.6). The story of the contretemps between Jeremiah and Pashhur is similar to that between Jeremiah and Hananiah (28) where two named individuals clash over a difference of proclaimed words about the immediate future. Where the Pashhur story differs is the lack of interest in what the priestly authority in the temple has to say. His actions against Jeremiah are the focus of the story, yet his fate is said to be due to his having 'prophesied falsely' (v. 6). In 28 Hananiah's words are given with Jeremiah's response to them; in 19.14 – 20.6 Jeremiah's words are given with Pashhur's reaction to them. In both stories the opponents of Jeremiah die – thereby demonstrating the truth of Jeremiah's word and position. However, the clash of prophets in 20.1–6 does not allow Pashhur to be heard. Perhaps his beating of Jeremiah represents his message: the words of Jeremiah are false and to demonstrate their falsity he is beaten and put in the stocks or confined to a cramped cell. 20.1–6 need not have originally stood here, so that 19.14–15 may give a misleading context for understanding it. Reconstructing Pashhur's prophecy from 20.1–6 (perhaps an unnecessary project if v. 6 is but a loosely used motif in the tradition for identifying those who are in the wrong, cf. the pseudoprophet epithet occasionally used in G traditions) suggests that he proclaimed the view that Babylon would not attack and evil would not come upon the temple-city. Such a reconstruction is simply based on the use of the Babylon and king of Babylon motifs in vv. 3–6 (cf. 21.2, 4, 7, 9–10; 25.9, 11–12; 29.19; 36.29). The response of Jeremiah to this is to incorporate Pashhur and his friends in the exposition of the significance of the king of Babylon's invasion of the land (cf. Amos 7.10–17 for a similar exchange between a prophesying person and a priest in charge of a sanctuary where opposition leads to the incorporation of the opponent into an oracular statement of the impending disaster). However, the fate of Pashhur need not be as a result of a false oracle; it could be a consequence of his disciplining of Jeremiah (cf. 29.24–28 with Jeremiah's oracular response in 29.32). Having Jeremiah beaten and restrained overnight constitutes a rejection of his message against Jerusalem and warrants the response of the prophet when released.

The oracle against Pashhur consists of two elements: a change of name and the deportation of all Judah by the king of Babylon. The name-change simply personalizes the judgment oracle against Jerusalem and Judah. Pashhur, the agent of Jeremiah's suffering, will become the occasion of his friends' destruction, and to symbolize this fate his name is changed from Pashhur (a name with connotations of violence, cf. Lam. 3.11 *wayᵉpaššᵉḥēnī*, 'and he tore me in pieces'; used of other officials in the book, cf. 21.1; 38.1) to Magor, 'terror'.

He is no longer to be the one imposing pain on others but to be its victim and the one in association with whom suffering comes to others: 'I will make you a terror to *yourself and to all your friends*' (v. 4). Not his opponents but his friends will find him a cause of terror. It is quite a neat transformation of name and role and echoes a fine emotional point that many a flogged victim of priestly overseers must have felt after that particular sacred duty had been carried out in the temple precincts. The text of v. 3 is more complicated in MT because it adds the word *missābīb*, 'all around', to *māgōr*, 'terror'. This element is appropriate in the context of the Babylonian invasion and the death of Pashhur's friends to which he is witness. However, the phrase occurs a number of times in the tradition (6.25; 20.10; 46.5; 49.29) and therefore may represent a redactional addition here in the transmission of the text (hence its absence in G). Of the five occurrences of the phrase three refer to the effects of the Babylonian attacks on different groups (Zion in 6.25; Egypt in 46.5; Kedar in 49.29) and two occur in block E with reference to Pashhur's new name and in the lament of 20.7–11. The lament allusion is similar to Ps. 31.12–14 (EV 11–13) and Lam. 2.22 (the effects of the Babylonian invasion on Jerusalem's inhabitants). As a victim of the king of Babylon's attack on the city, Pashhur represents an individualization of the motif which belongs in the tradition more to the general effects of the Babylonian onslaught than to particular individuals. The unit reflects later developments in the redaction of the tradition (typified by the motifs of Jeremiah the prophet and the king of Babylon).

The Babylonian onslaught will result in the slaughter of Pashhur's friends (fellow priests?), the capture of city and territory, the deportation of all Judah to Babylon and the execution of them there. Elements of hypberbole are present in v. 4, and the notion of the deportees being killed in Babylon is both an exaggeration and in conflict with other views of the fate of the exiles (e.g. 24.4–7; 29.1–9, 10–14). It probably represents the rhetoric of opposition to city and cult and may also reflect the antagonism directed against certain important figures in the exiled community (cf. 29.24–32; Thiel 1973, 227–8). If 20.1–6 and 28–29 belong to the same redactional strand, then the motifs of conflict, false prophesying and priestly authority shared by them are about the same thing. The true figure of authority in the community, whether in Palestine or in Babylon, is Jeremiah the prophet, and those who will not conform to his words must suffer the extreme penalty. This includes witnessing the death of their companions (e.g. Pashhur in 20.4 and Shemaiah in 29.32). The stories in this strand are about conflict between authority figures and the imposition of discipline or death: Jeremiah is beaten (20.1) or should be chastized (29.26–27). Because Jeremiah is the prophet of Yahweh, his opponents suffer death (Pashhur and friends, Hananiah, Shemaiah and his descendants) presumably in accordance with the Deuteronomistic decrees (cf. Deut. 18.19–22). Thus the stories are illustrations of the framework notion of Jeremiah *the prophet* (20.1; 28.5, 6, 10, 12, 15; 29.1, 29) and are shaped by it.

The plundering of the wealth of Jerusalem (see on 27.19–22; 28.1–4) is but one feature of the destruction attending the Babylonian victory. Part of that plunder will be the people and, in particular, Pashhur (note that the change of name is not in fact followed by the text in v. 6) with his family and friends. All who have listened to Pashhur's false prophesying will die; so that it is not only those who prophesy falsely who are doomed but also those who listen to them or are associated with them. Thus the king of Babylon motif (first mooted in v. 4, cf. 28.2, 4) is a device for singling out Jeremiah as the true prophet and associating alternative views with destruction (cf. 36.27–31).

20.7–13

7 O Lord, thou has deceived me,
  and I was deceived;
thou art stronger than I,
  and thou hast prevailed.
I have become a laughing-stock all the day;
  every one mocks me.
8 For whenever I speak, I cry out,
  I shout, 'Violence and destruction!'
For the word of the Lord has become for me
  a reproach and derision all day long.
9 If I say 'I will not mention him,
  or speak any more in his name,'
there is in my heart as it were a burning fire
  shut up in my bones,
and I am weary with holding it in,
  and I cannot.

10 For I hear many whispering.
Terror is on every side!
'Denounce him! Let us denounce him!'
say all my familiar friends
watching for my fall.
'Perhaps he will be deceived,
then we can overcome him,
and take our revenge on him.'
11 But the LORD is with me as a dread warrior;
therefore my persecutors will stumble,
they will not overcome me.
They will be greatly shamed,
for they will not succeed.
Their eternal dishonour
will never be forgotten.
12 O LORD of hosts, who triest the righteous,
who seest the heart and the mind,
let me see thy vengeance upon them,
for to thee have I committed my cause.
13 Sing to the LORD;
praise the LORD!
For he has delivered the life of the needy
from the hand of evildoers.

---

[7] MT *kullōh*, 'every one': G *dietelesa*, 'continuously, incessantly'. **[8]** MT *kī-middē ʾadabbēr ʾezʿāq*, 'for as often as I speak I cry out', cf. 48.27. G *hoti pikrō logō mou gelasomai*, 'for I will laugh because of my bitter speech'. For the motif of crying out 'violence' (*zʿq ḥāmās*), cf. Job 19.7. **[9]** G lacks 'heart', and for MT *ʿoṣur*, 'shut up', has *phlegon*, 'flaming (fire)'. **[10]** MT *māgōr missābīb*, 'terror is all around': G *sunathroizomenōn kuklothen* '(many) gathering around'. Bright, 132f., treats the phrase as a nickname for Jeremiah used by the crowd but the phrase may be a gloss from v. 3, which disrupts what the crowd is saying, cf. NEB. MT *haggīdū wenaggīdenū*, 'inform and let us inform', cf. JPSB: EVV 'against him' has to be supplied. Cf. Job 17.5 for the motif of informing against one's friends. G *episustēte kai episustōmen autō*, 'conspire and let us conspire against him'. MT *kōl ʾenōš šelōmī šōmerē ṣalʿī*, 'all my friends, watchers of my stumbling': cf. Ps. 35.15. Cf. *ʿaqēbay yišemōrū*, 'they watch my heels', Ps. 56.7 (EV 6); 71.10 (*šōmerē napšī*, 'watchers of my life'). The phrase 'man of my *šālōm*', i.e. 'friend', possibly means the one having to do with my welfare; cf. 38.22 (*ʾanšē šelōmekā*, 'your friends'); Obad. 7; Ps. 41.10 (EV 9). G *pantes andres philoi autou*, 'all his friends'; G has *epinoian autou*, 'his intention', for *ṣalʿī*, 'my stumbling'. **[11]** MT *rōdepay yikkāšelū welōʾ yukālū*, 'my persecutors will stumble, they will not overcome':

G *ediōxan kai noēsai ouk ēdunanto*, 'they persecuted but could not perceive' = *rādᵉpū wᵉhaśkēl lō' yākōlū*. **[12]** = 11.20 (*ṣadīq* for *ṣedeq*); BHS treats as addition here (cf. Rudolph, 132). MT *gillītī*, 'I make known, disclose', cf. 33.6; BHS reads *gallōtī*. **[13]** MT *'ebᵉyōn*, 'the poor': a technical term in the Psalms for the pious, cf. 'the righteous' of v. 12 (Volz, 209).

Baumgartner 1917, 48–51, 63–6; Clines and Gunn 1976; Fishbane 1979, 91–102; Polk 1984, 152–62

A lament and a hymn of confidence follow the exchange between Jeremiah and Pashhur (vv. 7–10, 11–13). The division of the unit is a much disputed matter and a wide range of possibilities has been opted for by commentators: vv. 7–9 (e.g. Baumgartner, Volz, Rudolph), vv. 10–13 (e.g. Baumgartner, Rudolph omitting v. 12); vv. 7–10, 11–13 (e.g. Condamin, Lundbom 1975, 45–6); vv. 7–9, 10–11, 12, 13 (e.g. Volz; cf. Duhm, 166: vv. 7–11, 12, 13); vv. 7–12 (e.g. Peake, Skinner); vv. 7–13 (e.g. Clines and Gunn, 394–8, Polk). Such diversity of opinions is indicative of the difficulties involved in the analysis and interpretation of vv. 7–13. Arguments and counter-arguments are available for each position and further variations allow for the incorporation of vv. 14–18 into the lament (cf. Vermeylen 1981, 267–8, who argues for a core of vv. 7–9, 14–18 from the post-exilic period with a second redactor adding vv. 10–13). Given so many different exegetical treatments of seven verses, the interpretation offered here is but one possible reading of the lament in vv. 7–13.

The plural form of address in v. 13 (*šīrū . . . halᵉlū*, 'sing . . . praise') makes a fitting communal closure for a lament which bemoans the lot of the righteous community facing the persecution of evildoers (cf. the other laments of this nature in 11.18–20; 12.1–3; 15.15–18; 17.14–18; 18.19–23). The individual lament (vv. 7–11) is the poem of a spokesman representing the pious in the post-exilic community, and the instruction to the group to praise Yahweh terminates the collection of such laments in the tradition. This appeal to the group makes v. 13 more an appropriate editorial conclusion than a part of the original individual lament with its solo voice. As v. 12 is a variation of 11.20 (see on 11.20) it is more likely an editorial contribution than an integral element of the lament itself. The note of confidence in v. 11 indicates that it is the response to vv. 7–10. Taking vv. 11–13 as a series of closures, editorial and response to a lament, would make vv. 7–10 the lament proper. The two pieces, vv. 7–10 and 11–13, belong together now, though vv. 11–13 may only have been composed or placed here at a time later than the composition of vv. 7–10 (cf. Lundbom 1975, 45).

The poem in vv. 7–10 is the familiar cry of outrage and suffering directed at the deity because of the persecuted state in which the speaker finds himself. On this occasion (cf. 12.1–2; 15.18; 17.17) the deity is part of the problem (some exegetes separate this motif from the persecution theme by treating vv. 7–9, 10–11 separately, e.g. Volz). He has deceived the speaker, overpowered him and made him a laughing-stock all day long to everybody. The precise nuance of meaning for the phrase *pittītanī*, 'you have deceived me' (v. 7) is debated: *pth* has connotations of deception (cf. II Sam. 3.25; Ezek. 14.9), seduction (cf. Ex. 22.15 [EV 16]), enticement (cf. Judg. 14.15; 16.5), persuasion (cf. Hos. 2.16 [EV 14]; Prov. 25.5). All of these shades of meaning have been suggested as the interpretation of v. 7 (cf. Clines and Gunn 1978). The combination of *pth*, 'seduce', and *ḥzq*, 'be strong, prevail' (with *tūkāl*, 'you have prevailed') in v. 7 has led some exegetes to understand the accusation to be one of 'rape': 'These terms used in immediate juxtaposition forcefully convey the complexity of the divine-human relationship: sweetness of enticement as well as violence of rape' (Heschel 1962, 114; cf. Carroll 1981, 125–6). In 15.18b the speaker accuses the deity of the deceit of being as failing waters; here the accusation is of overpowering or raping the suppliant. The use of *pth* in connection with the divine deception of prophets (I Kings 22.20; Ezek. 14.9; cf. DeVries 1978, 44) allows a further level of interpretation of v. 7 to be developed and facilitates that approach to the laments which sees them as the utterances of the *prophet* Jeremiah. Putting v. 7 into the mouth of Jeremiah raises many interpretative problems, and permits the possibility of contemplating the bizarre image of the *celibate* prophet (conventional interpretation of 16.2) accusing the deity of *rape*. Gianlorenzo Bernini may have been able to represent St Theresa in the grip of a mystical orgasm in his famous sculpture 'The Vision of St Theresa' (altar in Sta Maria della Vittoria, Rome), but a disgruntled prophet complaining about divine rape in a life devoted to ranting about his neighbours' sexual excesses (cf. 5.7–8) is an image too grotesque and modern to be the likeliest reading of the text. It *can* be derived from v. 7, but there are sufficient alternative interpretations available to allow more modest roles to hyperbole and rhetoric in the poem.

The evidence advanced for the claim that Yahweh has deceived and overpowered the speaker is given in two sets of images. In vv. 8–9 the effects of speaking and not speaking are both intolerable. If the speaker does speak he cries out, shouting 'Violence! Outrage!' (*ḥāmās wāšōd*): a conventional outcry of distress signalling oppression and violence being suffered by the complainant (cf. 6.7; Amos 3.10; Ezek. 45.9; Isa. 59.6, 7; 60.18; Hab. 1.3; 2.17). The term 'violence' (*ḥāmās*) is also a feature of the individual lament psalms, where it characterizes the behaviour of the enemies of the speaker and Yahweh (e.g. Ps. 7.17 [EV 16]; 18.49 [EV 48]; 25.19; 27.12; 35.11; 55.10 [EV 9]; cf. Marrow 1965). Although the precise meaning of the cry 'Violence! Outrage!' in v. 8 is disputed (e.g. Rudolph, 130, offers three different interpretations), the strong affinities between the lament psalms and the laments in the Jeremiah tradition suggest that the speaker is identifying Yahweh as the enemy (cf. Berridge 1970, 154; Clines and Gunn 1978). It may be an ironic use, but the deity as the enemy poses the problem of whence will come vindication (cf. Marrow 1965, 255, and his subtle allusion to I Sam. 2.25, suitably emended to reflect v. 8). The divine word of v. 8b need not necessarily be the prophetic word (the view taken by many exegetes) but may be that word which constitutes the delight of the pious (cf. Ps. 1; 119). It is because of fidelity to the divine word (i.e. Yahweh's law) that the pious regard themselves as being persecuted (cf. Vermeylen 1981, 268), but if that word is the cause of their suffering, then they must refrain from speaking it. Hence v. 9, where the speaker resolves not to mention Yahweh or to speak in his name any longer. Again, many exegetes prefer to interpret v. 9 of Jeremiah giving up his prophetic ministry, of his remaining silent (especially in view of vv. 1–6). However, that is only one possible understanding of v. 9. The interpretation of the silence as the retreat of the pious from public acknowledgment of Yahweh (e.g. Ps. 137.3–6) fits the general exegesis of the laments as the complaints of the pious against the persecution of the wicked (the closures of vv. 12, 13 make that opposition very clear). Yet because the pious are so bound up with Yahweh and the contemplation of his word, such silence is as painful as its alternative. It is a fire in the mind, imprisoned in the bones – it has to be released.

The other set of images which expresses the extent to which the deity has overpowered the speaker deals with his opponents. The whispering of the crowd (*dibbat rabbīm*) is a conspiracy against the speaker. The phrase *māgōr missābīb*, 'terror all around', is probably a gloss here, though it fits a lament psalm (e.g. Ps. 31.12–14 [EV 11–13]). It hardly expresses the object of 'Inform, let us inform', and it is absurd to imagine that the phrase refers to a popular attempt to catch Jeremiah the prophet speaking seditious words because no conspiracy would have been required for that, as vv. 1–2 make plain (Bright's view of the phrase as a nickname is imaginative but unpersuasive, because its use in the tradition is quite otherwise and its occurrence in v. 10, if not a gloss from the lament psalms, is most likely due to v. 3). The image in v. 10 is of a crowd (of evildoers? cf. v. 13) conspiring against the speaker, watching for his fall and its concomitant opportunity to overpower him and have revenge. The crowd hope to achieve what the speaker claims the deity already has achieved (vv. 7, 10 echo each other in a number of ways, e.g. the motifs of deception and overpowering). This note of persecution (paranoia?) is to be found in many of the laments in the Jeremiah tradition, but one new note is sounded in v. 10: among the crowd plotting against him are his friends. This motif has its place in the lament psalms (e.g. Ps. 41.9 [MT 10]; cf. Obad. 7; Zech. 13.6) and may represent the rhetoric of the lament rather than a literal conspiracy between the crowd and his friends (the influence of this formal feature of the lament on the NT story of the trial and passion of Jesus should not go unmarked).

The resolution of the speaker's complaint appears in v. 11. Yahweh, the dread warrior, is with the speaker, and so his persecutors stumble and are unable to overcome him. Permanent ignominy (23.40; cf. 3.25; 51.51) is the lot of those who persecute the speaker. The secondary closures which form an appendix to the note of confidence terminating the lament identify the conflict as one between the righteous and their opponents, a conflict in which the deity delivers the needy (cf. Ps. 107.41; 132.15) from the power of evildoers (cf. Ps. 9.18; 12.5; 40.17; 70).

The reading of the laments as utterances of Jeremiah is perhaps the most common interpretation of the poems offered by exegetes (e.g. Berridge, Bright, Clines and Gunn, Fishbane, Polk, Thompson, Wimmer 1978). In an area of such disagreement about meaning and interpretation it is a reading which cannot be ruled out on *a priori* grounds, but it poses more problems than it solves. None of the poems is introduced by a redactional formula attributing it to Jeremiah, yet the tradition has many such formulations for the poems and narratives in it. Hence the redactors did not read (or intend?) the poems to be read as Jeremiah's utterances. The holistic approach to the text which reads it as a totality of utterances by Jeremiah is therefore unwarranted and mistaken. The formal aspects of the laments, so akin to the lament psalms, suggest a generality of meaning rather than the particularity of the life of Jeremiah. Whenever an individual lament is applied to Jeremiah's life (a process arrived at by assuming the narratives describe a real historical set of attitudes and events) it lacks appropriateness of fit. This lack of fit might be accounted for by the formality of such laments, i.e. they are not to be taken literally, but if that is the case, then there is no point in trying to match them with Jeremiah's life in the first place. The formal nature of the psalms of lament makes them poor indices of real events and experiences.

The laments in the tradition may reflect conflict between the righteous (i.e. innocent) and the wicked who persecute them, but there is only a surface similarity between this conflict motif and the conflict between Jeremiah and other officials in the narratives. The reference to 'my familiar friends' in 20.10 ('the men of my *šālōm*') can hardly be an indictment of Pashhur the priest of vv. 1–2 (so Polk, 157), unless it is argued that Jeremiah and Pashhur had been fellow-priests working in the temple together and after the beating Jeremiah felt betrayed by his good friend. If this lament motif is given a literal meaning with reference to Jeremiah, then it must implicate such friends as Baruch (32.12; 36.4; 45) and Ahikam (26.24) in the conspiracy against him. The likelihood of this interpretation is again questionable. Furthermore, the conflict bemoaned in the laments is resolved by the confident expectation of the destruction of the opponents. This hope is a sensible outlook in a general conflict between pious and impious, but in the context of 597–587 it is quite unreal. The destruction of Jerusalem and the various deportations befell Jeremiah as much as his opponents. They may have ended their lives in Babylon, he ended his in Egypt. Where, then, is the divine vindication of the one over the others? This type of vindication is as inappropriate for the preacher of the word as is the lament genre for prophets.

20.14–18

14 Cursed be the day
on which I was born!
The day when my mother bore me,
let it not be blessed!
15 Cursed be the man
who brought the news to my father,
'A son is born to you,'
making him very glad.
16 Let that man be like the cities
which the LORD overthrew without pity;
let him hear a cry in the morning
and an alarm at noon,
17 because he did not kill me in the womb;
so my mother would have been my grave,
and her womb for ever great.
18 Why did I come forth from the womb
to see toil and sorrow,
and spend my days in shame?

---

[16] MT *wᵉhāyāh*, 'and (that man) shall be': G *estō*, 'let be . . .' = *yᵉhī*. BHS prefers *hayyōm*, '(that) day', cf. v. 14, to MT 'that man'. The cities overthrown (*hāpak*) by Yahweh are Sodom and Gomorrah. G has *en thumō*, 'in anger' (*bᵉʼap*), after *yhwh*. MT *wᵉšāmaʻ*: Vrs *yišmaʻ* 'let him hear'. **[17]** MT *mērāḥem*, 'from the womb', as in v. 18: G *en mētra*, 'in the womb' = *bᵉrāḥem*. Dahood 1963 vocalizes it as *mᵉruḥḥām*, 'enwombed'.

The block ends with a sudden outcry of despair. The speaker wishes that he had never been born and curses his birth day and the man who announced his birth to his father. Better that these events should not have happened than that he should have been born. Indeed his mother's uterus would have made a better grave for him because his life since he left it has been misery and agony (cf. 8.3a). His days pass in shame.

What does this curse mean here? The occurrence of a similar cursing of one's birth in Job 3 (a poem linguistically distinctive from 20.14–18) suggests a lament over a terrible disaster. It could therefore represent a cry of utter despair over the fate of people and city. Such a disaster might well evoke feelings of depression and thoughts of premature death. Another possibility is to read the poem as a conventional utterance in response to hearing bad news (cf. Hillers 1965). The bringer of good news is blessed (cf. II Sam. 4.10; 18.22), cursed is the bearer of bad tidings (by reversal of response to good news). Examples of the physical response to bad news occur in 6.22–23; 30.5–6; 23.9; 49.23; 50.43 (so Hillers) and 20.14–18 might be analogous to these (cf. Clines and Gunn 1976, 406–7).

As a response to the bad news of Jerusalem's destruction, vv. 14–18 represent a statement about the disaster mooted in the block and may be read as a preface to the first section of the next block (21.1–10; cf. Polk 1984, 159–62). The destruction of the city finds an echo in v. 16, where there is an allusion to the overthrow of the cities of Sodom and Gomorrah. The normal use of the Sodom and Gomorrah motif in the prophetic traditions is as a metaphor of the wickedness of the people of Jerusalem or its leaders (e.g. 23.14; Isa. 1.10; 3.9; Ezek. 16.45–46). Here the allusion refers to the more literal sense of the cities as the objects of divine wrath and is therefore more appropriate (cf. 49.18; 50.40).

A different interpretation of vv. 14–18 regards them as Jeremiah's self-curse (e.g. Polk). However, this approach raises all the difficulties already outlined about the linking of the laments to the life of the prophet. The man who spent his life preaching against the city, on occasion even welcoming the impending disaster, is not well represented as the one bemoaning its fate (it would make 'death shall be preferred to life' [8.3a] ironic!). To see Yahweh's vindication of the prophet in Jeremiah's survival of Jerusalem's defeat and to interpret that as the refusal to let the self-curse be the final word on his fate (Polk 1984, 162) is an inadequate reading of the tradition (especially for the holistic approach). Jeremiah's fate in Egypt (43–44) is the vindication of nobody. If vv. 14–18 are to be read in this fashion as a self-curse uttered by Jeremiah then the interpretation of the laments as 'confessions' is unravelled and the prophet left unvindicated and cursed. That may be a very good reading of the whole tradition, but it is not the one ever seriously offered by the advocates of this approach. Treating vv. 14–18 as a self-curse would make the poem a dire response to the disaster which befell the city.

F. 21.1 – 24.10

This block of material (an appendix to part I) consists of two cycles of poems and prose enclosed between a brief prose account of a meeting between Jeremiah and the king's delegation and a vision relating to the deportation of citizens to Babylon. Chronologically 24 takes place about a decade before 21. The presence of 21.1–10, using motifs employed in 34.1–7; 37.3–10, poses questions about its place at the head of this cycle and its relation to the other accounts of this period and such delegations to Jeremiah. As a preface to the cycle addressed to the royal house (22.11 – 23.6) it may be designed to associate the royal leadership with the fall of Jerusalem in such a manner that responsibility for the disaster may be laid at the door of the royal house (cf. 23.2). A similar intention may lie behind the inclusion of the cycle against the prophets (23.9–40) in this block. Kings and prophets are the guilty men. They are the ones responsible for what befell city and people. The vision set in the temple (24) belongs to a rather different strand in that it distinguishes between two groups, those deported in 597 and those who remained behind in the city (i.e. the people addressed by 21.6), and designates one group as Yahweh's specially favoured people (cf. 29.1–14). It introduces a radical shift in Yahweh's attitude to the nation and represents the pro-Babylonian community strand in the tradition. The appendix as a whole gathers together many discrete elements and provides two valuable commentaries on the kings and the prophets. The preface and conclusion to these two cycles function as links within the redaction of the tradition between what precedes and what follows the block.

21.1–10

21[1] This is the word which came to Jeremiah from the LORD, when King
Zedekiah sent to him Pashhur the son of Malchiah and Zephaniah the
priest, the son of Maaseiah, saying, 2 'Inquire of the LORD for us, for
Nebuchadrezzar king of Babylon is making war against us; perhaps the
LORD will deal with us according to all his wonderful deeds, and will make
him withdraw from us.'

3 Then Jeremiah said to them: 4 'Thus you shall say to Zedekiah, "Thus
says the LORD, the God of Israel: Behold, I will turn back the weapons of
war which are in your hands and with which you are fighting against the
king of Babylon and against the Chaldeans who are besieging you outside
the walls; and I will bring them together into the midst of this city. 5 I
myself will fight against you with outstretched hand and strong arm, in
anger, and in fury, and in great wrath. 6 And I will smite the inhabitants
of this city, both man and beast; they shall die of a great pestilence. 7
Afterward, says the LORD, I will give Zedekiah king of Judah, and his
servants, and the people in this city who survive the pestilence, sword, and
famine, into the hand of Nebuchadrezzar king of Babylon and into the hand
of their enemies, into the hand of those who seek their lives. He shall smite
them with the edge of the sword; he shall not pity them, or spare them, or
have compassion."

8 'And to this people you shall say: "Thus says the LORD: Behold, I set
before you the way of life and the way of death. 9 He who stays in this city
shall die by the sword, by famine, and by pestilence; but he who goes out
and surrenders to the Chaldeans who are besieging you shall live and shall
have his life as a prize of war. 10 For I have set my face against this city for
evil and not for good, says the LORD: it shall be given into the hand of the
king of Babylon, and he shall burn it with fire." '

---

[1] MT *haddābār ᵓᵃšer-hāyāh ᵓel-yirmᵉyāhū mēᵓet yhwh . . . lēᵓmōr*, 'the word which came to Jeremiah from Yahweh . . . saying': = 7.1; 11.1; 18.1; 30.1; 34.1; 35.1; cf. 32.1; 34.8; 40.1. **[2]** MT *nᵉbūkadreᵓṣṣar*, 'Nebuchadrezzar': lacking in G. First occurrence of the name in the Jeremiah tradition; this is its proper spelling (Akkadian *Nabū-kudurri-uṣur*), though it appears as Nebuchadnezzar in 27.6, 8, 20; 28.3, 11, 14; 29.1, 3. G lacks MT *ᵓōtānū*, 'us' ('will deal with us'), cf. NEB. **[3]** G *pros Sedekian basilea Iouda*, 'to Zedekiah king of Judah'. **[4]** G has a shorter verse because it lacks a number of phrases to be found in MT: 'the god of Israel', 'which are in your hands', 'the king of Babylon and', 'and I will gather them'. MT *wᵉᵓāsaptī ᵓōtām*, 'and I will gather them': RSV 'and I will bring them together (into the midst of this city)', cf. NEB. The phrase is ambiguous: does it refer to the weapons (Rudolph) or the Chaldaeans (Volz)? **[5]** MT *bᵉyād nᵉṭūyāh ūbizrōᶜa ḥᵃzāqāh*, 'with outstretched hand and strong arm': cf. variations in 27.5; 32.17, 21. Cf. the Deuteronomistic phrase *bᵉyād ḥᵃzāqāh ūbizrōᶜa nᵉṭūyāh*, 'with strong hand and outstretched arm' (Deut. 4.34; 5.15; 26.8; slight variations in 7.19; 11.2; cf. I Kings 8.42 = II Chron. 6.32; outside Deuteronomistic literature cf. Ezek. 20.33, 34; Ps. 136.12). **[6]** G '(. . .with a great pestilence) and they shall die' = *wāmētū* for MT *yāmatū*, 'they shall die (with a great pestilence)'. **[7]** MT *wᵉ'et-hāᶜām wᵉ'et-hanniš'ārīm*, 'and the people and those who remain . . .': some mss and Vrs lack *wᵉ'et*, hence EVV. MT *min-haḥereb* 'from the sword': many mss and Vrs represent *ūmin*, 'and from . . .'. As in v. 4, G has a shorter text and lacks 'into the hand of Nebuchadrezzar king of Babylon and', 'and into the hand of (those who seek)'. MT *wᵉhikkām*, 'and he will smite them': G *kai katakopsousin autous*, 'and they will smite them' = *wᵉhikkum* (the logic of lacking 'Nebuchadrezzar . . .'). MT *lō' yāḥūs . . . wᵉlō' yᵉraḥēm*, 'he will not pity . . . nor have compassion': G *ou pheisomai . . . kai ou mē oiktirēsō*, '*I* will not spare . . . nor will *I* have compassion'; G lacks *wᵉlō' yaḥmōl*, 'and he will not spare'. Cf. 13.14, where MT approximates to G here. **[8]** Cf. Deut. 30.15; vv. 8–10 are separate from vv. 3–7, as is evidenced by *tō'mᵉrun*, 'you (plur.) shall say' (v. 3) and *tō'mar* 'you (sing.) shall say' (v. 8), i.e. different speakers because the delegation is not addressed in vv. 8–10. **[9]** = 38.2 (with minor variations). G lacks 'and by pestilence'. MT *wᵉnāpal*, 'and surrenders': lacking in 38.2 (cf. 37.13 for *npl*, 'surrender, desert'). K *yḥyh*; Q *wᵉḥāyāh*, 'and shall survive': Vrs favour K *yiḥyeh*, 'shall survive', i.e. 'live'. G *kai zēsetai*, 'and shall live', at end of verse = *wāḥāy*, as in 38.2. For the motif 'possess one's life as a prize of war', cf. 38.2; 39.18; 45.5.

McKane 1982; Pohlmann 1978, 31–47; Thiel 1973, 230–7; Weippert 1971; 1973, 67–86

The blocks of material (A–E) in the tradition to this point have been undated, but from 21.1 onwards they, and individual narratives, tend to be dated either formally or with reference to certain events (the notable exceptions being the collection in 30–31 and the oracles against the nations in 46–51). The event referred to in 21.1, the delegation sent to Jeremiah by king Zedekiah, may be dated in the period 588–7 during the Babylonian attack on Jerusalem. It therefore belongs to the strand of stories told about delegations, consultations and interviews between the royal house and Jeremiah (e.g. 34.1–7; 37.1–10; 38.14–23). This is a strand which appears to be out of place in 21.1, though the lack of dating for what precedes 21.1 makes it appear less starkly anachronistic (yet it is a decade after 24.1!).

Commentators who insist on reading the text as a chronological unfolding of events and utterances (e.g. Holladay 1983) tend to date the undated texts in such a way that a historical sequence is created by the progress of the blocks. But even this approach recognizes that 21.1–10 is hardly the sequence to 20, especially if 20.1–6 is dated to the time of Jehoiakim (e.g. Bright, 133, 216, separates the treatment of the two units and deals with 21.1–10 in relation to 34.1–7). The problem is modified by recognizing that chronological sequences are not an editorial feature of the tradition so much as a factor within some of the blocks of material, and represent elements of the redactional framework more than integral features of the individual narratives. Yet some account is required of why a piece such as 21.1–10 is to be found so far from the other variations on the same theme and so apparently out of place in its present position.

Two different approaches may be singled out as characterizing the scholarly discussion about the present position of 21.1–10. These two courses of explanation entail looking at the unit in terms of what precedes it or what follows it. The first approach explains the placing of 21.1–10 after 20 because of the occurrence of the name Pashhur in 20.1–6 and 21.1 (the two Pashhurs are different persons, but the same name provides an associative link). This argument is developed by Rudolph in terms of the contrast the two passages make: in one story Jeremiah is abused and beaten by the priest Pashhur, in the other account the *king* sends his officials, including Pashhur, to consult Jeremiah. It is a contrast lost in the account in 38.1–6, where Pashhur ben Malchiah is among the princes who have Jeremiah thrown in the cistern, but it may reflect 37.3 with the substitution of Pashhur (because of 20.1–6?) for Jehucal ben Shelemiah. The other approach is typified by Thiel, who relates 21.1–10 to the following cycles as a Deuteronomistic introduction to them setting out the deity's attitude to king, city and people. Read together 21–23 now form a coherent whole, and 21.1–10 provides a necessary explanation of what the consequences are for a community served by such corrupt or pathetic leaders (i.e. kings and prophets). The editing of 21.11 makes such a connection between the introductory material and the cycle on the kings: '*and* to the house of the king of Judah say . . .' (cf. v. 8 'and to this people you shall say'). This approach is preferable in that the cycles require some spelling out of the consequences of such poor leadership, but imaginative exegesis may combine the two approaches in search of holistic analysis.

21.1–10 is not a unity but consists of vv. 1–2 as background information for the occasion of vv. 3–6; i.e. vv. 1–6 belong together, v. 7 as a variation on v. 6, and vv. 8–10 as an independent piece. McKane has suggested that the final editor of 21.1–10 may have intended to represent a sequence of events roughly corresponding to 52.4–16 (cf. 39.1–10; II Kings 25.1–12). It is an imperfect correspondence, but vv. 1–6 may reflect the eighteen-months-long siege, v. 7 the break-out of Zedekiah and his officials, and vv. 8–10 the fate of the people left in the city. There are, however, problems with such analysis (cf. McKane, 61–4) and the different accounts of delegations and interviews in the tradition do not permit the formation of a coherent and consistent story. This lack of agreement between the stories calls in question the view that 21.1–10 is based on 37.3–10. It also suggests that the different stories may be variations on a formal theme (the fate of the city and its inhabitants) rather than reflections on historical events. This would explain the peculiar material in 34.4–5 (see on 34.1–5). Each occurrence of the theme allows for a different development of the material, and the only other unifying factor is the role of Jeremiah. Thus Jeremiah may speak in response to a royal delegation (cf. 21.1–2; 37.3), a royal summons (38.14), a divine commission to the king (34.2), or be overheard by the princes (38.1). The theme is manipulated and transformed by different contexts, but the stabilizing element is Jeremiah the speaker. In this way the prefacing of the cycles against the kings and the prophets with a variation on the theme allows those cycles to be attributed specifically to Jeremiah. It is part of the redaction of the tradition designed to tie together the contents of the book with the identification of the speaker of the contents as Jeremiah.

It is tempting to analyse vv. 1–10 in terms of vv. 4–6 (minus the first introduction of v. 4) as the proclamation and vv. 1–3, 4a, vv. 7, 8–10 as subsequent developments of theme and redaction. Such an analysis would make the fate of city and people the subject of the statement. This is a statement using images drawn from holy war concepts (cf. Weippert 1971) but transformed in order to underline the divine animus against the city. Following G the opponents of the city are the Chaldaeans, expanded in MT to include the king of Babylon (a linking theme with 20.4). The weapons used by the Judaeans will be turned against themselves by the deity and the enemy brought into the city. The key concept in holy war terminology is the idea of the deity fighting *for* the people against their enemies.

Here it is transformed so that Yahweh fights against the people in the form of the Chaldaeans. Since this is a holy war, the fate of the defeated is complete annihilation (the technical term *ḥerem* 'sacred ban' is not used here, but its effects are present, cf.Weippert 1971, 400). Hence man and beast die (v. 6; cf. Deut. 20.16–17; I Sam. 15.3). The context of such an oracle must be the period when the Chaldaeans were attacking Jerusalem and its function the disheartening of the Judaean opposition (cf. 38.4). If the proclamation of holy war gave heart to the fighters, this reversal of the motif would achieve the opposite.

The present redaction of the oracle has linked it with the delegation sent by Zedekiah to Jeremiah (37.3–5), but because it introduces a new block of material it becomes the divine word for a specific occasion. The formulaic introduction is awkwardly interrupted by the specification of that occasion (cf. the introductory summary in 37.1–2). Jeremiah is represented as the one to whom important officials have recourse during crises, and the piety of the delegation is apparent in v. 2b. The context of the delegation is better set out in 37.3–10, in that a good reason is provided for the inquiry. In 21.1–2 only the occasion of the delegation is specified, but the notice includes references to Zedekiah and to Nebuchadrezzar king of Babylon (not in 37.3–10 but in the introductory 37.1) which suggests that v. 7 also belongs to this redactional stage. The oracle is further introduced as Jeremiah's reply to the delegation *and* as being addressed to Zedekiah (vv. 3, 4a). These editorial moves transform the oracle from being a general statement addressed to the nation (or its fighting men in the first instance) to a message for the king. The oracle then requires supplementation in order to include the king in particular – hence v. 7. The logic of v. 6 is that everybody, man and beast, king and dog, dies. Holy war language does not usually distinguish between classes of people, because annihilation is the lot of everybody. Thus the editorial addition of v. 7 is awkward as well as unnecessary. The phrase 'afterward' (*wᵉ'aḥᵃrē-kēn*) is a linking of vv. 6, 7, but the totality of destruction in v. 6 renders v. 7 otiose.

In v. 7 the complete annihilation of everybody is again announced. This superfluous verse is clearly a variation of v. 6, but expressing in greater detail and by means of the favoured triads of the tradition (e.g. 'pestilence, sword, famine', 14.12; 'pity, spare, compassion', 13.14) the totality of death facing the community. It also brings together the two royal figures of vv. 1–2, Zedekiah and Nebuchadrezzar, and comments on those who have survived the skirmishes of v. 4 and the deprivations of the siege. The presence of Deuteronomistic language in the unit indicates one source of editorial activity (analysis in Thiel), but some of the peculiarities in the Deuteronomistic phraseology (see Notes on v. 5) point to a greater degree of freedom within such circles than is sometimes allowed for in exegetical analysis (a different explanation is offered in Weippert 1973). The fate of Zedekiah in v. 7 is very different from that envisaged in 34.4–5 or described in 39.4–7. The differences may be due to variations in editorial function and intention, but also indicate the great difficulty with which any unit of the text may be related to historical circumstances. As the cycle on the kings will reveal (cf. 22.19, 30), the fate of kings is a theme full of discrepancies, contradictions and problems for the exegete.

A quite different piece appears in vv. 8–10, where the oracular statement is addressed to the people rather than to the delegation or Zedekiah (in contrast to vv. 3, 4a). It is also very different from the variants of vv. 6, 7 which proclaim the complete annihilation of the people. Here the people are offered a choice between life and death. Their situation is that of the siege rather than its termination in vv. 6, 7. The synchronic, rather than diachronic, use of material in the tradition makes vv. 8–10 less disjunctive than they might at first sight appear to be. The editing of the whole piece allows vv. 4–6, 7 to be read as a statement to the king and his counsellors and vv. 8–10 as a contingent offer to the people. No choice is offered to the authorities because their fate is sealed, but the common people may yet escape the fate of the city. That is how vv. 4–10 may be read. The internal contradictions of vv. 6, 7, 9 remain unresolved, but because they are caused by the editing together of three discrete units they do not affect the material substance of each unit. The holy war warrant applies only to vv. 4–6, 7 and not to vv. 8–10: the possibility of escape makes the situation less harsh and the war against the city less total than that entailed by a holy war (cf. Deut.20.10–18).

The choice offered between life and death, the two ways of v. 8, may reflect the Deuteronomistic motif of two possibilities (cf. Deut. 30.15–20; Thiel, 235) or the more general two ways of life advocated by wisdom sources (e.g. Prov. 4.10–19; cf. McKane, 69; 1970, 306–10). Whatever the origins of the motif (Berridge 1970, 204–5, strongly denies any Deuteronomistic influence here), its function is clear in v. 9. The two ways are defined as 'stay in the city – die' and 'surrender to the enemy – live'. The same options appear in 38.2. That there were other options (e.g. stay in the city and live as Jeremiah and many others did, cf. 39.9–10; 40.1–6; 52.15) is an ironic comment on vv. 8–10, but hardly affects the exegesis of the text. The fate of the city is certain and those who remain in it stand a good chance of sharing that fate. Those who abandon the city and surrender to the Chaldaeans may win their lives as booty. There is irony here in the text itself. One consequence of war for the individual is the opportunity to gain booty; but those who flee Jerusalem (always referred to as 'this city' in vv. 4–10) may acquire booty – their own lives! Survival is victory. Whether surrender to the Chaldaeans would have contributed to or militated against survival is a moot point not touched on by the text. Such unrealism is a feature of the traditions about the Babylonians (see on 39–40), but here it is dictated by the motif of the two choices. That choice is defined in Deut. 30.15 as 'life and good, death and evil', and these terms are used in vv. 8, 10. The good is a negative one, i.e. saving one's own life, because Yahweh has determined to do evil to the city (cf. 44.11, where the metaphor 'set my face against' also appears) rather than good. If good is to be found in the situation it can only be found outside the city. Thus the way of life, the good, is to desert the city and surrender to the enemy. The alternative is the way of death, the evil, and it is chosen by doing nothing or defending the city (see on 38.1–6).

The three stages in the redaction provide a number of responses to the royal invitation to Jeremiah to seek Yahweh in the hope that he may act on the people's behalf and cause Nebuchadrezzar (MT) to withdraw. In all of the responses the city is doomed, as are the king and his officials. But one response allows the possibility that some of the people may save themselves.

21.11 – 23.6 The cycle of texts on the kings

'Go, mouse, go nibble at Lenin in his tomb' (Wallace Stevens)

A collection of independent pieces is gathered together under the general heading 'concerning the house of the king of Judah' (21.11, *l^ebēt melek y^ehûdāh*, cf. 23.9). The collection is made up of poems and prose pieces which concern the general behaviour of the royal house, make statements about individual kings and comment on an unnamed city. They have been collected together because they have certain thematic features in common and here they display some of the editorial aspects characteristic of the tradition itself. They are not a statement about the royal house which sets out the grandiose image it had of itself, nor does the ideology of kingship contribute much to the cycle. In striking contrast to some of the biblical images of the king as Yahweh's son or the glorious nature of royal rule over the earth (cf. Ps. 2, 45, 72, 110, 132; Isa. 9.2–7; 11.1–9) is the modesty with which the kings are treated in the cycle. That royal ideology which Judah shared with the Egyptian and Mesopotamian cultures is notably absent here (on royal ideology cf. Bernhardt 1961; Johnson 1967). The cumulative effect of the discrete pieces is a desacralizing and demystification of royalty, its status and its achievements. The sacred city, seat of the great kings, is also subjected to criticism. The twin beliefs about city and king epitomized by Lam. 4.12, 20 are conspicuously missing from the assessment offered in the collection.

21.11–12

11 'And to the house of the king of Judah say, "Hear the word of the LORD,
12 O house of David! Thus says the LORD:
' "Execute justice in the morning,
and deliver from the hand of the oppressor
him who has been robbed,
lest my wrath go forth like fire,
and burn with none to quench it,
because of your evil doings." '

---

[11] G lacks 'and', which in MT connects what follows with what precedes it and identifies Jeremiah as the speaker. The whole verse may well be redactional: title and instruction. The plural *šim^e'û*, 'hear', indicates that the royal officials, rather than the king, are addressed. **[12]** MT *labbōqer*, 'in the morning': BHS *labb^eqorīm*, 'every morning', cf. Ps. 73.14 (*m* lost by haplography); for MT cf. Amos 4.4. MT *miyyad 'ōšēq*, 'from the hand of the oppressor': as in 22.3; Vrs '. . . of him that wrongs him' = *'ōš^eqō*, also in 22.3. G lacks last phrase: an addition from 4.4 (Rudolph). K *m'llyhm*, 'their deeds'; Q *ma'allēkem*, 'your deeds'; v. 12b = 4.4b. Rudolph, 138, omits 'thus says Yahweh' as unmetrical: either it or 11b is a redundant phrase overstressing the oracular nature of what follows.

The cycle is introduced by some editorial notes which identify the recipients of the collection as the royal house of David and the contents as oracular statements. The royal officials (cf. 26.10–11) are regarded as the ones responsible for the maintenance of justice in the community and their failure to defend the oppressed is made the grounds for divine wrath breaking out against them (cf. Isa. 1.10, 17). They are therefore advised to administer justice (NEB) on a regular basis (i.e. daily), a justice which is defined specifically as the deliverance of the robbed from the oppressor. The reference to 'morning' may reflect an ancient practice of legal disputes being engaged in during the early part of the day (cf. II Sam. 15.1–6) when all those who were party to the dispute would meet to thrash out the matter. The precise role of the royal house in the administration of justice is a much disputed matter and, although there are associations of the king with justice in proclamations of the royal ideology (cf. Ps. 72.1–4, 12–14; Isa. 11.3–5), it is far from clear to what extent state law is represented in the Bible (discussion in Boecker 1980, 40–9). The injunction to the royal house here reflects a strand of royal ideology which attributes to the collective the oversight of justice in the community. This attribution allows the cycle to begin and end with the same theme: the royal maintenance of justice (cf. 23.5–6). Its theoretical and ideological nature may be clear, but it opens the cycle with a statement of principle which is then linked to the motif of fire. That motif (cf. 4.4b; 17.4b, 27b) is echoed elsewhere in the cycle (e.g. v. 14; 22.7) and identifies the royal house as the cause of divine wrath in the community. If justice is not maintained then fire will sweep the officials away and it will not be quenched.

It may be reading too much into v. 12b to hold the royal house responsible for the outbreak of divine wrath (fire) against city and community. The statement of principle in v. 12a need have no necessary connection with the additional warning in the second part of the verse. Furthermore the editorial titles of vv. 11–12a have implicated the representatives of the royal house in the admonitions about the maintenance of justice in the community. Originally an oracular statement warning the community to protect the oppressed from the oppressor (contrast 9.2–6) may have been placed here (or constructed for this purpose) and should be related to the strand addressing those referred to in vv. 13b, 14a (12b may be included here or excluded on the grounds that it belongs to 4.4b). Similar motifs are developed in 22.1–5 with reference to the royal house, including the king, so a number of arguments are available for the presence of v. 12a (minus the editorial address) as part of the preface to that unit. It may anticipate the longer, Deuteronomistic sermon (Volz treats 21.11–12; 22.1–5 together as one piece). It may generalize a principle, applicable to everybody in the community, from the specific instructions to the royal house. 21.11–14 may represent a number of motifs used loosely to provide an introduction anticipating the sermon and therefore be part of a redactional development combining elements of executing justice, community behaviour and statements, and an address to an unnamed city. These elements are given firmer identity in the cycle when individual kings are specified as the subject of particular poems. This process of identification would account for 21.11, 12aα.

21.13–14

13 'Behold, I am against you, O inhabitant of the valley,
O rock of the plain,
says the LORD;
You who say, "Who shall come down against us,
or who shall enter our habitations?"
14 I will punish you according to the fruit of your doings,
says the LORD;
I will kindle a fire in her forest,
and it shall devour all that is round about her.'

---

[13] MT *yōšebet hā'ēmeq*, 'inhabitant of the valley': BHS suggests *hā'ōpel*, 'hill, Ophel', cf. Micah 4.8; Isa. 32.14 for 'valley'. Weiser, 182, understands the phrase as 'enthroned over the valley', i.e. the one overlooking the valley or plain; NEB 'who lie in the valley'. MT *ṣūr*, 'rock': G *Sor*, 'Tyre'. BHS reads *hammiśgāb*, 'height', for MT *hammīšōr*, 'plain', but *mīšōr* may refer to 'table land, plateau' (cf. Bright, 141). Volz, 217, reads *yōšebet ṣūr hā'ēmeq*, 'those dwellers of the rocks of the valley', i.e. 'the rocks over the valley', treating *'ēmeq* and *mīšōr* as variants. MT *yēḥat*, 'come down': *nḥt*, cf. Aramaic *neḥat*; G *ptoēsei*, 'alarm, frighten', understanding *yḥt* as from *ḥtt* 'be shattered, dismayed'. MT need not imply a descent from a height but can denote a penetration (of defences). **[14]** G lacks 14a: for MT cf. 23.2b. Changes of person and number in 13–14 indicate editorial combination of two distinctive pieces (sing. fem. = a city; plur. 'us', 'you' inhabitants), though some exegetes (e.g. McKane 1982, 70) allow the limits of poetic licence to tolerate the mixture as a reference to a city and its inhabitants. MT *bᵉya'rāh*, 'in her forest', cf. 22.6–7: Volz *bō'ᵃrāh*, 'blazing (fire)', cf. BHS. MT *wᵉ'ākᵉlāh kol-sᵉbîbêhā*, 'and it will devour all that is round her': BHS reads *subbᵉkāh* (with Cornill, 247), 'her thicket', from *smilaka*, 'yew-tree', G 46.14. This image balances 'forest' (cf. the similar images in Isa. 10.16–19).

An independent fragment addresses a stately inhabitant who dominates the plains, reigning over them in her regal splendour (cf. Weiser's reading of v. 13). Elements in the fragment are to be found in the oracles against Moab (cf. 48.8b, 21a, 28–29), and these suggest that a conventional denunciation of a foreign city-state has been used here to attack a proud and secure city. Unnamed it may be (a feature of the cycle is the way the poems seldom identify the object of attack), but in the fully edited collection of poetry and prose Jerusalem must be assumed to be the city singled out for divine opposition. This would make v. 13a an oblique parallel to v. 10. The influence of the conventional attack on foreign places may be detected in the cycle in the way it interpolates fragments and poems denouncing lofty places as expressions of hostility against an unnamed city (e.g. 21.13; 22.6–7, 23). Yet the name Jerusalem only appears once in the cycle and prefaces of 21.1 – 23.6 (i.e. 22.19).

The arrogance of the lofty dweller will be destroyed by fire (v. 14b), a motif this fragment shares with v. 12b and 22.7. The proud city (the feminine forms of address identify the object as a city) will be swept away by a fire which will engulf it. The reference to a fire devouring its forest and its surroundings may be a description of the conflagration destroying the city and its surrounding territory (e.g. woods and forests). It may, however, be an allusion to the firing of the city's wooden palaces and houses. According to I Kings 7.2 king Solomon built 'the house of the forest of Lebanon' using wood from the great cedars of Lebanon (cf. I Kings 5.6, 8–10). Such buildings may be the object of the burning which devastates the city and would justify the references to Lebanon in 22.6–7, 23 as an allusion to the city of Jerusalem. The allusive method of referring gives the poems a tension and a skill which the direct naming of the ill-fated city would lack.

The proud speakers referred to in v. 13b may be the inhabitants of the city or part of an independent strand interwoven here with the poetry strand (cf. Bright, 140; Thiel 1973, 238). However discrete the origins of the two strands (singular and plural) may have been, they complement each other in their combined form. The inhabitants of the proud city are arrogant and hubristic: they boast of their impregnable situation (v. 13b, cf. Lam. 4.12). They are beyond the reach of military penetration. But their nemesis is to hand because the deity is against them – he will fire the city. The gloss in v. 14a (absent in G) alludes to the punishment of these arrogant people but does not define the deeds which warrant the judgment (cf. the gloss in v. 12c). The combined strands allow for a statement to be made against city and inhabitants and provide a suitable parallel to the developed attack on city and citizens in vv. 4–10.

22.1–5

22 1 Thus says the LORD: 'Go down to the house of the king of Judah, and
speak there this word, 2 and say, "Hear the word of the LORD, O King of
Judah, who sit on the throne of David, you, and your servants, and your
people who enter these gates. 3 Thus says the LORD: Do justice and
righteousness, and deliver from the hand of the oppressor him who has been
robbed. And do no wrong or violence to the alien, the fatherless, and the
widow, nor shed innocent blood in this place. 4 For if you will indeed obey
this word, then there shall enter the gates of this house kings who sit on the
throne of David, riding in chariots and on horses, they, and their servants,
and their people. 5 But if you will not heed these words, I swear by myself,
says the LORD, that this house shall become a desolation." '

---

[1] MT *rēd*, 'go down': i.e. from the temple to the royal palace; cf. 26.10 *wayyaʿᵃlū*, 'and they went up', i.e. from the palace to the temple. **[2]** MT *šᵉmaʿ*, 'hear': the imperative sing. in an address to groups is odd in view of the plur. address *šimᵉʿū* in 21.11; but presumably concentrates on the king rather than his officials. MT *waʿᵃbādēkā*, 'and your servants': G *kai ho oikos sou*, 'and your house' = *ūbētᵉkā*. **[3]** MT *miyyad ʿāšōq*, 'from the hand of the oppressor': cf. Notes on 21.12. Vrs have 'and' before 'fatherless', 'do no violence'. **[4]** MT *hūʾ waʿᵃbādāw wᵉʿammō*, 'he, and his servants (Q), and his people': BHS treats as an addition, cf. v. 2b. K *wʿbdw*, 'and his servant'; Q *waʿᵃbādāw*, 'and his servants'. G *autoi*, 'they', for *hūʾ* = *hēmmāh*; *hoi paides autōn*, 'their servants' = *ʿabᵉdēhem*; *ho laos autōn*, 'their people' = *ʿammām*.

EVV follow G. **[5]** MT *tišᵉmᵉʿu*, 'hear, heed': G *poiēsēte*, 'do, perform' = *taʿᵃśu*.

The admonition of 21.12a is more fully developed in the sermon of 22.1–5. As a prose statement the sermon may well be based on an original poetic fragment preserved in 21.12 but here expanded in terms similar to other sermons in the tradition (e.g. 7.1–15; 17.19–27). It belongs to the redactional strand which presents the speaker as moving about the city (temple, palace, city gates) at the divine command and is identified with the Deuteronomistic editing of the text (e.g. Thiel) or source C (e.g. Rudolph). As in the sermons in the temple (7.3–7) and in the city gate (17.24–26), it is a proclamation of possibilities for the future. If those addressed will respond positively to the warnings given, then the future will be a secure one (contrast the sermons in 11.1–13; 19.3–9, where the possibility of change or positive action is not mooted). The maintenance of social justice is the condition upon which the future depends in vv. 1–5 (similar to 7.3–7; cf. 17.21–22, 24–26, where sabbath observances are the key to the future). Here it is spelled out more fully than in 21.12a (it differs from 7.3–7 only in that it says nothing about the pursuit of other gods). The essence of social justice here is the defence of the oppressed strata of society: the robbed, the resident alien, the orphan and the widow. It also includes the preservation of innocent lives. These general and rather conventional specifications (conventional in that they are to be found throughout biblical literature e.g. Ex. 22.21–24; Isa. 1.17; Job 31.16–23) constitute the meaning of 'do justice and righteousness' (v. 3 *ʿᵃśū mišpāṭ uṣᵉdāqāh*) and represent the maintenance of social well-being throughout the community.

The sermon is represented as being preached in the royal palace (to which the speaker has gone from his regular place in the temple, cf. 19.1, 14) and addressed to the king, his retinue and his people. Such is the redactional presentation of it, which qualifies it for inclusion in the cycle about kings and kingship. Because the sermon is rhetorical and Deuteronomistic in style (cf. Thiel 1973, 239; Nicholson 1970, 87) it is imprecise in its statements. The 'gates' motif appears in vv. 2, 4 (cf. 7.2; 17.19, 20, 21, 24, 25, 27) and the 'house, palace, temple' motif in vv. 1, 5 (*bayit* may refer to all three). It is therefore not clear whether the future which is contingent on the behaviour of king *and* people (v. 2 'you and your . . .') concerns the city, the palace and/or the temple. This lack of clarity is confirmed by v. 4 where the reward for the practice of justice is the same as that proclaimed for keeping the sabbath holy (17.25). The punishment is also similar in that the palace will become a desolation (v. 5) if justice is not maintained, and if the sabbath is not kept, the palaces (*'armᵉnōt* rather than *bayit*) of Jerusalem will be set on fire. The imprecision of the sermon is also evident in that it is addressed to the king as an individual (*šᵉma'*, 'hear'), but it is the community who must practice (*'ᵃśū*, 'do') justice. The plurality of address and generality of stipulations make the admonitions similar to 21.12a and suggest that their association with the royal house belongs to the editing of the cycle rather than to any original connection. 22.1–5 fits here as a development of 21.11–12, yet has links with 21.13 (in its present position) because of the similar images of descent (upon the city in 21.13; from temple to palace in 22.1).

22.6–7

6 'For thus says the LORD concerning the house of the king of Judah:
"You are as Gilead to me,
as the summit of Lebanon,
yet surely I will make you a desert,
an uninhabited city.
7 I will prepare destroyers against you,
each with his weapons;
and they shall cut down your choicest cedars,
and cast them into the fire." '

---

[6] MT *gilᵉ'ād 'attāh lī*, 'Gilead you are to me': EVV provide an element of comparison, cf. NEB 'Though you are dear to me as Gilead'; originally an oracle against Gilead reapplied here to Jerusalem? MT *'im-lō'*, 'yet surely': a formal element from an oath, cf. NEB 'I swear that . . .'. Cf v. 5, where *'im lō'* is followed by *nišba'tī*, 'I swear'. K *nwšbh*, '(not) inhabited (city)'; Q *nōšābū*, '(un)inhabited (cities)': K fits the sense of the verse better (Jerusalem will become a desert, an uninhabited city), but Q is grammatically correct for *'ārīm*, 'cities'; cf. MT 2.15. NEB 'a land of unpeopled cities'; Bright 'an abandoned town' = 'like a desert, the towns (of which) are abandoned'. **[7]** MT *wᵉqiddaštī*, 'and I will prepare': for this use of *qdš* see 6.4 (cf. 1.5), where it may have holy war connotations, i.e. ritually prepare for battle (cf. Bright, 141). MT *wᵉkēlāyw*, 'and his weapons': G *kai ton pelekun autou*, 'and his axe', i.e. a single weapon.

A brief poem using imagery similar to 21.14b curses foreign territory (Gilead – Lebanon) and threatens it with complete destruction. The fertile land of trees and forests will be turned into a desert (*midbār*, cf. *ḥorbāh*, 'a ruin', v. 5). This image of transformation is sustained in v. 7 by the figures of the ritually prepared raiders, each armed with a weapon (G more specific than MT), who advance on the forest and chop down the choicest cedars. The consignment of the trees to the fire completes the devastation of the territory. The destroyers (*mašḥitīm* cf. 6.28) may be demonic figures (cf. Ex. 12.23; II Sam. 24.16; Ezek. 9; 'the Angel of Death', Rudolph, 138) who move against the territory as an uncanny force which cannot be resisted. This interpretation of the hostile forces would fit the allusion to the holy war idea in the phrase 'I will prepare' (*qdš*), where a sacred act is involved in the preparation of the destroyers (cf. Weiser, 186). Something uncanny, irresistible is being released by the deity against the splendid territory and nothing will be able to prevent its destruction (cf. 8.17; Lindström 1983, 62 argues against the demonic interpretation of *mašḥitīm*).

The original poem may have been a curse (a divine oath) hurled against Gilead or Lebanon, but in its present context it is intended to refer to Jerusalem. The introductory editorial phrase in v. 6a relates it to the Judaean king's palace (linking it with the material introduced by v. 1 and concluded by the oath in v. 5), but it is more suited to a threat against a city – hence the phrase 'cities lacking an inhabitant'. The appropriateness of the terms 'Gilead' and 'Lebanon' as applied to Jerusalem must be seen in terms of the provision of wood from those territories for the building of palaces and houses in Jerusalem (cf. I Kings 5.1–10; Isa. 22.8). Just as trees are cut down in those areas for building purposes so will invaders cut down and fire the buildings of Jerusalem (for the image of the Babylonians, or some such invasive force, as woodchoppers cf. Ps. 74.4–7). Both activities reduce territories to wasteland. A different interpretation (cf. EVV) reads the poem as a statement about how even Jerusalem's favoured status will not protect it from destruction: even if it were Gilead or Lebanon (territories famous for forests and vegetation cf 8.22; Ps. 29.5–8) it would not be spared. The oath form gives the poem greater force – the threat against the city is as absolute as possible, Yahweh has sworn it (the conditionality of vv. 4–5 is gone), and its inevitability is certain (cf. 21.10, 13).

The fall of Jerusalem transformed holy war ideas and the thrust of the oracles against the nations. The enemy against which Yahweh acted was no longer the foreign nations but Judah and, in particular, the city of Jerusalem. The denunciation of the enemy by mantic voices hurling curses at the foe in the context of a holy war setting is directed against the capital of Judah. The old attitudes towards the nations have come home to roost and the manipulation of powers against them in the name of Yahweh have been rendered ineffective. In the catastrophe of 587 all values were transvalued and all cherished beliefs devastated. Not the least of the victims of this period were the royal house, family and palaces.

22.8–9

8 ' "And many nations will pass by this city, and every man will say to his neighbour, 'Why has the LORD dealt thus with this great city?' 9 And they will answer, 'Because they forsook the covenant of the LORD their God, and worshipped other gods and served them.' " '

---

[8] MT *gōyim rabbīm*, 'many nations': Volz and Rudolph prefer to translate *gōyim* as 'people' rather than 'nations'; cf. NEB 'Men of many nations'. The use of the word *gōyim* to describe the heathen is a sign of the lateness of the piece (Rudolph). Cf. Deut. 29.22, 24 (MT 21, 23) for similar images of the visiting foreigner (*nokrī*) and nations (*gōyim*).

A short prose commentary appears after the brief poem of vv. 6–7 and interprets the poem in relation to the city rather than to the royal house. This seems to be a more acute observation about the poem than the editorial introduction to it in v. 6a. The motif 'fire' is used in 21.14b; 22.7 to describe the fate of the unnamed city (cf. 21.12b, where 'fire' is just a general figure for divine wrath), a very apt image of the destruction of a city and its great wooden houses, and comment such as v. 8 is more appropriate to a city's fate than to that of just one building. The burning of the city would include the firing of its palaces and temple, but passers-by would be more likely to remark upon the burnt-out state of the city than to single out one of its buildings.

The question-and-answer style of the piece, providing a justification for what has happened, links it to other uses of the style in the tradition (e.g. 5.19; 9.12–14; 16.10–13; cf. Deut. 29.24–28; I Kings

9.8–9). This particular form of the question is used by foreigners rather than the people of Yahweh and therefore has more in common with Deut. 29.22, 24 (cf. 'everyone passing by it [the temple]', I Kings 9.8). It is a catechetical method of teaching from a later period (so Volz, 219n.) using a Deuteronomistic style of formulation (cf. Thiel 1973, 240), designed to account for the disaster which befell city and land in 587. In its dramatic presentation of people (foreign or homeland) asking themselves questions and providing the answers it uses what may have been a conventional mode of expressing propaganda. Thus in the annals of Ashurbanipal (668–633) a similar statement appears in the record of the campaign against the Arabs:

> Whenever the inhabitants of Arabia asked each other: 'On account of what have these calamities befallen Arabia?' (they answered themselves:) 'Because we did not keep the solemn oaths (sworn by) Ashur, because we offended the friendliness of Ashurbanipal, the king, beloved by Ellil!' (Pritchard 1969, 300).

The familiarity of the speakers with Deuteronomistic covenantal terminology should not be read as evidence that foreigners were well versed in such theology, but is to be understood as a conventional form of expression. It allows the editors to relate a specific disaster in terms which validate their own ideology (cf. Nebuzaradan's impeccably correct theological assessment of the fall of Jerusalem in 40.1–3).

The destruction of the great city demonstrates the truth of the explanation offered by the foreign peoples as they pass by its ruins. The broken city is evidence of the abandoned covenant – abandoned in terms of the worship of other gods. This reference to idolatry is the only occurrence of such an explanation in the whole cycle and, though it is indicative of the Deuteronomistic obsession with false forms of worship, hardly fits the tenor of the collected pieces. In so far as the cycle has an underlying theme it is focused on the practice and maintenance of justice (21.12a; 22.3, 13–17; 23.5) rather than modes of worship. However, the Deuteronomistic motif of the covenant, especially in its abandoned form (cf. Deut. 29.25–26), belongs to the conventional mode employed here. The Assyrian annal makes the Arabs confess that the reason their land lies in ruins is that they have broken a treaty with the Assyrian king. The Deuteronomistic use of the convention may not fit the cycle, but it certainly suits its theology of the covenant and reflects the way that particular circle responded to the fall of Jerusalem. The disaster of 587 helped significantly to underwrite the Deuteronomistic ideology which presented the land as the people's holding under the terms of an agreement (*bᵉrīt* conventionally translated as 'covenant') between nation and deity. Proof of such an arrangement, even if only in negative terms, is the ruined city and the response of foreigners to it.

22.10

10 Weep not for him who is dead,
    nor bemoan him;
but weep bitterly for him who goes away,
    for he shall return no more
    to see his native land.

---

[10] MT *lᵉmēt*, 'for the one who is dead': G *ton tethnēkota*, 'the dead' = *lammēt*. MT *kī lō' yāšūb 'ōd wᵉrā'āh*, 'for he shall not return again and see': Rudolph, 140, treats the two verbs as one 'for he shall not see again', cf. the use of *šūb*, 'to do something again' (with another verb) in 12.15; 18.4.

A very brief poem laments the departure of an unnamed person who is leaving his native land never to return to it again. His fate is such that it warrants bitter weeping and makes the dead one's fate pale into insignificance. The force of the poem is 'never mind the dead, mourn for the living because he will never return to his own land'. At least the dead one will have (or have had) a burial in his own land, in the family grave. The participial phrases, 'he who is dead' (*mēt*), 'he who goes away' (*hōlēk*), distinguish in terms of state or activity rather than identity (cf. the participles in 21.9; 22.13–14). The anonymity of the figures spoken of may be conventional (cf. vv. 13–14), but if spoken on a specific public occasion the immediacy of the utterance within that social context may have identified the subjects instantly.

22.11–12

11 For thus says the LORD concerning Shallum the son of Josiah, king of Judah, who reigned instead of Josiah his father, and who went away from this place: 'He shall return here no more, 12 but in the place where they

have carried him captive, there shall he die, and he shall never see this land again.'

---

[11] G^L *Iōachaz* for MT Shallum (G *Sellēm*). G lacks 'king of Judah'. **[12]** MT *kī bimᵉqōm ᵓᵃšer-higᵉlū*, 'for in a place where they took (him) into exile': G *ou metōkisa auton*, '(but in that place) where I took him into exile'.

A prose commentary on, or attached to, the poem explains its meaning. The explanation identifies the one who is dead as king Josiah and the one who goes away as his son and successor Shallum. Shallum, the fourth son of Josiah (I Chron. 3.15), whose throne name was Jehoahaz, succeeded his father on the throne at the instigation of the people of the land (*'am-hā'āreṣ*, II Kings 23.30; note the reference to the dead Josiah as *mēt* there). Josiah had been killed at Megiddo opposing the Egyptian forces of Pharaoh Neco, so the installation of his youngest son as king by the common people may have represented an anti-Egyptian gesture. After three months as king he was removed from the throne by Neco and put in bonds at Riblah (II Kings 23.31–3; cf. the fate of king Zedekiah's sons at the hands of the Babylonians at Riblah in Jer. 39.6). From there he was taken to Egypt and died there (II Kings 23.34b). In his place the Egyptians made his older brother Eliakim king and he proved more amenable to Egyptian control (II Kings 23.34a, 35). Eliakim's name was changed to the throne name Jehoiakim (note the Yahwistic piety of the Egyptians!), making him one of the kings in whose reign the tradition represents Jeremiah as having been active (1.3). Thus there were two kings of Judah alive at the same time (*c.* 609): one chosen by the people and in exile and the other chosen by the Egyptians and on the throne in Jerusalem. The extent to which this arrangement created divided loyalties in the community is not reflected in the relevant texts, but partisan conflict must have been one element in the political life of the period.

The prose explanation repeats the message of the poem, adding the point that Shallum would die in Egypt. Its force here may include the writing off of any hopes cherished that the king in exile might one day return and lead the anti-Egyptian elements in the land (cf. the similar dashing of hopes for Jehoiachin in vv. 24–30). Those people who remained loyal to the king in exile and who waited expectantly for a change in his status (cf. 52.31–4) are here doomed to bitter disappointment. Hence the point of the poem's 'weep not for the dead but for *him* who goes into exile . . .'. There will be no return for Shallum and therefore political expectations must not be bound up with his fate. With his exile his role in Judaean politics comes to an end.

The naming of Shallum in v. 11 marks a turning in the cycle from general, anonymous statements to a series of poems and comments associated with individual Judaean kings (vv. 11–30). Some of these identifications are editorial rather than integral to the poems with which they are linked (e.g. vv. 11, 18). That this is the case may be seen in vv. 10–12. The contrast between the dead one and the exiled one hardly reflects the respective fates of Josiah and Shallum: it was some three months before Shallum's deportation took place and the dead king's obsequies would have been completed by then. It is more likely that the poem is a contrast between two people, one of whom has been killed but the other deported. The point of the poem is then to drive home to the mourners that the fate of the exiled one is even worse than that of the dead. The dead one will be gathered to his fathers in accordance with the funeral rites of the community, but the deported one will languish in exile, die there and be buried without interment in the family tomb. He is therefore a much more fitting subject for bitter lamentation.

The editors have supplied a commentary on a brief, obscure poem which reflects their knowledge of II Kings 23.30–4. The need to explain it indicates their distance from its original setting (when it would have needed no such explanation) and the lack of fit demonstrates that matching poetry and prose did not require precision or exactitude. Given this framework of explanation the poem in v. 10 will be read with the meaning provided by vv. 11–12. But the writing down of the poem requires some such interpretation to accompany it because the context of the cycle is insufficient to make its meaning clear. Anonymity cloaks the whole cycle (with the notable exception of the material on Coniah in 22.24–30 and the editorial notes in 22.11, 18a): neither speaker nor spoken to is identified; not even those spoken of in v. 10 are named. If the poems were delivered on specific occasions the public forum would have provided their meaning, but removed from their original social context such utterances, given their oblique form in this cycle, lack specificity. This feature of the cycle provides a good example of the shift from oral to written communication and the concomitant need to provide additional written information to do what the original utterance did more efficiently within an oral culture (cf. Ong 1982 on such shifts). The prose explanation of v. 11 turns the short poem into an oracular statement by spelling out its meaning as a divine word. In the harnessing of anonymous poems to an oracular framework with the provision of specific information narrowing down the poetry's range of reference we may catch a glimpse of how a good deal of the Jeremiah tradition came into being and was developed along certain lines until it reached its canonical form.

22.13–17

13 'Woe to him who builds his house by unrighteousness,
and his upper rooms by injustice;
who makes his neighbour serve him for nothing,
and does not give him his wages;
14 who says, "I will build myself a great house
with spacious upper rooms,"
and cuts out windows for it,
panelling it with cedar,
and painting it with vermilion.
15 Do you think you are a king
because you compete in cedar?
Did not your father eat and drink
and do justice and righteousness?
Then it was well with him.
16 He judged the cause of the poor and needy;
then it was well.
Is not this to know me?
says the LORD.
17 But you have eyes and heart
only for your dishonest gain,
for shedding innocent blood,
and for practising oppression and violence.'

---

[13] MT *hōy*, 'woe': this is the only example of a woe oracle in the Jeremiah tradition, i.e. *hōy* as preparatory to a declaration of judgment and condemnation (much more typical of the Isaiah tradition, cf. Isa. 1.4; 5.8, 11, 18, 20, 21, 22; 10.1); cf. *'ōy*, 13.27. For other uses of *hōy* in Jeremiah cf. 23.1; 30.7; 47.6; as part of a funeral oration cf. 22.18; 34.5. On the prophetic woe oracle cf. Gerstenberger 1962; Janzen 1972; Westermann 1967, 190–2. **[14]** MT *hā'ōmēr 'ebᵉneh-lī*, 'who says, "I will build myself . . ." ': G *ōkodomēsas seautō*, 'you have built for yourself . . .'. MT *mᵉruwwāḥīm* 'spacious': the masc. plur. participal (Pual form) is odd with two fem. nouns (*middōt*, 'sizes', i.e. 'great'; *ʿaliyyōt*, 'roof-chambers, upper rooms') and a masc. noun (*bēt*, 'house'). Rudolph, 142, follows Cornill, 252, and revocalizes it as an active verbal form *merʿwāḥīm* (not an attested form), 'widen, make spacious', cf. BHS. MT *ḥallōnāy*, 'my windows': delete *y*, 'window', cf. BHS; or read *ḥallōnāw*, 'its windows'. MT *wᵉsāpūn*, 'and panelled': read active form *sāpōn*, 'panelling', cf. *ūmāšōaḥ*, 'and painting'; for *šāšar* 'vermilion' cf. Ezek. 23.14; Zimmerli 1979, 486f. **[15]** MT *hᵃtimᵉlōk*, 'do you reign?': Duhm, 175 reads as *hᵃtitᵉmallēk*, 'are you a king?', or, 'do you act as a king?' (Hithpael forms can have the force of play-acting cf. 29.24) with loss of *t* due to haplography, followed by Rudolph, cf. BHS. MT *mᵉtaḥᵃreh bā'ārez*, '. . . compete in cedar': cf. *tᵉtaḥᵃreh* in 12.5 for the sense of 'competing'; *ḥārāh*, 'burn, be angry', Hithpael 'heat oneself, hotly contend'. G *paroxunē en Achaz tō patri sou*, '(that you) are provoked with your father Achaz'; G^A has the proper name Achaab: a slightly different division of the line from MT. MT *'āz ṭōb lō*, 'then it was well with him': out of place here; G has it after 'drink' and relates it to doing justice. G vv. 15b, 16a are quite different: 'it is better for you to do judgment and righteousness; they do not know, they do not judge the case of the afflicted or the case of the poor; is not this that you do not know me?'. **[16]** MT *'āz ṭōb*, 'then it was well': an addition from v. 15? Cf. BHS. MT *hᵃlō-hī' hadda'at 'ōtī*, 'is not that *the* knowledge of me?': i.e. the real or true knowledge of Yahweh (so Rudolph), cf. 9.24. **[17]** MT *dam-hannoqī* 'blood of the innocent': the usual form of this phrase lacks the definite article (7.6; 22.3; cf. 2.34). MT *hammᵉrūṣāh*, 'violence, crushing': not from *rūṣ*, 'run', i.e. 'course' (cf. 8.6; 23.10), but *rṣṣ*, 'crush'; cf. G *phonon*, 'murder, slaughter, bloodshed'.

The woe saying is a feature of some prophetic traditions (e.g. Isa. 5.8–23; Amos 6.1–3, 4–6), but not of the book of Jeremiah. Woe sayings denounce practices which are unjust and disrupt the social order of the community. They are formal denunciations of anonymous groups introduced by the word 'Woe . . .' (*hōy*), and have their origins in the wise men's reflections about the conditions of the world (so Gerstenberger 1962, 256, 261; but cf. Janzen 1972). To denounce groups in this manner is to call down bad luck on them: 'bad luck (to those who practise) . . .' and is parallel to the curse (i.e. 'cursed is . . .'). The contents of a particular woe saying are determined by the practice being denounced (e.g. drunkenness, land-grabbing), and as it applies to a group practising such disruptive behaviour, those addressed are anonymous. The only woe saying in the Jeremiah tradition which belongs to this formal category occurs in vv. 13–15a (see on 23.1).

In vv. 13–15a the social practice condemned is the building of large houses using unpaid labour. The builder is not named, but the building of such houses without right or justice (*bᵉlōʾ mišpāṭ*, cf. the proverb in 17.11) is disruptive of social order. It creates conflict within the community because it exploits the labour of the builder's neighbours. For that reason it warrants the denunciation of a woe saying. The singular ('who builds . . . who says') is unusual in a form that normally employs the plural, but it may represent a variation (cf. *hōy bōneh*, 'woe to him who builds . . .', Hab. 2.12) or be used as a collective. Its placing here may reflect the participial forms of v. 10. The indictment of the unjust practice is developed in v. 14 by extending the description of the building project. It is a large, spacious house with upper rooms and a window, and well decorated with cedar panelling and vermilion paintings (cf. Ezek. 23.14 for vermilion decorations). It is a very fine building, but because it is built without right the builder must be denounced. The poem closes with a satirical question: 'Do you think you are a king that you compete in cedar?' The force of the question could be: 'Are you playing at being a king that you compete in cedar?' Cedar is the trademark of royal builders, so for such a builder to build a spacious house panelled in cedar at his neighbours' expense is for him to behave like a king. Kings may build on such a scale, but within the community grandiloquent building enterprises are to be condemned.

The rhetorical question which concludes the woe saying may have misled the editors into thinking that it referred to a king and was about royal building projects. Thus it is understood by v. 18a and many modern exegetes. That reading of it is facilitated by its presence within the royal cycle, but its original meaning may not have had a king in mind at all (kings are not usually the recipients of woe sayings). Woe sayings attack social groups which are seen as violating the rights of others in the community and disrupting the wellbeing of the whole people. If the question in v. 15a is treated as the beginning of a new statement (confining the woe saying to vv. 13–14), it could be read as an indictment of a king attached to the independent woe saying. This would spoil a very good closure to the woe saying, but the common motif 'cedar' might explain why the two pieces are attached together. In a context shaped by vv. 10–12, i.e. royal father and son, it is understandable that the editors should treat the two poems as having a similar point to make and read them as statements about the behaviour of Jehoiakim (the builder) and Josiah (his father). It is not the original meaning of either v. 10 or vv. 13–15a but a secondary, or applied, meaning created by the editing of the different texts and their insertion into the cycle about individual kings.

The poem added to the woe saying offers a contrast between father and son (cf. vv. 11–12). The transition from the one to the other is reflected in the distinctive MT and G readings and the awkwardness of the Hebrew in vv. 15b–16. The sense of the statements is that the father of the addressee enjoyed a balanced life of aesthetic pleasure and the practice of justice, whereas his son has behaved in a vicious manner and devoted himself to violent gain. The stark contrast between the two belongs to the hyperbole of rhetoric. The description of the father as a practitioner of justice and righteousness (contrast the claim in 5.1) and therefore as one who knew Yahweh (v. 16 is oracular in its present form) furnishes a further link in the royal identification of the persons described. For the editing of the cycle has combined the command to practise justice with reference to the royal house (21.12; 22.2–3), and so it is part of the logic of the additional material that vv. 15–16 should lead on to the interpretation of v. 18a. The formal contrast to the maintenance of the right of the poor is the practice of oppression. Here the son is accused of most vicious deeds which include the shedding of innocent blood (i.e. a violation of the ruling in v. 3). This is a far cry from the woe saying, which attacks a building project but on the grounds of exploitation rather than bloodshed. The motif of building with blood, i.e. through bloodshed, reflects a practice condemned in Micah 3.10; Hab. 2.12 (note woe saying here), but it is not used in vv. 13–15a. It may have influenced the editors who added vv. 15b–17 to the woe saying and thereby constructed a kerygmatic unit of vv. 13–19 (cf. Gerstenberger 1962, 253, on the way new elements develop a woe saying in this direction).

The accusation in v. 17 reflects II Kings 24.4, where Jehoiakim is condemned for filling Jerusalem with innocent blood (a secondary expansion of the text under the influence of II Kings 21.16) and is therefore a Deuteronomistic element here (cf. Seeligmann 1977, 282). The Deuteronomistic editing of Kings put a great deal of the blame for the exile on Manasseh (an echo of which is to be found in Jer. 15.4) and in II Kings 24.1–6 this level of redaction has linked Jehoiakim and Manasseh, giving the impression that both filled the city of Jerusalem with innocent blood (on this redactional stage cf. Weippert

1972, 333–4). Other Deuteronomistic elements in v. 17 include 'oppression and violence' (*'šq*, *rṣṣ*, cf. Deut. 28.33; I Sam. 12.3; Thiel 1973, 241–2). The contrast between the approved behaviour of the father and the appalling viciousness of the son is so far removed from the form and tenor of the preceding woe saying that vv. 15b–17 must be considered a quite different piece (cf. Wessels 1984, 63–7, 73–6). If it were not for the presence of Deuteronomistic elements in vv. 15b–17 and the editorial interpretation of v. 18a which confirms the concealed identities of the persons alluded to by them, it might be possible to argue for a conventional force to the meaning of the contrast. As a convention the contrast would simply compare father and son to the detriment of the son. In effect it would say: 'Your father was a very fine person who lived well and protected the poor; you are rubbish!' The protection of the poor motif indicates that those addressed have power in the community and belong to the ruling classes (cf. the discussion about the relative policies of father and son in I Kings 12.1–15). The piece would then be a formal way of comparing the relative merits of a family's execution of its duties in the community. However, the secondary nature of much of the piece suggests that it is a more specific condemnation of an individual than a conventional assessment of two generations.

22.18–19

18 Therefore thus says the LORD concerning Jehoiakim the son of Josiah, king of Judah:
'They shall not lament for him, saying,
"Ah my brother!" or "Ah sister!"
They shall not lament for him, saying,
"Ah lord!" or "Ah his majesty!"
19 With the burial of an ass he shall be buried,
dragged and cast forth beyond the gates of Jerusalem.'

---

[18] G prefaces the non-lament with the phrase *Ouai epi ton andra touton*, 'Woe to this man' = *hōy 'al-hā'îš hazzeh*: thus combining the two distinctive uses of *hōy*, i.e. funereal and critical (cf. Janzen 1972, 71–3). G lacks the second element in both the lament pairs (i.e. 'sister', 'majesty'). RSV 'saying' supplies a term not in MT, as does NEB; it is not necessary to supply it, cf. JPSB. The fourfold lamentation (twofold in G) may be a standard form of lamentation (so Gaster 1969, 604), but other examples are briefer cf 34.5; I Kings 13.30; so G may represent the more original form of the text. The difficult *hōdōh*, 'majesty' (normal form *hōd*), is changed to *hōrāh*, 'mother', by Dahood 1961, 462–4, who translates *'ādōn*, 'lord', as 'father', thereby representing the king as father, mother, brother, sister to his people. MT *'aḥī*, 'my brother': G *adelphe*, 'brother'; MT reflects the mourning formula of a sister who was the chief mourner for her dead brother (cf. Jahnow 1923, 63–5), whereas G standardizes the form (Janzen 1972, 71 n. 109). BHS suggests *dōd* for *hōdōh*, i.e. a reference to Adonis (Tammuz), 'beloved one'; cf. Rudolph, 142, who questions Dahood's treatment of the text.

The final link in the chain of vv. 13–19 is a brief funeral-type ode and an editorial note identifying the person spoken of in the various pieces. Such stitching together of independent pieces with editorial notes makes vv. 13–19 parallel vv. 10–12. In v. 10 a death notice shades into a lapidary lament for one who must suffer burial in an alien land. The redactional gloss on this makes it a contrast between father and son, in particular the fate of their respective corpses. The next set of units develops in a parallel way, though vv. 13–15a are quite different from anything in vv. 10–12, 15b–19. However, there is one element in vv. 13–15a which allows the general direction of the editing to justify itself. The woe saying (*hōy*) of v. 13 has links with the funeral woes of v. 18 (better linking between vv. 13, 18 is provided by G): both as shared linguistic elements and as an echo of ancient funerary rites.

The woe saying denouncing disruptive social practices is but one category of woes in the biblical traditions. It may have its roots in wisdom (Gerstenberger), but there is another category of woes which is associated with funerary lamentations (cf. Janzen 1972). In this category *hōy* (cf *'ōy*) is a mourning cry – the shriek over the corpse of the dead. The woe of mourning can shade into the woe of accusation when in a funerary lament the voice of the mourner becomes the cry of the accuser (e.g. over the body of a murderer's victim, cf. Jahnow 1923, 88). Here *hōy* belongs to a mourning-vengeance pattern (Janzen, 27–34). This pattern suggests a context for the use of *hōy* which permits the mourning cry to 'undergo a metamorphosis from grief and mourning to accusation, threat, and even curse' (Janzen, 39). This context may provide the emotive thrust behind the woes directed at behaviour which disrupts the equilibrium of society. Hence the attack on a particular mode of exploitative building projects in v. 13 is completed with an extract from a funerary lament. The *hōy* of v. 13 finds its echo in the formal *hōy* of v. 18 (even though it is the absence of the traditional *hōy* which is the point of v. 18).

The unknown builder (or builders) of v. 13 will suffer an ignominious burial in v. 19. Not for him the traditional cries of the mourning relative nor the rites of burial in the family vault but a disgraceful dragging of the corpse through the streets of the city and its disposal outside the gates. The phrase 'burial of an ass' (an oxymoron, cf. Watson 1984, 312–3) characterizes his fate and may reflect an ironic reversal of the grandiose building project which was the glory of his life. The original independence of the units makes it difficult to determine the extent to which vv. 18b–19 are a fitting end to the guilty party of vv. 13–15a. They may represent vengeance more than poetic justice. Furthermore the lament may owe its place here to an editorial attempt to shape vv. 13–19 as a parallel to vv. 10–12. Such an attempt would account for the father-son contrast in vv. 15b–17.

The interpretation of the text is made more complicated by editorial decisions: the incorporation of the kerygmatic unit of vv. 13–19 into the cycle concerning the royal house and the identification of the builder (v. 13) and son (v. 14) as Jehoiakim ben Josiah. The chronological pattern of vv. 10–30 makes the unit refer to Jehoiakim as well as the direct reference in v. 18a (i.e. Shallum-Jehoiakim-Coniah). From the Deuteronomistic history it is known that Josiah was a king much approved of and Jehoiakim a king disapproved of, like most of the kings, by the Deuteronomists (cf. II Kings 23.25; 24.1–7). So the referral of the poems to Jehoiakim and the additional material in vv. 15b–17 reflect Deuteronomistic influence in the cycle. The problem of complication arises from the fact that many commentators read vv. 13–19 as genuine statements about King Jehoiakim. Yet there is no corroborative information in Kings or Chronicles about his building projects (just or unjust). II Kings 23.33–35 represents him as having to tax the country in order to pay the tribute exacted of Jehoahaz, but this is hardly sufficient evidence to warrant the inference *therefore* he pursued his building programme without paying his workers. The anonymity of the accusations does not require a king as their subject, though if a king must be singled out for building projects or the shedding of blood other royal names suggest themselves before that of Jehoiakim's (e.g. Solomon or Josiah cf. I Kings 5–9; II Kings 23.4–20). Yet the very anonymity of the poems allows Jehoiakim to be specified as the culprit of such gross anti-social behaviour and fits the Deuteronomistic ideology of kingship.

According to 36.30 a divine oracle predicts lack of burial for king Jehoiakim ('his dead body shall be cast out to the heat by day and the frost by night'), so it is small wonder that the poem of vv. 18b–19 should be applied to Jehoiakim. But its conventional nature should warn against such a specific application. Conventional statements such as woe sayings represent powerful emotional outbursts which serve the most useful purpose of giving vent to anger and expressing feelings of revenge. As predictions they may not have any force, though their relation to the curse (cf. Gerstenberger 1962) may give them some predictive status. Denouncing a tyrant (king, rich man, great builder, one's opponent) with a woe saying such as vv. 18b–19 (G) may have entertained the hope that such would be his fate but it could hardly guarantee it. As a threat the saying may have some force, but treated as a prediction and applied to Jehoiakim it represents just one more failed prediction in the Bible. Failed predictions are a fact of life in biblical traditions and therefore not a problem (cf. Hyatt, 984; Carroll 1979), but they do highlight an interesting aspect of what may be called 'the fate of kings'.

The only information on the death of Jehoiakim available in the Bible is the conventional notice in II Kings 24.6, 'So Jehoiakim slept with his fathers' (*wayyiškab yᵉhōyāqīm ʿim-ʾᵃbōtāyw*: an expression referring to natural death, cf. Smit 1966). No burial notice is provided for him, though one may be implied by the convention used (G II Chron. 36.8 adds, 'and he was buried in the garden of Uzza with his fathers'; here were the tombs of Manasseh and Amon [II Kings 21.18, 26] and possibly those of Josiah and Jehoiakim, cf. Yeivin 1948, 32–5). The absence of a specific burial notice may allow space for the interpretation of vv. 18b–19 offered by v. 18a (cf. Harrison, 118; Thompson, 480), but it is most curious that neither Kings nor Chronicles know of such an unusual fate of a king. The various ingenious explanations offered by exegetes wishing to treat vv. 18–19 as historically accurate (cf. Feinberg, 158–9) are necessitated by reading the editorial gloss of v. 18a as a correct understanding of vv. 18b–19 and 36.30 as a precise prediction with actual fulfilment. That neither reading is necessarily correct is suggested by the lack of fit between such convention-bound predictions and the fate of kings. In 34.4–5 Zedekiah is reassured that he will die in peace and not by the sword. Yet in 39.4–7 he is taken captive by the Babylonians, sentenced by them, witnesses the slaughter of his sons, has his eyes put out and is taken to Babylon in fetters. If *šālōm*, 'peace, wellbeing', describes that fate, then it may be used to summarize *King Lear* and would appear to have lost all its semantic force. A similar problem exists for Huldah's prediction that Josiah would be gathered to his grave in peace (*šālōm*, II Kings 22.20). His death is shrouded in mystery but he appears to have met it violently at the hands of Pharaoh Neco (II Kings 23.29). In peace he may have been buried but that is to rescue a failed prediction by desperation rather than plain meaning. The extent to which the death of Josiah represents a problem for the Deuteronomists is debatable (cf. Frost 1968) but, apart from an indirect allusion in 22.10 according to v. 11, the Jeremiah tradition has nothing to say about it. That is to be expected if the tradition really does come from a period *after* Josiah's reign (see on 1.2).

The death of Josiah may not register as an ideological problem in the Deuteronomistic writings, though the Chronicler felt compelled to account for it in such a way that his ideology of retribution for bad deeds was maintained (II Chron. 35.20–5; cf. his treatment of king Manasseh for the same purpose, II Chron. 33.10–20), but the predictions about the treatment of Jehoiakim's dead body in the Jeremiah tradition (22.18–19; 36.30) point to the negative view of Jehoiakim in the book. Direct information on Jehoiakim is minimal (cf. 26.20–23; 36) and there is no contact whatsoever between Jeremiah and Jehoiakim (see on 26; 36). The redactional framework dates certain activities of Jeremiah to the reign of Jehoiakim (e.g. 25.1; 26.1; 35.1; 36.1; cf. 1.3), but the tradition never permits the two antagonists to encounter each other. The narratives present Jeremiah and king Zedekiah in terms of a sympathetic relationship (hence the oracle of *šālōm* in 34.5), but hostility is the dominant theme in those stories where Jeremiah *or* Jehoiakim is to the fore (26; 36). Whatever the basis of this hostility may have been (in point of fact according to the tradition Jeremiah suffered more in the time of Zedekiah than of Jehoiakim!) it is behind 22.18a. As such it allows vv. 13–19 to be read as an evaluation of Jehoiakim's reign. But to read the unit in this way as history is to be misled by ideology and hostility. Only v. 18a makes the connection, and the dominant ideology of the Deuteronomists is an unreliable guide for the purposes of history writing. Jehoiakim in the Jeremiah tradition is very much like the Macbeth of Shakespeare (also Verdi's *Macbeth*), a study in nastiness, but not to be confused with the historical king of the same name. About the historical Jehoiakim we know very little and 22.13–19 is not part of what we know.

22.20–23

20 'Go up to Lebanon and cry out,
and lift up your voice in Bashan;
cry from Abarim,
for all your lovers are destroyed.
21 I spoke to you in your prosperity,
but you said, "I will not listen."
This has been your way from your youth,
that you have not obeyed my voice.
22 The wind shall shepherd all your shepherds,
and your lovers shall go into captivity;
then you will be ashamed and confounded
because of all your wickedness.
23 O inhabitant of Lebanon,
nested among the cedars,
how you will groan when pangs come upon you,
pain as of a woman in travail!'

---

[20] MT *mē'ᵃbārīm*, 'from Abarim': G *eis to peran tēs thalassēs*, 'to the other side of the sea', i.e. 'across the sea' = *mē'ēber yām*, cf. Vrs. Abarim is the mountain area of Moab (Deut. 32.49; cf. Num. 27.12). **[21]** MT *bᵉšalōtaīk*, 'in your prosperity': G *en tē paraptōsei sou*, 'in your transgression' = *bᵉšālūtēk* (cf. Aramaic *šālū*, 'neglect, remissness', Dan. 6.5; BHS). G lacks MT *kī* 'for (you have not obeyed . . .)'. **[22]** MT *kol-rō'aīk tir'eh-rūaḥ*, 'all your shepherds the wind will shepherd': word-play on *r'h*, 'shepherd, feed'. MT *rā'ātēk*, 'your wickedness': G *tōn philountōn se*, 'your lovers', i.e. 'friends' = *rē'aīk*. **[23]** K *ysbty*; Q *yōšabt*, cf. 10.17 'dweller, inhabitant'; also K *mqnnty*; Q *mᵉqunnant*, 'nestler'. MT *mah-nēḥant*, 'how you are to be pitied': *nēḥant* from *ḥnn*, 'be gracious, show favour'. G *katastenaxeis*, 'you shall sigh' = *'nḥ*, 'groan' (*nēnaḥat* for *ne'ᵉnaḥat*, cf. BHS).

The section on specific kings (vv. 10–30) is interrupted by a poem addressed to an unnamed city (the feminine forms throughout the poem indicate the subject is a woman, i.e. a metaphor of the city). It has links with similar material in 21.13–14; 22.6–7 and the reference to shepherds in v. 22 is an allusion to the leaders of the community (cf. 23.1–4). Read in the context of the cycle the leaders may be regarded as royal and the city addressed as Jerusalem – the poem itself presupposes neither reading.

The woman is commanded to go up to the various mountainous regions about her and cry out because all her lovers are destroyed (cf. 7.29a). It is a lamentation for the death of lovers. Couched in language appropriate to such matters the imagery depicts a distraught woman abandoned by her lovers, whose security has been breached by the fate of her friends and upon whom pain has come as it does when giving birth (cf. 4.31). Within the poem the woman is blamed for what has happened to herself and her lovers: she has been in the habit of not listening to the speaker (her husband? the deity?), so when the wind sweeps away her leaders then her companions will be deported. That catastrophe will make her ashamed of her evil ways.

The identity of this woman is given in v. 23 as Lebanon, the nestler among the cedars. Lebanon, the epitome of height, mightiness, grandeur and security, is the victim of invasion, deportation and spoliation. The poem is about the reversal of fortunes, the transformation of the mighty into the weak and the humiliation of the arrogant. It is shaped by the form and content of the oracles against the nations (cf. 46–51). Such images of arrogance and security suddenly shaken and devastated are the heart of the oracle proclaiming destruction against individual nations (cf. the more generalized poem in Isa. 2.12–17). But what is such a poem doing here in the middle of a section on minor kings of Judah? The cycle itself contains a number of elements which attack a city for its lofty security using images of forests and cedars (21.13–14; 22.6–7; cf. 22.14–15) and it must be assumed that these statements about well defended cities which suffer unexpected defeat represent an instructive analogy of Jerusalem. The OAN genre contributes a set of images with which the editors of the cycle are able to criticize Jerusalem. Little is said in the tradition about Jerusalem's arrogance and self-confidence, but by using these motifs which are at home in the genre directed against other nations and cities (cf. Isa. 47) it becomes possible to expose the self-deluded state of the city and its citizens (cf. Lam. 4.12). Oracles directed against Lebanon or making reference to Lebanon function as statements about Jerusalem because of the association between the two places in trading and building enterprises. The secure city nestling among the cedars is an epithet which may be transferred to Jerusalem without undue difficulty.

Jerusalem is not named because it may not have been the original target of the poem, but within the context of the royal cycle we may interpret it *now* of Jerusalem. The speaker is not identified, nor are there any editorial additions which would transform the poem into an oracle (except implicitly by virtue of its oracle against the nations genre). The broken lovers of Jerusalem may be understood as its allies (cf. 2.18, 33, 36–7; 4.30; Hos. 8.9–10), trading or political, or, in view of v. 22a, the leaders of the community. The tone of vv. 21–22 is similar to that of the discourse in 2.5–37 where, at times, the deity complains about the community's preference for other lovers (cf. 2.25; 3.1–2). Temporal changes within the poem (e.g. v. 20, 'are broken', v. 22, 'will go') indicate a sermonizing element in vv. 21–22 which may owe something to the Deuteronomistic motif of disobedience (cf. Thiel 1973, 242). In this sermon the wind shepherds the shepherds (the association of 'wind' and 'shepherd' suggests a reference to the prophets, cf. 5.13, but perhaps that is too specific an understanding of such a general term as 'shepherds'), meaning that the leadership (including the prophets?) will be deported. Like all good word-plays the phrase is more impressive aesthetically than semantically. The imagery in v. 23 is very fine: the city, like a safely nested bird, is secure among its palaces, but it will be devastated just like a woman who is suddenly seized by labour pains. Images of safety and painful loss of control are blended to produce a picture of unexpected devastation. This is hardly a description of the deportation of 597 or 587, but the original force of v. 23 may not have had such historical events in mind.

22.24–27

24 'As I live, says the LORD, though Coniah the son of Jehoiakim, king of
Judah, were the signet ring on my right hand, yet I would tear you off 25
and give you into the hand of those who seek your life, into the hand of those
of whom you are afraid, even into the hand of Nebuchadrezzar king of
Babylon and into the hand of the Chaldeans. 26 I will hurl you and the
mother who bore you into another country, where you were not born, and
there you shall die. 27 But to the land to which they will long to return,
there they shall not return.'

[24] MT *'ett^eqenkā*, 'I will tear you off': V 'I will tear *him* off'. Rudolph treats v. 24 as poetry, so deletes 'the son of Jehoiakim, king of Judah' because it destroys the rhythm. Coniah: the abbreviated form of the name Jehoiachin (52.31); used in 22.24, 28; 37.1. The more frequently used form is Jeconiah (24.1; 27.20; 28.4; 29.2). **[25]** G has a shorter text (cf. G 21.4, 7), lacking 'into the hand (of those of whom you are afraid)', 'and into the hand of Nebuchadrezzar the king of Babylon'. Rudolph, 144, has an even shorter text consisting of 25a. **[26]** MT *'al hā'āreṣ 'aḥeret*, 'to the other land': G *eis gēn*, 'into a land'. **[27]** MT *hēm m^enaśś^e'īm 'et-nap^ešām lāšūb šām*, 'they lift up their souls to return there', i.e. 'eagerly expect, long for'. BHS deletes *šām*, 'there', and reads *šāmmāh*, 'thence', with the preceding clause, thus repunctuating MT.

A prose statement about Coniah ben Jehoiakim is cast as an oracular proclamation against the king (cf. vv. 11–12 for a less harsh statement about Shallum). Jehoiachin (Coniah) succeeded his father Jehoiakim on the throne but was displaced by the Babylonians after only three months (II Kings 24.8–9; note the error in II Chron. 36.9, where Jehoiachin is said to have been eight years old when he began to reign, thus making the judgment on him absurd). They deported him, the queen mother (Nehushta), his wives, officials and the chief men of the land to Babylon, and replaced him on the throne with his uncle Mattaniah (throne-name Zedekiah). He therefore became king in exile and appears to have left behind him in Jerusalem supporters who hoped for his eventual return (cf. 28.4; see on 52.31–34). The extent to which the deported king polarized the community into pro-Egyptian 'king in exile' versus pro-Babylonian 'king on the throne' (i.e. Zedekiah) factions is difficult to determine from the text, but some of the narratives in the Jeremiah tradition may reflect such a division of loyalties. Against a background of expectations focused on Jehoiachin (contrast similar hopes associated with Zedekiah in 23.5–6) the statement in vv. 24–27 should be read as a denunciation of any such hopes. A divine oath asserts that Coniah (the shortened form may reflect the affection felt for the young exile) will never return to his own land (he shares the same fate as Shallum – exile without return). Even if he were a signet ring on Yahweh's right hand (cf. Hag. 2.23), he would be torn off and hurled away into exile (*nātaq*, v. 24; *ṭūl*, v. 26, are violent words). There he and his group will perish, in spite of the deep longing they have to return to their native land.

The meaning of the piece is clear: in spite of being king, Coniah will go into exile, and any special relationship thought to exist between king and Yahweh will count for nothing. In strong imagery the deity is represented as swearing an oath and pulling the signet ring (i.e. the king) off his hand. Nothing can save the king. Given over to the Babylonians he, and his family, his retinue and many important officials of the land go into an exile whence they will not return. The same might have been said of Shallum (vv. 10–12), but why is so much more said about Coniah? Why is it said in such strong erms? Why does the prose statement have attached to it some poetic fragments which appear to make the same point? Among the kings of Judah neither Shallum nor Coniah could be considered significant, yet Coniah features in the cycle more prominently than any other *named* king. In order to relate vv. 13–19 to Jehoiakim an editorial note in v. 18a is required (who would read the verses as referring to him otherwise?), yet in vv. 24–30 Coniah is named twice. What is so special about him that so much material focuses on him? Why is he singled out for such treatment and why are the terms used of him so strongly expressed? To answer such questions requires incorporating vv. 28–30 into the discussion. (For a different approach to the Jehoiachin-problem cf. Hermisson 1980: the Jeremianic composition develops the original word of Jeremiah of v. 24 in vv. 28*, 29, 30a; connections with 13.18–19 are unlikely, though possible for 22.10; the model used for the composition [word of doom, lament, stronger word of doom] is drawn from 14.1–15.1; the Deuteronomistic redaction is based on II Kings 24.9; a new word of Yahweh on the subject is encountered in Haggai.)

22.28–30

28 Is this man Coniah a despised, broken pot,
    a vessel no one cares for?
  Why are he and his children hurled and cast
    into a land which they do not know?
29 O land, land, land,
    hear the word of the Lord!
30 Thus says the Lord:
  'Write this man down as childless,
    a man who shall not succeed in his days;

for none of his offspring shall succeed
in sitting on the throne of David,
and ruling again in Judah.'

[28–30] Opinions vary on whether these verses should be treated as poetry (RSV, JPSB) or prose (NEB). BHS arranges them as poetry (cf. Rudolph, 144; Volz, Bright; Thiel 1973, 244 reconstructs v. 28 as poetic). **[28]** G 'Jechonias is dishonoured as a vessel for which there is no use; for he is thrown out and cast forth into a land which he does not know.' MT *hū' wezar'ō*, 'he and his children': this hardly reflects II Kings 24.15, but is in agreement with I Chron. 3.17, so is probably a later gloss, cf. BHS. **[29]** MT *'ereṣ 'ereṣ 'ereṣ*, 'land, land, land': cf. similar triples in 7.4 (temple), Isa. 6.3 (holy), Ezek. 21.27 (ruin); G *gē gē* 'land, land'. For a similar incantation in Mesopotamian literature cf. *EN irṣitum irṣitum irṣitum dGilgameš bêl ma-mi-ti-ku-nu* 'earth, earth, earth, Gilgamesh casts a spell upon you!' (cited in Gaster 1969, 605, 707). **[30]** G lacks 'thus says Yahweh'. MT *'arīrī*, 'stripped': cf. Gen. 15.2; Lev. 20.20, 21. G *ekkērukton*, 'banished, proscribed' (lit. proclaimed by herald, banishment by public proclamation); cf *abdicatum* (Old Latin). NEB 'stripped of all honour'; Driver 1937–38, 115, 'The real meaning is "disgraced" (as stripped of honour) or perhaps rather "proscribed" (as stripped of all rights) . . .'. RSV, JPSB respectively 'childless', 'without succession': Coniah did not lack children, seven sons are listed for 'Jeconiah, *the captive* . . .' in I Chron. 3.17–18. If *kitebū*, 'write, register', indicates a census list background for v. 30 (cf. Bright, 143), it may mean 'childless' in the sense that none of his sons will ascend the throne. G lacks 'a man who shall not succeed in his days': a gloss in MT. It is unsuitable for a census list.

Two brief statements and an incantation consider the case of Coniah and write off his future. The three elements are related to one another by virtue of redactional activity but the state of the MT points to development within vv. 28, 30 and v. 29 may have no necessary connection with Coniah. Between G and MT there are differences which represent editorial developing of the text in the direction of the Chronicler's view of Jeconiah. Disagreement among exegetes about whether the text should be read as poetry or prose is partly caused by the extent to which explanatory glosses have been added to it. Without accompanying explication a series of brief phrases is too cryptic to be understood and the identification of Coniah as the one to whom the phrases apply may be part of the redaction of the unit here.

The image used in v. 28 is that of a vessel (pot), for which nobody has any further use, hurled to the ground and shattered. Such pots are too common a feature of domestic life for any attention to be paid to one more discarded vessel (cf. the reconstruction of v. 28 as a tricola in Thiel 1973, 244). Similar imagery used in 19.1, 10–11 demonstrates the way such pots may symbolize in their breaking the irreversibility of fate. This reconstruction (cf. Thiel's) of the original form of the poem in v. 28 presupposes a purely figurative statement lacking the explanatory extension of G and MT. MT's interrogative form may be rhetorical or require the answer 'yes' (G lacks the element of query). The further question 'why is he hurled to the ground?' (*maddūʿa hūṭal ʿal-hāʾāreṣ*) is not answered at any point in the cycle (cf. vv. 10–12, where no motive is provided for the exiling of Shallum, unlike v. 22, which offers a non-specific reason for the deportation of the community's leaders). In the development of the original image the deportation of Coniah *and his children* is made the subject of the poem. This weakens the imagery and makes the linking motif of 'land' (*ʾereṣ*) in vv. 26, 27, 28, 29 more uniform. The secondary expansion (cf. v. 30b) reflects the later controversy about the children of Jeconiah.

In v. 29 a strange incantation is heard: 'O land, land, land, hear the word of Yahweh!' This triple address introduces what follows as the divine word (unnecessary in view of present MT) and hints at a magical process behind the words. Like a curse released across the length and breadth of the land (cf. the talismanic cry about the temple in 7.4), what follows may be viewed as the words accompanying the hurling of the pot to the ground. Not that the text presents vv. 28–30 as a ritual incantation accompanied by a magical act (19.1, 10–11 do precisely that), but it allows for such an interpretation. The effect of v. 29 on vv. 28, 30 is to turn the material into an incantatory act. The statement in v. 30, 'Write this man down as stripped . . .', is hereby addressed to the whole land using the formulaic 'land, land, land'. It is a most solemn and impressive declaration to the whole land (cf. the oath form of v. 24). Oath and incantation combine to destroy Coniah's future. He is registered (in the book of life? cf. 17.13) as stripped of position and title – proscribed throughout the land. The land (of his birth) is a place to which he no longer has entitlement, hence the word is adddressed to the land itself. All who are born in the land have title to belong to it, but this native-born man is barred from it. If the image presupposes a land register, then this man's entry in that book represents him as stripped of all legitimate claims (whether the writing is also part of a magical performance is a moot point). The editorial development of v. 30 applies the ban to his children and thereby extends Coniah's proscription to all future generations of his family. As contenders for the throne of David the sons of Coniah are here proscribed by most solemn magical enactment. Land, land, land, hear this word of Yahweh: any claimant to the royal throne of Judah who can claim membership of Coniah's clan is herewith proscribed! No man belonging to that family has any legitimate right to the throne because *Yahweh* has proscribed all the members of that clan. And the magic worked!

The questions posed by the strong tones of vv. 24–27 are reinforced by the equally virulent vv. 28–30. Why such strength of feeling against Coniah? What could a young king three months on the throne have done to warrant such hostility? The fall of Jerusalem to the Babylonians in 597 may have been so traumatic that the remaining kings of the house of Josiah were the inevitable target for abuse. Coniah and his father represented the Egyptian control of the state and the hostility felt towards Egypt may have been exacerbated in the period after Babylonian hegemony was established in Jerusalem. The pro-Babylonian elements in the community (headed by Zedekiah and, according to the tradition, Jeremiah) reacted strongly against all vestiges of pro-Egyptian presence in the city, and Coniah may have been the focus of much aggressive opposition. This line of reasoning would make party politics the key to understanding the sense of outrage generated by vv. 24–30. The conflict between pro-Egyptian and pro-Babylonian politics in Jerusalem is evident from the narratives of 27–29, 34, 37–40, 44, and the attack on Coniah may represent one strand of this struggle. In writing off Coniah the pro-Babylonian party is underwriting its own position in terms of oracular statements.

However, the development of vv. 28, 30 to include Coniah's descendants in the absolute dismissal of the young king suggests a different perspective for interpreting vv. 24–30. The fact that the Jeremiah tradition concludes with a much more sympathetic picture of Coniah (52.31–34 = II Kings 25.27–30; cf. Zenger 1968) demonstrates that hostility towards Coniah is only *one* strand in the book. From the perspective of the hostile strand the attack on Coniah and his sons may represent a specific community struggle about leadership in the period of Jerusalem's reconstruction. The clue to this interpretation is to be found in the extravagance of his dismissal.

Shallum suffered the same fate but no abuse. Coniah *and* his offspring are damned in the strongest terms possible (divine oath, incantation, divine word). Now in the Persian period when there was a movement to reconstruct the city of Jerusalem, rebuild its temple and reorganize its economy, certain prophets linked the future well-being of the city to the destiny of Zerubbabel, the governor of Judah (Hag. 1.1, 12–14; 2.2–4, 21–23; Zech. 3.8; 4.6–10; 6.12–14). In the preaching of the prophets Haggai and Zechariah the governor Zerubbabel represents the community's manifest destiny and is Yahweh's servant, his chosen one, whom Yahweh will make as a signet ring (Hag. 2.23 *kaḥōtām*, 'like a signet ring'; cf. 22.24, where the same word is used of Coniah). This designation of Zerubbabel is set in a context of the shaking of the nations when Yahweh will destroy the foreign kingdoms. In that reversal of power Zerubbabel will emerge as the real power in the land, as Yahweh's servant and leader of the community. When it is realized that Zerubbabel is a grandson of king Jeconiah (I Chron. 3.17–18; on the father of Zerubbabel cf. Williamson 1982, 57) and has prophetically inspired claims to the throne, the *intensity of opposition* to the descendants of Coniah in vv. 28, 30 becomes more comprehensible. Either all of vv. 24–30 or the editorial expansion belongs to an anti-Zerubbabel movement. If the latter, then the original attack on Coniah (rather than his family) may have been intended as support for Zedekiah, *the king on the throne*, in opposition to Jeconiah, *the king in exile* (cf. 23.5–6). This contrast is lost by the development of the cycle in the time of Zerubbabel and the editing of the tradition which placed 23.1–4 between 22.24–30 and 23.5–6.

The interpretation of vv. 24–30 along these lines accounts for the strong invective used against Coniah. If Yahweh had sworn an oath in the past that Coniah would never return to his own land and, furthermore, that none of his sons would ever sit on the throne of David, then Zerubbabel's claim to the throne is ruled out in the most absolute way. Oath and incantation declare the illegitimacy of Zerubbabel's aspirations and condemn his supporters as false. Even the view of Zerubbabel as a signet ring is echoed in the dismissal of Coniah, which would explain why an oath is used. Such a solemn asseveration of divine attitude would help to combat an alternative prophetic party's view that the deity had designated Zerubbabel as his signet ring. Even if that claim were true, it would be invalid because Yahweh had torn from his finger Zerubbabel's grandfather and consigned him to perpetual exile. Not only did an oath and an incantation stand against Zerubbabel but the speaker of these terrible things was Jeremiah – a former prophet whose sayings had been confirmed by the fall of Jerusalem (cf. Zech. 1.4–6, 12; 7.7; II Chron. 36.12, 16, 20–1, 22). The clash of prophetically inspired parties in the Jerusalem community to which vv. 24–30 bear witness throws an ironic light on the collection of anti-prophetic polemical sayings in 23.9–40. In the pursuit of political power prophets could be found to support every party position in the community and to give to each programme the imprimatur of 'thus says Yahweh'. In the redaction of the tradition vv. 24–30 reveal that Jeremiah suffered such a fate and was made to be a supporter of partisan politics.

23.1–4

23[1] 'Woe to the shepherds who destroy and scatter the sheep of my pasture!'
says the LORD. 2 Therefore thus says the LORD, the God of Israel, concerning
the shepherds who care for my people: 'You have scattered my flock, and
have driven them away, and you have not attended to them. Behold, I will
attend to you for your evil doings, says the LORD. 3 Then I will gather the
remnant of my flock out of all the countries where I have driven them, and
I will bring them back to their fold, and they shall be fruitful and multiply.
4 I will set shepherds over them who will care for them, and they shall fear
no more, nor be dismayed, neither shall any be missing, says the LORD.'

[1–4] Holladay 1966c, 420–4, and Thompson, 485–6, treat the unit as poetry, cf. Condamin, 175; Volz, 228, finds poetry in vv. 2, 4, but regards v. 3 as secondary; Rudolph, 145–6, reads it as prose but takes v. 3 as a post-exilic gloss. **[1]** MT *mar'îtî*, 'my pasture': G^BS^ *nomēs autōn*, 'their pasture'. For the flock image cf. 10.21; 13.20; Ezek. 34. MT 'my pasture' may reflect Ezek. 34.31 (cf. 'Yahweh's flock' in Jer. 13.17). G lacks 'says Yahweh'. **[2]** MT *welō' peqadtem 'ōtām hinenī pōqēd 'alēkem*, 'and you have not *attended* them, look I am *attending* to you': word-play on *pqd* using negative and positive senses of *pqd*, 'attend, watch, visit, punish'; cf. NEB. The reversal process here (i.e. those who do something have that done to them) reflects a feature of the tradition, cf. 11.21–22; 12.14–5; 14.15; 50.15b, 29; 51.49. **[3]** MT *mikkōl ha'arāṣōt*, 'from all the lands': G *apo pasēs tēs gēs*, 'from every land', lit. 'from the whole earth'. On the relation of v. 3 to the Ezekiel school cf. Mendecki 1983. **[4]** G lacks 'neither shall any be missing'. MT phrase *welō' yippāqēdû* indicates a further meaning for *pqd*, 'missing, lacking', cf. I Sam. 20. 18–19; 25.7; Giesebrecht, 126, reads it as *welō' yiphādū*, 'neither shall any be afraid' (*pḥd*, 'be in dread').

The cycle closes with a number of short pieces which comment on the problems of leadership in the community (under the figure of 'shepherds') and look forward to a new king on the throne of David. In vv. 1–4 general criticisms are made of the leaders (cf. 22.22) and more efficient ones are promised to the community by Yahweh. An interpolated statement from the Ezekiel school (cf. Ezek. 34) in v. 3 interrupts the flow of imagery about leadership with a comment on the restoration of the flock (i.e. the people) to their own fold, where they will be fruitful and multiply. The punishment of the bad leaders and the appointment of new leaders are the main points of vv. 1–4.

In the context of the royal cycle a statement about shepherds may be taken to refer to the community's kings, but the term is broader than that and includes all the ruling elements charged with the oversight of the people. They are charged in v. 1 with the destruction and scattering of the flock, i.e. they are responsible for the deportation of the people. This accusation uses a woe saying but only in the most generalized way (cf. Amos 5.18–20) and possibly as an associative link word with 22.13–17 (cf. Janzen 1972, 73). No particular social evil is specified, but a rather general point about social disruption is made. The rulers of the community are blamed for the disintegration caused by the deportation of the people (contrast v. 3, where Yahweh is the cause of it). The piece is therefore a general condemnation of the leadership (as in 22.21–2) in vv. 1–2 and permits the contrast with the future good rulers of v. 4. That contrast is reinforced by the images of the scattered flock in v. 1 and the cared-for flock of v. 4 where not a single sheep is missing. The blaming of the rulers for what happened in 597/587 fits the cycle, but is in striking contrast to the poems (e.g. 5.1–5; 9.2–6) which make the people themselves the ones responsible for what befell the community. The imagery of vv. 1–2 is also strange in that it blames the shepherds for the fate of the sheep (a fair analogy given such language) and yet threatens them with the same fate. In reality the deportations which ruined the community exiled primarily the leaders and so the shepherd-sheep analogy is an inadequate image of the realities of the period. That suggests a source for vv. 1–2 of pious preaching which generalizes from a distance using conventional language rather than giving an analysis of a historical situation; though the text could be viewed as a pious summary of 22.13–17 parallel to 22.20–23 (cf. Thiel 1973, 247, who treats them as a résumé of the material from 21.11). The word-play of v. 2 is an expression of opposition to the leaders, but not in relation to the deportations, so it may reflect opposition to the community's leaders of a later period (cf. the suggested background to 22.24–30).

The mood of the piece changes in vv. 3–4, though the analogy of sheep and shepherds is a link to vv. 1–2. The gathering of the scattered people (or what remains of them, i.e. 'the remnant of my flock', *'et-šᵉ'ērīt ṣō'nī*) reflects motifs to be found in Ezek. 34 and late Deuteronomistic material (e.g. Deut. 30.1–10; cf. Hyatt, 988; Thiel 1973, 247–8; Herrmann 1965, 207–8; Lust 1981, 134–5). It disrupts the flow of images in vv. 1–2, 4 but sets the scene for v. 4. It may be a very late gloss (cf. Rudolph, 145), but because it is required to make sense of v. 4 (i.e. the scattered flock of vv. 1–2 need to be regathered before the shepherds of v. 4 can care properly for them) it is probable that the whole unit should be regarded as a late piece. The verse also disrupts the thought of vv. 1–2 because instead of the leaders driving the flock away in v. 3 it is Yahweh who has driven them into exile (*hiddaḥtī*, '*I* have driven away . . .', cf. 8.3; 16.15 = 23.8; 24.9; 27.10, 15; 29.14, 18; 32.37; Deut. 30.1). The theologizing of the exile in this manner allows for the possibility of return, i.e. he who drove out may also retrieve (the images and theology are much more developed in Ezek. 34), whereas blaming the community's leaders is to make the people's fate a permanent one. It is Yahweh who will gather together all the exiles, restore them to their own land (i.e. 'their fold'), and make them prosperous (i.e. 'and they shall be fruitful and multiply' *ūpārū wᵉrābū*, cf. 3.16; Ezek. 36.11; Gen. 1.28; similar images appear in Deut. 30.9). Responsible leaders will be set over the community (cf. 3.15), and these will maintain the welfare and unity of the people. Thus proper leadership is restored to Yahweh's flock.

23.5–6

5 'Behold, the days are coming, says the LORD, when I will raise up for David a righteous Branch, and he shall reign as king and deal wisely, and shall execute justice and righteousness in the land. 6 In his days Judah will be saved, and Israel will dwell securely. And this is the name by which he will be called: "The LORD is our righteousness." '

RSV treats the piece as prose but NEB, Volz, Rudolph, Bright, Weiser and others read it as poetry; cf. 33.15–16 for a similar oracle.

[5] MT *ṣemaḥ ṣaddīq*, 'a righteous branch' or 'legitimate growth'; i.e. a true or genuine shoot (from a tree), cf. G *anatolēn dikaian*, 'righteous rising', where *anatolē* (a figure used of heavenly bodies) is used of *ṣemaḥ*, 'branch', i.e. future ruler (Zech. 3.9; 6.12). **[6]** MT *w^{e}yiśrā'ēl*, 'and Israel . . .': 33.16; also G^S 'and Jerusalem'. MT *yiqr^e'ō*, 'one will call him': abnormal form, cf. BHS *yiqrā'ēhū*. MT *yhwh ṣid^{e}qēnū*, 'Yahweh our righteousness': cf. *ṣid^{e}qiyyāhū* (*ṣid^{e}qiyyāh*), 'Zedekiah' = a word-play on the king's name (and/or an allusion to it). G *kurios Iōsedek*, 'lord Iosedek' i.e. (the lord will call him) 'Yah is righteous', with duplication of *yhwh*.

The cycle is a mixture of prose and poetry, pieces about the city, leadership in general and specific kings. To balance the generality of vv. 1–4 a brief piece of poetry (cf. BHS) speaks about a future king of David's dynasty who will rule justly and wisely and also maintain the security of Judah and Israel. The name of this legitimate scion of the royal house will reflect his unimpeachable right to rule under the aegis of Yahweh. The expectation of such a future is given an oracular force. It is also to be found in 33.15–16 where it applies to Judah and Jerusalem rather than Judah and Israel (see on 33.14–16).

The word-play on Zedekiah's name in v. 6b, the placing of the oracle after 22.24–30, and the absence of any reference to Zedekiah (the dominant royal figure in the narratives) in the royal cycle all suggest that this oracle refers to Zedekiah. Its positive attitude towards the future king makes the oracle quite distinctive in its present context. The legitimacy motif is emphasized in the qualification of the scion and in his name and that motif is reflected in the name Zedekiah given by the Babylonians to Mattaniah (II Kings 24.17). In effect the Babylonians said 'Zedekiah is the right and proper king, not Jehoiachin'. This reading of the text would make it a reflection of community questions about which king (the puppet on the throne or the prisoner in exile) was the authentic ruler, the one to whom loyalty was owed (cf. Swetnam 1965). The oracle here legitimates Zedekiah and promises peace and security in his time (here 'Jerusalem' is better read with 33.16 for 'Israel'). Such a reading is consistent with the attitude shown by Jeremiah towards Zedekiah in the narratives and indicates the pro-Babylonian nature of his rule. The oracle may be understood as an inaugural celebration of Zedekiah's legitimate claim to be king.

Reading vv. 5–6 as a celebration of Zedekiah's assumption of the throne (cf. Isa. 9.2–7; 11.1–5 for the conventional oracle welcoming a new king) presupposes a historical occasion for the piece, whereas it is set in the future and rounds off the cycle (or is an appendix to it). Its positive note contrasts with the other individual king elements in the cycle. The logic of its position here, apart from its function as an appendix, is that it provides an instantiation of the good shepherds of v. 4. It also expresses the belief that there will emerge, after the exile of v. 2, in the land of Judah a practitioner of justice, thus fulfilling the command of 21.12 (different linguistic terms are used in relation to justice, but the particularity of 21.12 is included in the generality of 23.5). In that period justice and security will be enjoyed by the land. Thus the unit reflects the time of salvation expected in the post-exilic period (indicated by the term *ṣemaḥ*, 'branch', cf. Zech. 3.8; 6.12, where it is used of Zerubbabel). As such it can hardly be referred to Zedekiah *simpliciter*. The word-play on that king's name preserves the memory of Zedekiah and incorporates him into the future hope, but the historical Zedekiah is only an echo in that hope, an echo contributed by the Jeremiah tradition. This transformation of the significance of Zedekiah's name underlines the *kingly* and wise rule of the future scion and, set in this tradition, inevitably contrasts him with Zedekiah's status as a client king of the Babylonians and his behaviour as the leader who foolishly brought about the ruin of Jerusalem. The extent to which all this may be read from a word-play is debatable but it offers an alternative reading to the interpretation of vv. 5–6 as the celebration of Zedekiah's inauguration as king.

23.7–8

7 'Therefore, behold, the days are coming, says the LORD, when men shall no longer say, "As the LORD lives who brought up the people of Israel out of the land of Egypt," 8 but "As the LORD lives who brought up and led the descendants of the house of Israel out of the north country and out of all the countries where he had driven them." Then they shall dwell in their own land.'

[7–8] = 16.14–15 (see Comm. on 16.14–15). G places vv. 7–8 after 23.40. The unit is more suitable as an appendix to 23.1–4, 5–6 than as an interpretation of 16.10–13, 16–18, but it has no real connection with the cycle on leadership and the royal house (hence its position in G). It has links with 23.3 and Janzen 1973, 93, suggests that the original order at one time was 23.1–4, 7–8, 5–6. Lust 1981, 135, treats it as 'nothing but a marginal note'. **[7]** MT *w^e^lō-yō'm^e^rū 'ōd*, 'and they shall no longer say': 16.14 has passive sing., 'it shall no longer be said'. MT *b^e^nē yiśrā'ēl*, 'people of Israel': G *ton oikon Israēl*, 'the house of Israel', as in G 16.15. **[8]** G lacks 'brought up and who . . .'. 16.15 has *he'^e^lāh*, 'he brought up', but lacks *hēbī*, 'brought in from', RSV 'led'. G *hapan to sperma*, 'the whole seed' = *'et-kol zera'* (MT lacks *kol*); G '(seed of) Israel' better than MT '(seed of) the house of Israel'. MT *hiddaḥtīm*, 'I have driven them': G *exōsen autous*, 'he had expelled them' = *hiddīḥām*, 'he had driven them', as in 16.15. MT *w^e^yāš^e^bū*, 'and they will dwell': G *kai apekatestēsen autous*, 'and he has restored them', cf. 16.15 *wah^a^šibōtīm*, 'I will bring them back' = G *apokatastēsō autous*.

A brief oracle expresses the future hope that those carried away to Babylon (i.e. the north country) will be brought back to their own land by Yahweh. The return from Babylon motif (cf. 29.14) is expanded in v. 8 to include all the scattered groups of Israelites wherever Yahweh has driven them (i.e. the Diaspora). This expansion indicates that the unit is a very late one and presupposes a house of Israel scattered throughout many countries. The theme of the return is a late strand in the tradition (cf. 3.15–18; 16.14–15; see on 30–31) and interrupts the various contexts in which it appears (see analysis in Lust 1981, 133–6). In the use of it here it is given a hyperbolic expression so that the return motif takes on a mythic dimension similar to the original exodus motif. Its status as a national myth is indicated by its future function as an oath (cf. 4.2; 5.2) and such is the grandiose nature of the return that as an oath it will *replace* the exodus myth. The unit is highly rhetorical and expresses the belief or hope that in the future there would be a grand return of all exiles wherever they were. If that were to happen it would dwarf the original exodus and even eclipse it because it would be a much larger exodus than the first one. Exodus terminology shapes the language used here (e.g. *h'lh*, 'bring up', a technical term for the exodus, cf. Wijngaards 1965) and the scattering of the nation provides an exodus style context for the future divine act. Blotting out of the memory of the exodus may be a hyperbolic form of the return hope but it expresses well a belief which hardly allowed for a more positive view of the scattered nation (contrast 29.4–7).

The present position of vv. 5–6, 7–8 in this cycle functions as a closure of the royal material and an introduction to what follows. This is purely a reading of the verses in terms of the redaction and the fact that both units appear elsewhere in the tradition. Whether the editors intended them to be read this way is a matter of debate, and attention is drawn simply to how they may be understood in this light. Treating vv. 5–6 as a closure of the cycle on kings and kingship makes reference back not only to 21.11–12 but also to 21.1–10 in the present order of the tradition's redaction. The introduction to the block presents a doomed city under the rule of Zedekiah and the possibility of escape for individual citizens. In 23.5–6 royal house, land and city (cf. 33.16) are all secure again under the leadership of a Davidic figure, and the catastrophe of 587 (21.1–10) is not the permanent fate of city or nation. The house of David practises justice and therefore the future is secured. The terrible events of the closing decade of pre-exilic Judaean statehood are not the last word on the royal house.

Reading 23.5–6 as a closure is spoiled by the presence of vv. 7–8 (hence the virtue of G's positioning them after 23.40). Read as a preface to what follows they may be understood as necessary background information on the controversy with the prophets. These prophets prophesied *šālōm* rather than disaster, but vv. 7–8 make clear that the people were scattered abroad and therefore disaster did happen. How wrong the prophets were! Implicit in all that follows is that error and they stand under its condemnation.

23.9–40 The cycle of texts on the prophets

'Your prophets have seen for you false and deceptive visions'

A series of individual pieces concerning the prophets represents a statement against the prophets for their behaviour in supporting the evildoers in the community and the techniques used by them. Except for very general indications the prophets are not identified, and the period of their activity is not stated. It is generally assumed by most commentators that the pieces relate to the time before the fall of Jerusalem, but this is not a necessary conclusion dictated by the text itself. It may be a more probable reading of the material *if* the conflict with prophets of 27–29 reflects the period between 597 and 587, but the anti-prophetic polemic of Zech. 13.2–6 offers a later setting for reading the cycle. The editors have incorporated the collection into the tradition immediately following the cycle on the royal house, thus linking kings and prophets and implicating them in the responsibility for the catastrophe of 587. However, block F is an appendix to the blocks making up 2–20 and may represent further reflections on the period from a later time.

The subject of prophetic conflict and the attempt to construct a criteriology of validation which would distinguish between 'true' and 'false' prophets have engaged biblical scholars in recent years, and many studies have scrutinized the difficulties involved in delineating the processes by which one prophet could be distinguished from another (e.g. Carroll 1981, 158–97; Crenshaw 1971; DeVries 1978; Hossfeld and Meyer 1973; Kraus 1964; Meyer 1977; Osswald 1962; Overholt 1970; Reventlow 1963, 121–40; Seidl 1978; van der Woude 1969). The material in the cycle here does not set out criteria for determining which prophets are authentic but criticizes 'the prophets' for a number of different practices. The cycle is edited from a viewpoint which regards the prophets as one of the causes (at times *the* cause, cf. v. 15b) of disruption and evil in the community. No alternative prophetic standard is advocated nor is the cycle presented on behalf of a preferred view of prophecy (though the occasional clause may indicate certain preferences e.g. vv. 22, 28b). It is therefore unlike 27–29, where other prophets are criticized and condemned in opposition to Jeremiah *the prophet*. Deuteronomistic editing of the cycle is minimal (cf. Thiel 1973, 249–53), and contributes only a few observations to the collection (e.g. v. 17; see on v. 22b). As the cycle is not a unified whole but a collection of discrete elements, it is not possible to date it to any particular period, though the background to vv. 33–40 suggests a post-exilic setting for the cycle. Prophetic conflict of that period may have contributed to the creation of the cycle, and its incorporation into the Jeremiah tradition gives it the status of an authoritative ruling on a particular controversy. Lack of data on its background warrants caution in producing an overview of the cycle.

23.9–12

9 Concerning the prophets:
My heart is broken within me,
all my bones shake;
I am like a drunken man,
like a man overcome by wine,
because of the LORD
and because of his holy words.
10 For the land is full of adulterers!
because of the curse the land mourns,
and the pastures of the wilderness are dried up.
Their course is evil,
and their might is not right.
11 'Both prophet and priest are ungodly;
even in my house I have found their wickedness,
says the LORD.
12 Therefore their way shall be to them
like slippery paths in the darkness,
into which they shall be driven and fall;
for I will bring evil upon them
in the year of their punishment,
says the LORD.'

---

[9] MT *lannᵉbi'îm*, 'to, concerning, or about the prophets': cf. the common psalm title *lᵉdāwid*, 'to, for, or about David'. An editorial phrase indicating a collection of items dealing with the prophets. G *en tois prophētais*, 'in, among the prophets': because G has vv. 7–8 after the cycle there is a connection between the end of v. 6 and the beginning of v. 9 that allows the phrase to be read with v. 6 or v. 9. Cf. BHS. MT *šikkōr*, 'drunken (man)': G *suntetrimmenos* 'broken, destroyed' = *šābūr*. MT *dibᵉrē qodᵉšō*, 'the words of his holiness': G *euprepeias doxēs autou*, 'the excellence of his glory', suggests *hᵃdar kᵉbōdō*. **[10]** G lacks 'for the land is full of adulterers': Rudolph, 148, rejects G ending of v. 9, inserts 'evildoers and' before 'adulterers', deletes MT *kī*, 'for', and understands it as the beginning of the divine words, cf. BHS. Hos. 7.4, 'they are all adulterers' (but see BHS there) may be the source for MT, though the first two lines of v. 10 may be variants. BHS treats the second line of MT as an addition, whereas G lacks first line but has second line. MT *'ālāh*, 'curse': G *toutōn* 'these', i.e. things (prophets?) = *'ēlleh*. For MT cf. Isa. 24.6. MT *mᵉrūṣātām*, 'their course', i.e. 'running', cf. 8.6. **[11]** MT *bᵉbētī*, 'in my house': whoever the speaker of vv. 9–10 may be, the deity is now the speaker (hence *nᵉ'um yhwh*, 'says Yahweh', notation). **[12]** MT *yiddaḥū*, 'they will drive': a few mss read as *yiddāḥū* from *dḥh* but treated as from *dḥḥ* by some exegetes (cf. BDB, 191), 'will be thrust down', cf BHS. NEB 'they shall be dispersed in the dark'. Cf. 11.23b for v. 12b, 'for I will bring upon them (the men of Anathoth) evil, the year of their punishment', *kī-'abī . . . rā'āh šᵉnat pᵉquddātām.*

The first poem in the cycle appears to have little connection with the prophets but is a general statement about the speaker's reactions to the state of the land. Oracular elements in vv. 11–12 include the prophets as part of the cause of that state, hence, perhaps, the justification for including this poem in the collection. Yet even in v. 11 the prophet is not the only official blamed and vv. 10, 12 may represent the original sense of the poem, i.e. a broad statement about the state of the land because of evildoers. This reading of it would make the unit similar to the psalms in the tradition which complain about the behaviour of the wicked and the effect it has on the righteous. The speaker is not identified, so the assertion about mental suffering and shaking bones akin to drunkenness cannot be referred to a specific situation. The speaker of the laments also complains about pain and suffering caused by opposition (cf. 15.17–18; 17.14, 18; 20.9), but the similarities are too general to permit a close identification of speakers. The state of shock and pain also characterizes the city's response to the devastation of invasion (cf. 4.19–21; 8.18, 21–9.1) and v. 9 could be read as a similar response to the moral state of the nation. MT's 'because of Yahweh and because of his holy words' is also too general to provide a precise interpretation (especially as G has a different reading). Yahweh's words against evildoers may be the point, but a sense of Yahweh's awful majesty shaking the speaker is a perfectly good interpetation of v. 9 (cf. G). As a preface to the cycle it asserts the impact of Yahweh on the speaker, whether as an individual or as a figure of the community (cf. vv.23–24 for another statement about the nature of the deity's relation to the people).

Two variants in v. 10 offer different accounts of why the land is in such a state (MT): because there are so many adulterers and because of the curse. Both explanations require more information than the text affords at this point. The first explanation hints at widespread immorality or, if 'adultery' is a figure of involvement with other cults, religious apostasy. Such a general charge (cf. 9.2; Hos. 7.4) may combine both ideas (see on 5.7–8) and be the equivalent of the phrase 'this adulterous and sinful generation' (Mark 8.38; cf. Matt. 12.39;

16.4), i.e. a term of abuse not to be taken literally. The alternative explanation reflects a condition of drought in the land (cf. 12.4a; 14.1–6) and blames it on the curse. The cause of that curse is not given, but in the context of vv. 9–12 it may be implicit. The behaviour of those condemned has brought upon the community a divine curse which has resulted in drought. The guilty ones are not named but their course is described as evil and the power they have is not right (*kēn*, 'honest, true', cf. 8.6; 48.30). The generality of these descriptions suggests illegitimate rulers of society (appropriate for a poem placed after the cycle of royal texts) or the conventional complaint of the powerless (i.e. the poor, the righteous) against those with power (i.e. the wicked), reflecting the righteous-wicked opposition of the laments (12.1–3; 20.12–13).

The poem shifts in vv. 11–12 from speaker's complaint to divine sayings. Although v. 12 would make a very good conclusion to v. 10, v. 11 intervenes with a statement about the behaviour of the prophets and priests in the temple. The phrase 'prophet and priest' appears in a stereotyped manner in 6.13b = 8.10b and both are associated together in contexts of abuse (2.26b; 5.31a; cf. 2.8). As cult officials their sphere of activity was the temple, hence their official duties are here condemned as 'their evil' (cf. 11.15 for a more general condemnation of the nation's behaviour in the temple). The singling out of prophet and priest is a secondary element in the poem (a poem very much constructed by redaction and transmission) but one which gives it some claim to be in a cycle devoted to prophets. The divine saying against prophet and priest is too general to be tied down to any particular social context and may reflect post-exilic conditions as much as earlier periods.

Because the course of the unidentified group is evil and their power false their way will become like slippery paths (*ḥalaqlaqqōt*, as in Ps. 35.6; 73.18). Into the dark they will be driven (MT, cf. NEB; RSV takes dark with previous figure) where they will inevitably fall (for the combination of their way being dark *and* slippery cf. Ps. 35.6). All this will happen to them because Yahweh is bringing upon them the year of their visitation (i.e. the time of punishment). The terms used for the destruction of the wicked reflect the strand in the tradition which focuses on the righteous-wicked conflict (cf. 11.236 = v. 126) and which also appears in the book of Psalms (e.g. 35, 73). This strengthens the interpretation of the poem as a diatribe against the wicked on behalf of the righteous. The redactional history of the poem has turned it into an oracular statement, added v. 11 and, by prefacing the cycle against the prophets with it, contributed towards the facility with which exegetes read such poems as 'confessions' of Jeremiah about his mistreatment at the hands of the other prophets.

23.13–15

13 'In the prophets of Samaria
I saw an unsavoury thing:
they prophesied by Baal
and led my people Israel astray.
14 But in the prophets of Jerusalem
I have seen a horrible thing:
they commit adultery and walk in lies;
they strengthen the hands of evildoers,
so that no one turns from his wickedness;
all of them have become like Sodom to me,
and its inhabitants like Gomorrah.'
15 Therefore thus says the LORD of hosts concerning the prophets:
'Behold, I will feed them with wormwood,
and give them poisoned water to drink
for from the prophets of Jerusalem
ungodliness has gone forth into all the land.'

---

[13] MT *ūbinᵉbîʾē šōmᵉrōn*, '*and* in the prophets of Samaria': cf. v. 14, *ūbinᵉbîʾē yᵉrûšālaim*, '*and* in the prophets of Jerusalem'; thus making the two statements correspond to each other (lost in EVV). MT *tipᵉlāh*, 'unsavoury, tasteless, unseemly (object)'. MT *hinnabbᵉʾû*, 'prophesied': Hithpael with *t* assimilated. Rudolph treats 'Israel' as a gloss (a correct explanatory gloss). **[14]** MT *šaʿărûrāh*, 'horrible thing': cf. 5.30. MT *wᵉhālōk baššeqer*, 'and walk falsely'; NEB 'hypocrites'. Thompson, 494, 'and go after The Lie', i.e. Baal; this makes v. 14 = v. 13 rather than a comparison in which Jerusalem is worse than Samaria (cf. 3.11), so Bright, 151–2. The association of adultery and *šeqer*, 'falseness', appears in 29.23 also in relation to prophets. Cf. 38.4 for the opposite image of 'weakening the hands'. MT *lᵉbiltî-šābû*, 'they do not turn': cf. 27.18; grammatically incorrect (perfect after *biltî*), read *yāšubû* (cf. Ex. 20.20) or *šûb* (cf. Ezek. 13.22), G *apostraphēnai*, 'turn back'. MT *wᵉyōšᵉbehā*, 'and its inhabitants': there is no antecedent for 'its' in the poem. Rudolph, 150, proposes reading *wᵉyaḥdā(y)w*, 'all' (cf. BHS, JPSB) in place of MT. **[15]** Cf. 9.15. MT *ḥănuppāh*, 'profaneness, pollution': cf. v. 11; 3.1, 2, 9 (all verbal forms of *ḥnp*). The adj. *ḥānēp* refers to 'the godless, heathen' (frequently in Job, cf. Ps. 35.16; Isa. 33.14 [plur]), i.e. those who profane or are profane, the irreligious (even the religiose?).

One of the interpretative difficulties of the Jeremiah tradition is caused by having to decide where units finish and new units commence. Translators and commentators differ considerably in the decisions they make, and 23.9–32 is a cycle where such differences are very apparent (cf. EVV). In following a particular division of the chapter into vv. 9–12, 13–15, 16–22, 23–24, 25–32, other divisions are ruled out, but there are equally good reasons for adopting a different segmentation of the collection (apart from the separation of vv. 23–24 my choice follows that of Weiser and Rudolph among others). The frequency with which the redactors have sprinkled the text with oracular indices (*nᵉ'um yhwh*, 'says Yahweh') renders division by oracle difficult and often quite inappropriate (e.g. vv. 11, 12, 23, 24). So in following the exegesis of each section of the cycle allowance must be made for alternative interpretations which a different division would permit.

The first proper reference to the prophets in the cycle appears in vv. 13–14, where the prophets of Jerusalem are contrasted with the prophets of Samaria (i.e. compared with them to their detriment). Such a contrasting of Judaean and Israelite prophets is similar to the comparison made between the two nations in 3.6–10, 11, where also it is maintained that Judah is worse than Israel. The lateness of the material in 3.6–10, 11 suggests that the cycle against the prophets contains much late matter. Two points are made in the poem: the prophets of Jerusalem are just like the prophets of Samaria, only more so; and they have encouraged the evildoers in the community. In order to make the comparison between the two groups demonstrate the claim that the Judaean prophets are worse than the Samarian prophets subtle distinctions are made. What the northern prophets did was to lead Israel (i.e. Yahweh's people) astray by means of baalistically inspired prophecies. Their syncretistic form of religious inspiration (details not supplied) is described as something 'tasteless' or 'unsavoury'. A rather mild epithet for apostasy bordering on idolatry (the Deuteronomistic history takes a much stronger view of the matter). On the other hand the Judaean prophets are described as doing something 'horrible' (cf. 5.30): they commit adultery, follow or walk in falseness, strengthen the evildoers so that they do not turn (*šūb*) from evil, and have made the evildoers (or conceivably the community depending upon the force given to 'no one turns') like Sodom and Gomorrah to the deity. The pejorative force of the terms used of the Jerusalem prophets in comparison to those used of the Samarian prophets clearly makes the statements contrastive. The Jerusalem prophets are worse than those of Samaria.

The lack of realism in this claim is transparent and indicates a setting for the poem similar to the material in the discourse of 2–3, especially the curious development of 3.11 in the direction of 3.6–10. Only in such a polemic could northern apostasy be treated so lightly and the Jerusalem leadership so harshly denounced. We need not suppose that the poem implies an eirenic approach to Samaria, for Jerusalem is the target and the comparison is only used in order to serve a polemical purpose against a specific group. The strength of the denunciation of the Jerusalem prophets (maintained and developed in the rest of the cycle) is indicative of the hostility felt towards them. All of them have become like Sodom and Gomorrah, the legendary cities which Yahweh wiped out for unspeakable offences (Gen. 19). In Isa. 1.10 the leadership and people of Judah and Jerusalem are compared to Sodom and Gomorrah (cf. Ezek. 16.46, 48, where the Sodom epithet applies to Samaria's sister Jerusalem), so prophets and people may also be the meaning of Sodom and Gomorrah here (for the post-exilic date of Isa. 1.10–17 cf. Kaiser 1983, 28). If the Samarian prophets led the people astray, the Jerusalem prophets have made them Sodom and Gomorrah, i.e. the veritable enemies of Yahweh. This they have achieved by immorality and lies (*šeqer* may refer to baalistic tendencies or false beliefs: the term is used too frequently in the tradition for its occurrence here to have any precise meaning without further qualification in the text).

The strengthening of the evildoers (the term *mᵉrēʿīm* confirms the analysis of the cycle as a conflict between the righteous and the wicked, with the prophets functioning in the role of the evildoers at the redactional level of the cycle) by such undefined, but clearly disapproved of, behaviour (cf. v. 22) suggests a conspiracy between the prophets and other, unspecified, people. In 38.4 Jeremiah is accused of weakening the hands of the military and the people in their defence of Jerusalem against the Babylonians. The two metaphors, strengthening/weakening the hands, describe support of or attack against either specific policies or people. But whereas 38.1–6 provides a setting and explanation of the metaphor, 23.14 does not.

Its generality is part of the blanket charges against the prophets using pejorative descriptions. Some groups of people (here termed 'evildoers') receive support by the way the prophets behave and do not need to change their ways. Hence the prophets contribute to the brazenness of the community (cf. Isa. 3.9) rather than challenge it. It may be tempting for exegetes to move from this level of the text to a holistic approach to the complete book of Jeremiah and produce a complex cross-referencing of texts to show that here Jeremiah opposes the prophets who supported Jehoiakim and, later, Zedekiah (cf. 27–29). The temptation should be resisted.

An oracular judgment is appended to the poem in which the deity punishes the prophets because they have created the pollution which has spread throughout the land. The punishment is the poisoning of the prophets. The images of poisonous herbs and water are used in 9.15 (cf. 8.14) with reference to the people and their destruction, so must be considered to be a secondary level of application here (Thiel 1973, 250, attributes them to the Deuteronomistic redaction). If the redactional direction in v. 15a is omitted as secondary, then it is possible to read 'them' as a reference to the evildoers of v. 14 (MT's 'inhabitants'). However, the introductory phrase in v. 15a is correct and consistent with the rest of the poem: it is an attack on the prophets, so they must be punished for their wicked ways. They are the ones responsible for profaning the land with their irreligious ways (cf. v. 11, where the temple houses their profanity). Too much should not be read into the term 'ungodliness' because it simply represents the 'godless' (i.e. 'sinners', cf. Isa. 33.14, 'the sinners in Zion are afraid; trembling has seized the godless [*ḥanēpīm*]') as opposed to the 'godly' (the opposition is well illustrated by Isa. 33.13–16). Irreligion in this sense describes the beliefs and practices of groups other than the speaking group ('infidel' as used by mediaeval Christians and Muslims is a perfect example of the significance of *ḥānēp*). In using images of the people's destruction (8.14; 9.15) to condemn the prophets the redaction makes connections between the two sets of references. It reflects a stage in the development of the tradition when the independent cycle of material against the prophets was being incorporated into the larger work and tied into it by this means. Whereas in 9.12–16 the people are quite capable of deserving their fate, here it is the prophets' fault (to read the text in terms of its redaction).

23.16–22

16 Thus says the LORD of hosts: 'Do not listen to the words of the prophets
who prophesy to you, filling you with vain hopes; they speak visions of their
own minds, not from the mouth of the LORD. 17 They say continually to
those who despise the word of the LORD, "It shall be well with you"; and
to every one who stubbornly follows his own heart, they say, "No evil shall
come upon you." '

18 For who among them has stood in the council of the LORD
to perceive and to hear his word,
or who has given heed to his word and listened?
19 Behold, the storm of the LORD!
Wrath has gone forth,
a whirling tempest;
it will burst upon the head of the wicked.
20 The anger of the LORD will not turn back
until he has executed and accomplished
the intents of his mind.
In the latter days you will understand it clearly.
21 'I did not send the prophets,
yet they ran;
I did not speak to them,
yet they prophesied.
22 But if they had stood in my council,
then they would have proclaimed my words to my people,
and they would have turned them from their evil way,
and from the evil of their doings.'

RSV presents vv. 16–17 as prose, but other EVV and many commentators treat them as poetry. **[16]** MT *hannibbᵉʾīm lākem*, 'who are prophesying to you': lacking in G, deleted by BHS; according to Thiel 1973, 250, the phrase is an inset from the Deuteronomists. Omitting it helps to restore the metre of the line (Rudolph, 152). MT *mahbilīm hēmmāh ʾetᵉkem*, 'filling you with vain hopes': G *hoti mataiousin heautois horasin*, 'for they are seeing for themselves a trifling (vision)' i.e. lacking 'you'; G refers all the statements to the self-deluding activities of the prophets. The denominative verbal form of *hebel*, 'vapour, wind, breath, vanity' (Qoheleth's word) is not easily translated into English: 'to make vain, cause to become vain' (Hiphil), so MT = 'they are making you vain'. NEB 'who buoy you up with false hopes'; JPSB 'They are deluding you', cf. Bright, Thompson. **[17]** MT *ʾōmᵉrīm ʾāmōr*, 'who say continually': G *legousin*, 'they say', lacking *ʾāmōr*, 'continually (say)', MT overloads the metre (variant readings). MT *limᵉnaʾaṣay dibber yhwh*, 'to those who spurn me spoke Yahweh': G *tois apōthoumenois ton logon kuriou*, 'to those who reject the word of the lord' = *limᵉnaʾᵃṣē dᵉbar yhwh*. MT *wᵉkōl*, 'and all . . .'; perhaps it should be *ūlᵉkōl*, 'and *to* all . . .' (G *tois*). MT *hōlēk bišᵉrirūt libbō ʾāmᵉrū*, 'who walk in the stubbornness of his own mind they say . . .': G *tois poreuomenois tois thelēmasin autōn, panti tō poreuomenō planē kardias autou eipan*, 'to all who walk after their own will, every one who walks in the error of his own heart, they have said'; G^AS lack 'they have said'. **[18]** MT *mī ʿāmad*, 'who has stood?': RSV, 'who among them has stood . . .' understands MT with *mēhem*, 'from them', inserted (cf. BHS), also NEB. JPSB 'But he who has stood . . .', Bright retains MT. The justification for adding *mēhem* is to be found in v. 22 'but if *they* had stood . . . ?'. MT *wᵉyēreʾ wᵉyišᵉmaʿ*, 'that he might see and hear': G *kai eiden*, 'and saw . . .', lacking 'and hear'. Rudolph reads *wᵉyirʾēhū*, 'that he sees him (and hears his word)', cf. BHS. K *dbry*, 'my word'; Q *dᵉbārō*, 'his word'. BHS points *wyšmʿ wᵉyašᵉmiʿa*, 'and proclaimed it'. **[19–20]** = 30.23–24 (with minor variations). **[19]** MT *ḥēmāh*, 'wrath', may be an addition here; it turns one statement into two (cf. NEB with RSV); but Driver 1937–38, 115 argues for its retention and vocalizes it as *ḥēmmāh*, 'heat', i.e. 'anger of the Lord as "hot" '. MT *mitḥōlēl*, 'whirling' = *mitgōrēr*, 'sweeping, roaring' in 30.23 (which lacks *wᵉ* 'and' at beginning of phrase). **[20]** 30.24 has *ḥᵃrōn*, 'fierce', before *ʾap*, 'anger'. MT *titbōnᵉnū bāh bīnāh*, 'you will understand it *clearly*': 30.24 lacks *bīnāh*, as does G. **[22]** MT *wᵉyašᵉmiʿū*, 'and they would have proclaimed': G^AB *kai ei ēkousin*, 'and if they had listened . . .'. MT *ʾet-ʿammī*, 'to my people': G takes this phrase with next clause, 'and my people they would have turned . . .'. G lacks 'from their evil way and'.

A number of elements makes up this unit: a Deuteronomistically shaped statement in vv. 16–17 dismisses the prophets as speakers of their own mind, a floating oracle in vv. 19–20 (also in 30.23–24), and a poem denying the prophets any claim to a divine commission. The motif of the divine council (*sōd*) appears in vv. 18, 22, but the authenticity of v. 18 is questioned by some commentators (e.g. Volz, 235; cf. Rudolph, 152). In Job 15.8 Eliphaz the Temanite asks Job the rhetorical questions 'Have you listened in the council of god? And do you limit wisdom to yourself?', and these suggest a similar role for v. 18. It is a wisdom saying which the redaction has added to the unit, possibly under the influence of v. 22 (so Volz). The answer presupposed by the question is 'No! No one has!' (cf. Duhm, 187). However, in its present position it appears to provide an occasion for vv. 19–20 and some exegetes (e.g. Bright, 152) even understand vv. 19–20 as the word spoken in Yahweh's council. The highly edited unit (cf. the variations between MT and G) functions in the cycle as a general statement against the prophets. It precedes a series of criticisms directed against the techniques of the prophets (vv. 25–32) and emphasizes the inauthenticity of the speakers. Hence the introductory ruling, 'Do not listen to the words of the prophets . . .'.

The charges made against the prophets in vv. 16–17, 21 also appear in 14.13–15. The community is presumably the recipient of the command not to listen, though a specific group might be intended by the editors. The prophets (no identification is offered of who they may be, so the prohibition may function in different circumstances) are described as speaking their own words and this judgment is characterized as a divine word (i.e. a prophetic oracle announces that the prophets do not speak the divine word). From the standpoint of the tradition this proclamation is an authentic one, though it can only be substantiated by processes which are not apparent in the text. The words spoken come only from the mind of the prophets (contrast 12.2 where the opposite is cause for complaint) and create empty possibilities (*mahbilīm* is difficult to translate here). Their visions are conjured up out of their own minds rather than constructed from Yahweh's words and they reassure those who despise Yahweh's words. Thus the prophets are identified with a class of people in the community which rejects visions based on the divine word. If this claim is more than an ideological point made by the Deuteronomists it may reflect some quarrel in the community between different groups (cf. v. 28). The polarization of the people into righteous (i.e. pious) and wicked (i.e. those who differ from the pious) is probably reflected in vv. 16–17, hence the condemnation of the prophets by associating them with a class of people who are said to despise Yahweh's words. Here the prophets support such people but in 4.10 divine deception via the prophets achieves the destruction of the people (whatever their attitude to the divine word may be). The charge of supporting evildoers is made in vv. 14, 17, 22 (with variations) and clearly whoever the material is directed against is being condemned by association with such people.

The presence of vv. 19–20 here indicates the hopelessness of proclamations of *šālōm* because the divine storm is about the break on the heads of the wicked. When that happens the people (i.e. those addressed in v. 16) will understand the falseness of the prophets. The latter days of v. 20 must refer in this context to the immediate future which will expose the wicked (i.e. the prophets), rather than to any eschatological future (the original intention of the phrase but out of place here). The clear distinction between the wicked and those who will understand as two classes of people renders the material a statement about the righteous-wicked controversy and *not* about prophetic clashes before 587. In the tradition the fall of Jerusalem demonstrates the guilt of everybody and not the vindication of any group or class of people. The contextual reading of vv. 19–20 makes the storm the vindication of the speaker and those who do not despise Yahweh's words, as much as it is the punishment of the wicked. Thus the prophets are condemned by being classified with the wicked.

Further charges are made against the prophets in v. 21. They have performed as prophets but without divine authorization. They run without commissioning; they speak but have no divine words to use (cf. 14.14). The theoretical nature of these charges is apparent: how could the speaker have known such inner matters as divine commissioning and speaking with references to *other* minds? If the holistic approach to the book of Jeremiah is taken, then the question may be asked in stronger terms. How could the person who admitted that the human mind is too crafty for anyone to understand it (17.9) make statements about other people's minds? How could he possibly know what went on in one other person's mind if he had such difficulty knowing what went on in his own? How could he make such statements as appear in vv. 16, 21? To ask such questions is to expose the defects of the holistic approach rather than to touch more than the surface of the text. In the text such judgments can be made because the ideology of the editors presents the speaker as being in the right and his opponents as being in the wrong. From that vantage point all else follows and internal contradictions may be attributed to the contiguities of discrete material without being incorporated into the exegesis. However, the unit does offer evidence for the falseness of the prophets and this may permit some justification for the unknowable claim that Yahweh did not speak to or send those prophets.

In v. 22 it is argued that the prophets have not stood in the divine council because if they had they would have proclaimed the divine words to the people. The result of this proclamation would have turned (*šūb*) the people from their evil ways. So the fact that the people have not turned from doing evil is evidence that the prophets have not had access to the divine council. The lack of turning from evil in the community *demonstrates* the claim that the prophets were not commissioned by Yahweh and did not speak his words. This reading of v. 22 allows some exegetes to understand v. 18 not as a rhetorical question, later wisdom gloss or a statement of impossible human achievement but as a question directed to finding out which prophet has had access to the council. 'Who is it that has stood in Yahweh's council? How can you tell him?' (Bright, 152). To understand v. 18 in this way is to reject the RSV reading of it in favour of MT and to separate v. 18 from v. 22. No longer do they both mean the same thing (i.e. the prophets have not stood in the council), but v. 18 conceals a claim for the speaker. Such a reading of v. 18 is less likely to be correct than the alternative interpretations offered already, but it does illustrate how vague and general are the assertions of vv. 16–22.

The motif of the divine council only appears in the Jeremiah tradition in vv. 18, 22, though there may be traces of it behind other texts (see on 5.1–5). The idea of an assembly where the gods meet to confer is clearly a mythological one (cf. Mullen 1980), though its role in biblical literature may be less mythological than metaphorical (cf. Cross 1953; Robinson 1944; Polley 1980; Kingsbury 1964). The polytheism explicit in the concept of a council of the gods is necessarily modified in Israelite thought to a meeting place where Yahweh and superhuman beings discuss matters affecting the earth. In this council decisions are made and then carried out in the human sphere. Examples of such matters include the creation of humankind (Gen. 1.26), the deception of a king in affairs of war (I Kings 22.19–23), the destruction of a nation (Isa. 6.8–11), the determining of the fate of Job (Job 1, 2) and the proclamation of forgiveness to Jerusalem (Isa.40.1–2). In material which has some association with Deuteronomistic editing a link between prophets and the council is mooted (e.g. Amos 3.7; Jer. 23.18, 22) and certain prophetic 'call' narratives can be read against a background of the council (cf. Isa. 6.1–11; Ezek. 1–3; Zimmerli 1979, 97–100). In the light of these stories vv. 18, 22 posit such a council to which prophets may have access. At least v. 22 may be read in this way. But if the motif is understood to be a metaphorical element in biblical literature it would be unwise to treat it as anything other than a literary device designed for telling certain kinds of story. These stories do have an affinity with prophetic tales because they both share certain common features: e.g. decisions made by the deity requiring communication to the parties concerned, hidden agendas which explain historical events, and differentiations between those who know and those who do not.

The force of v. 22 is simply: if the prophets had had access to the council their message would have been different from the empty visions with which they encouraged the wicked. They would have spoken the divine words and the people would have turned from their evil ways. The charge that they supported evildoers is evidence that they had not stood in the council. There appears to be a claim here that support for a particular group or order of things allied to a failure to change people's behaviour constitutes proof that the prophets were not sent by Yahweh. Many exegetes understand v. 22 in this fashion, and among older writers on Jeremiah much is made of this analysis in defining 'false' prophecy (e.g. Peake; Skinner 1922; Calkins 1930). However, the analysis is not without serious defects. The claim in v. 22 cannot be substantiated because there is no inherent connection between preaching the divine words and turning the people from the evil of their doings. A simple *tu quoque* argument will demonstrate this. The holistic approach to the tradition makes Jeremiah the speaker of these oracles, yet in the summary of Jeremiah's twenty-three years of preaching it is quite clear that he failed to turn the people or to persuade them to turn (25.1–7). If failure to turn the people is evidence of not having stood in the council then Jeremiah had no more stood in that council than had the other prophets. The argument of v. 22 lacks cogency as well as coherence (cf. Carroll 1976a). This may only further call into question the holistic approach to interpreting Jeremiah but it has a serious point to make. The arguments used against the prophets are ideological ones and, like all ideological argumentation, only achieve what is already believed to be the case. If they are reversed in a *tu quoque* manner they undermine the ideologists as effectively as their opponents.

23.23–24

23 'Am I a God at hand, says the LORD, and not a God afar off? 24 Can a man hide himself in secret places so that I cannot see him? says the LORD. Do I not fill heaven and earth? says the LORD.'

[23] MT *ha'elōhē miqqārōb 'ānī*, lit., 'Am I the god of from near': the phrase 'god of from near(by)' balances *'elōhē mērāḥōq*, 'god of from afar'. G *theos eggizōn egō eimi, legei kurios, kai ouchi theos porrōthen*, 'I am a god at hand, says the lord, and not a god afar off'. MT's interrogative form is lacking in G which asserts the opposite to MT. Ehrlich 1912, 304, reads *ha'elōhīm qārōb*, 'the near god', *'elōhīm rāḥōq*, 'the far god'. **[2]** G lacks first occurrence of *ne'um yhwh*, 'says Yahweh'.

Herrmann 1983; Lemke 1981

Three oracular fragments appear between vv. 22, 25. Translators and commentators differ as to their form and whether they should be attached to the preceding section (e.g. NEB) or the following (e.g. RSV). Treating them as separate fragments (cf. JPSB) not only avoids making such a decision, it permits them to be scrutinized in relation to both vv. 16–22 and vv. 25–32. The brevity of the three sayings prevents the necessity of a discussion about their poetic or prosaic form. The threefold *ne'um yhwh*, 'says Yahweh', presents the independent disputation as a divine speech, initiated and terminated by this formulaic phrase (cf. 3.1; Rendtorff 1954, 33).

Minor variations between MT and G (e.g. two questions and two oracle formulas in G whereas MT has three of each) highlight interpretative difficulties in the text. According to MT Yahweh is a distant god rather than a near god and this distance allows him to see everything because of his transcendence. G makes v. 23 a statement rather than a rhetorical question and asserts that Yahweh is near and not a distant god. This nearness allows him to see everything because he is an immanent god. In both versions Yahweh fills the heavens and the earth. The theological perspectives behind the texts are immanentist (G) and transcendental (MT): though some exegetes read the Hebrew *ha . . . welō'* as 'not only . . . but also' rather than 'either . . . or' (e.g. Meyer 1977, 130), which would allow MT to combine both perspectives. In theological discourse immanence and transcendence are pairs which belong together but seldom are they held in balance without one or the other dominating the discussion about the nature of the divine. It is therefore difficult to determine what v. 23 means and which version should be followed.

The interpretative difficulties of v. 23 are created by the difference between MT and G, the brevity of the two halves of the verse, and the connotative range of the two words 'near' (*qārōb*) and 'far' (*rāḥōq*).

The lapidary nature of the three sayings, especially of v. 23, inevitably increases the scope for interpretation because it conceals the information necessary for delimiting the possible meanings of phrases. It also filters out clues to gestures and tone which assist interpretation (here MT's interrogative inflection of v. 23 makes ambiguous G's straightforward assertion). As the first edition G represents a simple statement that Yahweh is not a distant god but one at hand. He is therefore in a good position to observe the prophets and, because no one can hide from him, to hear what they are saying (v. 25). If taken with v. 22 it asserts that though the prophets have not had access to the divine council, Yahweh is close to them. They may not know what is going on in the assembly, but the deity knows what is going on among them. The immanentist theology of G provides the background for the dismissal of the prophetic techniques discussed in vv. 25–32. Yahweh as the nation's near god is one of the features of Israel's special relation to Yahweh which make it unique (Deut. 4.7 note *'elōhīm qerōbīm*, 'near gods'; cf. the nearness of the divine word-commandment in Deut. 30.11–14 and the nearness of Yahweh to the pious, Ps. 119.151). That Yahweh is not a distant god is the point of v. 23; from it stem the subsequent criticisms of the prophets.

What appears to be a straightforward piece of theological introduction to the next unit is, however, more complicated when MT is considered. It puts the assertion into the interrogative form and thereby makes it rather difficult to interpret. 'Am I a god at hand . . . and not a god afar off?' What is the tone of this question? Where do the stresses appear? Is it saying 'I am not near but far off' or 'I am not only near but far off'? Ambiguity of this type makes the exegete's task harder because it permits a wider range of meaning to be explored but without checks on the exegesis. If MT is taken to be an assertion that Yahweh is not near but far away then v. 23 may be an anticipation of v. 24. Because Yahweh is not parochial but transcendent he sees all and, by implication, is aware of what the prophets are doing and saying. The interrogative form may then reflect the theology of the prophets who believe in a near god to whom they have access (i.e. the god of the national shrine, cult, palace). On the contrary, asserts v. 23: Yahweh is a distant god, beyond your reach and control. The distant god is the one which cannot be manipulated or with which one cannot horse-trade (cf. Lemke, 554). As vv. 25–32 set out a series of techniques about manipulating the prophetic role, this is a fair way of understanding

v. 23. The near god is the local deity from which one may safely hide (cf. v. 24; Bright, 152), the one who cannot see all. Yahweh is the transcendent one who fills the heavens and the earth and from whom no one can hide (cf. Amos 9.2–4; Ps. 139.7–12).

The word *qārōb*, 'near', can be interpreted spatially or temporally. Its temporal sense with reference to gods appears in Deut. 32.17 where the nation's fathers are accused of sacrificing to new-fangled gods, 'to new gods that had come in of late (*ḥᵃdāšîm miqqārōb bā'ū*), whom your fathers had never dreaded' (cf. Deut. 13.8 [EV 7], where 'near' and 'far' have a spatial reference to the gods). In this temporal sense the distant god is the ancient one, not the alien new gods, and v. 23 asserts a radical difference between Yahweh and the god of the prophets. Here there may be a hint of associating the prophets with other gods or, at least, a condemnation of their understanding of Yahweh. The question is therefore in keeping with the elements in the cycle which associate the prophets with godlessness in the community (vv. 11, 14, 15). It does not state that the prophets are idolaters but, if the god who is near is an allusion to more recent gods than Yahweh, it insinuates that there is some connection between them and heterodox (from the editorial viewpoint) cults. This reading of the oracular fragment points to a period akin to that of Zech. 13.2–6 where prophets are clearly associated with idols and the unclean spirit in the land (cf. Duhm, 185, who attributes vv. 16–40 to the editors and relates the material to the period of Zech. 13.2–6; Isa. 13–23). The techniques of the prophets which are then condemned are but the products of such illicit religion.

A third category of interpretation is offered by exegetes who wish to read v. 23 as combining two truths about Yahweh: he is *both* near and far (cf. Lemke, Meyer). This approach would rule out understanding *qārōb* to refer to 'local deity' or 'recently acquired novel deity' because neither can be applied to Yahweh. The near god is a fundamental theological truth about Yahweh which has become perverted by being absolutized and subjected to the manipulations of the prophets (Lemke, 554). Yahweh *is* a god who is near, but he cannot be manipulated – in that sense he is a god who is distant. Too much should not be presumed about him. The distinction between man and Yahweh must be maintained; the distance between god and man cannot be ignored (Weiser, 208). Yahweh is distant (especially from the prophets) and his word invades human experience from outside it (cf. v. 29). The deity's immanence is limited by his transcendence, which should correct any misconceptions about the god who is near.

A different way of reading v. 23, but which combines the 'near' and 'far' motifs, is to interpret it in terms of the righteous-wicked conflict. Elements of the conflict inform the cycle, especially in the presentation of the prophets as companions and supporters of evildoers (vv. 14, 17, 22). In 12.2b (cf. 9.8) it is said of the wicked that Yahweh is near (*qārōb*) in their mouth but far (*rāḥōq*) from their feelings. So the god who is near their mouths (cf. v. 31) is in reality the god who is far from the prophets. This reading interprets v. 23 as a fragment from that controversy which is an important strand in the tradition. The prophets are religiose but not genuine pietists. That is perhaps too allusive a reading of v. 23, too sophisticated a view of the text as a shorthand extract from the tradition. But the fragmentary nature of the question assists the proliferation of interpretations.

If the terms 'near' and 'far' which are used to qualify 'god' in the text are understood theologically rather than as references to the inner-outer states of the prophets, then they may refer to divine activity in relation to salvation or destruction. Such a theological reading of v. 23 would suit both the cycle and the fragments in it. The god who is near is the one who saves (cf. Isa. 55.6; note Isa. 46.12–13, where Yahweh's salvation is near but scoffers [?] are far from it). The saviour god is the central theological platform of the prophets (v. 17; cf. 28.2–4). But Yahweh is also a distant god, i.e. one who does not save but destroys (hence v. 19 in the cycle), whose word is a fire and a hammer (i.e. destructive, v. 29). It is this god who is distant which is opposed to the near god of the prophets. In the debate about salvation and destruction v. 23 sides with the destruction party. The god proclaimed by the prophets is not the one active on behalf of the community but the distant one operating against the people (v. 16 indicates lack of distance). The fragment is a counter-claim to the salvation principle advocated by the prophets. The word for now is 'look, the storm of Yahweh has gone forth!' (v. 19).

The hiding motif of v. 24 reflects the idea of the transcendent deity who sees all and from whom none can hide (cf. Gen. 3.8; 4.14; Job 34.22; Amos 9. 2–4; Ps. 139.7–12). The omnipresence of Yahweh (v. 24b) exposes the prophets to his scrutiny (hence the exposure of their techniques in vv. 25–32). Yet the inability of humankind to hide from Yahweh is but one element in an important theological strand of biblical thought: the hiddenness of god (cf. Perlitt 1971; von Rad 1965, 374–8; Barth 1957, 179–204). 'All true knowledge of God begins with the knowledge of his hiddenness' (von Rad 1965, 377; cf. Isa. 45.15). The god who cannot be hidden from is at the same time the god who is hidden from mankind. His accessibility is strictly limited: an important point in the debate with the prophets and one which prophetic manipulation and confidence appear to have forgotten. The fragments therefore represent an extract from a theological perspective diametrically opposed to the prophetic behaviour which can manipulate the deity or is at ease in the divine presence. The hiddenness of Yahweh (even as the saviour god) calls into question human activities, pretensions and claims and counteracts the frenzied performances of those who would speak for God (not the god but God!). In reality the theological framework of the fragments draws attention not to the god who is near and/or distant, but to the one who is hidden.

How suited is this theological framework to the cycle in which it appears? The rhetorical questions can only loosely be attached to the arguments of vv. 25–32 (cf. Brueggemann 1973, 369), and their presence there is entirely an editorial placement. The god who speaks (v. 29) is hardly the hidden one, for such an unmediated action has a directness about it which is lacking in the concept of hiddenness (the context of Isa. 45.14–15 illustrates the obliqueness of the idea). When Yahweh is hidden, even the prophetic word ceases to speak (cf Isa.8.16–22; Carroll 1980, 131–2). Thus the hiddenness of Yahweh may function in a *tu quoque* manner even against favoured prophets, so that the very claim to speak in Yahweh's name is evidence of falseness (this criterion would falsify Jeremiah as much as the other prophets!). The shaping of the section with these questions therefore suggests a theological context where *all* prophets were regarded with suspicion and this would constitute another link between the cycle and Zech. 13.2–6. It is a profound irony, however, that such a controversy should have found its way into the tradition of Jeremiah *the prophet*.

23.25–32

25 'I have heard what the prophets have said who prophesy lies in my name,
saying, "I have dreamed, I have dreamed!" 26 How long shall there be lies
in the heart of the prophets who prophesy lies, and who prophesy the deceit
of their own heart, 27 who think to make my people forget my name by their
dreams which they tell one another, even as their fathers forgot my name
for Baal? 28 Let the prophet who has a dream tell the dream, but let him
who has my word speak my word faithfully. What has straw in common
with wheat? says the LORD. 29 Is not my word like fire, says the LORD, and
like a hammer which breaks the rock in pieces? 30 Therefore, behold, I am
against the prophets, says the LORD, who steal my words from one another.
31 Behold, I am against the prophets, says the LORD, who use their tongues
and say, "Says the LORD." 32 Behold, I am against those who prophesy
lying dreams, says the LORD, and who tell them and lead my people astray
by their lies and their recklessness, when I did not send them or charge
them; so they do not profit this people at all, says the LORD.'

EVV and the majority of commentators treat vv. 25–32 as prose, even Condamin, 184–5. BHS, Rudolph take vv. 28b, 29 as poetry (Bright vv. 28–29), whereas Holladay 1966c, 424–33, sets out the whole unit as poetry (cf. Thompson, 500, who sees the unit as 'originally poetic in form'). **[25]** MT *šeqer*, 'falsehood, deception, deceit, lie': RSV, NEB 'lies', JPSB 'prophesy falsely'; the plural *šiq^{e}rēhem*, 'their lies', is used in v. 32, so a singular meaning is better in v. 25. **[26]** MT *'ad-mātay h^{a}yēš b^{e}lēb hann^{e}bi'īm nibb^e'ē haššāqer*, 'how long will there be in the heart of the prophets prophecies of falsehood?': Duhm, 191 reads *'ad-mātay* as *ḥālamtī*, 'I have dreamed', making the word a triple phrase with *ḥālamtī ḥālāmtī* of v. 25 (cf. 7.4; 22.29 for other triples), followed by Rudolph (BHS). Meyer 1977, 132, rejects this in favour of translating MT as 'making plans' (cf. KB, 340), i.e. *ḥšb*. Duhm redistributes *hyš blb* as *h^{a}yāšub lēb*, 'when will the heart (of the prophets) turn . . .?' MT *ūn^{e}bī'ē tarmit libbām*, 'and prophets of the deceit of their own hearts': BHS *w^{e}nibb^e'ē*, 'and prophecies of . . .'. Rudolph, 154, reads *h^{a}yēš* as *hašš^{e}mī*, 'is my name (in the heart of . . .)', cf. Ex. 23.21; BHS. **[27]** MT *l^{e}haškkīaḥ 'et-'ammī š^{e}mī*, 'to cause my people to forget my name': for *š^{e}mī* G has *tou nomou mou*, 'my law', G* *tou epilathesthai tou onomatos mou*, 'to forget my name'; S 'to lead my people astray in my name' cf. BHS. Meyer deletes 'my people' as a double reading in MT (lacking in G). **[28]** MT *y^{e}sappēr ḥ^{a}lōm* '(the prophet who has a dream) let him tell a dream': G *to enupnion autou*, '*his* dream' = *ḥ^{a}lōmō* (cf. '*my* word'); MT due to haplography. **[29]** MT *h^{a}lō kōh d^{e}bārī kā'ēš*, 'is not thus my word like fire?': G has a double reading (cf. Janzen 1973, 12) *houtōs hoi logoi mou legei kurios. ouchi hoi logoi mou hōsper pur phlegon*, 'so are my words, says the lord. Are not my words as a *blazing* fire?'

i.e. reading *kōh* as *kōweh*, 'blazing, burning, scorching', cf. BHS. **[31]** MT *hallōqeḥīm lešōnām*, 'who take their tongues', i.e. 'use their tongues': NEB 'concoct words of their own', cf. JPSB 'who wag their tongues'. Driver 1937–38, 115, treats it as ' "who conceive (with) their tongues," namely who give birth to all kinds of false prophecies'. G *tous ekballontas prophēteias glōssēs*, 'who put out prophecies of the tongue'. MT *wayyinᵃmū neʾum*, 'and say "says Yahweh" ': the word-play here is a coinage from the formulaic *neʾum yhwh*, 'says Yahweh', which is very difficult to put into English; cf. Bright, 153, 'and "oracle an oracle" '. This is the only occurrence of the verbal form of *neʾum* and presumably apes prophetic jargon. A few mss have *neʾum yhwh*, 'says Yahweh', in place of the word-play. G *kai nustazontas nustagmon autōn*, 'and sleep their sleep' = *wayyānūmū nūm* (missing the word-play because of the dream theme in vv. 25–27, 32). **[32]** MT *hinenī ʿal-nibbeʾē ḥᵃlōmōt šeqer neʾum yhwh*, 'look, I am against the prophecies of dreams of falsehood, says Yahweh': many mss have 'the prophets of . . .'; G . . . *pros tous prophētas tous propheteuontas* . . . '. . . against the prophets who prophesy . . .'. BHS inserts *hannebīʾīm*, 'the prophets', into MT (following G). MT *ūbepaḥᵃzūtām*, 'and by their recklessness': *paḥᵃzūt* means 'wantonness, extravagance, boastful tales, loose talk, recklessness'. Bright translates as 'mendacious claptrap', taking *paḥᵃzūt* and *šeqer* together, cf. NEB 'wild and reckless falsehoods'. MT *wehōʿēl lōʾ-yōʿīlū*, 'and they do not profit at all . . .': cf. 2.8; some Q mss read *wehōʿēl*.

Carroll 1981, 173–9; Holladay 1966c, 424–33; Meyer 1977, 132–40

The unit in vv. 25–32 appears to pick up from v. 21 and to continue the divine attack on the prophets (the redaction has sprinkled liberally the rhetorical phrase 'says Yahweh' throughout vv. 28–32). The theme of the unit is the proclamation of the prophets that they 'have a dream'. This dream is announced in Yahweh's name and has the effect of misleading the people. Opposed to the dream is the divine word. The two modes of divine revelation are sharply distinguished from each other in a number of different ways and the message of the heavily edited unit is the oracular statement 'I am against the prophets, says Yahweh, who . . .' (cf. 'Do not listen to the prophets . . .', 27.9, 14, 16, 17).

The element of conflict is clearly part of the unit but the divine word versus the dream factor is only on the surface of it and not the heart of the matter. Analysing the text reveals that the conflict is between word and word and the basis of the opposition is the acquisition of the divine word. A summary of the unit shows that

Yahweh is against the prophets who 'prophesy in *my* name . . . to make *my* people forget *my* name . . . steal *my* words . . . use their tongues . . .'. These are all verbal activities referring to actions and effects. The dream is simply one technique for acquiring the word which is also condemned. In fact the techniques of acquiring the divine word are the target of the attack: dreams, self-deceit, stealing of oracles, mimicry of oracular speech, and reckless talk. If the dream appears to be singled out it may be because it is one of the dominant features of the group under attack or, more likely, the term 'dream' (*ḥ*ᵃ*lōm*) is assonantally close to 'peace' (*šālōm*). These prophets proclaim *šālōm šālōm* (6.14; 8.11; 23.17; cf. 4.10), which is really *ḥ*ᵃ*lōm ḥ*ᵃ*lōm*, 'dream dream (I have dreamed)' or even *ḥ*ᵃ*lōm šālōm*, 'dream of peace'. The repeated phrase (cf. the triple talismanic phrase in 7.4; BHS on 23.25–26) is part of the ritual gesture accompanying the declaration of a divine revelation (considered to be false by the editors of the tradition). The message proclaimed is false (*šeqer*) because it is acquired in the wrong way: either because dreams are disapproved of in the context of this unit or, more likely, because the divine word is acquired by false means. They tell each other their dreams, they steal each other's words, and they use their tongues to ape authentic prophetic techniques.

The prophets are false (*šeqer*), i.e. pseudo-prophets (neither MT nor G uses this good Greek word or its equivalent here), because of the techniques they use. They *do* use the divine word (cf. 'my words', v. 30), but they have no title to it because of the means they have used to acquire it. The false dreams (cf. 'lying vision' of 14.14) are the equivalent of the Samarian prophets prophesying in the name of Baal (v. 13), yet they are uttered in the name of Yahweh. MT is confusing in vv. 25–27 (cf. G v. 27 which lacks 'my people') because it accuses the prophets of prophesying falsehood (*šeqer*) in Yahweh's name and thereby causing the people to forget Yahweh's name, just as their fathers forgot the divine name for Baal. But how could prophesying *in Yahweh's name* make people forget Yahweh? Explaining the difficulty in terms of Yahweh's 'essential character' (e.g. Bright, 153) is unsatisfactory because name and character are bound up together, not separated in this fashion in Hebrew thought. The incoherence (lessened in some G versions) is best accounted for by recognizing the highly rhetorical nature of the attack and the patchwork-quilt phraseology of the unit (for Deuteronomistic influence cf. v. 32; Thiel 1973, 252–3). These features of the polemic also account for the curious discrepancy between the admission that the prophets are using the divine words (v. 30 'who steal *my words* from each other') and the polarity between divine word and dream asserted by v. 28.

The poetic kernel in vv. 28b–29 may be the mid-point of the poem (so Holladay, 424), but it really disrupts the flow of the sermon by introducing a quite disjunctive note into the unit. If false acquisition of the word is the theme, then the contrast between word and dream of v. 28a (with implicit backing of metaphors in vv. 28b–29) is irrelevant. As vv. 30–31 make clear, the prophets *are* speaking the *word* so v. 28a is beside the point. They are condemned for the ways they have acquired the word (e.g. stealing it or mimicry of it) rather than for not having it. The dream-word polarity is part of the unit but only because vv. 28–29 form an element in the poem. The poetic images in vv. 28b–29 have no inherent connection with word or dream but are similes introduced into the unit to construct a differentiation between word and dream. They therefore reflect an ideological position which approves of the word but not of dreams (a reversal of the terms will demonstrate this). The content of the prophetic dream is never specified, so it cannot be shown that the dream is not like a fire or hammer (cf. the chief baker's dream interpreted by Joseph in Gen. 40.16–19!). The poetic fragment 'What has straw in common with wheat?' (*mah-latteben 'et-habbār*, cf. Holladay's reconstructed addition 'my word/dream') may function for any contrast whatsoever between an approved of term and one disapproved of by whoever is speaking. The dynamic and destructive images of the word in v. 29 suggest that the dream concerns *šālōm* and future well-being. This would fit the previous units where the *šālōm* preaching of the prophets is contrasted to the divine storm bursting on the heads of the wicked. In such a polarized discussion dream is equivalent to straw and word to wheat, but only for the purposes of party polemics.

The use of the images in vv. 28–29 slews the argument in the direction of a straightforward contrast between those who use words and the producers of dreams. This then produces a false dichotomy between the word and the dream as media of divine revelation. It is false because the dream is as much a legitimate form of divine communication in biblical traditions as the word is (cf. Gen. 20.3, 6; 28.10–17; 31.10–13; 37.5–10; 40.5–23; Num. 12.6; Judg. 7.13–15; I Kings 3.5–15; Dan. 1.17; 2.25–30). However, the dream does not appear to have a major place in the prophetic traditions, so its attribution to the prophets here undermines their activity. Actions, visions, gestures and words are all used to describe standard prophetic behaviour, and the singling out of dreams may be due to a particular controversy in a time when dreams and visions were being denounced by anti-prophetic sources (cf. Zech. 10.2; 13.4). The sharp antithesis between word and dream cannot be sustained as a general critique of certain prophets because dreams and visions are as much the inspiration of Yahweh as words and signs (e.g. Num. 12.6; Deut. 13.1–3). All may be true *and* all (including words Deut. 13.3) may be false. The forms of revelation are not defective in themselves, though they may become false when used in certain ways or by certain people (cf. Lindblom 1962, 201). In the future age the outpouring of the divine spirit will result in young people prophesying and seeing visions and old people dreaming dreams (Joel 2.28 [MT 3.1]), so the forms of inspiriting cannot be regarded as false *per se*. Oneiromancy may not have been approved of by some circles or by the individuals incorporated into the prophetic traditions but that is a matter of ideology, aesthetics or prejudice. The young Samuel became a prophet through some incubatory process which involved sleeping in the temple and receiving a revelatory dream or visitation (I Sam. 3.1–14; cf. Wilson 1980, 171). Although v. 28 may appear to rule out such a possibility, it should not be read as a general principle but only as a pejorative remark in a party political dispute. It also distracts from the main argument about the improper acquisition of the word (see on 31.26).

The accusations hurled in the dispute denounce the techniques of the prophets who proclaim what is false. It is the falseness of what they say (determined from the standpoint of their critics) which makes their techniques false. Words, dreams, oracles are all false because they come from the minds of the speakers and not from Yahweh. This cannot mean that words, dreams, oracles are false *per se*, because that would falsify the whole range of inspirational techniques used even by those of whom the editors approved (e.g. Jeremiah and the canonical prophets of a later period; cf. Job. 33.14–16, where it is acknowledged that God speaks through dreams and night-visions). It can only mean that legitimate techniques in the hands of people who are false become false themselves. It is the false consciousness (an ideological point) of the prophets which falsifies their use of proper channels of inspiration. Yahweh has not spoken to them *therefore* what they say must come from their own minds (vv. 16, 26). If they do speak the divine word it is because they have *stolen* those words (*m^e gann^e bē d^e bāray*, 'stealers of my words', v. 30) or so wield their tongues that they 'oracle an oracle', i.e. mouth the right words. But right words, formulas and techniques do not make true prophets. What is false is false within, and the external modes, though correct, only mislead the people and profit them not at all.

There is no criteriology here but an ideology which determines truth or falsehood. If the unit could be read as affording criteria of validation it would falsify every prophet in the canon! For who among them never borrowed an oracle or used correct formulas, never had dreams and visions, or never spoke softly on occasion with words of comfort (e.g. Isa. 40.1–2; 42.1–4)? The divine word is not always a fire or a hammer, so v. 29 cannot function as the criterion of the authentic word. However, if the unit is not read as criteriological but as the output of an ideological conflict either between prophetic parties or against prophets its inconsistencies cease to be such and it may be read as a contribution to the construction of the tradition. In the context of the cycle it gives the impression of being the true versus the false but in point of fact the cycle is *only* concerned with the false. All the prophets under consideration are false! This fact rather confirms the analysis of the cycle belonging to that late period when prophets were banned as false *per se* (Zech. 13.2–6). Prophecy and word may well be opposed in v. 28 (the Hebrew will allow this interpretation, though the word *hannābī'* may be distributed to both parts of the verse). The speaker of the word (neither identified: prophet? *tōrāh*? tradition?) may point to a higher authority than prophets (note the contrast between prophets and Moses in Num. 12.6–8).

23.33–40

33 'When one of this people, or a prophet, or a priest asks you, "What is the burden of the LORD?" you shall say to them, "You are the burden, and I will cast you off, says the LORD." 34 And as for the prophet, priest, or one of the people who says, "The burden of the LORD," I will punish that man and his household. 35 Thus shall you say, every one to his neighbour and every one to his brother, "What has the LORD answered?" or "What has

the LORD spoken?" 36 But "the burden of the LORD" you shall mention no
more, for the burden is every man's own word, and you pervert the words
of the living God, the LORD of hosts, our God. 37 Thus you shall say to the
prophet, "What has the LORD answered you?" or "What has the LORD
spoken?" 38 But if you say, "The burden of the LORD," thus says the LORD,
'Because you have said these words, "The burden of the LORD," when I
sent to you, saying, "You shall not say, 'The burden of the LORD,' " ' 39
therefore, behold, I will surely lift you up and cast you away from my
presence, you and the city which I gave to you and your fathers. 40 And I
will bring upon you everlasting reproach and perpetual shame, which shall
not be forgotten." '

---

[33] Rudolph treats 'or a prophet, or a priest' as an addition from v. 34,
cf. BHS. MT *wᵉ'āmartā ᵃlēhem 'et-mah-maśśā'*, 'and you shall say to them,
"the what burden?" ': the consonants may be redistributed to produce an
intelligible reply *'attem hammaśśā'*, 'you are the burden'. Many exegetes see
a word-play in *maśśā'*, 'oracle', and *maśśā'*, 'burden', (e.g. Bright, Meyer,
Nicholson, Thompson, Weiser). McKane 1980a, 35–40, sets out the arguments and concludes that the words are homonyms in which there is no
nuance of 'burden' attached to '(oracular) utterance'. The homonymic
character of the two words is exploited in the question 'what is Yahweh's
utterance?' and its answer 'you are the burden' (McKane, 44). [36] MT
tizkᵉrū, 'you shall remember (no more)': G *onomazete*, 'you shall name' =
tazᵉkkirū, 'you shall mention'. Rudolph reads *hᵃmaśśā'* for MT *hammaśśā'*,
'shall his word be a burden for anybody?', cf BHS. Gᴮˢ lack vv. 36b–37a
from 'and you pervert . . .' to '. . . answered you?', this may represent the
'accidental loss of a line' (cf. Janzen 1973, 223–4). MT *'ᵉlōhīm ḥayyīm*, 'living
god', cf. 10.10. [38] G* lacks 'but if you say "The burden of Yahweh" '.
[39] MT *wᵉnašītī 'etkem nāśō'*, 'I will really forget you': Vrs suggest *wᵉnāśītī*,
'I will lift up' (word-play on *maśśā'*, 'burden'); MT a marginal variant
according to Janzen 1973, 99. G* lacks *'etkem nāśō'*, though SV read *nāśō'*.
G lacks *mēʿal pānāy*, 'from my presence', at the end of the verse; according
to Janzen 1973, 44, 'The phrase makes no sense following *wnṭšty*', where *nṭš*
is taken to mean 'desert, abandon, forsake' but not 'cast away', but cf. *nṭš*
as a synonym of *ʿzb*, 'forsake, leave', in Neh. 5.10; 10.32 (cf. McKane, 43–4).
NEB 'I will carry you like a burden and throw you down, casting out of my
sight . . .'. McKane, 50–1, regards G's lack of 'from my presence' as
evidence that it is an addition to MT, the phrase is appropriate with 'I will
cast you out' but not with 'I will cast out the city' (where *nṭš* is better
understood as 'desert'). The divine desertion of the city is a secondary
elaboration. [40] After v. 40 G has vv. 7–8. In this position they balance
the terrible and permanent destruction of people in that they speak of a
return.

McKane 1980a; Petersen 1977, 27–33

The final unit in the cycle touches on prophets at certain points but not directly in the way that other units focus on them. It ends with a word of judgment against the people which envisages them being cast away and suffering permanent shame (a suitable ending for a cycle which begins with an attack on the wicked who have ruined the land?). The speaker appears to be Yahweh in v. 33, but the person spoken to is not identified. If Jeremiah is assumed to be the one addressed (an assumption nowhere indicated in the cycle but made by many exegetes), then he is presented as a figure in society consulted by individuals and officials (cf. 21.1–2; 42.1–6). However, the undefined addressee should be allowed to remain anonymous because what follows is set out as a series of variations on a standard response to a question. Word-play runs through the piece, and some of it is concerned with the prophetic role in society. Only in v. 37 is the prophet singled out, but in vv. 33–34 the prophet is one of the groups specified in a very general way. Allowing for the variations between MT and G the key to understanding the unit is the word *maśśā* which in biblical Hebrew can mean 'burden, load, lifting, tribute' and also 'utterance, oracle'. It is a formal term for a prophetic statement (cf. Hab. 1.1; II Kings 9.25–26; Isa. 14.28–31; Ezek. 12.10–16) and is often used in a titular way to introduce a series of oracular pronouncements (e.g. Isa. 13.1; 15.1; 17.1; 19.1; 21.1, 11; 22.1; 23.1; Nahum 1.1; Zech. 9.1; 12.1; Mal. 1.1). The homonyms 'burden', 'oracle' provide the word-play element in v. 33. When the speaker is asked the question 'What is the *oracle* of Yahweh?' he replies 'you are the *burden* which Yahweh will abandon!'

This question-and-answer routine is an exchange between speaker and people, the reference to 'or a prophet or a priest' being a secondary addition as a result of the development of the saying by the variations on it in vv. 34–40 (Weiser, Rudolph). As vv. 38–40 show, the saying is related to the people; they (i.e. *'attem*, 'you') are the burden, and their casting off will be a devastating one. The brevity of the exchange allows for a wide range of interpretations of the word-play (exhaustive textual exegesis in McKane), and the switch of meanings of *maśśā* may hint at a note of mocking in the original question (cf. McKane, 44–5). In dismissing the people's inquiry with a clever turn of phrase the speaker indicates anger and impatience with such jaded or derisory questions. Hence the statement reflects a rather different background from that of the preceding units. There the prophets are attacked and denounced for their values, attitudes and practices; here the people are denounced for questioning the speaker (a prophet?) in such a manner. Yet the attitude behind the question or the intonation with which it is posed can only be surmised from its answer. If we may assume many things about v. 33 it is possible to decode it as: 'What is the (latest) utterance of Yahweh?', 'you are and it is a burden Yahweh will carry no longer but cast away!'. That reading of it will be spelled out in vv. 38–40.

In vv. 34–38 the phrase *maśśā' yhwh*, 'utterance of Yahweh', appears five times (with a slight variation on a further occasion cf. v. 36 *hammaśśā' yihyeh*, 'the burden will be', a clear allusion to the Leitmotif). But whereas in v. 33 it is used in a punning way, in vv. 34–38 the phrase becomes the thing itself, and any use of it by anybody will result in Yahweh's judgment. As the variations unfold it becomes clear that the formulaic words *maśśā' yhwh* must never be used on any account. It is the phrase itself that incriminates its user rather than any defect in the speaker of it (though v. 38 allows that the very use of the phrase indicates obduracy on the part of the user). This treatment of the phrase is quite different from its uses in v. 33, so the view that vv. 34–40 are not part of v. 33, held by most commentators and exegetes, is incontestible. They have been added to the fragmentary v. 33 at some stage in the editing of the cycle and represent a treatment of *maśśā' yhwh* in a variety of ways which reflect social developments of a later period. They may not be consistent with v. 33, but they are not entirely out of place in a cycle dealing with prophets who are regarded as false. The concentration on a particular formal phrase even allows for some affinity with v. 31, which condemns prophets for using formal terminology.

As the differences between MT and G indicate, there are variations in vv. 34–40 which reflect the development of the text (cf. McKane, Janzen 1973). In v. 34 people (not 'this people' of v. 33), prophet, priest are represented as potential speakers of the phrase which in v. 33 is a question addressed to a quite different person. So the setting is somewhat distinct from that of v. 33, and it is only those who use the banned phrase who will suffer (in v. 33 'this people', i.e. the nation, is Yahweh's burden which he will slough off). In fact the individual and his house will be punished (prophetic, priestly or lay). In v. 35 everybody is permitted to use certain formal phrases when inquiring about Yahweh's word, but they must never use that phrase *maśśā' yhwh*. In a social context where inquiries are made about the divine word, every formal phrase is permitted except a certain banned phrase. In v. 36 word-play on *maśśā' yhwh* appears as a reflection on what people say: the burden is every man's own word (cf. the variation on this word-play proposed by Rudolph, Bright following Ehrlich, 'is Yahweh's word a burden to anybody?'). The addition to v. 36 (cf. G) refers to the overturning (*h^a^paktem*, 'you pervert') or perversion of the divine words, an allusion that probably reflects some social dispute about the words of the living god. Lack of information prevents any more precise identification of the parties to the dispute (e.g. '*you* . . . *our* god'). By v. 37 the subject has changed again and this time the speaker (one of the classes listed in v. 34?) addresses the prophet using the correct forms of inquiry laid down in v. 35. Here the variation suggests that the real subject of these verses is the proper form of appeal to a prophet. If the instructions of vv. 35, 37 are conformed to, all will be well. But if *they* (who? people in general? the classes of v. 34? lacking in G) dare to speak the unspeakable, then because they have uttered the forbidden phrase, in spite of the warning (the divine sending of v. 38b), the deity will lift them up (word-play on *nś-maśśā'*) and cast them away. In the development of the tradition the punishment includes the city. Permanent shame will be the result of this catastrophe – and all because they said *maśśā' yhwh*!

The incongruity of the destruction of the people over the use of a cliché, especially when it appears in a tradition which attributes the nation's destruction to its own gross immorality, social oppressiveness, idolatry and as a result of its history, has been commented on by many exegetes. Some have regarded vv. 34–40 as a very late development of v. 33 and have dismissed the piece as 'completely worthless, a gross misunderstanding' (Volz, 245; cf. Duhm, 194–6). This dismissal of the value of the piece is characteristic of older treatments of the text, the spirit of which is perfectly characterized by the following quotation of the complete exegesis of vv. 34–40 taken from a minor commentary:

> The previous verse became unintelligible to some readers. And a faithful but unintelligent person, standing in the tradition of Jeremiah, evolved the idea that Jeremiah meant that the term *massa'* was utterly offensive. Provided you did not use the term,

> you could say exactly the same thing; but if the people used the term *massa'*, then God would forget and cast off and shame his people. This legalistic pedantry has nothing to do with the mind of Jeremiah or with any true religion (Cunliffe-Jones, 164).

Such an evaluation of vv. 34–40 may be understandable, but it is rather short-sighted in that it does not explore possible explanations of the prohibition (cf. 3.16 'they shall no more say, "The ark of the covenant of the LORD" '; the prohibition of carrying loads into Jerusalem on the sabbath, 17.19–27) in terms of later social practices or as reflections of communal conflicts.

Interpretations of vv. 34–40 along the lines of conflict between prophets or in relation to prophecy are offered by McKane and Petersen. The reinterpretation of v. 33 affords an opportunity for the author to rule out any claim to the possession of new oracles from Yahweh: 'to prohibit the use of prophetic formulae and thereby to prohibit the prophetic enterprise as we know it from the classical prophets' (Petersen, 28). The words of former prophets may be used, i.e. cited, but nobody may ask for a new oracle or claim to give one. This prohibition allows the traditionists who preserved and edited the oracles of former prophets to control contemporary 'false' prophecy by ruling out the possibility of any such proclamation. *Now* the distinction between the genuine and the false is determined by the pastness of the utterance and all contemporary speaking becomes by definition 'false'. A somewhat different explanation is offered by McKane, who focuses on the line, 'I will punish that man and his household' (v. 34b):

> . . . it is likely that from v. 34 on we have to reckon with attempts of later generations, living in historical circumstances greatly different from those of the late pre-exilic period, to elucidate the conflict between Jeremiah and the prophets, in the course of which they seek to identify themselves with the pre-exilic prophet of doom (53).

Both these approaches have the virtue of relating vv. 34–40 to prophetic conflict and therefore of suggesting a tie-in between the development of the word-play in v. 33 and the cycle 'concerning the prophets'.

The rapid shifts between speakers and the concentration on 'utterance of Yahweh' point to conflict over prophetic authority and possibility. The wicked people who suffer the rejection of Yahweh (vv. 33, 38–40) provide a further link between the prophets and the parallels with the wicked which the cycle uses to condemn them (hence v. 40, *ūkᵉlimmūt ʿôlām ʾᵃšer lōʾ tiššākēaḥ*, 'and perpetual shame which shall not be forgotten'; cf. 20.11, *kᵉlimmat ʿôlām lōʾ tiššākēaḥ* '[their] perpetual shame shall not be forgotten'). Here people who pay any attention to the prophet(s) will be destroyed along with the prophet(s). Thus the cycle ends with the working out of a pun (such word-play is very characteristic of the tradition) which becomes the word of judgment against those who dare to behave verbally like prophets. It is both a warning and a closure of the cycle. That it may reflect a period similar to Zech. 13.2–6, when prophets and their behaviour had become too outrageous to be tolerated any longer, is quite likely, though not capable of demonstrable proof (cf. Petersen, 33–8; he treats the two units as deutero-prophetic texts reflecting negative assessments of prophecy). The unforgettable and permanent reproach and shame of v. 40 (cf. 20.11) is the last word on the prophets. Like the wicked they face the wrath of Yahweh, and in that devastating judgment (cf. the storm of v. 19) may be heard the echo of an implicit vindication of Jeremiah (starkly absent throughout the cycle), implicit by virtue of the cycle's incorporation into the tradition bearing his name (cf. 1.1, 5, 8).

24.1–10

24[1] After Nebuchadrezzar king of Babylon had taken into exile from
Jerusalem Jeconiah the son of Jehoiakim, king of Judah, together with the
princes of Judah, the craftsmen, and the smiths, and had brought them to
Babylon, the LORD showed me this vision: Behold, two baskets of figs placed
before the temple of the LORD. 2 One basket had very good figs, like first-
ripe figs, but the other basket had very bad figs, so bad that they could not
be eaten. 3 And the LORD said to me, 'What do you see, Jeremiah?' I said,
'Figs, the good figs very good, and the bad figs very bad, so bad that they
cannot be eaten.'

4 Then the word of the LORD came to me: 5 'Thus says the LORD, the
God of Israel: Like these good figs, so I will regard as good the exiles from
Judah, whom I have sent away from this place to the land of the Chaldeans.
6 I will set my eyes upon them for good, and I will bring them back to this
land. I will build them up, and not tear them down; I will plant them, and
not uproot them. 7 I will give them a heart to know that I am the LORD;

and they shall be my people and I will be their God, for they shall return to me with their whole heart.

8 But thus says the LORD: Like the bad figs which are so bad they cannot be eaten, so will I treat Zedekiah the king of Judah, his princes, the remnant of Jerusalem who remain in this land, and those who dwell in the land of Egypt. 9 I will make them a horror to all the kingdoms of the earth, to be a reproach, a byword, a taunt, and a curse in all the places where I shall drive them. 10 And I will send sword, famine, and pestilence upon them, until they shall be utterly destroyed from the land which I gave to them and their fathers.'

---

[1] The temporal clause with which RSV opens the chapter is in fact a subsidiary clause in MT (rightly followed by NEB, JPSB): 'Yahweh showed me and look, two baskets of figs placed before the temple of Yahweh'. For MT *hir'anī*, 'he caused me to see, showed me', cf. Amos 7.1, 4, 7; 8.1, where the phrase *kōh hir'anī*, 'thus he showed me', appears; Duhm, 197, followed by Rudolph, 156, inserts *kōh* here (cf. BHS). MT *mū'ādīm*, 'placed': i.e. 'arranged, set', Hophal participle form only occurs here and in Ezek. 21.21 (EV 16); some exegetes emend to *'ōmᵉdīm*, 'standing', or *mā'omādīm*, 'placed' (cf. BHS). Thomas 1952b, 55, suggests a stem *wd'* (Arabic *wada'a*), 'put, deposit, place'. MT *wᵉ'et-hammasgēr*, meaning uncertain, but RSV, JPSB, 'smiths', may imply 'locksmiths' (*sgr*, 'shut, closed') or goldsmiths (*sāgūr*, an epithet applied to gold, cf. Job. 28.15); G *kai tous desmōtas*, 'and the prisoners' = *sgr*. NEB margin 'the smiths: *or* the harem' reflects the lengthy discussion in Driver 1937–38, 116–8: 'it may be inferred that *msgr* in the list of deported persons denotes the "harem" containing all the women (below the regular *nšy hmlk*) kept in the palace for the service of the king, his princes and his courtiers' (118), cf. 38.22. **[1b]** = II Kings 24.14 (minus the last clause), cf. 29.2; II Kings 24.14–16. After 'the smiths' G has *kai tous plousious* 'and the rich'. **[5]** Rudolph deletes 'Thus says Yahweh the god of Israel . . .', as the formal messenger speech introduction does not fit the private nature of the communication given to Jeremiah by Yahweh (v. 4); the same argument applies to v. 8. **[6]** MT *'ēnī*, 'my eye': a few mss, GV 'my eyes' = RSV. The motifs 'build', 'tear down', 'plant', 'uproot' belong to the inner exegesis of the tradition (cf. 1.10; 12.14–17; 18.7–10; 31.28, 40; 42.10; 45.4; see on 1.10; cf. Bach 1961). **[7]** MT *lāda'at 'ōtī*, 'to know me': cf. *hadda'at 'ōtī*, 'the knowledge of me', 22.16; *wᵉyādō'a 'ōtī*, 'that he knows me', 9.23 (EV 24). MT *wᵉhāyū-lī lᵉ'ām wᵉ'ānōkī 'ehyeh lāhem lē'lōhīm*, 'and they shall be my people and I shall be their god': cf. 31.33 *wᵉhāyītī lāhem lē'lōhīm wᵉhēmmāh yihyū lī lᵉ'ām*, 'and I shall be their god and they shall be my people'. **[8]** MT *kī-kōh 'āmar yhwh*, 'for thus says Yahweh': a redactional addition cf. BHS; see Notes on v. 5. RSV is misleading in placing it at the beginning of the verse (correct order in JPSB) when MT has it after '. . . so bad they cannot be eaten'. **[9]** MT *lᵉzaʿᵃwāh lᵉrāʿāh*, 'a horror for evil': K *lzwʿh*, Q *lᵉzaʿᵃwāh*; *zwʿ*, 'tremble, quake', noun 'object of trembling, terror, fright', cf. 15.4; 29.18; 34.17; (K–Q), also Deut. 28.25; Ezek. 23.46. G *eis diaskorpismon* '(I will give them) into dispersal abroad', lacking 'evil'. Volz, 247, transfers *lᵉrāʿāh*, 'for evil', to the end of v. 8, thus balancing *lᵉṭōbāh*, 'for good' at the end of v. 5. MT *lᵉḥerpāh ūlᵉmāšāl lišᵉnīnāh wᵉliqᵉlālāh*, 'a reproach, a byword, a taunt, and a curse': NEB 'a reproach, a by-word, an object-lesson and a thing of ridicule'; *šᵉnīnāh* (derived from *šēn*, 'tooth') means 'a sharp word, taunt' (cf. *šinnan*, 'teach incisively', Deut. 6.7) cf. Deut. 28.37; I Kings 9.7 = II Chron. 7.20. BHS regards 'in all the places where I shall drive them' as an addition from Deut. 28.37; it is inconsistent with v. 10 (Rudolph). **[10]** G lacks 'and to their fathers'.

Niditch 1983, 53–72; Pohlmann 1978, 19–31; Reventlow 1963, 87–94; Thiel 1973, 253–61; Zimmerli 1982, 109–14

The block concludes with a unit making a sharp contrast between two groups of Judaeans and thus makes a companion piece with 21.8–10 where a similar, though much more modest, opposing fate distinguishes between those who remain in the city and those who escape from it. With little concern for chronological sequences the editors preface the block with contrasting images of 588–7 and close it with a visionary contrast ostensibly reflecting 597. Allusions have been made to the lateness of some of the contents of the two cycles included in the block (e.g. 22.24–30; 23.34–40), and the vision of 24 provides further evidence for detecting late strands in the block (and the tradition). The contrast between those who were taken into exile by Nebuchadrezzar in 597 and those who were left behind (cf. 29.16–19) develops into a theological evaluation of both groups in terms of Yahweh's action 'for good' and 'for evil'. This theologizing of the respective fates of the two groups is propaganda on behalf of one group and is therefore a partisan statement (cf. 29; 42–44). In its present form the propaganda is not only directed against the Palestinian community (including Jerusalem) but also against Palestinian refugees in Egypt (v. 8b). These refugees probably fled Jerusalem after its fall or in the aftermath of Gedaliah's assassination (41–42; cf. Nicholson 1970, 110), and to find them attacked in a piece supposedly on behalf of the 597 deportees indicates the fact that 24 must be dated to a period after 587. The use of the motifs in v. 6 is further evidence for assigning the vision to a late stage in the development of the tradition (cf. 1.10). That Jeconiah, his court, harem, craftsmen and others, should be viewed so sympathetically by the deity runs counter to 22.24–30 (but is in line with 52.31–34) and reflects an independent strand in the tradition.

The independent strand of which 24 (also 29) is a part constitutes one of the many puzzling features of the Jeremiah tradition. The tradition knows of two attacks on Jerusalem and two deportations (i.e. 597, 587), yet only presents a developed account of one attack (587) and focuses on only one deportation (597). The deportation of 587 is mentioned briefly (39.7–10; cf. 40.1, 4), but of its fate or future nothing is ever said in the tradition (52 reflects II Kings 25 but without reference to the killing of Gedaliah, which appears in 41.1–3). Of the Babylonian march on Jerusalem and Jeconiah's capitulation the tradition has nothing to say (the allusions in 22.24–28 do not represent a treatment of the events). But commentators and exegetes read many of the poems in 2–20 against a backdrop of the events of 597, a feature the narratives know nothing about. The poems may be read that way, but they may be as easily read in terms of 587. The narratives are remarkably parsimonious in their treatment of two sets of defeats and deportations. The material in the Deuteronomistic history (II Kings 24–25) may account for some of this reticence, but the focus of the strand which concentrates exclusively on the Jeconiah deportation points in the direction of propaganda for a particular group of deportees. The vision of 24 does not mean that all deportees in Babylon are the hope for the future, but only that group which can be identified with (i.e. trace their ancestry to) those who went into captivity with Jeconiah. It is an echo of seniority claims and differentiations made by returned groups wishing to gain power in Jerusalem during its reconstruction (cf. the Ezra-Nehemiah traditions). Thus it is not simply the voice of *gālūt yᵉhūdāh* ('the exile of Judah', v. 5; cf. 28.4; 29.22; 40.1; i.e. *'am haggōlāh*, 'the people of the exile') against *'am hā'āreṣ* ('the people of the land', cf. Gunneweg 1983), but a specific vintage of it. Those who went to Babylon in 587 would have found themselves outsiders and inferiors to those associated with Jeconiah and lacking a decade's experience of creating and maintaining new power relations. In view of 24.8–10 they would also be regarded as 'rubbish', without legitimation or divine approval. This would account for why the deportation of Jeconiah is presented by II Kings 24.10–16 in terms of almost complete depopulation of Judah (e.g. '*none* remained, except the poorest of the land', v. 14b). As the same hyperbolic approach is used of the deportation of Zedekiah (II Kings 25.8–12; cf. Jer. 39.8–10) too much should not be made of either report that but for those who went to Babylon with Jeconiah only the dregs remained (e.g. Zedekiah, *Jeremiah*, princes, craftsmen . . .!). The historicity of these reports may be dubious, but the narrative and theological factors are what concern the editors and the presentation by the Deuteronomists of the two events as mirror-images of each other is noteworthy. It helps to explain why it is so difficult to disentangle history from theology in the book of Jeremiah. Whatever the cause of this puzzlement in the tradition it is important to note that only the Jeconiah deportation counts as something positive for the future.

The declaration of Yahweh's special care for those deported in 597 is made the subject of a vision. It is a special kind of vision because two elements appear in it and the negative-positive aspects of these constitute the divine message. It is a vision with complicated explanations attached to it, rather than the simpler visions where an object has a direct meaning (cf. 1.11–12, 13–14; Amos 7.1–8; 8.1–3). There is about the symbols in this vision an unpredictability which makes them quite obscure as to meaning (cf. the night visions of Zechariah which are equally obscure; Niditch, 69–70). This is a vision which will require complex interpretation. Now the visionary element is not a feature of the Jeremiah tradition, but appears briefly in the later stages of its redaction (e.g. 1.11–14; 24). This in itself is an argument for the lateness of chapters 1 and 24. Auditory rather than visual experiences dominate the tradition, though verbal pictures are used frequently and magical actions dominate. The vision belongs to the realms of magic as well (cf. Niditch), but certain traditions seem to be dominated by the word (e.g. Hosea, Jeremiah, Second Isaiah) and others by the vision (e.g. Ezekiel, Zechariah, Daniel; cf. Zimmerli, 114–6). To find a couple of vision strands in Jeremiah is a pointer in the direction of editing from a specific source (hence the peculiarity of 24 in the tradition). The authorization of certain theological claims is grounded in the vision (e.g. Amos 7.1–8; 8.1–3; not for nothing is this visionary sequence thought to be interrupted by Deuteronomistic elements in 7.10–17, with both sections contributing to a claim on behalf of Amos's authenticity), and 24 is most certainly a polemic on behalf of one group as much as it is an attack on another.

The form of the vision in 24.1 is not the same as the introduction to the things seen in 1.11, 13, though the questions are. Here it is Yahweh who shows Jeremiah the objects; in 1.11, 13 Jeremiah sees them for himself; in each instance the deity provides the meaning of the thing seen. If the absurd temporal clause in v. 1 is omitted (it is only absurd in the light of the fact that it uses a reference which according to II Kings 24.14 left hardly anyone in the land), the vision may be given due consideration. It consists of two baskets of figs set in front of the temple. That suggests a temple vision which would place 24 with those narratives which represent Jeremiah as a temple official located there and working from there (cf. 1.1; 7.2; 17.12; 19.1, 14; 22.1; 35.1–2). However, the temple element may not be significant (Cornill, 277, deletes the phrase; Volz, 249, argues that 'temple' is not the meaning of *hēkal* here but 'Yahweh's dwelling place' in the heavens; Niditch, 67, denies any cultic setting and relates the baskets to good and bad agricultural products [cf. Gen. 41.1–8]). It may just be local colour providing a background for the two baskets. Zimmerli, 114, suggests that the original report of a visionary experience may have been about two baskets of figs which had been brought to the sanctuary as offerings, one of which had been acceptable and the other unacceptable (cf. Mal. 1.7–9). From that differentiation follows the explanation when applied to the events of 597. The precise role in the story of the phrase 'set before the temple of Yahweh' must be left open because it is too unintegrated in what follows to control the reading of the text. The vision is about Yahweh's plans for good and evil (i.e. salvation and destruction), and these flow forth from his holy temple (cf. 25.30; Amos 1.2; Joel 3.16). Among the punishments of the bad is a curse (v. 9), and the temple setting of the vision would fit such a ritual gesture with its magical activity setting in motion the punishments predicated of the rejected group. All these elements suggest that a ritual context of the vision is a warranted reading of the story (cf. Reventlow), but to be dogmatic about it is unwise.

The explanation of the state of the figs in the baskets, one lot being excellent, first-ripe figs, the other too rotten for human consumption, is in terms of an analogy. This analogy is drawn between 'the exiles of Judah' and 'the remnant of Jerusalem', hence the redactional dating in v. 1b (MT). The temple priest would look on one basket with relish, but the other would disgust him. So Yahweh would regard the two baskets in a similar fashion: he would look on the one for good, the other for evil. The figs represent the two communities: one still in the land, the other gone into exile. What was the status of the deportees? In this vision they are given a special status as Yahweh's favoured group, and to reinforce that the Judaeans are written off as disgusting rubbish. A similar discussion is to be found in Ezek. 11.14–21, and it displays the same attitude. The deportation has in some magical way turned the wicked king and his equally evil retinue into something fine and good and now only those who remain behind are to be viewed as wicked. The deportees will be returned to their own land (cf. 29.10–14), and there they will be built up into a community enjoying normal conditions of peace and prosperity. Furthermore, the deity will give them a mind to know Yahweh and with that new mind they will turn (*yāšubū*) to him (cf. 29.13). Thus the deportees will become Yahweh's people and he their god (cf. 31.33, where similar language is used of a new covenant rather than a new mind; for the new mind motif cf. Ezek. 36.24–28). The image of the basket of good figs is therefore part of the salvation strand in the tradition (cf. 30–31).

The identity of the bad figs is specified as Zedekiah, his princes, the remnant of Jerusalem *and* those who live in Egypt (cf. 44); in other words, everybody else apart from Jeconiah's group. The spaciousness of the salvation oracles (e.g. 30.18–22; 31.2–6, 16–20; 31.31–34) is not to be found in this vision. Everybody outside a small group in Babylon is to be hounded until wiped out as a sign of Yahweh's rejection of those left behind when Nebuchadrezzar took away Jeconiah and his companions (contrast 22.24–30). Formal Deuteronomistic elements appear in the story (cf. 1.18; 2.26; 8.1; 17.25; 32.32; 44.17, 21; Thiel, 256), and these account for the sweeping judgment against the different strata of society, including the reference to those who now live in Egypt (see on 44; it is unnecessary to delete the phrase from v. 8b because the tradition displays immense hostility towards the Egyptian communities and such a late strand as 24 would naturally attack them also). The dismissal of the Judaeans in vv. 9–10 uses motifs to be found in Deuteronomistic sources (analysis in Thiel, 257–8) and used in the Jeremiah tradition (cf. 8.3; 29.17–19; 35.15). The hyperbole of vv. 9–10 should be noted as well as the rhetorical style characteristic of Deuteronomistically influenced texts. Not only will Zedekiah and all those associated with him perish, but those who are deported (i.e. driven by Yahweh into foreign countries) will become an object lesson wherever they go. People will use their experience as verbal forms of abuse (cf. 18.16; 25.18, where hissing is a protective device):

they, i.e. the deportees, will become legends and proverbs in their own lifetime! The destruction of v. 10 gives the impression that it pursues the exiles wherever they go (cf. 20.3), but is in reality a statement about the fate of those who live in the land. Those who are deported will remain cursed (v. 9), but in Palestine the land will be cleared completely of the remnant of Jerusalem (for the triad 'sword, famine, pestilence' cf. 14.12; 21.7, 9; 27.13; 29.17; 32.24, 36; 34.17). Thus will the land be cleared of them all and become vacant for the returning good figs. The essential points of vv. 8–10 are made again in 29.16–19, but with an explanation of why Yahweh is so bent on destroying Zedekiah's community.

The vision and the meanings attached to it are quite clear, but the place of this strand in the tradition is difficult to assess. Due allowance for rhetoric hardly reduces the tensions between it and so many other strands in the book. It is impossible to recognize in the description of Jeconiah and his companions the wretched king dismissed so contemptuously in 22.24–30. The fate of Pashhur and his friends when deported to Babylon (20.1–6) also conflicts with this idyll. If the basket of bad figs really represents Zedekiah, his companions and their fate, then the narratives where Jeremiah and Zedekiah are presented in friendly terms strangely conceal this judgment. A more realistic interpretation of the chapter is to be found in reading it as propaganda. It is a partisan account on behalf of the deportees presenting them as Yahweh's special group and reassuring them of their claims to live in and control Jerusalem. Some commentators attribute the story to a Babylonian setting for the tradition (cf. 29) and see it as propaganda for the exiles there. However, a Palestinian provenance of the story is more likely, because vv. 5–6 indicate that the land is spoken of from the vantage point of Palestine ('back to *this* land – sent away from *this* place'). The temple setting (or reflection) of the two baskets and the vision category of the story both point to a Jerusalem location rather than a Babylonian one. If the claim on behalf of the deportees emanates from Jerusalem (whether from the temppe may be a moot point), then it must represent an attempt to legitimate that claim over against other claimants to power in Jerusalem. Those of the *gālut yᵉhūdāh* who returned to Jerusalem (cf. the traditions of Haggai, Zech. 1–8, Ezra, Nehemiah) would appear to have had their claim and its legitimation incorporated into the Jeremiah tradition, and some of the subtlety of their propaganda here should be noted. The fall of 587 wrote off all associated with it (those who remained *and* those who left), but there had been a previous deportation which did not come under that ruling. So the descendants of Jeconiah's deportation had the *only* legitimate claim to live and rule in Jerusalem and Judah. A vision (an alien element in the tradition) attributed to Jeremiah incorporates precisely that claim.

SUMMARY 25.1–14

25.1–7

25[1] The word that came to Jeremiah concerning all the people of Judah, in the fourth year of Jehoiakim the son of Josiah, king of Judah (that was the first year of Nebuchadrezzar king of Babylon), 2 which Jeremiah the prophet spoke to all the people of Judah and all the inhabitants of Jerusalem: 3 'For twenty-three years, from the thirteenth year of Josiah the son of Amon, king of Judah, to this day, the word of the LORD has come to me, and I have spoken persistently to you, but you have not listened. 4 You have neither listened nor inclined your ears to hear, although the LORD persistently sent to you all his servants the prophets, 5 saying, "Turn now, every one of you, from his evil way and wrong doings, and dwell upon the land which the LORD has given to you and your fathers from of old and for ever; 6 do not go after other gods to serve and worship them, or provoke me to anger with the work of your hands. Then I will do you no harm." 7 Yet you have not listened to me, says the LORD, that you might provoke me to anger with the work of your hands to your own harm.'

---

[1] G lacks the final clause 'that was the first year of Nebuchadrezzar king of Babylon'. For formulaic similarities of the reception of the divine word motif cf. 14.1; also 32.1; 34.1; 35.1. **[2]** G lacks 'the prophet'. **[3]** G has 'in' for 'from', lacks *hāyāh d*^{e}*bar-yhwh 'ēlāy*, 'the word of Yahweh came to me', and *w*^{e}*lō' š*^{e}*ma'tem*, 'but you have not listened'. MT *'aškēm*, 'I rose early and spoke': some mss, Cairo geniza fragment have the standard *haškēm*, 'rising early and speaking', cf. 7.13, 25. Weiser, Rudolph delete from 'but you have not listened' to 'his servants the prophets' (v. 4) as additions from 7.13, 25–26; 11.7–8; this makes v. 5 the message of v. 3. G *en*, 'in', for 'from' reflects 1.2. **[4]** MT *w*^{e}*šālaḥ yhwh*, 'and Yahweh sent . . .': G *kai apestellon*, 'and sending' (cf. *kai apesteila*, 7.25). MT *kol-'*^{a}*bādāyw*, 'all his servants': G *tous doulous mou*, 'my servants'. G lacks *lišmō'a*, 'to hear'. **[5]** MT *nātan yhwh*, 'Yahweh has given': G *edōka*, 'I gave' = *nātattī*. **[6]** Weiser, Rudolph delete v. 6 as a later addition (cf. 35.15). MT *w*^{e}*lō' 'āra'*, 'and I will do no harm': G *kakōsai humas*, 'to do you harm' = *l*^{e}*hāra'*. **[7]** G lacks *n*^{e}*'um-yhwh*, 'says

Yahweh'; its brevity *kai ouk ēkousate mou*, 'but you did not listen to me', in contrast with longer MT suggests a misplaced variant of v. 6b in MT v. 7b (cf. Bright, 157; Janzen 1973, 13). K *hk'swny*; Q *hak'isēnī*, 'to provoke me'.

Thiel 1973, 262–75

25.1–14 constitute the summary and the closure of Part I of the tradition. Part II, the oracles against the nations (cf. Isa. 13–23; Ezek. 25–32), begins in v. 15, but after v. 38 is interrupted by Part III in MT (not the case in G). The summary consists of two parts: vv. 1–7 are a Deuteronomistically influenced summary of Jeremiah's work from 627 to 605; vv. 8–11, 13, are a post-Deuteronomistic construction reflecting on the period of Babylonian domination, and vv. 12, 14 attack Babylon (analysis in Thiel). The variations between MT and G in the summary indicate the rather different developments of the text, especially the role of 'Nebuchadrezzar king of Babylon' (vv. 1, 9, 11; absent in G). The shorter G text allows the expansion of MT in the direction of developing Jeremiah's role as '*the* prophet' (v. 2; cf. 'says Yahweh', v. 7) to be noted.

The summary of Jeremiah's preaching from 627 to 605 is given in language derived from the same strand as 7.1–8.3; 11.1–13; 44.2–6 (on similarities between 25.3b–6a and 35.14b–15, cf. Thiel, 267). Jeremiah is presented as having begun to preach in the thirteenth year of king Josiah (i.e. 627) and as having gone on preaching for twenty-three years until king Jehoiakim's fourth year (i.e. 605). MT notes that this was also the *beginning* of Nebuchadrezzar's regency (the redaction attaches similar datings to 26.1; 27.1; 28.1, so historical accuracy should not be insisted upon in such framework matters). G lacks all allusions to the Babylonian king and represents the earlier edition of the tradition. 605 was a noteworthy year because in it Nebuchadrezzar came to power and defeated the Egyptians at Carchemish (Neher 1960, 59, calls this battle his Rubicon). The association of the two, the word spoken by Jeremiah in Jehoiakim's fourth year and Nebuchadrezzar's first year, allows the edited MT to make connections between vv. 3–7 and vv. 8–11. The proclamation of vv. 3–7 becomes a writing down of all the words spoken over the twenty-three years in 36.2 (the closure to block III).

25.1 reflects the latest stage of the tradition in that it represents Jeremiah as having started his work in the year 627 (cf. 1.2). It also presents Jeremiah as the receiver of the divine word and the epithet 'the prophet' (v. 2) confirms the lateness of the block (G lacks this description). The clichéd image of the deity rising early and sending his servants the prophets incorporates Jeremiah into the Deuteronomistic representation of history as the history of the divine word mediated by prophets (MT v. 3 allows Jeremiah to do the early rising and speaking roles). The history of the prophetic proclamation is also the history of the people's rejection of that word (cf. 7.13, 25–26; 11.7–8; 26.4–5; 32.33; 35.14b–15; 44.4–5). The content of that preaching is given in v. 5: 'Turn now (*šūbū-nā'*), every one of you, from his evil way and the evil of your deeds, and dwell (*ūšᵉbū*, word-play with *šūbū*, 'live – turn') upon the land . . .'. So the preaching of Jeremiah over more than two decades is presented as late Deuteronomistic 'turning' theology. Here is not the figure denouncing the corruption (moral, social, religious) of the city and its people but a preacher of repentance, including the denunciation of false cults. This is the Jeremiah of a later stage of the tradition: one who belongs to a long line of divinely sent messengers who announced the possibility of turning rather than the inevitability of destruction (contrast Amos 5.2; and the figure of Jeremiah arrived at by attaching the poems of Part I to him). The incorporation of redactional elements into the Deuteronomistic clichés makes Jeremiah a prophetic figure of a particular kind. The late editorial element in v. 1b (lacking in G) allows a connection to be made between the consistent rejection of Jeremiah's preaching and the rise of Nebuchadrezzar.

25.8–14

8 'Therefore thus says the Lord of hosts: Because you have not obeyed my
words, 9 behold, I will send for all the tribes of the north, says the Lord,
and for Nebuchadrezzar the king of Babylon, my servant, and I will bring
them against this land and its inhabitants, and against all these nations
round about; I will utterly destroy them, and make them a horror, a hissing,
and an everlasting reproach. 10 Moreover, I will banish from them the
voice of mirth and the voice of gladness, the voice of the bridegroom and
the voice of the bride, the grinding of the millstones and the light of the
lamp. 11 This whole land shall become a ruin and a waste, and these nations
shall serve the king of Babylon seventy years. 12 Then after seventy years
are completed, I will punish the king of Babylon and that nation, the land
of the Chaldeans, for their iniquity, says the Lord, making the land an

everlasting waste. 13 I will bring upon that land all the words which I have uttered against it, everything written in this book, which Jeremiah prophesied against all the nations. 14 For many nations and great kings shall make slaves even of them; and I will recompense them according to their deeds and the work of their hands.'

---

[8] MT *lō' šᵉmaʿtem 'et-dᵉbāray*, 'you have not heard my words': G *ouk episteusate tois logois mou*, 'you did not believe my words'. **[9]** MT *'et-kol-mišpᵉḥōt ṣāpōn*, 'all the families of the north': cf. 1.15; i.e. 'clans'. G *ten patrian apo borra*, 'a family from the north'. G lacks *nᵉ'um yhwh*, 'says Yahweh'; also 'and for Nebuchadrezzar the king of Babylon, my servant', cf. 27.6; 43.10. Weiser, Rudolph follow G and delete these phrases (cf. BHS). MT *wᵉʿal kol-haggōyim hā'ēlleh sābīb*, 'and against all *these* nations round about': an addition which reflects and anticipates vv. 15–26 (cf. Rudolph, 160). G lacks 'these'. MT *wᵉhaḥᵃramtīm*, 'and I will utterly destroy them': i.e. 'I will put them to the sacred ban'; *ḥerem* indicates a holy war practice of the complete annihilation of the population (cf. Josh. 7–8; I Sam. 15.1–9). MT *wᵉlišrēqāh*, 'and for a hissing': cf. 18.16; Lam. 2.15. Such hissing may have been derisive, or it may have been part of an action performed to ward off the evil which had befallen others (cf. JPSB on 18.16). Hissing motifs appear in 19.8; 25.9, 18; 29.18; 49.17; 50.13; 51.37. MT *ūlᵉḥorᵉbōt ʿōlām*, 'and for permanent ruins': *ḥorbāh*, 'waste, ruin, desolation'. G *kai eis oneidismon aiōnion*, 'and into an everlasting reproach', reading *ūlᵉḥerpat . . .*; Driver 1937, 118–19, retains *ḥrbh*, 'idle gossip', cf. NEB, 'a scandal for ever.' **[10]** MT *qōl rēḥayim*, 'the sound of the millstones': i.e. the handmill, the noise of which is indicative of normal family life. G *osmēn murou*, 'the fragrance of myrrh, perfume' (*murou* = a corruption of *mulou*, 'mill, handmill'?); the reference to sweet oil extracted from plants (*muron*) may reflect *rēaḥ mōr* (cf. BHS). **[11]** G lacks MT *hazzō't lᵉḥorbāh*, 'this (land) a ruin'; cf. 7.34, *kī lᵉḥorbāh tihyeh hā'āreṣ*, 'for the land shall become a waste' (vv. 10–11 share elements of 7.34). G *kai douleusousin en tois ethnesin ebdomēkonta etē*, 'and they shall serve among the nations seventy years', lacking any reference to the king of Babylon. **[12]** Weiser, Rudolph delete this verse as not original, cf. 29.10 (Rudolph links 12a with 29.10 and 12b with 51.26, 62). G lacks *ʿal-melek-bābel wᵉ*, 'against the king of Babylon and', and *nᵉ'um yhwh . . . kaśdīm* 'says Yahweh . . . of the Chaldaeans'. MT *'ōtō*, 'it, him', but *'ōtāh*, 'it, her' (*'ereṣ* is fem.) cf. BHS. **[13]** K *whb'yty*; Q *wᵉhēbē'tī*, 'and I will bring' (K a mistake for Q or for *wᵉhēbē'tī*). MT *hahī*, 'that': i.e. the land of vv. 12, 14, but BHS *hazzō't*, 'this', makes v. 13 refer to the land of Israel; BHS regards MT *'ᵃšer-nibbā' yirmᵉyāhū ʿal-kol-haggōyim*, 'which Jeremiah prophesied against all the nations' as an addition due to vv. 15–38 (cf. on v. 9; Rudolph, 162), lacking in G. MT *kol-hakkātūb bassēper hazzeh*, 'all that is written in this book': a possible reference to the book of oracles written against Babylon (51.60); it could be an oblique allusion to the scroll containing Jeremiah's words (36.2), making vv. 1–13a the conclusion to Baruch's scroll (cf. Hyatt, 1001). The section ends here in G, lacking vv. 13b–14. **[14]** G lacks v. 14, but its 25.14 – 32.38 represents the oracles against the nations of MT 46–51; 25.15–38, though in a different order. MT *kī 'ābᵉdū-bām gam hēmmāh gōyim rabbīm*, 'for they served among them, even these great nations': obscure but a possible reference to 'that nation' of v. 12, though influenced by adjustments to the nations of vv. 15–38. BHS reads *ya'abᵉdū*, 'they will be made to serve' (cf. 22.13 *'bd b*), cf. 27.7b for 14a; 50.29 for 14b (Rudolph).

The words of Jeremiah (1.1) are brought to a conclusion with a statement spelling out the consequences of the decades of rejecting the divine word spoken by him (cf. Thiel 1973, 272–3). The first edition of this statement knows only of an enemy from the north which will invade the land of Judah, subjugate it, make it a terrible warning to everybody, cut off from it normal domestic activities (i.e. weddings, the preparation of grain for meals and oil for lamps), and disperse the population among the nations for seventy years. In the second edition (MT) the enemy is more closely identified as Nebuchadrezzar the king of Babylon and the eventual punishment of the king of Babylon, after seventy years, is mooted. The more expanded MT also makes connections with the following section directed against the nations.

The two parts of the closure are connected by the motif of Yahweh's sending (*šlḥ*, vv. 4, 9): the refusal to hear the prophets who were *sent* now leads on to the *sending* for the family from the north which will come and devastate the land. Thus the message of Part I of the book of Jeremiah, as constructed by various redactions (especially the Deuteronomistic one), anticipates the theme of Part III. Part IV is anticipated by vv. 9–11 and vv. 12, 14 link with Part II. There is therefore in the closure of 25.1–14 a nexus of connections between the different parts of the whole tradition which is indicative of the lateness of the material in the two units. That lateness is fully demonstrated by the reference to 'seventy years' in vv. 11, 12 (see on 29.10).

The phrase 'seventy years' (also in 29.10) is capable of many interpretations. If the year 605 (cf. v. 1) is taken as the starting point, then the seventy years may be understood as a literal figure for the period of Babylonian domination as an empire (605–539; cf. Duhm, 230; Orr 1956; Volz, 265, makes the period 605–536). This would fit the general sense of the reference in 25.11, 12; 29.10 without taking into account the different editorial datings for both texts. As a *vaticinium ex eventu* (Volz) the editorial context becomes unimportant for dating the period, and the approximation of seventy years to the time of Babylonian power permits the editors to use it. Dissatisfaction with this explanation has led Whitley to argue for a different period as the meaning of the phrase (1954, 72; 1957, 416–18). He prefers the period 586–516 when the temple lay desolate as the referent of seventy years (cf. Isa. 60.7, 13 for the role of the nations in restoring the glory of the temple). This period makes the phrase an exact figure rather than a round number (with varying degrees of accuracy). It also posits a very late element in the tradition, one which reflects the reconstruction of the temple in 516 and identifies the real significance of the Babylonian invasion with the destruction of the Jerusalem temple. There is no hint of this connection in either of the strands which refer to the seventy years, though a strand which focuses on the temple as important (e.g. 17.12; the movements of Jeremiah from the vantage point of the temple) is to be found in the tradition. The historical accuracy of the duration of the period (Whitley) is only an important argument if such a concern with precision can be shown to be a feature of the book. But the two periods, 605–539/6 and 586–516, cannot be ruled out as possible meanings of 'seventy years'; they fit and therefore are perfectly good interpretations.

A different approach to understanding the phrase is to move from historical accuracy to literary artistic forms (cf. Cornill, 291). In Ezek. 4.6 (cf. 29.13 with reference to Egypt) the period of Judah's punishment is given as forty years where a literal interpretation of the number is quite problematic. The phrase should be understood according to the pattern of forty years 'as a period of punishment, in which one generation of grown men passed away and a new generation arose, who were not twenty years old before the beginning of the forty years or who were still unborn then' (Zimmerli 1979, 166–7). If a patterned meaning is assigned to 'seventy years' it may represent a combination of three generations (i.e. twenty years for each generation) and the magical connotations of the number seven. In 27.7 the period of Babylonian domination is given as three generations (Nebuchad*n*ezzar, his son and grandson), so this would fit the interpretation of the seventy years as three generations (see on 27.7). Isa. 23.15, 17 uses the motif of 'seventy years' to describe the period Tyre will be forgotten. It should not be taken as a chronological reference but as an allusion to a lifespan or a whole generation (cf. Clements 1980, 195; Ackroyd 1958, 23–5; see Kaiser 1974, 169–72, for a possible historical interpretation). So the reference to the same period in 25.11, 12 should be read as a statement about the duration of the land's desolation being for a whole generation which would see at least three individual generations disappear (cf. Weiser, 219). A whole generation would pass before the deity turned the punishment of the land – a possibility not touched on in the unit (implicit in vv. 12–14?).

In conjunction with this alternative approach to the interpretation of the seventy years it should be noted that an Esarhaddon inscription contains a reference to a seventy-year period during which Babylon would lie desolate (cf. Weinfeld 1972a, 143–6). The god Marduk decrees seventy years against Babylon until such time as he becomes reconciled with the land he has punished (cf. 29.10). This looks like 'the conventional numerical typology of the period, which appears to have been particularly employed by Mesopotamian scribes' (Weinfeld, 146). As such the motif may be a scribal convention in Jeremiah, and the Deuteronomistic formulation of it here may have transformed the three generations reference into a conventional allusion to a period of the god's anger with his land (cf. Weinfeld, 146).

It cannot be determined whether a literal, metaphorical or conventional meaning should be understood as the meaning of the phrase 'seventy years'. All are possible categories for it and its use in a number of traditions outside Jeremiah (cf. Zech. 1.12; 7.5; II Chron. 36.21; Dan. 9.2) is indicative of its flexibility of meaning and reference. It would therefore be unwise to insist on only one specific narrow meaning for its occurrence in 25.11, 12. What may be insisted on is the function of the phrase in its present context. As part of the word of judgment against Judah for not hearing the divine word (however late it may be) it stresses the fullness of that judgment. For seventy years, i.e. a long time during which generations will come and go, the land must bear its punishment. This will be no short or momentary setback but a complete cycle of years (whatever its literal length). A long history of rebellion merits a long period of punishment. If the word has not been heard through the decades of its proclamation, then the land will have to go through a period when there will be nobody there *not-to-listen-to-it*. Any mistaken beliefs about the brevity of Babylonian domination must be abandoned.

This point is not relevant for 25.1–14 but is a key issue in 29.10 (especially in the context of 27–29). It is therefore quite likely that the motif comes from the addition of 29.10–14 to 29.1–9 and appears in 25.8–14 as part of the late editing of Part I. The optimistic element in the motif is implicit in 29.10 and positively developed in II Chron. 36.21–22; cf. Ezra 1.1. 25.11, 12 use both the negative and positive aspects of the motif, but only v. 11 concerns the word of judgment.

The motifs in v. 10 appear in 7.34; 16.9, but there are two minor additions to the cessation of merrymaking and marriage customs. 'I will destroy from them . . . the grinding of the millstones and the light of the lamp.' A similar malediction is to be found in the vassal treaties of Esarhaddon where occur the lines 'May the sound of the mill and oven not be heard in your houses' (cited in Weinfeld 1972a, 141–2, who understands *nēr*, 'lamp', in the sense of oven [*tannūr*, cf. Isa. 31.9]; cf. Wiseman 1958, 62 line 444). The gathering together in vv. 9–11 of various motifs and phrases which appear throughout 1–25 is indicative of the closure structure of the unit. Part I is essentially the indictment of the nation and its punishment, spelled out here in two highly edited units (vv. 1–7, 8–11) which close the collection and editing of the first part of the tradition.

Part II has influenced the ending of Part I because vv. 12–14 anticipate what follows in vv. 15–38 (the oracles against the nations). Only v. 13 may be said to belong to vv. 8–11 and only if the last clause is deleted as a title to vv. 15–38. The land referred to is Judah and not Babylon. The book is the alternative account of vv. 1–11 given in 36 (cf. v. 29) and not the book written against Babylon (51.59–64). As MT now stands vv. 12–14 open a window on the future (cf. Rudolph, 162).

PART TWO

Oracles against the Nations

25.15–38; 46–51

The tripartite structure of the three major prophetic anthologies consists of judgment material, oracles against the nations (OAN), and salvation elements (cf. Isa. 1–12; 13–23; 40–55; Ezek. 1–24; 25–32; 34–39). In spite of significant differences the Jeremiah tradition retains this structure, but there are marked variations between MT and G. In the developments between the two editions the OAN (i.e. Part II) have been separated from their beginnings in 25 and appear in MT after Part IV in 46–51. In G everything concerning the nations is in the one place, but the order of the nations is different (G 25.14–19; 26–32 = MT 46–51; 25.15–38 with minor variations and a distinctive sequence of the nations listed in MT).

The existence of many discrete and disparate strands, books and traditions within the larger Jeremiah tradition points to the diverse forms which originally gave rise to the construction of the book. If these all existed in earlier independent forms, then the OAN also would have circulated in separate form. When they were added to the developing tradition they were probably attached to 25.13a in conformity to the tripartite pattern reflected in Isaiah and Ezekiel. The extent to which they were *added* to or *inserted* into existing manuscripts will have depended upon the state and scope of such manuscripts. The differences between MT and G testify to the flexibility of development and suggest the circulation of manuscripts of both kinds once the OAN were attached to the tradition (i.e. the OAN after 25.13a or appended after 45.5). Between the two editions the order of the oracles has been brought into conformity to the listing in MT 25.15–26 (to some extent) and this points to the originality of G's order (cf. Janzen 1973, 116). For lack of firm information it is only possible to speculate about the different placings of the OAN and such speculations may be consulted in the standard commentaries. (On the shape, substance and interpretation of the OAN see the introduction to 46–51 after Part IV.)

25.15–29

15 Thus the LORD, the God of Israel, said to me: 'Take from my hand this
cup of the wine of wrath, and make all the nations to whom I send you drink
it. 16 They shall drink and stagger and be crazed because of the sword
which I am sending among them.'
17 So I took the cup from the LORD's hand, and made all the nations to
whom the LORD sent me drink it: 18 Jerusalem and the cities of Judah, its
kings and princes, to make them a desolation and a waste, a hissing and a
curse, as at this day; 19 Pharaoh king of Egypt, his servants, his princes, all
his people, 20 and all the foreign folk among them; all the kings of the land
of Uz and all the kings of the land of the Philistines (Ashkelon, Gaza, Ekron,
and the remnant of Ashdod); 21 Edom, Moab, and the sons of Ammon; 22
all the kings of Tyre, all the kings of Sidon, and the kings of the coastland
across the sea; 23 Dedan, Tema, Buz, and all who cut the corners of their
hair; 24 all the kings of Arabia and all the kings of the mixed tribes that
dwell in the desert; 25 all the kings of Zimri, all the kings of Elam, and all
the kings of Media; 26 all the kings of the north, far and near, one after
another, and all the kingdoms of the world which are on the face of the
earth. And after them the king of Babylon shall drink.
27 'Then you shall say to them, "Thus says the LORD of hosts, the God
of Israel: Drink, be drunk and vomit, fall and rise no more, because of the
sword which I am sending among you." '
28 'And if they refuse to accept the cup from your hand to drink, then
you shall say to them, "Thus says the LORD of hosts: You must drink! 29
For behold, I begin to work evil at the city which is called by my name, and
shall you go unpunished? You shall not go unpunished, for I am summoning
a sword against all the inhabitants of the earth, says the LORD of hosts." '

[25.15–29] = G 32.1–24. G prefaces the section with 25.13b as a title: *hosa eprophēteusen Ieremias epi panta ta ethnā*, 'which Jeremiah prophesied against all the nations'. Rudolph, 164, uses 25.13b as a preface to vv. 15–29. **[15]** MT *kī*, 'for . . .': a secondary linking of vv. 14, 15 (JPSB translates it but not RSV, NEB); lacking in G. MT *'ēlay*, 'to me': lacking in G and some Vrs. MT *qaḥ 'et-kōs hayyayin haḥēmāh hazzō't miyyādī*, 'take the cup of wine, this wrath from my hand': lit. '. . . the cup of the wine, the wrath this . . .'.

G *tou oinou tou akratou*, 'of unmixed wine' = *yayin haḥemer*, cf. Ps. 75.9; Driver 1937–38, 119, reads *hayyain haḥōmeh*, 'strong wine'. MT 'this cup of wine, wrath' may represent variants (Bright, 158); Rudolph deletes 'of wrath', cf. BHS. MT *wᵉhišᵉqîtāh 'ōtō*, 'and cause to drink *it*': *kōs*, 'cup' is fem., *yayin*, 'wine', is masc., so 'it' must refer to the wine rather than the cup; *'ōtō* lacking in G. **[16]** MT *wᵉšātu wᵉhitgōʿᵃšu*, 'and they shall drink and stagger': G *kai piontai kai exemountai*, 'and they shall drink and vomit', cf. NEB 'When they have drunk it they will vomit'; *yitgōʿᵃšū* is used of the waters of the Nile in 46.8 'like rivers whose waters surge', an image better conveyed by the term 'vomit' than 'reel to and fro' (?), cf. 5.22b for similar images. McKane 1980b, 491, regards 'vomiting' as the meaning of *htgʿšw* rather than 'reeling'. 16b (from 'because of the sword . . .') is omitted by Rudolph as an addition from v. 27b; it spoils the image created by 16a (Duhm, 203): the wine makes them dizzy, crazed, not the sword. **[17]** MT *wā'ašᵉqeh*, 'and I made drink': EVV '. . . drink it' imply *wā'ašᵉqehā* (cf. Duhm, 204). **[18]** G lacks 'and a curse, as at this day'. What does *'ōtām*, 'them', refer to in v. 18? Only cities, not kings or princes, can be a ruin or a desolation; but the context requires officials (to drink the wine), not places. As the unit is directed against foreign nations, v. 18 should be deleted as an addition derived from vv. 1–14 (cf. Bright, 161). Rudolph treats it as an addition reflecting vv. 9b, 11a; 44.6, 22; cf. BHS. **[20]** MT *wᵉ'ēt kol-hāʿereb*, 'and all the mixed company': NEB 'and all his rabble of followers'; G *kai pantas tous summeiktous autou*, 'and all *his* mixed (people)', understanding it as a continuation of v. 19 and referring to those under the Pharaoh's control (cf. Ex. 12.38). G lacks 'and all the kings of the land of Uz', cf. Lam. 4.21 for the association of Uz and Edom (the phrase may belong to v. 21). Rudolph deletes also 'and all the kings of the land of the Philistines'. The absence of Gath from the formal listing of the Philistine Pentapolis (also absent in 47) is curious; the reference to 'the remnant of Ashdod' may reflect the Egyptian campaign of Psammetichus I against the town which destroyed it after a long siege (cf. Herodotus II, 157 which refers to a twenty-nine year siege). G lacks 'and' before the towns (MT *wᵉ'et*), thus making them a new set for visiting with the cup (cf. v. 19 *'et-parʿōh*). **[22]** MT *malᵉkē hā'ī*, 'kings of the coast, islands': NEB 'kings of the coasts and islands'; the coasts which are across the sea, i.e. the regions beyond the sea, are the Phoenician colonies and islands. G *basileis tous en tō peran tes thalassēs*, 'kings in (the region) beyond the sea'. Rudolph treats v. 22 as secondary in his translation. **[23]** MT *būz*, 'Buz': G *rōs*, 'Ros'. MT *wᵉ'ēt kol-qᵉṣūṣē pē'āh*, 'and all who cut the edge (of their hair)'; cf. 9.25 (EV 26), a reference to the desert tribes (G 'all who shave round their face'). **[24]** MT *wᵉ'ēt kol-malᵉkē ʿᵃrāb*, 'and all the kings of Arabia': cf. v. 20a; lacking in G. MT repeats the phrase (vocalizing *ʿrb* as *ʿᵃrāb*, 'Arabia', in the first instance and *ʿereb*, 'mixed company', in the second); G lacks the dittography and reads *ʿrb* as 'mixed (people)'. Both phrases in MT are probably glosses on v. 23b (cf. Bright, 158); Rudolph retains only 'who dwell in the desert' of v. 24 which he reads with v. 23. **[25]** MT *zimrī*, 'Zimri': the place or territory is unknown; G lacks the phrase 'all the kings of Zimri'. Rudolph reads Zimki as an athbash (see on v. 26) for *'ēlām*, 'Elam' (*zmk* for *'lm*), so that the following clause is a gloss on it ('all the kings of Zimki'). An athbash followed by its decoded form may be possible but is unlikely. Volz, 387–8, reads the name as Simri, in the neighbourhood of Elam and Media. **[26]** MT *kol-hammamᵉlᵉkōt hā'āreṣ*, 'all the kingdoms of the earth': G lacks 'earth'; MT *hā'āreṣ*, a variant of 'upon the face of the earth'; one version is sufficient. BHS repoints MT as *hammamᵉlākōt*. MT *ūmelek šēšak*, 'and the king of Sheshak': *šēšak* is an athbash – a cryptographic device whereby letters of the alphabet in reverse order are substituted for letters in the proper order (' becomes *t*, *b š* etc. in Hebrew). Hence MT *ššk* = *bbl* (Babylon). Sheshak may have been a genuine name for Babylon used by the Babylonians (cf. Nicholson, II, 222–3; see on 51.1, 41). As a cipher athbash need not imply secrecy or contribute to dating v. 26 before 539 (cf. Bright, 161), but in the context of vv. 15–29 (and OAN) may be an echo of magical rituals of an incantatory nature. G lacks the phrase; T has 'Babylon'. G also lacks 'shall drink after them' (i.e. all of MT after '. . . on the face of the earth'). Rudolph treats vv. 25–26 as secondary. **[27]** MT *ūqᵉyū* (K[Mss] *wqww*): Rudolph vocalizes as *wᵉqīyyū* (= *wᵉqī'ū*, stem *qy'*, 'vomit, disgorge, spew up'), '(drink and be drunk) and vomit'. **[29]** G lacks 'says Yahweh of hosts'.

Brongers 1969; McKane 1980b, 487–92

Three stages form this unit: a trial by ordeal procedure contributes an image introducing the motif of the judgment of the nations, a list of the kings of the nations provides the victims of this judgment, and the drinking image is developed to give a justification for the destruction of the nations. The three elements do not form an original unity but are used to build up an attack on the nations. Even though the drinking metaphor appears in vv. 15–17 and vv. 27–28, the two pieces are quite distinct. They encapsulate the list of kings and peoples within a context of ritual magic which guarantees the downfall of all those named in the list. The present position of the unit is linked to vv. 8–11, 12–14 by the parallel motifs of 'sending' and 'taking' (*šlḥ*, *lqḥ*, vv. 9, 15): in the word of judgment against Judah Yahweh sends for and takes a family (MT 'families' makes a better parallel with the nations of vv. 18–26) from the north, in the cup metaphor Jeremiah (assuming the continuity of vv. 1, 2, 15) takes from Yahweh's hand the fatal cup and is sent to all the nations. Thus in the redaction of 25 a certain symmetry is obtained and the commonalty of all the nations, including Judah, stressed.

The action of vv. 15–17 is not easily understood. The divine command and the response to it of the speaker suggest the magical action category encountered in 13.1–7; 19.1–2, 10–11. But whereas obtaining a girdle or a ceramic flask and travelling to a specific place with either are coherent ideas with quite feasible possibilities of execution, taking a cup *from Yahweh's hand* and making *the nations* drink are far from clear notions. Rudolph treats the unit as a vision (this approach is used by him for 13.1–8 as well and doubles the amount of visionary material in the tradition) and thereby resolves the problem of staging the action. Interpreting the images as part of a literary production would also avoid the difficulties entailed by envisaging a literal event. Clearly no literal meaning can be posited of vv. 15–17: a cup handed by Yahweh to Jeremiah and then taken around the nations, from Egypt to Babylon and from the bedouins of Arabia to the islands beyond the sea, cannot be interpreted literally. A dramatic performance with various individuals playing the parts of the kings of the nations is possible (cf. Carroll 1981, 133), but unlikely. It is unlikely because part of the problem is caused by the addition of the list of nations to the image of the cup and also because the development of the unit has turned a metaphor into a dramatic representation of magical significance. If an original poem has been reworked here into a more complicated literary piece (cf. DeRoche 1978) or the original image has been extended by the list (cf. Isa. 3.16–24 where simple transformations of beauty into ugliness have been extended by a lengthy list of garments and ornaments), then it is futile seeking to reconstruct an original setting for a hypothesized action. As a unit vv. 15–17, 19–26 may give the appearance of a sustained action (magical or symbolic), but that is the effect of reading the different elements as a coherent whole. The action only takes place in the redacted material; in its constituent parts there are only discrete images.

The image of the cup of wine, identified as Yahweh's anger, is a common metaphor (cf. 51.7; Obad. 16; Ezek. 23.31–4; Isa. 51.17, 22; Hab. 2.16; Zech. 12.2; Lam. 4.21; Ps. 75.9; analysis in Brongers). Drinking from this cup is a way of expressing the view that somebody or something is the recipient of divine wrath. Behind the metaphor may be one of two background settings: a banquet or a trial by ordeal (cf. McKane). In the trial by ordeal (Num. 5.11–31) the wife suspected of adultery must submit to a magical ritual operated by the priest: in the sacred precincts she must drink the water of bitterness containing holy water, dust from the sacred floor, and the curses washed from the book in which they have been written. This act of drinking is the final element in a series of ritual gestures, and its outcome determines her state (i.e. whether she has committed adultery or not) and therefore her fate. It is an ordeal which may demonstrate her guilt or her innocence. In so far as the images of vv. 15–17 portray judgment, elicit a verdict, prove guilt and impose a penalty, they may be said to reflect the trial by ordeal (McKane, 490–1). But that ceremony only provides the metaphor of the cup: the nations are not on trial but are already guilty and the wine is their execution (hence the addition of v. 16b explaining the meaning of the images of drunkenness). The woman's fate in the ritual drinking of the curse-laden water is not predetermined but may be settled either way depending upon whether her guilt or innocence is established (cf. Brongers, 183). The fate of the nations is determined and when they drink from the cup they vomit. Hence they are doomed. The cup divines their future (cf. Volz, 389; Gen. 44.5 for the divining cup).

The banquet imagery may also contribute to the understanding of the metaphors in vv. 15–16. In 8.14; 9.15; 23.15 Yahweh is represented as supplying a banquet of poisonous substances for the people and prophets of Judah. The same idea may be behind the giving of the cup to the nations (what McKane, 491, calls a 'banquet of death'), only wine rather than poison is the drink served. The great wine feasts, drunken orgies associated with funerary cults (cf. 16.5, 7; Amos 6.7), may be the setting here. On this occasion of the feast, however, it is Yahweh who serves (via his messenger) the wine, and the terrible drunkenness and vomiting which follow represent the divine judgment against the nations. Those who have caused Judah such appalling suffering must now take their turn at drinking the wine of Yahweh's wrath. This reversal is better expressed in Hab. 2.15–16, where the sense of reciprocation is plainly asserted. Both the trial by ordeal and the wine banquet settings may provide elements of the images used in vv. 15–17.

The various secondary features of vv. 18–26 (details in Rudolph, 164; see Notes) indicate how the second stage of the unit has been built up to include all the nations, the mighty enemies of Judah and the lesser tribes which had never had any contact with it. The presence of v. 18 makes the whole sequence a movement of the divine wrath from original target (vv. 8–11) to original instrument (vv. 9, 26). Such a universalization of Yahweh's anger is evidence of an apocalyptic development in the unit and confirms the lateness of the redaction. This apocalyptic feast for the nations reverses the image of a divine wine feast for them in Isa. 25.6 but can hardly include v. 18 (cf. Isa. 51.22–3 for the necessary adjustment of the image of Yahweh's bowl of wrath). The listing of the nations in vv. 19–26 is much more comprehensive than in the oracles against the nations of 46–51 and the order, although quite similar, is not the same (closer in MT than G). That the final point of the list is Babylon may be deduced from the oracles against the nations, but the use of Sheshak in v. 26 (cf. 51.41) may indicate a cipher for whatever the great power of the period may have been (e.g. Greek or Roman; cf. Duhm, 206). In 51.41 the cipher has no concealment force but the manipulation of letters may be a trace of the ritual magic inherent in the OAN. Its occurrence in 25.26 within a context of magical rituals and curses is evidence for reading it as an incantatory device – whether against Babylon or Babylon's successor (cf. Rev. 18.2, 10, 21) is a moot point.

The third stage returns to the cup image but develops it in terms of an explanation of why the nations must suffer. The presentation of the cup to the nations is not an invitation to drink but a command. No option is offered them. Thus the image is developed by means of a discussion between messenger and nations. The lack of choice provides an explanation in v. 29. The nations must consume the wine because Jerusalem has suffered Yahweh's wrath already and the nations can be no exception to that movement of anger. There is a transformation here which turns the destruction of Jerusalem (the theme of 2.5 – 25.11, 13a) from being Yahweh's punishment for its long history of oppression and offences against Yahweh into the first act (i.e. 'I am beginning . . .') of Yahweh's doing evil against *all* the inhabitants of the earth. A quite radical reinterpretation of the tradition appears here and the apocalyptic character of the unit is quite marked (cf. Peake's view of the cipher as an apocalyptic fondness for mysterious designations). A hint of this reinterpretation is to be found in v. 12 where the Babylonians are to be punished 'for their iniquity', presumably because they had attacked Jerusalem (cf. 51.49, 'Babylon must fall for the slain of Israel'). However, in

v. 29 it is not only Babylon but all the nations who must suffer – if Jerusalem is punished, why should any nation go unpunished? Yet there is no hint of this idea in the first part of the tradition (cf. 30. 7; 45.5). Jerusalem and its people suffer for many reasons, but never as an instalment of a universalized divine wrath (a motif more at home in the later apocalyptic movements). The development of the cup metaphor may reflect the images associated with the divine day of vengeance in Isa. 63.1–6, where the deity tramples down the people in his anger just as he has trodden the wine press. The transference of the deity's bowl of wrath from Jerusalem to its tormentors (Isa. 51.21–23) is part of this imagery but is not used in the unit here. With the incorporation of the different units into the redaction of 25, the word of judgment dominates the whole chapter and therefore there is no place for such a transference motif. But if judgment begins at Jerusalem it will most certainly not end there.

25.30–38

30 'You, therefore, shall prophesy against them all these words, and
say to them:
"The LORD will roar from on high,
and from his holy habitation utter his voice;
he will roar mightily against his fold,
and shout, like those who tread grapes,
against all the inhabitants of the earth.
31 The clamour will resound to the ends of the earth,
for the LORD has an indictment against the nations;
he is entering into judgment with all flesh,
and the wicked he will put to the sword,
says the LORD."
32 Thus says the LORD of hosts:
Behold, evil is going forth
from nation to nation,
and a great tempest is stirring
from the farthest parts of the earth!
33 And those slain by the LORD on that day shall extend from one
end of the earth to the other. They shall not be lamented, or
gathered, or buried; they shall be dung on the surface of the ground.
34 Wail, you shepherds, and cry,
and roll in ashes, you lords of the flock,

for the days of your slaughter and dispersion have come,
and you shall fall like choice rams.
35 No refuge will remain for the shepherds,
nor escape for the lords of the flock.
36 Hark, the cry of the shepherds,
and the wail of the lords of the flock!
For the LORD is despoiling their pasture,
37 and the peaceful folds are devastated,
because of the fierce anger of the LORD.
38 Like a lion he has left his covert,
for their land has become a waste
because of the sword of the oppressor,
and because of his fierce anger.'

[MT 25.30–38] = G 32.30–38. **[30]** MT *ūmimm*^{e}*ʿōn qod*^{e}*šō*, 'and from his holy habitation': G *apo tou hagiou autou*, 'from his sanctuary' = *miqqod*^{e}*šō*. The motif of Yahweh roaring from his sanctuary (in Zion) also appears in Amos 1.2; Joel 3.16 (MT 4.16); cf. Isa 66.6. MT *hēdād k*^{e}*dōr*^{e}*kīm yaʿ*^{a}*neh*, 'a shout like treaders will answer': cf. NEB 'an echo comes back like the shout of men treading grapes'; for the imagery cf. 48.33; 51.14; Isa. 16.9f. Rudolph, 166, reads the final clause 'against all the inhabitants of the earth' with v. 31 (cf. BHS; G); Bright, 162, takes 'the clamour will resound' of v. 31 with v. 30. Rudolph regards vv. 30–31, 33 as secondary. **[31]** MT *n*^{e}*tānām*, 'he will give them (to the sword)': G *edothēsan*, 'are given' = *nitt*^{e}*nū*; V *tradidi* = *nātatti*, 'I have given'. For the motif of a quarrel between Yahweh and the nations (*kī rīb layhwh baggōyim*, 'for Yahweh has a dispute with the nations') cf. 2.9; Isa. 3.13, where the quarrel is with Judah (reversed in 50.33–34). Both motifs are metaphors and have no necessary connections with a covenant lawsuit. **[33]** MT *bayyōm hahū'*, 'on that day': G *en hēmera kuriou*, 'in the day of the lord' = *b*^{e}*yōm yhwh*. G lacks 'they shall not be lamented, or gathered'. The verse is a prose expansion using motifs to be found elsewhere in the tradition (cf. 8.2b; 12.12; 16.4) but here reapplied to the nations; it interrupts the connection between vv. 32, 34. **[34]** MT *w*^{e}*hitpall*^{e}*šū*: an act of mourning – 'roll in ashes' (RSV), 'sprinkle yourselves with ashes' (NEB), 'strew (dust) on yourselves' (JPSB); cf. 6.26 ('ashes' expressed); Micah 1.10; Ezek. 27.30; G *koptesthe* 'mourn, lament', by striking oneself as a sign of grief. MT *ūt*^{e}*pōṣōtīkem*, 'and your dispersal': lacking in G; exegetes regard the word as unintelligible (e.g. Weiser, Rudolph, Bright). Weiser, 222 n. 1, suggests *w*^{e}*nippaṣtīkem*, 'and I shatter you' (*npṣ*, 'shatter'; cf. *pṣṣ*, 'shatter'). MT *kik*^{e}*lī ḥemdāh*, 'like choice vessel': the two verbs *pūṣ*, 'scatter'; *npl*, 'fall', may be variants, one referring to sheep (the dominant metaphor of vv. 34–7), the other to vessels; G *hōsper hoi krioi hoi eklektoi*, 'like choice rams' = *k*^{e}*'ēlē ḥemdāh* (?). Ehrlich 1912, 309, reads as *bib*^{e}*lī ḥem*^{e}*lāh*, 'without mercy'. **[37]**

Bright, 160, omits the phrase 'because of the fierce anger of Yahweh' as it duplicates the last clause of v. 38 (where G lacks it). **[38]** MT *kakkᵉpīr . . . kī*, 'like a lion . . . for': BHS deletes *k . . . kī* as dittographies. MT *mippᵉnē ḥᵃrōn hayyōnāh ūmippᵉnē ḥᵃrōn 'appō*, 'because of the anger of the oppressor(s) and because of his fierce anger': G *apo prosōpou tēs machairas tēs megalēs*, 'before the great sword'. EVV read 'sword' with G (cf. Vrs), treating 'anger' as a dittography from the final clause; cf. 46.16, where *mippᵉnē ḥereb hayyōnāh*, 'because of the sword of the oppressor', may represent what MT should be here (but see on 46.16).

Whatever the taking of the cup of wine around the listed nations sequence may refer to, it is provided with a commentary (Rudolph) in vv. 30–38. A series of poetic sayings grouped together is presented as a prophetic statement ('and *you* shall prophesy against them', v. 30). The words of this statement spell out the message of the cup and conclude the introduction to the oracles against the nations. These poems would fit anywhere in the tradition because they are about the fierce wrath of Yahweh destroying the nations of the earth, the wicked and the leaders of the peoples. Nothing precise or particular is to be found in vv. 30–38, but images of destruction and anger (already pervasive throughout 2–20). The dominant metaphors are drawn from the language of sheep-herding: shepherds, sheep, pastures and sheep-folds (cf. 6.1–3; 23.1–4). The repeated references to 'shepherds' and 'lords of the flock' parallel the subject of 'kings' in vv. 19–26. It is the leaders of the nations who are addressed, but the devastation will include their peoples. If the language of the poems repeats images found throughout Part I and the rest of the tradition (e.g. v. 32, 'the farthest parts of the earth', cf. 6.22; 32.8; 50.41), it would be unwise to attribute it to any one particular speaker (e.g. Jeremiah; to whom Rudolph attributes vv. 32, 34–8). It is a dominant feature of the book of Jeremiah that many of its strands (metaphors and poetry) are shifted around throughout the tradition without any firm location within a specific section. Such shifts point to redactional influences rather than indicate authentic Jeremiah speeches. The metaphors which describe Yahweh's destruction of the nations do double service in the tradition; they refer as much to Judah as to the nations (which direction the influence goes is a moot point).

The commentary or, better, appendix is a prophetic utterance (reflecting the late strand of Jeremiah *as* prophet implicitly if not explicitly) introduced by the announcement of Yahweh's war against the inhabitants of the earth. This is the language of apocalyptic doom rather than of military campaigns. Although v. 30 is similar to Amos 1.2 and Joel 3.16 (the nations are the context of all three occurrences), there are subtle differences between them. Zion is the stated centre of divine action in Amos and Joel but is only implied in v. 30 (but NEB 'roars from Zion on high' makes it explicit). The transcendental atmosphere of apocalyptic language is more direct here because it allows for the divine roaring (the lion of v. 38) to be done from the heavens in contradistinction to its effects being felt to the ends of the earth (MT 31). The sanctuary (G) may well refer to the temple (cf. Ex. 15.17), so the interpretation of v. 30 should allow for a dual reference to heavenly and earthly sanctuaries. But the judgment of Yahweh against the nations starts from the holy place and spreads out across the earth (note the similar images of temple and destruction of the nations enclosing the work of Haggai). Only the Joel reference counterbalances the divine roaring with a statement about the protected status of the people of Israel, but there is nothing in vv. 30–38 which militates against reading such a notion as being implicit in all the material directed against the nations. In v. 27 there is the beginning of a reversal of Judah's fate (cf. vv. 12, 14); the oracles which follow (G ends the collection with vv. 15–38) in 46–51 contain further statements to this effect.

Yahweh's roar is like the shout of those who tread the grapes (cf. Isa. 16.9–10), i.e. the riotous pleasure of those who enjoy what they are doing and anticipate the consumption of their labours. It has about it a furious strength, a full-blooded engagement in the task at hand, that is well characterized by the reference to treading the grapes in the winepress (cf. 48.33). The roar of those who trample the grapes and stain their garments red easily becomes a metaphor for the appalling slaughter of war (Isa. 63.1–3). Commotion, confusion, enthusiasm, liquefaction processes and social encounter are the common elements shared by making wine or waging war. But the deity's form of wine-making is blood-letting. The noise will be heard throughout the earth because Yahweh has a quarrel (*rīb*) with the nations (cf. 2.9). The divine quarrel with which Part I begins has been transferred from Judah to the nations by Part II, but in neither case is it necessary to construct a complex theology of covenantal forms to explain such a quarrel. There is no covenant between Yahweh and the nations, yet he has a *rīb* against them. Why, then, should a *rīb* against Judah necessarily entail a covenant? Yahweh's evil (cf. v. 29), i.e. his storm (cf. 23.19; 30.23), goes forth from nation to nation (just like the cup in v. 17), and disaster befalls all. The leaders of the nations are commanded to go into mourning because there can be no escape from this disaster. It is like a lion leaving its lair and going among the sheep – terrible destruction follows. The metaphors of sheep-herding dominate vv. 34–38. Hence the shepherds fall like choice rams and what they should be protecting, namely the sheep-folds, are devastated. Yahweh's anger wipes out the nations.

PART THREE

Miscellaneous Narratives and Cycles

26–36

The second half of the book of Jeremiah poses serious problems of division and classification. The long stretch of chapters from 26 to 45 is broken into smaller collections and discrete narratives, but commentators differ on how they should be grouped. No central organizing theme can be detected in the twenty chapters which would allow them to be treated as a unity or give them a unifying title. Bright's 'Incidents from the life of Jeremiah' as a title is only a loosely accurate description which requires the extraction of 30–33 from the collection and incorporates into it units from other parts (e.g. 19.1–2, 10–11, 14–15; 20.1–6; 21.1–10; 24; 32.1–15; 51.59–64b). It also ignores the absence of Jeremiah from 40.7–41.18. If the word of judgment dominates 2.5–25.11 as an overarching concept (with only a few fragments of salvation material), there is no equivalent organizing principle for 26–45. The closest element to such a unifying feature is the notion of the word of Yahweh proclaimed by Jeremiah (26–36) and its fulfilment in the destruction of Jerusalem and the fate of those who survived that catastrophe (37–45; cf. Ackroyd 1968b). Jeremiah as the servant of the word holds together most of the narratives (with the exception of 39.1–10; 40.7–41.18) rather than incidents from his life and this theme may be used to organize the material in a number of ways (cf. Kessler 1968, 83–7).

The precise division of 26–45 into two parts (i.e. Parts III and IV in this commentary) is equally a matter for disagreement among exegetes. 26.1 ('the reign of Jehoiakim') and 37.1 (Zedekiah as replacement of Jehoiakim) indicate the most natural division of 26–45 into two blocks. If 26–45 are not divided up into parts, decisions of this kind may be avoided, but the subtle shifts of emphasis which appear in the redaction will be missed. Commentators organize the sections of the book in many different ways (e.g. Volz, Hyatt, Thompson), but the scheme followed here is essentially the four-part division proposed by Rudolph, with minor variations (cf. Rudolph, 1). The variations include the classification of 1 and 52 as prologue and epilogue and the precise division of 26–45. Rudolph divides parts C and D into 26–35 and 36–45 (cf. Rietzschel 1966, who also follows this division). Rudolph's title for part C is 'prophecies of salvation for Israel' (Rudolph, 168). The presence of doom material in 26–29; 32.26–35; 34.8–22 hardly justifies Rudolph's title, and a less one-sided category is required to describe the contents of Part III. A further disagreement with Rudolph concerns the actual division of the two parts. A better case can be made for dividing the collection at 36 than at 35 (cf. Kessler 1968). 36 functions in relation to 26–35 in the same way as 25.1–11 relates to 2–20: it summarizes and acts as a closure of the section. It concludes what is begun by 26. It therefore belongs with 26–35 much more than it does with 37–45 (see on 37.1–2).

In Part III 26 and 36 act as preface and conclusion: 26 raises the question of turning, but 36 demonstrates the rejection of that possibility. Two distinctive cycles are included in Part III: an independent treatment of prophetic conflict (27–29), with its own peculiar features, and a book of salvation oracles (30–31), with prosaic appendices (32–33). Two independent narratives (34–35) complete the collection in III.

26.1–24

261 In the beginning of the reign of Jehoiakim the son of Josiah, king of
Judah, this word came from the LORD, 2 'Thus says the LORD: Stand in the
court of the LORD's house, and speak to all the cities of Judah which come
to worship in the house of the LORD all the words that I command you to
speak to them; do not hold back a word. 3 It may be they will listen, and
every one turn from his evil way, that I may repent of the evil which I intend
to do to them because of their evil doings. 4 You shall say to them, "Thus
says the LORD: If you will not listen to me, to walk in my law which I have
set before you, 5 and to heed the words of my servants the prophets whom
I send to you urgently, though you have not heeded, 6 then I will make this
house like Shiloh, and I will make this city a curse for all the nations of the
earth." '

7 The priests and the prophets and all the people heard Jeremiah speaking
these words in the house of the LORD. 8 And when Jeremiah had finished
speaking all that the LORD had commanded him to speak to all the people,
then the priests and the prophets and all the people laid hold of him, saying,
'You shall die! 9 Why have you prophesied in the name of the LORD, saying,
"This house shall be like Shiloh, and this city shall be desolate, without
inhabitant?" ' And all the people gathered about Jeremiah in the house of
the LORD.

10 When the princes of Judah heard these things, they came up from the
king's house to the house of the LORD and took their seat in the entry of the
New Gate of the house of the LORD. 11 Then the priests and the prophets
said to the princes and to all the people, 'This man deserves the sentence of
death, because he has prophesied against this city, as you have heard with
your own ears.'

12 Then Jeremiah spoke to all the princes and all the people, saying, 'The
LORD sent me to prophesy against this house and this city all the words you
have heard. 13 Now therefore amend your ways and your doings, and obey
the voice of the LORD your God, and the LORD will repent of the evil which
he has pronounced against you. 14 But as for me, behold, I am in your
hands. Do with me as seems good and right to you. 15 Only know for certain
that if you put me to death, you will bring innocent blood upon yourselves
and upon this city and its inhabitants, for in truth the LORD sent me to you
to speak all these words in your ears.'

16 Then the princes and all the people said to the priests and the prophets,
'This man does not deserve the sentence of death, for he has spoken to us
in the name of the LORD our God.' 17 And certain of the elders of the land
arose and spoke to all the assembled people, saying, 18 'Micah of Moresheth
prophesied in the days of Hezekiah king of Judah, and said to all the people
of Judah: "Thus says the LORD of hosts,

Zion shall be ploughed as a field;
 Jerusalem shall become a heap of ruins,
 and the mountain of the house a wooded height."

19 Did Hezekiah king of Judah and all Judah put him to death? Did he not
fear the LORD and entreat the favour of the LORD, and did not the LORD
repent of the evil which he had pronounced against them? But we are about
to bring great evil upon ourselves.'

20 There was another man who prophesied in the name of the LORD,
Uriah the son of Shemaiah from Kiriath-jearim. He prophesied against this
city and against this land in words like those of Jeremiah. 21 And when
King Jehoiakim, with all his warriors and all the princes, heard his words,
the king sought to put him to death; but when Uriah heard of it, he was
afraid and fled and escaped to Egypt. 22 Then King Jehoiakim sent to
Egypt certain men, Elnathan the son of Achbor and others with him, 23

and they fetched Uriah from Egypt and brought him to King Jehoiakim, who slew him with the sword and cast his dead body into the burial place of the common people.

24 But the hand of Ahikam the son of Shaphan was with Jeremiah so that he was not given over to the people to be put to death.

[MT 26] = G 33. **[1]** MT *hāyāh haddābār hazzeh*, 'this word came . . .': S adds *'l 'rmy'*, 'to Jeremiah', cf. 27.1; Rudolph inserts it into the text (cf. BHS), also Volz, 92. MT *bᵉrē'šīt mamᵉlᵉkūt yᵉhōyāqīm*, 'in the beginning of the reign of Jehoiakim': cf. 27.1; 28.1, which both start with the same formulaic 'in the beginning of the reign of . . .' (with the variation *mamᵉleket*, 'reign'). Such stereotypical introductions to 26.1; 27.1; 28.1 are indicative of redactional activity rather than accurate historical datings (see on 27.1). The accession year (cf. Akk. *rēš šarrūti*) of Jehoiakim refers to the period between the king's accession and the following new year, i.e. c. Sept 609 – April 608 (Bright, 169). **[2]** Cf. 7.2. MT *'al-tigra' dābār*, 'do not withhold a word': cf. Deut. 4.2; 13.1 (EV 12.32); Janzen 1981 for the concept of withholding the word (i.e. diminishing it). Cf. 50.2 for the sense of hiding the message (also 38.25). **[5]** MT *wᵉhaškēm wᵉšālōaḥ*, 'and rising early and sending': cf. 7.25; 25.4; 29.19; 44.4 (variations in 7.13; 11.7; 35.15); delete first 'and' with many mss and Vrs. MT *wᵉlō' šᵉma'tem*, 'but you did not listen': the phrase is virtually a Leitmotif in Part III (cf. the variations on it in 27.9, 14, 16, 17; 29.19; 32.33; 34.17; 35.14, 15, 16, 17; 36.31). **[6]** K *hz'th*; Q *hazzō't*, 'this': K a scribal error, but Driver 1951, 244–5, regards the rare pronominal form as a remnant of colloquial or local idiom; G lacks 'this (city)'. For the city as a curse (*qᵉlālāh*) cf. 25.18; more often used of remnants who survive the defeat of the city (24.9; 42.18; 44.8, 12). Used of the land (44.22), Bozrah (49.13), and a general curse (29.22). **[8]** MT *kol-'ᵃšer-ṣiwwāh yhwh*, 'all which Yahweh had commanded': Vrs read . . . *ṣiwwāhū* . . . '. . . commanded *him* . . .', cf. BHS. MT *wᵉkol-hā'ām*, 'and all the people': BHS regards the phrase as an addition from v. 7a; Rudolph, 170, deletes it because only the priests and prophets are prosecutors, whereas the people belong with the judges in vv. 11, 16. The fluctuating role of the people is one of the problems of the interpretation of 26 (Bright, 170, takes it to mean 'various of the people' rather than literally). MT *mōt tāmūt*, 'you will surely die': a variation of the formal legal ruling *mōt yūmat*, 'he will surely die' (cf. Schulz 1969, 71–83, on the legal terminology and its sacral background and 118–23 on 26.7–19). **[9]** MT *nibbētā*, 'you have prophesied': some mss have the more usual form *nibbē'tā*. MT *wayyiqqāhēl kol-hā'ām 'el-yirmᵉyāhū*, 'and all the people gathered to Jeremiah': some mss, Vrs have *'al*, 'against', for *'el*, 'to', cf. NEB; see BHS for the *'el*/*'al* variations in 26. The use of *qhl* may reflect a formal religious assembly (cf. v. 17b), which would suit the sacral language used in the story (cf. Schulz, 122). **[10]** MT *wayyu'ᵃlū*, 'and they came up':

cf. 22.1; the temple was at a higher level than the royal residences. MT *bᵉpetaḥ ša'ar-yhwh heḥādāš*, 'at the door of the gate of Yahweh, the new one': many mss, Vrs read *bēt*, 'house of' before 'Yahweh', cf. 36.10. **[12]** G lacks 'all' before princes; cf. v. 16. **[13]** Cf. 7.5; the notion of Yahweh's repentance (cf. v. 19) is mooted as a general principle in 18.7–10. **[17]** MT *wayyāqumū ʾᵃnāšīm mizziqᵉnē hāʾāreṣ*, 'and *men* from the elders of the land stood up'. **[18]** K *mykyh*; Q *mīkāh*, 'Micah'; cf. Micah 1.1. The citation in v. 18b is from Micah 3.12. G lacks *hāyāh nibbā'*, 'was prophesying'. MT *'iyyīm*, 'ruins' (*'iyyīn* in Micah 3.12), cf. Ps. 79.1; EVV 'heap of ruins' is justified as a parallel to *lᵉbāmōt yā'ar*, 'forest heights', lit. 'high places of a wood, forest', cf. NEB 'rough heath'; JPSB 'a shrine in the woods' (G *alsos drumou*, 'a grove [sacred] of oaks', i.e. 'a thicket grove'). Rudolph, 172, reads *lᵉbahᵃmōt*, 'for beasts of (the forest)', as in Micah 5.7 (EV 8), fulfilled in Lam. 5.18 (cf. BHS); cf. Janssen 1956, 89. **[19]** MT has '*they* put to death . . . *he* feared . . . *he* appeased . . .', Vrs sing . . . plur . . . plur. MT *wayᵉḥal*, 'and he appeased (the face of Yahweh)': *ḥillāh*, 'appease, mollify, entreat the favour of, pacify'; NEB 'seek to placate'. The anthropomorphism ('soften the face') is a vestige of ancient rituals relating to the idol of the god in the cult (cf. Bright). **[20]** G lacks 'against this city and'. Kiriath-jearim: about six miles north-west of Jerusalem. **[21]** G lacks 'and all his warriors . . . and he was afraid and fled'. MT *wayᵉbaqqēš hammelek*, 'and the king sought': G *kai ezētoun*, 'and they sought'. **[22]** MT *ʾᵃnāšīm miṣrāyim*, 'men Egypt': cf. v. 17; an unnecessary addition (cf. BHS) in view of 22b (lacking in G); cf. 36.12 for Elnathan. **[23]** MT *qibᵉrē bᵉnē hā'ām*, 'the graves of the sons of the people': i.e. the common burial ground (probably in the Kidron valley, cf. II Kings 23.6). G *to mnēma huiōn laou autou*, 'the memorial of the sons of his people': i.e. his family grave.

Hossfeld und Meyer 1974; Reventlow 1969

The second half of the book of Jeremiah opens with a story which attempts to present Jeremiah as the speaker of the authentic word of Yahweh, a role which is recognized and acknowledged by important social strata in the community. Part III will end with a story in which very powerful strata of society will reject that role and seek his execution (36). If in the first story he escapes for reasons which are far from clear (see on v. 24), in the second he escapes because he has gone into hiding (36.26). In 26 he openly proclaims his message of doom against temple and city, in 36 he does it by sending a deputy speaker to read a written account of his oracles. Both proclamations (in person and delegated) take place in the temple precincts. Between the two stories subtle shifts in Jeremiah's temerity may be imagined to have taken place but the text allows no insight into them (see on 36.5). In point of fact, the two stories should be read as parallel and paradigmatic. In 26 Jeremiah is fully present and Jehoiakim completely absent (the redaction in vv. 1a, 20–23 makes that absence palpable); in 36 Jeremiah absents himself while Jehoiakim is very much present. The tradition knows of no encounter between Jeremiah and Jehoiakim. A few incidents are dated to the reign of Jehoiakim but Jeremiah never confronts him nor addresses him directly. The only contact between Jeremiah and a king allowed by the tradition is that in which Jeremiah and Zedekiah meet or that king consults Jeremiah. Even the formal dating of certain speeches to the time of Jehoiakim (e.g. 25.1; 26.1; 36.1) may be questioned as to historical accuracy and these passages are probably to be treated as redactional notes making connections between the tradition and 605, the date of Carchemish and Nebuchadrezzar's rise to supreme power (see on 1.2–3). The two formidable characters, Jehoiakim and Jeremiah, never meet because they only belong together as elements in the structured narratives. It is in the redaction of the tradition and the creation of the story in 36 that the two approach, but only as shadows. The absence of the one is the presence of the other – both cannot occupy the stage at the same time.

In the original story of 26 there is no place for Jehoiakim and the absence of the king from matters of sacral law is to be expected. Some Deuteronomistic influence may be detected in 26 (e.g. vv. 3–5, 12–15 show traces of Deuteronomistic reflection, cf. Thiel 1981, 3–4; Nicholson 1970, 52–6), especially in the presentation of what looks like a formal trial without any recourse to the king (Deut. 16.18; 17.8–12 allow no place for the king in relation to the dispensation of justice; cf. Boecker 1980, 40–9; de Vaux 1965, 150–2). Given the nature of the debate in 26 there is no role for the king to play and, although it may well be asked how the princes became involved without the king knowing about it (especially in view of vv. 20–23), therefore he is absent. Yet his absence may be accounted for also on the grounds that the narrative is a story constructed to make certain points and not an account of a historical incident in the life of Jeremiah (cf. Hossfeld und Meyer; Schulz 1969, 122–3). As a fictional story the narrative cannot be expected to answer questions asked about historical matters. Questions such as 'Why is the king absent throughout the trial?', 'Why are vv. 20–23 included in the story?', 'Why should there be such a reaction to Jeremiah's preaching in 609 when, according to 2–20, he has been saying such things for decades?', 'What coherent role do the people play in the story?', 'If the princes and *all* the people acquitted him (v. 16) what does v. 24 mean?', 'If Jeremiah was acquitted as one who genuinely spoke in Yahweh's name, in what sense may the people be said to have rejected the divine message?', and many others cannot be asked because they all presuppose that 26 is about a real event. The story is not the record of what happened to Jeremiah as a result of his preaching vv. 4–6 in the temple precincts. It is a complex of different strands of redaction which has developed an original story about a public procedure for establishing Jeremiah's authenticity in a number of different ways (cf. Hossfeld und Meyer; Reventlow, 341–51). As a result of these diverse interferences the final form of the story mystifies the modern reader as to its meaning. The redactional levels provide a surfeit of meaning without clarifying their aim by ending the narrative at v. 16.

Many commentators treat 26 as a real event in the life of Jeremiah and their work may be consulted for an alternative handling of the text (e.g. Bright, Thompson). There are similarities between the edited version of 26 and the temple sermon as presented in 7.1–15 (cf. vv. 2, 4–6, 13), but these represent strands added to 26 rather than another version of 7.1–15 giving occasion and response. The tensions between conditional and absolute elements in the sermon (e.g. 7.3–7, 8–15) are not so apparent in 26 but may be discerned in vv. 3–6, 13 (contingent word) and vv. 9, 11–12 (absolute word). But the editing of the story makes it impossible to separate out conditional from absolute elements because the Deuteronomistic schema of the sending of the prophets, and their rejection seals the fate of the city whatever the response of one particular generation. Jerusalem's fate is inevitable, not only because it happened but as a result of a long history of the rejection of the prophetic word (v. 5). This is such a dogma of the tradition that it skews any presentation of Jeremiah as a preacher of repentance (the radical nature of 18.7–10 is post-Deuteronomistic and late). A call to repentance would hardly have sparked off the riot of a lynching mob (cf. vv. 8–9, 24), nor would it have led to Uriah's extradition and execution (vv. 20–3).

The formal structures of the story should be noted. Jeremiah stands in the temple courtyard and announces the word to all the cities of Judah as they congregate there. He utters a curse against the city – in the environment of the temple an uttered curse is a most powerful and fateful act. It releases aweful forces against its object. Small wonder then that those who heard it should seize (v. 8 *tpś*, 'lay hold of, arrest', cf. 2.8; 34.3; 38.23) the speaker of it. Priests, prophets and people arrest Jeremiah and charge him with a capital offence. The crowd milling around him (v. 9b) may give the impression of a near riot, but there may be an element of a formal religious gathering against him (*qahal*, v. 17; cf. v. 9, may refer to the sacred congregation). Temple precincts, destruction of a sanctuary (Shiloh), curse, cultic officials, and the sacred congregation all point in the direction of a sacral procedure in which the accused is liable to face the penalty for blasphemy. Temple and city have been cursed and the charges of blasphemy against god and people (king?, cf. I Kings 21.10, 13) are implicit in the demand for the death penalty. The story does not explain why this should be so, but the reaction of priests, prophets and people clearly indicates that cursing the temple (vv. 6, 9, 12) or the city (vv. 6.9, 11, 12, 20) warrants such punishment. This can only be explained on the grounds that an ideology of the sacred site and city existed which made both the property of the deity (e.g. Ps. 46; 48; Lam. 4.12). So to speak against either was to blaspheme Yahweh of hosts, *the* god of Israel. What justification can there ever be for such blasphemy?

The story changes in v. 10 with the introduction of the princes. What are they doing in a case involving sacral matters? They have no jurisdiction here. This is a matter for priests. The Deuteronomic regulations allow for cases which are too difficult for local judgments to be taken to the divinely chosen place and there to be heard by the priests (Deut. 17.8–12; cf. Mayes 1979, 268–9). Difficult decisions are to be determined not by the royal house and certainly not by the king but by sacral means. Now the king is rightly absent from the story, but what are the princes doing here? They are introduced into the story to turn the proceedings into a kind of trial. Sufficient evidence is already available to convict Jeremiah of blasphemy, but the shaping of the story by the redaction is in a different direction from that charge. The commotion or a report brings the princes up from the royal residences to the temple gate, where they take their seat (thus combining the ancient village practice of judgment in the gate with the sacral proceedings in the temple; on the old practice cf. Köhler 1956, 149–75). There are now five parties to the dispute; Jeremiah, priests, prophets, people and the princes: accused (Jeremiah), accusers (priests, prophets, people) and judges (princes).

But another switch is introduced in v. 11, when the people appear to become part of the judges (so Rudolph), or certainly cease to be among the accusers (contrast v. 24). A symmetrical structure is developing here: priests and prophets on one side, princes and people on the other side, and Jeremiah in the middle. The charge is repeated in v. 11, though the claim 'as you have heard with your own ears' can only loosely include the princes in view of v. 10.

Now Jeremiah speaks in his own defence (cf. Ramsey 1977, 51). This self-defence speech contains a number of elements: he claims as his warrant for what has been said Yahweh's sending – a formal claim to the right to prophesy (cf. Amos 7.15) – a call to the amendment of life, thus rendering the judgment a contingent one and raising the possibility of Yahweh's repentance – the city is not yet doomed – a complete submission of the speaker to his judges' power – a magnificent gesture of self-humbling which indicates a lack of arrogance – and a warning that a death sentence executed against him will bring innocent blood upon the city. These elements constitute a formidable set of claims which is summed up in v. 15b: 'for in truth Yahweh sent me to you to speak in your ears all these words'. It is an impressive performance by a man facing death at the hands of a mob screaming for his blood and, even more dangerous, a tribunal with the power to execute him. The editors have penned the portrait of a very brave man.

Having duly considered his defence (vv. 12–15), the princes and the people answer his accusers with what appears to be the verdict: 'this man does not warrant the sentence of death (*mišpaṭ-māwet*) because he has spoken to us in the name of Yahweh our god' (v. 16). The story should end here with everybody returning to their homes. Jeremiah has been vindicated by the 'court' on his own testimony and has neutralized the power of the priests and prophets by gaining the sympathy of the princes and the people. He has also acquired public recognition of his authenticity as one who speaks the words of Yahweh (the verdict emphasizes that point '*in the name of Yahweh our god* he has spoken to us'). The decision of the princes and the people has affirmed his innocence and he has escaped from death.

The narrative should end at v. 16 because Jeremiah has been vindicated and had his claim to be sent by Yahweh accepted by the nation. If the purpose of the story is to present Jeremiah before the tribunal and its outcome, then it has been achieved. However, in vv. 17–19 a further element is added to the story: men from the senior representatives of the rural areas (i.e. elders, cf. 19.1) arise and address the sacred congregation. In a most unusual fashion they cite another prophetic saying from a previous century. The citation from Micah of Moresheth-gath (cf. Micah 1.14; Mays 1976, 37), a countryman from the area south-west of Jerusalem, provides a precedent for Jeremiah's attack on the city and the temple-hill (cf. Micah 3.12). It also indicates a history of attacks on the city from non-residents (cf. 1.1, which locates the family home of Jeremiah at Anathoth, a town to the north of Jerusalem). The introduction of Micah's prediction about the destruction of Jerusalem, city and temple, may afford a precedent but the real concern of the elders' speech is with the community's response to it. In the light of Micah's terrible words what was the response of king and nation? Did they put Micah on trial and execute him? No! they most certainly did not. They listened to him, took him seriously, feared Yahweh, and appeased the deity. In turn the deity repented and the evil predicted against the city was withdrawn from it (cf. 18.7–8). The final element of their appeal relates to the trial of Jeremiah: if the community proceeds to execute Jeremiah (after v. 16!), then it will bring upon itself even greater evil (cf. v. 15).

There are a number of strange features in vv. 17–19. The direct citation of another speaker's work and its use as an argument are unique in the prophetic traditions. The availability of such a quotation suggests a collection of Micah's oracles (at least those which may be regarded as authentic in Micah 1–3) and therefore a period when such a record had some authority (i.e. after the fall of Jerusalem in 587). The conclusions drawn from Micah's utterance (the citation in v. 18 is prefaced by the oracular 'thus says Yahweh of hosts', whereas Micah 1.2–3.12 hardly ever use such indicators) are most unusual. The modern reader of Micah 3.12 would conclude that Micah had been unduly pessimistic and wrong (cf. von Rad 1965, 150 n. 5). But an entirely different conclusion is taken from the failure of his prediction in the eighth century. The elders see in its non-fulfilment the rescinding of the threat by Yahweh because king and people respond in the proper fashion to such threats. There is no evidence for such a view in Micah 1–3 because the charges levelled against the community are not the kind that ritual gestures (e.g. the appeasement of Yahweh referred to in v. 19) can dissipate. The context of Micah's prediction is an attack on the leaders of Zion (rulers, priests, prophets cf Micah 3.9–11) and the city's fate is caused by those leaders (Micah's 'therefore because of *you*' is notably absent in v. 18). Having built Zion in blood, how could they change that past? But Micah 3.12 is only inappropriate in the context of 26.7–16 because of the argument based on it in v. 19. It does provide a precedent for Jeremiah's preaching, but it does not warrant the use made of it in v. 19 by the redactors.

The function of the Micah citation in v. 19 belongs to the editorial strand which presents the story as a call to change (vv. 3, 13). There is no evidence for Hezekiah's change of heart, and in the Deuteronomistic history he is presented as an incomparable king: 'there was none like him among all the kings of Judah after him, nor among those who were before him' (II Kings 18.5; Hezekiah's piety and rectitude are unimpeachable, cf. II Kings 18–20; only the Chronicler hints at a blemish in terms of his pride after his illness [II Chron. 32.24–26. cf. II Kings 20.12–19], and that reflects the fact of the Babylonian exile [cf. Williamson 1982, 386]). Yet if Micah was a genuine speaker of the divine word, and his utterance of 3.12 did not come to pass (cf. the regulation in Deut. 18.20–22), then some account must be provided which will justify his status. That justification is amply supplied in v. 19 and any dissonance arising from a falsified prediction is avoided (cf. Carroll 1976b). However that is but an incidental by-product of v. 19. A more important feature of v. 19 is the implicitly prescriptive nature of its description of Hezekiah's response to the word of absolute doom. Reference to Hezekiah (whether it reflects a memory of Micah playing a role similar to Isaiah's in II Kings 19.1, 14–28 [cf. Mays 1976, 92] is a moot point) inevitably transforms 26 into a statement for king and people. Hence the editorial allusions to Jehoiakim in vv. 1, 20–23 in spite of his complete absence from the story.

The story in vv. 20–23 has nothing to do with the structured confrontation of vv. 7–16 but is a response to v. 19. It also functions as background information on the situation facing Jeremiah, but lacks cogency here because, even if it represented an accurate historical account of a particular event rather than a further editorial creation, it neither reflects a trial nor the beginning of Jehoiakim's reign (v. 1). Some exegetes read it as an illustration of what might have happened to Jeremiah (e.g. Bright, 172; Thompson, 528), but the absence of Jehoiakim from the story of Jeremiah renders that less than likely. Jehoiakim and his court are introduced to make a formal contrast with Hezekiah and his people. Both are represented as hearing the prophetic word proclaimed against the city: Micah in the time of Hezekiah and Uriah ben Shemaiah (also from outside Jerusalem) in the time of Jehoiakim (see on 36 for further paradigmatic parallels). Hezekiah and his people responded by appealing to and appeasing Yahweh, thereby changing the deity's mind (thus confirming the principle expressed in v. 13). Jehoiakim and his people, on the contrary, responded to Uriah by seeking to kill him (just like priests, prophets, people in v. 8). Like a fool Uriah fled to Egypt, where (could he have not known?) the authorities supported Jehoiakim because he was their vassal. Uriah was extradited from Egypt (as he must have known he would be, unless he was an exceptionally ignorant prophet!), returned to the court and was there executed. His burial may have been ignominious (but cf. G; is this the origin of the application of 22.18–19 to Jehoiakim by way of revenge for Uriah?). Jehoiakim's response to Uriah could not be more different from Hezekiah's reaction to Micah. Thus vv. 19–23 provide two paradigms of response to the word of absolute judgment: the prescriptive nature of v. 19 and the disapproved of behaviour of vv. 20–23 are implicit features of the narrative.

What about Jeremiah? What happened to him? His absence in vv. 17–23 is noteworthy, though his implied presence may cast a shadow over the material here. In v. 24 the editors return to him and observe that he escaped death at the hands of the people because Ahikam ben Shaphan enabled him to do so. How odd! In v. 16 the people, as well as the princes, acquit Jeremiah of the charge of blasphemy (or treason as vv. 20–23 seem to imply). So why should he be given to them for stoning? (For stoning as the penalty cf. Deut. 13.6–11; 21.18–21; I Kings 21.13–15.) Have the people changed sides yet again? What power did they have that could override that of the princes? These questions, like so many other questions raised by the editing of this chapter, cannot be answered because we are not dealing with a historical account which provides accurate information. Too many discrete strands make up the story for a coherent account to be derived from it. The theological shaping of Part III (cf. 36) is such that the word proclaimed by Jeremiah must be heard by all (e.g. 26.2, 7; 36.6, 10), yet also rejected (36.31; cf. 37.1–2). Jeremiah must be acquitted of blasphemy or else his authenticity will not be established (hence v. 16), but if he is acknowledged as being sent by Yahweh the people will have to pay attention to him and believe his words. How to achieve both his legitimation *and* his rejection is the real problem for the editors. It cannot be achieved because it involves a logical contradiction, but the editing of the story using many discrete strands allows the contradiction to be glossed over by separating the verdict from the conclusion. 26 may be heard now as if it were a coherent story rather than an amalgam of very different elements all doing quite separate things in the narrative. 587 and the theology of some of the redactors are responsible for that state of affairs.

This analysis of 26 represents an attempt to allow each separate strand to contribute to the story without ignoring the way so many discrete elements have ruined whatever may have been the original story. The fate of Jeremiah is hardly an interest of the editors (cf. Hossfeld und Meyer, 48), but as the introduction to the second half of the book the story points to opposition between Jeremiah and different strata of society. As the bearer of the divine word his social role is important, but his own personal fate lacks all significance for the editors (e.g. the tradition lacks both birth and death notices for him). Conflict with the prophets (27–29) and the upper classes (36, 38) will characterize many of the narratives, and all these elements are in 26. The passing references to Micah and Uriah are strange, but exemplify the diverse elements forming the narrative. The switches and shifts in the narrative underline the discrete nature of much of the material but also frustrate the interpretative task of making sense of the whole text.

The transformation of Micah into a preacher of doom leading to repentance is one of the most remarkable features of 26. Such a reversal indicates the distance the tradition has travelled from Micah of Moresheth-gath in the direction of Jonah ben Amittai. Jonah is the paradigmatic figure of the prophet preaching a message of absolute doom and achieving repentance by it. The people of Nineveh repent by means of ritual gestures and appease the deity by fasting, dressing in sackcloth, crying to God, and turning from their evil ways (both man *and beast*, cf. Jonah 3.5–10). Thus their imminent doom is averted. King Hezekiah and his people are presented as responding to Micah's proclamation of imminent catastrophe in a similar way and with equal success. Elements of the prophet as the preacher of repentance by means of the absolute word of destruction appear in 26. But whereas Micah and Jonah are successful transformations of doom into salvation, Jeremiah remains as an example of an unsuccessful reversal. Real disasters (e.g. 587) cannot be so averted.

In point of fact the reversals of Micah and Jonah were but holding actions, because Jerusalem and Nineveh later were destroyed. However, that is hardly the point of the stories. The reversal of Micah in 26.17–19 is of a piece with the many reversals of material within the Jeremiah tradition itself (see on 27.16–22; 32.36–41; 33.10–11; 52.31–4) and illustrates just how radically elements could be handled and transformed in relation to their original meanings.

Another late element in 26 is the notice about the pursuit and execution of Uriah ben Shemaiah (vv. 20–3). Apart from its contribution to doing down Jehoiakim (cf. 22.17, which is associated with Jehoiakim by virtue of the redactional note in 22.18a), it is one of only two such notices in the Bible (cf. II Chron. 24.20–22 where Zechariah ben Jehoiada, in whom the divine spirit clothes itself, speaks out against the people in an oracular fashion and is stoned for his moment of inspiration) where the prophetic activity is punished by execution. The traditions earlier than the Chronicler's know nothing of the killing of prophets. The people of ancient Israel were not in the habit of executing their prophets (the legendary Jezebel may have tried to introduce the practice into Israelite culture but such 'folly in Israel' never caught on) – the motif of the persecuted and murdered prophet is a dogma of a later time (cf. Steck 1965) and its appearance in 26.20–23 reflects that late belief. If the later dogma had any truth in it, Jeremiah would not have lived as long as the tradition (cf. 1.1–3) represents him as having done so. He would quickly have met the fate said to have befallen Uriah (in post-biblical literature he is stoned by the people in Egypt!). That he lived such an active life for so long undermines the dogma and exposes it as a later romantic glossing of the prophets as so many Ishmaels (i.e. 'his hand against every man and every man's hand against him', Gen. 16.12). Yet the editing of the Jeremiah tradition contributed to the making of that dogma, and the midrash of Uriah ben Shemaiah especially reflects its development. However, the people of ancient Israel are maligned enough in 2–20, and should be spared this further libel against their collective memory. They may not have listened to their prophets: they certainly did not refuse to listen to the point of killing them.

Jeremiah against the prophets: an independent cycle 27–29

A series of stories about Jeremiah is set in and around 597 in a cycle of narratives. These stories portray Jeremiah's attitudes to all the other prophets, whether Judaean or foreign, Jerusalem-based or active in Babylon, and to Babylon. He is against *all* the prophets and for Babylon. The cycle is an independent one in the tradition, as its distinctive style demonstrates (cf. Rudolph, 172). In it Jeremiah is described as *the* prophet (28.1, 5, 6, 10, 11, 12, 15; 29.1; lacking in G), and some of his prophetic opponents are named (e.g. Hananiah, Shemaiah; cf. Ahab and Zedekiah 29.21–23). The theoretical nature of the attack on the prophets in 23.13–32 is replaced in this cycle by specific situations in which the prophets are presented as opponents of Jeremiah. Distinctive features of the cycle are the spelling variations which indicate its discrete origins and circulation. The regular spelling of Jeremiah is *yirmᵉyāhū* (e.g. 1.1, 11; 7.1; 11.1), but in the cycle it is the variant form *yirmᵉyāh* (27.1; 28.5, 6, 10, 11, 12, 15; 29.1; reverting to regular spelling in 29.27, 31). A similar variation is to be found for Zedekiah's name: *ṣidᵉqiyyāhū* is the regular form (e.g. 21.1, 4, 7; 32.1; 37.1; 39.1), but it is *ṣidᵉqiyyāh* in the cycle (27.12; 28.1; 29.3; cf. 49.34). The proper form of the Babylonian emperor's name is Nebuchad*r*ezzar (e.g. 25.9; 32.1; 34.1; 37.1), but it appears as Nebuchad*n*ezzar in the cycle (27.6, 8, 20; 28.3, 11, 14; 29.1, 3; except for 29.21), a form to be found in other biblical traditions (e.g. II Kings 24.1, 10, 11; 25.1, 8, 22; Ezra 1.7; Dan. 1.1; 2.1). Such spelling variations are only minor matters, but they indicate the independent origins of the cycle.

The three chapters of the cycle share a number of motifs, and 28 may be considered a variant story of 27.16, 18–22. The treatment of Shemaiah in 29.31–32 parallels that of Hananiah in 28.15–16, and the denunciation of the Judaean prophets in Babylon (29.8–9) is a variant of the attack on the foreign prophets (27.9–10). Such shifts of motifs point to the literary origins of the cycle. The cycle is a literary creation rather than historical records or reflections. The legendary role of Jeremiah is quite apparent and, although dating the cycle is not possible, there are a number of similarities between the way he behaves and the Chronicler's portrayal of prophets. Furthermore, the discussion about the fate of the temple furnishings (27.16–28.4) is akin to views held about them in Chronicles, Ezra and Daniel. The Nebuchadrezzar of the cycle is very much the Nebuchadrezzar of the legends of Daniel. All these connections *suggest* a provenance in the fifth century (if not later) for the cycle. The expansion of 29 with material about the restoration of the people from exile (vv. 10–14) spoils the force of the cycle as a statement about life under Babylonian rule and 29 as a strategy for *permanent* community life in Babylonia. As such, the cycle probably represents the legitimation of life outside Palestine, though it has been glossed by a Judaean redactor at some point.

The cycle is tied into the larger tradition by means of redactional introductions at the beginning of each chapter. These are similar to the introductory note in 26.1, except for 29.1–3 where a more complicated preface introduces the story. Nothing in the stories which follow these redactional notes is necessarily dependent upon the dating or setting, and the stories may be regarded as quite independent of their present presentations. They are in this way similar to the stories of Daniel and his companions in Babylon, which are set in the period immediately after Jeconiah's deportation by Nebuchadrezzar. Although the cycle is stitched into the tradition by various means, its distinctive character and outlook cannot be overlooked. It is pro-Babylonian in a fundamental way and rejects the belief that there would be a return of the temple furnishings to the shrine in Jerusalem (MT 27.22 modifies this attitude). In the light of the campaign to return the furnishings to Jerusalem in the book of Ezra it is possible that the cycle retains traces of a particular controversy about the temple of which 27–28 represent an anti-Ezra movement. Analogous to this reading of the cycles is the one offered on 22.24–30, where it is suggested that the categorical rejection of Coniah in the oracles there is directed against the Haggai-Zechariah campaign to make one of his descendants the new Davidic leader of the community. The stress on the theme of Jeremiah against all the other prophets overshadows this other strand but it may still be discerned in the cycle. The balance to the view that Babylon is now the centre of Yahwistic life is to be found in the next cycle (30–31) and other elements throughout the tradition.

27.1–22

27[1] In the beginning of the reign of Zedekiah the son of Josiah, king of
Judah, this word came to Jeremiah from the LORD. 2 Thus the LORD said
to me: 'Make yourself thongs and yoke-bars, and put them on your neck. 3
Send word to the king of Edom, the king of Moab, the king of the sons of
Ammon, the king of Tyre, and the king of Sidon by the hand of the envoys
who have come to Jerusalem to Zedekiah king of Judah. 4 Give them this
charge for their masters: "Thus says the LORD of hosts, the God of Israel:
This is what you shall say to your masters: 5 'It is I who by my great power
and my outstretched arm have made the earth, with the men and animals
that are on the earth, and I give it to whomever it seems right to me. 6 Now
I have given all these lands into the hand of Nebuchadnezzar, the king of
Babylon, my servant, and I have given him also the beasts of the field to
serve him. 7 All the nations shall serve him and his son and his grandson,
until the time of his own land comes; then many nations and great kings
shall make him their slave.'

' "8 But if any nation or kingdom will not serve this Nebuchadnezzar
king of Babylon, and put its neck under the yoke of the king of Babylon, I
will punish that nation with the sword, with famine, and with pestilence,
says the LORD, until I have consumed it by his hand. 9 So do not listen to
your prophets, your diviners, your dreamers, your soothsayers, or your
sorcerers, who are saying to you, "You shall not serve the king of Babylon."
10 For it is a lie which they are prophesying to you, with the result that you
will be removed far from your land, and I will drive you out, and you will
perish. 11 But any nation which will bring its neck under the yoke of the
king of Babylon and serve him, I will leave on its own land, to till it and
dwell there, says the LORD." '

12 To Zedekiah king of Judah I spoke in like manner: 'Bring your necks under the yoke of the king of Babylon, and serve him and his people, and live.
13 Why will you and your people die by the sword, by famine, and by pestilence, as the LORD has spoken concerning any nation which will not serve
the king of Babylon? 14 Do not listen to the words of the prophets who are
saying to you, "You shall not serve the king of Babylon," for it is a lie which
they are prophesying to you. 15 I have not sent them, says the LORD, but
they are prophesying falsely in my name, with the result that I will drive you
out and you will perish, you and the prophets who are prophesying to you.'

16 Then I spoke to the priests and to all this people, saying, 'Thus says
the LORD: Do not listen to the words of your prophets who are prophesying
to you, saying, "Behold, the vessels of the Lord's house will now shortly be
brought back from Babylon," for it is a lie which they are prophesying to
you. 17 Do not listen to them; serve the king of Babylon and live. Why
should this city become a desolation? 18 If they are prophets, and if the

word of the LORD is with them, then let them intercede with the LORD of hosts, that the vessels which are left in the house of the LORD, in the house of the king of Judah, and in Jerusalem may not go to Babylon. 19 For thus says the LORD of hosts concerning the pillars, the sea, the stands, and the rest of the vessels which are left in this city, 20 which Nebuchadnezzar king of Babylon did not take away, when he took into exile from Jerusalem to Babylon Jeconiah the son of Jehoiakim, king of Judah, and all the nobles of Judah and Jerusalem – 21 thus says the LORD of hosts, the God of Israel, concerning the vessels which are left in the house of the LORD, in the house of the king of Judah, and in Jerusalem: 22 They shall be carried to Babylon and remain there until the day when I give attention to them, says the LORD. Then I will bring them back and restore them to this place.'

[MT 27] = G 34. G is considerably shorter than MT and illustrates well how the second edition (MT) developed from a shorter text by way of many expansions as well as a different recension (analysis and exegesis of differences in Tov 1979). **[1]** G lacks this redactional introduction; MT is presumably modelled on 26.1 (cf. 28.1). MT *b*ᵉ*rē'šīt mam*ᵉ*leket y*ᵉ*hōyāqim*, 'in the beginning of the reign of *Jehoiakim*': a few mss, S have 'Zedekiah' for 'Jehoiakim'. The inaugural year of Jehoiakim (see on 26.1) is wrong for what follows (e.g. Zedekiah is mentioned in vv. 3, 12 and implied in vv. 16–22). The mistaken MT raises the question of the extent to which 26.1 may not also be wrong. 26.1; 27.1; 28.1 all appear in MT as stories set in the inaugural years of kings (see on 28.1), but their errors and redactional nature suggest that they are most unreliable guides. BHS reconstructs the dating as 'in the fourth year' following 28.1 (cf. Rudolph, 176, where it is mooted that this may be the heading for 27–29; perhaps 26.1 has influenced 27.1); cf. 28.1 'in that year', i.e. the same year (Zedekiah's fourth year). The formulaic reception of the divine word phrase is the same here as in 26.1 *hāyāh haddābār hazzeh . . . mē'ēt yhwh*, '*this* word came . . . from Yahweh' (cf. Neumann 1973 for the formulaic variations in 1–25); both occurrences of '*this* word' indicate the redactional influence linking the two chapters. **[2]** MT *kōh-'āmar yhwh 'ēlay*, 'thus said Yahweh to me': the formula also occurs in 13.1; 19.1, where Jeremiah is ordered to go and purchase items; cf. 25.15 (expanded divine title), where the item acquired by Jeremiah is that with which he is sent to the nations (as here). **[3]** MT *w*ᵉ*šillaḥtām*, 'and send them': this is the logic of such magical-symbolical acts (cf. 25.15–17); EVV delete 'them' (cf. JPSB margin), BHS reads *w*ᵉ*šālaḥtā*, 'and you send', cf. G^L. 28.10 shows Jeremiah to be wearing the yoke-bars, hence he could hardly have sent them to the nations (cf. Rudolph), but as 28 is a variant story, such logic may not apply in this case. MT *mal'ākīm*, 'messengers': G *aggelōn autōn*, 'their messengers' = *mal'*ᵃ*kēhem* (so BHS); Tov, 81, regards *autōn* as an addition rather than a variant reading. G *eis apantēsin autōn* '(who have come) to meet them (at Jerusalem)' = *liqrā'ōtām* (cf. BHS). Tov, 82, treats the shorter MT as more original here than G. **[4]** MT *yhwh ṣᵉbā'ōt 'ᵉlōhē yiśrā'ēl*, 'Yahweh of hosts, the god of Israel': G lacks 'of hosts', as it frequently does in Jeremiah. Out of nineteen occurrences of the phrase 'of hosts' in 'thus says Yahweh of hosts', G lacks fifteen; it never registers *ṣᵉbā'ōt* in the thirty-two instances of the longer phrase 'Yahweh of hosts, the god of Israel'; *ṣᵉbā'ōt* is therefore a divine epithet almost entirely added in the second edition (cf. Tov, 82; Janzen 1973, 75–80). **[5]** G lacks 'with man and beast on the face of the earth' due to homoioteleuton (i.e. the scribe's eye may have jumped from the first *hā'āreṣ*, 'the earth', to the second *hā'āreṣ*). MT *yāšar bᵉ'ēnāy*, 'right in my eyes': cf. 26.14 *wᵉkayyāšār bᵉ'ēnēkem*, 'and as right in your eyes'. The phrase 'by my great power and my outstretched arm' may reflect Deuteronomistic influence (cf. Thiel 1981, 7); it occurs in a similar form in 32.17; Deut. 9.29 ('your' for 'my'); II Kings 17.36 but is not to be confused with the Deuteronomistic cliché 'with mighty hand and outstretched arm' (and its variations). **[6]** G lacks the introductory phrase *wᵉ'attāh 'ānōkī*, 'but now I . . .'; cf. Tov, 82–3 for discussion of the textual fluidity of the two editions here. MT *'et-kol-ha'ᵃrāṣōt hā'ēlleh bᵉyad nᵉbūkadne'ṣṣar melek-bābel 'abdī*, 'all these lands into the hand of Nebuchadnezzar, the king of Babylon, my servant': G *tēn gēn tō Nabouchodonosor basilei Babulōnos douleuein autōn*, 'the earth to Nebuchadnezzar, the king of Babylon, to serve him'. G^S lacks 'Nebuchadnezzar' and 'to serve him'. The spelling Nebuchad*n*ezzar is peculiar to the cycle 27–29 in the Jeremiah tradition (normal spelling in 29.21). The phrase 'Nebuchadnezzar, my servant' also occurs in 25.9; 43.10 (lacking in G but see on 43.10); there are some problems in establishing whether the first edition knew this phrase or not (*'abdī*, 'my servant', is conspicuously absent in G 25.9; 50.10 [MT 43.10]), cf. Tov, 83–4; Lemke 1966; Overholt 1968; Zevit 1969. Tov, 84, concludes that MT here reflects the original text rather than G; but G is the original text in the other two references. Nebuchadrezzar's oversight of the beasts of the field is ironic in view of the legend about Nebuchadrezzar's vision, the meaning of which entailed his being driven from among men to have his dwelling *with the beasts of the field* (Dan. 4.25 [MT 22]). 'Yahweh gives and Yahweh takes away' (Job 1.21); but there are times when he gives – he *really* gives! **[7]** G lacks v. 7 (discussion of speculations as to why in Tov, 84–5). The fact that Nebuchadrezzar did not have a grandson who ruled over the empire need not count against MT, as the biblical writers were not historians and did not necessarily have access to such historical knowledge. Nebuchadrezzar's line was superseded in 560 (Bright, 200, thinks it possible that G dropped it in view of this fact and that v. 7 is conceivably original). The triple stages of the phrase 'N . . . son . . . grandson' may refer to three generations or may be an idiomatic way of referring to 'many generations', i.e. 'an indeterminable period of time' (Weinfeld 1972a, 144 n. 5. cf. Tov, 85). If this latter view is taken, then the question of historical inaccuracy does not arise. MT may have developed the time factor by adding '. . . and his son . . . and the son of his son . . .' retrospectively, after 539 (cf. Tov). As in the interpretation of the 'seventy years' of 25.11; 29.10, there is a wide range of possible meanings for v. 7 (whether it is original or secondary). MT *bō*, 'him': this must refer to Nebuchadrezzar, hardly his grandson (cf. *wᵉʿābᵉdū ʾōtō*, 'they will serve *him*': *wᵉʿābᵉdū bō*), cf. 25.14. The reversal of the fate of the Babylonians requires a different sense for *bō* which does not fit 'many nations and great kings'; BHS reads *bāh* '(they will make) it (serve)', i.e. the country of Babylon, rather than Nebuchadrezzar (or his descendants, if they are not a further addition to v. 7). MT *gam-hūʾ*, 'even he': this phrase suggests that the first form of v. 7 applied only to Nebuchadrezzar and envisaged his defeat (cf 28.2–4). **[8]** For 'nation or kingdom' regulations cf. 18.7–10. MT *ʾᵃšer lōʾ-yaʿabᵉdū . . . wᵉʾet ʾᵃšer lōʾ-yittēn ʾet-ṣawwāʾrō*, 'which will not serve . . . and which will not yield its neck . . .': the two phrases are variants: G lacks the whole sentence up to '. . . king of Babylon' (due to homoioteleuton according to BHS). MT *ʿad-tummī ʾōtām bᵉyādō*, 'until I have consumed them by his hand': *tmm*, 'complete, finish', is seldom used as a transitive verb, so commentators emend to *tittī*, 'I will give (into his hand)', cf. S, T; if MT is retained a word may have fallen out (cf. Bright, 200). The familiar triad 'sword, famine, pestilence' (cf. v. 13; 14.12; 21.7, 9; 24.10; 29.17–18; 32.24, 36; 34.17; 38.2; 42.17, 22) also appears in 44.13 in combination with the verb *pqd*, 'punish, visit upon'. **[9]** MT *ḥᵃlōmōtēkem*, 'your dreams': the list is of agents rather than instruments, so *ḥōlᵉmēkem*, 'your dreamers', is read with Vrs; NEB 'your wise women' suggests a reading of *ḥᵃkamōtēkem* (but cf. Brockington 1973, 208). **[10]** G lacks 'and I will drive you out, and you will perish': the phrase appears in v. 15. It is out of place here because the activity of the agents of v. 9 is distancing (*harḥīq*) the people from their land, rather than Yahweh. **[11]** G lacks *nᵉʾum-yhwh*, 'says Yahweh'. **[12]** MT *bᵉʿōl melek-bābel*, 'under the yoke of the king of Babylon': repeated from vv. 8, 11; lacking in G. Cf. Neh. 3.5 for the idiom 'bringing the neck under', i.e. 'submitting to'. **[13–14]** G lacks v. 13 and part of v. 14, including the ending of v. 12 (homoioteleuton due to *wᵉʿibᵉdū ʾōtō . . . taʿabᵉdū ʾet-melek bābel*, 'and serve him . . . do [not] serve the king of Babylon', 12b–14a); cf. the discussion in Tov, 87. Rudolph, 177, treats v. 13 as an addition from v. 8. **[15]** MT *lᵉmaʿan hiddīḥī ʾetkem*, 'in order that I might drive you out': cf. v. 10; suffix lacking in G and deleted by BHS 'to drive you out'. Bright here and v. 10 translates 'which will only serve to . . .' as the force of *lᵉmaʿan*. G reflects a doublet at end of v. 15 ('and your prophets who are prophesying to you, false lies', where *adikō pseudē* represents *šeqer* twice and in a different sequence). **[16]** MT *wᵉʾel-hakkōhᵃnīm*, 'and to the priests': G *humin*, 'to you' (*lākem* from v. 15 in doublet), with reversal of order of people and priests. 16b can hardly be a divine speech in view of

v. 18, where Yahweh is referred to in the third person. Heb. *k^{e}lī*, 'articles, vessels, utensils, objects, implements, apparatus, instruments, equipment': 'vessels' does not quite fit the furnishings and equipment of temples and palaces which include furniture and appliances, i.e. any and all movable objects (cf. Bright, 200, 'furnishings'). MT *'attāh m^{e}hērāh*, 'now quickly': lacking in G; in 28.3, 11 'within two years' is the expected return period (lacking in G but G^A has it in 28.3). The first edition (G) is concerned with the general question of *whether* the furnishings will be returned, whereas the second edition debates *when* (cf. Tov, 88). Bar. 1.1–3.8 deals, at length, with the story (cf. Tov 1976). MT *kī šeqer hēmmāh nibb^e'īm lākem*, 'for it is falsehood which they are prophesying to you': G + *ouk apesteila autous*, 'I did not send them', cf. end of v. 15; Tov, 88. G lacks v. 17. **[17]** BHS treats v. 17 as an addition as G lacks it; it disrupts the flow of vv. 16, 18 on the subject of the (temple) furnishings. **[18]** MT *bayhwh ṣ^{e}bā'ōt*, 'with Yahweh of hosts': G *moi*, 'me' = *bī*, 'with me' (*bī* may represent an abbreviation of the tetragrammaton, cf. Driver 1960, 119–21). G ends v. 18 at this point, MT continues with an expanded account of the fate of the furnishings. G knows of temple furnishings, but MT includes palace materials as well, cf. 52.13. **[19–22]** A much shorter text appears in G: 'For thus says the lord – and as for the remaining implements which the king of Babylon did not take, when he carried Iechonias from Jerusalem, they shall go to Babylon, says the lord.' Cf. Tov, 89–90, on MT expansions. **[22]** Cf. Ezra 1.7–11; Dan. 5.2–3; discussion of 'vessels' theme in Ackroyd 1972, 176–7.

Tov 1979

The linking motif between the three chapters of the cycle 27–29 is the prophets and their relationship to Babylon. The failure of their position on Babylon is reflected in 29 where the material concentrates on the community of exiles there and only in passing touches on a further example of prophets behaving in a false way. The triple strata of 26, priests, prophets and people, are present in all three chapters of the cycle and allow 26 to be considered as a preface to 27–29. Yet the difference in the roles of the priests in 26 and 27–29 should be noted. They are not the hostile figures of 26 but an important element in the organization of the community, whether in Jerusalem or Babylon.

Differences between MT and G not only point to developmental variations between the two editions but also indicate independent treatments of particular motifs (e.g. the fate of the vessels in 27.16–22; the use of the term *pseudoprophetēs* in G to describe the prophets in 26.7, 8, 11, 16; 27.9; 28.1; 29.1, 8; cf. 6.13; Zech. 13.2). Among the themes of 27 is a general rejection of the prophets and their preaching against the Babylonians (vv. 9, 14, 16, 17, 'Do not listen to your prophets'). In view of this central theme its instantiation in 28 is odd in that a specific conflict between two individual named prophets over the issue is unnecessary. However, in the interests of the story in 28 the general ruling 'do not listen to your prophets' is suspended so that a debate between Jeremiah and Hananiah may be presented. 27, 28, therefore, are doublets rather than two historical incidents and should be treated as variations on a theme.

In 27 a number of elements are combined in relation to the central theme of 27–29, 'reaction to Babylon'. The redactional dating at the beginning of each chapter is questionable, but the MT focus on 597/3 is understandable as an attempt to locate the material in some historical context. But the difficulties of demonstrating a specific set of events which would account for a coalition against Babylon *after* 597 (Driver 1963, 83–8; cf. Wiseman 1956, 32–7) must raise questions about the historicity of 27–28. That Zedekiah, a vassal of Neubchadrezzar and presumably also pro-Babylonian in outlook and policy, should even entertain the idea of a rebellion against his overlord *and* at the beginning of his reign (corrected MT 27.1) is too unlikely to be realistic. The already noted phenomenon of the tradition's blending together of 597 and 587 (see on 24.1) may account for the confusion here, but even that cannot resolve all the difficulties. These are created by the editing of the different themes together so that the impression is given that Zedekiah may be contemplating revolt or that he is under pressure from his prophets (where did they come from after the deportation of 597?) to join in a coalition of rebellion represented by the embassy of five kings and their representatives (cf. Driver 1963, 87–8, who dates this visitation to 596). The historical problems may be put to one side in order to pursue the exegesis of 27 as they only bear on the question of the redaction of the text and the genre of the material presented.

Chapter 27 consists of a magical act performed by Jeremiah with reference to the messengers of the five kings of neighbouring countries, an attack on their soothsayers, diviners and prophets who are preaching resistance to Babylon, a statement along similar lines to king Zedekiah, and a denunciation of the Judaean prophets over the matter of the fate of the temple furnishings (cf. the analysis in Seebass 1970 for different emphases). These thematic elements include a number of features which are to be found throughout the tradition (on Deuteronomistic factors cf. Thiel 1981, 5–10; for others cf. Wanke 1971, 19–36, 73–7). The combination of a magical act with direct reference to a list of foreign powers makes vv. 2–11 similar to the cup of wine given to the nations material in 25.15–27. However, here the performance of the divine command is intended to persuade certain nations not to resist Babylon, whereas the wine cup act refers to their destruction (most likely by Babylon). The delegated nature of the message in v. 4 is parallel to the delegated word sent to Babylon in 51.59–64 (on prophetic delegation cf. Schmidt 1982). The one distinctive feature of vv. 2–11 is the fact that the five nations are appealed to rather than informed of their destruction. It is an illustration of the late motif of Jeremiah as a 'prophet to the nations' (1.5) and reflects a somewhat more positive attitude to other nations, characteristic of the cycle 27–29 (cf. 29.7). The making and wearing of the yoke-bars are part of the strand of performative behaviour in the tradition (cf. 19.1–2, 10–11; Wanke 1971, 75; also 13.1–7; 25.15–17; 43.8–13; 51.59–64) but in 28.10–12 the motif has a variable function. If in 27.2–3 the yoke-bars are a message to the foreign nations, in 28.10–12 they are treated as a statement about the fate of Judah (cf. 28.13–14).

The focus on Babylon, one of the distinctive features of the whole cycle, in MT 27 includes the phrase 'Nebuchad*n*ezzar, my servant' (*'abdī*, v. 6, cf. 25.9; 43.10). This expression 'my servant', in which Yahweh is represented as acknowledging the pagan emperor to be his devotee, has occasioned debate. Very different views have been taken of the phrase: it is an accidental error in the textual transmission of the book and represents an addition from a later period when, according to Dan. 2.47; 3.28–4.3, 34–37, 'the famous pagan king has now become a conscious worshipper of the only true God' (so Lemke 1966, 50). Overholt disagrees with Lemke's instrument – servant distinction, argues that 'the basic perception of Nebuchadnezzar is a theological one' (1968, 45) and attributes the phrase to Jeremiah as a statement about Yahweh's instrumental use of the foreign power (cf 50.17; Isa. 10.5). Another approach treats *'ebed*, 'servant', as a diplomatic term meaning 'vassal', so that Jeremiah in using this phrase asserts that the king of Babylon is Yahweh's vassal (Zevit 1969, 77). Various exegetes regard the term as Jeremiah's own invention (e.g. Weiser, Rudolph, Hyatt), even allowing that it is a 'bold thought' (Hyatt, 1011). Comparisons with the designation of the Persian emperor Cyrus as *māšîaḥ*, 'anointed one' (Isa. 45.1), are also made.

The instrumental view of other nations as the deity's way of punishing Israel is a feature of the tradition (e.g. 25.9) and is clearly represented by the metaphors of 50.17 where Assyria and Babylon form an enclosure of such activity. But 'my servant' goes beyond the notion of instrumentality (cf. Assyria as the *rod*, not the servant, in Isa. 10.5) to a level of relationship between deity and emperor more characteristic of Second Isaiah's view of Cyrus. The Jeremiah tradition knows a formal servant-Yahweh relationship but only of the prophets (e.g. 7.25; 25.4; 26.5), and that is a late Deuteronomistic strand. Chapters 27–29 have distinctive features as a cycle, but the phrase is found outside it (25.9; 43.10), so its genuineness cannot be argued for on the grounds of its appearance in a special cycle (though all three references may reflect a common strand or addition to such a strand). G is ambiguous in 27.6 (cf. Tov, 83–4), though it lacks the phrase in 25.9; 43.10. The presentation of Babylon in 27, 29 points to a pro-Babylonian strand (especially 29.7) and reflects the interests of a particular party. For the exiles in Babylon are presented as Yahweh's special concern in 24.4–7; 29.4–7, 10–14 and all the other communities (e.g. Zedekiah's people, the refugees in Egypt) are dismissed from being recipients of Yahweh's favour. The hidden agenda of this strand is to bolster the claims of the *gālūt yᵉhūdāh* (the exile party), and the representation of Nebuchadrezzar as the servant of the living god, who carried them into exile, would contribute to those claims. This argument works whether the epithet reflects the later development of Nebuchadrezzar into a pious worshipper of Yahweh or a theology of him as Yahweh's vassal. The treatment of Cyrus in Second Isaiah points to a similar development and suggests a post-exilic date for the cycle. It should be read not so much as a claim for those in Babylon as one on behalf of the few who have returned from Babylon and who wish to gain power in the reconstructed Jerusalem (cf. Ezra-Nehemiah). Nebuchadrezzar and Jeremiah, *both* servants of Yahweh, underwrite that claim. Part of the Babylonian contribution to Judaean theology may be seen in 27.5 where the designation of Nebuchadrezzar is set in the context of Yahweh as the creator of the earth (the exiles learned much about the creator gods in Babylon, cf. Saggs 1978, 41–52; note how the material on Cyrus in Isa. 44.24–45.1, 12–13 is structured by references to Yahweh the creator god). The singling out of the animals in vv. 5, 6 as part of Yahweh's creation and also his gift to Nebuchadrezzar allows for reflection on the irony of Nebuchadrezzar's dream in Dan. 4.4–37 (MT 1–34).

The report of the command to make and wear yoke-bars is not developed to the point where Jeremiah's act of carrying out the command is reported (contrast 13.2, 5, 7; 25.17; cf. 19.14), but the variant in 28.10 implies that he did so. The yoke-bars are thought to symbolize the sovereignty given to Nebuchadrezzar by Yahweh, though such performances carry a much stronger force than that. Hananiah's breaking of them is more than a symbol of their reversal, it is an act designed to reverse their significance. By wearing the yoke-bars Jeremiah *asserts* (by doing) the domination of Babylon. Although the act would have more direct relevance to Judah it is presented in 27.3 as a message for the five nations (listed in the same order as in 25.21–2) and therefore resembles the reading of the scroll in 36 in having a delegated status. Two strands appear to be mixed here: the magical act which destroys Judah (cf. 36.23, where the king tries to prevent it) and the delegated message against the nations (cf. 51.59–64). In v. 8 the message is universalized as a principle of national action in relation to Babylon in a manner similar to the disruption of the visit to the potter's house by the regulations of 18.7–10. The five nations' prophets, diviners, dreamers, soothsayers and sorcerers are dismissed as telling lies with their programme of 'you shall not serve the king of Babylon' (a strange reversal of Jeremiah's message, cf. 28.14; 36.29). The application of so many elements from the tradition to foreign nations is part of the peculiarity of the cycle and is indicative of a secondary usage of conventional motifs quite distinctive in the book of Jeremiah. It may display the logic of the creator god who rules over all the nations (as in 18.7–10 which is a very late element), but it looks more like the misapplication of terms due to the redactional history of the unit.

In vv. 12–15 the same message is proclaimed to Zedekiah (hence the tendency of EVV to substitute his name for Jehoiakim's in v. 1). The essence of the yoke-bars performance is 'submit to Babylon and live' (vv. 12, 17). How very different a view is taken of Zedekiah's kingdom in 24.1–3, 8–10 where no such option is offered to it but it is written off as worthless and doomed! Now it is the Judaean prophets who are described as prophesying 'you shall not serve the king of Babylon' (in v. 14 the plural form of address makes the community rather than Zedekiah the recipient of the message, though it is formulaic in 27). These prophets are dismissed in the language of 23.25, 26, 32 and are blamed for the potential expulsion of the people. The vagueness of the material in 27.2–15 (even allowing for considerable editorial activity cf. Thiel 1981, 7–8) does not permit the exegete sufficient, clear information to determine whether any particular historical occasion is part of the background to the story (e.g. 605, 597, 587). What appears to be the case is the fact that the cycle uses conventional motifs (e.g. the triad in vv. 8, 13; the attack on prophets) drawn from the larger tradition to construct a very distinctive view of Babylon and the causes of the destruction of the nation(s). There is in 27 a radical handling of traditional material which cannot be squared with other parts of the tradition and which therefore points to the independent origin and development of the whole cycle.

In vv. 16–22 the subject matter changes and the speaker addresses the priests and the people (no longer the king). They are not to listen to the prophets (the combination 'priests and prophets' so frequent in the tradition, e.g. 2.8, 26b; 5.31; 6.13b; 8.10b; 26.7, 8, 11, 16 is here broken). This time the falsehood being prophesied by the prophets is different, though it may be regarded as a variation on the previous ie (this is unlikely). What is *šeqer* on this occasion is the proclamation that the temple vessels (i.e. furnishings) will be returned to Jerusalem from Babylon. So the temple has been raided and the Babylonians are in control. That at least means that the attack on Jerusalem of 597 is in the past (implied by MT v. 1). The parallel story in 28.2–4 (with 27.20) sets the temple furnishings motif in the period following the first attack on Jerusalem. But why prophetic activity about the temple furnishings? Why not a more direct claim for the return of the king and the deportees (as in 28.4, but note order of precedence)?

The reference to the temple furnishings (extended in vv. 18, 21 to include palace and other furnishings in Jerusalem) signals the discussion of a topic of controversy at some stage in the rebuilding of Jerusalem (cf. Ezra 1.5–11; 5.14–16; 6.5; analysis of all the relevant texts in Ackroyd 1972). The subject is controversial because according to 52.17–23 and II Kings 25.13–17, when Nebuchadrezzar took Jerusalem in 587 the large furnishings were all broken up and therefore were not in a fit condition to be restored. The matter is more complicated than that because in II Kings 24.11–17 when Nebuchadrezzar captured Jerusalem in 597 he deported Jehoiachin, the leading strata of society, and *all* the treasures of the *temple* and the king's *palace*. The temple vessels were cut in pieces (for transportation purposes and as a ruination of their sacral functions because the god of that temple cult had been defeated). That there are problems with these double accounts of the same event can hardly be doubted, and the temple-furnishings motif is an excellent illustration of the view that the biblical traditions regularly confuse and conflate the invasions, defeats and deportations of 597 and 587. In 27.18–21 there is a recognition that the furnishings in the temple and palaces are those which Nebuchadrezzar *left* after the first penetration of the city. II Kings 24.13 leaves no room for any such residue, and the account of the fall of Jerusalem in 587 in 39.2–10 makes no reference to any temple or palace treasures being taken. There is therefore a variety of very different traditions about the fate of the city's treasures, a multiplicity of viewpoints which cannot be harmonized (cf. Ackroyd 1972, 175). The variety of disparate positions includes the views that in 597 the temple furnishings were destroyed and taken to Babylon as loot, that some were left behind and taken in 587 as loot, that the sacral objects were taken to Babylon and housed in a Babylonian shrine (Ezra 1.7) and therefore were available for transportation back to Jerusalem. The Chronicler's view agrees with that found in Ezra 1: the furnishings were taken in 597 and housed in Nebuchadrezzar's palace; other furnishings were taken to Babylon in 587 (II Chron. 36.7, 10, 18; cf. Dan. 1.2; 5.2–4), and there is no knowledge of their being cut up and rendered useless by the Babylonians (the legend of Belshazzar's feast in Dan. 5 would be spoiled by such a knowledge).

27.16–22 as a discussion of the fate of the temple furnishings belongs to the world of Ezra and the Chronicler. It bears on the social controversy behind the rebuilt temple and the rebuilding of Jerusalem relating to power in the community and the right to reorganize the cult. When will the furnishings return from Babylon and whose party is in the right with reference to them? The struggle to answer such questions is reflected in the conflict between prophets in 27.16–28.9. The importance of the cultic furnishings, their survival in Babylon and their return to Jerusalem *after* having been preserved for a long time in exile are the central issues in the dispute. Those traditions which know an end to the temple and the breaking up of the valuable sacral furnishings (e.g. Micah 3.12; II Kings 24.13; 25.13; Jer. 52.17) are an alternative approach to the debate, but are essentially irrelevant to it. Only the stories which claim that the furnishings went intact to Babylon, survived there but not as loot, and therefore were available for return (e.g. 27–28; II Chron. 36; Ezra 1; Dan. 1; 5) are germane to the discussion about power and legitimation in the second temple period. The key feature of the furnishings motif is continuity with the past – the sacral vessels and temple furniture provide the only link with the first temple (note the disappearance of the ark in 3.16). Those who possess them and bring them back from Babylon have strong claims to a legitimacy other claims lack. The furnishings confer on the new temple power and an identification with the old temple. 'Clearly restoration of the vessels implies re-establishment of that continuity of the cultus which was in some measure interrupted by the disaster of 597.' (Ackroyd 1972, 175).

Verses 16, 18–22 should be read against this background. The two deportations are recognized: implicitly in the preaching of the prophets about the return of the furnishings and in v. 18, where the remaining vessels are mentioned. The listing of furnishings left behind by Nebuchadrezzar reflects the list of sacral objects taken to Babylon in 587 (v. 19; cf. 52.17; II Kings 25.13), but ignores the fact that they were broken up (this is in keeping with the presentation of the story as an event taking place before 587). There is an element of irony in v. 18, where it is suggested that evidence of being prophets who possess the divine word would be for the prophets to intercede with Yahweh on behalf of the furnishings which are left in the temple and palaces. 'Never mind the furnishings which were taken away to Babylon, pray for what the Babylonians left behind!' (cf. 22.10). The notion of residual furnishings allows for two deportations rather than there being the need to assume the acquisition of new furnishings after 597 in order that there might be furnishings available for capture in 587 (even though such a notion does conflict with the plain meaning of II Kings 24.13).

The very repetitive MT vv. 19–22 (in contrast to the brevity of G) reveals a development of the tradition in a quite different direction from G. In the first edition the attack on the prophets is a straightforward reversal of their message. Instead of the furnishings returning from Babylon, those which were left behind will go to Babylon. The second edition of the story hints at the possibility that the furnishings need not be deported (v. 19), then repeatedly asserts that furnishings from the temple, the royal palace and the city will be taken to Babylon, and ends on a note of restoration to 'this place' (v. 22). G is a doom oracle, but MT introduces the notion of restoration. The furnishings are now a symbol of restoration and therefore of continuity: 'we have a theme of restoration built into a theme of exile; the idea of continuity with the previous temple is maintained by the promise of the restoration of the temple vessels.' (Ackroyd 1972, 177). The viewpoint of G is continued in 28, but the effect of this restoration theme in 27.22 is to reverse that note of doom. In a subtle way v. 22 vindicates Hananiah, but because 27 and 28 are independent variations on a theme, there is no conscious acknowledgment of that vindication (see on 29.10). In MT v. 22 Yahweh's attention (*pqd* is a frequently used motif in the tradition, even though its use with reference to objects here is unusual) in the future will be on the furnishings and he will bring them up (*'lh* indicates a sacral procession, but is not used in the allusions to the restoration of the furnishings in Ezra) and restore them to the temple. So the prophets of v. 16 were right after all but were wrong about the timing! MT's expansion of the material produces a programme of deportation and restoration which allows for the passage of time between the destruction of Jerusalem and the events of Ezra's period.

28.1–17

28[1] In that same year, at the beginning of the reign of Zedekiah king of
Judah, in the fifth month of the fourth year, Hananiah the son of Azzur, the
prophet from Gibeon, spoke to me in the house of the LORD, in the presence
of the priests and all the people, saying, 2 'Thus says the LORD of hosts, the
God of Israel: I have broken the yoke of the king of Babylon. 3 Within two
years I will bring back to this place all the vessels of the LORD's house,
which Nebuchadnezzar king of Babylon took away from this place and
carried to Babylon. 4 I will also bring back to this place Jeconiah the son
of Jehoiakim, king of Judah, and all the exiles from Judah who went to
Babylon, says the LORD, for I will break the yoke of the king of Babylon.'
5 Then the prophet Jeremiah spoke to Hananiah the prophet in the
presence of the priests and all the people who were standing in the house of
the LORD; 6 and the prophet Jeremiah said, 'Amen! May the LORD do so;
may the LORD make the words which you have prophesied come true, and
bring back to this place from Babylon the vessels of the house of the LORD,
and all the exiles. 7 Yet hear now this word which I speak in your hearing
and in the hearing of all the people. 8 The prophets who preceded you and
me from ancient times prophesied war, famine, and pestilence against many
countries and great kingdoms. 9 As for the prophet who prophesies peace,
when the word of that prophet comes to pass, then it will be known that the
LORD has truly sent the prophet.'

10 Then the prophet Hananiah took the yoke-bars from the neck of
Jeremiah the prophet, and broke them. 11 And Hananiah spoke in the
presence of all the people, saying, 'Thus says the LORD: Even so will I break
the yoke of Nebuchadnezzar king of Babylon from the neck of all the nations
within two years.' But Jeremiah the prophet went his way.
12 Sometime after the prophet Hananiah had broken the yoke-bars from
off the neck of Jeremiah the prophet, the word of the LORD came to Jeremiah:
13 'Go, tell Hananiah, "Thus says the LORD: You have broken wooden
bars, but I will make in their place bars of iron. 14 For thus says the LORD
of hosts, the God of Israel: I have put upon the neck of all these nations an
iron yoke of servitude to Nebuchadnezzar king of Babylon, and they shall
serve him, for I have given to him even the beasts of the field." ' 15 And
Jeremiah the prophet said to the prophet Hananiah, 'Listen, Hananiah,
the LORD has not sent you, and you have made this people trust in a lie. 16
Therefore thus says the LORD: "Behold, I will remove you from the face of
the earth. This very year you shall die, because you have uttered rebellion
against the LORD." '
17 In that same year, in the seventh month, the prophet Hananiah died.

[MT 28] = G 35. Lys 1979 provides a structural analysis of the chapter which permits the various inner relations between the elements of the story to be seen clearly. **[1]** MT *baššānāh hahī'*, 'in that year': i.e. the same year as 27; lacking in G. MT encloses the whole story between two occurrences of the phrase. MT has two dates for the story: 1. in the beginning of Zedekiah's reign (cf. 26.1; 27.1 for formal structure); 2. in the fifth month of the fourth year. Both cannot be right and exegetes vary in the options exercised: e.g. BHS (i.e. Rudolph, 178) reads 'in the fourth year, in the fifth month' (cf. Oded 1977, 472); Driver 1963, 84–7, dismisses the fourth year as impossible and opts for the fifth month of the first year (the textual fourth year he explains as being due to an erroneous reading of an abbreviated text); Bright, 200, appears to accept the fourth year following G's 'in the fourth year', but his argument about the factual correctness of 'in the same year' is confused because only MT has that phrase and it refers back to 27.1, which Bright recognizes as not original (Bright's echo Thompson, 537 n. 1, uses the same confused argument). Some such note as 'in the same year' is required in order to point out that Jeremiah did not spend years wearing the yoke-bars! Part of the confusion is caused by the redactional fondness in 26–28 for using the same formulaic introductions; the rest is supplied by 28 being a variant of 27 (28.1 has the seams showing). K *bšnt*, 'in the year of'; Q *baššānāh*, 'in the (fourth) year'. MT *'ēlay*, 'to me': in 28 Jeremiah is a third-person character (e.g. v. 5), so this first-person reference is either an error or an abbreviation for *'el-yirmᵉyāh* (cf. BHS). As in 27.9; 29.1, 8 G uses *pseudoprophetēs* to describe a prophet other than Jeremiah, hence Hananiah 'the false prophet' (G). This is not consistently carried out in 28 because G lacks MT's persistent contrasting of the two as 'Hananiah the prophet' (vv. 1, 5, 10, 12, 17) and 'Jeremiah the prophet' (vv. 5, 6, 10, 11, 12, 15). The location of Gibeon is disputed cf. 41.12, 16; Blenkinsopp 1972, 98–100. It would be ironic if the Gibeon from which Hananiah came were the Benjaminite Gibeon (cf. Volz, 260); for the purposes of the story Gibeon might be the great high place used by Solomon (I Kings 3.4–5) where sacrifices were offered and dreams received. **[3]** MT *beʿōd šenātayim yāmīm*, lit. 'in yet two years days', i.e. 'within two years time'. G has a shorter text of vv. 3–4: 'In two years time (*hēmerōn*, 'days') I will bring back to this place the vessels of the house of the lord and Iechonias and the colony of Judah, for I will break the yoke of the king of Babylon.' MT demonstrates how the second edition expanded the text in many small ways. **[5]** G has an inverted order of 'priests . . . people'. Throughout the story MT presents the two characters as 'Hananiah *the prophet*' and 'Jeremiah *the prophet*'; apart from the formal aspect of the redaction the phrase is indicative of the later second edition. **[6]** MT *yāqēm yhwh 'et-debārekā*, 'may Yahweh establish your words': i.e. fulfil them; some mss, G, T, read 'your word'. **[7]** MT *haddābār hazzeh*, 'this word': G *ton logion kuriou*, 'the word of the lord'. **[8]** MT *ūlerāʿāh ūledāber*, 'and disaster and pestilence': G lacks what looks like an addition in MT (the phrase closes v. 8). G makes a fine contrast in vv. 8, 9 between 'prophesying war' and 'prophesying *šālōm*' which is lost in MT. Many mss read 'famine' (*rāʿāb*) for 'disaster' (*rāʿāh*); the triad fits the general redaction of the tradition, but is not one actually used in Jeremiah (cf. 27.8, 13). For 'many countries and great kingdoms' cf. 'many nations and great kings' (25.14; 27.7). **[9]** MT *ʾašer-šelāḥō yhwh be'emet*, '(the prophet) whom Yahweh has sent in truth': i.e. truly sent, cf. *be'emet šelāḥanī yhwh*, 'in truth Yahweh sent me' (26.15). Note the rather different principles behind the similar phrases: in 26.15 the self-asseveration must be taken at face value; in 28.9 a more empirical form of verification is formulated. The regulation in Deut. 18.22 may be modified here or even narrowed down (cf. Davidson 1964, 414). **[10]** MT *'et-hammōṭāh*, 'the yoke-bar': cf. NEB 'the yoke', JPSB 'the bar'; G plur., cf. RSV. The plur *mōṭōt* is used in v. 13; 27.2, but sing. in v. 12. MT *wayyišberēhū*, 'and he broke it': masc. suffix (referring to *ʿōl*, 'yoke', in v. 11, where the meaning of the action is stated?); BHS suggests changing it to fem. *-rehā* (*w* of MT a dittography from next word). **[11]** G lacks 'Nebuchadnezzar', 'within two years'. **[12]** RSV 'sometime' is not represented in the text but may be a fair interpretation of *wayehī . . . 'aḥarē*; Bright, 198: 'But then, sometime after . . .'. Cf. 42.7 for a definite period of waiting before the divine word was heard. **[13]** MT *weʿāśītā*, 'but you will make': G *kai poiēsō*, 'but I will make'; RSV follows G, NEB and JPSB follow MT. MT may be read as meaning Hananiah's action has only had the effect of making the servitude harder. **[14]** G lacks 'these', 'Nebuchadnezzar', 'and they shall serve him and also the beasts of the field I have given him'. The last part of v. 14 is probably an addition from 27.6b (cf. BHS). **[15]** Cf. 14.14–15; 23.21, 25–7, 32; 27.14–16. **[16]** MT *hinᵉnī mᵉšallēḥᵃkā*, 'look, I am sending you': i.e. dismissing you from the land of the living (to death). There is a word-play here with *lō'-šᵉlāḥᵃkā yhwh*, 'Yahweh did not send you', in v. 15 in which, although Yahweh *did not* send him, he *will* send him now (two senses of *šlḥ*). MT *kī-sārāh dibbarta 'el-yhwh*, 'because you have spoken rebellion against Yahweh': G lacks the phrase. Cf. *kī dibber-sārāh 'al-yhwh*, 'for he has spoken rebellion against Yahweh', Deut. 13.6 (EV 5). Deut. 18.20–21 uses a different criterion from this one (i.e. to speak a word Yahweh has not spoken is to speak presumptuously [*bᵉzādōn*]) which, though similar, is quite distinct from the charge in 28.16; Deut. 13.6 (EV 5). The absence of the charge in G suggests that MT has been expanded under Deuteronomistic influence (cf. Thiel 1981, 10) in the second edition; the same charge is made against Shemaiah in 29.32 (also lacking in G). Davidson 1964, 415, suggests that in the two places where the Deuteronomistic charge is made it may be the case that Jeremiah is accusing the representatives of Deuteronomic orthodoxy of being themselves in a state of rebellion against Yahweh. **[17]** G simply reads 'and he died in the seventh month', i.e. a couple of months after his original proclamation. Cf. Ezek. 11.13 for a death notice but with 'no element of direct encounter' (Zimmerli 1979, 260); Acts 5.1–6, for the death of another Ananias (Hananiah) due to a lie.

Lys 1979; Mottu 1975

The variant account of 27.16–22 provided by 28 introduces into the tradition a fascinating conflict between two named prophets in which Jeremiah behaves in a very distinctive fashion. He appears as a quite different character from the more dominant presentation of him in the major strands of the book. Part of that difference is due to the heterogeneous origins of the cycle 27–29 and part to the nature of the story told in 28. Yet in 27 Jeremiah is represented as denouncing *all* the prophets who proclaim the kind of message which is typified by Hananiah's declaration of the divine word. In reality the position adopted by Jeremiah in 27.12–15, 16–22 renders his response to Hananiah both unnecessary and incomprehensible. Why should Jeremiah listen to a particular instantiation of a message he already has dismissed as false? If what the prophets say is a lie (*šeqer*), then Hananiah, who says the same thing and in the same way (i.e. in the name of Yahweh, cf. v. 2; 27.14–15, 16), is a liar. Why should Jeremiah treat a liar with such sensitivity? Why should he respond in a dignified manner instead of heaping abuse on Hananiah's head? Why should he wish Hananiah to be right? Why should he accept the breaking of his own performative message and go his way? All these questions may be answered in terms of the structure of the story. It is an independent story and only owes to 27 certain features necessary for it to be a variant account (e.g. the conflict of prophets, the performance with the yoke-bars, the expectation of an imminent return of temple furnishings, king and people). To understand the story it needs to be heard (read) as quite independent of its present context and treated as an exchange between two prophets complete in their independence of what precedes and follows the story of their encounter. The holistic approach which insists on integrating each individual story with all the other traditions in the collection will only expose the contradictions between 28, its present context and the rest of the tradition.

In this analysis of 28 the encounter between Hananiah of Gibeon and Jeremiah is treated as a story rather than a historical account of a real event (in contrast to Koch 1969, 204 who regards it as the report of an eye witness who is completely reliable; formal analysis of story in Koch, 200–10). It is a story in which some of the details necessary for understanding it are provided by its present context but its main thrust is concerned with asserting yet again (i.e. in the context of Part III) the truth of the word proclaimed by Jeremiah *the prophet* (a subtle development in MT). This assertion is achieved in an indirect way by focusing on another prophet and allowing the *deity* to distinguish between them. If princes and people have validated Jeremiah's message in 26, now Yahweh himself puts the seal of approval on Jeremiah's preaching in relation to the king of Babylon motif. Hananiah serves this purpose (cf. Uriah in 26.20–3) and is of no other importance in the story. At the end of the account his dead body will invalidate his message and also vindicate Yahweh's word as spoken by Jeremiah (hence v. 14). In 26, 28 two dead prophets are introduced into the tradition, but both only serve to highlight the word of Yahweh as uttered by Jeremiah.

Hananiah ben Azzur from Gibeon is introduced in v. 1 as a prophet who encounters Jeremiah the prophet in the temple on a particular occasion (MT's overload of dating information is indicative of redactional problems of fitting the story into its present context). Nothing more is known about Hananiah (like Uriah ben Shemaiah he is only known because his story has been put into Jeremiah's story). He shares with Jeremiah a number of features: he is a Yahwistic prophet who speaks the word of Yahweh; he comes from outside Jerusalem (wherever Gibeon may be located); he addresses Jeremiah in the presence of the priests and people *in the temple* (cf. 7.2; 26.2). In some ways he is the mirror image of Jeremiah. The only discernible difference between the two men is the ideology of each. Hananiah is presented as a *šālōm* prophet (by implication of v. 9), Jeremiah is a prophet of war (cf. v. 8). The story is therefore a clash of ideologies (Mottu rightly discerns the ideological nature of the conflict but fails to scrutinize Jeremiah's ideology). It is difficult to delineate the ideological holdings of Hananiah because the story only provides two pieces of information about his work: his message in vv. 2–4 and his action in vv. 10–11. If these are sufficient for analysing his theory and his praxis (an unlikely possibility), it may be said of him that he represented the anti-Babylonian element in Judaean society. His position is close to that behind 24.4–7; 27.22; 29.10–14, except that he appears to have believed in a more imminent implementation of such a programme. In the context of 27–29 the only point separating him from the presentation of Jeremiah is a matter of timing.

Too much is said about Jeremiah in the tradition and too little about Hananiah for a satisfactory analysis of the differences between the two prophets. G's use of *pseudoprophetēs* to qualify Hananiah may be an idiosyncrasy of that edition, but it does expose the ideology of the redactors. Whatever Hananiah's status and belief system may be, they cannot be explicated from the story because he is essentially the foil for a presentation of Jeremiah as the 'true' prophet. This is a presentation much assisted by the story's opposing of two prophets in which one appears to be very self-assertive and the other a quiet listener and humble servant of Yahweh (cf. the analysis in Lys). One speaks and acts, the other listens, responds, goes away, listens to Yahweh and *then* speaks the divine word. A story of subtle relationships and movements which is remarkably different from all the other stories in the tradition where Jeremiah never listens to anybody but denounces and asserts all the time. In such stories the other prophets are silent or have words put in their mouths, but always they are denounced from the moment Jeremiah opens his mouth. Chapter 28 is so different from those accounts that it is necessary to draw attention to its eirenic presentation of the two prophets in order not to overemphasize the significance of the representation of

Jeremiah here (many exegetes use 28 as if it were a picture of the normal Jeremiah approach to other people – it is not). The peculiarities of 28 should warn the exegete against treating it as anything other than a disjunctive story in the tradition. It is in the unfolding of the story that the eirenic features appear but by its conclusion death and destruction have put an end to such pleasantries.

Hananiah's initial statement declares that Yahweh has broken (*šābartī*, 'I have broken', v. 2) the yoke of the king of Babylon. This announcement allows the story to be linked to the yoke-bars motif of 27 (it is further linked in v. 10). So Hananiah may be viewed as a representative of those in Judah who opposed the Babylonians and who believed that Yahweh would break their power. As evidence of his claim Hananiah says that in two years time the temple furnishings will return to the temple. This verification element links the story with the controversy in 27.16, 18–22 and associates Hananiah with the prophets who make such a claim (27.16). It is a mistake to accuse Hananiah of making the temple vessels into a fetish and belonging to a world where such commodities are viewed as prior to people (*contra* Mottu, 62–3). With the furnishings the king and people will return to Jerusalem. Temple and people belong together (cf. Haggai, Malachi), and not as commodities or fetishes, but as symbols of the creator Yahweh's rule of the world (cf. Levenson 1984b). Hananiah's concern with the furnishings is part of the contextualization of the discussion in the cycle, and not evidence of his involvement on the side of the subjective interests of the ruling class against the objective interests of the Judaean people (*contra* Mottu). The controversy in 27.16, 18–22; 28.2–4 is about the return of the furnishings as the symbol of Yahweh's breaking the imperial power of the empire which has enslaved the peoples of the region. Hananiah sides with those aspirations of the people, hence he addressses Jeremiah in the temple in the presence of priests *and people*. If Zedekiah is on the throne (v. 1) and Hananiah announces that Jeconiah *king of Judah* will return to Jerusalem, then he cannot be accused of serving the interests of the ruling class. He is in defiance of Zedekiah, the court and the Babylonians. Against the might of Babylon he risks his own personal safety by opposing the word of Yahweh to the present state of power politics in Jerusalem. Small wonder that he is dead by the end of the story!

Jeremiah the prophet responds to Hananiah in similar circumstances to the delivery of the original divine word: in the presence of the priests and the people in the temple. His reaction to the divine word is paradigmatic: 'May Yahweh do so' (*kēn ya'aśeh yhwh*). He listens quietly and then he speaks. He speaks to affirm Hananiah's words: 'May Yahweh indeed fulfil your words. Far be it from him that he should appear to oppose the return of the exiles to this place.' The formality of the speech probably represents the correct response to the utterance of the divine word (cf. 26.19). A similar soft answer appears in 26.12–14 and on both occasions Jeremiah adds a rider to his response – 'but, howbeit, only' (*'ak*). General agreement with a situation or belief is expressed, *but* a few dissenting points may yet be made (cf. *'ak* in 12.1). These points usually constitute the heart of the matter and have a tendency to reverse the agreement expressed with the sentiments just enunciated. Jeremiah's reservation is spoken to Hananiah and to all the people and represents a pertinent contrast between the long tradition of war prophets and the innovative word of the *šālōm* prophet (vv. 8–9). It is a strong riposte to Hananiah. It calls into question Hananiah's position by raising doubts about its backing warrants. In opposing Hananiah (if that is what Jeremiah is doing in vv. 8–9) Jeremiah sides with tradition against innovation; with the word of judgment against the word of salvation. Yet it could be said that in the terms of v. 8 Hananiah was in fact proclaiming war, i.e. Yahweh's war, against a great kingdom. Yahweh's breaking of Babylon would fit a tradition of his mighty acts against the nations on behalf of his own people (cf. Isaiah on Assyria in Isa. 10.12–19). Jeremiah's criterion for *šālōm* oracles in v. 9 is an interesting adaptation of Deut. 18.20–2, but it is not the Deuteronomistic criterion of fulfilment. It is not so much a narrowing down of Deut. 18.22 as a separation of war oracles from *šālōm* oracles. Oracles announcing war against the nations have the backing of a very long, and therefore honourable, tradition; oracles proclaiming *šālōm* lack any such warrant and must therefore justify themselves. The only backing warrant suggested for them is their fulfilment. When they happen they authenticate their speaker. Thus Jeremiah's response to Hananiah achieves a stalemate. The people must wait and see whether Hananiah is right or not; whether Yahweh has sent him or not.

As a blocking move it is a brilliant reply: full of subtle nuances and interesting possibilities. It appears to leave the issue open, but it has really closed it because the weight of tradition is now against

Hananiah. What can he do? He cannot just wait two years, for that would expose him to ridicule and an empty career. He could return to Gibeon and become yet another prophet from the Benjaminite territory who had gone to Jerusalem and been destroyed by the opposition there. But had not Yahweh of hosts spoken to him, and what could he do but obey (cf. Amos 3.8)? So he acted – the time for words being over, he backed his words with an appropriate action. He took the yoke-bars from Jeremiah's neck (here we need 27.2 because the necessary information is lacking in 28.1, cf. Rudolph, 172–3) and broke them. Accompanying his action are the words used on such occasions: 'Thus says Yahweh: even so (*kākāh*, cf. 13.9; 19.11; 51.64) will I break the yoke of the king of Babylon' (v. 11). If we assume an original setting of Jeremiah making and wearing the yoke as an act creating the servitude of Judah to Babylon (distorted in its present position in 27.2–4, 11) Hananiah now destroys that act with a divinely willed performance. Word and act match, and the prophet is the performer of both. Furthermore, the possibility of one prophetic performance cancelling out another prophet's act is raised here, but not developed (see on 36.23; cf. I Kings 13; 22.5–28). Jeremiah also acts. He goes his way (from the temple, but whither is not stated). The first encounter is over and the two prophets part. Silence develops between the two figures.

The extent to which the second part of the story (vv. 12–16) mirrors the first (Lys, 474–5) may be disputed. The direct intervention of Yahweh is absent in vv. 1–11 (contrast 26.1; 27.1, but cf. 29.1–29) but appears in v. 12. Both figures respond to each other in the first part whereas Hananiah is inert in vv. 12–16. The divine word comes to Jeremiah in v. 12 but is singularly absent in vv. 1–11 (except as reported by a prophet). In the first part Jeremiah is acted upon, but he acts in vv. 13, 15 ('go, tell Hananiah . . . and Jeremiah . . . said to . . . Hananiah'), whereby Hananiah is acted upon by the deity. Activity and passivity are elements in the two parts, but Jeremiah is never a completely inert figure in the way that Hananiah is in part two. Mirror-imaging is not the best description of the two parts of the story, except in so far as it is a broken mirror. This fracture inverts some of the elements, but part two picks up the disjunctive element introduced by *'ak* in v. 7 and develops that in a way not foreseen in vv. 1–11.

If Jeremiah has no real answer to Hananiah's claim (cf. von Rad 1965, 209–10) and has to go his way, v. 12 resolves his dilemma by introducing the divine word directly into the story. After the events of vv. 10–11 the word comes to Jeremiah in private (at least no public place is denoted in contrast to vv. 1, 5, 7). By himself Jeremiah cannot refute Hananiah, though he may make some canny observations; he must receive the divine word in order to do that. This feature of the story links it with the explanation of the vision in 24 and Jeremiah's role in the community in 42.1–7. No longer the one who initiates the action or speaks the word directly to a given situation, he requires a divine response to a situation before he may speak freely. Now the familiar form of the word comes to him: 'Go, tell Hananiah, "Thus says Yahweh . . ." '. At last the strains of an old sound are heard and Jeremiah may act and speak with confidence. The message for Hananiah (cf. the Pashhur incident in 20.1–6 following the act of 19.1–2, 10–11) reverses his act of vv. 10–11 but increases the severity of what the performance represents. Hananiah may have broken wooden bars, but iron ones will replace them (G, MT differ on who makes the new bars). The divine speech ends there, perhaps because it has affirmed Jeremiah's act of wearing the bars. The editors wish to press on in the matter of Hananiah versus Jeremiah, so v. 15 skips over a number of necessary moves and has Jeremiah confront his opponent. No longer does he speak in reasonable tones, though he does repeat his opening gambit 'listen now . . .' (vv. 7, 15 *šᵉmaʿ-nā'*). But the open question of v. 9 about whether a prophet of *šālōm* might have been sent (*šlḥ*) by Yahweh is a closed assertion in v. 15: 'Yahweh has not sent you (*lō'-šᵉlāḥᵃkā*)'. Instead of bringing *šālōm* to the people he has made them trust in falsehood (*šeqer*). He will, however, be sent (*šlḥ*) by Yahweh, but in the sense of *sent* from this life into death – 'you will die' (v. 16, *'attāh mēt*). In v. 11 Jeremiah had gone his own way after the first encounter with Hananiah; now after the second encounter Hananiah goes the way of all flesh. He dies because he is in rebellion against Yahweh (cf. Deut. 13.6; a similar charge is made against Shemaiah in 29.32). Between the true sending of Yahweh (v. 9) and Hananiah stands the lie (*šeqer*) spoken by him. The editors record his death in the seventh month of that year and thus round off the story in a neatly symmetrical way (cf. Pelatiah's fate in Ezek. 11.13).

The story ends there without comment on Hananiah's fate. There is none to mourn him or to bury him (contrast I Kings 13.29), but then the tale is not about Hananiah as much as it is about the confirmation of Yahweh's word as spoken by Jeremiah. In effect the story says: there will be no return of the temple furnishings or of Jeconiah and the exiles to Jerusalem. That is the point of the first edition of 27 (G) and 28 affirms it. The complication of the matter in 27.22 (MT) has no direct bearing on 28. The prophet from Gibeon who supported the belief that furnishings and exiles would return from Babylon has been executed by Yahweh of hosts (or the Babylonians?) and with his execution that party political scheme is at an end. Yahweh has spoken through his prophet Jeremiah and there is an end to the matter. The redactors pass on to a different subject.

Chapter 28 has been analysed without remainder and its interpretation appears to be unproblematical. Some of the things said by Hananiah will resurface elsewhere in the tradition and will be noted when they do (see on 29.10), but the story is straightforward by the standards of the book of Jeremiah. However, the chapter has attracted much special attention, especially in relation to questions about false prophecy and criteria for evaluating different prophets (cf. Hossfeld und Meyer 1973, 90–103; Kraus 1964; Lys, 477–82; Overholt 1970, 24–48; Wolff 1983, 67–73). The chapter offers no criteria for distinguishing between prophets because it is set in a tradition where Jeremiah is already established as the true prophet (e.g. 26.15–16) and in the confrontation between Jeremiah and Hananiah there are no differentiating marks which single out one of the prophets as true or false. The implication of II Kings 18.19–25 that when there are rival claimants to divine revelation one of them is probably lying would appear to be the point behind 28 (cf. De Vries 1978, 72). But identifying the liar is beyond the wit of man and, if even Jeremiah required a subsequent revelation to know that Hananiah was lying, therefore the story does not set out criteria for making such judgments. All the subtle exegesis of many commentators on 28 should not be allowed to conceal that lack of a criteriology. Distinguishing between prophets who proclaim radically different divine words may be an existential problem rather than an academic one (rightly Lys, 478), but sophisticated exegesis which reads into the story many elements from other ideologies will not provide what is already lacking in the text (*contra* Lys, Mottu). A careful exegesis of 28 will not produce evidence to back Jeremiah against Hananiah because there is no such evidence either in the text or in the world at large. Because Yahweh is not at hand but is the hidden god who is afar off (23.23), 'there could be no standard method of any sort by which he granted revelation' (von Rad 1965, 209). That factor may help to explain why Jeremiah is 'so much at sea' (von Rad's phrase) in his encounter with Hananiah. The irony of 23.28 should not be overlooked in the analysis of 28: 'let the prophet who has a dream tell the dream, but let him who has my word speak my word faithfully'. Hananiah speaks that divine word, yet it is declared a lie. So when the divine word may be a lie, prophecy itself becomes an activity in which true and false are indistinguishable. Without a redactional framework which can provide the necessary theological guidance for reading reality, prophecy is a mute witness.

Reading 28 as a clash between a central prophet (Hananiah) and a peripheral prophet (Jeremiah) in which the accusation of being a false prophet functions as the equivalent of witchcraft accusations in other cultures (cf. Wilson 1980, 247–51; 1984, 74–80) is an interesting approach to the material, but founders on being incoherent as a conceptual analysis of Jeremiah. Apart from his speaking in the temple, an activity much more frequently posited of Jeremiah, there is no evidence for Hananiah being a central prophet. Jeremiah has much better claims to that role, but the amassing of discrete traditions about Jeremiah make it impossible to determine his status in relation to central or peripheral prophecy (cf. the fluctuating analysis of Isaiah in Wilson 1980, 270–4). The concept of a peripheral prophet with support from members of the central establishment (Wilson 1980, 248) indicates the incoherence of such an analysis and the way the tradition represents Jeremiah as freely moving about the temple and the royal residence, with many powerful supporters, hardly supports the thesis of his peripheral status. The suggestion that Hananiah was Jeremiah's replacement after the death of Josiah (Johnstone 1967, 55) cannot be sustained by the text. If Hananiah had been a central prophet since Josiah's death he would most certainly have been deported by the Babylonians or so discredited by the collapse of the pro-Egyptian party that he would never have survived the changeover of power in 597. There is insufficient evidence in 28 to provide any account of Hananiah's social status, and therefore the encounter between the two prophets cannot be analysed using sociological factors or be assumed to be anything other than a paradigmatic story.

The Marxist analysis of 28 undertaken by Henri Mottu is an interesting approach to the text, but it collapses under the weight of its own ideological jargon. It has to posit of Hananiah so many things which are neither in the text nor necessarily held by Hananiah as to render the exposition almost worthless. Hananiah is set up as a straw man and then knocked down and buried under the Marxist terminology of Althusser, Gramsci, Sartre and others. None of this is justified by the text, which is quite capable of denigrating Hananiah but chooses not to attack his character, history or associations. Hananiah cannot even be identified from the text as a proponent of that Zion-orientated ideology which van der Woude identifies as the mark of the pseudo-prophet (van der Woude 1969). So when Mottu attacks Hananiah for being on the side of the powerful he is reading into the text what his theory tells him must be there. But consider the setting: in the temple of Zedekiah's day, i.e. with Babylonian overlords exercising the real power through their vassal, this prophet from Gibeon (not Jerusalem), this outsider or peripheral figure, proclaims the judgment of Yahweh on Babylon. How does that make Hananiah a participant in the power relationships of his time? If the authorities hear Hananiah, he will be executed (cf. 29.21–23). Hananiah risks all with his future-orientated faith that Yahweh will bring back furnishings, king and people. He may be wrong but not on the grounds that he lacks faith or praxis, is not open to the future, serves the powers that be or is trapped in the past. Jeremiah's response to him is far more anchored in the past than the future, yet many commentators praise him as being innovative in 28. This is a complete misreading of the text. Exegetes are generally so eager to praise Jeremiah and denigrate Hananiah that they read into the text much that is simply not there. To say that Yahweh will bring back the king, i.e. displace the present occupant of the throne, is an act of brave faith, however mistaken it may be. It is both radical and revolutionary in its political context and cannot be construed as support for the ruling classes. It is quite the opposite! Mottu accuses Hananiah of stealing Isa. 9.4 (the breaking of the yoke of the oppressor; but cf. 30.8!) and making a commodity of it (Mottu, 62; cf. 23.30 for the motif of stealing the divine words). Hananiah is also accused of 'parrotry of Isaiah' (Lys, 480) because in the sixth century he repeats what Isaiah said in the eighth (but what about the argument in v. 8 which uses the ancient tradition of the prophets of war? – is that not parrotry also?). Yet there is nothing in all these accusations which cannot be made of the Jeremiah represented in the tradition.

The point of representing these criticisms of Hananiah is simply to contrast the exegetical superstructure of so much modern analysis of 28 with what the text itself actually says about him. If so much extraneous material must be imported into the text in order to damn Hananiah, the resultant eisegesis is doing something other than explaining the text. Such misguided readings of 28 are based on the presupposition that it is history and that Hananiah's falseness is being demonstrated by the text. Neither is the case. 28 may be a cleverly constructed story (cf. Lys' structuralist analysis) but its point is very simple: the temple furnishings are not coming back (nor is the king). Babylon rules!

The cycle in which Hananiah's story is set has as its dominant motif the falseness (*šeqer*) of what *all* the prophets say (27.10, 14, 15, 16; 28.15; 29.9, 21, 23, 31), and in such a context Hananiah *the prophet* is inevitably a speaker of what is false. As the figure opposite Jeremiah his is the role characterized by the term *šeqer*. It is unnecessary, however, to construct a closely argued account of just why Hananiah of Gibeon is false. His falseness is part of the given in the story (demonstrated by Yahweh's only contribution in vv. 13–14) because in conjunction with Jeremiah he must be false. If he takes a different view from the bearer of the tradition he must be wrong. The redaction is committed to Jeremiah, *therefore Hananiah is false*. As Wilson rightly observes: 'the observer can decide which of the prophecies to believe only if he has already recognized the authority of one prophet or the other' (1980, 250). The process of authentication is prior to the encounter between the two prophets and is determined at the redactional level of the tradition. So it is futile to seek to demonstrate the falseness of Hananiah's position or to justify his condemnation as *šeqer*. Nor is it necessary for the modern exegete to join in the editorial excoriation of Hananiah with further denunciations of lying prophets who manipulate divine words for their own ends. The matter of prophecy is not so simple that the term *šeqer* may be bandied about with such certitude, and the remarks of Dodds on the Pythia's trance in relation to her priests' interpretation of her words hold good for this aspect of biblical prophecy:

> We cannot see into the minds of the Delphic priesthood, but to ascribe such manipulation in general to conscious and cynical fraud is, I suspect, to oversimplify the picture. Anyone familiar with the history of modern spiritualism will realise what an amazing amount of virtual cheating can be done in perfectly good faith by convinced believers (1973, 74).

29.1–23

29 1 These are the words of the letter which Jeremiah the prophet sent from Jerusalem to the elders of the exiles, and to the priests, the prophets, and all the people, whom Nebuchadnezzar had taken into exile from Jerusalem to Babylon. 2 This was after King Jeconiah, and the queen mother, the eunuchs, the princes of Judah and Jerusalem, the craftsmen, and the smiths had departed from Jerusalem. 3 The letter was sent by the hand of Elasah the son of Shaphan and Gemariah the son of Hilkiah, whom Zedekiah king of Judah sent to Babylon to Nebuchadnezzar king of Babylon. It said: 4 'Thus says the LORD of hosts, the God of Israel, to all the exiles whom I have sent into exile from Jerusalem to Babylon: 5 Build houses and live in them; plant gardens and eat their produce. 6 Take wives and have sons and daughters; take wives for your sons, and give your daughters in marriage, that they may bear sons and daughters; multiply there, and do not decrease. 7 But seek the welfare of the city where I have sent you into exile, and pray to the LORD on its behalf, for in its welfare you will find your welfare. 8 For thus says the LORD of hosts, the God of Israel: Do not let your prophets and your diviners who are among you deceive you, and do not listen to the dreams which they dream, 9 for it is a lie which they are prophesying to you in my name; I did not send them, says the LORD.

10 For thus says the LORD: When seventy years are completed for Babylon, I will visit you, and I will fulfil to you my promise and bring you back to this place. 11 For I know the plans I have for you, says the LORD, plans for welfare and not for evil, to give you a future and a hope. 12 Then you will call upon me and come and pray to me, and I will hear you. 13 You will seek me and find me; when you seek me with all your heart, 14 I will be found by you, says the LORD, and I will restore your fortunes and gather you from all the nations and all the places where I have driven you, says the LORD, and I will bring you back to the place from which I sent you into exile.

15 Because you have said, "The LORD has raised up prophets for us in Babylon," – 16 Thus says the LORD concerning the king who sits on the throne of David, and concerning all the people who dwell in this city, your kinsmen who did not go out with you into exile: 17 "Thus says the LORD of hosts, Behold, I am sending on them sword, famine, and pestilence, and I will make them like vile figs which are so bad they cannot be eaten. 18 I will pursue them with sword, famine, and pestilence, and will make them a horror to all the kingdoms of the earth, to be a curse, a terror, a hissing, and a reproach among all the nations where I have driven them, 19 because they did not heed my words, says the LORD, which I persistently sent to you by my servants the prophets, but you would not listen, says the LORD." – 20 Hear the word of the LORD, all you exiles whom I sent away from Jerusalem to Babylon: 21 "Thus says the LORD of hosts, the God of Israel,

concerning Ahab the son of Kolaiah and Zedekiah the son of Maaseiah, who are prophesying a lie to you in my name: Behold, I will deliver them into the hand of Nebuchadrezzar king of Babylon, and he shall slay them before your eyes. 22 Because of them this curse shall be used by all the exiles from Judah in Babylon: 'The LORD make you like Zedekiah and Ahab, whom the king of Babylon roasted in the fire,' 23 because they have committed folly in Israel, they have committed adultery with their neighbours' wives, and they have spoken in my name lying words which I did not command them. I am the one who knows, and I am witness, says the LORD." '

[MT 29] = G 36. **[1]** MT *w*^{e}*'ēlleh dib*^{e}*rē hassēper*, 'and these are the words of the document': *w*^{e}, 'and', connects 29 with 28. Weiser, 249, translates the phrase as a title: 'This is the story of the letter.' 51.60 represents Jeremiah as writing a book and sending it to Babylon; for the idea of a prophet writing (a letter) to somebody cf. Elijah's writing (*miktāb*) to king Jehoram (II Chron. 21.12–15). The letter may not be authentic (cf. Williamson 1982, 306–7), but it reflects a period when 'Prophetic words are gaining canonical status' (Ackroyd 1973, 154), cf. Zech. 1.5–6. MT *yeter ziq*^{e}*nē haggōlāh*, '(to) the rest of the elders of the exile': G lacks *yeter*, followed by RSV. MT may reflect the result of the trouble referred to in v. 22 or *yeter* may be out of place and belong with 'all the people' (cf. Nicholson, 44; for the second view cf. Volz, 266). Rudolph, 182, suggests the sense of 'preeminence' for *yeter* as in Gen. 49.3, meaning the most prominent elders. **[2]** A parenthetical insertion based on II Kings 24.14–16; cf. 24.1. For 'queen mother' see on 13.18. MT *w*^{e}*hassārīsīm*, 'and the eunuchs': not necessarily castrates (unless in charge of the harems, cf. on 24.1), cf. Potiphar (Gen. 39.1), who was married (though his wife's behaviour with Joseph may suggest a certain lack in her husband!); cf. 38.7. MT *śārē y*^{e}*hūdāh wirušālaim*, 'princes of Judah and Jerusalem': G *kai pantos eleutherou*, 'and every freeman'. **[3]** MT *b*^{e}*yad*, 'by the hand of . . . ': v. 3 continues from v. 1 after the interruption of v. 2; the means of sending the letter is not clear. Perhaps by diplomatic bag (Thompson, 545), but cf. 51.60 (an ancient subversive practice?): Jeremiah is here a man of power with access to diplomatic dispatches. Elasah may have been a brother of Ahikam (26.24), and Gemariah (cf. 36.12?) may have been a son of Josiah's high priest (II Kings 22.4, 8). G lacks 'Nebuchadnezzar'. MT *lē'mōr*, 'saying': RSV 'It said'. **[4]** MT *'*^{a}*šer-hig*^{e}*lētī*, 'whom I have exiled': the shift from third person to first is awkward (cf. v. 7); BHS suggests emending with S to *hogl*^{e}*tāh*, 'who have been exiled'. The contents of the letter appear in vv. 4–7. **[6]** MT *w*^{e}*tēlad*^{e}*nāh bānīm ūbānōt*, 'and let them give birth to sons and daughters': lacking in G. MT *w*^{e}*'al-tim'āṭū*, 'and do not become few': cf. *pen-tam'iṭēnī*, 'lest you make me few', 10.24. **[7]** MT *hā'īr*, 'the city': G *tēs gēs*, 'the country' = *hā'āreṣ*. Unless taken in a distributive sense MT is unlikely and exegetes prefer G (e.g. Weiser,

Rudolph, Bright). Loss of cult and deportation have not ruled out prayer to Yahweh in a foreign land; some exegetes read the text as evidence of the replacement of the temple cult by the synagogue (Volz, 270; Janssen 1956, 109–10). The notion of praying for a heathen land is unique in the Hebrew Bible, even if self-interest is the ground for such activity (*kī biš^elōmāh yihyeh lākem šālōm*, 'for in its well-being is your own well-being'). Yet if there is to be no return from Babylon (G 27.19–22; MT 28), it makes sense to pray for the well-being of the new (home) land. **[8–9]** Rudolph reads these verses after v. 15; they have no place in the letter but belong to the highly edited section which separates the letter from responses to it (vv. 24–29). These additions belong to the cycle's twin foci of Babylon and 'false' prophets. Bright, 208, regards vv. 8–9 as giving needed reinforcement to the preceding piece and leading into vv. 10–14. **[8]** MT *'el-ḥ^alōmōtēkem*, 'to your dreams': BHS reads 'their dreams' with G[26]. MT *'attem maḥl^emīm*, '(which) you cause to be dreamed': Rudolph treats as a textual error; G *ha humeis enupniazesthe*, 'which you dream', i.e. *hēm ḥōl^emīm*, 'they dream' (cf. v. 9). **[9]** MT *b^ešeqer*, 'with a lie': Vrs *šeqer*, 'it is a lie, a falsehood'. **[10]** Cf. 25.11–12, where 'seventy years' is also mentioned. The secondary nature of vv. 10–14 should be obvious from the fact that both places refer to seventy years, yet each is dated quite differently (25 = 605; 29 = 597). Here the addition corrects the view that exile in Babylon is to be permanent, a view easily deduced from vv. 4–7 and corresponding to the subseuqent experience of millennia of Jewish life in Babylon! See on 25.11–12 for discussion of range of meaning of 'seventy years'. **[11]** MT *'ānōkī yāda'tī 'et-hammaḥ^ašābōt '^ašer 'ānōkī*, '*I* know the plans which I': lacking in G (probably due to homoioteleuton: *'ānōkī . . . 'ānōkī* with the translator's eye moving from the first to the second *'ānōkī*). G lacks *n^e'um yhwh*, 'says Yahweh'. MT *'aḥ^arīt w^etiqwāh*, 'a latter end and a hope': i.e. a hoped-for future (cf. Bright, 209 hendiadys); cf. 31.17 for these two terms. G *tauta* 'these things'. **[12]** MT *wah^alaktem*, 'and you will go'; meaning? Perhaps spoken from the second temple and therefore an allusion to worship in a rebuilt shrine. Treated as secondary by many commentators; lacking in G. S lacks 'and I will hear you' (BHS). MT may include variants in vv. 12–13. **[13]** Cf. Deut. 4.29 of which this verse is virtually a citation (cf. Thiel 1981, 15). G^S lacks 'and you will find when you seek me' (MT). **[14]** MT *w^enimṣē'tī lākem*, 'and I will be found by you': G *kai epiphanoumai humin*, 'and I will manifest myself to you'. G ends verse at this point (cf. BHS). What follows in MT has little to do with Babylon in particular but refers to widespread dispersion among many nations. MT *w^ešabtī 'et-š^ebūt^ekem* (Q) 'and I will restore your fortunes': K *š^ebīt^ekem*, 'your captivity'. The phrase *šūb š^ebūt*, 'restore the fortunes', occurs in 30.3, 18; 31.23; 32.44; 33.7, 11, 26; 48.47; 49.6, 39; Lam. 2.14; Deut. 30.3; for its meaning cf. Baumann 1929; Dietrich 1925; Holladay 1958, 110–15; Johnson 1962, 67 n. 4. **[15]** Cf. Deut. 18.15, 18. **[16–20]** G lacks these verses (except for G^L which has the order 14, 16–20, 15, 21–23); they are another addition to the letter sequence and have no relevance to the Babylonian community (cf. 24.8–10 for similar sentiments but a different use of the figs metaphor). Note vv. 15, 20 both end with the word *bābelāh*, 'to Babylon', but vv. 16–20 are too long and different for G's lack to be due to homoioteleuton. **[17]** 'I will make them *like* disgusting figs (*katt*ᵉ*'ēnīm haššō'ārīm*)': cf. 24.2, 3. The vision of the two baskets of figs in 24 may have contributed the root metaphor here but in v. 17 it is Yahweh who *makes* the citizens uneatable figs, whereas 24 offers no explanation for the equation of the community with bad figs. If 24 is behind this usage then the writer has not grasped its meaning (cf. Rudolph, 186) and uses a masc. qualifier for a fem. noun (contrast 24.2, 3). **[18]** Cf. 15.2–4, where many of these terms are used, especially the triad sword, famine, pestilence (reversed order). Cf. note on 27.8 for listing of the triad references. K *lzw'h*; Q *l*ᵉ*za'*ᵃ*wāh*, 'a horror', as in 15.4. MT *w*ᵉ*lišrēqāh*, 'and for a whistling, hissing', cf. 18.16; 19.8; a few mss read *w*ᵉ*liq*ᵉ*lālāh*, 'and for a curse' (BHS). **[19]** MT *haškēm w*ᵉ*sālōaḥ*, 'rising early and sending': see on 7.13, 25. Some mss read *'*ᵃ*lēhem*, 'to them', as *'*ᵃ*lēkem*, 'to you', probably in view of *š*ᵉ*ma'tem*, 'you would (not) listen', which is the clichéd form of this motif throughout the tradition (Rudolph attributes it to a mechanical copying of the phrase cf. 25.3–4; 26.5). G^OL, S = *šāma'tū*, 'they would (not) listen'. **[21]** G lacks 'the son of Kolaiah', 'the son of Maaseiah', 'Nebuchadrezzar' (only example of normal spelling in 27–29), 'who are prophesying a lie to you in my name'. **[22]** MT *'*ᵃ*šer qālām*, 'whom he roasted': a possible word-play on *ben-qōlāyāh*, 'the son of Kolaiah' – but his name is as close to *qll*, 'curse', so the word-play might be with *q*ᵉ*lālāh*, 'curse' (cf. Carroll 1981, 191). *qlh*, 'roast'; *qll*, 'curse', *qōlāyāh*, 'Kolaiah' all share word-play elements, though MT lacks *qōlāyāh* in v. 22 (note defective spelling of *'eḥāb* for *'aḥ'āb*). **[23]** MT *ya'an 'ᵃšer 'āśū n*ᵉ*bālāh b*ᵉ*yiśrā'el*, 'because they have committed folly in Israel': 'to commit folly in Israel' is an idiomatic phrase for some outrageous act contrary to the good order of the community, hence its use even here to describe acts perpetrated in Babylon! Certain heinous activities are associated with the idiom: rape (Gen. 37.7); premarital loss of virginity discovered after marriage, indicative of an active sex life before marriage (Deut. 22.21); vicious rape (Judg. 20.6, 10); breach of the holy war rules applying to sacred property (Josh. 7.15); violation of a woman (cf. II Sam. 13.12–13). Apart from sacrilege, wanton sexual acts appear to be the meaning of 'folly in Israel'; cf. Gerleman 1974; Phillips 1975. Whether the wives referred to here were Babylonian cannot be inferred from the text, but Nebuchadrezzar's penchant for roasting people (Dan. 3) may have been sufficient reason for the fate of the two prophets. Bright, 209, attributes their execution to their seditious words but that also is only an inference from the context of the cycle. G lacks *šeqer*, 'falsehood, lie'. K *hwyd'*; Q *hayōdē'a*, 'the one who knows' (K *hū ' yōdē'a*, 'he who knows');

lacking in G. A dittography due to *wā'ēd*, 'and witness'; BHS reads *'ānōkī* . . . *(hā) 'ēd*, 'I am . . . (the) witness'. Adultery is a secret practice but Yahweh witnesses it, so its inherent falseness (*šeqer*) is exposed by the fate of the two prophets — This accusation makes the command in v. 6 'take wives' appear quite ironic!

The third chapter in the cycle is a much expanded account of an exchange of letters between Jerusalem and Babylon (vv. 3–7, 25–29, 31–32). The deportation of 597 has taken place and there appears to be a state of normal communication between the two communities (cf. v. 3). Jeremiah the prophet is presented as a figure of authority writing letters to the leaders of the deportees in Babylon, setting out the strategy for survival there. In this cycle he is clearly the leader of both communities, advising, condemning and encouraging the social leaders of the people in Jerusalem and Babylon. Even at so great a distance as that between the two territories he may command and send the divine word (cf. 51.59–64; Bright treats the book of oracles against Babylon as a magical act after 29.32). Like the legendary Elijah (II Chron. 21.12–15), Jeremiah can react at a distance to events by means of the written word. This role of the writing prophet is a major feature of Part III (e.g. 29.1; 30.2; 36.2; cf. 51.60) and reflects the later development of the prophet in the direction of becoming a canonical figure. In the story of this letter he is associated with important Jerusalem people (v. 3 Elasah and Gemariah) who are part of a royal delegation to Babylon (not to be confused with 51.59). His role, therefore, in the cycle is that of an authoritative figure moving about Jerusalem, advising foreign nations on foreign policy (27), confronting an anti-Babylonian prophet (28), and proclaiming a policy of co-operation with the Babylonians to the Judaeans now living in Babylon. The interests behind the cycle are clearly Babylonian, though whether on behalf of the communities in Babylon or those descendants of the original deportees who returned to Palestine after the fall of Babylon cannot be determined from the text (the redactional notes of vv. 1–2 would be unnecessary in earlier times).

In spite of the disjunctive additions which appear to be part of the contents of the letter, the letter itself is brief and straightforward. It advises the deportees to settle down to permanent exile. This is the clear message of its contents (vv. 5–7) and agrees with the view expressed in 28 that there would be no return from Babylon. The oracular format of the letter (v. 4) makes the policy expressed in it the word of Yahweh. It therefore provides divine sanction for the way of life of the Babylonian communities and is quite unique in the biblical traditions. The people who have moved to the new territory are counselled to settle down to a normal social life (cf. similar instructions relating to Palestinian territory in 32.15). Such an existence consists of building houses, planting gardens for the production of food, marrying and giving in marriage in order to reproduce the community's stock of people and increase its population. These are all long-term projects which produce a firmly established society with an open-ended future. It can go on developing as long as it does not diminish its stock (v. 6b). The well-being (*šālōm*) of this community is however bound up with the well-being (*šālōm*) of the city (MT) or country (G) of Babylon, hence the people must intercede (*hitpalᵉlū* in contrast to 7.16; 11.14; 14.11) with Yahweh on behalf of the well-being of their new home. This is civil religion at its very best, and virtually unique in the Bible: domesticity and devotion, hard work and prayer all contributing to *šālōm*. After the terrible events of invasion, deportation and life in an alien land, *šālōm* is to be found in a blend of normal existence and prayerful conformity to Babylonian life. Unique though the prescriptions may be in the Bible, they are a remarkably acute assessment of the situation and a blueprint for millennia to come.

The strategy for survival in a foreign land is completed in v. 7. The fate of the exiles is bound up with the fate of their new territory and the *šālōm* element in the strategy is a relational one between deportees and overlord culture. This makes the *šālōm* feature quite unique in the tradition in that it affects others (i.e. foreigners) and is not directed by Yahweh solely towards Judah (contrast v. 11). However, the letter is supplemented by a number of additions which have nothing to do with its contents but which reflect the present context of that letter. These are supplementary expositions designed to balance the letter and link it with the anti-prophetic theme of the cycle.

An oracular statement in vv. 8–9 denounces the prophets and diviners. These are not identified in the text, but the redaction's placing of the piece after vv. 5–7 permits, rather than necessitates, identifying them as deported prophets and diviners (cf. v. 1; G *pseudoprophētai*). Commentators interpret the attack on their activities as a further polemic against the prophetically inspired view that the exile would be a short one (cf. 27.16; 28.3). This is a possible interpretation based on inference but not on what the text says. It simply warns against being deceived by prophets and dreamers (i.e. those who divine by dreams). Such agents do not come from Yahweh and what they prophesy is false (*šeqer*). These are clichéd charges in the tradition and without further clarification in the text could mean anything. If the oracle is taken at face value it asserts what is stated so often in the polemic against the prophets: they deceive (cf. 4.10) by means of what they prophesy and dream (cf. 23.25–32). Nothing more is said about them, whether they are Judaean or foreign, in Judah or Babylon. What they do is false and Yahweh has not sent them (cf. 28.15). The reference to diviners (v. 8 *qōsᵉmīm*) only occurs elsewhere in 27.9 (but the prophets attacked in 14.14 produce worthless divination [*qesem*]), which raises the question whether 29.8 is a displacement of 27.9 or vice versa (27.9–11 is odd in its address to foreign prophets, but then 27–29 is an odd cycle). In 27–29 there appears to be a steady shift of a few elements to cover a wide diversity of situations and these movable phrases consequently lose their semantic force. The present position of vv. 8–9 taken in the context of 27–29 may imply prophetic and divinatory processes which claimed that there would be no exile or a short one. The letter explaining the permanence of the new life in an alien land is then a counterbalance to such behaviour. The point could have been made much more clearly in the text, if that is indeed what vv. 8–9 purport to be.

A further addition to the text occurs in vv. 10–14. It also appears to be a counterbalance to what precedes it (if Rudolph is followed in reading vv. 8–9 after v. 15 then the counterbalancing effect of vv. 10–14 to vv. 5–7 becomes quite apparent). For if vv. 5–7 assert the permanence of the exile, vv. 10–14 speak of a return to the homeland (v. 10 ‘this place’ i.e. Jerusalem or the temple, cf. 27.22; 28.3). These two motifs do not necessarily contradict each other but vv. 10–14 look suspiciously like the message of the prophets in the cycle who are declared to be prophesying falsehood. It only differs from what they say in having a longer time sequence – seventy years instead of two years. The seventy years motif which appears also in 25.11–12 indicates the end of Babylonian rule (cf. 27.7 where three generations or a long time is given as the duration of that domination) and presumably identifies the unit as a post-exilic creation. As the return to the homeland never became a very popular movement the strategy for building a permanent life in Babylon proved to be very wise counsel.

The presence of the seventy years motif in v. 10 set in the cycle of 27–29 produces an unintended irony. In 28.9 a prophecy of *šālōm* requires fulfilment before it can be determined whether Yahweh sent the prophet or not. Although Hananiah is not condemned on the grounds of the failure of his prediction (28.9 does not function as a criterion in 28), his two years look very modest beside seventy years. A prediction of seventy years time would be absurd if either 28.9 or Deut. 18.22 was imposed as a test of authenticity. Nobody would be alive after another seventy years to be able to verify the speaker's genuineness and hence the criterion is not designed for long term predictions (if such were conceived of in biblical times). The speaker of vv. 10–14 need not be charged with being a false prophet because there are no grounds for considering the statement to be anything other than an after the event proclamation. Its function in 29 is to correct the impression rightly given by vv. 5–7 that exile would be permanent. There may be very few Jews in Iraq today, but the Jewish presence in Babylonia has been a permanent one. The restoration motif of v. 10 reflects that return to Palestine which a few descendants of the exiles made. This point needs to be underlined: those who went into exile in 597 were not those who returned in the century following the fall of Babylon in 539. Few, if any, of the original exiles lived so long that they could even contemplate returning to a land which they had left in their youth. The bulk of those who 'returned' had never known life in Palestine – it was a new and risky venture for them.

The restoration of the exiles in vv. 10–11 is given an oracular grounding and made the fulfilment of Yahweh's 'good word' (*dᵉbārī haṭṭōb*). For Yahweh has plans of well-being (*maḥšᵉbōt šālōm*, contrast 18.11) rather than disaster for the people. The future hope planned by Yahweh is developed in vv. 12–14 along pietistic lines and fused in v. 14 with the much more general return from the diaspora of all the scattered exiles. The influence of Deuteronomistic language here indicates redactional development of the piece in a direction quite distinct from vv. 10–11. There Yahweh restores the exiles from Babylon, after which they call upon him when they go (to the temple? MT v. 12) and pray to him. But in vv. 13–14 the restoration takes place after the scattered ones have sought Yahweh. The two different sequences of events probably reflect the two distinctive views of future restoration: an act of divine grace in which the deity initiates the movement (cf. 31.33–4) and a situation in which the people turn to Yahweh and he responds graciously (cf. 3.12; 4.1–2, 3–4; Deut. 30.1–10). In the first the return is Yahweh keeping his word (cf. NEB 'I will take up your cause and fulfil the promise of good things I made you'); in the second the deity restores the diaspora as a result of their response to him. As they both refer to rather different returns they should not be confused (cf. Emmerson 1984, 9–55, for analysis of the two distinctive strands as they affect the editing of the book of Hosea). The expansion of the unit in terms of the restoration of the diaspora has the effect of making v. 14 contradict the motif in v. 18. The post-exilic hope that the diaspora would return to Palestine conflicts with those elements in the tradition which write off any exilic community outside Babylon or any deportation other than that of 597.

The attack on the prophets is resumed in vv. 15, 21–23 but MT interrupts it with an onslaught on the Jerusalem community (lacking in G). This interpolation in vv. 16–19 would be better read after vv. 10–14 where it would afford a strong contrast between the different futures posited for the exiles of 597 (and all the diaspora) and those who remained behind in the land of Judah. The sequence vv. 15, 21–3 (G) identifies the prophets under attack as ones in the Babylonian community (if vv. 8–9 were to be incorporated into this section that would solve the problem of identification there). Apparently once the deportees settled down in various parts of Babylonia they developed normal social structures which included the emergence of prophets (v. 15 hardly refers to the prophets of the redactional heading in v. 1 as the community would not then have spoken of Yahweh raising up for them prophets). These prophets are recognized as coming from Yahweh, presumably in fulfilment of Deut. 18.15, 18 (the late addition to the Deuteronomistic law parallels the lateness of this material in 29). Because they are accepted as such by the people, an oracle is given against them (v. 20, lacking in G, is required in MT to provide an introduction to vv. 21–2 because of the disruption of vv. 16–19 which have isolated v. 15). In vv. 21–23 these prophets are identified as Ahab and Zedekiah (a peculiarity of the cycle is the naming of prophets against whom Jeremiah speaks). They also are accused of prophesying falsehood (*šeqer*) in the divine name. Nothing of what they say is given in the text, so again the redactional context may be to taken to imply that they are prophesying against Babylonian rule (like Second Isaiah?). Such an implication is in keeping with the charge against Hananiah (28) and the foreign prophets (27.9–10) but is *not* a necessary reading of the text. The redaction of 29 is particularly poor in the provision of adequate information which would allow each unit to be understood clearly.

The fate of the two prophets at the hands of Nebuchadrezzar is proof of their falseness and their adultery. In the attack on prophets of 23.14 adultery is one of the charges but there it is probably some involvement in illicit cults (see on 5.7–8); here the accusation of adultery concerns sexual activities with the wives of their neighbours. How could Jeremiah living in Jerusalem have known what was going on in secret (cf v. 23b) so many hundreds of miles away? To ask that question is to answer it. He could not have known such matters, unless they were common gossip in Babylon of the kind that would be mentioned in dispatches back to the homeland. This seems highly unlikely as it presupposes that vv. 21–23 belong to the letter and that adultery was tolerated at such a level. While it may be encouraging to discover that normal domestic concourse had been resumed to the point that adultery could be practised among the exilic communities, it might be wiser to assume that either a story is involved here or one further example of the denigration of the prophets so typical of the cycle is intended by the allusion. If the story is read as having any historical content then it must be treated as a product of the Babylonian exilic communities and not as the output of Jeremiah or the Jerusalem people.

The legends about Nebuchadrezzar collected and circulated in the Aramaic half of the book of Daniel include stories about his predilection for roasting people, so the tale about Ahab and Zedekiah may belong to the same provenance. They are a famous couple roasted by Nebuchadrezzar (the elements of word-play in v. 22 make the story a macabre example of gallows humour in the Bible), indeed so well-known is the tale that the exiles use it as a curse. Such a curse is used to explain their falseness. They are a famous example of sexual behaviour which is characterized as 'folly in Israel', i.e. 'deluded ignorance' (von Rad 1962, 267), a class of acts which bring appalling suffering in their wake because they disrupt the sexual harmony of the community. As prophets they would have had greater access to married women because of their special holy status as men of god (e.g. II Kings 4.11–17; cf. Isa. 8.3). Yet such adultery would require great secrecy, or else all the parties to it (note no women are mentioned as victims of the same fate) would have suffered whatever the consequences of the great sin were at that time and in that society. Falseness (*šeqer*) is the essence of adultery, hence the connection between prophesying falsehood and being adulterers. From the charge of prophesying falsehood it is but a step to accusing the 'false' prophet(s) of committing other kinds of false behaviour. The roasting of the prophets is *proof* of their falseness (whether due to sedition, *šālōm* preaching or just the story line) and whatever else may be charged against them. The reference to Yahweh as witness suggests a legal analogy: cf. Deut. 19.15, where two or three witnesses are required for a charge to be sustained; presumably the deity as witness would outrank this demand! But adultery in secret would only have the deity as witness, and his execution of the criminals by the hand of his vassal Nebuchadrezzar must be taken as proof of guilt (cf. the later rabbinic interpretation of disease and sickness as proof of sinfulness).

The question may be asked whether such a charge of adultery might not be a technique for controlling prophets. To be accused of the deed would certainly curtail a prophet's activities and either silence him or make him cautious. There is no evidence to confirm this analysis, though the biblical traditions use the charge as a metaphor of idolatry when they wish to denounce particular communities (cf. 2.20–25; 3.1; Hos. 3; Ezek. 23). However, the charge of not having been sent by Yahweh and of speaking falsehood in the divine name may have had a controlling function in the community, so the additional accusation of adultery may not have been necessary. It is the execution of Ahab and Zedekiah which allows the interpretation of their fate to be made in terms of having committed adultery. The story of their wretched fate at the hands of the cruel despot Nebuchadrezzar highlights a feature of the cycle: the death of prophets. Hananiah, Ahab and Zedekiah all die, and presumably because of opposition to Nebuchadrezzar (cf. Uriah in 26.23, who dies at the hands of Jehoiakim). Being a prophet in opposition to the Babylonians is a very risky calling, and those who embraced such a ministry must have been very brave, if perhaps foolish, Yahwists. Small wonder that Jeremiah the prophet was a supporter of Babylon and lived, according to the tradition, to be an old man. It is a wise prophet who knows which side to support and who does not allow nationalistic fervour to displace self-interest.

What is curious, however, is the number of commentators who praise Jeremiah endlessly for his bravery and equally condemn out of hand the other prophets for kowtowing to authority. According to the cycle of 27–29, all the risks being taken were by those prophets who preached against Babylon and encouraged resistance to Babylon at home. No risks were taken by those who praised the Babylonians and encouraged submission to their cruel yoke. Conformity to imperialist power was no doubt the wise thing to encourage, but such pusillanimity should not be praised by exegetes as risk-taking. As the oracles against Babylon (50–51) show, there is an alternative position to conformity.

The interpolated attack on the Jerusalem community in vv. 16–19 (not in G) allows a striking contrast to be made between the exiles in Babylon (vv. 5–7) and those who did not go into exile. The future for the exiles is one of settled domesticity and well-being (*šālōm*), whereas Jerusalem's king and people face a horrible future of destruction. Invasion, with its concomitant death by butchery, starvation and disease, will attend them and the deity will make them like rotten fruit. The figs metaphor may be derived from 24.1–3, but it is used in a quite different way from the vision of the two baskets of fruit (perhaps the influence is from 29.17 and 24.1–3 represent a further development). In the vision the figs represent the status of the two communities (exiled and domestic), here the deity turns the home community into something resembling (v. 17 '*like* disgusting figs') rotten figs (rotten in the sense of being too bad to eat – fruit gone off). The people will be driven from their homeland and wherever they are exiled the deity will pursue them with the triad of devastations. Thus wherever they go they will be an object of horror and the nations will hiss them, use them as a curse (v. 18, cf. v. 22), an occasion of appalment and a reproach (cf. 25.9, 18; 42.18; 44.8, 12, 22; also 49.13, 17; 51.37). This terrible pursuit by Yahweh is caused by the people's rejection of the prophetic word.

The horrific fate of Jerusalem and its people in contrast to the *šālōm* of the exiles (in spite of the fact that those exiled in 597 are accused of the same rejection of the divine word in 25.4; 26.5) is not only hyperbolic but also has a political function. It serves the interests of the Babylonian groups. It promotes those who can trace their ancestry to the exiles of 597 over those who remained in the land or who were deported at a later period. The deportation of 597 represents the *Mayflower* of the reconstructed Jerusalem community. All those who were not a part of that event are the special enemies of Yahweh and will be hunted down by him until completely annihilated. Yahweh's future plans (vv. 10–11) only concern the exiles in Babylon, and the myth of the extinction of all other occupants of Palestine (cf. II Chron. 36.20–1) facilitates this belief.

To read the various units in 29 in this way represents an attempt to explain why the tradition should contain strands (such as 24; 29.16–19; 44) where every community, except those in Babylon, is written off in relation to Yahweh's good pleasure for the future. Why is such undisguised hatred of the Jerusalem community so rampant in these strands? Is it simply hyperbole? Ought the exegete not to ask the question 'whose interests are served by such denunciations?'? According to Ezra and Nehemiah political elements came from the Persian court to reorganize Jerusalem, its economy and religion. Are, then, the strands in the Jeremiah tradition which display kindness towards the Babylonian groups and abuse the Jerusalem community in such vilifying terms not evidence of party bias reflecting a situation in which there was conflict between representatives of both communities? Such an explanation, however tentatively it may be advanced here, would help to account for a hostility towards everything non-Babylonian which cannot be explained in any other way.

29.24–32

24 To Shemaiah of Nehelam you shall say: 25 'Thus says the LORD of hosts, the God of Israel: You have sent letters in your name to all the people who are in Jerusalem, and to Zephaniah the son of Maaseiah the priest, and to all the priests, saying, 26 "The LORD has made you priest instead of Jehoiada the priest, to have charge over every madman who prophesies, to put him in the stocks and collar. 27 Now why have you not rebuked Jeremiah of Anathoth who is prophesying to you? 28 For he has sent to us in Babylon, saying, 'Your exile will be long; build houses and live in them, and plant gardens and eat their produce.' " '

29 Zephaniah the priest read this letter in the hearing of Jeremiah the prophet. 30 Then the word of the LORD came to Jeremiah: 31 'Send to all the exiles, saying, "Thus says the LORD concerning Shemaiah of Nehelam: Because Shemaiah has prophesied to you when I did not send him, and has made you trust in a lie, 32 therefore thus says the LORD: Behold, I will punish Shemaiah of Nehelam and his descendants; he shall not have any one living among this people to see the good that I will do to my people, says the LORD, for he has talked rebellion against the LORD." '

[24] MT *w^e'el-š^ema'yāhū hanneḥ^elāmī l'omar lē'mōr*, 'and to Shemaiah the Nehelamite you shall say saying': NEB deletes 'you shall say, saying', G lacks 'saying'; Rudolph, 186–7, treats as a title 'Concerning Shemaiah from Nechlam'. Nehelam is unknown as a place name in the Bible. The gentilic form may refer to a place name or a family; the uncertainty about the name suggests that its form here is part of the literary creation of the story and is opposed to Jeremiah the Anathothite (another gentilic form, v. 27). Yaure 1960, 306–9, understands the name to be Shemaiah the dreamer (cf. v. 8; 27.9; 23.17; 14.14), a prototype of Barjesus, i.e. Elymas the magician, in Acts 13.6–12. He is a prophet inspired by dreams; the Niphal form of *ḥlm*, 'dream', hardly supports this suggestion. **[25]** G lacks 'Thus says Yahweh of hosts, the god of Israel, saying'. MT 24, 25 overload the piece with forms of *'mr*, 'say'. G 'I did not send you in my name; and to Sophonias son of Maasaios the priest say' is a much shorter text than MT, which has developed the story to make it refer the prophetic statement to the priests and people as well. G lacks any reference to a letter at this point (cf. v. 29), whereas MT has *s^epārīm*, 'letters', here but *sēper*, 'letter', in v. 29. **[26]** MT *lihyōt p^eqidīm*, 'to be overseer*s*': G *genesthai epistatēn*, 'to be overseer'. MT *bēt yhwh*, 'house of Yahweh': many mss, Vrs *b^ebēt*, 'in the house'. MT *l^ekol-'īš m^ešuggā' ūmit^enabbē'*, 'over every man who is mad and plays the prophet': i.e. crazy prophesying; 'madman', *m^ešuggā'*, is a synonym for prophet (II Kings 9.11; Hos. 9.7). Cf. 20.2 for the overseer priest with the authority to beat unruly prophets. **[27]** MT *lō' gā'artā*, 'you not rebuke': G *suneloidorēsate*, '(why do) you (plur.) rebuke'. G is quite different from MT in that the piece is directed against the two named characters rather than against Jeremiah. Hence they are challenged about rebuking Jeremiah (G), whereas MT demands of Zephaniah (the brother of Zedekiah in v. 21?) that he should have beaten Jeremiah of Anathoth. MT *hammit^enabbē'*, 'who is playing at being a prophet': cf. NEB 'who poses as a prophet'. **[28]** MT *kī 'al-kēn šālaḥ*, 'for therefore he sent': G^V *dia tou mēnos toutou*, 'during the course of this month'. **[31]** A few mss, G* lack 'the exiles' (BHS); note *lākem* 'to you' here and in v. 27 where the two communities and their prophets are contrasted. Cf. 28.15 for the motif 'making the people trust to what is false'. **[32]** MT *w^elō'-yir'eh*, 'and he will not see': G *tou idein*, 'to see' = *lir'ōt*. G *humin*, 'to you' = *lākem*, for MT *l^e'ammī*, 'to my people'. G lacks 'for he has uttered rebellion against Yahweh', cf. 28.16; Deut. 13.6 (EV5).

In a rather confused section dealing with exchanges of letters between Babylon and Jerusalem the theme of false prophets is continued. MT and G differ in their presentation of the story: in the Hebrew the priest Zephaniah ben Maaseiah (cf. 21.1; 37.3; 52.24) is challenged about his failure to control Jeremiah who is posing as a prophet (cf. NEB), whereas in the Greek the priest is berated for rebuking Jeremiah. In MT *letters* are sent from Babylon concerning the behaviour of the (pseudo-) prophet Jeremiah (cf. II Kings 10.1 for the motif of sending letters to stir up trouble), but in G the material is oracular rather than epistolary. The section appears to be an exchange of abuse between Shemaiah (cf. Uriah ben Shemaiah 26.20) the Nehelamite and Jeremiah the Anathothite (the only occurrence of this gentilic form in the tradition; for similar gentilic forms of Anathoth, cf. I Chron. 12.3; 27.12; II Sam. 23.27 = I Chron. 11.28). As such it is an argument between two prophets, each accusing the other of being wrong. In MT it would appear that this form of mutual abuse is carried on via letters and at a great distance. However, the exchange incorporates the temple priest in charge of madmen who play at being prophets (i.e. act the part of a prophet). In Shemaiah's letter the priest is upbraided for not keeping Jeremiah of Anathoth in check, thus implying the temple location of Jeremiah's activity. The view of Jeremiah as a crazy play-acting prophet is interesting in that it demonstrates the ease with which prophets may abuse each other. This type of abuse, i.e. accusations of posing as a prophet, telling lies, not being sent, making people trust in falsehood, is the stock-in-trade of prophetic conflict. There is no good reason for treating the language used as anything other than the fulminations against one another of members of the *same* profession. That the exchanges are so vituperative and defamatory is part of the process of denunciation common to all prophets. It is the rhetoric of prophecy.

The cause of Shemaiah's attack on Jeremiah is his view of the length of the exile (v. 28, *'arukkāh hī'*, 'it is long', refers to the exile, though the phrase lacks an object, because the rest of the verse is a citation of v. 5). Whereas Jeremiah's letter says nothing about the length of the exile because it does not admit of an end to it, Shemaiah's inference from it is not incorrect. From the standpoint of there being an end to the exile (i.e. Shemaiah's position) the logic of the letter from Jeremiah would entail a lengthy period before any such change in fortunes. Also from Shemaiah's viewpoint such discouraging information coming from Jerusalem must have militated against his own endeavours to maintain the deportees' courage and confidence that soon they would return to their own land. Hence his letter(s) to Zephaniah demanding to know why the overseer had not chastized Jeremiah for such irresponsible behaviour (cf. 20.1–2 for what Shemaiah would have considered the proper response to an irresponsible prophet).

Because Jeremiah is a temple prophet in this cycle (cf. 28.1, 5) it is natural in this story that he should be present for Zephaniah's reading of the letter. Perhaps the overseer summoned him so that he could listen to the complaint about his attitude and behaviour coming from Babylon. Zephaniah's role in the story is minimal: he receives the letter(s) and conveys its (cf. v. 29, 'this letter', in contrast to MT v. 25) contents to Jeremiah. He is part of the story because the priests are one of the main elements in the cycle (27.16; 28.1, 5; 29.1, 25) and much of what happens in the various stories takes place in the presence of the priests. Whether he disciplines Jeremiah or not is not mentioned in this story because its concern is with the exchange between the two prophesying figures. In vv. 30–31 Jeremiah's response is oracular. Yahweh replies to letters yet! The reply to Shemaiah is a public one addressed to all the exiles. Because he has misled the people by making them trust a lie (presumably *šeqer* refers to an implicit proclamation that the exile would be a short one, cf. 27.16; 28.2–4; though no statement of Shemaiah's to that effect appears in the unit) he will be punished by the deity. The reference to Yahweh's visitation (*pqd* v. 32, cf. v.10) ironically mirrors the divine visit of v. 10 and contrasts the fate of Shemaiah and his descendants with that of the descendants of the exiles. When the restoration does take place Shemaiah and his people will have no part in it (cf. 23.34 for the notion of the punishment of a man and his household). Shemaiah's fate is due to his having spoken rebellion against Yahweh (cf. Hananiah's fate 28.16 and the ruling in Deut. 13.5). Thus the Shemaiah story is a fragmentary variant of Hananiah's story and we must assume that the similarities imply that Shemaiah was a preacher of a short exile (a point not stated in the text though perhaps hinted at in v. 28).

What is most curious about the stories in this cycle is the fact that in spite of Hananiah and Shemaiah making the people trust in a lie (cf. the role of Ahab and Zedekiah among the exiles 28.21), only these prophets are punished and the people are not condemned for believing their falsehoods. In the context of the cycle this may not be particularly remarkable but within the tradition it is noteworthy. That Ahab and Zedekiah could commit adultery (29.23) without the community being condemned for adulterous behaviour is peculiar. It is odd in the light of the whole tradition and that oddity justifies the analysis of the material in the cycle as literary creations rather than historical events. The many peculiarities of 27–29 are best explained as being due to the independent origins of the cycle, which have produced a quite late and legendary image of Jeremiah the prophet whose status as the source of the divine word in the community makes him the dominant figure, whether in the Jerusalem temple or among the communities in Babylon. He now bestrides both countries like a prophetic colossus, and opposition to his viewpoint is evidence of being false. More than that, a prophet whose divine word differs from Jeremiah is guilty of 'having uttered rebellion against Yahweh' (Deuteronomistic influence on MT here, cf. Deut. 13.5). Thus to oppose Jeremiah is to be in rebellion against Yahweh. That is the main point of the cycle in its most fully developed form, though the attack on certain views about the duration of the exile is an important element in that presentation. Because certain ideological points dominate the cycle, there is no concern with denouncing the communities which have followed the false proclamations of the condemned prophets (29.16–19 is no exception to this point).

This interpretation of the letter(s) of 29 as fabrication(s) within the cycle of 27–29 differs considerably from that of many exegetes who regard the letter of Jeremiah as a genuine historical document (e.g. Dijkstra 1983). That a prophet might communicate the divine word by written form (tablet or letter) is known from the Mari archives and Akkadian sources (cf. Moran 1969; Pritchard 1969, 623–7), but the biblical traditions do not present the prophets as communicating by such means. The occasional writing of a message for the future is indicated in Isa. 8.1–2; 30.8, but only the Chronicler appears to attribute letter writing to a prophet (Elijah in II Chron. 21.12–15). As the Chronicler has a more developed role for prophets such as Elijah and Jeremiah (cf. II Chron. 35.25 where Jeremiah utters a lament for the dead Josiah, a lamentation conspicuously absent from the book of Jeremiah!), his work cannot be regarded as corroborative evidence of the *historicity* of the story in 29. Dijkstra's claim that 'we may have in Jer xxix 24–32 a complete copy of a real *document humaine*' (1983, 321) is a misreading of the tangled elements in 29.24–32 and fails to take into account the complex traditions forming the cycle of 27–29. In the context of 27–29 the dominant motif is Jeremiah's denunciation of the prophets 'who are prophesying lies' (cf. 27.10, 14, 15, 16; 28.15; 29.9, 21, 23, 31, where *šeqer* is the evaluation of what *all* the other prophets have to say) and, by means of the letter device, that polemic is extended to include the prophets in Babylon in 29. Such a fabrication serves the cycle's main thrust better as an interpretation of 29 than the vain search for evidence of a real letter submerged beneath the surface of the heavily edited narrative.

The book of the restoration of the fortunes: 30–31

A feature of the Jeremiah tradition is the presence of fragments of future hopes scattered throughout the book but lacking a coherent structure and presentation (e.g. 3.14–18; 12.14–17; 16.14–15; 17.24–26; 22.2–4; 23.5–6, 7–8; 24.4–7; 29.10–14; 42.7–12). This lack of a sustained hope is made good with an independent cycle in 30–31 which gathers together numerous poems about the restoration of the nation to its own land and the rebuilding of people, cities and economy. To these poems are added two narrative collections which develop the theme of the restoration of the fortunes (32–33). The central motif of these chapters is future salvation, though the occasional sour note can be detected (e.g. 30.5–7, 23–24; 31.22a, 29–30; 32.3–5, 23–24, 28–35). The hopes expressed by the restoration of the fortunes motif (30.3, 18; 31.23; 32.44; 33.11, 26; cf. 29.14) are modest ones and envisage a future of bucolic pleasures, political and economic security and the reversal of the bitter experiences of the past.

Following on, in the present redaction of the tradition, from Jeremiah's letter to Babylon, the cycle is represented as another of his writings. On four different occasions Jeremiah is said to have written things: 29.1; 30.2; 36.2 (this occasion is developed into the work of his amanuensis Baruch); 51.60. Two of these writings were sent to Babylon and two were addressed to the nation in Palestine – two were destroyed (51.63; 36.23–26, though this scroll was rewritten, 36.32) and two, presumably, were preserved. These different acts of writing should be interpreted as symbolic gestures – as adding something to the spoken word. In 36 and 51.59–64 the significance of the written form lies in its eventual destruction: Jehoiakim condemns himself by his act and Babylon is destroyed by the sinking of the book in the waters of the Euphrates. The letter of 29.4–7 clearly had to be written in order to be sent to Babylon. Only the writing of the book of the restoration of the fortunes remains unexplained. If, however, the writing of the word is part of the magical gesture (cf. Num. 5.23), then the collection of salvation poems in written form is itself one of Jeremiah's performative acts whereby the future is brought into existence. He who is so associated with the destruction of city and nation is here made the one who proclaims the reversal of the word of judgment and the dawn of a new age of restoration. The Book of Consolation affirms a good future for the people of Yahweh: a future not only spoken by Jeremiah but written in a book at the command of Yahweh.

If the cycle adds a dimension lacking in the tradition (cf. the building and planting motifs of 1.10), it also raises problems about its origins and connection with Jeremiah. Apart from the redactional 30.1–3 there is nothing in the cycle which would associate it with him, though there are a number of editorial elements which link it with the book of Jeremiah (e.g. 30.12–14, 23–24). Many commentators attribute it to the prophet Jeremiah, either after the collapse of Jerusalem or in the days of Josiah (e.g. Rudolph; cf. Raitt 1977, 106–27). Since he had proclaimed the complete destruction of city, land and people without residue it is difficult to see how Jeremiah could perform such a volte-face as is entailed in attributing 30–31 to him (see also on 31.1–6). As the cycle shows the marked influence of Hosea and Second Isaiah in places (e.g. 30.9, 10–11; 31.2–6, 7–9; 10–14, 18–20) and shares some common elements with the Ezekiel tradition (e.g. 31.29–30, 33, 38–40), it is preferable to attribute it to the anonymous circles during and after the exile which cherished expectations of restoration (the descendants of the prophets of *šālōm*?). The vagueness of this attribution is balanced by the lack of information available for determining the issue in a reliably historical manner and the contradictions inherent in crediting Jeremiah with the authorship of the cycle.

Deuteronomistic and post-Deuteronomistic influences on the cycle are minimal (cf. 31.31–34), though Böhmer, Herrmann and Thiel find numerous examples and traces of such activity in the text. If the Deuteronomistic outlook on the future may be summarized as the possibility of restoration on the grounds of the nation's turning (*šūb*), then there is little of such influence in the poems (cf. 31.21–22a). The alternative to such a view of future hope is the belief that a divine act of reversal and restoration will create the new age. This is the driving force of the poems in the cycle. Yahweh's love for his people will bring them back from afar and set them up in their own land, and never again shall they be disturbed (cf. Hos. 11.8–9). Apart from the fragments in the tradition already noted, this view of divine action is quite foreign to the spirit of Jeremiah as represented in the poetry and prose sections of the book. There Yahweh's hatred of his people, his fierce wrath and his overwhelming determination to destroy them for ever is the opposite of the love, compassion and tenderness which breathe through 30–31. Here the spirit is more akin to Hosea's and Second Isaiah's, and the cycle must be viewed as having its home in the circles which developed the Hosea-Second Isaiah outlook on the future in the Persian period. That such a cycle is incorporated into the Jeremiah tradition may be due to the redaction of the tradition at a time when such poems were in circulation, and their attachment to Jeremiah gave them a setting they would otherwise have lacked. It also gave them that authority which by now the figure of Jeremiah had acquired. To attribute them to the Jeremiah of the tradition was to underwrite their significance. Thus Jeremiah also became associated with the bucolic hopes for the future and even was made responsible for them. This process suggests a period when material required to be attached to more authoritative work in order to gain a hearing (cf. Ezek. 40–48; Zech. 9–11; 12–14; Malachi). Only the developed theological figure of the tradition could provide this status, and not the rejected 'historical' individual dimly discernible in the text (*contra* Raitt 1977, 126). The attribution of 30–31 to Jeremiah rounds off the development of the paradigmatic figure of the prophet: he now bestrides the culture like a colossus and determines both fate and future of Judah, whether in exile (29.1, 4–7) or its own land (30–31), of the deportees and remnant of 597 (24), of the refugees who flee to Egypt (44), and even of mighty Babylon (50–51). Not only is this achieved by word of mouth (note the almost liturgical quality of 'says Yahweh' in parts of 30–31), but it is also accomplished by the power of his pen.

30.1–4

30 1 The word that came to Jeremiah from the LORD: 2 'Thus says the LORD,
the God of Israel: Write in a book all the words that I have spoken to you.
3 For behold, days are coming, says the LORD, when I will restore the
fortunes of my people, Israel and Judah, says the LORD, and I will bring
them back to the land which I gave to their fathers, and they shall take

possession of it.' 4 These are the words which the LORD spoke concerning Israel and Judah:

[MT 30] = G 37. **[3]** MT *wᵉšabtî 'et-šᵉbût 'ammî yiśrā'ēl wîhûdāh*, 'and I will restore the fortunes of my people Israel and Judah': for the idiom *šûb šᵉbût*, 'restore the fortunes', cf. 29.14 (Notes). BHS treats 'Judah' as an addition to the text here and in v. 4 (cf. Rudolph, 189). This is unnecessary unless 'Israel and Judah' are to be understood as an explanatory gloss on 'my people'; cf. 31.1, 'all the families of Israel'.

The cycle opens with a lengthy redactional introduction which represents the collected poems, sayings and prose pieces in 30–31 as the words of Yahweh spoken to Jeremiah and written by him in a book. The book constituted by this collection is often referred to by scholars as 'the Book of Consolation' because virtually all its contents refer to the salvation of the community. It is therefore in striking contrast to the bulk of the Jeremiah tradition.

The introductory sentence of v. 1 is the standard formulaic preface to the various blocks of material in the tradition (e.g. 7.1; 11.1; 18.1; 21.1; 32.1; 34.1, 8; 35.1; 40.1) and its use here integrates the independent cycle of 30–31 into the book of Jeremiah. Its secondary nature is also evidenced by the fact that what follows in vv. 2–4 contains an overload of further redactional material stressing the oracular nature of the cycle, to which v. 1 adds yet another assertion of the divine origin of Jeremiah's work. The representation of Jeremiah writing all the divine words in a book reflects a period when the spoken word has become the written word and there has been a significant shift in the role of the prophetic figure. By attributing all that follows to Jeremiah, the salvation oracles of a later period are given an authority which they would not have had by themselves. This book written by Jeremiah becomes a statement about the future (cf. 51.60; Isa. 30.8) which is summarized by v. 3. The fortunes of Yahweh's people will be restored (the idiom *šûb šᵉbût* may contain a word-play on *šûb*) in the future when Yahweh brings back (*hᵃšîbōtîm* an important use of *šûb* in the tradition) the people to the land given to their fathers. The least that is presupposed by this introduction is the exile of 587. To delete 'Judah' from vv. 3–4 in order to make the cycle refer to northern Israel and therefore represent the preaching of the young Jeremiah in the time of Josiah (cf. Rudolph, 188–9; Lohfink 1981) is quite unwarranted. The expansion of the term 'my people' as 'Israel and Judah' may reflect the recognition of the widespread dispersal of various tribal elements over a long period of time and the hope that in the future they would all be reunited in their own land (cf. 2.4; 31.1; Ezek. 37.15–23; contrast Zech. 11.7–14). This is more akin to the Chronicler's work with its programmatic appeal to all Israel, and it may be the case that the Book of Consolation is intended to be part of the argument for a unified and inclusive community in the future (cf. Williamson 1977b for such an analysis of Chronicles). Given Jeremiah's backing the collection of discrete materials is presented as the divine word in oracular form (hence the repeated 'says Yahweh', using different forms in v. 3 and the further introductory title in v. 4). All these hopes for the future are Yahweh's word to Jeremiah and, in a period when that figure had acquired either legendary status in the community or had become the focal point of the tradition, therefore authoritative.

When so many diverse elements are collected together and presented as the work of one person yet clearly contain the influences of other circles (e.g. Second Isaiah's), it becomes very difficult for the modern exegete to tease out the different strands and attribute them to specific sources with any degree of accuracy. The Book of Consolation poses this problem in its most extreme form (cf. the oracles against the nations in 46–51), and in the following analysis it will be argued that the collection is both anonymous and contains many disparate elements. Similarities between 30–31 and the poems in Second Isaiah cannot be demonstrated to be the influence of Jeremiah on the anonymous prophet of the exile (*contra* Paul 1969), without too many assumptions being made in one direction. Only in the final redaction is the cycle incorporated into the Jeremiah tradition and therefore attributed to him by means of the editorial vv. 1–4. Constructing complex accounts of how the one person could be prophet of judgment and *also at the same time* speaker of salvation (e.g. Raitt 1977 and many exegetes) involves too many major presuppositions to be a correct analysis and applies to the finished work of redaction rather than the supposed figure behind the tradition (cf. Kaiser 1975, 223, for similar strictures about treating Isaiah as a preacher of repentance).

The position of 30–31 as an independent cycle following on immediately from another independent cycle in 27–29 may be explained in terms of the associative links between the dominant motif of the good Yahweh will do to his people in 30–31 and the reference to that motif in 29.32. There Shemaiah of Nehelam is denied a share in that good, whereas in 30–31 the substantive elements in that good fortune are illustrated in a series of poems. From all these benefits Shemaiah and his descendants will be excluded. Furthermore, 30–31 focus on the restoration of the fortunes of Israel and Judah where 27–29 concentrate on the subjugation and dispersal of the community. What is taken away to and by Babylon is restored to the land of Israel in 30–31. Thus the two cycles work quite well together as a balanced account of judgment and destruction on the one hand and salvation and restoration on the other hand. Their origins and central motifs are very different, but together they form a dialectical element in the tradition which links past (judgment) and future (restoration) through the proclamation of the word of Yahweh by Jeremiah (the prophet).

30.5–7

5 'Thus says the LORD:
We have heard a cry of panic,
of terror, and no peace.
6 Ask now, and see,
can a man bear a child?
Why then do I see every man
with his hands on his loins like a woman in labour?
Why has every face turned pale?
7 Alas! that day is so great
there is none like it;
it is a time of distress for Jacob;
yet he shall be saved out of it.'

---

[5] MT *kī-kōh 'āmar yhwh*, 'for thus says Yahweh': a redactional addition which turns the report of the nation's distress into a divine oracle and typifies the overload of redactional indicators of oracularity in vv. 1–5a. MT *šāmā'nū*, 'we have heard': G *akousesthe*, 'you will hear'. Rudolph, 188, reads *šāma'tī*, 'I have heard', to balance *rā'ītī*, 'I have seen' in v. 6b; cf. Volz, 281, who reads 'I have heard' and accounts for MT as being due to the influence of 6.24. Böhmer 1976, 57, also reads *šāma'tī*. MT *paḥad*, 'terror': a term associated with the day of Yahweh motif (cf. Isa. 2.10–17; Amos 5.18–20; Zeph. 1.18; Böhmer, 57–8); this motif does not appear in the Jeremiah tradition (apart from in 46 and 47). **[6]** G has a double reading of the line 'why do I see every man with his hands upon his hips?' which represents in part an inner-Greek corruption (Janzen 1973, 29). MT *kayyōlēdāh*, 'as a woman giving birth': cf. 31.8; Micah. 5.2 (EV 3); lacking in G in spite of its double reading, hence a late gloss in MT (Rudolph, 190; Janzen, 49). MT *l*ᵉ*yērāqōn*, '. . . to paleness': i.e. every face turns green (cf. *yereq*, 'green, grass'). G *eis ikteron egenēthē*, 'to become pale', reading *hwy* (v. 7) as *hyw* (*hāyū*); cf. BHS, which incorporates it into v. 6. G (Ziegler, 350; cf. Ziegler 1958, 97; Janzen, 29) represents inner-Greek corruption and a number of doublets here. **[7]** MT *hōy*, 'woe, alas': cf. G, BHS; Janzen, 73. MT *ūmimmennāh yiwwāšē'a*, 'and from it he shall be saved': before the addition of vv. 10–11 the original form of this phrase may have been 'and will he be saved from it?', cf. Bright, 297; Holladay 1962b, 53–4; Lundbom 1975, 33.

The first poem in the collection has very little to do with the introductory phrase in v. 5a or v. 4. The poem is a description of human response to the terrible day of Yahweh. Panic seizes the people, and even the men are terrified to the point where they are behaving like pregnant women giving birth (MT). The effect of the occasion on the men is to make them act pregnant: hands on hips and faces turning green! Such a transformation of men (see on 31.22b) into creatures caught in the agonies of childbirth indicates the aweful terror of that day. Trembling and horror without any wellbeing (*šālōm*) seize the community and the state of the men is graphic evidence of the disaster. The day is so great that there is none to match it. Such a nonpareil day is described as 'a time of distress for Jacob'. Nothing in this report of public reaction to the terrifying time of suffering suggests an oracular announcement, though the last phrase in v. 7 may represent a hint of (divine) salvation or a word of despair. It is this terrible scene which raises the curtain on the restoration of the fortunes cycle.

The image of destruction as comparable to a woman giving birth, i.e. the sudden onslaught of pains over which the person has no control, is to be found in 4.31; 13.21b; 49.24; 50.43, but here it is used in a different way. As a metaphor of the community suffering invasion the image is striking, but in the poem here it is used to convey something beyond that experience. The men of the community, i.e. members of the nation rather than a metaphor of it, are the ones seized by pains as if they were pregnant women. It is the transformation, even the transmogrification, of the normal patterns of life which characterizes this particular day (cf. 31.22 for a different transformation). Depicted in this manner the day cannot simply be 597 or 587 for, apart then from the inappropriateness of v. 7b, 'he shall be saved out of it' (but see Notes), there is something preternatural about it. Only the almost apocalyptic catastrophe of 4.23–26 comes close to the mood of this poem, and its significance must be sought in that direction. What the poem is about is the day of Yahweh. This is a motif to be found in many prophetic traditions (e.g. Isa. 2.10–17; 13.6–16; Obad. 15–21; Joel 2.1–11, 30–32 [MT 3.3–5]; Zeph. 1.14–18), though it is lacking in the Jeremiah tradition (apart from elements in the oracles against the nations e.g. 46.10; 47.4). Whatever the motif may have contributed to understanding various historical disasters (cf. Amos 5.18–20), its real function is to point forward to a time when all the nations which have opposed Israel for so long will be destroyed by the deity. In that destruction Zion and Jacob will escape (cf. Joel 2.32; Obad. 17, 18; Zeph. 3.11–20). As a preface to the collection of salvation oracles the poem creates the atmosphere for the development of that point.

30.8–9

8 'And it shall come to pass in that day, says the LORD of hosts, that I will
break the yoke from off their neck, and I will burst their bonds, and strangers
shall no more make servants of them. 9 But they shall serve the LORD their
God and David their king, whom I will raise up for them.'

---

[8] MT *'ullō mē'al ṣawwā'rekā*, 'his yoke from your neck': = Isa. 10.27; who is 'you' here? G *autōn*, 'their', i.e. the people; Rudolph, 190, reads 'his' (BHS), i.e. Jacob's. MT *ūmōsrōtekā*, 'and your bonds': G 'their', cf. BHS, RSV. MT *w^{e}lō'-ya'ab^{e}dū-bō*, 'and they shall not serve him': cf. *'bd b* in 22.13, 'they shall not use him as a servant' (24.14; 27.7). G 'they shall no longer serve foreigners'; *autoi*, 'them', for *bō*, 'him'. **[9]** Cf. Hos. 3.5, '. . . and they shall seek Yahweh their god and David their king': both texts use the same Hebrew phrases *'et(-)yhwh '^{e}lōhēhem w^{e}'et dāwid malkām*. On the relationship between the two references cf. Emmerson 1984, 101–13, who allows for the possibility that Hos. 3.5 belongs to the primary stratum of Hosea.

A brief prose unit speaks of the future in terms of a divine liberation of the people from servitude to foreigners (contrast the divine imposition of such servitude in 27–28; for a different use of these images cf. 2.20; 5.5). This futuristic hope is also found in Isa. 10.27a (cf. Isa. 9.4). Its position here is as an explanation of the phrase 'but he shall be saved out of it'. Jacob, i.e. Judah-Israel, will be freed from foreign domination (cf. v. 3), and the only servitude it will know in the future is to Yahweh and its own king (cf. Amos 9.11 for the figure of the deity raising up [*'āqīm*, 'I will raise up'] the fallen booth of David). No longer will the nation serve foreign kings but their own Davidic king will be their ruler. This belief in the restoration of the deposed dynasty of David also appears in 23.5–6 where it is an appendix to the cycle on royal matters. It represents a hope which was kept alive in certain circles after 587 (cf. 33.14–16, 17, 21–22, 26; Ezek. 34.23–24; 37.24–25), a hope which *never* materialized. The belief that Yahweh would break the yoke of foreigners is also to be found elsewhere (e.g. Nahum 1.13, where Assyria's domination is brought to an end by Yahweh). But the combination of the two hopes in vv. 8–9 reflects some circle which identified the defeat of the foreigners as the occasion when expectations about the revival (*qūm*) of the royal house would be realized.

The distance between different parts of the tradition can be seen in a comparison of 30.8–9 with 2.25; 3.13 where 'strangers' have a rather different meaning. In the pious discourses of 2–3 'strangers' refer to alien cults among which the people pursue their own goals. In the cycles represented by 25.8–14; 27–29; 30–31, 'strangers' and 'servitude' belong to the experience of foreign domination. The resolution of such servitude will mean the service of their own god and king, a very different concept from that condemned in the discourses. The common elements of 30.9 and Hos. 3.5 point to the shared streams of tradition which the book of Jeremiah has in common with so many other biblical traditions. It is therefore unnecessary to maintain that the hope for David refers to Jeremiah's early preaching (*contra* Weiser, 269; cf. Böhmer 1976, 60), because the association of Jeremiah with the time of Josiah is a very late strand in the tradition which does not represent an actual preaching ministry before 609. The raising up of a king for the people (cf. the raising up of a prophet in 29.15; Deut. 18.15, 18) indicates the non-existence of a king of their own and therefore points to a period when the Davidic house was no longer a sovereign power in the land (cf. Amos 9.11). Domination by foreigners characterizes the post-587 period (especially after 539, when the Persians did not permit independent kings in the provincial areas of the empire). Although Hos. 3.5 may be an authentic element in the Hosea tradition (cf.

Emmerson), its use in 30.9 would not necessarily indicate the same hope as expressed by Hosea, though if applied to Judah it would presumably reflect the loss of monarchy (cf. Hos. 3.4). The presence of similar elements in different traditions raises difficult questions about interpretation. The most difficult of these concerns the precise relationship between original meaning and present setting. In the cycle of 30–31 the restoration of the fortunes of Israel and Judah is the controlling motif which determines the meaning of the various elements in the collection. The elements have their own specific meanings but those are subordinated to the central thrust of the cycle. Discrete strands contribute to that cycle but lose much of their original force by being associated with so many different elements. Thus the near apocalyptic sense of distress in 30.5–7 is developed by the addition of vv. 8–9 in the direction of a much more mundane outlook on the future as a time when foreign domination will disappear and the Davidic house will rule again.

30.10–11

10 'Then fear not, O Jacob my servant, says the LORD,
nor be dismayed, O Israel;
for lo, I will save you from afar,
and your offspring from the land of their captivity.
Jacob shall return and have quiet and ease,
and none shall make him afraid.
11 For I am with you to save you, says the LORD;
I will make a full end of all the nations
among whom I scattered you,
but of you I will not make a full end.
I will chasten you in just measure,
and I will by no means leave you unpunished.'

[10–11] = 46.27–28. G lacks them here because the oracles against the nations precede the cycle of 30–31 in G. G usually lacks such doublets, though whether by reason of omitting repeats or because such repeats are a feature of the second edition represented by MT divides scholars (the latter is the more likely case). **[10]** 46.27 lacks *nᵉ'um yhwh*, 'says Yahweh'. MT *'abdī ya'ᵃqōb*, 'my servant Jacob': cf. 'Jacob my servant', Isa. 44.1; 45.4; also 48.20. Throughout Second Isaiah the names Israel, Jacob, Judah, Jerusalem, Zion are used interchangeably to refer to the exiles or those living around and in Jerusalem (e.g. 40.1–2, 27; 41.8, 21, 27; 42.24; 43.14–15; esp. 48.1–2). **[11]** Cf. 46.28, where the first line repeats the first line of the previous verse and the phrase *kī-'itt^ekā 'anī*, 'for I am with you' (v. 11; cf. 1.8) is at the end of the first line. MT *h^apiṣōtīkā*, 'I have scattered you': 46.28 *hiddaḥtīkā*, 'I have driven you'. MT *'ak 'ōt^ekā*, 'only of you': 46.28 *w^e'ōt^ekā*, 'but you'. For the motif 'discipline with justice' cf. 10.24. Cf. 4.27; 5.10, 18 for the motif 'not make a full end'.

This brief poem expresses hope for the people's return from captivity in terms derived from the circles which produced Second Isaiah and added elements to the Jeremiah tradition. It combines the motif of the return with the belief in the destruction of the nations. If Yahweh has not spared his own people, then the nations will suffer even more than Israel (cf. 25.29). Again the context of the piece is Israel's exile and the nations' domination over the people, and its content concerns the reversal of these factors. The tendency of the poems to refer to the people as Israel or Jacob rather than Judah (apart from redactional and additional strands, e.g. 30.3, 4; 31.23–24, 27, 31) is not a reflection of the northern origins of the poems but indicates the use of a wide variety of terms for Judah in the exilic and later periods (hence Zion in 30.17; 31.6, 12, 38–40). This kind of language is at home in the Second Isaiah tradition and reflects the development of the patriarchal stories in the sixth century as a means of bypassing the problems of history in favour of theological constructs (cf. Van Seters 1975). In a context of salvation the patriarchal image of Jacob is more congenial than the historical images of the nation. Thus it is that the community may be called 'Jacob my servant' in a cycle far removed from the other use of 'servant' in the tradition (e.g. 2.14). The god who is far off (cf. 23.23) will save the nation which is afar in captivity and return it to its homeland, where it will enjoy peace and quiet (without the panic referred to in v. 5). The saviour god will annihilate the enemies of Jacob (*kālāh*, cf. Nahum 1.9) among whom the exiles have been scattered.

In a period of such divine annihilation (cf. v. 7) it is important to be able to make a distinction between the nations and Israel. That differentiation is made in terms of a partial destruction of Israel in contrast to the complete wiping out of the other nations. This division between the divine punishment of Israel and destruction of the nations makes vv. 10–11 fit the cycle of 30–31 better than the cycle of 46–51 (cf. 46.26). The view of Israel's sufferings in the period described by v. 11 is that of just (*mišpāṭ*) discipline. Such an understanding of the nation's appalling experience is the same as that expressed in the communal prayer of 10.24–25. There the community prays for Yahweh's just measure (*mišpāṭ*) of correction lest he make them too few to survive (cf. 29.6; 30.19), but also appeals to him to pour out his anger on those nations who not only do not know him but also have laid *Jacob* waste. Part of the function of the coming great apocalyptic destruction of the nations will be Yahweh's just annihilation of all those who have destroyed Israel. In that terrible period Israel will again suffer, but will survive, and in returning to the homeland will face a secure future because there will be none left to induce any further panic (v. 10).

The priestly oracle of salvation (an important form in the construction of the oracles of Second Isaiah, cf. Isa. 41.10, 13, 14; 43.1, 5; 44.2; 54.4; Westermann 1969, 68–9, 71–3) provides the initial motif of the poem 'fear not'. Often it announces the assuring word of confidence after a lament has stated the individual or communal complaint about present circumstances. As such vv. 10–11 would make a fitting response to vv. 5–7, where the terrible day of Jacob's distress may be regarded as equivalent to a formal lament (vv. 8–9 interrupt the connection and must be regarded as secondary additions to the cycle). The great liturgical songs of confidence which characterize much of Second Isaiah provide a fitting note of comfort for the community enduring Jacob's distress. 'Fear not my servant Jacob, you will be saved and will return from distant lands to enjoy peace and quiet in your own land without hindrance from others.' This reassurance of salvation, i.e. return to the homeland, necessarily contains a reference to the destruction of the other nations because from 597 onwards the foreign powers have plagued Jacob's existence. Although suffering greatly at the hands of these nations, Jacob has not undergone complete annihilation. In the coming destruction of the nations Jacob will survive still to enjoy a good future. Hints of this belief can be found in Part I of the tradition (cf. 4.27b; 5.10, 18) and, although ambiguous, give rise to certain tensions within the text there. The different streams which feed the tradition provide the formal elements of these contradictions, but the communities which developed the traditions were no doubt able to resolve the difficulties to their own satisfaction.

30.12–17

12 'For thus says the LORD:
Your hurt is incurable,
and your wound is grievous.
13 There is none to uphold your cause,
no medicine for your wound,
no healing for you.
14 All your lovers have forgotten you;
they care nothing for you;
for I have dealt you the blow of an enemy,
the punishment of a merciless foe,
because your guilt is great,
because your sins are flagrant.
15 Why do you cry out over your hurt?
Your pain is incurable.
Because your guilt is great,
because your sins are flagrant,
I have done these things to you.
16 Therefore all who devour you shall be devoured,
and all your foes, every one of them, shall go into captivity;
those who despoil you shall become a spoil,
and all who prey on you I will make a prey.
17 For I will restore health to you,
and your wounds I will heal,
says the LORD,
because they have called you an outcast:
"It is Zion, for whom no one cares!" '

---

[12] MT *'ānūš lᵉšibrēk*, 'incurable is your fracture': G *anestēsa suntrimma*, 'I have brought destruction'; *lᵉ* may be emphatic here (Nötscher 1953, 380) cf. 9.2 (EV 3), but Rudolph, 190, reads it as *lāk šibrēk* (cf. BHS). For *'ānūš*, 'incurable', cf. v. 15a; 15.18; 17.9, 16. **[13]** MT *'ēn-dān dīnēk lᵉmāzōr*, 'there is none who pleads your cause, concerning injury': for *māzōr*, 'injury', cf. Hos. 5.13; 'oozing infection' (Andersen and Freedman 1980, 413) from *zūr*, 'squeeze pus', cf. Isa. 1.6. MT is either a failure to understand the metaphor or a variant (cf. Bright, 271); Rudolph reads *rikkukīm*, 'soothings, alleviation' (cf. *rukkᵉkāh baššāmen*, 'soothing with oil', Isa. 1.6). NEB 'there can be no remedy for your sore, the new skin cannot grow'; RSV 'no medicine for your wound, no healing for you'. MT *rᵉpu'ōt*, 'healings'; Rudolph treats as a gloss, though it correctly interprets *tᵉ'alāh*, 'comes up', i.e. 'new skin coming on the wounded flesh' (NEB); cf. 46.11. **[14]** MT *mūsar 'akzārī*, 'the discipline of a cruel one': cf. 6.23; 50.42; if the absolute form *mūsār* is read, then the phrase means 'cruel discipline'. The lines 'because your guilt is great, because your sins are flagrant' are probably a repetition from v. 15b (G lacks v. 15, which may be due to the repeated lines in 14–15). **[15]** MT *tiz'aq*, 'you cry out': masc. form, but the whole poem uses fem. forms because it refers to the city Zion. MT *'āśītī 'ēlleh lāk*, 'I have done these things to you': cf. 4.18 *'āśō 'ēlleh lāk* 'he has done these things to you' (see BHS). **[16]** MT *lākēn kol*, 'therefore all': but there is no logical connection between vv. 15, 16 which would justify *lākēn*; Rudolph, 192, treats as a dittography and reads *wᵉkol*, 'and all' (BHS). MT *kullām baššᵉbī yēlēkū*, 'all of them will go into captivity': G *kreas autōn pan edontai*, 'all eat their own flesh' = *kullōh bᵉśārām yō'kēlū*. MT probably represents variants: 'all your foes, all of them'. K *s'syk*; Q mss *šōsaik* = *šōssaik* (BHS), 'your plunderers' (*šāsas* a form of *šāšāh* cf. BDB, 1042): K an Aramaized form. Some G recensions produce v. 15b in the middle of v. 16. **[17]** Rudolph reverses the first two clauses as being more appropriate and transfers *nᵉ'um yhwh*, 'says Yahweh', to the end of the verse. G has 'from the grievous wound' for MT 'from your wound'. MT *ṣiyyōn*, 'Zion': G *thēreuma hēmon*, 'our prey' = *ṣēdēnū*.

This longer poem describes the condition of the nation or city (the personification is feminine) in metaphors drawn from illness and injury. Some of the metaphors appear in poems in Part I (cf. 8.18–22; 10.19; 14.17). If the poem appears to be out of place in a collection of salvation oracles its inclusion in the cycle may be justified by the concluding vv. 16–17 (added for that purpose?). The community has suffered greatly because of its own shortcomings (cf. Isa. 1.5–6) and has been abandoned by its lovers (cf. 2.25, 33; 3.1–2). It is a wretched sight – battered and broken, bleeding and oozing pus, untreated and without medical attention. Different meanings may be given to these metaphors, but within the cycle the dominant significance of the poem is probably as a lament for the terrible damage done to the nation by invasion and deportation. The savage attacks on it by the Babylonians have destroyed the body politic and the desperately wounded woman lies there bleeding to death. The images and their significance are suddenly reversed in vv. 16–17 and the broken flesh becomes whole again. The deity provides the healing which is lacking in the community. He turns the tables on the enemy and they go into captivity because they have despised the outcast Zion.

The poem summarizes the community's recent history in terms which identify the causes of its terrible condition as the number and strength of its sins (vv. 14b, 15b) and yet permit the transformation of its state. There is in the poem a fluctuating explanation which makes Yahweh the enemy because of the community's sinfulness and yet blames the external enemies for what has happened. If the terrible wounds are really self-inflicted (vv. 12–15), the possibility of healing comes about because the deity acts against the adversaries of the city. The two different kinds of explanation belong to separate sections of the poem (vv. 12–15, 16–17) and are only loosely connected (*lākēn*, 'therefore', in v. 16 lacks logical force). But without a reversal of the community's state the poem would have no place in this cycle. The identification of the victim as Zion in v. 17 (different in G) accounts for the feminine forms used throughout the poem and confirms the view that the cycle is about Judah and Jerusalem, whatever names are used in the different sections. The enemy is not identified in specific terms, though elsewhere the destruction of the Babylonians is justified on the grounds of their treatment of Judah, Israel and Zion (50.28, 33–34; 51.6, 10, 24, 35, 49; cf. the reversal of fates in Isa. 49.25–26; 51.22–23).

30.18–22

18 'Thus says the LORD:
Behold, I will restore the fortunes of the tents of Jacob,
and have compassion on his dwellings;
the city shall be rebuilt upon its mound,
and the palace shall stand where it used to be.
19 Out of them shall come songs of thanksgiving,
and the voices of those who make merry.
I will multiply them, and they shall not be few;
I will make them honoured, and they shall not be small.
20 Their children shall be as they were of old,
and their congregation shall be established before me;
and I will punish all who oppress them.
21 Their prince shall be one of themselves,
their ruler shall come forth from their midst;
I will make him draw near, and he shall approach me,
for who would dare of himself to approach me?
says the LORD.
22 And you shall be my people,
and I will be your God.'

---

[18] MT *hinᵉnī-šāb šᵉbūt*, 'look, I will restore the fortunes': cf. 29.14; 30.3;

31.23; 32.44; 33.7, 11, 26; 48.47; 49.6, 39 for this concept. G lacks 'of the tents': a pastoral image balancing 'dwellings' in the Hebrew poetry. For *raḥēm*, 'have compassion', in a positive sense in the Jeremiah tradition, only here and 31.20; 33.26; cf. 12.15; Isa. 49.10, 13, 15; 54.8, 10; 55.7; 60.10. G *kai aichmalōsian autou*, 'and his prisoners', for MT *ūmiškᵉnōtāyw*, 'and his dwellings' = *ūšᵉbītō* (BHS). MT *'īr 'al-tillāh*, 'the city upon its tell', i.e. the mound of the ruins of a city; the sing. may refer to Jerusalem or be a collective referring to the rebuilding of the towns of Judah. MT *wᵉ'armōn 'al-mišpāṭō*, 'and the citadel upon its accustomed place': *mišpāṭ* here may mean 'plan' (cf. BDB, 1049), 'proper place' (JPSB), 'familiar household' (NEB), 'accustomed place' (Rudolph), 'rightful place' (Weiser), 'where it used to be' (RSV). **[19]** G lacks *wᵉhikbadtīm wᵉlō' yiṣ'ārū*, 'and I will make them honoured and they will not be insignificant': cf. Job 14.21 for the contrast between being honoured and being despised. Cf. 10.24; 29.6 for the motifs of population and depopulation. **[20]** MT *wᵉhāyū bānāyw kᵉqedem*, 'and their sons shall be as of old': G *kai eiseleusontai hoi huioi autōn hōs to proteron*, 'and their sons shall go in (= *ūbā'ū*?) as before'; cf. 46.26b; Lam. 5.21. MT *wa'ᵃdātō*, 'and its assembly': i.e. its sacred congregation (cf. 26.9, 17, where *qhl* is used). The sacral protected status of the community is demonstrated by the divine punishment (*pqd*) of its oppressors. **[21]** MT *wᵉhāyāh 'addīrō mimmennū*, 'and its leader shall be from it': Rudolph reads this as *wᵉhāyāh 'addīr mēhem*, 'and their leader shall be from them', i.e. one of their own rather than their oppressors, cf. vv. 8–9. Cf. 14.3; 25.34–36 for *'addīr*, 'leader, chieftain, noble'; for *mōšēl*, 'ruler' cf. 22.30; 33.26; Micah 5.2 (MT 1). Deut. 17.15 stipulates that the king should come 'from the midst of your brethren'; here the leader is a cultic figure rather than a king, as 21b makes clear. G *kai sunaxō autous, kai apostrepsousin pros me*, 'and I will gather them, and they shall return to me', for *wᵉhiqrabtīw wᵉniggaš 'ēlāy*, 'and I shall bring him near and he shall approach me'. MT *'ārab 'et-libbō*, lit. 'he gives his mind in pledge': i.e. who would dare risk giving his mind as security to be so bold as to approach me? Cf. NEB 'no one ventures of himself'. **[22]** G lacks this verse; it may be a pious addition here summing up the force of vv. 18–21 or reflecting 31.1. The shift in person indicates its secondary nature.

The devastations caused by invasion and defeat reduced the Judaean territory to a landscape of ruins and greatly depopulated areas. Any restoration of the fortunes of the people (vv. 3, 18) would have to focus on programmes of rebuilding and repopulation. These are therefore the concern of this poem. The reconstruction of the community, in particular the towns, strongholds, population and organization of the sacred assembly, is the core of the restoration of the people's fortunes. The key to this concept is *šûb*, the 'turning' or 'reversal' of what the long years of destructive neglect have entailed for Judaean society. The divine anger and hatred are turned to compassion (*rḥm*), the mounds of ruins are transformed into cities as used to be the case (*mišpāṭ*), the funerary laments and bitter weeping (cf. 9.17–22; 14.17; Lamentations) are changed to songs and sounds of merrymaking, and the pathetically few people become many and weighty with honour. Things will become the way they used to be (v. 20 'as they were of old'). The sacred congregation will once again be constituted before the divine presence and will have a protected status (cf. 2.3). And instead of being dominated by foreigners (cf. v. 8; 27.12–15), their leader will be one of their own people. Furthermore, access to the divine presence will be permitted to the leader (G different) so that the assembly will be a properly constituted and represented cultic community. The absence of a king here (contrast v. 9; 23.5; 33.17, 21) indicates a programme of rebuilding the community as a theocratic assembly in which the royal status of the leaders is not an important element (cf. Ezek. 40–48). Yet the main features of the poem are to be found in a number of sources elsewhere: e.g. rebuilding of the cities of Judah (Isa. 44.26–28; 49.17; Ezek. 36.10, 33–36), repopulation of the nation (3.16; Isa. 49.20–21; 54.1–3; Ezek. 36.8–15), and the setting of the divine sanctuary in the midst of the people (Ezek. 37.26–28). All these shared elements are indicative of the restoration programme of the Persian period.

The glossator's addition of v. 22 makes an admirable summary of the poem by spelling out the implications of the great restoration of the nation's fortunes. The people will become Yahweh's people and he their god (cf. 31.1, 33; 32.38). They will become a theocracy in which the ruler will be one of their own people (cf. Micah 5.2) and foreign oppression will disappear under divine protection. All the defective institutions of the past will be put right and a harmonious community will enjoy in the future a mythical past (cf. v. 20). Elements of this hope betray the influence of Deuteronomistic ideas in which the historical plan of Yahweh is designed to produce the result specified in v. 22 (cf. Deut. 7. 6; Herrmann 1965, 221–2). The great upheavals of the sixth century have created the conditions in which, with the restoration of Israel's fortunes, the plan may be realized. The destruction of the old institutions has cleared the ground for rebuilding a new community which will combine the old and the new in the proportions believed to be desirable. Then the reciprocal relationship of v. 22 will be achieved.

30.23–24

23 Behold the storm of the LORD!
Wrath has gone forth,
a whirling tempest;
it will burst upon the head of the wicked.
24 The fierce anger of the LORD will not turn back
until he has executed and accomplished
the intents of his mind.
In the latter days you will understand this.

[23–24] = 23.19–20 (see Notes there).

The occurrence of these verses in two rather different contexts raises questions about the appropriateness of the unit in either place. It would be difficult to demonstrate that one context is better than the other (polemic against the prophets cycle in 23 or Book of Consolation cycle in 30), though some commentators (e.g. Bright, 152) think that the verses make a splendid fit in 23.19–20. Here the image of the divine storm breaking on the heads of the wicked may seem inappropriate contextually, but if the oppressors of Jacob are understood as the wicked a case may be made for reading vv. 23–24 as a reminder of the divine wrath about to fall upon the foreign nations (cf. vv. 8, 11, 16, 20b). It is not a strong case, but neither placement of these verses is contextually felicitous. 31.1 picks up the final line of the unit and identifies the turning back of the divine anger (*šūb*) with the restoration of the people to their own land. This use of *šūb*, 'turn', provides a closure for vv. 18–22 (cf. *šāb šᵉbūt*, 'turn the fortunes') and also with v. 3, so that a case could be argued for greater integration of the unit in 30 than 23. Only in the future, i.e. the latter days, will the people understand that Yahweh's destruction of the wicked is the prelude to the nation's restoration of fortunes in the homeland. The terrible day of Jacob's distress (v. 7) is also the time when Yahweh will turn the people's fate. In the cycle in 23 the wicked are identified with the prophets; here they are the oppressors of Israel. G has the repeat also, so the placing of the unit here (as well as in 23.19–20) reflects the double use of it in the first edition. Such floating units, of which the Jeremiah tradition has a considerable number, demonstrate the flexibility of the redactional construction of the book without contributing to the exegete's task of understanding why doublets should be used.

31.1–6

311 'At that time, says the LORD, I will be the God of all the families
of Israel, and they shall be my people.'
2 Thus says the LORD:
'The people who survived the sword
found grace in the wilderness;
when Israel sought for rest,
3 the LORD appeared to him from afar.
I have loved you with an everlasting love;
therefore I have continued my faithfulness to you.
4 Again I will build you, and you shall be built,
O virgin Israel!
Again you shall adorn yourself with timbrels,
and shall go forth in the dance of the merrymakers.
5 Again you shall plant vineyards
upon the mountains of Samaria;
the planters shall plant,
and shall enjoy the fruit.
6 For there shall be a day when watchmen will call
in the hill country of Ephraim:
"Arise, and let us go up to Zion,
to the LORD our God." '

[MT 31] = G 38. **[1]** MT *lᵉkōl mišpᵉḥōt*, 'to all the families of': G *tō genei*, 'to the family'. The plur. may represent the development of the second edition in terms of the widespread diaspora; cf. 'all the families of the house of Israel', 2.4; 'all the families of the kingdom of the north', 1.15; 'all the families of the north', 25.9 (see Notes on 1.15; 25.9). This verse functions as a heading to the collection in 31 (cf. 30.3, 4); 30.22 is a simpler form of v. 1. **[2]** MT *māṣā' ḥēn bammidbār 'am śᵉrīdē ḥāreb*, lit. 'he found grace in the wilderness the people survivors of the sword': G *euron thermon en eremō meta olōlotōn*, 'I found him warm in the desert with them that were slain by the sword'; cf. Ex. 32.12–17 for the motif 'find grace, favour'. Rudolph, 192, reads *kammidbār*, 'as in the wilderness', i.e. not in the wilderness as such but *like* finding in the desert a survivor from a battle. The oracular introduction *kōh 'āmar yhwh*, 'thus says Yahweh', is formal here, as the divine speech does not begin until v. 3b (cf. Bright, 280; Rudolph). MT *hālōk lᵉhargīʿō yiśrā'ēl*, lit. 'going to find him rest Israel': BHS reads *hōlēk lᵉmargōʿō* (with A, Symm; cf. 6.16) 'going for his rest'; cf. *lō' targīʿa*, 'you will not find rest', Deut. 28.64. **[3]** MT *mērāḥōq yhwh nir'āh lī*, 'from afar Yahweh appeared to *me*': G *autō*, 'to him', and lacking *wᵉ*, 'and', of next word suggests *lō*, 'to him', is what MT should be. MT *'ᵃhabtīk*, 'I have loved *you*'; fem. object here refers to 'virgin Israel' of v. 4 rather than the 'he' of v. 2. MT *mᵉšaktīk ḥāsed*, lit. 'I drew you (with) loving devotion': cf. the similar metaphor in Hos. 11.4 *māšak ḥesed*, 'draw (with) loving devotion' (this is a reconstructed reading of MT there, cf. Andersen and Freedman 1980, 580–1; BHS); the parallel use of *'hb*, *ḥsd* allows 'love' to translate either or both words (cf. Ps. 36.11 [EV 10] for *māšak ḥesed* metaphor). G *eis*, '(I drew you) in (compassion)'. In v. 3 the sense of *māšak*, 'drew', is strengthened by the reference to 'from afar' at the beginning of the verse (cf. 30.10 'I will save you from afar'): the magnetic pull of love, even from far away. **[4]** MT *bᵉtūlat yiśrā'ēl*, 'O virgin Israel': for the epithet cf. v. 21; 18.13; Amos 5.2. MT *bimḥōl mᵉśaḥᵃqīm*, 'in the dance of the merrymakers': G *meta sunagōgēs paizontōn*, 'with the company of those who play', i.e. dance; cf. v. 13; 30.19 (different terms are used in 33.11 for merrymaking). The motif of building (29.5; 30.18; 31.4, 38) used in Part III contributes to its listing in 1.10 (cf. the planting motif also in 29.5; 31.5, 12). Note the triple *ʿōd . . . ʿōd . . . ʿōd*, 'again . . . again . . . again' (vv. 4–5). **[5]** MT *nāṭʿū nōṭʿīm wᵉḥillēlū*, 'the planters planted and they will profane': *ḥillēl*, 'profane', here means to treat something as common by using it (cf. Deut. 20.6; 28.30 for profaning by use; Lev. 19.23–25 for rules about the uncircumcised fruit of trees [i.e. fruit with foreskins] becoming available for food in the fifth year). Rudolph, 194, follows Cornill, 333, and reads *nōṭʿē nᵉṭāʿīm yᵉḥallēlū*, 'the planters of plants will profane', i.e. those who do the planting will enjoy the fruit themselves rather than others (cf. Isa. 65.21–22; contrast Amos 5.11). Rudolph treats the phrase as an additional gloss from Deut. 28.30 (cf. BHS); it differs in person and number from *tiṭṭᵉʿī*, 'you (fem.) will plant'. G *phuteusate kai ainesate*, 'plant and praise' (i.e. *hll* for *ḥll*). The phrase 'the mountains of Samaria' only occurs here and Amos 3.9 (cf. 'the mountain of Samaria', I Kings 16.24; Amos 4.1; 6.1). **[6]** MT *qār'ū nōṣrīm*, 'the watchman cried out': G *klēseōs apologoumenōn*, 'those who plead in defence cry out'.

A collection of poems in 31.2–22 is given a unifying theme by the addition of the titular v. 1. The introductory phrase 'at that time' connects with 30.24b. In the future (i.e. the time of understanding according to 30.24b) Yahweh will become the god of all the families of Israel and they shall become his people. Such a reference to 'all the families' (MT not G) reflects the diaspora with its many scattered communities of Israelites and Judaeans throughout the Persian and Greek empires. The restoration of fortunes in the future will include the reunification of all the clans, and these together will constitute the people of Yahweh. As a preface to the bucolic poems in the collection v. 1 indicates how the poems were understood by the editors.

The poems in 31.2–22 differ from those in 30.5–7, 10–21 in a number of ways, though both collections share the same theme of restoration. One minor difference is the use of the term 'Ephraim' (31.6, 9, 18, 20) to describe the territory of the people. Except for 4.15 and 7.15, the word is not used in the Jeremiah tradition, so its repeated employment in these poems has persuaded some commentators that the poetry represents the early preaching of the young Jeremiah to northern Israel in the period when king Josiah was extending his territory to include what had been the kingdom of Israel (e.g. Volz, Rudolph). This viewpoint has influenced some exegetes (cf. Bright, 285), but is unlikely to be correct. The eroticism of some of the language used (e.g. v. 3), the deeply emotional and idyllic images of pastoral life (worthy of a Breughel), and the strong links between the poetic expressons and the traditions of Hosea and Second Isaiah all point in directions other than the author of the bitter denunciations of Judaean life which dominate the tradition. To imagine that Jeremiah bottled up these feelings until some forty years later and then gave expression to them after 587 (e.g. Lindars 1979) is as unnatural as it is unlikely. The poems breathe an air of delight, are bucolic idylls which rejoice in life lived in a rural setting punctuated by occasional visits up to Jerusalem (cf. Zech. 3.10; 8.3–8); they are hardly the utterances of a man depicted throughout the tradition as sour and alienated from all communal activities and as incapable of speaking kindly without adding even more words of judgment (e.g. 28.7–9, 15–16; 42.9–12, 13–22). These representations of Jeremiah may only be creations of different strands put together by the redactors, but they do not assist in producing an image of Jeremiah which would make him the most likely speaker of the poems in 31. The fictional Jeremiah created by the tradition is temperamentally incapable of uttering such images of love and merrymaking – the last representations of him in the tradition are of his haranguing the communities in Egypt (44) and cursing the Babylonians (51.59–64). Those are characteristic poses of the man

Jeremiah and it is against a backdrop of such images that the sudden shift to love poetry and songs supportive of the people is so unlikely. These are poems which delight in how communities live; they bless and praise rather than damn and curse. They are at home in the world of Second Isaiah and later (e.g. Isa. 60.1–62.12; 65.17–25; 66.7–14, 22–3), though they may imitate some elements in Hosea (cf. Lindars 1979, 51).

The foregoing argument is an attempt to account for the radically different atmosphere and world of the poems in 30–31 (cf. the prose appendices in 31.23–34, 38–40; 32; 33). The only grounds for attributing the poems to Jeremiah are the redactional introduction in 30.1, which has no necessary connection with the contents of the book, and the late reference to building and planting in 1.10. All exegetes recognize the artificiality of these editorial features, and the denial of the poems to Jeremiah does not detract from their meaning, power or importance. The inclusion of these idylls of salvation in the tradition represents one aspect of Judaean society in the Persian period: its hopes for the future. By being attributed to a book written by Jeremiah their incorporation into the tradition is facilitated and they are given the kind of authority associated with Jeremiah by the makers of the book of Jeremiah.

The first poem in 31 is presented as an oracular statement, though the deity does not speak until v. 3b. Israel is represented as somebody (MT a people) who has escaped the sword, like a man finding nourishment in the desert. The images suggest a miraculous escape from destruction, though without defining what the catastrophe may have been (the exile? the terrible storm of Yahweh? the time of Jacob's distress?). From afar (cf. 30.10; 23.23) Yahweh appears to him (G) and speaks words of great love to the nation. Here the image changes to that of a woman much beloved of the speaker, and he reassures her of his love which is such that it draws her to him. What this declaration of love means is set out in vv. 4–6. She, the virgin Israel, will be built again and, adorned with tambourines, she will join the dance of the merrymakers celebrating victory (cf. Ex. 15.20; Judg. 11.34; I Sam. 18.6). The vineyards will be replanted and those who planted them will enjoy their produce. The old ways will come back ('again . . . again . . . again') and there will even be days when in the hill country of Ephraim the guardians will summon the people to go on pilgrimages to Yahweh in Zion.

It is a wonderful idyll of restoration which spells out what it is to be a woman loved by Yahweh. Its links with Hosea and the late elements in Isaiah point to a continuing poetic tradition which depicts the restoration of the fortunes of Yahweh's people (*šūb š*^{e}*būt*) in terms drawn from simple rural life in which the divine blessing produces fertility, prosperity, security and merrymaking. This future is danced (cf. v. 13) and sung, and what the villagers produce they enjoy. No longer does the shadow of the invader frustrate all their work or rapacious troops curtail travelling to the shrine in Jerusalem. The rebuilt community is one in which work and worship are integrated; past and future have become as one (cf. 2.2–3). The pilgrimage to Jerusalem is part of the restoration (cf. Ps. 120–34, esp. 122, 126, 127, 133), and suggests a unified land which no longer knows north and south as rival kingdoms. This is more than an idyllic reconstruction of the past, for no such past ever really existed (the so-called split after Solomon's time demonstrates the non-unity of the clans). The use of Ephraim in these poems takes up the old name of Israel but applies it to a territory of which Zion is the cult centre and outside Jerusalem is the rural area of Israel. The nation living in its own land as an agricultural economy with Zion as its centre is an idyll which has no past, though it may well have a future (cf. 41.5 for a very different pilgrimage to Jerusalem).

31.7–9

7 For thus says the Lord;
'Sing aloud with gladness for Jacob,
  and raise shouts for the chief of the nations;
proclaim, give praise, and say,
  "The Lord has saved his people,
  the remnant of Israel."
8 Behold, I will bring them from the north country,
  and gather them from the farthest parts of the earth,
among them the blind and the lame,
  the woman with child and her who is in travail, together;
  a great company, they shall return here.
9 With weeping they shall come,
  and with consolations I will lead them back,
I will make them walk by brooks of water,
  in a straight path in which they shall not stumble;

for I am a father to Israel,
  and Ephraim is my first-born.'

---

[7] G lacks *śimḥāh*, 'gladness'. MT *b*e*rō'š haggōyīm*, 'at, for the head of the nations': cf. *rē'šīt haggōyīm*, 'the first of the nations', Amos 6.1. The raucous public commotion (*rnn, ṣhl*, cf. Isa. 24.14) may be an expression of chauvinistic pride or may represent an imaginary procession of the nations, at the head of which is Jacob; for the shrill neighing (*ṣah*a*lū*) of public performances cf. 5.8. BHS suggests *hārīm*, 'mountains', for 'nations'. MT *hōša' yhwh 'et-'ammekā*, 'save O Yahweh your people': G *esōsen kurios ton laon autou*, 'the lord *has* saved *his* people'; i.e. *hōšī'a . . . 'ammō*. The final phrase *'et š*e*'erīt yiśrā'ēl*, 'the remnant of Israel', may be an additional gloss (Rudolph, 195), cf. 23.3; it is in G. **[8]** MT *bām 'iwwēr ūpissēaḥ*, 'among them the blind and the lame': G *en heortē phasek*, 'in the feast of passover' = *b*e*mō'ēd pēsaḥ*; for the blind and lame cf. II Sam. 5.6, 8; Isa. 35.5–6. MT *hēnnāh*, 'hither, here': Rudolph reads *hinnēh*, 'look, behold', and takes it with v. 9 (BHS). The imagery of vv. 8–9 is shared with Isa. 35; 40.3–5; 41.17–19; 42.16; 43.5–6; 44.3–4; 48.20; 49.9–13. **[9]** MT *yābō'ū*, 'they shall come': G *exēlthon*, 'they went forth' = *yāṣ'ū*. MT *ūb*e*taḥ*a*nūnīm* 'and with supplication for favour': cf. 3.21; Dan. 9.18. G *kai en paraklēsei*, 'and with consolation', suggests *ūb*e*tanḥūmīm*; cf. EVV. This makes a better contrast with 'weeping' than MT: they went out weeping but will be led (back) with 'consolations'.

In this poem great joy and much noise is caused by the return of the diaspora from the north (cf. Isa. 43.6) and everywhere else (cf. 6.22). This great return mimics the terrible invasion route of the cruel enemy which had brought about the original scattering of the people (e.g. *miyyark*e*tē-'āreṣ*, v. 8; 6.22, 'from the farthest parts of the earth'). It reverses the fate of the nation in the past. But it does so in subtly different ways: the mighty army which came down from the north and destroyed Judah-Jerusalem was an appallingly fierce and vicious force (4.13; 5.15–17; 6.22–26), whereas the army of people which now returns to its own land includes the blind and the lame, as well as the pregnant and those who have given birth recently. One is a very human procession of the weak and those who carry the promise of new life for the nation; the other an almost superhuman force of mighty warriors whose weaponry was like an open grave (5.16). The first brought death with it and left behind it a dead kingdom. The second brings with it life and the remaking of the land into a place full of joy and prosperity (cf. vv. 12–14). The feminine images in these poems are characteristic of the restoration theme: a land filled with overflowing life. In the poems about the destruction of city and nation the feminine is an image of the raped and violated nation – the victim. Now the great reversal (*šūb šᵉbūt*) transforms the feminine back into its active state of that which gives life and sustains it. From the passivitiy of destruction to the activity of giving birth and drawing love from the other (v. 3), the feminine imagery in the tradition demonstrates the polarities of the life of the community.

The return from other lands is heralded in v. 7 as a procession for the chief of the nations and explained in v. 9 on the grounds that Yahweh is the father of the nation, Ephraim is his first-born (Volz takes v. 9 with v. 6, and other exegetes suggest reading vv. 7, 9c with v. 6 as the conclusion to vv. 2–6). The old pride in the nation has been reawakened with the return of the exiles from so many different lands (this is not the return from Babylon but a later diaspora's regathering to the land). This is the head of the nations, this is Yahweh's first-born son (cf. Ex. 4.22). That the old name Ephraim is used in this fashion suggests an allusion to the story of how Ephraim, who was not the first-born son, *became* the first-born in reality (cf. Gen. 48.8–20; it is a moot point whether Jeremiah reflects Genesis or vice versa, cf. Brodie 1981, 46–51). Thus the nation which suffered the humiliation and devastation of defeat and scattering to the ends of the earth is brought back in triumph as Yahweh's heir to the land. The nation's fecundity and good fortune are due to Yahweh being its father. The shift in the gender of the metaphors used of the relationship between Yahweh and Israel is characteristic of the biblical writers' use of images drawn from family and communal life for describing the shared life of deity and people. Israel is both Yahweh's mistress (wife) and son – the one loved by him. The multiplicity of metaphors used, masculine and feminine, positive and negative, should warn the modern exegete to exercise caution when reading the text from a contemporary ideological viewpoint (see on 4.30–31).

The great assembly (*qāhāl gādōl*) which comes in triumph from so many parts of the world and which travels with such ease along well-watered, straight paths is an image shared by the poem and the poetry of Second Isaiah. This common poetic tradition may also account for the positive feminine images which abound throughout the cycle (on Second Isaiah cf. 49.8–23; 51.17–20; Gruber 1983). With the fall of Babylon great hope developed among some of the exiles, and in the subsequent centuries the many scattered communities focused on Zion as their centre and made pilgrimages there (in reality and in fantasy). The poems in the cycle represent some of these hopes as well as the reconstruction of urban and rural areas in the Persian period.

31.10–14

10 'Hear the word of the LORD, O nations,
and declare it in the coastlands afar off;
say, "He who scattered Israel will gather him,
and will keep him as a shepherd keeps his flock."
11 For the LORD has ransomed Jacob,
and has redeemed him from hands too strong for him.
12 They shall come and sing aloud on the height of Zion,
and they shall be radiant over the goodness of the LORD,
over the grain, the wine, and the oil,
and over the young of the flock and the herd;
their life shall be like a watered garden,
and they shall languish no more.
13 Then shall the maidens rejoice in the dance,
and the young men and the old shall be merry.
I will turn their mourning into joy,
I will comfort them, and give them gladness for sorrow.
14 I will feast the soul of the priests with abundance,
and my people shall be satisfied with my goodness,
says the LORD.'

---

[10] MT *bā'iyyīm*, 'in the coastlands, among the islands': cf. 2.10; Isa. 41.1, 5; 42.4, 10, 12; 49.1; 51.5; 59.18; 60.9; 66.19; Ps. 97.1; Zeph. 2.11. MT *wᵉ'imrū*, 'and say': an unnecessary gloss? (cf. BHS); but cf. v. 7. MT *ūšᵉmārō kᵉrōʿeh ʿedrō*, 'and will keep him as a shepherd his flock': cf. Isa. 40.11 *kᵉrōʿeh ʿedrō yirʿeh*, 'as a shepherd his flock he will feed'. **[11]** MT *kī-pādāh . . . ūgᵉ'ālō* 'for he has ransomed . . . and redeemed him': these are terms which appear frequently in Isa. 40–55 but, apart from 31.11; 15.21; 50.34, not at all in the Jeremiah tradition. **[12]** MT *bimrōm-ṣiyyōn*, 'on the height of Zion': Rudolph treats this as a Judaean correction (as he does for 30.17b) of *behārīm*, 'on the mountains', deleting *ṣiyyōn*. MT *wᵉnāhᵃrū*, 'and they shall shine, be radiant': cf. 51.44b; Isa. 60.5; Ps. 34.6 (EV 5), the only other occurrences of the verb. MT *ʿal-dāgān wᵉʿal-tīrōš wᵉʿal yiṣhār*, 'over the new grain, the new wine, and the oil': this list of the triple products of the fertile land of Canaan occurs frequently in Deuteronomy (e.g. 7.13; 11.14; 12.17;

14.23; 18.4; 28.51); also Hos. 2.10 (EV 8); Joel 1.10; 2.19; Hag. 1.11. The terms refer to the products 'in an unmanufactured state' (Driver 1896, 193), and relate Yahweh's goodness (*ṭūb yhwh*) to the new growth of the land. G *epi gēn sitou . . .*, 'to a land of corn . . .'. MT *keгan rāweh*, 'as a watered garden': cf. Isa. 58.11 (Ezek. 36.35 likens the new land to the garden of Eden). G *hōsper xulon egkarpon*, 'like a fruitful wood'. **[13]** MT *bemāḥōl ūbaḥurīm*, '. . . in the dance, and young men . . .': G *en sunagōgē neaniskōn*, 'in the assembly of youth', cf. v. 4. MT *yaḥdāw*, adv., 'together': G *charēsontai*, 'shall rejoice' = *yaḥdū* (*ḥādāh*, 'rejoice'). The scene represented by G is that of virgins (*betūlōt*, *parthenoi*; MT collective?) enjoying the dance of youth and old men rejoicing. MT *wehāpaktī*, 'and I will overturn', i.e. 'transform'. G lacks *weniḥamtīm*, 'and I will comfort them'. MT *migōnām*, 'from sorrow': G *megalunō*, 'I will make great', taken with next verse where it appears as a doublet of *weriwētī*, 'I will make great (i.e. *ribbītī*, cf. BHS) and cheer with wine (*methusō*) . . .' **[14]** MT *weriwwētī nepeš hakkōhanīm dāšen*, lit. 'I will saturate the appetite of the priests with fatness', i.e. satiate the priests with food and drink: G 'sons of Levi' in place of *dāšen*, 'fatness'.

The poem in vv. 10–14 is linked to vv. 7–9 by the use of similar terms in vv. 7, 10 (cf. the triple verbs 'proclaim, give praise, and say', v. 7; 'hear, declare, say' v. 10; the use of 'nations' in both poems). Subject matter is also shared, as both pieces celebrate the return of the scattered people to their own land. Where they differ is in the more strongly pastoral imagery of vv. 10–14 and the focus on the fertility of the land to which the dispersed return (cf. vv. 4–5). Fewer metaphors are used and the dominant image is of Yahweh the shepherd gathering his scattered flock (a dispersal caused by Yahweh himself, v. 10) and tending it as a responsible shepherd. The basis of both poems is the declaration that Yahweh has saved, ransomed and redeemed his people (vv. 7b, 11). In vv. 12–14 the exiles return to Zion and become radiant over the goodness of Yahweh: this goodness is the agricultural products of the land. The new grain, grape and olive proclaim the goodness of Yahweh in the abundance of food, wine and oil and in the harvest celebrations of such productivity great joy is experienced by the community. With this fertility of land and animals the life of the people (i.e. its spirit, *nepeš*) is like a watered garden, knowing no further dearth of anything. The young virgins join in the dance of youth (G) and the old men make merry (cf. v. 4), and Yahweh transforms mourning and sorrow into joy and happiness (cf. 33.11). As in v. 6, prosperity and cultic life belong together, so that the priests are sated with food and drink.

All the scarcities of the past have disappeared in the great transformation of restoration to the homeland (cf. Second Isaiah's imagery and message). Thus the evil intended and executed by Yahweh in the past is overturned (*hpk*) by his shepherding of the people back to a fecund land of prosperity.

31.15–20

15 Thus says the LORD:
'A voice is heard in Ramah,
lamentation and bitter weeping.
Rachel is weeping for her children;
she refuses to be comforted for her children,
because they are not.'
16 Thus says the LORD:
'Keep your voice from weeping,
and your eyes from tears;
for your work shall be rewarded,
says the LORD.
and they shall come back from the land of the enemy.
17 There is hope for your future,
says the LORD,
and your children shall come back to their own country.
18 I have heard Ephraim bemoaning,
"Thou hast chastened me, and I was chastened,
like an untrained calf;
bring me back that I may be restored,
for thou art the LORD my God.
19 For after I had turned away I repented;
and after I was instructed, I smote upon my thigh;
I was ashamed, and I was confounded,
because I bore the disgrace of my youth."
20 Is Ephraim my dear son?
Is he my darling child?
For as often as I speak against him,
I do remember him still.
Therefore my heart yearns for him;
I will surely have mercy on him,'
says the LORD.

---

[15] The formulaic introduction 'thus says Yahweh' does not introduce a divine saying (v. 16 begins the divine speech), but (cf. v. 3) indicates a redactional unit, vv. 15–20, which is to be treated as the divine word by the receiving community (hence the additional *nᵉ'um yhwh*, 'says Yahweh', in vv. 16, 17). MT *bᵉrāmāh*, 'in Ramah, in the upland, on the height': BHS reads *bārāmāh* because Ramah always has the article. MT *bᵉkī tamrūrīm*, 'bitter weeping': cf. 6.26; Hos. 12.15. The use of Rachel as a figure of the community weeping for its dead children may be an allusion to the story of Rachel's death in childbirth (Gen. 35.16–20). It is possble that *rāḥēl*, 'ewe-lamb', is the sense here rather than Rachel, one of the wives of Jacob (cf. Gaster 1969, 605–6). According to I Sam. 10.2 Rachel's tomb is at Zelzah in Benjaminite territory, not far from Ramah (I Sam. 8.4); Gen. 35.19 places it near Bethlehem, on the way from Bethel. Whether these different accounts agree is a matter of debate. The image of the mother weeping for the dead children may be an echo of the folk belief that women who die in childbirth haunt the earth in search of their babies (cf. Gaster 1969, 605). **[16]** G lacks *nᵉ'um yhwh*, 'says Yahweh'. **[17]** G *monimon tois sois teknois*, 'a lasting (place) for your children': a shorter text than MT which stresses the children's (future) stability. MT emphasizes the return of the children (*bānīm*, 'children', rather than EVV '*your* children'): *wᵉšābū . . . wᵉšābū*, 'and they shall return . . . and they shall return' (vv. 16, 17). Delete *nᵉ'um yhwh*, 'says Yahweh'. **[18]** MT *šāmōa' šāma'tī . . . yissartanī wā'iwwāsēr*, 'I have really heard . . . you have disciplined me and I was disciplined': cf. the repeats in 17.14. MT *hᵃšībēnī wᵉ'ašūbāh*, 'bring me back that I may come back': word-play on *šūb*; *šūb* is used in vv. 16, 17, 18, 19. The image of Ephraim as an untrained calf (*kᵉ'ēgel lō' lummād*) reverses the figure of Ephraim as a trained heifer (*'eglāh mᵉlummādāh*) in Hos. 10.11 (note the gender variations with reference to Ephraim). **[19]** MT *kī-'aḥᵃrē šūbī niḥamtī*, 'for after my turning I repented': exegetes think a word has fallen out of this sentence; Rudolph reads *šabtī*, 'I turned', after *šūbī* (lost by haplography) and translates 'after my going astray I turned back' (cf. BHS; Bright). G *aichmalōsias mou* 'my captivity' = *šibyī*; Driver 1937–8, 119–20, follows G and Rudolph to read 'for after my captivity (I turned) (and) repented'. He treats *hiwwād'ī* ('I was instructed') as from *yd'*, 'was humbled', rather than *yd'*, 'know'. G *estenaxa eph' hēmeras aischunēs*, 'I groaned for the days of shame' = *'ānaqtī 'al-yᵉmē bōšet* rather than 'I smote upon my thigh; I was ashamed'. **[20]** MT *hᵃbēn yaqqīr* 'is a precious son . . . ?': G lacks the interrogative *hᵃ-* and the linking *'im*, 'is (he a darling child)?'. MT *kī-middē dabbᵉrī bō*, 'for as often as I speak about him'. RSV translates *bō* as 'against him', but cf. Bright, 282; Driver, 120, understands *dbr b* as 'to turn the back on' or 'reject' (followed by NEB; cf. JPSB's 'turned against him'). Rudolph reads *dabbᵉrī* as *hinnākᵉrī*, 'I estrange myself against him' (cf. Ecclus. 11.34; BHS). MT *hāmū mē'ay lō*, 'my inward parts (i.e. emotions or intestines) thrill for him': cf. BDB, 242; EVV 'heart' may be a fair translation here if the physical and emotional senses of 'innards' are understood. The visceral feelings referred to describe the physically powerful urges a mother feels for her son or lovers for each other. Bright, 275, translates as 'I am filled with yearning for him'. The parallel phrase *raḥēm ʾaraḥamennū* may also have an equally physical sense beyond the standard translation of 'I will surely have compassion'; cf. Trible 1978, 45, 'motherly-compassion'.

Anderson 1978; Lindars 1979; Trible 1976; 1978, 40–50

The poem in vv. 15–20 is made up of a number of distinctive elements, vv. 15–17, 18–19, 20 (cf. Weiser, 279–82), bound together by the redactional markers 'thus says Yahweh', 'says Yahweh' (vv. 15, 20). These elements are independent of each other but have been forged into a poem by the incorporation of v. 15 as an oracular statement, though it clearly is not one, into what looks like a series of dialogue poems. Ephraim and Yahweh are the main speakers in vv. 18–20, though the figure of Ephraim can hardly be posited of the speaker of v. 15 or the female addressed in vv. 16–17. The terrible mourning of v. 15 is responded to by Yahweh in vv. 16–17, and the bemoaning oneself (*mitnōdēd*) of vv. 18–19 is replied to by the deity in v. 20. In vv. 15–17 the mother is the speaker and addressee; in vv. 18–20 the son is speaker and addressee. The connection between the two is redactional because each element is about something quite distinctive. The lamenting Rachel of v. 15 is a distraught mother who mourns the disappearance of her children – 'for they are not' (*kī ʾēnennū*). The divine response in vv. 16–17 is shaped by v. 15 (whether by association or in terms of cannot be determined) to the extent that images of weeping are common to both pieces, but it deals with the return of the exiled children, whereas v. 15 is about the death of the mother's children. Her children no longer exist, and that is why she refuses to be comforted. It is not a case of her children having gone away but of their annihilation. The fragment constituted by v. 15 does not fit this context, and would be better treated by exegetes as an independent poem. However, the context of the cycle allows the response to transform the utter despair of the mother into a word of hope for the future. The juxtapositioning of the two pieces modifies the meaning of v. 15. In vv. 18–19 the nation speaks as a man complaining about his youth and the deity responds in very strongly maternal and visceral terms in v. 20. The tone and images of vv. 18–20 are very different from those of vv. 15–17. Many exegetes also include vv. 21–22 in the poem (e.g. Anderson, Bright, Condamin, Duhm, Hyatt, Thompson), but speaker and addressee are quite distinctive in these verses, and the deity's position is also sufficiently different for the unit to be treated in isolation from what precedes it (following Weiser, Rudolph).

The redactional unit formed by associating different poems together produces a number of striking images in which the bitter feelings of the community as mother are balanced by the erotic-maternal urgings of the deity as mother. Between these two sets of images the community as son struggles to come to terms with a regretted past by appealing to the deity to turn him back. Some of the metaphors used in vv. 18–20 reflect similar images used in the Hosea tradition (e.g. Hos. 4.16; 10.11; 11.8–9), and both the cycle and Hosea share the representation of Yahweh's very emotional involvement with the community. It is that overwhelming love (cf. 31.3; Hos. 11.8) which warrants the hope that Ephraim will not be destroyed (Hosea) or will find mercy and turning (31.18, 20). As a woman the community is shattered by the loss of its people (wiped out in the cruel invasions, sieges, killings and executions), as a man the community bemoans its disgraceful youthful past, and as a mother the deity's innards heave with maternal feelings whenever she considers her son. In the strength of such feelings and emotions the future of the community lies and the idyllic elements of the cycle are of a piece with such representations of the relationship between Yahweh and the people.

Rachel weeping for her children in Ramah is a strange metaphor in the independent v. 15. Its precise meaning is not clear, especially as the word *rāḥēl* may be understood as 'ewe-lamb'. Rachel, the wife of Jacob, is hardly ever mentioned outside the stories of Jacob (apart from the grave notice in I Sam. 10.2 and as part of a simile in Ruth 4.11), though there are some associations between the cycle 30–31 and the Genesis stories which would make the allusion to her appropriate here (cf. Brodie 1981). The term Ramah may combine a reference to Rachel's burial mound and the transit camp of 40.1 where the Judaean captives were herded on their way to exile in Babylon. Again, it is quite possible that *rāmāh* means 'height' here, and the image is one of a mother sheep lamenting on the highlands the loss of her lambs. Whichever figure is understood by the metaphor, the meaning remains the same: the mother of the community bitterly laments the loss of her children. The verse is a lament in response to the complete destruction of the community and represents a word of judgment in the cycle. Only in combination with vv. 16–17 is the judgment aspect transformed.

Yahweh's answer to the lament is given by the redaction which appends vv. 16–17 to v. 15. It commands the woman not to weep because her children will return (*šābū*) from the land of the enemy. There is a reward for all her labours on behalf of her children. The content of this response is repeated in v. 17. If a core is to be sought for the cycle, it might be found in the sentence *w*ᵉ*yēš-tiqwāh l*ᵉ*'aḥ*ᵃ*rītēk*, 'and there is hope for your future' ('and' links the hope with *yēš śākār*, 'there is reward', of v. 16; G has a shorter v. 17). The reward for the woman's work is the hope for the future. Finding the right nuance for *'aḥ*ᵃ*rītēk* is difficult: it may refer to the future (RSV) or what happens *afterwards*, i.e. after the mother's death. In this latter sense it is an allusion to the woman's posterity (cf. NEB margin; also 29.11 NEB); she will leave descendants after her (NEB). This may make a better connection between v. 17 and the reference to Rachel in v. 15 because Rachel died in childbirth, and to a woman dying in childbirth the only comfort that may be given is that of reassurance about the welfare of the child. However, the metaphorical representation of the community as a mother weeping for her children in vv. 16–17 should not be taken to the point where it is the community which is dying but its children are surviving. The weeping of v. 16 refers to the exile of some of the people and the reassurance of vv. 16–17 applies to the return of those exiles. The mother's children will return to her, and thus the despair of v. 15 is reversed. In reality of course the children died, but later generations were able to return to the old homeland. The metaphors of vv. 15, 16–17 refer to different things; hence their redactional combination tends to obscure what is being said about each situation. However, the hope for the future is the return, which is a dominant motif in 31 (e.g. vv. 8–9, 10–12, 16–17, 21).

The subject matter of vv. 18–19 is really quite different from vv. 16–17. There is no talk about a return of the children but a penitential confession by Ephraim (cf. 3.21–23 for this kind of liturgical statement). Ephraim moves to and fro in lamentation about his condition and confesses to having been disciplined like an untrained calf. The image is that of a domesticated animal which has not yet been trained properly, so it has wandered away and has to be flogged in order to make it return. Ephraim, i.e. the community, appeals to Yahweh to turn him back effectively. He acknowledges having gone astray and confesses to having repented (*nḥm*). After instruction he admits his shame and humiliation caused by his youthfulness (or in his youth? contrast 2.2–3). The reference to repentance is unusual in the cycle as all the images of salvation are of the divine initiative irrespective of human response, so this extract from a confessional lament is quite out of place in the cycle. Set within this poem it may be read as a transformed element in the dialogic exchanges between Yahweh and community, but it reflects a very different notion of potential salvation from the rest of the cycle. In 30–31 repentance is not a prerequisite of salvation (cf. Hos. 11.8–9).

The divine response to this confession is an expression of the deity's powerful feelings for her son. Mother Yahweh speaks affirmatively (G but interrogatively in MT) of Ephraim as her son who is very precious (*yaqqīr*) and an absolute delight (*šaʿᵃšuʿīm*, cf. Isa. 5.7; Prov. 8.30–1) to her. Every time she speaks of him she remembers just what he means to her and her insides moan for him (cf. Trible 1978, 45, 'my womb trembles for him'). So she most surely will have mercy on him. The images of overwhelming feminine love for her son characterize the deity's view of the community and bespeak a glowing future for it. What that future may be is not spelled out in the divine answer to the lament, but within the context of the whole poem and the cycle may be deduced to be either the return to the homeland or the prosperous building up of the community in the fertile land of their ancestors. Yahweh's love for Ephraim is so strong, so visceral, that the child will encounter mercy in spite of his foolish youthfulness. The Hosea tradition and the Book of Consolation belong together at this point, and in order to express the intensity of Yahweh's feelings for the people feminine metaphors are employed. The community as mother (cf. vv. 15, 16) becomes the people as son and Yahweh as mother (vv. 18–19, 20), and the bitter weeping of the bereaved mother is transformed by Yahweh's uterine love. The different units contribute various images to the development of this metaphoric statement about the community's future as the child of the powerful and possessive mother deity, and that compulsive love will guarantee the future. The rhetoric of the poem is 'replete with female semantics' (Trible 1978, 50) and should be noted as such (see on 4.30–31). It should not, however, be over-elaborated in theological terms because the words used are but metaphors and the tradition contains a wide range of variable figures of speech which may contribute to the construction of a sensibly balanced theology of divine-human interaction using both masculine and feminine terminology.

31.21–22

21 'Set up waymarks for yourself,
make yourself guideposts;
consider well the highway,
the road by which you went.
Return, O virgin Israel,
return to these your cities.
22 How long will you waver,
O faithless daughter?
For the LORD has created a new thing on the earth:
a woman protects a man.'

---

[21] MT *ṣiyyunīm*, 'sign-posts, markers': G *Siōn*, 'Zion'. MT *tamrūrīm*, cf. v. 15, where the same word means 'bitter' (from *mrr*), but here must be derived from *tmr*, 'palm-tree, post', cf. 10.5, i.e. 'sign-posts' (NEB). Giesebrecht, 169, reads it as *timōrīm*, 'posts', i.e. artificial palms; cf. BHS *tīmōrīm*, 'palm-like columns'. G *timōrian*, a transliteration of the Hebrew. MT *lamᵉsillāh*, 'the highway': a motif used in Isa. 40.3; 49.11 to describe the return from exile (cf. Isa. 62.10); G *eis tous ōmous*: 'to the path' (reading *oimous*). MT *'ēlleh*, 'these': cf. v. 8 *hēnnāh*, 'here'; G *penthousa*, 'mourning' = *'ᵃbēlāh* (BHS). **[22]** MT *habbat haššōbēbāh*, 'faithless daughter': cf. 3.14, 22, 'faithless sons'; *šūb* has the sense of waywardness here (cf. NEB) and balances *tithammāqīn*, 'twisting and turning'. MT *nᵉqēbāh tᵉsōbēb gāber*, 'a female . . . a man': perhaps the most difficult half-line in the book of Jeremiah. G *en sōtēria perieleusontai anthrōpoi*, 'in safety men shall go about'. For the motif of Yahweh doing something new (*'ōśeh ḥᵃdāšāh* rather than *bārā' ḥᵃdāšāh*), cf. Isa. 43.19. The crux of the matter is the translation of *tᵉsōbēb* (assonant word-play with *šōbēbāh*?): 'protects' (RSV), 'turned into' (NEB), 'courts' (JPSB), 'shall compass' (AV). Duhm, 251 emends it to *tissōb*, 'turned into', cf. Zech. 14.10 (cf. NEB), and suggests that the phrase is probably a proverb which can be used in a number of different ways. Here its function may be that of a mocking gloss which points out that Israel appears first as a son, then as a woman (a post-exilic gloss). Volz, 278, 283, treats v. 22b as an addition which is quite incomprehensible, reads *bᵉ'ereṣ tᵉšūbāh*, 'in the land of return', and treats *nᵉqēbāh*, *gāber* as glosses to v. 27b, which he reads as part of v. 22. Giesebrecht, 170, relates *tᵉsōbēb* to *sbb* in

Deut. 32.10 with the meaning 'protect', i.e. the woman protects the man; cf. Ehrlich 1912, 322. Cornill, 342, follows Duhm's emendation and reads v. 26 immediately after v. 22. Condamin, 225, 227–8, reads . . . *tāšūb l^{e}geber*, '(the woman) returns to her husband', i.e. Israel returns to Yahweh, making the new thing reflect 3.1. Hyatt, 1034, appears to agree with Condamin. Weiser, 282, understands the phrase as 'the woman surrounds the man' and sees in it a hint of the renewal (i.e. the new thing created by Yahweh in the land) of the creation blessing of fruitfulness in Gen. 1.28; cf. Jer. 31.27. Both Weiser and Rudolph, 198, admit that the phrase is completely mysterious as to its meaning, though each offers some clarification of it. Rudolph, 199, suggests *n^{e}qabbāh t^{e}sōbab g^{e}birā(h)*, 'the cursed one changes to queen', cf. 30.20–21. Bright, 282, provides a literal translation: 'a female shall compass a man', but comments, 'the meaning is wholly obscure, and it might have been wiser to leave the colon blank . . . Quite possibly we have here a proverbial saying indicating something that is surprising and difficult to believe, the force of which escapes us.' Anderson 1978, 477, 'encompass, enfold', i.e. will be the agent of new life in the new age. Holladay offers a rather different account of v. 22, treating it in relation to 30.6, where the men behave like women; now the sex roles will be reversed again and the female will have priority, initiative, dominance over the male. 'Your warriors have become female? Look: the female will surmount the warrior! Take heart; come home' (1966b, 239). Lundbom 1975, 33–4, treats the line as ironic, expressing shock and surprise at the defeat of Israel's soldiers: 'My, a new thing on earth! The woman must protect the soldier.' This forms an *inclusio* for the core of the cycle with 30.6, which Lundbom regards as saying the same thing as 31.22b (cf. Holladay 1962b, 53–4, for the view that 30.7, 'yet he shall be saved out of it', is an ironic question with an implicit negative answer). The wide range of opinions on v. 22b is indicative of the difficulties of interpreting the phrase; it is both lapidary and over-rich in possible meanings (e.g. *sbb* means 'surround', 'encompass', 'enclose', 'encircle', 'march around', 'turn around'). Sexual connotations may well be present in view of v. 20, and the proverbial nature of the saying (a view taken by many exegetes; cf. Carroll 1981, 327 n. 25) may allude to this aspect of community life by means of an oblique reference to future fertility: 'the woman encircles, i.e. wraps herself around, the man' (perhaps 'the vagina envelops the penis'). This reference to vigorous sexual intercourse is shorthand for the renewal of the community (cf. v. 8). As a bawdy proverb it may not suit the metaphorical role it has to play in vv. 21–22 (hence the problems of understanding it), but it provides a fine closure of the cycle with 30.6, where the mimicry of pregnancy by men in a time of trouble will be replaced by the real thing when Yahweh creates something new in the land. Not role reversal (cf. Isa. 4.1) is the point of the saying, but an affirmation that when Yahweh acts creatively women will be women and men will be men – and ever the twain shall meet and become one flesh! Hence the repopulation of the community.

The cycle of poems is concluded with a short poem which provides a closure with 30.5–7 but transforms the terrible gloom of the prefatory poem. Speaker and figure change from vv. 15–20, though the community is still addressed. The masculine image of Ephraim in vv. 18–20 becomes the feminine figure of the virgin daughter, but the deity probably retains a parental role in the poem without specification of gender. The scattered exiles are commanded to make preparations for returning home by marking out their route. Milestones and signposts will assist them to return by the highway along which they went into exile. The woman here addressed is not the mother figure of vv. 15–17 but the people in exile. They are described in v. 22a as wavering, i.e. turning to and fro without making any real progress, and faithless (a use of *šūb* which links the poem to the circle which produced 3.12, 14, 21–23; cf. Hos. 14.1 [MT 2]). In tone the poem is quite different from the more idyllic pieces of vv. 2–6, 7–9, 10–14 and suggests a reluctance on the part of the exiles to return to the cities. This failure to return to the homeland is what earns Israel the epithet 'faithless' (*šōbēbāh*) and hints at some of the problems in the Persian period, when returning to the land of Israel must have represented a quite unpleasant prospect for many families living outside that land. Yet nothing should prevent their return, because Yahweh has created something new in the land (MT *bā'āreṣ* is better translated 'in the land' than 'in the earth' with EVV). What that new thing may be is far from clear, but in its present context it is presented as an argument for returning home.

Much has been written already on the meaning of v. 22b, and little of it will bear repeating. The mystification expressed by various exegetes as to its meaning is quite understandable and the terseness of the three-word half-line allows great scope for speculative interpretations. Two points are worth making: as the closure of the cycle the verse may be more influenced by 30.5–7 than by v. 21 and the use of a punning word-play (*šōbēbāh – tᵉsōbēb*) reduces the semantic content of the statement because paronomasia inevitably narrows down meaning in favour of sound or *double entendre*. Both these points should warn against over-confidence in seeking a definitive meaning for the phrase 'a female encompasses the virile'. If the saying is also proverbial (e.g. Duhm and others), then its significance may be lost to us because such aphorisms are often confined to particular cultures and without further explication may be meaningless to outsiders. The bawdy interpretation of the words (cf. the mocking style of 30.6) underlines a further obscurity because, in spite of its universal character, obscene and ribald language is highly particularized in individual cultures (this is even true of euphemisms: e.g. feet, knees, hand are terms for genitals in Hebrew but not in English).

Many of the explanations offered entail emending the text or involve exegesis which only succeeds in terms of what is known as using the form *obscurum per obscurius* (i.e. explaining what is obscure by something which is more obscure). The temptation to use this form is strong when such a difficult half-line presents itself in a context where explanations must be provided. It is tempting to pick up words and phrases in the immediate context and to build them into an exegesis which is coherent and interesting. Thus the stress may be put on Yahweh's new creation, and role(?) reversal may be emphasized so as to explain v. 22b in terms of the Genesis creation stories (connections between the cycle and the stories of Genesis have been noted and the two sets of stories may have come into existence together or have been recited in the same liturgical circles). In the first Genesis account Yahweh creates male and female (Gen. 1.27) and in the second story he creates the man, puts him to sleep, takes a rib from his body and builds it into a woman (Gen. 2.7, 21–23; note the sleep motif in Jer. 31.26). Now, where once the rib encircled the man and woman was made from it, things will be reversed and the woman will encircle the man. The brief saying may reflect such a meditation on the story of how men and women came to be the way they are, especially in terms of their sexual passions for each other. This explanation would fit the tenor of the context about the rebuilding of the community by means of repopulation and would harvest the various nuances of gender in the poems. It is, however, purely a speculative reconstruction of a possible setting for a proverbial half-line.

The wiser course for the exegete is to admit ignorance and acknowledge that ancient texts occasionally do baffle the modern hermeneut. 31.22b is one such baffling text. It may have been a witty gloss or addition to the poem when it was first produced but the humour eludes the modern mind. Perhaps the amount of exegetical activity aroused by the text is equivalent to those lengthy explanations of jokes indulged in by the humourless – and with as much point! In the final analysis I must admit that I do not know what v. 22b means.

31.23–26

23 Thus says the LORD of hosts, the God of Israel: 'Once more they shall use these words in the land of Judah and in its cities, when I restore their fortunes:

"The LORD bless you, O habitation of righteousness,
O holy hill!"

24 And Judah and all its cities shall dwell there together, and the farmers and those who wander with their flocks. 25 For I will satisfy the weary soul, and every languishing soul I will replenish.'

26 Thereupon I awoke and looked, and my sleep was pleasant to me.

---

[23] G *eulogēmenos kurios epi dikaion oros to hagion autou*, 'blessed be the lord on his righteous holy mountain'. Bright, 282, treats the terms *ṣedeq*, 'righteous', and *qōdeš*, 'holy', as titles of Yahweh rather than epithets of the temple mount. **[24]** MT *w^enās'ū*, 'and they shall wander (with the flock)': BHS follows Vrs and reads *w^enōs'ē*, 'and those who wander . . .', i.e. shepherds. NEB deletes 'Judah and all his cities' as an addition. MT *bāh*, 'in her': RSV 'there'; probably a reference to *'ereṣ*, 'land', in v. 23, rather than the temple region. **[25]** MT *w^ekol-nepeš dā'^abāh*, 'and every soul languishes': i.e. every one who is hungry, cf. v. 12; either the relative *'^ašer* should be understood or the adjectival form *d^e'ēbāh* should be read. **[26]** MT *wā'er'eh*, 'and I saw': BHS suggests *w^e'erweh*, 'and I was refreshed' (cf. Rudolph, 200); cf. v. 14. The line is enigmatic and may be a marginal comment on the utopian nature of the collection (i.e. the hopes are merely a dream). Some exegetes (e.g. Weiser, 283–4; Rudolph) treat *'al-zō't*, 'for this reason', as indicative of a citation and translate what follows as a quotation of a well-known song. It may represent an editorial note indicating a prediction of future pastoral well-being using incubatory techniques or revelation through dreams (cf. John Bunyan's sojourn in Bedford gaol which produced *The Pilgrim's Progress*). JPSB treats 'sleep' as 'the vision in the preceding verses'. Bright, 283, confesses to being baffled by the verse.

To the collection of poems in the cycle 30–31 have been added five units which expand the theme of restoration by a series of reversal motifs (vv. 23–26, 27–30, 31–34, 35–37, 38–40). These deal with specific sayings (cf. vv. 23, 26, 29, 34) and motifs and have the effect of defining more clearly the future awaiting the nation in its own land. As they are discrete units, it is difficult to locate them in any particular period or social setting. They concern the restoration of Judah and Israel in terms of repopulation around the cult centre, the reversal of the divine maleficence towards the nation, the making of a new covenant to replace the old broken agreement, a divine guarantee of the permanence of the people analogous to the fixity of the heavenly bodies, and the rebuilding of the city as a reversal of its profanation referred to in 7.30 – 8.3. Each of these motifs may represent a specific social issue in the Persian period.

The first of the five additions hints at the restoration of the temple mount when Yahweh restores the people's fortunes. When the great instauration happens, then the nation will once more be able to use the old blessing, 'blessed be Yahweh on the true (*ṣedeq*, i.e. legitimate) habitation (*nāweh*, cf. Ex. 15.13; but see 50.7), the holy mountain' (cf. G). It will be a time of solidarity between farmers and shepherds when both will live together in the land. At the same time those who are weary with thirst and languish from hunger will be refreshed and fed. It will be a time of plenty which will reverse the harsh experiences of the present era. The dream of peace and prosperity in the land with Yahweh's presence on the sacred temple mount is recognized in v. 26 as the product of sleep. Waking up from sleep the speaker acknowledges the pleasantness (*'ārbāh*, contrast 6.20) of what he has seen. The enigmatic quality of v. 26 makes it difficult to determine the precise meaning of the text (as the exegetical opinions in the commentaries indicate). As a marginal gloss it may represent the editor's response to the idyll, without necessarily implying a scepticism about the difference between the harsh reality of his own world and the dream-like qualities of the future hope. If the vision of such a benign state is the product of dream techniques used by seers (apocalyptic?) to foresee the future, it is ironic to find it included in the Jeremiah tradition which includes material so hostile to the use of dreams (cf. 23.25, 27–28, 32; 27.9; 29.8). However, the irony need only be noted as a possible reflection on the text and the indeterminate meaning of the statement renders all particular interpretations subject to dispute. The hope expressed in the images of vv. 23–25 is closely related to the bucolic joys of the poems in 30–31, with the additional element of the temple mount from whence the blessing of Yahweh (cf. the development of this motif in MT) will characterize the life of the restored communities throughout the land of Judah. If there is to be a resurgence of an old saying indicative of Yahweh's presence in the (rebuilt is implied though not stated) temple it should be contrasted with 3.16–17, where a different saying (relating to the ark of the covenant) will no longer be used. Both motifs have the same meaning: there will come a time when the presence of Yahweh in the land (Jerusalem in 3.17) will be so palpable that territory and people will thrive in the most wonderful of ways. Small wonder that the hope of vv. 23–25 should be viewed as the product of a most pleasant sleep.

31.27–30

27 'Behold, the days are coming, says the LORD, when I will sow the house of Israel and the house of Judah with the seed of man and the seed of beast.
28 And it shall come to pass that as I have watched over them to pluck up and break down, to overthrow, destroy, and bring evil, so I will watch over them to build and to plant, says the LORD. 29 In those days they shall no longer say:

"The fathers have eaten sour grapes,
and the children's teeth are set on edge."

30 But every one shall die for his own sin; each man who eats sour grapes, his teeth shall be set on edge.'

---

[27] MT *wᵉzāraʿtī*, 'and I will sow': for *zrʿ* as a figure of repopulating the land cf. Hos. 2.25 (EV 23); as a metaphor of scattering the people from their land cf. Zech. 10.9. The term is used in Num. 5.28 for the insemination of a woman which is analogous to sowing a field; so Yahweh will inseminate the communities with people and animals. **[28]** MT *šāqadtī*, 'I have watched': a positive use of *šqd*, cf 44.27 for its negative application (see on 1.12 for a neutral use of the term). G *kathairein kai kakoun*, 'to pull down and to maltreat', lacking two of the four terms in MT used to describe Yahweh's evil actions against the nation. The six metaphors of divine action only occur here and in 1.10, though various selections of them appear in 12.14–17; 18.7, 9; 24.6; 31.40; 42.10; 45.4 (for meanings see on 1.10; cf. Bach 1961). **[29]** MT *lōʾ-yōʾmᵉrū ʿōd*, 'they shall no longer say': = 3.16; 23.7; cf. 16.14. The phrase is the opposite of *ʿōd yōʾmᵉrū* 'once more they shall say' in v. 23, but both statements refer to the reversal of the nation's contemporary misfortunes. The use of *bayyāmīm hāhēm*, 'in those days', links an independent citation to the future hope of v. 27. MT *bōser*, 'unripe, sour grapes': cf. Isa. 18.5; Ezek. 18.2; Job 15.33. The proverb cited here and rebutted in v. 30 also appears in Ezek. 18.2, where it is debated at much greater length (18.1–32; cf. Zimmerli 1979, 378–87, for discussion). Lam. 5.7 touches on the same point without using the gnomic saying. **[30]** Cf. Deut. 24.16 for the same sentiment and reversal of the dogma of inherited retribution set out in the Decalogue (Ex. 20.5; Deut. 5.9); cf. II Kings 14.6. Mayes 1979, 326, relates the Deuteronomic law to the human administration of justice and argues that it is therefore not directly comparable with the divine justice of the Decalogue. The discussion of the matter in Ezek. 18.25, 29 suggests that divine rulings may be behind the debate (e.g. 'the way of Yahweh is not just'), but here vv. 29–30 hardly afford sufficient information to determine whether divine or only human justice is involved.

The first of the three future hopes ('look, the days are coming', vv. 27, 31, 38) for reversals of the past concerns the repopulation of the land by the two communities, Israel and Judah. Yahweh is represented as the virile progenitor who will sow the two houses with people and animals. This striking figure (cf. Hos. 2.23 [MT 25]) reflects the relationship between deity and land in the nature cults, where the maintenance of fertility is sustained by the cult in terms of the divine insemination of the earth and of humans. The terrible losses of human and animal life in the invasions of the land and the destruction of the cities (cf. 7.20) will be reversed in the future. This divine sowing of the communities will be a direct reversal of his previous policy of watching over them for evil purposes (cf. 18.11; 21.10). That policy was characterized by the disruption of all civilized life and the deity's negative attitude towards his people (summarized by the use of the four redactional motifs used throughout the tradition: 'pluck up', 'break down', 'overthrow', 'destroy'). These four negative terms are reversed by the two positive redactional figures 'build', 'plant'. The arid and deserted landscapes produced by Yahweh in his anger will now be cultivated again and human civilization will flourish in the future. The scrutiny (*šqd*) of evil with which Yahweh destroyed the nation will become a scrutiny of building and planting which will result in the great reversal of the nation's fate.

To this oracular proclamation of Yahweh's future transformation of man and beast in Israel and Judah has been added a further citation (cf. vv. 23, 26) which may also be found in Ezek. 18.2. Apparently as a result of the preaching of certain parties about the causes of the invasion, destruction and exile of the community being due to the long history of idolatry and rebellion (typical of the sermons in 7; 11; 25.1–7; 26. 2–6; Ezek. 16; 20; 23), there had grown up in the land a proverb to the effect that the fathers had eaten ssour grapes but the children's teeth have been set on edge (cf. 2.5,9). The proverb summarizes in the most succinct way the belief in inherited guilt and punishment – it is later generations who must pay for the sins of the fathers (cf. Job 21.19). The Ezekiel tradition attempts to combat this claim with assertions of the opposite belief. Here the addition to vv. 27–28 regards the future as a time when such a saying will have no validity. In that future each individual (cf. Ezek. 18.25–29; 33.17–20) will die for his own guilty actions. As part of a much debated controversy (cf. Lam. 5.7; Deut. 24.16) after the fall of Jerusalem such a fragment as vv. 29–30 has a rightful place in the Jeremiah tradition, though perhaps not here in a cycle of poems and prose additions about future salvation. For it introduces into the images of a great and prosperous future a chill note about the human condition (cf. Isa. 65.20b). Although in the future nobody will suffer for any misdeeds other than their own, there will be those who misbehave to the point of being executed! Everybody will bear the responsibility of their own actions. As a note of realism among the golden dreams of the utopian future it is quite out of place. In view of the next addition with its equally utopian image of a time when nobody will need to teach his neighbour divine knowledge because everybody will automatically possess that knowledge, it is even more inappropriate (see on v. 34). However, in this reversal of a popular saying of the time an old criticism is being transformed and the further implications of v. 30 should perhaps not be scrutinized too closely.

31.31–34

31 'Behold, the days are coming, says the LORD, when I will make a new covenant with the house of Israel and the house of Judah, 32 not like the covenant which I made with their fathers when I took them by the hand to bring them out of the land of Egypt, my covenant which they broke, though I was their husband, says the LORD. 33 But this is the covenant which I will make with the house of Israel after those days, says the LORD: I will put my law within them, and I will write it upon their hearts; and I will be their God, and they shall be my people. 34 And no longer shall each man teach his neighbour and each his brother, saying, "Know the LORD," for they shall all know me, from the least of them to the greatest, says the LORD; for I will forgive their iniquity, and I will remember their sin no more.'

[31] Rudolph, 201, deletes 'and the house of Judah' because it is lacking in v. 33; he understands 'house of Israel' to refer to the northern kingdom and not the whole people north and south. The reference to Judah may be an expansion (cf. v. 27; Bright, 283), but in that case 'Israel' should be understood as the whole nation and not the northern kingdom. **[32]** MT *hēpērū 'et-bᵉrītī*, 'they broke my covenant': cf. 11.10; 14.21; 33.20; Thiel 1970. MT *wᵉ'ānōkī bā'altī bām*, 'but I was their husband': *bā'al* may also be translated 'lord, baal', cf. 3.14. G *egō ēmelēsa autōn*, 'I loathed them' = *gā'altī* (cf. Heb. 8.9), which makes a better divine response to the broken covenant. **[33]** MT *bēt yiśrā'ēl*, 'house of Israel': a few mss *bᵉnē*, 'children . . .'. MT *'aḥᵃrē hayyāmīm hāhēm*, 'after those days': a curious phrase in the light of the formal 'days are coming' of v. 31; cf. v. 29; Martin-Achard 1974, 156 n. 49. Bright, 277, 'when that time comes', makes the two phrases equivalent (cf. Rudolph, 202–3). Perhaps the writer has synthesized two motifs: the coming days of restoration *after which bᵉrīt ḥᵃdāšāh*, 'a new covenant' (or divine obligation) will be enacted; it being a further event in the programme of restoration'; cf. Perlitt 1969, 180 who refers it to the 'dark present'. Weiser, 288, refers the strange phrase to the extension of the historical horizon into the eschatological. Many mss read *wᵉnātattī*, '*and* I will put (my *tōrāh* in their midst)'. The formulaic 'I will be their god and they shall be my people' appears in various forms in 7.23; 11.4; 13.11; 24.7; 30.22; 31.1; 32.38. The inscribing of the *tōrāh* on the mind (*lēb*, EVV 'heart') is a metaphorical transformation of an external practice whereby what the law stands for is interiorized; cf. the similar transformation of the figure of circumcision in 4.4 (enjoined upon the people as something they must do for themselves); Deut. 30.6 (a divine enactment). 9.25–26 represent a rather different strand of tradition. **[34]** MT *kī 'eslaḥ la'ᵃwōnām*, 'for I will forgive their iniquity': for the motif of forgiveness in the Jeremiah tradition see 5.1, 7; 33.8; 36.3; 50.20 (cf. Amos 7.2; Isa. 55.7). In Num. 14.18–20 Yahweh's forgiveness (*nś'*, *slḥ*) of the people's iniquity (*'āwōn*) is seen as a history of continual forgiveness (*nś'*), from the exodus to the time when the prayer of Moses was written ('even until now'); cf. Solomon's prayer for forgiveness in I Kings 8.30–50.

Anderson 1964; Bright 1966a; Buis 1968; Herrmann 1965, 179–85, 195–204; Martin-Achard 1974; Weippert 1979

The third addition to the cycle envisages the making of a *new bᵉrīt* (the only occurrence in the Hebrew Bible where *bᵉrīt*, 'covenant' [?] 'obligation' [?], is qualified by *ḥᵃdāšāh*, 'new') in the future indicated by the formulaic 'look, days are coming' (cf. vv. 27, 38). A reversal motif is incorporated in the piece in that the new *bᵉrīt* will replace the old one broken by the community's fathers in the past. That broken *b^e rīt* had reversed the relationship of Yahweh with the people by making him disgusted with the nation (v. 32 G), but when the new *b^e rīt* is instituted the house of Israel will become Yahweh's people and he their god (once more?). If the motif *b^e rīt* is a common one in Dueteronomistically influenced traditions, the concept of newness associated with it here is less clear. This particular instantiation of *b^e rīt* interiorizes the divine *tōrāh* in the minds of the people, and such interiorization may constitute the *new* element in *b^e rīt* (cf. Swetnam 1974 for the interpretation of the new feature as the making available in the synagogues [or wherever Israelites are to be found] of copies of the Mosaic Law). As a consequence of such internalization there will be 'the cessation of tradition' (Westermann 1964, 219); i.e. the human teaching of the knowledge of Yahweh will cease because each person will know Yahweh (already). Every class of persons in the nation ('from the least of them to the greatest') will know the deity, and this state of knowledge will reverse the accusations made in 5.1–5; 8.7. A further consequence of the new *b^e rīt* will be the divine forgiveness of the nation's iniquity (contrast 5.1, 7a). So in the future to which this oracular statement looks forward the dire straits into which the fathers of the community had brought the nation in 587 will be reversed by the making of an *unbreakable* new *b^e rīt* (as in the discourses of 2–3, only two generations are described: the past and the future, though a third one [i.e. the one receiving this declaration] may be discerned, cf. 2.9).

The *b^e rīt* motif is not a dominant element in the Jeremiah tradition, though it appears in that strand often identified as Deuteronomistic (cf. Herrmann; Thiel 1981, 23–28). A number of different *b^e rīt* feature peripherally in the traditions: e.g. the ark of the covenant (3.16), the covenant preached by Jeremiah (11.2, 3, 6, 8), the *new* covenant appended to the cycle of 30–31 (31.32, 33), Yahweh's covenant with day and night which affords an analogue of the future covenant between Yahweh and the dynasy of David (33.20–2, 25), a covenant made between king Zedekiah and the people of Jerusalem (34.8, 10, 13, 15, 18), the covenant of the exodus period (34.13; cf. 31.32) and the covenant of the future whereby the people will join themselves to Yahweh permanently (50.5; cf. 32.40). These mainly refer to future hopes about the organization of the community, though a few are allusions to the past. In envisaging a new *b^e rīt* the author of this oracle ignores the problems of the past and foresees a form of relationship between Yahweh and nation which will avoid the defects of the old system of *b^e^rît* by virtue of internalizing the divine instructions (*tôrāh*). It is a pious hope rather than a programme of social organization and it may be described quite fairly as utopian. Such utopianism is a feature of the futuristic elements in the prophetic anthologies (cf. Blenkinsopp 1983, 105) and represents a fundamental weakness of biblical prophecy. The individuals within the nation will not need to teach one another the knowledge of Yahweh (is this awareness and experience of the deity [cf. 5.4–5; 9.24] or the practice of justice [cf. 22.15–16] or something quite undefined?) because each one will know it already and the nation's iniquity will be forgiven. Bright rightly asks important questions of this utopian outlook: 'And what of the still further future? Will the people thereafter sin no more?' (1966a, 195). His answer to these queries is correct without being penetrating: 'That is a question that lies beyond Jeremiah's field of vision. The new covenant is God's final, gracious provision for his people; the question of its continuing endurance does not enter his mind.' That is the very nature of utopian thought – it predicts a splendid future but is unable to show how such a state may first be achieved and then maintained permanently without disintegration into the chaos which preceded it. The old covenant may have been broken, but it is assumed that the new one will not be (on the analogy of the tables of the law only being broken once?). If the people will really know Yahweh in such an interior manner then the future will be sinless – a veritable utopia and the triumph of hope over experience. Such coming days have yet to come, and it is worth pondering again some words of Immanuel Kant on the difficulty of producing a just society: 'from so crooked wood as man is made out of, nothing completely straight can be built' (Kant 1963, 18).

Whatever the problems of utopian visions of the future, the exegesis of vv. 31–34 is straightforward and the interpretation of the piece would be simple were it not for the fact that many commentators insist on reading 31.31–34 as 'one of the profoundest and most moving passages in the entire Bible' (e.g. Bright, 287; cf. Thompson, 579–80). This Christian appreciation of a minor and prosaic hope for the future, often identified with the new covenant of the New Testament (cf. Heb. 8.8–13; 10.15–17), while irrelevant for the meaning of the text, complicates the treatment of the section because there is a large literature devoted to its interpretation from the viewpoint of Christian theology. In this reading of the new *b^e^rît* passage the future hope for the house of Israel becomes a prediction of the Christian gospel:

> So we must go beyond Jeremiah's word, and beyond B.C. We must follow Jeremiah's word ahead to the gospel, for it is to the gospel that it points us and drives us; and until it has driven us there it has not discharged its function. We hear Jeremiah's word, '. . . I will make a new covenant . . .' – and that is promise. We also hear the gospel word, 'This cup is the new covenant in my blood' – and that is fulfillment (Bright 1966a, 204).

Part of this perspective on the text is a striving to demonstrate that it comes from Jeremiah (e.g. Bright, 287; 1966a, 192–3; discussion in Martin-Achard, 149–52), though the question of authorship can hardly affect the meaning of the statement. If Bright clamours for Jeremiah's responsibility for its sentiments, others regard it in varying degrees as coming from the prophet of Anathoth (probably the majority of exegetes: e.g. Martin-Achard, 151, attributes its paternity to Jeremiah; Rudolph, 201, assigns it to his early preaching to the northern kingdom). The Deuteronomistic shaping of the language and thought allows some scholars to associate it with that redaction of the tradition rather than with Jeremiah (e.g. Böhmer, Herrmann, Nicholson, Thiel). Others attribute it to a disciple of Jeremiah (e.g. Coppens 1963; Mowinckel 1942, 93–6) or a post-exilic scribe (Duhm, 255). Among those exegetes who assign it to Jeremiah himself, some regard it as including his response to Deuteronomistic views (Martin-Achard, 163) or his reaction to the failure of the reform of 621 (Anderson, 229). Deuteronomistic influence must be acknowledged in the passage, but in view of the fact that the Deuteronomists do not themselves at any point in their writings propose a new covenant, not even in the late piece on the restoration of Israel in Deut. 30.1–10, it must be questioned whether they are responsible for this addition to the cycle. The attribution of authorship in the Jeremiah tradition is a moot point, especially in relation to 30–31, and, though I favour a post-exilic dating for 31.31–34, a dogmatic position is to be avoided. However, I would regard the relation between 31.31–34 and the Deuteronomistic strand in the tradition to be one of critical dialogue (cf. Wisser 1983, 223–4). The Deuteronomists believed that the covenant had been broken and therefore had become inoperable. Late additions to their work allow for the possibility of Yahweh's restoration of the nation and the divine circumcision of its mind after it has turned back to him (Deut. 30.1–10). But of a new covenant the Deuteronomists know nothing (cf. Buis, 13 for the possible connections between 31.31–34 and Deut. 30.1–10). The author of 31.31–34 transcends that limitation by asserting the divine initiative beyond human turning and the making of a new *b^erît*. It is a post-Deuteronomistic hope but one which has learned its theology from Deuteronomism and made the leap of hope into the utopian future. In that future the broken *b^erît* would be transformed in the creation of a new *b^erît* which would transpose *tôrāh* from the stones of the Mosaic legend or the documents of scribes to the mind of the community. This movement from literal to symbolical indicates the metaphorical status of *b^erît* in 31.31–34 (cf. the new mind and spirit of Ezek. 36.26). The *b^erît* motif, asserts this future hope, did not come to an end with 587 as the logic of Deuteronomism demands, but has a future when Yahweh will act to transform the nation.

The use of *b^erît* as a metaphor to describe a state where the community will automatically keep the divine *tôrāh* must be considered a postscript to Deuteronomistic uses of *b^erît* because it transforms those uses in a very radical way. This future *b^erît* is not an obligation between two parties with national and moral regulations which may be kept or broken, but a metaphor of an arrangement with an imaginary community (what Bultmann 1955 calls an 'eschatological concept') which rescues a resonant word (*b^erît*) from oblivion. The utopian society characterized by this metaphor of *b^erît* does not and cannot exist, yet like all the additions to the cycle vv. 31–34 utilize motifs and sayings from the past to construct an idyll of the future. Transformations of such an idyll may produce fertile soil for new movements to develop in ways unimaginable by the author (e.g. the rise of Christian communities), but in terms of the Jeremiah tradition the images and language of the piece reflect upon and transform motifs of a disintegrating and fragmented society to be found in chapters 4–21. In the restoration of the nation the deity will act to create the kind of society which previous generations failed so miserably to achieve.

31.35–37

35 Thus says the LORD,
who gives the sun for light by day
and the fixed order of the moon and the stars for light by night,
who stirs up the sea so that its waves roar –
the LORD of hosts is his name:
36 'If this fixed order departs
from before me, says the LORD,
then shall the descendants of Israel cease
from being a nation before me for ever.'
37 Thus says the LORD:
'If the heavens above can be measured,
and the foundations of the earth below can be explored,
then I will cast off all the descendants of Israel
for all that they have done,
says the LORD.'

---

[35] NEB treats this verse as a prose introduction to the oracular poem in v. 36 and v. 37 as a prose conclusion to it. G has v. 37 before vv. 35, 36. MT *ḥuqqōt*, 'fixed orders': cf. *ḥuqqīm*, v. 36; *ḥuqqōt*, 33.25; *ḥoq-'ōlām*, 'permanent limit', 5.22; these are what von Rad (1972, 107 n. 7) calls ' "orders" in creation . . . orders of heaven and earth'. In 33.20, 25 the orders of night and day are described as Yahweh's *berīt* with day and night. Volz, 283, reads *ḥōqēq*, 'fixed' (moon), followed by Rudolph, 204 (cf. BHS). MT *rōga' hayyām wayyehemū gallāyw yhwh ṣebā'ōt šemō*, 'he disturbs the sea so that its waves roar – Yahweh of hosts is his name' = Isa. 51.15b; G *kai kraugēn en thalassē*, 'and a roaring in the sea . . .'. **[36]** MT *'im-yāmušū haḥuqqīm hā'ēlleh*, 'if these fixed orders depart': i.e. are removed or fail. As the fixed orders of creation exist before Yahweh's presence, so does the seed (*zera'*, i.e. descendants) of Israel; both are permanent. **[37]** G lacks 'thus says Yahweh', and has *hupsōthē*, 'be raised' (= *yārumū*) for MT *yimmaddū*, 'be measured'. MT *weyēḥāqrū*, 'and (they) be searched out, explored': G *kai ean tapeinōthē*, 'and if (they) be sunk'. G lacks 'all' (*kol*) before 'seed of Israel'.

The fourth addition is a hymnic poem which affirms the permanence of the seed (i.e. race NEB; offspring JPSB; descendants RSV) of Israel and Yahweh's maintenance of it for ever. Yahweh of hosts (cf. Isa. 51.15) is the one who has provided the sun to give light during the day and the moon and stars to light up the night (cf. Gen. 1.14–18), and these permanent orders of creation are analogues of Israel's permanence as a nation before Yahweh. This late hymn is the only element in vv. 23–40 which does not directly reverse a saying or past event and it may once have been a hymnic conclusion to the cycle before vv. 23–34, 38–40 were added (cf. Bright, 286–7). It summarizes the word of restoration which dominates 30–31 using cosmic figures as metaphors of Israel's guaranteed future and reflects the late glossing of prophetic texts with allusions to the power of *Yahweh of hosts* (cf. Amos 4.13; 9.5–6; Crenshaw 1975). The hymn presents Israel's descendants as having a permanent existence before the divine presence (contrast the more negative use of created orders in 5.20–25) and contrasts quite strikingly with much of the Jeremiah tradition which emphasizes the doom-laden future of the nation because of its past sins or its current state. In the oracles about the prosperous future the possibility of sin and destruction is almost entirely absent (see on 31.30). The optimism of the dogma of permanent favoured status before Yahweh gives the book of Jeremiah a tension between present misery and future prosperity which reverses the usual dialectic of absolute judgment and contingent hope analysed by the theological scrutineers of the tradition. After 587 the word of absolute destruction began to give way to words of hope (though see on 44, where destruction remains decreed of the communities in Egypt) and these are to be found concentrated in 30–33. The permanence of Israel through its descendants on the basis of created orders of the universe (i.e. Israel's existence is equivalent to such a fixed order of nature; cf. Second Isaiah's equivalences between the creation of the world and the creation of Israel through the exodus and the return from exile) is a parallel motif to the new *bᵉrīt* of 31.31–34 which implies, without specific articulation, a permanent future without sin in which the whole nation will know Yahweh. These additions to the cycle (vv. 23–40) point to the development of beliefs (in the Persian period?) in the absoluteness of Israel's restoration and prosperity in the future. No such disaster as 587 would ever again destroy the nation, for its future existence is of the order of one of Yahweh's decrees of creation, i.e. permanent (cf. 32.40; 33.17–26; 50.4–5, 20). And this Yahweh himself says – oracular indicators are used four times in MT to stress the intensity and importance of this hymnic affirmation.

31.38–40

38 ‘Behold, the days are coming, says the LORD, when the city shall be rebuilt for the LORD from the tower of Hananel to the Corner Gate. 39 And the measuring line shall go out farther, straight to the hill Gareb, and shall then turn to Goah. 40 The whole valley of the dead bodies and the ashes, and all the fields as far as the brook Kidron, to the corner of the Horse Gate toward the east, shall be sacred to the LORD. It shall not be uprooted or overthrown any more for ever.’

---

[38] MT *hinnēh yāmīm*, ‘look, days . . .’, lacks *bā’īm* (supplied masoretically by Q reading in text): lack of representation in K may be due to haplography of *n’m*, ‘says’ (cf. BHS); Vrs read ‘are coming’ (*bā’īm*). MT *hā‘īr lyhwh*, ‘the city for Yahweh’: or ‘the city of Yahweh’, cf. NEB ‘in the Lord’s honour’ (analogous to *l*^{e}*dāwid*, ‘for David’, in the titles in the book of Psalms). Rudolph, 206, suggests ‘by’ Yahweh, cf. 31.4. For the two locations ‘tower of Hananel’ (Neh. 3.1; 12.39) and ‘corner gate’ (II Kings 14.13; II Chron. 26.9) cf. Zech. 14.10; ‘(from) . . . *to*’ may be represented in MT by *hpnh* with *he locale* (so Driver, 1937–38, 120) or *l* ‘to’ lacking due to haplography (cf. BHS). **[39]** K *qwh*; Q *qāw*, ‘line’ (K construct form *q*^{e}*wēh*, cf. BDB, 876). MT *negdō*, ‘in front of *it*’: G *autōn* ‘ . . . *them*’; *w*^{e}*nāsab gō‘ātāh*, ‘and shall turn to Goath’: G *kai perikuklōthēsetai kuklō ex eklektōn lithōn*, ‘and it shall be encompassed with a circle of choice stones’. The locations ‘hill of Gareb’, ‘Goath/Goah’ are unknown; Bright, 283, relates them to the west on the grounds that v. 38 refers to the north and v. 40 to the south and east. **[40]** G lacks ‘and the whole valley of the dead bodies and the ashes’: the ‘valley’ (*‘ēmeq*) may be an allusion to the fire-cult practised in the valley (*gay’*, 7.31–32) but need not be so understood. It may simply refer to an area where terrible slaughter once took place. K *hšrmwt*; Q *hašš*^{e}*dēmōt*, ‘fields’ (K incomprehensible): a possible reference to *š*^{e}*dēh māwet*, ‘field of death’, i.e. cemetery (cf. V *regionem mortis*; Ug. *šd mt*, ‘field of Mot’; Lehmann 1953), though here it may just mean ‘fields’ for cultivation (cf. Croatto und Soggin 1962); G = K. MT *‘ad . . . ‘ad* ‘as far as (the brook Kidron), as far as (the corner)’: Rudolph, Bright follow Volz, 283, and read *‘al*, ‘above’, for the first *‘ad* (MT due to scribal miscopying). MT *lō’-yinnātēš w*^{e}*lō’ yehārēs ‘ōd l*^{e}*‘ōlām*, ‘it shall not be uprooted or overthrown again for ever’: *ntš*, *hrs* belong to the thematic list of 1.10.

The final addition to the cycle is the third of the ‘days are coming’ series which reverses old sayings, practices and occurrences. In this piece the rebuilding of Yahweh’s city, i.e. Jerusalem, is described in terms of the area which will be reconstructed so as to represent the sacred territory that will remain inviolable for ever. The plucking up *(ntš)* and overthrowing *(hrs)* of the city in the past (587 and subsequently?) will be reversed in the future building of the area, and its special relation to Yahweh *(qdš)* will make it the holy city (this motif appears in Isa. 48.2; 52.1). Such sacred status will afford the city permanent protection. The images of the city in 7.30 – 8.3 are here reversed, and the rebuilding of the city is given an oracular justification which may have been intended to provide backing for a particular building project (cf. Zech. 14.10–11; Ezek. 40–48). So the coda to the cycle ends with the rebuilt Jerusalem, Yahweh's city, facing a prosperous future under permanent divine protection (cf. Isa. 4.5–6), with its terrible past completely reversed.

32.1–15

32[1] The word that came to Jeremiah from the LORD in the tenth year of
Zedekiah king of Judah, which was the eighteenth year of Nebuchadrezzar.
2 At that time the army of the king of Babylon was besieging Jerusalem,
and Jeremiah the prophet was shut up in the court of the guard which was
in the palace of the king of Judah. 3 For Zedekiah king of Judah had
imprisoned him, saying, 'Why do you prophesy and say, "Thus says the
LORD: Behold, I am giving this city into the hand of the king of Babylon,
and he shall take it; 4 Zedekiah king of Judah shall not escape out of the
hand of the Chaldeans, but shall surely be given into the hand of the king
of Babylon, and shall speak with him face to face and see him eye to eye; 5
and he shall take Zedekiah to Babylon, and there he shall remain until I
visit him, says the LORD; though you fight against the Chaldeans, you shall
not succeed"?'

6 Jeremiah said, 'The word of the LORD came to me: 7 Behold, Hanamel
the son of Shallum your uncle will come to you and say, "Buy my field
which is at Anathoth, for the right of redemption by purchase is yours." 8
Then Hanamel my cousin came to me in the court of the guard, in
accordance with the word of the LORD, and said to me, "Buy my field which
is at Anathoth in the land of Benjamin, for the right of possession and
redemption is yours; buy it for yourself." Then I knew that this was the
word of the LORD.

9 And I bought the field at Anathoth from Hanamel my cousin, and
weighed out the money to him, seventeen shekels of silver. 10 I signed the
deed, sealed it, got witnesses, and weighed the money on scales. 11 Then I
took the sealed deed of purchase, containing the terms and conditions, and
the open copy; 12 and I gave the deed of purchase to Baruch the son of

Neriah son of Mahseiah, in the presence of Hanamel my cousin, in the presence of all the Jews who were sitting in the court of the guard. 13 I charged Baruch in their presence, saying, 14 "Thus says the LORD of hosts, the God of Israel: Take these deeds, both this sealed deed of purchase and this open deed, and put them in an earthenware vessel, that they may last for a long time. 15 For thus says the LORD of hosts, the God of Israel: Houses and fields and vineyards shall again be bought in this land." '

[MT 32] = G 39. **[1]** K *bšnt*; Q *baššānāh*, 'in the (tenth) year': cf. 28.1 for this K–Q variation. The introductory formula for the reception of the divine word is the same as that in 21.1; 34.1, 8; 35.1; 40.1; and similar to 7.1; 11.1; 18.1, which have *lē'mōr*, 'saying', instead of a temporal clause indicating the occasion on which the word was received. For the eighteenth year of Nebuchadrezzar, cf. 52.29, which places the deportation of 587 then (counting his first year as 604/3), but 25.1; 52.12; II Kings 25.8 (counting from 605) refer the deportation to his nineteenth year; cf. Soggin 1984, 251, on the discrepancy, which can hardly be attributed to two different chronological systems in Jer. 52 (*contra* Malamat 1968, 150). **[2]** Verses 2–5 are a redactional parenthesis setting out the reason for Jeremiah's imprisonment (cf. 37.11–14 for a different account; 34.2–3 for a summary of the charge here). MT *hannābî'*, 'the prophet': lacking in G. **[3]** Cf. 37.21 for the imprisonment motif and 34.2 for the message of v. 3. **[4]** Cf. 34.3; K *'ynw*; Q *'ēnāw*, 'his eyes': MT lit. 'and his mouth will speak with his mouth and his eyes will see his eyes', cf. NEB 'he will speak with him face to face and see him with his own eyes'. **[5]** MT *'ad-poqᵉdî 'ōtō*, 'until I visit him': cf. 15.15; 27.22; 29.10 where *pqd* means 'to visit graciously' (cf. Ruth 1.6; Ps. 65.10 [EV 9]) and that would appear to be the meaning here (hence the motif of peaceful death in 34.4–5). G lacks second half of verse from after 'and remain there' (*kai ekei kathieitai*); G^A *apothaneitai*, 'and die' (cf. 22.12, 26). Zedekiah died in prison (52.11); some exegetes think that the editor has here confused Zedekiah with Jehoiachin (cf. 52.31–34; Duhm, 261; Volz, 299; Hyatt, 1043–4). **[6]** MT *wayyō'mer yirmᵉyāhû hāyāh*, 'and Jeremiah said . . . came . . .': G *egenēthē* = *wayᵉhî*; MT *'ēlay*, 'to me': G *pros Ieremian*, 'to Jeremiah' (cf. 'to me', v. 8). This is not Jeremiah's response to Zedekiah but the beginning of the symbolical-magical act of vv. 6–15, of which vv. 1–5 are the editorial setting of the transaction. The text does not indicate to whom Jeremiah spoke (MT), hence G is better as an introduction to the divine word. **[7]** Hanamel ben Shallum: cf. Hananel in 31.38. MT *mišpaṭ haggᵉ'ullāh*, 'the right, duty, custom of redemption': cf. Lev. 25.25–28 for some of the rules about kin obligations to purchase land in the family. For the divine word as anticipating the future behaviour of people cf. 13.12–13. **[8]** MT *ben-dōdî*, lit. 'the son of my uncle', i.e. 'cousin'. G lacks *kidᵉbar yhwh*, 'according to the word of Yahweh'. BHS treats 'which is in the land of

Benjamin' as additional (a superfluous gloss Rudolph, 208); G has the phrase before 'which is in Anathoth'. MT *ûlᵉkā haggᵉʾullāh qᵉnēh-lāk*, 'and to you belongs (the right of *mišpaṭ*?) the redemption, buy for yourself': G *kai su presbuteros*, 'and you are the oldest', i.e. the closest of kin (?). MT *mišpaṭ hayᵉruššah*, 'the right of possession', varies the form of v. 7. MT *wāʾēdaʿ kī dᵉbar-yhwh hūʾ*, 'then I knew that this was the word of Yahweh': a most unusual example of confirmation of the divine word in the tradition. **[9]** Apparently the land was bought unseen by Jeremiah! Cf. 37.12, where he takes the opportunity to visit it during a lull in the siege (see on 37.11–15). G lacks 'which was in Anathoth' and '(weighed out to him) the silver'. It is not possible to determine the value of this transaction since we do not know the size of the field or the exchange rate of the silver shekel. As it stands the story presents a Jeremiah who has both money and property. **[11]** MT *hammiṣwāh wᵉhaḥuqqīm*, 'the order and the statutes': lacking in G, NEB; JPSB, 'according to rule and law'; 'the contract and the prescriptions', Bright, 237. The legal terminology may indicate the rules governing contracts: the sealed copy was for a permanent record and the open copy was for consultation (cf. Hyatt, 1045; Bright, 237–8; the Elephantine Letters [Porten 1968]). **[12]** Baruch ben Neriah ben Mahseiah: cf. 36.4–32; 43.3–7; 45. MT *ḥᵃnamʾēl dōdī*, 'Hanamel my uncle': some mss, Vrs read 'son of my uncle', i.e. 'cousin', as in vv. 8, 9. MT *ûlᵉʿênē hāʿēdīm hakkōtᵉbīm*, 'and in the sight of the witnesses who wrote . . .': G 'and in the sight of those standing and writing . . .'. **[14]** Rudolph treats the opening phrase as a mechanical gloss after 'saying' (cf. BHS). G lacks 'these deeds', 'the sealed'. The storing of the deeds in a ceramic jar may be for their protection over a long period, which hardly suggests that the open copy was for consultation.

The story of Jeremiah's purchase of a field in Anathoth belonging to his kin appears in a heavily edited chapter which develops a number of themes at great length (vv. 1–5, 16–25, 26–35, 36–41, 42–45). It is complicated by being placed after an introductory account of Zedekiah's arrest and imprisonment of Jeremiah during the siege of Jerusalem in 588–7. This particular theme is presented a number of times in the tradition, though on each occasion there are significant variations in the story of the encounter between Jeremiah and Zedekiah (or his delegation) which make a complex pattern of motifs (cf. 21.1–7; 32.1–5; 34.1–7; 37.1–15, 16–21; 38.1–6, 14–28). These constitute a major theme in the narratives of the book of Jeremiah. However, it is not happily presented as an introduction to the buying of the family plot in Anathoth as it represents an occasion when access to the city from the north was freely available to Jeremiah's relative in spite of Jerusalem being *under siege* at the time! Jeremiah's visit to Benjaminite territory is explained in 37.12 as occurring during a tactical withdrawal by the Babylonians but no such explanation is offered in 32.1–5. Rather Jeremiah is depicted as being shut up in the courtyard at a time when the Babylonians had shut up the city so as to prevent exit or access. If the story of the land purchase is read apart from its present redactional position sense may be made of it (to a certain degree), yet its placing here must be taken into account on two counts. The story is a positive statement about the future (cf. v. 15), hence belongs with the additions to the cycle of 30–31. It is a statement of Jeremiah's actions, rather than words, for the future which, because of their magical nature, create that future. The second count concerns the contrast set up between Jeremiah's constricted circumstances in vv. 1–5 and the great freedom with which he manipulates the future so as to secure it for the nation. His actions while under open arrest preserve for the Jews a future of conventional buying and selling.

There are other problems with the story of Jeremiah's purchase of family land which undermine treating it as a historical event and demonstrate it to be a paradigmatic account of how the future was secured by Jeremiah *the prophet* (MT). In 11.21–23 the men of Anathoth are represented as seeking Jeremiah's life (the interpretation taken by most conventional exegetes), yet in 32.7–8 a relative from Anathoth offers him land. Had the quarrel, in spite of its lethal potentialities, been settled between the two parties? If it had not been amicably solved, what likelihood was there that Jeremiah could ever make use of his piece of land among people who wished to kill him? The purchase of land during a harsh siege by the Babylonians may be presented as hope for the future in the text, but in real-life terms such an action would be the most foolhardy of treasonous acts. Consider the matter. In a time of invasion and siege why buy land that might never be occupied? Might it not be the case that a man who was prepared to make such a purchase was in fact a traitor, a collaborator with the enemy who stood to gain after the nation's defeat? It is not a fanciful argument – it is similar to the accusation made against Jeremiah in 37.13. A man who proclaimed that the Babylonians would capture the city and the king, yet who at the same time bought up land, must have come under suspicion immediately. The tradition knows no such accusation but does emphasize that the seizure of Jeremiah was due to his opposition to Judah in favour of the enemy *in a time of war* (the most absolute form of high treason). For this treachery he was arrested (cf. 32.3; 37.13–15; 38.1–6). It therefore seems most unlikely that the story of the purchase of family land should be understood as a literal act of Jeremiah's; it should be read as one more presentation of *Jeremiah the prophet* behaving in a paradigmatic manner with reference to the community's future. *The* prophet here *creates* the positive future spoken of in his oracles in 30–31 by means of a piece of family business in which he secures property against the distant future ('many days', v. 14) when once more (*'ōd*, cf. 31.23, 29) houses, fields and vineyards will be bought and sold in the land.

The encounter between Jeremiah and Zedekiah reflects the one constant in that theme – the Babylonians will prevail against city and king. If in 21.6–8 nobody escapes the savage butchery of the Babylonians, here Zedekiah is reassured that he will be taken to Babylon after confronting Nebuchadrezzar and there he must remain until Yahweh visits him (cf. 27.22). In 34.5 Zedekiah is apprised of his own death in Babylon, a death which will be 'in *šālōm*' (Yahweh's gracious visit of 32.5?), with the proper funeral arrangements following. Here the precise details of the divine visitation are left unstated because the redactors' concern is with a rather different future. In Babylon there is no future (but horror and death), whereas in the land of Palestine there is a future. That future is now secured by Jeremiah's actions. What is spoken and written in 30–31 is here made good by the first act of the future.

For reasons unstated in the text, Jeremiah's cousin Hanamel offers him family land as his to purchase by right. The divine word does not command Jeremiah to go and buy land but simply informs him that land will be offered for sale to him. When Hanamel appears, Jeremiah knows that what he had heard was indeed Yahweh's word (an unusual point of confirmation in the tradition, cf. I Sam. 10.1–7). Here we have *the prophet* (MT) whose every anticipation and action is governed by the divine word and whose knowledge of what is happening in the world is mediated to him by that word (cf. 11.21–23; 13.12–13). So Hanamel's offer of land is accepted by Jeremiah, and for seventeen shekels of silver (seven ounces) he buys family territory in the land of Benjamin. It would be pointless to speculate on Jeremiah the man of means and property because the tradition provides no hints as to how someone so universally spoken against could also be so well appointed as to buy land with silver on the spur of the moment. The paradigmatic prophet is always adequately equipped and furnished, no matter what the emergency (cf. the stories of Elijah and Elisha). The transaction of buying and selling land is scrupulously observed: written deeds, sealed and open, witnesses in particular and in general (the Jews in the court reveal how open Jeremiah's arrest is, though their presence is fundamentally important because what they are observing is *their* title-deed to land in the future). Baruch ben Neriah, appearing in the tradition for the first time, becomes the custodian of the deeds which are placed in a ceramic jar for preservation. In the presence of this assembled host Jeremiah proclaims the meaning of his action: 'houses and fields and vineyards shall again be bought in this land'. This is Yahweh's word, and the prophet's action will one day, a long time from now, create Judah's future because it is the first purchase of land in and for that future.

The family land bought by Jeremiah is like the field of Ephron which Abraham bought in order to bury his dead (Gen. 23), an earnest of the future and a land claim legitimately acquired. The small plot of land in Anathoth will become a symbol of the whole land and the prophet is the first man to own property in the new age when Yahweh restores the fortunes of Israel. Ironically Jeremiah will be dead by then, and as a childless man (the conventional interpretation of 16.1–2) his piece of property will have passed on to others. However, the niceties of legal requirements have been observed and the act is more important than the fact that Jeremiah will never see that land. Its purchase by *the* prophet is what matters because it stakes a claim to the future *in the land* for the people. The future is not in Babylon (*contra* 24.4–7; 29.4–7) but here in Judah – which is why the story is set in the period of Jeremiah's arrest during the siege by Babylon. The terrifying present is reversed by his act in buying Palestinian land. Zedekiah may go to Babylon (with his courtiers, supporters and other citizens), but Yahweh has a future for the land of Judah (cf. 42.7–12). The jar containing the title deeds to that field in Anathoth, wherever it may be hidden (did it survive the fall of Jerusalem? foolish question because it is not that kind of story), contains Judah's future and the divine word acting through *the prophet* has already created that future. The Babylonians may lay siege to the city, take it and raze it to the ground, but the future has been secured.

32.16–25

16 'After I had given the deed of purchase to Baruch the son of Neriah, I
prayed to the LORD, saying: 17 "Ah Lord GOD! It is thou who hast made
the heavens and the earth by thy great power and by thy outstretched arm!
Nothing is too hard for thee, 18 who showest steadfast love to thousands,
but dost requite the guilt of fathers to their children after them, O great and
mighty God whose name is the LORD of hosts, 19 great in counsel and
mighty in deed; whose eyes are open to all the ways of men, rewarding every
man according to his ways and according to the fruit of his doings; 20 Who
hast shown signs and wonders in the land of Egypt, and to this day in Israel
and among all mankind, and hast made thee a name, as at this day. 21
Thou didst bring thy people Israel out of the land of Egypt with signs and
wonders, with a strong hand and outstretched arm, and with great terror;
22 and thou gavest them this land, which thou didst swear to their fathers
to give them, a land flowing with milk and honey; 23 and they entered and
took possession of it. But they did not obey thy voice or walk in thy law;
they did nothing of all thou didst command them to do. Therefore thou hast
made all this evil come upon them. 24 Behold, the siege mounds have come
up to the city to take it, and because of sword and famine and pestilence
the city is given into the hands of the Chaldeans who are fighting against
it. What thou didst speak has come to pass, and behold, thou seest it. 25
Yet thou, O Lord GOD, hast said to me, 'Buy the field for money and get
witnesses' – though the city is given into the hands of the Chaldeans." '

---

[16] MT *wā'etpallēl 'el-yhwh*, 'and I prayed to Yahweh': contrast the presentation of Jeremiah in 7.16; 11.14; 14.11. **[17]** MT *lō'-yippālē' mimm^{e}kā kol-dābār*, 'nothing is too difficult for you': this half-line links the prayer to the oracular sermon in vv. 26–35 by virtue of the similar half-line in v. 27b; cf. the question in Gen. 18.14a, *h^{a}yippālē mēyhwh dābār*, 'is anything too difficult for Yahweh?'. G *apokrubē*, 'hidden', for *pl'*, 'wonderful, difficult, extraordinary'. The occurrence of *hinnēh*, 'look', may be linked to *hinnēh* in v. 24, where the prayer may be said to continue after the extolment of Yahweh in vv. 18–23 (cf. Bright, 294). Deuteronomistic elements are to be found in the prayer (cf. Thiel 1981, 31–4). **[18]** G lacks 'of hosts is his name', and links *yhwh* with 'great' in v. 19, where the occurrence of *pantokratōr* indicates a displaced *ṣ^{e}bā'ōt*, 'hosts', i.e. 'all-powerful'. The recital of Yahweh's favour and vengeance (cf. Ex. 20.5–6; Deut. 5.9–10) contrasts with 31.29–30 but indicates the rhetorical nature of such liturgical recitations. **[19]** This verse appears to contradict the principle of extended guilt in v. 18, but prayers such as this one (cf. Neh. 9.6–37; Dan. 9.3–19) are made up of many clichés and conventional lines, so should not be scrutinized for precision of principle or thought. G lacks 'and according to the fruit of his doings'. **[20]** MT *'ad-hayyōm hazzeh*, 'to this day': i.e. the present time, whenever the speech may be given (cf. Childs 1963 on this formulaic phrase); cf. v. 31; 3.25. JPSB understands the phrase to mean 'with lasting effect', whereas RSV, NEB provide 'and' (added to MT by BHS) before it as the logic of the statement demands. MT *kayyōm hazzeh*, 'as at this day': i.e. 'like today' or 'this very day', cf. 11.5; 25.18; 44.6, 23; DeVries 1975, 52 n. 78. **[21]** Cf. Deut. 4.34; 26.8–9. **[23]** K *wbtrwtk*; Q *ūbᵉtōrātᵉkā*, 'and in your law'; cf. 30.3 where the taking possession of the land is also posited of the future. The sense of v. 23 is to be found in 9.13; 11.8; 44.10, 23. **[24]** MT *hassōllōt bā'u hā'īr*, 'the siege ramps have come to the city': G *ochlos*, 'a mob, crowd', for 'mound, siege rampart' (33.4; cf. 6.6); it presupposes the success of the siege. G lacks *wᵉhinnᵉkā rō'eh*, 'and look, you see': i.e. the deity may observe his handiwork of the destroyed city. **[25]** MT *wᵉhā'ēd 'ēdīm*, 'and make witnesses': i.e. get witnesses. G follows v. 10 instead here: 'and I wrote the deed (*biblion*, 'book') and sealed it and got witnesses'. The command 'buy the field for silver' is not part of vv. 7–8, but reflects the ultimate lesson drawn from the story in v. 44, 'fields shall be bought for silver'.

The twin motifs of vv. 1–15, the siege and Jeremiah's purchase of the field for silver, are developed in various ways in the additional material appended in 32. In vv. 16–25 Jeremiah is represented as making a great prayer of praise to Yahweh and recital of the nation's disobedient past in order to point up the absurdity of buying land during a siege. The juxtaposition of the two motifs allows for a meditation on the theme that nothing is too marvellous (i.e. impossible) for the deity, and hence out of the most unlikely circumstances he will create the possibility of a good future (developed in the other sections). The language of the prayer is very conventional, Deuteronomistic and reflects the great litanies of the Persian period and later (e.g. Neh. 9.6–37; Dan. 9.3–19). It is more akin to the prayers used by groups in worship than by individuals (cf. Volz, 300) and is only loosely integrated with the theme of buying the field (thus Bright, 289–91, reads vv. 16–17a, 24–25, as Jeremiah's prayer and vv. 17b–23 as an insertion). As the leader of the prayer Jeremiah is presented as a major liturgical figure and the addition indicates a significant development in the treatment of the prophetic stories in the tradition.

32.26–35

26 The word of the LORD came to Jeremiah: 27 'Behold, I am the LORD, the
God of all flesh; is anything too hard for me? 28 Therefore, thus says the
LORD: Behold, I am giving this city into the hands of the Chaldeans and
into the hand of Nebuchadrezzar king of Babylon, and he shall take it. 29
The Chaldeans who are fighting against this city shall come and set this
city on fire, and burn it, with the houses on whose roofs incense has been
offered to Baal and drink offerings have been poured out to other gods, to
provoke me to anger. 30 For the sons of Israel and the sons of Judah have
done nothing but evil in my sight from their youth; the sons of Israel have
done nothing but provoke me to anger by the work of their hands, says the
LORD. 31 This city has aroused my anger and wrath, from the day it was
built to this day, so that I will remove it from my sight 32 because of all the
evil of the sons of Israel and the sons of Judah which they did to provoke
me to anger – their kings and their princes, their priests and their prophets,
the men of Judah and the inhabitants of Jerusalem. 33 They have turned
to me their back and not their face; and though I have taught them
persistently they have not listened to receive instruction. 34 They set up
their abominations in the house which is called by my name, to defile it. 35
They built the high places of Baal in the valley of the son of Hinnom, to
offer up their sons and daughters to Molech, though I did not command
them, nor did it enter into my mind, that they should do this abomination,
to cause Judah to sin.'

---

[26] G 'to me' for MT 'to Jeremiah', cf. v. 16, where Jeremiah is the speaker. What follows in vv. 28–35 is an entirely different oracular attack on the nation, which is quite inappropriate in this context of appendices to 30–31. This formula is found in 33.19, 23; cf. 31.1; 35.12; 37.6. **[27]** Cf. v. 17; the spelling out of this claim does not appear until vv. 37–41. MT *yhwh ᵉlōhē kol-bāšār*, 'Yahweh, the god of all flesh': cf. *'ēl ᵉlōhē hārūḥōt lᵉkol-bāśār*, 'El, the god of the spirits of all flesh', Num. 16.22; said of Yahweh in Num. 27.16. G *krubēsetai*, 'be hidden', for MT *yippālē'*, 'difficult, wonderful' cf. v. 17. **[28]** Cf. v. 36. MT *hinᵉnī nōtēn 'et-hā'īr hazzō't*, 'I am giving this city': G *dotheisa paradothēsetai*, 'shall certainly be given' = *hinnātōn tinnātēn* (cf. BHS); cf. 34.2. G lacks 'the Chaldaeans and into the hands of Nebuchadrezzar'; cf. the shorter MT of v. 3. **[29]** Cf. 37.10 for the motif of the Chaldaeans burning the city (not in 32.3–5); cf. 34.2; 39.8 for the burning of the city or parts of it. Cf. 19.13 for the motif of offerings to other gods on the roofs. **[30]** A summary of Israel's and Judah's idolatrous history is provided in vv. 30–35; for v. 30 cf. 7.30. The two nations contrast with the essential orientation of 32.44 on Judaean and southern territory, but this is part of the Deuteronomistic glossing of the tradition (cf. Thiel 1981, 33–4). The phrase 'work of their hands' refers to idols, cf. 1.16; cf. 7.18–19 for the provocation of Yahweh to anger by involvement in other cults. G lacks the second half of v. 30. **[31]** MT *w*^e^*'ad hayyōm hazzeh*, 'and to this day': cf. v. 20. The hyperbolic nature of this harangue should be apparent from the reference to the day Jerusalem was built – a period long before Judah took possession of the city. However, 'from that day to this day' makes a fine rhetorical point. Cf. 7.25–26 for a similar piece of rhetoric about the exodus. The syntax of v. 31 is most awkward and quite similar to 52.3 (cf. Bright, 296). **[32]** Cf. the gloss in 2.26b. **[33]** MT *w*^e^*lammēd*, 'and taught': if read as an infinitive absolute it may have the force of *wā'*^a^*lammēd* 'and I taught', so Rudolph, 210 (cf. BHS). The idiom *haškēm w*^e^*lammēd*, 'rising early and teaching', is a variation of a form which appears frequently in the sermons of the tradition (e.g. 7.13, 25; 11.7; 25.4; 26.5; 29.19; 35.14, 15; 44.4). Many of these idioms refer to the prophets, but the teaching process is not identified here, though in view of the cultic matters criticized it might refer to the priestly role of teaching (*tōrāh* is normally used to describe that function of the priests, cf. Deut. 33.10). For the turning of the back on the deity, though here it is a metaphor of the rejection of the divine teaching, cf. the cult act described in Ezek. 8.16 (the language is quite different from 32.33). **[34]** Cf. 7.30. **[35]** Cf. 7.31; 19.5; see on 7.30–34 for interpretation of the fire-cult (*contra* Bright, 296). MT *l*^e^*ha'*^a^*bīr*, 'to pass': i.e. to dedicate to Molech rather than 'to offer up' (RSV); Bright, 296 translates correctly 'in order to cause to pass [through the fire]', i.e. 'to devote', but spoils his treatment by insisting 'But sacrifice of sons and daughters is meant'. The phrase 'to cause Judah to sin' is an additional point here to those made in 7.31; 19.5. S adds 'in Tophet' after 'Baal' (BHS); G has *Moloch basilei*, 'king Moloch'. K *hḥṭy*; Q *haḥ*^a^*ṭī*, 'to cause to sin'.

The prayer of Jeremiah gives way to a lengthy oracular harangue of the city and then of Judah and Israel. In spite of the repetition of the claim that nothing is impossible for Yahweh, the point of this affirmation of divine omnipotence is postponed yet again by editors who wish to make further comments on the Babylonian siege of Jerusalem and to recite extracts from a monothematic history of the two communities. In this outburst the burning of the city after the siege is accounted for in terms of the long history of idolatry in Israel and Judah. Not because Zedekiah failed to surrender was the city burned (cf. 38.17–18) nor because of the evil done by Zedekiah and Jehoiakim (52.2–3), but as a result of a continous history of barbarous and idolatrous practices. Also the city had aroused divine anger since its very foundation! Thus the fall of Jerusalem is more than accounted for in this oracular sermon. In spite of being quite out of place in the development of the field buying motif, the sour note of vv. 28–35 (some exegetes would limit the harangue to vv. 29b–35) betrays the influence of the circles which edited the Jeremiah tradition by means of attacks on pagan practices (e.g. 1.16; 7.16–20, 30–34; 9.12–16; 11.1–13; 19.3–9, 11b–13). These attacks represent a dismissal of the religious practices favoured by other groups in the city and the land in favour of a more Yahwistic type of religion which concentrated solely on Yahweh as the cult and national god. Hence the pejorative descriptions of cultic life and the association of such worship with the destruction of Jerusalem. Yahweh gave the city into the hands of the Babylonians, thereby demonstrating his anger against such cults. Curiously his wrath is said to have been aroused since the city was first built, long before the Judaeans had taken possession of it, though such a view may simply be the hyperbole of outrage against groups with different cultic outlooks. Sermons of denunciation should not be regarded as models of accurate description or fair comment: the producers of these harangues may have believed that Jerusalem had always been part of their history and that some profound explanation was required to account for its destruction (the syntax of v. 31 is awkward, see on 52.3). The events of 588–7 were too good an opportunity for the Yahweh-alone party not to use them in its ideological battles with other parties favouring different cultic arrangements.

32.36–41

36 'Now therefore thus says the LORD, the God of Israel, concerning this city of which you say, "It is given into the hand of the king of Babylon by sword, by famine, and by pestilence". 37 Behold, I will gather them from all the countries to which I drove them in my anger and my wrath and in great indignation; I will bring them back to this place, and I will make them dwell in safety. 38 And they shall be my people, and I will be their God. 39 I will give them one heart and one way, that they may fear me for ever, for their own good and the good of their children after them. 40 I will make with them an everlasting covenant, that I will not turn away from doing good to them; and I will put the fear of me in their hearts, that they may not turn from me. 41 I will rejoice in doing them good, and I will plant them in this land in faithfulness, with all my heart and all my soul.'

---

[36] G lacks 'therefore'. MT *'attem 'ōmᵉrīm*, 'you say': G sing. *su legeis*; a transformation of vv. 3, 28, whereby Yahweh's claim to be giving the city to the Babylonians is made out to be a claim by the people (MT) or the prophet (G). G *kai en apostolē*, 'and by banishment', for MT *ūbaddāber* 'and by pestilence'; the triad 'sword, famine, pestilence' appears throughout the later prose sections of the tradition (e.g. v. 24; 14.12; 21.7; 24.10; 27.8, 13; 29.18; 42.17, 22; 44.13). **[37]** MT *mikkol-hā'arāṣōt*, 'from all the lands': G *ek pasēs tēs gēs*, 'out of all the land'; MT refers to the diaspora rather than the exile to Babylon. MT *'el-hammāqōm hazzeh*, 'to this place': possibly the temple, though the city or the land may be intended, if the speaker was in the cult place. **[38]** Cf. 7.23; 11.4; 24.7; 30.22; 31.1, 33. **[39]** MT *lēb 'eḥād wederek 'eḥād*, 'one mind and one way': Bright, 290, 'singleness of mind and of purpose'; G *hodon heteran kai kardian heteran*, 'another way and another heart', i.e. reading *'eḥād* as *'aḥēr*; S *ḥdt'* = *ḥādāš*, 'new', cf. Ezek. 11.19; 36.26. MT *kol-hayyāmīm*, 'all the days', i.e. permanently; for the sentiments here cf. Deut. 4.10; 5.29; 6.24; 14.24; 31.13; Thiel 1981, 35. **[40]** MT *berīt 'ōlām*, 'a permanent covenant': Ezek. 16.60; 37.26; cf. the new covenant of 31.31; Weippert 1981b, 95–102, for a treatment of 32.36–41; 31.31–34 as variations on a theme. MT *lō'-'āšūb mē'aḥarēhem lehētībī 'ōtām*, 'I will not turn from following them to do them good': NEB 'to follow them unfailingly with my bounty'; G lacks 'to do them good'. **[41]** MT *weśaśtī 'alēhem*, 'and I will rejoice over them': G *kai episkepsomai*, 'and I will visit (to do good to them)'; cf. Deut. 30.9 for the motif of Yahweh's joy (*lāśūś*) over his people. The planting (*nṭ'*) motif is a further occurrence of the set of motifs used in 1.10 to summarize the message of the tradition. The Deuteronomistic phrase 'with all my heart and all my soul' is uniquely applied to Yahweh here.

The excoriation of the community finally gives way to a more positive oracular statement whereby the deity reverses the terrible destruction wrought by the Babylonians (it is the people who claim that the city has been given over to the king of Babylon) and promises to gather all the dispersed exiles from all the countries to which he has driven them in his fierce anger (described in a triad of 'anger, wrath and indignation'). The editors have almost got around to developing the buying of the field motif! The great reversal of the diaspora will involve the return of the exiles to a safe homeland where the deity will genuinely (*be'emet*, 'in truth', cf. 26.15) plant them (cf. 21.7; 31.28; 42.10; Amos 9.15). Part of this restoration process will be the making of a permanent *berīt* with the people which will guarantee them perpetual protection by the deity. The binding of Yahweh in a permanent obligation to do good to his people will make good the most obvious defects in previous *berīt* arrangements which regularly broke down in outbursts of divine anger. The future permanent agreement between Yahweh and people is characterized by a tenderness, joy and concern implemented by the deity with 'all his mind and being' which contrasts significantly with his bouts of brutal anger in the past (cf. Deut. 28.16–68). The dream of the Deuteronomists that the people should fear Yahweh all the days of their life will also be realized in the future because Yahweh will put that fear within them (cf. the interiorization of *tōrāh* in 31.33) so that they do not turn away from him. Permanent loyalty will exist between both parties, and the deity will not desist from doing good to his people. The motif of the permanent *bᵉrīt* is a feature of the future expectations of various traditions (e.g. Ezek. 16.60; 37. 26; Isa. 55.3; 61.8; cf. Raitt 1977, 200–6), and is indicative of a profound desire for perpetual security, based on divine protection, without having to have recourse to the kind of human behaviour which would placate the deity (except in so far as the deity makes such behaviour automatic). It is a utopian dream of a time when the flawed character of human communities will disappear for ever, a time when deity and community will delight in each other without the prospect of disintegrating forces producing tears in paradise.

32.42–44

42 'For thus says the LORD: Just as I have brought all this great evil upon this people, so I will bring upon them all the good that I promise them. 43 Fields shall be bought in this land of which you are saying, It is a desolation, without man or beast; it is given into the hands of the Chaldeans. 44 Fields shall be bought for money, and deeds shall be signed and sealed and witnessed, in the land of Benjamin, in the places about Jerusalem, and in the cities of Judah, in the cities of the hill country, in the cities of the Shephelah, and in the cities of the Negeb; for I will restore their fortunes, says the LORD.'

---

[42] Cf. 19.15; 35.17, where the evil is spoken of; the good promised (*dōbbēr*, '[I] speak') to the people is that to which vv. 37–41 allude. Cf. the similar reversal in 31.28. **[43]** Cf. v. 36. MT plur., G sing. 'say': for the land without man or beast cf. 9.10. In v. 36 the popular saying refers to the city (cf. v. 28); here it refers to the land which is more appropriate for the field buying motif. MT *haśśādeh*, 'the field': sing. as collective for land, fields. **[44]** MT *hāhār . . . haššᵉpēlāh*, 'the hill country . . . the lowland': cf. Deut. 1.7; Josh. 9.1 for these technical terms describing areas of the territory according to the compass points. This listing appears in 17.26; 33.13. These two terms refer to the mountains and the lowland, i.e. to wherever there are cities in the land of Judah and Benjamin. The restoration of the fortunes (of the cities) motif is an important feature of the cycle 30–31 with its prose appendices (cf. 30.3, 18; 31.23; 33.26; also 29.14).

The heavily expanded chapter finally reflects on the significance of the story of Jeremiah's buying family land (adequately stated in v. 15). The emphasis on there being nothing that is impossible for Yahweh (vv. 17b, 27) is presumably intended to anticipate objections to the assertion that Yahweh will restore the land and the fortunes of the cities of Judah. From the standpoint of the land during the Babylonian period such a restoration must have seemed very unlikely, hence affirmations of Yahweh's power are very necessary (though they are not directly linked to the restoration motif). The oracular statement of vv. 42–44 reverses the evil brought upon the people by Yahweh and their forlorn observation of a land from which man and beast have been banished. How can there be hope in such a time? Will normal life ever return to Judah? To these questions the editors proffer the answer 'yes'. Yes: because Yahweh's great No to land and people has been reversed and he now speaks 'yes' to their hopes. But the guarantee of such positive expectations is not simply the oracles of promise but the transactions carried out by the prophet Jeremiah in the very days when the Babylonians were besieging Jerusalem. The Babylonians will not dominate the land for ever, but there will come a time when the buying and selling of land for silver will again be part of life in the land. Jeremiah's act of familial loyalty creates the future. All the things he did – signed and sealed deeds, acquired witnesses, bought land for silver – will take place when Yahweh restores the fortunes of the cities of Judah. These cities are listed in geographical regions: around Jerusalem, throughout Judah, in the highlands and the lowlands, and in the south and north (land of Benjamin). So the restoration of the fortunes of the people (cf. 30.3) includes the resumption of property deals throughout the cities of Judah (cf. 31.23), in all its territories (cf. 17.26; 33.13). These property transactions, of which Jeremiah's act is the great sign and portent, are indicative of the restoration of normal living conditions no longer subjected to foreign overlords, invasions or sieges. The frightful experiences of the cities during the sixth century will be reversed in the future. Thus Jeremiah's divinely inspired (vv. 6–8) response to his cousin's invitation to buy family land resonates beyond his own time, beyond the era of ruined cities and deserted landscapes into a future when all Judah will once again be able to move freely about their own land buying and selling property. Such images are not utopian but betoken the very stuff of community life.

33.1–13

33[1] The word of the LORD came to Jeremiah a second time, while he was still shut up in the court of the guard: 2 'Thus says the LORD who made the earth, the LORD who formed it to establish it – the LORD is his name: 3 Call to me and I will answer you, and will tell you great and hidden things which you have not known. 4 For thus says the LORD, the God of Israel, concerning the houses of this city and the houses of the kings of Judah which were torn down to make a defence against the siege mounds and before the sword: 5 The Chaldeans are coming in to fight and to fill them with the dead bodies of men whom I shall smite in my anger and my wrath, for I have hidden my face from this city because of all their wickedness. 6 Behold, I will bring to it health and healing, and I will heal them and reveal to them abundance of prosperity and security. 7 I will restore the fortunes of Judah and the fortunes of Israel, and rebuild them as they were at first. 8 I will cleanse them from all the guilt of their sin against me, and I will forgive all the guilt of their sin and rebellion against me. 9 And this city shall be to me a name of joy, a praise and a glory before all the nations of the earth who shall hear of all the good that I do for them; they shall fear and tremble because of all the good and all the prosperity I provide for it.

10 Thus says the LORD: In this place of which you say, "It is a waste without man or beast," in the cities of Judah and the streets of Jerusalem that are desolate, without man or inhabitant or beast, there shall be heard again 11 the voice of mirth and the voice of gladness, the voice of the bridegroom and the voice of the bride, the voices of those who sing, as they bring thank offerings to the house of the LORD:

"Give thanks to the LORD of hosts,
for the LORD is good,
for his steadfast love endures for ever!"

For I will restore the fortunes of the land as at first, says the LORD.

12 Thus says the LORD of hosts: In this place which is waste, without man or beast, and in all of its cities, there shall again be habitations of shepherds resting their flocks. 13 In the cities of the hill country, in the cities of the Shephelah, and in the cities of the Negeb, in the land of Benjamin,

the places about Jerusalem, and in the cities of Judah, flocks shall again pass under the hands of the one who counts them, says the LORD.'

[MT 33] = G 40. **[1]** MT *šēnīt*, 'a second time': i.e. subsequent to the word of 32.6–8 or 32.26, thus making 33.1–13 (a series of such divine words) a supplement to 32 (cf. Thiel 1981, 37); cf. 1.13 for *šēnīt*. 32.2b; 33.1b are redactional notes providing the same setting in the life of Jeremiah for 32–33, but much of the material presupposes a devastated Judah and Jerusalem (e.g. 32.43; 33.10, 12), hence the siege context is thematic rather than historical (cf. Rudolph, 215). **[2]** MT *'ōśāh yhwh yōṣēr 'ōtah* 'who made it, Yahweh who formed it': G *poiōn gēn kai plassōn autēn*, 'who made the earth and formed it'. Rudolph, 214 reads *'ōśeh w^{e}hāyāh*, 'who made and it is there', and *'ōtiyyāh*, 'what is to come' (cf. Isa. 41.23; 44.7): 'what has happened', i.e. the past, and 'what is to come', i.e. the future. 'Yahweh is his name': cf. 32.18b. **[3]** MT *ūb^{e}ṣurōt*, 'and inaccessible (things)': *bṣr* is often used of cities to describe their fortified impregnability (cf. 15.20, where it refers to a wall); a few mss read *nṣr*, 'guarded, secret', cf. Isa. 48.6 *ūn^{e}ṣurōt w^{e}lō' y^{e}da'tām*, 'and hidden things which you have not known', virtually the same phrase as here. **[4f.]** MT *malkē*, 'kings of': G *basileōs*, 'king of', cf. 22.18, 21. MT seems to suggest that there were many royal palaces in the city. The text of vv. 4b, 5a is hopelessly corrupt in MT (cf. Bright, 296; Rudolph, 214): lit. 'which were torn down to the siege ramparts and to the sword 5 coming to fight the Chaldaeans and to fill them (with) the corpses . . .'. G lacks 'coming' and reads 'bulwarks, ramparts' for 'sword', but otherwise is the same as MT. Some description of fortifying the city against the siege may be behind the present text (cf. Isa. 22.10), but without rewriting the whole piece coherence must remain lost. **[5]** MT *mēhā'īr hazzō't*, 'from this city': G *ap' autōn*, 'from them' = *mēhem*. The hiding of the divine face is a metaphor of anger and destruction, of Yahweh's withdrawal of his protection and favour cf. Isa. 8.17; 54.8; 64.6. **[6]** MT *'^{a}rukāh*, 'healing': lit. 'lengthening', i.e. the new flesh which replaces the wound; cf. 8.22; 30.17; Isa. 58.8; used of repairing the temple (II Chron. 24.13) and rebuilding the walls of Jerusalem (Neh. 4.1 [EV 2]). Some Vrs read *lāhem*, 'to them', i.e. the houses for *lāh*, 'to her', i.e. the city. MT *'^{a}teret*, 'abundance': this form only appears here (from *'tr*, 'be abundant'); G *kai poiēsō*, 'and I will make', suggests *w^{e}ābadtī* (an Aramaism cf. 7.29 G). Duhm, 272, reads *'^{a}tidōt*, 'treasures' (cf. Isa. 10.13); Rudolph, 214, suggests *'ēt rewaḥ*, 'a time of refreshment' (cf. BHS); cf. *'^{a}ṭeret* 'crown of (peace and truth)'. MT *šālōm we'^{e}met*, 'peace and truth': if treated as a hendiadys, 'true peace', 'genuine well-being'. **[7]** Some G mss have 'Jerusalem' for 'Israel', which fits the context of 32–33 better (cf. Rudolph). **[8]** K *lkwl*; Q *l^{e}kol*, 'all': K a scribal error. **[9]** MT *w^{e}hāy^{e}tāh*, 'and it will be': i.e. she, the city, will be . . . cf. v. 6. MT *lī l^{e}šēm śāśōn*, 'to me a name of joy': G *eis euphrosunēn*, 'for joy'; NEB 'This city will win me a name', deleting 'joy' as an addition. Volz, 308, reads the consonants *lylšm* as an abbreviation for Jerusalem, followed by Rudolph (cf. Bright, 292): 'Jerusalem shall be a source of joy.' MT *'ōtām*, 'them': i.e. the citizens of Jerusalem rather than the nations; BHS deletes or would read *'ōtāh*, 'her', cf. *lāh*, 'to her', at the end of the verse. **[10]** MT *bammāqōm-hazzeh*, 'in this place': i.e. Jerusalem. Cf. 32.36, 43. **[11]** Cf. 7.34; 16.9; 25.10. MT *tōdāh*, 'praise': G *dōra*, 'gifts'; cf. 17.26 for the bringing of thank-offerings (*tōdāh*) to the (rebuilt) temple. The liturgical chant of v. 11b is formulaic (cf. Ps. 106.1; 107.1; 118.1; 136). Cf. Job 42.10 for the motif of 'restoring the fortunes', though there Job is given twice as much as he had before; here inevitably the land can only be restored 'as at first' – nothing has been lost by its terrible destruction! **[13]** Cf. 17.26; 32.44; the formal listing of territorial areas has a different purpose in each reference (e.g. temple offerings, the buying of land, the pasturing of flocks) and a different order of areas. MT *'al-yᵉdēmōneh*, 'under the hands of him who counts': i.e. the tally-keeper (Bright, 296) who counted the sheep returning to the fold at night; whatever its precise meaning the phrase indicates a period when sheep would safely graze and always be accounted for by the shepherds.

If the expansion of 32 shows much Deuteronomistic editorial influence, the supplement to it in 33 is a post-Deuteronomistic postscript to the cycle of salvation expectations in 30–31 (cf. Thiel 1981, 37). This supplement is made up of two collections of oracular pieces, one dealing with the reconstruction of Jerusalem and the land (vv. 2–9, 10–11, 12–13) and the other devoted to the revival of the Davidic dynasty (vv. 14–16, 17–18, 19–22, 23–26).

33 is linked to 32 by means of a redactional note which places Jeremiah's reception of the divine word in the same situation as that of his buying Hanamel's field (v. 1; 32.2, 8). However unsuitable such a context may be for this material, it indicates the editorial concern to pack all the positive elements into the siege period, so that even before the city had fallen its future rise should be announced. The restoration of commercial deals in the land (32) and the rebuilding of Jerusalem and the cities of Judah (33) are underwritten by allusions to Yahweh as creator (e.g. 32.17; 33.2). Thus creation and redemption are bound together (cf. the fusing of these two motifs in Second Isaiah). In both supplements the figure of Jeremiah is developed in ways different from other strands in the tradition, e.g. he makes lengthy prayers typical of the post-exilic period (32.17–23) and he is invited to call upon the deity for the revelation of great mysteries (33.3; cf. the figure of Daniel to whom Yahweh reveals

such matters as are hidden from others concerning the future). In 33.4–9 the inaccessible things concern the rebuilding of a Jerusalem partially knocked down to fight off the Chaldaeans (assuming vv. 4b–5a refer to the siege defences project) and destroyed by the enemy. The future holds healing, i.e. rebuilding, for the city: a metaphor used in the poems to describe precisely the one thing lacking in the community (cf. 8.22). In the restoration of the fortunes of Judah and Jerusalem (Israel in present texts) the rebuilding of the nation will reproduce the conditions prevailing at the beginning of its history (contrast 32.31). And in this restoration sin and guilt will be cleansed and forgiven (cf. 31.34).

The modern reader may feel that the destruction of city and land, the death of so many people and the deportation of various citizens would constitute both punishment and cleansing-forgiveness, especially as the guilty generations all would have been dead when this reconstruction began. However, these sermons and meditations on restoration should not be read as realistic descriptions of social history, but as theological reflections on abstract notions which have to do with cultic matters in the period of the second temple. Only with the forgiveness of the past and the cleansing of guilt and rebellion could the renewed city and temple become again a place which would yield joy, praise and glory to Yahweh. The various generations between the events of 597–87 and the speaker's period (cf. 'this very day', 32.20, 31) are invariably absent in the tradition's handling of destruction and restoration (cf. 2.9; 7.25–26; 32.21–23). So the generation of the reconstruction period requires forgiveness and cleansing for the crimes of their distant ancestors (cf. 31.32–34). When the past is completely reversed then the renewed community will become a repository of Yahweh's goodness. The bounty enjoyed in this period will shake and terrify the nations, and thus will the new age reverse that period when the Chaldaeans were breaking down the walls of Jerusalem and butchering its inhabitants. Yahweh's restoration of the fortunes of Judah and Jerusalem in the future will be everything the present is not – hence the setting of the material in the period of the siege.

Two further oracular statements embellish this reconstruction expectation: vv. 10–11 are a variation on 32.36, 43 or, perhaps, one of three treatments of a popular saying about the desolation of city (32.36) and land (32.43); vv. 12–13 also deal with the same view of the city or land as a wasteland, but envisage a return of shepherds and flocks. These future expectations are based on reversals of the past (and contemporary?) experiences of the community. Where once no human or animal sounds were heard (cf. 9.10), now shall be heard all the normal sounds of human activity, typified by weddings (cf. the merrymaking of the maidens and young men in 31.4, 13) and liturgical processions to the temple. The resurgence of these noisy human encounters reverses the note of their cessation in 7.34; 16.9; 25.10. In a few lines denoting sexual activity and worship v. 11 reconstructs the communal life of the nation without expansive details of rebuilding the temple (contrast Ezek. 40–48). The sounds of animals throughout the land are implied (without articulation) in vv. 12–13, when the culture will become once again a thriving pastoral civilization. Once all the cities are rebuilt and reinhabited in the listed districts (cf. 17.26; 32.44), pastoral life will thrive again. These are all simple images of the restoration of a way of life disrupted and destroyed by the Babylonian incursions into Palestine. They are neither profound nor utopian, but represent the return to normal urban and rural life after the disappearance of the Babylonians in the Persian age. The loss of stability and security after the emergence of Babylon in 605 is apparent from these hopes about the future, and most of the elements in 30–33 provide a very simple but clear meaning for the dominant motif of 'the restoration of the fortunes of Judah' (i.e. Israel).

33.14–26

14 'Behold, the days are coming, says the LORD, when I will fulfil the
promise I made to the house of Israel and the house of Judah. 15 In those
days and at that time I will cause a righteous Branch to spring forth for
David; and he shall execute justice and righteousness in the land. 16 In
those days Judah will be saved and Jerusalem will dwell securely. And this
is the name by which it will be called: "The LORD is our righteousness."

17 For thus says the LORD: David shall never lack a man to sit on the
throne of the house of Israel, 18 and the Levitical priests shall never lack a
man in my presence to offer burnt offerings, to burn cereal offerings, and to
make sacrifices for ever.'

19 The word of the LORD came to Jeremiah: 20 'Thus says the LORD: If
you can break my covenant with the day and my covenant with the night,
so that day and night will not come at their appointed time, 21 then also
my covenant with David my servant may be broken, so that he shall not

have a son to reign on his throne, and my covenant with the Levitical priests my ministers. 22 As the host of heaven cannot be numbered and the sands of the sea cannot be measured, so I will multiply the descendants of David my servant, and the Levitical priests who minister to me.

23 The word of the LORD came to Jeremiah: 24 'Have you not observed what these people are saying, "The LORD has rejected the two families which he chose"? Thus they have despised my people so that they are no longer a nation in their sight. 25 Thus says the LORD: If I have not established my covenant with day and night and the ordinances of heaven and earth, 26 then I will reject the descendants of Jacob and David my servant and will not choose one of his descendants to rule over the seed of Abraham, Isaac, and Jacob. For I will restore their fortunes, and will have mercy upon them.'

G lacks vv. 14–26. They should be regarded as an addition to the second edition of Jeremiah (MT). Cf. 23.5–6, of which vv. 14–16 are a development. **[14]** MT *'et-haddābār haṭṭōb*, 'the good word': i.e. the promise cf. 29.10; this may refer to 23.5–6, though curiously Israel appears in 23.6 but not here in vv. 15–16 (see on 23.5–6). **[15]** Cf. 23.5, where the language of v. 14, is used, hence the terms here are different: *'aṣmīaḥ . . . ṣemaḥ ṣᵉdāqāh*, 'I will cause to sprout . . . a true shoot'; word-play on *ṣmḥ* lacking in 23.5 ('and he shall reign as king and deal wisely' does not appear in 33.14–16; though many mss add it). **[16]** MT *bayyāmīm hāhēm*, 'in those days': 23.6 'in his days'. MT *wirūšālaim tiškōn*, 'and Jerusalem will dwell': 23.6 *wᵉyiśrā'ēl yiškōn*, 'and Israel will dwell'; in spite of Israel in v. 14 the use of Jerusalem here reflects the modification of 23.6. In 23.6 the branch is named using a pun on Zedekiah's name (appendix to royal cycle), in 33.16 the context of the rebuilding of Jerusalem (vv. 6–13) may have infleunced the text's development into a statement about the name of the city. A few mss, S read *šᵉmō*, 'his name' (cf. 23.6); Rudolph, 216, inserts *haššēm*, 'the name', following G^O,L, Theod, V (cf. BHS). Cf. Ezek. 48.35 for a different name of the city (*yhwh šāmmāh*, 'Yahweh is there'). The significance of the phrase 'this (is the name) which one will call her "Yahweh is our vindication" ' probably refers to the reconstruction of land and city, as much as the reemergence of the Davidic dynasty. MT may represent the transition of the name from the branch to the city. **[17]** MT *lō'-yikkārēt lᵉdāwid*, 'there shall not be cut off for David': i.e. there shall never be lacking for David an occupant of the throne; note 'house of Israel', where Israel stands for Judah and Israel (v. 14). **[18]** MT *wᵉlakkōhᵃnīm halᵉwiyyim*, 'and for the priests, the levites': i.e. the levitical priests, a typically Deuteronomistic phrase (Deut. 17.9, 18; 18.1; 24.8; 27.9; Josh. 3.3; 8.33; cf. Ezek. 43.19; 44.15). The same idiom (*lō'-yikkārēt*) is used of the appointment of priests as for the occupant of the throne. **[19]** Cf. v. 23; 32.26; 35.12; 43.8 for this shortened form of the reception of the divine word formula (slight expansion in 43.8). **[20]** MT *'im-tāpērū 'et-b^{e}rîtî hayyōm*, 'if you could break my *b^{e}rît* of the day': for this unusual grammatical form of an absolute with suffix in a construct chain cf. MT Lev. 26.42; Num. 25.12; v. 21 uses the normal form *b^{e}rîtî . . . 'et-dāwid*, 'my *b^{e}rît* . . . with David'. The creation of the day and night by Yahweh (cf. Gen. 1.5; 8.22) is here described by the term *b^{e}rît*, indicating its meaning as a fixed obligation rather than an agreement between two parties (cf. the fixed orders of 31.35–36). **[21]** MT *w^e'et-hal^{e}wiyyim hakkōh^{a}nîm*, 'and with the levites, the priests': a transposition of the normal order (cf. vv. 18, 22; either of which should be read here, cf. BHS). **[22]** Cf. Gen. 22.17 for similar images of the stars and sand as figures of the multitudinous descendants of Abraham; here they apply to the royal and priestly houses. MT *m^{e}šār^{e}tē 'ōtî*, 'who minister to me': governs only the priests; Rudolph, 218, reads *m^{e}šār^{e}tay 'ittō*, 'my ministers with him' (BHS). **[24]** The two families here presumably refer to Israel and Judah (v. 14), though it is possible that David and Levi (vv. 17–22) are intended, or even Jacob and David (v. 26). MT *lipnēhem*, 'before them'; who are 'them'? The same question may be asked of *hā'ām hazzeh*, 'this people', i.e. those who acknowledge that Yahweh has rejected the two families. Perhaps they are Jews who agree with the critique offered by Jer. 2–20 and who are attacked here by supporters of a different ideology. **[25]** Cf. v. 20. MT *b^{e}rîtî yômām*, 'my *b^{e}rît* by day': perhaps *yôm*, 'day' (BHS on vv. 20, 25); Rudolph follows Duhm, 277, in reading *bārā'tî*, 'did I not create day?'. MT *ḥuqqōt*, 'the ordinance of': cf. 31.35, 36. **[26]** MT *mōš^{e}lîm*, 'ruling': plur. i.e. rulers; $G^{O,L}$, Theod, S read sing. K *'šwb*; Q *'āšîb*, 'I will restore': cf. 32.46 for conclusion of supplement (see also 33.11; 49.39). The phrase *dāwid 'abdî*, 'David my servant' (vv. 21.26) should be compared to 'Nebuchadrezzar my servant' (25.9; 27.6).

Notably absent from the future expectations listed in the cycle of 30–31 and its supplements is any detailed account of the restoration of the royal house of David (touched on in 30.9, 21). When the fortunes of Judah are restored by Yahweh, peace and prosperity will descend upon the land and its cities, but what about the royal and priestly houses? The expectations hint at the rebuilt temple and the services which will take place there (cf. 30.20–21; 31.23, 40; 33.11), and assert the divine forgiveness and cleansing (31.34; 33.8). But no clear statement appears about the revival of the royal house (apart from 30.9) or the organization of the cult. It is hardly surprising, then, that these lacunae should be made good in a supplement to the cycle and its supplements in the second edition of the tradition (MT).

The additional supplement provides four oracular statements

which assert the revival of the house of David in conjunction with the levitical priesthood as *permanent* elements of social organization in the future. Never again will David's dynasty lack an occupant on the throne (or, presumably, suffer the humiliation of deposed kings and puppet client kings as happened during the Babylonian period). Never again will the temple be destroyed (implicit in v. 18) nor will the levitical priests be excluded from sacral duties there (cf. Ezek. 44.15–27). The future envisaged here is one ruled over by a Davidic figure on the throne (the word 'king' is not used, but *mōlēk*, 'reign', is in v. 21; cf. 23.5) and a levitical priest officiating in the temple. Permanent royal leadership and perpetual levitical sacrifice will characterize this future. The order of that permanency is given in terms of the created orders of day and night (cf. 31.35–36) and guaranteed by means of the fertility of the royal and priestly houses – they will multiply the way the legends of the patriarchal stories envisage the nation increasing. These hopes (vv. 14–22; 23.5–6; 30.9) represent a minority report in the Jeremiah tradition and reflect sources in the Persian period which still hoped for a revival of the Davidic house. They were unsuccessful, though the expectations about a levitical organization of the temple cult reflect the reality of the Chronicler's time (perhaps he also entertained hopes of a restoration of the Davidic monarchy, cf. Williamson 1977a).

The devastations of the sixth century persuaded some people that Yahweh had rejected the two families (cf. Amos 3.2), but the saying to this effect (v. 24) would be reversed when Yahweh restored the fortunes of the nation. The final word in the cycle and its supplements is *w^eriḥamtīm*, 'and I will have mercy upon them'. That divine mercy will reverse all the devastations of the past and revive the destroyed institutions in a new age when the seed of Abraham, Isaac, and Jacob will enjoy all the expectations ever entertained for the nation. Only in Yahweh's mercy could that happen.

34.1–7

34[1] The word which came to Jeremiah from the LORD, when Nebuchadrezzar king of Babylon and all his army and all the kingdoms of the earth under his dominion and all the peoples were fighting against Jerusalem and all of its cities: 2 'Thus says the LORD, the God of Israel: Go and speak to Zedekiah king of Judah and say to him, "Thus says the LORD: Behold, I

am giving this city into the hand of the king of Babylon, and he shall burn
it with fire. 3 You shall not escape from his hand, but shall surely be
captured and delivered into his hand; you shall see the king of Babylon eye
to eye and speak with him face to face; and you shall go to Babylon." 4 Yet
hear the word of the LORD, O Zedekiah king of Judah! Thus says the LORD
concerning you: "You shall not die by the sword. 5 You shall die in peace.
And as spices were burned for your fathers, the former kings who were
before you, so men shall burn spices for you and lament for you, saying,
'Alas, lord!' " For I have spoken the word, says the LORD.'
6 Then Jeremiah the prophet spoke all these words to Zedekiah king of
Judah, in Jerusalem, 7 when the army of the king of Babylon was fighting
against Jerusalem and against all the cities of Judah that were left, Lachish
and Azekah; for these were the only fortified cities of Judah that remained.

[MT 34] = G 41. **[1]** The formulaic reception of the divine word introductory note here is of the expanded kind which includes the occasion of its reception, cf. 21.1; 32.1; 34.8; 35.1; 40.1 (simple form, i.e. lacking occasion, 7.1; 11.1; 18.1; 30.1). Cf. 21.1–2; 32.2; 37.3–5 for the siege and variations on this encounter between Jeremiah and Zedekiah; v. 7 gives further details of the occasion. G *kai pasa hē gē archēs autou*, 'and all the country of his dominion': MT expanded by 'and all the peoples', 'kingdoms'. These represent the military contingents from the subjugated states of the empire. MT *we'al-kol-'āreha*, 'and against all her cities': i.e. the towns of Judah associated with Jerusalem, cf. 19.15; G *kai epi pasas tas poleis Iouda*, 'and against all the cities of Judah'. **[2]** 'Go and speak to Zedekiah': the only version of the Jeremiah encounter with Zedekiah series of stories which has Jeremiah initiating the contact (by divine command). MT *hinenī nōtēn 'et*, 'look, I am giving': G *paradosei paradothēsetai*, 'shall certainly be delivered', cf. 32.28. G has *kai sullēmpsetai autēn*, 'and he shall take it' (= *ūlekādāh*) after 'the king of Babylon', cf. 32.3. Rudolph, 218 treats 'and he shall burn it with fire' as a *vaticinium ex eventu* added to the text. **[3]** Cf. 32.4; 39.5–7; Ezek. 17.11–21. Zedekiah's rebellion against his overlord is the reason for this personal confrontation with the king of Babylon. Rudolph regards 'and you shall go to Babylon' as a later *vaticinium ex eventu* which conflicts with the death notice of v 5. G* lacks 'and his mouth shall speak with your mouth' (BHS). **[4]** G lacks 'you shall not die by the sword'. Bright, 216, reads this verse as a conditional offer that if Zedekiah heeds Yahweh's word and surrenders, then Nebuchadrezzar will spare his life (cf. 38.17–18); cf. Rudolph, 220. **[5]** MT *bešālōm tāmūt*, 'you will die in peace': hardly captures the essence of Zedekiah's experiences at Riblah, where he witnesses the execution of his sons, is blinded and taken to Babylon (39.5–7). Rudolph transposes 'in Jerusalem' from the end of v. 6 (where it is superfluous) to here and reads *bešālōm* as *bīrūšālāim*. The promise to Zedekiah then becomes one of death in his own city rather than Babylon. For the mourning rites specified here cf. 22.18; II Chron. 16.14; 21.19. The burial honours afforded the king confirm the view that interment in Jerusalem is intended. MT *ūkᵉmiśrᵉpōt ʾᵃbōtekā*, 'and as the burnings of your fathers': i.e. the kindling of fires for your ancestors (cf. NEB); spices are not necessarily implied by the term used (cf. RSV, JPSB, Bright, 214). G *eklausan . . . klausontai*, 'they wept . . . they shall weep': a free translation of mourning rites (cf. BHS). **[6]** 'Jeremiah *the prophet*': cf. 32.2; 'the prophet' is lacking in G. Bright, 214, deletes 'the prophet', 'of Judah' (with G) as redundant. **[7]** G lacks 'which were left': G^A = MT. If only Lachish and Azekah were left, the campaign must have been nearing its climax; cf. Lachish Letters IV on the fate of Azekah (Pritchard 1969, 321–2). On the relation of the Lachish ostraca and 34.7 cf. Migsch 1981, 246–53 (with analysis of vv. 1–7 on 99–111).

The theme of Jeremiah and Zedekiah during the Babylonian campaign against city and land appears in a variety of different forms in the tradition: a delegation sent by Zedekiah to Jeremiah (21.1–7; 37.3–10), a summons of Jeremiah to an interview with the king (37.16–21; 38.14–27), and a divine sending of Jeremiah *to* Zedekiah (34.1–7). The Babylonian presence is a constant of the stories, though in 37.5 it has withdrawn temporarily, but the situation of Jeremiah varies considerably. He may be at large somewhere in the city (probably the temple if he can be found with such ease), in prison for the offence of speaking in such terms to the king (32.3–5), secretly summoned from the cells (37.16–17), or summoned from constraint to the temple (38.13–14). The response to the delegation is always a word of unmitigated destruction (21.6; 37.8–10), but in his encounters with the king Jeremiah allows for the possibility that Zedekiah may save his own life, and that of his house, by surrendering to the Babylonians (38.17–23; cf. 34.4–5; but not in 37.17).

These variations on a theme indicate how a few motifs may be used in the tradition in a number of different ways to put across certain theological perspectives. The absolute word of judgment against the city and the contingent possibility of survival are combined in these stories in accordance with the pattern of absolute-contingent elements used in the prose sections of the tradition (e.g. 7.1–15; 21.3–7, 8–10; 25.3–7, 9–11; 26.2–6; 36). Hence the various accounts of Jeremiah's encounter with Zedekiah, or his delegation, shift between a declaration of Zedekiah's inevitable fate (along with that of the city and citizens) at the hands of the Babylonians and an affirmation of the possibility of king and city avoiding that fate.

Intransigence in the face of the enemy will lead to the destruction of everybody (21.6–7), whereas surrender to the princes of the king of Babylon will entail survival for city, king and his house (38.17). The peculiarity of 34.2–5, apart from its distinctive element of the prophet being sent by Yahweh to the king rather than receiving a delegation from the king or a summons to speak to him, is its combination of an announcement of the fate of city and king with an oracle of deliverance addressed to Zedekiah (vv. 2–3, 4–5). An editor has fused together two halves of quite discrete pieces to produce a strange amalgam of material which, as it stands, requires substantial rewriting in order to become coherent.

The two elements of vv. 2–3, 4–5 formally contradict each other. In the first piece the burning of the city is announced and Zedekiah's deportation to Babylon after confrontation with the Babylonian king is asserted. In the second oracular statement a personal word of reassurance is addressed to Zedekiah (v. 4) in which the king is assured of a proper and conventional royal burial in his own land. He will not be killed in battle but will die in peace (*bešālōm*, i.e. well-being) and his body will be accorded the full honours of a royal funeral (cf. II Chron. 16.14; contrast 22.18–19). Such a funeral ceremony could only take place in his own land (contrast the fate of Shallum 22.11–12) and hardly at the termination of a siege. If 38.17 were to be read here it could be argued that vv. 4–5 imply a call to surrender with a promise of a quiet life leading eventually to a traditional burial. The present text of 34.4–5 does not make that connection but in order to make sense of what are contradictory accounts some such background explanation is required.

The prediction of the death of kings and their subsequent obsequies would appear to be a problematical feature of certain biblical traditions. The contrast between 34.4–5 and 39.5–7 is considerable because by no stretch of the imagination can Zedekiah's fate be described as 'dying in peace'. The term *šālōm* cannot be said to cover the experiences of witnessing the execution of one's sons, the blinding of oneself, deportation in fetters to a foreign land, and one's eventual death there (52.10–11). It is also highly unlikely that such a wretched prisoner should then be accorded the full state funeral honours of a foreign country after his death in prison. Thus the oracle of 34. 4–5 must be regarded as an utterance with reference to peaceful demise in Jerusalem and read *as if* it contained an *implicit* conditional force (cf. Bright, 216) which would contrast it to vv. 2–3. This is not a necessary reading of the text, because the two oracles may be understood as contradictory on the grounds that predictions about the fate of kings are problematic in the Hebrew Bible. Thus the prophetess Huldah predicts a gathering to his grave in peace (*b^ešālōm*) for king Josiah (II Kings 22.20), whereas he was slain by Pharaoh Neco at Megiddo (II Kings 23.29). Problems of interpreting the prediction of Jehoiakim's lack of proper burial in 22.18–19 have been noted already, so allowance must be made for a considerable gap between conventional oracles of the death and burial of kings and the actual fate of those kings. The combination of two discrete oracles in 34.2–5 without adequate editing to relate them to each other (along the lines of 38.17–18) provides the exegete with a range of possible explanations, but only the pattern of stories about Jeremiah in relation to Zedekiah may justify an exegetical approach.

The oracular material is enveloped in contextualizing notes about the siege of Jerusalem under the king of Babylon (vv. 1, 6–7). Nebuchadrezzar's campaign in the land of Judah had reached the point where only two other towns, Lachish and Azekah, remained uncaptured. Thus the fate of Jerusalem was virtually sealed. Once those towns were taken the Babylonians could devote their whole attention to breaching Jerusalem and then confront king Zedekiah with the consequences of his breach of vassalage to Nebuchadrezzar (see on 39.5). Hence the urgency of Jeremiah's commission to speak to Zedekiah. Time was short and the king's fate hung in the balance.

34.8–22

8 The word which came to Jeremiah from the LORD, after King Zedekiah
had made a covenant with all the people in Jerusalem to make a proclamation
of liberty to them, 9 that every one should set free his Hebrew slaves, male
and female, so that no one should enslave a Jew, his brother. 10 And they
obeyed, all the princes and all the people who had entered into the covenant
that every one should set free his slave, male or female, so that they would
not be enslaved again; they obeyed and set them free. 11 But afterward they
turned around and took back the male and female slaves they had set free,
and brought them into subjection as slaves. 12 The word of the LORD came
to Jeremiah from the LORD: 13 'Thus says the LORD, the God of Israel: I
made a covenant with your fathers when I brought them out of the land of
Egypt, out of the house of bondage, saying, 14 "At the end of six years each
of you must set free the fellow Hebrew who has been sold to you and has

served you six years; you must set him free from your service." But your fathers did not listen to me or incline their ears to me. 15 You recently repented and did what was right in my eyes by proclaiming liberty, each to his neighbour, and you made a covenant before me in the house which is called by my name; 16 but then you turned around and profaned my name when each of you took back his male and female slaves, whom you had set free according to their desire, and you brought them into subjection to be your slaves. 17 Therefore, thus says the LORD: You have not obeyed me by proclaiming liberty, every one to his brother and to his neighbour; behold, I proclaim to you liberty to the sword, to pestilence, and to famine, says the LORD. I will make you a horror to all the kingdoms of the earth. 18 And the men who transgressed my covenant and did not keep the terms of the covenant which they made before me, I will make like the calf which they cut in two and passed between its parts – 19 the princes of Judah, the princes of Jerusalem, the eunuchs, the priests, and all the people of the land who passed between the parts of the calf; 20 and I will give them into the hand of their enemies and into the hand of those who seek their lives. Their dead bodies shall be food for the birds of the air and the beasts of the earth. 21 And Zedekiah king of Judah, and his princes I will give into the hand of their enemies and into the hand of those who seek their lives, into the hand of the army of the king of Babylon which has withdrawn from you. 22 Behold, I will command, says the LORD, and will bring them back to this city; and they will fight against it, and take it, and burn it with fire. I will make the cities of Judah a desolation without inhabitant.'

---

[8] Cf. v. 1 for introductory formula. G lacks 'all', 'which are in Jerusalem', 'to them'. MT *liqrō' lāhem d^erōr*, 'to proclaim to them liberty': cf. vv. 15, 17; Isa. 61.1; Ezek. 46.17; Lev. 25.10. In Ezek. 46.17; Lev. 25.10 the use of *d^erōr* refers to the year of jubilee, but no such connection applies here, though Sarna 1973, 148–9, makes 588–7 a sabbatical year (cf. BDB, 204). Heb. *d^erōr*, 'freedom, emancipation, liberty', cf. Akk. *andurāru* (Weinfeld 1972a, 153). **[9]** MT *ḥopšîm l^ebiltî ʿ^abād-bām bîhūdî 'āḥîhū 'îš*, '. . . free, so that none should serve among them, of a Jew, his brother, anyone': Heb. awkward (part of this line is repeated in v. 10); cf. 22.13; 25.14 for *ʿbd b*, 'to make serve'. **[10]** MT *wayyišm^eʿū*, 'and they obeyed': G *kai epestraphēsan*, 'and they turned' = *wayyāšūbū* (cf. v. 11). G lacks *ḥopšîm . . . way^ešallēḥū*, 'free, so that they would not be enslaved again; they obeyed and released'. **[11]** G lacks most of v. 11; its shorter text reads *kai eōsan autous eis paidas kai paidiskas*, 'and gave them over to be men-servants and maid-servants'. K *wykbyšwm*; Q *wayyikb^ešûm*, 'and they subdued them': i.e. 'brought them into bondage (again)'; K represents Hiphil use, Q the more normal Qal. The uses of *šûb*, 'turn, change, repent' (vv. 11, 15, 16) should be noted. Bright, 221, relates the change of policy to the lifting of the siege (cf. vv. 21–2; 37.5); this may be implied by v. 21, but the editor has not presented the story in such terms. **[12]** Two introductory formulae are used here to indicate the reception of the divine word: 'and the word of Yahweh came to Jeremiah' + '(the word which came to Jeremiah) from Yahweh'; cf. vv. 1, 8; 33.1; 32.26; G lacks 'from Yahweh'. **[13]** Cf. 7. 22; 'out of the house of bondage', cf. Ex. 20.2; Deut. 5.6. **[14]** MT *miqqēṣ šebaʿ šānīm*, 'at the end of seven years': following Deut. 15.1, 12; G *hex etē*, 'six years', followed by RSV. It is *in* the seventh year (Ex. 21.2; Deut. 15.12), rather than at the end of it (Deut. 15.1), that the debt bondage comes to an end. MT *ʾ^{a}šer-yimmākēr l^{e}kā*, 'who has been sold (or has sold himself) to you': indicates the servitude was due to debt bondage. The Deuteronomistic concluding sentence (cf. Thiel 1981, 42) about the fathers refusing to obey Yahweh (cf. 7.24, 26; 11.8), apart from being stereotypical, may indicate a tendency for the law on manumission to be ignored (cf. Mendelsohn 1949, 85–91); cf. Neh. 5.1–13. **[15]** MT *wattāšubū ʾattem hayyōm wattaʿ^{a}śū*, 'but you turned, you, today, and you did . . .': G lacks *ʾattem* and reads the verbs as third person plur. The use of *hayyōm*, 'today', is curious but it may be a contrast between the right action of the people *now* and the failure of the fathers *b^{e}yōm*, 'on the day', when Yahweh commanded them to keep his covenant (cf. DeVries 1975, 241–3). The technical language for making a covenant *krt b^{e}rīt* (cf. McCarthy 1978, 91–5) appears in vv. 8, 13, 15, 18; cf. II Kings 23.3, where king Josiah also makes a covenant. In a Deuteronomistically influenced text it is hardly surprising to find a king 'cutting' a *b^{e}rīt*. Cf. 7.10, 11, 14 for 'in the house which is called by my name.' **[16]** MT *ʾ^{a}šer-šillaḥtem ḥopšīm l^{e}napšām*, 'whom you had set free to their desire': cf. Deut. 21.14, *w^{e}šillaḥtah l^{e}napšah*, 'and you will release her to her desire'. RSV 'you shall let her go where she will'; *npš* here may mean 'to do what one wishes' or 'to go where one wishes'. Though where the released slaves could have gone after Zedekiah had freed them during a siege is a moot point (to their own land after Nebuchadrezzar's withdrawal? Cf. v. 21; 37.11–12). They must have remained in, or close to, the city for them to have been taken back into debt bondage! G* lacks 'and you brought them into subjection to be'. **[17]** A word-play on *d^{e}rōr*: you did not proclaim *d^{e}rōr*, 'freedom', to your brother (G only has one variant here); look, I am proclaiming *d^{e}rōr* to sword, pestilence and famine (a dominant triad in the prose sections of the tradition). K *lzwʿh*; Q *l^{e}zaʿ^{a}wāh*, 'for a horror': cf. 15.4; 24.9; 29.18 where the same phrase appears. **[18]** MT *w^{e}nātattī ʾet-hāʾ^{a}nāšīm . . . hāʿēgel ʾ^{a}šer kār^{e}tū liš^{e}nayim wayyaʿb^{e}rū bēn b^{e}tārāyw*, 'and I will make the men . . . the calf which they cut in two and passed between its parts': EVV, Ehrlich 1912, 331, read *kāʿēgel*, 'like the calf'; this strange statement may mean that the deity will treat the people like the animal they cut up, i.e. kill them. Driver 1937–38, 121–2, alters *l^{e}pānāy* to *lipnē*, 'like', i.e. 'like the calf'. Here the ritual is an acted-out curse where the animal is a substitute for the parties to the *b^{e}rīt*, and those who breach it suffer the same fate (cf. Rudolph, 225; McCarthy 1978, 94; Weinfeld 1972a, 102–4). It reflects a ceremony of self-cursing (Rudolph); cf. Gen. 15.7–18 for a similar ritual of cutting up an animal and passing between the pieces in the making of a *b*^e^*rīt*. Bright, 220, transposes 'the young bull' after 'they cut' and makes v. 20 the continuation of the main verb (*ntn*). G quite different here: *epoiēsan ergazesthai autō*, '(which) they made to serve it', i.e. (presumably) to sacrifice the calf, a rather vague rendering of MT *krtw . . . btryw*. Whether G did not understand the ritual alluded to in MT, confused the two occurrences of *krtw*, found the ceremony offensive or had a Hebrew text which lacked any reference to the calf practice is a moot point. G (= *'ašer 'āb*^e^*dū lišrātō*) may point to a reading of the phrase as an allusion to the golden calf incident, but this is unlikely (cf. Giesebrecht, 192). **[19]** G has a shorter text than MT: 'the princes of Judah, and the powerful men, and the priests, and the people'. MT *hassārisīm*, 'officials': not necessarily 'eunuchs', cf. JPSB, 'the officials'; 29.2; 38.7; 52.25. MT *w*^e^*kōl 'am hā'āreṣ*, 'and all the people of the land': hardly the rabble or peasants but the landed gentry who might have possessed debt slaves; cf. 1.18 where 'its princes, its priests and the people of the land' may refer to the leading classes of society. **[20]** MT *w*^e^*nātattī 'ōtām*, 'and I will give them': refers back to the beginning of v. 18, with 'them' identified in vv. 18a, 19. G lacks 'and into the hand of those who seek their lives': for the phrase cf. 21.7. Cf. 7.33; 16.4; 19.7b for v. 20b; also Deut. 28.26. **[21]** G lacks 'and into the hand of those who seek their lives'. MT *hā'ōlīm mē'ălēkem*, 'who are going up from you': i.e. 'withdrawing', cf. 21.2. Only vv. 21–22 provide a setting for the *b*^e^*rīt* ceremony (cf. vv. 6–7, which are hardly suitable for what follows). **[22]** A combination of 37.8 and 9.11b.

David 1948; Lemche 1976; Sarna 1973

The word of salvation to Zedekiah (34.4–5) is followed by a Deuteronomistically edited attack on him in relation to a specific ritual act which the king, and his officials, has failed to carry through to its proper and permanent conclusion. Thus the word of assurance to the king – fulfilled in the going up of the Babylonians from the city (v. 21) – is arrested and changed to the command of destruction. Such may be the purport of this strange tale of the royal edict which the leading classes failed to sustain by subsequent public actions.

The king's proclamation of freedom to the slaves is a story unique in biblical traditions (cf. Neh. 5.1–13, where Nehemiah the governor persuades the nobles and officials to return to the people the mortgaged properties, goods and interest charges they have exacted from them). It betrays the Deuteronomists' interest in the making and breaking of *b^e^rīt*, and relates the destruction of the city of Jerusalem to the abrogation of this particular *b^e^rīt* (cf. 17.19–27, where the burning of Jerusalem is a punishment for breaking sabbath regulations). In a tradition where so many poems denounce the community for incorrigible corruption and prose sermons harangue the people about the nation's long history of idolatry and rebellion against Yahweh, these specific examples of what caused Jerusalem's destruction are redundant as well as difficult to explain. They appear to be midrash-type explanations added to the tradition which reflect the exegetical activity of communities in the Persian period rather than accounts of historical events prior to the fall of Jerusalem. As such they use the catastrophe of a previous age to underline the importance of keeping sabbath or ceremonial agreements between people.

The grounds for this interpretative approach to vv. 8–22 are manifold. In the midst of a terrible siege, with most of the outlying towns devastated (cf. vv. 6–7), why should the king and his nobles suddenly decide to liberate their slaves? Many different explanations have been offered by various exegetes: for military reasons (e.g. David, Rudolph); out of self-interest so as not to have to feed them (cf. Volz, 318; Duhm, 280); as an act of repentance (cf. v. 15; Weiser, 312); because it was the sabbatical year and, besides, an Egyptian force had relieved the siege temporarily (cf. v. 21; 37.5; Sarna). This appearance of a relief force from Egypt may have occasioned the Babylonian withdrawal, thereby allowing the leading classes to rescind their agreement (Sarna, 144). Many such rationalizing explanations may be provided to make good the absence of an editorial account of *why* Zedekiah should behave so out of character (in terms of the Jeremiah tradition cf. 38.19, 24–27) in the middle of the Babylonian onslaught. But they fail to carry conviction because they read the story as historical rather than as midrashic (Duhm treats vv. 12–22 as midrash and the product of the later supplementer of the tradition). If the community's fathers had not practised the manumission rules (v. 14), why should Zedekiah's generation suddenly institute them during a time of war? Where would the slaves have gone once they were released? What if they had refused to go, on the grounds that they preferred to stay with their masters (cf. Ex. 21.5–6; Deut. 15.16–17)? What space of time had elapsed between the making of the *b^e^rīt* and the turning (*šûb*) of the leading citizens to renege on it? What were the freed people doing during that period? The lull in the siege caused by the withdrawal of the Babylonians is represented as the occasion for Jeremiah to leave the city and head for home (37.11–13); would the newly released slaves have done the same? Did the ruling citizens lavish on their erstwhile slaves the bounty the law demanded of them (Deut. 15.13–14) and, if they did (what kind of *berīt* based on Deut. 15.12–18 could have avoided providing such compensation?), where did they acquire such provisions during a siege?

Many questions, no answers! The text offers no explanations nor the kind of information which would permit the careful exegete to recreate the events behind the story. Yet the questions must be asked in order to justify a different reading of the account and to explain why the exegete must view sceptically the temptation to read the story as if it were to be taken literally. As the story appears in its edited form in vv. 8–22 it is an amalgam of various strands and motifs. It uses the ruling of Deut. 15.12 but read in terms of Deut. 15.1, so that a specific regulation about individual debt slaves becomes a general proclamation of liberty to *all* slaves *at the same time*. Behind this confusion of regulations there may be some notion of a sabbatical year or even the year of jubilee (cf. Lev. 25.10, 25–28; Ezek. 46.17; Lemche), but not in any coherent form. The freeing of the slaves may be explained by modern exegetes in terms of *Realpolitik*, which would account for the act of general liberation, but the editor attributes it to the law on the release of slaves whose debt has been paid off by six years of servitude. These are two very different things. No connection with sabbatical or jubilee years is made by the redaction of the text, though vague notions of these (theoretical?) institutions may not be far from that process (depending upon the social setting of the editors of these midrashic elements in the Jeremiah tradition). The *berīt* ceremony is represented as a temple ritual (v. 15), though the regulations for releasing slaves have no specifications for a cultic setting of the rite (except for those slaves who do not wish to go free! Ex. 21.6). Here a parallel with Josiah's *berīt*-making in the temple should be noted (II Kings 23.1–3) and an explanation found for the general nature of the act. Like king Josiah, king Zedekiah also made a *berīt*. He, too, made it with *all* the people (v. 8 MT; II Kings 23.3). The similarities end there, but if 34.8–22 is midrashic at all, it is so because so much of the story is made up of allusions to and citations of other writings on the subject of slaves and their release and from the Deuteronomistic corpus. In v. 9 the motivation of the proclamation of liberty to the slaves is given as 'that no one should enslave a Jew, his *brother*'. Now this is *not* the law on the release of slaves as set out in Ex. 21.1–11; Deut. 15.12–18 because that does not contemplate the ending of bondage but the regulation of the practice. It is closer to the spirit of Lev. 25.39, which also aspires to preventing the enslavement of 'your *brother*' (cf. Deut. 15.1b). Thus the story in vv. 8–11 should be read as a midrash on slave rulings set into the Jeremiah tradition and reflecting the teaching programme of later communities (cf. 7.5–7; 17.19–27). The reversal of the *bᵉrīt* in v. 11 allows for a Deuteronomistically shaped sermon (cf. Nicholson 1970, 64–5) to teach its lessons by making connections between the abrogated *bᵉrīt* and the destruction of Jerusalem and the cities of Judah.

The story in vv. 8–11 is but the background to the divine word which comes to Jeremiah as a response to the turning of the princes and the people (vv. 8, 12). What follows in vv. 13–22 is Yahweh's word to Jeremiah without any instructions for its delivery to the king and his nobles or the people (nor any report of his so delivering it – though that is also absent for vv. 2–5). In the sermon the *bᵉrīt* between Yahweh and the people who came out of Egypt is stated in terms of the ruling about the release of slaves in the seventh (MT) year. Although this follows Deut. 15.12 inflected by v. 1, as befits the Deuteronomistic influence on the redaction, Ex. 21.1–6 would fit the point better as it is the first of the ordinances (*mišpāṭīm*) prefacing the making of that *bᵉrīt* (cf. Ex. 24.3–8). In keeping with the view expressed in the prose sermons in the tradition (e.g. 7.22–26; 11.7–8; 17.21–23), it is asserted that the exodus generation did not keep that *bᵉrīt* (v. 14b; cf. 31.32). The people of Zedekiah's time are represented as having been different from that generation because they had turned (v. 15, *šūb*) and behaved rightly in the divine eyes (contrast 7.25–26; 16.11–12). This right behaviour consisted of making a *bᵉrīt* in the temple – a different matter, perhaps, from the original *bᵉrīt* between Yahweh and people in that it was between the people and their slaves or, more likely, between the king and the slave-owning people (cf. vv. 8, 15, 16). However, the making of such *bᵉrīt* counts as virtue. It constitutes turning (in spite of all the assertions in Part I about the incapacity of the people to turn!) and is therefore to be praised. Unfortunately, however, the turning did not last and soon (how soon?) the people had profaned the name (v. 16) by subjugating the freed slaves again (profaned because the proclamation of liberty was carried out as a sacral act in the temple).

This turning back from the *b^{e}rīt* to which they had turned occasions a divine word-play (v. 17): the people failed to proclaim liberty to their neighbours (the slaves or more general?), so Yahweh proclaims liberty to 'sword, pestilence, famine' against them. Those who transgressed the *b^{e}rīt* will bear the curse implicit in the ritual making of that *b^{e}rīt* – the hacked animal becomes an analogue of their fate (cf. Judg. 19.29; I Sam. 11.5–11). All those involved in the ceremony will be given over to the enemy and their corpses will provide food for the birds and beasts. At this point the story alludes to the withdrawal of the Babylonians, but not by way of explaining the occasion of the *b^{e}rīt*. The retiral of the siege army is a necessary condition of Yahweh commanding them to come back and destroy the city with fire after capturing it. Thus the fate of Jerusalem is directly related to the abrogated *b^{e}rīt*, and Zedekiah's fate is bound up with that treachery (a very different account from vv. 2–5; 38.17–23). To the question 'why did Jerusalem fall?' this particular story answers: 'because Zedekiah and his companions (listed in v. 19) turned from the *b^{e}rīt* and profaned the divine name'. Could a better story be told to teach the community the importance of making *and keeping b^{e}rīt*? I doubt it. If great Jerusalem fell because Zedekiah and his lords broke faith with the common people and discarded solemn agreements, then the community must pay careful attention to these matters because even *one* of the *mišpāṭīm*, if broken, could lead to terrible destruction (cf. Neh. 5.13).

35.1–19

35[1] The word which came to Jeremiah from the LORD in the days of
Jehoiakim the son of Josiah, king of Judah: 2 'Go to the house of the
Rechabites, and speak with them, and bring them to the house of the LORD,
into one of the chambers; then offer them wine to drink.' 3 So I took
Jaazaniah the son of Jeremiah, son of Habazziniah, and his brothers, and
all his sons, and the whole house of the Rechabites. 4 I brought them to the
house of the LORD into the chamber of the sons of Hanan the son of Igdaliah,
the man of God, which was near the chamber of the princes, above the
chamber of Maaseiah the son of Shallum, keeper of the threshold. 5 Then
I set before the Rechabites pitchers full of wine, and cups; and I said to
them, 'Drink wine.' 6 But they answered, 'We will drink no wine, for

Jonadab the son of Rechab, our father, commanded us, "You shall not drink wine, neither you nor your sons for ever; 7 you shall not build a house; you shall not sow seed; you shall not plant or have a vineyard; but you shall live in tents all your days, that you may live many days in the land where you sojourn." 8 We have obeyed the voice of Jonadab the son of Rechab, our father, in all that he commanded us, to drink no wine all our days, ourselves, our wives, our sons, or our daughters, 9 and not to build houses to dwell in. We have no vineyard or field or seed; 10 but we have lived in tents, and have obeyed and done all that Jonadab our father commanded us. 11 But when Nebuchadrezzar king of Babylon came up against the land, we said, "Come, and let us go to Jerusalem for fear of the army of the Chaldeans and the army of the Syrians." So we are living in Jerusalem.'

12 Then the word of the LORD came to Jeremiah: 13 'Thus says the LORD of hosts, the God of Israel: Go and say to the men of Judah and the inhabitants of Jerusalem, Will you not receive instruction and listen to my words? says the LORD. 14 The command which Jonadab the son of Rechab gave to his sons, to drink no wine, has been kept; and they drink none to this day, for they have obeyed their father's command. I have spoken to you persistently, but you have not listened to me. 15 I have sent to you all my servants the prophets, sending them persistently, saying, "Turn now every one of you from his evil ways, and amend your doings, and do not go after other gods to serve them, and then you shall dwell in the land which I gave to you and your fathers." But you did not incline your ear or listen to me. 16 The sons of Jonadab the son of Rechab have kept the command which their father gave them, but this people has not obeyed me. 17 Therefore, thus says the LORD, the God of hosts, the God of Israel: Behold, I am bringing on Judah and all the inhabitants of Jerusalem all the evil that I have pronounced against them; because I have spoken to them and they have not listened, I have called to them and they have not answered.'

18 But to the house of the Rechabites Jeremiah said, 'Thus says the LORD of hosts, the God of Israel: Because you have obeyed the command of Jonadab your father, and kept all his precepts, and done all that he commanded you, 19 therefore thus says the LORD of hosts, the God of Israel: Jonadab the son of Rechab shall never lack a man to stand before me.'

[MT 35] = G 42. **[1]** Cf. 21.1; 32.1; 34.8; 40.1 for the introductory formula with note of the occasion of Jeremiah's reception of the divine word, though in this instance 'the days of Jehoiakim' is a very general notice (cf. 26.1; 36.1 for other narratives purportedly set in the period of Jehoiakim). **[2]** MT *'el-bēt*, 'to the house': *bēt* can mean 'household' or 'community, members of a clan', cf. vv. 3b, 5a, *bēt hārēkābīm*, 'the Rechabite community'. However, here it probably refers to the house in the city to which they moved when the Babylonians invaded the land (v. 11) rather than the community (*contra*

Rudolph, 224; Bright, 189). Had they been living in tents in the city, the text would have stated it to demonstrate their fidelity to the ancestral command, but then the contrast between vv. 10–11 would have been lost. Here Jeremiah goes (*hālōk*; hardly Bright's 'Seek out') to the *house* where they stay in order to take them to Yahweh's *house* (*bēt yhwh*). Neither the irony of the Rechabites living in the city (in a house at that!) nor their visiting a house where the deity lives is apparent to the writer. **[3]** MT *ben-yirmᵉyāhū*, 'the son of Jeremiah': one of the *three* Jeremiahs mentioned in the tradition, cf. 1.1; 52.1; G *Ieremin*, 'Jeremin'. **[4]** MT *bᵉnē ḥānān ben-yigdalyāhū 'īš hāᵉlōhīm*, 'the sons of Hanan ben Yigdaliah, the man of god': i.e. the prophetic guild of Hanan . . . the prophet. This is the only occurrence of the term 'man of god' to describe a mantic figure in the Jeremiah tradition; the phrase is used of Samuel, Elijah, Elisha and various anonymous figures (e.g. I Sam. 2.27–36; I Kings 13.1–10). Jeremiah's relationship with this guild is not known. On Hanan's name cf. Hananiah 28.1, 5, 10, 12, 13, 15, 17; a few minor Vrs read *bᵉnē*, 'guild', as *ben*, 'son of (Hanan)'. G *Godoliou* = *gᵉdalyāh* (cf. 40.7) for Yigdaliah. 'Maaseiah ben Shallum, keeper of the threshold': cf. 52.24, where such a post appears to be an important one; this may be the same Maaseiah father of Zephaniah the priest in 29.25; 52.24. **[5]** G has 'a jar of wine' for MT's 'jars, pitchers or bowls of wine'. **[6]** Jonadab ben Rechab, the founder of the community, appears in II Kings 10.15–17, 23; the group is related to the Kenites in I Chron. 2.55. Only the story in Jer. 35 tells of their anti-cultivation (viticulture, agriculture and house-building) outlook which rejects the values of urban and farming cultures (in favour of a pastoralist economy?). It cannot therefore be determined whether 35 is a fabrication of the writer or reflects an actual separatist group in Judaean life; the point of the story is not affected, whichever may be the case. **[7]** G *kai ampelōn ouk estai humin*, 'and a vineyard you shall not have': for MT *lō'-tiṭṭā'ū wᵉlō' yihyeh lākem*, '(a vineyard) you shall not plant nor shall you have'. MT *'attem gārīm šām*, 'you shall wander as aliens there': i.e. having no fixed abode and therefore behaving like aliens (*gērīm*) in Judaean society. **[9]** MT *wᵉśādeh wāzera'*, 'or field or seed': perhaps this should be read with Ehrlich 1912, 332, as *ūśᵉdēh-zera'*, 'and fertile soil', as in Ezek. 17.5 (cf. Rudolph, 226; BHS). **[11]** MT *ḥēl 'ᵃrām*, 'the army of the Syrians': G *dunameōs tōn Assuriōn*, 'the might of the Assyrian'; S 'Edom'. MT *wannēšeb bīrūšālāim*, 'and (so) we live in Jerusalem': some explanation is required for their infidelity to the communal rule about not living in houses and therefore a fortiori not in cities. Cf. I Macc. 2.29–41 for a similar breach of faith due to military pressure. The story-teller does not appear to be aware of the irony of the situation or the contradiction between Rechabite principle and practice in v. 11. **[12]** G has 'to me' for MT 'to Jeremiah': cf. 1.4, 11, 13; 2.1; 34.12 for this short introductory formula for the reception of the divine word. **[14]** MT *hūgam 'et-dibrē yᵉhōnādāb*, 'the words of Jonadab have been upheld': i.e. observed, obeyed. G lacks 'to this day, for they have obeyed their father's command'. MT *haškēm wedabbēr*, 'rising early and speaking': i.e. urgently speaking (7.13; 25.3; cf. urgently sending 7.25; 25.4; 26.5; 29.19; 35.15; 44.4; II Chron. 36.16; urgently witnessing 11.7; urgently teaching 32.33); RSV 'persistently . . .'. **[15]** MT *haškēm wešālōaḥ*, 'rising early and sending': i.e. urgently sending (7.25; 25.4; 26.5; 29.19; 44.4; II Chron. 36.15). The stereotypical phrase 'all my servants the prophets' (7.25; 26.5; 29.19; 44.4; cf. 'his servants . . .' 25.4) has no specific meaning other than as a blanket approval of prophets. It lacks identification of what prophets are considered to be Yahweh's and only identifies their message in terms of general warnings against evil ways and idolatry (cf. the negative generality of 28.8). **[17]** G lacks 'because . . . not answered' explanation in MT. **[18]** G has a shorter introduction than MT: 'therefore thus says the lord' and a slightly different description of the Rechabite behaviour. **[19]** G lacks MT introductory phrases and ends the chapter with the phrase *pasas tas hēmeras tēs gēs*, 'all the days of the earth' (cf. *kol-yemē hā'āreṣ*, Gen. 8.22). MT *lō'-yikkārēt*, 'shall not be cut off': i.e. lacking, cf. 33.17–18, where the house of David and the levitical priesthood are assured of a similar future to the Rechabites. The propinquity of these two sections in the tradition, though quite independent in origins, underlines the irony of a belief in the one case (Rechabites) that continuity and permanence are the reward for fidelity to principles and in the other (David and Levi) the confidence that such a reward may be gifted by Yahweh in spite of infidelity in the past.

Part III closes with two stories set in the reign of king Jehoiakim, thus forming a closure with 26. The strange tale of the Rechabites in 35 provides a positive contrast to the infidelity of the nation and Zedekiah's community in 34.8–22. If the abrogated *berīt* of that story accounts for the Babylonian destruction of Jerusalem and the cities of Judah, the narrative of the Rechabite fidelity to its cultural past points up the way communities could survive.

The story is set about ten years before the *berīt* ceremony of 34.8–11, presumably in the last year of king Jehoiakim, when the Babylonians invaded the land and eventually deported Jehoiachin. This invasion forced the Rechabite community to move into the city of Jerusalem, thus making them betray their cultural heritage of having nothing to do with settled modes of life. To this end they had shunned cultivating vineyards, working arable land or building houses. The definition of their way of life in negative terms emphasizing their rejection of urban civilization and the values of sedentary culture is attributed to their loyalty to their clan ancestor Jonadab (a figure associated with one of Jehu's political and religious bloodbaths, II Kings 10.15–27). In obedience to his command they had maintained a community which rejected urban and agrarian ways in favour of what may only be surmised to be pastoralist quasi-nomadic ways (reflecting the values of the desert culture?). Apart from this story, we know nothing about this group and it would be idle to speculate on how they lived or what their relation to the urban areas (e.g. Jerusalem) may have been. Their living in tents and refusing to drink wine appear in 35.6–10 to symbolize their rejection of viticulture and the building of permanent houses. But did they also not eat anything which might be produced by agriculture? Were they purely a meat-eating group or were leguminous plants permitted? The story only focuses on the matter of their not drinking wine and the explanation for it. Whether there were internal contradictions in their way of life is not the concern of the editor of this account.

Jeremiah is brought into contact with the Rechabites by means of an oracular instruction to perform a symbolic action (of all the dramatic actions presented in the tradition this one is the most symbolical and the least performative). He is sent (*hālōk*, 'go', cf. 13.1; 19.1) to the house in the city where the Rechabites are staying (whether he is sent from the temple is not made clear) in order to take them and bring them to Yahweh's house. Again it would be futile to speculate on what the Rechabites might have thought of a deity who dwelled in a magnificently built house but, presumably, they would have rejected such a religion. However their thoughts on the matter are not part of the story. There in the temple he is to offer the Rechabite clan wine to drink. Jeremiah carries out these instructions and takes the Rechabites to a chamber of a prophetic guild in the temple (MT). His access to such a place may imply friendliness between him and the *b^enē* Hanan or a shared working area. The story shows Jeremiah as one having access to the temple (contrast 36.5), influence there and the kind of authority which can command groups of people such as the Rechabites (cf. 19.1; 32.12). These may be features only of the story and should not be used to construct images of the historical Jeremiah. In the temple room he sets out pitchers of wine and cups and commands the Rechabites to drink. They refuse to drink wine and explain why they behave in such a peculiar manner. They are being faithful to their ancestor's command. They must, however, excuse their residency in Jerusalem as the Babylonian invasion has forced them to break faith in the matter of where and how they live.

The divine word explaining the significance of this act now follows (vv. 12–17). The key to understanding what has taken place is the refusal of the Rechabites to drink wine (whether they now live in a house or simply in Jerusalem is not the focus of the story). That refusal demonstrates their fidelity to the ancestral command and such obedience to commands is one of the demands of the prose sermons in the book of Jeremiah (for Deuteronomistic influence in 35 cf. Thiel 1981, 44–8). Jeremiah is now to go (*hālōk*, v. 13) to the men of Judah and the citizens of Jerusalem (cf. 4.4; 11.2, 9; 17.25; 18.11; 32.32) and declare to them the significant contrast between the loyalty of the Rechabites to their cultural values and the disloyalty to Yahweh of their own behaviour. The evidence for that infidelity is the rejection of the prophetic mission sent by Yahweh to the people (v. 15; 7.25; 25.4; 26.5; 29.19; 44.4; cf. II Kings 9.7; 17.13, 23; 21.10; 24.2; Ezra 9.11; Dan. 9.10; Amos 3.7; Zech. 1.6). In this explanation it is assumed that the people have been witnesses of the incident with the Rechabites or have had the matter explained to them at some point in Jeremiah's speech. The text offers no evidence of this, and it must be assumed that vv. 12–17 belong to the editorial explanation of the Rechabite refusal to drink wine in the temple. The Rechabite culture is presented as the outcome of obedience to an ancient command and thus affords a contrasting image of Judaean society which is represented as the opposite. That refusal to obey the prophetic warnings to turn and amend their way of life (cf. 7.5–7; 25.3–6; 26.3–5; 36.3, 7) will bring upon the communities great evil (cf. 6.19; 11.11, 23; 19.3, 15; 32.42; 36.31; 42.17; 44.2; 45.5).

In contrast to the word condemning Judah and Jerusalem is the word given to the Rechabites (vv. 18–19): their fidelity to the past is rewarded with the guarantee of their continual survival in the future. The phrase used to assert this, 'Jonadab . . . shall never lack a man . . .', is a post-Deuteronomistic one (cf. 33.17–18) in that the normal form of the Deuteronomistic statement is a conditional assertion (cf. I Kings 2.4; 8.25; 9.5; II Chron. 6.16; 17.8). That the second edition of Jeremiah contains 33.17–18 is ironic in view of 35.19 being a reward for faithful duty done in the past (not the Deuteronomistic motif which speaks of future fidelity). Yet David and the levitical priests are also rewarded in the same way as the Rechabites in spite of past infidelities. The editing of 35 has produced a number of ironies by setting the story in the days of Nebuchadrezzar's invasion against Jehoiakim. Thus the residency of the Rechabites in a city has to be ignored in the claim that they have been faithful to their ancestor's rules and only their refusal to drink wine is made the test of their loyalty (would eating bread have been an equally good test?). The Rechabites do not figure in any of the stories of the fall of Jerusalem, so perhaps 35 should be treated as a fabricated story rather than a historical account.

The curious tale of the Rechabites appears here after the story of Zedekiah's abrogated *b*^{e}*rīt* and, to some degree, makes an effective contrast. Disloyalty to the past brings destruction (34.15–16), and its opposite (35.8–10) guarantees a permanent future. The parallels between the Rechabite culture and the nation's history are far from exact but the traditionists use a simple parallel to offer yet again a theologized account of why city and country were destroyed by the Babylonians. Hints as to how the future might have been secured are contained in both stories.

36.1–32

36 1 In the fourth year of Jehoiakim the son of Josiah, king of Judah, this
word came to Jeremiah from the LORD: 2 'Take a scroll and write on it all
the words that I have spoken to you against Israel and Judah and all the
nations, from the day I spoke to you, from the days of Josiah until today. 3
It may be that the house of Judah will hear all the evil which I intend to do
to them, so that every one may turn from his evil way, and that I may
forgive their iniquity and their sin.'

4 Then Jeremiah called Baruch the son of Neriah, and Baruch wrote
upon a scroll at the dictation of Jeremiah all the words of the LORD which
he had spoken to him. 5 And Jeremiah ordered Baruch, saying, 'I am
debarred from going to the house of the LORD; 6 so you are to go, and on a
fast day in the hearing of all the people in the LORD's house you shall read
the words of the LORD from the scroll which you have written at my dictation. You shall read them also in the hearing of all the men of Judah who
come out of their cities. 7 It may be that their supplication will come before
the LORD, and that every one will turn from his evil way, for great is the
anger and wrath that the LORD has pronounced against this people.' 8 And
Baruch the son of Neriah did all that Jeremiah the prophet ordered him
about reading from the scroll the words of the LORD in the LORD's house.

9 In the fifth year of Jehoiakim the son of Josiah, king of Judah, in the
ninth month, all the people in Jerusalem and all the people who came from
the cities of Judah to Jerusalem proclaimed a fast before the LORD. 10 Then,

in the hearing of all the people, Baruch read the words of Jeremiah from the scroll, in the house of the LORD, in the chamber of Gemariah the son of Shaphan the secretary, which was in the upper court, at the entry of the New Gate of the LORD's house.

11 When Micaiah the son of Gemariah, son of Shaphan, heard all the
words of the LORD from the scroll, 12 he went down to the king's house, into
the secretary's chamber; and all the princes were sitting there: Elishama
the secretary, Delaiah the son of Shemaiah, Elnathan the son of Achbor,
Gemariah the son of Shaphan, Zedekiah the son of Hananiah, and all the
princes. 13 And Micaiah told them all the words that he had heard, when
Baruch read the scroll in the hearing of the people. 14 Then all the princes
sent Jehudi the son of Nethaniah, son of Shelemiah, son of Cushi, to say to
Baruch, 'Take in your hand the scroll that you read in the hearing of the
people, and come.' So Baruch the son of Neriah took the scroll in his hand
and came to them. 15 And they said to him, 'Sit down and read it.' So
Baruch read it to them. 16 When they heard all the words, they turned one
to another in fear; and they said to Baruch, 'We must report all these words
to the king.' 17 Then they asked Baruch, 'Tell us, how did you write all
these words? Was it at his dictation?' 18 Baruch answered them, 'He
dictated all these words to me, while I wrote them with ink on the scroll.'
19 Then the princes said to Baruch, 'Go and hide, you and Jeremiah, and
let no one know where you are.'

20 So they went into the court to the king, having put the scroll in the
chamber of Elishama the secretary; and they reported all the words to the
king. 21 Then the king sent Jehudi to get the scroll, and he took it from the
chamber of Elishama the secretary; and Jehudi read it to the king and all
the princes who stood beside the king. 22 It was the ninth month, and the
king was sitting in the winter house and there was a fire burning in the
brazier before him. 23 As Jehudi read three or four columns, the king would
cut them off with a penknife and throw them into the fire in the brazier,
until the entire scroll was consumed in the fire that was in the brazier. 24
Yet neither the king, nor any of his servants who heard all these words, was
afraid, nor did they rend their garments. 25 Even when Elnathan and
Delaiah and Gemariah urged the king not to burn the scroll, he would not
listen to them. 26 And the king commanded Jerahmeel the king's son and
Seraiah the son of Azriel and Shelemiah the son of Abdeel to seize Baruch
the secretary and Jeremiah the prophet, but the LORD hid them.

27 Now, after the king had burned the scroll with the words which Baruch
wrote at Jeremiah's dictation, the word of the LORD came to Jeremiah: 28
'Take another scroll and write on it all the former words that were in the
first scroll, which Jehoiakim the king of Judah has burned. 29 And
concerning Jehoiakim king of Judah you shall say, "Thus says the LORD,
You have burned this scroll, saying, 'Why have you written in it that the

king of Babylon will certainly come and destroy this land, and will cut off from it man and beast?' 30 Therefore thus says the LORD concerning Jehoiakim king of Judah, He shall have none to sit upon the throne of David, and his dead body shall be cast out to the heat by day and the frost by night. 31 And I will punish him and his offspring and his servants for their iniquity; I will bring upon them, and upon the inhabitants of Jerusalem, and upon the men of Judah, all the evil that I have pronounced against them, but they would not hear." '

32 Then Jeremiah took another scroll and gave it to Baruch the scribe, the son of Neriah, who wrote on it at the dictation of Jeremiah all the words of the scroll which Jehoiakim king of Judah had burned in the fire; and many similar words were added to them.

[MT 36] = G 43. **[1]** G has *pros mē*, 'to me', for 'to Jeremiah', cf. 32.26; 35.12. The fourth year of Jehoiakim was 605, the year of the battle of Carchemish, though the drama about to unfold is set in 604 (v. 9). The standard reception of the divine word introductory formula is used in v. 1b with the occasion specified first, cf. 16.1; 27.1. **[2]** MT *'al-yiśrā'ēl*, 'against Israel': G^BS have 'Jerusalem', G^A 'Israel'. MT represents the later edition which knows Israel, Judah, nations as the tripartite objects of Jeremiah's preaching, but the content of the scroll suggests that 'Jerusalem and Judah' are the target of what follows (cf. vv. 9, 31). The aim of the scroll is to turn the house of Judah (v. 3), though the normal order is 'Judah and Jerusalem' in the other prose sermons; cf. Wanke 1971, 61. Duhm, 289, regards 'and against all the nations' as a superstitious (i.e. 'touch wood') rounding off of the introduction. MT *m^egillat-sēper*, 'a book-scroll': only here, v. 4 and Ps. 40.8 (EV 7); Ezek. 2.9; on its constitution cf. Hicks 1983. The force of *'al*, 'against' or 'concerning', is debatable in v. 2: the summary of 36 in v. 29 favours 'against' (cf. Rietzschel 1966, 130; Rudolph, 228); other exegetes prefer 'concerning' (e.g. Weiser, 320, 323; Bright, 176, 179). **[3]** MT *'ūlay*, 'perhaps, it may be': cf. v. 7; 26.3; Amos 5.15. Thiel 1981, 49–51, regards vv. 3, 7, 31 as the Deuteronomistic redaction of the story; v. 31 shows that the possibility mooted in vv. 3, 7 is lost by the king's attitude, though the scroll is directed to the people. In this strand forgiveness (*slḥ*) is determined by turning (*šūb*), rather than a divine gift (contrast 31.31–34; 33.8). The scroll is addressed to 'the house of Judah' (*bēt y^ehūdāh*), but the syntax of v. 3 is plural rather than collective. **[4]** MT *wayyiqrā' . . . 'et*, 'and he summoned . . .'; cf. v. 18, where MT has *'el*; a few mss here have *'el*. 'Baruch ben Neriah': cf. 32.12, 13; of all the references to Jeremiah writing something (29.1; 30.2; 51.60), this is the only case of his using an amanuensis. It must reflect a strand in the tradition which elevates Baruch's importance (cf. 43.3; 45). MT *'^ašer-dibbēr 'ēlāyw*, 'which he spoke to him': ambiguous phrase meaning either 'which he (Yahweh) spoke to him (Jeremiah)' or 'which he

(Jeremiah) spoke to him (Baruch)'. **[5]** MT *'ᵃnī 'āṣūr 'ūkal lābō' bēt yhwh*, 'I am restrained, I am unable to enter the house of Yahweh': why? Cf. *'āṣūr*, 33.1; but hardly this kind of constraint if he may go into hiding (vv. 19, 26). See Comm. **[6]** G lacks *ūbā'tā 'attāh*, 'you go, you yourself', and reads *en tō chartiō toutō*, 'in *this* scroll', for MT 'in the scroll which you have written at my command the words of Yahweh'. MT *bᵉyōm ṣōm*, 'on a fast day': presumably the next time a fast is observed in the temple, unless a specific future event is in mind – according to v. 9 it was virtually another year before a fast was proclaimed. **[7]** MT *tippōl tᵉḥinnānām*, 'their supplication will fall': cf. 37.20; 38.26; 42.2, 9 for this idiom (also Dan. 9.18, 20). **[8]** MT *yirmᵉyāhū hannābī'*, 'Jeremiah *the prophet*': G lacks 'the prophet'. Cf. v. 10, where a similar statement indicates Baruch's carrying-out of Jeremiah's command. As a summary v. 8 completes the first telling of the story; are vv. 9.26 a variant account of vv. 4–8? (cf. vv. 9–10, 11–19, 20–26, where the scroll is read on three separate occasions). **[9]** MT *baššānāh haḥᵃmišīt*, 'in the fifth year': G^BS^ *en tō etei tō ogdoō*, 'in the eighth year'; G^A^ = MT. G 'all the people in Jerusalem and the house of Judah' for MT 'and all the people who came from the cities of Judah to Jerusalem'. The people can hardly be the subject of 'they proclaimed a fast before Yahweh'; presumably the cultic authorities called the fast (cf. Rudolph, 230). **[10]** Cf. 35.4 where the chamber of the *bᵉnē* Hanan is used by Jeremiah. The chamber here was either extremely large or an open area for 'all the people' to have heard the reading. The combination of motifs drawn from large-scale temple gatherings for public speeches (cf. 7.2; 26.2) and the more intimate meetings in rooms (cf. 35.4; 36.10, 12, 20) has made the story confusing at this point. Gemariah ben Shaphan: cf. 26.24; II Kings 22.3 for Shaphan the secretary; as v. 12 makes clear, Gemariah was not the secretary (*hassōpēr*, lit. 'the scribe'). Cf. 26.10 for reference to the New Gate; I Kings 7.12 for the various courts of the temple. **[12]** MT *wayyēred bēt-hammelek*, 'and he went *down* to the house of the king': cf. 22.1; 26.10. The named individuals here are the council or, what Bright, 180, calls, 'the cabinet ministers'. Whether Hananiah (*ḥᵃnanyāhū*) the father of Zedekiah here is the prophet Hananiah (*ḥᵃnanyāh*) cannot be determined from the text. G has variations of some of the names in v. 12 (cf. BHS). **[14]** Yehudi *ben* Nethaniah *ben* Shelemiah *ben* Cushi: the listing of three generations suggests a very important figure, but as Yehudi is an unknown person otherwise, it is possible that *wᵉ'et*, 'and . . .', has dropped out before the name of Shelemiah (even Baruch does not warrant such an ancestry, cf. 32.12); cf. Rudolph, Bright, Wanke, etc. MT *wayyābō*, 'and he came . . .': G *katebē*, 'went down', an accurate understanding of Baruch's movement. **[15]** MT *šēb*, 'sit down': G *palin*, 'again' = *šūb*, i.e. 'read it again'. Bright treats MT as evidence of the courtesy with which the princes treated Baruch and further proof of their friendliness towards him. **[16]** MT *pāḥᵃdū 'īš 'el-rē'ēhū wayyō'mᵉrū 'el-bārūk*, 'they were afraid to one another and they said to Baruch': syntax awkward; G lacks 'to Baruch' which eases the text. If 'and they said' were transposed to before 'to one another' (cf. Volz, Rudolph, Bright), good sense would follow. The fear expressed by the princes may be dictated by Josiah's response to a similar reading of a book (II Kings 22.11; Volz, 328), but they may be afraid simply on behalf of Baruch (and Jeremiah once they establish his hand in the matter vv. 17–19); cf. McKane 1965b, 118–21. Why they should express surprise or fear if what they had just heard had been Jeremiah's preaching for the previous twenty years (v. 2) is difficult to imagine. Their reaction would make more sense if this were the first occasion on which they had heard such dire warnings of imminent destruction (hence the reaction in 26.7–9). **[17]** MT *'ēk*, 'how': G* *pothen*, 'whence' (*mē'ayin*); G^B *pou*, 'where' (*'ayyēh*). MT *mippīw*, 'from his mouth': lacking in G; it anticipates v. 18 and belongs to Baruch's knowledge rather than what the princes know. RSV 'Was it at his dictation?' assumes something like *h^amippīw*, 'was it from his mouth?', and suggests an awareness of Jeremiah's presence 'in absence' among the princes. **[18]** G has 'Jeremiah' after 'to me': this makes better sense as it identifies the source and authority for Baruch's scroll without the over-subtle allusions of MT. G lacks *badd^eyō*, 'with ink': Giesebrecht, 199; Ehrlich 1912, 334, treat the original as 'by my hand' (*b^eyādī*, 'by my hand', or *b^eyād*, 'by hand'). **[20]** MT *ḥaṣērāh*, 'to the court(yard)': hardly in winter when it would have been too cold for such sessions! Giesebrecht, 200, suggests *ḥadrāh*, 'inner chamber' or 'his cabinet'. Many mss, G, Vrs have 'these' after 'all the words'. Presumably the scroll was left behind to facilitate giving the king a modest summary of its contents suitably toned down or perhaps to heighten the tension of the story by delaying the moment when king and scroll would encounter each other. **[22]** G lacks 'in the ninth month'. MT *bēt haḥōrep*, 'autumn-house': cf. Amos 3.15; NEB 'winter apartments'. MT *w^e'et-hā'āḥ l^epānāyw m^ebō'āret*, 'and the brazier before him was burning': Vrs read *w^e'ēš*, 'a fire'; G lacks 'burning'. **[23]** MT *šālōš d^elātōt w^e'arba'āh*, 'three or four columns': on the nature and substance of these cf. Hicks 1983, 49–57; *delet*, 'door', only occurs here in the Hebrew Bible in the sense of 'column' or 'writing board'. MT *yiqrā'ehā b^eta'ar hassōpēr*, 'he would cut it with a penknife': the 'he' is ambiguous, but presumably refers to the king (cf. v. 25). **[24]** MT *w^elō' pāḥ^adū w^elō' qār^e'ū 'et big^edēhem*, 'but they did not fear nor did they rend their garments': cf. v. 16; a word-play contrast appears here using *qr'*, 'cut, rend', to describe the king's response to the scroll and his failure to respond properly (cf. Josiah's rending, *qr'*, of his garments when he heard the words of the book found in the temple, II Kings 22.11). This verse condemns the king and his courtiers (G *hoi paides autou*, 'his servants', possibly 'his youths', i.e. his children) and it is unlikely that a distinction is being made, by using *kol-'^abādāyw*, between them and the princes (*śārīm*) of vv. 12–16. Neither servants nor princes rend their garments. **[25]** 'Delaiah': G *Godolias*; G^BS lack the negative element *mē*, hence make the named individuals persuade the king to burn the scroll! G lacks the final clause 'but he would not listen to them'. Cf. 26.22 for Elnathan ben Achbor. The mildly sympathetic picture presented of some of the princes in this story may reflect the motif of the support of Jeremiah by the princes in 26.16. However, the point of v. 25 may be to stress Jehoiakim's obduracy rather than the opposition of the princes. **[26]** G lacks 'and Shelemiah ben Abdeel': perhaps due to homoioteleuton (BHS). MT *wayyastirēm yhwh*, 'but Yahweh hid them': G *kai katekrubēsan*, 'but they were hidden' (= *wayyissātērū*, 'but they had hidden themselves'?). MT is probably a false dittography due to *wayᵉhī* in v. 27 (Rudolph, 232) and represents a miraculous development of the text which is quite unique in the book of Jeremiah. **[27]** MT *wᵉ'et-haddᵉbārīm*, '*and* the words': G *pantas tous logous*, '*all* the words', i.e. (the scroll), all the words. For the introductory reception formula cf. 33.1; 35.12 (lacking occasion); 43.8. **[28]** G lacks 'former' and 'first' as qualifications of the scroll. **[29]** G lacks 'and concerning Jehoiakim the king of Judah': possibly due to homoioteleuton (cf. end of v. 28; BHS). MT is emphatic *'attāh śāraptā*, 'you, you have burned . . .'. The king's summary of the scroll reflects the destruction of 587! Cf. 9.10–11; 32.43 for the devastation of 'man and beast'. **[30]** Cf. 22.18–19 for the casting out of the corpse of Jehoiakim. The fate of the king's body may reflect ironically the image of him sitting in his winter quarters heating himself beside the brazier (v. 22). In 22.30 similar language describes Jehoiachin's lack of a successor 'to sit upon the throne of David'; ironically Jehoiachin himself, for the few months he was king, falsifies this threat of Jehoiakim lacking a successor on the throne! For the problem of 'the predicted fate of kings' see on 22.18–19; 34.4–5. **[31]** G lacks MT *'et-ʿᵃwōnām*, 'their guilt, iniquity': the use of *pqd* is sufficient to indicate punishment (cf. 29.32). The introduction of 'the inhabitants of Jerusalem and . . . the men of Judah' (cf. vv. 3, 9) by the editor here (Thiel's Deuteronomists) is the only hint given of the people's reaction to the reading of the scroll. It is out of place in a denunciation of the royal house. Cf. 19.15; 35.17 for the judgment against the nation. **[32]** MT *wᵉyirmᵉyāhū*, 'and Jeremiah': G *kai . . . Barouch*, 'and . . . Baruch'; MT has Jeremiah carry out the instruction of v. 28 (cf. vv. 2, 4), whereas G assumes Baruch made the arrangements (the divine word shows no awareness whatever of Baruch's existence). It is idle to speculate on what additional material the second scroll may have contained (for such speculations cf. Holladay 1976a, 169–74; 1983, 149), but the supposed difference between the two scrolls implies a passage of time between the event of vv. 20–26 and the response of v. 32.

Kessler 1966; Nicholson 1970, 39–45; Wanke 1971, 69–69

Part III ends as it begins with a confrontation between Jeremiah and the community in the time of Jehoiakim. But there are subtle differences between 36 and 26. In 26 Jeremiah is present all the time but king Jehoiakim never appears. His absence is palpable, however, because of the redactors' dating of the story and their supplement (26.20–3) about the killing of the prophet Uriah ben Shemaiah. In 36 Jeremiah is only present for the preparation of the scroll (vv. 4–7) and in the aftermath of its burning (vv. 27–32). For the three readings of the scroll he is absent. The third reading takes place in the king's chamber (v. 20), and his presence is sensed in the second reading (v. 16). Throughout the readings of the scroll Jeremiah is present in his absence, i.e. awareness of him shapes the responses to the scroll (e.g. vv. 17–19, 26). The going into hiding of Jeremiah and Baruch (vv. 19, 26; cf. I Kings 17.3; 18.13) reflects the motif of a king who is prepared to kill prophets. In the editing of the two stories the purpose of the public declaration or reading of Jeremiah's words is the same: the attempt to persuade the community to turn (*šūb*, 26.3; 36.3, 7). The roles of the various strata of society differ in the two stories: in 26 the priests and prophets are ranged against Jeremiah, the princes and elders appear to support him, and the people fluctuate in their loyalty. In 36 no response is given for the people (v. 10, cf. v. 31b), the princes are sympathetic towards Baruch, the king is completely hostile towards the two creators of the scroll, and there is no mention of the priests and prophets. How Jeremiah avoids trouble is unclear in both stories, but survive he does, no matter what the king intends.

The most important differences between 26 and 36 concern Baruch and the fate of the king. If 26 represents the vindication of Jeremiah without clarifying precisely what happens to him, in 36 his presence is no longer necessary for the divine word to be heard in society. Between the two stories the motif of the divine word itself has come to the fore, and that is symbolized by Baruch's role as a scribe writing down what Jeremiah says and then reading it out in various chambers of the temple and palace. The written word has *replaced* Jeremiah. The scroll may be burned in the story (v. 23), but it can be rewritten (v. 32) in a way that an executed Jeremiah could not be repeated. If 26 ends in some confusion about what happened to Jeremiah, 36 is very clear on what happened to the divine words. *They were burned.* They were rejected by the king and, implicitly according to v. 31, by all the people. It is not necessary for the story to emphasize the rejection of the word by the people and the princes. The readings of the scroll in the presence of the worshippers in the temple and before the princes in the palace are the means whereby the scroll arrives in the chamber of the king for its third and fateful reading. The failure of all the groups to respond properly (i.e. by repentance and rendering of garments, v. 24) condemns them outright. Thus the writing of the words and the delegation of their reading to Baruch the scribe are symbolic actions whereby the community is exposed to the divine words and the various responses seal the fates of king, princes and people. By the end of Part III the fate of Jerusalem and Judah is determined by the ashes of that scroll lying under the king's brazier.

The dating of the story in 605–4 (vv. 1, 9, or 601, cf. G) may be a purely redactional matter, but it makes a close connection between Jehoiakim's action in burning the scroll and the emergence of Babylon as the dominant power in international politics (hence the summary of the scroll's contents in v. 29). As the scroll is read out to the people thronging the temple at the fast, and as it moves through the various echelons of Judaean society on its way to the king, the nation's destiny is determined. When the king dismisses its claims by burning it, he seals the fate of himself and his people. The threats and curses in the scroll are not destroyed by the king's apotropaic act but released by it. All that follows in Part IV is but the working out of that fate (cf. 52.2–3). Symbolic of that fact is the way the story ends with a brief account of the process of rewriting the scroll and developing its venomous message with further additions (v. 32). The king may burn the scroll, but he cannot prevent its contents becoming operative (cf. the broken flask of 19.1–2, 10–11; the drowned book of 51.59–64). In this story of a prophetic act the irony lies in the fact that it is the king himself who releases the fatal word rather than the prophet. Jeremiah delegates his authority to Baruch, but the king brings down upon himself and his people the destruction of the nation at the hands of the king of Babylon. The king may have been opposing the power of the spoken word with his own undoubted power in the community, but the point of the story is that such royal power is inferior to the prophetic word. Against Yahweh's word there is no effective power, not even that of a prophet-killing king.

Apart from forming a closure with 26, 36 should be read in conjunction with II Kings 22 (cf. Isbell 1978). The story of king Josiah's response to the finding of the book of the law in the temple is the counterpart to the tale of Jehoiakim's burning of the scroll.

Both stories belong together and, Deuteronomistic editing apart, provide paradigms of how to respond to the hearing of the divine word (or not as the case may be). Josiah's reaction to the reading of the book by Shaphan the scribe (hence Baruch in Jer. 36) is to rend his garments (II Kings 22.10–11; which explains why Jehoiakim and his courtiers are condemned in such terms as 36.24). His next response is to send his servants to inquire of Yahweh on behalf of himself, the people and all Judah because the nation is in dire trouble over their failure to obey the words of the book. This inquiry takes the form of a consultation with the prophet Huldah who assures the delegation that the words mean what they say and that the nation is doomed (II Kings 22.14–17). She also conveys an individual message for king Josiah which promises him a peaceful death because of his reaction to the curses of the book (II Kings 22.18–20). Josiah's weeping and torn garments, his concern for the nation and his consultation with a prophet represent the correct way to respond to the divine word in its written form. That story cannot be ignored in reading the account of the scroll of Jeremiah's words delivered by Baruch to the people, the princes and, finally, to the king. In spite of the apparent concern of the princes for the safety of Baruch and Jeremiah (vv. 16–19), they do not respond to the actual words read out to them. Throughout 36 there is no response to the scroll's contents: people, princes, king and courtiers *all* are represented as ignoring the contents of the scroll. Thus 36 reverses the paradigmatic response of Josiah to the words of the book.

The parallels between 36 and II Kings 22 contribute to accounting for Jeremiah's absence in vv. 9–26 and Baruch's presence in the story. In the Josiah story the source of the book is veiled, but its contents are validated by a prophetic source at some distance from the palace. It is read to the king by Shaphan the secretary. Chapter 36 also presents a story of a king being read to by a secretary from a scroll which has been validated by a prophetic authority outside the palace. As Josiah's book comes from the temple, we would expect Jeremiah to have lodged the scroll of his sayings in the sacred house from which he did so much of his work. However, if this had been the case, the pattern of II Kings 22 would have been broken and the king would have heard the words from Jeremiah himself rather than from a scribal figure. Furthermore, the editing of the book of Jeremiah invariably presents the prophet and king Jehoiakim as two figures who never encounter one another (hence the king's inexplicable absence from 26). By absenting Jeremiah from the temple, a role is created for Baruch the scribe and the parallel maintained to II Kings 22. Such structural symmetry is impressive, though v. 5 attempts to explain why Jeremiah could not go to the temple. Exegetes have offered various explanations for his debarment from the cult centre: e.g. he is banned on the grounds of levitical impurity (Duhm, 290), or because the temple priesthood opposed him for his behaviour on previous visits to the temple (e.g. 20.1–6; 26.2–15; cf. Volz, 328; Weiser, 325; Bright, 179). The view of Jeremiah as a trouble-maker simply does not explain how he moves so freely about the temple (e.g. 22.1; 29.24–29; 35.2–11). If he had been barred after 20.1–6 or 26.2–15 (assuming either story to be historical), then surely he would have been excluded even more categorically after Baruch's performance in 36. Yet a few years later (?) in 35.2–11 we find him introducing a group of Rechabites into the temple! The text offers no reason for the temple being inaccessible to him, but the story requires him to be debarred, otherwise there will be no role for Baruch the scribe. So Jeremiah is excluded from going to the temple to speak his words and therefore has to write them and delegate Baruch to deliver them at the next large public gathering.

The introduction of Baruch as a companion and amanuensis of Jeremiah has persuaded many scholars that 36 affords clues as to how the book of Jeremiah came to be written, and Baruch has been credited with the production of 'memoirs' which are to be found in many of the prose sections of Jeremiah (e.g. Duhm; Mowinckel 1914; Muilenburg 1970; cf. Rietzschel 1966; Wanke). There is little warrant for this reading of 36, and it should be noted that only in 36 is the writing of Jeremiah's work attributed to Baruch. Elsewhere Jeremiah writes his own material or, at least, nobody is credited with writing it for him (29.1; 30.2; 32.10; 51.60). These references may not reflect historical events, but they do not attribute Jeremiah's scribal activities to Baruch. Furthermore, the parallel account of 36.1–3 which appears in 25.1–7 does not present Jeremiah's summary of his twenty-three years of preaching in written form (hinted at in 25.13?), but as a further proclamation. The turning of the spoken word into writing occurs in 36 as part of a symbolic act and Jeremiah's use of Baruch is not a necessary element of the divine command (i.e. Yahweh does *not* order Jeremiah to acquire for himself a scribe to whom he may delegate the writing of the divine words). Baruch's role may be accounted for by the pattern of II Kings 22, but the thesis that 36 represents the taking over of the tradition by the Deuteronomistic scribal school (as II Kings 22 provides a possible legitimation of the book of Deuteronomy) cannot be ruled out altogether (cf. Carroll 1981, 15–16). There is a Baruch strand in the tradition (e.g. 32.12–13, 16; 36; 43.3, 6–7; 45) which, although brief and obscure, may reflect the beginning of an independent figure within the book which develops significantly in post-Jeremiah literature. Here, as the writer of the sayings of Jeremiah (36.4, 32), Baruch lays claim to authority by association and delegation, but too much should not be made of this claim because it is registered only in 36 and not elsewhere in the blocks of material in the book (though the other references to him confirm the degree of his association with Jeremiah). To focus on Baruch in 36 is to miss the point of the story:

> . . . it may be concluded that the central concern of this narrative is not with a description of how the book of Jeremiah had its beginnings, much less with a mere recording of an incident, albeit an important one, in the prophet's life, but rather with the manner in which Yahweh's Word as proclaimed by the prophet was rejected by Israel as personified in the king and actualized in his deeds (Nicholson 1970, 45).

The story of the fate of the scroll in 36 is one of the finest pieces of writing in the book. It is an example of Judaean storytelling at its best and, especially in vv. 11–19, 20–26, creates a number of striking dramatic moments which brilliantly illuminate scenes of potential conflict and disaster. (An alternative and undramatic account of the story may be implied by v. 8!) Suspense is built up and maintained by a sequence of three very different readings of the scroll. These are encapsulated by two introductory pieces (vv. 1–3, 4–8) and two concluding sections (vv. 27–31, 32). At the end of the story the fate of the nation is sealed, and yet Jeremiah and Baruch have only just written the scroll (again). The introductory material sets the scene for Baruch's visit to the temple whenever a suitable occasion presents itself. Thereafter Jeremiah disappears from sight and is replaced by the scroll. At a great public fast the temple is crowded with people seeking to appease Yahweh because of the Babylonians or a terrible drought (the reason for the fast is not given, but exegetes relate it to the military threat of Babylon or the terrible drought of 14.2–6; cf. Holladay 1981, 71–2, for the linking of both motifs). At this gathering Baruch gives his first public reading of the scroll. Nothing is recorded of its reception, but Micaiah ben Gemariah hears it and goes down to the palace where the princes are gathered. Thus the word is about to penetrate further into the corridors of power

Baruch is summoned to the palace, and there he gives a second reading of the scroll. What the princes hear (cf. v. 29, the force of which is lost by the redactional introduction of vv. 1–3) makes them afraid, and they recognize the fact that the king must hear these words. Once they have elicited from Baruch the source of the scroll, they counsel him to hide and they go to the council chamber where the king is. So the scene is set for the third reading, and this time only the scroll is present. Neither the presence of Baruch nor that of Jeremiah can distract from that document. The king is warming himself by a fire because it is winter. Jehudi reads the scroll to him. As the sections are read the king cuts them off with a knife and casts them into the fire. Thus king and court condemn themselves. Even though urged by some of the princes not to burn the scroll, the king refuses to listen. Instead he issues orders for the seizure of Jeremiah and Baruch, but they have hidden themselves (G). So at the end of the *third* reading of the *short* scroll, it is in ashes, the authors of it are in hiding and the king remains in his chamber unopposed.

Why did the king burn the scroll? To show his contempt for it? To counteract its terrible power? To frustrate the onslaught of the Babylonians of which it spoke? To show where the real power in the kingdom lay? The text offers no answers to these questions. The presentation of Jehoiakim in Jeremiah and the Deuteronomistic history is such that the burning of scrolls and the execution of prophets are to be expected of him. However, as the leader of the country, what else could he do to turn back the power of Babylon? Clearly neither he nor his councillors believed that the prophetic word provided any defence against the Babylonians (cf. McKane 1965b, 118–30). However much some of the princes may have felt that the scroll should not have been burned, none of them acted correctly according to the story-teller (v. 24). If v. 29 is a fair summary of the scroll's contents, then it offered no means of resisting the invaders. The redactional setting of the story within a pattern of proclamation and turning (vv. 3, 7, 31) obscures the absoluteness of the word of judgment (whether the scroll is imagined to have contained the oracles in 4–6 or not). Against the power of the written-spoken word (cf. 51.59–64) Jehoiakim exercised his royal authority to destroy it by burning the scroll.

Is that the end of the prophetic word? Does a king outrank a prophet? Is royal power the effective word in the kingdom? What of

Yahweh's word? Is that also hidden with those who cannot face the king's wrath? What now? The divine word strikes again (v. 27) and Jeremiah is ordered to repeat the process as before. This time there will be a special word for Jehoiakim (vv. 29–31): the image of the king sitting there by the fire burning the scroll is picked up in the cursing of the king. He will die without a successor on the throne and his body will be flung out (cf. the fate of Hananiah 28.16) to face heat by day and cold by night (cf. 22.19). The redactor uses this opportunity to include the nation in the word of judgment (v. 31b). Finally, the instructions of v. 28 are carried out (v. 32, cf. v. 8) and once more the scroll of words exists in Jerusalem. The written words of Yahweh are not easily destroyed, not even by a king!

With the disintegration of the nation brought about by the fall of king, city, and land and the development of the prophetic word in a written form, it becomes possible to discern the emergence of the idea of the word over against society. Committed to writing, the word has a permanence beyond the exigencies of human existence and can survive even the absence of its original bearer. The written word begins to transcend time and place and, in 36, we may catch a glimpse of an important transformation of theological thought in the exilic and later periods. George Steiner makes a similar point:

> The locus of truth is always extraterritorial; its diffusion is made clandestine by the barbed wire and watch-towers of national dogma . . . The mortal clash between politics and verity, between an imminent homeland and the space of the transcendent, is spelt out in *Jeremiah* 36–39. King Jehoiakim seizes the scroll dictated by God's clerk and bookkeeper. He cuts out the offending columns and casts the entire text into the consuming flame (governments, political censors, patriotic vigilantes burn books). God instructs the prophet: 'Take thee again another scroll and write on it all the words that were written on the first.' The truth will out. Somewhere there is a pencil-stub, a mimeograph machine, a hand-press which the king's men have overlooked. 'So Jeremiah abode in the court of the prison till the day that Jerusalem was taken; and he was *there* when Jerusalem was taken.' The formulaic specification is magnificent in meaning. The royal city, the nation are laid waste; the text and its transmitter endure, *there* and *now*. The Temple may be destroyed; the texts which it housed sing in the winds that scatter them (1985, 21).

PART FOUR

The Fall of Jerusalem and Aftermath

37–45

The rejection of the divine word in 36 determines the fate of Jerusalem and the people. Part IV spells out the consequences of that act and presents an image of Jeremiah as a passive figure undergoing maltreatment at the hands of various social groups. Jeremiah's passivity is intimated in 36 by his delegation of Baruch to write and read out the scroll of his words to the people. It is further developed throughout 37–45 (with the exception of 39.15–18; 43.8–13), though the delegated status of Baruch is limited to 36. Neither figure is the central focus of the tradition, and it is therefore not possible to develop a reading of Part IV as the passion narrative of Jeremiah (*contra* Kremers 1953; Zimmerli 1981; cf. Welten 1977). This is not possible because, as in 36, the figure of Jeremiah fades from view at certain points of the narrative (e.g. 40.7 – 41.18; 45.3–5). Only the word counts, and the bearer of that may be Jeremiah, Baruch (36) or, even, Seraiah (51.59). Jeremiah's sufferings are incidental in Part IV and provide opportunities for further proclamations of that divine word (hence the repetitions in 37–38). When the word is not present Jeremiah is absent (as in 40.7 – 41.18). 37.2b summarizes the first half of Part IV: king, officials and people 'did not listen . . . to the words of Yahweh which he spoke *by means of* Jeremiah the prophet'. Jeremiah is simply the instrument of the divine word or its expression (cf. Ackroyd 1968b, 52). Even in Egypt (43.8–13; 44) his only function is the declaration of the word.

Part IV consists entirely of prose narratives (with the exception of the poetic couplet in 38.22b) dealing with Jeremiah's imprisonment in the dungeons (37) or cistern (38), the fall of Jerusalem (39.3–10), the rescue of Jeremiah from prison by the Babylonians (39.11–14) or from among the deported Judaeans at Ramah (40.1–6), the community under Gedaliah's governorship, including the governor's assassination and the rebellion of Ishmael ben Nethaniah (40.7 – 41.18), the leadership of Johanan ben Kareah and Jeremiah's consultative role among the remnant of Judah (42.1 – 43.3), the flight to Egypt of that remnant (43.4–7), Jeremiah's performative magic against Egypt (43.8–13), a lengthy and highly edited sermon with responses directed against the Jewish communities in Egypt (44), and a brief lament with reply relating to Baruch (45). Nothing unifies these stories except the unfolding of the divine word as it shapes the fate of the community. The element of hope to be found in Part III (e.g. 29.4–7, 10–14; 30–31; 32.6–15, 36–44; 33) is almost entirely absent in Part IV. It can be detected in a few places: e.g. 39.15–18; 40.7–12; 42.9–12; 45.5. But these are all very modest expressions of potential well-being set into contexts of overwhelming destruction. The militancy with which the Egyptian connection is denounced (42–44) contrasts with the pro-Babylonian tendency of 27–29 (counteracted by 30–31) and hints at ideological conflict between the different Jewish communities in Palestine, Babylon and Egypt from the sixth century onwards. Apart from a consistent attitude to Egypt, the figure of Jeremiah supports the Palestinian community in Part IV and both Palestinian and Babylonian in Part III.

37.1–2

37[1] Zedekiah the son of Josiah, whom Nebuchadrezzar king of Babylon made king in the land of Judah, reigned instead of Coniah the son of Jehoiakim. 2 But neither he nor his servants nor the people of the land listened to the words of the LORD which he spoke through Jeremiah the prophet.

[MT 37] = G 44. **[1]** MT *wayyimᵉlāk-melek ṣidqiyyāhū*, 'and Zedekiah reigned as king': G lacks *malek* – a dittography in MT unless read as *hammelek*, '(Zedekiah) the king'; cf. 23.5 for MT idiom. G lacks 'Coniah ben Jehoiakim', thereby making v. 1 the fulfilment of 36.30; i.e. Zedekiah becomes king instead (*antitaḥat*) of Jehoiakim. **[2]** MT *wᵉlō'šāma'*, 'but he did not listen': this is the central point of 37–39, but it is expanded in the title here to emphasize the collective responsibility of the leadership: '*he* and his servants and the people of the land'. This third group appears in 1.18;

34.19, where they refer to the landed gentry, though some exegetes regard them as the people in general (e.g. Rudolph, 236). If they are the common people, then 37.2 follows 36 by indicting the three strata of king, princes and people (36.10, 24, 31). MT *dibber bᵉyad yirmᵉyāhū hannābī'*, 'he spoke by means of Jeremiah the prophet': G lacks 'the prophet'; *bᵉyad*, lit. 'by the hand of', frequently means 'by the agency of', 'instrumentality of', cf. II Kings 9.36; 17.13, 23 (often of prophets).

Part IV is introduced by a titular statement to the effect that Zedekiah took over from Jehoiakim (G), but he *too* did not listen to Yahweh's words delivered by Jeremiah. This title summarizes the content of 37–39 and anticipates by way of explanation the fall of Jerusalem. It opens the final part of the book (G order) with a clear statement to the effect that even a change of king did not avert the nation's fate (sealed in 36). Zedekiah continues his predecessor's policy of ignoring the words of Jeremiah. All that follows will unfold the consequences of that attitude, and again the words of Jeremiah (i.e. Yahweh's word) will dominate the narratives. In the second edition (MT) Jeremiah's prophetic status is emphasized (cf. 34.6). In spite of the stories which appear in Part IV and elsewhere in the tradition (e.g. 21.1–7; 34.8–22), nothing needs to be known about Zedekiah's reign beyond the dismissive preface to the block in 37.2. As the fall of Jerusalem comes into focus, it is sufficient to know that the Babylonian replacement on the throne proved to be no more receptive to the divine word mediated through the agency of Jeremiah than all the other kings. The destruction of Jerusalem may be heard through the filter of the motif of a leadership which failed to grasp the significance of the prophetic ministry of Jeremiah. That summary judgment is unique among the parts which make up the book in that it anticipates what is to happen by offering an account of the reason why before allowing the story to unfold in its own way.

37.3–10

3 King Zedekiah sent Jehucal the son of Shelemiah, and Zephaniah the priest, the son of Maaseiah, to Jeremiah the prophet, saying, 'Pray for us to the LORD our God.' 4 Now Jeremiah was still going in and out among the people, for he had not yet been put in prison. 5 The army of Pharaoh had come out of Egypt; and when the Chaldeans who were besieging Jerusalem heard news of them, they withdrew from Jerusalem.

6 Then the word of the LORD came to Jeremiah the prophet: 7 ‘Thus says
the LORD, God of Israel: Thus shall you say to the king of Judah who sent
you to me to inquire of me, “Behold, Pharaoh’s army which came to help
you is about to return to Egypt, to its own land. 8 And the Chaldeans shall
come back and fight against this city; they shall take it and burn it with fire.
9 Thus says the LORD, Do not deceive yourselves, saying, ‘The Chaldeans
will surely stay away from us,’ for they will not stay away. 10 For even if
you should defeat the whole army of Chaldeans who are fighting against
you, and there remained of them only wounded men, every man in his tent,
they would rise up and burn this city with fire.” ’

---

[3] MT *wayyišlaḥ hammelek ṣidqiyyāhū*, ‘and Zedekiah the king sent . . .’: = v. 17; 38.14; cf. 21.1. Jehucal is Jucal in 38.1. Zephaniah ben Maaseiah appears in 21.1; 29.25. The delegation here (Jehucal, Zephaniah) differs from that given in 21.1 (Pashhur [cf. 38.1], Zephaniah). G lacks ‘the prophet’ as a qualifier of Jeremiah. MT *hitpallel-nā’ ba‘*^{a}*dēnū*, ‘pray on our behalf’: cf. *d*^{e}*rāš-nā’ ba‘*^{a}*dēnū*, ‘inquire on our behalf’, 21.2. **[4]** MT *bā’ w*^{e}*yōṣē’ b*^{e}*tōk hā‘ām*, ‘coming in and going out among the people’: G *ēlthen kai diēlthen dia mesou tēs poleōs*, ‘came and went through the midst of the city’. K *hkly’*; Q *hakk*^{e}*lū’*, cf. 52.31 for K–Q: *hakkele’*, ‘prison, confinement’, vv. 15, 18. This verse anticipates vv. 13–15; cf. 32.2–5. **[5]** G lacks ‘who were besieging Jerusalem’. Cf. 34.21–22 for the Babylonian withdrawal. **[6]** G lacks ‘the prophet’. **[7]** MT *kōh tō’m*^{e}*rū*, ‘thus will *you* (plur.) say’: i.e. the delegates; G sing. which, with *pros se*, ‘to you’, for MT *’etkem ’ēlay*, ‘you to me’, refers to Jeremiah. **[8]** MT *ūś*^{e}*rāpuhā bā’ēš*, ‘and burn it with fire’: cf. 34.2; 38.3. It is regarded as an additional gloss (Rudolph, 238; cf. BHS); see v. 10 also. **[10]** MT *’īš b*^{e}*’oh*^{o}*lō*, ‘each in his tent’: G *hekastos en tō topō autou*, ‘each in his place’. BHS treats ‘burn . . . with fire’ as a possible gloss. Cf. II Chron. 24.23–24 for the motif of the defeat of the Judaeans by a *few* enemies; II Sam. 5.6–8 for the element of contempt in this verse.

The first block of material in Part IV is 37.3 – 38.28 (analysis in Migsch 1981, 125–80; Pohlmann 1978, 49–93; Wanke 1971, 95–102). It consists of a series of variations on encounters between Jeremiah and Zedekiah. These encounters take two very different forms: in one set Zedekiah sends a delegation to the prophet (21.1–2; 37.3), in the other set he summons Jeremiah for an interview (37.17; 38.14). One group of stories relates to a prophet who has his freedom to move about the city (37.4 G), the other focuses on an imprisoned Jeremiah (37.15; 38.13; cf. 32.2–3). All the stories must be regarded as variations on a theme rather than as historical accounts of independent events in the intertwined lives of Zedekiah and Jeremiah (cf. Bright, 233; Skinner 1922, 258 n. 1 on 37–38 as two accounts of the *same* story). Apart from 38.17, every encounter between the king and the prophet, whether by delegation or summons, has the same result. The message remains the same throughout: the king of Babylon or the Chaldaeans will take the city (34.4–5 may be regarded as a modification of the harsh forecast). The severity with which the enemy will treat the occupants of the city varies in the telling (cf. the gradations of 21.5–6, 7, 8–10), but only 38.17 affords any escape for king and city. The theme, with all its variations and its outworking in 39.1–10, is the only point of contact between Jeremiah and Zedekiah (just as 36 is the only story where Jeremiah and Jehoiakim almost encounter each other). This underlines the dominant motif of parts III and IV – the movement of the divine word in Jerusalem. The tradition has little interest in the story of Jeremiah or the activities of the kings; only the encounter with the word is the concern of the redactors who have put together these stories.

The variation on the delegation motif in 37.3–10 (see on 21.1–7) sets the event in the lull caused by the Babylonian withdrawal from the siege of Jerusalem to meet the Egyptian force (v. 5; 34.8–22 is set in this period too). 21.2 has the delegation approach Jeremiah so that his intercession with the deity may lead to a Babylonian withdrawal. 38.3 does not make it clear why Jeremiah should intercede with the deity, but the motif reflects the theme of Jeremiah *the prophet* (MT). An explanation is required here because Jeremiah ought to have been under arrest during the siege (cf. 32.2–5). The king had had him arrested for his treasonous proclamation about the triumph of the Chaldaeans, but in anticipation of vv. 12–15 in this telling of the story he is at liberty. In 34.21–22 the withdrawal of the Babylonians is made to coincide with the *b^e^rīt* releasing the debt slaves, and their return is viewed as the punishment for the profanation of that obligation. Here the raising of the siege is accounted for in terms of an Egyptian military expedition against the Babylonians. The possibility of hope facilitates the sending of the delegation to the intermediary. However, the message remains what it has always been. The Chaldaeans will return and take the city. The Egyptian intervention will peter out and no confidence is to be placed in it. Furthermore, even if the Babylonian army were to be defeated by the Judaeans (never mind the Egyptians), it would not help the city. Here the prophet uses irony to make his point: a defeated army would still conquer Jerusalem because even its wounded soldiers would rise from their beds to capture the city (cf. the irony in II Sam. 5.6–8 with reference to the taking of Jerusalem). If 21.1–7 in its treatment of the delegation theme asserts the inevitability of the city's defeat and the death of everybody in it, 37.7–10 reasserts that lesson but reinforces it by relating it to the false hopes raised by the appearance of the Egyptians on the horizon. Even under such circumstances there is no hope for Jerusalem.

37.11–16

11 Now when the Chaldean army had withdrawn from Jerusalem at the approach of Pharaoh's army, 12 Jeremiah set out from Jerusalem to go the land of Benjamin to receive his portion there among the people. 13 When he was at the Benjamin Gate, a sentry there named Irijah the son of Shelemiah, son of Hananiah, seized Jeremiah the prophet, saying, 'You are deserting to the Chaldeans.' 14 And Jeremiah said, 'It is false; I am not deserting to the Chaldeans.' But Irijah would not listen to him, and seized Jeremiah and brought him to the princes. 15 And the princes were enraged at Jeremiah, and they beat him and imprisoned him in the house of Jonathan the secretary, for it had been made a prison. 16 When Jeremiah had come to the dungeon cells, and remained there many days.

---

[12] MT *laḥaliq miššām betōk hā'ām*, lit. 'to divide from there among the people': the last phrase appears in v. 4, where it is used as a reference to this incident, but in order to place vv. 6–10 before what transpires in vv. 13–15; cf. II Kings 4.13, where the phrase *betōk 'ammī*, 'among my own people', indicates one's kinsfolk (hardly its meaning in v. 4). The expression 'to divide' (Piel *ḥillēq*) can refer to apportioning land (cf. Josh. 19.51; Micah 2.4; Joel 4.2 [EV 3.2]; Dan. 11.39), but Jeremiah hardly was a distributor of land. G *tou agorasai*, 'to buy': an attempt to understand *ḥlq*. The word may refer to his inheritance (cf. Rudolph) as described in 32.6,15 (so Bright, 229), but that transaction took place when Jeremiah was under arrest and the tradition knows nothing of his release until 39.14! **[13]** MT *ba'al peqidut ūšemū yir'īyyāyh*, lit. 'master of the guard and his name (was) Irijah': G *kai ekei anthrōpos, par' hō kateluen, Sarouias*, 'and there a man with whom he lodged, Saruia'; a rather different account of the matter. Cf. 20.2 for the Benjamin Gate. G lacks 'the prophet' as in vv. 2, 3, 6. **[14]** G Saruia for Irijah (S Neriyah as in v. 13). The Heb. word for 'desert' in vv. 13–14 is *nōpēl*, i.e. 'fall away, go over to'; cf. 21.9. **[15]** G lacks MT *bēt hā'ēsūr*, 'prison' (cf. JPSB; other EVV 'imprisoned'). MT's two 'houses' (prison, Jonathan's) represent variants, as *bēt hā'ēsūr* is unnecessary in view of the final clause.

[16] MT *kī bā'*, 'when he went . . .': G *kai ēlthen*, 'and he came' = *wayyābō'*. RSV is a poor translation here (other EVV superior) and necessitates reading v. 16 as the beginning of the next piece rather than the end of this section. MT *'el-bēt habbōr we'el-haḥanuyōt*, lit. 'to the house of the pit (i.e. dungeon, cistern), and to the cells': hendiadys 'dungeon cells'; cf. the variant story in 38.6 where Jeremiah is put in a pit or cistern (*bōr*). G *chereth* for *haḥanuyōt*. 'And he remained there many days': end of this particular story; cf. v. 21; 38.13, 28.

A rather different story is now set in the period of the Babylonian withdrawal from the siege. In 32.2–5 Jeremiah had been put under house arrest in the guard court for his proclamation of the Chaldaean destruction of Jerusalem. In this version of that motif he is stopped as he attempts to leave the city and thrown into the dungeons. Thus there are two different traditions in the book about Jeremiah's fate during the siege. In one he is restricted severely in his movements but may receive visitors and transact business (32.6–15; very much like Socrates waiting for hemlock). In the other he is at liberty to move about the city (37.4) and preach sedition to the people (38.1). The variants of this tradition give different reasons for his incarceration in the dungeons and for his eventual escape from them. All the variations of the two traditions allow the redactors to drive home the primary message of the Babylonian destruction of everything, though even here variants appear in the fate of Zedekiah (34.4–5; 38.17) and the city (38.17).

Jeremiah in his freedom chooses to leave the city to go to his homeland in Benjaminite territory. The text (v. 12) is not clear about his reason for doing this, but relates it to the division of land. This may refer to Jeremiah's purchase of land in 32.6–15, though no such connection is made directly by the editors. It is much more likely that the story is told in order to explain why Jeremiah was thrown into the cells. He chose to leave the city when the opportunity presented itself and suffered the consequences of his actions. Such an explanation requires Jeremiah to have had his freedom at the time and also necessitates the withdrawal of the Babylonians. The editions differ about the precise details of the story: G presents his experience as the result of a citizen's arrest by the man with whom he lodged, whereas MT has him arrested by an officer of the guard. He is charged with deserting to the enemy. This charge he denies as being false (*šeqer*, 'it is false', v. 14). In 21.8–10; 38.2 he advocates desertion to the citizens so it is hardly surprising that he should now suffer arrest for appearing to be following his own advice. Enraged by his disloyalty the princes beat him (different princes from 26.16; 36.19?) and imprison him in the dungeons (variants obscure v. 15). There he remains a long time.

37.17–21

17 King Zedekiah sent for him, and received him. The king questioned him secretly in his house, and said, 'Is there any word from the LORD?' Jeremiah said, 'There is.' Then he said, 'You shall be delivered into the hand of the king of Babylon.' 18 Jeremiah also said to King Zedekiah, "What wrong have I done to you or your servants or this people, that you have put me in prison? 19 Where are your prophets who prophesied to you, saying, "The king of Babylon will not come against you and against this land"? 20 Now hear, I pray you, O my lord the king: let my humble plea come before you, and do not send me back to the house of Jonathan the secretary, lest I die there.' 21 So King Zedekiah gave orders, and they committed Jeremiah to the court of the guard; and a loaf of bread was given him daily from the bakers' street, until all the bread of the city was gone. So Jeremiah remained in the court of the guard.

---

[17] MT *wayyiqqāḥēhū*, 'and he received him': G *kai ekalesen auton*, 'and he called him'. Contrast the secret meeting here in the palace with the meeting in the temple of 38.14. **[18]** MT *wayyō'mer*, 'and he said': cf. NEB 'Then . . . said'; better than RSV 'also'. Jeremiah's question is naive in the extreme (contrast 26.14–15) in the context of deserting in a time of war, but the interview strand should be read independently of its present context. G sing. '*you* put me in prison', i.e. the king is responsible for his imprisonment (cf. 32.3). **[19]** K *w'yw*; Q *w*^{e}*'ayyēh*, 'but where . . .?': Thiel 1981, 53–4 treats v. 19 as a redactional verse from the Deuteronomistic editing; cf. 27.9, 16; 29.8. **[20]** Cf. 36.7 for the supplication motif (*t*^{e}*ḥinnāh*). **[21]** Cf. 32.2 for the court of the guard. In 52.6–7 the breaching of the city wall coincides with the exhaustion of the food supply. MT *wayyēšeb yirm*^{e}*yāhū baḥ*^{a}*ṣar hammaṭṭārāh*, 'and Jeremiah remained in the court of the guard': = 38.13, 28; cf. 37.16b. Volz, 332; Rudolph, 243, transpose 38.24–28 to follow 37.21 (cf. BHS).

Jeremiah's incarceration in the dungeons is terminated in this version of the story by a summons from the king (v. 17; cf. 38.14, but contrast 38.7–13; 34.2). No details are given about how the king knew that Jeremiah had been thrown into the cells, nor are the stages of his release noted in the text. The text passes in silence over the movements required to transfer Jeremiah from his erstwhile prison to the king's palace, though it notes that the interview was 'in secret' (v. 17, *bassēter*). Curiously the king blithely inquires about a divine oracle, as if vv. 7–10 were unknown or all that had passed between king and prophet on other occasions had been forgotten. This minor point confirms the view that there is only a set of motifs which is used repeatedly in different ways to construct variations on a theme rather than a historical event behind the variant accounts. In this particular version of the interview motif Jeremiah reasserts his message of the king's deliverance into the hand of the Babylonian king and adds a plaintive question about his own imprisonment (v. 18). The question may be naive in the light of Jeremiah's constant preaching of sedition, but here it reflects the independent interview motif rather than the integrated strands of 37–38.

The main feature of the interview motif (37.17–21; 38.14–28; cf. 34.2–5) is the eirenic exchange between king and prophet. Death is much spoken of (37.20; 38.15–16, 19–20, 24–26) and there is between the two men a sympathy which is strikingly absent from much of the tradition. Zedekiah is presented as a person quite prepared to ease Jeremiah's position, but also as a man somewhat afraid of his official advisors. As a man afraid he appears to be quite human (38.19, 24–27) and rather different from the redactional material which blames him for the fall of Jerusalem (37.1–2; 52.1–3; cf. May 1956, 103–5 on Zedekiah). He is susceptible to Jeremiah's pleas and capable of overriding the wishes of his princes. Thus he accedes to Jeremiah's entreaty and releases him from the dungeon in which he would inevitably have died. He can save the prophet's life by freeing him and by assigning him a daily food allowance; an allowance facilitated by confining him to the court of the guard. There Jeremiah would have lived out the siege and have been in a better position than the citizens, not confined, but exposed to the hazards of finding food in a time of war. Yet no credit is granted to the king in the tradition (cf. Obadiah's role in I Kings 18.13). The story of how Jeremiah survived the terrible siege of Jerusalem is told a number of times in 37.17–21; 38.7–13, 24–28. But his survival is hardly a concern of the tradition; rather, it is more interested in recording how the purveyor of the divine word came to be alive after the catastrophe and to be still the bearer of that word. The irony of vv. 18–19 raises an interesting point (attributed to Deuteronomistic influence according to some exegetes), but the text does not develop it.

38.1–6

38[1] Now Shephatiah the son of Mattan, Gedaliah the son of Pashhur, Jucal
the son of Shelemiah, and Pashhur the son of Malchiah heard the words
that Jeremiah was saying to all the people, 2 'Thus says the LORD, He who
stays in this city shall die by the sword, by famine, and by pestilence; but
he who goes out to the Chaldeans shall live; he shall have his life as a prize
of war, and live. 3 Thus says the LORD, This city shall surely be given into
the hand of the army of the king of Babylon and be taken.' 4 Then the
princes said to the king, 'Let this man be put to death, for he is weakening
the hands of the soldiers who are left in this city, and the hands of all the
people, by speaking such words to them. For this man is not seeking the
welfare of this people, but their harm.' 5 King Zedekiah said, 'Behold, he
is in your hands; for the king can do nothing against you.' 6 So they took
Jeremiah and cast him into the cistern of Malchiah, the king's son, which
was in the court of the guard, letting Jeremiah down by ropes. And there
was no water in the cistern, but only mire, and Jeremiah sank in the mire.

[MT 38] = G 45. **[1]** G lacks 'and Pashhur the son of Malchiah': cf. 21.1 for Pashhur ben Malchiah; 37.3 for Jehucal ben Shelemiah. Is Gedaliah the son of the Pashhur of 20.1? **[2]** = 21.9. Rudolph, 240, treats the verse as a marginal gloss (cf. BHS); Bright, 230, thinks of it as a genuine citation by the princes. K *yḥyh*; Q *w*^{e}*ḥāyāh*: 'and shall live': an addition forming a doublet with *wāḥāy*; 21.9 lacks *wāḥāy*, 'and live'. **[3]** Cf. 21.7; 32.28; 34.2. **[4]** G 'and they said' for MT 'and the princes said': Rudolph suggests *hā'ēlleh*, 'these', has dropped out after 'princes' due to haplography (cf. BHS). For the idiom 'weakening the hands' cf. Lachish Letter VI for the same phrase; the opposite idiom appears in 23.14. Cf. 29.25–28 for other complaints about Jeremiah's defeatist attitude. **[5]** MT *hinnēh-hū' b*^{e}*yed*^{e}*kem*, 'look, he is in your hands': cf. *wa'*^{a}*nī hin*^{e}*nī b*^{e}*yed*^{e}*kem*, 'but as for me, look, I am in your hands', 26.14. MT *kī-'ēn hammelek yūkal 'et*^{e}*kem dābār*, 'for the king can do nothing against you': G *hoti ouk ēdunato ho basileus pros autous*, 'for the king was not able to withstand them'. MT stresses the king's weakness, G the power of the princes. **[6]** G lacks 'and they took Jeremiah', 'Jeremiah by ropes', and reads 'and he was in the mire' for MT 'and Jeremiah sank in the mire'.

The second account of Jeremiah's adventures during the events leading up to the sacking of Jerusalem follows the pattern of the first story in 37. He is arrested by the princes, thrown into a cistern, rescued from there, granted an interview with the king and has his conditions of restraint ameliorated. The pattern may be similar, but the details are quite different: the circumstances of his arrest are no longer the attempt to leave the city to visit Benjaminite territory but one of the occasions when Jeremiah was trying to persuade the citizens to desert to the Babylonians. This time when arrested, Jeremiah is thrown into a cistern in the court of the guard (contrast 37.15) by permission of the king. He is rescued from there by an Ethiopian official with the king's permission, whereas in 37.17 a royal summons appears to have gained him his release from the dungeons. The royal interview now takes place in the temple rather than the palace, and the exchanges between Zedekiah and Jeremiah are much longer than in 37.17–20. As variations on a theme there are inevitably divergent elements in the accounts which cannot be harmonized (*contra* Bright, 234). Such disharmonious features point to the development (independently?) of doublets in the tradition about the fate of Jeremiah during the siege (cf. the two stories of his release by the Babylonians in 39.11–14; 40.1–6). These doublets allow for considerable interplay between different motifs in the tradition: e.g. the occasion of Jeremiah's arrest in 37.12–14 is linked to property in the land of Benjamin (cf. 32.6–15), whereas in 38.1 it is related to his public preaching which permits an editorial citation in 38.2. In the first account of the interview with the king an ironic point is made about the other prophets (37.18–19); in the second interview a symmetrical connection is made between Jeremiah's experience in the cistern and the fate of the king's harem at the hands of the Babylonians (38.6b, 22).

The charge of desertion in the first story becomes one of seditious preaching in the second account (37.13; 38.4). 21.9 is cited in 38.2 (cf. 45.4 for the idiom 'having one's life as a prize of war'), and Jeremiah is charged with weakening the war effort against the Babylonians (in 21.8–10 the desertion motif is a redactional development of an original statement about complete destruction, hence the appearance of 21.9 in 38.2 points to editorial activity). It is Jeremiah's preaching *to all the people* (v. 1) which attracts the attention of certain princes rather than his arrest by Irijah (37.14b). In a time of war such seditious preaching must be regarded as a capital offence, and Jeremiah is to be considered fortunate that he was not executed summarily (cf. 26.20–23). Once more the prophet appears in a situation which could lead to his death (cf. 26.8, 11, 15, 16, 24; 36.19, 26), but as usual he leads a charmed existence. He may have to hide or be smuggled out of danger, but he always survives. He may even, as on this occasion, be flung into a dungeon or cistern where death is inevitable and only a matter of time. Yet out of these depths also he is rescued. A charmed existence is how his life appears in the different stories in the tradition. But the charge of treason should be noted not only as an element in this version of 37–38 but especially by exegetes who insist on reading the tradition as the representation of an *imitatio jeremiae* (e.g. Polk 1984). At no point is this type of reading more problematical than on the issue of Jeremiah as a traitor (cf. Schoneveld 1976, 194–205; Carroll 1981, 276). The clash of ideologies behind 38.2–4 is not articulated in the story, but the modern exegete would be well advised not to side with one or the other ideology too easily. Jeremiah's stance in this story is acutely criticized by the princes, and his contribution to the defeat of Jerusalem, though unquantifiable, quite notable. Such treachery is well defined by the princes in the charge 'this man is not seeking the welfare (*šālōm*) of this people, but their harm (*rā'āh*)' (v. 4b).

In the exchange between the princes and the king Zedekiah is exposed as a ruler who cannot control his officials. This may be a correct reading of the story, but Zedekiah could hardly have defended Jeremiah against such a charge of treason without revealing himself to be a traitor as well. In the set of stories he clearly has sufficient power to modify the actions of the princes (37.17; 38.10, 14), but even the king cannot release a traitor like Jeremiah and permit him to undermine further the attempt to repulse the Babylonians. The variation in the pattern whereby it is Zedekiah who imprisons Jeremiah for his treasonous talk should be noted (32.3). However, the presentation of some of the princes in 36; 37–38 is quite unsympathetic, and the king appears in the stories as a foil to them. If they are hostile and cruel towards Jeremiah then the king will be represented as kind and sympathetic towards him. These are but the structures of the story-telling techniques and reflect motifs within the tradition. They should not be extrapolated into a psychological profile of either king or princes.

The princes succeed in their attempt to silence Jeremiah by persuading the king that the man is too dangerous for the community's well-being (*šālōm*). He concedes to their wishes and Jeremiah is thrown into an *empty* (cf. 2.13b?) cistern (in a full one he would have drowned!). The princes are more interested in preventing him from damaging the war effort than in killing him (MT v. 6, 'letting Jeremiah down *by ropes*'!). However, the possibility of his death may be mooted by his confinement to an empty cistern (cf. v. 9; 37.20); though such a place also facilitates his being rescued. By confining him there the princes make Jeremiah available for any interviews the king may wish to grant his obdurate prophet. To have killed him outright would have been the ruination of a good story!

38.7–13

7 When Ebed-melech the Ethiopian, a eunuch, who was in the king's house, heard that they had put Jeremiah into the cistern – the king was sitting in the Benjamin Gate – 8 Ebed-melech went from the king's house and said to the king, 9 'My lord the king, these men have done evil in all that they did to Jeremiah the prophet by casting him into the cistern; and he will die there of hunger, for there is no bread left in the city.' 10 Then the king commanded Ebed-melech, the Ethiopian, 'Take three men with you from here, and lift Jeremiah the prophet out of the cistern before he dies.' 11 So Ebed-melech took the men with him and went to the house of the king, to a wardrobe of the storehouse, and took from there old rags and worn-out clothes, which he let down to Jeremiah in the cistern by ropes. 12 Then Ebed-melech the Ethiopian said to Jeremiah, 'Put the rags and clothes between your armpits and the ropes.' Jeremiah did so. 13 Then they drew Jeremiah up with ropes and lifted him out of the cistern. And Jeremiah remained in the court of the guard.

---

[7] G lacks *'îš sārîs*, 'a eunuch': cf. 29.2, where *sārîsîm* may refer to officials rather than eunuchs (cf. Rab*saris* in 39.3, 13). In 39.16 Ebed-melech is not qualified in this manner, though he may have been a eunuch (cf. Bright, 231) because he appears to be part of the king's household. MT *'ebed-melek*, 'Ebed-melech', i.e. 'servant of the king': cf. Obadiah 'servant of Yahweh' (I Kings 18.3–16), a man in charge of the king's household and also given to rescuing prophets in trouble. The king is placed at the Benjamin Gate, cf. 37.13 (an echo of the other story?). **[9]** G lacks introductory 'my lord the king' and has a different reading from MT: G 'you have done evil in what you have done to kill this man with hunger'. MT accuses the princes as if vv. 4–5 were not part of the story; it also has variants *'ēt kol-'ašer 'āśû*, 'all that they did', and *'ēt 'ašer-hišlikû 'el-bōr*, 'their casting into the cistern', which are both the object of *hērē'û*, 'they did evil'. G inevitably lacks 'Jeremiah the prophet'. MT *wayyāmāt*, 'and he has died': a trace of Jeremiah's death notice? Revocalize to *w^eyāmut*, 'that he may die' (BHS). MT *mipp^enē hārā'āb kī 'ēn hallehem 'ōd bā'īr*, 'because of starvation, for there is no more bread in the city': a curious explanation when Jeremiah's plight is more one of suffocation or exposure than lack of food. If the bread supplies in the city had been exhausted, hauling him from the cistern would not have made him any the less hungry! Exegetes regard this clause as a mistaken gloss (Bright, 227n.) or an addition from 37.21 (BHS; Volz). According to 52.6–7 the siege ended with the exhaustion of the food supply; 38.9 reflects a different viewpoint. **[10]** MT *š^elōšīm 'anāšīm*, 'thirty men': generally regarded as a mistake by commentators (G *triakonta*, 'thirty') and corrected to *š^elōšāh*, 'three', following one ms (cf. Hitzig, 301; II Sam. 23.13). G lacks 'Jeremiah the prophet', reading only *auton*, 'him'; also 'the Ethiopian'. **[11]** MT *b^eyādō*, 'with him': lacking in G. MT *'el-tahat hā'ōṣār*, 'to under the storehouse': G *tēn hupogeion*, 'the underground'; read with Ehrlich 1912, 304, *meltaḥat*, 'wardrobe', cf. II Kings 10.22 (followed by most commentators). K *hsḥbwt*; Q *s^eḥābōt*, 'rags, clouts': K definite article from v. 12. G lacks *baḥ^abālīm*, 'by ropes': MT influenced by v. 6 (it is unnecessary for the rags to be lowered by rope; they can be thrown down the cistern!). **[12]** G has a shorter text: 'and he said, Put these under the ropes. And Jeremiah did so.' **[13]** G *auton*, 'him', for MT 'Jeremiah'. MT *wayyēšeb yirm^eyāhū baḥ^aṣar hammaṭṭārāh*, 'and Jeremiah remained in the court of the guard' = v. 28; 37.21.

The one novel section in the second version of Jeremiah's imprisonment and interview with the king is 38.7–13. The story of Ebed-melech's rescue of the prophet is the only element in the two variant accounts which explains *how* Jeremiah was extricated from the cistern down which the princes had put him. 37.17 passes over the logistics of the matter, but the development of the cistern element (*bēt habbōr*, 'the house of the cistern', 37.16) in 38.6 requires some account of the transition of Jeremiah from that parlous position to his encounter with the king. A new character is introduced into the story: Ebed-melech an Ethiopian (conceivably a eunuch), who served in the king's household (cf. Obadiah's role as overseer of Ahab's household, I Kings 18.3). His intervention with the king on behalf of Jeremiah indicates that the story is quite independent of its present context in that the king's participation in Jeremiah's plight (vv. 4–5) is incompatible with his orders to rescue the prophet (v. 10). The king has consented to Jeremiah's death ('let this man be put to death . . . he is in your hands', vv. 4–5) and can hardly be expected to change his mind now (G v. 9 is more aware of vv. 4–5 than MT). In 37.12–14 Jeremiah is arrested at the Benjamin Gate; here in v. 7b

Ebed-melech finds the king there. As the story unfolds, Ebed-melech is represented as making a number of journeys: from the king's house to the Benjamin Gate, back to the king's house and then to the cistern in the court of the guard. He is a busy but conscientious official who clearly has access to the king and can sway his actions and decisions. His representations on behalf of Jeremiah are successful, and in some detail the story explains how he rescued the incarcerated prophet (vv. 11–13; briefer in G).

No explanation is offered in the text of the reasons for Ebed-melech's actions towards Jeremiah, though 39.15–18, which also refers to him, may allude to one possible reason – his trust in Yahweh. The two pieces are not connected (39.18 may echo 38.2; cf. 45.5, though the editors have not chosen to place the motifs together). Perhaps Ebed-melech represents that strand of sympathy between Jeremiah and the princes which occurs at various points in the tradition (e.g. 26.16; 36.17–19). On occasions an official figure is presented in the text as assisting the prophet during a crisis in his career (cf. 26.24; 38.7–13; even Baruch in 36.5). The introduction of Ebed-melech into 37–38, with the intimation of his fate in 39.15–18, may point in the direction of the development of the tradition. Variant stories allow for development and embellishment, and the figures of Baruch and Ebed-melech represent examples of this creative aspect of the growth of the book (much developed in post biblical literature). The story of Ebed-melech introduces a new character into a set of stories and permits mediation between certain features of the basic story. Balancing the hostility of the princes is the concern of the Ethiopian official and the three men who assist him (v. 10). The king's decision to supply Jeremiah with his daily bread (37.21) becomes Ebed-melech's pointing out to the king the prophet's lack of food. The same motifs are manipulated in different ways, and the historical fantasy (cf. Pohlmann 1978, 79–80) of the Ethiopian official becomes a third account of how Jeremiah came to be under arrest in the court of the guard during the final days of the siege. Such scope for variation belongs to the art of story-telling and that art is a dominant feature of Part IV (especially in 37–41).

38.14–23

14 King Zedekiah sent for Jeremiah the prophet and received him at the
third entrance of the temple of the Lord. The king said to Jeremiah, 'I will
ask you a question; hide nothing from me.' 15 Jeremiah said to Zedekiah,
'If I tell you, will you not be sure to put me to death? And if I give you
counsel, you will not listen to me.' 16 Then King Zedekiah swore secretly
to Jeremiah, 'As the Lord lives, who made our souls, I will not put you to
death or deliver you into the hand of these men who seek your life.'
17 Then Jeremiah said to Zedekiah, 'Thus says the Lord, the God of
hosts, the God of Israel, If you will surrender to the princes of the king of
Babylon, then your life shall be spared, and this city shall not be burned
with fire, and you and your house shall live. 18 But if you do not surrender
to the princes of the king of Babylon, then this city shall be given into the
hand of the Chaldeans, and they shall burn it with fire, and you shall not
escape from their hand.' 19 King Zedekiah said to Jeremiah, 'I am afraid
of the Jews who have deserted to the Chaldeans, lest I be handed over to
them and they abuse me.' 20 Jeremiah said, 'You shall not be given to them.
Obey now the voice of the Lord in what I say to you, and it shall be well
with you, and your life shall be spared. 21 But if you refuse to surrender,
this is the vision which the Lord has shown to me: 22 Behold, all the women
left in the house of the king of Judah were being led out to the princes of the
king of Babylon and were saying.

"Your trusted friends have deceived you
  and prevailed against you;
now that your feet are sunk in the mire,
  they turn away from you."

23 All your wives and your sons shall be led out to the Chaldeans, and you
yourself shall not escape from their hand, but shall be seized by the king of
Babylon; and this city shall be burned with fire.'

---

[14] MT *wayyiqqaḥ 'et-yirm^e yāhū hannābī' 'ēlāyw*, 'and Jeremiah the prophet was brought to him': G *kai ekalesen auton pros heauton*, 'and called him to himself'. The third entrance (G 'the house of Aselisi', cf. G^AS) of the temple is unknown; but yet again the text associates Jeremiah with the temple. Duhm, 305, follows Giesebrecht, 208, and reads *mābō' haššālīšīm* (MT *hašš^e līšī*, 'third'), 'the entrance of the officers', cf. II Kings 11.4–8. MT *šō'ēl 'anī 'ōt^e kā dābār*, 'I will ask you something': cf. NEB, JPSB; better than RSV 'question'. The force of *dābār* here may be 'oracle', i.e. 'prophetic word' (cf. Bright, 231); this would parallel 37.17, where a divine oracle is sought. The phrase 'hide nothing from me' (cf. v. 25; I Sam. 3.17; II Sam. 14.18) may reflect the motif of the reluctant speaker withholding the divine word (e.g. 26.2; 42.4b; cf. Janzen 1981, 97–105). The word sought by the king is given in vv. 17–18. **[15]** The exchange here is similar to the rational conversation between the two parties in 37.18–20. The storyteller's art focuses on a realistic aspect of the encounter, rather than the more frequent stereotypical clichés which characterize the tradition. **[16]** MT *bassēter*, 'in secret': cf. 37.17; lacking in G here. It may well be asked 'what is swearing in secret'?, but the motif belongs to the pattern of the stories in 37–38 and occurs here for that reason. 16b contradicts v. 5. MT *ḥay-yhwh 't ʾašer ʿāśāh-lānū ʾet-hannepeš hazzōʾt*, lit. 'as Yahweh lives who has made for us this life': Q omits K *'t* (a scribal error). Cf. v. 9 for 'these men' (note 'this man', v. 4; 'these men', vv. 9, 16). G lacks 'who are seeking your life': the phrase reflects the option motif of 21.7; cf. 34.20, 21. **[17]** G lacks 'the god of hosts, the god of Israel'. MT *ʾim-yāṣōʾ tēṣēʾ*, 'if you will really go out', i.e. surrender. Whether the Babylonians would have spared king and city after a lengthy siege is a matter of speculation, but the king's surrender hardly would have made good his breach of trust against Nebuchadrezzar in the first place. The options of vv. 17–18 reflect the motif in v. 2; 21.8–9, but with the added element of the king's surrender sparing the city. **[18]** Cairo geniza fragments lack 'the princes of'; G lacks 'from their hands'. **[19]** Jeremiah's campaign to persuade people to desert is represented by v. 19 as a successful one. Zedekiah's pliability has limits, and this reason may be an excuse for not following Jeremiah. Whichever course of action Zedekiah follows he faces a nasty future – whether from the Babylonians (39.5–7) or from those who feel betrayed by him. **[20]** Cf. the *šālōm* oracle of 34.4–5 for a similar word of well-being (*weyīṭab lekā*, 'it shall be well with you'). MT *lōʾ yittēnū*, 'they will not give': i.e. it will not happen, they will not hand you over to the Jews who have deserted. **[21]** MT *zeh haddābār ʾašer hirʾanī yhwh*, 'this is the thing which Yahweh has showed me': not a vision as such (cf. 24.1), though it may be an imaginative conjuring up of a scene typical of invaded cities and the fate of the harems of defeated kings. **[22]** Cf. Obad. 7 for the poem. MT *ʾanšē šelōmekā*, 'your trusted friends': cf. 20.10 for a similar motif of treachery among familiar friends. The sinking of the foot (MT, but many mss 'feet') into the mire parallels Jeremiah's sinking into the mire in v. 6b. **[23]** G lacks 'all', 'from their hand', 'with fire'; MT *tiśrōp*, 'burn': a few mss *tiśśārēp*, 'shall be burned'; cf. G *katakauthēsetai*.

The extended interview between Zedekiah and Jeremiah in the ch. 38 version of their encounter has a number of distinctive points. It is conducted in the temple complex rather than in the royal palace. A secret oath is sworn by the king to protect Jeremiah, and the prophet (MT) offers Zedekiah the possibility of escaping his fate by surrendering to the Babylonians. The king explains his reluctance to surrender because of the threat posed by the citizens who have surrendered already. Jeremiah repeats and expands his message about the fate of king and city in terms of what will happen to the royal harem. A brief piece of poetry is used to portray the king's plight. These additional features make for a more interesting exchange of opinions between king and prophet and indicate some of the story-teller's skills. The dialogue between Zedekiah and Jeremiah (also in vv. 24–26) presents the king as pusillanimous in his relations with other people, though only up to a point in that he refuses to kow-tow to Jeremiah's threats about the future. This characterization of him also appears in vv. 4–5, where he allows the princes to act against Jeremiah. The Zedekiah of the interviews strand is a man trapped between the Babylonians and his own princes: he cannot resolve his problems because whichever way he turns he faces disaster. Even though v. 17 may hint at a resolution of his difficulty, it can hardly be taken seriously. The Babylonians are besieging the city (the withdrawal of 37.11 is not represented in 38); the princes are determined to defend Jerusalem, and Zedekiah cannot oppose them. Whether he surrenders or fights, he faces the anger of the Babylonians as their vassal, and if he surrenders he must bear the wrath of the betrayed people and princes as well as that of those who are outside the city already. Jeremiah's advocacy of such betrayal can hardly be palatable to him. It does, however, represent the motif of choice epitomized by v. 2 and it is used in vv. 17–18 to offer Zedekiah the option available to the citizens. Yet what Zedekiah appears to want from Jeremiah is a divine oracle (37.17; 38.14): a word which will transform his situation (cf. 21.2b; 37.3). That transformation would entail the withdrawal of the Babylonians, not his surrender to them. Surrendering to the king of Babylon could only bring about his destruction because he would have to face charges of disloyalty (hence 39.5b). Jeremiah fails to persuade Zedekiah to surrender because it is not a proper option open to him. The unrealistic assurances of the prophet cannot convince him. Elements of his dilemma are well presented by the developed dialogue of vv. 14–23.

The novelty of the surrender offer in v. 17 illustrates the freedom with which the writers develop the theme of the interview and the motifs of that theme. It is part of the logic of the siege-surrender material but extended to the king it breaks down. The king cannot surrender in the way an ordinary citizen might, because he is the one responsible for the siege in the first place. Since he is Nebuchadrezzar's vassal, the termination of the siege will bring about his own downfall. Sympathy towards Jeremiah permits the interview, control of the princes allows him to promise protection; but his pliability has limits, and he compromises with both prophet and princes by pleasing neither. Jeremiah's final word to him is an oracular one (v. 21 is not necessarily a vision, though the force of 'Yahweh has shown me' will allow for a visionary element) depicting the outcome of his failure to surrender. This word depicts the fate of the royal women and children. The harem will go to the victorious army, as is the inevitable fate of women in war: rape, concubinage, abuse and exploitation. Their treatment symbolizes the defeat of the kingdom, as does the leading out of the royal sons to their captors (it is not specified in v. 23, but execution would be their most probable end, cf. 39.6). Pathos is added to this picture of the fall of Jerusalem by the placing of the brief poem of v. 22b in the mouths of the women as they are led out to endure the lot of women wherever men gain complete power over them. They mock Zedekiah with a conventional poetic outcry, castigating him for his deception by his companions and sneering at his plight. The snatch of poetry also makes connections between Jeremiah's erstwhile internment in the cistern (v. 6b) and Zedekiah's figurative position. The *seizing* of Jeremiah by the princes (37.14) is reprised now by the *seizing* (*tpś*) of Zedekiah by the king of Babylon (v. 23b). This terrible picture of what lies in store for the king constitutes Jeremiah's last word in the interview strand (what follows in vv. 24–28 represents no exchange between king and prophet) and reiterates the harshness of 21.7 (cf. 37.17b for much greater brevity of sentiment). In refusing the possibility of surrender Zedekiah has not only sealed his own fate but also guaranteed the destruction of the city (v. 18). Thus the extended interview of 38 allows the king's responsibility for the fate of Jerusalem to be fully demonstrated, and the interview strand may be regarded as serving just this precise purpose in the tradition (cf. 37.2).

38.24–28

24 Then Zedekiah said to Jeremiah, 'Let no one know of these words and you shall not die. 25 If the princes hear that I have spoken with you and come to you and say to you, "Tell us what you said to the king and what the king said to you; hide nothing from us and we will not put you to death," 26 then you shall say to them, "I made a humble plea to the king that he

would not send me back to the house of Jonathan to die there." ' 27 Then all the princes came to Jeremiah and asked him, and he answered them as the king had instructed him. So they left off speaking with him, for the conversation had not been overheard. 28 And Jeremiah remained in the court of the guard until the day that Jerusalem was taken.

---

[24] Cf. v. 16; this section would fit better after 37.20, especially in view of the reference to 'the house of Jonathan' in v. 26 (cf. 37.15). It would then not appear to be a modification of Zedekiah's promise in v. 16. The section vv. 24–28 may well be a variant of 37.20–21 added at the end of the interview section and inverting the speakers. **[25]** MT *mah-dibbartā 'el-hammelek . . . ūmah-dibber 'ēlekā hammelek*, 'what you said to the king . . . and what the king said to you': G *ti elalēsen soi ho basileus . . . kai ti elalēsen pros se ho basileus*, 'what the king said to you . . . what the king said to you'! BHS transposes 'and what the king said to you' to immediately after 'what you said to the king', cf. Volz, 332–3; Rudolph, 242. RSV, NEB assume this rearrangement of the MT (JPSB follows its order). The story variants have placed together conflicting offers to spare Jeremiah's life, thus rendering neither of the parties guilty of planning his death. **[26]** Cf. 37.20. **[27]** MT *ṣiwwāh hammelek*, 'the king commanded': some mss, Vrs *ṣiwwahū*,' (the king) commanded *him*'. MT *wayyaḥarišū mimmennū kī lō'-nišma' haddābār*, lit. 'and they were silent for him because the thing (word) had not been heard': G *kai apesiōpēsan, hoti ouk ēkousthē logos kuriou*, 'and they were silent because the word of the lord was not heard'. **[28]** = 37.21; 38.13b + 'until the day that Jerusalem was taken': this addition links with the next section which in MT begins in v. 28b with a repeat of 'that Jerusalem was taken' (see Notes on 39.1). Bright, 229, reads 39.15–18 immediately after 38.28a. This transposition makes sense as the completion of Jeremiah's activities in the court of the guard, but the MT order has the advantage of associating Ebed-melech's deliverance with Jeremiah's release when the Babylonians freed him.

The final element in the collection of pieces constituting the Jeremiah-Zedekiah interview motif explains how Jeremiah is confined to the court of the guard rather than returned to the cistern. In 37.20 the transference from the dungeons to the court is effected by Jeremiah's own request, whereas 38.24–28a do not explain precisely how the change came about but emphasizes the way Jeremiah escaped from death at the hands of king *and* princes. According to v. 26 the request of 37.20 is employed, but it is put in the king's mouth rather than Jeremiah's. This change of speaker reflects the inversion of activity between 37.20–21 and 38.24–26. In the first account of Jeremiah's escape from the dungeons and interview with the king, Jeremiah does the speaking (from v. 18) and the king acts in accordance with what he says (v. 21). In the second account the king and Ebed-melech speak, with Ebed-melech and Jeremiah acting (38.9–13). But in the third account the king does all the speaking; Jeremiah says nothing yet acts according to the king's commands. The effect of 38.24–28 on the whole story is ironic in that the section reverses the role of the princes and presents the king as seeking Jeremiah's protection. In v. 27 the princes, who had sought his death in v. 4, are now happy to accept from his lips the explanation provided by the king. Gone is all hostility against Jeremiah, and the one who throughout the story faces death in various forms without the protection of the authorities protects the king from his princes! Only 38.7–13 provides a mediating position between these two versions with the presentation of Ebed-melech as a supportive third party. His role in the story saves Jeremiah from the embarrassing situation of having to prevaricate about his conversation with the king into which he is put by vv. 24–27.

Irony abounds in the final exchange between Zedekiah and Jeremiah: in order not to die Jeremiah must not speak a truth which the tradition represents him as constantly speaking. He must equivocate with the princes and use an explanation concocted by the king which happens to be Jeremiah's own words in the first version of the story (37.20)! The irony of 38.25 may be modified by viewing the statement as the king's imaginative projection on to the princes, but in v. 27 they appear to be satisfied by the request for a transfer to a more congenial place of confinement. Jeremiah is protected by the king by protecting the king from the princes. Conscious irony on the writer's part may be discernible here. At the same time it would be inadvisable to take Jeremiah's 'white' lie in vv. 24–27 too seriously, though recent writers on prophetic conflict have noted it carefully (e.g. Crenshaw 1971, 59). If moral issues are to be imported into the scrutiny of prophecy then it may be of some importance, but in the context of a story variation it is only an element used by a storytelling technique to explain how Jeremiah overcame the hostility of king and princes. The image of the ranting prophet reduced to 'lying' to protect the king or himself from the hostility of the princes is ironic within the context of the whole tradition, but hardly so from the viewpoint of the exchanges between king and prophet in 37.17–20 or 38.14–23. It is hardly the intention of the writers to present

Jeremiah as a liar by their development of the theme of his interview with the king.

The varied material in 37.3 – 38.28a represents the growth of a section of the tradition in terms of reworking a limited number of motifs in a number of different ways. The creation of stories about the fate of Jeremiah during the siege and the way he survived the twin rigours of starvation and royal opposition subtly illustrates the storyteller's art in the book of Jeremiah and leads up to the final collapse of Jerusalem. Apart from securing a food supply for Jeremiah nothing is changed by the stories, though the introduction of Ebed-melech provides a concrete example of the truth of Jeremiah's preaching about the possibility of survival (38.2; 39.15–18). The word spoken and read out in the time of Jehoiakim (36) remains as the background to 37–38 (in spite of a slight modification in 38.17), and the network of variations on Jeremiah in the dungeons and in encounters with the king allows a certain suspense to be maintained before the fate of king and city is unfolded.

39.1–14

39[1] In the ninth year of Zedekiah king of Judah, in the tenth month, Nebuchadrezzar king of Babylon and all his army came against Jerusalem and besieged it; 2 in the eleventh year of Zedekiah, in the fourth month, on the ninth day of the month, a breach was made in the city. 3 When Jerusalem was taken, all the princes of the king of Babylon came and sat in the middle gate: Nergal-sharezer, Samgar-nebo, Sarsechim the Rabsaris, Nergal-sharezer the Rabmag, with all the rest of the officers of the king of Babylon. 4 When Zedekiah king of Judah and all the soldiers saw them, they fled, going out of the city at night by way of the king's garden through the gate between the two walls; and they went toward the Arabah. 5 But the army of the Chaldeans pursued them, and overtook Zedekiah in the plains of Jericho; and when they had taken him, they brought him up to Nebuchadrezzar king of Babylon, at Riblah, in the land of Hamath; and he passed sentence upon him. 6 The king of Babylon slew the sons of Zedekiah at Riblah before his eyes; and the king of Babylon slew all the nobles of Judah. 7 He put out the eyes of Zedekiah, and bound him in fetters to take him to Babylon. 8 The Chaldeans burned the king's house and the house of the people, and broke down the walls of Jerusalem. 9 Then Nebuzaradan, the captain of the guard, carried into exile to Babylon the rest of the people who were left in the city, those who had deserted to him, and the people who remained. 10 Nebuzaradan, the captain of the guard, left in the land of Judah some of the poor people who owned nothing, and gave them vineyards and fields at the same time.

11 Nebuchadrezzar king of Babylon gave command concerning Jeremiah through Nebuzaradan, the captain of the guard, saying, 12 'Take him, look after him well and do to him no harm, but deal with him as he tells you.' 13 So Nebuzaradan the captain of the guard, Nebushazban the Rabsaris, Nergal-sharezer the Rabmag, and all the chief officers of the king of Babylon 14 sent and took Jeremiah from the court of the guard. They entrusted him to Gedaliah the son of Ahikam, son of Shaphan, that he should take him home. So he dwelt among the people.

[MT 39] = G 46. G lacks vv. 4–13, possibly due to homoioteleuton (vv. 3, 13 have virtually the same list of Babylonian officers' names). MT 39.1–10, cf. 52.4–16; II Kings 25.1–12 for essentially the same material. 39.1–2 interrupt the connection between 38.28b ('when Jerusalem was taken' transposed by RSV to 39.3a; cf. JPSB n. i) and 39.3 (Rudolph, 243, treats them was a parenthetical summary from 52.4–7aα). **[1]** Cf. 52.4; G^BS^ 'ninth *month*' for MT 'ninth year'. According to most of the texts the siege of Jerusalem started in January 588 and finished in July 587 (see on 52.12). The MT phrase *wᵉhāyāh ka'ᵃšer nilkᵉdāh yᵉrūšālāim*, 'now when Jerusalem was taken', in 38.28b should be followed by 39.3 'and all the princes came . . .', but the editors provide vv. 1–2 as a background to the events of 39 (everything in 37.3–38.28a is set in this period). G^BS^ lack 'in the tenth month'. **[2]** Cf. 52.5–7a. MT 'fourth': a few mss, S 'fifth'. MT *hobqᵉ'āh hā'īr*, 'the city was breached': i.e. the city wall was penetrated, cf. 52.7a; II Kings 25.4a. As a redactional title to 39, vv. 1–2 constitute a summary of the siege, but the other accounts of the matter are ambiguous because they associate the breaching of the city (*wattibbāqa' hā'īr*) with the breaking out of the besieged rather than the penetration of the city by the Babylonians. RSV circumvents any misunderstanding by prefixing 38.28b to v. 3, whereas in MT v. 3 looks like the next stage of the siege after the breaching of the wall. **[3]** MT *bᵉša'ar hattāwek*, 'in the middle gate ':unknown location. Bright, 241, reads 38.28b; 39.3, 14 together after 39.1–2, 4–10 and before 39.11–13. The list of Babylonian officers is confused in MT, cf. v. 13; Rudolph, 245; Bright, 243. Nergal sar-ezer occurs twice in MT: the four names of v. 3 become three in v. 13 and in the emended list of many modern exegetes appear as Nergalsarezer, the prince of Sin-magir (a district), the Rabmag (a high official), Nebushazban the Rabsaris (a diplomatic or military rank rather than chief eunuch, cf. 29.2; 34.19; [38.7?]), cf. Rudolph, 245. MT *wᵉkol-šᵉ'rīt śārē*, 'and all the rest of the princes of': 'rest' may be a gloss due to dittography (cf. BHS); it is lacking in v. 13. Cf. Ehrlich 1912, 342: *yeter*, 'rest', would be more suitable, cf. v. 9. **[4]** MT *wayᵉhī ka'ᵃšer rā'ām ṣidqiyyāhū*, 'and when Zedekiah saw them': Volz, 342–3, reads *rā'āh*, 'saw it', i.e. the breach of

v. 2; MT represents an adjustment of the text to v. 3. MT *wayyēṣē derek hā'arābāh*, 'and *he* went out in the direction of the Arabah': i.e. towards the Jordan valley (cf. v. 5). Only Zedekiah acts according to MT, but v. 5; 52.7 indicate the action was taken by him and his warriors; various mss, Vrs read plur., cf. BHS *wayyēlᵉkū*, 'and they went', as in 52.7. **[5]** S, a few mss read 'and all his army was scattered from him' after 'in the plains of Jericho' as in 52.8; II Kings 25.5. 'Riblah, in the land of Hamath': cf. II Kings 23.33; on the river Orontes it was the Syrian headquarters of Nebuchadrezzar from which he conducted his campaign against Judah. MT *wayᵉdabbēr 'ittō mišpāṭīm*, lit. 'and he spoke with him judgments': i.e. pass sentence upon, cf. 1.16. NEB understands Zedekiah to be the subject of the verb 'and he pleaded his case before him'; JPSB 'and he put him on trial' conveys the sense of the idiom entirely adequately. **[8]** MT *bēt hā'ām*, 'the house of the people': cf. 52.13, where temple, palace and all the houses of Jerusalem are burned; S *bāttē*, 'houses of . . .'. Cf. II Kings 25.9. Rudolph inserts 'of Yahweh and the houses of', cf. BHS. No 'house of the people' is known for Jerusalem nor is there any evidence in the Hebrew Bible that the temple was ever called by such a demotic title. Bab. Talmud *Megillah* 27a understands the phrase to refer to the synagogue; cf. Landsberger 1949 for the temple as the meaning of *bēt hā'ām*. **[9]** MT repeats *wᵉ'ēt yeter hā'āmōn*, 'and the rest of the artificers' (see on 52.15), cf. Prov. 8.30; followed by Rudolph, Bright. MT *nᵉbūzar-'adān rab-ṭabbāḥīm bābel*, 'Nebuzaradan, the chief of the butchers of Babylon': an archaic title but meaning marshal or captain. Nebuzaradan, '(the god) Nabu has given seed', is regarded as having become a proselyte in later years (tractate *Sanhedrin* 95a–96b): small wonder in view of 40.2–5! The irony of v. 9 should be noted: both those who deserted and those who remained in the city were deported, whereas the options proclaimed by Jeremiah offered survival only to those who deserted and death to those who remained in the city (cf. 21.8–9; 38.2). **[10]** MT *wīgēbīm*? cf. 52.16; II Kings 25.12: of uncertain meaning; ST 'fields', V 'cisterns' (*gēbīm*); perhaps '(vineyards) and cisterns' but other texts *ūlᵉyōgᵉbīm*, 'and ploughmen, field labourers'. MT *bayyōm hāhū'*, 'on that day': i.e. the same day; it may represent an editorial link between v. 10 and v. 11 (Bright, 243, takes it with v. 11). **[11]** Rudolph suggests transposing vv. 11–12 to before 40.2a, 1b, 2b (cf. BHS). MT *bᵉyad*, 'by means of (Nebuzaradan)': cf. 37.2. Two stories are told about the release of Jeremiah (39.11–14; 40.1–6): in this one the emperor himself plays a role; in both Nebuzaradan is the main actor. **[12]** MT *wᵉ'ēnekā śīm 'ālāyw*, lit. 'and put your eyes on him': i.e. look after him. **[13]** Cf. 40.2; an attempt to harmonize vv. 11–12 with vv. 3, 14; cf. Rudolph, 246, where his rearrangement of the text eases some of the problems. **[14]** Rudolph, 245, regards 'to Gedaliah ben Ahikam ben Shaphan' as an addition from 40.6 (cf. Weiser, 345); it is an attempt to harmonize rather different accounts of Jeremiah's release from prison or rescue from deportation. MT *wayyēšeb bᵉtōk hā'ām*, 'and he remained among the people': cf. 37.4; 40.6. G lacks 'to the house'; RSV 'home', NEB 'the Residence'.

———

Textual confusions abound in 39.1–14 and most commentators rearrange the text to make better sense of it (e.g. Rudolph reads 38.28b; 39.3, 11–12, 14 with 39.1–2, 4–10, 13 bracketed as redactional and secondary). The details of the fall of Jerusalem are to be found in 52.4–16 and II Kings 25.1–12 so they are unnecessary here except as background to the account of what happened to Jeremiah when the city fell. Appended to the various accounts of how Jeremiah fared during the siege and his residence in the court of the guard are two stories of how the Babylonians liberated him (39.3, 11–12, 14; 40.1–6). These stories are the equivalent of the variations on the interview motif and indicate the variety of story-telling used to portray Jeremiah in 37–40.6; 42–45. The stories cannot be harmonized, but they share central themes: Nebuzaradan the commander freed Jeremiah, and once freed Jeremiah elected to stay in Judah rather than go to Babylon. The details and circumstances of each story are different. The image of Jeremiah in Part IV is that of a man who belongs 'among the people' (37.4, 12; 39.14c; 40.6) and, the imprisonment stories and 40.7–41.10 apart, he is so represented in all the stories (typified by 42.1–2).

The fall of Jerusalem results in the devastation of the city and its great buildings (v. 8; cf. 32.29), the capture and execution of all the nobles and the deportation of the citizens (see on 52.4–16). According to v. 10 all that is left in the land are a few poor people who are allowed to take over the vineyards and fields. However, this assertion is in conflict with v. 14, where some important people remain behind to govern the land. It also conflicts with the information given about Gedaliah's community in 40.7–41.18 (see on 41.10). The contradictions between the different accounts in 39–41 are more obvious because the redactors have placed 39.4–10 in this context. Discrete traditions contribute to making the picture of Judaean life in the aftermath of the fall of Jerusalem rather confused; though the confusion is no greater than exists for any block of biblical literature measured against its historical background (e.g. the exodus and Ex. 1–24; settlement of the land in Joshua and Judges: the origins of the monarchy and I Samuel). The deportation of all the people, deserters from the city and survivors of the siege, to Babylon undermines the claim attributed to Jeremiah that remaining in the city would lead to death whereas deserting would secure life. Again the discrepancy is brought to our attention by the editing which places in close proximity the two different traditions. The contradiction is hardly an important one, but it does underline the nature of the material in the book as a collection of diverse stories associated with Jeremiah but lacking a coherent and harmonious unity.

In the first account of Jeremiah's release from the court of the guard he is made the special object of concern of *Nebuchadrezzar* (whether v. 11 imagines the emperor to be present in Jerusalem or at Riblah is a moot point because v. 6 is not part of the rescue operation). Thus the one who had advocated the Babylonian cause for so long is rewarded by his sponsors (?) with special consideration after a harrowing siege. This is in keeping with the view of Jeremiah as the friend of Babylon (cf. 27–29; but contrast 50–51) and belongs to the logic of that strand of tradition. It is hardly necessary to speculate on whether the story is realistic or otherwise (cf. the idyll of 40.1–6), but the element of choice offered in 40.4–5 is absent here. Jeremiah is to be looked after in general terms, and Nebuzaradan is to implement whatever the friend of Babylon wishes to be done in particular. After release from confinement Jeremiah is given into the keeping of Gedaliah ben Ahikam (cf. 26.24) ben Shaphan and so remains among the people. This story of his residing in the land does not belong to a deportation tradition (which is why the editorial placement of 39.4–10 is so confusing), but reflects a rather different account of the organization of life in the land after the fall of Jerusalem. Those who supported Babylon in the period before the destruction of Jerusalem and the people are allowed to live in the land (40.4–5 offers an account of Jeremiah's release in relation to the deportation). Jeremiah now becomes part of Gedaliah's group (cf. 40.6). The tradition knows nothing more about Jeremiah in relation to Gedaliah and therefore can only assert that he was a member of it. As a last word on the matter it is noted that 'he remained among the people' (cf. 37.4, 12; 40.6). This point is hardly compatible with v. 10, but presupposes a quite different tradition of life after the loss of Jerusalem as the centre of life in the land. Jeremiah 'among the people' is one of the dominant images of the stories in Part IV and is a rather distinctive element in the book.

39.15–18

15 The word of the LORD came to Jeremiah while he was shut up in the
court of the guard: 16 'Go, and say to Ebed-melech the Ethiopian, "Thus
says the LORD of hosts, the God of Israel: Behold, I will fulfil my words
against this city for evil and not for good, and they shall be accomplished
before you on that day. 17 But I will deliver you on that day, says the LORD,
and you shall not be given into the hand of the men of whom you are afraid.
18 For I will surely save you, and you shall not fall by the sword; but you
shall have your life as a prize of war, because you have put your trust in me,
says the LORD." '

---

[15] The introductory formula word-order is peculiar in MT: 'and to Jeremiah came the word of Yahweh'. G lacks 'while he was shut up': this makes better sense than emphasizing the constraints upon him in relation to the command of v. 16 'Go'! **[16]** MT *hālōk*, 'go': cf. 13.1; 19.1; 35.1. If the redactional note in v. 15 is taken at face value then the command of v. 16 is absurd (cf. Duhm, 312; but Bright, 232, feels it should not be taken literally: 'Either he sent the message, or Ebed-melek came to visit him'). Rationalizations apart, vv. 15–16 represent stereotypical language-usage by the editors without thought for content. Jeremiah is a prophet who comes and goes (cf. BHS b–b on 39.14) by divine command and so the word here is given such an introduction even though it is unsuitable for the circumstances indicated by MT. K *mby*; Q *mēbī*, 'bringing', i.e. fulfilling: cf. 19.15; 21.10 for the motifs used here. G lacks *w^{e}hāyū l^{e}pānekā hayyōm hahū'* lit. 'and they shall be before you on that day': i.e. the words will be performed in your presence the same day; cf. v. 10 for *bayyōm hahū'*; dittography from v. 17? (cf. BHS; Cornill, 410–11). **[17]** MT *w^{e}lō' tinnātēn b^{e}yad hā'^{a}nāšīm '^{a}šer-'attāh yāgōr mipp^{e}nēhem*, 'and you shall not be given into the hand of the men of whom you are afraid': this assurance would fit the Zedekiah of 38.19–20 better than the Ebed-melech of 38.7–13. The men who are feared cannot be the princes (*contra* Bright, 232) because 'on that day' they either would be killed or would have to flee for their lives. If Ebed-melech had anything to fear from them it would have been before the Babylonian penetration of the city. Cf. 22.25 for the affirmative form of this sentence (i.e. the giving of Coniah into the power of those whom he fears). **[18]** Cf. 21.9; 38.2; 45.5b for the metaphor 'your life as a prize of war', but here it does not refer to deserting from the city (see on 45.5). MT *kī mallēṭ '^{a}malleṭ^{e}kā*, 'for I will surely deliver you': lit. let you escape.

Inserted between the two accounts of Jeremiah's release from confinement by Nebuzaradan is an oracular statement given to

Ebed-melech before the siege was terminated. Like so much else in 37–39 it is out of place in the logical scheme of things, but the editors may have wished to link together the fate of both men. The imprisoned Jeremiah and the Ethiopian official both would survive the siege and its aftermath. Although the oracle given to Ebed-melech would be more appropriate after 38.7–13, its present position (like an afterthought) emphasizes the fulfilment of the divine word and the relation between deliverance and trust in Yahweh.

39.15–18 is virtually a midrash built out of phrases and motifs from the whole tradition (cf. Duhm, 312–13). The way these are put together suggests a late source developing the tradition by means of concrete examples which demonstrate the truth of Jeremiah's preaching (Ebed-melech here and Baruch in 45 are prime instances of this technique). As evidence of this reading of the text the awkwardness of vv. 15–18 may be adduced. Jeremiah is confined to the court of the guard (a form of house arrest), yet is *sent* (*hālōk*, 'go') to the king's house where Ebed-melech works (where else would he be sent?). This is a perfectly good idiom from the tradition (cf. 13.1; 19.1; 35.1) and reflects the presentation of Jeremiah as an actor who responds to cues from Yahweh (e.g. 'go', 'go down', 'stand'). But it does not fit Jeremiah's situation during the siege. Ebed-melech is then made a witness of the fulfilment of the divine word ('*before you* on that day', v. 16) and incorporated into the message (vv. 17–18; cf. Baruch in 45.4–5). The motif of being given into the power of the enemy is one used to describe the Babylonians (cf. 21.7; 22.25) but can hardly have that meaning here. Why should the Chaldaeans wish to harm Ebed-melech in particular? Fear of other Jews is introduced in 38.19, but different language is used so v. 17 is not citing that motif. As an official of the king Ebed-melech may have had the same enemies as Zedekiah, and his escape after the breaching of the city wall may be the point of vv. 17–18. The view that he feared the princes who were Jeremiah's enemies because he had assisted the prophet to escape from the cistern and had accused the princes of doing evil (38.9; Bright) is an unlikely meaning of v. 17. The princes could have killed him at any stage in the siege until the Babylonians breached the wall, and then they would have had to devote their energies to escaping rather than to the settling of old scores. Furthermore, to interpret v. 17 in this fashion is to assume a historicity to 38.7–13 and to ignore the lack of hostility between the princes and Jeremiah in 38.27. All the elements in 37–39 should be read as stories rather than history and their lack of compatibility with each other should be noted as evidence for that reading of them.

Jeremiah and Ebed-melech are two figures who did not desert to the Babylonians during the siege, yet survived the ordeal of those days. 39.11–14; 40.1–6 deal with Jeremiah's fate as a 'friend of Babylon'. 39.15–18 present a rather different account of how survival was possible: as the result of a divine oracle. The extent to which this oracle is to be linked to Ebed-melech's action in rescuing Jeremiah in one of the stories about the siege is difficult to determine. According to v. 18 Ebed-melech's deliverance is due to his putting his trust in Yahweh (cf. 17.7–8, where such trust rules out fear). No direct connection is made between the rescue of Jeremiah and Ebed-melech's own escape from danger (that lack of connection is much facilitated by the separation of 39.15–18 from 38.7–13). Not his attitude towards Jeremiah but his trust in Yahweh underwrites Ebed-melech's fate. In the fall of Jerusalem the Ethiopian will survive (i.e. have his life as a spoil of war) because of his trust. Thus is the man who trusts in Yahweh blessed (17.7), and Ebed-melech becomes an example of the pious whose survival in whatever circumstances depends only upon their trust in Yahweh. Gone is the option of 38.2, and now only trust in Yahweh is required. This is the lesson drawn by a pious editor from the stories of Jeremiah in the siege of Jerusalem.

40.1–6

40[1] The word that came to Jeremiah from the LORD after Nebuzaradan the
captain of the guard had let him go from Ramah, when he took him bound
in chains along with all the captives of Jerusalem and Judah who were being
exiled to Babylon. 2 The captain of the guard took Jeremiah and said to
him, 'The LORD your God pronounced this evil against this place; 3 the
LORD has brought it about, and has done as he said. Because you sinned
against the LORD, and did not obey his voice, this thing has come upon you.
4 Now, behold, I release you today from the chains on your hands. If it
seems good to you to come with me to Babylon, come, and I will look after
you well; but if it seems wrong to you to come with me to Babylon, do not
come. See, the whole land is before you; go wherever you think it good and
right to go. 5 If you remain, then return to Gedaliah the son of Ahikam, son
of Shaphan, whom the king of Babylon appointed governor of the cities of
Judah, and dwell with him among the people; or go wherever you think it
right to go.' So the captain of the guard gave him an allowance of food and

a present, and let him go. 6 Then Jeremiah went to Gedaliah the son of Ahikam, at Mizpah, and dwelt with him among the people who were left in the land.

[MT 40] = G 47. **[1]** The text is in disorder here. The formulaic introduction of a divine oracle appears without the oracle itself following (unless vv. 2–3 are it). Cf. 32.1; 34.1, 8; 35.1 for the formula. Rudolph, 247, rearranges the text: 39.11f.; 40.2a,1b, 2b–6a, 1aβ, 6b, deleting 1aα (cf. BHS); Bright, 244 regards v. 2 as resuming 39.11–13aα, with 40.1b as a parenthesis explaining the circumstances under which Jeremiah was found. Ramah: cf. 31.15; the assembly point for the deportation of the citizens (the modern *er-Rām* five miles north of Jerusalem?). MT *wᵉhū'-āsūr*, 'and he was bound': lacking in G. Q *bā'ziqqīm*, 'in manacles': K *ba'ᵃziqqīm* (? cf. BHS; Judg. 9.41 MT). The image of Jeremiah 'among the people' (37.4, 12; 39.14; 40.5, 6) is here matched by 'Jeremiah among all the exiles' (*bᵉtōk kol-gālūt*). **[2]** MT *wayyiqqaḥ rab-ṭabbāḥīm lᵉyirmᵉyāhū*, 'and the captain of the guard *took* Jeremiah': *lᵉ* an Aramaism; NEB 'set him free', JPSB 'took charge of'; Bright, 241 'had . . . brought'. Cf. 39.14, where Jeremiah is taken (*lqḥ*) from the court of the guard rather than from among the deportees at Ramah. The speech made by Nebuzaradan in vv. 2b–3 is in impeccable Deuteronomistic language (cf. Thiel 1981, 58–61). This is typical of speeches put into the mouth of foreigners (cf. 22.8–9; Rahab the whore in Josh. 2.8–14 makes such a theologically correct speech). **[3]** G has a shorter text: 'the lord has done it because you sinned against him and did not listen to his voice.' In v. 2 'you' is sing., but plur. in v. 3 (a characteristically Deuteronomistic number shift). K *dbr*; Q *haddābār*, '*the* word': cf. Lam. 2.17 for the motif of the fulfilled word. **[4]** MT *min-hā'ziqqīm 'ᵃšer 'al-yādekā*, 'from the manacles (cf. v. 1) which are on your hand': many mss, Vrs read 'your hands'; *ydk* may be dual form (cf. Wanke 1971, 105), cf. 38.22. G lacks v. 4b (from 'but if it seems wrong'): MT is due to dittography (cf. Volz, 346); cf. BHS for adjustments with v. 5. **[5]** MT *wᵉ'ōdennū lō'-yāšūb wᵉšubāh*: unintelligible. G *ei de mē, apotreke kai anastrepson*, 'but if not, go away and return' (translating MT yields lit. 'but he was still not turning, and turning'): Rudolph, 246, follows Volz, 346, *'im ṭōb bᵉ'ēnekā lāšebet šubāh*, 'if it be pleasing in your eyes to return, return' (cf. BHS). Rudolph refers this to 39.14 and understands it as a reference to freedom of movement rather than returning (cf. BHS b–b on 39.14). MT *'ᵃšer hipqīd melek-bābel bᵉ'ārē yᵉhūdāh*, 'whom the king of Babylon appointed over the *cities* of Judah': surely the Judaean cities had been destroyed by the Babylonians! Cf. 34.22b. G has *en gē Iouda*, 'in the land of Judah' (= *bᵉ'ereṣ* for *bᵉ'ārē*), which makes sense of the material in the context of its setting (i.e. the aftermath of the fall of Jerusalem). MT *'ᵃruḥāh ūmaś'ēt*, 'an allowance and a position': G *dōra*, 'a gift'; *maś'ēt* can refer to a present from a superior person (cf. Gen. 43.34; II Sam. 11.8) or largesse in general.

Cf. 52.34 for the continual *'ᵃruḥāh* given to Jehoiachin by Evil-merodach; here the 'allowance' may refer to 'a meal for the journey' (*'rḥ*, 'travel, journey'). Nebuzaradan's actions may represent simple courtesy in terms of hospitality or the lavish treatment of a special person. **[6]** Mizpah: the location of Mizpah is uncertain. A number of exegetes favour *tell en-naṣbe* (e.g. Bright, 244; Thompson, 653) about eight miles north of Jerusalem (41.4–6, 12–16), though *nebī samwīl* (five miles to the north of Jerusalem) and *tell el-bīre* also have advocates (cf. Rudolph, 246). 41.17–18; 42.1–2 suggest that Jeremiah was in Bethlehem! MT *wayyēšeb 'ittō bᵉtōk hā'ām hanniš'ārīm bā'āreṣ*, 'and he remained with him among the people who were left in the land': cf. 37.21; 38.13, 28; 39.14 for the motif of Jeremiah remaining in a particular place and 37.4, 2; 39.14; 40.5, 6 for the image of Jeremiah 'in the midst of the people'.

The second account of Jeremiah's rescue by the Babylonians is very different from the story which has him released from the court of the guard (39.14). In this version Jeremiah is taken into exile among the other deportees (*gālūt yᵉrūšālaim*, 'the exile of Jerusalem' v. 1) and is in chains. At Ramah where the prisoners are stockaded before the long journey to Babylon he is discovered by Nebuzaradan and released. This is a very different story from the instructions to the guard to look after him by releasing him from the courtyard where he has spent the siege (39.11–12, 14). It is unnecessary to harmonize these two stories as if they could be merged together to produce a sequential account of two releases, one in Jerusalem and the other in Ramah after having been picked up wandering about the streets of Jerusalem (cf. 'while not exactly harmonious . . . not necessarily contradictory', Bright, 245–6). In the present state of the text MT presents an absurd picture of the preacher going into exile and being made the recipient of a sermon preached to him by the pagan military commander Nebuzaradan. At some point in the redaction an oracular statement by Jeremiah about the fall of the city given in Deuteronomistic language has been turned into a pious outburst by the Babylonian soldier. Once again the biblical writers present the heathen as first-class Deuteronomists, and only the Judaeans appear to be theologically illiterate (cf. 22.8–9). If the two strands are untangled, a story of Jeremiah's deportation with the exiles is found to be mixed up with a proclamation about the city's fall. In spite of a shorter text G contains the confusion.

The two stories of how Jeremiah escaped death in the burning city are based on similar motifs: release by the Babylonians, his remaining in the land of Judah instead of going to Babylon (what price 24 now?), and his association with Gedaliah ben Ahikam ben Shaphan. 40.1–6 develops these motifs more fully than the story in 39.11–12, 14. Nebuzaradan gives Jeremiah the option to go to Babylon or remain in the land of Judah (G). He accepts Jeremiah's decision to stay in Judah and sends him to Gedaliah. The parting gift (v. 5b) need not be understood as Babylonian homage to the great man, but may only be a courteous provision of food for the journey to Mizpah from Ramah. That the Babylonians took pains to look after Jeremiah may be interpreted as the storyteller's art, but it could reflect the belief that Jeremiah had been a Babylonian agent and therefore deserved to be rewarded now that his activity had been successful in demoralizing the citizens of Jerusalem (38.4; cf. Winckler 1903, 170, for the now unfashionable view that the prophets were agents of or friendly towards foreign powers). In both stories the Babylonians are represented as knowing about Jeremiah and as being concerned for his welfare.

Both accounts of Jeremiah's association with Gedaliah run counter to the motif of the destruction of the land with only the poor remaining (39.10; 52.16; II Kings 25.12; II Chron. 36.17–21; cf. Ezra 1.3–4). On the contrary, a thriving community developed around Gedaliah, who was himself an important official figure in Jerusalem society (cf. 40.9–12; 41.10). It is therefore from this group that the association with Jeremiah must be derived, and the stories are to be read as reflecting the discrete motif of 'survival *in the land of Judah*'. This strand is technically in conflict with other strands in the tradition which denounce the Palastinians (e.g. 24) or regard only the community in Babylon as the recipients of divine care (e.g. 29.4–7). The presentation of Jeremiah as actively *choosing* to stay in Judah and associate himself with Gedaliah underwrites the legitimation of the community with its centre at Mizpah. Thus the stories provide an ironic reflection on many of the elements in the book of Jeremiah.

Gedaliah's community 40.7 – 41.18

The traditions in 40–44 about the aftermath of the fall of Jerusalem have a unique section in 40.7 – 41.18 where Gedaliah's governorship of the settlements which survived the Babylonian onslaught is depicted (cf. II Kings 25.22–26). Its uniqueness lies in the fact that Jeremiah is completely absent from the story until 42.1–2. In the series of crises faced by the community during and after the assassination of the Babylonian appointed governor Gedaliah *Jeremiah plays no part*! He is entrusted to Gedaliah in 39.14, and in 40.6 goes to Gedaliah from Ramah, but in the material on Gedaliah's community he disappears until the crises are over. His absence is inexplicable except on the grounds that II Kings 25.22–26 has no place for him either. In the story of Gedaliah Jeremiah has no role and therefore must disappear from the picture until the hostages move to Bethlehem. He then becomes instrumental in guiding the community and goes to Egypt with them (42–43). However, his disappearance in a time of crisis is noteworthy, especially in the book which purports to tell his story. Part IV stresses the image of Jeremiah 'among the people', but in the disintegration of Gedaliah's community he is nowhere to be found (an extension of his imprisonment theme?). When Jerusalem fell and when Gedaliah was assassinated Jeremiah is out of harm's way or absent (cf. David when Saul fell on Mount Gilboa). The tradition makes no observations about these factors and may even be unaware of the significance of the fact that Jeremiah is absent in 40.7–41.18.

The story of Gedaliah's assassination and the break-up of his community is told without reference to Jeremiah because the editors had it in this form. They know nothing of Jeremiah's involvement with the community until it is ready to flee to Egypt. Thus the tradition links Jeremiah with the beginning and end of the community, but cannot find a place for him during the crises of that community. This is all the more remarkable in that the tradition presents Jeremiah as 'the prophet for all seasons'. Yet as the hopes for reconstructing communal life in Judah blossom and fade *Jeremiah is conspicuously absent.* How can this be? If the book of Jeremiah were a historical work, there would be insuperable problems here, but in a collection of stories constructed around the bearer of the word the absence of that bearer in 40.7 – 41.18 is less problematic. Apart from inheriting stories which lacked Jeremiah in them, his absence in the critical period of the rise and collapse of Gedaliah's community facilitates the subsequent disintegration of the survivors. When Jeremiah does reappear it is too late for him to prevent the headless rush to Egypt (42–44). Hence his absence which strikes the modern reader as inexplicable may not have been such an enigma for the ancient editors. The historical-critical approach which scrutinizes the text very closely may note anomalies of which the writers of that text may have been unaware. These may make for poor history, but they can contribute to the storyteller's art. In telling the story of Gedaliah's community are the editors blithely unaware that they have left out Jeremiah?

In Jeremiah's absence other figures come to the fore. Gedaliah as governor of the community is central until his tragic assassination. In his place Ishmael ben Nethaniah emerges briefly as the focus of the story and his banditry threatens to remove the people from Judah. But he is quickly displaced by Johanan ben Kareah, who behaves like the community's natural leader by rescuing the hostages and making decisions about the future of the people. Only after the crisis is over does Jeremiah reappear in order to perform his prophetic role and give guidance to the people. The general pattern of Part IV is resumed in 42–43 where Jeremiah is presented as warning the community against going to Egypt and having his warning rejected. His passivity, so characteristic of Part IV and typified by his absence from the story of Gedaliah's community, is reinforced as a motif in the tradition by the account of his being taken to Egypt (presumably against his own wishes). Briefly in 42.10–12 Jeremiah announces the possibility of divine mercy to the community on condition they remain in the land of Judah (cf. Ackroyd 1968b, 37–54). This moment of possibility is rejected and the work begun by Ishmael is continued by Johanan. The people go into exile in Egypt and thus reverse the legendary history of the nation as the movement of people from Egypt to the land of Canaan. At the same time the story of Jeremiah in part IV which began with him in the empty cistern (cf.

37.16; 38.6) ends with him in Egypt, just like part of the story of Joseph whose brothers put him in an empty cistern (*bōr*, Gen. 37.22–24) and then sold him to Midianites (or Ishmaelites!) who took him to Egypt (Gen. 37.25, 28, 36).

40.7–12

7 When all the captains of the forces in the open country and their men
heard that the king of Babylon had appointed Gedaliah the son of Ahikam
governor in the land, and had committed to him men, women, and children,
those of the poorest of the land who had not been taken into exile to Babylon,
8 they went to Gedaliah at Mizpah – Ishmael the son of Nethaniah, Johanan
the son of Kareah, Seraiah the son of Tanhumeth, the sons of Ephai the
Netophathite, Jezaniah the son of the Maacathite, they and their men. 9
Gedaliah the son of Ahikam, son of Shaphan, swore to them and their men,
saying, 'Do not be afraid to serve the Chaldeans. Dwell in the land and
serve the king of Babylon, and it shall be well with you. 10 As for me, I will
dwell at Mizpah, to stand for you before the Chaldeans who will come to
us; but as for you, gather wine and summer fruits and oil, and store them
in your vessels, and dwell in your cities that you have taken.' 11 Likewise,
when all the Jews who were in Moab and among the Ammonites and in
Edom and in other lands heard that the king of Babylon had left a remnant
in Judah and had appointed Gedaliah the son of Ahikam, son of Shaphan,
as governor over them, 12 then all the Jews returned from all the places to
which they had been driven and came to the land of Judah, to Gedaliah at
Mizpah; and they gathered wine and summer fruits in great abundance.

[40.7–9] Cf. II Kings 25.22–24. **[7]** MT *kol-śārē haḥ^{a}yālīm '^{a}šer baśśādeh*, 'all the princes of the armies which were in the field': i.e. the forces in the open country which had not been destroyed by the Babylonians. G^{BAS} *kai parekatethento autō andras kai gunaikas autōn*, 'and they committed to him the men and their wives', for MT *hipqīd 'ittō '^{a}nāšīm w^{e}nāšīm wāṭāp ūmiddallat hā'āreṣ*, 'and had committed to him men, women, and children, those of the poorest of the land'. MT influenced by 39.10; 52.16; it represents a harmonization of two discrete views of the aftermath of the fall of Jerusalem. **[8]** G lacks 'and Jonathan' due to haplography of Johanan: lacking in a few mss, Vrs, II Kings 25.23; also RSV but see other EVV. It therefore follows that many Vrs read *ben qārēaḥ*, 'son of Kareah', for MT *b^{e}nē-qārēaḥ*, 'sons of Kareah'. K *'wpy*; Q *'ēpay*, 'Ephai' (K Opay): G, V follow K. MT *wīzanyāhū*: a few mss, II Kings 25.23, *w^{e}ya'^{a}zanyāhū*; Jezaniah – Jaazaniah. **[9]** MT *mē'^{a}bōd*, 'of serving': II Kings 25.24, *mē'ab^{e}dē*, 'of the servants of', i.e. the

Chaldaean officials; G *apo prosōpou tōn paidōn tōn*, 'before the children of'. Cf. Lam. 5.8. **[10]** MT *yōšēb*, 'dwell': G *kathēmai enantion humōn*, 'dwell in your presence'. Cf. 15.1 for the motif of standing before. With Gedaliah as mediator between people and Babylonians there is no role for Jeremiah in the community! MT *beʿārēkem*, 'in your cities': G *en tais polesin*, 'in the cities' = *beʿārīm*; cf. v. 5. The seizure (*tpś*) of towns may represent the successes of the military in the field (v. 7). **[11]** MT *bekol-hāʾarāṣōt*, 'in all the lands': EVV, 'other countries'; G *en pasē tē gē*, 'in all the land'. **[12]** G lacks 'then all the Jews came from all the places to which they had been driven'.

The images presented of Gedaliah's community in vv. 7–12 depict a society beginning to re-establish itself after the disasters of 588–7. No dating is provided in the text so it is not possible to determine whether the events of 40–41 took place immediately after the fall of Jerusalem or some years later (see on 52.30). Once Gedaliah is established as the Babylonian appointed leader of the community and governor of Judah the various factions in the land rally to him. Military leaders, their forces with them, join him, among whom are notable individuals (named in v. 8). Jews who had fled during the invasion and siege now return to their homeland. They are all prepared to associate with Gedaliah ben Ahikam as their legitimate leader. Thus Gedaliah finds himself in charge of many people, including military forces, with Mizpah as his centre. In v. 10 he is represented as the community's mediator with the Babylonians. One ostensible reason put forward by the text for the gathering together of the people to Gedaliah and their resettlement in the land is the need for the ingathering of the harvest. A good summer had produced abundant fruit, grapes and oil and there was a pressing need for them all to be harvested. Gedaliah could deal with political matters but he needed workers for the fields and vineyards (cf. 32.15). So the community begins to emerge in relation to the tasks facing it, and stability is created in response to nature's prodigality (cf. 31.5, 12).

The story of Gedaliah's community represents a different account of the aftermath of the fall of Jerusalem from the view that all the people were deported and only some of the poorest left to look after the land (39.9–10; 52.15–16; II Kings 25.11–12). Many people, including those important enough to have their names registered in terms of their families, remained in the land and these were joined by others who recognized Gedaliah's authority. The fertility of the land hardly suggests a recent invasion and siege. Such foreign intrusions into a country usually devastate all food resources and leave behind them the consequences of a scorched earth policy. However, the products listed, vines ('wine' presupposes vineyards and the due processes of wine-making), summer fruits and oil, represent crops which may not have required the constant supervision which the invasion and siege will have destroyed. Furthermore, the time-gap between the ending of the siege and the period depicted in 40.7–12 may have been sufficiently long for the vineyards to have been tended. But images of a devastated land occupied by the huddled masses of the poor are completely absent from the depiction of the circumstances prevailing under Gedaliah's governorship. For him and the people under his command a new age is beginning – one of stability and plenty. As presented in 40.7–12 there is an idyllic quality about the new community. The exiles driven away from home in recent years come flocking back to their homeland (vv. 11–12) and participate in the great harvesting: 'and they gathered wine and summer fruits in great abundance' (v. 12b).

40.7–12 reads like the fulfilment of the future hopes expressed in the poems of 30–31 or the idylls of Second Isaiah (cf. Baltzer 1961, 33–7). It certainly suggests a very different view of life in the land of Judah after 587 from other strands in the book of Jeremiah which denounce the Judaeans in favour of the deportees in Babylon (e.g. 24.4–7; 29.16–19). With the emergence of Gedaliah's community, hope returns to the land and the future of the many people who associate themselves with him begins to look bright.

40.13 – 41.3

13 Now Johanan the son of Kareah and all the leaders of the forces in the open country came to Gedaliah at Mizpah 14 and said to him, 'Do you know that Baalis the king of the Ammonites has sent Ishmael the son of Nethaniah to take your life?' But Gedaliah the son of Ahikam would not believe them. 15 Then Johanan the son of Kareah spoke secretly to Gedaliah at Mizpah, 'Let me go and slay Ishmael the son of Nethaniah, and no one will know it. Why should he take your life, so that all the Jews who are gathered about you would be scattered, and the remnant of Judah would perish?' 16 But Gedaliah the son of Ahikam said to Johanan the son of Kareah, 'You shall not do this thing, for you are speaking falsely of Ishmael.'

41 1 In the seventh month, Ishmael the son of Nethaniah, son of Elishama, of the royal family, one the chief officers of the king, came with ten men to

Gedaliah the son of Ahikam, at Mizpah. As they ate bread together there at Mizpah, 2 Ishmael the son of Nethaniah and the ten men with him rose up and struck down Gedaliah the son of Ahikam, son of Shaphan, with the sword, and killed him, whom the king of Babylon had appointed governor in the land. 3 Ishmael also slew all the Jews who were with Gedaliah at Mizpah, and the Chaldean soldiers who happened to be there.

---

[13] Johanan ben Kareah: cf. v. 8. 40.13 – 43.5 refer to him in this fashion, hence MT *b^enē qārēaḥ* (v. 8) may be incorrect. **[14]** Baalis, king of the *b^enē Ammon*: cf. 27.3; Ezek. 21.18–32 [MT 23–37] for Ammonite opposition to Babylon. The plot against Gedaliah may be part of this campaign against the Babylonians. MT *l^ehakkōt^ekā nepeš*, 'to strike you mortally': cf. v. 15; NEB 'to assassinate you'. G lacks 'ben Nethaniah' and 'ben Ahikam'. **[15]** MT *bassēter*, 'in secret': as in 37.17; 38.16. This would appear to be a literary device in 37–40 used to convey a dramatic sense of the conspiratorial nature of the meetings and interviews delineated. MT *š^e'ērīt y^ehūdāh*, 'the remnant of Judah': cf. v. 11. **[16]** K *t'š*; Q *ta'^ašēh*, 'you shall (not) do'. MT *kī-šeqer 'attāh dōbēr 'el*, 'for you are speaking falsely of': cf. 43.2 *šeqer 'attāh m^edabbēr*, 'you are telling a lie'. **[MT 41]** = G 48. **[1]** Cf. II Kings 25.25; 'in the seventh month': the year is not identified, but the sequence in II Kings 25 implies that it was the same year as the fall of Jerusalem (cf. 'in the fourth month', 39.2). Zech. 7.5; 8.19 refer to a fast in the seventh month which may be associated with the assassination of Gedaliah (or is the assassination dated to this month because of the fast?). G *Elasa* for Elishama. G lacks 'and the chiefs of the king', MT *w^erabbē hammelek*, i.e. one of the king's chief officers: also lacking in II Kings 25.25, NEB; a dittography in MT (cf. Rudolph, 250; BHS). **[2]** G lacks 'the son of Ahikam, son of Shaphan, with the sword and killed him'. MT *wāyyamet 'ōtō*, 'and he killed him': Vrs 'they killed him'. **[3]** MT *'et-g^edalyāhū bammiṣpāh*, 'with Gedaliah at Mizpah': G lacks 'with Gedaliah'; a gloss identifying the Jews who were killed. As all the Jews at Mizpah were not killed (v. 10), the word *bammiṣpāh* is problematic (G has it). Duhm, 317, considers it a gloss to *šām*, 'there'; Rudolph, 250, reads *bammišteh*, 'at the feast' (cf. BHS). MT consists of a series of direct object indicators *w^e'ēt . . . 'et . . . w^e'et . . . 'ēt* governed by the final two words of v. 3, *hikkāh yišmā'ē'l*, 'Ishmael smote'.

A second account of the gathering of the military leaders with their forces to meet with Gedaliah at Mizpah is given in 40.13–16 (this is lacking in the II Kings 25 version). In this story there is no influx of refugees from foreign lands or great gathering of fruits and the vintage, but the commanders gather to inform Gedaliah of a conspiracy against his life. This conspiracy is organized by the

Ammonites and centres on Ishmael ben Nethaniah (cf. 36.14). Johanan ben Kareah also informs the governor of the plot in a secret session with Gedaliah. In this private interview (modelled on the Zedekiah-Jeremiah interviews?) Johanan volunteers to assassinate Ishmael and thereby save the community of the remnant of Judah. As a would-be champion of the governor Johanan emerges as the military leader of the new community (cf. 41.11). However, Gedaliah refuses to believe that there is a conspiracy against him and declines permission for an assassination attempt. Thus he appears to be a good, eirenic leader who is not prepared to allow Judaeans to slaughter each other on the strength of rumours.

41.1–3 (cf. II Kings 25.25) provides a brief account of Ishmael's successful assassination of Gedaliah, his companions and the Babylonian soldiers stationed at Mizpah. Apparently this slaughter takes place in the 'seventh month', some three months after the fall of Jerusalem. This may seem too brief a period to cover the return of the foreign exiles and the great harvest ingathering, but the account in II Kings 25 knows nothing of these developments which appear exclusively in the Jeremiah tradition. Yet Ishmael must have been well-known to Gedaliah to have shared a meal with him, especially after the warning issued by Johanan. As a member of the royal family Ishmael would have had some standing in the land, though not necessarily in Gedaliah's community. Perhaps behind his animosity towards Gedaliah (why would Gedaliah not realize this?) lay loyalty to the family of Zedekiah which had been outrageously butchered by the Babylonians (cf. 39.6–7; 52.10–11). Gedaliah by his association with Babylon and his acceptability to Nebuchadrezzar as a governor would have been a traitor to the people of Judah in Ishmael's eyes. In killing him and all those in league with him Ishmael may have struck a blow against the Babylonian domination of Judah. This explanation would make the assassination one further act in the long conflict between pro-Babylonian and anti-Babylonian forces in Judaean politics since the Babylonians first penetrated the land in 597. Other possibilities may be mooted also: Ishmael may represent anarchic guerilla forces operating against the Babylonian settlements in Judah or, as 40.14 suggests, he may have been part of other conspiracies against the Babylonians (cf. 41.10b). The simple story of Gedaliah's assassination may be read in many different ways for political motives, but the text affords little serious information to account for it. As the story appears in II Kings 25 it could hardly be simpler or briefer. Developed at some length in 40.7 – 41.18 the story becomes no clearer in spite of added details. With ten men Ishmael is able to kill governor, companions and the Babylonian soldiers! The eleven men are then able to take captive all the other people in Mizpah and transport them towards Ammonite territory (41.10). The lack of realism in the story becomes more obvious in 41.11–18 when Johanan's forces reappear (from where?), chase Ishmael, and retrieve the captives. It is difficult to read the stories making up the account of Gedaliah's community as realistic descriptions of history or as serious accounts of what happened. At best they may be regarded as tales told about the assassination of the Babylonian appointed governor Gedaliah. They expand the much briefer account in II Kings 25.22–26 and prepare the way for further stories about Jeremiah among the people (cf. 42.1–6).

With the assassination of 41.2 the story of Gedaliah comes to an end. The fate of his community (cf. II Kings 25.26) remains in suspense for some further time (cf. 41.4 – 43.7). The future which dawned so brightly with Gedaliah, the return of the exiles and the ingathering of the harvest is snuffed out by a malcontent of the royal house. The innocent and good Gedaliah, the mediator and spokesman of the community in its relations with Babylon, becomes one more murdered victim of a brutal age (cf. Baltzer 1961, 35, who sees a striking similarity between the stylization of Gedaliah and the figure who suffers so starkly in Isa. 53). With his death the stability of the community is wrecked and hopes of a good future in Judah are shaken. Ishmael's act of defiance against a hated enemy (i.e. the Babylonians and one of their collaborationists) now threatens the security of the renascent country and it remains to be seen whether those who survive the attack can control Ishmael and persuade their Babylonian overlords of their own lack of complicity in the conspiracy.

41.4–10

4 On the day after the murder of Gedaliah, before any one knew of it, 5
eighty men arrived from Shechem and Shiloh and Samaria, with their
beards shaved and their clothes torn, and their bodies gashed, bringing
cereal offerings and incense to present at the temple of the LORD. 6 And
Ishmael the son of Nethaniah came out from Mizpah to meet them, weeping

as he came. As he met them, he said to them, 'Come in to Gedaliah the son of Ahikam.' 7 When they came into the city, Ishmael the son of Nethaniah and the men with him slew them, and cast them into a cistern. 8 But there were ten men among them who said to Ishmael, 'Do not kill us, for we have stores of wheat, barley, oil, and honey hidden in the fields.' So he refrained and did not kill them with their companions.

9 Now the cistern into which Ishmael cast all the bodies of the men whom he had slain was the large cistern which King Asa had made for defence against Baasha king of Israel; Ishmael the son of Nethaniah filled it with the slain. 10 Then Ishmael took captive all the rest of the people who were in Mizpah, the king's daughters and all the people who were left at Mizpah, whom Nebuzaradan, the captain of the guard, had committed to Gedaliah the son of Ahikam. Ishmael the son of Nethaniah took them captive and set out to cross over to the Ammonites.

---

[4] MT *way^{e}hī bayyōm haššēnī l^{e}hāmīt 'et-g^{e}dalyāhū*, lit, and it came to pass on the second day with reference to the killing of Gedaliah'. **[5]** Shiloh: G Salem; cf. 7.14; 26.6. The three towns Shechem, Shiloh, Samaria appear in MT in alphabetical rather than geographical order. MT *ūmitgōd^{e}dīm*, 'and gashed', i.e. their bodies cut: cf. 5.7; 16.6; 47.5; 48.37; I Kings 18.28; the funeral rites described here are forbidden by Deut. 14.1. Such a late (cf. Mayes 1979, 238) prohibition may reflect a rejection of the self-laceration custom of mourning associated with pagan religion. MT *ūl^{e}bōnāh*, 'and frankincense'. It is generally assumed that *bēt yhwh* refers to the temple in Jerusalem because to posit a temple in Mizpah would be an over-subtle reading of the text (cf. Giesebrecht, 216); cf. Ackroyd 1968a, 25–8; Jones 1963, 14–16, on the relation of v. 5 to the question about cultic practices in Jerusalem during the exile. **[6]** MT *hōlēk hālōk ūbōkeh*, idiomatic for 'weeping as he went': G *autoi eporeuonto kai eklaion*, 'they were going along weeping'. MT makes Ishmael dissemble by weeping, whereas G follows the logic of the story and has the pilgrims weep. Why Ishmael should weep *and* invite the pilgrims to meet Gedaliah is less than clear. G lacks MT's *way^{e}hī kip^{e}gōš 'ōtām*, 'and when he encountered them'. **[7]** MT *'el-tōk habbōr*, 'to the midst of the cistern': G lacks *tōk*; a dittography of (*'el-*)*tōk* (*hā'īr*), '(to) *the midst of* (the city)'. The lack of a verb is supplied by S (= *wayyašlīkēm*, 'and he cast them') before 'to the midst of the cistern'. The cistern (*habbōr*) motif of 37–38 appears here and reflects storytelling techniques used in Part IV. G lacks 'he and the men with him'. **[8]** MT *bām*, 'among them': G *ekei*, 'there' = *šām*. The story told by the ten men is presumably a lie to buy off Ishmael, for what would mourning pilgrims be doing with supplies buried in the fields! However, realism should not be expected in such stories as make up the account of Gedaliah's community. **[9]** G lacks 'the bodies of the men'. MT *b^{e}yad-g^{e}dalyāhū*, 'by the hand of Gedaliah': G *phrear mega touto estin*, 'this is the great cistern' = *bōr gādōl hū'*. Cf. I Kings 15.22 for king Asa's association with Mizpah. **[10]** MT *wayyišbᵉ*, 'and he took captive': G *kai apestrepsen*, 'and he brought back' = *wayyāšeb*. G lacks 'all the people who were left in Mizpah', 'Nebuzaradan', 'and Ishmael ben Nethaniah took them captive'. A few mss, G^OL read *wayyaškēm*, 'and he rose early', for *wayyišbēm*, 'and he took them captive' (cf. BHS).

———

The supplements attached to the story of Gedaliah's assassination are so tantalizingly brief and disconnected that it is difficult to determine what is happening or why. On the second day, i.e. the day after, of the murder eighty pilgrims arrive from a variety of famous cultic cities on their way to the Jerusalem temple. Their long pilgrimage is endured in a state of mourning – beards removed, clothes torn, bodies gashed – and it must be presumed that they are responding to the fall of the city and the destruction of the temple. As 41.1 sets the stories in the seventh month, the pilgrimage may be associated with the great pilgrimages of that season (cf. Lev. 16.29 for the setting of the Day of Atonement ritual in the seventh month). Whether as response to 587 or as an annual pilgrimage to Jerusalem in the seventh month, it is a curious affair and not referred to elsewhere in the Hebrew Bible. Ishmael persuades the pilgrims to meet Gedaliah in Mizpah, and there he kills seventy of them. How realistic an account the story may be is hard to imagine, because the eleven killers massacred seventy pilgrims while the rest of the people (v. 10) stood and watched. Yet they spared ten pilgrims on the grounds that they had hidden stores of wheat, barley, oil and honey in the fields. Then, having dumped the corpses in a large cistern, killers and captives all left to go to the Ammonites. Put together like this the elements in vv. 4–8, 9–10 hardly make any sense, but part of the incoherence may be due to the combination of discrete strands in the chapter (e.g. 1–3, 10; 4–9 are quite independent of one another, cf. Pohlmann 1978, 115–8). With v. 8 the ten pilgrims spared disappear from the story, and in v. 10 the people who were not present at Gedaliah's meal (v. 1) are taken captive. Not much coherence is gained by separating the strands, because in each story the community appears to be passive in the extreme as Ishmael and his ten men terrorize governor, town, garrison and people. It is a most remarkable story and, considering that Gedaliah represented Babylonian authority in a recently subjugated land and therefore must have had ample troop support, quite unreal.

Even as a fiction Ishmael ben Nethaniah is a difficult character to understand. His killing of Gedaliah and the Babylonian soldiers is the act of a patriot, but his slaughter of the pilgrims is an outrage and suggests a psychotic bandit. Put together, the stories are unconvincing because they mix two very different types of activity. The bandit story might well fit the period in which it is set, but in that case the pilgrims would have had an armed escort or would not have been wandering about in a land only beginning to recover from the depredations of invasion and the consequences of so many plundered cities. That the stories may reflect aspects of the period need not be denied, but they should not be read as historical accounts of the aftermath of Jerusalem's destruction. They are better understood as stories used to fill in the interstices of the account given in II Kings 25.22–26 and built around the characters of Ishmael ben Nethaniah (villain) and Johanan ben Kareah (hero).

41.11–15

11 But when Johanan the son of Kareah and all the leaders of the forces with him heard of all the evil which Ishmael the son of Nethaniah had done,
12 they took all their men and went to fight against Ishmael the son of Nethaniah. They came upon him at the great pool which is in Gibeon. 13
And when all the people who were with Ishmael saw Johanan the son of Kareah and all the leaders of the force with him, they rejoiced. 15 So all the people whom Ishmael had carried away captive from Mizpah turned about and came back, and went to Johanan the son of Kareah. 15 But Ishmael the son of Nethaniah escaped from Johanan with eight men, and went to the Ammonites.

---

[12] MT *'et-kol-hā'ᵃnāšîm*, 'all the men': *to stratopedon autōn*, 'their army'. MT *'el-mayim rabbîm 'ᵃšer bᵉgib'ōn*, 'at the great waters which are in Gibeon': cf. II Sam. 2.13; for Gibeon cf. 28.1. Rudolph, 252, favours reading *bᵉgeba'*, 'in Geba'. In view of Ishmael's flight to the Ammonites these details favour identifying Gibeon with *nebī samwīl* rather than *tell en-naṣbe* (cf. Blenkinsopp 1972, 100). Bright, 255, allows for the possibility that Ishmael may have followed a circuitous route, so that *tell en-naṣbe* may still be indicated; see on 40.6. **[13]** G lacks 'and they rejoiced' (*wayyiśmāḥū*). Bright, 249, reads vv. 13a, 14aβ, 13b, 14aαb, transposing the MT for the sake of clarity. **[14]** G is much shorter than MT, reading only *kai anestrepsan pros Iōanan*, 'and they returned to Johanan'.

The reappearance of Johanan ben Kareah, the military leaders and their forces in vv. 11–12 prompts the question 'where were they during the assassination of Gedaliah?'. Their absence during the crisis is most curious and remarkable. Such a military force would have protected Gedaliah, especially as 40.14 indicates that Johanan knew about the plot. Yet he seems to disappear, taking his men with him, until it is too late to sustain the community's existence. Then after the kidnapping of the remnant of the community in v. 10 (note the presence of the king's daughters among Gedaliah's charges in spite of 38.22–23; 39.9), Johanan and his forces return in order to rescue them. Like Jeremiah's absence throughout the crisis, the temporary disappearance of Johanan and his troops is another mystery of 40.7 – 41.18.

The mere appearance of Johanan and troops is sufficient to rescue the kidnapped people. Once they are informed (by whom?) about Ishmael's activities, the military commanders and their troops pursue the bandits and overtake them by the great pool of Gibeon (another story motif like the great cistern made by king Asa). Ishmael loses control of the hostages once military opposition appears, and the kidnapped people easily elude their captors and turn to Johanan. In the ensuing confusion Ishmael and *eight* of his men escape (v. 15; does this imply that two of his men were killed? cf. v. 2). They join the Ammonites and disappear from the story. Ishmael's contribution to 40.7 – 41.18 is to have struck the death-blow of Gedaliah's community.

41.16–18

16 Then Johanan the son of Kareah and all the leaders of the forces with him took all the rest of the people whom Ishmael the son of Nethaniah had carried away captive from Mizpah after he had slain Gedaliah the son of Ahikam – soldiers, women, children, and eunuchs, whom Johanan brought back from Gibeon. 17 And they went and stayed at Geruth Chimham near Bethlehem, intending to go to Egypt 18 because of the Chaldeans; for they were afraid of them, because Ishmael the son of Nethaniah had slain Gedaliah the son of Ahikam, whom the king of Babylon had made governor over the land.

---

[16] MT *ʾašer hēšīb mēʾēt yišmāʿēʾl*, 'which he recovered from Ishmael': cf.

NEB, JPSB. RSV follows an emended text reading *šābāh 'ōlām*, 'he took them captive' (cf. Hitzig, 320; Rudolph; BHS). Johanan did not rescue the people 'from Mizpah'. G lacks 'the son of Kareah from Mizpah after he had slain Gedaliah the son of Ahikam'. MT *g^ebārīm 'anšē hammilḥāmōh* 'men' i.e. 'soldiers': G *dunatous andras en polemō*, 'men mighty in battle'; understanding *gbrym* as *gibbōrīm* 'warriors' (a few mss read this form); cf. 43.6. It is unlikely that Ishmael took captive soldiers along with all the other people listed in vv. 10, 16b. MT *w^esārisīm*, 'and eunuchs': cf. 38.7; it is possible that these were eunuchs in the service of the princesses (cf. Rudolph, 252) rather than high-ranking officials. MT *w^eṭap*, 'and children': lit. 'toddlers'; G *kai ta loipa*, 'and the residue'. Cf. 43.6. **[17]** MT *b^egērūt kimhām*, 'at Gerut-kimham': K *kmwhm*; Q *kimhām*; Vrs have different forms of a place name. Cf. II Sam. 19.37–38 for the proper name Chimham. The hapax legomenon *gērūt* may refer to a lodging-place, inn or khan (cf. BDB, 158).

The final element in this stage of the story of the disintegration of Gedaliah's community represents Johanan's return with the captives. He does not, however, return to Mizpah but settles at some lodging area near Bethlehem. There the remnant of the community regroup in order to emigrate to Egypt. Sound reasoning is behind this decision: once the Babylonian authorities discover what has happened to the garrison at Mizpah and to Gedaliah their representative they will act harshly against the occupants of the area. In spite of the propaganda about the generous nature of the Babylonians in 39.11–14; 40.1–5, their reactions to Ishmael's activities would have been a good deal less kind. Those who had failed to fight off Ishmael and his *ten* men and thereby protect Gedaliah or even their own interests could hardly have expected much support from a retaliatory Babylonian expedition (such a campaign may account for the deportation of 583, cf. 52.30). One minor absurdity may be noted in v. 16b, where reference is made to 'men, men of war' as being among the captives taken by Ishmael. How a handful of bandits captured such soldiers (cf. v. 3) is beyond imagination, though in keeping with the style of storytelling in 41. If it is a mistaken interpretation of 'men', it is a mistake maintained by both editions (G, MT).

With the disappearance of Ishmael Johanan ben Kareah emerges as the dominant figure in the community. But having failed to prevent the assassination of Gedaliah and not having captured Ishmael he is not able to hold the people together in the land of Judah. Ishmael has effectively killed off any positive future in the homeland.

42.1–6

42[1] Then all the commanders of the forces, and Johanan the son of Kareah
and Azariah the son of Hoshaiah, and all the people from the least to the
greatest, came near 2 and said to Jeremiah the prophet, 'Let our supplication
come before you, and pray to the LORD your God for us, for all this remnant
(for we are left but a few of many, as your eyes see us), 3 that the LORD your
God may show us the way we should go, and the thing that we should do.'
4 Jeremiah the prophet said to them, 'I have heard you; behold, I will pray
to the LORD your God according to your request, and whatever the LORD
answers you I will tell you; I will keep nothing back from you.' 5 Then they
said to Jeremiah, 'May the LORD be a true and faithful witness against us
if we do not act according to all the word with which the LORD your God
sends you to us. 6 Whether it is good or evil, we will obey the voice of the
LORD our God to whom we are sending you, that it may be well with us
when we obey the voice of the LORD our God.'

[MT 42] = G 49. **[1]** MT *wizanyāh*, 'Jezaniah': cf. 40.8; G *Azarias*, 'Azariah', cf. 43.2; here and in 43.2 (G 50.2) G makes Azariah the son of *Maasaeas* rather than of Hoshaiah. **[2]** 'Jeremiah the prophet': one of the very few occurrences in G of the epithet 'the prophet'. Cf. Gen. 20.7 for the association of prophet and intercession. The supplication (*t^{e}ḥinnāh*) motif appears in 36.7; 37.20; 38.26. G lacks *ba'^{a}dēnū*, 'for us'; S lacks 'for all this remnant'; MT has both variants. MT *miqqāṭōn w^{e}'ad-gādōl*, 'from the smallest to the greatest': cf. variations in 6.13; 8.10; 16.6; 31.34; 42.8. **[3]** MT *'^{e}lōhekā*, 'your god': a few mss, S '*our* god', cf. 37.3. **[4]** G lacks 'the prophet' and reads 'our god' for MT 'your god'. MT *'^{a}šer-ya'^{a}neh yhwh 'etkem*, 'which Yahweh shall answer you': Volz, 354, reads *'^{e}lōhēkem*, 'your god', for *'etkem*, 'you', on the grounds that Yahweh answers the prophet, not the people (followed by Rudolph, cf. BHS); G lacks 'you'. Cf. 26.2; 38.15 for the motif of withholding the divine word. **[5]** MT *'^{a}šer yišlāḥ^{a}kā yhwh*, 'with which Yahweh sends you': cf. v. 21; 43.1 for this sending (*šlḥ*) motif. **[6]** K *'nw*; Q *'^{a}naḥnū*, 'we' (K *'^{a}nū*, 'we', is common in post-biblical Hebrew but only appears in the Hebrew Bible here). Thiel 1981, 64, regards v. 6 as a pious repetition of v. 5 explaining it in Deuteronomistic terms; cf. Pohlmann 1978, 126–7.

The last stage in the story of the fate of Gedaliah's community unfolds in 42.1 – 43.7 (analysis in Pohlmann 1978, 123–59; Wanke 1971, 116–33). Jeremiah returns to the centre of the stage but displays an utter unawareness of recent events and alludes not at all to the assassination of Gedeliah. The crises of the community are not referred to him until the disappearance of Ishmael and the retreat of the refugees to near Bethlehem (if 42.1 is read as linked to 41.16–18 by virtue of 'then', it may be assumed that the meeting of 42.1–2 takes place near Bethlehem). Then he emerges as the prophetic figure in the community to whom all may seek for guidance. The figure of 37–38 who makes humble supplication to the king becomes the one who may intercede with the deity for all the people. This is not only a case of role reversal but also a contrast with the figure of Part I (cf. 7.16; 11.14; 14.11) who is forbidden to intercede on behalf of the people. This presentation of Jeremiah as the prophet of the community no longer forbidden to pray for it reveals a significant change in the status of that community before Yahweh. Jeremiah can behave like an authoritative prophetic figure because the community is acceptable to Yahweh. With the fall of Jerusalem the hostility of the deity against the people of Judah (cf. 40.2–3) has been dissipated, and the community constituted by the remnant now enjoys his favour to the extent that Yahweh is prepared to listen to the prophet. In the strands of the tradition where intercession is prohibited Jeremiah is not represented as a prophet, but here he is *Jeremiah the prophet* (v. 2 both editions; 4 MT). Thus 42 reflects a quite distinctive element in the book of Jeremiah and one which differs significantly from that strand which identifies the divine pleasure exclusively with the exiles in Babylon (cf. 24.4–7; 29.4–7, 10–14). Not in Babylon but in Judah lies the real hope for the future (cf. Ackroyd 1968a, 57; 1968b, 37–54). Whether that hope can be sustained is the question under discussion in this chapter, and the assassination of Gedaliah appears to be irrelevant to the answer.

The whole community, its military leadership and all its ranks, gathers to Jeremiah to seek help from the deity. Jeremiah's prowess as a prophet is tacitly recognized by the formal request for his mediation with the deity. He agrees to intercede with the deity on their behalf and to convey to them everything said to him by Yahweh. They in turn agree to act in conformity with whatever the divine answer may be. An editorial note (v. 6) reinforces that affirmation.

42.7–17

7 At the end of ten days the word of the LORD came to Jeremiah. 8 Then he summoned Johanan the son of Kareah and all the commanders of the forces

who were with him, and all the people from the least to the greatest, 9 and said to them, 'Thus says the LORD, the God of Israel, to whom you sent me to present your supplication before him: 10 If you will remain in this land, then I will build you up and not pull you down; I will plant you, and not pluck you up; for I repent of the evil which I did to you. 11 Do not fear the king of Babylon, of whom you are afraid; do not fear him, says the LORD, for I am with you, to save you and to deliver you from his hand. 12 I will grant you mercy, that he may have mercy on you and let you remain in your own land. 13 But if you say, "We will not remain in this land," disobeying the voice of the LORD your God 14 and saying, "No, we will go to the land of Egypt, where we shall not see war, or hear the sound of the trumpet, or be hungry for bread, and we will dwell there," 15 then hear the word of the LORD, O remnant of Judah. Thus says the LORD of hosts, the God of Israel: If you set your faces to enter Egypt and go to live there, 16 then the sword which you fear shall overtake you there in the land of Egypt; and the famine of which you are afraid shall follow hard after you to Egypt; and there you shall die. 17 All the men who set their faces to go to Egypt to live there shall die by the sword, by famine, and by pestilence; they shall have no remnant or survivor from the evil which I will bring upon them.'

---

[7] MT *wayᵉhī . . . wayᵉhī*, 'and it happened . . . that (the word) came': an unusual variation on the formulaic reception of the divine word introduction. Apart from the double *wayᵉhī* caused by the temporal phrase preceding the formal statement, the passage of time indicator is unique in the book of Jeremiah (cf. 28.12, where the precise amount of time is *not* indicated). Cf. 33.1; 35.12; 43.8 for the formulaic phrase and 1.4, 11, 13; 2.1; 16.1 for its variant form. **[8]** Cf. v. 2; 6.13; 8.10; 16.6; 31.34 for variations of the phrase 'from the smallest to the greatest'. **[9]** G much shorter: *kai eipen autois outōs eipe kurios*, 'and he said to them Thus says the lord'. **[10]** MT *'im-šōb tēšᵉbū*, 'if you will surely stay': correcting MT scribal error *šōb* to *yāšōb*, cf. Vrs. The verbs 'build' (*bnh*), 'pull down' (*hrs*), 'plant' (*nṭ'*), 'pluck up' (*ntš*) are those of 1.10; cf. 18.7–9, where they are also employed in conjunction with divine repentance (*nḥm*). **[11]** Cf. 40.9 for the motifs of fearing the Chaldaeans and serving the king of Babylon. The motif of the divine presence in deliverance appears in 1.8, 19b. **[12]** MT *wᵉriḥam 'etkem*, 'and he will have mercy on you': G *kai eleēsō humas*, 'and I will have mercy on you'. MT *wᵉhēšīb 'etkem 'el-'admatkem*, 'and he will restore you to your land': G *kai epistrepsō* . . . 'and *I* will restore . . .'; this may reflect an exilic perspective (cf. Bright, 256) but could also be a statement about the displacement of the people at Bethlehem (cf. 41.17–18; Rudolph, 254). **[14]** G lacks MT *lē'mōr lō'*, 'saying No'. **[16]** Cf. 39.5 (*wayyaśśigū*) for the image of the sword *overtaking* (*taśśīg*) those who flee away. MT *wᵉhārā'āb . . . šām yidbaq 'aḥᵃrēkem*, 'and the hunger . . . there shall cleave after you': i.e. cling to you wherever you go. BHS reads *w^e^hāyāh* for *w^e^hay^e^tāh* and suggests *b^e^miṣraim*, '*in* Egypt', for MT *miṣraim* '(to?) Egypt'. **[17]** MT *w^e^yihyū*, 'and they (died)': better as BHS *w^e^hāyāh*, 'and it shall be', i.e. come to pass (cf. v. 16). G also has 'and all the strangers' after 'all the men' = *w^e^kol-hazzārīm* (cf. *hazzēdīm*, 'the insolent', 43.2). Cf. Thiel 1981, 63, on v. 17 as a Deuteronomistic element; for the triad sword, famine, pestilence, cf. 14.12; 21.7, 9; 24.10; 27.8, 13; 29.17–18; 32.24, 36; 34.17; 38.2; 42.22; 44.13.

The passivity of Jeremiah is a dominant element in Part IV (broken only in 39.16, where the command is anomalous), and nowhere is it more obvious than in 42.7, where Jeremiah waits ten days for the divine word to come to him. The figure who moves about so much in Part I becomes quite passive in Part III and almost inert in Part IV. Things happen to him more frequently and he is more the victim of circumstances than an activist. This representation of him reflects his status as bearer of the divine word: a word whose bearer is rendered otiose, once it has been rejected (cf. 36.23–26; 37.1–2). Even in this story of the community's consultation with him, he must wait for the word to come to him instead of being the one who possesses it and delivers it without delay (cf. 28.12, where his passivity is also an element in the story). No details are given about his techniques for receiving the word (contrast Num. 22.38–23.5; 24.1–3; II Kings 3.14–16); only the length of time it took for the communication to occur (cf. the passage of time in the visions of Daniel: Dan. 8.15–17, 27; 9.1–2, 20–3; 10.1–21). Speculations about the time factor in v. 7 would be too eisegetical for sound interpretation, but the movement away from the presentation of Jeremiah as the one to whom the word comes before he acts towards the figure of the one who seeks the word in order to speak to a particular situation should be noted. It is not a movement developed in the tradition in an articulated way, but here it is consonant with the passivity of Jeremiah as a major feature of Part IV.

On reception of the divine word Jeremiah summons the community along with its leaders and addresses a sermon to all of them. The sending (*šlḥ*) motif which plays a large part in the tradition is used in v. 9 in a rather different manner: it is the community which *sends* Jeremiah to Yahweh with its supplication (cf. v. 21, where Yahweh *sends* Jeremiah with the answer; 43.1). The answer to that inquiry is set out in vv. 10–17 in terms of possible alternatives. Yahweh's intention towards the community is positive – he will create the conditions for normal life in the land (using the motifs of 1.10, 'building', 'planting', to convey this message). This change of attitude towards the community is due to divine repentance (*nḥm*), which reveals a change of mind by Yahweh. Recent devastations of the community ('pulling down', 'plucking up', cf. 1.10) belong to the past of which the deity repents. Such a figure as repentance used of Yahweh simply asserts a change of attitude and policy (cf. 18.8, 10) and represents the standard anthropomorphic language used of the deity by biblical writers. It is unwise to single out the repentance motif for a criticism of such language and it is unnecessary for exegetes to be peculiarly sensitive to this particular metaphor (I Sam. 15.11, 29, 35 suggest that such sensitivity is an ancient problem). All language about god is metaphorical and problematic, but no biblical exegesis would be possible if certain metaphors were singled out for criticism. Repentance is a human activity also posited of the deity, and one means of expressing the view that the past need not be overdeterminative of the future. It is the language of possibility and renewal, and when used of the deity indicates such changes in his attitude towards the community that its future becomes an open one. A good future is now possible for the people.

The conditionality of this future is an important element in the sermon. *If* is the opening word of v. 10. *If* the people are prepared to remain (*šūb*) in their own land, then a positive future is a possibility. The factors operating against that future are dismissed as inconsequential: divine hostility is gone (cf. 29.11); fear of the emperor is to be displaced by divine protection and mercy (v. 12: G and MT differ about *who* shows mercy and *who* permits residence in the land). If the people can overcome their legitimate fears about the consequences of the Babylonian reaction to the assassination of Gedaliah (whether this is the point of v. 11 is difficult to determine, but may be understood implicitly to be so because of the present editing of 41–42), then a secure residence in Judah is possible. If, on the other hand, the people are determined to flee to Egypt, then their future will be disastrous, even though there are very good reasons for leaving Judah: safety, food and security. There in Egypt they will encounter all the evils they had left Judah to avoid (v. 16). The familiar triad – sword, famine, pestilence – will destroy them in Egypt. Thus the sermon is typical of the sermons in the tradition (e.g. 7.3–7; 11.3–5; 18.7–10; 22.3–5) which present the future in terms of either-or: *either* the people must behave in a particular fashion *or* they face destruction. In this form of the sermon the alternatives are: *either* stay in Judah and live *or* go to Egypt and perish (a reversal of the options offered in 21.8–10!). The positive future lies in the land of Judah or nowhere. Yahweh's repentance only holds good for life in Judah – elsewhere his intention is evil (v. 17).

42.18–22

18 'For thus says the LORD of hosts, the God of Israel: As my anger and my
wrath were poured out on the inhabitants of Jerusalem, so my wrath will
be poured out on you when you go to Egypt. You shall become an execration,
a horror, a curse, and a taunt. You shall see this place no more. 19 The
LORD has said to you, O remnant of Judah, "Do not go to Egypt." Know
for a certainty that I have warned you this day 20 that you have gone astray
at the cost of your lives. For you sent me to the LORD your God, saying,
"Pray for us to the LORD our God, and whatever the LORD our God says
declare to us and we will do it." 21 And I have this day declared it to you,
but you have not obeyed the voice of the LORD your God in anything that
he sent me to tell you. 22 Now therefore know for a certainty that you shall
die by the sword, by famine, and by pestilence in the place where you desire
to go to live.'

---

[18] G lacks 'of hosts'. Cf. 44.12 for the same four epithets 'execration', 'horror', 'curse', 'taunt'; three of the four appear in 29.18; and two in 24.9; 25.18 (all these references use four epithets). The outpouring of the divine anger motif occurs in 7.20; 44.6; cf. 32.31; 33.5; 36.7. For the curses of Egypt cf. Deut. 28.15–68. **[19]** Because Rudolph, 256, and Bright, 252, read 43.1–3 between 42.18 and 19, they insert the phrase 'and Jeremiah said' at the beginning of v. 19 (cf. BHS). G has *kai nun*, 'and now', before 'know for a certainty', i.e. surely know (*yādo'a tēdeʿū*). G lacks 'that I have warned you this day'. **[20]** K *ht'tym*; Q *hit'ētemy* 'you have erred' (K a scribal error); MT *hit'ētem benapšōtēkem*, lit. 'you have erred at the cost of your lives'. G *eponēreusasthe en psuchais humōn*, 'you have done wickedness in your souls' = *harē'ōtem* for *hit'ētem*. G lacks 'to the lord your god', 'our god', and 'our god so declare to us'. The sending (*šlḥ*) motif dominates the chapter, cf. vv. 5, 6, 9, 20, 21; cf. 43.1, 2. **[21]** G lacks 'and I have declared to you this day', 'your god', and *ulekol*, 'and concerning everything'. **[22]** G lacks 'know for a certainty that'. See Notes on v. 17, for the triad sword, famine, pestilence.

Some commentators favour transposing 43.1–3 between 42.18 and 19 in order to sharpen the force of the dialogue (e.g. Bright, 258), but the expansion of the prose of 42 is such that it is hardly necessary to rearrange the chapter to improve its logic. 42.18–22 appears to anticipate the people's refusal to listen to Jeremiah and their determination to go to Egypt. These points are not made until 43.1–3, but the editors have already introduced the going to Egypt motif in 41.17 and have expanded it in 42.13–17. The attention of the hearers of the tradition is therefore well prepared for the people's response in 43.2–3. In devising and expanding the sermon of 42.9–22 the editing has focused on the choice between staying in the land of Judah and going to the land of Egypt. 42.18–22 is a further statement about the journey to Egypt which describes Egypt in terms drawn from the tradition about the fate of Jerusalem. 43.4–7 will deal with the actual flight to Egypt, but 42.18–22 hammers out the consequences of that possibility. Thus 42.9–22 is made up of three verses about the benefits of remaining in the land of Judah and ten verses about the horrors of going to Egypt (cf. the proportion of blessings to curses in Deut. 28).

In vv. 18–22 Jeremiah is presented as a faithful warner of the community. He addresses the people: 'O remnant of Judah – Do not go to Egypt' and this warning is reinforced by reassurances that such a journey will most certainly (vv. 19, 22) result in the forfeiture of the people's lives. The horror expressed about going to Egypt reflects the anti-Egyptian outlook behind Deut. 28 (cf. Mayes 1979, 348–51, for discussion of the post-Deuteronomistic aspects of this chapter) and the antipathy towards all things Egyptian held by certain circles in Judah. In going to Egypt the people would appear to be reversing the original divine act of redemption which brought the people out of Egypt. In Deuteronomistic circles such an apostate act was unthinkable, and contrary to divine command (cf. Deut. 17.16b; 28.68a). Hence to go to Egypt was to enter into the realm of the curse and to become an execration oneself (vv. 18b; 44.12). Merely by fleeing to Egypt the people would bring down upon their own heads the wrath of Yahweh; that very wrath which had destroyed Jerusalem so recently.

The emphasis by the people on their willingness to obey (vv. 5–6) can now be seen to be a literary device of the editors whereby the enormity of the people's disobedience is underlined (vv. 13, 21). In going to Egypt they will never see the land of Judah again (v. 18), but they will die (vv. 16, 17, 20, 22) without any survivors (v. 17b). Thus the remnant of Gedaliah's community is presented as tottering on the brink of annihilation. Will they be so foolhardy as to go to Egypt?

43.1–7

43[1] When Jeremiah finished speaking to all the people all these words of the LORD their God, with which the LORD their God had sent him to them, 2 Azariah the son of Hoshaiah and Johanan the son of Kareah and all the insolent men said to Jeremiah, 'You are telling a lie. The LORD our God did not send you to say, "Do not go to Egypt to live there"; 3 but Baruch the son of Neriah has set you against us, to deliver us into the hand of the Chaldeans, that they may kill us or take us into exile in Babylon.' 4 So Johanan the son of Kareah and all the commanders of the forces and all the people did not obey the voice of the LORD, to remain in the land of Judah. 5 But Johanan the son of Kareah and all the commanders of the forces took all the remnant of Judah who had returned to live in the land of Judah from all the nations to which they had been driven – 6 the men, the women, the children, the princesses, and every person whom Nebuzaradan the captain of the guard had left with Gedaliah the son of Ahikam, son of Shaphan; also Jeremiah the prophet and Baruch the son of Neriah. 7 And they came into the land of Egypt, for they did not obey the voice of the LORD. And they arrived at Tahpanhes.

[MT 43] = G 50. **[1]** G lacks both occurrences of 'their god'. Cf. 42.5 for the motif of Yahweh sending (*šlḥ*) Jeremiah to the people. **[2]** Cf. 42.1 for these two figures (G Azariah the son of *Maasaeas*). MT *wᵉkol-hā'ᵃnāšîm hazzēdîm*, 'and all the insolent men': G lacks 'insolent'; MT anticipates the community's answer to Jeremiah. MT *'ōmᵉrîm*, '(they) say': G *hoi eipantes*, 'who say' = *hā'ōmᵉrîm* (MT lit. 'and Azariah . . . said . . . and all the men . . . say'); Giesebrecht, 220, reads as *wᵉhammōrîm* '(insolent) and rebellious' cf BHS. G has *legontes*, 'saying', after 'to Jeremiah'. MT *šeqer 'attāh mᵉdabbēr*, 'falsehood you are speaking': G lacks 'you are speaking'; cf. 40.16 for a similar accusation. MT *'ᵉlōhēhû*, 'our god': G *pros hēmas*, 'to us' = *'ēlēhû*. **[3]** MT *massît 'ōtᵉkā bānû*, 'has incited you against us': *sût* instigated or seduced, cf. 38.22; Deut. 13.7 (EV 6); Job 2.3. NEB better than RSV. **[5]** G lacks 'from all the nations to which they had been driven there' and reads *en tē gē*, 'in the land', for MT *bᵉ'ereṣ yᵉhûdāh*, 'in the land of Judah'; cf. 40.12. **[6]** MT *'et-haggᵉbārîm* 'the men': G *tous dunatous andras*, 'the mighty men', cf. 41.16b. MT *wᵉ'et-bᵉnôt hammelek*, 'and the daughters of the king': as in 41.10, i.e. the princesses. Both MT and G read 'Jeremiah *the prophet*'. **[7]** Tahpanhes (*taḥpanḥēs*): cf. 2.16; 44.1; Daphne, modern tell Defneh, in north-east Egypt.

The response of the community to Jeremiah's presentation of the options available to them contains a fine irony. They accuse him of telling a lie (*šeqer*). This accusation against Jeremiah is highly ironic in a book which represents him as constantly accusing other people of speaking lies (*šeqer*, e.g. 8.8; 9.4 [EV 5]; 14.14; 23.25, 26, 32; 28.15; 29.21). It also demonstrates how easily the accusation may be made against any speaker and how prejudiced a judgment it may be. Further irony may be glimpsed in the explanation offered in v. 3 that behind Jeremiah's false speaking is the figure of Baruch ben Neriah. This accusation that Baruch has incited (*sūt*) Jeremiah to lie is ironic in that throughout the book of Jeremiah the prophet is always presented as a man quite capable of acting on his own initiative (i.e. at Yahweh's command). Yet the irony is in keeping with the depiction of Jeremiah as a passive figure in Part IV. Only at the instigation of some other person may he be regarded as becoming active in these stories. A conspiracy is detected behind his advocacy of staying in Judah rather than fleeing to Egypt. That conspiracy is attributed to Baruch, and the accusation itself may represent the suspicion that Jeremiah and Baruch have plans for self-aggrandisement in advocating such a policy. They certainly could be expected to benefit from the Babylonian reaction to the assassination of Gedaliah because they were not implicated in it (hence their complete absence from that part of the story?). Johanan and Azariah would most likely face the wrath of the Babylonians and could expect to die for their failure to protect the Babylonians' appointee. The other people would have to face deportation to Babylon (cf. v. 3). These legitimate fears account for the rejection of Jeremiah's warnings against going to Egypt, though they do not explain why Baruch is accused of inciting Jeremiah to adopt such a standpoint.

The sudden appearance of Baruch in this story is inexplicable. Up to this stage of Part IV he is completely absent from the story of Jeremiah, but now he is introduced into the story in order to explain why the prophet is so hostile towards the plan to go to Egypt. Jeremiah's claim to be speaking Yahweh's words is rejected as falsehood (*šeqer*), and the hand of Baruch is detected behind his words. Why should that be? Where was Baruch during the fall of Jerusalem? Where has he been during the period when Gedaliah was organizing the community and after the assassination? Where was he when the people consulted Jeremiah? Chapter 45 attempts to answer the question about Baruch's survival of the destruction of

Jerusalem, but all the other questions (like so many questions raised by a serious reading of the tradition) cannot be answered *from the text*. Baruch appears very infrequently in the book of Jeremiah and his appearance in 43.3 (cf. v. 6) may be regarded as part of that process whereby the tradition created and developed a subsidiary figure to accompany Jeremiah at certain points of the story (e.g. 32.12–13, 16; 36; 45). What Baruch represents in the story-telling pattern of the tradition is a debatable matter (cf. Wanke 1971, 154–6; Pohlmann 1978, 198–204), but, rejecting the theory that he is the author of much of the book, whatever view is taken of him he remains a very *minor* figure in the story of Jeremiah. His surfacing in that story at 43.3, 6 reflects the creation of a secondary character whose role is far from being well defined and who therefore remains an aleatory figure in the book.

The outcome of the rejection of Jeremiah's stand against going to Egypt is the journeying of everybody, including Jeremiah and Baruch, to the land of the curses. Although v. 5 represents the whole community, i.e. all the remnant of Judah, as going to Egypt, this should be read as an ideological rather than a literal statement. It can hardly be maintained that the land of Judah was completely denuded of people and that everybody went to Egypt. The groups of people associated with Johanan ben Kareah may have fled to Egypt, but all the other groups of people left throughout the land of Judah must have remained (cf. Lam. 5). This analysis would appear to be confirmed by the deportation of seven hundred and forty-five people to Babylon in 582 (52.30); a deportation which may have been the result of the assassination of Gedaliah. The impression is given in 40.7 – 43.7 that everybody in the land associated themselves with Gedaliah and that therefore the whole remnant of Judah went into exile to Egypt. If such an impression is intentional, then it must reflect the ideology of the editors, who wish to write off all the people left in Judah (cf. 39.9–10; 52.15–16). Such an ideological presentation is in keeping with the sermon of 42.9–22, which offers divine protection to the remnant of Judah and then in 43.1–3 indicts the remnant for rejecting that offer. The actual people (among whom it may be supposed were those who would be deported in 582) who went on living in the land of Judah are of no interest to the editors. Jeremiah and Baruch go to Egypt or, more precisely, are taken to Egypt, and the editorial attention focuses on that area. What remains behind in Judah ceases to have any significance for the tradition and may be deemed not to exist. But this non-existence should not be confused with social reality; it is but an ideological blank space in the tradition.

With the descent of the people to Egypt the story of Gedaliah's community comes to an end. What follows in 43.8–13 and 44 is a number of statements against Egypt and the Jewish commun*ities* in Egypt, but the groups which constituted Gedaliah's community are no longer the subject of the tradition. The great hopes associated with Gedaliah are dead, and the possibility of a renewed people in the land of Judah is now in the past. As if to emphasize the passivity of Jeremiah, he is not only accused of being Baruch's puppet (or ventriloquist's dummy) but is taken to Egypt (presumably cf. 42.13–22) against his wishes. Thus he becomes a pathetic victim of other people's fears and plans and is branded a liar into the bargain. Those who go to Egypt, including Jeremiah and Baruch, now enter the area of the curses and cannot hope for anything other than a miserable life under Yahweh's curses – 'and you shall become an execration, a horror, a curse, and a taunt' (42.18b). This, then, is the fate of Jeremiah – the victim of other men's incompetence and plans. But the tradition is not concerned with his fate – this is not a biography of Jeremiah – so the account of the people's flight to Egypt only mentions the taking of Jeremiah and Baruch there in passing (e.g. v. 6c). All those who go to Egypt are enclosed in the editorial condemnation 'they did not obey the voice of Yahweh' (v. 7). Thus under disobedience and the aweful power of the curses uttered by Jeremiah against going to Egypt Gedaliah's community face a future without hope after the shattering of their hopes for life in the land of Judah.

43.8–13

8 Then the word of the LORD came to Jeremiah in Tahpanhes: 9 'Take in your hands large stones, and hide them in the mortar in the pavement which is at the entrance to Pharaoh's palace in Tahpanhes, in the sight of the men of Judah, 10 and say to them, "Thus says the LORD of hosts, the God of Israel: Behold, I will send and take Nebuchadrezzar the king of Babylon, my servant, and he will set his throne above these stones which I have hid, and he will spread his royal canopy over them. 11 He shall come and smite the land of Egypt, giving to the pestilence those who are doomed to the pestilence, to captivity those who are doomed to captivity, and to the sword

those who are doomed to the sword. 12 He shall kindle a fire in the temples of the gods of Egypt; and he shall burn them and carry them away captive; and he shall clean the land of Egypt, as a shepherd cleans his cloak of vermin; and he shall go away from there in peace. 13 He shall break the obelisks of Heliopolis which is in the land of Egypt; and the temples of the gods of Egypt he shall burn with fire." '

---

[8] Cf. 33.1; 35.12; 42.7 for this form of the reception of the divine word formulaic introduction. Jeremiah's reception of the word in Egypt maintains his prophetic status there and is a form of the OAN strand in the tradition (cf. 46; 51.59–64). **[9]** MT *qaḥ*, 'take': cf. 25.15; 36.2; negative command (*lō'-tiqqaḥ*, 'do not take') in 16.2. MT *bammeleṭ bammalbēn ᵓašer*, 'in the cement, in the brick-mould which': lacking in G; meaning of Hebrew uncertain, cf. NEB 'in cement in the pavement'; JPSB 'in mortar in the brick structure'. The word *meleṭ* only occurs here and may mean 'mortar, cement', cf. Bright, 259, 'in the clay flooring [?]'; *malbēn* appears in II Sam. 12.31, where it may refer to 'brick-making', and Nahum 3.14 'brick-mould', where it may mean 'terrace of bricks' (cf. KB, 527; KB³ II, 555f.; Driver 1937–38, 122; 'quadrangle', BDB 527); The two words are variants in MT; G *en prothurois*, 'in the vestibule'. A, Theod. *en tō kruphiō*, 'in secret'. Rudolph, 258, regards *malbēn* as a dittography of *meleṭ*, 'clay soil' (cf. BHS). MT *lᵉʿênê ᵓanāšîm yᵉhûdîm*, 'in the sight of the men of Judah': lit. 'to the eyes of the men, the Jews'; cf. 28.1, 5, 11, where words and actions are performed *in the sight of* various social strata. **[10]** G lacks 'of hosts, the god of Israel'. G lacks 'my servant' in the phrase 'Nebuchadrezzar the king of Babylon', cf. 25.9; 27.6, where the fullest form of the phrase appears in MT but the whole phrase is lacking in G 25.9. G 34.6 lacks 'my servant', but has *douleuein autō*, 'to serve him', which may reflect MT (cf. Tov 1979, 83–4) which, in turn, probably influenced 43.10 (se Notes on 27.6). MT *wᵉśamtî*, 'and *I* will place': G *kai thēsei*, 'and *he* will place' = *wᵉśām*. MT *ṭāmāntî*, '*I* have hid': G *katekrupsas*, '*you* have hid'. K *šprwrw*; Q *šaprîrô*: the word only occurs here and is of doubtful meaning; possible meanings are 'canopy, pavilion, carpet' (cf. BDB, 1051). **[11]** K *wb'h*; Q *ûbā'*, 'and he will come'. Cf. 15.2 for the incantatory words *ᵓašer lammāwet lammāwet waᵓašer laššebî laššebî waᵓašer laḥereb leḥāreb*, 'those who are for death to death, those who are for captivity to captivity, and those who are for the sword to the sword'. Rudolph suggests the last motif (sword) may be an addition (cf. BHS), as there is no essential difference between death and the sword. RSV, JPSB translate *māwet* respectively as 'pestilence', 'plague', which distinguishes it from 'sword' = death. The terms in the list are stereotypes, cf. 15.2 (death, sword, hunger, captivity) and reflect the magical performance of Jeremiah. **[12]** MT *wᵉhiṣṣattî*, 'and *I* will kindle': Vrs 'and *he* will kindle' = *wᵉhiṣṣît*; cf. other verbs '*he* will burn them' or '*he* will carry them captive'. Here 'them' must refer to the gods (i.e. the idols) rather than the temples in which the fires are kindled. MT *wᵉʿāṭāh*, 'and he will wrap himself up': i.e. as a shepherd wraps himself up in his garment, so king Nebuchadrezzar will wrap himself up in the land of Egypt. This is a graphic image of Babylon's complete domination of Egypt, cf. JPSB. G *phtheiriei*, 'search for lice': i.e. as a shepherd searches his garment for lice, cf. RSV, NEB; this suggests *ʿāṭāh*, 'grasp, pick' (cf. Isa. 22.17), rather than *ʿāṭāh*, 'wrap oneself'. Rudolph favours 'delouse', cf. BHS. The image of Nebuchadrezzar departing in peace (*bᵉšālōm*) may favour G imagery. **[13]** MT *ʾet-maṣṣᵉbōt bēt šemeš*, 'the standing stones of Beth-shemesh': i.e. the sacred pillars of the house of the sun; G *tous stulous Hēlioupoleōs*, the pillars of Heliopolis. MT *ʾᵃšer bᵉʾereṣ miṣrāyim*, 'which is in Egypt': written from a Palestinian perspective. G *tous en Ōn*, 'which are in On': a double rendering Heliopolis – On. Giesebrecht, 221, treats MT as a late gloss to distinguish the *bēt šemeš* which is in Egypt from the Palestinian one. MT *wᵉʾet-bātē ʾᵉlōhē-miṣrayim*, 'and the houses of the gods of Egypt': i.e. the temples, but G *kai tas oikias autōn*, 'and their houses' (= *bātēhem*), may be a more general reference to the houses of the town, as the burning of the temples is referred to in v. 12 (cf. Giesebrecht).

In Egypt the divine word comes to Jeremiah and he becomes active once more in the performance of a magical act. He is commanded to take large stones and hide them somewhere in the area of the door of the Pharaoh's house (i.e. his official residence when visiting that part of Egypt) in Tahpanhes. This strange performance is to be carried out in the sight of the Jews who fled with Jeremiah to that town. The words accompanying this magic act are given in vv. 10–13 so that the witnesses understand what is happening. The dramatic actions of carrying large stones and burying (?) them in the brick terracing outside the royal residence must have bewildered the onlookers. Whether the performance should be regarded as a literal one (how would the Egyptian guards have responded to a foreigner digging up their premises?) or an enactment elsewhere with theatrical overtones is a moot point. But the spoken words explaining the meaning of the action clarify whatever obscurities cloak the action depicted in v. 9. Jeremiah's transportation of stones to the royal residence in Tahpanhes signifies Yahweh's sending (*šlḥ*) and taking of Nebuchadrezzar (Yahweh's servant in MT) to Egypt where he will set up his throne on the very spot where Jeremiah hid the stones. Thus Jeremiah brings Nebuchadrezzar to Egypt by his performative magic. To this explanation of the drama vv. 11–13 add a number of details: the Babylonian invasion of Egypt will devastate the land and its people will be consigned to death or deportation (cf. 15.2). This incantation chanted over the land of Egypt effectively brings about the destruction of the people (cf. 51.59–64, where Babylon is similarly spoken against). The temples of the gods of Egypt will be fired and Nebuchadrezzar will have complete control over Egyptian territory (cf. G and MT images in v. 12). The obelisks of Heliopolis will be shattered also and the houses burned. These details are only given in the spoken part of the ritual action – they are the meaning of the incantatory aspects of Jeremiah's performance.

Thus the first act of Jeremiah in Egypt is to bring about its destruction. Such ritual magic (cf. 46) is characteristic of the presentation of Jeremiah in certain strands of the tradition (e.g. 13.1–11; 19.1–2, 10–11; 25.15–17; 51.59–64). He creates and presides over the annihilation of the enemy (e.g. Judah, Jerusalem, Egypt, Babylon) by his performance of certain acts accompanied by incantation, curses and magical utterances. Each of the victims of his actions in due course undergoes the fate conjured up for it. The extent to which Egypt suffered a devastating invasion by the Babylonians is debatable because the evidence for the Babylonian incursion into Egypt suggests a military campaign to curb Egyptian interference in Babylonian matters rather than a punitive campaign of destruction (e.g. Pharaoh Amasis appears to have retained his throne and to have established friendly relations with Babylon; cf Pritchard 1969, 308). However, the important thing in the tradition is not the historicity of these acts but the power of the word manipulated by Jeremiah and linked to his performative magic. The condemnation of Egypt epitomized by the act of v. 9 is part of the strong anti-Egyptian strand in the book at this point (42.13–22; 43.8–13; 44; 46). By presenting this strand in conjunction with one of Jeremiah's formidable magic acts accompanied by incantation (v. 11), the editors increase the force of the rejection of the community which fled to Egypt. No sooner have they fled from the potential threat of Babylon in the land of Judah (42.11–12) than they must face Yahweh's sending for Nebuchadrezzar to invade the very land to which they fled in order to avoid him! Their disobedience against the warnings of Jeremiah has trapped them in a place where Yahweh's wrath is about to descend.

44.1–14

44 1 The word that came to Jeremiah concerning all the Jews that dwelt in
the land of Egypt, at Migdol, at Tahpanhes, at Memphis, and in the land
of Pathros, 2 'Thus says the LORD of hosts, the God of Israel: You have seen
all the evil that I brought upon Jerusalem and upon all the cities of Judah.
Behold, this day they are a desolation, and no one dwells in them, 3 because
of the wickedness which they committed, provoking me to anger, in that
they went to burn incense and serve other gods that they knew not, neither
they, nor you, nor your fathers. 4 Yet I persistently sent to you all my
servants the prophets, saying, "Oh, do not do this abominable thing that I
hate!" 5 But they did not listen or incline their ear, to turn from their
wickedness and burn no incense to other gods. 6 Therefore my wrath and
my anger were poured forth and kindled in the cities of Judah and the streets
of Jerusalem; and they became a waste and a desolation, as at this day. 7
And now thus says the LORD God of hosts, the God of Israel: Why do you
commit this great evil against yourselves, to cut off from you man and
woman, infant and child, from the midst of Judah, leaving you no remnant?
8 Why do you provoke me to anger with the works of your hands, burning
incense to other gods in the land of Egypt where you have come to live, that
you may be cut off and become a curse and a taunt among all the nations
of the earth? 9 Have you forgotten the wickedness of your fathers, the
wickedness of the kings of Judah, the wickedness of their wives, your own
wickedness, and the wickedness of your wives, which they committed in the
land of Judah and in the streets of Jerusalem? 10 They have not humbled
themselves even to this day, nor have they feared, nor walked in my law
and my statutes which I set before you and before your fathers.

11 Therefore thus says the Lord of hosts, the God of Israel: Behold, I will
set my face against you for evil, to cut off all Judah. 12 I will take the
remnant of Judah who have set their faces to come to the land of Egypt to
live, and they shall all be consumed; in the land of Egypt they shall fall; by
the sword and by famine they shall be consumed; from the least to the
greatest, they shall die by the sword and by famine; and they shall become
an execration, a horror, a curse and a taunt. 13 I will punish those who
dwell in the land of Egypt, as I punished Jerusalem, with the sword, with
famine, and with pestilence, 14 so that none of the remnant of Judah who
have come to live in the land of Egypt shall escape or survive or return to
the land of Judah, to which they desire to return to dwell there; for they
shall not return, except some fugitives.'

[MT 44] = G 51. 1–30. **[1]** Cf. 25.1 for the reception of the divine word formula. The site of Migdol is uncertain, but it may be near Tahpanhes (to the east of it, cf. Rudolph, 258; Ex. 14.2). MT *ūb*^{e}*nōp*, 'and in Memphis': cf.

2.16; lacking in G. Memphis was the capital of Lower Egypt. Pathros was in Upper Egypt. These towns and areas represent Jewish communities which had settled in Egypt over a long period and 44.1 should not be read as a continuation of 43.8–13. **[2]** G lacks 'this day' and 'of hosts'. The representation of the cities of Judah as a waste or ruin (*ḥorbāh*) reflects the belief that during the exile there were no people living in the land of Judah (cf. II Chron. 36.21; but cf. Lam. 5). This belief favoured the exiles in Babylon (24.4–7) because it left the land vacant for their return. Cf. 25.11; 34.22; 35.17; 36.31; 40.2–3 for the motifs of evil and desolation in operation against Jerusalem and Judah. **[3]** G lacks 'to serve': MT *leqaṭṭēr laʿabōd*, 'to burn to serve', is overloaded. It is better to understand *qṭr*, 'burn', as in 'offer sacrifice', cf. NEB, JPSB, rather than 'burn incense', cf. 1.16; 7.9. MT *ʾašer lōʾ yedāʿūm*, 'which they did not know them': G *hois ouk egnōte*, 'which you did not know'. MT adds *hēmmāh ʾattem waʾabōtēkem*, 'they, you, and your fathers': cf. 2.5–9, where different generations are accused of such behaviour. It is an absurd feature of these sermons that the nation is accused of persistent idolatry throughout their existence yet always in terms of gods which they have not known! Either they worshipped them constantly or they did not know them, but hardly both. Cf. 7.9; 19.4 for the unknown gods motif. **[4]** Cf. 7.25; 26.5; 29.19; 35.15 for the motif of sending Yahweh's servants the prophets (*haškēm wešālōaḥ*, 'rising early and sending'). Here the function of the prophets is reduced to warnings against 'this matter of abomination' (*ʾet debar-hattōʿēbāh hazzōʾt*), i.e. idolatry; cf. 7.10; 32.35; 44.22 for the motif 'doing this (these) abomination(s)'. **[5]** Cf. 7.13b, 26; 11.8; 25.4, 7; 29.19; 34.14; 35.14, 15 for the motif of not listening. The point made about *qṭr* in v. 3 applies throughout 44 (e.g. vv. 5, 8, 15, 17, 18, 19, 21, 24). **[6]** Cf. v. 2. MT *leḥorbāh lišmāmāh*, 'a ruin a waste': possibly variants, but some mss, Vrs read 'a ruin *and* a waste'. Cf. 42.18 for the pouring out of the divine wrath on Jerusalem; also 7.20 where the burning motif is associated with the outpouring of anger. Cf. 7.17, 34; 11.6; 33.10; 44.6, 9, 17, 21 for the phrase 'in the cities of Judah and in the streets of Jerusalem'. MT *kayyōm hazzeh*, 'as at this day': cf. vv. 22–23; 11.5; 25.18; 32.20. **[7]** MT *yhwh ʾelōhē ṣebāʾōt ʾelōhē yiśrāʾēl*, 'Yahweh god of hosts, god of Israel': G *kurios pantokratōr*, 'lord almighty', i.e. Yahweh of hosts. The evil (*rāʿāh*) committed here is different from that of v. 2 (Yahweh's evil); it refers to the moral injury that is self-inflicted through idolatry rather than the destruction caused by Yahweh (cf. Thiel 1981, 72). Cf. 27.13, 17 for the why question motif. MT *lebiltī hōtīr lākem šeʾērīt*, 'in order not to leave for yourselves a remnant': the motif of complete annihilation runs through this chapter (cf. vv. 12, 14, 27). **[8]** MT *lemaʿan hakrīt lākem ū*, 'in order to cut off yourselves and': an addition from v. 7? (cf. Rudolph, 260; BHS). Cf. 25.18; 42.18 for the motifs 'curse', 'taunt'; 7.18b–19 for the notion of provoking the deity to anger; 26.6, 'a curse for all the nations of the earth'; 25.6; 32.30 for provoking Yahweh to anger by the work of your/their hands (cf. Deut. 31.29; I Kings 16.7; II Kings 22.17 = II Chron. 34.25). The theme of settling in Egypt appears in vv. 8, 12, 14, 28; 42.15, 22. **[9]** MT *wᵉ'ēt rā'ōt nāšāyw*, 'and the evil of his wives': *nᵉšēhem*, 'their wives', is assumed by EVV; cf. BHS. I Kings 11.4; 15.13 indicate a plurality of wives; G *kai tōn kakōn tōn archontōn humōn*, 'and the evil of your princes', cf. vv. 17, 21. G lacks 'and your own evil'; S lacks 'and the evil of your wives'. For the rhetorical question of v. 9 cf. 3.6; 7.17. **[10]** MT *lō' dukkᵉū*, 'they were not crushed': cf. *mᵉdukkā'īm*, 'crushed', Isa. 19.10; meaning crushed by remorse, cf. NEB. G *kai ouk epausanto*, 'and have not ceased': = *niklᵉ'ū*? Vrs have different readings which suggest MT is uncertain; Rudolph, 260, *nik'ū* (*k'h*, Niph., 'be disheartened, cowed'), cf. Dan. 11.30; Ps. 109.16. G lacks 'nor have they feared'. MT *bᵉtōrātī ūbᵉḥuqqōtay*, 'in my law and in my statutes': G *ton prostagmatōn mou*, 'my ordinances' = *bᵉḥuqqōtay*. G lacks 'before them' and reads '*their* fathers' for MT '*your* fathers'. Cf. 9.13; 26.4; 32.23, for the motif of not walking in Yahweh's *tōrāh*. **[11]** G is briefer than MT: 'therefore thus says the lord behold I set my face'. Cf. 21.10 for the motif of setting the face against (city/people) for evil. **[12]** MT *baḥereb bārā'āb*, 'by sword, by famine': many mss, Vrs 'by sword *and* by famine', so RSV but cf. NEB, JPSB. Cf. vv. 18, 27 for the consumption (*tmm*) motif; 42.17, 18 for many of the elements in v. 12; also 21.9; 27.13; 38.2; 42.16, 22. In v. 11 Yahweh sets his face, in v. 12 the people set their faces (*śīm pānīm*, 'to set faces', idiom for determination); the same behaviour of deity and remnant leads to confrontation and only one party can win, cf. v. 28b 'whose word shall stand' (G, cf. MT, which spells out the point further). Cf. 42.18b for the fourfold designation of the remnant 'execration, horror, curse, taunt'. G has three terms rather than four. **[13]** Cf. 42.18a; the triad sword, famine, pestilence are to be found throughout the tradition, cf. Notes on 42.17. This verse forms a conclusion to Jeremiah's sermon by making an equation between the sins of the remnant in Egypt and those of the people of Jerusalem (cf. Thiel 1981, 73). G^BS lack 'pestilence'. **[14]** Cf. 42.17; a citation and paraphrase of 42.17b. G lacks *šām*, 'there' (to live in the land of Egypt) and 'to live', *lāšebet*. MT *kī lō'-yāšūbū kī 'im-pᵉlēṭīm*, 'for they shall not return except fugitives': the last phrase contradicts 14a, 'there shall be no fugitive (*pālīṭ*) or survivor (*śārīd*) belonging to the remnant of Judah'. It is regarded as a gloss by many commentators (e.g. Duhm, Volz, Rudolph, Bright); an addition to v. 14 in view of v. 28a, which asserts that a few will escape from Egypt and return to Judah. Cf. 22.27 for the phrase *'ᵃšer-hēmmāh mᵉnaśśᵉ'īm 'et-napšām lāšūb . . . lō'-yāšūbū*, 'to which they desire (lit. they lift up their souls) to return . . . they shall not return'.

A prolix sermon in 44 concludes Part IV in such a manner that it forms a closure with the equally long diatribe against idolatrous practices which opens Part I (i.e. chapter 2; 1 and 45 are parallel additions to the blocks forming the tradition). The long-winded discourse against involvement with other gods is addressed to the fugitive communities of Jews in the land of Egypt (both upper and lower parts of that land). Thus v. 1 is not a continuation of 42.13–22 but a more general attack on communal religion similar to the discourses of 2–3 which are addressed to 'all the families of the house of Israel' (2.4b). That so many communities should be scattered throughout the land of Egypt reflects a period when the Jews were well settled in Egypt and not the immediate aftermath of the fall of Jerusalem. Ideologically 44 sets out to deny divine favour to such communities and the sermon must be read as reflecting the interests of other groups. Whether those interests belong to the Jerusalem community (second temple period?) or the exiles in Babylon (cf. 24.4–7) cannot be determined from the text. The hostility towards Egypt is a feature of 42–44 which is shared by Deuteronomistic circles, and many elements in 44 point to a Deuteronomistic influence on the construction of the sermon (analysis in Thiel 1981, 69–81; cf. Pohlmann 1978, 166–82). The sermon is a mosaic of phrases and motifs drawn from many of the prose discourses in the book of Jeremiah, and there is little in 44 which represents an independent tradition (with the possible exception of v. 1).

Despite the prolix nature of the sermon it may be divided into a number of sections. In vv. 2–14 Jeremiah makes a lengthy statement, though hardly to all the different communities of Jews living throughout the land of Egypt (contrast v. 15b). This statement may be divided into three parts: vv. 2–6, 7–10, 11–14 (cf. Pohlmann 1978, 168–72). These parts consist of a review of the idolatrous past of Judah and Jerusalem which brought about the disaster of 587, an indictment of the people to whom the sermon is addressed, and a statement of Yahweh's punishment of the remnant of Judah now living in the land of Egypt. Each part is filled out by citations and paraphrases of pieces from elsewhere in the tradition. The key motifs in the sermon include the burning (*qiṭṭēr*) of sacrifices to other gods (vv. 3, 5, 8, 15, 17–19, 21, 23, 25), the fate of the remnant of Judah in Egypt (vv. 12, 14, 28), the lack of any survivors of the coming judgment (vv. 7, 11, 14, 27, 28), and the attack on the familial cults of the people (vv. 7, 9, 14, 20–21, 24–25). All these motifs may be found in the prose collections of 7.1–8.3; 11.1–13; 19.1–13; 25.1–7; 26.2–6; 32.23–35; 42.13–22, and only the setting of the sermon in

Egypt allows for nuances of variation in the handling of so many clichés.

There is no reason to assume that 44 represents an authentic sermon of Jeremiah preached to the many communities scattered throughout Egypt (*contra* Bright, 265). Such an assumption fails to recognize the redactional nature of v. 1 (cf. 7.1; 11.1; 18.1; 21.1; 30.1; 32.1; 34.1, 8; 35.1; 40.1) which renders what follows impossible as a literal performance. It also refuses to acknowledge the clichéd nature of the material constituting the sermon as an ideological rejection of 'unreal' situations, in the sense that the communities criticized are constructs of the tradition itself. There is nothing in 44 which permits a glimpse of the historical Jewish communities in Egypt, communities which were to be so important in the following centuries for the development of the Jewish religion. The fact that everything said about these communities in Egypt is also said at length about the people of Judah and Jerusalem is indicative of the ideological nature of 44. Ideology reduces all distinctions to the same level of unreal similarity in order to condemn discrete entities in blanket terms. Such an ideology can be detected in the writings of the Deuteronomistic school and other writings influenced by them (cf. Thiel 1981, 93–115). The central feature of Deuteronomistic ideology is the claim that the states of Israel and Judah were destroyed because of cultic and idolatrous practices. This claim is dominant in 44 and the prose sermons of the tradition, and it is difficult to deny a Deuteronomistic influence at some level in the construction of the book of Jeremiah. Even if the influence belongs to a post-Deuteronomistic level of tradition construction, the ideological handling of cultic malpractices and idolatrous beliefs owes much to the influence of the Deuteronomists.

To underline the importance of cultic purity and the avoidance of rituals tainted with paganism the sermon in 44 extends the critique of Judah and Jerusalem to the communities living in Egypt. The catastrophe of 587 is not viewed as the end of Yahweh's wrath (contrast 42.10–12) but a major instantiation of it. That wrath continues to burn against similar cultic practices, and no matter where they are cultivated the devotees of such cults are exposed to summary judgment. Two strands run through the sermon in its present form; v. 1 applies the sermon to all the communities in Egypt and vv. 11–14 refer it to the remnant (cf. 40.11 – 43.7) which fled to Egypt. To these two strands is added a midrashic section in vv. 15–29, 20–23, 25 which develops 7.17–19 as a particular example of idolatry leading to destruction. Throughout the sermon the state of the land of Judah is represented as a place where nobody lives any more (e.g. vv. 2, 6, 22). Such desolation is the result of idolatry, and it will befall the Jews who now live in Egypt. Thus the disasters of the past are used by the editors to present a case for their own ideological outlook. The association of the past with idolatry and disaster makes connections between ideology and history which must be viewed as part of a complex of arguments about the nature of cultic worship in the Persian period when the second temple became the focus of rival claims about power and control (cf. Haggai, Zechariah, Chronicles, Ezra-Nehemiah and Isa. 56–66).

The three parts of the sermon outline the history of the past (vv. 2–6) in terms of offering sacrifices to other gods, the persistent sending of the prophets, and the rejection of such messengers and the destruction of Jerusalem 'as at this day' (v. 6). The present is represented by vv. 7–10, which accuse those addressed of having forgotten such matters because they behave in the same way as their fathers and therefore endanger their own lives to the point of being cut off (*krt*) without any remainder (*šᵉʾērīt*, v. 7). The future (vv. 11–14) uses a word-play on the divine setting of the face against those who set their face to go to Egypt (vv. 11–12). That fate which befell Jerusalem will befall them (v. 13), and none will escape (v. 14). An additional phrase allows for a few fugitives to survive.

44.15–19

15 Then all the men who knew that their wives had offered incense to other gods, and all the women who stood by, a great assembly, all the people who dwelt in Pathros in the land of Egypt, answered Jeremiah: 16 'As for the word which you have spoken to us in the name of the Lord, we will not listen to you. 17 But we will do everything that we have vowed, burn incense to the queen of heaven and pour out libations to her, as we did, both we and our fathers, our kings and our princes, in the cities of Judah and in the streets of Jerusalem; for then we had plenty of food, and prospered, and saw no evil. 18 But since we left off burning incense to the queen of heaven and pouring out libations to her, we have lacked everything and have been consumed by the sword and by famine.' 19 And the women said, 'When we burned incense to the queen of heaven and poured out libations to her, was it without our husbands' approval that we made cakes for her bearing her image and poured out libations to her?'

[15] MT *qāhāl gādōl*, 'a great assembly': cf. 31.8 (26.17, *qᵉhal hā'ām*, 'assembly of people'); a great crowd or, more likely, the sacred congregation of worshippers. BHS suggests *qōl*, 'voice', for *qāhāl*. The clause 'and all the people who dwelt in the land of Egypt, in Pathros' is regarded as an addition (e.g. Rudolph, Bright, BHS) because it is most unlikely that all the people throughout Egypt attended Jeremiah's sermon. Rudolph, 260, regards it as a gloss to 'a great assembly'. S '*and* in Pathros': i.e. in (Lower) Egypt and Pathros (Upper Egypt), cf. Rudolph. **[16]** Cf. 43.1–2, where all the people also refuse to listen to Jeremiah. **[17]** MT *'et-kol-haddābār 'ᵃšer-yāṣā' mippīnū*, lit. 'everything which comes out of our mouth': idiomatic for vowing, cf. Num. 30.3, 13; 32.24; Judg. 11.36. Cf. v. 25, where *ndr*, 'vow', is used. MT *limᵉleket haššāmayim*, 'to the hosts of the heavens': many mss *lml'kt*; G *tē basilissē tou ouranou*, 'to the queen of heaven' = *lᵉmalkat* . . . cf. 7.18. The queen of heaven probably refers to some form of the Ishtar cult or Isis as she would be known in Egypt. **[18]** Cf. v. 17 for vocalization of 'queen of heaven'. G lacks 'and poured out libations to her'. MT *tāmᵉnū*, 'have consumed us': cf. vv. 12, 27 for this motif (*tmm*). **[19]** MT *wᵉkī-'ᵃnaḥnū*, 'and when we': G^{L} *kai hai gunaikes eipon hote kai*, 'and the women said and when', cf. S; = *wᵉhannāšīm 'āmᵉrū wᵉkī*. Cf. RSV, NEB but JPSB = MT. Vocalization of 'queen of heaven' as in vv. 17, 18. MT *lᵉha'ᵃṣibāh*, lit. 'to fashion': *h* lacks a mappiq, which would make the word mean 'to fashion *her*', i.e. shaping her image on the cakes or making the cakes in the shape representative of her.

The response to Jeremiah's sermon comes from a great assembly of people from *all over Egypt* (cf. S). MT identifies the location of the people as Pathros, i.e. Upper Egypt, but it is unlikely that people travelled from so far afield to hear a recent immigrant preach. This aspect of the response is part of the editorial story which represents Jeremiah as preaching a sermon on proper techniques of worship and the people as responding to him. In typical fashion (cf. 43.1–2) they refuse to listen to what he says (v. 16) and thereby condemn themselves as obdurate as well as apostate. The sermon requires no response as such, so the reply of the people in vv. 15–19 should be regarded as a development of the sermon along different lines. It singles out the motif of burning (*qṭr*) sacrifice to other gods (cf. vv. 3, 5, 8, 21, 23, 25) and has the men of the assembly defend the cultic practices of their wives (v. 15; cf. v. 9, where the behaviour of wives is also part of the indictment of history). However, vv. 17–18 represent the cult of the queen of heaven as a communal matter whereas vv. 15,19 (cf. S) present it as a feminine cult performed by the women with their men's approval (cf. v. 25). The discrepancy between these two viewpoints may be due to the rhetoric of the edition, especially in v. 17, where stereotypical language predominates.

At first sight vv. 15–19 look like a midrash on 7.17–18, but a scrutiny of both pieces will reveal significant differences. In 7.17–18 a familial cult involving all the members of the family is condemned, but in 44.15, 19 a feminine cult of devotion to the queen of heaven is singled out as an example of sacrificing to other gods. The two pieces have in common the queen of heaven motif and the pouring out of libations to her accompanied by cakes (*kawwānīm*) bearing her image (only in 44.19). They are clearly about the same cult, but the treatment of that cult is different in both places. The midrashic quality of the treatment is such that a common core may be presupposed for the story, but disparate contexts determine some of the differences. In 7.1 – 8.3 a collection of responses to cultic abuses prefaces an independent sub-block of material; in 44 a highly edited attack on idolatrous worship throughout history focuses in particular on the cult of the queen of heaven (e.g. vv. 17–19, 25). Like so many parallel accounts in the tradition (e.g. 7.1–15; 26 or 37–38) a common feature may be discerned in the stories, but on each occasion the form of the story is significantly different from other treatments of the material. In 7.17–18 the family cult devoted to the goddess is an example of the outrageous behaviour of the people in 'the cities of Judah and the streets of Jerusalem' and it provokes the deity to great anger (v. 20; in spite of the subtle argument of v. 19 about the self-injury of idolatry). In 44.17 the same cult is spoken of, but from the viewpoint of its participants. It refers to the past, to the time when the people practised such things 'in the cities of Judah and the streets of Jerusalem'. But in v. 18 there is a confession that the cult has not been active since those days. Thus the cult of vv. 17–18 has nothing to do with the charge in v. 8 of offering sacrifices to other gods in the land of Egypt! The tie-in between the two may be v. 15, but v. 19 is ambiguous in that it may refer to current activity or past behaviour (the participial form *mᵉqaṭṭᵉrīm* allows either, cf. 33.18). Reference to the men's knowledge of their wives' behaviour (v. 15. *hᵃmibbalʿᵃdē*, 'was it apart from?', in v. 19 is more oblique, but it implies that the men knew about the practice) makes the cult an exclusive female one, but implicates the men in the guilt attached to involvement with such other gods. It is, however, quite a different presentation from

7.17–18, where men and children are as involved in the cult of the queen of heaven as the women. Inconsistent editing is a major feature of the Jeremiah tradition (cf. McKane 1981), and evidence of that inconsistency may be detected in a comparison of 7. 17–18 and 44. 15, 19, 17–18.

In v. 17 the men (cf. v. 15 where MT is clearer than RSV 'then all the men answered Jeremiah') affirm that they will go on doing what they did when they lived in Judah. The break with the past of v. 18 is a temporary one, interrupted by the destruction of Jerusalem and the flight to Egypt no doubt, but the people are determined (v. 16 have vowed) to return to the old cultic ways which had worked so well in the past. A very interesting argument is put forward in vv. 17–18. In the past when the cult of the queen of heaven was in operation the community enjoyed prosperity (*ṭōbīm*), i.e. they had food and never saw disaster. But having desisted from the practice of that cult they have lacked everything (*kōl*), i.e. they have been consumed by sword and famine. The argument is essentially a *post hoc ergo propter hoc* one, but implicit in its presentation is the view that the cult of the queen of heaven guaranteed prosperity. Proof of that claim is to be found in the recent terrible disasters which befell the community when they abandoned the goddess. No account is given of that change, so it is not possible to determine whether a new cult policy had been adopted or the old practice allowed to fall into desuetude. Some exegetes (e.g. Weiser, 372; cf. Thiel 1981, 75) relate the period of prosperity to the long reign of Manasseh (695–641) when pagan cults were tolerated, and the change of fortunes to the time of Josiah when such cults were annihilated in the savage massacres of the reform instituted by that king (cf. II Kings 23.4–20). The sudden death of Josiah (II Kings 23.29) was the beginning of Judah's decline into disaster and exile. This reading of 44.17–18 identifies the reforming zeal of Josiah with the cause of Judah's run of disasters and Manasseh's toleration of many cults as the basis of Judah's prosperity. It is an interesting reading of the text, but by no means a necessary interpretation of it (e.g. Volz, 365, relates the cessation of the cult to the time of Zedekiah and not to Josiah's reform). To read 44.17–18 against a background provided by II Kings 22–23 is to assume a historicity for the Josiah story which is by no means warranted by the Deuteronomistic stories (cf. Hoffmann 1980). Yet if the hand of the Deuteronomists is to be detected in 44 (cf. Thiel 1981, 74), then it may well be the case that vv. 17–18 are intended to be a reflection on that Deuteronomistically constructed reform. However, there are no direct connections between vv. 17–18 and the story of Josiah's reform of the cult (of either a linguistic or a theological nature). The generality of the contrast in vv. 17–18 is such that the argument may be read simply as a statement of justification for resuming an old cultic practice without representing a confirmation of the Deuteronomistic history. It is an *ad hoc* argument put in the mouths of the people by the editors in order to demonstrate the incorrigibility of the people no matter what they have suffered. As v. 22 indicates, a different interpretation of the 'facts' may be offered, so v. 17 underlines the obduracy of the community.

An interesting feature of the argument of vv. 17–18, whatever its origins or editorial nature may be, is the similarity it bears to the thesis offered by David Hume in his *The Natural History of Religion.* In this work Hume argues that the original religion of mankind is polytheism, out of which arises monotheism. But because of 'a kind of flux and reflux in the human mind' nations move from polytheism to theism and then back again (Hume 1976, 51–57; cf. Mackie 1982, 188–90). 44.17–18 illustrates Hume's 'flux and reflux' thesis to some extent, though v. 18 may not warrant the inference that the people shifted from polytheistic to monotheistic practices. The Deuteronomistic history's presentation of the nation's long history of shifting loyalties from Yahweh to the gods and back to Yahweh (or from the gods to Yahweh to the gods) is a fine example of what Hume had in mind. A further interesting point about the argument of vv. 17–18 is its *post hoc* nature. It appears to argue from experience in order to make connections between events and beliefs (though the reverse form of the argument is offered in vv. 21–22). It is therefore a very good example of the unsatisfactory nature of such arguments. The interpretation of experience depends upon prior (or even *a priori*) beliefs which are then confirmed by experience. But the same set of experiences will confirm different beliefs because of the primacy of belief over experience. Thus the editors use one set of experiences (disaster) to ground two different sets of beliefs. Neither set of beliefs is warranted by the evidence offered for it because such beliefs are originally independent of experience. Belief in Yahweh or the queen of heaven is prior to the prosperity or disaster associated with such commitment. In 44 logic is on the side of neither the community nor the editors, though the sermon illustrates this principle very well. Perhaps the Deuteronomists (or the editors of 44 and other sermons in Jeremiah) really did think that logic and experience were on their side because so much in the book of Jeremiah uses the fall of Jerusalem to argue for certain beliefs and practices, but as the author of Job knew only too well, the logic of belief can be a very poor interpreter of experience.

44.20–23

20 Then Jeremiah said to all the people, men and women, all the people who had given him this answer: 21 'As for the incense that you burned in the cities of Judah and in the streets of Jerusalem, you and your fathers, your kings and your princes, and the people of the land, did not the LORD remember it? Did it not come into his mind? 22 The LORD could no longer bear your evil doings and the abominations which you committed; therefore your land has become a desolation and a waste and a curse, without inhabitant, as it is this day. 23 It is because you burned incense, and because you sinned against the LORD and did not obey the voice of the LORD or walk in his law and in his statutes and in his testimonies, that this evil has befallen you, as at this day.'

---

[20] MT *hā'ōnīm 'ōtō dābār*, lit. 'who answer him a word': i.e. who made the response of vv. 16–19. **[21]** MT *hᵃlō' 'et-haqqiṭṭēr 'ᵃšer qiṭṭartem*, 'is it not the burning which you burned?': i.e. the sacrifices made in the cities of Judah and the streets of Jerusalem; cf. *qṭr* in vv. 3, 5, 8, 15, 17–19, 23, 25. Burning incense (RSV) is too narrow an application of *qṭr*. MT *wᵉ'am hā'āreṣ*, 'and the people of the land': cf. 1.18; 34.19; 37.2. Whether it refers to the landed gentry or the common people here is difficult to determine. In Jeremiah it often refers to the wealthy (e.g. 34.19) but most of these were supposed to have been deported to Babylon, so Jeremiah could hardly have been addressing them in Egypt. However, 44 is built up out of phrases from the tradition and does not represent a historical reflection of life in Egypt. The people in general may be meant in v. 21; cf. 37.2. MT *'ōtām zākar yhwh*, '*them* Yahweh remembered': G lacks 'them'; some exegetes read *'ōtāh*, 'it' (e.g. Rudolph, 262; cf. BHS), in agreement with following verb. MT *watta'ᵃleh 'al-libbō*, 'and it came into his mind': for the idiom (all in the negative) cf. 7.31; 19.5; 32.35; the negative form may be understood here by virtue of the introductory *hᵃlō'*, 'did not . . .?'. **[22]** G lacks *mē'ēn yōšēb*, 'without inhabitant': cf. v. 2 *wᵉ'ēn bāhem yōšēb*, 'and there is no inhabitant in them' (i.e. in the cities). MT *kᵉhayyōm hazzeh*, 'as is the case this day': cf. vv. 6, 23. For the evil doings as a motive for divine destruction cf. 4.4b; 21.12b; 26.3; Deut. 28.20; vv. 22–23 have an apologetic character in the sermon and constitute an explanation for Yahweh's judgment (cf. Thiel 1981, 75). **[23]** G lacks *kayyōm hazzeh*, 'as is the case this day': cf. vv. 6, 22. Cf. 16.10; 40.3 for the motif of sinning against Yahweh; the motif of not walking in his testimonies only appears here. Cf. v.10 for the motif of not walking in Yahweh's *tōrāh* or his statutes. The image of evil befalling (*qr'*) the nation occurs in 32.23; Deut. 31.29.

Two responses to the people's response to Jeremiah are attributed to Jeremiah (vv. 20–23, 24–28). Thus the sermon is turned into a debate, with both sides responding to each other in an antiphonal manner (cf. the two strands of response in vv. 15, 19, 17–18), by its present editing. In his first answer (v. 20, cf. v. 15 for the men and women to whom he replies) Jeremiah responds to the point about the people having offered sacrifice in the land of Judah in the past, but makes no acknowledgment of the queen of heaven cult (that occurs in his second answer in v. 25). He offers an entirely different explanation of the fate of the people. It was because Yahweh remembered such sacrifices and was unable to go on bearing them any more that he destroyed the land. So the popular explanation of the connection between worship and fate is inverted by Jeremiah to account for the present desolate state of the land of Judah. Both parties to the dispute accept the same principle: fate of land is bound up with worship of the god. The people claim that their abandoning of their god (i.e. the queen of heaven) caused the terrible experiences of the past. Jeremiah in principle agrees with that explanation but offers it on behalf of a different god. In strongly anthropomorphic language he represents Yahweh as remembering the past behaviour of the community and the various social strata and becoming unable to put up with the burden of evil deeds any longer. For these reasons the land became 'a desolation and a waste and a curse' (cf. v. 12) and not for the reasons offered by the people.

The different claims made by the people and Jeremiah using the same data underline the hopelessness of using experiences and 'facts' to explain ideological positions. Jeremiah's response in vv. 21–23 embodies a distinctive conception of history and an alternative account of the destruction of Judah to that of the people (cf. Thiel 1981, 75–6, who describes this account as Deuteronomistic). Without such a prevenient theology the 'facts' of 587 would remain uninterpreted and both people and Jeremiah would share the same experiences without disagreeing about the meaning of what had happened to them. The Deuteronomistically influenced theology of 44 provides an alternative explanation to that of the people, but the case for both positions is determined by the ideologies of the parties to the dispute and cannot be decided independently of one ideology or the other.

44.24–30

24 Jeremiah said to all the people and all the women, 'Hear the word of the
LORD, all you of Judah who are in the land of Egypt, 25 Thus says the LORD
of hosts, the God of Israel: You and your wives have declared with your
mouths, and have fulfilled it with your hands, saying, "We will surely
perform our vows that we have made, to burn incense to the queen of heaven
and to pour out libations to her." Then confirm your vows and perform
your vows! 26 Therefore hear the word of the LORD, all you of Judah who
dwell in the land of Egypt: Behold, I have sworn by my great name, says
the LORD, that my name shall no more be invoked by the mouth of any man
of Judah in all the land of Egypt, saying, "As the Lord GOD lives." 27
Behold, I am watching over them for evil and not for good; all the men of
Judah who are in the land of Egypt shall be consumed by the sword and by
famine, until there is an end of them. 28 And those who escape the sword
shall return from the land of Egypt to the land of Judah, few in number;
and all the remnant of Judah, who came to the land of Egypt to live, shall
know whose word will stand, mine or theirs. 29 This shall be the sign to
you, says the LORD, that I will punish you in this place, in order that you
may know that my words will surely stand against you for evil: 30 Thus
says the LORD, Behold I will give Pharaoh Hophra king of Egypt into the
hand of those who seek his life, as I gave Zedekiah king of Judah into the
hand of Nebuchadrezzar king of Babylon, who was his enemy and sought
his life.'

---

[24] G lacks 'all Judah who are in the land of Egypt'. Some exegetes delete 'to all the people and' because in v. 25 only the women are addressed (*watt*^{e}*dabbērnāh*, 'and you [fem.] said'), cf. Rudolph 262; Pohlmann 1978, 176–7; BHS; Bright, 262. **[25]** G lacks 'of hosts'. MT *'attem ūn*^{e}*šēkem*, 'you and your wives': G *humeis gunaikes*, 'you women' = *'attēnāh hannāšīm*; MT represents v. 20 and the editing of the chapter as Jeremiah's responses to *all* (vv. 1, 15, 20, 24) the people. MT *'et-n*^{e}*dārēnū*, 'our vows': cf. v. 17 where an idiom is used instead of *ndr* for vowing. The homologation (cf. G *has hōmologēsamen*, 'which we have agreed to') of vows in v. 25 reads v. 19 as a declaration of intent rather than a statement of past historical actions. MT *l*^{e}*qaṭṭēr lim*^{e}*leket haššāmayim*, 'to burn to the works of the heavens': see on v. 17

for the queen of heaven cult (G) and on v. 3 for *qṭr* as 'burn', meaning to sacrifice. MT *tāqīmnāh*, 'confirm': regarded as an abnormal form (cf. GK 72k), perhaps *tāqēmnāh* or *t^eqīmenāh* (cf. BHS). MT *w^e'āśōh ta'^aśenāh 'et-nidrēkem*, 'and really perform your vows': a few mss read *niskēkem*, 'your libations'; this reading fits better in that vows *and* libations are part of the affirmation. G lacks the word; Bright, 262, reads 'By all means perform them'; NEB 'and make your words good' (cf. BHS). **[26]** Cf. vv. 1, 15 for the address to all (Judah) who live in Egypt; cf. 22.5 for the divine swearing by himself. Duhm, 333, treats this verse as ironic. Cf. 4.2; 5.2; 12.16; 16.14, 15; 23.7, 8; 38.16 for the oath *ḥay-yhwh* 'as Yahweh lives'; here *ḥay-'^adōnāy yhwh*, 'as the lord Yahweh lives' (G *zē kurios kurios*, G^B *zē kurios*). **[27]** MT *hin^enī šōqēd '^alēhem*, 'look, I am watching over them': the watching (*šqd*) motif appears in 1.12; 31.28 (cf. 5.6); for evil here but for good in 31.28. Cf. 21.9; 39.16 for the phrase 'for evil and not for good'; cf. v. 12 for consummation by sword and famine. **[28]** G lacks *mimmennī ūmēhem*, 'mine or theirs'. BHS treats 'who came to the land of Egypt to live there' as a 'false addition' (Rudolph, 262). It hardly fits the annihilation of the community in Egypt referred to at the end of v. 27 or the few fugitives who escape to Palestine. Cf. 42.15, 19; 44.12, 14 for the attack on the remnant; the association of the remnant with knowing (*yd'*) appears in 42.19, 22. Cf. Deut. 18.21 for knowing (*yd'*) the word which Yahweh has *not* spoken; here the survivors *know* that Yahweh has spoken (i.e. his word stands) because the community has been annihilated. Hence some survivors are needed in order to act as witnesses to the confirmation (*qūm*) of Yahweh's word. Cf. v. 14b where a few fugitives survive from the destruction of the remnant (cf. discussion in Thiel 1981, 77–81; Ehrlich 1912, 351). **[29]** MT *w^ezō't-lākem hā'ōt*, 'this is the sign for you': this is the only occurrence of sign in this sense in the book of Jeremiah (cf. 10.2; 32.20, 21). G has a shorter reading: 'and this (is) the sign to you that I will visit you for evil'; BHS explains the lack of 'in this place in order that you may know that my words shall surely stand against you' in terms of homoioteleuton (*'^alēkem . . . '^alēkem*). Perhaps this is correct, but the briefer G text introduces v. 30 more succinctly than MT's repetition of the idea in v. 28b (with the addition of *n^e'um-yhwh*, 'says Yahweh'). Cf. vv. 11, 27 for the motif *l^erā'āh* 'for evil'. **[30]** G lacks 'Pharaoh': due to haplography? MT *'et-par'ōh ḥopra'*, 'Pharaoh Hophra': this king ruled Egypt 589–570 and was killed in a rebellion. He was succeeded by Amasis (570–526). Hophra's troubles are here made the sign of the destruction of the remnant or so understood by the editors. The parallel between Hophra and Zedekiah is made in stereotypical language, cf. 19.7; 21.7; 22.25; 34.20, 21; thus the remnant will suffer a fate similar to the end of Jerusalem when Zedekiah was given into the hand of his enemy – Nebuchadrezzar.

The second response of Jeremiah to *all* the people (cf. v. 20) is a development of a reply to the women involved in the cult of the queen of heaven (cf. v. 19). In the editing of the sermon the women's cult is combined with the address to all the people of the Jewish communities in Egypt so that a particular cultic practice is generalized as the behaviour of all the communities. This permits the editorial ideology to condemn all the exogenous groups outside Palestine (i.e. Egypt, though presumably not Babylon) by means of a sermon and a debate in which Jeremiah acts as the divine mouthpiece for dismissing as idolatrous Yahwistic practices in the land of Egypt (cf. v. 26). The mixing together of discrete elements in 44 constitutes an ideological dismissal of thriving communities elsewhere.

Jeremiah responds to the women's cult of the queen of heaven with biting irony (e.g. v. 25b). This is achieved by turning the statement of practice in v. 19 into a declaration of intent on the women's part in v. 25. The implication of the men in the women's cult (cf. vv. 15–19, 20, 24) allows the condemnation of a special ritual (cf. Ezek. 8.14) to become a wholesale rejection of 'all Judah who dwell in the land of Egypt'. It also facilitates the divine forswearing of even the practice of Yahwism in Egypt (v. 26). The swearing by the name of Yahweh is a mark of the genuine worship of Yahweh (cf. 4.2), but here it is ruled out as a permissible way of life in Egypt (cf. 5.2 for the practice as a mask for false behaviour). Such a blanket condemnation of the cult of Yahweh in Egypt must represent an ideological conflict between Palestine (?) and Egypt over cultic matters at some period after the fall of Jerusalem (e.g. in the second temple era? Cf. the tensions between the two areas in matters cultic as evinced by the Elephantine documents, Porten 1968, 105–50, 278–98). The complete writing off of the Jewish communities in Egypt betrays xenophobic prejudices against rival groups practising Yahwism outside the 'holy land' of Palestine, and Jeremiah is used to give these prejudices respectability. Their fate is to be the same as befell Jerusalem in 587 and is expressed in terms of the divine watching (*šqd*) for evil rather than good (e.g. v. 27a; 31.28; cf. 1.12). Whether the voice of the pro-Babylonian exiles (cf. 24.4–7; 29.10–14) strand in the tradition should be detected in 44 is a moot point.

The annihilation of the remnant of Judah in the land of Egypt is a dominant motif in 42.13–22 and 44. This motif is expressed most clearly in 44.27b, where the whole community ('all the men of Judah who are in the land of Egypt') is to be wiped out by sword (i.e.

invasion) and famine. A lack of survivors is one of the features of this motif (cf. 42.17, 22; 44.14). It is therefore strange to read in v. 28a that there will be survivors who will escape the slaughter and return to the land of Judah (cf. v. 14 'except some fugitives'). Having put an end (*'ad-k^e^lōtām*, 'until there is an end of them') to the remnant in v. 28b it is odd to find survivors making their way *back to Judah*! This returning motif (*šūb*) is such a feature of the tradition that its occurrence here is in keeping with the book of Jeremiah as a whole, though out of place in 44.27–28. It may be regarded as an editorial addition to the attack on the Egyptian communities (cf. the addition to v. 14). Whether it represents an addition in the light of historical experience (i.e. Jews from Egypt returned to Palestine over the years) or a literary motif added to the story in order to highlight the complete destruction of the communities in Egypt in terms of surviving witnesses to it is a debatable matter. Without survivors there could be no meaning to the claim 'in order that you may know that my words will surely stand against you for evil' (v. 29b: lacking in G; cf. Ezek. 6.8–10 for a similar argument).

The concluding point of the sermon is the establishment (*qūm*) of the divine word. In the destruction of the Jewish communities in Egypt that word (v. 28; words in MT, v. 29) will stand as confirmed by events (the competition between 'mine or theirs' in v. 28 belongs only to MT). As a sign of the fulfilment of the divine word v. 30 refers to the defeat of Pharaoh Hophra (though the reference is presented as a prediction). This suggests a date after 570 for the editing of the sermon (or the addition of v. 30 to it). In the events surrounding the fall of Hophra the editors detect the establishment of the divine word against the Jewish communities throughout Egypt. Thus his fall is described in stereotypical language from the tradition and compared with the defeat of Zedekiah by Nebuchadrezzar. So the divine word against the remnant in Egypt is of the same order as the word against Jerusalem (cf. 42.18). Strictly speaking a holistic reading of the book of Jeremiah would arrive at the conclusion that all the Jewish communities, apart from the one in Babylon, are written off as the objects of Yahweh's implacable wrath. That may well be the point of 44. However, the voice behind 44 may be that of the cultic community in Jerusalem, among whom may be exiles returned from Babylon (hence v. 28). In Jeremiah's attitude to the people in Egypt there may be detected a strong anti-Moses parallel (cf. Alonso Schökel 1981).

45.1–5

45[1] The word that Jeremiah the prophet spoke to Baruch the son of Neriah, when he wrote these words in a book at the dictation of Jeremiah, in the fourth year of Jehoiakim the son of Josiah, king of Judah: 2 'Thus says the LORD, the God of Israel, to you, O Baruch: 3 You said, "Woe is me! for the LORD has added sorrow to my pain; I am weary with my groaning, and I find no rest." 4 Thus shall you say to him, Thus says the LORD: Behold, what I have built I am breaking down, and what I have planted I am plucking up – that is, the whole land. 5 And do you seek great things for yourself? Seek them not; for, behold, I am bringing evil upon all flesh, says the LORD; but I will give you your life as a prize of war in all the places to which you may go.'

[MT 45] = G 51.31–35. **[1]** Cf. 36.1–4. The introductory phrase *haddābār ᵓᵃšer dibber yirmᵉyāhū hannābîᵓ ᵓel-bārûk ben-nērîyyāh*, 'the word which Jeremiah the prophet spoke to Baruch ben Neriah', is quite different from the formulaic reception of the word introductions used throughout the book (cf. 51.59). MT *bᵉkātᵉbō ᵓet-haddᵉbārîm hāᵓēlleh*, 'when he wrote *these words*': what words? In its present position 45.1 gives the impression that 44 is the content of Baruch's writing. This makes no sense, as the dating of 45.1 to 605 (Jehoiakim's fourth year) places the writing at least twenty years before the supposed event of 44. Although 45 should follow 36, where 'these words' would have a logical force (cf. Bright, 184), its placing after 44 removes any reference to 36 and makes it a more general reference to 'the well-known words' (Rudolph, 262) of Jeremiah. The dating in 1b confuses that point (cf. Skinner 1922, 346). **[2]** G lacks 'the god of Israel'. **[3]** G begins the verse with *hoti*, 'because' = *kî*; lacking in MT due to haplography (*bārûk* in v. 2). G repeats *oimmoi oimmoi*, 'woe, woe'. **[4]** MT *kōh tōᵓmar ᵓēlāyw*, 'thus you will say to him': a change of person from v. 3 (him – you) which suggests the phrase is a later addition (cf. Wanke 1971, 133). Cf. 1.10 for the motifs used in v. 4. MT *wᵉᵓet-kol-hāᵓāreṣ hîᵓ*, 'that is, the whole earth': *hîᵓ* makes the meaning of this phrase uncertain (cf. JPSB); G lacks the clause. Rudolph, 264, reads *ᵓakkeh*, 'I will smite'; Driver 1937–38, 122–3, reads *ᵓᵃnî makkeh*, 'I am smiting'. MT is a gloss (cf. Giesebrecht, 226) relating the divine action to the land rather than the people (as in v. 5). **[5]** MT *kol-bāśār*, 'all flesh': i.e. mankind, cf. 12.12; 25.31; 32.27; not the land but all mankind will undergo the destruction brought about by Yahweh – why then should Baruch complain or seek great things for himself? Cf. 39.16, where Yahweh is bringing evil upon the city. MT *wᵉnātattî lᵉkā ᵓet-napšᵉkā lᵉšālāl*, 'and I will give you your life for booty': i.e. 'but you shall save your life and nothing more' (NEB). Cf. the idiom *hāyᵉtāh . . . nepeš . . . lᵉšālāl*, 'to have (one's) life for booty', 21.9. 38.2; 39.18. This is an ironic figure of speech which assures the recipient of survival but nothing else, using an image drawn from the aftermath of battle when the victors divide the booty (*šālāl*). In 21.9 = 38.2 it is linked to survival (*ḥāyāh*), in 39.18 it is associated with escape (*mallēṭ*), and here it is related to survival wherever Baruch goes (*tēlek*). 21.9; 38.2 are general offers to the community; 39.18; 44.5 are directed to named individuals (Ebed-melek, Baruch). After the onslaught the only booty such people will possess will be their own lives! Thiel 1981, 86, regards 44.5 as basic and 21.9; 38.2; 39.18 as imitations used by the Deuteronomists (cf. Duhm, 336).

Part IV ends surprisingly with a short piece about Baruch's lament which is dated to the year 605. Coming immediately after the lengthy section on the aftermath of the fall of Jerusalem (39.11 – 43.7) and the denunciations of the Jewish communities in Egypt (44), it appears to make connections with 36 which are out of place after 44. The editorial arrangement of it here may be parallel to the concluding of Part III with 35–36, which do not follow chronologically from 32–34. Chronological sequence is seldom followed by the editors of the book of Jeremiah and it is arguable that 45 makes an appropriate ending to Part IV by alluding to 36 and 26, where the material is set also in Jehoiakim's reign (cf. discussion in Thiel 1981, 82–90). As the closing story it concludes the block of material rather than continues the theme of 42, 44. Furthermore, the redactional presentation in vv. 1–2 reflects the standard treatment of the stories in the tradition by giving them settings which have no original connection with the material in the first place. The unit of 45 is the lament with response in vv. 3–5 (cf. Wanke 1971, 135), and the editorial introduction is precisely what raises the problem of appropriateness. An original lament with response is quite appropriate as a closure of Part IV because the denunciations of the communities in Egypt have introduced the question of survival (cf. 44.7, 14, 27, 28). The oracular response to this question appears in 45.4–5 and asserts the divine gift of survival. Survival and nothing else is the point of the metaphor in v. 5b. The editing which transforms the generality of this oracular declaration into a personal oracle to Baruch ben Neriah breaks the connection between 45.3–5 and 44 but links it to 36. That transformation uses a concrete example to make the point about the futility of seeking self-aggrandizement (v. 5 *geḏōlōt*, 'great things') in the period characterized by 44 (vv. 3–5) or 'these words' (i.e. 605 if v. 1b is read in terms of the final form of the text or 587 if this phrase is understood as a general reference to Jeremiah's preaching). A different interpretation of *g^e dōlōt* is offered by de Boer (1973, 33–5), who treats it as a reference to divine, superhuman acts (cf. 33.3), and the complaint as an attempt by Baruch to persuade Yahweh to change his mind about destroying his people.

The presence of 45 at the end of Part IV may be compared to the addition of 1 as a prologue to Part I. In the first edition of Jeremiah (G) the four parts are enclosed by lengthy discourses against idolatry (2, 44). To this collection have been added a prologue (1) and an epilogue (52 = II Kings 24.18–25.30). It is possible that 45 represents a parallel development to 1. In 1 the individual figure of Jeremiah is introduced as the speaker of the tradition which follows and the prologue ends with a divine promise of protection (1.19b). 36 introduces the figure of Baruch as the amanuensis of Jeremiah and credits him with the writing of Jeremiah's words. Now in 45 as a parallel to I Baruch is addressed and given a promise of survival. The connecting link between the two chapters is signalled by 1.10 and 45.4 which share similar motifs. If 45 is a good deal less substantial than 1 that reflects the minor role played by Baruch in the book of Jeremiah. The effect of 45 as a conclusion to the book (before the addition of the epilogue in 52) is to make Baruch the last figure in the tradition (a role played by Jehoiachin in 52) rather than Jeremiah (cf. Bogaert 1981a, 172–3). This irony is achieved by the development of a brief strand in the tradition which provides Jeremiah with Baruch as a companion or assistant. Those exegetes who maintain the theory that Baruch is the *author* or *writer* of the book of Jeremiah (or parts of it) may regard 45 as a kind of author's colophon by means of which the writer puts himself into his work. A more likely explanation is to read 45.1–2 as the editorial development of the figure of Baruch in the tradition by associating him with a saying of (or attributed to) Jeremiah (cf. Wanke 1971, 133–6).

The introductory formula in v. 1a is a very distinctive one in the book of Jeremiah, though 51.59 is virtually the same and shares the structure of 45.1 (cf. 46.13; 50.1, where a similar formulaic introduction is used but with Yahweh as the speaker). Jeremiah *the prophet* (epithet also in G) makes an oracular proclamation in response to his companion Baruch's lament. These two elements, Jeremiah *as* prophet and Baruch, reflect late developments of the tradition and the association of the oracle with 605 allows the editors to respond to 36. Without that editorial point (v. 1b) the piece could be read as a response to the plight of Baruch in 43.3, 6 (cf. Wanke 1971, 141) and as forming a closure with 43.1–7. The reason for Baruch's lamentation can only be speculated about (cf. Bright, 185–6) because there is nothing in the tradition to suggest that Baruch was anything other than an inert figure who did Jeremiah's bidding. 43.3 may hint at activity on his part, but that may be attributable to the paranoia of the community's leaders. The lament of 45.3 would fit the laments in Part I and it may therefore reflect a further development of the character of Baruch by attributing to him sentiments which Part I at times appears to associate with Jeremiah, though the language of v. 3 is quite different from that of the laments in 11–20 (cf. Wanke 1971, 134 n. 6).

In a time characterized by the breaking down of what the deity had built and his plucking up of what he had planted (cf. the reversal of these motifs in 31.28), the individual may not hope for the realization of his ambitions. Each use of the motifs listed in 1.10 is distinctive in the tradition (cf. 12.14–17; 18.7, 9; 24.6; 31.40; 42.10) and here Yahweh, who is always the actor implementing these terms (with the exception of 1.10 where Jeremiah takes that role), is represented as reversing his former policy. The terms of 45.4 which view the past as a period of divine building and planting (!) and the present as a change in the deity's attitudes therefore constitute a different view of life from that represented by 42.10 (the dating in v. 1b may preserve the deity from the charge of being peculiarly fickle in his dealings with the community). Rapid changes in the fortunes of the people are assimilated into the theological outlook of the editors by the use of the metaphors set out in 1.10. These cover the positive and negative aspects of the period and enable a wide range of assessments of events and social trends to be incorporated into a coherent theological perspective. Behind everything which happens is the deity establishing the conditions of normal life or destroying the bases of communal living. Prosperity and disintegration are his doing, and the proper response of communities (or even individuals as 45.4–5 suggest) to his activity is to align themselves with whatever is the current mode of that action (e.g. 12.16–17; 42.10). If seeking great things for oneself in a time of great destruction for all flesh (v. 5; cf. 12.12; 25.31) is a futile aspiration, the response to the lament is not entirely negative. It allows the speaker the reassurance of survival. Using a metaphor which is also used in 21.9; 38.2; 39.18 Baruch is promised survival wherever he goes. As the figure of speech is ironic this may be cold comfort but it is a better alternative to being dead! The metaphor describes the gift of survival in terms drawn from the practice of war. After the fighting the victorious troops plunder the corpses, towns and whatever they can lay their hands on in order to take away with them the spoils of war. In the terrible evil coming upon everybody Baruch also will receive war booty – his own life. Devastation will be so great that just surviving may be described as acquiring the plunder of war. The sweep of the destruction, i.e. 'evil upon *all flesh*', is so complete that we may detect in 45.5 an allusion to the suprahistorical war against all the nations (cf. 12.12; 25.31; 30.5–7) associated in prophetic forecasts with the end of time. In such a time surviving is the most that can be hoped for (cf. 30.7b), and Baruch is reassured of such survival. Thus the ironic metaphor corrects his grandiose expectations by drawing his attention to the period in which he lives and warning him to adjust his aspirations to a more realistic perspective.

The parallel between Baruch's prospects for the future and the reassurance of deliverance given to Ebed-melech (39.15–19) is strengthened by the use of the same ironic metaphor. Ebed-melech is assured that he will not be slain in the siege or destruction of Jerusalem but will be rescued (*mlṭ*) by the deity. The figurative statement 'you shall have your life as booty' (39.18) is more positive in his case because it is related to his trust in Yahweh and to a situation less overwhelming than the evil befalling all flesh in 45.5. Apart from the fact that they share the same metaphor the relative positions of the two pieces in the tradition should be noted. Both are technically out of place and ought to be attached to other points of the book. However, the editors have placed both of them immediately after stories of great destruction. In 39.3–10 a version of the destruction of Jerusalem is given and followed by two accounts of Jeremiah's escape from imprisonment in the fallen city. Sandwiched between these accounts is the promise of deliverance to Ebed-melech. All three stories contribute to toning down the story of Jerusalem's destruction by focusing on those who survive it. So in 45 the word of survival addressed to Baruch is placed immediately after the prolix sermon of destruction directed against the communities of Jews in Egypt. The complete annihilation of those communities is emphasized in 44, but the placing of 45 serves to modify the note of doom to some extent by announcing the possibility of survival to Baruch who in 43.6 is taken down to Egypt. So a moment of hope (strictly delimited) is allowed to penetrate the utter gloom. Communal devastation cannot be avoided, but in all the great slaughter named individuals survive as the booty of war. That hope is not articulated any further (except in the book of 30–31), but the beginnings of a pattern may be detected in the editing of Part IV (cf. the juxtaposing of doom and salvation elements in the arrangement of Isa. 1–12). In 45 Baruch symbolizes such hope, though whether as an earnest of the future or as a survivor whose very survival emphasizes the dimensions of the destruction is more difficult to determine. Governed by anxiety, caution and modesty, the Jeremiah tradition makes few sweeping gestures in the direction of a positive future (even 30–31 are modest in comparison with other traditions). Thus the figure of Baruch is quite unrealized in the book of Jeremiah.

The concluding of Jeremiah's work with this brief glimpse of Baruch (G but not MT) draws attention to the son of Neriah and reminds the reader of the half-glimpsed association between Jeremiah and Baruch. In 32.12–13 Baruch is party to Jeremiah's purchase of land, but the significance of that involvement is neither stated nor developed. He is Jeremiah's companion in the flight to Egypt (43.6) and is even held responsible for Jeremiah's advocacy of living in the land of Judah (43.2–3). 36 presents him as the prophet's amanuensis and delegated authority in the matter of writing and reading out the scroll of Jeremiah's life's work. The glimpses of him are too enigmatic and inchoate for a theory of them to be established or even a pattern detected. In two pieces he is associated with the future: mere (?) survival in 45.5 and the reconstruction of the land in 32.12–15. The other two glimpses of him *hint* at his replacement of Jeremiah *as if* in the development of the tradition's redaction he represents the next generation (of the community?). In later literature the relationship between Jeremiah and Baruch is that of father and son (metaphorically speaking).

He is the means whereby Jeremiah's words are passed on to the future. The structure of 45.1 is essentially the same as 51.59 (cf. 46.13; 50.2) and both introduce sons of Neriah. Baruch and Seraiah are probably brothers, and both are used in similar ways by Jeremiah. Baruch is used to convey the written word of doom to the people and king Jehoiakim; Seraiah is commissioned as a delegate of Jeremiah's written word of doom to deliver it to Babylon in the fourth year (cf. 45.1b) of Zedekiah's reign. If the structural particularity of 45.1

and 51.59 is significant, even if only to the extent of allowing both stories to be read together, then the pieces may be read as statements about the future in which the tentativeness of 45 becomes the definite affirmation of 51.59–64 (cf. Wanke 1971, 140–3). Seraiah enacts and thereby creates the destruction of Babylon and therefore the deliverance of Israel (cf. 50.17–20). His brother is less creative in this respect but his survival in 45.5 may be an oblique allusion to a future beyond Yahweh's bringing of evil upon all flesh.

This reading of the few references to Baruch in the book of Jeremiah is necessarily a tentative one. It cannot be regarded as *the* meaning of the texts or even perhaps as the most likely reading of them. The most precise interpretation of the data on Baruch would be a restatement of what each text says about him, but that would fail to elicit the significance of Baruch in the tradition. More grandiose theories about him as the author of the book of Jeremiah go beyond the evidence by reading 36 as a paradigm of the tradition and as a historical account without allowing for the literary creativeness of the editors. Baruch remains an enigma in the tradition, and that is a fitting role for the figure whose survival became his spoils of war!

PART TWO

46.1 – 51.64

The oracles against the nations 46–51

> The prophets who preceded you and me from ancient times prophesied war, famine, and pestilence *against many countries and great kingdoms* (28.8).

Formal oracles against the nations (OAN) are to be found in the major prophetic anthologies (Isa. 13–23; Ezek. 25–32) and the smaller collections associated with prophetic figures (Amos 1.3–2.3; Nahum; Obadiah; cf. Joel 3; Zeph. 2–3). The book of Jeremiah is no exception to this pattern, though the two editions vary in their placing of the collection and the order of the nations denounced.

The conventional nature of these oracles is established by their widespread occurrence in so many different prophetic traditions, but the origins of the OAN form are unknown. Comparative material from Mari demonstrates the existence of the practice of prophesying against foreign nations in a culture other than those represented by the Bible (cf. Malamat 1966; Moran 1969). This evidence only indicates the popularity of the practice in the ancient Near East, it affords no information about the origins or development of the form. However, it may lend weight to the view that the OAN are the oldest form of prophetic oracle (cf. Hayes 1968, 86–7), a point echoed in the statement attributed to Jeremiah in 28.8. If the origins of the form are beyond our knowledge, there is no lack of scholarly speculation about the setting in life out of which it may have arisen (e.g. Christensen 1975; Clements 1975, 58–72; Hayes 1968; Reventlow 1962, 56–75).

The story of the prophet Balaam being summoned by Balak, king of Moab, to curse Israel (Num. 22–24) suggests a ritual of cursing (and blessing) which could be operated against foreign enemies in a period of potential conflict. No such ritual appears elsewhere in the Bible, but the OAN may reflect cultic activity directed against the nation's enemies as a means of encouraging the people and defeating the foe (cf. Isa. 7.7–9; 8.9–10). A ritual of blessing and cursing in which the king is assured of his triumph over the national enemy (cf. Ps. 2; 110) might well include the cursing of the adversary in the form of an oracle delivered by the cult prophet. Such oracles accompanied by the magical rituals of the cult may have determined foreign policy by encouraging the kings to make war or to desist from ill-advised campaigns (cf. I Kings 22; II Kings 13; Fohrer 1967, 257–61; Christensen 1975). The context of this activity is seen by some scholars as the covenant festival (e.g. Reventlow 1962, 65), though the complete lack of information in the text should render such specificity open to serious questioning. Mowinckel associates the OAN with the enthronement of Yahweh festival but not as part of the festal ritual proper:

> . . . they mark extempore inspirations and improvisations of the cult prophet, only loosely connected with the festival, and taking place before the crowd, which was eating and drinking and playing in the temple courts (1962, I, 154).

The incorporation of collections of OAN into the traditions of Amos, Isaiah, Jeremiah, and Ezekiel raises a number of problems. If the form represents threats against the enemy or veiled assurances for Judah, it does not sit well with the denunciatory oracles directed against Israel and Judah in these traditions. This combination of disparate forms may require modifying the account of OAN as oracles supporting the nation to include the notion that they may occasionally serve to disabuse the people of false notions of security (cf. Clements 1975, 64). Amos 1–2, in their present redaction, illustrate this function by combining attacks on the nations with a thoroughgoing vilification of Israel. However, it cannot be shown that the same speaker uttered both OAN *and* diatribes against Israel of Judah. The association of the two is a feature of the redaction of the traditions, and it may represent the marriage of incompatible partners rather than a modification of the OAN. Different forms of activity may have been incorporated into the same tradition without requiring a rationalization of the role of the eponymous figure associated with it. Yet if the OAN cannot be related to a specific setting in the life of the community, their significance becomes much more difficult to determine. Clements is undoubtedly right in his assessment:

> That any one sphere of Israel's life, the royal court, the cultus or the military organization of the state with its inheritance of holy war ideology, formed the exclusive setting of the category of the oracles against foreign powers cannot be regarded as established. Rather we must regard these prophecies as a distinctive genre of their own which drew from many aspects of Israel's life (1975, 72).

As a distinctive genre the OAN are independent of the contexts in which they now appear, and this inevitably causes problems of interpretation in relation to the larger traditions into which they have been integrated by the editorial processes which created those traditions.

A comprehensive account of the OAN cannot be given in a commentary, but the central problem of the OAN for the interpretation of the book of Jeremiah is the relation between them and the Jeremiah of the other strands in the book. How can the preacher of the destruction of Jerusalem and Judah also be the speaker of the OAN in 46–51? The simplest answer to that question is – he cannot be the speaker of all the different levels of tradition in the book. That would appear to be the correct response to such a question. However, many exegetes attribute 46–51 to Jeremiah (in varying proportions), and so the obvious becomes a matter of dispute. Leaving aside convoluted theological arguments (cf. Raitt 1977) which argue for a shift in the prophet's outlook after 587, the crux of the matter focuses on the role of Babylon in 27–29 and the attitude expressed towards Babylon in 50–51. It is difficult to reconcile the proclamation of submission to Babylon in 27–29 and the announcement of its destruction as the work of the same speaker when both sets of material are dated to the same period (cf. 27.1; 28.1; 51.59). The representation of Babylon (Nebuchadrezzar) as Yahweh's servant (27.6) *and* as the dragon (51.34) indicates the incompatibility of the imagery as well as authorship. Neither tradition may be attributable to Jeremiah; both cannot be so attributed. The separation of the OAN into two distinct collections, 46–49 and 50–51, may ease the problem of attribution because the nations denounced in 46–49 represent opposition to Babylon as well as opponents of Judah and a nationalistic prophet might well speak out against them (cf. Bardtke 1935; 1936). However, all attempts to attribute the OAN of 46–51 to Jeremiah depend upon the prior theory that the book represents the utterances of the historical Jeremiah rather than the construction of the editorial framework. Only in that framework does such an attribution appear (e.g.; 46.1, 13; 47.1; 49.34; 50.1) and nothing in the poems necessitates identifying the speaker as Jeremiah (see on 50.1). If Jeremiah's connection with the OAN is the creation of the editing processes, then the whole debate about how the authorship of 27–29 and 50–51 is to be reconciled is beside the point. The editorial presentation of Jeremiah is as a prophet to the nations (1.5, 10) and 46–51 provide the OAN which warrant such a description.

46–51 contain some of the finest, as well as the most difficult, poetry in the book of Jeremiah (e.g. 46.3–12, 14–24; 48.1–10; 50.35–38a; 51.20–23). Similarities between the poems of 46–51 and those in 4–6, 8–10 raise the question of whether the two collections of poetry have a common source or one is modelled on the other. If the latter is the case, then an argument may be mounted for viewing 4–6, 8–10 as imitated OAN describing the (Babylonian) destruction of Jerusalem. This would support the view of Jeremiah as a nationalistic prophet speaking against the nations (Bardtke): a dominant element in the tradition which has been extended in Part I to make him a speaker against Jerusalem. This is simply one interpretation among many of the implications of the shared poetic elements of 46–51 and 4–6, 8–10. 46–51 also share common features with the OAN of Isaiah, Amos and Obadiah and poetry elsewhere in the Bible (e.g. cf. 48.45–46 with Num. 21.28–29; see Notes on 46–51 for parallels) and such shared aspects point to the stereotyping of OAN in the different collections throughout the Bible. They also weaken the arguments for a specific authorship of any single tradition. The genre OAN must be regarded as independent of the traditions into which they have been incorporated and as *one more level* of tradition within those books. Hence the editorial links which connect the poems of 46–51 with Jeremiah (46.1, 13; 47.1; 49.34; 50.1) are necessary in order to relate this specific collection to the redactional framework governing the book of Jeremiah.

The division of 46–51 into two parts, 46–49 and 50–51, permits certain differences between the collections to come into focus. The nations denounced in 46–49 (excluding 49.28–39) represent Judah's neighbours and belong to the socio-political history of the nation over a number of centuries. These poems may therefore reflect encounters between Judah and its neighbours during the eighth to the sixth century (cf. Rudolph 1963; Ogden 1982) rather than the onslaught of the Babylonians against Judah's traditional opponents from 605 onwards. But the defeat of Egypt by Babylon at Carchemish in 605 (cf. 46. 2, 6) must be regarded as an important element in the poems and it is possible to read the collection in the light of Babylonian dominance in the sixth century. Bardtke's interpretation of the poems as Jeremiah's preaching against the enemies of Josiah's expansionist plans in the years 617–615 (1935, 236–9; 1936, 242) cannot be ruled out *a priori*, but is too precise an identification of the background of stereotypical poems and too dependent on the redactional presentation of Jeremiah as a prophet in the time of Josiah (1.2; 25.1, 3). It does, however, illustrate one approach to 46–49 as war oracles determining foreign policy (cf. Christensen 1975, 208–49). Christensen's analysis of 46–49 divides them into genuine OAN of Jeremiah (46.2–12, 13–24; 47.1–7; 49.28–33, 34–39) and archaic OAN (48.1–47; 49. 1–6, 7–22, 23–27). This division allows the stereotypical and distinctive elements in the OAN of 46–49 to be related to the Jeremiah tradition without furnishing arguments for attributing them to Jeremiah. In 50–51 a different spirit may be detected (termed 'eschatological orientation' by Christensen 1975, 208) as well as a different enemy, namely Babylon. The length of the oracular collection against Babylon in conjunction with a number of distinctive features in it justifies the separate treatment of 50–51 (cf. Christensen 1975, 249–80; Wiklander 1978, 43–5). Apart from the lengthy material against Moab in 48 with its depiction of a hubristic enemy of Yahweh, the foe attacked in 50–51 is at times less the historical Babylon than a mythical creature (cf. the dragon of 51.34) symbolizing opposition to Yahweh (cf. the representation of Babylon in Isa. 13–14 and Tyre in Ezek. 28). Such a presentation of the destroyer of Jerusalem slips history and moves in the direction of apocalyptic (Christensen). Babylon becomes a symbol of the oppressor of Yahweh's people and the fully redacted 50–51 ceases to be solely the product of the sixth century. Zion as victim is an important feature of this cycle which distinguishes it from 46–49 (with the exception of 48.27): e.g. 50.6–7, 17–20, 28, 29, 33–34; 51.10, 11, 24, 34–37, 49–51. Whether this motif is an integral part of the cycle or a later glossing of 50–51 (cf. Fohrer 1981, 50–2) is a moot point and does not affect the interpretation of the work as it now stands. With the destruction of Babylon (whether as

Nebuchadrezzar's kingdom or as a cipher of whatever imperial power dominates the people of Israel) the vindication of Zion and Israel is guaranteed and the cycle reflects the worshipping community's liturgy of triumph. Such a reflection is quite lacking in 46–49, especially in view of the grace notes scattered throughout these OAN (e.g. 46.26b; 48.47; 49.6, 39).

The hubris of the enemy (Moab in 48, Babylon in 50–51) which attracts the wrath of Yahweh (48.26, 29–30, 35, 42; 50.24–27, 31–32; 51.6, 11, 25–26, 56) is a motif to be found in other OAN (e.g. Isa. 13–14 against Babylon; Ezek. 28 against Tyre) and suggests that some OAN transcended their origins in xenophobic curses against other nations to become statements of a theological nature against hubris of any form (cf. Isa. 2.12–17). Yahweh's vengeance reflects Yahweh's imperium which may be the background to the developed use of the OAN (on *nāqām*, *n^eqāmāh*, 'vengeance, vindication' in the Bible and especially the book of Jeremiah cf. Mendenhall 1973, 69–104). Against the imperial dominance of the empire (in particular Babylon) the OAN pose Yahweh's power on behalf of his people. This opposition makes 46–51, 50–51 especially so, very different from the other levels of tradition in the book of Jeremiah which are so scathing against Yahweh's people and more akin to the cycle of salvation oracles in 30–31. The two cycles 30–31, 50–51 may be read together because, though having different origins and interests, they share the motif of the restoration of Israel. In 30–31 that restoration is focused on without much emphasis on external enemies (apart from 30.12–16), whereas in 50–51 the enemy is the main focus with minor allusions to the vindication of Zion and the return of the exiles. The differences between the cycles are more significant than the shared motif of restoration, but both traditions contribute to the more positive aspects of the book of Jeremiah.

A full treatment of the themes of 46–51 can only arise out of the exegesis of the poems, but two further features of the OAN may be noted here. Many exegetes detect the influence of holy war concepts in the poems (e.g. Bach 1962; Christensen 1975, 184–93) as well as elsewhere in the Jeremiah tradition (cf. 4.5–8; 6.1–5; 15.7–9). Such concepts are not a distinctive feature of Israelite religion but represent the general beliefs of ancient Near Eastern societies that their gods intervened on their behalf against their enemies (cf. M. Weippert 1972). In the OAN Yahweh fights against Israel's enemies, especially against Egypt (46.10, 15, 25), Philistia (47.4, 7), Moab (48.26, 35,

44), Ammon (49.5), Edom (49.10, 13, 15–16), Damascus (49.27), Elam (49.35–38), and Babylon (50.13–15, 24–25, 31–32, 34, 45; 51.1–2, 11, 12, 24, 25–26, 29, 36–37, 40, 44, 52–53, 55–57). This motif is reversed in Part I (4–6), where the enemy comes against Jerusalem at Yahweh's bidding (e.g. 5.15–17; 6.6). Such a reversal of a traditional form suggests that the fall of Jerusalem was justified in the development of the tradition by the use of the OAN genre in a transformed mode, and this may warrant the view that the relevant poems in Part I reflect a later stage of the development of the book. The other notable feature of the OAN is the allusion to magical practices in 51.59–64 with reference to Babylon and the use of ciphers in 50–51 (e.g. 51.1, 41). Incantation and prestidigitation with a background in magical activity are important elements in the book of Jeremiah (e.g. 13.1–7; 19.1–2, 10–11; 25.15–17; 43.9–13) and may be presupposed for the OAN. The ciphers used (cf. 25.26) can hardly be intended to conceal the identity of the victim (clearly stated throughout 50–51), so must be accounted for in terms of magical tricks designed to bring about the downfall of specific opponents through the creation of ill omens against them. Prophecy and magic are particularly associated in the OAN (cf. Fohrer 1967, 257–61) and the manipulation of oracles (as in 51.59–64) makes a fitting conclusion to the cycle in MT. Gesture, word, incantation and ritual activity combine in the OAN to bring about the downfall of the imperial enemy and the termination of the words of Jeremiah at this point (only in MT 51.64b) concludes the story impressively with the doom of Babylon.

This analysis of 46–51 inevitably brings to the fore the considerable differences between the two editions of Jeremiah (G and MT). In the MT positioning of 50–51 it is difficult to avoid the impression that the editors have deliberately concluded their work with the ritual dismissal of Babylon as the last word of Jeremiah. G, with its very different order, represents a less impressive editorial arrangement and conclusion. MT ends on a dramatic note; G is much more modest in concluding with the story of Baruch's worries about his future. Whether the defeat of Babylon (in the past?) accounts for the difference cannot now be determined, but the different editions point to divergent editorial presentations of the OAN. In G they are where they would be expected to be – as Part II of the tradition (cf. Isaiah, Ezekiel) and integrated with the cup of the wine of wrath story (G 32.15–29 = MT 25.12–29). MT separates them from that story and turns 25.15–38 into a closure of Part I rather than the beginning of Part II. The motif of the cup (*kōs*) is common to 25.15–17, 27–29 and some of the OAN (49.12; 51.7), but is used quite differently in each instance. In 25.15–17, 27–29 *all* the nations drink it (including Jerusalem and Judah according to the addition in v. 18) because Yahweh's work of evil begins at Jerusalem but will not finish there. Thus all the nations (Babylon as well) share in the wrath of Yahweh which the events of 587 presage. In the development of the OAN against Edom the victim must drink the cup because those who did not deserve to drink it have had to partake of it. Who are these? Most likely 49.12 refers to Judah and this allusion is very different from 25.29. 51.7 represents Babylon as the golden cup in Yahweh's hand which has made the whole earth drunk. The metaphor is the same as in 25.15–17, but here it is Babylon rather than Jeremiah who administers the deadly vinous potion to the nations. However, the cup metaphor is only a passing reference to Babylon because the point of the poem in 51.6–10 is the sudden transformation in the fortunes of Babylon; from being Yahweh's golden cup one moment to being broken herself the next moment (how are the mighty fallen!). So the cup metaphor holds together a cluster of different motifs.

The difference between G and MT is compounded by a different order of nations attacked in the respective presentations of the OAN:

G	MT (EVV)
Elam	Egypt
Egypt	Philistia
Babylon	Moab
Philistia	Ammon
Edom	Edom
Ammon	Damascus
Kedar	Kedar
Damascus	Elam
Moab	Babylon

G places the material in MT 25.15–38 at the end of the OAN whereas in MT this section is separated from the OAN by Parts III and IV. The order of MT approximates more closely to the list of nations in 25.19–26 (it is *not* the same order) than does G (i.e. G 32.5–12), but little may be deduced from that approximation except that there may have been an *attempt* in the second edition to make the order conform (cf. Janzen 1973, 116). Some exegetes have discerned a geographical (e.g. Pfeiffer 1941, 487) or chronological (e.g. Hyatt, 1104) order in MT, but no discernible order can be detected in G. The position of the OAN in G, with its list of nations in no particular order, must be regarded as original and the arrangement of them in MT as a secondary development of the tradition.

46.1

46[1] The word of the LORD which came to Jeremiah the prophet concerning the nations.

[MT 46] = G 26. **[1]** MT *ʾašer hāyāh dᵉbar-yhwh ʾel-yirmᵉyāhū hannābīʾ ʿal*, lit. 'what came (as) the word of Yahweh to Jeremiah the prophet concerning': this curious form of a stereotypical introduction also appears in 14.1; 47.1; 49.34 (14.1 lacks *hannābīʾ*, 'the prophet'); cf. 1.2. G lacks v. 1 because it integrates the OAN with 25.15–38 in G 25.14–32.24 and therefore has no need of a separate title like MT. MT *ʿal-haggōyim*, 'concerning the nations': many mss 'against *all* the nations'; cf. 25.13b, *ʾašer-nibbāʾ yirmᵉyāhū ʿal-kol-haggōyim*, 'which Jeremiah prophesied against all the nations'. Rudolph, 264, 268, adds 'in the fourth year of Jehoiakim the son of Josiah, king of Judah' from v. 2b because he regards 46.1 – 49.33 as oracles belonging to the fourth year of Jehoiakim (49.34 is dated to the beginning of Zedakiah's reign). Cf. 45.1b.

A formulaic reception of the divine word notice functions as a title to the collection of OAN. As an editorial note it uses the form which occurs in 14.1; 47.1; 49.34 and, to some extent, in 1.2. It has three elements: the divine word, Jeremiah *the prophet*, and the nations. These explain the general description of Jeremiah in 1.5c as 'a prophet to the nations' (*nābīʾ laggōyim*). In denouncing the enemy nations Jeremiah functions as a nationalistic prophet.

46.2

2 About Egypt. Concerning the army of Pharaoh Neco, king of Egypt, which was by the river Euphrates at Carchemish and which Nebuchadrezzar king

of Babylon defeated in the fourth year of Jehoiakim the son of Josiah, king of Judah:

---

[2] MT *l^emiṣrayim*, 'concerning Egypt': section title, cf. 23.9; 48.1; 49.1, 7, 23; the longer title here is also to be found in 47.1; 49.28; cf. 49.34; 50.1. The section title may be separated from the occasion notice which follows: as a general title to 46 and because the detailed specifications of the rest of v.2 apply only to vv.3–12 (cf. v. 13). The occasion is 605 when Babylon defeated Egypt at Carchemish. Cf. 25.1; 36.1; 45.1 for this date. Whether Rudolph, 268, is justified in shifting the date notice to v. 1 in order to make 46.1 – 49.33 a block of material parallel to 25.1ff. and 36.1ff. is a moot point, but MT does not present it in this fashion. The dating owes something to 25.1 in that 25.19 identifies the Egyptians as the first of the recipients of the cup of Yahweh's wrath.

Egypt

The first nation addressed is Egypt (cf. 25.19, but G puts Elam first in 25.14–20; cf. Isa. 19; Ezek. 29–32). As all the OAN are declarations of defeat and destruction (though allowance is made for subsequent recovery in certain cases, cf. 46.26b; 48.47; 49.6, 39), the editorial dating of v. 2 may reflect an attempt to relate some poems to specific historical events. 605 was a fateful year for Egypt because its defeat by the Babylonians at Carchemish established Babylon's power throughout Palestine and curtailed effectively Egyptian control of Palestine. The denunciation of Egypt in 46 may be read in conjunction with 25.1–11, but in view of 50–51 is better read in the light of 25.15–17, 19–26. Were it not for 45, which has links with 46.2, the condemnation of Egypt in 46 would follow in MT immediately after the denunciations of Egypt in 43.8–13 and the Jewish communities there in 44. The enormous hostility felt towards Egypt and evidenced by 42.13 – 44.30 as much as 46 reflects political as well as ideological factors in the tradition. Between 609 and 587 pro-Egyptian elements in Judaean politics contributed significantly to national policy and, to some extent, were behind the revolts against Babylonian imperial power which brought Jerusalem to ruins. Deuteronomistic ideology viewed Egypt with extreme hostility and regarded any form of involvement with it, be it political, religious or residential, as apostasy against Yahwism and betrayal of the nation's history. After 605 the emergence of pro-Babylonian forces in Judaean political life created factions within the body politic. The extent to which the oracles against Egypt in 46 represent the output of such factions or the standard responses to the misfortunes of foreign nations is difficult to determine. Various strands in the book of Jeremiah reflect the partisan politics of both parties (cf. 26.20–23; 37.7–10 for traces of pro-Egyptian sentiments; 27–29, 39–40 for pro-Babylonian attitudes) but the oracles of 46–51 run counter to both outlooks in that they treat all foreign nations as the intended victims of Yahweh's wrath.

46.3–12

3 'Prepare buckler and shield,
and advance for battle!
4 Harness the horses;
mount, O horsemen!
Take your stations with your helmets,
polish your spears,
put on your coats of mail!
5 Why have I seen it?
They are dismayed
and have turned backward.
Their warriors are beaten down,
and have fled in haste;
they look not back –
terror on every side!
says the LORD.
6 The swift cannot flee away,
nor the warrior escape;
in the north by the river Euphrates
they have stumbled and fallen.
7 Who is this, rising like the Nile,
like rivers whose waters surge?
8 Egypt rises like the Nile,
like rivers whose waters surge.
He said, I will rise, I will cover the earth,
I will destroy cities and their inhabitants.
9 Advance, O horses,
and rage, O chariots!
Let the warriors go forth:
men of Ethiopia and Put who handle the shield,
men of Lud, skilled in handling the bow.

10 That day is the day of the Lord GOD of hosts,
a day of vengeance,
to avenge himself on his foes.
The sword shall devour and be sated,
and drink its fill of their blood.
For the Lord GOD of hosts holds a sacrifice
in the north country by the river Euphrates.
11 Go up to Gilead, and take balm,
O virgin daughter of Egypt!
In vain you have used many medicines;
there is no healing for you.
12 The nations have heard of your shame,
and the earth is full of your cry;
for warrior has stumbled against warrior;
they have both fallen together.'

---

[4] MT *wa'alū happārāšīm*, 'and mount the stallions: cf. Watson 1984, 380; *pārāš* means 'horse, steed' as well as 'horseman' (4.29) or 'charioteers'. G lacks 'and', and this lack gives the commands of the Egyptian officers a more realistic staccato manner, cf. EVV. MT *mirqū hārᵉmāpḥīm*, 'polish the lances': G *probalete ta dorata*, 'advance the spears', i.e. raise the spears; Rudolph, 266, follows Ehrlich 1912, 352, in reading it as *hērīqū*, 'empty', i.e. draw, unsheath (cf. Ps. 35.3) the lances (BHS *hāriqū*). **[5]** MT *madoū'a rā'ītī*, 'why do I see?': i.e. what is it that I see?; lacking in G due to 'simple scribal lapse' (Janzen 1973, 109). MT *ūmānōs nāsū*, lit. 'and the fleeing they flee': the noun *mānōs*, 'flight', may reflect an enclitic *m* (so Watson 1984, 380), so the phrase is to be understood as if it were an infinitive absolute with finite verb (i.e. *nōs nāsū*), 'really fleeing' or 'fleeing to and fro', cf. Rudolph, 266; Bright, 301, 'they flee pell-mell'. MT *māgōr missābīb*, 'terror on every side': cf. 6.25; 20.3, 4, 10; 49.29; Lam. 2.22; Ps. 31.13 (MT 14); Bach 1962, 51 n. 3, translates it as 'ambush' (cf. Watson). **[6]** MT *'al-yānūs*, 'do not flee': the jussive force here expresses the view that the swift *cannot* flee cf. GK 107p. G lacks 'river'; BHS deletes it. **[7]** MT *kannᵉhārōt yitgā'ašu mēmāyw*, 'like rivers whose waters surge': plurals of amplification (Watson 1984, 381); cf. v. 8a. **[8]** The answer to the question in v. 7; deleted by Rudolph as unnecessary (cf. BHS). G lacks part of the line (8a); it also lacks 'city and' in v. 8b. **[9]** MT *wᵉyēṣᵉ'ūsᵉ'u haggibbōrīm*, 'and let the warriors go forth': G *exelthate* . . . 'go forth . . .' = *ṣᵉ'ū*, cf. NEB; Bright, 302; BHS. 'Put': G *Libues*, 'Libyans'; but Put is hardly Libya (cf. Nahum 3.9). It is more likely to be Punt on the Somali coast (cf. Rudolph, 268). MT *wᵉlūdīm*, 'and Ludim': not the Lydians of Asia Minor but an African people under the control of Egypt (cf. Gen. 10.13). Cf. Nahum 3.9 *puṭwᵉlūbīm*, 'Put and the Libyans'; see comments in Thompson, 689. MT *tōpᵉśē dōrᵉkē qāšet*, lit. 'handlers of, benders of the bow': variants or, more likely, an erroneous repetition of *tōpᵉśe* from previous clause *tōpᵉśē māgēn*, 'handlers of the shield'; most exegetes delete it (cf. BHS). **[10]** G lacks *ṣᵉbā'ōt*, 'of hosts'. MT *ḥereb*, 'the sword': but perhaps *ḥarbō*, 'his sword', should be read due to haplography (cf. BHS); G *hē machaira kuriou*, 'the sword of the lord'. There may be a hint or element of word-play in the word *miṣṣārāyw*, 'on his foes', in an oracle about *miṣrāyim*, 'Egypt', though Egypt does not occur in v. 10; cf. v. 11; Watson. **[11]** K *hrbyty*; Q *hirbêt*, 'you have multiplied': K represents the old feminine ending, cf. 2.33; 3.4. Watson 1984, 382–3, detects rootplay and pun in *ʿalī gilᵉʿād*, 'go up (to) Gilead', and *ṣōrī*, 'balsam, balm, storax', and *miṣrāyim*, 'Egypt'; word-play may be detected in *ʿalī*, 'go up', and *tᵉʿālāh*, 'healing' (lit. the new flesh which *comes up* in the healing of a wound). Cf. 8.22 for the association of Gilead with healing. For the epithet 'virgin daughter' personifying a nation cf. 18.13; 31.4,21; Amos 5.2 ('virgin Israel'); Jer. 14.17 ('virgin daughter my people'); Isa. 47.1 ('virgin daughter Babylon'); Isa. 23.12 ('virgin daughter Sidon'). **[12]** MT *qᵉlōnēk*, 'your cry': cf. G. *phōnen sou*, 'your voice' (= *qōlēk*). NEB. RSV, JPSB, 'your shame', is a poor match for *ṣiwḥātēk*, 'your outcry'. In late Heb. *qōlan* means 'shouter, crier': unattested in biblical Hebrew but possible here or *qōl*, 'voice' with afformative – (*ā*)*n* (cf. Watson 1984, 382 n. 62); cf. Bright, 302 n.

A brilliant poem in vv. 3–12 fits the redactional introduction in v.2. It is one of the finest poems in the book of Jeremiah, and skilfully uses word-play, assonance, simile, metaphor, personification and certain structural patterns (cf. analysis in Watson 1984, 379–83). Dominant motifs include uses of *ʿālāh*, 'go up, rise' (vv. 4, 7, 8, 9, 11), *gibbōr*, 'warrior' (vv. 5, 6, 9, 12), and *'ereṣ*, 'earth' (vv. 8, 10, 12). The poem moves from a graphic depiction of the call to war to the complete rout of the Egyptian army as its warriors flee from the enemy – an enemy never directly identified because in the background of the disastrous encounter 'in the north (country) by the river Euphrates' (vv. 6, 10) lurks the figure of Yahweh (v. 10a). The real enemy is Yahweh, hence the Babylonians do not appear in the poem. Egypt's defeat is the focus, and from the Judaean perspective of the poet the lord Yahweh is the host at the slaughter of the ancient enemy (cf. v. 10). Behind the ideology of the poem may be detected elements of the holy war motif (cf. Bach 1962) used to construct this oracle of doom.

Whether the oracle was uttered before, during or after the defeat of the Egyptian army at Carchemish cannot be determined from the text because the conventional nature of such oracles allows them to be interpreted as curses against the enemy by way of debilitating their campaign or as celebrations of their defeat. The battle between Egypt and Babylon at Carchemish was not one involving Judah, so the poem can hardly be read as a determinative of Judaean policy. It does, however, cleverly represent the *real* enemy of Egypt as being Yahweh and therefore the Babylonian defeat of the Egyptian army as the triumph of Yahweh's vengeance over *his* adversaries. Thus an event of international significance is drawn into the realm of Judaean ideology and made to conform to the domestic theology of a minor state on the edges of the two empires engaged in the struggle for dominance. Describing the encounter at Carchemish in the *north* (cf. 1.13–14; 4.5; 6.1, 22; 25.9 for the reverberations of this motif in the tradition) as Yahweh's day, i.e. a day of vengeance (*yōm n^eqāmāh*) belonging to him, and as the time of the lord Yahweh's sacrifice (*zebaḥ la'dōnāy yhwh*), the poem domesticates international affairs in terms of Judaean religious matters (cf. Isa. 34.5–8; Ezek.39. 17–20; Zeph. 1.7 for similar motifs.)

In vv. 3–4 the Egyptian officers are heard barking commands at their troops to mount up in preparation for battle, but in vv. 5–6 the warriors are beaten back and flee, only to fall by the river (MT v.5a has the poet witness the rout of the Egyptians). Having summarized the battle in vv. 3–6 the poet describes it further in 7–9 and explains it in vv. 10–12. The mighty power and, even, hubris of Egypt is depicted in vv. 7–8 as the rising of the waters of the Nile – an image which captures admirably the essence of Egypt. Behind the repetitions of vv. 7–8a (MT) may be an allusion to the cosmic mythology of the waters of chaos shared by many nations in the ancient Near East (cf. Gen. 1.2; Bright, 306; Christensen 1975, 218; May 1955, 16). The surging of the Nile becomes a figure of the Egyptian army's pursuit of conquest and power and at the same time alludes to the destructive forces released by the waters of chaos which threaten to engulf the civilized world. Egypt is chaos and its war aims are a hubristic endeavour to cover the earth and destroy (cf. Isa. 10.5–16 for a description of Assyria as a destructive form of hubris). So the Egyptian warriors and their auxiliary troops go forth to do battle in the north (v. 9). But the day of battle belongs to Yahweh as his day of vengeance (cf. Isa. 2.12–17 for Yahweh's day against all hubristic attitudes and enterprises). The confident march of the Egyptians is but to the place of Yahweh's sacrifice, and his sword (cf. G) will devour the Egyptians. So the military expedition becomes a scene of ritual slaughter and there is no hope for the Egyptians. Against Yahweh's slaughter there can be no healing, in spite of all the efforts made by Egypt to find a cure for disaster (v. 11; cf. 8.21–22).

46.13

13 The word which the LORD spoke to Jeremiah the prophet about the coming of Nebuchadrezzar king of Babylon to smite the land of Egypt:

---

[13] Cf. 37.2; 50.1 for similar elements of the formulaic reception of the divine word introduction. G *en cheiri*, 'by the hand of': MT *'el*, 'to' (Jeremiah) = *bᵉyad*, 'by means of', as in 37.2; 50.1. G lacks *hannābīʼ*, 'the prophet'.

The redactional introduction to the poem in vv. 14–24 identifies the occasion of that utterance as Nebuchadrezzar's invasion of Egypt. In view of the poem's reference to 'a gadfly from the north' (v. 20) and 'a people from the north' (v. 24), that identification would appear to be a reasonable one. However, Nebuchadrezzar did not invade Egypt until 568–7, some forty years after the defeat of Egypt at Carchemish, so the appropriateness of the attribution of the poem to Jeremiah is questionable. The association of the two poems together is justifiable on the grounds that they represent two periods of Egyptian defeat by the Babylonians and define Egypt's fate in terms of Babylonian domination. Commentators who wish to attribute vv. 14–24 to Jeremiah do so on the grounds that he may have uttered it in 604 when the invasion of Egypt by Babylon appeared likely to happen (cf. Bright, 308; Thompson, 691; Rudolph, 271). A date *c.* 587 may be indicated by 37.6–10 which would make the poem an attack on the pro-Egyptian party in Jerusalem by denouncing their hopes of Egyptian support with an oracle of doom against Egypt. The most likely period for the poem is the two decades after the fall of Jerusalem (cf. Cornill, 450–1). This would make vv. 14–24 similar to the denunciation of Egypt in 43.8–13 (cf. Hyatt, 1107; Ezek. 29–32). Apart from the images of invasion in the poem, the word-play on the Pharaoh's name in v. 17 reflects the fact that Hophra (Apries) was in power then (Cornill, 451). The force of the word-play should not be exaggerated: it is over-subtle and may be more imaginary than real (G specifically identifies Necho as the Pharaoh and therefore relates it to 605 rather than after 589).

Such difficulties in dating a poem are characteristic of all biblical interpretations because the highly metaphorical and allusive language of biblical poetry permits a wide range of meaning. The problem of meaning is compounded in the book of Jeremiah by the editorial framework, which may have no necessary connection with the poetry and prose attached to it. Part of the difficulty with 46.13 is the conventional dating of Jeremiah's ministry to the 620s, so that by 566–7 he would have been very old indeed (i.e. in his eighties cf Duhm, 239). Exegetes who do not place Jeremiah's work as early as 1.2 indicates are relieved of this minor problem and may envisage Jeremiah prophesying twenty years after his arrival in Egypt. However, only the editorial note attributes vv. 14–24 to Jeremiah, and that may be regarded as more schematic or formal than accurate (cf. Volz, 395). A dating of the poem to 605–4 is necessary only if v. 13 reflects v. 2 and is judged to be a continuation of the defeat of Egypt depicted in vv. 3–12. The most natural reading of v. 13 is to relate the poem which follows to the invasion of Egypt by Nebuchadrezzar and therefore to the period of 568–7. No editorial dating is given, so v. 13 should be read as the redactors' introduction by way of commentary on vv. 14–24. As the *prophet* (lacking in G) of the tradition Jeremiah is credited with the oracle against Egypt, so that the poem describing the collapse of Egypt against the onslaught from the north becomes an oracular utterance. The occasion of the oracle is given in the most general terms in v. 13 but without sufficient detail (stereotyped or otherwise, cf. v. 2) to permit the modern reader to determine the precise intention of the editors. Such editorial glossing of the text is part of the development of the tradition, but has the effect of historicizing what may have been originally a quite different type of utterance (i.e. the curse against the enemy). The poem may *now* be read as a commentary on Nebuchadrezzar's campaign against the Egyptians rather than the calling down on the Egyptians of bad luck and misfortune in the future.

46.14–24

14 'Declare in Egypt, and proclaim in Migdol;
proclaim in Memphis and Tahpanhes;
Say, "Stand ready and be prepared,
for the sword shall devour round about you."
15 Why has Apis fled?
Why did not your bull stand?
Because the LORD thrust him down.
16 Your multitude stumbled and fell,
and they said one to another,
"Arise, and let us go back to our own people
and to the land of our birth,
because of the sword of the oppressor."
17 Call the name of Pharaoh, king of Egypt,
"Noisy one who lets the hour go by."
18 As I live, says the King,
whose name is the LORD of hosts,
like Tabor among the mountains,
and like Carmel by the sea, shall one come.
19 Prepare yourselves baggage for exile,
O inhabitants of Egypt!
For Memphis shall become a waste,
a ruin, without inhabitant.
20 A beautiful heifer is Egypt,
but a gadfly from the north has come upon her.
21 Even her hired soldiers in her midst
are like fatted calves;
yea, they have turned and fled together,
they did not stand;
for the day of their calamity has come upon them,
the time of their punishment.
22 She makes a sound like a serpent gliding away;
for her enemies march in force,
and come against her with axes,
like those who fell trees.
23 They shall cut down her forest,
says the LORD,
though it is impenetrable,
because they are more numerous than locusts;
they are without number.
24 The daughter of Egypt shall be put to shame,
she shall be delivered into the hand of a people from the north.'

[14] G lacks 'in Egypt and proclaim', 'and in Tahpanhes': MT, cf. 44.1; Isa. 11.11. Cf. 4.5 for the three verbs 'declare' (*higīd*), 'proclaim' (*hašmi'a*), 'say' (*'āmar*). MT *sᵉbībekā*, 'round about you': G *tēn smilaka sou* 'your yew tree' = *subbᵉkēk* cf. 21.14; MT changes gender here (cf. *lāk*, 'yourself'), BHS corrects it and in v. 15 (cf. Rudolph, 270). **[15]** MT *maddū'a nisḥap 'abbīrekā*, lit. 'why are your bulls prostrated?': i.e. why are your mighty ones (warriors?) prostrate? G *dia ti ephugen ho Apis*, 'wherefore has Apis fled?' (G^B *apo sou*, 'from you'). G represents *nisḥap* read as two words, *nās ḥap*, 'Hapfled', where Hap is Apis the sacred bull reverenced as the incarnation of the Egyptian god Ptah. Giesebrecht, 231, reads *nās ḥap 'abbīrᵉkā lō' 'āmad*, '(why) has Apis fled . . . your bull not stood?' (cf. Cornill, 452); Rudolph, 270, prefers MT (cf. BHS) with suffix gender of 'mighty ones' adjusted. **[16]** MT *hirbāh kōšēl*, lit. 'he increased one stumbling': G *kai to plēthos sou ēsthenēsen*, 'and your multitude has fainted' = *wahᵃmōnᵉkā kāšal*, 'and your crowd has stumbled'; Rudolph suggests *rahab hārab kāšal*, 'the mighty Rahab has stumbled' (cf. BHS), i.e. Egypt has stumbled (cf. Isa. 30.7 for Rahab [the mythical sea monster] as an epithet of Egypt). Giesebrecht, 231, reads *'erbᵉkā*, 'your mixed multitude', i.e. the foreign troops among them (cf. 50.37; Ezek. 30.5; see also 25.20). Christensen 1975, 218–19, offers the conjectural emendation *rābbᵉ(kā)*, 'your champion', based on *rīb* as an epithet applied to the deity (cf. 50.34; 51.36). MT *wayyō'mᵉrū*, 'and they said': transpose to beginning of clause (cf. G *hekastos . . . elalei*, 'each . . . said'). MT *mippᵉnē ḥereb hayyōnāh*, 'because of the sword of the oppressor': cf. 25.38; G *apo prosōpou machairas Hellēnikēs*, 'from the Greek sword' = . . . *hayyᵉwāniyyāh*. **[17]** MT *qārᵉ'ū šām par'ōh*, 'they called there, "Pharaoh . . ." ': G *kalesate to onoma Pharaō Nechaō* . . . 'call the name of Pharaoh Necho . . .' = *qirᵉ'ū šēm* . . .; BHS treats 'king of Egypt' as an addition to the text. MT *šā'ōn heᶜᵉbīr hammō'ēd*, lit. 'battle noise who lets pass the appointed time': meaning uncertain, but possibly a reference to mistimed battle strategy (cf. 25.31; 48.45, where *šā'ōn* represents the noise of war). The Pharaoh is the *din* of war no doubt, but to little effect. Bright, 306, conjectures a pun on his personal name or royal titles; NEB 'King Bombast, the man who missed his moment'; JPSB 'Braggart who let the hour go by'; Christensen 1975, 218, 'Big Noise, who missed his chance!' The use of *heᶜᵃbīr* may be a pun on Pharaoh Hophra's name Apries, i.e. *w'ḥ-ib-r'* (cf. Thompson, 692), G transliterates *Saōnesbiemōēd*. **[18]** MT *hammelek yhwh ṣᵉbā'ōt šᵉmō*, 'the king Yahweh of hosts is his name': G *kurios ho theos*, 'the lord god'. MT '*the* king' (cf. 48.15b) contrasts with v. 17 'king of Egypt', thus emphasizing Yahweh as the real, i.e. effective, king, so unlike the windbag who cannot seize the right moment for action. Rudolph, 270, inserts *gibbōr*, 'warrior', after *kī* in v. 18b and adds *'ōyēb*, 'foe', to the end of it (cf. BHS): *'ōyēb* is lacking due to haplography and *gibbōr* because of homoioteleuton. **[19]** MT *yōšebet bat-miṣrāyim*, lit. 'inhabitress, daughter Egypt': cf. 'virgin daughter Egypt', v. 11; and the more frequent 'daughter my people' (e.g. 8.19, 21, 23 [EV 9.1]). It represents a personification of the people of Egypt as a woman. Cf. 2.15; 9.10 (EV 11) for similar motifs of the Judaean cities and Jerusalem becoming ruins without inhabitants. **[20]** MT *yᵉpēh-piyyāh*, 'pretty': better with many mss, *yᵉpēpiyyāh*. MT *qereṣ miṣṣāpōn bā' bā'*, lit. 'a fly from the north has come, has come': *qereṣ* (a hapax leg.) is of uncertain meaning, 'fly, gadfly' (stem *qrṣ*, 'nip, pinch', cf. Prov. 6.13; 10.10; 16.30; Job 33.6); G *apospasma*, 'shred, something torn off'. Cf. Isa. 7.18 for a direct entomological allusion as a figure of invasion and defeat. Many mss, GS read *bā' bāh*, 'has come upon her'; some exegetes delete the second *bā'* as a dittography. **[21]** MT *kᵉʿeglē marbēq*, 'like calves of the stall': i.e. stall-fed, fat calves as a simile of well-fed, fat warriors (cf. Isa. 10.16 for fatness as a figure of soldiers); the hired ones in her midst are mercenaries. The phrase *ʿēt pᵉquddāh* (suffix variable), 'time of ... punishment', appears in 6.15; 8.12; 10.15; 49.8; 50.27, 31; 51.18 (cf. 'year of ...' 11.23; 23.12; 48.44). **[22]** MT *qōlāh kannāḥāš yēlēk*, 'her voice like the snake it goes': G *phōnē hōs opheōs surizontos*, 'their voice is like a hissing snake'; Bright, 304 reads 'Hear her hiss like a snake', following G (*šōrēq*). Rudolph, 270, reads *kᵉnaham yōlᵉdāh*, 'like the groaning of one giving birth' (cf. BHS); Christensen 1975, 219–20, suggests *qalāh kᵉnāḥāš zāḥal*, 'quickly like a snake she glides away' (cf. Micah 7.17, where *nāḥāš* and *zāḥal* occur in parallel). MT *bᵉḥayil*, 'in force': G *en ammō*, 'in the sand' = *bᵉḥōl*. MT *lāh*, 'against her': many mss *lāk*, 'against you'. **[23]** MT *kārᵉtū*, 'they have cut down': G *ekkopsousin*, 'they will cut down'. MT *kī lō' yēḥāqēr*, 'for it cannot be searched': i.e. it is impenetrable; Rudolph favours reading plur here, '*they* cannot be searched' (cf. BHS). Cf. 21.14; 22.7 for the forest (trees) image in terms of destruction (Isa. 10.33–34 have similar figures); some exegetes see in the figure of woodmen chopping down an impenetrable forest the continuation of the snake imagery of v. 22 (i.e. they cut down the forest in order to attack the snake, e.g. Bright, 306). This is unlikely, as the image changes in v. 22b and v. 23 stresses the *numerical* force of the invaders by virtue of which they can cut down even impenetrable forests. MT *kī rabbū mē'arbeh*, 'for they are more numerous than locusts': a hint of word-play on *rābāh* 'to be many', and *'arbeh*, 'locust-swarm', cf. Nahum 3.15 (a different image is used in relation to locusts). **[24]** MT *hōbīšāh bat-miṣrāyim*, 'daughter-Egypt is put to shame': Egypt personified as a young woman is raped by her invaders from the north. Christensen 1975, 220, treats the two occurrences of *bat*, 'daughter' (vv. 19, 24), as *bᵉtūlat*, 'virgin', cf. v. 11. Cf. 13.22, 26 for sexual violence as an image of the shaming of a people.

The second poem on Egypt's defeat focuses on the Egyptian experience of and response to invasion from the north (like the poems in 4.5 – 6.26 the foe from the north is not identified, except for the editorial 46.13). In the Egyptian towns the people are warned (cf.

v. 14; 4.5) to prepare for destruction. Behind the invasion is Yahweh's defeat of Egypt (MT) or his rout of the Egyptian god Apis (G). As expressions of that triumph are the incompetence of the Pharaoh (v. 17) and the failure of the Egyptian mercenaries to withstand the invading forces (v. 21). Thus the poem depicts the invasive defeat of Egypt in terms of Yahweh's activity and thus reflects the holy war motif also apparent in vv. 3–12. Contrasts are made between Yahweh, the Egyptian god Apis (G) and the king of Egypt. Yahweh is the effective power behind the political events of the period, whereas the bull-god of Egypt cannot stand against him nor can the Egyptian king act effectually. In vv. 17, 18 the king of Egypt is represented as a noise (windbag?) who cannot seize the opportune moment (a reflection on 37.7–10?), but the king, identified as Yahweh of hosts (cf. 48.15b; 51.57; also 8.19; 10.7, 10), who acts with power, is the very one who will bring the invader against Egypt. Behind Babylon's defeat of Egypt is Yahweh, and therefore the kudos accruing from that triumph belongs to the Judaean god. In Egypt's destruction is the vindication of Judaean ideology, and the fate of the people of Egypt is the same as that of Judah and Jerusalem (v. 19; a compensation for the fall of Jerusalem or just shared misery?).

In vv. 20–24 a series of theriomorphic metaphors describes Egypt's plight. Egypt is a beautiful heifer savaged by a nipper (the literal meaning of *qereṣ*) from the north. This graphic image of a cow plagued by a vicious species of insect is very appropriate to Egypt because of its theriomorphic cult of the gods. The inroads made by the Babylonians destroy Egypt's beauty. Even her mercenaries (cf. v. 9), like well-fed cattle, have fled in the face of the enemy. The imagery changes in v. 22 to depict Egypt's response to the invasion by means of a simile: she is like a snake hissing at (NEB) or gliding away (RSV) from attack. The snake image again reflects the Egyptian use of serpents as symbols of the gods and insignia of royalty. But Egypt as a snake is a figure of impotent reaction to threatened existence. The invading forces are powerful and numerous (vv. 22–23), and come against her with axes (cf. Ps. 74.5). Again the images change (though some exegetes relate the felling of the trees to the snake metaphor), and like a forest Egypt is chopped down by the axe-men. No matter how impenetrable that forest may be, the invading army is too numerous to be deterred from complete destruction of Egypt. An entomological image, locusts, is used to indicate the sheer numbers of soldiers penetrating the Egyptian territory. That image may appropriately reflect Egyptian uses of insects in religion, but the connection should not be exaggerated, as the point of v. 23 concerns vast numbers rather than locusts as such. The final image of Egypt's defeat is that of a young woman (daughter) violated by the invading troops. Behind the metaphor of national defeat is the all too real practice of occupying armies raping the women of conquered territories. Given over to the northern invader Egypt is a woman (cf. virgin, v. 11) violently ravished.

The Judaean perspective of this poem may be detected in v. 18, where the invader is described in terms reflecting geophysical features of the land of Israel. Two mountains, Tabor and Carmel, regarded as magnificent and impressive sights, are used to depict the enemy who 'shall come' (*yābō'*). These form part of a divine oath that Egypt will be invaded most surely and are rather strange and fantastic images of such an event (cf. Duhm, 340). To the poet's satisfaction Egypt will be exiled and Memphis become a waste (in contrast to Carmel's fertile aspect).

46.25–26

25 The LORD of hosts, the God of Israel, said: 'Behold, I am bringing punishment upon Amon of Thebes, and Pharaoh, and Egypt and her gods and her kings, upon Pharaoh and those who trust in him. 26 I will deliver them into the hand of those who seek their life, into the hand of Nebuchadrezzar king of Babylon and his officers. Afterward Egypt shall be inhabited as in the days of old, says the LORD.'

---

[25] G has a shorter text: 'Behold, I will avenge Amon her son on Pharaoh, and upon them that trust in him.' MT introductory formula is unusual in that it lacks *kōh*, 'thus' (cf. 48.1, 40; 50.18; 51.33). MT *'āmōn minnō'*, 'Amon of Thebes': cf. *minnō' 'āmōn*, Nahum 3.8; Amon was the chief god of Thebes, the capital of Upper Egypt (cf. Ezek. 30.14–16). Rudolph, 272, detects a type of word-play in the two words and suggests that *wᵉ'al-par'ōh*, 'and against Pharaoh', might be *wᵉ'al-pārōh*, 'and against his bull' (but cf. BHS); he also treats the absence of 'and Egypt . . . upon Pharaoh' from G as due to homoioteleuton (BHS; Bright, 305, rightly regards the phrase as an expansion in MT). NEB prints vv. 25–26 as poetry (followed by Thompson, 694), whereas most translations and exegetes treat them as prose. **[26]** G lacks v. 26; cf. 21.7; 44.30 for the motifs in v 26a. MT *wᵉ'aḥᵃrē-kēn tiškōn kimē-qedem*, 'afterwards it will dwell as in the days of old': i.e. Egypt will be inhabited as of old. Cf. 48.47; 49.6, 39 for a similar note of recovery in the oracles against the nations.

A brief prose statement (contrast NEB) summarizes the preceding poem as Yahweh's punishment of Egypt, her gods and institutions. Those Egyptians who trust in these things will be delivered into the power of Nebuchadrezzar and his troops. Thus the poem in vv. 14–24 is enclosed in two editorial comments identifying the enemy of Egypt as Nebuchadrezzar and the power behind him as Yahweh. The final sentence in v. 26 reverses the judgment of Egypt by hinting at a restoration of its inhabitation in the future just like the old days (cf. the more stereotypical restoration of the fortunes of Moab, the Ammonites, and Elam in 48.47; 49.6, 39). Whether this is a realistic note caused by Egypt's survival of the Babylonian invasion of 568 or a modification of the word of judgment because of the Jewish communities living there cannot be determined due to the brevity of the statement. It probably reflects a more positive view of Egypt than is to be found elsewhere in the book of Jeremiah (cf. the prose additions to the oracle denouncing Egypt in Isa. 19.18–25).

The oracles against Egypt conclude with the prosaic summary of vv. 25–26. These brilliant poetic denunciations of Egypt reveal how the oracles against the nations appropriate the political victories of Babylon in order to make statements about Yahweh's activities. Defeated themselves by Babylon, the Jewish communities can only claim the Babylonian achievements as triumphs of their own god. Yet the military might of Babylon (itself to be challenged in 50–51) occasions some very fine poems in the tradition. These assimilate events from international politics to internal ideology and use a combination of oracles of doom and holy war motifs to forge a statement about the *reality* of what is happening in the world at large.

46.27–28

27 'But fear not, O Jacob my servant,
 nor be dismayed, O Israel;
for lo, I will save you from afar,
 and your offspring from the land of their captivity.
Jacob shall return and have quiet and ease,
 and none shall make him afraid.

28 Fear not, O Jacob my servant,
says the LORD,
for I am with you.
I will make a full end of all the nations
to which I have driven you,
but of you I will not make a full end.
I will chasten you in just measure,
and I will by no means leave you unpunished.'

[46.27–28] = 30.10–11 with minor variations: 30.10 has *n^e'um yhwh*, 'says Yahweh', which appears in 46.28 where v. 27a is repeated (lacking in 30.11). 46.28a is necessarily different from 30.11a, which ends with an additional *l^ehôšî'ekā*, 'to save you'. For the motif 'I will not make a full end' cf. 4.27; 5.10, 18. Cf. Notes on 30.10–11.

The appearance of this poem here and in 30.10–11 raises questions about its original location (G only has it here) and its function in the oracles against the nations (see on 30.10–11). In MT the verses are between the oracles against Egypt and Moab, whereas in G they follow Egypt but *precede* the material against Babylon (G 27–28). Israel's return from captivity is a motif used in the oracles against Babylon (e.g. 50.4–5, 17–20; cf. vv. 33–34), so 46.27–28 may originally have been a marginal gloss on 50.2–5 which became displaced by editorial activity (cf. Hitzig, 348; Janzen 1973, 93–4). G represents the verses as a preface to the Babylon collection (cf. Isa. 14.1–3 for a similar prefatory approach to anti-Babylon material), whereas the changed order of MT vitiates that function of the piece. If the verses are read as a postscript to the oracles against Egypt they may be understood as making a contrast between the fate of Egypt and the future of Israel. However this is an inappropriate reading in the light of the final sentence of 46.26 where Egypt's restoration is alluded to because v. 28 refers to the complete annihilation (*kālāh*) of the nations. Such a reference suits 50–51 better than 46.25–26, though it is arguable that these verses are a late addition to the poems in 46. What 46.26b and 27–28 share is the motif of restoration and that link may be sufficient for the present position of vv. 27–28.

The editorial differences between G and MT entail distinctive interpretations of the material in terms of the discrete development of the tradition in its two editions. In 30.10–11 the oracle of salvation contributes to modifying the word about 'a time of distress for Jacob' (lacking in G) by using a poem belonging to the circle from which the poems of Second Isaiah emanated (cf. 30.4–7). Such a function is less clear for 46.27–28 (MT) and the superiority of G here must be acknowledged.

47.1

47[1] The word of the LORD that came to Jeremiah the prophet concerning the Philistines, before Pharaoh smote Gaza.

[MT 47] = G 29. **[1]** G lacks all this verse except for the titular phrase *epi tous allophulous*, 'against the Philistines' = MT *'el-pᵉlištīm*; this looks like the original title (cf. 46.2; 48.1; 49.1, 7, 23, 28; Rudolph, 272–5), perhaps a variation of *lipᵉlištīm*, 'concerning the Philistines'. Katzenstein 1983, 250, regards MT as authentic in spite of G lacking the expansion (cf. Bright, 311, who allows for the possibility that the addition is 'factually correct and furnishes us with the actual occasion of the prophecy'; Janzen 1973, 114, regards G as original). Cf. 14.1; 46.1; 49.34, for this form of the reception of the divine word notice.

Philistia

A short poem against the Philistines (cf. Amos 1.6–8; Isa. 14.29–32; Ezek. 25.15–17; Zeph. 2.4–7; Zech. 9.5–7 for other oracles against Philistia) is prefaced by an editorial introduction which identifies it as an oracular utterance of Jeremiah *the prophet* and its occasion as the period before the Egyptians attacked the Philistine city of Gaza (all this information belongs to the second edition of Jeremiah). The phrase 'before Pharaoh smote Gaza' raises a problem because the poem speaks of the threat to the Philistines as coming from the north (v. 2; cf. Isa. 14.31) rather than the south, whence an Egyptian campaign would come. It is arguable that the secondary introduction is not a statement about an Egyptian attack but an indication that the poem refers to a defeat inflicted on the Philistines *before* the more recent Egyptian onslaught on Gaza. Apart from the general principle that prose introductions have no necessary connection with the poems to which they are attached, the poems themselves are of such a general nature that it is difficult to discern in them precise information about specific historical events. The editors represent Jeremiah as uttering an oracle against the Philistines and provide further background detail by means of a reference to an Egyptian invasion of Philistine territory. Exegetes disagree about the occasion of this attack on Gaza: it may refer to Pharaoh Necho's defeat of the city Kadytis (probably Gaza) in 609 (cf. Herodotus II, 159; Oded 1977, 468), to Babylonian conquests in Palestine after the defeat of Egypt in 605 (cf. Wiseman 1956, 68–73), to the period of Necho's defeat of Nebuchadrezzar in 601 (cf. Katzenstein 1983, 250). The first edition of the text lacks this editorial material and therefore leaves the occasion of the poem to be deduced from the poetry itself. Such a deduction is hardly facilitated by the allusive phrases in the poem, some of which have been interpreted in relation to a rebellion of Ashkelon against Esarhaddon the Assyrian emperor (cf. Tadmor 1966, 100). The wisest course here may be to admit to ignorance and uncertainty (cf. Bright, 312, 'we cannot be sure') rather than to date the occasion of Jeremiah's oracle to the fourth year of Jehoiakim and 47.1 to *c.* 600 (*contra* Katzenstein's confidence).

47.2–7

2 'Thus says the LORD:
Behold, waters are rising out of the north,
and shall become an overflowing torrent;
they shall overflow the land and all that fills it,
the city and those who dwell in it.
Men shall cry out,
and every inhabitant of the land shall wail.
3 At the noise of the stamping of the hoofs of his stallions,
at the rushing of his chariots, at the rumbling of their wheels,
the fathers look not back to their children,
so feeble are their hands,
4 because of the day that is coming to destroy
all the Philistines,
to cut off from Tyre and Sidon
every helper that remains.
For the LORD is destroying the Philistines,
the remnant of the coastland of Caphtor.
5 Baldness has come upon Gaza,
Ashkelon has perished.
O remnant of the Anakim,
how long will you gash yourselves?

6 Ah, sword of the LORD!
How long till you are quiet?
Put yourself into your scabbard,
rest and be still!
7 How can it be quiet,
when the LORD has given it a charge?
Against Ashkelon and against the seashore
he has appointed it.'

---

[2] Cf. 46.7–8 for the rising waters motif; it is combined with the overflowing (*šṭp*) motif in Isa. 8.7–8. MT *'ereṣ ūmᵉlō'āh 'īr wᵉyōšᵉbē bāh*, 'the land and its fullness, the city and those who dwell in it': = 8.16b. MT *kōl yōšēb hā'āreṣ*, 'every inhabitant of the land': many mss, Vrs read *yōšᵉbē*, '(all the) inhabitants of . . .'. **[3]** MT *mēripᵉyōn yādāyim*, lit. 'because of sinking of hands': i.e. terror-induced feebleness, cf. 6.24. Rudolph, 272, relates 3a to v. 2 and 3b to v. 4 (cf. BHS); cf. Christensen 1975, 212, who reads *'al-hayyōm*, 'in that day' at the end of v. 3. **[4]** MT *lᵉṣōr ūlᵉṣīdōn kōl śārīd 'ōzēr*, 'Tyre and Sidon every remaining helper': i.e. (cutting off) every last defender of Tyre and Sidon. G (*kai aphaniō*) *tēn Turon kai tēn Sidōna kai pantas tous kataloipous tēs boētheias autōn*, '(and I will destroy) Tyre and Sidon and all the rest of their allies': a prophecy against the Phoenician cities is strange in a poem about the Philistines, but the line may represent an expansion of the original poem (Christensen deletes *ūlᵉṣīdōn kōl* as an expansionary gloss). Cf. 27.3 for Tyre and Sidon in relation to Palestinian struggles against Babylon. G lacks 'the Philistines' in 4c. MT *'ī kaptōr*, 'the isle of Caphtor': G *tōn nēsōn*, 'the islands' = *hā'iyyīm*; for the belief that the Philistines came from Caphtor (i.e. Crete and adjacent islands) cf. Amos 9.7. Cf. 11.23; II Sam. 14.7 for the notion of wiping out a group so that not even a remnant (*šᵉ'ērīt*) is left. **[5]** Cf. 16.6; 41.5 for baldness or beards shaved off as signs of mourning. MT *nidmetāh*, 'destroyed' (EVV *dmh*) or 'silenced' (*dmm*): 'silenced' suits the context of mourning better than 'destroyed' (cf. Rudolph, Bright). G *aperriphē*, 'cast away'. MT *šᵉ'ērīt 'imqām*, 'the remnant of their valley': hardly intelligible; G *kai hoi kataloipoi Enakim*, 'and the remnant of the Anakim', cf. Josh. 11.22; RSV. The Anakim are a legendary race of giants believed to have inhabited Canaan before Israel moved there, remnants of which were associated with Gaza, Gath and Ashdod. Condamin, 309; Rudolph, 272, add 'Ashdod' to the text: 'Ashdod, the remnant of Anakim'. Cf. Zeph. 2.4 for the three place-names (Gaza, Ashkelon, Ashdod). Bright, 310, explains *'imqām* as 'strength' on the basis of Ugaritic *'mq* (cf. 49.4); followed by Christensen 1975, 212–13: i.e. 'the remnant of their strength'. MT *titgōdādī*, 'will you gash yourselves?': cf. 5.7; 16.6; 41.5 for the practice of self-laceration; Christensen emends the text to *titgōrārī* with 2QJer fragment 'will you whirl about' because it 'renders better sense here than the root *gdd*, "cut", of MT' (1975, 213). The funerary ritual of MT makes perfectly good sense in this context. **[6]** G lacks *hôy*, 'woe, ah'; cf. 51.35–37 for the sword image. **[7]** MT *'ēk tišqōṭī*, 'how can *you* rest?': Vrs 'How can *it* rest?' i.e. the sword. MT continues the address of v. 6a, but in v. 7 the sword is spoken of in the third person.

The poem against the Philistines has two parts: an oracle of doom in vv. 1–5 and a song of Yahweh's sword in vv. 6–7 (cf. the analysis in Christensen 1975, 213–15). Waters rise in the north (Babylon?) against the inhabitants of Philistia and this symbol of invasion (cf. Isa. 8.7–8) denotes such a devastating onslaught that the Philistines and their towns are swept away completely. It is such a frightening day of destruction that even the fathers will be too terrified (or weak) to turn to assist their children. The reference to Tyre and Sidon in v. 4 (if not an expansion of the text) may allude to an alliance between the Philistine and Phoenician cities, though no evidence survives of such a treaty. When the Babylonians swept into Palestine they would have attacked the Phoenician cities as well as the Philistine territory, so this allusion may be a trace of such a campaign (cf. Ezek. 26.28; 29.18–20 for the devastation of Tyre; the oracles against the nations in the Jeremiah tradition lack a section on Tyre). The responses of the Philistine citizens to the destruction are the inevitable funeral rites of baldness, silence and self-laceration (v. 5). In the hymn to Yahweh's sword (vv. 6–7) the identity of the warrior who fights against Philistia is given as Yahweh, and his sword is represented as being insatiable (cf. the hymn in 51.35–37).

The short poem against the Philistines is similar to much else in the poems of the OAN. Terrible slaughter befalls a people and, whatever the invading force may be in reality, behind it is inevitably the figure of Yahweh. Babylon is *not* identified as the invading enemy, but the holy warrior Yahweh is the one who wields the bloodthirsty sword against the designated victim. It is Yahweh who marches from the north to cut off the Philistines and the actual army (i.e. the stallions and chariots of v. 3a) is but the means he uses to vent his spleen against the foreign nations. Against the Philistine towns and the seacoast he has commanded and appointed his sword.

48.1–10

481 Concerning Moab.
Thus says the LORD of hosts, the God of Israel:
'Woe to Nebo, for it is laid waste!
Kiriathaim is put to shame, it is taken;
the fortress is put to shame and broken down;
2 the renown of Moab is no more.
In Heshbon they planned evil against her:
"Come, let us cut her off from being a nation!"
You also, O Madmen, shall be bought to silence;
the sword shall pursue you.
3 Hark! A cry from Horonaim,
"Desolation and great destruction!"
4 Moab is destroyed;
a cry is heard as far as Zoar.
5 For at the ascent of Luhith
they go up weeping;
for at the descent of Horonaim
they have heard the cry of destruction.
6 Flee! Save yourselves!
Be like a wild ass in the desert!
7 For, because you trusted in your strongholds and your treasures,
you also shall be taken;
and Chemosh shall go forth into exile,
with his priests and his princes.
8 The destroyer shall come upon every city,
and no city shall escape;
the valley shall perish,
and the plain shall be destroyed,
as the LORD has spoken.
9 Give wings to Moab,
for she would fly away;
her cities shall become a desolation,
with no inhabitant in them.
10 Cursed is he who does the work of the LORD with slackness; and
cursed is he who keeps back his sword from bloodshed.'

[MT 48] = G 31 (lacking vv. 45–47). **[1]** G lacks 'of hosts, the god of Israel' and the first occurrence of *hōbîšāh*, 'shamed' (a repetition in MT from next line). MT *hōbîšāh hammiśgāb wāḥāttāh*, 'shamed is the fortress and broken down': the feminine forms of the verbs suggest that *miśgāb* was understood as a place name (Rudolph, 274, corrects them, cf. BHS); cf. vv. 20, 38, 39, where this general confusion persists. In 46.24 *hōbīšāh* is used correctly because Egypt is personified as a young woman. **[2]** MT *tᵉhillat mōʾāb*, 'the renown of Moab': cf. 49.25; 51.41; G *iatreia Mōab*, 'healing for Moab' = *tᵉʿālat*. MT *bᵉḥešbōn ḥāšᵉbū*, 'in Hesbon they plot': word-play on *ḥšb*; G *agauriama en Esebōn*, 'glorying in Esebon' = *tᵉhillāh*. G lacks *lᵉkū*, 'come'. MT *gam-madmēn tiddōmmī*, 'also Madmen you shall be silent': Madmen is unknown but Dibon may be meant (Rudolph), cf. Isa. 15.9 where Dimon may be a word-play on Dibon (cf. BHS; Kaiser 1974, 69). In Isa. 25.10 *madmēnāh*, 'dung-pit' (cf. *dōmen*, 'dung', Jer. 8.2; 9.21; 16.4; 25.33) is used in a simile about Moab. Word-play on *dmm*, 'be silent', may be detected in the phrase, cf. G *kai pausin pausetai*, 'and she shall be completely silent', reading *mdmn* as *dāmōm* (infin. absol.). Kuschke 1961, 185; Dahood 1962b, 70 translate *gam* as 'with a loud voice (Madmen shall *wail*)', followed by Christensen 1975, 238. Silent (*dmm*) wailing with a loud voice introduces an oxymoron into the text! **[3]** MT *mēḥōrōnāyim*, 'from Horonaim': cf. v. 5; Isa. 15.5; Cornill, 463, reads *mēʿᵃbarīm*, 'from Abarim', cf. 22.20 (*ṣʿq*, 'cry', is used in both places), influencing Rudolph to read *mēhar ʿᵃbārīm*, 'from mount Abarim' (cf. BHS). MT *šōd wāšeber gādōl*, 'desolation and great destruction': cf. Isa. 59.7; 60.18, for the two terms together (without *gādōl*); 'great destruction' occurs in 4.6; 6.1. **[4]** MT *hišᵉmīʿū zᵉʿāqāh ṣᵉʿīrehā*, 'her little ones make a cry': cf. 49.20; 50.45 for *ṣᵉʿīrīm*, 'little ones', i.e. the insignificant or helpless ones (children). K *ṣʿwryh*; Q *ṣᵉʿīrehā*, cf. 14.3. G *anaggeilate eis Zogora*, 'proclaim to Zogora': lacking 'cry', cf. Isa. 15.5, *ʿad-ṣōʿar*, 'to Zoar'; followed by RSV, NEB, BHS and many exegetes. **[5]** K *hlḥwt*; Q *halluḥīt*, 'Luhith', cf. Isa. 15.5 (K 'tablets, planks' makes no sense). MT *bibᵉkīya ʿᵃleh-bekī*, 'with weeping one goes up weeping': cf. Isa. 15.5 *bibᵉkī yaʿᵃleh-bō*, 'with weeping one goes up *on it*' (i.e. the ascent); BHS, Bright and others follow Isa. 15.5. MT *ṣārē ṣaʿaqat-šeber*, 'the distresses of the cry of destruction': G lacks *ṣārē*, cf. RSV, NEB, BHS, Isa. 15.5. Driver 1937–38, 123, translates *ṣārē* as 'shrill cry', and deletes *ṣaʿᵃqat* as an explanatory gloss on it. **[6]** MT *wᵉtihyeynāh kaʿᵃrōʿēr bammidbār*, 'and be like Aroer in the desert': the meaning of this phrase is unintelligible. The fem. plur. (*hyh*) is odd but may be explained as second masc. plur. (cf. Bright, 314n.); *ʿᵃrōʿēr* may be a corruption of *yᵉʿōʿērū*, 'raise, rouse', in Isa. 15.5 (a variant in place of *šāmēʿū*, 'they have heard', in v. 6, but misplaced here?). G *hōsper onos agrios*, 'like a wild ass': i.e. *ʿārōd*, 'wild ass' (Job 39.5), cf. *pere'* 2.24(MT); Rudolph deletes the word (cf. BHS); also Christensen. Duhm, 346, reads *ūtᵉḥayyunhā kᵉʿarʿār bammidbār*, 'and eke out an existence as a juniper tree in the desert', cf. 17.6. Rudolph reads *wthynh* as *wᵉtaḥᵃnū*, 'and encamp (in the desert)', cf. BHS. **[7]** MT *bᵉmaʿᵃśayik ūbᵉʾōṣᵉrōtayik*, 'in your works and in your treasures': G *en ochurōmasin sou*, 'in your stronghold' = *bᵉmāʿuzzayik* or *bimᵉṣudōtayik* or some such word; MT *maʿᵃśayik* may represent a general term 'works' covering any defence work (cf. Janzen 1973, 19–20), but the doublet overloads the line. As variants MT may be an attempt to decipher an unreadable word (Volz, 405; cf. Weiser, 392); Christensen 1975, 238, deletes the second word. Note that Moab is personified as a woman here. K *kmyš*; Q *kᵉmôš*, 'Chemosh': K is a scribal error. K *yḥd*; Q *yaḥdāyw*, 'together': Q is a variation on the more usual *yaḥdāw*; cf. 46.12, 21; 49.3; K 'together' lacks *w* due to haplography (cf. v. 8). Many mss represent Q forms. **[8]** G lacks the second occurrence of *'îr*, 'city'. MT *hā'ēmeq . . . hammîšōr*, 'the valley . . . the plain': perhaps not collectives for 'valleys' and 'plains' but specific Moabite areas. Rudolph, 285, identifies the valley as the territory east of the Jordan and north of the Dead Sea (cf. Josh. 13.27) and the plain as the plateau north from the Arnon to the area of Heshbon (cf. Weiser, 392; Schottroff 1966). MT *'ᵃšer 'āmar yhwh*, 'which Yahweh has said': as if v. 8 were a citation of 33.22; Rudolph deletes as a dittography (cf. BHS). **[9]** MT *tᵉnū-ṣîṣ lᵉmō'āb*, 'give ? to Moab': meaning of *ṣîṣ* is dubious: G *sēmeia*, 'signs, marks', suggests *nēs*, 'standard' (4.6) or *ṣiyyûn*, 'road-mark' (31.21; cf. 'grave-mark,' II Kings 23.17; Giesebrecht, 236; BHS). RSV highly unlikely; NEB 'Let a warning flash to Moab': following G 'Set up a monument for Moab', i.e. her grave marker will indicate her complete destruction. A different approach is advocated by Moran 1958, 69–71, who argues for *ṣîṣ*, 'salt', on the basis of Ugaritic glosses in Akkadian texts: 'give salt for Moab' means 'salt her cities', a figure symbolizing the utter annihilation of a city by sowing its ruins with salt (cf. Judg. 9.45; Ecclus. 43.19). Hence NEB margin, 'Doom Moab to become saltings'. Cf. Gevirtz 1963 for the practice of sowing cities with salt. MT *nāṣō' tēṣē'*, Hebrew obscure: word-play or confusion may explain MT. Two verbs, *nṣh*, 'collapse in ruins', and *yṣ'*, 'go out', are combined when two forms of the one verb may be intended, cf. G *haphē anaphthēsetai*, 'kindling she shall be kindled' (*yṣt*, cf. 2.15; 9.9, 11 [EVV 10, 12]; 46.19). Rudolph, 275, reads *nāṣōh tiṣṣeh*, 'she shall surely fall in ruins' (cf. BHS; 4.7). MT may conceal an alternative reading *yāṣō tēṣē'*, 'she shall surely surrender' (cf. I Sam. 11.3; Isa. 36.16 for *yṣ'*, 'surrender'). **[10]** G lacks the repeat of *'ārûr*, 'cursed be . . .': v. 10 is regarded by many exegetes as a prose comment on the preceding poem (e.g. Duhm, Volz, Rudolph, Bright, Christensen); cf. 50.25; Judg. 5.23 for the motifs of Yahweh's work and human involvement in it.

Moab

A series of poems with prose comments constitutes the oracle against Moab (cf. Isa. 15–16; Amos 2.1–3; Zeph. 2.8–11; Ezek. 25.8–11 for similar oracles directed against Moab). Apart from the poems about Babylon in 50–51, there is nothing in the collection of 46–51 to match the length of the material on Moab (48 is longer than all the oracles against Moab in the other prophetic to be disrupted in a most violent manner: the deity will send against Moab those who will violently disturb the wines by tipping them over (the word-play is difficult to capture in English), emptying the drinking vessels, and smashing the jars (cf. 13.12–14) containing the wines. Such a brawl in the taverns (if this more modern image may be used of v. 12) will destroy Moab. A pious editor has added v. 13 in order to draw the religious lesson from the images of vv. 11–12. The destruction of Moab will cause disillusionment with the national god Chemosh. Such dissatisfaction with the god is likened to Israel's loss of faith in Bethel. It is hardly necessary to see in this simile a pre-exilic note, though such a dating cannot be ruled out. A Judaean editor could hardly have referred to the fall of Jerusalem as occasioning disillusionment with Yahweh (cf. 44.17–19), hence an allusion to the northern kingdom's syncretistic ways is appropriate here. Yahweh no less than Chemosh or Bethel failed to protect his nation but such a sensitive issue has other explanations in the tradition. As a passing comment on Moab's rude awakening from a tranquil past the point of v. 13 makes connections with Israel's past, but the shadow of 587 may be detected throughout the oracles against the nations whatever the precise dating of any individual poem or verse.

The images change completely in vv. 14–17 and return to the theme of vv. 2–9. Moab's destroyer (unidentified as is characteristic of all the poems in the OAN) has come up against its cities and fortresses and has destroyed its mighty warriors. The destroyer *comes up* and the young men (i.e. the troops) *go down* to slaughter (v. 15). In v. 16 the ruin of Moab is envisaged as being about to happen ('near at hand', 'hastens quickly') rather than as having happened already. This change of perspective depicts the slaughter as a process moving swiftly to its completion and is but a change of pace in the poetry. As the Moabites collapse against the enemy those, who are familiar with Moab's great reputation (cf. vv. 29–30) are invited to shake their heads in mourning (v. 17 *nudū*, cf. 15.5; 16.5; 18.16; 22.10; 31.18) at its loss and the attendant reversal of its powerful status.

48.18–28

18 'Come down from your glory,
and sit on the parched ground,
O inhabitant of Dibon!
For the destroyer of Moab has come up against you;
he has destroyed your strongholds.
19 Stand by the way and watch,
O inhabitant of Aroer!
Ask him who flees and her who escapes;
say, "What has happened?"
20 Moab is put to shame, for it is broken;
wail and cry!
Tell it by the Arnon,
that Moab is laid waste.
21 Judgment has come upon the tableland, upon Holon, and Jahzah, and
Mepha-ath, 22 and Dibon, and Nebo, and Beth-diblathaim, 23 and
Kiriathaim, and Beth-gamul, and Bethmeon, 24 and Keri-oth, and Bozrah,
and all the cities of the land of Moab, far and near. 25 The horn of Moab
is cut off, and his arm is broken, says the LORD.
26 Make him drunk, because he magnified himself against the LORD; so
that Moab shall wallow in his vomit, and he too shall be held in derision.
27 Was not Israel a derision to you? Was he found among thieves, that
whenever you spoke of him you wagged your head?
28 Leave the cities, and dwell in the rock,
O inhabitant of Moab!
Be like the dove that nests
in the sides of the mouth of a gorge.'

---

[18] K *yšby*; Q *ûšᵉbî*, 'and sit': K is a scribal error. MT *rᵉdî . . . ûšᵉbî*, 'come down . . . and sit': cf. Isa. 47.1, where the dethroned daughter Babylon is spoken to in the same way. Rudolph, 276, favours reading *baṣṣō'āh*, 'in the filth' (vomit or excrement), for *baṣṣāmā'*, 'dry ground', in order to make a sharp contrast between her former glory and her present state (cf. the image of vomit in v. 26); cf. Bright, 315. G *en hugrasia*, 'in a damp place' (cf. S). MT *yōšebet bat-dîbōn*, lit. 'inhabitress, daughter Dibon': cf. 46.19; G lacks 'daughter' (omitted by Christensen 1975, 238 with G). Cf. the suggestion in BHS that *bat* is a dittography of (*ywš*)*bt*. Dibon is the city north of the river Arnon where the Moabite Stone (Mesha's inscription) was found. Cf. v. 15a for v. 18bα. **[19]** Cf. 6.16 for a similar instruction. The subtle gender shift of MT (*nās*, 'him who flees' – *nimᵉlāṭāh*, 'her who escapes') is lost in the Vrs, which read both words as masc. MT may be an expression of the totality of the fleeing population. Cf. 21.13; 22.23 for the epithet *yōšebet*, 'inhabitress', describing a town or location. **[20]** Cf. v. 1; 46.24. MT *kī-ḥattāh*, 'for *she* is broken': read *ḥat*, '*he* is broken', i.e. *it* (Moab); MT due to dittography. K *hylyly wz'qy* (cf. G); Q *hēlīlū ūzᵉ'āqū*, 'wail and cry': K sing., Q plur. Either is possible, as *yōšebet* is a collective. **[21]** K *mwp't*; Q *mēpā'at*, 'Mephaath': Vrs follow Q but G has K (*Mōphath*). 21–24 are a prose expansion which interrupts the poem. **[25]** G lacks *nᵉ'um yhwh*, 'says Yahweh'. The words 'horn' (*qeren*) and 'arm' (*zᵉrō'a*) are metaphors of strength (cf. Lam. 2.3 for *qeren* with reference to Israel). This may be the answer of the refugees to the question asked in v. 19b (cf. Rudolph, 278). **[26]** MT *wᵉsāpaq mō'ab bᵉqī'ō*, lit. 'and Moab shall *slap* in his vomit': *spq* means 'slap' (cf. Job 34.26) or 'clap' hands in anger or mockery (cf. Num. 24.10; Lam. 2.15; Job 27.23); also 'slap' the thigh in remorse and sorrow (cf. 31.19; Ezek. 21.17). Its occurrence here is difficult: RSV 'shall *wallow* in his vomit', NEB 'until he *overflows* with his vomit', JPSB 'shall vomit till he is drained'; G *kai epikroussei Mōab en cheiri autou*, 'and Moab shall *clap* his hands'. The figure may be one of splashing about in vomit or falling with a splash into vomit (cf. BDB, 796); though some connect *spq* with slapping the thigh out of rage and disgust with vomiting (*bᵉ* 'on account of', KB, 665; *spq* II, 'to vomit, be sick', KB^3 III, 722, following Rudolph, 278). Syr. *spq*, 'throw up', i.e. 'spew forth his vomit' (cf. NEB; Driver 1950, 62): delete *bᵉ* as dittography (cf. BHS). The images of drunkenness reflect a standard metaphor of the divine anger (cf. 25.15–29; Isa. 49.26; 51.21–23; 63.6; also the imagery of 13.12–14). **[27]** K *nmṣ'h*; Q *nimᵉṣā'*, '*he* was found' (K fem.). G lacks *middē dᵉbāreykā*, 'as often as your words': Rudolph and others revocalize with Symm. *middē dabberᵉkā*, 'as often as you speak' (cf. BHS). MT *titnōdād*, 'you shook' (your head in derision); cf. 18.16; 31.18: a mocking or bewildered gesture. 26–27 are another prose expansion breaking up the flow of the poem and developing very different images from vv. 18–20. **[28]** Cf. 13.4; Isa. 2.21 for the image of hiding in the rocks. MT *bᵉ'ebᵉrē pī-pāḥat*, lit. 'on the sides of the mouth of the pit': cf. v. 43; i.e. make your refuge in the precarious places where birds make their nests – on the edges of chasms or gorges (contrast the nesting image of 22.23 as a figure of security).

A brief poetic section on the transmogrification of Moab (v. 18a) is expanded by two prose insertions (vv. 21–24, 26–27). In the poem the descent of Moab (from the throne, cf. Isa. 47.1) to sit on the dry ground (or in the excrement cf v. 26; Rudolph) is attested by questioning those who flee (vv. 19–20). Moab's power is broken (v. 20) and its inhabitants are advised to leave the cities in order to find protection in the steep sides of the gorges where birds make their nests (v. 28). The poem graphically conveys the sense of Moab's collapse by focusing on the fleeing inhabitants and the telling of the sad tale by the river Arnon (v. 20).

The flow of the poem is interrupted at two points: vv. 21–24 list the cities upon which judgment (*mišpāṭ*) has come (the names do not appear to be in any particular order, cf. Rudolph, 281), and vv. 26–27 describe Moab's plight in images more akin to vv. 11–12 than their present position. Both these pieces are in prose (though NEB, JPSB and some exegetes treat vv. 26–27 as poetry) and make observations about Moab which are tangential to the poem in vv. 18–20, 25, 28. The imagery of v. 26 shares with vv. 11–12 a setting in the world of brewing and wine-making, but the metaphors are used differently. Moab is to be made drunk (cf. 25.15–17; 51.6, 39) because it has opposed (*higdîl*, i.e. vaunted himself against) Yahweh (the how is not explained, but cf. v. 27). In such drunkenness Moab will be humiliated: wallowing about in vomit (cf. 25.27) is a figure of military destruction drawn from the experiences of being drunk and incapable. As in all human communities such degrading behaviour makes the victim an object of hilarity (*śᵉḥōq*, 'derision') to those who observe the floundering about and eventual collapse in the vomit and excrement produced by such drunkenness. Thus Moab is to be humiliated for its opposition to Yahweh by its attitude to Israel (v. 27). This is a rather different explanation of Moab's fate from the hubris and overweening self-confidence of vv. 7, 11, 14, 29–30 (cf. v. 42, where Moab's opposition [*higdîl*] to Yahweh is not linked to its attitude towards Israel). It reflects antagonism between Israel and Moab but does not identify the occasion (if occasion it be) of the hostility between the two nations. As neighbouring states Israel and Moab (and all the other small states) must have watched each other jealously over the centuries, and the fall of one would have been an occasion of great joy for the other (the OAN reflect the nationalistic envy in a most thorough-going fashion). Moabite taunts against Israel are viewed as grounds for the destruction of Moab (cf. Zeph. 2.8–11), and such taunts may have been a particular feature of Israelite-Moabite relations during the period when Babylon devastated Judah in 597 and 587. Nothing definite may be deduced from v. 27, but Moab's constant mocking of Israel (quite unjustified from an Israelite viewpoint) is turned around in v. 26 so that Moab also (*gam-hû'*, '*he* also') becomes an object of mockery. Israel's innocence is protested in the question 'was he found among thieves?'. Was this why every time Moab mentioned him there was a shaking of the head at him? How different this protestation of innocence or assertion of *amour-propre* is from the denunciations of the nation throughout the Jeremiah tradition! The shaking of the head (cf. 18.16) is quite justified in the poems and sermons making up the bulk of the book, but here in the OAN such criticism is out of place. Nationalistic pride turns the enmity of the nations into opposition against Yahweh and therefore into grounds for the divine judgment to fall on the mockers of Israel *and* Yahweh (cf. 50.29; 51.5, 11, 24, 35, 49–51).

48.29–39

29 'We have heard of the pride of Moab –
he is very proud –
of his loftiness, his pride, and his arrogance,
and the haughtiness of his heart.
30 I know his insolence, says the LORD;
his boasts are false,
his deeds are false.
31 Therefore I wail for Moab;
I cry out for all Moab;
for the men of Kir-heres I mourn.
32 More than for Jazer I weep for you,
O vine of Sibmah!
Your branches passed over the sea,
reached as far as Jazer;
upon your summer fruits and your vintage
the destroyer has fallen.
33 Gladness and joy have been taken away
from the fruitful land of Moab;
I have made the wine cease from the wine presses;
no one treads them with shouts of joy;
the shouting is not the shout of joy.
34 Heshbon and Elealeh cry out; as far as Jahaz they utter their voice, from
Zoar to Horonaim and Eglath-shelishiyah. For the waters of Nimrim also
have become desolate. 35 And I will bring to an end in Moab, says the
LORD, him who offers sacrifice in the high place and burns incense to his
god. 36 Therefore my heart moans for Moab like a flute, and my heart
moans like a flute for the men of Kir-heres; therefore the riches they gained
have perished.
37 For every head is shaved and every beard cut off; upon all the hands

are gashes, and on the loins is sackcloth. 38 On all the housetops of Moab and in the squares there is nothing but lamentation; for I have broken Moab like a vessel for which no one cares, says the LORD. 39 How it is broken! How they wail! How Moab has turned his back in shame! So Moab has become a derision and a horror to all that are round about him.'

---

[29] MT *šāma'nū*, '*we* have heard': G *ēkousa*, 'I have heard'; this is the only we-style form in 48 (v. 14 is reported speech), cf. Bardtke 1936, 245, for analysis. Cf. vv. 29–33 and Isa. 16.6–10; v. 36a and Isa. 16.11; v. 35 and Isa. 16.12; v. 34 and Isa. 15.4a, 5a, 6a. On Isa. 15–16 see Rudolph, 281–2; 1963, 130–43; Clements 1980, 150–6; Kaiser 1974, 57–75; v. 29 = Isa. 16.6 with variations (MT *gāb*ᵉ*hō ū*, 'his loftiness and', is lacking in G; Isa. 16.6; *w*ᵉ*rum libbō*, 'and the haughtiness of his mind', is not in Isa. 16.6, which has *lō'-kēn baddāyw*, 'his boasts are false' cf. v. 30). **[30]** MT *'eb*ᵉ*rātō w*ᵉ*lō'-kēn*, 'his arrogance and (is) not right': MT should be repunctuated (i.e. *atnah* shifted back a phrase) in order to read *w*ᵉ*lō'-kēn* with next word (cf. Isa. 16.6; BHS as in Rudolph, 280); G *erga*, 'works', for MT 'arrogance'. G lacks *n*ᵉ*'um yhwh*, 'says Yahweh'. MT *baddāyw*, 'his idle talk': i.e. empty boastings, cf. 50.36; Job 11.3; G *ouchi to hikanon autou*, 'is it not his sufficiency?', i.e. 'is it not enough for him?' = *dayyō*. MT *lō'-kēn 'āšū*, lit. 'not right *they* do'. **[31]** Cf. Isa. 16.7. MT *'el-'anšē qīr-ḥereś yehgeh*, 'for the men of Kir-heres *he* moans': Isa. 16.7 *la'*ᵃ*šīšē*, 'for the raisin-cakes of (Kir-heres)', i.e. delicacies (cf. S. of Sol. 2.5; Hos. 3.1; II Sam. 6.19) associated with Kir-heres; *yehgeh* is the indefinite 'one' (a mistake for *'ehgeh*, 'I moan', cf. Bardtke 1936, 245; Q^{Or}). G lacks *ūl*ᵉ*mō'āb*, 'and for Moab', and duplicates '(Kir-)*ḥereś*' as *auchmou*, 'drought', i.e. dry place (?). **[32]** Cf. Isa. 16.8–9; v. 32 is shorter and uses only some of the lines from Isa. 16. MT *mibb*ᵉ*kī*, lit. 'from weeping': idiomatic for greater weeping *than* . . . but Isa. 16.9 *bib*ᵉ*kī ya'zēr*, '*with* the weeping of Jazer (I weep)'; G *hōs klauthmon Iazēr*, '*as* the weeping of Jazer' = *kib*ᵉ*kī*. Rudolph, 282, suggests *mabb*ᵉ*kē*, 'springs' (*nbk*), cf. Job 38.16; i.e. springs of Jazer. Landes 1956, 31, connects *bky* with Ug. *npk*, 'fountain, well, source' (cf. Christensen 1975, 239); there may be an element of word-play here (Bright, 321). MT *haggepen śibmāh*, 'the vine Sibmah': G, Isa. 16.9 lack article; cf. 2.21; 6.9 for *gepen* as a figure of Israel. Christensen deletes the phrase for metrical reasons as a secondary conflation from Isa. 16.8 (though the citation is from 16.9!). MT *'ad yām ya'zēr*, 'as far as *the sea of* Jazer': *yām* repeated from previous clause (lacking in Isa. 16.8; G). MT *w*ᵉ*'al-b*ᵉ*ṣīrēk*, 'and upon your vintage': a few mss, Isa. 16.9, *w*ᵉ*'al-q*ᵉ*ṣīrēk*, 'and upon your harvest'. MT *šōdēd nāpāl*, 'the destroyer has fallen': Isa. 16.9, *hēdād nāpāl*, 'the shout has fallen', cf. v. 33; 25.30; 51.14. **[33]** Cf. Isa. 16.10. MT *mikkarmel ūmē'ereṣ mō'āb*, 'from Carmel *and from* the land of Moab': RSV, NEB combine these terms, though G lacks the first and Isa. 16.10 the second. They are clearly variants combined here in 48.33. MT *w*ᵉ*yayin* *mīqābīm hišbattī*, 'and the wine from the presses I have made to cease': Isa. 16.10, *lō' yayin bayᵉqābīm*, 'there is no wine in the presses'; G lacks negative force because it reads *prōi* 'early' (= *haškēm*?) for *hišbattī*, cf. G Isa. 16.10. MT *lō'-yidᵉrōk hēdād*, 'the shout does not tread'! Isa. 16.10 *lō'-yidᵉrōk haddōrēk*, 'the treader does not tread': i.e. the grapes are not trodden into wine. MT *hēdād lō' hēdād* lit. 'a shout not a shout': a too subtle word-play, a mistake, or a gloss; Isa. 16.10, *hēdād hišbattī*, 'I have caused to cease shout'; i.e. the shouting associated with grape-treading is gone. Cf. 25.30, where *hēdād* alludes to the battle shout as well as the jubilant noise of workers producing the new season's wine. In Isa. 16.9 the shout (*hēdād*) which falls is that of battle (v. 32 *šōdēd*, 'destroyer'); thus the pun here may reflect 'the shouting (is of battle) not the shouting (of drunken grape-treaders)' in a context where images of grapes, wine, and drunkenness can mean disaster (vv. 12, 26, 33; 25.15–17, 27; 51.39). The same images may denote great joy (31.5, 12), but v. 33a clearly indicates that the context is not one of gladness and joy. Cf. 51.14 for the battle shout (*hēdād*). G *oude deilēs, ouk epoiēsan aidad*, 'nor in the evening, they did not make shouting': not helpful, but an attempt at translating an awkward text. Rudolph favours reading a verbal form of the second *hēdād*, i.e. *yᵉhōdād* or *yᵉhuddād*, 'burst into (song)', cf. BHS; Bardtke 1936, 246n. deletes the phrase as a gloss. Christensen 1975, 239, attaches the *m* of the next word (v. 34) to *hēdād* (i.e. *hyddm*) as an enclitic and reads 'The shout of harvest is no longer voiced'. **[34]** Cf. Isa. 15.4–6. RSV corrects to 'Heshbon and Elealeh cry out' from Isa. 15.4a: MT 'from the cry of Heshbon *to* Elealeh *to* Jahaz . . .'. 34–39 are prose, though v. 37 may be regarded as poetry (cf. Bright, 318), with vv. 34–36 as a conglomerate formed from Isa. 15.2–6; 16.11–12 (cf. Schottroff 1966, 184–7; Bardtke 1936, 246–7). **[35]** MT *maʿᵃleh bāmāh*, lit. 'the one who raises a high place': something is missing here; G *anabainonta epi bōmon*, 'going up *on* high place', may be considered an improvement. Rudolph inserts *ʿōlāh* (cf. T) *ʿal* (with G) *hab(bāmāh)*, i.e. '(one who offers up) a sacrifice upon the (high place)'; a double loss of *ʿlh*, but cf. Driver 1937–38, 124. Cf. Notes on 44.3, 5, 8, 15, 17–19, 21, 23, 25 for *qṭr* as 'burn' sacrifice in general rather than RSV's more limited 'burn incense'. Cf. Isa. 16.12 for reference to a different Moabite practice in the cult; the offering of sacrifice to the god(s) here is more in keeping with the Jeremiah tradition. **[36]** Cf. Isa. 16.11; 15.7. MT *yitrat ʿāśāh 'ābādū*, lit. 'the abundance he has gotten they are destroyed': i.e. the accumulated riches have gone; the similar phrase (*yitrāh ʿāśāh*) in Isa. 15.7 is developed in a different way. Christensen 1975, 239, transposes 'for the waters of Nimrim have become desolate' (v. 34; cf. Isa. 15.6) to the end of v. 36. **[37]** Cf. Isa. 15.2b–3. G *en panti topō*, '(every head) *in every place* (shall be shaved)'. Many mss, Vrs read 'all' before *mātᵉnayim*, 'loins', i.e. on *every* waist is sackcloth. Cf. 16.6; 41.5; 47.5 for the ritual marks of mourning. **[38]** Cf. Isa. 15.3. G lacks *kullōh mispēd*, 'all of it (is) mourning': i.e. nothing but mourning. MT *kikᵉlī 'ēn-ḥēpeṣ bō*, 'as a vessel for which no one cares': cf. 22.28, where the same phrase (*'im* instead of *kᵉ*) is used of the discarded Coniah. NEB treats 'says Yahweh' as addition. **[39]** MT *'ēk ḥattāh hēlīlū* 'how it is broken, they wail': cf. v. 20, where *ḥat* also should be read (BHS); A, Symm lack *hēlīlū* ('they howl' or 'howl'). Rudolph, 282, treats as an addition from v. 20 (cf BHS). Cf. v. 26 for *wᵉhāyāh . . . liśḥōq*, 'and (Moab) shall become a derision'; 17.17 for *mᵉḥittāh*, 'terror', i.e. object of terror.

The second part of 48 (dividing the chapter into vv. 1–28, 29–47 is an alternative way of reading the poem to its division into various parts) consists of poems and prose statements which continue the denunciation of Moab intertwined with laments for its fall. Much of vv. 29–38 is based on Isa. 15.2–7 and 16.6–11, and part two of the poem may be regarded as secondary development of vv. 1–28 (cf. Christensen 1975, 244). A comparison of vv. 29–38 and Isa. 15–16 will reveal a wide diversity of influence, usage and placement of the phrases and motifs of Isa. 15–16 in 48 and the question of originality of source, if raised at all, is perhaps not as easily answered as many exegetes think it is. An early dating of Isa. 15–16 (cf. Rudolph 1963, 142) would settle the matter in favour of the Isaiah tradition, but the problems of determining origin, date and reference of Isa. 15–16 must counsel the wise exegete to exercise a cautious agnosticism about the relation between the two different uses of the material on Moab (cf. Kaiser 1974, 60–65).

The hubris of Moab is stressed in v. 29 (cf. Isa. 16.6; G *hubrin Mōab*), and in v. 30 that arrogance is denounced by the deity (only in MT) as false. As in Isa. 16.6–7, the response to such hubristic arrogance is lamentation and mourning, though in 48.31 it is the speaker who wails for Moab rather than Moab who is invited to wail over its own plight. The focus of the mourning is the destruction of the land, in particular the cessation of the great wine-making production of Sibmah (hence the epithet '*vine* Sibmah'). The late summer harvesting reaches its climax in the vintage when a good season's hard work is crowned with the pleasures of the grape. Now mourning must descent upon Moab because the joy and pleasure of that occasion are gone, and the noise of drunken celebration (*hēdād*) is in reality the din of battle (*hēdād*, cf. 25.30–31). The mourning spreads throughout Moab (v. 34): everybody is shaved, gashed and dressed in sackcloth, everywhere there is lamentation, and even the speaker's heart wails like a flute for the Moabites. Yahweh has broken Moab like a discarded ceramic pot and, in fulfilment of v. 26, it has become an object of derision and terror to its neighbours. The section may well be secondary (cf. Rudolph, 280–2), but its images graphically lament the destruction of a proud people.

48.40–47

40 For thus says the LORD:
'Behold, one shall fly swiftly like an eagle,
and spread his wings against Moab;
41 the cities shall be taken
and the strongholds seized.
The heart of the warriors of Moab shall be in that day
like the heart of a woman in her pangs;
42 Moab shall be destroyed and be no longer a people,
because he magnified himself against the LORD.
43 Terror, pit, and snare
are before you, O inhabitant of Moab!
says the LORD.
44 He who flees from the terror
shall fall into the pit,
and he who climbs out of the pit
shall be caught in the snare.
For I will bring these things upon Moab
in the year of their punishment,
says the LORD.
45 In the shadow of Heshbon
fugitives stop without strength;
for a fire has gone forth from Heshbon,
a flame from the house of Sihon;
it has destroyed the forehead of Moab,
the crown of the sons of tumult.
46 Woe to you, O Moab!
The people of Chemosh is undone;
for your sons have been taken captive,
and your daughters into captivity.
47 Yet I will restore the fortunes of Moab
in the latter days, says the LORD.'
Thus far is the judgment on Moab.

---

[40] G lacks all of v. 40 except 'for thus says the lord'. Cf. 49.22 for elements of vv. 40–41. Many exegetes follow G and delete the rest of v. 40 as secondary from 49.22 (e.g. Rudolph, 283; contrary view in Weiser, 401 n. 3, based on the theory that G omits doublets, but against this position cf. Janzen 1973, 94–5). Cf. Ezek. 17.3 for the eagle image; Isa. 8.8b for the wings motif as a figure of invasion (or is it protection?). **[41]** MT *nitpāśāh*, 'is seized': Q^{Or} plur., but for plur. nouns with sing. verbs cf. Rudolph, 284. G lacks v. 41b: cf. 49.22 where the line occurs with Edom in place of Moab; some exegetes delete it here as an addition from 49.22 (cf. BHS). Cf. 4.31 for the birth-pangs seizing a woman and 30.6 for the transformation of men (*geber*, warriors?) into women in a time of awesome trouble. **[42]** Cf. v. 26 for *kī 'al-yhwh higdīl*, 'because he magnified himself against Yahweh'. Bardtke 1936, 249, concludes the poem with v. 42 (omitting vv. 37–41, 43–47) and uses this line as the theological grounding of the trilogy of poems in 48 (explained in the light of the Deuteronomistic reform, cf. Bardtke, 247–8). **[43]** Cf. Isa. 24.17 (*hā'āreṣ*, 'of the earth', instead of 'of Moab'; lacking *n^{e}'um yhwh*, 'says Yahweh'). G lacks 'says Yahweh'. MT *paḥad wāpaḥat wāpāḥ*, 'terror and pit and trap': fine example of assonance in Heb. **[44]** Cf. Isa. 24.18. K *hnys*; Q *hannās*, 'he who flees' (as Isa. 24.18, but lacking *w^{e}hāyāh*, 'and it shall be . . .'), K = ? (refugee perhaps). If Isa. 24 belongs to the post-exilic period (cf. Kaiser 1974, 173–9; Miller 1976, 108), then this section of 48 must be from an equally late era (i.e. post-catastrophe of 587). The argument of v. 44a,b is essentially that of Amos 5.19. Minor variations between v. 44 and Isa. 24.18 include *mipp^{e}nē*, 'from' – *miqqōl*, 'from the sound of', and *min*, 'from' – *mittōk*, 'from the midst of'; the third line is quite different in both places. MT *kī-'ābī' 'ēleyhā*, 'for I will bring *upon her*': G *hoti epaxō tauta*, 'for I will bring *these things*' = *'ēlleh*; MT *'ēleyhā* and *'el-mō'āb*, 'against Moab', are probably variants. **[45]** Cf. Num. 21.28; 24.17b. S lacks v. 45a. MT *'ēš yāṣā'*, 'a fire has gone forth': many mss, Num. 21.28 read *yāṣ^{e}'āh* (correct gender matching). MT *w^{e}lehābāh mibbēn sīḥōn*, lit. 'and a flame from between Sihon': a few mss read *mibbēt*, 'from the house of' (i.e. the capital city, cf. Bright, 319; NEB 'the palace of Sihon'); Num. 21.28 *miqqiryat*, 'from the town of'. MT *p^{e}'at mō'āb*, 'the temples of Moab': i.e. the hair (lit. 'corner') on the side of the head (cf. 9.25 [EV 26]; 25.23; 49.32 where the phrase describes tribes who practise cutting their side locks); a personification of Moab as a man whose head has been destroyed by fire. Cf. Num. 24.17b. **[46]** Cf. Num. 21.19. MT *'ābad 'am-k^{e}mōš*, 'the people of Chemosh is destroyed': or 'he has destroyed'; some Vrs, Num. 21.29 *'ābadtā*, 'you have destroyed'. **[47]** Cf. 30–31 for the 'restoration of the fortunes' motif (see Notes on 29.14); applied here to Moab and elsewhere to the Ammonites (49.6) and Elam (49.39). A hint of mercy towards Moab may be detected in Isa. 16.1–5 (contrast Zeph. 2.8–11). The phrase 'in the latter days' refers to the future (i.e. when all the destruction is over) without eschatological overtones (cf. Rudolph, 284), cf. 23.20; 30.24; Num. 24.1. It is equivalent to 'afterward' (*'aḥ^a rē-kēn*) in 46.26; 49.6. MT *'ad-hēnnāh mišpāṭ mō'āb*, 'thus far the judgment of Moab': cf. 51.64. The sheer length of the oracle against Moab has constrained an editor to add a note indicating its termination.

A further section comprising vv. 40–42, 43–44, 45–46, 47 concludes the lengthy poem against Moab and is presented as an oracular utterance (G is considerably shorter). The poem effectively ends at v. 42 (cf. Bardtke 1936, 249; Rudolph, 284, treats vv. 40b, 41b, 43–47 as secondary) with a theological explanation for Moab's destruction: *against Yahweh he magnified himself* (cf. v. 26). This assertion is neither explained nor spelled out, but it equates the fate of Moab with its hubris (cf. v. 29), and hubris is always regarded as a fatal defect in human communities (cf. Isa. 2.12–17; 10.5–15). Whether Moabite arrogance against Judah during the Babylonian slaughter of the Judaeans and the destruction of Jerusalem or long-standing antagonism between the neighbouring states is behind this accusation cannot be determined, but the OAN genre is clear testimony to the hostility felt by Judaeans towards their neighbours. Any defeat of or setback to the surrounding states would be a cause for Judaean celebration and yet fully in line with the fundamental religious outlook shared by Judah *and* Moab. The Moabite Stone (cf. Pritchard 1969, 320–1) provides evidence of the close affinity between Israelite and Moabite beliefs, and indeed the inscription 'reads almost like a chapter from the Bible' (Gibson 1971, 71). This shared religious outlook permits the defeat of the one to be the work of the other's god, hence the destruction of Moab becomes the triumph of Yahweh (just as Jerusalem's destruction in 587 may have been regarded as Chemosh's defeat of an old enemy) and Moab's offence self-aggrandizement against Yahweh (i.e. against Yahweh's people, cf. vv. 26–27; Zeph. 2.8, 10).

The concluding poems in vv. 43–46 contain elements to be found in Isa. 24.17–18b and Num. 21.19, 28; 24.17b. They therefore can hardly be considered original to 48, but reflect the many strands of anti-Moabite material in the Bible. Added to the poem of 48 they extend the denunciations of Moab (though vv. 43–44 must be regarded as a free-floating piece because in Isa. 24.17–18b it has no connections with Moab). These codas depict the ruination of Moab but add nothing of a serious nature to the argument of the poem. The shorter G edition lacking vv. 45–47 ends the poem on the note of terror for all the inhabitants of Moab in the year of divine judgment for them (MT adds oracular indicators).

The apparent reversal of the poem in v. 47 (cf. 49.6, 39) may surprise the modern reader but, in the light of 30–31, should not. After the destruction of Moab there will come a time when Yahweh (Judaean perspective) will restore the fortunes (*šūb šᵉbūt*) of the devastated nation. This penultimate postscript simply asserts a future recovery of Moab. Nothing miraculous or wonderful is posited of this revival of Moab's fortunes – only a recognition of that nation's survival after the devastations depicted in the poem. A similar explanation may be offered for 30–31 (developed at greater length because the book is the product of Judaean communities which survived the destructions of the sixth century) and the use of the restoration of the fortunes motif throughout the book of Jeremiah. The motif is a statement about survival. Here it refers to Moab which, in spite of the depredations described repeatedly in the poem, survived at least to the period when 48 was edited in its final form (MT). The fact that similar motifs are used of different nations (e.g. Judah, Moab, Ammon, Elam, even Egypt) indicates a fair degree of stereotyping in the language of the tradition and demands a conventionalist interpretation of such motifs. Disaster is brought about by Yahweh (whatever the means may appear to be in the sphere of social reality) and the subsequent survival of such catastrophes represents his restoration of the fortunes of the nation so devastated. This restoration consists of the rebuilding of the community and the renewal of traditional modes of living (cf. 1.10; spelled out in 30–31). A further example of the conventionalist nature of many of the motifs in the tradition may be seen in the mourning language used of Moab in vv. 31–32, 36 (cf Isa. 16.7–10). The speaker (the 'I' of the poem) mourns for the destruction of Moab, just as the speaker of 4.19–21, 8.18–9.1; 10.19–20 bewails the disasters which have overtaken city and people. Whether these are the utterances of the nation or city personified or of the poet on behalf of either, they are conventional expressions of lamentation. It is therefore unnecessary to develop, in the case of the poems lamenting Jerusalem's fall, a theory of the prophet Jeremiah's self-identification with his people because such a theory then would be required for his self-identification with Moab! This would be an absurd theory. It is better exegesis to recognize how conventional these mourning songs are and to understand *all* of the poems as expressions of grief traditionally uttered over the fallen.

A wise editor has noted the excessive length of the poem about Moab and has brought it to a final conclusion (cf. G) with a note to the effect that 'here ends the sentence on Moab' (NEB). A similar editorial point is provided for the even longer attack on Babylon (cf. 51.64), but there it has a different effect. The meaning of the line 'thus far . . .' (*'ad-hēnnāh*) is not entirely clear: it is understood here to be a closing notice terminating the poem (just as 51.64 indicates the end of Jeremiah's words), but there are other interpretations of it. It has been seen as a temporal note indicating that until this point (i.e. the editor's notation) judgment (*mišpāṭ*) has been Moab's experience (e.g. Rothstein, 796). Thus things may be about to change for Moab. Until the new age of restoration dawns Moab must face destruction, but 'in the latter days' the nation will be rebuilt by Yahweh. A different explanation allows for the possibility that the phrase is a marginal note originally intended to mark off one oracle from another in older manuscripts, perhaps before the titular information was added to the poems (cf. Duhm, 352). Such marginal glosses may get displaced in the transmission of manuscripts and allowance must be made for this note being out of place (perhaps originally after v. 42 or v. 44).

49.1–6

1 Concerning the Ammonites.
Thus says the Lord:
'Has Israel no sons?
Has he no heir?
Why then has Milcom dispossessed Gad,
and his people settled in its cities?
2 Therefore, behold, the days are coming,
says the Lord,
when I will cause the battle cry to be heard
against Rabbah of the Ammonites;
it shall become a desolate mound,
and its villages shall be burned with fire;
then Israel shall dispossess those who dispossessed him,
says the Lord.'
3 'Wail, O Heshbon, for Ai is laid waste!
Cry, O daughters of Rabbah!
Gird yourselves with sackcloth,
lament, and run to and fro among the hedges!

For Milcom shall go into exile,
with his priests and his princes.
4 Why do you boast of your valleys,
O faithless daughter,
who trusted in her treasures, saying,
"Who will come against me?"
5 Behold, I will bring terror upon you,
says the Lord GOD of hosts,
from all who are round about you,
and you shall be driven out, every man straight before him,
with none to gather the fugitives.
6 But afterward I will restore the fortunes of the Ammonites, says
the LORD.'

[MT 49.1–6] = G 30.1–5 (Rahlfs 1935, 30. 17–21). **[1]** MT *malkām*, 'their king': Vrs Milkom, i.e. Molech, patron deity of Ammon, depicted here as acquiring Israelite territory by conquest. A good example of the religious ideas and language common to Israel, Moab and Ammon and typical of 48; 49.1–6. G 'Gilead' for 'Gad': cf. Num. 32.29 for Gad's possession of Gilead. **[2]** Rudolph, 286, regards v. 2a as an addition (cf. BHS) to be deleted as in 48.12; the line is in G. G lacks *b^{e}nē-ʿammōn*, 'of the Ammonites': Rabbah (cf. v. 3) is the capital of the territory (cf. modern-day Amman, capital of Jordan). Cf. 4.19 for 'the battle cry'; 30.18 for mound (*tēl*). MT *ūb^{e}nōteyhā* lit. 'and her daughters': i.e. the outlying villages dependent upon Rabbah; G *kai bomoi autēs*, 'and her high places' = *ūbāmōteyhā* (but cf. v. 3). Rudolph, 289 treats v. 2d as an addition based perhaps on Zeph. 2.9b; cf. Cornill, 474, but Weiser, 404 n. 2, discerns a different logic in Zeph. 2.9b from Jer. 49.2b. MT *w^{e}yāraš yiśrāʾēl ʾet-yōr^{e}šayw*, 'then Israel shall dispossess *those who dispossessed him*': G *kai paralalēmpsetai Israēl tēn archēn autou*, 'and Israel shall take possession of *his dominion*'. G lacks *ʾāmar yhwh*, 'said Yahweh': cf. 48.8, where *ʾ^{a}šer ʾāmar yhwh* suggests a citation; perhaps MT alludes here to the belief expressed by Zeph. 2.9b. **[3]** MT *hēlīlū ḥešbōn kī šudd^{e}dāh-ʿay*, 'Howl, Heshbon, for Ai is laid waste': Heshbon, though near the border, is a Moabite town (cf. 48.2, 34, 45) and no Ammonite Ai is known; Volz, 411, reads *šōdēd ʿālāh*, 'the destroyer has come up' (cf. 48.18), followed by Rudolph (cf. BHS); Duhm, 353, and Cornill, 475, favour reading *hāʿīr*, 'the city (i.e. the capital) is destroyed'. MT *w^{e}hitšōṭaṭ^{e}nāh bagg^{e}dērōt*, 'and rush to and fro among the walls (i.e. hedges or sheep-folds)': lacking in G. NEB 'and score your bodies with gashes': *šūṭ*, 'rove about', but *šōṭ*, 'scourge, whip', as verb would support NEB translation (cf. Driver 1937–38, 124–5). Giesebrecht, 241, and other exegetes (e.g. Duhm, Rudolph) favour reading *gdd* for *gdr* (cf. *d-r* shift in 48.37), i.e. *mitgōd^{e}dīm* (41.5) 'gashing yourselves' or *big^{e}dudōt* (BHS) 'with gashes', cf. the funeral rites of 16.6; 41.5; 48.37.

MT is incomprehensible. MT *malkām*, 'their king': cf. v. 1 (G *Melchol*); cf. 48.7 for 'his priests and his princes together (shall go into exile)'; also Amos 1.15. **[4]** MT *bāʿᵉmāqīm zāb ʿimᵉqēk*, lit. 'in the valleys flowing your valley': G *en tois pediois*, 'in the plains'. Duhm, 353, explains *zb* as *z* (= *zeh*) *bᵉ* 'that is, in your valley' (explaining 'valleys'); followed by Rudolph (deleting 'valleys' cf. BHS) and others (cf. Driver 1937–38, 125). A different explanation is offered by Dahood 1959, 166–7, who understands *ʿmq* to mean 'strength' as in Ugaritic and reads MT as 'Why boast of your strength (enclitic *m*), your ebbing strength?'; followed by Bright, 324–5, and Christensen 1975, 225. Cf. 47.5. MT *habbat haššōbēbāh*, 'O faithless daughter': epithet used of virgin Israel in 31.22; G *thugatēr atimias*, 'dishonoured daughter' = *bat habbūšāh*. Duhm prefers *habbat haššaʾᵃnannāh*, 'O complacent daughter', cf. 48.11 (*šaʾᵃnan mōʾāb*), followed by Rudolph (cf. BHS). Cf. 48.7 for the same image of trusting in treasures (i.e. strongholds?). A few mss, Vrs have 'who says' before 'Who will come against me?' (cf. Lam. 4.12 for the conviction of impregnability). **[5]** MT *paḥad . . . mikkol-sᵉbībāyik*, 'terror . . . from every side': i.e. from all around; cf. *māgor missābīb*, 'terror on every side' (6.25; 20.3, 10; 46.5; 49.29; cf. Christensen 1973). G *eipe kurios*, 'says the lord': lacking *ʾᵃdōnāy . . . ṣᵉbāʾōt*, 'lord . . . hosts'. Rudolph deletes the whole phrase as an addition. G lacks *lannōdēd*, 'the wanderers', i.e. the stragglers (cf. NEB). **[6]** Lacking in G. Cf. 46.26 for the 'afterward' motif and 48.47; 49.39 for the 'restoration of the fortunes' idea. A prose addition to the poem against the Ammonites representing the subsequent revival of Ammonite fortunes (contrast Zeph. 2.9, which envisages a permanent wasteland for Moab and the Ammonites).

Ammon

The lengthy collection of material on Moab is followed by a series of much shorter pieces against neighbouring and more distant nations. In the first poem the Ammonites are the target of divine punishment (cf. Amos 1.13–15; Zeph. 2.8–11; Ezek. 21.20, 28–32; 25.1–7 for other anti-Ammonite statements). Rabbah, the chief town of the territory, is the focus of the oracular announcement and, as in all the OAN, its fate represents great destruction with concomitant mourning, exile and the reversal of national hubris. Nemesis pursues Ammon in this poem because of Ammonite domination of Gileadite territory. The Ammonite god Milcom having dispossessed Israel will in turn be dispossessed by Israel when the Ammonite towns are burned and Rabbah reduced to a mound (*tēl*). Echoes of the poems against Moab can be detected in vv. 1–5 (e.g. the reference to Heshbon in v. 3), especially the hubristic attitude of the nation (v. 4, cf. 48.7, 29). The brevity of the piece allows for no development of theme, variations or speaker's responses: great mourning comes upon the people (v. 3), but the poet does not join in the lamentation (contrast 48.31–35). An additional note in v. 6 recognizes the revival of Ammonite fortunes in a period after the devastations celebrated in the poem.

Some exegetes date the poem to *c.* 617 in the time of Josiah (e.g. Bardtke 1936, 251; Christensen 1975, 227), when Judaean nationalistic policy was one of territorial expansion. There is little in the poem to confirm or deny such an interpretation, and its stereotypical elements divorce it, to a great extent, from a specific situation, though v. 1 may point to some Ammonite infiltration of Judaean land. Ammon's defeat is inevitably the work of Yahweh, just as Gilead's loss is expressed in terms of Milcom's possession of land and cities. Theomachy, i.e. the battle of the gods, is an important element behind many of the poems in the collection of oracles against the nations because the defeat of a nation is the defeat of its god. Thus the fluctuating fortunes of Judah and its neighbours represent the flux of divine power and loss, though Judaean theology hardly permits the entertaining of the notion that Yahweh's defeat is entailed in Judaean disasters. Each nation presumably exempts its god from defeat but allows credit to be taken for the defeat of other nations (cf. Moabite Stone, the oracles of Second Isaiah). The brevity of vv. 1–5 does not allow for the development of themes and motifs found in the longer poems, so it is difficult to determine the extent to which the speaker is hostile towards Ammon or 'seems almost to express sympathy for the Ammonites' (Hyatt, 1117). That hint of sympathy may be the contribution of the editor who appended v. 6 to the poem and allowed for Yahweh's revival of the fortunes of Ammon, but in view of 46.26b; 48.47; 49.39 sympathy may be too strong a word for such stereotypical notes.

49.7–11

7 Concerning Edom.
Thus says the LORD of hosts:
'Is wisdom no more in Teman?
Has counsel perished from the prudent?
Has their wisdom vanished?

8 Flee, turn back, dwell in the depths,
O inhabitants of Dedan!
For I will bring the calamity of Esau upon him,
the time when I punish him.
9 If grape-gatherers came to you,
would they not leave gleanings?
If thieves came by night,
would they not destroy only enough for themselves?
10 But I have stripped Esau here,
I have uncovered his hiding places,
and he is not able to conceal himself.
His children are destroyed, and his brothers,
and his neighbours; and he is no more.
11 Leave your fatherless children, I will keep them alive;
and let your widows trust in me.'

[MT 49.7–11] = G 29.8–12. **[7]** G lacks 'of hosts'. The interrogative of MT (*ha'ēn 'ōd*, 'is there no longer . . . ?) is a simple assertion in G (*ouk estin eti*, 'there is no longer . . .'). MT *nisr^eḥāh ḥokmātām*, '(has) their wisdom been let loose': *srḥ*, 'go free, be unrestrained'; Rudolph, 288, 'rancid', cf. modern Heb. *srḥ*, 'stink'. NEB 'decayed'; Bright, 328, 'gone stale'. Cf. 7.28 for a similar structure to 'counsel has perished . . .'. **[8]** MT *hop^enū*, 'be turned back': Hophal imperative; Ehrlich 1912, 360, reads *hiṣṣāp^enū*, 'hide yourselves'. MT *'ēd 'ēśāw*, 'the calamity of Esau': G *duskola epoiēsen*, 'he has done (i.e. *'āśāh*) peevishly'; i.e. behaved badly. **[9]** Cf. Obad. 5. The image of gleaning appears in 6.9. MT *hišḥītū dayyām*, 'they would destroy their sufficiency': i.e. they would destroy no more than they needed for themselves; G *epithēsousi cheira autōn*, 'they shall lay their hands on' = *yāšītū yādām*. **[10]** Cf. Obad. 6. MT *ḥāśaptī*, 'I have stripped bare': cf. 13.26; Obad. 6, *neḥp^eśū*, 'is searched out', i.e. exposed. MT *w^eneḥbāh*, lit. 'and is hidden': GV and modern exegetes (e.g. Ehrlich, Rudolph and others) read infin. absol. *w^enaḥbōh*, 'to hide (themselves)'. MT *šuddad zar'ō w^e'eḥāyw*, 'his seed is destroyed and his brothers': Rudolph regards 'and his brothers' as incomprehensible, deletes it and transposes *w^e'ēnennū*, 'and he is no more', to follow 'his seed is destroyed' (cf. Bardtke 1936, 253). Christensen 1975, 230 understands *zr'* as *z^erō'a*, 'arm' (cf. G *epicheira adelphou autou*, '*forearm* of his brother') in the sense of 'strength', cf. 17.5, and reads the line as 'The strength of his allies is shattered'. MT *w^e'ēnennū*, 'and he is no more': cf. Symm, G^L, *ouk estin hos erei*, 'there is none who speaks', followed by Rudolph (also Bardtke) as *w^e'ēn 'ōmēr* (cf. BHS). Driver 1937–38, 125, transfers *'āz^ebāh* from v. 11 and reads *w^e'ēnām 'ōz^ebō*, 'and there was none to help him'. **[11]** MT *tib^eṭāḥū*, 'let them trust': masc. ending for fem. = *tib^eṭāḥnāh* (BHS).

Edom

Moab, Ammon, and now Edom (cf. different order in 25.21 and G) are grouped together in MT (the piece on Damascus interrupts G 29–31). The Edom piece is more like the Moab poem than the Ammon one in that it has been extended by prose material and shares common elements with OAN in other traditions (e.g. Obadiah and Isa. 34.5–15). Hostility towards Edom is to be found in many biblical sources and especially in relation to the Babylonian destruction of Judah (cf. Lam. 4.21–22; Ps. 137.1; Isa. 11.14b; 21.11–12; 63.1–6; Amos 1.11–12; Ezek. 25.12–14; 32.29; 35; Ps. 60.9–10 [MT 10–11]; Mal. 1.2–5; Ogden 1982). However, the degree of such antagonism is not reflected in the length of the poem which, though long, is by no means as developed as the material against Egypt, *Moab* and Babylon. The expansion of 49.7–11 owes much to other sources and therefore the length of the anti-Edomite piece is more a redactional matter, drawing together discrete strands of comparable material, than an indication of particular hostility towards Edom.

The poem itself is typical of the collection and, apart from the individual details of names and places which identify the antagonist, calls upon Edom (using the names of its towns Teman and Dedan) to flee from the enemy. Like the Ammonite poem it opens with questions, but these are about the state of wisdom in Edom. If the people of Edom still possess understanding and insight they will flee from the calamity of Esau. In the genealogical legends of Israel the nation's eponymous forebear has a brother called Esau: he lived in Edomite territory and indeed was known as Edom (Gen. 25.31; 32.3; 36.8–9, 43). Thus Israelites and Edomites were believed to be closely related kin groups. Common origins and common territorial interests would explain much of the mutual hostility between the two nations (cf. Gen. 19.30–38 for similar connections between Israel, Moab, and the Ammonites). The ferocity of Esau's (i.e. Edom's) destruction is explained in vv. 9–10 using figures which appear also in Obad. 5–6. Unlike the gleaning of the vineyards (cf. 6.9; 8.13) or the consideration of thieves, neither of which actions completely removes everything, the punishment of Esau has been a stripping of him naked. Nothing is left (the deity being less kind and more thorough than humans). No hiding places, no people nor neighbours: nothing remains to protect Edom or to afford the nation help. Such terrible devastations may reflect Babylonian incursions into Edomite territory, but any particular destruction of Edom may be included in such a brief poem.

The ending of the poem in v. 11 is strange: the nation is summoned to abandon its orphans and widows to Yahweh. He, the Judaean god, will protect the Edomite victims of his wrath. Such concern for the oppressed suggests a lack of serious hostility against Edom in the poem (cf. vv. 6, 39 for other eirenic attitudes towards foreign nations) and a possible allusion to the belief in Yahweh's protection of widows and orphans (cf. Deut. 10.18 and the epithets of Ps. 68.5, 'father of the fatherless and protector of widows'). Those among the Edomite widows who are prepared to trust Yahweh will find protection from him (cf. 17.7–8; 39.18 for the trust motif). It is a strange statement because Yahweh's role as a caring and protective figure is seldom applied to members of foreign nations. Whether such a note of concern for foreigners reflects a pre- or post-587 setting is a moot point.

49.12–22

12 For thus says the Lord: 'If those who did not deserve to drink the cup
must drink it, will you go unpunished? You shall not go unpunished, but
you must drink. 13 For I have sworn by myself, says the Lord, that Bozrah
shall become a horror, a taunt, a waste, and a curse; and all her cities shall
be perpetual wastes.'

14 I have heard tidings from the Lord, and a messenger has been
  sent among the nations:
'Gather yourselves together and come against her,
  and rise up for battle!'
15 For behold, I will make you small among the nations,
  despised among men.
16 The horror you inspire has deceived you,
  and the pride of your heart,
you who live in the clefts of the rock,
  who hold the height of the hill.
Though you make your nest as high as the eagle's,
  I will bring you down from there,
    says the Lord.

17 'Edom shall become a horror; every one who passes by it will be horrified
and will hiss because of all its disasters. 18 As when Sodom and Gomorrah
and their neighbour cities were overthrown, says the Lord, no man shall
dwell there, no man shall sojourn in her. 19 Behold, like a lion coming up

from the jungle of the Jordan against a strong sheepfold, I will suddenly make them run away from her; and I will appoint over her whomever I choose. For who is like me? Who will summon me? What shepherd can stand before me? 20 Therefore hear the plan which the LORD has made against Edom and the purposes which he has formed against the inhabitants of Teman: Even the little ones of the flock shall be dragged away; surely their fold shall be appalled at their fate. 21 At the sound of their fall the earth shall tremble; the sound of their cry shall be heard at the Red Sea. 22 Behold, one shall mount up and fly swiftly like an eagle, and spread his wings against Bozrah, and the heart of the warriors of Edom shall be in that day like the heart of a woman in her pangs.'

---

[12] G is shorter here: 'for thus says the lord They who were not appointed to drink the cup, have drunk; and you shall by no means be cleared'. MT *'ēn mišpāṭām*, lit. 'there was no obligation on them': cf. 25.28–29; this deviates from the sense of 25.15–27, where Jerusalem and Judah are obligated to drink the cup, though v. 18 should be deleted as an addition to 25.15–29. In this context the forcing of the cup is made to apply to Edom. **[13]** Cf. 22.5; 44.26; 51.14 for the divine swearing by himself. MT *leḥōreb*, 'a waste': lacking in G; possibly a dittography of *leḥorebōt*, 'waste places'. Cf. 42.18b; 44.12 for similar fourfold execrations. 'Bozrah': cf. v. 22; the chief city of Edom (modern el-Busreiah). G *en mesō autēs*, 'in the midst of her' = *betōkāh*. Bozrah is probably a figure for the whole land (cf. Isa. 34.6b) as Teman is in v. 7. **[14]** Cf. Obad. 1. **[15]** Cf. Obad. 2. **[16]** Cf. Obad. 3–4. MT *tipelaṣtekā*: hapax legomenon, meaning uncertain; *plṣ*, 'shudder' (BDB, 814); *tplṣt*, 'shuddering, horror' (cf. KB, 1037, 'the horror caused by thee?'). NEB 'Your overbearing arrogance', cf. *mipeleṣet*, 'horrid thing', used of some idolatrous object (I Kings 15.13); Bright, 331, thinks the two words may have the same sense (i.e. 'your horrible idol') and that *tplṣt* may be a contemptuous epithet for the Edomite god. Christensen 1975, 228, translates it as 'Your reputation for ferocity'; Driver 1937–38, 125, 'shuddering', i.e. 'Edom has mistaken men's shuddering horror of her misdeeds for fear of her prowess.' MT *hiššī' 'ōtāk*, 'has deceived you': many exegetes read *hiššī'atekā* (cf. Ehrlich 1912, 361; Rudolph, 288). G lacks *ne'um yhwh*, 'says Yahweh'. Cf. 22.23 for the image of nesting as a figure of security. **[17]** Cf. 19.8. Much of vv. 17–22 is a patchwork of elements to be found throughout the book of Jeremiah. **[18]** = 50.40 with minor variations. G has *kurios pantokratōr* for MT *yhwh*, i.e. 'lord almighty'. Cf. Zeph. 2.9, where Moab and Ammon become like Sodom and Gomorrah (20.16 is more allusive). Christensen treats vv. 17–18 as secondary prose elements (also vv. 13a, 22b), but the rest as poetry. Cf v. 33b for v. 18b. **[19]** 49.19–21 = 50.44–46 (*mutatis mutandis*). MT *migge'ōn hayyardēn*, 'from the jungle of the Jordan': see Notes on 12.5b; G *ek mesou tou Iordanou*, '*from the midst of* the

Jordan' = Aram. *miggō'* (BHS). MT *'el-nᵉwēh 'ētān*, 'to the perennial pastures': cf. NEB; i.e. permanent pasturage, here suddenly depopulated by the enemy (under the figure of a lion). Rudolph refers the phrase to the oases of the Jordan desert territory. MT *kī*, 'for': BHS *kēn*, 'so', follows Duhm, 336. MT *'argī'āh 'ᵃriṣennū mē'āleyhā*, 'I will in a moment chase *him* from her': 50.44; Vrs 'them' (RSV margin); Rudolph, 288 reads *'ergᵉ'āh 'et-ṣō(')n mar'ītō*, 'I will startle the sheep of his flock' (BHS). MT *ūmī bāḥūr 'ēleyhā 'epqōd*, lit. 'and who is chosen? Over her I will appoint': Cornill, 482, and followed by many (e.g. Rudolph, Bright) *ūmibḥar 'ēleyhā 'epqōd*, 'and the choicest of her rams I will single out'. **[20]** MT *'īm-lō . . . 'īm-lō'*, 'surely . . . surely': the asseverative force reflects the formal oath style. MT *yisḥābūm*, 'they shall drag them': Rudolph, 290, reads *yissāḥᵃbū gam*, 'they will be dragged also' (BHS); Kselman 1970, 580, treats it similarly but reads the *m* as enclitic (followed by Christensen 1975, 230). MT *yaššīm 'ᵃlēhem nᵉwēhem*, lit. 'he shall devastate their fold on account of them': Rudolph reads *yiššōm* (cf. v. 17) 'shall be devastated' (BHS); MT Hiphil may have the force of the Qal. Kselman treats *'lyhm* as *'ullēhem*, 'nurslings' (cf. Gen. 33.13). **[21]** MT *ṣᵉ'āqāh bᵉyam-sūp nišma' qōlāh*, lit. 'cry is heard by the sea of reeds her voice': many mss read '*their* voice'; G, 50.46 lack *qwlh*. Rudolph reads *ṣā'ᵃqāh*, 'the cry from it'; Driver 1937–38, 126, interprets the line as 'the crying thereof (i.e. of the earth) is heard in the Red Sea: hark to it!'. The sea of reeds (*yam-sūp*) refers to the Egyptian border territory associated with the legend of the exodus (Ex. 14) and not the Red Sea (as in EVV but not JPSB). **[22]** Cf. 48.40–41. G 48.40 lacks 'shall mount up and'. MT *'al-boṣrāh*, 'against Bozrah': G *ep' ochurōmata autēs*, 'over her strongholds' = *'al-mibᵉṣārehā*. Rudolph, 290, deletes 'in that day' for metrical reasons.

The oracle against Edom (original form consists of vv. 7–8, 22a, 10–11 [Bardtke] or vv. 7–8, 10–11, 22 [Rudolph]) is expanded considerably by secondary material in vv. 12–21. These expansions reflect Obad. 1–4 and the anti-Babylonian collection in 50.44–46, but also use 19.8 and elements from 25.15–29. The fate which befell Judah in 587 (cf. 25.18) now becomes the destiny of Bozrah (v. 13). To some extent the development of the poem in vv. 7–11 may be due to post-587 considerations and the use of so many different strands from other contexts suggests common material against the nations available for such constructions. Apart from the occasional place name in a poem or the redactional introduction which provides a key to the interpretation, many of the poems have a generality of reference which permits them to be used interchangeably of different nations (e.g. vv. 14–16 could refer to any state, and its present application to Edom is determined by the context of vv. 7–22 and influenced by the title in Obad. 1a). This feature of the OAN may be detected also in the poems directed against Jerusalem in Part I.

The cup metaphor in v. 12 refers to the cup of the wine of the wrath of Yahweh sequence in 25.15–29, where all the nations are forced to drink the wine in order to be destroyed. Jerusalem and the cities of Judah are included in that list (perhaps not originally) and two points are developed from that inclusion (25.29; 49.12). The first reflection makes the punishment of Jerusalem the grounds for the destruction of the nations. In the second the fate of Jerusalem is recognized as being unwarranted (i.e. lacking justification, *'ēn mišpāṭ*), but, since it has happened, the punishment of Edom is *a fortiori* inevitable. 587 becomes the warrant for the annihilation of the nations and the OAN show a remarkable shift from the arguments of Parts I, III–IV, which elucidate good reasons for the destruction of Jerusalem. Hence the same language is used of Jerusalem and Edom (v. 13; cf. v. 17; 19.8; 42.18b; 44.12). The bitter lessons taught by 597 and 587 (cf. Lam. 4.12) have become the inspiration for denouncing the nations and exposing their hubristic outlook (v. 16; cf. 48.29–30; 49.4, 31; 50.31–32). Whether the enemy addressed in v. 14 is Babylon or some other foe cannot be determined from vv. 14–16, but the more developed vision of Obadiah suggests that Babylon is the force summoned to destroy Edom (cf. Obad. 10–14). Edom's fate comes from Yahweh and will involve a reversal of its standing among the nations; instead of being much feared it will become small and inferior to the other states (vv. 15–16). The first line of v. 16 is ambiguous in that the opening word is an obscure one which may refer to Edom's attitude or its effect on others (cf. EVV). But Edomite arrogance (*zᵉdōn lēb*) allied to this other feature of its existence has deceived the nation (cf. 4.10 for Jerusalem's deception), and its secure position in the rocks cannot protect it (cf. 21.13; 22.23) from Yahweh.

Further images are used to describe Edom's fall in vv. 17–22. Like Jerusalem, those who pass through it will be shaken by what they see. Unlike Jerusalem (cf. Isa. 1.9), Edom will become like Sodom and Gomorrah, the legendary cities of the plain overthrown by the deity (Gen. 19.24). The invading army is described as a lion coming up from the lush growth of the Jordan area and savaging the sheepfolds (v. 19). These images are continued in v. 20 as an explanation of Yahweh's plan against Edom. The young sheep are dragged away by the lion and the slaughter is such that the community (sheepfold) are appalled by the massacre, the report of which reaches as far as the border of Egypt. In v. 22 (cf. 48.40–41) the enemy is like an eagle attacking Bozrah, and the Edomite warriors become like women (cf. 51.30), unable to fight back.

49.23–27

23 Concerning Damascus.
'Hamath and Arpad are confounded,
for they have heard evil tidings;
they melt in fear, they are troubled like the sea
which cannot be quiet.
24 Damascus has become feeble, she turned to flee,
and panic seized her;
anguish and sorrows have taken hold of her,
as of a woman in travail.
25 How the famous city is forsaken,
the joyful city!
26 Therefore her young men shall fall in her squares,
and all her soldiers shall be destroyed in that day,
says the Lord of hosts.
27 And I will kindle a fire in the wall of Damascus,
and it shall devour the strongholds of Ben-hadad.'

[MT 49.23–27] = G 30.12–16. **[23]** 'Hamath and Arpad': petty states in central and northern Syria respectively (cf. Isa. 10.9; 36.19; 37.13). MT *nāmōgū bayyām d*^{e}*'āgāh*, lit. 'they melt in the sea (is) anxiety': Volz, 415, reads *nāmōg libbām midd*^{e}*'āgāh*, 'their hearts melt from anxiety', and is followed by many exegetes (e.g. Rudolph, Bright). Christensen 1975, 245–6, uses a conjectural emendation *nmg (k)ym d'g(w)* and translates 'they melt away (in terror) like Yamm, they quiver in fear'. G represents the line with two verbs: *exestēsan*, *ethumōthēsan* 'they are amazed, they are angry'. Cf. 6.24 for the hearing of a report motif. **[24]** MT *w*^{e}*reṭeṭ heḥ*^{e}*zīqāh*, 'and *she* has seized panic': read with Giesebrecht, 244, and others *-āh*, i.e. 'and panic has seized *her*'; *rt̤t̤* is a hapax legomenon in MT, cf. Aram. *r*^{e}*ṭēṭ*, 'tremble'. G lacks v. 24b and it is deleted by many exegetes (e.g. Bardtke, Rudolph, Christensen); cf. 6.24b; 50.43b where a similar phrase occurs expressing a state of collapse in terms of a pregnant woman's seizure with birth pangs. **[25]** MT *'ēk lō' 'uzz*^{e}*bāh 'īr t*^{e}*hillāh*, lit. 'how *not* deserted (is) she, the city of praise': i.e. the city of renown is *not* deserted but the context demands an assertion of forsakenness rather than its denial; only V lacks *lō'*, 'not'. Some exegetes delete 'not' (cf. BHS), others explain *lō'* as a mistake for the emphatic *lamed* (*lᵉ*, cf. Nötscher 1953, 374; Christensen 1975, 246); Driver 1937–38, 126, treats *'zb* as 'helped'. Rudolph, 292, regards it as a marginal note of a reader who would award such a title only to Jerusalem. Q *tᵉhillāt* = *tᵉhillātī*, '*my* praise', parallel to *qiryat mᵉśōśī*, 'city of *my* joy', i.e. my joyful city (Jerusalem); most Vrs lack suffix. **[26]** = 50.30 with the addition of *ṣᵉbā'ōt*, 'of hosts' (lacking in G). **[27]** Cf. Amos 1.14; v. 27b = Amos 1.4b. Ben-hadad represents the name of the Syrian dynasty in the ninth-eighth centuries (BCE) and also the names of individual kings (cf. I Kings 20).

Damascus (Syria)

The shortest oracle in the collection is the one against Damascus (the town stands for Syria) and in MT it belongs to a group of three pieces which deal with territories further afield than Judah's neighbouring states. The title 'concerning Damascus' (*lᵉdammeśeq*) reflects the identification of Syrian territory with its main city (cf. Amos 1.3–5; Isa. 17.1–3; Zech. 9.1), though the oracle also alludes to the cities of nearby states Hamath (cf. Zech. 9.2a) on the Orontes and Arpad near Aleppo. Reference to areas so far away from Judah (incorporated into the Assyrian empire in the late eighth century) is strange in oracles attributed to Jeremiah and has been explained as a reflection of the Assyrian conquests of a previous age using an archaizing tendency characteristic of epigonic literature of the fifth century (cf. Pfeiffer 1941, 508). It is less likely that the piece represents an anonymous eighth-century poem reapplied to Damascus in relation to a campaign of Nebuchadrezzar's against that area (though allowance must be made for this possibility, cf. Bright, 337). A reference to Syrian troops in II Kings 24.2 associates them with the curbing of Jehoiakim's activities *c.* 597, but the oracle against Damascus hardly belongs to such an anti-Judaean strand in the Deuteronomistic history.

The poem is very brief and consists of vv. 23, 24a, 25 (Bardtke 1936, 255), with v. 26 an addition from 50.30 and v. 27 a concluding appendix from Amos 1.4, 14 (cf. Rudolph, 292; Christensen 1975, 245–6, excludes much less). It depicts Damascus panic-stricken and routed – a famous city abandoned. The report of this catastrophe makes Hamath and Arpad extremely anxious. No account is given of the cause of the panic and no specific historical situation can be discerned at all in the poem (though Christensen, 248, relates it to the period of Josiah's political expansion). Rather it is Yahweh who destroys Damascus, hence the extract from Amos 1. Stereotypical phrases identify Yahweh as the opponent of the foreign nations, and it is possible to detect here a hint of apocalyptic orientation (cf. Pfeiffer).

49.28–33

28 Concerning Kedar and the kingdoms of Hazor which Nebuchadrezzar
king of Babylon smote.
Thus says the LORD:
'Rise up, advance against Kedar!
Destroy the people of the east!
29 Their tents and their flocks shall be taken,
their curtains and all their goods;
their camels shall be borne away from them,
and men shall cry to them: "Terror on every side!"
30 Flee, wander far away, dwell in the depths,
O inhabitants of Hazor!
says the LORD.
For Nebuchadrezzar king of Babylon
has made a plan against you,
and formed a purpose against you.
31 Rise up, advance against a nation at ease,
that dwells securely,
says the LORD,
that has no gates or bars,
that dwells alone.
32 Their camels shall become booty,
their herds of cattle a spoil.
I will scatter to every wind
those who cut the corners of their hair,
and I will bring their calamity
from every side of them,
says the LORD.
33 Hazor shall become a haunt of jackals,
an everlasting waste;
no man shall dwell there,
no man shall sojourn in her.'

[MT 49.28–33] = G 30.6–11. **[28]** MT *ūlᵉmamlᵉkōt ḥāṣōr*, 'and the kingdoms of Hazor': G *tē basilissē tēs aulēs*, 'the queen of the courtyard' =

l^emalkat ḥāṣēr. MT hardly makes sense with a reference to Hazor in an oracle about the bedouins of the eastern desert (vv. 30, 33 make it a place name), and most modern exegetes translate 'the kingdom of Hazor' quite differently. Cf. Isa. 42.11, *ḥ^aṣērīm tēšēb qēdār*, 'the villages Kedar inhabits'. Thus Bardtke, Rudolph, Christensen among others treat *ḥṣr* as 'encampments'; *maml^ekōt* may mean 'chieftains' (cf. 1.15) and the phrase can be translated as 'village chieftains' (cf. Bright, 336). Cf. 2.10 for Kedar as a designation of the eastern desert region. K *nbwkdr'ṣwr*; Q *n^ebūkadre'ṣṣar*, 'Nebuchadrezzar': K a scribal error perhaps under the influence of Hazor (*ḥṣwr*). Bardtke 1936, 255, and Christensen 1975, 209, delete 'which Nebuchadrezzar king of Babylon smote' as unoriginal (an expansionary gloss). MT *w^ešād^edū*, 'and destroy': G *kai plēxate*, 'and fill', i.e. destroy? (cf. *apolesai* in 29.4 [MT 47.4]; BHS). **[29]** Cf. 4.20; 10.20 where the destruction of bedouin encampments provides images of the disaster befalling the speaker's people. MT *māgōr missābīb*, 'terror on every side': cf. 6.25; 20.3, 4, 10; 46.5 (see on 19.14 – 20.6). **[30]** Cf v. 8a for v. 30a. MT *nudū m^e'ōd*, 'wander greatly': G lacks *nudū*. Rudolph, 292, treats 'dwell in the depths' as an addition from v. 8 (cf. Rothstein). MT *yōš^ebē ḥāṣōr*, 'inhabitants of Hazor': G *kathēmenoi en tē aulē*, 'those who live in the courtyard', cf. v. 28. G lacks *n^e'um yhwh*, 'says Yahweh'. Rudolph regards 'king of Babylon' as an addition because it disrupts the metre; it may be an expansionary gloss (Christensen); G lacks 'Nebuchadrezzar'. Cf. v. 20a for plan (*'ēṣāh*) and purpose (*maḥ^ašābāh*) with Yahweh as subject. K *'lyhm*, 'against them'; Q *'^alēkem*, 'against you' (lacking in G^{BS}). **[31]** Cf. Ezek. 38.10–11. G lacks *n^e'um yhwh*, 'says Yahweh': deleted by Rudolph (cf. BHS) because Nebuchadrezzar is the speaker. **[32]** MT *q^eṣūṣē pē'āh*, 'those who cut the corner (of their hair)': cf. 9.25 (EV 26); 25.23; i.e. the Arabs of the desert who clip the hair of their temples. MT *ūmikkol-'^abārāyw* 'and from every side of *him*': Vrs have plur. suffix '. . . of them'; Rudolph reads the unsuffixed *'^abārīm*, i.e. '(from every) side'. **[33]** MT *ḥāṣōr*, 'Hazor': G *hē aulē*, 'the courtyard', as in vv. 28, 30. 33 appears to consist of phrases from the book of Jeremiah: cf. 9.10 (EV 11); 10.22; 51.37 for 'haunt of jackals', 'desolation' (33a); 33b = v. 18b. It is an editorial conclusion to the poem.

Kedar

The redactional introduction to the poem associates the oracle with Nebuchadrezzar's campaign against the Arabian tribes of Kedar and the kingdoms of Hazor (MT). Hazor is a common name for cities in Palestine (e.g. Josh. 11.1; 12.19; 15.23, 25; 19.36), but in this context it either refers to an Arabian locality in the eastern desert or should be translated as the 'unwalled villages' (cf. v. 31b) of that area (cf. G). The bedouin settlements of the desert are to be swept away by the onslaught of the Babylonian emperor. Exegetes differ in their analysis of the limits of the poem (e.g. vv. 28*, 29, 31, 32 [Bardtke]; vv. 28a, 30–32 [Rudolph]), but vv. 28a, 33 may be recognized as secondary.

The oracle against Kedar is the only one in the collection to contain an identifying reference to the destroyer, but that line in v. 30 may well be secondary. It does, however, indicate how the generality of the poems in the OAN may be identified with the Babylonian domination of the ancient Near East (cf. the redactional notes in 46.2, 13; 49.28, 34). The poems themselves do not identify the foe but use conventional terms to describe invasion and defeat, flight and panic. Behind the plight of each nation is Yahweh rather than the Babylonian emperor, but Nebuchadrezzar may be regarded as a convenient historical point of reference for poems belonging to Judaean cultic life. Kedar's destruction is facilitated by the unprotected nature of bedouin settlements and their unawareness of danger which renders them complacent (v. 31). The shout 'terror on every side' (v. 29b) is a characteristic shocked response to invasion and destruction, and echoes through a number of different places in the book of Jeremiah (cf. the development of it in MT 20.3). As in so many other parts of the tradition, the desert settlements will become an uninhabited place where no one will live again, a haunt of jackals (cf. 10.22; 51.37). No reason is given for Kedar's destruction, and the poem may be an echo of Assyrian campaigns in the mid-seventh century or a reference to Nebuchadrezzar's attack on the Arabs in 599–8 (cf. Wiseman 1956, 31–2). As with all the poems in 46–51, if there is a historical setting behind the poem it cannot be detected.

49.34

34 The word of the LORD that came to Jeremiah the prophet concerning Elam, in the beginning of the reign of Zedekiah king of Judah.

[MT 49.34] = G 26.1. **[34]** G lacks this redactional title to the oracle on Elam but concludes that piece (G 25.14–19) with part of it: *en archē basileuontos Sedekiou basileōs egeneto ho logos outos peri Ailam*, 'in the beginning of the reign of king Zedekiah, there came this word concerning Elam'. The different order of the oracles against the nations in G has Elam as the first piece, and because it starts the collection G uses MT 25.13b as a title – *ha eprophēteusen Ieremias epi ta ethnē ta Ailam*, 'which Jeremiah prophesied against the nations: against Elam'. MT *'ᵃšer hāyāh dᵉbar-yhwh 'el-yirmᵉyāhū hannābî',el-'ēlām*, 'what came (as) the word of Yahweh to Jeremiah the prophet concerning Elam': cf. 1.2; 14.1; 46.1; 47.1 for this fractured form of the reception of the divine word formula. MT *bᵉrē'šît malᵉkūt ṣidᵉqiyyāh*, 'in the beginning of the reign of Zedekiah': i.e. his accession year; the period between the deportation of Jehoiachin and 1 Nisan 597 (cf. 26.1; 52.28; Rudolph, 295; Bright, 336). Cf. v. 35, where *rē'šît*, 'beginning, first, chief', also occurs.

Elam

An editorial introduction prefaces the piece on Elam (vv. 35–38) and attributes it to an oracular utterance of Jeremiah *the prophet* *c.* 597 at the beginning of Zedekiah's reign (contrast 46.2, 'the fourth year of Jehoiakim'). Rudolph uses these two dating points to divide the oracles against the nations into two parts: 46.2 – 49.33 belong to the fourth year of Jehoiakim and 50.1 – 51.64 are to be assigned to the fourth year of Zedekiah. 49.34–38 would therefore represent a transition between the two sets of oracles. Symmetrical though this division may be, it is scarcely warranted by the text. *If* the redactional notices are to be taken at face value then they may be applied only to the nations named in each note (i.e. Egypt and Elam) and may not be extended indefinitely to cover every oracle within either set (cf. 46.13).

Why Elam should be identified with the beginning of Zedekiah's reign is beyond our knowledge (Bardtke 1936, 257, deletes this element of the notice), though there may have been conflict between the Elamites and the Babylonians *c.* 596–5 (cf. Wiseman 1956, 36, 72–3). After a long history of conflict with the Assyrians Elam was conquered by Assyria under Asshurbanipal in 640. It appears to have regained independence *c.* 625 (cf. Wiseman 1956, 8–10, 50–1) and contributed to the defeat of Babylon in 540–39. The Elam oracle is like all the others in 46–51 in that it contains no specific historical information and its vague, stereotypical phrases are capable of an a-historical explanation. Whether vv. 35–38 are poetry or prose is difficult to determine, though the prosaic nature of some of the elements in them are recognized by most exegetes. RSV and JPSB treat them as prose, but many commentators regard the oracle as being essentially poetic (e.g. NEB, Rudolph, Bardtke, Christensen).

49.35–39

35 Thus says the LORD of hosts: 'Behold I will break the bow of Elam, the mainstay of their might; 36 and I will bring upon Elam the four winds from the four quarters of heaven; and I will scatter them to all those winds, and there shall be no nation to which those driven out of Elam shall not come.
37 I will terrify Elam before their enemies, and before those who seek their life; I will bring evil upon them, my fierce anger, says the LORD. I will send the sword after them, until I have consumed them; 38 and I will set my throne in Elam, and destroy their king and princes, says the LORD.'
39 'But in the latter days I will restore the fortunes of Elam, says the LORD.'

[MT 49.35–39] = G 25.14–19. **[35]** G lacks 'of hosts'. Cf. Isa. 22.6 for Elam's association with archery. MT *rē'šīt gᵉbūrātām*, lit. 'first of their strength': i.e. chief (weapon) of their power (NEB); the occurrence of *rē'šīt* here may account for the dating of the editorial note in v. 34 (*bᵉrē'šīt*, 'in the beginning of . . .'). **[36]** The second part of v. 36 is regarded as a prosaic addition by many exegetes (e.g. Rudolph, Bright, Christensen but not Bardtke). MT *haggōy*, '*the* nation': *ha* due to dittography (lacking in G, T). Some mss and Vrs read *yābō'ū*, '*they* shall come,' for MT *yābō'*, 'it shall come'. K *'wlm*; Q *'ēlām*, 'Elam': K 'permanently', perhaps influenced by v. 13b. **[37]** G *kai ptoēsō autous*, 'I will put them in fear': lacking 'Elam'. Cf. 21.7; 44.30; 46.26 for the motif 'those who seek (their) life'. G lacks *nᵉ'um-yhwh*, 'says Yahweh'. Cf. 9.15 (EV 16) for v. 37c. **[38]** MT *wᵉha'ᵃbadtī miššām*, 'and I will destroy from there': G *kai exapostelō ekeithen*, 'and I will send forth thence', i.e. expel; G may be a corruption of *exapolesō* 'I will destroy utterly', (cf. BHS). G lacks *nᵉ'um-yhwh*, 'says Yahweh'. **[39]** Cf. 48.47. K *'šwb 't šbyt*, Q *'āšīb 'et-šᵉbūt* 'I will restore the fortunes': probable reading should combine K and Q as *'āšūb 'et-šᵉbūt* (cf. Rudolph, 294); but Q = 49.6.

The oracle asserts Yahweh's campaign against Elam's power characterized by the bow (cf. Isa. 22.6). Elam will be scattered to the four winds by some great force which is not identified, but v. 37 hints at invasion (though G's 'my sword' may continue the motif of divine power exercised against the Elamites, cf. Ezek. 32.24–25). Scattering and slaughtering are two rather different fates, but the language of vv. 35–38 is too stereotyped to afford precise identification of meaning. Elam will be annihilated by Yahweh and the divine throne will be placed there (cf. 3.17; 17.12 where the throne motif has different meanings). The destruction of the Elamite leadership and its replacement by Yahweh's throne reflect the belief that in the future Yahweh's suzerainty will displace the power of the foreign nations and Judah's god will rule over the empires (cf. Zech. 14.16–19). A new realm of 'history' is envisaged – what some exegetes would call 'eschatological' (cf. Christensen 1975, 223). The oracular assertion of Elam's annihilation is reversed to some extent by the addition of a brief oracle in v. 39 which recognizes a revival of Elamite fortunes in the future (cf. 46.26b; 48.47; 49.6). Such an appendix indicates how rhetorical the language of vv. 35–38 is.

50.1

58[1] The word which the LORD spoke concerning Babylon, concerning the land of the Chaldeans, by Jeremiah the prophet:

[MT 50] = G 27. **[1]** MT *haddābār 'ᵃšer dibber yhwh 'el-bābel*, 'the word which Yahweh spoke to (concerning) Babylon': cf. 46.13 (45.1 with Jeremiah as speaker; 37.2 with variations) for this formal introduction; G *logos kuriou, hon elalēsen epi Babulōna*, 'word of Yahweh which he spoke against Babylon', cf. 51.1. MT develops the introduction 'and (with many mss, Vrs) concerning the land of the Chaldaeans, by means of (*bᵉyad*) Jeremiah the prophet'; cf. 37.2.

Babylon

The final section of the OAN consists of two very lengthy chapters of oracular utterances against Babylon. These are almost as long (110 verses) as the material against the other nations in 46–49 (121 verses). Their length indicates the obsessional antagonism felt towards Babylon as the national enemy which had destroyed Jerusalem and ruined the nation (cf. Isa. 13–14; 21.1–10; 47; Ps. 137). Two themes dominate the poems: the fall of Babylon and the restoration of the exiles to their own land (cf. the similar themes in Isa. 40–55) and these are interwoven together without any marked degree of progress of thought. Within a framework of Babylon's fall (50.2–3; 51.54–58) many poetic and prosaic elements depict the downfall of the enemy intercut with pieces about Judah-Israel (cf. analysis in Fohrer 1981, 50–1).

The structural analysis of 50–51 is the most difficult problem in the exegesis of the text and few commentators agree on how to divide the poems into units. From the one extreme of about fifty oracles and fragments (e.g. Robinson 1918) to the other extreme of 'a well-ordered complex of structurally related elements' (e.g. Aitken 1984, 26), exegetes have puzzled over how best to treat the text. The problem may be avoided by a continuous verse-by-verse commentary (e.g. Cornill, Duhm, Giesebrecht, Hyatt) or more realistically side-stepped by dividing the material into units for exegetical convenience (e.g. Bright, Thompson). Other commentators more confidently discern a varying number of poems in the collection: three (Christensen 50; 51.1–40, 41–58), four (Condamin 50.2–20, 21–46; 51.1–37, 38–58), five (Volz 50.2–16, 21–32, 35–38; 51.1–26, 27–58 with additions and citations), six movements (Aitken 50.4–20, 21–32, 33–46; 51.1–33, 34–44, 45–53), fifteen units (Rudolph 50.2–7, 8–20, 21–28, 29–32, 33–40, 41–46; 51.1–19, 20–26, 27–33, 34–40, 41–43, 44–46, 47–48, 49–57, 58) and even more units (cf. Fohrer, Weiser). Whatever their disagreement about unit division, many of these exegetes would agree on the poorly organized state of the collection, its thematic poverty and exorbitant length. It is regarded as a purely artificial literary production, more interested in quantity than quality and monotonous to the point that only a commentator could read it through (Duhm, 360). Dismissive judgments such as '. . . a prolix, disjointed, vacuous literary exercise . . . this inane poem . . .' (Pfeiffer 1941, 507) convey well the opinions of many commentators of the older schools of thought on biblical literature. More recent approaches to the Bible are less caustic and more prepared to detect structure and coherence where once all was thought to be shapeless and incoherent (cf. Aitken, Christensen). The repetitiveness of the thematic material may be attributable to the emotions aroused by Babylon and to circles which celebrated the downfall of the great enemy in terms of its potential for the return of the exiles to their homeland (cf. the hymns of Second Isaiah, where so few ideas are repeated in so many units). Aitken postulates a deep structure for the poem consisting of the matrix 'situation – intervention – outcome' (1984, 28), and these three ground-elements may be found throughout 50–51 in various pairings. Although tending to abstraction, this approach has the advantage of descrying unifying features in the poem which may account for the final form of the text redaction. However many units make up the poem, the creative hand of the editors must be allowed a shaping influence.

In MT the oracular utterance against Babylon is attributed to Jeremiah *the prophet* (contrast G). As part of the redactional framework this attribution cannot be regarded as historically reliable, though from the viewpoint of the holistic approach to the book of Jeremiah the created persona of Jeremiah may be viewed as the speaker of this lengthy poem against Babylon. In such an approach fundamental contradictions are less important than they are for historical reconstructions. If such a poem were to be attributed to the 'historical Jeremiah', it would raise the insuperable problem of reconciling the speaker of this anti-Babylonian outburst with the image of Jeremiah as the friend of Babylon portrayed in 27–29, 39–40. Babylon would not have trusted a man who could utter such things *against* Babylon, even if on other occasions he was credited with the view that Nebuchadrezzar was the servant of Yahweh (25.9; 27.6). Emperors may be very susceptible to flattery, but they are not at all impervious to criticism. Utterances of the calibre of 50–51 lead to death sentences rather than honourable treatment under the patronage of the empire (39.12–14; 40.4–6). It is difficult to see how Jeremiah could have been advocating submission (27) or surrender (38) to the Babylonians and yet *at the same time* (cf. 51.59) have been proclaiming 51.1–14 or 51.25–40 (these oracles are dated to *c.* 590–580 by Christensen 1975, 278–9, and attributed to Jeremiah). The mental reservations required to hold both views together (never mind the problems of confusing the people!) are hardly eased by proposing a sequential aspect to the beliefs (cf. 25.11–14). 50–51 present a very different view of Judah from that given in 2–20 or Parts III and IV, and to attempt to reconcile all these aspects of the tradition is to produce a chimerical Jeremiah.

A better approach to the contradictory elements in the tradition is to recognize that inconsistency is a major feature of the editing of the book of Jeremiah and to accept that the various strands present irreconcilable images of Jeremiah *the prophet*. It is as a prophet that he is represented as a speaker to the nations (cf. 1.5), and this role comes to the fore in MT's presentation of the oracles against the nations (46.1, 13; 49.34; 50.1). As a prophet Jeremiah combines all the disparate attitudes incorporated into the tradition and thus he represents the Jews of Palestine and even Babylon in their quarrels with the Jewish communities in Egypt and also the pro- and anti-Babylon parties of the sixth century. Real, historical people cannot be such representative figures, nor can they speak for every party in the community, but the cumulative effect of the many discrete traditions making up the book of Jeremiah is to produce a figure who transcends all the limitations of history and society and becomes a paradigmatic prophet to the nations. Nowhere is this transcendence of all human limitations so clearly seen as in the material on Babylon. In 27–29 the pro-Babylonian stance is taken by Jeremiah and the anti-Babylonian prophet Hananiah is dismissed (a case of premature anti-Babylonism?). Co-existence with Babylon and even settlement in Babylon is advocated (29), and the well-being of both Jews and Babylonians is bound up together in the religious activity of the Jews in Babylon (29.7). After 597 and especially in view of the destruction of Jerusalem in 587, Babylon becomes the target of great hostility as well as the place where many Jews lived. So in 50–51 the voice of that hostility is given full range – needless to say that voice is Jeremiah's! In his capacity as prophet Jeremiah articulates the great hatred of Babylon felt by its many victims and gives expression to the feelings of countless Judaeans who saw Babylon only as the destroyer of Jerusalem, temple and people.

50.2–3

2 'Declare among the nations and proclaim,
  set up a banner and proclaim,
  conceal it not, and say:
"Babylon is taken,
  Bel is put to shame,
  Merodach is dismayed.
Her images are put to shame,
  her idols are dismayed."
3 For out of the north a nation has come up against her, which shall make her land a desolation, and none shall dwell in it; both man and beast shall flee away.'

---

[2] Cf. 51.54–58. MT *uśᵉʾū-nēs hašᵉmîʿū*, 'and raise the signal, proclaim': cf. 4.6; Isa. 13.2; lacking in G. 'Bel . . . Merodach': Bel (= *baʿal*) was originally the patron god of Nippur but became an epithet of the patron god of Babylon, Marduk (cf. Rudolph, 300); hence these are not two gods but different names of the one god (cf. 51.44; Isa. 46.1). G *katēschunthē (Bēl) hē aptoētos, hē truphera (pareluthē Marōdach)*, 'confounded (Bel) the fearless, the voluptuous (Marodach is destroyed)': an inner Greek doublet (cf. Janzen 1973, 20, 28; Ziegler 1958, 96) with later correction to MT (in brackets). MT variant 'shamed are her images, shattered her idols' is lacking in G:*gillūlîm* may be translated 'godlets' (Bright), 'fetishes' (JPSB) or 'godlings' – lit. 'balls of dung', it is a scatological reference to foreign gods/idols frequently used in Ezekiel but only here in Jeremiah. **[3]** MT *mē'ādām wᵉ'ad bᵉhēmāh nādū hālākū*, lit. 'from man and to beast they have fled, they have gone': i.e. both man and beast have fled and gone away. G lacks the two verbs; they appear together in 9.9 (EV 10) which may have influenced 50.3bβ or they may be variants here.

The poems and prose pieces constituting 50–51 are enclosed in a framework of 50.2–3; 51.54–58. This framework announces the destruction of the great enemy Babylon and reflects (though according to some exegetes it may anticipate) the defeat of Babylon in 539. The gap between the historical reality of the power shift from Babylonian to Persian forces without the destruction of the city of Babylon and the depiction of the overthrow of Babylon in terms of destruction and desolation (e.g. 50.13, 15, 23, 30, 39–40; 51.2–4, 26, 29, 32, 37, 43, 58) has led many exegetes to argue that the poems must belong to the period before the actual defeat of Babylon. Whatever force this argument may have, it is not necessarily a persuasive one. The language of the poems is conventional and influenced by other parts of the book of Jeremiah; it may not therefore be a description of what actually happened but a celebration of Babylon's defeat. Emotion is the key here rather than historical accuracy. For those living in Palestine the defeat of Babylon would have been a great joy, and the details of the event could be supplied from traditional songs of triumph over the enemy. Taunt songs furnish their own emotional charge independent of the actual course of events and, like the folk songs of so many cultures, often are a preferred surrogate to the more mundane reality they celebrate. A different argument detects in the dissonance arousing gap between expectation and reality as constituted by the fall of Babylon evidence for reading 50–51 as an 'eschatological poem' (cf. Christensen 1975, 263, for the phrase and 249–80 for the connections between 50–51 and early apocalyptic; my argument here is not Christensen's). By that weasel-word description (i.e. 'eschatological') is meant a poem in which Babylon is less the historical city-enemy of the sixth century and more the epitome of the antagonist of Yahweh's people in all subsequent ages. As such the fall of Babylon in 539 is the starting point for the development of the belief in a catastrophic overthrow of all the forces believed to be arranged against Jerusalem and the people of Israel (cf. Ezek. 38–39; Isa. 24–27; Joel 3.1–21 [MT

4.1–21]; Zech. 14). The mythic roots of this belief may belong to the temple cult of the pre-587 period but the defeat of Babylon in 539 gave it the boost necesssary to remove it from the sphere of ancient myth to that of potential historical reality. That defeat may not have been as grandiose as expected but in the future there would be a mighty devastation of Babylon (or whatever it stood for) which would dwarf the changeover of power in the time of Cyrus.

The preface to the collection sets out the theme of 50–51: 'Babylon is taken' (*nilkᵉdāh bābel*). This slogan links all the poems and comments in the collection and underwrites its significance. The alternation between Babylon (vv. 2–3, 8–15, 21–27, 29–32, 35–38) and Israel (vv. 4–7, 17–20, 28, 33–34) demonstrates the twin themes arising from this announcement: Babylon's defeat as *punishment* and the restoration of Israel. These themes are also to be found in Second Isaiah which suggests the period (*c.* 550–539?) when the poems were edited, but the language of 50–51 reflects the Jeremiah tradition and must be attributed to the redaction of Jeremiah rather than associated directly with the circles which produced Isa. 40–55. Arising out of the same period the two traditions developed quite distinctive responses to the (impending?) fall of Babylon and the prospects for the exiles emerging from that catastrophe (cf. Isa.47; also sa. 40.1–2; 44.24–28; 48.17–21; 49.24–26; 51.17–23; 52.1–2, 11–12). The primary consequence of the capture of Babylon drawn by the preface is the humiliation of the Babylonian deity Marduk (Bel; cf. Isa.46.1). The defeat of Babylon is the defeat of the god and the triumph of Yahweh – a logic not used in the tradition with reference to Jerusalem's defeat in 587 but mooted in the lament psalms (e.g. 44.23–26; 74.18–23; 79; 89.38–48) within the constraints of the chauvinistic theology of the national cult (cf. the Moabite Stone for the theologization of defeat and victory). In effect the defeat of the god Marduk means the humiliation of the cult's idols (cf. Isa. 44.9–20; 46.1–2), though Cyrus's praise of Marduk (cf. Pritchard 1969, 315–16) should lend perspective to this pro-Judaean understanding of the fall of Babylon (cf. v. 38b for the view of Babylon as 'a land of images'). In v. 3 the universal proclamation of v. 2 is explained in more prosaic terms (many exegetes, NEB, JPSB treat v. 3 as poetry). Out of the north has come up against her a nation which shall destroy her and render her land uninhabited. How ironic this assertion is in the light of the proclamation of the very same motif against Jerusalem in 6.22 (cf. 1.14; 4.6; 10.22)! The tradition has come full circle with this announcement that the destroyer is the destroyed.

50.4–20

4 'In those days and in that time, says the Lord, the people of Israel and the people of Judah shall come together, weeping as they come; and they shall seek the Lord their God.
5 They shall ask the way to Zion, with faces turned toward it, saying, "Come, let us join ourselves to the Lord in an everlasting covenant which will never be forgotten." '

6 'My people have been lost sheep; their shepherds have led them astray, turning them away on the mountains; from mountain to hill they have gone, they have forgotten their fold.
7 All who found them have devoured them, and their enemies have said, "We are not guilty, for they have sinned against the Lord, their true habitation, the Lord, the hope of their fathers." '

8 'Flee from the midst of Babylon, and go out of the land of the Chaldeans, and be as he-goats before the flock.
9 For behold, I am stirring up and bringing against Babylon a company of great nations, from the north country; and they shall array themselves against her; from there she shall be taken. Their arrows are like a skilled warrior who does not return empty-handed.
10 Chaldea shall be plundered; all who plunder her shall be sated, says the Lord.'

11 'Though you rejoice, though you exult,
O plunderers of my heritage,
though you are wanton as a heifer at grass,
and neigh like stallions,
12 your mother shall be utterly shamed,
and she who bore you shall be disgraced.
Lo, she shall be the last of the nations,
a wilderness dry and desert.
13 Because of the wrath of the Lord she shall not be inhabited,
but shall be an utter desolation;
every one who passes by Babylon shall be appalled,
and hiss because of all her wounds.'
14 'Set yourselves in array against Babylon round about,
all you that bend the bow;
shoot at her, spare no arrows,
for she has sinned against the Lord.
15 Raise a shout against her round about,
she has surrendered;
her bulwarks have fallen,
her walls are thrown down.

For this is the vengeance of the LORD:
take vengeance on her,
do to her as she has done.
16 Cut off from Babylon the sower,
and the one who handles the sickle in time of harvest;
because of the sword of the oppressor,
every one shall turn to his own people,
and every one shall flee to his own land.'
17 'Israel is a hunted sheep driven away by lions. First the king of Assyria
devoured him, and now at last Nebuchadrezzar king of Babylon has gnawed
his bones. 18 Therefore, thus says the LORD of hosts, the God of Israel:
Behold, I am bringing punishment on the king of Babylon and his land, as
I punished the king of Assyria. 19 I will restore Israel to his pasture, and
he shall feed on Carmel and in Bashan, and his desire shall be satisfied on
the hills of Ephraim and in Gilead. 20 In those days and in that time, says
the LORD, iniquity shall be sought in Israel, and there shall be none; and
sin in Judah, and none shall be found; for I will pardon those whom I leave
as a remnant.'

---

[4] G lacks *nᵉ'um yhwh*, 'says Yahweh': 4QJer[b] agrees with MT in reading it (cf. Janzen 1973, 184). Rudolph, 298, treats *ubᵉnē-yᵉhūdāh yaḥdāw*, 'and the people of Judah together', as an addition to the text; it is an unnecessary gloss on *bᵉnē-yiśrā'ēl*, 'people of Israel', which includes Israel *and* Judah (cf. vv. 17, 19). Cf.v.20; 33.15 for the double phrase *bayyāmīm hāhēmmāh ūbā'ēt hahī'*, 'in those days and in that time' (parallel but separate in 3.17, 18). **[5]** MT *ṣiyyōn yiš'ālū derek hēnnāh pᵉnēhem*, lit. 'Zion they shall ask (the) way hither their faces': i.e. they ask the way to Zion with their faces turned hither. MT *bō'u wᵉnilᵉwū*, 'they came and they shall cleave': G *kai hēxousi kai katapheuxontai*, 'and they shall come and flee for refuge'; many exegetes read *wᵉnillāweh*, 'and let us cleave' with S (cf. BHS) and some read *ūbā'ū*, 'and they shall come', with G (cf. Bright, 340, retaining MT; Rudolph). Cf. 32.40; Ezek. 37.26 for the motif *bᵉrīt 'ōlām*, 'a permanent *bᵉrīt*', i.e. an everlasting covenant (or obligation). **[6]** K *hyh*; Q *hāyū*, 'they have been': K treats *'ammī*, 'my people', as a collective requiring a sing. verb; cf. Gen. 30.43 for Q. MT *hārīm šōbᵉbūm* (Q; K *šōbēbīm*), lit. 'mountains recusant': i.e. (on the) mountains they wander (apostatize); G *epi ta orē*, 'upon the mountains' = *'al-hārīm* (Driver 1937–38, 126, prefers *behārīm*). Christensen 1975, 250, reads *šwbbw* with the next line. Duhm, 361, detects a playful use of 3.23 here. Cf. 23.1–2 for the motif of shepherds (i.e. rulers) who scatter the flock; BHS suggests *mōrēhem*, 'their leaders' (teachers) as a possible reading of *hārīm* (*m* lost by haplography; cf. Rudolph, 298). **[7]** MT *lō' neᵉšām*, 'we are not guilty': cf. 2.3 for' *šm*, 'acquire guilt'; G *mē anōmen autous*, 'let us not leave them alone' = *lō' niśśā'ēm*. G lacks *yhwh* at end of v. 7; cf. 14.8 (G); 17.13 for Yahweh as

Israel's hope (*miqwēh*). The true habitation (*nᵉwēh-ṣedeq*) here is Yahweh, but in 31.23 the phrase refers to the sacred hill of the temple. **[8]** Volz, 421, reads MT *yhwh* at end of v. 7 as *hōy* at the beginning of v. 8 (cf. BHS); cf. Zech.2.10–11 (EV 6–7) for this use of *hōy* as a prefix to a command to flee (translated as 'listen' by Petersen 1985, 172–3). K *yṣ'w*, 'they go out'; Q *ṣᵉ'ū*, 'go forth': MT places *atnah* here but many exegetes transpose it to *kaśdīm*, 'Chaldaeans', cf. NEB, BHS. MT *kᵉ'attūdīm*, 'like he-goats': i.e. like the sheep which lead the flock; 'bellwethers' (Bright, 340). G *hōsper drakontes*, 'like dragons, serpents': perhaps a corruption of *archontes*, 'rulers' (cf. *arxantes* = *'attūdē*, Isa. 14.9; BHS) or *tragoi*, 'he-goats' (Streane 1896, 288; cf. *eriphoi* = *'attūdīm*, 'he-goats', in 28.40; MT 51.40). **[9]** G lacks *ūmaʿᵃleh*, 'and bringing up', and *gᵉdōlīm*, 'great (nations)': both words may be MT dittographies (cf. BHS). MT *kᵉgibbōr maškīl*, 'like a bereaving warrior': i.e. a soldier who makes childless, cf. JPSB margin; many mss, A, T, V read *maśkīl*, 'successful', i.e. skilful warrior, cf. RSV, NEB. **[10]** MT *kaśdīm*, 'Chaldaeans': here it must refer to the land (hence fem. *hāyᵉtāh*, 'shall be') as in 51.24, 35 (*yōšᵉbē kaśdīm*, 'inhabitants of Chaldaea'). G lacks *nᵉ'um yhwh*, 'says Yahweh'. **[11]** K *tśmḥy . . . tʿlzy*, fem.sing.; Q *tiśᵉmᵉḥu . . . taʿᵃlᵉzū*, masc.plur., 'you rejoice . . . you exult': both are possible in Heb., as is the case for K *tpwšy . . . wtṣhly*; Q *tāpūšū . . . wᵉtiṣᵉhᵃlū*, 'you spring about . . . and you neigh'. MT *kᵉʿeglāh dāšāh*, 'like a cow threshing': G *hōs boidia en botanē*, 'like calves in grass' = *kᵉʿeglē baddeše'*, cf. Mal. 3.20 (EV 4.2). **[12]** MT *ḥāpᵉrāh yōladtᵉkem*, 'ashamed is she who bore you': G *mētēr ep' agatha*, 'mother for good', i.e. (the one who bore you) for good. G lacks *hinnēh*, 'look': BHS suggests *hī*, 'that is (the end of the nations)', cf. Rudolph, 300; cf. NEB 'the mere rump of the nations' as the meaning of *'aḥᵃrīt gōyim*. G only has *erēmos*, 'desert', for MT's three synonyms *midbār ṣiyyāh waʿᵃrābāh*, 'wilderness dry land and desert', cf. 2.6. **[13]** Cf. 19.8; 49.17. **[14]** MT *yᵉdū*, 'shoot': a few mss *yᵉrū*, 'shoot'; both variations convey the same idea. G lacks 'for against Yahweh she has sinned': a pious gloss. **[15]** G lacks *sābīb*, 'round about'. MT *nātᵉnāh yādāh*, lit. 'she has given her hand': i.e. a gesture signalling surrender (cf. I Chron. 29.24; II Chron.30.8; Latin *manum dare*); G *parelu-thēsan hai cheires autēs*, 'her hands are weakened', cf. v. 43. T 'she is given into their hand' (BHS). MT *'āšyōteyhā*, 'her bulwarks': hapax legom. Q presupposes a noun *'āšyāh*; K *'šwytyh* is uncertain (cf. BHS); G *hai epalxeis autēs*, 'her battlements'. Cf. Aram. *'uššayyā'*, 'the foundations' (Ezra 4.12). **[16]** Rudolph, 302, prefers Hiphil form *hakritū* (*h* lost due to haplography) to Qal *kirtū*, 'cut off', as better linguistic usage (cf. G *exolethreusate*, 'completely destroy'). MT *zōrēʿa*, 'sower': G *sperma*, 'seed' = *zeraʿ*. Cf. 46.16 for the phrase *mippᵉnē ḥereb hayyōnāh*, 'because of the sword of the oppressor', and see Notes there for G reading of 'Grecian sword'; cf. 25.38 for a similar phrase. 16bβγ = Isa. 13.14b. **[17]** MT *'ᵃrāyōt hiddīḥū*, 'lions have driven away'; a suffix is required, perhaps *hiddīḥūhū*, 'have driven *him* away'; cf. G *leontes exōsan auton*, 'lions have driven *him* out'. G lacks 'Nebuchadrezzar'. MT *'iṣṣ^emō*, lit. 'he has boned him': the verb is a denominative from *'eṣem*, 'bone', and only occurs here, presumably with the sense 'gnaw off bones' (cf. KB, 727; EVV). **[18]** G lacks 'of hosts, god of Israel'. **[19]** G lacks 'and Bashan'. **[20]** G lacks *n^e'um-yhwh* 'says Yahweh'.

The first section of 50 consists of at least six units (vv. 4–5, 6–7, 8–10, 11–13, 14–16, 17–20), which are here treated together because vv. 4 and 20 form a closure. Within vv. 4–20 the attack on Babylon is celebrated in three poems and the fate of Israel encloses these poems. At the time of Babylon's fall (cf. vv. 2–3) the people of Israel will return to their own land and seek Yahweh in Zion. This weeping procession presents the return in liturgical terms as a pilgrimage back to Jerusalem *and to Yahweh* (cf. 3.21–23). Israel (i.e. Judah, cf. v. 17, though the larger diaspora may be envisaged here) will return to Yahweh in a permanent *b^erīt*. This motif links the view of Judah-Israel in 50–51 with that of 30–31 and their expansion in 32–33. In both collections the restoration of the people to their homeland includes notes about the renewal of the community's relationship with Yahweh as a permanent arrangement. Where the collections differ is in the emphasis put solely on Judah-Israel in 30–33, whereas the central feature of 50–51 is Babylon the enemy, and Judah's restoration is but a concomitant of the Babylonian defeat. Included in the introductory pieces about Yahweh's people is the recognition that the nation has been served poorly by leaders (v. 6, cf. 23.1–2), but that is the most critical the collection ever becomes of Judah. All the other pieces present Israel as the innocent victim of vicious opponents, and 50–51 breathe a very different atmosphere from the trenchant critique of Judah and Jerusalem presented in 2–20. Verses 6–7 present the nation, under the figure of sheep, as wandering aimlessly across the mountains and being savaged by their enemies. These enemies hide behind the excuse that their victims sinned against Yahweh (MT). Such a belittling of Judah's offences is indicative of the attitude taken towards the nation's past in 50–51. 'More sinned against than sinning' is the cliché which well summarizes the presentation of Judah-Israel in the OAN, and it makes a very interesting contrast with other strands incorporated into the book of Jeremiah.

The flock metaphor reappears in v. 8 in a brief poem (prose in RSV, but apart from v. 9a the piece would appear to be poetic) as a figure of the fugitives (exiles?) fleeing from doomed Babylon like he-goats prancing at the head of the flock. Ironically Babylon's enemy comes from the north, that fateful direction from whence came Jerusalem's doom. If the first Babylon poem addresses those who must flee from the ill-fated city, the second one (vv. 11–13) denounces Babylon herself and explains why she will become a complete desolation. Mother Babylon (cf. 10.20; 15.10; 31.15 for the maternal metaphor) will be disgraced because her children plundered Yahweh's territory. That pillaging of the land of Judah is represented in further animal terms as a cow gambolling in the fields and stallions neighing. In v. 13 the cause of Babylon's downfall is identified as Yahweh's wrath (cf. the gloss in v. 14, 'because she has sinned against Yahweh'), though elsewhere in the poems the more specific charge of attacking Israel is stated as Babylon's crime (cf. vv. 17bβ, 28; 51.11, 24, 49). The striking feature of this element in 50–51 is its ignorance of the tradition's claim in other strands that *Yahweh himself* destroyed Judah by means of his servant Nebuchadrezzar and the Babylonians as a punishment for their gross sins, apostasy, oppression and idolatry. 50–51 clearly represent a radically different theological perspective on the exile which cannot be integrated with some of the other perspectives in the book of Jeremiah. Such diversity of opinion on the causes and theologization of 587 is not a problem in the interpretation of the Jeremiah tradition, but it is a serious obstacle to a holistic reading of the book because any holistic approach entails a trimming process whereby the integrity of each individual tradition in the book is seriously diminished. From the perspective of 50–51 Judah was hunted down and destroyed by the king of Babylon (cf. 50.17) and for that outrageous campaign Yahweh will destroy Babylon – 'Babylon must fall for the slain of Israel' (51.49; cf. 50.15, 29 'do to her as she has done').

The poem of vv. 14–16 addresses the attackers of Babylon and stresses the cause of the attack as Yahweh's vengeance against the one who has sinned against himself. The great enemy of so many nations must now face the poetic justice of falling before her own enemy (v. 15a, cf. 51.44). With her destruction all the exiles are freed to flee to their own lands and the section returns to the position of the Judaean exiles (cf. vv. 8, 16). This motif allows the section to conclude with some observations on Israel's past and future (vv. 17–20: a mixture of poetry and prose with vv. 17b–19 as a prose commentary on v. 17a). In the most general way v. 17 summarizes

Israel's history over the previous two centuries under the figure of a scattered sheep (*śeh pᵉzūrāh*) driven away by lions. These lions are then identified as the king of Assyria and the king of Babylon, and the effects of their campaigns against Israel as the devouring of the sheep followed by the gnawing of its bones. Between them Assyria and Babylon have destroyed Israel and *therefore* (v. 18) must be punished. Assyria had been punished already (cf. Isa. 10.5–19; ironically Babylon had had a hand in Assyria's downfall), so now it is Babylon's turn. The corollary of Babylon's defeat is the restoration of Israel to its own land. This return to the old territories – the fertile land of Carmel and Bashan (MT) and the hills of Ephraim (cf. 31.6) and Gilead – will satisfy the nation's appetite (*nepeš*). Here is the same dream as is delineated in 31.2–14; it represents the natural longings of any exiled group or people dominated by foreign powers to find satisfaction once more in their own land, free of the unwelcome attention of foreigners. The idyllic nature of v. 19 is of a piece with the dreams of 30–31, and the prerequisite for their achievement is the destruction of Babylon. Beyond Babylon's fall lies a glorious future. A further note adds the observation that in such a future in their own land the sins (past, present or future?) of Israel and Judah will be undetectable because the deity will have pardoned them (cf. 31.34b). Even here there is no concentration on the sins of the people; the subject is only raised in order to emphasize the prospect of Yahweh's forgiveness in the future. Thus the past with its sinfulness and the present with Babylon the arch-enemy will be transformed in the future when the remnant (for that is all the lions left!) settle down in their own land.

50.21–40

21 'Go up against the land of Merathaim,
    and against the inhabitants of Pekod.
  Slay, and utterly destroy after them,
                    says the LORD,
    and do all that I have commanded you.
22 The noise of battle is in the land,
    and great destruction!
23 How the hammer of the whole earth
    is cut down and broken!

How Babylon has become
a horror among the nations!
24 I set a snare for you and you were taken, O Babylon,
and you did not know it;
you were found and caught,
because you strove against the LORD.
25 The LORD has opened his armoury,
and brought out the weapons of his wrath,
for the Lord GOD of hosts has a work to do
in the land of the Chaldeans.
26 Come against her from every quarter;
open her granaries;
pile her up like heaps of grain, and destroy her utterly;
let nothing be left of her.
27 Slay all her bulls,
let them go down to the slaughter.
Woe to them, for their day has come,
the time of their punishment.'
28 'Hark! they flee and escape from the land of Babylon, to declare in
Zion the vengeance of the LORD our God, vengeance for his temple.'
29 'Summon archers against Babylon, all those who bend the bow.
Encamp round about her; let no one escape. Requite her according to her
deeds, do to her according to all that she has done; for she has proudly
defied the LORD, the Holy One of Israel. 30 Therefore her young men shall
fall in her squares, and all her soldiers shall be destroyed on that day, says
the LORD.'
31 'Behold, I am against you, O proud one,
says the Lord GOD of hosts;
for your day has come,
the time when I will punish you.
32 The proud one shall stumble and fall,
with none to raise him up,
and I will kindle a fire in his cities,
and it will devour all that is round about him.'
33 'Thus says the LORD of hosts: The people of Israel are oppressed, and
the people of Judah with them; all who took them captive have held them
fast, they refuse to let them go. 34 Their Redeemer is strong; the LORD of
hosts is his name. He will surely plead their cause, that he may give rest to
the earth, but unrest to the inhabitants of Babylon.'
35 'A sword upon the Chaldeans, says the LORD,
and upon the inhabitants of Babylon,
and upon her princes and her wise men!

36 A sword upon the diviners,
    that they may become fools!
  A sword upon her warriors,
    that they may be destroyed!
37 A sword upon her horses and upon her chariots,
    and upon all the foreign troops in her midst,
    that they may become women!
  A sword upon all her treasures,
    that they may be plundered!
38 A drought upon her waters,
    that they may be dried up!
  For it is a land of images,
    and they are mad over idols.'
39 'Therefore wild beasts shall dwell with hyenas in Babylon, and ostriches shall dwell in her; she shall be peopled no more for ever, nor inhabited for all generations. 40 As when God overthrew Sodom and Gomorrah and their neighbour cities, says the LORD, so no man shall dwell there, and no son of man shall sojourn in her.'

---

[21] MT *'al-hā'āreṣ m^{e}ratāyīm '^{a}lēh 'āleyhā*, 'against the land, Merathaim, go up against her': many exegetes (but not Christensen) read *'^{a}lēh* (*'al*) *'ereṣ* . . ., 'go up (against) the land of . . .'. The command is addressed to the sword rather than to an invading people (Nötscher, 337). Rudolph, 302, reads *r^{e}dōp*, 'pursue', after *p^{e}qōd*, 'Pekod', and transposes *'aḥ^{a}rēhem*, 'after them', to follow it: 'and against the inhabitants of Pekod pursue after them'. Word-play may be detected in the use of the names Merathaim (the district of *marratim* at the head of the Persian Gulf), 'double rebellion' (*mrh*, 'rebel'), and Pekod (*puqudu*, a people in East Babylonia), 'doom' (*pqd*, 'punish'), cf. Bright, 354. MT *ḥ^{a}rōb*, lit. 'put to the sword': a denominative verb from *ḥereb*, 'sword', cf. v. 27; G *machaira*, 'sword': G reads *pqd* with *ḥrb* and translates 'avenge, O sword . . .'. MT *w^{e}haḥ^{a}rēm*, 'and utterly destroy': i.e. put to the sacred ban by annihilation, cf. v. 26. **[22]** Cf. 4.6; 6.1; 48.3 for the phrase *w^{e}šeber gādōl*, 'and great destruction'; G 'in the land of the Chaldaeans', cf. v. 25. **[23]** Cf. 51.41 for v. 23b. The metaphor of hammer (*paṭṭīš*), here used to describe Babylon's domination of the land, appears in 23.29 as a figure of the equally destructive power of Yahweh's word. **[24]** MT *yāqōštī lāk*, 'I have set a snare for you': lacking in G; as Yahweh is spoken of in the third person in v. 24b (*bayhwh* 'against Yahweh'), *yāqōštī* should be read as a second person fem. form, '*you* set a snare (for yourself)'; cf. the forms in 2.20, 33. The nature of the trap is not easily discerned but, avoiding an Aulenesque theologization of v. 24, it is probably just a figure of speech for Babylon's defeat. S lacks 'you were found and also seized' (BHS). MT *kī bayhwh hitgārīt*, 'for against Yahweh you engaged in strife':

whether this refers to Babylon's hubristic campaign of world domination or its attack on Jerusalem is a moot point (cf. Volz, 424; Nötscher, 338, who favour the first view, which fits the context of vv. 23–27; the other possibility is indicated by the notes in the poems attacking Babylon for its treatment of Jerusalem). **[25]** G lacks 'of hosts': its *tō kuriō theō* may represent *yhwh ᵉlōhīm* rather than MT's *ᵃdōnāy yhwh*, i.e. 'Yahweh god' instead of 'lord Yahweh', cf. Christensen 1975, 252. Cf. v. 13 for the wrath theme. **[26]** MT *bō'ū-lāh miqqēṣ*, 'come against her without end': read with 51.31, Symm, and many exegetes (e.g. Giesebrecht, Rudolph, Christensen) *miqqāṣeh*, 'from all sides'; cf. G *hoi kairoi autēs*, 'her times (have come)'. MT *kᵉmō-ʿᵃrēmīm*, 'like heaps': i.e. like heaps of grain (cf *maʾᵃbusīm*, 'granaries') or of rubbish or even of ruins; cf. v. 16a for the harvesting motif. G *hōs spēlaion*, '(search her) as a cave' = *kᵉmō-mᵉʿārāh*; Rudolph reads *bᵉmō-* 'in . . .' (cf. BHS); Christensen 1975, 252, 256, conjectures *km ʿ(mr)ym*, 'as a swath of grain' (cf. A *hōsper sōreountes*, 'like those heaping up' = *kamᵉʿammᵉrīm*). Cf. Isa. 14.22 for the cutting off of Babylon's remnant (*šᵉʾār*); *šᵉʾērīt*, 'remnant, is used here. **[27]** MT *ḥirᵉbū kol-pāreyhā*, 'put to the sword all her bulls': i.e. slay her warriors, cf. NEB; G *anaxēranate pantas tous karpous autēs*, 'dry up all her fruits' = *ḥārᵉbū kol*, continuing the harvesting motif of laying waste the agricultural products of v. 26 (taken by Christensen with v. 26 and following G). Cf. 48.15 for the motif of going down (*yrd*) to slaughter; *ʿēt pᵉquddātām*, 'the time of their punishment', appears in 6.15 (see Notes); 8.12; 10.15; 46.21; 51.18; cf *šᵉnat pᵉquddātām*, 'the year of their punishment', 11.23; 23.12; 48.44. **[28]** G lacks *niqᵉmat hēkālō*, 'vengeance of his temple': possibly a gloss from 51.11 defining Yahweh's vengeance in terms of Zion's ideology; cf. Ps. 79.1. **[29]** MT *rabbīm*, 'crowd, host': many exegetes read *rōbīm*, 'archers', cf. Gen. 49.23; G *pollois* = MT. K *'l-yhy*; Q *'al-yᵉhī-lāh*, 'let there not be to her': cf. G *mē estō autēs*; v. 26. Cf. v. 15 for the notion of retaliatory behaviour; also Lev. 24.19b; Judg. 1.7, where the talionic principle is similarly expressed (cf. Miller 1982, 94). MT *kī 'el-yhwh zādāh*, 'for against Yahweh she has acted insolently': cf. the insolent men (*zēdīm*) in 43.2; the insolent one (*zādōn*) of vv. 31, 32; and Edom's insolence of mind (*zᵉdōn lēb*). It is difficult to determine the precise connotation of *zūd* here: whether insolence (i.e. insult NEB), presumption, arrogance or hubris (cf. the accusation against Moab in 48.26, 42); perhaps simple defiance of Yahweh (a concomitant of being a foreign nation) is intended, cf. G *autestē*, 'opposed'. The designation of Yahweh as 'the holy one of Israel' (*qᵉdōš yiśrā'ēl*) is a particular feature of the Isaiah tradition and only occurs here and in 51.5 in Jeremiah. **[30]** = 40.26 minus *ṣᵉbā'ōt*, 'of hosts'; G lacks 'in that day'. **[31]** MT *zādōn*, 'O Insolence': G *tēn hubristian*, 'the overbearing one', cf. the similar charge of hubris against Moab in 48.29 (G 31.29). G lacks *ᵃdōnāy . . . ṣᵉbā'ōt*, 'lord . . . of hosts'. MT *ʿēt pᵉqadtīkā*, 'the time when I punish you': cf. 6.15 for this form; a few mss, Vrs *pᵉquddātekā*, 'your punishment' = the standard form of this cliché, cf.

v. 27 (Notes). **[32]** In vv. 31–32 masc. forms are used, but throughout the poems Babylon, as a city, is personified in fem. terms (normal Hebrew usage). V. 32b = 21.14b except that *bᵉyaʿrāh*, 'in her forest', is used instead of *hᵉʿārāyw*, 'in his cities'; G *en tō drumō autēs*, 'in his forest' = *bᵉyaʿᵃrō*, cf. 21.14b. MT *sᵉbībōtāyw*, 'his environs': a few mss, 21.14b read *sᵉbībāyw*. **[33]** G lacks *ṣᵉbāʾōt*, 'of hosts'. **[34]** MT *gōʾᵃlām*, 'their redeemer': Yahweh as *gōʾēl* is the kinsman obligated to act on behalf of Israel his kin (cf. 31.11); this designation of Yahweh is a dominant epithet in Second Isaiah (41.14; 43.14; 44.6, 24; 47.4; 48.17; 49.7, 26; 54.5, 8) and later strands of Isaiah (e.g. 59.20; 60.16; 63.16). G *kai ho lutroumenos autous* = *wᵉgōʾᵃlām*, '*but* their redeemer', makes a better contrast with v. 33. MT *rīb yārīb ʾet-rībām*, 'he will surely plead their cause': cf. Isa. 34.8; the punning assonance of MT cannot be captured in English. Christensen 1975, 253, deletes *ʾet-* and translates *rībām* as 'their Champion'. **[35]** G lacks *nᵉʾum-yhwh*, 'says Yahweh'. **[36]** G lacks v. 36a, perhaps due to homoiarkton. MT *ʾel-habbaddīm*, 'upon the empty talkers': i.e. windbags, cf. 48.30; Isa. 44.25; NEB 'false prophets'. Vrs 'her empty talkers' = *baddeyhā* (cf. BHS). Bright, 355, thinks *baddīm* is meant to be a pun on *bārīm* (i.e. the *bāru* priests who practised divination in Babylonian culture). **[37]** MT *ʾel-sūsāyw wᵉʾel-rikbō*, 'upon *his* horses and upon his chariot': possibly a gloss from 51.21a (the suffixes are wrong, though corrected by RSV, NEB, cf. JPSB; G *autōn*, 'their'). MT *wᵉhāyū lᵉnāšīm*, 'and they shall become as women': cf. 30.6; 48.41; 49.22 for the motif of warriors turning into women as a figure of fear and devastation caused by invasion and defeat. MT *wᵉʾel-kol-hāʿereb*, 'and upon all the rabble': cf. 25.20; 46.16; a heterogeneous body of mercenaries and auxiliary troops most prone to weakening against fierce opposition. **[38]** MT *ḥōreb*, 'drought': lacking in G but *ḥereb*, 'sword', is better read here with G^OL, S; with the sword (i.e. invasion) will come neglect of the Babylonian irrigation system and drought will ensue. MT *ūbāʾēmīm yithōlālū*, 'and they behave like madmen over terrors': i.e. dreadful gods, numina which frighten (cf. the Emim of ancient folklore, Gen. 14.5; Deut. 2.10–11), V *portenta*; 'bogeymen', cf. Bright's 'hoodoos', 'bogies'. MT Hitpolel *hll*, 'behave like madmen over': Vrs *hll*, 'boast', cf. NEB. Rudolph, 304, treats v. 38b as an addition to the text because the context makes Babylon the sword's target for its treatment of the exiles (vv. 33–34) rather than because of its iconic religion. **[39]** MT *ṣiyyīm ʾet-ʾiyyīm*, 'desert-dwellers with inhabitants of the desert': EVV treat as desert animals: 'wild beasts with hyenas' (RSV), 'marmots and jackals' (NEB), 'wildcats and with hyenas' (JPSB); as usual word-play (cf. Cornill, 505–6) sacrifices meaning to cleverness and obscures the semantic force of the phrase. Perhaps animals are not meant but uncanny or demonic beings associated with the desert (cf. Bright, 355, 'goblins and ghouls'); this would match v. 38b quite well. Both terms appear in Isa. 34.14, and each one appears respectively in Isa. 13.21, 22. Isa. 13.20a = v. 39b (plus *ʿōd*, 'no more'); for vv. 39–40 cf. Isa. 13.19–22. The use of *yšb* three times in MT may not be original; *škn*, 'dwell', probably should be read for the second occurrence of *yšb* (cf. BHS). **[40]** Cf. 49.18; Isa. 13.19 for the Sodom and Gomorrah allusion. 40b = 49.33b.

The second section of 50 consists of a number of units (at least seven: vv. 21–27, 28, 29–30, 31–32, 33–34, 35–38a, 39–40) enclosed by the motif of utter destruction (vv. 21, 40), though vv. 39–40 are essentially an appendix to v. 38b. The invasion and defeat of Babylon are the central elements, and Israel only appear infrequently (e.g. vv. 28, 33–34). Yahweh is the one who attacks Babylon, the one who releases the sword against the hammer of the whole earth (vv. 21, 35–38a). Yet the invading forces can be discerned at certain points as also commanded by Yahweh to destroy Babylon (e.g. vv. 26–27, 29). Babylon's role as devastator of so many countries is reversed in these poems and her overweening arrogance (like Moab, hubris is the flaw in her make-up) is such that she has been trapped into striving against Yahweh. This hubristic attitude of Babylon's is not developed in 50–51, though it is repeatedly referred to, but in Isa. 14.12–20 it gives rise to the splendid satire on Helel ben Shachar (the morning star which via V becomes Lucifer and then is transformed into the devil in gothic theology). Throughout this section the view of Babylon reflects that of all the states devastated by the tyrannical imperium – now it is her turn to experience what she herself has imposed on others (cf. vv. 15, 29). Now it is Yahweh who opens his arsenal, brings forth the weapons of his wrath, and lays waste the land of the Chaldaeans. In brilliant images the poet makes the deity summon up the invading forces to tear apart the enemy Babylon. The metaphors are derived from the harvesting process (vv. 26–27a; cf. v. 16a) and represent Babylon as a land replete with its ingathered harvest. Granaries bursting with produce are to be torn open and the precious grain spilled out in heaps. Gathered fruit is to be ruined (G) or, to vary the image, her bulls are to be slaughtered (MT). Such a reversal of the harvest is the death of a culture (rather different images of the *failure* of the harvest make the same point against Jerusalem in 8.13, 20). Yet how well the images of destroyed granaries convey the idea of a powerful and politically sated empire such as Babylon being overrun and devastated by invaders!

As a dramatic counterpoint to this picture of the reversal of the fortunes of Babylon, v. 28 depicts refugees fleeing from the fallen city and defeated land to announce in Zion the unfolding of Yahweh's vengeance. A glossator anticipates 51.11 by spelling out the nature of that vengeance – it is the vindication of Zion's temple. How bitterly painful had been that perfidious destruction of the sacred house of Yahweh in 587, and now, fifty years later, sweet revenge is gained by Yahweh's defeat of the blasphemers. The sentiment, gloss though it may be, is in keeping with the view of the temple expressed throughout the Jeremiah tradition (e.g. 3.17; 17.12; 31.40; implicit in the placing of Jeremiah in the temple as the centre of his work 7.2; 19.14; 22.1; 26.2; 35.2; it is likely that 7.12–15 represents not so much a denigration of the temple as a criticism of the people who use it). Babylon's crimes may be many, but her destruction of the temple is singled out here in order to define Yahweh's vengeance. A more general account is given in v. 29, where all Babylon's actions are made the grounds of her defeat (cf. v. 15). But these are seen as constituting opposition to Yahweh, the holy one of Israel (an echo of the Isaiah tradition). How different this accusation is from the presentation of Babylon as Yahweh's servant in 27–29, 39–40! And how more realistic it is also from the viewpoint of all those oppressed by the imperial power (cf. Ps. 109; 137).

An independent poem in vv. 31–32 (the gender is different from the standard presentation of city and country as feminine forms) attacks one whose hubris is such that he may be addressed 'O insolent one' (*zādōn*). Babylon is not named here, and the anonymity of the target indicates the conventionality of the poem (vv. 31b, 32b use forms found elsewhere in Jeremiah). But in the context of the edited vv. 21–40 Babylon may be regarded as the hubristic one intended here (cf. Isa. 13–14; 47.7–10; in OAN Babylon is not the only nation guilty of hubris, cf. 48.29 for Moab; Isa. 10.7–14 for Assyria; Ezek. 27–28 for Tyre). Against the hubris of nations and individuals (cf. 17.5–6; Isa. 2.12–17) Yahweh is the implacable opponent, and thus Babylon the great must fall before his wrath.

The exiled Israelites appear for the first time directly in this section (v. 28 is an oblique reference to them) in vv. 33–34 and are represented as being held fast by their captors who refuse to let them go. To this state of affairs Yahweh responds and is thus justly described as their kinsman (redeemer is conventional English). As kinsman he meets his obligations to act on behalf of his kinsfolk by taking up their quarrel (*rīb*, 'case, suit') and vindicating them. This vindication will bring rest to the earth but turmoil to Babylon (contrast 25.31, where Yahweh's *rīb* is directed against the nations and all flesh). Attached to this oracular proclamation of Yahweh's activity on behalf of the exiles is a fine poem about the sword against Babylon, which may be understood as the means whereby the captives will be liberated. The sword motif appears in vv. 21, 27 (used as a verb), but in vv. 35–38a the noun *ḥereb*, 'sword', is used five or six times (cf. Notes) in brief statements delineating the classes of its Babylonian victims. Whether the sword stands for Yahweh's uncanny defeat of Babylon or for the invading (Persian) forces or both is unclear from the text, but the sword's crusade against the Chaldaeans effectively ruins people and land.

38b offers a different explanation for the destruction of Babylon from vv. 33–34: it is a land of images (*pᵉsilīm*, cf. 10.2–5, 8–9, 14–15), and the people behave like madmen over dreadful gods. Appropriately then the land of such wild, superstitious behaviour will be depopulated and become the haunt of wild animals (EVV) or, more likely, the place of 'ghouls and ghosties' (Bright). What the people have worshipped will take over the uninhabited territory, and Babylon will become an unsalubrious place forever (v. 39). So great will be Babylon's devastation that the fate of Sodom and Gomorrah (Gen. 19.24–25, 28) comes to mind as the best analogy of it (v. 40; cf. Isa. 13.19). Here Babylon has a mythical status and its annihilation is so complete that never again will the land (or is it the city only?) be inhabited. Apart from the rhetoric of these poems and comments, the depiction of Babylon's fall is given in such grandiloquent terms that the actual changeover of power between the Babylonians and the Persians is dwarfed into insignificance. This is hardly evidence of a pre-539 setting for 50 (cf. v. 28; or 51), though elements may belong to that period, but indicates the development of Babylon as the symbol of hubristic opposition to Yahweh. After 539 such a symbol became independent of the actual Babylonia where people continued to live, even to this day (i.e. modern Iraq).

50.41–46

41 'Behold, a people comes from the north;
a mighty nation and many kings
are stirring from the farthest parts of the earth.

42 They lay hold of bow and spear;
they are cruel, and have no mercy.
The sound of them is like the roaring of the sea;
they ride upon horses,
arrayed as a man for battle
against you, O daughter of Babylon!
43 The king of Babylon heard the report of them,
and his hands fell helpless;
anguish seized him,
pain as of a woman in travail.'
44 'Behold, like a lion coming up from the jungle of the Jordan against a
strong sheepfold, I will suddenly make them run away from her; and I will
appoint over her whomever I choose. For who is like me? Who will summon
me? What shepherd can stand before me? 45 Therefore hear the plan which
the LORD has made against Babylon, and the purposes which he has formed
against the land of the Chaldeans: Surely the little ones of their flock shall
be dragged away; surely their fold shall be appalled at their fate. 46 At the
sound of the capture of Babylon the earth shall tremble, and her cry shall
be heard among the nations.'

[50.41–43] = 6.22–24 with minor variations: in v. 42 the target is daughter Babylon whereas in 6.23 it is daughter Zion; in v. 43 it is the king of Babylon who responds to the invasion as a helpless, pregnant woman but in 6.24 it is the citizens of Jerusalem who respond in this fashion. **[50.44–46]** = 40.19–21 with the necessary changes made for Babylon rather than Edom (see Notes on 49.19–21) and minor variations: v. 44 K *'rwṣm*; Q *'ᵃrīṣēm*, 'I will make them run away'; v. 45 the divine plan is against *Babylon* rather than Edom (49.20) and the land of the Chaldaeans instead of the inhabitants of Teman: v. 46 the nations hear the outcry of Babylon, whereas in 49.21 the cry of Edom is heard at the sea of reeds. Cf. BHS for further minor variations between both sets of texts and MT-G variations in 50.41–46.

Two common pieces conclude this part of the collection of material against Babylon with v. 46 forming a closure with 50.2. The interchangeability of material in the book of Jeremiah indicates the conventional nature of the poetry used to construct the tradition (see on 6.22–26). Jerusalem-Babylon or Edom-Babylon or Jerusalem community-the Jewish communities in Egypt may all be the recipients of the same poem, indictment or saying. Material is freely created and applied to different groups, with the necessary adjustments for identification. Hence the tradition has a high degree of formal construction and a correspondingly low degree of semantic content. The enemy in 4–6 and 46–51 is therefore anonymous, the language rhetorical, and the semantics difficult to determine. Yet a glimpse of irony (unintentional perhaps) may be discerned in the interpretation of 6.22–26 as a statement about the Babylonian attack on Jerusalem and the recognition that in 50.41–43 Babylon herself becomes the victim of that very process she implemented against Zion. Thus is it done to her as she has done to others (vv. 15,29). The revenge afforded to the Jews by the downfall of Babylon must have been very sweet and a good liturgy of the events of the sixth century would read 50–51 *after* the reading of the book of Lamentations.

The destruction of Babylon is described in vv. 44–46 using a piece also used in the denunciations of Edom (49.19–21). It is a mixture of prose and poetry (cf. EVV, BHS, various exegetes) and illustrates the variations with which the same material may be applied to different nations. Echoes of the incomparability of Yahweh theme (v. 44b) appear in it, and this motif works well in 50 with its emphasis on the hubristic nature of Babylon's domination of the world. Against the incomparable one even the hammer of the earth cannot prevail, and Babylon is like a flock of sheep against which a lion comes up from the jungle of Jordan. *Among the nations* is heard the outcry of her devastation, and this motif (v. 46) provides a fine conclusion (or midpoint) to the poem's prefatory exclamation 'declare *among the nations* . . . Babylon is taken!' (50.2). 'So perish all thine enemies, O Lord!' (Judg. 5.31a).

51.1–33

511 Thus says the Lord:
'Behold, I will stir up the spirit of a destroyer
against Babylon,
against the inhabitants of Chaldea;
2 and I will send to Babylon winnowers,
and they shall winnow her,
and they shall empty her land,
when they come against her from every side
on the day of trouble.
3 Let not the archer bend his bow,
and let him not stand up in his coat of mail.

Spare not her young men;
utterly destroy all her host.
4 They shall fall down slain in the land of the Chaldeans,
and wounded in her streets.
5 For Israel and Judah have not been forsaken
by their God, the LORD of hosts;
but the land of the Chaldeans is full of guilt
against the Holy One of Israel.'
6 'Flee from the midst of Babylon,
let every man save his life!
Be not cut off in her punishment,
for this is the time of the LORD's vengeance,
the requital he is rendering her.
7 Babylon was a golden cup in the LORD's hand,
making all the earth drunken;
the nations drank of her wine,
therefore the nations went mad.
8 Suddenly Babylon has fallen and been broken;
wail for her!
Take balm for her pain;
perhaps she may be healed.
9 We would have healed Babylon,
but she was not healed.
Forsake her, and let us go
each to his own country;
for her judgment has reached up to heaven
and has been lifted up even to the skies.
10 The LORD has brought forth our vindication;
come, let us declare in Zion
the work of the LORD our God.'
11 'Sharpen the arrows!
Take up the shields!
The LORD has stirred up the spirit of the kings of the Medes,
because his purpose concerning Babylon is to destroy it, for that
is the vengeance of the LORD, the vengeance for his temple.
12 Set up a standard against the walls of Babylon;
make the watch strong;
set up watchmen;
prepare the ambushes;
for the LORD has both planned and done
what he spoke concerning the inhabitants of Babylon.
13 O you who dwell by many waters,
rich in treasures,

your end has come,
  the thread of your life is cut.
14 The Lord of hosts has sworn by himself:
Surely I will fill you with men, as many as locusts,
  and they shall raise the shout of victory over you.'
15 'It is he who made the earth by his power,
  who established the word by his wisdom,
and by his understanding
  stretched out the heavens.
16 When he utters his voice there is a tumult of waters in the heavens,
  and he makes the mist rise from the ends of the earth.
He makes lightnings for the rain,
  and he brings forth the wind from his storehouses.
17 Every man is stupid and without knowledge;
  every goldsmith is put to shame by his idols;
for his images are false,
  and there is no breath in them.
18 They are worthless, a work of delusion;
  at the time of their punishment they shall perish.
19 Not like these is he who is the portion of Jacob,
  for he is the one who formed all things,
and Israel is the tribe of his inheritance;
  the Lord of hosts is his name.'
20 'You are my hammer and weapon of war:
with you I break nations in pieces;
  with you I destroy kingdoms;
21 with you I break in pieces the horse and his rider;
  with you I break in pieces the chariot and the charioteer;
22 with you I break in pieces man and woman;
  with you I break in pieces the old man and the youth;
with you I break in pieces the young man and the maiden;
23 with you I break in pieces the shepherd and his flock;
with you I break in pieces the farmer and his team;
  with you I break in pieces governors and commanders.'
24 'I will requite Babylon and all the inhabitants of Chaldea before
your very eyes for all the evil that they have done in Zion, says
the Lord.'
25 'Behold, I am against you, O destroying mountain,
says the Lord,
  which destroys the whole earth;
I will stretch out my hand against you,
  and roll you down from the crags,
  and make you a burnt mountain.

26 No stone shall be taken from you for a corner
    and no stone for a foundation,
  but you shall be a perpetual waste,
    says the LORD.'
27 'Set up a standard on the earth,
    blow the trumpet among the nations;
  prepare the nations for war against her,
    summon against her the kingdoms,
    Ararat, Minni, and Ashkenaz;
  appoint a marshal against her,
    bring up horses like bristling locusts.
28 Prepare the nations for war against her,
    the kings of the Medes, with their governors and deputies,
    and every land under their dominion.
29 The land trembles and writhes in pain,
    for the LORD's purposes against Babylon stand,
  to make the land of Babylon a desolation,
    without inhabitant.
30 The warriors of Babylon have ceased fighting,
    they remain in their strongholds;
  their strength has failed,
    they have become women;
  her dwellings are on fire,
    her bars are broken.
31 One runner runs to meet another,
    and one messenger to meet another,
  to tell the king of Babylon
    that his city is taken on every side.
32 The fords have been seized,
    the bulwarks are burned with fire,
    and the soldiers are in panic.
33 For thus says the LORD of hosts, the God of Israel:
  The daughter of Babylon is like a threshing floor
    at the time when it is trodden;
  yet a little while
    and the time of her harvest will come.'

[MT 51] = G 28. **[1]** MT *wᵉ'el-yōšᵉbē lēb qāmāy*, lit. 'and against the inhabitants of the heart of those who rise up against me': or perhaps the territory of Leb-Qamay, i.e. Kambul (NEB) or an allusion to Gambuli (cf. Rudolph, 306). Many exegetes treat it as an athbash (see Notes on 25.26) or cipher for Chaldaea (*lb qmy = kśdym*): G *Chaldaious*, 'Chaldaeans', cf. T. Rudolph deletes 'against Babylon and' because it ruins the metre: a cipher is hardly needed if Babylon is named in 1a, though such ciphers (cf. v. 41) may be no more than a vestige of incantatory practices directed against the enemy using poems such as make up 50–51. MT *rūaḥ mašḥīt*, 'spirit of destruction/destroyer': Heb. is ambiguous cf. vv. 11 (destroyer addressed), 25 (mountain of destruction/destroyer); cf. G *anemon kausōna diaphtheironta*, 'a destructive burning wind'. **[2]** MT *zārīm*, 'strangers': vocalize as *zōrīm*, 'winnowers', with A, Symm, V. MT *kī-hāyū 'āleyhā missābīb*, 'and they shall be against her round about': some exegetes follow Volz, 428, *kī yaḥᵃnū*, 'for they will encamp (against her round about)', cf. BHS; G *ouai epi Babulōna kuklothen*, 'woe to Babylon round about'. Cf. 4.11–12 for a different use of the winnowing image; 19.7 for the emptying (*bqq*) of the plans of Jerusalem, a motif used more literally here for the emptying (*bqq*) of the land of inhabitants. **[3]** K *'l ydrk ydrk hdrk qštw*; Q *'el-yidrōp haddōrēk qaštō*, 'to let bend (let bend K) the bowman his bow': unintelligible; G lacks *'l*; many mss, Vrs read *'al*, 'not . . .'; G^L *ep' autēs 'eleyhā* = 'against her'. These corrections yield 'let the bowman bend his bow against her', cf. JPSB or 'let not the bowman bend his bow', cf. RSV, NEB (with reference to Babylon's inability to defend herself). MT *wᵉ'el-yit'al bᵉsiryōnō*, 'and to let him rise up in his armour': some mss, Vrs *wᵉ'al*, 'and not . . .'; Rudolph, 306, reads *'al-yiyga' lᵉbuš siryōnō*, 'let him not be weary of wearing his armour' (to balance his reading of *'al-yerep haddorēk qaštō*, 'let him not cease from wielding his bow'), cf. BHS. Christensen 1975, 263, 268, treats *'l* as El, 'god' (cf. v. 56; 32.18) in both places (and emends *hyw* in v. 2 to *yhwh*, 'Yahweh'), so that it is El who treads down (*drk*) and rises up wearing armour. Cf. 50.21, 26 for the motif of total war (*ḥrm*). **[5]** MT *kī lō'-'almān yiśrā'ēl wīhūdāh*, lit. 'for Israel and Judah have not been *widowed*': i.e. Yahweh has not killed the husbands of Israel and Judah; a figure of desolation and abandonment. This is a curious image which suggests that the verse is intrusive here (cf. Bright, 356). MT *kī 'arṣām māl'āh 'āšām*, 'for *their* land is full of guilt': whose land? If the land of Babylon is intended, then v. 5b should precede 5a (cf. Cornill, 508–9; Nötscher, 342; Rudolph, 306–7); cf. 50.29 for the holy one of Israel as the one offended by Babylon. 51.5 and 50.7 provide an antithesis: the nations regard Israel as guilty (*'āšām*), but it is their own land (i.e. Babylon's) which is really guilty; cf. 2.3. Isa. 47.8–9 presents the fall of Babylon in terms of widowhood; the assertion that Israel and Judah have not been widowed is strange in view of 721 and 587, when the kingdoms fell to external forces. **[6]** Cf. 50.8. The phrase *ūmallᵉṭū 'īš napšō*, 'and let each man save his life', occurs in v. 45 (cf. 48.6) and may be an addition here (cf. Cornill, 509; Rudolph, 307). **[7]** Cf. 25.15–17 for the cup metaphor; the metaphor is used differently here and some exegetes delete 'in Yahweh's hand' as a gloss from 25.15ff. (e.g. Duhm, Giesebrecht, Cornill, Rudolph). Vrs lack the second occurrence of *gōyīm*, 'nations'. **[9]** K *rp 'nw*; Q *rippinū*, 'we treated' (K *rp'*, original form; for Q cf. 3.22). MT *'izᵉbūhā*, 'abandon her': in this context 'let us abandon her'; cf. G *egkatalipōmen autēn*. **[10]** MT *hōṣī yhwh 'et-ṣidᵉqōtēnū*, 'Yahweh has brought forth *our* vindication': the defeat of Babylon from the perspective of Zion cf. v. 11; 50.28; G . . . *to krima autou*, '. . . *his* judgment'. **[11]** MT *mil'ū haššᵉlāṭīm*, lit. 'fill the shields/quivers': meaning of *šeleṭ* uncertain; EVV favour 'quiver', modern exegetes 'shield' (e.g. Rudolph, Christensen); cf. II Sam. 8.7; II Kings 11.10; Ezek. 27.11; G *plēroute tas pharetras*, 'fill the quivers' (translation or interpretative gloss?). The sense of *ml'* appears to be 'make ready' (cf. Rudolph, 308); Driver 1937–38, 127, understands it as 'make full ready the shields'. Cf. Thomas 1952a on *ml'* as a military term; Zech. 9.13 for *ml'* with *qešet*, 'bow'. 11a is continued in v. 12 and 11b should be regarded as an additional comment explaining the battle against Babylon as Yahweh's vengeance (*niqmat hēkālō*, 'vengeance of his temple', cf. 50.28); cf. Fohrer 1981, 50–1, who treats all the references to Zion, Israel, temple and cult as redactional. G has *basileōs*, 'king of' for *malᵉkē*, 'kings of'. **[12]** MT *kī gam-zāmam yhwh gam-'āśāh*, 'for Yahweh has both planned and done': cf. Lam. 2.17: *'iāśāh yhwh 'ᵃšer zāmam*, 'Yahweh has done what he planned'; the destruction of both Jerusalem and Babylon are divine acts of the same type. **[13]** K *šknty*; Q *šōkantᵉ*, 'you who dwell': cf. 22.23 (K old fem. ending). MT *'al-mayim rabbīm*, 'by many waters'; reference to the Euphrates and the irrigation canals of Babylon, with a possible allusion to the mythological waters which undergird the earth (cf. May 1955). MT *'ammat biṣ'ēk*, lit. 'the cubit of your unjust gain': uncertain meaning; possibly a metaphor from the weaving trade (cf. Isa. 38.12), 'the cubit of your cutting off', i.e. your cubit (thread of life cf. RSV) is cut off; cf. NEB 'your destiny is certain'. G *hēkei to peras sou alēthōs eis to splagchna, sou* 'your end is truly come to your bowels' = . . . *'ᵉmet bᵉmē'āyik*. The obscurity of MT (partly caused by *bṣ'* as noun, 'unjust gain', or infinitive, 'cut off') would appear to have a simple meaning: 'your end has come' (cf. *bā' qiṣṣēk*), your length of cloth is cut off. **[14]** MT *nišba' yhwh ṣᵉbā'ōt bᵉnapšō*, 'Yahweh of hosts has sworn by himself': for the unusual use of *šb' bnpš* with Yahweh as subject cf. Amos 6.8; the normal forms of self-swearing by Yahweh appear in 22.5; 44.26; 49.13. G *hoti ōmose kurios kata tou brachionos autou*, 'for the lord has sworn by his arm': cf. Isa. 62.8 for this idiom; Rudolph inserts *'ᵉlōhē yiśrā'ēl*, 'the god of Israel' before 'by himself' for metrical reasons (cf. BHS). MT *'ādām kayyeleq*, lit. 'mankind as locusts': perhaps 'men like locusts', i.e. countless men (EVV); Rudolph substitutes *'ōyᵉbīm*, 'foes', for *'ādām* because 'men' is too universal. Cf. II Kings 5.20 for the positive use of *kī 'im*; Nahum 3.15–17 for the locust imagery. It is possible to read the Hebrew as *kī 'ᵃmallē' 'ōtāk*, 'for I *will* fill you', thus resolving the problem of MT's 'I *have* filled you' (Giesebrecht, 256; cf. Cornill, 511); or to translate the line as 'even if you were filled with people (*kᵉ'ādām*) as with locusts, yet would they (i.e. the invaders) chant the triumph shout over you'. **[15–19]** = 10.12–16 with minor variations (cf. Notes there; BHS). **[20]** MT *mappēṣ*, lit. 'shatterer':

variously translated as 'hammer' (RSV; contrast 50.23 *paṭṭīš*, 'hammer': a figure of Babylon), 'battle-axe' (NEB), 'war club' (JPSB), 'mace' (Bright); derived from *npṣ*, 'shatter' (cf. Ps. 137.9), a figure used in 13.14 for the shattering of the inhabitants of Jerusalem. G *diaskorpizeis su moi*, 'you scatter for me': treating Heb. as a verbal form from *pūṣ*, 'scatter'. MT *keᵉlē*, 'weapons of': read sing. *keᵉlī*, 'weapon of (war)', as *bᵉkā*, 'with you', in vv. 20–23 indicates. **[21]** MT repeats *wᵉrōkᵉbō*, 'and its rider': Duhm, 369, changes the second occurrence to *rakkābō*, 'his charioteer', followed by Rudolph, 310, for variety (BHS); also Bright, 348. **[22]** MT may have one clause too many: G lacks 'with you I break in pieces the old man and the youth' (deleted by BHS); Christensen 1975, 269, deletes 'with you I break in pieces the young man and the maiden' as a variant reading; Rudolph also omits this clause. **[23]** Rudolph deletes the third clause as an addition from v. 28 (BHS); whereas Christensen adds 'with you I shatter princes and wise men' as a conjectural emendation from 51.57 to balance the third colon. **[24]** MT *'ašer-'āśū bᵉṣiyyōn lᵉ'ēnēkem*, 'which they did in Zion in your sight': i.e. those who saw the destruction of Jerusalem in 587 will witness Babylon's defeat in 539; those addressed are the defeated of 587. However, some exegetes link 'in your sight' to 'I will requite' (e.g. RSV, Rudolph, Bright), thus limiting the reference to the witnesses of Babylon's destruction. Cf. v. 11; 50.28 for the same explanation of 587 as the cause of Babylon's punishment. **[25]** MT *har hammašḥīt*, 'mountain of destruction': G *to oros to diephtharmenon*, 'the destroyed mountain' = *har hammāšḥāt*. Bright, 357, translates MT as 'mountain of raiders', cf. I Sam. 13.17; 14.15. The phrase 'the destroyer of the whole earth' may be an explanatory gloss (cf. BHS). G lacks *nᵉ'um-yhwh*, 'says Yahweh'. The metaphor of rolling a mountain from the rocks is a mixed one and 'from the rocks' is deleted by Rudolph, who translates *wᵉgilgaltīkā* as 'and make you a heap of stones'. Rudolph reads *lᵉtannur*, 'fire-pot, stove', for *lᵉhar*, 'mountain (of burning)'. The transformation of the mountain into a fireplace will render its stones useless for building purposes (v. 26). **[26]** Contrast Isa. 28.16. **[27]** 'Ararat, Minni, and Ashkenaz': territories (in modern Armenia) under the control of the Medes (v. 28); probably an explanatory gloss here (cf. Rudolph). MT *qaddᵉšū*, 'prepare for war': lit. 'sanctify'; perhaps begin war with a sacred ritual, cf. 6.4; 22.7. MT *ṭipsār*, 'scribe, marshal': Akk *tupšarru*, 'tablet writer'; a high ranking officer, cf. Nahum 3.17, where it occurs also in a context of locust imagery. MT *kᵉyeleq sāmār*, 'like bristling locusts': G *hōs akridōn plēthos*, 'like a multitude of locusts', reading *mispār* for *sāmār* (a word of uncertain meaning and used only here). **[28]** Cf. v. 11; G 'king of the Medes' for MT 'kings of the Medes'. MT *memᵉšaltō*, 'its dominion': *-tām*, 'their (dominion)', cf. BHS. A gloss on v. 27 reflecting the Median control of territory at some stage in the sixth century. **[29]** MT *qāmāh . . . maḥšᵉbōt*, 'the purposes of . . . stand': sing. verb with plur. noun; a few mss, G, S read 'purpose of . . .'; Q^Or *qāmū* makes number agree. **[30]** MT *hayū l^enāšîm*, 'they have become women': cf. 30.6; 48.41; 49.22; 50.37 for this motif. **[32]** MT *w^e'et-hā'^agammîm*, lit. 'and the swamp-reeds': i.e. the marshes where fugitives might hide (cf. Bright, 357); RSV, Rudolph 'bulwarks'; NEB 'guard-towers'. Christensen 1975, 269, follows G in reading *miqqāṣeh* (v. 32, 'on every side') with v. 33 as qualifying the fords, i.e. 'remote fords'. MT *nibhālū*, 'are terrified': G *exerchontai*, 'are going forth' = *hāl^ekū*. **[33]** G lacks 'of hosts, the god of Israel' and has *oikoi basileōs Babylōnos*, 'the houses of the king of Babylon', for MT *bat-bābel*, 'daughter Babylon'. In preparation for harvesting the threshing floor was tamped to make it hard. The personification of Babylon as a woman here in conjunction with images drawn from agricultural techniques of stomping and threshing may have sexual overtones of rape and pillage (cf. Job 31.10 for a similar use of *ṭḥn*, 'grind'). The savage rape of a young woman is a universal image of the depradations of war which reduce a land and its cities to a bloody, bowed mess. Vrs lack second occurrence of *'ēt*, 'time of . . .'; *qāṣîr*, 'harvest', is a common metaphor of destruction, whether military or otherwise (cf. Hos. 6.11; Joel 4.13 [EV 3.13]).

The first section of 51 is made up of a number of units (e.g. vv. 1–5, 6–10, 11–14, 15–19, 20–23, 24, 25–26, 27–33) and, although few exegetes agree on how to divide the chapter intosections, would appear to consist of vv. 1–33 because vv. 2, 33 form a closure using harvesting motifs. The mixture of motifs and pieces is similar to 50 and there are elements in 51 which may not have originally applied to Babylon's destruction (e.g. vv. 15–19 belong more appropriately to 10.1–16, and vv. 20–23 may have been spoken of Babylon as the destroyer rather than the victim). However, the central theme of the section is unmistakably the defeat of Babylon: a defeat either celebrated (v. 8) or imminently anticipated (vv. 6, 33). Glosses within the poems identify some of the military action against Babylon as Median (e.g. vv. 11b, 27bY, 28; cf. Isa. 13.17), but whether these indicate a period before 550 for the editing of the poem is difficult to determine. The section must be considered independent of such glosses, and therefore pre-Cyrus opposition to Babylon is hardly a feature of the poems. Yet like all the poetry sections of the book of Jeremiah, 51 is too general to be pinned down to a specific time before or after the fall of Babylon in 539. Only a few fragments deal with Zion in this section (vv. 10, 11b, 24), and these simply equate Babylon's defeat with the vindication of Zion. Retribution has come to Babylon – 'let us declare in Zion the work of Yahweh our god' (v. 10). That retribution is Yahweh's vengeance for what happened in Zion, in particular the destruction of the temple (vv. 24, 11b). There is in 50–51 no sense of the justifications offered throughout the book of Jeremiah for the fall of Jerusalem or even of the temple sermon with its analogy between Shiloh and the cult centre in Jerusalem (7.12–14). These are quite foreign to the spirit of the anti-Babylonian material (v. 5 can be read as an acknowledgment of the sinfulness of the land of Israel and Judah, but such a reading depends upon the ambiguity of the Hebrew text; cf. 50.7). Clearly the producers and editors of 50–51 did not share the belief that Babylon had been the servant of the living god when it massacred the people of Judah and destroyed both city and temple in 588–7. Babylon was the enemy, and remained so throughout the decades after the catastrophe, and its defeat is celebrated in poem after poem in 50–51.

The residual incantatory cipher in v. 1 (MT) indicates something of the magical function of the collection of poems in 50–51. Babylon is denounced by various means, including special words which conceal the name of the enemy (cf. 25.26 *Sheshak* for Babylon), and therefore render the spells incapable of being counteracted. Repetitive chantings of these poems (note how little development is achieved from 50.2–3 to 51.54–57) may have been intended to bring about the fate of the enemy celebrated or, in conjunction with various military campaigns against the foe, to encourage every sign of opposition to the Babylonian empire. The agricultural metaphors which enclose the section (vv. 2, 33; cf. 50.26) represent the destruction of Babylon as a great harvesting operation which will empty the land. Within this representation various voices (defined as oracular by v. 1) are heard encouraging the exiles to flee, bemoaning the defeat of Babylon (vv. 8–9), summoning the enemy to attack (vv. 11–12, 27–28), praising Yahweh as the incomparable portion of Jacob, addressing an unidentified power (vv. 20–23), speaking against the mountain of destruction (v. 25 only identifiable as Babylon by virtue of the context of 50–51), and describing the panic induced in the Babylonians by their defeat (vv. 30–32). Such a comprehensive defeat of the great enemy reflects the earlier destruction of Jerusalem (cf. 4–6, 8–10) and must be judged as compensation for that disaster. Total war (vv. 3, 13, 25–26) against Babylon is the theme of the section, and the extermination of the violator of Jerusalem becomes the vindication of Zion and temple.

Interpretative questions arise from the ambiguity of certain verses: e.g. vv. 5, 7, 14, 20–23. The assertion that Israel and Judah have not been widowed is difficult to understand in the light of 587, but given the chauvinism of 50–51 may reflect an optimism arising out of the defeat of Babylon (cf. the similar spirit of Second Isaiah). It is intrusive here, and the ambiguity of '*their* land' may indicate a displaced polemic about the status of Israel and the land (cf. 50.7; Isa. 50.1). Babylon as a golden cup in Yahweh's hand with which he made the nations mad (cf. 25.15–17, where the cup imagery is used differently to represent Jeremiah as the dispenser of the poisonous brew) is a metaphor out of place in a poem about Babylon's destruction. The notion of Babylon as Yahweh's instrument *and* the object of his wrath for behaving as such an instrument raises theological problems (cf. the similar set of motifs in Isa. 10.5–15, but there Assyria is blamed for over-reaching its commission by excessive zeal in conquering nations; here no such charge is made against Babylon). The inconsistency of the two motifs may be resolved by a sharp separation of the different strands which use them: Babylon as the servant of Yahweh and Babylon as the violator of Zion and the nations. But the theological problems of Yahweh using an *idolatrous* nation to do his bidding against another *idolatrous* nation (Judah) remain. How can Babylon's idolatry be overlooked in order to punish Judah for religious deviations? Is this not to strain at a gnat and to swallow a camel on the deity's part? The use of 10.12–16 in 51.15–19 indicates an awareness of Babylon's idolatrous status (cf. 50.2c, 38b–39; 51.47, 52), but the incongruity of the matter is not grasped by the text. For Yahweh to use an idolatrous power so blithely is a serious problem of theological integrity in the tradition and, although diversity of sources in the book may explain why the problem is not recognized, the fundamental incoherence of the belief should be noted. The beginnings of a critique are attempted in a different context in II Chron. 28.9–11, where the prophet Oded berates the invading Israelites for their savage treatment of the Judaeans with the pertinent question: 'Have you not sins of your own against Yahweh your god?'. How much more rigorously might the question be posed to idolatrous nations invading Judaean territory: 'Are not your own idols an affront to Yahweh?'. It would appear to be the case that the notions of Judah as idolatrous (a feature of Part I) and the idolatrous Babylon as the enemy of Judah are quite separate elements in the tradition. Reading the book holistically raises serious problems such as this, but if its redactional history is stressed the difficulties may be modified.

The sympathetic attitude towards Babylon hinted at in vv. 8–9 must be regarded as purely rhetorical, perhaps even satirical. It hardly implies an attempt on the part of the Judaean exiles to save their enemy from destruction, but represents conventional expressions of concern over the wounded (cf. 8.22; 46.11). The sick woman cannot be healed, and the only practical course of action is to abandon her to her fate and flee to the homeland. Just as Zion was once stricken without healing, so Babylon is now mortally wounded. The divine oath in v. 14 is ambiguous in that it is not clear whether the deity will fill the city with the very men who will shout the victory song over it or whether in spite of the city being filled with men like locusts (a figure of troops or number?) the invaders will still chant the shout of triumph over it (cf. Notes). The ambiguity is hardly a significant one. It is not obvious what the shattering imagery of vv. 20–23 refers to: 'with you' could be Babylon (cf. 50.23), Babylon's enemy, or something mythical (cf. Yahweh's weapons, 50.25, or the sword of 50.35–38a). Elements of holy war terminology in 50–51 and the mythical dimensions of Babylon as the hubristic opponent of Yahweh suggest that the poem of vv. 20–23 may be an expression of Yahweh's direct attack on Babylon without the use of intermediaries. The poem would then be a parallel to the song of the sword in 50.35–38a. In a series of ten statements (MT) the weapon of war is unleashed against an unnamed enemy and shatters it. A prose note in v. 24 identifies the victim of this shattering defeat as Babylon and the inhabitants of Chaldaea and explains why Yahweh behaves in such a fashion. It is because of the evil done in Zion that Babylon is destroyed. Again the text is ambiguous because the phrase 'before your eyes' qualifies 'in Zion'. This might mean that those who saw the tragic events of 587 would see Babylon's destruction (though not necessarily in 539) or those who are witnesses of the present state of Jerusalem (the result of Babylonian activity) will see the defeat of the national enemy or, perhaps more likely, those to whom these poems were recited would see Yahweh's requital (*šillam*) of Zion's evil (cf. RSV). It is a minor point, but 'before your eyes' may indicate that v. 24 is a fragment from a liturgy of revenge against Babylon used by the worshipping community during the sixth century (cf. Ps. 137).

51.34–44

34 'Nebuchadrezzar the king of Babylon has devoured me,
he has crushed me;
he has made me an empty vessel,
he has swallowed me like a monster;
he has filled his belly with my delicacies,
he has rinsed me out.
35 The violence done to me and to my kinsmen be upon Babylon,'
let the inhabitant of Zion say.
'My blood be upon the inhabitants of Chaldea,'
let Jerusalem say.
36 Therefore thus says the LORD:
'Behold, I will plead your cause
and take vengeance for you.
I will dry up her sea
and make her fountain dry;
37 and Babylon shall become a heap of ruins,
the haunt of jackals,
a horror and a hissing,
without inhabitant.'
38 'They shall roar together like lions;
they shall growl like lions' whelps.
39 While they are inflamed I will prepare them a feast
and make them drunk, till they swoon away
and sleep a perpetual sleep
and not wake, says the LORD.
40 I will bring them down like lambs to the slaughter,
like rams and he-goats.'
41 'How Babylon is taken,
the praise of the whole earth seized!
How Babylon has become
a horror among the nations!
42 The sea has come up on Babylon;
she is covered with its tumultuous waves.
43 Her cities have become a horror,
a land of drought and a desert,
a land in which no one dwells,
and through which no son of man passes.
44 And I will punish Bel in Babylon,
and take out of his mouth what he has swallowed.
The nations shall no longer flow to him;
the wall of Babylon has fallen.'

[34] K *'klnw hmmnw*; Q *'ᵉkālanī hᵃmāmanī*, 'he has devoured me he has vexed *me*' (K '. . . *us* . . . *us*'): *hmm*, 'discomfit, confuse', cf. Aramaic *hmm*, 'exhaust, debilitate'; G *emerisato me*, 'he divided me'. Rudolph, 312, deletes 'Nebuchadrezzar', because it spoils the rhythm (BHS). K *hṣygnw* . . . *bl'nw* . . . *hdyḥnw*; Q *hiṣṣīganī* . . . *bᵉlā'anī* . . . *hᵉdīḥānī*, 'he has set *me* aside as . . . he has swallowed *me* up . . . he has rinsed *me* out' (K '*us*'). A slight change of pointing (*hᵉdīḥānī* to *hiddīḥānī*) would yield 'he has driven me from my Eden (*mē'ᵃdānāy*)', i.e. from Palestine (cf. Rudolph, 312). For the mythical connotations behind the swallowing up motif (*bl'*) cf. the Jonah legend; Day 1985, 109–11: *kattannīn*, 'like the dragon or sea-monster': cf. Isa.27.1; 51.9; Ezek.29.3; 32.2 (mostly of Egypt); Job 7.12; Ps.74.13; G *hōs drakōn*, 'as a dragon'. **[35]** MT *ḥᵃmāsī ūšᵉ'ērī 'al-bābel*, lit. 'my violence and my flesh upon Babylon': meaning uncertain, but it may have the sense of 'let my violated flesh be on Babylon' (cf. Bright, 358), i.e. Babylon is to be held responsible for the violence done to Zion's flesh. RSV, JPSB treat *šᵉ'ēr*, 'flesh', as blood-relation, i.e. 'kinsmen, kindred' (cf. Lev. 18.12, 13, 17; 20.19 for this use of *šᵉ'ēr*). G puzzled by the Hebrew reads *exōsan me hoi mochthoi mou kai hai talaipōriai mou eis Babulōna*, 'my hardships and my afflictions have driven me out to Babylon'. Rudolph, 312, reads *šō'ātī*, 'my devastation', for *šᵉ'ērī* (cf. BHS). Cf. 50.10; 51.24 for the motif of retribution against the Chaldaeans, here given a liturgical style (cf. Weiser, 436; Ps. 118.2–4; 124.1; 129.1). **[36]** Cf. 50.34. The term 'sea' (*yam*) may refer to the Euphrates (cf. Isa. 18.2; 19.5, where *yam* refers to the Nile), though a mythological allusion cannot be ruled out. **[37]** Cf. 9.11 (MT 10); 10.22. G much shorter, lacking 'the haunt of jackals, a horror and a hissing'. **[38]** G lacks 'they shall roar' and reads *nā'ᵃrū*, 'they growl', as *exegerthēsan*, 'they rose up' = *nē'ōrū*. Cf. 49.19; 50.44 for different use of lion imagery. **[39]** MT *lᵉma'an ya'ᵃlōzū*, 'in order that they may rejoice': read *yᵉ'ullāpū*, 'they may be stupefied', with Vrs (cf. G *methusō*). Rudolph transposes v. 40 to follow *ya'ᵃlōzū* and treats *nᵉ'um yhwh*, 'says Yahweh', as the formal ending of the unit; Driver 1937–38, 127–8, understands *'lz* as 'to have colic'. **[41]** Cf. 50.23. MT *šēšak*, 'Sheshak': a cipher (athbash) for Babylon, cf. 25.26; lacking in G. It is unnecessary as a cipher because Babylon is specified in vv. 41, 42, 44 and it may represent traces of the use of magical spells against Babylon in MT. **[43]** Cf. 2.6c. MT *'ereṣ lō'-yēšēb bāhēn kol-'īš*, 'a land *in them* no man dwells': G lacks 'a land'; MT erroneously repeats *'ereṣ*, 'land', and, as *bāhēn*, 'in them', indicates, the cities should be understood as the places lacking inhabitants. **[44]** G lacks 'Bel in' and vv 44bβ-49a (from *gam* . . . to *gam*); cf. 50.2 for Bel. MT *wᵉlō'-yinhᵃrū 'ēlāyw 'ōd gōyim*, 'and the nations shall no longer flow to him': cf. Isa.2.2 for the motif of the nations flowing (*nhr*) to a specific place (Zion). This treatment of *nhr 'l* as an idiom derived from *nhr* I, 'flow', is disputed by a number of exegetes who prefer to relate it to *nhr* II, 'shine, radiate with joy', cf. JPSB 'And nations shall no more gaze on him with joy'; Ehrlich

1912, 10, 320; Wiklander 1978, 61–3; 31.12. The fall of Babylon's wall is referred to in v. 58; 50.15.

Wiklander 1978

A shorter section, enclosed by the motifs of gorging and disgorging (vv. 34, 44), is composed of vv. 34–35 with a divine response in vv. 36–37 and further units in vv. 38–40, 41–43, 44. Jerusalem is the speaker in the first instance and laments her experiences at the hands of Nebuchadrezzar, king of Babylon. Like a dragon Babylon has swallowed her, gorging itself on her (flesh) as one might empty a container or devour delicacies. Zion has been wiped off the face of the earth (the final image of v. 34 is less than clear). The sea-monster image (cf. Gen. 1.21) is one derived from ancient mythology (Babylonian and Canaanite; cf. Day 1985) and used to described different things in the biblical traditions: cosmic forces (e.g. Ps. 74.13; Isa. 51.9) controlled by Yahweh in the past or in the future (Isa. 27.1) or as a figure of the national enemy (e.g. Egypt in Ezek. 29.3; 32.2). Babylon warrants the epithet 'dragon' (*tannīn*) because of its cruel destruction of land, city and people in the period 597–582. The image is not only a fitting description of the imperial bully but echoes the imagery of the section which uses a variety of water metaphors (e.g. vv. 36, 42, 44). A liturgical-style (Weiser) response to this outrageous behaviour occurs in v. 35, where Zion encourages her people to chant their curse on Babylon in order to bring about its downfall. To this call for retribution the deity himself responds with asseverations of Babylon's destruction. Its water supplies will be cut off (thereby destroying the sea-monster's habitat?) and the land will be depopulated. Just as Zion's territory had been evacuated of people, so will Babylon become a haunt of jackals (cf. 9.11; 10.22). Poetic justice as well as rhetorical symmetry links the fates of Jerusalem and Babylon (analysis of section in Wiklander, 50–6).

Very different images are used in vv. 38–40 to depict the complete destruction of the people of Babylon. Raging like lions the people (cf. 12.8, or are these images of warriors cf. 49.19–20; 50.44–45?) will be treated to a banquet of Yahweh's (cf. the banquet of death in 9.15; 25.15–17) and, in a drunken stupor, they shall sleep a permanent sleep from which they shall never wake (cf. v. 57). A change of images in v. 40 makes the same point (cf. 50.27).

In vv.41–43 a lament is the response to Babylon's downfall. The world-famous and much-envied Babylon has been transmogrified by the turn of events. Swamped by the sea and lapped by the heavy waves, she is destroyed. Chants (v. 35) and incantations (v. 41 'Sheshak') have had their effect and the imperial enemy is reduced to the very state to which she had brought so many other nations. That the sea images are metaphors is made clear by the drought and desert figures of v. 43. The section ends in v. 44 (Lundbom 1975, 92–5, concludes it with v. 45) with a return to the images of v. 34, but reverses them: what Babylon has gorged herself on she must now disgorge (i.e. the exiled nations and Zion in particular, cf. vv. 34–35; v. 45 of next section). No longer shall the nations flow to (as a river: *nhr*, cf. Isa. 2.2; Micah 4.1) or rejoice in him (i.e. Bel the Babylonian god, but G 'her' refers to Babylon) because the city's walls are down. In v. 45 the flow is reversed as the people flee *from* the doomed city. Thus the monster Babylon represented by its king Nebuchadrezzar (v. 34) yields up its prey (Zion's exiles) to Yahweh.

The reference to Bel in MT v. 44 hints at an ideological interpretation of the destruction of Babylon. In the downfall of Zion the god Bel had defeated the god Yahweh; now in the fall of Babylon Yahweh reasserts himself and demonstrates his superiority by retrieving from the mouth of the monster that which it had swallowed. G lacks this theomachy element, but at some stage in the development of the second edition the theological significance of the downfall of Babylon appears as the triumph of Yahweh over Bel – the reversal of 587. Bel ceases to be an attraction for the nations because Babylon's wall has fallen and the god is clearly no longer able to protect his property. That would appear to be the meaning of v. 44:

> Bel, the god of Babylon, worshipped by its inhabitants and the supreme representative of the city, has taken dominion over the world including Zion-Jerusalem; the nations praise him and cheer him as supreme god. Thus he has committed an offence against YHWH, the Lord of the universe who bestowed world power on Babylon. What is more, Babylon has oppressed Zion-Jerusalem, i.e. the place where YHWH is worshipped and the people who worship him. Therefore YHWH shall take vengeance for Bel-Babylon's haughtiness; he shall take away his power and glory and then the nations will no longer cheer him as supreme god nor praise Babylon's glory (Wiklander, 61).

51.45–53

45 'Go out of the midst of her, my people!
Let every man save his life
from the fierce anger of the LORD!
46 Let not your heart faint, and be not fearful
at the report heard in the land,
when a report comes in one year
and afterward a report in another year,
and violence is in the land,
and ruler is against ruler.'
47 'Therefore, behold, the days are coming
when I will punish the images of Babylon;
her whole land shall be put to shame,
and all her slain shall fall in the midst of her.
48 Then the heavens and the earth,
and all that is in them,
shall sing for joy over Babylon;
for the destroyers shall come against them out of the north,
says the LORD.
49 Babylon must fall for the slain of Israel,
as for Babylon have fallen the slain of all the earth.'
50 'You that have escaped from the sword,
go, stand not still!
Remember the LORD from afar,
and let Jerusalem come into your mind:
51 "We are put to shame, for we have heard reproach;
dishonour has covered our face,
for aliens have come
into the holy places of the LORD's house." '
52 'Therefore, behold, the days are coming, says the LORD,
when I will execute judgment upon her images,
and through all her land
the wounded shall groan.
53 Though Babylon should mount up to heaven,
and though she should fortify her strong height,
yet destroyers would come from me upon her,
says the LORD.'

The lack of vv. 44β–49a in G may be due to haplography (the translator's eye skipping from the first *gam* to the third *gam*), though the similarity of language between vv. 44b–49a and 49b–53 suggests that they are variants conflated in MT (cf. Janzen 1973, 119). **[45]** Cf. 50. 8; 51.6; Isa. 52.11–12.

[46] A prose transition from the exhortation of v. 45 to the oracle of vv. 47–48 (Bright), though understood by some exegetes as an eschatological, rather than historical, statement (e.g. Rudolph, 313; Volz, 433). **[47]** Cf. v. 52; 50.38 for the attack on Babylonian images (*pᵉsīlîm*). **[48]** Cf. 50.3, 41 for the motif of the foe from the north coming against Babylon; Isa. 49.13 for the idea of the heavens and the earth singing because of the release of the exiles. **[49]** MT *ḥallē yiśrā'ēl*, 'the slain of Israel': read with many exegetes *lᵉḥlly* . . . '*for* the slain . . .' (cf. BHS). **[50]** MT *mēḥereb hilᵉkū*, 'from the sword, go': unusual imperatival form (*lᵉkū* is normal form); a redivision of the words yields *mēḥarbāh lᵉkū*, 'from *her* sword, go', cf. G *ek gēs, poreuesthe*, 'from the land, you who escape'. MT *mērāḥōq*, 'from afar': remembering Yahweh from afar indicates the exilic context of the refugees (cf. 30.10) and the Zion orientation of the exhortation. **[51]** Cf. 3.24–25 for the confession of shame and covering with dishonour. MT *'al-miqdᵉšē bēt yhwh*, 'to the sanctuaries of the house of Yahweh': G *eis ta hagia hēmōn, eis oikon kuriou*, 'into our sanctuary, into (the) house of the lord'; read *miqdašēnū*, 'our sanctuary', as the plur. form is unusual for referring to the temple (*miqdāš*). It is possible that Heb. *mqdšy* represents *miqdaš y(hwh)*, 'sanctuary of Yahweh', and *byt yhwh* is a variant or explanatory gloss (cf. Bright, 352 n.). Cf. 50.28; 51.11 for the temple motif in 50–51; Ps. 74.1–8 for the invasion of the sanctuary by Yahweh's foes. **[52]** MT *ye'ᵉnōq*, 'shall groan': G *pesountai*, 'shall fall' = vv. 4, 49; here MT refers *ḥll* to the wounded, whereas G consistently relates it to the dead. Cf. v. 47; 50.38 for the polemic against images.

———

A number of brief elements constitutes the final section before the framework conclusion of vv. 54–58. Exhortations (vv. 45, 46, 50), a confession (v. 51), two variant oracles on Babylon's destruction (vv. 47–48, 52–53), and an assertion of the necessity for Babylon to suffer the same fate as it imposed on Israel and the slain of all the earth (v. 49) bring together a number of themes to be found throughout 50–51. As a result of the divine punishment of Babylon the Judaean exiles ('my people', v. 45) must flee from Yahweh's anger. A variant exhortation encourages the people to flee from the invading forces and to return to Jerusalem (v. 50). The confession in v. 51 represents a view of the Babylonian conquest of the temple as an occasion of great shame for the worshippers of Yahweh, but lacks any of the sense of responsibility for the event which characterizes other parts of the Jeremiah tradition (contrast the confession in 3.24–25). It does, however, identify the humiliation of Yahweh's house as one of the central charges against Babylon (cf. 50.28; 51.11), and the appearance of this motif in 50–51 indicates a temple orientation in the editing of the poems. The two oracles (introduced by the editorial 'days are coming') about the punishment of Babylon focus on the idols used in Babylonian worship (cf. 50.38b) and may be read as a contrastive comment on the cultic practices of both nations (i.e. Jerusalem's sanctuary and Babylon's images). This is closer to the polemic against other national cults in 10.1–16 than to the discourses on syncretistic worship in 2–3.

Other elements in the section include the encouragement of the exiles in a time of rumours and political intrigue (v. 46: a prose reference to the steady disintegration of Babylonian society after the death of Nebuchadrezzar in 562?) and the universal rejoicing caused by the overthrow of Babylon by the destroyers from the north (v. 48). This note of joy brings the movement of the tradition full circle from the enemy out of the north which destroys Jerusalem (1.13–15?; 4.5–8; 6.22–26) to the enemy from the north which devastates Babylon (50.3, 9, 41; 51.48b). Such symmetry is explicitly expressed in v. 49, where Babylon's fate is sealed by its treatment of Israel and the other nations. As Babylon has done, so it shall be done to her (cf. 50.15, 29) – small wonder that the heavens and the earth sing for joy over her fall!

51.54–58

54 'Hark! a cry from Babylon!
The noise of great destruction from the land of the Chaldeans!
55 For the LORD is laying Babylon waste,
and stilling her mighty voice.
Their waves roar like many waters,
the noise of their voice is raised;
56 for a destroyer has come upon her,
upon Babylon;
her warriors are taken,
their bows are broken in pieces;
for the LORD is a God of recompense,
he will surely requite.
57 I will make drunk her princes and her wise men,
her governors, her commanders, and her warriors;
they shall sleep a perpetual sleep and not wake,
says the King, whose name is the LORD of hosts.'

58 'Thus says the LORD of hosts:
The broad wall of Babylon
shall be levelled to the ground
and her high gates
shall be burned with fire.
The peoples labour for naught,
and the nations weary themselves only for fire.'

---

[55] MT *gallēhem k^e^mayim rabbīm*, '*their* waves like many waters': i.e. the invading army (cf. v. 53) roars like crashing billows; some exegetes favour reading *galleyhā*, '*her* waves' (cf. G°, A, Symm), i.e. the din of Babylon is destroyed by Yahweh (cf. G; BHS). **[56]** Rudolph, 314, deletes the first line as a marginal comment on v. 55a (BHS); G *talaipōriai*, 'hardship', suggests *šōd*, 'destruction', rather than MT *šōdēd*, 'destroyer' (cf. Bright, 353). MT *ḥitt^e^tāh qaššᵉtōtām*, 'their bows are shattered': intransitive Piel should perhaps be read as Qal *ḥattāh qaštām*, 'their bow is broken' (Giesebrecht, 260; cf. BHS; G *to toxon autōn*, 'their bow'). Cf. Isa. 59.18 for the sentiments of v. 56b. **[57]** A prose variation on v. 39 with a list of the high-ranking victims of Yahweh's campaign against Babylon. **[58]** MT *ḥōmōt bābel hārᵉḥabāh*, 'the broad walls of Babylon': many mss, G, V *ḥōmat*, 'wall of . . .'. MT *'ar'ēr tit'ar'ār*, lit. 'stripped utterly bare': i.e. razed to the ground. **[58b]** = Hab. 2.13b (with the order of *bᵉdē-rīq*, 'for naught', and *bᵉdē-'ēš*, 'for fire', reversed); MT *wᵉyā'ēpū*, 'and they weary themselves': read by many exegetes as *yī'āpū*, 'will weary themselves' (MT is repeated by error in v. 64). G negates the force of MT by reading *kai ou kopiasousi laoi eis kenon*, 'and the people shall *not* be exhausted in vain'; it also reads *bᵉdē-'ēš* as *en archē*, 'in dominion' = *bᵉrō'š* (*d-r* confusion). Bright, 207n., 359, reads here 'thus far the words of Jeremiah' from v. 64 which, according to him, has been displaced by the insertion of vv. 59–64.

The collection of material against Babylon is concluded by vv. 54–58 forming a framework with 50.2–3. A cry is heard from Babylon which indicates great destruction in the land of the Chaldaeans. The noise is Yahweh laying waste the great enemy and stilling her voice for ever (so G; MT represents a slightly different sense of v. 58: much of the noise is caused by the invading forces). This reversal of Babylon's great prowess is the work of Yahweh who is a god of retributions (*'ēl gᵉmulōt*, v. 46; cf. Isa. 59.18) and the compensation or recompense he will surely extract (*šallēm yᵉšallēm*) from Babylon is the avenging of the defeat of his people by the hubristic foe (cf. vv. 6, 11, 24, 35–37, 49, 53; cf. 25.14b). It is because Yahweh is a god of such recompenses that the catastrophe of 587 is balanced in these poems by the exultation caused by Babylon's defeat (whether imagined, anticipated or celebrated). Her officials, warriors and important people will all sleep a permanent sleep (of death) brought about by Yahweh making them drunk (vv. 39, 57; cf. Isa. 49.26; 51.22–23). It is the king, i.e. Yahweh not Nebuchadrezzar (cf. v. 34), who pronounces this verdict on the enemy (cf. 8.19; 10.7,10; 46.18; 48.15 for the motif of Yahweh as king). A final oracular note in v. 58 declares that Babylon's wall will be razed to the ground and her massive gates burned (cf. 50.2, 'Babylon is taken'). The meaning of v. 58b is ambiguous: it is either a citation from Hab. 2.13b or, more likely, the use of a saying from a common source used by both traditions. It appears to mean that people weary themselves in vain opposing Yahweh or pursuing different goals from his (cf. Hab. 2.12–14), but in its present context other meanings are possible. The destruction of Babylon renders the activity of the nations otiose – over Babylon, which is no more, the people wearied themselves pointlessly (ie a great fuss about nothing!). If the understanding of G is followed, then the negative reading means that the attack on Babylon by the nations has not been in vain. Whatever its precise meaning it is essentially an observation on the futility of the activities of the nations which end in fire, i.e. destruction, in particular Babylon the mighty with its great wall and high gates (cf. Ps. 2.1 for such futility). Hubris has met with nemesis!

All empires disintegrate, collapse and perish – the Assyrian, Persian, Greek, Roman, Holy Roman and British – and Babylon is no exception to this general principle of the fate of large conglomerates of political power and organization. The songs, chants, incantations, poems, diatribes and observations collected together in 50–51 represent Judaean responses to the experience of Babylonian rule in the sixth century. It is not possible to determine the precise relationship of the collection to historical events of the period. Like so much in the book of Jeremiah, parts of 50–51 may be related to the period before the Persian takeover of power in 539, but the poems need not be read in this manner. There is a fair degree of fantasy and stereotypical language in 50–51 and it is not necessarily the case that the poems *must* be derived from before the changeover of power because the fall of Babylon was, in fact, nothing like the descriptions given of razed walls and burning gates. These are clichéd accounts of the fall of Jerusalem and, in positing them of Babylon, the poets have maintained a symmetry of justice against the great enemy for its sacrilegious treatment of the sacred city. Emotionally Babylon was destroyed in this manner – of what importance could the mere details of what happened so many hundreds of miles away be to those who knew at first hand the ruins of Jerusalem! Beyond the political events of the sixth century it is possible to discern in these poems the emergence of Babylon as a mythical entity standing for the hubristic enemy of Yahweh and his people (cf. Rev. 18–19). The outrage generated by Babylon with regard to the sacking of Jerusalem outlived the passing of the Babylonian empire, and 'Babylon' became a catchword for describing *the enemy*.

51.59–64

59 The word which Jeremiah the prophet commanded Seraiah the son of Neriah, son of Mahseiah, when he went with Zedekiah king of Judah to Babylon, in the fourth year of his reign. Seraiah was the quartermaster. 60 Jeremiah wrote in a book all the evil that should come upon Babylon, all these words that are written concerning Babylon. 61 And Jeremiah said to Seraiah: 'When you come to Babylon, see that you read all these words, 62 and say, "O Lord, thou hast said concerning this place that thou wilt cut it off, so that nothing shall dwell in it, neither man nor beast, and it shall be desolate for ever." 63 When you finish reading this book, bind a stone to it, and cast it into the midst of the Euphrates, 64 and say, "Thus shall Babylon sink, to rise no more, because of the evil that I am bringing upon her." '

Thus far are the words of Jeremiah.

---

[59] MT *haddābār ʾašer-ṣiwwāh yirmeyāhū hannābīʾ ʾet-śerāyāh*, 'the word which Jeremiah the prophet commanded Seraiah': cf. 46.13; 50.1 for this introductory formula (*dbr*, 'spoke', for *ṣwh*, 'commanded'; Yahweh for Jeremiah); G *ho logos hon eneteilato kurios Ieremia tō prophētē eipein tō Saraia*, 'the word which the lord commanded Jeremiah the prophet to speak to Saraia'. Cf. 32.12 for the family of Seraiah, brother of Baruch. MT *belektō ʾet-ṣidqiyyāhū*, 'when he went *with* Zedekiah': G *hote eporeueto para Sedekiou*, 'when he went *from* Sedekia' (*ʾet* = *mēʾēt*); in MT Seraiah accompanies Zedekiah, in G he is sent by him (as a delegate). MT *śar menūḥāh*, lit. 'official of (the) resting place': i.e. the one in charge of the bivouacking of troops, etc.; G *archōn dōrōn*, 'chief of gifts' = *menāḥōt*, i.e. the one in charge of tribute (to the foreign overlord). **[60]** Cf. 25.13. The motif of Jeremiah writing appears in 29.1; 30.2 and is implied by 25.13; in 36.2 it is combined with the motif of delegation (Jeremiah is commanded to write but delegates the writing to

Baruch). Here the book (*sēper 'eḥād*, '*one* book'; in contradistinction to other books written by him or the indefinite 'a book'?) is a book of ill omen (*kol-hārā'āh*, 'all the evil') spoken against Babylon (cf. 25.13, where the words in the book may be those spoken against *all* the nations, but see Comm.). 60b may be an attempt to link the delegation process of vv. 59–64 with the material in 50.1 – 51.58 (cf. Bright, 210); 59b–60 are essentially parenthetical and v. 61 resumes v. 59a (cf. Rudolph, 316). **[62]** MT *kī-šimmōt 'ōlām tihyeh*, 'for it shall be permanent ruins': Vrs sing., 'a ruin'. Note how the conventional phrase *hammāqōm hazzeh*, 'this place', so characteristic of the prose of Jeremiah, here refers to Babylon (normally it indicates the temple or Jerusalem [e.g. 7.3, 7; 16.2, 3, 9; 19.3, 4, 6, 7, 12]). G *kurie kurie*, 'lord, lord', for MT *yhwh*. **[63]** MT *'et-hassēper hazzeh*, 'this book': cf. 25.13 *bassēper hazzeh*, 'in this book'. **[64]** MT *kākāh*, 'thus': the standard formula accompanying special actions, cf. 13.9; 19.11; 28.11. MT adds *w^eyā'ēpū*, 'and they shall weary themselves', after 'the evil that I am bringing upon her': lacking in G; it is repeated from the end of v. 58. MT *'ad-hēnnāh dibrē yirm^eyāhū*, 'thus far the words of Jeremiah': cf. 48.47 for the formulaic termination of a lengthy section – i.e. 46–51 the OAN and here (cf. Duhm, 377); Job 31.40 uses a similar device to indicate the end of of Job's speeches. The statement would be better after v. 58 (Rudolph, Bright), as Jeremiah hardly stopped speaking in the fourth year of Zedekiah! It is lacking in G because the oracles against Babylon (G 27–28) are not at the end of the collection of OAN; its present position in MT, though displaced, may be due to the addition of 52 to the book of Jeremiah and thus it indicates a separation of Jeremiah's work from what follows.

The collection of anti-Babylonian materials in 50–51 is terminated by the report of a magical act of Jeremiah's dated to the fourth year of king Zedekiah (*c.* 594–3). This act is more appropriately associated with the period depicted in 27–29 (cf. Bright's treatment of it after 29.32) than with the post-587 responses to Babylon. However, it is placed here in order to attribute 50–51 to Jeremiah (cf. 50.1) and to demonstrate how the prophet conveyed the words of ill omen to the land of Babylon. Thus he who advocates submission to Babylon in 27–29 here reverses the act of wearing yoke-bars and by his delegated act dooms Babylon to eternal destruction. The question of treason mooted in the treatment of 27–29, 37–40 is balanced by this magical act of speaking, writing, sending and disposing of Babylon. Normally the evil word spoken against the foreign opponent was simply uttered and allowed to take effect accordingly, but in the case of the arch-enemy Babylon more than the spoken word would appear to have been required. Hence the words uttered are written down by Jeremiah (cf. 25.13) in *one* of the books he wrote (cf. 30.2), transported to Babylon by a delegated official (Baruch's brother) who may have been travelling there with the vassal king's tribute to his suzerain lord (cf. G; how ironic that the diplomatic bag which carried such wealth also contained the book of curses!), read out over the land, and then destroyed as an act whereby Babylon is annihilated and the ill omens placed beyond retrieval. Nothing can now prevent Babylon's defeat – just as the smashing of the ceramic vessel outside Jerusalem's gates had destroyed that city (19.1–2, 10–11). The delegated authority of Jeremiah carries the same power as his spoken word (cf. Schmidt 1982), and the magic behind the act of drowning the book is just as effective for Seraiah ben Neriah as for Jeremiah. With this displaced report Babylon's fate is sealed.

51.59–64 should be read in parallel with 36 where there is also a case of Jeremiah delegating a task to another person (i.e. Baruch the brother of Seraiah). Jeremiah speaks the words, has them written down (a unique element in the tradition, because in all other instances Jeremiah does his own writing), and they are delivered by Baruch orally to the people, the princes and the king. At the end of Baruch's mission the scroll is destroyed by the king, but Jeremiah dictates it again and Baruch inscribes it once more. The word cannot be destroyed so easily, though those who oppose it are set aside with ease. In 51.59–64 a similar process is intended to lead to the destruction of the written word and, on this occasion, there is no need for the word to be rewritten. Since its destruction is intentional, nothing can preserve it. It is perhaps too subtle a reading of the text to see in the survival of Baruch's scroll through rewriting and the destruction of Seraiah's book of ill omen the relative difference between Judah and Babylon. One survives; the other does not: the word to Judah can be rewritten, reshaped, even reformulated (cf. 1.10; 29.11); but there is only one word for Babylon – destruction – and that requires no restatement. When the book sinks beneath the waters of the river Euphrates, Babylon sinks with it – never to rise again. Underlining this point is the fact that MT represents Jeremiah as playing Yahweh to Seraiah (e.g. 'the word which Jeremiah *commanded*'; see on 1.10) and speaking from a position (*the prophet*) of established power in the tradition. It is his last word (MT), and it carries the doom of Judah's enemy.

EPILOGUE 52.1–34

52.1–3a

52[1] Zedekiah was twenty-one years old when he became king; and he reigned eleven years in Jerusalem. His mother's name was Hamutal the daughter of Jeremiah of Libnah. 2 And he did what was evil in the sight of the LORD, according to all that Jehoiakim had done. 3 Surely because of the anger of the LORD things came to such a pass in Jerusalem and Judah that he cast them out from his presence.

[MT 52] = G 52. **[52.1–3a]** = II Kings 24.18–20a; G lacks vv. 2–3. **[1]** K *ḥmyṭl*; Q *ḥ^a^mûṭal*, 'Hamutal': cf. II Kings 23.31; I Chron. 3.15–16. 'Jeremiah from Libnah' (*yirm^e^yāhû millibnāh*): the third Jeremiah mentioned in the tradition (cf. 1.1; 35.3). **[2]** A stereotypical Deuteronomistic phrase which indicates the editorial disapproval of the king more than it specifies his faults; in that Zedekiah was a vassal of the Babylonians he can hardly be said to have behaved in the same fashion as Jehoiakim the vassal of Egypt. Cf. 37.1–2 for a similar sweeping rejection of Zedekiah; 15.4 for the identification of Jerusalem's fate with the dealings of a former king (Manasseh). **[3]** MT *kî 'al-'ap yhwh hāy^e^tāh bîrûsalaim wîhûdāh 'ad-hišlîkō 'ōtām mē'al pānāyw*, lit. 'for upon the anger of Yahweh was against Jerusalem and Judah until he cast them from his presence': cf. 32.31 for similarly awkward syntax; this statement makes Yahweh's anger the cause of the deportation, but this was hardly the opinion the Deuteronomists wished to convey (cf. Rudolph, 318); Gray 1977, 762, however, views II Kings 24.20a as meaning that Yahweh consented to Zedekiah's sin because he had already doomed Israel for earlier sins.

The book of Jeremiah does not end with words or actions of Jeremiah (hence the note at the end of MT 51.64), but with an appendix taken from the Deuteronomistic history of the kings of Israel and Judah (i.e. II Kings 24.18 – 25.30). Why this should be the case is not known – the rabbinic view which credited Jeremiah with having written Kings as well as the book of Jeremiah is not an explanation but a deduction from the shared material and the common Deuteronomistic style. 52 and II Kings 25 are not exactly the same: 52 omits the section on the assassination of Gedaliah (II Kings 25.22–26) and has an additional extract from a register of the numbers of people deported to Babylon (vv. 28–30). A similar sharing of material is to be found in the Isaiah tradition, where Isa. 36–39 form a conclusion to Isa. 1–35 drawn from II Kings 18–20. But in this common material the prophet Isaiah is one of the dominant figures, whereas Jeremiah is completely absent in Jer. 52 and II Kings 24.18–25.30. The effect of concluding Jeremiah with an appendix from II Kings is to form a closure with the Deuteronomistic history and reflects the editorial history of the book of Jeremiah. This closure feature is somewhat obscured by the subsequent development of Hebrew Bibles whereby the book of Isaiah now stands at the head of the prophetic collection (replacing Jeremiah, the largest volume in that collection). The editors may have wished to conclude their work with an appendix emphasizing the fall of Jerusalem as the vindication of the work of the prophet Jeremiah and the confirmation of his vision of the overturned pot signalling the northern invasion (1.14–16; but see Comm.). In the tradition's end is its beginning!

The first part of the appendix sets the background to the fall of Jerusalem with a few details about the accession to the Judaean throne of Zedekiah (cf. 37.1). These consist of Zedekiah's age when he became king, the length of his reign, and his mother's name (Hamutal or Hamital, cf. Q–K). A brief homily follows which, in characteristically Deuteronomistic fashion, condemns Zedekiah out of hand without specific reasons. The allusion to the evil he did in terms of 'according to all that Jehoiakim had done' is a mark of the Deuteronomistic concern to underline the continuity of evil maintained by the kings of Judah (esp. Manasseh) which led to the destruction of Jerusalem. Even the details of Zedekiah's reign are modelled on those provided for Jehoiakim (cf. II Kings 23.36–37). Whether the similarity between the reigns of the two vassal kings should be extended to include their rebellion against Nebuchadrezzar their overlord (cf. II Kings 24.1, 20b) is difficult to determine, but both kings are presented as suffering the consequences of the actions of former kings in Jerusalem (Jehoiakim for Manasseh – Zedekiah for Jehoiakim, II Kings 24.3, 19). The syntax of v. 3 is difficult and the meaning far from clear: the fate of Jerusalem is determined by

Yahweh's anger rather than Zedekiah's activities. That would appear to be the most sensible understanding of MT, though the EVV differ considerably in the way they translate it (JPSB at least acknowledges the uncertain meaning of the Hebrew). It is as a consequence of Yahweh's anger that Zedekiah behaves so foolhardily against Babylon (v. 3b). Such an account of his reign is rather different from the presentation of the interviews between him and Jeremiah in 37–38 (where the prophet attempts to persuade him to change his mind but does not denounce him for evil practices), though the end-result is the same in both traditions.

52.3b–11

3b And Zedekiah rebelled against the king of Babylon. 4 And in the ninth year of his reign, in the tenth month, on the tenth day of the month, Nebuchadrezzar king of Babylon came with all his army against Jerusalem, and they laid siege to it and built siegeworks against it round about. 5 So the city was besieged till the eleventh year of King Zedekiah. 6 On the ninth day of the fourth month the famine was so severe in the city, that there was no food for the people of the land. 7 Then a breach was made in the city; and all the men of war fled and went out from the city by night by the way of a gate between the two walls, by the king's garden, while the Chaldeans were round about the city. And they went in the direction of the Arabah. 8 But the army of the Chaldeans pursued the king, and overtook Zedekiah in the plains of Jericho; and all his army was scattered from him. 9 Then they captured the king, and brought him up to the king of Babylon at Riblah in the land of Hamath, and he passed sentence upon him. 10 The king of Babylon slew the sons of Zedekiah before his eyes, and also slew all the princes of Judah at Riblah. 11 He put out the eyes of Zedekiah, and bound him in fetters, and the king of Babylon took him to Babylon, and put him in prison till the day of his death.

[52.3b–11] = II Kings 24.20b – 25.7 (with minor variations); cf. 39.1–2, 4–7 (see Notes and Comm. there). **[4]** G^BS *enatō*, 'ninth'; G^A *hebdomō*, 'seventh', for MT, G 'tenth (month)'. MT *wayyibᵉnū ʿālеyhā dāyēq sābīb*, 'and they built against it siegeworks round about': *dāyēq* occurs here and in II Kings 25.1; Ezek.4.2; 17.17; 21.27 (EV 22); 26.8; it may be translated as 'siegeworks', 'siege wall', 'siege towers', cf. NEB watch-towers, JPSB towers; Gray 1977, 763–4, 'a wall of circumvallation' cf. Aramaic *zāqa*, *yāzīq* ('to put a collar on to a shirt'), i.e. a rampart (like a collar) round the city. In spite of the explicit statement here, Nebuchadrezzar did not himself besiege

Jerusalem but remained at his headquarters at Riblah on the Orontes (cf. vv. 9–10, 26–27; 39.5–6). **[6]** G, II Kings 25.3 lack 'in the fourth month'. MT *'am hā'āreṣ*, 'the people of the land': here this term refers to the general populace (cf. 37.2; 44.21) rather than the landed gentry (cf. 34.19; see on 1.18). **[7]** 39.4 reads 'and when *Zedekiah* . . . and all the men of war *saw* . . .': Rudolph, 320, supplies *wayyar' hammelek*, 'and the king saw', from there because some such reference is required to account for the king being among the fugitives of v. 8 (cf. Bright, 363). G lacks 'they fled' and 'from the city'. MT *bēn-haḥōmōtayim*, 'between the two walls': cf. Isa. 22.11, where the term indicates a reservoir area at the convergence of two of the city's walls (for possible location, cf. Gray 1977, 765). A more graphic depiction of this escape by night is given in Ezek. 12.12–14. **[8]** MT 'pursued the king and overtook Zedekiah': cf. 39.5 'pursued them and overtook Zedekiah'; but G, II Kings 25.5, 'pursued the king and overtook him'. MT *be'arebōt yerēhō*, 'in the plains of Jericho': i.e. the arid, semi-desert plains south of Jericho; G *en tō peran Ierichō*, 'in the (area) beyond (= *be'ēber*) Jericho'. MT *wekol-ḥēlō nāpōṣū mē'ālāyw*, 'and all his troops were scattered from him': whether they abandoned him (cf. Gray) or fled when the Chaldaean troops arrived (cf. Bright) is difficult to determine; G *pantes hoi paides autou*, 'all his servants' (= *kol-'abādāyw*), suggests that his personal retinue was dispersed. **[9]** MT *riblātāh be'ereṣ ḥamāt*, 'to Riblah in the land of Hamath': G, II Kings 25.6 lack 'in the land of Hamath'; see Notes on 39.5 for Riblah and the idiom *dibbēr* . . . *mišpāṭīm* (G, II Kings 25.6 *mišpāṭ*), 'to pass . . . sentence', or 'to put on trial' (cf. Gray 'he took process with him'); cf. 1.16. **[10]** Cf. 39.6 'nobles' (*ḥōrē*) for 'princes' (*śārē*) here; 'all' need only govern the princes taken to Riblah rather than all the princes of the realm (cf. Bright, 367, 'various of the princes'); II Kings 25.7 lacks any reference to the slaying of the princes. **[11]** K *bbyt*, '*in* the house of', Q *bēt*, 'the house of': *happequddōt*, 'punishments', i.e. prison; G *eis oikian mulōnos*, 'in the mill-house'.

The summary of the siege and fall of Jerusalem (cf. 39.1–2, 4–7) is brief and partial. It picks out a few details of the eighteen-month campaign by the Babylonians to penetrate the city and seize the rebellious vassals. That the siege took such a length of time may be attributed to the unwelcome attentions of the Egyptians elsewhere (cf. 37.5–7) rather than to the skill of the Judaeans or the effectiveness of the city's fortifications. The brief account (cf. II Kings 25.1–7) is less interested in the events of the siege (causes and course) than in the fall of the city and the consequences of that for its rulers and citizens. Hence the story of the breach of the city wall is told from the viewpoint of the besieged rather than the besiegers and the impression is given that the starving citizens broke down the wall rather than the Babylonians (less the case in 39.2–3). Instead of the attacking army pouring into the breached city the Judaean soldiers and the royal party fled through the broken wall *by night* (the dominant escape motif). They successfully eluded the Babylonian army but were overtaken in the plains of Jericho. From there they were taken to Nebuchadrezzar's headquarters in Syria and king Zedekiah faced trial for disloyalty to his overlord. His sons and his princes were executed and he was treated cruelly before being deported to Babylon where he was imprisoned until his death. It is not clear why he was not executed at Riblah along with his family and counsellors, but Nebuchadrezzar may have had political motives for not killing his rebel vassal. Zedekiah's imprisonment in Babylon meant that two Judaean kings were detained there during the same time, and a striking contrast is afforded between the treatment of both kings in this chapter (cf. vv. 31–34). Whatever may have been Jehoiachin's experience of confinement, it cannot have been as wretched as the blinded Zedekiah's. As presented in this epilogue Zedekiah's fate is blinding, imprisonment and death, whereas eventually Jehoiachin is released from prison and enjoys a royal pension until his death in exile. The contrast may be only structural (i.e. part of the story-telling process) but it is possible that the fate of each king represents an observation on the consequences of a life lived in opposition to the prophet's warnings. Although Jeremiah is conspicuously absent in this epilogue, the appending of it to the book of the words of Jeremiah may reflect the wish to underline the fate of king, people and city which did not listen to those words. Jehoiachin could hardly be accused of rejecting the prophet's advice (though 22.24–30 hardly flatter that king), hence he is the only one spoken kindly to in this appendix. That may be an oversubtle reading of the contrast between the kings, but it is not an unreasonable inference from the similar but distinctive fates of the last two monarchs of the city of Jerusalem.

52.12–16

12 In the fifth month, on the tenth day of the month – which was the nineteenth year of king Nebuchadrezzar, king of Babylon – Nebuzaradan the captain of the bodyguard who served the king of Babylon, entered Jerusalem. 13 And he burned the house of the LORD, and the king's house

and all the houses of Jerusalem; every great house he burned down. 14 And all the army of the Chaldeans, who were with the captain of the guard, broke down all the walls round about Jerusalem. 15 And Nebuzaradan the captain of the guard carried away captive some of the poorest of the people and the rest of the people who were left in the city and the deserters who had deserted to the king of Babylon, together with the rest of the artisans. 16 But Nebuzaradan the captain of the guard left some of the poorest of the land to be vinedressers and ploughmen.

[52.12–16] = II Kings 25.8–12 (with minor variations); cf. 39.8–10. **[12]** MT 'tenth day': II Kings 25.8 'seventh day'. G lacks 'which was the nineteenth year of king Nebuchadrezzar, king of Babylon'. The nineteenth year of Nebuchadrezzar was 587, counting from 605 the year when he came to power (II Kings style); v. 28 gives the year of the deportation after the fall of Jerusalem as Nebuchadrezzar's *eighteenth* year! This may follow the Babylonian style of reckoning (cf. Bright, 369), but the Bible is notoriously unreliable in matters of dating and numbers, so the two verses may simply illustrate the complexity of chronological issues and the discrepancies which can appear even within the same chapter. MT *'āmad lipᵉnē melek-bābel bîrûšālāim*, lit. 'he stood before the king of Babylon in Jerusalem': this is quite ambiguous, and gives the impression that Nebuzaradan arrived (*bā'*) and stood before Nebuchadrezzar in Jerusalem. As the king was at Riblah this can hardly be the sense of the statement, and it may be intended to qualify Nebuzaradan's special status as one who stands (revocalized *'ōmēd* cf. G) before the great king (cf. 15.19; I Kings 10.8; 17.1 for the idiom); II Kings 25.8 makes Nebuzaradan the 'servant' (*'ebed*) of the king of Babylon and lacks 'in' (Jerusalem). **[13]** The phrase 'and every great house he burned down' may be an addition to the text (cf. BHS); it is unnecessary in view of the previous statement. **[14]** 39.8; II Kings 25.10 lack 'all' (the walls); G lacks 'all' (the army). **[15]** G lacks v. 15: perhaps due to haplography, as vv. 15–16 both begin with *ûmiddallôt* (*hā'ām*?, cf. 39.10), 'and some of the poor (of the people)'; cf. Janzen 1973, 20–1. This phrase may not be original to v. 15, as it is lacking in 39.9; II Kings 25.11; it belongs to v. 16 and its deletion here makes v. 15 virtually equivalent to 39.9 (with the addition of *wᵉ'ēt yeter hā'āmōn*, 'and the remainder of the master-workmen'). MT *hā'āmōn*, 'master-workmen': cf. Prov. 8.30; EVV 'artisans', JPSB 'craftsmen'; yet according to II Kings 24.14 all the craftsmen were deported in 597! II Kings 25.11 has *hehāmōn*, 'the multitude'; 39.9 *hā'ām*, 'the people'; some exegetes favour reading *hā'ommān* (cf. Akkadian *ummānu*; S. of Sol.7.2), 'skilled artisans' (e.g. Rudolph, Bright). **[16]** G *kai tous kataloipous tou laou*, 'and the remnant of the people', for MT 'and some of the poorest of the land'. G, II Kings 25.12 lack 'Nebuzaradan'. MT *ûlᵉyōgᵉbîm*, 'and for ploughmen': meaning of Hebrew uncertain (see on 39.10); G *kai eis geōrgous*, 'and to be labourers, tillers of the ground'.

A month after the breach made in the city wall Nebuzaradan the commander of the Babylonian troops enters Jerusalem and razes the city to the ground. Why a month should pass between the breach being made and the penetration of the city is unknown. Perhaps the troops waited for their commander to arrive (cf. Bright) or they waited to see who else would dare to venture forth through the breach and be slaughtered. These possibilities are derived from the story-teller's presentation of the breach as something made by the besieged rather than by the besiegers. If the Babylonians made the breach (cf. 39.2) they would hardly have waited another month before entering the beleaguered city. Furthermore, the association in v. 6 of the severity of the starvation in the city with the breach made in v. 7 does not really allow a further month for the citizens to linger in a state of such hunger (unless the Babylonians were sadists and the inhabitants of Jerusalem a peculiar form of masochists). However the delay of a month is explained it remains a curious feature of the story.

The variations in the stories told about the Babylonian penetration and destruction of Jerusalem (39.2–10; 52.6–16; II Kings 25.3–12) indicate the lack of a detailed account of what really happened when the city fell to the onslaught of the Babylonians. Dates and figures vary, even though one basic account appears to be the source of the stories, but these variations are typical of biblical narratives which are unreliable in matters of precise dates or numbers. The destruction of the city is followed by the deportation of various groups of people (details are far from clear) and the leaving behind of the poorest to work the land. This arrangement would appear to have emptied the land of people – vv. 15–16 refer to the city and the land but the story is essentially about the fate of Jerusalem rather than the land of Judah (otherwise 40.7 – 41.18 would be inconceivable). However, the figures given in vv. 28–30 for the various deportations of the Jews to Babylon made in the reign of Nebuchadrezzar do not warrant the claim that the land was emptied of its population apart from those of the poor left behind to till the land (cf. Lam. 5). The myth of an empty land is part of the ideology of the Chronicler and others (cf. II Chron. 36.20–21), developed in a period when it became necessary to distinguish sharply between the returning exiles and those who were outside the pale (i.e. the people of the land, cf. Ezra 4.1–5). Such a differentiation belongs to the power politics of the fifth century, when the reestablishment of city and temple polarized various factions in Judaean territory. The account of Nebuzaradan leaving only the dregs of Judaean society behind after the burning of Jerusalem and the deportation of all the important people (though MT v. 15 even includes some of the poorest elements in the deportation!) provides a warrant, however unfounded in reality, for the ideological conflict of the fifth century. One final curiosity in the story may be noted in passing: those who remained in the city were deported by Nebuzaradan and those who fled from the city were executed (v. 10). Yet in the preaching of Jeremiah the potential fate of the different groups appears to be the reversal of this experience (cf. 21.9; 38.2, 17–18). It is an unimportant point and may be modified by stressing the survival of those who did surrender (v. 15). But ironically those who survived the hardships of the siege and did *not* surrender to the Chaldaeans would appear to have gained their lives as prizes of war, even though they may have been deported. Thus even in the best constructed stories prophets do not predict the future with any degree of reliability!

52.17–23

17 And the pillars of bronze that were in the house of the LORD, and the
stands and the bronze sea that were in the house of the LORD, the Chaldeans
broke in pieces, and carried all the bronze to Babylon. 18 And they took
away the pots, and the shovels, and the snuffers, and the basins, and the
dishes for incense, and all the vessels of bronze used in the temple sevice;
19 also the small bowls, and the firepans, and the basins, and the pots, and
the lampstands, and the dishes for incense, and the bowls for libation. What
was of gold the captain of the guard took away as gold, and what was of
silver, as silver. 20 As for the two pillars, the one sea, the twelve bronze
bulls which were under the sea, and the stands, which Solomon the king
had made for the house of the LORD, the bronze of all these things was
beyond weight. 21 As for the pillars, the height of the one pillar was eighteen
cubits, its circumference was twelve cubits, and its thickness was four
fingers, and it was hollow. 22 Upon it was a capital of bronze; the height of
the one capital was five cubits; a network and pomegranates, all of bronze,
were upon the capital round about. And the second pillar had the like, with

pomegranates. 23 There were ninety-six pomegranates on the sides; all the pomegranates were a hundred upon the network round about.

[52.17–23] = II Kings 25.13–17 (a briefer version). An account of the construction of the temple furnishings is to be found in I Kings 7.15–50. **[17]** MT *wayyiśᵉʾū' et-kol-nᵉḥuštām bābelāh*, 'and they carried all *their* bronze to Babylon': II Kings 25.13, G lack 'all'. **[18–19]** G, II Kings 25.14–15 are briefer; cf. BHS for variations between MT and G in v. 19. **[20]** II Kings 25.16 lacks 'the twelve bronze bulls which were under (the sea)'; cf. II Kings 16.8, 17, where king Ahaz removed these in order to pay the Assyrians to attack his enemies – the editor of Jer. 52 may have forgotten this point (so Gray 1977, 767; cf. Rudolph, 320). G lacks 'all these furnishings (*hakkēlīm*)' at the end of v. 20. I Kings 7.27 has *ten* stands: added here by some exegetes (cf. BHS). **[21]** II Kings 25.17 lacks 'and the pillars'. G *triakonta pente pēchōn*, 'thirty-five cubits' (cf. II Chron. 3.15), for MT 'eighteen cubits'. K *qwmh*; Q *qōmat*, 'height' (both mean the same). II Kings 25.17 lacks 'its circumference was twelve cubits, and its thickness was four fingers, and it was hollow'. MT *wᵉḥūṭ šᵉttēm-ʿeśrēh ʾammāh yᵉsubbennū*, lit. 'and a line of twelve cubits surrounded it'. **[22]** II Kings 25.17 gives the height of the capital as 'three cubits'; here it is 'five cubits'. The last word in MT *wᵉrimmōnīm*, 'and pomegranates', is odd in that such a motif is included in the phrase 'and the second pillar (had) the like of these (*kāʾēlleh*)', i.e. the same; II Kings 25.17, 'upon the network'. G *oktō rhoai to pēchei tois dōdeka pēchesi*, 'eight pomegranates to a cubit for the twelve cubits'. **[23]** II Kings 25 lacks the equivalent of v. 23. MT *rūḥah?*, 'windwards': perhaps *rwḥ*, 'spaced', i.e. at intervals, should be read here, cf. *rewaḥ*, 'a space', in Gen.32.17 (EV 16); Bright, 365n. According to I Kings 7.20, 42, each capital had *two* hundred pomegranates, in two rows.

The executions and deportations of vv. 9–16 might appear to be the end of the story, but 52 is derived from the summarizing account of the Deuteronomistic historians and there remain a number of itemized observations on the fall of Jerusalem. The Deuteronomistic interest in the temple provides a list of the valuable furnishings which the Babylonians took as loot to Babylon. II Kings 24.13 and 25.13–17 give accounts of the two lootings of the temple in 597 and 587. Now it may be thought that the Babylonians would have done a thorough job of ransacking the temple the first time and have left very little for subsequent invasions (see on 27.19–21), but the historians appear to work with an idealized notion of the temple. Each time a foreign power attacked Jerusalem the Judaean king would buy it off by using the temple furnishings of gold and silver as tribute or Danegeld.

Perhaps only the movable items were ever taken and then replaced at a later time, ready to be used to buy protection for the city when necessary. Yet each invasion would appear to have successfully plundered the temple without seriously depleting its contents. Hence in 597 *and* 587 the Babylonians could raid it *twice*. However these accounts are to be rationalized, they reflect quite different themes melded together: in some cases the Babylonians break up the furnishings because they are valuable and these must cease to function as sacral utensils. In other cases the furnishings are transported wholesale and these become the source of legends about their return or their misuse (cf. 27.22; 28.3; II Chron. 36.18; Ezra 1.7; Dan. 1.2; 5.2–4). Apart from an additional note to 27.22 the Jeremiah tradition has no interest in the temple furnishings – their loss is simply the judgment of Yahweh against a corrupt nation. The temple is important and respected in the tradition (e.g. 7.11; 17.12), but 52.17–23 reflect the interests of the Deuteronomistic historians rather than those of the other levels in the book of Jeremiah.

52.24–27

24 And the captain of the guard took Seraiah the chief priest, and Zephaniah the second priest, and the three keepers of the threshold; 25 and from the city he took an officer who had been in command of the men of war, and seven men of the king's council, who were found in the city; and the secretary of the commander of the army who mustered the people of the land; and sixty men of the people of the land, who were found in the midst of the city. 26 And Nebuzaradan the captain of the guard took them, and brought them to the king of Babylon at Riblah. 27 And the king of Babylon smote them, and put them to death at Riblah in the land of Hamath. So Judah was carried captive out of its land.

[52.24–27] = II Kings 25.18–21. **[24]** G lacks the personal names of the officials: cf. I Chron. 5.39–41 (EV 6.13–15) for Seraiah the grandson of Josiah's high priest Hilkiah; Zephaniah may be the priest of the same name referred to in 29.24–29; 37.3. MT *šōmᵉrē hassap*, 'keepers of the threshold': i.e. door-keepers, an important temple function (cf. 35.4); G *tous phulassontas tēn hodon*, 'keepers of the way'. **[25]** G lacks 'and from the city'. MT *sārîs 'eḥād*, 'one official': i.e. a certain official; as in 29.2; 34.19; 38.7; 39.3, 13; 41.16 *sārîs* means 'official' and not necessarily 'eunuch'; here it denotes a military officer. II Kings 25.19 has 'five men', whereas here 'seven men':

such discrepancies are typical of the two accounts but hardly significant degrees of error warranting analytical investigation. MT *sōpēr śar haṣṣābā'*, 'a secretary of the commander of the army': II Kings 25.19 *hassōpēr*, '*the* secretary . . .'; G lacks *śar*, 'commander'; cf. 36.12 for the association of the two terms. NEB makes *sōpēr* 'adjutant-general' and treats *śar haṣṣābā'*, 'commander-in-chief', as an addition to the text. MT *wᵉšiššîm 'îš mē'am hā'āreṣ*, 'and sixty men of the people of the land': *'am hā'āreṣ* is a technical phrase which may mean 'the ordinary peasantry of the country' or 'the landed gentry'; it is ambiguous here and may refer to the conscripted peasants or the landowners forming part of the army. **[27]** MT *wayyakkeh 'ōtām . . . wayᵉmitēm*, 'and he smote them . . . and he put them to death': i.e. had them flogged and then executed (cf. NEB; Rudolph, 322); Nebuchadrezzar will not have carried out this treatment himself but will have given orders for the beatings and executions. G lacks 'and he put them to death' and 'so Judah was carried captive out of its land'.

The impression given by vv. 7–16 is that all the various strata of Judaean society had been punished by the Babylonians, but vv. 24–27 single out a number of specific officials for execution. This may be an alternative account to vv. 8–10 or, perhaps on balance more likely, a supplementary story accounting for the fate of those considered to have been responsible for the events leading up to the siege and for its maintenance over a long period. Again it is noteworthy that the accounts know nothing of Jeremiah – hence the stories told about him in 39.11–14; 40.1–6. He is not part of the official records made of the period and his role in the siege must be presumed to be a part of the fiction of the tradition. A list of 'guilty men' is drawn up: *two* very senior priests, *three* important temple officials, *one* officer who organized the army, *seven* men who had had immediate access to the king (his inner cabinet?), a secretary to the army commander, and *sixty* men found in the city (whether important officers or conscripts or even non-combatants is not clear from the text). These seventy-four men are then taken by Nebuzaradan to Riblah (on the same trip as v. 9?). There they encounter the wrath of king Nebuchadrezzar, are beaten, and then executed. That there were so many executions at Riblah increases the sense of wonderment that king Zedekiah was not also summarily executed there. He was, after all, the one most responsible as king for the policy pursued by Judah, though he may have found his imprisonment a crueller fate than death. The executions and the cruel treatment of the king will have served *pour encourager les autres* and will also have removed the threat of resistance from those deported. All who had escaped during or after the siege (the seventy-four men were probably those important officials who had *not* escaped) were another matter, but the Babylonians do not appear to have taken them seriously (cf. 40.7 – 41.18). In crushing the revolt Nebuchadrezzar effectively exiled Judah, and the section ends with a note making that point. Here may well be 'the climax and conclusion of the theme of the Deuteronomic redactor's continuation of the historical narrative of the Deuteronomic compiler of Kings' (Gray 1977, 769). What follow are two appendices which bring up to date the story of Jerusalem's destruction and the exile of Judah.

52.28–30

28 This is the number of the people whom Nebuchadrezzar carried away captive: in the seventh year, three thousand and twenty-three Jews; 29 in the eighteenth year of Nebuchadrezzar he carried away captive from Jerusalem eight hundred and thirty-two persons; 30 In the twenty-third year of Nebuchadrezzar, Nebuzaradan the captain of the guard carried away captive of the Jews seven hundred and forty-five persons; all the persons were four thousand and six hundred.

G, II Kings 25 lack 52.28–30. **[28]** Rudolph, 322–5, inserts *'eśrēh*, 'ten', i.e. the seventeenth year, and thus makes v. 28 refer to the deportation of Judaeans and v. 29 to the exiling of the citizens of Jerusalem: cf. 34.7. MT refers to 598–7; cf. II Kings 24.10–16, where the figures given are 18, 000 for the number of deported people. **[29]** Cf. v. 12, where the year is given as Nebuchadrezzar's nineteenth. Some mss and Vrs supply *hegᵉlāh*, 'exiled, took captive' (as in vv. 28, 30). **[30]** MT *kol-nepeš 'arba'at 'ᵃlāpīm wᵉšēš mē'ōt*, 'all the persons (were) four thousand and six hundred': it is unlikely that *nepeš*, 'person', should be restricted to male Jews, in spite of *yᵉhūdīm*, 'Judaeans, Jews' being masculine (e.g. would the one hundred and twenty thousand persons of Nineveh in Jonah 4.11 necessarily be male because they are described as *'ādām*, 'human'?). The discrepancy between the total here and II Kings 24. 14, 16 can hardly be resolved by distinguishing between males and others (*contra* Bright, 369), though Rudolph's proposal dissolves the problem by relating the figures to different events and periods.

The only information available for the numbers deported by the Babylonians appears in vv. 28–30 (II Kings 24–25 only record figures for 597). The source of this register is not known and the accuracy of its information cannot be vouched for. As with all statistical accounts in the Bible there are discrepancies between it and the relevant parallel material in II Kings 24.14, 16 (cf. discussion in Ackroyd 1968a, 23). Such discrepancies are better not harmonized but accepted as evidence for the lack of definitive information available to the editors of the biblical stories. The impression given by v. 30 is that the total refers to *all* the persons (*nepeš*) who were exiled to Babylon, rather than just to the males (Bright). The point could be argued, but probably only for the purpose of harmonizing the different accounts, and that would entail some dubious exegesis (Rudolph's solution depends upon interfering with the text), without necessarily resolving the problems.

The deportation of four thousand and six hundred persons over a sixteen year period does not represent a drastic shift in population, though considerable social changes will have been effected by the loss of the landed gentry, the priests, officials and important citizens of the territory (general assessment in Ackroyd 1968a, 20–31). Without knowing the general population figures of Judah and Jerusalem in the early sixth century it is impossible to determine the proportion of deported people or the extent to which the land was populated after 582. The onslaught of the Babylonians certainly devastated the population in many different ways: starvation from the famine caused by invasion and siege, disease as a concomitant product of war and siege, slaughter and executions, deportations and emigration (40.11–12). All these factors changed the face of life in Judah for those who remained after the Babylonians had returned home from their spoliations of the cities and the land. But the deportations were probably only a small part of the changes brought about in social organization in the sixth century, and the impression given by Jer. 52 and II Kings 25 of a radical, large-scale depopulation of Judah (e.g. 52.27b) should be regarded as a distortion of the facts for ideological reasons.

The reference in v. 30 to a third deportation dated to the year 582 is enigmatic, but may refer to the Babylonian reprisals for the assassination of Gedaliah. Too much remains unknown about this period (587–582) for such an interpretation to be anything other than speculation. If the Gedaliah story (40.7 – 41.18) reflects historical events in any sense, then Babylon must have responded in a retaliatory fashion and a further deportation (after slaughter) would have been characteristic of their foreign policy. The fact that, according to vv. 29–30, the numbers of deportees are so similar for 587 and 582 (i.e. a difference of only eighty-seven) should lend perspective to the dimensions of the 587 deportation (taking the text as it stands). However, the similarity of the two sets of figures for two very different events (siege and punishment of land and city in revolt as opposed to retribution for a small-scale assassination) lends weight to Rudolph's reading of v. 28 as a reference to the deportation of the inhabitants of the Judaean territory in 588–7 (cf. 34.7).

52.31–34

31 And in the thirty-seventh year of the captivity of Jehoiachin king of Judah, in the twelfth month, on the twenty-fifth day of the month, Evil-merodach king of Babylon, in the year that he became king, lifted up the head of Jehoiachin king of Judah and brought him out of prison; 32 and he spoke kindly to him, and gave him a seat above the seats of the kings who were with him in Babylon. 33 So Jehoiachin put off his prison garments. And every day of his life he dined regularly at the king's table; 34 as for his allowance, a regular allowance was given him by the king according to his daily need, until the day of his death as long as he lived.

[52.31–34] = II Kings 25.27–30 (with minor variations). **[31]** G has *Iōakim*, 'Ioakim' (= Jehoakim?) for MT's Jehoiachin. II Kings 25.27 'twenty-seventh day' for 'twenty-fifth day' here; G 'twenty-fourth'. MT *ʾᵉwīl mᵉrōdak*, 'Evil-merodach': a corruption (deliberate?) of Awel (Amēl)-marduk, 'man of Marduk', Nebuchadrezzar's son (ruled 561–560); *ʾᵉwīl*, 'foolish, stupid', suggests Judaean mockery of the Babylonian king. MT *bišᵉnat malᵉkutō*, 'in the year of his reign': i.e. when he became king (II Kings 25.27, *malᵉkō*); the amnesty for Jehoiachin may have been due to the accession of the new king when such acts of kindness were appropriate. G^B *kai ekeiren auton*, 'and shaved him', after the raising of his head (cf. Gen. 41.14). K *hklyʾ*; Q *hakkᵉlūʾ*, '(house of) restraint', i.e. prison; cf. 37.4. **[32]** K *mlkym*, 'kings'; Q *hammᵉlākīm*, '*the* kings': i.e. the other kings also detained in Babylon. **[33]** MT *wᵉʾākal leḥem lᵉpānāyw tāmīd kol-yᵉmē ḥayyāw*, 'and he ate bread (i.e. dined) in his presence continually all the days of his life': this is ambiguous in that it is not clear whether 'all the days of *his* life' refers to Jehoiachin or Amel-Marduk; as the king died *c.* 560 (whether naturally or by intrigue is not known, cf. Wiseman 1956, 38) the phrase should refer to him (Cornill, 529; Rudolph, 322), though it is possible Jehoiachin predeceased his overlord (cf. Gray 1977, 773), or the biblical writer, being only concerned with Jehoiachin, refers to the Judaean 'king-in-exile'. **[34]** Pritchard 1969, 308, gives details of the Babylonian allowance to Jehoiachin (cf. Gray 1977, 774–5), but vv. 31–34 represent a rather different story from that suggested by the Babylonian administrative documents, where Jehoiachin is the recipient of a state pension. MT *mē'ēt melek-bābel*, 'by the king of Babylon': RSV, II Kings 25.30 lack 'of Babylon' (= *mē'ēt hammelek*). II Kings 25.30 lacks 'until the day of his death'; G lacks 'all the days of his life': MT represents a combination of two variants. Cf. 40.5 for the motif of a special allowance (*'aruḥāh*).

The appendix does not conclude with the stark listing of the number of deportees but closes the book of Jeremiah (and Kings) on a happier note. A story is told about the release of the exiled king Jehoiachin from prison and the kindness shown to him by Nebuchadrezzar's successor Amel-Marduk. This touching story reverses the treatment handed out to Jehoiachin's successor Zedekiah (vv. 9–11) and suggests that, with the death of Nebuchadrezzar, things may have changed for the better for the Judaean exiles (cf. the opposite reversal for the people of Israel when the king who knew Joseph died and a new king arose over Egypt 'who did not know Joseph', Ex. 1.8–10). In v. 9 Nebuchadrezzar speaks judgments (*dbr mšpṭym*, i.e. passes sentence) on Zedekiah, but in v. 32 Amel-Marduk speaks kindly (*way^edabbēr 'ittō ṭōbōt*, lit. 'and he spoke with him good things') to Jehoiachin. Zedekiah is treated in the most vicious manner and imprisoned until his death (v. 11). Whereas whatever harsh treatment Jehoiachin may have suffered in the past (implicit in the story of his imprisonment) is now ended with his release, his elevated status above the other 'kings-in-exile', his kind reception by the king and the permanent allowance he receives until his death. The contrast between the two kings is almost symmetrical, and in their respective fates it may be possible to detect a subtle statement about the different futures of their family line. Zedekiah's immediate family is cut down before his eyes, so the blinded, imprisoned king brings to an end with his own death any hopes of a dynasty arising from his family. Nothing is said about Jehoiachin's family, but his emergence from prison into the king's favour bodes well for their future. This may be an over-subtle reading of the contrasting stories, but the implicit note of hope makes a better ending to an appendix so full of woeful tales than yet a further word of doom. It also provides a postscript to the tradition which expresses an attitude towards

Jehoiachin which is singularly lacking in the Jeremiah tradition proper (cf. 22.24–30). The hostility with which Jehoiachin is dismissed in the material attributed to Jeremiah is absent in this note from a different tradition appended to the book. Furthermore, the great cruelty of Nebuchadrezzar towards Judah appears to die with his death and his successor behaves in a much more humane fashion towards a deposed monarch who has suffered a very long imprisonment.

Excavations of Babylon have yielded cuneiform tablets which set out, among other things, the allocations for Jehoiachin and his sons (Weidner 1939; Pritchard 1969, 308; cf. Oded 1977, 481) and these may be regarded as confirming v. 34 (cf. Gray 1977, 774–5). However, such discoveries do not confirm the status of Jehoiachin as a prisoner nor do they present him in terms parallel to the story in vv. 31–34. He and his sons receive an allowance from the Babylonian authorities, and this provision (which in no sense singles them out as important or different) may be said to lie behind the story developed by the Deuteronomists. For them Jehoiachin had been incarcerated (*throughout* Nebuchadrezzar's reign?) but released during an amnesty associated with Amel-Marduk's accession year, and this liberation is presented in glowing terms. Questions about how the 'king-in-exile' came to be in jail or how such an exile could behave in such a fashion without being executed can be raised but not answered because they presuppose a real history behind the story. However, the story must be considered in terms of the editors' purpose in shaping their account along the lines of an imprisonment followed by a release at a specific juncture of Babylonian history. Are vv. 31–34 designed to make a statement about the Judaean royal house with which to conclude the Deuteronomistic history of the kings of Israel and Judah?

There are two dominant views of the significance of the release of king Jehoiachin from prison: it is simply the alleviation of the unpleasant lot of the captive king (e.g. Gray 1977, 773–5), or it is a Deuteronomistic statement that Jehoiachin's rehabilitation bears on the fate of the whole house of David as presented throughout the books of Kings (cf. Zenger 1968). The difference between the two views is determined by reading vv. 31–34 as a simple observation of a change in Jehoiachin's fortunes in order to end the book of Kings on an auspicious note rather than to blight the future under the evil influence of a despondent ending (Gray). Alternatively, the story may be read in conjunction with the Deuteronomistic theology of kingship running through the history, of which II Sam. 7 may be regarded as the linchpin. Either reading may be supported from the text but one depends upon a wider reading of the books of Kings in a holistic manner. The Deuteronomistic history of the royal house demonstrates the failure of the monarchy to maintain fidelity to Yahweh, a failure which culminated in the deportation of the king in 597 and the destruction of city, palace and temple in 587. The Deuteronomistic theme epitomized by II Sam. 7 represents a different word active in history, namely that of salvation anchored in the promise to David of a permanent throne and dynasty (cf. von Rad 1962, 343–4). In the light of 587 what had happened to this word? Did the humiliation of king Zedekiah and the massacre of his family extinguish for ever the hope vested in the house of David? Perhaps by ending the history of the royal house with a story about Jehoiachin, rather than Zedekiah, the Deuteronomists wished to leave open the question of the fate of David. The door closed by Zedekiah's tragic end is reopened by a story in which the alternative 'king-in-exile' is made the recipient of Babylonian kindness. Thus the future of the royal house becomes a vital question rather than a dead letter.

If an optimistic reading of vv. 31–34 is to be entertained, it must be done in modest terms. The transformation of Jehoiachin's allowance into a story of his release from prison and his elevation *above* the other 'kings-in-exile' indicates a preparedness to read too much into the king's new status among the exiles in Babylon. But this willingness goes no further than to present Jehoiachin as enjoying some degree of comfort in his declining years. No direct statement is made about the future of his family or the prospects for the dynasty of David. That silence may indicate realistic modesty or cautious optimism; but the Deuteronomists do not show their hand. All that may be said with certitude is that, 'The last verses of Kings announce, in a cautious, nuanced way, that a scion of David, king of Israel, is yet alive and well' (Levenson 1984a, 361). The future is left pregnant with possibility, yet nothing is said or implied which could expose the Deuteronomists to the charge of speaking presumptuously or prophesying falsely. The wise reader of vv. 31–34 may prefer to understand the story as simply the alleviation of Jehoiachin's circumstances, but as the last statement in the lengthy story of the adventures of the house of David it is open to being read as a word to the wise and a nod in the direction of the future.

Thus the book of Jeremiah *as we now have it* ends on an ambiguous note. The original ending represented by the second edition (MT) anticipates the utter destruction of Babylon and, therefore, implicitly asserts the restoration of Judah. The first edition (G) ends with the more modest word of hope to Baruch which represents the possibility of survival for individuals in a time of evil inflicted on all flesh. With the addition of the appendix from the Deuteronomistic history the book of Jeremiah, so characterized by anger, destruction, horror and pain, ends on a kindlier note. So all three endings (or stages in the ending) of the book of Jeremiah reverse the dominant trend of the tradition which rants and rages against the communities of Jews in Palestine and Egypt. Do these endings constitute the prelude to the building and planting of the community in its own land – motifs used throughout the tradition, but related to the nations in the prologue of 1.5, 10? Perhaps they are symptomatic of those elements which form a minor aspect of the book (e.g. 24.4–7; 29.10–14; 30–33) and reflect the more positive outlook of the post-catastrophe period. Whatever they represent, the final element in the appendix closes the book on a brief note of quietness and, dare one say, grace (human, of course). 'Calm of mind all passion spent' – the book ends with a touching depiction of human kindness enacted between human beings. It may even be a beginning . . .